Spanish-English
English-Spanish
Medical Dictionary

Diccionario Médico
Español-Inglés
Inglés-Español

Spanish-English English-Spanish Medical Dictionary

Diccionario Médico Español-Inglés Inglés-Español

Second Edition

Onyria Herrera McElroy, Ph.D.

Lola L. Grabb, M.A.

Foreword by Vincent A. Fulginiti, M.D.
Chancellor/Professor of Pediatrics
University of Colorado School of Medicine

Introducción por la Dra. Beatriz Varela
Professor of Spanish
University of New Orleans, New Orleans

LIPPINCOTT WILLIAMS & WILKINS
A **Wolters Kluwer** Company
Philadelphia · Baltimore · New York · London
Buenos Aires · Hong Kong · Sydney · Tokyo

Library of Congress Cataloging-in-Publication Data

McElroy, Onyria Herrera.
   Spanish-English, English-Spanish medical dictionary = Diccionario médico, español-inglés, inglés-español / Onyria Herrera McElroy, Lola L. Grabb ; foreword by Vincent A. Fulginiti ; introduccion por Beatriz Varela.—2nd ed.
     p. cm.
   ISBN 0-316-55448-0
   1. Medicine—Dictionaries. 2. English language—Dictionaries— Spanish. 3. Medicine—Dictionaries—Spanish. 4. Spanish language— Dictionaries—English. I. Grabb, Lola L. II. Title.
   [DNLM: 1. Dictionaries, Medical—Spanish. W 13 M478s 1996]
R121.M488 1996
610'.3—dc20
DNLM/DLC
for Library of Congress   96-20619
                                            CIP

For more information write Lippincott Williams & Wilkins, 530 Walnut Street, Philadelphia, PA 19106

This is a facsimile of the original edition. All material contained in the original is included in this edition

Printed in the United States of America

10

Editorial: Jo-Ann T. Strangis, Suzanne Jeans
Production Services: Beckwith Bookworks
Production Supervisor/Designer: Cate Rickard

Contents / Contenido

Contents / Contenido

Foreword

Non-Spanish-speaking physicians are frustrated when attempting to communicate with their Spanish-speaking patients. Not only is there an obvious language barrier, but also the precise definitions of some words that the physician may acquire from dictionaries may not be correct in the medical context. Additionally, patients are uncomfortable with those who do not share their language, and facility with the language may be an incentive to full disclosure. Most of us who are not mutlilingual pick up phrases and terms that we use loosely in attempting to explore history or reactions to our physical examinations. Now McElroy and Grabb have provided us with a handy reference that will facilitate our ability both to understand our patients and to communicate with them with greater precision and ease.

They have assisted us by providing a well-written, well-structured volume that will provide ready reference to the words, phrases, and constructions that we need. Their use of side by side English-Spanish throughout facilitates ready reference in both directions and can help persons other than the health-care worker and the primarily Spanish speaker to move between the two languages. A unique feature is the inclusion of accepted abbreviations, which I have seen in no other text of this type. The abbreviations are placed in context, which makes learning and transition quick and easy. The conversion tables explain the roots of words, meanings of prefixes and suffixes, and orthographic changes in the two languages.

Finally, the appendixes include a matrix for the physician-patient encounter, with very useful phrases that are commonly employed in gathering historical information and in informing patients of the physician's recommendations and interpretations.

A health-care worker armed with this text will find that he or she is more capable of communication than with most other aids to Spanish-English equivalents. I find this a most useful treatment of this important area in medicine for those whose daily professional and personal lives are dependent on accuracy in communication.

Vincent A. Fulginiti, M.D.

Introducción

La importancia del español y del inglés en el mundo de hoy es obvia, no sólo por el número tan considerable de hablantes que posee cada lengua sino también por las contribuciones culturales llevadas a cabo por ambas civilizaciones y con las cuales se ha venido enriqueciendo y beneficiando la humanidad desde hace muchos siglos. La medicina, por ejemplo, se halla entre los campos que cuentan con más adelantos: técnicas nuevas, innovaciones en la cirugía y los tratamientos, conceptos desconocidos que hay que expresar con neologismos y muchas novedades en el diagnóstico y la prevención de enfermedades. Las autoras McElroy y Grabb acertaron, pues, en publicar este diccionario médico-bilingüe en estos momentos tan propicios. Desde luego que la habilidad de escoger el tiempo oportuno no es el único acierto de estas escritoras. Nos encontramos ante un diccionario de calidad, que usa definiciones breves, claras y precisas—en inglés y en español—y que además, en secciones que no he visto en otros diccionarios, estudia las abreviaturas médicas más conocidas, las tablas de conversión con los cambios ortográficos propios de cada lengua y la formación de términos médicos por medio de raíces, prefijos y sufijos. También ofrece orientaciones sencillas para la pronunciación de los sonidos que causan más dificultades al anglo y al hispano respectivamente y una gramática simplificada con las estructuras que contrastan en las dos lenguas. Hay asimismo, cuatro apéndices en los cuales se traducen pesos y medidas, la temperatura, los números, las tablas de conversión, las frases más comunes que se emplean en el ejercicio de la medicina y los signos y síntomas del paciente. En todas estas divisiones del contenido, las traducciones de cada voz o frase se encuentran una al lado de la otra, de manera que no hay necesidad de acudir a ninguna otra referencia. Cuando se busca una voz en el diccionario, bien sea en español, bien en inglés, aparece en primer lugar el cognado (cuando lo hay) y después la connotación del mismo, expuesta en forma sencilla para que la entienda tanto el científico como el vulgo que nada sabe de estas voces médicas. Se incluye, además, si existe, el vocablo popular de la enfermedad o el tratamiento.

Lo expuesto comprueba que este diccionario médico-bilingüe ha de ser una fuente indispensable no sólo para médicos, trabajadores sociales y enfermeros dedicados a problemas de la salud, sino también para los pacientes y las personas que deseen documentarse sobre distintos aspectos de la medicina contemporánea. Por último, conviene subrayar que la obra ha de beneficiar lo mismo al ciudadano de una nación anglohablante que al de todo país de habla española.

Dra. Beatriz Varela

Preface

Since the first edition of the *Spanish-English/English-Spanish Medical Dictionary*, we have seen a growing interest in improving communication between English-speaking health-care providers and Spanish-speaking patients seeking care. Thus, the use of the dictionary is now more important than ever. To our satisfaction, the dictionary has been accepted by educators and translators in addition to health-care professionals who use it in hospital and clinical settings, and in doctor's offices. It has also become a resource for Spanish-speaking medical professionals who wish to learn medical English vocabulary and grammar.

The second edition continues and expands the primary bilingual value of the first edition and adds some new tools for the dictionary's better use. There are of course new terms, and these are defined as clearly and concisely as possible in both languages. We have also created for this edition illustrations and charts to facilitate comprehension of concepts and structures. Furthermore, additional sections of useful terms and phrases have been created: Care of the Newborn, Childhood Contagious Diseases, Diagnostic Testing, Emergency Situations, Foods and Nutrition, Physical Fitness, and the vocabulary of terms and phrases for existing sections has been augmented. Examples of the use of cognates have been added to Table of Conversion I to capitalize on the reader's knowledge of medical terms and to expedite the acquisition of vocabulary. In Communicating with the Patient, instructions have been added that will help users formulate more definite questions to suit their specific needs. We hope that all these improvements to the bilingual value of the dictionary will benefit the user's ability to communicate in these two languages and to feel confident to work independently. Undoubtedly, English will remain—as it has been for some years now—the principal international means of communication in medical research and health care around the world. At the same time, the Spanish-speaking population of the United States continues to grow, and the need for bilingual communication skills will also surely increase. The *Spanish-English/English-Spanish Medical Dictionary*, because of its balance between practical features and completeness, will be a useful tool in meeting that increasing need for Spanish-English/English-Spanish communication in the medical and health fields.

O.H.M.
L.L.G.

Prólogo

Desde la primera edición del *Diccionario Médico Español-Inglés Inglés-Español* hemos visto que el interés de mejorar la comunicación entre los angloparlantes que ofrecen servicios médicos y los pacientes hispanoparlantes ha aumentado. El uso del diccionario se hace, pues, más importante que nunca. Para nuestra satisfacción, el diccionario ha sido aceptado por educadores y traductores además de profesionales médicos que lo usan en el hospital, así como en otras situaciones clínicas y en los consultorios médicos. También ha resultado ser un instrumento de gran valor para los profesionales médicos hispanoparlantes que deseen aprender el vocabulario médico y la gramatica en inglés.

La segunda edición continúa y expande el carácter bilingüe del diccionario, valor primordial de la primera edición, y añade nuevas maneras de darle mejor uso. Por supuesto, hay términos nuevos, y éstos se definen en la forma más breve y precisa posible en ambos idiomas. También hemos añadido a esta edición cuadros gráficos para facilitar la comprensión de conceptos y estructuras. Además, hay secciones adicionales de términos y frases útiles: Cuidado del recién nacido, Enfermedades infantiles contagiosas, Pruebas de diagnóstico, Situaciones de emergencia, Comidas y nutrición, y Acondicionamiento físico. Se ha aumentado el vocabulario de términos y frases en secciones que ya aparecen en la primer a edición. Se ha añadido el uso de cognados a la Tabla de conversión 1 para sacarle provecho al conocimiento que el lector ya tenga de términos médicos, y apresurar la adquisición de nuevo vocabulario. En la sección Comunicación con el paciente, se han añadido instrucciones para ayudar a formular preguntas más definidas que se ajusten a cada situación específica. Esperamos que todas estas adiciones al valor bilingüe del diccionario aumente la facilidad de comunicación entre estos dos idiomas y que le dé al usuario mayor habilidad para trabajar independientemente.

Sin duda, el inglés seguirá siendo, como lo ha sido durante algunos años hasta la fecha, el medio principal de comunicación en investigaciones médicas y cuidado de la salud en el mundo. Al mismo tiempo, la población hispanoparlante de los Estados Unidos continúa creciendo, y la necesidad de incrementar la comunicación bilingüe también aumenta. *El Diccionario Médico Inglés-Español Español Inglés* reune las características necesarias para satisfacer esta creciente necesidad.

Acknowledgments

In addition to those institutions and persons acknowledged in the first edition of our dictionary, to whose beneficial assistance we here pay tribute again, we would also like to express our gratitude to Silvio Aristizabal, Estelle Bornhurst, Leyla Catán, Robert Croese, Peggy C. Ferry, Semantha Guthrie, Steve Nash, L. Claire Parsons, Julius Pietrzak, Ronald P. Spark, and Arnulfo Trejo for their encouraging reception and promotion of the first edition and for their generous help in preparing this revised edition.

How to Use the Dictionary

Main entries

The main entries are printed in **boldface,** in slightly larger type than the rest of the text set flush to the left hand margin. The main entry may consist of:

1. one word: **abdomen**
2. words joined by a hyphen: **cross-eyed**
3. descriptive phrases: **sympathetic nervous system**

The main entries are listed in alphabetical order according to the initial letter of the entry. Two kinds of entries appear: a) strictly medical words and b) common words related to general communication with patients.

When the main entry is a medical term, a simple definition is given with the most important facts pertaining to it. When the main entry has different meanings which are identified as the same part of speech, they are itemized numerically and labeled with an abbreviation if it is needed for clarification (1). When the main entry is a non-medical word or a common term, synonyms are used to define it. If a main entry has more than one meaning, a word or phrase between brackets is given, in italics, in the same language as the entry to clarify its meaning, or in some cases the entry is used in a phrase to clarify its use (2). We have listed new technical words designating programs, products, instruments, or treatments and defined them by following the general rules of language usage.

(1)
> **absorption** *n.* absorción. 1. la acción de un organismo de absorber o pasar líquidos u otras sustancias; 2. *psic.* ensimismación.

(2)
> **fit** *n.* ataque, convulsión; *a.* [*suitable*] adecuado-a; *v.* [*to adjust to shape*] ajustar, encajar.

In some cases, when there is a slight difference in the spelling of words with the same meaning, both spellings are entered together, and the most common one of the two is entered first (3).

(3)
> **exophthalmia, exophthalmus** *n.* exoftalmia, exoftalmus, protrusión anormal del globo del ojo.

Only words that would pertain to communication in a medical situation and to needs related to patients or medical personnel are included in the glossary.

Subentries

Subentries under main entries of medical words in the same language as the entry are printed in **boldface type** (4); subentries under main entries of common words and phrases and idiomatic expressions are printed in **boldface type** (5). A slash (/) separates the translation of the subentries from English to Spanish or Spanish to English, while a double space (__) stands for the main entry. Subentries generally are not defined. Their plural forms are indicated by adding **-s** or **-es** after the double space.

(4)   **dislocation** *n.* luxación, desplazamiento de una articulación; **closed** ___ / ___ cerrada; **complicated** ___ / ___ complicada; **congenital** ___ / ___ congénita.

(5)   **around** *prep.* cerca de; en; *adv.* alrededor de, cerca; a la vuelta; más o menos; ___ **here** / ___ aquí; *v.* **to look** ___ / buscar; **to turn** ___ / dar la vuelta; voltear; voltearse.

Popular Names

When an entry refers to a sickness which is known by more than one name, only one definition is given. The abbreviation *V.* (See) will guide the reader to the term defined (6).

(6)   **chickenpox** *n.* varicela. *V.* **varicella.**

Parts of Speech

All main entries, simple or combined, are identified as to part of speech. When the main entry has more than one word, the combined phrase is also identified (7).

(7)   **robust** *a.*
role model *n.*
radioactive iodine excretion test *n.*

The meanings of a word used as more than one part of speech are indicated in the following order of forms: **noun** *n.;* **adjective** *a.;* **verb** *v.;* **irregular verb** *vi.;* **reflexive verb** *vr.;* **adverb** *adv.* (2).

In the English section of the dictionary, the glossary includes nouns, adjectives, infinitives of verbs, the past participle (classified as an adjective), comparatives and superlatives, prepositions and adverbs. Idiomatic expressions involving the main entry are included following the definitions. Other parts of speech such as pronouns and verb forms can be found in the grammar section of the dictionary.

In the Spanish section nouns and adjectives are identified by their gender (*m., f.*). In the English section, the translations into Spanish of nouns and adjectives indicate their gender (masculine or feminine) by adding the feminine ending **-a,** accordingly, to nouns and adjectives ending in **-o** that are inflected. In example (8) **rápido-a** means that the masculine is **rápido,** and the feminine is **rápida.** When the adverb is indicated by the ending **-mente,** it means that this ending has to be added to the feminine ending of the adjective, or just added to it if the adjective ends in a consonant.

(8)   **fast** *n.* ayuno; *a.* [*speedy*] rápido-a; ligero-a; **color** ___ / resistente a un colorante; *v.* [*not to eat anything*] ayunar; **to break one's** ___ / dejar de ayunar; *adv.* aprisa; rápidamente; **to walk** ___ / andar ___; ___ **asleep** / profundamente dormido-a.

When entries are spelled alike but have a different classification (homographs), the part of speech is indicated by its corresponding abbreviation, definitions follow separated by semicolons without using numerals, as is the case when the entry has the same classification regarding part of speech (9).

(9) | **mucoid** *n*. mucoide, glucoproteína similar a la mucina; *a*. de consistencia mucosa.

Eponyms are entered alphabetically according to last names (10).

(10) | **Babinski's reflex** *n*. reflejo de Babinski, dorsiflexión del dedo gordo al estimularse la planta del pie.

Plurals

Irregular plurals in English, and the plurals of Latin and Greek nouns used in medical terminology are indicated in parentheses after the entry.

(11) | **woman** *n*. (*pl*. **women**) mujer.

(12) | **septum** *L*. (*pl*. **septa**) septum, tabique o membrana que divide dos cavidades o espacios.

Consult the grammar section of the dictionary to find the rules that apply to the formation of plurals in each language.

Capitalization

Most entries in English begin with a lowercase. Capitalization is used in eponyms and trade names of medications; names of plants and animals are capitalized, printed in italics, and given in the singular if referring to the genus, and in the plural if referring to the class, order, family, or phylum (13).

(13) | **Salmonella** *n*. Salmonela, género de bacterias de la familia *Enterobacteriaceae* que causan fiebres entéricas, otras infecciones gastrointestinales y septicemia.

Medical Abbreviations and Conversion Tables

To save space and facilitate their use, medical abbreviations and prefixes, suffixes, and roots have been listed in separate sections entitled **Most Common Medical Abbreviations** and **Conversion Tables.**

Communicating with Patients

This section is intended to satisfy the simplest daily communications that a health professional who speaks either Spanish or English may need to have with a patient who speaks the other language. It is also intended that this section will have the effect of increasing the reader's ability to use the other language in non-clinical contexts as well, such as reading medical literature, attending conferences, and communicating orally and in writing with fellow health professionals in the other language.

Appendixes

Numerals, measures, words related to time, words related to signs and symptoms, as well as practical charts on contagious diseases, emergency care, medical tests, nutrition, physical fitness, idioms and vocabulary for conducting interviews with patients and giving them instructions are found in separate appendices.

Word to the Reader

In the second edition, new additions have been made, some of them following the suggestion of our readers. We hope that our new readers will do the same, forwarding via Little, Brown and Company recommendations for improving this dictionary in future editions.

Uso del diccionario

Entradas principales

Las entradas principales aparecen impresas en letra **negrita** formando el margen izquierdo. La entrada principal puede consistir en:

1. una sola palabra: **abdomen**
2. una palabra compuesta: **intra-abdominal**
3. una frase descriptiva: **cuello uterino**

Las entradas principales siguen un orden alfabético de acuerdo con la primera letra de la palabra. Hay dos tipos de entradas: (a) palabras estrictamente médicas, (b) palabras del lenguaje común necesarias para la comunicación con los pacientes.

Cuando la entrada principal es un vocablo médico, a éste le sigue una definición simple que señala los aspectos más importantes del mismo. Si el vocablo tiene más de una acepción para una misma parte de la oración (sustantivo, adjetivo, etc.), a cada acepción se le atribuye un número y una abreviatura adicional para mayor claridad (1). Cuando la entrada principal es un vocablo común, no médico, se hace uso de sinónimos para traducirla. Si tiene más de un significado, se hace uso de alguna palabra o frase entre corchetes ([]), en *bastardilla* y en el mismo idioma de la entrada, para aclarar su significado, o se emplea la misma entrada en una frase para aclarar su uso (2). En algunos casos incluimos nuevas palabras técnicas que designan programas, productos, instrumentos y tratamientos; estas palabras están definidas de acuerdo con las reglas generales del uso del idioma.

(1)
> **absorción** *f.* absorption, uptake. 1. taking up of fluids and other substances by an organism; 2. *psych.* self-centeredness.

(2)
> **apagar** *v.* [*luces*] to turn off; [*fuego*] to put out.

En algunos casos, cuando hay una pequeña diferencia en la forma escrita de dos palabras con el mismo significado, ambas palabras se presentan en la misma entrada, y se registra primero la palabra de uso más común (3).

(3)
> **fibrocístico-a, fibroquístico-a** *a.* fibrocystic, cystic and fibrous in nature; **enfermedad ___ de la mama / ___** disease of the breast.

En el glosario de este diccionario se han incluido solamente términos relacionados con una situación médica, ya sea para la comunicación con los pacientes o para la atención a sus necesidades.

Entradas subalternas

Las entradas subalternas que aparecen bajo la entrada principal están impresas en letra **negrita** si están en el mismo idioma que ésta; asimismo, ya refiriéndose a la terminología no médica o a expresiones idiomáticas en el mismo. Una línea inclinada (/) separa la traducción del español al inglés y del inglés al español en las entradas subalternas, y un doble guión (___) sustituye la entrada principal; el plural se indica con una -s o con -es después del doble guión. Las entradas subalternas generalmente no se definen (4).

(4) | **cuidado** *m.* care, attention; ___ **intensivo** / intensive ___; ___ **postnatal** / postnatal ___; **estar al ___ de** / to be under the ___ of; **tratar con ___** / to handle with ___. **febril** *a.* febrile, having a body temperature above normal, **convulsiones ___-es** / ___ convulsions.

Términos populares

Cuando un término médico tiene más de un nombre, solamente se define uno de los términos; la abreviatura V. (Véase) en la entrada del otro término guía al lector a la entrada que aparece definida (5).

(5) | **glucopenia** *f.* V. **hipoglicemia.**

Partes de la oración

Después de cada entrada, consista de una o de más palabras, se indica la parte correspondiente de la oración (6).

(6) | **emulsión** *f.* **enajenamiento mental** *m.* **brazalete de identificación** *m.*

Cuando una misma entrada tiene más de una clasificación como parte de la oración, se sigue el siguiente orden: nombre *m.*, *f.*; adjetivo *a.*; verbo *v.*; verbo irregular *vi.*; verbo reflexivo *vr.*; adverbio *adv.* Las terminaciones -a y -mente indican la terminación que se añade a la entrada para formar el adjetivo y el adverbio respectivamente (7).

(7) | **elástico** *m.* elastic; **-a** *a.* elastic, that can be returned to its original shape after being extended or distorted. **natural** *a.* natural; **-mente** *adv.* naturally.

En la sección del diccionario en español, el glosario incluye sustantivos, adjetivos, infinitivos de verbos, el participio pasado (clasificado como adjetivo), preposiciones y adverbios. Las expresiones idiomáticas aparecen como entradas subalternas a continuación de las definiciones. Otras partes de la oración, pronombres y distintas formas de los verbos aparecen en la sección de gramática del diccionario.

En la sección del diccionario en español, los sustantivos y adjetivos se identifican por su género (*m.*, *f.*) En la sección en inglés, la traducción de sustantivos y adjetivos al español indica el género de los mismos (masculino o femenino) mediante el uso de la terminación -a añadida a los sustantivos y adjetivos terminados en o (8).

> (8)   **métrico-a** *a*. metric, rel. to meter or the metric system.

Cuando a una misma entrada se le atribuye más de una clasificación (términos homógrafos) cada parte de la oración se indica con su correspondiente abreviatura, y las definiciones siguen a cada clasificación, separadas por un punto y coma pero sin asignarles números como se hace en los casos en que un mismo término tiene más de una acepción pero mantiene la misma clasificación (véanse ejemplos 1 y 7). Los epónimos están registrados alfabéticamente por apellido (9).

> (9)   **Babinski, reflejo de** *m*. Babinski's reflex, dorsiflexion of the big toe on stimulation of the sole of the foot.

Plurales

Los plurales de vocablos incorporados del latín y del griego, así como los plurales irregulares, se indican entre paréntesis a continuación de la entrada (10).

> (10)   **septum** *L*. (*pl*. **septa**) septum, partition between two cavities.

En la sección de gramática del diccionario se encuentran las reglas que gobiernan la formación de los plurales en cada idioma.

Letras mayúsculas

La mayoría de las entradas en inglés y en español aparecen en letra minúscula. Las letras mayúsculas se usan en los epónimos y en nombres comerciales de medicinas. Los nombres de plantas y animales se presentan con letra mayúscula, en bastardilla, en singular si se refieren al género y en plural si se refieren a la clase, orden, familia o filo (11).

> (11)   **Salmonela** *f*. Salmonella, a gram-negative bacteria of the *Enterobacteriaceae* that causes enteric fever, gastrointestinal infection and septicemia.

Abreviaturas médicas y tablas de conversión

Para abreviar y facilitar su uso, las abreviaturas médicas y los prefijos, sufijos y raíces aparecen en secciones aparte tituladas **Abreviaturas médicas mas usuales** y **Tablas de conversión**.

Comunicación con los pacientes

Esta sección tiene como propósito facilitar la comunicación entre el profesional médico y el o la paciente cuando el inglés o el español no es el idioma común. Puede, además, servir de ayuda en situaciones no clínicas como en la lectura de literatura médica, durante la asistencia a conferencias o en la comunicación oral con colegas.

Apéndices

Los apéndices que se encuentran al final del diccionario comprenden: números, pesos y medidas, palabras relacionadas con el tiempo, síntomas y signos, enfermedades contagiosas, cuidado de emergencia, pruebas médicas, nutrición, acondicionamiento físico, y una sección de vocabulario y frases, **Communicación con los pacientes.**

Palabras a los lectores

En esta segunda edición hemos hecho varias adiciones, algunas de ellas siguiendo la sugerencia de nuestros lectores. Esperamos que los nuevos lectores del diccionario hagan lo mismo, enviándonos sus recomendaciones por vía de Little, Brown and Company, para seguir mejorando ediciones futuras.

Abbreviations / Abreviaturas

English		Spanish	
a.	adjective	*a.*	adjetivo
abbr.	abbreviation	*abr.*	abreviatura
adv.	adverb	*adv.*	adverbio
approx.	approximate	*aprox.*	aproximadamente
art.	article	*art.*	artículo
aux.	auxiliary	*aux.*	auxiliar
Cast.	Castilian	*Cast.*	castellano
comp.	comparative	*comp.*	comparativo
cond.	conditional	*cond.*	condicional
conj.	conjunction	*conj.*	conjunción
dem.	demonstrative	*dem.*	demostrativo
esp.	especially	esp.	especialmente
f.	feminine	*f.*	femenino
		fam.	familiar
Fr.	French	*Fr.*	francés
		form.	formal pronoun
gen.	generally	gen.	generalmente
Gr.	Greek	*Gr.*	griego
gr.	grammar	*gr.*	gramática
H.A.	Hispanic America	*H.A.*	Hispanoamérica
imp.	imperative	*imp.*	imperativo
impf.	imperfect	*impf.*	imperfecto
ind.	indicative	*ind.*	indicativo
indef.	indefinite	*indef.*	indefinido
inf.	infinitive	*inf.*	infinitivo
infl.	inflammation	infl.	inflamación
int.	interjection	*int.*	interjección
interr.	interrogative	*interr.*	interrogativo
L.	Latin	*L.*	latín
m.	masculine	*m.*	masculino
Mex.	Mexico	*Mex.*	México
Mex.A.	Mexican-American	*Mex.A.*	Mexicano-americano
n.	noun	*n.*	nombre
neut.	neuter	*neut.*	neutro
obj.	object	*obj.*	objeto
pop.	popular	*pop.*	popular
pp.	past participle	*pp.*	participio de pasado
p.p.	present participle	*p.p.*	participio de presente
pref.	prefix	*pref.*	prefijo
prep.	preposition	*prep.*	preposición
pres.	present	*pres.*	presente
pret.	preterite	*pret.*	pretérito
pron.	pronoun	*pron.*	pronombre
psych.	psychology	*psic.*	psicología
ref.	reflexive	*ref.*	reflexivo
rel.	relative	rel.	relativo
subj.	subjunctive	*subj.*	subjuntivo
sup.	superlative	*sup.*	superlativo
surg.	surgery	*cirg.*	cirugía

English		*Spanish*	
U.S.A.	United States of America	E.U.A.	Estados Unidos de América
usu.	usually	usu.	usualmente
V.	see	V.	véase
v.	verb	v.	verbo
vi.	irregular verb	vi.	verbo irregular
vr.	reflexive verb	vr.	verbo reflexivo

Most Common Medical Abbreviations /
Abreviaturas médicas más usuales

Abbreviations in English are commonly used in oral communication as well as in written medical reports. In Spanish, however, they are generally only used in written reports.

Las abreviaturas en inglés se usan comúnmente como medio de expresión oral y escrita. En español, las siglas indicadas sólo se usan generalmente en la forma escrita.

Abbr.	English / Inglés	Abreu	Spanish / Español
AA	Alcoholics Anonymous	—	Alcohólicos Anónimos (asociación de)
AA	auto accident	—	accidente de automóvil
A&B	apnea and bradycardia	—	apnea y bradicardia
Ab	abortion; antibody	—	aborto; anticuerpo
ABC	artificial beta cells	CBA	células beta artificiales
abd	abdomen	—	abdomen
ABE	acute bacterial endocarditis	EIA	endocarditis infecciosa aguda
ABG	arterial blood gases	GSA	gases de sangre arterial
ABMT	autologous bone marrow transplantation	TAMO	transplante autólogo de médula ósea
ac (*ante cibum*)	before meals	—	antes de las comidas
ACBP	aorto-coronary-bypass	DAC	derivación aorto-coronaria
ACG	angiocardiography	—	angiocardiografía
ACTH	adrenocorticotropic hormone	HACT	hormona adrenocorticotrópica
ad (*ad*)	until	—	hasta
AD	right ear	OD	oído derecho
ADD	attentive deficit disorder	DDA	desorden de falta de atención
ad effect (*ad effectum*)	until it is effective	—	hasta que produzca efecto
ADH	antidiuretic hormone	HAD	hormona antidiurética
ADHD	attention deficit hyperactivity	DAHD	desorden de falta de atención por hiperactividad
ADL	activities of daily living	AVD	actividades de la vida diaria
AE	above elbow	EC	por encima del codo
AF	auricular fibrillation	FA	fibrilación auricular
AFB	aorto-femoral bypass	DAF	derivación aorto-femoral
Afeb.	afebrile	—	afebril
AFP	alphafetoprotein	—	alfafetoproteína
AG	albumin globulin ratio	IAG	índice de albúmina y globulina
agit (*agitatum*)	shake	—	agítese
AHF	antihemophilic Factor VIII	FAH	Factor VIII antihemofílico
AI	aortic insufficiency	IA	insuficiencia aórtica
A.I.D.	artificial insemination by donor	I.A.D.	inseminación artificial por donante
AIDS	acquired immunodeficiency syndrome	SIDA	síndrome de inmunodeficiencia adquirida

continued

Latin expressions (in *italics*), and abbreviations that are the same in both languages appear only on the left.

Las expresiones en latín (en letra *bastardilla*), y las abreviaturas comunes a ambos idiomas aparecen a la izquierda solamente.

Abbr.	*English / Inglés*	*Abreu*	*Spanish / Español*
A.I.H.	artificial insemination by husband	I.A.E.	inseminación artificial por esposo
AK	above knee	ER	por encima de la rodilla
AL	left ear	AU	oído izquierdo
ALB	albumin	—	albúmina
ALL	acute lymphocytic leukemia	LLA	leucemia linfocítica aguda
ALS	amyotrophic lateral sclerosis	ELA	esclerosis lateral amiotrófica
ALT	serum alanine aminotransferase	ALAT	alanina aminotransferasa sérica
a.m.	routine care in the morning	a.m.	cuidado rutinario del paciente por la mañana
AMA	against medical advice	CRM	en contra de la recomendación médica
A.M.A.	American Medical Association	A.M.A.	Asociación Médica Americana
amnio	amniocentesis	—	amniocentesis
ANA	antinuclear antibody	—	anticuerpo antinuclear
Anes.	anesthesia	—	anestesia
AO	aorta	—	aorta
AP	anteroposterior	—	anteroposterior
APTT	activated partial thromboplastin time	APTP	tiempo de tromboplastina activado parcialmente
AR	aortic regurgitation	RA	regurgitación aórtica
ARC	AIDS related complex		complejo del SIDA
arf	acute rheumatic fever	fra	fiebre reumática aguda
ARF	acute renal failure	IRA	insuficiencia renal aguda
as	aortic stenosis	EA	estenosis aórtica
AS	left ear	OI	oído izquierdo
ASAP	as soon as possible	LAP	lo antes posible
ASC	ambulatory surgery center	CCA	centro de cirugía ambulatoria
ASCVD, ASVD	arteriosclerotic vascular disease	ASV	arteriosclerosis vascular
ASD	atrial septal defect	DTA	defecto del tabique auricular
ASHD	arteriosclerotic heart disease	ASC	arteriosclerosis cardíaca
AST	aspartate aminotransferase	—	aspartato aminotransferasa
ATB	antibiotic	ATB	antibiótico
ATP	adenosine triphosphate	—	trifosfato de adenosina
ATR	Achilles tendon reflex	RTA	reflejo del tendón de Aquiles
AV	arteriovenous	—	arteriovenoso
AV	atrioventricular	—	auriculoventricular
AVM	arteriovenous malformation	MAV	malformación arteriovenosa
AVR	aortic valve replacement	RVA	reemplazo de la válvula aórtica
AVS	arteriovenous shunt	DAV	derivación arteriovenosa
AZT	Azidothimidine	—	Azidotimidina
BB	blood bank	BS	banco de sangre
BBB	bundle branch block	BR	bloqueo de rama
BE	bacterial endocarditis	EB	endocarditis bacteriana
BE	barium enema	EB	enema de bario
BF	breast feeding	LM	lactancia materna
BI	bacterial infection	IB	infección bacteriana
bid (*bis in die*)	twice a day	—	dos veces al día
BIL	bilateral		bilateral
BKA	below knee amputation	ADR	amputación debajo de la rodilla
BL	bleeding time	TS	duración de sangramiento
BM	bowel movement	EF	evacuación, defecación, eliminación fecal
BMR	basal metabolic rate	IMB	índice metabólico basal
BP	blood pressure	PA	presión arterial
BPD	bronchopulmonary dysplasia	DBP	displasia broncopulmonar
BPH	benign prostatic hyperplasia	HBP	hiperplasia benigna de la próstata
BSO	bilateral salpingo-oophorectomy	SOB	salpingo-ooforectomía bilateral

Most Common Medical Abbreviations / Abreviaturas médicas más usuales

Abbr.	*English / Inglés*	*Abreu*	*Spanish / Español*
BUN	blood urea nitrogen	US	urea sanguínea
Bx	biopsy	—	biopsia
c.	with	—	con
CA, Ca	cancer, carcinoma	—	cáncer, carcinoma
CAD	coronary artery disease	—	enfermedad de la arteria coronaria
CAH	congenital adrenal hyperplasia	HCS	hiperplasia suprarrenal congénita
CAPD	continuous ambulatory peritoneal dialysis	DPAC	diálisis peritoneal ambulatoria continua
cap(s)	capsule(s)	cap(s)	cápsula(s)
CATH	catheterize	CAT	cateterizar
CBC	complete blood count	CSC	conteo sanguíneo completo
CBD	common bile duct	CBC	conducto biliar común
CC	chief complaint	QP	queja principal
cc	cubic centimeter	—	centímentro cúbico
CCU	coronary care unit	SCC	sala de cuidado coronario
CDC	Centers for Disease Control	CCE	Centros de Control de Enfermedades
CDC	congenital dislocation of the hip	DCC	dislocación congénita de la cadera
CF	cystic fibrosis	FC	fibrosis cística
CHF	congestive heart failure	ICC	insuficiencia cardíaca congestiva
CHOL	cholesterol	COL	colesterol
cl	clear	—	claro
CM	continuous murmur	CM	soplo continuo
CMV	cytomegalovirus	—	citomegalovirus
CNS	central nervous system	SNC	sistema nervioso central
CO	cardiac output	GC	gasto cardíaco
COPD	chronic obstructive pulmonary disease	EPCO	enfermedad pulmonar crónica obstructiva
C.P.	chest pain	D.P.	dolor de pecho
CPR	cardiopulmonary resuscitation	RCP	resucitación cardiopulmonar
CRF	chronic renal failure	IRC	insuficiencia renal crónica
C&S	culture and sensitivity	—	cultivo y sensibilidad
CS	cesarean section	OC	operación cesárea
CSF	cerebrospinal fluid	LCR	líquido cefalorraquídeo
CSP	carotid sinus pressure	PSC	presión del seno carotenoide
CT	computerized tomography	TC	tomografía computada
CV	cardiovascular	—	cardiovascular
CVA	cerebrovascular accident	AP	apoplejía
CVD	cardiovascular disease	ECV	enfermedad cardiovascular
CVI	cerebrovascular insufficiency	ICV	insuficiencia cerebrovascular
CVP	central venous pressure	PVC	presión venosa central
CVS	chorionic villus sampling	MC	muestra coriónica
CXR	chest X-ray	TXR	radiografía del tórax
cysto	cystoscopic examination	cisto	cistoscopía
d.	dose	—	dosis
D	delivery	P	parto
D&C	dilation and curettage	—	dilatación y curetaje
DC	discontinue	SP	suspéndase
DD	differential diagnosis	—	diagnóstico diferencial
ddC 2′, 3′	dideoxycytidine	—	dideoxitidina
dd in d	from day to day	dd in d	de un día a otro día
dE 2′3′	dideoxyinosine	—	dideoxiinosina
DGI	disseminated gonoccochal infection	IGD	infección gonocócica diseminada

continued

Most Common Medical Abbreviations / Abreviaturas médicas más usuales

Abbr.	English / Inglés	Abreu	Spanish / Español
DIC	disseminated intravascular coagulopathy	CID	coagulopatía intravascular diseminada
DIFF	differential blood count	CSD	conteo sanguíneo diferenciado
DJC	degenerative joint disease	EDA	enfermedad degenerativa de las articulaciones
DKA	diabetic ketoacidosis	CE	cetoacidosis diabética
DM	diabetes mellitus	—	diabetes mellitus
DM	diastolic murmurs	SD	soplos diastólicos
DNA	deoxyribonucleic acid	ADN	ácido desoxirribonucleico
DOB	date of birth	FDN	fecha de nacimiento
DOE	dyspnea on exertion	DDE	disnea de esfuerzo
DPT	diphtheria, pertussis, tetanus	—	difteria, pertusis, tétano
DRG	drainage	—	drenaje
DTP	diphtheria, tetanus, and pertussis vaccine	DTP	vacuna contra difteria, tétano y pertusis
DTR	deep tendon reflexes	RTP	reflejos tendinosos profundos
Dx	diagnosis	—	diagnóstico
EBL	estimated blood loss	PES	pérdida estimada de sangre
ECG, EKG	electrocardiogram	ECG	electrocardiograma
EEG	electroencephalogram	—	electroencefalograma
EFW	estimated fetal weight	PEF	peso estimado del feto
EIA	enzyme immunoassay	IEE	inmunoensayo de enzimas
ELISA	enzyme-linked immunosorbent assay	—	prueba inmunosorbente enzimática
EM	ejection murmur	SE	soplo de eyección
EMG	electromyogram	—	electromiograma
ENT	ear, nose, and throat	NGO	nariz, garganta, y oídos
EOM	extraocular muscles	MEO	músculos extraoculares
ER	emergency room	SE	sala de emergencia
ES or clic	expulsion sound or clic	SE	sonido de expulsión o clic
ESR	erythrocyte sedimentation rate	IES	índice de eritrosedimentación
ESRD	end-stage renal disease	ERTF	etapa final de enfermedad renal
EST	electric shock therapy	ECH	electrochoque
ESWL	extracorporeal shock wave lithotripsy	LEOCH	litotripsia extracorpórea con ondas de choque
EXT	extremity	—	extremidad
f	female	SF	sexo femenino
FBS	fasting blood sugar or glucose		glicemia en ayunas
FCF	fetal cardiac frecuency	FCF	frecuencia cardíaca del feto
FFP	fresh frozen plasma	PFC	plasma fresco congelado
FHR	fetal heart rate	FCF	frecuencia cardíaca fetal
fl	fluid	—	fluido líquido
FMH	family medical history	HMF	historia médica de la familia
FSH	follicle stimulating hormone	HFE	hormona de folículoestimulante
FTND	full term normal delivery	PAT	parto a término (normal)
FTT	failure to thrive	DC	déficit en el crecimiento
FUO	fever of unknown origin	FOD	fiebre de origen desconocido
F / U	follow-up	S / C	seguimiento del caso
Fx	fracture	—	fractura
G	gonorrhea	—	gonorrea
GA	gastric analysis	AG	análisis gástrico
GB	gallbladder	VB	vesícula biliar
GC	gonococcus	—	gonococo
gen	general	—	general
GEN	genetics	—	genética
GGT	gamma-glutamyl transferase	—	gamma glutamil transferasa
GH	growth hormone	HC	hormona del crecimiento
GI	gastrointestinal	—	gastrointestinal

Most Common Medical Abbreviations / Abreviaturas médicas más usuales

Abbr.	English / Inglés	Abreu	Spanish / Español
GIT	gastrointestinal tract	TGI	tracto gastrointestinal
GLUC	glucose	—	glucosa
GnRH	gonadotropin liberating hormone	HLH	hormona liberadora de gonadotropina
Grx	gravida	—	grávida
GTT	glucose tolerance test	PTG	prueba de tolerancia a la glucosa
Gtt., gtt (guttatim)	drops	—	gotas
GU	genitourinary	—	genitourinario
GYN	gynecology	GIN	ginecología
h	hour	—	hora
HB	hepatitis B vaccine	VHB	vacuna B de hepatitis
HCG	human chorionic gonadotropin	GCH	gonadotropina coriónica humana
HCT	hematocrit	—	hematócrito
HCVD	hypertensive cardiovascular disease	ECVH	enfermedad cardiovascular hipertensiva
HD	hemodialysis	—	hemodiálisis
HD	hip disarticulation	DC	desarticulación de la cadera
HDL	high density lipoprotein	LAD	lipoproteína de alta densidad
HGT	height	—	altura
HIB	haemophilus b conjugate vaccine	HBI	vacuna conjugada de hemofilo b
HIV	human immunodeficiency virus	VIH	virus inmunodeficiente humano
HLA	human lymphocitary antigen	ALH	antígeno linfocitario humano
HM	health maintenance	MS	mantenimiento de la salud
H₂O	water	—	agua
HNP	herniated nucleous pulposus	—	hernia del núcleo pulposo
HR	heart rate	IC	índice cardíaco
hs (hora somni)	at bedtime	—	a la hora de acostarse
hypo	hypodermically		inyectado
Hyst	hysterectomy	Hist	histerectomía
ICF	intracellular fluid	LIC	líquido intracelular
ICH	intracerebral hematoma	HIC	hematoma intracerebral
ICH	intracraneal hemorrhage	HIC	hemorragia intracraneana
ICSH	interstitial cell-stimulating hormone	HECI	hormona de estimulación de célula intersticial
ICU	intensive care unit	SCI	sala de cuidado intensivo
I&D	incision and drainage	—	incisión y drenaje
ID	identification	—	identificación
id	infectious disease		enfermedad contagiosa
IDDM	insulin-dependent diabetes mellitus	DMID	diabetes melitus insulinodependiente
IE	infective endocarditis	EI	endocarditis infecciosa
IgG	immunoglobulin G	—	inmunoglobulina G
IgM	immunoglobulin M	—	inmunoglobulina M
II	icteric index	—	índice ictérico
im	intramuscular	in	intramuscular
Imp	impression	—	impresión
INFO	information	—	información
I&O	intake and output	AG	absorción y gasto
IOL	intraocular lens	LIO	lente intraocular
IPD	intermittent peritoneal dialysis	DPI	diálisis peritoneal intermitente
IPPB	intermittent positive pressure breathing	RIPP	respiración intermitente con presión positiva
IPV	polio vaccine shots	VPI	vacunas de polio inyectadas
IQ	intelligence quotient	CI	cociente de inteligencia
ISE	ion selective electrodes	EIS	electrodos de iones seleccionados

continued

Abbr.	English / Inglés	Abreu	Spanish / Español
ISG	immune serum globulin	GSI	globulina sérica inmunológica
ITP	idiopathic thrombocytopenic purpura	PTI	púrpura trombocitopénica idiopática
IU	international unit	UI	unidad internacional
IUD	intrauterine device	DIU	dispositivo intrauterino
IUM	intrauterine monitoring		monitoreo intrauterino
IUP	intrauterine pregnancy	EIU	embarazo intrauterino
IUT	intrauterine transfusion	TIU	transfusión intrauterina
IV	intravenous	VIV	vía intravenosa
IVC	intravenous cholangiogram	CIV	colangiograma intravenoso
IVP	intravenous pyelogram	PIV	pielograma intravenoso
K	potassium	—	potasio
KCL	potassium chloride	—	cloruro de potasio
KD	knee disarticulation	DR	desarticulación de la rodilla
KUB	kidney, ureter, bladder	RUV	riñón, uréter, vejiga (placa simple de abdomen)
KVO	keep vein open	MVA	mantener la vena abierta
L	left	Iz.	izquierdo-a
L	leukoplakia	L	leucoplaquia
LA	left atrium	AI	aurícula izquierda
LAB	laboratory	—	laboratorio
LAP	laparotomy	—	laparotomía
LBBB	left bundle branch block	BRI	bloqueo de rama izquierda
LDH	lactic dehydrogenase	DHL	deshidrogenasa láctica
LDL	low density lipoprotein	LBD	lipoproteína de baja densidad
LE	lupus erythematosus	—	lupus eritematoso
LE	left eye	OI	ojo izquierdo
LFT	liver function test	PFH	prueba de función hepática
LH	luteinizing hormone	HL	hormona luteinizante
LLE	left lower extremity	EIIz	extermidad inferior izquierda
LLQ	left lower quadrant	CIIz	cuadrante inferior izquierdo
LM	last menstrual period	UPM	último periodo menstrual
LP	lumbar puncture	PL	punción lumbar
LRF	luteinizing releasing factor	FLE	factor luteinizante de descargo
LS	liver scan	EH	escán del hígado
LS	lumbar spine	EL	espina lumbar
LUE	left upper extremity	ESIz	extremidad superior izquierda
LUQ	left upper quadrant	CSIz	cuadrante superior izquierdo
L&W	living and well	V y S	vivo y saludable
MAE	moves all extremities	MTE	mueve todas las extremidades
MAT	multifocal atrial tachycardia	TAM	taquicardia auricular multifocal
mc	millicurie	—	milicurie
MCA	middle cerebral artery	ACM	arteria cerebral media
MCB	medium corpuscular volume	VCM	volumen corpuscular medio
MCH	mean corpuscular hemoglobin	ICH	índice corpuscular de hemoglobina
MCNS	minimal change nephrotic syndrome	SN	síndrome nefrótico de cambio mínimo
MCV	mean corpuscular index	IVC	índice de volumen corpuscular
MD	medical doctor	DM	doctor en Medicina
ME	middle ear	OM	oído medio
MED	medicine	—	medicina
MHCM	medium hemoglobin corpular concentration	CCHM	media de concentración corpuscular de hemoglobina
MI	myocardial infarction	IC	infarto cardíaco
mi	mitral insufficiency	IM	insuficiencia mitral
min	minute	dim	diminuto-a
MM	mucous membrane	—	membrana mucosa

Abbr.	English / Inglés	Abreu	Spanish / Español
MMR	measles, mumps, and rubella vaccine	VSPR	vacuna triple de sarampión, paperas y rubeola
MR	mitral regurgitation	RM	regurgitación mitral
MRI	magnetic resonance imaging	IRM	imagen de resonancia magnética
MS	multiple sclerosis	EM	esclerosis múltiple
MS	mitral stenosis	EM	estenosis mitral
MT	medical technologist	TM	técnico médico
MVI	multivitamins	—	multivitaminas
mx	mixture	—	mezcla
NA	nursing assistant	AE	asistente de enfermería
N / A	not applicable	—	no aplicable
Na	sodium	—	sodio
NEC	necrotizing enterocolitis	EC	enterocolitis
neurol	neurology	—	neurología
NG	nasogastric	—	nasogástrico
NH	neonatal hyperthyroidism	HN	hipertiroidismo neonatal
NK	no known allergies	SAC	sin alergia conocida
NPO	nothing by mouth	NPB	nada por la boca
NS	nephrotic syndrome	SN	síndrome nefrótico
NST	nonstress test	PSE	prueba sin esfuerzo
NSR	normal sinus rhythm	RSN	ritmo sinusal normal
NTG	nitroglycerin	—	nitroglicerina
N&V	nausea and vomiting	—	náusea y vómitos
NVD	neck, vein distention	DVY	distensión de las venas yugulares
OA	osteoarthritis	OA	osteoartritis
OB, Obs	obstetrics	—	obstetricia
OC	oral contraceptive	AO	anticonceptivos orales
od	once a day	—	una vez al día
omn hor (omni hora)	every hour	—	cada hora
on (omni nocte)	every night	—	todas las noches
O&P	ova and parasites	P	parásitos
op	operation	—	operación
OPV	oral poliovaccine	VPO	vacuna oral de poliomielitis
OR	operating room	—	sala de operaciones, quirófano
ORTHO	orthopedic	ORTO	ortopédico
OS,RE	right eye	OD	ojo derecho
OS,LE	left eye	OI	ojo izquierdo
OT	occupational therapy	TO	terapia ocupacional
OU	both eyes	—	ambos ojos
P	prognosis	—	prognosis
P	pulse	—	pulso
p (post)	after	—	pasado (el tiempo de), después de
P.A.	pernicious anemia	AP	anemia perniciosa
PA	pulmonary artery	AP	arteria pulmonar
PAC	premature atrial contraction	CAP	contracción auricular prematura
Pap	Papanicolaou	—	Papanicolaou
PAT	paroxysmal atrial tachycardia	TAP	taquicardia auricular paroxística
PATH	pathology	PAT	patología
PA view	posteroanterior view (radiology)	VPA	vista postero-anterior (radiología)
pc (post cibus)	after meals	—	después de las comidas
PCO$_2$	carbon dioxide content of blood	—	contenido de dióxido de carbono en la sangre
PCP	Pneumocystis Carinii pneumonia	—	Pneumocistis Carinii pneumonia
PD	pulse deficit	DP	déficit de pulso
PDR	pulse volume recorder	RVP	registro del volumen del pulso

continued

Most Common Medical Abbreviations / Abreviaturas médicas más usuales

Abbr.	English / Inglés	Abreu.	Spanish / Español
PE	physical examination	EF	examen físico
pe	pulmonary embolism	ep	embolia pulmonar
PERRLA	pupils equal, round, and equally reactive to light and accommodation	PIRRLA	pupilas iguales y redondas de igual reacción a la luz y acomodación
PFC	persistent fetal circulation	CFP	circulación fetal persistente
PGH	pituitary growth hormone	HPC	hormona pituitaria del crecimiento
pH	hydrogen ion concentration (acidity)	—	concentración de iones de hidrógeno (acidez)
PH	pulmonary hypertension	HP	hipertensión pulmonar
PI	present illness	EF	enfermedad actual
PICU	pediatric intensive care unit	SPCI	sala pediátrica de cuidado intensivo
PID	pelvic inflammatory disease	EIP	enfermedad inflamatoria de la pelvis
PKU	phenylketonuria	CF	cetonuria fenil
PLTS	platelets		plaquetas
pm (*post meridien*)	afternoon	—	pasado meridiano
PMH	past medical history	HM	historia médica
PMN	polymorphonuclear	—	polimorfonuclear
PND	paroxysmal nocturnal dyspnea	DPN	disnea paroxística nocturna
PNH	paroxysmal nocturnal hemoglobinuria	HPN	hemoglobinuria paroxística nocturna
PNS	peripheral nervous system	SNP	sistema nervioso periférico
PO (*per os*)	by mouth	—	por vía oral
PO$_2$	oxygen content of blood		contenido de oxígeno en la sangre
POS	positive	—	positivo
Post-OP	after operation	—	post operatorio
p.p.m.	pulses per minute	i.p.m.	pulsaciones por minuto
PR	per rectum	PVR	por vía rectal
PR	pulse ratio	FP	frecuencia del pulso
Pre-op	before operation	—	anterior a la operación
prn (*pro re nata*)	as needed	—	cuando sea necesario
PSA	prostatic specific antigen	AEP	antígeno prostático específico
psych	psychiatry	psiq	psiquiatría
P.T.	physical therapy	TF	terapia física
PT	prothrombin time	TP	tiempo de protrombina
PTA	prior to admission		pre-admisión
PTCA	percutaneous transluminal coronary angioplasty	ACPT	angioplastia coronaria percutánea transluminal
PTH	parathyroid hormone	HP	hormona paratiroidea
PTH	pseudohypoparathyroidism rickets	—	pseudohipoparatiroidismo
PTT	partial thromboplastia time	TPT	tiempo parcial de tromboplastia
PUD	peptic ulcer disease	UP	úlcera péptica
PV	peripheral vision	VP	visión periférica
PVC	premature ventricular contraction	CVP	contracción ventricular prematura
q (*quaque*)	every	—	cada; todo
QA	quality assurance	SC	seguridad de calidad
QC	quality control	CC	control de calidad
qd (*quaque die*)	every day	—	diariamente
q.h. (*quaque hora*)	every hour	—	cada hora
qhs	at hour of sleep	—	a la hora de dormir

Most Common Medical Abbreviations / Abreviaturas médicas más usuales

Abbr.	English / Inglés	Abreu.	Spanish / Español
qid (*quater in die*)	four times a day	—	cuatro veces al día
qod	every other day	—	días alternos
qns (*quantum non suffict*)	quantity not sufficient	—	cantidad insuficiente
q.q.h. (*quaque quarta*)	every quarter of an hour	—	cada cuarto de hora
QS (*quantum suffict*)	enough amount	—	en suficiente cantidad
q 2h	every two hours	—	cada dos horas
R	respiration	—	respiración
RA	right atrium	AD	aurícula derecha
rad	radiation absorbed dose	dra	dosis de radiación absorbida
RAM	rapid alternating movements	MAR	movimientos alternos rápidos
RAP	recurrent abdominal pain	DAR	dolor abdominal recurrente
RBC	red blood cells	GR	glóbulos rojos (hematíes)
RDS	respiratory distress syndrome	SDR	síndrome de dificultad respiratoria
RE	right eye	OD	ojo derecho
REM	rapid eye movement	MRO	movimientos rápidos oculares
RF	renal failure	IR	insuficiencia renal
RF	rheumatoid factor	FR	factor reumatoideo
Rh	blood factor	RH	factor sanguíneo
RHD	rheumatic heart disease	ERC	enfermedad reumática cardíaca
RI	respiratory insufficiency	IR	insuficiencia respiratoria
RIA	radioimmunoassay	ERI	estudio radioinmunológico
RK	radial keratotomy surgery	CQR	cirugía de queratotomía radial
RLE	right lower extremity	EID	extremidad inferior derecha
RLL	right lower lobe	LID	lóbulo inferior derecho
RLQ	right lower quadrant	CID	cuadrante inferior derecho
RM	regurgitation murmur	SR	soplo de regurgitación
RM	*rigor mortis*	RM	*rigor mortis*
RNA	ribonucleic acid	ARN	ácido ribonucleico
R / O	rule out		elimínese
ROM	range of motion		alcance en el movimiento
ROS	review of systems		interrogatorio por aparatos
RPR	rapid plasma reagin test	PRP	prueba de reagina de plasma
RR	respiratory rate	IR	índice respiratorio
RT	radiation therapy	TR	terapia de radiación
RTA	renal tubular acidosis	ATR	acidosis tubular renal
RU	routine urinalysis	AO	análisis de orina
RUL	right upper lobe	LSD	lóbulo superior derecho
RUP	right upper extremity	ESD	extremidad superior derecho
RV	right ventricle	VD	ventrículo derecho
RVH	renovascular hypertension	HRV	hipertensión renovascular
Rx	prescription	—	receta, prescripción
s (*sine*)	without	—	sin
s. (*signetur*)	label	—	desígnese
S&A	sugar and acetone	A y A	azúcar y acetona
SA	spontaneous abortion	AE	aborto espontáneo
SBE	subacute bacterial endocarditis	EBS	endocarditis bacteriana subaguda
SBO	spina bifida occulta	EBO	espina bífida oculta
SCD	sequential compression devices	DCS	dispositivos de compresión en secuencia
SE	Status Epilepticus	SE	estado o condición epiléptica
SEM	systolic ejection murmur	SSE	soplo sistólico de eyección

continued

Abbr.	English / Inglés	Abreu.	Spanish / Español
SGOT	serum glutamic oxaloacetic transaminase	TGOS	transaminasa glutámica–oxaloacética del suero
SGPT	serum glutamic pyruvic transaminase	TGPS	transaminasa glutámicopirúvica del suero
SH	serum hepatitis	HS	hepatitis sérica
SI units	international system of units	SIun	sistema internacional de unidades
SIADH	syndrome of inappropriate antidiuretic hormone secretion	SSHAI	síndrome de secreción hormonal antidiurética insuficiente
SIDS	sudden infant death syndrome	SMIS	síndrome de muerte infantil súbita
SLUD	salivation, lacrimation, urination, and diarrhea	SLOD	salivación, lagrimeo, orina y diarrea
SM	systolic murmurs	SS	soplos sistólicos
SOB	short of breath	FDR	falta de respiración
sol (solutio)	solution	—	solución
sp.gr.	specific gravity	gr.esp.	gravedad específica
SRM	systolic regurgitant murmurs	SSR	soplo sistólico regurgitante medio-a
ss	half		
staph	staphylococcus		estafilococo
stat (statim)	immediately	—	inmediatamente
STD	sexually transmitted disease	ETS	enfermedad de transmisión sexual
strep	streptococcus	estrep	estreptococo
subcu, SC	subcutaneously	—	subcutáneo-a
surg.	surgery, surgical	cirg.	cirugía
SVR	systemic vascular resistance	SVR	resistencia vascular sistémica
SVT	supraventricular tachycardia	TSV	taquicardia supraventricular
Sx	symptoms	—	síntomas
T	temperature	—	temperatura
T&A	tonsillectomy and adenoidectomy	T y A	tonsilectomía y adenoidectomía
TAB	tablet	—	tableta
TB	tuberculosis	TB	tuberculosis
TFT	thyroid function tests	PFT	pruebas funcionales de la tiroides
THR	total hip replacement	RTC	reemplazo total de la cadera
TI	tricuspid insufficiency	IT	insuficiencia tricuspídea
tid (ter in die)	three times a day	—	tres veces al día
TORCHES syndrome	toxoplasmosis, rubella, cytomegalovirus, herpes simplex, syphilis	—	síndrome de toxoplasmosis, rubeola, citomegalovirus, herpes simple, sífilis
TPR	temperature, pulse, and respiration	TPR	temperatura, pulso y respiración
TR	transrectal ultrasonography	UT	ultrasonografía transrectal
TR	tricuspid regurgitation	RT	regurgitación tricuspídea
TRH	thyrotropin-releasing hormone	HLT	hormona liberadora de tirotropina
TSH	thyroid-stimulating hormone	HTE	hormona tirostimulante
TSS	toxic shock syndrome	SCHT	síndrome de choque tóxico
TURBT	transurethral resection of bladder tumor	RTUTV	resección transuretral de tumor vesical
TURP	transurethral resection of prostrate	RTUP	resección transuretral de la próstata
TV	tricuspid valve	VT	válvula tricúspide
TWE	tap water enema	E	enema de agua de pila
TX	transplant	trans	transplante
Tx	treatment	—	tratamiento
U	units	—	unidades
UA	urinalysis	—	examen de orina

Abbr.	English / Inglés	Abreu	Spanish / Español
UC	uterine contractions	CU	contracciones uterinas
UC	ulcerative colitis	—	colitis ulcerativa
UCD	usual childhood diseases	ECI	enfermedades comunes de la infancia
UGI	upper gastrointestinal tract	TGA	estudio del tracto gastrointestinal alto
ung	ointment	—	ungüento
ur	urine		orina
URI	upper respiratory infection	ITRS	infección del tracto respiratorio superior
US	ultrasound imaging	IUS	imagen de ultrasonido
UTI	urinary tract infection	IVU	infección de las vías urinarias
Vag	vaginal	—	vaginal
VD	veneral disease	EV	enfermedad venérea
VHD	ventricular heart disease	EVC	enfermedad ventricular del corazón
VLDL	very low density lipids	LBD	lípidos de baja densidad
VPC	ventricular premature contractions	CVP	contracciones ventriculares prematuras
VR	ventricular hypertrophy	HV	hipertrofia ventricular
vs	vital signs	sv	signos vitales
VSD	ventricular septal defect	DVS	defecto ventricular septal
WBC	white blood cells	GB	glóbulos blancos
WC	wheel chair	—	silla de ruedas
WR	Wassermann reaction	RW	reacción de Wassermann
Wt	weight	P	peso
y / o	years old	Ed	edad
Z	zone	—	zona

Conversion Tables

The **Conversion Tables** facilitate vocabulary building in both languages. They also instruct the reader in the recognition of the fundamental orthographic differences between Spanish and English and in the etymological analysis of words.

Consult the **Conversion Tables** when building a vocabulary of medical words or interpreting medical words either in Spanish or in English.

Table 1: Rules for orthographic changes and differences in spelling between English and Spanish words.

Table 2: Most commonly used roots.

Table 3: Most frequently used prefixes.

Table 4: Most frequently used suffixes in surgical procedures, diagnoses, and symptoms.

The three components listed in Tables 2, 3, and 4 may or may not be together at the same time in a medical term.

Start in Table 1 by learning the orthographic changes and differences in spelling between English and Spanish words. This practice will help you to independently increase your vocabulary in Spanish and English.

When forming or interpreting a medical term it is advisable to find the meaning of the **suffix** first. For example, given the medical term **gastropathy / gastropatía,** the meaning of the suffix (in Table 4) **-pathy / -patía** is **disease / enfermedad;** the root of the term (in Table 2) is **gastr-, stomach / estómago.** The vowel **o** is added to the root to join another term which begins in a consonant. The interpretation of the medical word results in: **disease of the stomach / enfermedad del estómago.** When interpreting or building a medical term keep in mind that a word root is the main element of the term, often indicating a body part. A medical term may contain more than one root element.

A **prefix** used at the beginning of a medical term either changes its meaning or makes it more specific. In the term **hypodermic,** for example, the three components or elements are present:

prefix	word root	suffix
hypo	derm	-ic (adjective ending)
(under)	(skin)	(pertaining to)

The meaning of the word root becomes more specific after the **prefix,** while the **suffix** indicates, in this case, how the term relates to the root's meaning.

Tablas de conversión

Las **Tablas de conversión** facilitan el aprendizaje continuado del vocabulario en ambos idiomas. Al mismo tiempo, enseñan al lector a reconocer las diferencias ortográficas fundamentales entre el español y el inglés, así como a analizar los vocablos etimológicamente.

Consulte las **Tablas** cuando trate de crear nuevos términos médicos o de interpretar el significado de un término no conocido, ya sea en español o en inglés.

Tabla 1:   cambios ortográficos y diferencia en la escritura de palabras entre el inglés y el español.
Tabla 2:   raíces más comunes.
Tabla 3:   prefijos usados con más frecuencia.
Tabla 4:   sufijos usados con más frecuencia en cirugía, síntomas y diagnósticos.

Estos tres últimos elementos (raíces, prefijos y sufijos) pueden o no estar presentes al mismo tiempo en un término médico.

Comience en la Tabla 1 para ver los cambios ortográficos que ocurren entre las palabras inglesas y las españolas. Al componer o interpretar un término médico, es aconsejable encontrar primero el significado del sufijo si se está haciendo su composición o interpretación en inglés. Por ejemplo, dado el término médico **gastropatía / gastropathy,** el significando del sufijo -patía / -pathy (V. la Tabla 4) es **enfermedad / disease,** la raíz o radical (V. la Tabla 2) es **gastr-, estómago / stomach.** En este caso, la vocal **o** se ha añadido a la raíz para unirla a otro vocablo que empieza con una consonante. El significado del término médico es: **enfermedad del estómago / disease of the stomach.** Cuando se crea o interpreta un término médico, se debe tener en cuenta que la raíz es el elemento principal del vocablo y que se refiere generalmente a una parte del cuerpo humano. Un mismo término médico puede tener más de una raíz.

El **prefijo** es un elemento que va delante de la raíz y cuya presencia modifica el significado de la misma o lo hace más específico. Tomemos, por ejemplo, la palabra **hypodermic / hipodérmico.** Si separamos los tres elementos o componentes tendremos:

prefijo	*raíz*	*sufijo*
hipo-	derm-	-ico (terminación adjectiva)
(bajo)	(piel)	(referente a)

El **prefijo** hace más específico el significado de la raíz, mientras que el **sufijo** indica a que se refiere el término o simplemente califica la parte definida por la raíz.

Conversion Table 1 / Tabla de conversión 1

Orthographic Changes / Cambios ortográficos

English / Inglés	Spanish / Español	English / Inglés	Spanish / Español
cc	c	accommodate	acomodar
cc[1]	cc before e and i	accessory	accesorio
		accident	accidente
ch	c	character	carácter
ch before e and i	qui	chemistry	química
		chiropractor	quiropráctico
comm-	com-	commissure	comisura
im-	in-	immersion	inmersión
qu	cu	quart	cuarto
r[2]	l	paper	papel
s	es[3]	special	especial
		gastrospasm	gastroespasmo
ph	f	phlebitis	flebitis
pn[4]	pn or n	pneumonia	pneumonía, neumonía
ps	ps or s	psychology	psicología, sicología
rh	r	rheumatic	reumático
th	t	therapy	terapia
y[5]	i	typhoid	tifoidea

[1]In Spanish words only two double consonants are used: cc and nn. The ll and the rr are considered to be single characters in the Spanish alphabet.
En español sólo hay dos consonantes dobles: cc y nn. La ll y la rr se consideran letras separadas en el alfabeto español.
[2]May change to l at the end of a word.
Puede combiar a l al final de palabra.
[3]Only before consonants p and t, including compound words.
Sólo delante de las consonantes p y t incluso en palabras compuestas.
[4]pn and ps may drop the initial p in Spahish.
En español se puede omitir la p inicial en las palabras que comienzan en pn o ps.
[5]When y is not at the end of the word.
Cuando la y no es final.

Conversion Table 1 / Tabla de conversión 1

Orthographic Changes and Cognates / Cambios ortográficos y cognadas

	Examples	
1. There are only two double consonants in Spanish words: **cc** and **nn**	acción accidente innovación	
2. Change **mm** to **m** except when preceded by **i**	co**mm**unicate co**mm**unication	co**m**unicar co**m**unicación
3. **ch changes to c** except when it is before **e** or **i** then, it changes to **qu**	me**ch**anic **ch**oleric **ch**imera **ch**emotherapy	me**c**ánico co**l**érico **qu**imera **qu**imioterapia
4. Drop the **h- inside words** except in *alcohol**	t**h**erapy aut**h**orization hemo**rrh**age	terapia autorización hemorragia
5. **ph becomes f** Many English words with **ph** at the beginning or in the middle of the word correspond to **f** in Spanish.	**ph**armacy **ph**ase dip**h**theria	**f**armacia **f**ase difteria
6. Drop one **-s,** there are no words with double **ss**es in Spanish.	nece**ss**ity di**ss**ect fi**ss**ura	nece**s**idad di**s**ecar fi**s**ura
7. English words that begin in **s + consonant** have corresponding Spanish words beginning in **es-**.	**s**pecial **s**cene **s**can	**es**pecial **es**cena **es**cán
8. The **y** in the middle of a word may change to **-i**.	cr**y**stal s**y**philis tr**y**psin	cr**i**stal s**í**filis tr**i**psina
9. **gram** + **-a = grama** **Add** -a to words ending in **-gram**.	**diagram**	diagra**ma**
10. The suffix *-um* drops and is substituted by **-o** in Spanish.	stadi**um** pendul**um** rostr**um**	estadi**o** péndul**o** rostr**o**
11. The suffix *-osis* refering** to condition or disease remains the same in Spanish.	dermat**osis** lymphocyt**osis** anisocyt**osis**	dermat**osis** linfocit**osis** anisocit**osis**
12. **-ty becomes -dad** Many words in English ending in *-ty* have a corresponding Spanish word ending in *-dad*.	fideli**ty** communi**ty** reali**ty**	fideli**dad** comuni**dad** reali**dad**
13. **-ous becomes -oso or -osa** Many words ending in *-ous* in English have a corresponding word in Spanish ending in **-oso** or **osa**.	vigor**ous** numer**ous** por**ous**	vigor**oso** numer**oso** por**oso**
14. *-tion* becomes *-ción* in Spanish	educa**tion** communica**tion** administra**tion**	educa**ción** comunica**ción** administra**ción**
15. ***Exact cognates?*** Words in Spanish and English that are spelled exactly the same way have the same root and mean the same: **control, factor, local**	However, there are other cognates that have similar or the same spelling and are misleading, because the meaning could be different: **real** can be translated **real** or **royal; actual** can mean **current;** asistir can be translated as **to attend** or **to help;** while **atender** in Spanish means to **pay attention** or **to take care of.**	

*and other words of Arabic origin
**See table of conversions 2–4 for other word changes in prefixes and suffixes in English and Spanish.

Conversion Table 2 / Tabla de conversión 2

A **root** is the main part or element of a term. In medicine, it generally refers to a body part. Compound words (words with more than one root) are common in medical terminology.

   La **raíz** o **radical** es el elemento principal de la palabra. En medicina la **raíz** se refiere generalmente a órganos o partes del cuerpo. En la terminología médica abundan palabras compuestas (palabras formadas por más de un elemento o raíz).

Most Commonly Used Roots / Raíces más frecuentes

English / Inglés	Spanish / Español	Meaning / Significado	Example / Ejemplo[1]
acou-	acu-	hearing / sonido	acoustics / acústica
aden-	aden-	gland / glándula	adenoids
aer-	aer-	air / aire	aerogenic / aerogénico
angi-	angi-	vessel / vaso	angiotitis
ankyl-, anchyl-	anquil-	immobility, stiffness / inmovilidad, rigidez	anchylosis / anquilosis
arth-	art-	joint / articulación	arthritic / artrítico
brachi-	braqui-	arm / brazo	brachialgia / braquialgia
bronchi-	bronqui-	bronchi / bronquios	bronchopathy / broncopatía
bucca-	buca-	mouth / boca	buccal / bucal
cardi-	cardi-	heart / corazón	cardiodynia / cardiodinia
carpo-	carpo-	wrist / carpo	carpal
cephal-	cefal-	head / cabeza	cephalitis / cefalitis
cerebr-	cerebr-	brain / cerebro	cerebral
cerv-	cerv-	neck / cerviz, cuello	cervical
cheil-	queil-	lip / labio	cheilectomy / queilectomía
cost-	cost-	rib / costilla	costal
crani-	crane-	skull / cráneo	cranial / craneal
cysto-	cisto-	bladder / vejiga	cystocele / cistocele
dactyl-	dactil-	finger, toe / dedo	dactylitis / dactilitis
derm-	derm-	dermis / piel	dermatitis
duoden-	duoden-	duodenum / duodeno	duodenohepatic / duodenohepático
encephal-	encefal-	brain / cerebro	encephaloma / encefaloma
enter-	enter-	intestine / intestino	enteritis
fibro-	fibro-	fiber / fibra	fibroma
gastr-	gastr-	stomach / estómago	gastritis
genu-	genu-	knee / rodilla	genuflexion / genuflexión
gloss-	glosa-	tongue / lengua	glossalgia / glosalgia
glyco-	glico-	sugar / glucosa, azúcar	glycogen / glicógeno
hem-, hemo-	hem-, hemo	blood / sangre	hematoxic / hematóxico
hepat-	hepat-	liver / hígado	hepatitis
histo-	histo-	tissue / tejido	histoma
homo-	homo-	same, equal / igual	homologous / homólogo
hydr-	hidro-	water / agua, líquido	hydrocele / hidrocele
hypn-	hipno-	sleep / sueño	hypnosis / hipnosis
hyster-	hister-	uterus / útero	hysterectomy / histerectomía
ili-	ili-	flank / ilíaco	iliocostal
luek-	leuc-	white corpuscle / leucocito	leukemia / leucemia
lingu-	lingu-	tongue / lengua	lingual
lip-	lip-	fat / grasa	lipoide
lith-	lith-	stone / cálculo	lithotriptor / litotriturador
mening-	mening-	membrane / membrana	meningitis
metr-	metr-	uterus / útero	metrorrhagia / metrorragia
my-	mi-	muscle / músculo	myocardium / miocardio
myel-	miel-	marrow / médula	myelitis / mielitis

[1]When the words have an identical spelling and meaning in both languages, the Spanish translation is not given.
Cuando las palabras tienen igual significado y se escriben igual en ambos idiomas, la traducción al español se omite.

English / Inglés	Spanish / Español	Meaning / Significado	Example / Ejemplo
narc-	narc-	sleep / sueño	narcotism / narcotismo
naso-	naso-	nose / nariz	nasopharynx / nasofaringe
ne-, neo-	neo-	new, recent / nuevo, reciente	neonatal
nephr-	nefr-	kidney / riñón	nephritis / nefritis
neur-	neur-	nerve / nervio	neurotripsy / neurotripsia
noct-	noct-	night / noche	nocturia
nucle-	nucle-, nucleo-	nucleous / núcleo	nucleic / nucleico
oculo-	oculo-	eye / ojo	ocular
oo-	oo-, ovo-	ova, egg / óvulo, huevo	ooplasm / ooplasma
oste-	oste-	bone / hueso	osteosis
oto-	oto-	ear / oído	otodynia / otodinia
ovari-	ovari	ovary / ovario	ovariectomy / ovariectomía
ox-	ox-	oxygen / oxígeno	oxygenation / oxigenación
path(o)	pato-	disease / enfermedad	pathology / patología
ped-	ped-	child / infante	pediatrics / pediatría
phleb-	fleb-	vein / vena	phlebitis / flebitis
pleur-	pleur-	pleura / pleura	pleuritis
pneum-	pneum-, neum-	air, lung / aire, pulmón	pneumothorax / neumotórax
prostat-	prostat-	prostate / próstata	prostatic / prostático
psych-	psic-, sic-	mind, spirit / mente	psychology / psicología
pupill-	pupil-	pupile / pupila	pupillometer / pupilómetro
pyel-	piel-	renal / renal	pyelitis / pielitis
ren-	ren-	kidney / riñon	renal
retin-	retin-	retina / retina	retinitis
rhin-	rin-	nose / nariz	rhinoclesis / rinoclesis
sarco-	sarco-	flesh / carne	sarcoma
semi-	semi-	half, partial / parcial, medio	semiflexion / semiflexión
sinus-	sinus-	cavity / cavidad	sinusitis
spermat-	espermat-	sperm, semen / esperma, semen	spermatoid / espermatoide
spondylo-	espondilo-	vertebra / vértebra	spondylous / espondiloso
strepto-	estrepto-	twisted / torcido	streptococcal / estreptocócico
techno-	tecno-	skill / técnica	technology / tecnología
teno-	teno-	tendon / tendón	tendonitis
thoraco-	torac-	chest, thorax / pecho, tórax	thoracic / torácico
thrombo-	trombo-	clot / coágulo	thrombosis / trombosis
toxic-	toxic-	toxic / tóxico	toxicity / toxicidad
ur-, uro-	ur-, uro-	urine / orina	urinary / urinario
vas-	vas-	vessel, duct / vaso	vascular
ventro-	ventro-	abdomen, anterior part / abdomen, porción anterior	ventroscopy / ventroscopía
xeno-	xeno-	foreign, strange / extranjero, extraño	xenophthalmia / xenoftalmia

Conversion Table 3 / Tabla de conversión 3

Prefixes are placed at the beginning of words; in medical terms the **prefix** is the element which changes the meaning of the term or makes it more specific. Prefixes are generally formed by one or two syllables. Most medical prefixes, roots, and suffixes are derived from Latin and Greek.

Los **prefijos** se colocan al principio de la palabra; en términos médicos el **prefijo** es el elemento que cambia el significado del término y lo hace más específico. Los prefijos tienen generalmente una o dos sílabas. La mayor parte de los prefijos, raíces y sufijos se derivan del latín y del griego.

Most Commonly Used Prefixes / Prefijos de uso más frecuente

English / Inglés	Spanish / Español	Meaning / Significado	Example / Ejemplo[1]
a-, an-	a-	lack of, without / falta de, sin	apathy / apatía
ab-	a-	away from / lejos de, sin	abnormal / anormal
ad-	ad-	toward, near to / hacia, con respecto a	adduction / aducción
ambi-	ambi-	both / ambos	ambidextrous / ambidextro
amphi-	anfi-	on both sides, double / en los dos lados, doble	amphibious / anfibio
ana-	ana-	up, back, again / sobre, otra vez, excesivo	anadipsia
ante-	ante-	before / antes de	antenatal
anti-	anti-	against, reversed / contra, reversión	antibiotic / antibiótic
bi-	bi-	twice, double / dos, doble	bifocal
brady-	bradi-	slow / despacio	bradycardia / bradicardia
circum-	circun-	about, around / alrededor de	circumcision / circuncisión
com-	co-	together, with / junto a, con	commisure / comisura
con-	con-	with, together / junto a, con	congenital / congénito
contra-	contra-	against, opposite / opuesto a, en contra de	contraceptive / contraceptivo
de-	de-, des-	away from, to suppress / separación, suprimir	dehydrated / deshidratado-a
dia-	dia-	through, across / por medio, a través	diaphragm / diafragma
diplo-	diplo-	double / doble	diplocardia
dis-	dis-	away, apart / separado	distention / distensión
dys-	dis-	bad, improper / malo, impropio	dysentery / disentería
e-, ex-	ex-	out, away from / fuera, lejos de	excrete / excretar
ecto-	ecto-	external, outside / afuera, sin	ectoderm / ectodermia
em-	em-	in / adentro de	embolic / embólico
endo-	endo-	inside, within / dentro, entre	endometrium / endometrio
epi-	epi-	upon, on / sobre, encima	epidermia
extra-	extra-	outside / fuera de	extracardial / extracardíaco
hemi-	hemi-	half / medio	hemisphere / hemisferio
hyper-	hiper-	excessive / excesivo	hypertensive / hipertensivo
hypo-	hipo-	under, deficient / falta de, deficiente	hypoglycemia / hipoglicemia
im-, in-	in-	in, into / dentro, junto	infiltration / infiltración
infra-	infra-	below / debajo	infraorbital
intra-	intra-	between / entre	intraglobular
intro-	intro-	into, within / dentro de	introversion / introversión
lingu-	lingu-	tongue / lengua	lingual
mal-	mal-	bad, abnormal / malo, anormal	malocclusion / maloclusión

[1]When the words have identical spelling and meaning in both languages, the Spanish translation is not given.
Cuando las palabras tienen igual significado y se escriben igual en ambos idiomas, la traducción al español se omite.

English / Inglés	Spanish / Español	Meaning / Significado	Example / Ejemplo[1]
meso-	meso-	in the middle / en el medio	mesocardia
meta-	meta-	beyond / más allá, extendido	metastasis / metástasis
micro-	micro-	small, minute / pequeño, diminuto	micrococcus / micrococo
neur-	neur-	nerve / nervio	neurosis
para-	para-	beside, near / al lado, cerca	paracardiac / paracardíaco
per-	per-	through, excessive / través, excesivo	perforation / perforación
peri-	peri-	around / alrededor de	perithelial / peritelial
poly-	poli-	many, several / varios	polyacid / poliácido
post-	post-	after, behind / después, detrás	postfebrile / postfebril
pneum-	neum-	lung / pulmón	pneumonia / neumonía
pre-	pre-	before, in front / antes, en frente	prediastole / prediástole
psych-	psico-	soul, mind / alma, mente	psychotherapy / psicoterapia
pyro-	piro-	heat, fire / calor, fuego	pyrogen / pirógeno
re-	re-	back again / de regreso otra vez	revive / revivir
retro-	retro-	backward; behind / en retroceso, detrás	retrolingual
schizo-	esquizo-	division / división	schizophrenia / esquizofrenia
semi-	semi-	partly, half / medio, parcial	semiflexion / semiflexión
sub-	sub-	under / debajo	subneural
super-	super-	above, upper / encima de, superior	supercentral
supra-	supra-	above / encima de	supranasal
sym-, syn-	sin-	together, with / junto, con	synovia / sinovia
tachy-	taqui-	accelerated, fast / rápido, acelerado	tachycardia / taquicardia
tetra-	tetra-	four / cuatro	tetralogy / tetralogía
therap-	terap-	treatment / tratamiento	therapeuetic / terapéutico
thromb-	tromb-	clot / coágulo	thrombosis / trombosis
trans-	trans-, tras-	across, through / transversal, a través	transurethral / transuretral
trauma-	trauma-	wound, trauma / herida, trauma	traumatism / traumatismo
tri-	tri-	three / tres	tridimensional
un-	in-, no	against, reversal / contrario, opuesto	unconscious / inconsciente
ultra-	ultra-	beyond, excess / más allá, excesivo	ultrasonic / ultrasónico

Conversion Table 4 / Tabla de conversión 4

Suffixes are endings attached to the root or stem of a word to modify its meaning. In medical terminology **suffixes** are added to the root to define terms according to operative, diagnostic, and symptomatic meanings.

Los **sufijos** son terminaciones que al añadirse a la raíz de una palabra modifican el significado de la misma. En la terminología médica los **sufijos** se añaden a la raíz para dininir términos usados en cirugía, diagnosis y síntomas.

Surgical Procedure Suffixes / Sufijos referentes a procedimientos quirúrgicos

English / Inglés	Spanish / Español	Meaning / Significado	Example / Ejemplo
-centesis	-centesis	aspiration, puncture / aspiración, punción	thoracentesis / toracentesis
-cision	-cisión	cut / corte	incision / incisión
-ectomy	-ectomía	excision, removal / excisión, extirpación	tonsillectomy / tonsilectomía
-desis	-desis	binding, fixation / ligar, fijar	arthrodesis / artrodesis
-oclasis	-oclasis	to break down / romper, quebrar	osteoclasis
-olysis	-olisis	separate, destroy / separar, destruir	enterolysis / enterolisis
-ostomy	-ostomía	forming an opening / crear un boquete o abertura	colostomy / colostomía
-otomy	-otomía	incision, cut into / incisión, piquete	lithotomy / litotomía
-pexy	-pexia	suspension, fixation / suspensión, fijación	hysteropexy / histeropexia
-plasty	-plastia	rebuilding, molding / reformando, moldeando	osteoplasty / osteoplastia
-rrhaphy	-rrafia	suture, closure / sutura, cierre	perineorrhaphy / perineorrafia
-stomy	-ostomía	new opening / apertura nueva	enterostomy / enterostomía
-tomy	-tomía	incision, section / incisión, sección	laparectomy / laparectomía
-tripsy	-tripsia	to crush / triturar	lithotripsy / litotripsia

Suffixes Relating to Diagnoses and Symptoms / Sufijos referentes a diagnósticos y síntomas

English / Inglés	Spanish / Español	Meaning / Significado	Example / Ejemplo
-algia	-algia	pain / dolor	cephalalgia / cefalalgia
-capnia	-capnia	carbon monoxide / monóxido de carbono	hypercapnia / hipercapnia
-cele	-cele	hernia, swelling / hernia, inflamación	metrocele
-chalasis	-calasia	relaxation / relajación	achalasia / acalasia
-dynia	-dinia	pain / dolor	metrodynia / metrodinia
-ectasis	-ectasia	dilation, expansion / dilatación, expansión	bronchiectasis / bronquiectasia
-emesis	-emesis	vomit / vómito	hematemesis / hematemesis
-emia	-emia	blood / sangre	hyperglycemia / hiperglicemia
-iasis	-iasis	condition, presence / condición, presencia	lithiasis / litiasis
-itis	-itis	inflammation / inflamación	dermatitis
-logy	-logía	study of / estudio de	dermatology / dermatología
-malacia	-malacia	softening / reblandecimiento	osteomalacia
-mania	-manía	obsession / obsesión	kleptomania / cleptomanía
-megaly	-megalia	enlargement / engrosamiento	hepatomegaly / hepatomegalia
-oid	-oide	resembling / de tipo similar	lipoide
-oma	-oma	tumorous / tumoroso	nephroma / nefroma
-osis	-osis	abnormal condition / condición anormal	dermatosis
-pathy	-patía	disease / enfermedad	gastropathy / gastropatía
-penia	-penia	decrease, deficiency / disminución, deficiencia	leukopenia / luecopenia
-phagia	-fagia	to eat / comer	dysphagia / disfagia
-phasia	-fasia	speech / habla	aphasia / afasia
-phobia	-fobia	fear / miedo, temor	acrophobia / acrofobia
-plegia	-plejía	paralysis, stroke / parálisis, ataque	hemiplegia / hemiplejía
-poiesis	-poyesis	formation / formación	hematopoiesis / hematopoyesis
-praxia	-praxia	activity, action / actividad, acción	apraxia
-rrhage	-rragia	bursting forth, flooding / derramamiento	hemorrhage / hemorragia
-rrhea	-rrea	discharge / flujo, descarga	diarrhea / diarrea
-sclerosis	-esclerosis	hardening / endurecimiento	arteriosclerosis / arterioesclerosis
-spasm	-espasmo	contraction / contracción	gastrospasm / gastroespasmo
-sthenia	-estenia	strength / fuerza	myasthenia / miastenia
-thymia	-timia	mind / mente	cyclothymia / ciclotimia
-uria	-uria	urine / orina	hematuria / hematuria

Notes:
1. When the suffix begins with a vowel, the wood root is directly added to the suffix: **cephalalgia / cefalalgia.**
2. When the suffix begins with a consonant, a connecting vowel is placed between the word root and the suffix (**-o** in the majority of cases): cardiogram / cardiograma.

Notas:
1. Cuando el sufijo comienza con una vocal, la raíz se añade directamente al sufijo: **cefalalgia / cephalalgia.**
2. Cuando el sufijo comienza en consonante se coloca una vocal, gen. una **-o-**, entre la raíz y el sufijo: cardiograma / cardiogram.

Conversion Table 4 / Tabla de conversión 4

Suffixes that Form a Noun / Sufijos que forman un nombre

English / Inglés	Spanish / Español	Meaning / Significado	Example / Ejemplo
-cide	-cidio	destruction, killing / destrucción, muerte	suicide/suicidio
-clysis	-clisis	irrigation / irrigación	venoclysis / venoclisis
-coccus	-coco	berry-shaped / en forma de baya	streptococcus / estreptococo
-cyte	-cito	cell / célula	oocyte / oocito
-gram	-grama	record made by an instrument / trazo de un instrumento	cardiogram / cardiograma
-graph	grafo-a	device for recording / dispositivo para grabar	polygraph / polígrafo
-graphy	-grafía	description made by an instrument / descripción hecha por un instrumento	radiography / radiografía
-ia	-a, -ia, -ía	condition or disease / condición o enfermedad	pneumonia / neumonía
-ician	-ico, -ica	person associated with a given speciality / persona asociada a una especialidad	technician / técnico
-ics	-ia	an art or science / un arte o ciencia	orthopedics / ortopedia
-ine	-ina	substance / sustancia	quinine / quinina
-is, -ism	-is, -ismo	abnormal condition / condición anormal	alcoholism / alcoholismo
-ist	-ista	specialist / especialista	dentist / dentista
-lysis	-lisis	setting free / liberar	dialysis / diálisis
-ologist[1]	-ólogo-a	specialist / especialista	cardiologist / cardiólogo
-ology	-ología	study, knowledge / estudio, conocimiento	pathology / patología
-oma	-oma	tumor	adenoma
-osis	-osis	condition, formation / condición, formación	tuberculosis
-osmia	-osmia	smell / olor	anosmia / anosmia
-pathy	-patía	disorder, disease / enfermedad, anomalía	myelopathy / mielopatía
-penia	-penia	deficiency / deficiencia	osteopenia
-phagic	-fágico	rel. to eating / rel. a comer	esophagic / esofágico-a
-philia	-filia	tendency, abnormal liking / tendencia, atracción mórbida	hemophilia / hemofilia
-phylaxis	-filaxis	protection / protección	prophylaxis / profilaxis
-ty	-dad	condition / condición	senility / senilidad
-y	-ia, -ía	condition or process / condición o proceso	myopathy / miopatía

[1]If -log precedes -ist in English, -ist is omitted in Spanish, and the ending -o (m.) or -a (f.) is added: **psychologist / psicólogo-a.**
Si en una palabra inglesa -log precede a -ist, esta terminación se omite en español y se añade -o (m.) o -a (f.) a log: **psicólogo-a / psychologist.**

Conversion Table 4 / Tabla de conversión 4

Suffixes that Form an Adjective / Sufijos que forman un adjetivo

English / Inglés	Spanish / Español	Meaning / Significado	Example / Ejemplo
-iac	-iaco, -iaca	pertaining to, one affected by / en relación a, afectado por	cardiac / cardíaco[1]
-al	-al	related to / que trata de	visual / visual
-ant	-ante	pertaining to, with characteristics / en relación a, con características	abundant / abundante
-ate	-ado, -ada	condition / condición	delicate / delicado
-cidal	-cida	destructive, that kills / destructivo, que mata	bactericidal / bactericida
-ic	-ico, -ica	affected by / afectado por	asthmatic / asmático
-ile	-il	state of being / estado	senile / senil
-prandial	-prandial	meal / comida	postprandial / postprandial

[1]Adjectives ending in -o change the -o to -a to form the feminine.
Los adjectivos que terminan en -o cambian la terminación a -a para formar el femenino.

Suffixes that Form a Verb / Sufijos que forman un verbo

English / Inglés	Spanish / Español	Example / Ejemplo
-ate	-ar	accommodate / acomodar
-e	-ar	cure / curar
-fy	-ficar	verify / verificar
-ize	-izar	revitalize / revitalizar

Simplified Spanish Grammar

Gramática española simplificada

The Spanish Alphabet / El alfabeto español

A, a	B, b	C, c	Ch, ch	D, d	E, e	F, f	G, g	H, h	I, I
a	be	ce	che	de	e	efe	ge	hache	i

J, j	K, k	L, l	Ll, ll	M, m	N, n	Ñ, ñ	O, o	P, p	Q, q
jota	ka	ele	elle	eme	ene	eñe	o	pe	cu

R, r	rr	S, s	T, t	U, u	V, v	W, w	X, x	Y, y	Z, z
ere	erre	ese	te	u	ve	uve doble	equis	ye, i griega	zeta

The Spanish alphabet has four more characters than the English alphabet: **ch, ll, ñ, rr**. In alphabetizing Spanish words or syllables, those beginning with **ch, ll,** and **ñ** follow words that begin in **c, l, n.** (In Spanish **rr** never begins a word.) The Spanish alphabet, like the English alphabet, has five vowels: **a, e, i, o, u.** The consonant **y** is pronounced like the vowel **i** at the end of a word. It is also pronounced like **i** when it is used by itself as the word **and.**

Unlike English vowels, each vowel in Spanish has, with few exceptions, a single sound.

Vowel	Sound	Example / Meaning
a	**ah** as in father	gasa / gauze
e	**eh** as in bed (without the glide)	leche / milk
i	**ee** as in me (without the glide)	mi / my
o	**oh** as in spoke	ojo / eye
u	**oo** as in food	cura / cure

The Spanish consonants that differ most from English pronunciation are described below. In the Pronunciation Chart the descriptions of sounds are approximations and do not indicate exact equivalence between English and Spanish sounds. The authors of this dictionary believe that a basic understanding of the pronunciation of Spanish and English will better serve the needs of the dictionary users than any attempt to represent the entire phonetic complexities of the two languages. Readers can develop their pronunciation skills apart from the dictionary by imitating native speakers and using pronunciation tapes available in many libraries.

Spanish Consonants That Differ Most from English Pronunciation

Letter	Approx. English Sound	Example / Meaning
c before e, i (Cast.)	**th** as in think	**círculo** / circle
c before e, i (H.A)	**s** as in sick	**centro** (sentro)[1] / center
c before a, o, u	**k** as in cancer	**cáncer** / cancer
ch	**ch** as in check	**leche** / milk
d between vowels	like **th** in weather	**medio** / half
d after n or l	like **d** in dart	**donde** / where
g before e, i	harsher than **h** in hemoglobin	**germen** / germ
gue, gui	hard **g** as in guest	**guisado** / stew
güe, güi	**gwe**, as in Gwen	**ungüento** / ointment
h	always silent as in hour	**hora** / hour
j	more forcefully than in ham	**jamón** / ham
ll (Cast.)	**lli** as in million	**millón** / million
ll (H.A)	same as **y** in yes	**millón** (miyón)
ñ	**ny** as in canyon	**muñeca** / wrist
p	not aspirated, less explosive than in patient	**paciente** / patient

(cont.)

[1] Phonetic spellings in brackets indicate how the word is pronounced in Hispanic America.

3

Letter	Approx. English Sound	Example / Meaning
q	always pronounced as **k**	**queso**[2] / cheese
r	1. inicial: multiple thrill, roll **r** more than in dia**rrh**ea	**reuma** / rheum
r	2. not initial, sound produced by the tip of the tongue against the alveolar ridge	**cirugía** / surgery
rr	same as initial **r**	**diarrea** / diarrhea
v as in **b** labial	as in **b**owl	**vacuna** (bacuna) / vaccine
x	**ks, gs** as in oxygen	**oxígeno** / oxygen **excelente** / excellent
y	same as **y** in yes like **j** in injection	**yeso** / plaster **inyección** / injection
y	by itself or at the end of a word, like **e** in me	**soy** / I am
z (*Cast.*)	like **th** in **th**umb	**zumo** / juice
z (*H.A.*)	as **s** in soft	**zumbido** (sumbido) / buzz

[2] In the letter combination **qu** the **u** is always silent in Spanish before **e** and **i**.

Linking Words

In Spanish, words are spoken in breath-groups of two or more words pronounced as if they were one. Breath-groups are formed when the ending of one word and the beginning of the following word meet these conditions:

The First Word Ends with	*The Next Word Begins with*
1. a consonant	a vowel
el	estudiante

e-**les**-tu-dian-te

2. consonant	the letter **h**
el	hospital

e-**lhos**-pi-tal

3. vowel	the same vowel
enfermera	asistente

en-fer-me-**ra**-sis-ten-te (longer a)

4. strong vowel (a, e, o)	weak vowel (i, u)
persona	interesante

per-so-**nain**-te-re-san-te

5. strong vowel (a, e, o)	strong vowel
la	otra

lao-tra

Comprehensive Example:

La otra medicina es mejor. / The other medicine is better.
lao-tra (stop) me-di-ci-**naes** (stop) me-jor.

Dividing Words into Syllables

A Spanish word has as many syllables as it has vowels and diphthongs. (A diphthong is the combination of an unstressed **i** or **u** with **a, e,** or **o**. A diphthong is dissolved, however, if the **i** or the **u** carries a written accent mark as shown in item 4.)

4

How to Separate Syllables

1. An initial vowel in a word is a syllable if it is followed by two consonants the second of which is **l** or **r**.

   aplicar / to apply   a-pli-car

2. The consonants **b, c, f, g, p, t** combine with **l** or **r** to form a syllable with the following vowel. (The letter **d** combines only with **r**.)

   flema / phlegm   fle-ma

3. Any consecutive consonants apart from the combinations described in the preceding rule mark a division between syllables.

   parte / part   par-te
   consultar / consult   con-sul-tar

4. The vowels that make up a diphthong are never separated.

   arteria / artery   ar-te-ria
   anatomía / anatomy   a-na-to-mí-a.

5. Two strong vowels form two separate syllables.

   monitoreo / monitoring   mo-ni-to-re-o.

Accentuation

Ending / Terminación	Stress / Sílaba acentuada	Examples / Ejemplos
vowel: **a e i o u**	next-to-the-last syllable	bac-**te**-ria
consonant: **n** or **s**	next-to-the-last syllable	**cu**-ran
consonant other than n or s	on the last syllable	o-fi-**cial**
		a-c-o-mo-**dar**

All infinitives are stressed on the last syllable. Any words that are exceptions to these rules carry a *written accent mark* (′) over the stressed vowel.

coffee / café   lung / pul**món**   easy / **fá**cil   lamp / **lám**para

A written accent mark is also used to distinguish two words that are written alike but have different meanings, such as demonstrative adjectives and pronouns (this / **este** paciente (*adjective*), this one / **éste** (*pronoun*)) and interrogatives and relative pronouns (what / ¿**qué**?, that / **que**). The same thing happens with yes / **sí** and if / **si**. All interrogatives require a written accent mark.

Punctuation / Puntuación

(.)	punto	(ü)	diérisis o crema
(;)	punto y coma	(*)	asterisco
(:)	dos puntos	(-)	guión
(¿)	interrogación abierta	(_)	raya
(?)	interrogación cerrada	()	paréntesis
(¡)	admiración abierta	(" ")	comillas
(!)	admiración cerrada	(. . .)	puntos suspensivos

The Article / El artículo

The article (definite or indefinite) precedes the noun. Spanish articles agree with the noun in gender and number.

The Definite Article (the)		
	Feminine (1)	Masculine (2)
Singular	la	el
Plural	las	los

1. the chronic infection / **la infección crónica**
   the chronic infections / **las infecciones crónicas**
2. the extreme case / **el caso extremo**
   the extreme cases / **los casos extremos**

Note: Singular feminine nouns that begin with stressed **a** or **ha** require the masculine form **el.**

the water / **el agua**
the speech / **el habla**

When **de** / of precedes **el,** they contract to **del;** and when **a** / to precedes **el,** they contract to **al.**

The Indefinite Article (a, an, some)		
	Feminine (1)	*Masculine (2)*
Singular	una	un
Plural	unas	unos

1. a complicated situation / **una situación complicada**
   some complicated situations / **unas situaciones complicadas**
2. an asthmatic boy / **un niño asmático**
   some asthmatic boys / **unos niños asmáticos**

In the first two examples of the definite article, the nouns **infección,** which is feminine, and **caso,** which is masculine, determine the gender and number of the article that precedes them. The descriptive adjectives that follow the nouns have the same gender and number as the noun they modify. The same rules of agreement apply in the examples for the indefinite article.

Uses of the Definite Article / Usos del artículo definido

1. To refer to parts of the body and articles of clothing.

   Antonia raises her arm. / **Antonia levanta el brazo.**
   The patient puts on her robe. / **La paciente se pone la bata.**
2. To refer to days of the week, dates, and seasons.

   Check into the hospital on Thursday. / **Ingrese en el hospital el jueves.**
3. With nouns of rate, weight, and measure.

   Take half of the pill. / **Tome la mitad de la pastilla.**
4. With titles when speaking about a person or persons.

   Dr. Ruiz is famous. / **El doctor Ruiz es famoso.**
5. With cardinal numbers to tell time (feminine forms **la** and **las** only).

   I'll see you at one. / **Te veo a la una.**
   Come back tomorrow at eleven. / **Vuelva mañana a las once.**

Uses of the Indefinite Article / Usos del artículo indefinido

1. To indicate some, any, a few, about (meaning approximately).

   The patient is about twenty years old. / **El paciente tiene unos veinte años.**
2. To stress a person's identity.

   Who is he? He is a famous doctor. / **¿Quién es él? Es un médico famoso.**
3. To identify objects or persons after **hay** (there is, there are).

   There are a book, a glass, and some medicines on the table. / **Hay un libro, un vaso y unas medicinas en la mesa.**

Note: The indefinite article is generally omitted after the verb **ser** with an unmodified noun referring to profession, religion or nationality:

He is a doctor. / **Él es médico.**

6

Nouns / Nombres

Gender / Género

In Spanish, nouns are either masculine or feminine. There are no neuter nouns.

Nouns referring to female beings and certain things are classified as feminine; they have the following endings.

Endings of Feminine Nouns / Terminaciones de nombres femeninos

Most Common	*Example*	*Exception*
-a	**hora** / hour	**el día** / day
Others		
-ad	**enfermedad** / sickness	
-ión	**atención** / attention	**el avión** / airplane
-is	**flebitis** / phlebitis	—
-ud	**salud** / health	—
-umbre	**costumbre** / custom	—

Nouns referring to masculine beings, days of the week, and names of languages are usually classified as masculine, as are the names of things having the following endings.

Endings of Masculine Nouns /
Terminaciones de nombres masculinos

Most Common	*Example*	*Exception*
-o	**brazo** / arm	**la mano** / hand
Others		
-or	**doctor**	
-ma*	**sistema** / system	**la flema** / phlegm
-pa*	**mapa** / map	

*Only nouns of Greek origin ending in **-ma, -pa** are masculine. This rule applies to most scientific names having these endings.

Adjectives / Adjetivos

Gender / Género

Adjectives are used in both the masculine and feminine genders. Change the ending **-o** of a masculine adjective to **-a** to form the feminine.

the anemic boy / **el niño anémico**
the anemic girl / **la niña anémica**

Add **-a** to an adjective of nationality ending in a consonant to form the feminine. The written accent on the last syllable drops when the feminine ending is added. However, the stress remains on the vowel **e**.

el estudiante francés / the French student
la estudiante francesa / the French student

7

Adjectives ending in **-e** or the consonant **l** remain unchanged for both the masculine and feminine forms:

la niña inteligente / the intelligent girl
el niño inteligente / the intelligent boy
la pregunta fácil / the easy question
el examen fácil / the easy examination

Adjectives ending in **-án, -ón,** and **-or** (except comparatives), add **-a** to form the feminine. The written accent is omitted when the feminine ending is added.

reductor / **reductor, reductora**   lazy / **haragán, haragana**

Note: The adjective may follow or precede the noun; however, nouns and adjectives that have the same endings are inflected alike.

Number / Número

Nouns and Adjectives / Nombres y adjetivos

Plural Endings

add	**-s**	if the noun or adjective ends in an unaccented vowel or diphthong, or stressed **é:**

microbio / microbe	**microbios**
café / coffee	**cafés**
amargo / bitter	**amargos**

add	**-es**	if the noun or adjective ends in a consonant:

pulmón / lung	**pulmones**
especial / special	**especiales**

add	**-es**	**if the noun or adjective ends in z,** change **z** to c before adding **-es.**

luz / light	**luces**
feliz / happy	**felices**

Note: Nouns ending in unstressed **-is** or **-es** remain unchanged in the plural. Their number is indicated by the preceding article.

la crisis	las crisis
el jueves	los jueves
el análisis	los análisis

Adjectives That Precede the Noun / Adjetivos que preceden al nombre

Demonstratives / Demostrativos

Demonstratives indicate location. A demonstrative adjective indicates persons, animals, or objects in relation to the speaker.

Near the speaker

	Singular *this*	Plural *these*
Masculine	este	estos
Feminine	esta	estas

8

this medicine / **esta medicina**   these medicines / **estas medicinas**
this doctor / **este médico**   these doctors / **estos médicos**

Not far from the person addressed or the speaker (in time or space)		
	Singular *that*	Plural *those*
Masculine	ese	esos
Feminine	esa	esas

that white robe / **esa bata blanca**   those white robes / **esas batas blancas**
that week / **esa semana**   those weeks / **esas semanas**

Distant from the speaker and person addressed		
	Singular *that*	Plural *those*
Masculine	aquel	aquellos
Feminine	aquella	aquellas

that lady (over there) / **aquella señora**   those ladies (over there) / **aquellas señoras**
that case (that was treated) / **aquel caso**   those cases (that were treated) / **aquellos casos**

Demonstrative Pronouns / Pronombres demostrativos

Demonstrative adjectives and pronouns have the same form except that the pronouns always carry an accent mark that distinguishes them from the adjectives: **éste, ése, aquél, ésta, ésa, aquélla; éstos, ésos, aquéllos, éstas, ésas, aquéllas.**

Adjective: This patient has a fever. / **Este paciente tiene fiebre.**
Pronoun: That one is anemic. / **Aquél es anémico.**

When referring to a concept, situation, or object of unknown gender, the forms **esto, eso,** and **aquello** are used:

Why do you say that? / **¿Por qué dice eso?**
What is this? / **¿Qué es esto?**
That was awful! / **¡Aquello fue terrible!**

Possessive Adjectives / Adjetivos posesivos

Possessive adjectives agree in gender and number with the thing possessed (the noun they modify). The following forms precede the noun.

Singular	Plural	English
mi	mis	my
tu	tus	your (*fam.*)
su	sus	his her
		its, your (*form.*)
nuestro -a	nuestros -as	our
vuestro -a	vuestros -as	your (*fam. Cast.*)
su	sus	their, your

my patient / **mi paciente**   my patients / **mis pacientes**
our evaluation / **nuestra evaluación**   our patients / **nuestros pacientes**

Note: To clarify **su** (which can refer to more than one possessor), substitute the preposition **de** and the subject pronoun for **su:**

9

article + noun + **de** + pronoun

His temperature is normal. / **Su temperatura es normal.**
La temperatura de él es normal. [*m. sing.*]
Their temperature is normal. / **Su temperatura es normal.**
La temperatura de ellas es normal. [*f. pl.*]

Other Possessive Forms

Other possessive forms that are stressed and placed after the noun are inflected in their endings like adjectives.

Singular	Plural	English
mío -a	míos -as	my, of mine
tuyo -a	tuyos -as	your (*fam.*), of yours
suyo -a	suyos -as	his, her, your, its, of his, of hers, of yours
nuestro -a	nuestros -as	our, of ours
vuestro -a	vuestros -as	your (*fam.*), of yours
suyo -a	suyos -as	their, your, of theirs, of yours

this patient of mine / **este paciente mío**
that patient of ours / **ese paciente nuestro**

Note: To clarify the meaning of **suyo, suya** (*sing.* or *pl.*) replace it with the preposition **de** and the corresponding personal pronoun, as explained in the case of **su.**

her temperature / **la temperatura suya** / **la temperatura de ella**

The stressed forms of the possessive adjectives can be used as possessive pronouns.

Adjective: Your medicine is here / **La medicina suya está aquí.**
Pronoun: Yours is here / **La suya está aquí.**
Adjective: Our treatment finishes today / **El tratamiento nuestro termina hoy.**
Pronoun: Ours finishes today / **El nuestro termina hoy.**

Limiting Adjectives / Adjetivos que limitan al nombre

Numbers and indefinite adjectives that indicate quantities usually precede the noun.

Singular	Plural	English
mucho-a	muchos-as	many, a lot, much
otro-a	otros-as	another
todo-a	todos-as	all, ever
algún, alguna	algunos-as	some, any
ningún, ninguno-a	ningunos-as	not any, none
primer, primero-a	primeros-as	first
tercer, tercero-a	terceros-as	third

Note: **Ninguno** changes to **ningún, primero** to **primer,** and **tercero** to **tercer** when placed in front of a masculine singular noun; **ningunos** and **ningunas** are rarely used.

Go down to the first floor. / Baje al **primer** piso.

Descriptive Adjectives / Adjetivos descriptivos

In Spanish, descriptive adjectives are most frequently placed after the noun, except adjectives denoting quantity, size, or order, which are generally placed before the noun.

You have high blood pressure. / Tiene la presión **alta.**
That sickness has many complications. / Esa enfermedad tiene **muchas** complicaciones.

It is the third time. / Es la **tercera** vez.

Some descriptive adjectives change in meaning depending on whether they precede or follow the noun:

bueno -a	**un médico bueno** / a good doctor (compared to others)
	un buen médico (he is excellent, worth recommending)
grande	**un hombre grande** / a big man (in a physical sense)
	un gran hombre / a great man (in a moral, spiritual, or intellectual sense)
malo -a	**una dieta mala** / a bad diet (of bad quality)
	una mala dieta / a bad diet (as compared to a good one)

Note: The adjectives **bueno** and **malo** drop the ending **-o** before a masculine singular noun; **grande** drops the ending **-de** before a singular noun, masculine or feminine.

Comparisons of Inequality

> **más** / more + the adjective + **que** / than

John is taller than Joe. / **Juan es más alto que Pepe.**

> **menos** / less + the adjective + **que** / than

Joe is shorter than John. / **Pepe es menos alto que Juan.**

Comparisons of Equality

> **tan** / as + an adjective or adverb + **como** / as

This pill is as effective as that one. / **Esta pastilla es tan eficaz como ésa.**

> **Tanto -a, -os, -as** / as much, as many + noun + **como**

He has as much fever as yesterday. / **Tiene tanta calentura como ayer.**

Irregular Comparatives

Adjectives	*Comparative*	*Superlative*
bad / **malo**	worse / **peor**	worst / **el, la peor**
big / **gran, grande**	bigger / **más grande**	the greatest / **el, la mayor**
good / **bueno**	better / **mejor**	the best / **el, la mejor**
young / **joven**	younger / **más joven**	youngest / **el, la menor**
low / **bajo**	lower / **inferior**	the lowest / **ínfimo**
much / **mucho**	more / **más**	the most / **el, la más**
old / **viejo**	older / **más viejo**	oldest / **el, la mayor**

Note: The forms oldest / **mayor** and youngest / **menor** usually refer to persons.
Translate **la mayor parte de** as *most (of)*.

La mayor parte de los pacientes son adultos. / Most of the patients are adults.

Article and adjective agree with the noun in gender and number.

This is the best treatment. / **Este es el mejor tratamiento.**
These are the best pills. / **Estas son las mejores pastillas.**

Note: In Spanish the preposition **de** is generally used after the superlative; before numerals, **de** is the translation of the English *than.*

The sickest of all. / **El más enfermo de todos.**
There are more than ten cases. / **Hay más de diez casos.**

The absolute superlative refers only to a quality possessed by a person or object to a high degree, without comparison to others. To form the absolute superlative, the ending **-ísimo** or **-ísima** is added to the radical of the adjective:

mucho → muchísimo	rápido → rapidísimo
excelente → excelentísimo	inteligente → inteligentísimo

Note: Adjectives ending in **-co** and **-go** change the **c** to **qu** and the **g** to **gu** before adding **-ísimo:**

poco → poquísimo	largo → larguísimo

Adverbs	*Superlatives*
well / **bien**	better, best / **mejor**
bad, badly / **mal**	worse, worst / **peor**
much / **mucho**	more, most / **más**
little / **poco**	less, least / **menos**

Do you feel well today? / **¿Se siente bien hoy?**
I feel better. / **Me siento mejor.**
I feel worse today. / **Me siento peor hoy.**

Pronouns / Pronombres

A pronoun is a word that takes the place of a noun. Different types of pronouns may replace the same noun according to how the noun is used.

Subject Pronouns / Pronombres personales

Subject pronouns tell who is performing the action of the verb. They are often omitted in Spanish since the form of the verb indicates person and number. Subject pronouns are used in Spanish for clarification and emphasis. The familiar **tú** is used when speaking to a friend, a relative, or a child. **Vosotros -as** is rarely used in Hispanic America, where **ustedes** is used for the plural of **tú.** There is no translation in Spanish for the English subject pronoun *it.*

It is a complicated case. / **Es un caso complicado.**
It is I. / **Soy yo.**

Direct Object Pronouns / Pronombres de objeto directo

A direct object pronoun replaces a noun object of the verb:

Did you bring the sample? / **¿Trajo la muestra?**
Yes, I brought it. / **Sí, la traje.**

Indirect Object Pronouns / Pronombres de objeto indirecto

An indirect object pronoun replaces a noun indirect object of the verb.

Did you give María (to her) the prescription? / **¿Le dio la receta a María?**
Yes, I gave it to her. / **Sí, se la di.**

Note: When two object pronouns are used together, the indirect object pronoun generally precedes the direct. **Se** replaces **le, les** when preceding **lo, la, los, las.**

First and Second Person (Familiar)

Subject Pronouns	Direct Object Pronouns	Indirect Object Pronouns
I / yo	me / me	to me, for me / me
you / tú	you / te	to you, for you / te
we / nosotros -as	us / nos	to us, for us / nos
you / vosotros -as	you / os	to you, for you / os

Note: **Me, te, nos** and **os** may be used as direct and indirect object pronouns, or as reflexive pronouns.

Third and Second Person (Formal)

Subject Pronouns	Direct Object Pronoun	Indirect Object Pronouns
you / usted	you / lo, la	to you, for you / le
he / él	him / lo	to him, for him / le
she / ella	her / la	to her, for her / le
	it / lo, la	to it, for it / le
you / ustedes	them / los, las	to you, for you / les
they / ellos	them / los	to them, for them / les
they / ellas	them / las	to them, for them / les

Note: The subject pronoun is sometimes used with the preposition **a** either for emphasis or clarification in addition to the indirect object pronoun.

El doctor le recetó esta pastilla a ella. / The doctor prescribed this pill for her.

Note: **Le** and **les** are also used in Spain as direct object pronouns for the second person: **usted, ustedes,** and for the third person masculine. In Hispanic America this usage is less frequent.

Reflexive Pronouns / Pronombres reflexivos

A reflexive pronoun is used when the subject acts upon itself. The forms **me, te, nos,** and **os,** are also used in the reflexive, meaning myself, yourself, ourselves, and yourselves. For the other persons **se** is used, meaning yourself (for **usted**), herself, and himself for the singular forms; yourselves (for **ustedes**), and themselves for the plural forms.

Subject Pronouns	Reflexive Pronouns
I / yo	myself / me
you / tú	yourself / te
you / usted	yourself / se
he / él	himself / se
she / ella	herself / se
we / nosotros -as	ourselves / nos
you / vosotros -as	yourselves / os
you / ustedes	yourselves / se
they / ellos -as	themselves / se

She washed her hands. / **Ella se lavó las manos.**
They get up early. / **Ellos se levantan temprano.**

13

Relative Pronouns / Pronombres relativos

A relative pronoun (**que; el (la) cual; quien** / that, who; that, which; who) introduces an adjective clause that refers back to an antecedent noun; it can be the subject or direct object of the clause's verb, or the object of a preposition.

I know a nurse who can assist you. / **Conozco a una enfermera que puede asistirlo.**
The medicine (that) you took. / **La medicina que usted tomó.**
The case which we are talking about . . . / **El caso del cual estamos hablando . . .**
The patient, to whom you gave the pill . . . / **El paciente, a quien le diste la pastilla . . .**

Possessive pronouns and **demonstrative pronouns** were explained under Adjectives.

Verbs / Verbos

In Spanish as in English, the mood of a verb states

1. a fact.

Indicative

> The doctor is in his office. /
> **El doctor está en su consulta.**

2. a condition expressed by the speaker involving some doubt, wish, hope, or possibility.

Subjunctive

> I hope you feel better tomorrow. /
> **Espero que se sienta mejor mañana.**

Expressions of willing that are generally followed by the infinitive in English are followed by the subjunctive in the dependent clause in Spanish:

I want you to come next week. / **Quiero que venga la semana próxima.**

The subjunctive is generally used when the subject of the dependent clause is not the subject of the main clause. The subjunctive is more frequently used in Spanish than it is in English. It appears in the main clause to express a formal command, after certain adverbs implying uncertainty (**tal vez, quizás**), or after interjections that introduce nonfactual statements.

Perhaps he can leave tomorrow. / **Quizás él pueda salir mañana.**

3. what might happen, without establishing when it would or could happen:

Conditional

> I would call the doctor. / **Yo llamaría al médico.**

4. a command or a request:

Imperative

> Take the medication now. / **Tome la medicina ahora.**

14

Verb Tenses / Tiempos del verbo

Tense means the time when the action takes place: present, past, or future. See how the verb changes in the following examples using a regular verb in the indicative.

Present   The doctor is speaking to the patient now. /
               La doctora habla con el paciente ahora.
Past   The doctor spoke to the patient. /
               La doctora habló con el paciente.
Future   The doctor will speak to the patient. /
               La doctora hablará con el paciente.

To indicate the tense of the verb in Spanish, add to the stem of the verb—or to its infinitive in the case of the future tense and the conditional mood—the ending that belongs to the appropriate tense, person, and number:

Present   **habl** + **-a** (third person singular) → **habla**
Past   **habl** + **-ó** (third person singular) → **habló**
Future   **hablar** (infinitive) + **-á** (third person singular) → **hablará**
Conditional   **hablar** (infinitive) + **-ía** (third person singular) → **hablaría**

The Spanish tenses are divided into simple and compound. The compound tenses of the indicative and subjunctive are formed with a simple tense form of the auxiliary verb **haber** and the past participle of the conjugated verb. In the indicative and the conditional, the compound tenses are generally translated as follows:

Simple Tenses

To examine / **examinar** has the following forms in the third person singular:

Present	**examina**	he, she examines; he, she is examining; he, she does examine
Imperfect	**examinaba**	he, she examined; he, she was examining; he, she did examine
Preterit	**examinó**	he, she examined; he, she did examine
Future	**examinará**	he, she will examine
Conditional	**examinaría**	he, she would (could) examine

Compound Tenses

Perfect	**ha examinado**	he, she has examined
Pluperfect	**había examinado**	he, she had examined
Future perfect	**habrá examinado**	he, she will have examined
Conditional perfect	**habría examinado**	he, she would (could) have examined

Note: See the Verb Tables in Appendix C for complete conjugation of compound tenses of the indicative, subjunctive, and conditional.

Conjugation of Verbs / Conjugación del verbo

The infinitive of verbs in Spanish end in: **-ar** (**tomar** / to take, to drink), **-er** (**comer** / to eat), and **-ir** (**admitir** / to admit). The letters preceding the infinitive ending are the root or stem of a Spanish verb. The tenses of regular verbs are formed by adding endings to the root, except for the future and the conditional tenses, which use the whole infinitive as a root. Only the most common verbs and irregularities are shown here.

Moods / Modos del verbo

INDICATIVE / INDICATIVO:
Present / Presente

To form the present tense, drop the infinitive ending and add to the root of the verb the following endings:

Verbs Ending in -ar

Singular		Plural	
I / yo	-o	we / nosotros -as	-amos
you / tú (fam.)	-as	you / vosotros -as	-áis
you / usted	-a	you / ustedes	-an
he / él	-a	they / ellos	-an
she / ella	-a	they / ellas	-an

Example: (tomar)

Yo tomo la medicina. / I take the medication.
Tú tomas la medicina. / You take the medication.

Verbs Ending in -er

Using the same procedure, change the vowel **-a** to **-e**:

Singular: -o, -es, -e; Plural: -emos, -éis, -en.

Example: (comer)

Usted come muy bien. / You eat very well.
Ellos comen muy bien. / They eat very well.

Verbs Ending in -ir

The singular endings are the same as for verbs ending in **-er.** The plural endings are also the same, except for the first person (**nosotros -as**) **-imos,** and the second person (**vosotros -as**) **-ís.**

Example: (vivir)

Vivimos en California. / We live in California.
Ella vive en California. / She lives in California.

Imperfect and Preterit / Imperfecto y Pretérito

There are two tenses of the indicative that refer to the past. The imperfect is one of them, frequently called the past descriptive because it describes actions and conditions which took place in a continuous or customary way.

I used to work from 8 A.M. until 3 P.M. / Yo **trabajaba** desde las ocho de la mañana hasta las tres de la tarde.

The preterit refers in a narrative way to an action in the past which ended at a definite time. Historical facts are generally narrated in the preterit.

Yesterday I worked from 2 P.M. until 10 P.M. / Ayer **trabajé** desde las dos de la tarde hasta las diez de la noche.

Imperfect / Imperfecto

Verbs Ending in -ar

Singular		Plural	
I / yo	-aba	we / nosotros -as	-ábamos
you / tú (fam.)	-abas	you / vosotros -as	-abais
you / usted	-aba	you / ustedes	-aban

Singular		Plural	
he / él	-aba	they / ellos	-aban
she / ella	-aba	they / ellas	-aban

Example: (tomar)

Yo tomaba la medicina. / I was taking the medication.
Tú tomabas la medicina. / You were taking the medication.

Verbs Ending in -er

Using the same procedure, add the following endings.

Singular: -ía, -ías, -ía;   **Plural: -íamos, -íais, -ían.**

Example: (comer)

Usted comía muy bien. / You were eating very well.
Ellos comían muy bien. / They were eating very well.

Verbs Ending in -ir

The singular and plural endings are the same as for verbs ending in **-er.**

Example: (vivir)

Vivíamos en California. / We were living in California.
Ella vivía en California. / She was living in California.

Note: The only irregular verbs in the imperfect indicative are: **ser, ver,** and **ir: yo era, yo veía, yo iba.** See the verb tables in Appendix C for complete conjugation.

Preterit / Pretérito

Verbs Ending in -ar

Singular		Plural	
I / yo	-é	we / nosotros -as	-amos
you / tú (fam.)	-aste	you / vosotros -as	-asteis
you / usted	-ó	you / ustedes	-aron
he / él	-ó	they / ellos	-aron
she / ella	-ó	they / ellas	-aron

Example: (tomar)

Yo tomé la medicina. / I took the medication.
Tú tomaste la medicina. / You took the medication.

Verbs Ending in -er

Using the same procedure, add the following endings.

Singular: -í, -íste, -ió;   **Plural: -imos, -isteis, -íeron.**

Example: (comer)

Usted comió muy bien. / You ate very well.
Ellos comieron muy bien. / They were eating very well.

Verbs Ending in -ir

The singular and plural endings are the same as verbs ending in **-er.**

Example: (vivir)

Vivimos en California. / We lived in California.
Ella vivió en California. / She lived in California.

Note: The first person plural of the present and the preterit have the same verb form.

17

Future / Futuro

The Spanish future expresses not only actions that will take place in the future, but often probability or speculation.

> She will be here at 9 A.M. / **Estará aquí a las nueve de la mañana.**
> I wonder what time it is? / **¿Qué hora será?**
> It is probably one o'clock. / **Será la una.**
> I wonder if the surgery will take a long time. / **¿Durará mucho la operación?**

The present tense is also used to express the immediate future.

> He will arrive at 10 A.M. / **Llega a las diez de la mañaua.**

Note: When translating English expressions in which *will* refers to willingness of someone to do something, use the verb **querer** and not the future tense: Will you please bring me some water? / **¿Quieres traerme agua, por favor?**

All verbs use the same endings to form the future tense. **Comer** and **vivir** take the same endings as **tomar,** shown here.

Infinitive + Endings	*Singular*	*Endings*	
tomar +	I / **yo**	-é	tomar**é**
comer +	you / **tú** (*fam.*)	-ás	tomar**ás**
admitir +	you / **usted**	-á	tomar**á**
	he, she / **él, ella**	-á	tomar**á**
	Plural	*Endings*	
	we / **nosotros-as**	-emos	tomar**emos**
	you / **vosotros-as**	-éis	tomar**éis**
	you / **ustedes**	-án	tomar**án**
	they / **ellos-as**	-án	tomar**án**

Conditional

All verbs use the same endings to form the conditional. The conditional is formed by adding to the infinitive the same endings used to form the imperfect indicative of **-er** and **-ir** verbs.

The conditional often refers to probability in the past:

> Joey felt bad last night. Could it be something he ate? /
> Pepito se sintió mal anoche. **¿Sería** algo que comió?

Infinitive + Endings	*Singular*	*Endings*	
tomar +	**yo**	-ía	tomar**ía**
comer +	**tú** (*fam.*)	-ías	tomar**ías**
admitir +	**usted**	-ía	tomar**ía**
	él, ella	-ía	tomar**ía**
	Plural	*Endings*	
	nosotros-as	-íamos	tomar**íamos**
	vosotros-as	-íais	tomar**íais**
	ustedes	-ían	tomar**ían**
	ellos-as	-ían	tomar**ían**

Note: Use the infinitive to form the future and the conditional. Only twelve verbs have irregularities in their radical in the future and the conditional: **caber / cabr-; haber / habr-; saber / sabr-; poder / podr-; poner / pondr-; salir / saldr-; tener / tendr-; valer / valdr-; venir / vendr-; hacer / har-; decir / dir- querer / querr-.** See the verb tables in Appendix C for complete conjugation.

Present Subjunctive

All persons of the present subjunctive have the same root as the first person singular of the present indicative except for the verbs: **dar, ser, estar, haber, ir, saber.** To form the present subjunctive, drop the **-o** of the first person singular of the present indicative before adding the endings of the subjunctive.

For verbs ending in **-ar,** start with the first person of the present indicative: **tomo.** Drop the **-o** and add the endings of the present subjunctive.

tomar	*Singular*		*Endings*	
tom- +	I / **yo**	-e	tome
	you / **tú** (*fam.*)	-es	tom**es**
	you / **usted**	-e	tome
	he, she / **él, ella**	-e	tome

	Plural	*Endings*	
	we / **nosotros-as**	-emos	tom**emos**
	you / **vosotros-as**	-éis	tom**éis**
	you / **ustedes**	-en	tom**en**
	they / **ellos, ellas**	-en	tom**en**

Verbs ending in **-er** and **-ir** have the same endings in the present subjunctive.

com- + *Endings*

comer	*Singular Endings*	*Plural Endings*	
I / **yo**	coma	we / nosotros	com**amos**
you / **tú**	comas	you / vosotros	com**áis**
you / **usted**	coma	you / ustedes	com**an**
he, she / **él, ella**	coma	they / ellos, ellas	com**an**

viv- + *Endings*

vivir	*Singular Endings*	*Plural Endings*	
I / **yo**	viva	we / **nosotros-as**	viv**amos**
you / **tú** (*fam.*)	vivas	you / **vosotros-as**	viv**áis**
you / **usted**	viva	you / **ustedes**	viv**an**
he, she / **él, ella**	**viva**	they / **ellos, ellas**	viv**an**

Note: Observe that the subjunctive endings are the reverse of the indicative endings, except for the first person singular.

Imperfect Subjunctive / Imperfecto de subjuntivo

The subjunctive has only one simple past tense, **el imperfecto de subjuntivo.** The endings are identical for all the verbs with infinitives ending in **-ar, -er,** or **-ir.** However, the endings are not added to the root of the verb, but to the third person plural of the preterit indicative, after dropping the ending **-on.**

Singular	*Endings*	*Plural*	*Endings*
I / **yo**	-a	we / **nosotros-as**	-amos
you / **tú** (*fam.*)	-as	you / **vosotros-as**	-ais
you / **usted**	-a	you / **ustedes**	-an
he / **él**	-a	they / **ellos**	-an
she / **ella**	-a	they / **ellas**	-an

I was hoping that he would eat more. / **Esperaba que él comiera más.**

Giving an Order or Making a Request

Imperative / El imperativo

A command is given generally to a second person, the person spoken to. There are two forms of addressing a second person in Spanish: a familiar way, **tú,** and a formal way, **usted.** A physician or health care professional addresses his or her patients in a formal way unless the patient is a child or a friend. A command is often followed by the polite phrase **por favor** (please).

Command Forms for **usted** and **ustedes** with Regular Verbs

Infinitives ending in **-ar** add **-e** to form the command with **usted** and **-en** to form the command with **ustedes.** Infinitives ending in **-er** or **-ir** add **-a** to form the command with **usted** and **-an** to form the command with **ustedes.**

19

Infinitive	Drop ending	Add	usted	ustedes (+n)
tomar / to take, to drink	-ar	-e	tome	tom**en**
comer / to eat	-er	-a	coma	com**an**
vivir / to live	-ir	-a	viva	viv**an**

Command Forms of Irregular Verbs

To form the **usted** command of irregular verbs, use the first person singular of the present indicative and drop the **-o** ending. Add **-e** to **-ar** verbs and **-a** to **-er** and **-ir** verbs. To form the **ustedes** command, add **-n** to the command form of **usted.**

Command Forms

Infinitive	1st p. sing.	usted	ustedes (+n)
to say, tell / **decir**	digo	diga	dig**an**
to do, make / **hacer**	hago	haga	hag**an**
to put / **poner**	pongo	ponga	pong**an**
to leave / **salir**	salgos	alga	salg**an**
to have / **tener**	tengo	tenga	teng**an**
to bring / **traer**	traigo	traiga	traig**an**
to come / **venir**	vengo	venga	veng**an**
to think / **pensar**	pienso	piense	piens**en**
to move / **mover**	muevo	mueva	muev**an**
to sleep / **dormir**	duermo	duerma	duerm**an**

Exceptions: Special Forms of Commands

Infinitive	usted	ustedes
to give / **dar**	dé	den
to be / **estar**	esté	estén
to have / **haber**	haya	hayan
to go / **ir**	vaya	vayan
to know / **saber**	sepa	sepan
to be / **ser**	sea	sean
to see / **ver**	vea	vean

Formal commands of root-vowel changing verbs (**e-ie, o-ue, e-i**) have the same root form as the first person singular of the present indicative.

to sleep / **dormir**   duerma Ud.   to think / **pensar**   piense Ud.

Verbs ending in **-car, -gar,** and **-zar** require spelling changes to keep the same sounds of the **c, g,** and **z** in the infinitive.

c → qu
to look for / **buscar**   Look for the prescription. / **Busque la receta.**

g → gu
to pay / **pagar**   Pay the bill / **Pague la cuenta.**

z → c
to begin / **empezar**   Begin now. / **Empiece ahora.**

Negative Formal Commands

Negative formal commands are formed by placing **no** before the command.

Take the medicine. / **Tome la medicina.**   Don't take the medicine. / **No tome la medicina.**

Negative tú Commands

No + command of usted + s
No + tome   **+ s → No tomes** (tú).

Affirmative **tú** Commands

Use an informal command with persons whom you address by their first name, using the same form as the third person singular of the present indicative.

tomar   Take the medicine. / **Toma (tú) la medicina.**
comer   Eat less. / **Come (tú) menos.**
dormir Sleep more. / **Duerme (tú) más.**

Special Forms of Commands of **tú** in the Affirmative

to say / **decir**   Tell me. / **Dime.**
to do, to make / **hacer**   Do it. / **Hazlo.**
to go / **ir**   Go home. / **Ve a la casa.**
to put / **poner**   Put your hand here. / **Pon la mano aquí.**
to leave / **salir**   Leave now. / **Sal ahora.**
to be / **ser**   Be attentive. / **Sé atento.**

Plural of **tú** Commands

Affirmative commands with **vosotros** are formed by substituting **-d** for the final **-r** of the infinitive. In Hispanic America, the plural form of the formal command is used for the plural of **tú** commands.

Nosotros Commands

Translate **let us** in either of two ways:

1. **Vamos a** + infinitivo:
   Let's examine her. / **Vamos a examinarla.**
2. Using the present subjunctive of the first personal plural:
   Let's study the case. / **Estudiemos el caso.**

Root-Vowel Changing Verbs and Spelling Change Verbs /
Verbos de cambio vocálico y ortográfico

1. **Root-vowel changing verbs** are classified according to the pattern of changes in the root vowel.
   a. **First class:** Verbs with infinitive ending in **-ar** and **-er.** When the root is stressed, root vowel **e** changes to **ie,** and **o** changes to **ue,** in all the forms of the present indicative and present subjunctive except the first and second person plural. **Apretar, entender, mostrar, volver,** and others belong to this class. See chart for conjugation of these verbs after spelling change verbs.
   b. **Second class:** Verbs with the infinitive ending in **-ir.** When the root is stressed the changes occur in the same tenses as verbs in the first class: **e** changes to **ie,** and **o** changes to **ue,** in the singular and the third person plural of the present indicative and the present subjunctive. They also occur in the first and second person plural of the present subjunctive but not the indicative. The **e** changes to **i,** and the **o** to **u,** in the third person singular and plural of the preterit and in the present participle (gerund). Examples of the second class are **sentir (ie)** and **dormir (ue).**
   c. **Third class:** Verbs ending in **-er** and **-ir.** When the root is stressed, the change is **e** to **i,** in the same forms in which changes take place in the second class. See the conjugation of **repetir** as a model verb for this class.
2. **Spelling change verbs:** Changes in spelling occur in Spanish in certain verbs to keep the sound of the final consonant of the root.

Note: When followed by **e** in the tenses indicated, these verb endings change as shown.

Verbs with Infinitive Ending in -ar

Ending	Change	Tenses
car	c-qu	1st. person pret., and
gar	g-gu	all persons pres. subj.
guar	gu-gü	for all these endings
zar	z-c	

Examples

Verb	Preterit	Pres. Subj.
buscar / to look for	busqué	busque
		busques
		busque
pagar / to pay	pagué	pague
		pagues
		pague
averiguar / to find out	averigüé	averigüe
		averigües
		averigüe
abrazar / to embrace, to hug	abracé	abrace
		abraces
		abrace

Note: The following changes occur when the consonant in the ending precedes **a** or **o** or when **i** falls between two vowels in a conjugated form.

Verbs with Infinitive Ending in -er and -ir

Ending	Change	Tenses
cer	c-z	1st. person sing. pres. indic.,
cir	c-z	
ger	g-j	all persons pres. subj.,
gir	g-j	
guir	gu-g	3rd person sing. and plural preterit,
eer	i-y	all persons imperf. subj.,
ocer	+z before c	all persons pres. subj.
ucir		

Tenses	conocer / to know	reducir / to reduce	proteger / to protect	creer (creyendo) / to believe
Present Indicative	conozco	reduzco	protejo	
Preterit Indicative	——	——	——	creyó
				creyeron
Present Subjunctive	conozca	reduzca	proteja	
	conozcas	reduzcas	protejas	
	conozca	reduzca	proteja	
Imperfect Subjunctive	——	——	——	creyera
				creyeras
				creyera

Note: Tenses not listed are regular. Only the singular forms are given.

Perfect Forms

Verb haber / to have

Indicative Tenses				Subjunctive Tenses		Conditional
Present	Imperfect	Preterit	Future	Present	Imperfect	
he	había	hube	habré	haya	hubiera	habría
has	habías	hubiste	habrás	hayas	hubieras	habrías
ha	había	hubo	habrá	habas	hubiera	habría
hemos	habíamos	hubimos	habremos	hayamos	hubiéramos	habríamos
habéis	habíais	hubisteis	habréis	hayáis	hubiérais	habríais
han	habían	hubieron	habrán	hayan	hubieran	habrían

Combine **haber** with the past participle to form the **perfect tenses.**

Indicative

Present perfect: present of **haber** + past participle of the conjugated verb.	**He tomado**
Past perfect: imperfect of **haber** + past participle of the conjugated verb.	**Había comido**
Preterit perfect: preterit of **haber** + past participle of the conjugated verb.	**Hube venido**
Future perfect: **haber** in the future + past participle of the conjugated verb.	**Habré dormido**

Note: In spoken Spanish the simple preterit replaces the preterit perfect.

Subjunctive

Present perfect: present of **haber** + past participle of the conjugated verb.	**Yo haya tomado**
Past perfect: imperfect of **haber** + past participle of the conjugated verb.	**Yo hubiera comido**

Conditional

Conditional perfect: conditional form of **haber** + past participle of the conjugated verb.
Yo habría dormido

List of Useful Verbs / Lista de verbos útiles

English	Spanish	English	Spanish
to abort	abortar, acortar, impedir	to arrive	llegar; [*on time*]
to abstain, to refrain	abstenerse de		llegar a tiempo
		to ask for	pedir (i)
to accelerate, to speed up	acelerar	(*to request*)	
		to ask (*to question*)	preguntar
to accept	aceptar	to aspirate	aspirar
to accompany, to go with	acompañar	to aspire to	aspirar a
		to assimilate	asimilar
to accumulate, to gather	acumular	to associate	asociar
		to assume	asumir
to ache, to hurt	doler (ue)	to assure	asegurar
to acquire	adquirir (ie)[1]	to astonish	asombrar
to add	añadir, agregar	to attack	atacar
to admit	admitir	to attend	asistir
to advise	aconsejar	to attract	atraer
to age	envejecer	to bathe	bañarse
to affect	afectar	to be	estar; ser
to aggravate	empeorar, agravar	to be able, can	poder (ue)
to aid	ayudar	to be absent	estar ausente
to alleviate	aliviar	to be afraid	tener miedo
to amputate	amputar	to be at fault	tener la culpa
to anesthetize	anestesiar	to be born	nacer
to announce	anunciar; informar; (*to warn*)[2] avisar	to be [*hot, cold*] [*weather*]	tener calor, tener frío hacer (calor, frío)
to annoy	molestar	to be hungry	tener hambre
to appear	aparecer	to be in a hurry	tener prisa
to apply for	solicitar	to be long [*time*]	tardar
to approach, to draw near	acercarse	to be lucky	tener suerte
		to be quiet	callarse; (*to calm down*)
to approve	aprobar (ue)		calmarse
to arouse	excitar	to be silent	callarse
to arrange	arreglar	to be right	tener razón
to arrest	arrestar; (*to stop*) parar	to be sick	estar enfermo -a

1. Vowels between parentheses indicate root-changing verbs.
2. Brackets clarify the meaning of the verb. Parentheses indicate a synonym.

23

English	Spanish	English	Spanish
to be sleepy	tener sueño	to diet	estar a dieta; hacer una dieta
to be . . . years old	tener . . . años		
to become (*adj.*)	hacerse; ponerse (+ *adj.*)	to discharge [*secretion*]	tener secreciones
to begin	empezar (ie), comenzar (ie)	to discharge [*a patient*]	dar de alta
to behave	portarse	to disinfect	desinfectar
to belch	eructar	to do, to make	hacer
to believe	creer	to doubt	dudar
to bend, to flex	doblar; doblarse	to dream	soñar (ue)
to bite	morder (ue)	to dress [*with clothes*]	vestir; vestirse (i)
to blame	culpar		
to bleed	sangrar	to dress [*a wound*]	vendar
to blink	parpadear	to drink	beber; tomar
to bother, to annoy	molestar	to earn	ganar
to break	romper; quebrar	to eat	comer
to breast-feed	amamantar, dar el pecho	to eat breakfast	desayunar
to breathe	respirar	to eat dinner	cenar
to bring	traer	to eat lunch	almorzar (ue)
to buy	comprar	to ejaculate	eyacular
to bruise	magullarse; amoratarse	to enter	entrar
to brush	cepillar	to examine	examinar
to burn	quemar; quemarse	to exercise	hacer ejercicio
to burp	eructar; repetir (i)	to exist	existir
to call	llamar	to expect	esperar
to carry, to wear	llevar	to explain	explicar
to cause	causar	to fail	dejar de
to change [*one's clothes*]	cambiarse (de ropa)	to fall asleep	dormirse (ue, u)
		to fall down	caerse
to chat	charlar	to fear	temer; tener miedo
to check [*to examine*]	examinar, revisar	to feel	sentir (ie, i)
		to follow	seguir (i)
to choke	atragantarse; ahogar; sofocar	to forget	olvidar
		to form	formar
to choose	escoger, elegir (i)	to fracture	fracturar; quebrar; romper
to clean	limpiar		
to climb up	subirse	to function	funcionar
to close	cerrar (ie)	to gargle	hacer gárgaras
to come	venir	to get	obtener, conseguir (i)
to complain [*of, about*]	quejarse (*de*)	to get angry	enfadarse, enojarse
		to get better	mejorarse
to complete	completar	to get up	levantarse
to conceive	concebir (i)	to get well	curarse, sanarse, ponerse bien
to consider	considerar		
to contain	contener	to give	dar
to continue	continuar, seguir (i)	to go	ir; salir
to convalesce	convalecer; recuperarse	to go away	irse
to cost	costar (ue)	to go to bed	acostarse (ue)
to count	contar (ue)	to grow	crecer
to cough	toser	to happen, to turn out	suceder
to create	crear		
to cry	llorar	to hand over	entregar
to cut	cortar	to have	tener; [*aux.*] haber
to deliver [*to give birth*]	dar a luz; estar de parto;. *pop.* aliviarse	to hear	oír
		to heat	calentar
to deny	negar (ie)	to help	ayudar
to depend on	depender de	to hide	esconder; esconderse
to develop	desarrollar; [*a photo*] revelar	to hope	esperar
		to hurry	apurarse, darse prisa
to die	morir (ue, u)	to hurt	doler (ue); lastimar

English	Spanish	English	Spanish
to immobilize	inmovilizar	to put on	ponerse
to improve	mejorar	[clothing]	
to incline	inclinar, inclinarse	to put to bed	acostar (ue)
to increase	aumentar	to qualify	capacitar
to inform	informar	to question	preguntar
to inject	inyectar	to raise	levantar
to insert	insertar, introducir, meter	to react	reaccionar
to itch	picar	to read	leer
to kill	matar	to receive	recibir
to know	saber; [to be acquainted	to recover	recobrar
	with] conocer	to recuperate	recuperar, recobrar
to lack	faltar	to rejuvenate	rejuvenecer
to leak	gotear	to relax	relajar, aflojar
to lean on	apoyarse en	to release	soltar (ue), librar,
to learn	aprender		desprender
to leave	salir	to relieve	aliviar, mejorar
to let	dejar, permitir	to remain	quedar
to lie	mentir (ie, i)	to remember	recordar (ue)
to lie down	acostarse (ue)	to remove, take off	quitar; quitarse
to lift	levantar, alzar	to repeat	repetir (i)
to like	gustar	to reply	contestar, responder
to listen	escuchar, atender (ie)	to resolve	resolver (ue), solucionar
to live	vivir	to respond	responder
to look at	mirar	to rest	descansar
to look for	buscar	to restore	restaurar, reparar
to lose	perder (ie)	to restrict	restringir, confinar
to love	amar; querer (ie)	to return	volver (ue)
to lower [arm, leg]	bajar	to run	correr
to marry	casarse	to say	decir
to masturbate	masturbarse	to scratch	arañar
to menstruate	menstruar	to seat	sentar
to miscarry	abortar	to see	ver
to move	mover (ue)	to seem	parecer
to need	necesitar	to send	mandar
to nurse [a baby]	amamantar	to serve	servir (i)
to nurse [the sick]	cuidar	to shake	agitar
to nurture	nutrir	to shout	gritar
to obtain	conseguir (i), obtener	to show	mostrar (ue), señalar,
to obstruct	obstruir		enseñar
to open	abrir	to shower	ducharse
to oppose	oponerse	to sit down	sentarse (ie)
to order	ordenar, mandar	to smoke	fumar
to owe	deber	to sneeze	estornudar
to palpate	palpar	to solve	resolver (ue)
to pant	jadear	to speak	hablar
to paralyze	paralizar	to spend	gastar; [time] pasar
to participate	participar	to spit	escupir
to pay	pagar	to sprain	torcer (ue)
to penetrate	penetrar	to spray	rociar
to permit	permitir, dejar	to stand up	levantarse
to plan	planear	to stimulate	estimular
to practice	practicar	to study	estudiar
to prefer	preferir (ie)	to suck	chupar, absorber
to prescribe	recetar, prescribir	to suffer	sufrir
to promise	prometer	to suppose	suponer
to push	pujar	to surprise	sorprender
[downward]		to swallow	tragar
to put	poner	to sweat	sudar
to put in	poner; meter	to sweeten	endulzar

English	Spanish	English	Spanish
to swell	hinchar	to urinate	orinar
to take	tomar	to use	usar, emplear
to take off	quitar, quitarse	to visit	visitar
to talk	hablar	to vomit	vomitar
to teach	enseñar	to wait	esperar
to tell	decir	to wake up	despertarse (ie)
to think	pensar (ie)	to want	querer (ie), desear
to throw [into]	echar	to wear	llevar
to tighten	apretar, ajustar	to wheeze	resollar (ue) con ruido sibilante
to try	tratar de; probar (ue)		
to turn	virar; virarse	to wish	querer (ie), desear
to turn around	dar vuelta; voltearse	to work	trabajar
to turn down	rechazar	to write	escribir

Spanish Verbs with Irregular Past Participles

Infinitivo / Infinitive	Past Participle
abrir / to open	abierto
bendecir / to bless	bendito
cubrir / to cover	cubierto
descubrir / to discover	descubierto
encubrir / to hide, to cover up	encubierto
decir / to say	dicho
predecir / to predict	predicho
despertar / to awake	despierto, despertado
dividir / to divide	dividido, diviso
escribir / to write	escrito
inscribir / to inscribe	inscrito
prescribir / to prescribe	prescrito
subscribir / to subscribe	subscrito
expresar / to express	expresado, expreso
freír / to fry	frito
sofreír / to refry	sofrito
hacer / to do, to make	hecho
deshacer / to undo	deshecho
rehacer / to redo	rehecho
satisfacer / to satisfy	satisfecho
imprimir / to print	impreso
juntar / to join	junto, juntado
oprimir / to oppress	oprimido, opreso
poner / to put	puesto
componer / to fix	compuesto
disponer / to dispose	dispuesto
exponer / to expose	expuesto
imponer / to impose	impuesto
oponer / to oppose	opuesto
reponer / to improve	repuesto
suponer / to suppose	supuesto
prender / to apprehend	preso, prendido
proveer / to provide	proveído, provisto
pudrir / to rot	podrido
absolver / to absolve	absuelto
disolver / to dissolve	disuelto
resolver / to resolve	resuelto
romper / to break	roto
soltar / to release	suelto
torcer / to twist	torcido, tuerto
ver / to see	visto
prever / to foresee	previsto

Infinitivo / Infinitive	*Past Participle*
volver / to return	vuelto
devolver / to give back	devuelto
envolver / to wrap around	envuelto
revolver / to stir, to agitate	revuelto

Note: Verbs in **boldface** serve as models for the derivate compound forms that do not appear in this list. / Los verbos en **negrita** sirven de modelo para los derivados que no aparecen en esta lista.

Spanish-English Vocabulary

Vocabulario Español-Inglés

a *abr.* **absoluto** / absolute; **acidez** / acidity; **acomodación** / accommodation; **alergia** / allergy; **anterior** / anterior; **aqua** / aqua; **arteria** / artery.

a *prep.* [*hacia*] to, **voy ___ la farmacia** / I am going to the drugstore; [*dirección*] to, **___ la derecha** / to the right, **___ la izquierda** / to the left; [*hora*] at, **voy ___ las tres** / I'm going at three o'clock; [*frecuencia*] a, per, **tres veces al día** / three times a day.

abajo *adv.* below, down.

abandonar *v.* to abandon, to neglect.

abarcar *vi.* to contain, to include; **___ mucho** / to cover a lot of ground.

abasia *f.* abasia, uncertainty of movement.

abastecer *v.* to supply.

abastecimiento *m.* supply; **artículos para ___** / supplies.

abatido-a *a.* depressed, dejected.

abdomen *m.* abdomen; *pop.* belly; **___ de péndulo** / pendulous ___; **___ escafoideo** / scaphoid ___.

abdominal *a.* abdominal, rel. to the abdomen; **cavidad ___** / **___ cavity**; **distensión ___** / **___** distention; **respiración ___** / **___** breathing; **retortijón, torsón ___** / **___** cramp; **rigidez ___** / **___** rigidity; **traumatismos ___-es** / **___** injuries; **vendaje ___** / **___** bandage.

abdominocentesis *f.* abdominocentesis, abdominal puncture.

abdominoplastia *f. surg.* abdominoplasty, plastic surgical repair of the abdominal wall.

abdominovaginal *a.* abdominovaginal, rel. to the abdomen and the vagina.

abducción *f.* abduction; separation.

abeja *f.* bee.

aberración *f.* aberration. 1. deviation from the norm; **___ cromática** / chromatic ___; 2. mental disorder; **___ mental** / mental ___.

aberrante *a.* aberrant, departing from the usual course; wandering.

abertura *f.* opening.

abierto-a *a. pp.* of **abrir**, open.

abiotrofia *f.* abiotrophy, premature loss of vitality.

ablación *f.* ablatio, ablation, detachment, removal; **___ de la placenta** / **___** placentae; **___ de la retina** / **___** retinae.

ablandar *v.* to soften.

abofetear *v.* to slap.

abogado *m.* lawyer, attorney.

aborrecer *vi.* to abhor, to hate.

abortar *v.* to abort, to interrupt the course of a pregnancy or to stop an illness.

abortivo *m.* abortifacient, stimulant to induce abortion.

aborto *m.* abortion; miscarriage; **___ criminal** / criminal ___; **___ electivo** / elective ___; **___**

espontáneo / spontaneous ___; **___ incompleto** / incomplete ___; **___ inducido** / induced ___; **___ inevitable** / imminent ___; **___ por succión** / suction ___; **___ provocado** / induced ___; **___ terapéutico** / therapeutic ___.

abotonar *v.* to button up.

abrasión *f.* abrasion, damage to or wearing away of a surface by injury or friction; **círculo de ___** / **___** collar, circular trace left on the skin by gunpowder.

abrasivo-a *a.* abrasive, rel. to or that causes abrasion.

abrazadera *f.* brace.

abrazar *vi.* to embrace.

abrazo *m.* hug, embrace.

abrebocas *m.* gag, jaw-lever, device used to keep the patient's mouth open.

abreviar *v.* to reduce, to shorten; **para ___** / in short.

abreviatura *f.* abbreviation.

abrigarse *vr., vi.* to put on warm clothing; to keep warm.

abrigo *m.* overcoat; cover; **buscar ___** / to look for shelter.

abrir *v.* to open; **___ de nuevo** / to reopen.

abrochar *v.* to fasten.

abrumar *v.* to overwhelm; to tax.

abrupción de la placenta *f.* abruptio placentae, premature detachment of the placenta

abrupto-a *a.* abrupt, brusque.

absceso *m.* abscess, accumulation of pus gen. due to a breakdown of tissue; **___ agudo** / acute ___; **___ alveolar** / alveolar ___; **crónico** / chronic ___; **___ de drenaje** / drainage ___; **___ enquistado** / encysted ___; **___ de las encías** / gingival ___; **___ hepático** / hepatic ___; **___ mamario** / mammary ___; **___ pélvico** / pelvic ___; **___ pulmonar** / pulmonary ___.

absoluto-a *a.* absolute, unconditional.

absorbente *a.* absorbent.

absceso	*abscess*
agudo	acute
alveolar	alveolar
crónico	chronic
cutáneo	cutaneous
de drenaje	drainage
de la pelvis	pelvic
de la uña	paronychial
de las amígdalas o anginas	peritonsilar
de las encías	gingival
enquistado	encysted
facial, de la cara	facial
hepático	hepatic
mamario	mammary
pulmonar	pulmonary
retrofaríngeo	retropharyngeal

absorber *v.* to absorb, to take in.

absorción *f.* absorption, uptake. 1. taking up of fluids and other substances by an organism; ___ **bucal** / mouth ___; ___ **cutánea** / cutaneous ___; ___ **entérica** / intestinal ___; ___ **estomacal** / stomach ___; ___ **externa** / external ___; ___ **parenteral** / parenteral ___; ___ **percutánea** / percutaneous ___; 2. *psych.* self-centeredness.

abstemio-a *m., f; a.* abstemious.

abstenerse *vr., vi.* to abstain, to refrain; ___ **de relaciones sexuales** / ___ from sexual intercourse.

abstinencia *f.* abstinence, voluntary restraint.

absurdo-a *a.* absurd.

abuelo-a *m., f.* grandfather; grandmother.

abulia *f.* abulia, loss of will power; ___ **cíclica** / cyclic ___.

abultado-a *a.* bulky, massive; swollen.

abundancia *f.* abundance.

abundante *a.* abundant, plentiful.

aburrido-a *a.* bored.

aburrirse *vr.* to become bored.

abusado-a *a.* abused; beyond the limits.

abusar *v.* to abuse, to mistreat.

abuso *m.* abuse, overuse; ___ **de medicamento** / overuse of medication; ___ **emocional** / emotional ___; ___ **físico** / physical ___; ___ **verbal** / verbal ___.

acabar *v.* to finish, to complete; ___ **de llegar** / to have just arrived; ___ **con eso** / to put an end to that; **acabarse** *vr.* to be finished; [*una sustancia*] to run out.

acalasia *f.* achalasia, inability to relax, esp. in reference to the sphincter muscles.

acantoide *a.* acanthoid, thornlike shape.

acantosis *f.* acanthosis, skin condition manifested by thick and warty growth.

acapnia *f.* acapnia, state produced by a decrease of carbon dioxide in the blood.

acariasis *f.* acariasis, skin disease caused by acarids.

ácaro *m.* acarid, parasite, mite.

acatarrarse *vr.* to catch a cold.

acceso *m.* 1. access, attack, seizure; ___ **de asma** / an asthma attack; 2. entrance.

accesorio *m.* accessory.

accidentado-a *m., f.* an injured person.

accidental *a.* accidental, unexpected.

accidente *m.* accident; ___ **automovilístico** / car ___; ___ **de trabajo** / work-related ___; ___ **de tráfico** / traffic ___; **víctima de un** ___ / casualty.

acción *f.* action.

aceite *m.* oil; ___ **de hígado de bacalao** / cod liver ___; ___ **de oliva** / olive ___; ___ **de ricino** / castor ___.

aceituna *f.* olive.

aceleración, aceleramiento *f., m.* acceleration.

acelerador *m.* accelerator, substance or agent acting as an accelerant; **-a** *a.* having the property of accelerating a process.

acelerar *v.* to accelerate, to quicken, to speed up; ___ **la cura** / to speed the healing process.

acento *m.* accent.

acentuado-a *a.* accented, accentuated.

acentuar *v.* to accentuate, to emphasize.

aceptable *a.* acceptable.

aceptación *f.* acceptance.

aceptar *v.* to accept.

acera *f.* sidewalk.

acerca (de) *adv.* about, concerning; ___ **de eso** / about that.

acercar *vi.* to bring closer; **acercarse** *vr.* to approach, to get close.

acertado-a *a.* right; **un diagnóstico** ___ / a correct diagnosis.

acertar *vi.* to be right; to guess.

acetábulo *m.* acetabulum, hip socket.

acético-a *a.* acetic, sour, rel. to vinegar or its acid.

acetona *f.* acetone, fragrant substance used as a solvent and found in excessive amount in diabetic urine.

acetonemia *f.* acetonemia, excess acetone in the blood.

acetonuria *f.* acetonuria, excess acetone in the urine.

acidemia *f.* acidemia, excess acid in the blood.

acidez *f.* acidity, sourness.

ácido *m.* acid; **-a** *a.* bitter; ___ **acético** / acetic ___; ___ **ascórbico** / ascorbic ___; ___ **bórico** / boric ___; ___ **butírico** / butyric ___; ___ **clorogénico** / chlorogenic ___; ___ **cólico** / cholic ___; ___ **desoxirribonucleico** / deoxyribonucleic ___; ___ **fólico** / folic ___; ___ **gástrico** / gastric ___; ___**-s grasos** / fatty ___**-s**; ___ **láctico** / lactic ___; ___ **nicotínico** / nicotinic ___; ___ **nucleico** / nucleic ___; ___ **resistente** / ___ fast; ___ **ribonucleico** / ribonucleic ___; ___ **salicílico** / salicylic ___; ___ **sulfónico** / sulfonic ___; ___ **sulfúrico** / sulfuric ___; **a prueba de** ___ / ___ proof.

ácido clorhídrico, hidroclórico *m.* hydrochloric acid, a constituent of gastric juice.

ácido glicocólico *m.* glycocholic acid, a compound of glycine and cholic acid.

ácido glucurónico *m.* glucuronic, glycuronic acid, acid that acts as a disinfectant in human metabolism.

ácido hialurónico *m.* hyaluronic acid, acid present in the substance of the connective tissue that acts as a lubricant and connecting agent.

acidosis *f.* acidosis, excessive acidity in the blood and tissues of the body; ___ **diabética** / diabetic ___; ___ **metabólica** / metabolic ___.

ácido úrico *m.* uric acid, a product of protein breakdown present in the blood and excreted in the urine.

acinesia *f.* akinesia, acinesia, partial or total loss of movement.

aclaramiento *m.* clearance, elimination of a given substance from the blood plasma of the kidneys.

aclarar *v.* to clarify, to explain.

aclimatación *f.* acclimatization.

aclimatarse *vr.* to acclimate; to get used to a condition or custom; to adjust.

acloropsia *f.* achloropsia, inability to distinguish the color green.

acné *m.* acne, inflammatory skin condition; ___ rosáceo / ___ rosacea; ___ **vulgar o común** / ___ vulgaris, common acne.

acolia *f.* acholia, absence of bile.

acomodación *f.* accommodation, adjustment.

acomodar *v.* to accommodate, to adjust.

acompañante *m., f.* companion.

acompañar *v.* to accompany.

acondicionamiento *m.* conditioning; ___ **físico** / physical fitness.

acondroplasia *f.* achondroplasia, dwarfism, congenital osseous deformity.

aconsejar *v.* to advise, to recommend; ___ **mal** / to misguide.

acontecer *v.* to transpire, to occur.

acordar *vi.* to agree; **acordarse** *vr.* to remember, to recall.

acortar *v.* to shorten.

acosamiento *m.* harassment.

acosar *v.* to harass.

acostado-a *a.* reclining; lying down.

acostar *vi.* to lay down, to put to bed; **acostarse** *vr.* to go to bed; to lie down; **hora de** ___ / bedtime.

acostumbrado-a *a.* accustomed, used to; **no** ___ / unaccustomed.

acostumbrarse *vr.* to get used to.

acre *a.* acrid, sour.

acreción *f.* accretion, growth; accumulation.

acreditado-a *a.* accredited, certified; **no** ___ / unlicensed.

acreditar *v.* to credit, to accredit, to certify.

acrocianosis *f.* acrocyanosis, Raynaud's disease, bluish discoloration and coldness of the extremities due to a circulatory disorder gen. brought about by exposure to cold or by emotional stress.

acrodermatitis *f.* acrodermatitis, infl. of the skin of hands and feet; ___ **crónica atrófica** / ___ chronica atrophicans.

acrofobia *f.* acrophobia, excessive fear of heights.

acromasia *f.* achromasia, lack or loss of pigmentation in the skin, characteristic of albinos.

acromático-a *a.* achromatic, lacking in color.

acromatopsia *f.* achromatopsia, color blindness.

acromegalia *f.* acromegaly, chronic disease common in middle age, manifested by progressive enlargement of the bones of the extremities and of certain head bones, gen. caused by a malfunction of the pituitary gland.

acromion *m.* acromion, part of the scapular bone of the shoulder.

actina *f.* actin, protein in muscle tissue that to-gether with myosin makes possible muscle contraction.

actitud *f.* attitude, disposition.

activar *v.* to activate.

actividad *f.* activity.

actividades de resistencia *f.* endurance activities.

activo-a *a.* active.

acto *m.* act; deed; **en el** ___ / right away.

actual *a.* actual, present, true, real; **-mente** *adv.* actually, presently.

actuar *v.* to act.

acuclillarse *vr.* to squat.

acuerdo *m.* agreement; **estar de** ___ / to be in agreement, to agree.

acumulación *f.* accumulation; pile, heap.

acumular *v.* to accumulate, to pile up, to amass.

acuoso-a *a.* aqueous; **humor** ___ / ___ humor; **intoxicación** ___ / water intoxication, condition caused by excessive retention of water in the body.

acupuntura *f.* acupuncture, method of inserting needles into specific points of the body as a means of relieving pain.

acústico-a *a.* acoustic, rel. to sound or hearing.

achacoso-a *a.* sickly, ailing.

achaque *m.* ailment, infirmity.

achicar *vi.* to reduce.

Adán, nuez de *f.* Adam's apple.

adaptabilidad *f.* adaptability; compliance. 1. the ease with which a substance or structure can change its shape, such as the ability of an organ to distend; 2. the degree to which a patient follows a prescribed regimen.

adaptación *f.* adaptation, adjustment.

adaptar *v.* to adapt, to fit, to accommodate; **adaptarse** *vr.* to adapt oneself.

Addison, enfermedad de *f.* Addison's disease, insufficiency or nonfunction of the adrenal glands.

adecuado-a *a.* adequate, suitable.

adelantado-a *a.* advanced, ahead; **por** ___ / in advance.

adelantar *v.* to advance, to move ahead; ___ **la fecha** / to move up the date.

adelante *adv.* forward, ahead; **más** ___ / later on; **de hoy en** ___ / from now on.

adelanto *m.* improvement, progress.

adelgazar *vi.* to lose weight, to get thin.

además *adv.* besides, in addition.

adenectomía *f. surg.* adenectomy, removal of a gland.

adenitis *f.* adenitis, infl. of a gland.

adenoacantoma *m.* adenoacantoma, slow-growing cancer of the uterus.

adenocarcinoma *m* adenocarcinoma, malignant tumor arising from a gland or organ.

adenocistoma *m.* adenocystoma, benign gland tumor formed by cysts.

adenofibroma *m.* adenofibroma, benign fibrous glandular tumor seen in the breast and uterus.

adenoide *m.* adenoid, gland-like; accumulation

of lymphatic tissue located in the throat behind the nose.

adenoidectomía *f. surg.* adenoidectomy, excision of the adenoid.

adenoiditis *f.* adenoiditis, infl. of the adenoid.

adenoma *m.* adenoma, glandular like tumor; __ **basófilo** / basophil __; __ **sebáceo** / sebaceous __; __ **tóxico** / toxic __.

adenomioma *m.* adenomyoma, benign tumor usu. seen in the uterus.

adenopatía *f.* adenopathy, a lymph gland disease.

adenosarcoma *m.* adenosarcoma, malignant tumor.

adenosis *f.* adenosis, enlargement of a gland.

adentro (de) *adv.* inside; inside of.

adherencia *f.* adhesion, attachment.

adherir *vi.* to adhere, to attach.

adhesivo-a *a.* adhesive.

adicción *f.* addiction, dependency, propensity; **dejar la** __ / *pop.* [*droga*] to kick the habit.

adictivo *m.* addictive, rel. to or causing addiction.

adicto-a *a.* addicted, physically or psychologically dependent on a substance such as alcohol or a narcotic.

adiós *int.* goodbye.

adiposo-a *a.* adipose, fatty; **tejido** __ / __ tissue.

adjetivo *m.* adjective.

adjuntar *v.* to enclose; to include.

adjutor *m.* adjuvant, helper; substance added to a medication to heighten its action.

administración *f.* administration, management.

administrador-a *m., f.* administrator, manager.

admisión *f.* admission.

admitir *v.* to admit.

adolescencia *f.* adolescence, puberty.

adolescente *m., f.* adolescent.

adolorido-a *a.* sore.

adopción *f.* adoption.

adoptar *v.* to adopt.

adoptivo-a *a.* adoptive.

adormecer *vi.* to put to sleep, [*un nervio*] to deaden; **adormecerse** *vr.* to drowse.

adquirir *vi.* to acquire.

adquisición *f.* acquisition.

adrede *adv.* on purpose.

adrenal *a.* adrenal. *V.* **suprarrenal.**

adrenalectomía *f. surg.* adrenalectomy, removal of the adrenal gland.

adrenalina *f.* adrenaline, epinephrin, hormone secreted by the adrenal medulla, commonly used as a cardiac stimulant.

adrenalismo *m.* adrenalism, inadequate function of the adrenal glands.

adrenocorticotropina *f.* adrenocorticotropin, hormone secreted by the pituitary gland that has a stimulating effect on the adrenal cortex.

adrenogénico-a *a.* adrenogenous, originating in the adrenal glands.

aducción *f.* adduction, 1. movement toward the

midline of the body or toward a limb or part; 2. movement toward a common center.

aductor-a *a.* adductor, a muscle that draws a part towards the median line.

adueñarse *vr.* to take possession.

adulterado-a *a.* adulterated, changed from the original; **no** __ / unadulterated.

adulterar *v.* to adulterate, to change the original.

adulterio *m.* adultery.

adulto-a *a.* adult.

adverbio *m. gr.* adverb.

adverso-a *a.* adverse, unfavorable.

advertencia *f.* warning, forewarning; advice.

advertir *vi.* to warn; to advise.

adyacente *a.* adjacent, next to.

aeróbic *f.* aerobics, a system of physical fitness combining calisthenics and a dance routine intended to promote cardiovascular endurance.

aeróbico-a *a.* aerobic, 1. rel. to an aerobe; 2. rel. to an exercise coordinated as a physical activity; **baile** __ / __ dance; **ejercicio** __ / __ exercise; 3. that lives or occurs in the presence of oxygen.

aerobio *m.* aerobe, organism that requires oxygen to live.

aeroembolismo *m.* aeroembolism, condition caused by a release of bubbles of nitrogen into the blood gen. due to a sudden change in atmospheric pressure; *pop.* the bends.

aeroenfisema *m.* aeroemphysema, condition caused by a sudden ascent in space without adequate decompression; *pop.* the chokes.

aerofagia *f.* aerophagia, excessive swallowing of air.

aerogénico-a *a.* aerogenic, gas-producing.

afán *m.* eagerness, desire.

afasia *f.* aphasia, inability to coordinate word and thought in speaking.

afebril *a.* afebrile, without fever.

afección *f.* affection, fondness; condition, sickness.

afectado-a *a.* affected.

afectar *v.* to affect; to cause change.

afectivo-a *a.* affective; **síntoma** __ / __ symptom; **trastornos** __-s / __ disorders.

afeitar *v.* to shave; **afeitarse** *vr.* to shave oneself.

afemia *f.* aphemia, loss of speech gen. due to a cerebral hemorrhage, a blood clot or a tumor.

afeminado *a.* effeminate.

aferente *a.* afferent, directing toward the center.

afibrinogenemia *f.* afibrinogenemia, deficiency of fibrinogen in the blood.

afinidad *f.* affinity; similarity.

afirmación *f.* affirmation.

afirmar *v.* to affirm, to make certain.

aflicción *f.* affliction, sorrow, grief, distress; **reacción de** __ / grief reaction.

afligido-a *a.* afflicted, distressed, sorrowful, grief-stricken, troubled.

afligir *vi.* to afflict, to cause pain; **afligirse** *vr.* to lament, to be grieved.

aflojar *v.* to loosen, to slacken; **aflojarse** *vr.* to become weak; to lose courage.

afonía *f.* aphonia, loss of voice due to an affliction of the larynx.

afónico-a *a.* aphonic, without voice or sound.

afortunado-a *a.* fortunate, lucky.

afrodisíaco *m.* aphrodisiac, any agent that arouses sexual desire.

afrontar *v.* to confront.

afta *f.* aphtha, a small ulcer, sign of fungal infection of the oral mucosa.

afuera *adv.* outside.

agacharse *vr.* to bend; to stoop, to squat.

agallas *f. pl.* tonsils; *pop.* **tener ___** / to have guts, to be bold.

agalorrea *f.* agalorrhea, cessation or lack of milk in the breasts.

agammaglobulinemia *f.* agammaglobulinemia, deficiency of gamma globulin in the blood.

agarrar *v.* to grab, to grip.

agenesia, agenesis *f.* agenesia, agenesis. 1. congenital failure of an organ to grow or develop; 2. sterility or impotence.

agente *m.* agent, factor.

ágil *a.* agile, nimble; mentally sharp.

agilidad *f.* agility; **___ mental** / mental **___**.

agitación *f.* excitement, agitation.

agitar *v.* to stir up, to shake; **___ la botella** / to shake the bottle; **agitarse** *vr.* to become agitated or excited.

aglomeración *f.* agglomeration.

aglutinación *f.* agglutination, the act of binding together.

aglutinante *m.* agglutinant, agent or factor that holds parts together during the healing process.

agobiar *v.* to weigh down; to burden.

agonía *f.* agony, anguish. 1. extreme suffering; 2. state preceding death.

agonizar *vi.* to agonize.

agorafobia *f.* agoraphobia, fear of being alone in a wide open space.

agotado-a *a.* exhausted, tired.

agotador-a *a.* exhausting, tiring.

agotamiento *m.* exhaustion, extreme fatigue; wasting.

agotar *v.* to exhaust; **___ todos los recursos** / to **___** all means.

agradable *a.* pleasant.

agradecer *vi.* to be grateful, to be thankful.

agradecido-a *a.* grateful, thankful.

agrafía *f.* agraphia, loss of ability to write due to a brain disorder.

agrandamiento *m.* enlargement.

agrandar *v.* to enlarge.

agranulocitosis *f.* agranulocytosis, acute condition caused by the absence of leukocytes in the blood.

agregar *v.* to add.

agresivo-a *a.* aggressive, hostile.

agriarse *vr.* to turn sour.

agrietado-a *a.* chapped; **labios ___-s** / **___** lips; **manos ___-as** / **___** hands.

agrio-a *a.* sour.

agua *f.* water; **abastecimiento de ___** / **___** supply; **___ alcanforizada** / camphor julep; **___ corriente o de pila** / tap **___**; **___ de rosa** / rose **___**; **___ helada** / ice **___**; **___ oxigenada** / hydrogen peroxide; **bolsa de ___ caliente** / hot **___** bottle; **cama de, colchón de ___** / **___** bed; **contaminación del ___** / **___** pollution; **ingestión o toma de ___** / **___** intake; **purificación del ___** / **___** purification; **soluble en ___** / **___** soluble.

aguado-a *a.* watered down.

aguantar *v.* to hold; to endure.

agudo-a *a.* acute, piercing, sharp.

agüero *m.* omen.

aguja *f.* needle; **___ hipodérmica** / hypodermic **___**.

agujero *m.* hole.

ahí *adv.* there.

ahijado-a *m., f.* godchild.

ahogamiento *m.* drowning.

ahogar *vi.* to drown; to smother, to extinguish; **ahogarse** *vr.* to drown oneself; to choke.

ahora *adv.* now, presently.

ahorcarse *vr., vi.* to hang oneself.

ahorita *adv.* right away.

ahorrar *v.* to save; to spare; **___ tiempo** / **___** time.

aire *m.* air, wind; breath; **___ acondicionado** / **___** conditioned; **___ contaminado, viciado** / contaminated **___**, pollution; **___ de ventilación** / ventilated **___**; **___ respiratorio** / tidal **___**; **bolsa de ___** / **___** pocket; **burbujas de ___** / **___** bubbles; **cámara de ___** / **___** chamber; **conducto de ___** / airway, air passage; **enfriado por ___** / **___**-cooled; **falta de ___** / **___** hunger; **falto de ___** / shortness of breath.

airear *v.* to aerate, to ventilate. 1. to saturate a liquid with air; 2. to change the venous blood into arterial blood in the lungs; 3. to circulate fresh air.

aislado-a *a.* isolated.

aislamiento *m.* isolation; **___ protector** / protective **___**; **sala de ___** / **___** ward.

aislar *v.* to isolate.

ajo *m.* garlic.

ajustado-a *a.* tight-fitting; adjusted.

ajustar *v.* to tighten; to adjust.

ala *m.* wing.

alambre *m.* wire.

alargado-a *a.* elongated, as the digestive tract.

alargar *vi.* to lengthen; to prolong.

alarma *f.* alarm; danger signal; **___ de fuego** / fire **___**.

alarmante *a.* alarming.

alarmar *v.* to alarm; **alarmarse** *vr.* to become alarmed.

albahaca *f.* sweet basil.

alberca *f.* swimming pool; pond; tank.

albinismo *m.* albinism, lack of pigment in the

Sin agregaciones pulmonares – without crepitations

skin and hair.

albino-a *m., f.* albino, person afflicted with albinism.

albúmina *f.* albumin, protein component.

albuminuria *f.* albuminuria, presence of albumin or globulin in the urine.

alcaloide *m.* alkaloid, one of a group of organic, basic substances found in plants.

alcalosis *f.* alkalosis, physiological disorder in the normal acid-base balance of the body.

alcance *m.* reach; span; **al ___ de** / within ___.

alcanfor *m.* camphor, camphor julep.

alcanzar *vi.* to reach; to catch up.

alcohol *m.* alcohol; **___ etílico** / ethyl ___.

alcohólico-a *m., f.* an alcoholic; *a.* alcoholic.

alcoholismo *m.* alcoholism, excess intake of alcohol.

aldosterona *f.* aldosterone, hormone produced by the adrenal gland.

aldosteronismo *m.* aldosteronism, anomaly caused by excessive secretion of aldosterone.

alegre *a.* cheerful, joyful, merry.

alelo, alelomorfo *m.* allele, any one of a series of two or more genes situated at the same place in homologous chromosomes that determined alternative characteristics in inheritance.

alentar *vi.* to encourage, to reassure.

alérgenos *m. pl.* allergens, allergy causing agents; **___ ambientales** / environmental ___.

alergia *f.* allergy.

alérgico-a *a.* allergic; **reacción ___** / ___ reaction; **rinitis ___** / ___ rhinitis.

alergista *m., f.* allergist.

alerta *a.* alert, vigilant.

aleteo *m.* flutter, cardiac arrhythmia characterized by fast auricular contractions that simulate the flutter of the wings of birds; ___ **auricular** / ___, atrial, auricular; **___ ventricular** / ___, ventricular; **___ y fibrilación** / and fibrillation.

aleucemia *f.* aleukemia, absence or deficiency of leukocytes in the blood.

alexia *f.* alexia, inability to understand the written word.

alfiler *m.* pin.

alfombra *f.* rug.

álgido-a *a.* algid, cold.

algodón *m.* cotton.

algor *m.* algor, chill.

algoritmo *m.* algorithm, arithmetical and algebraic method used in the diagnosis and treatment of a disease.

aliento *m.* 1. breath; **sin ___** / breathless; **mal ___** / bad ___. 2. encouragement.

aligeramiento *m.* lightening, descent of the uterus into the pelvic cavity in the final stage of pregnancy.

aligerar *v.* to lighten, to ease.

alimentación *f.* feeding, alimentation, nourishment; **___ enteral** / enteral ___; **___ forzada** / forced ___; **horario de ___** / feeding schedule;

___ **intravenosa** / intravenous ___; **___ por sonda** / tube ___; **___ rectal** / rectal ___; **requisitos de la ___** / food requirements.

alimentar *v.* to nourish, to feed.

alimenticio-a *a.* alimentary, nourishing; **aditivos ___-s** / food additives; **intoxicación ___** / food poisoning; **tracto ___** / ___ tract.

alimento *m.* food, nourishment, nutrient; **___-s enriquecidos** / ___ supplements; **manipulación de ___-s** / ___ handling.

aliviado-a *a.* relieved, alleviated.

aliviar *v.* to relieve, to alleviate; [*un dolor*] to lessen.

alivio *m.* relief; **¡qué ___!** / what a relief!

almacenamiento *m.* storage; [*toma*] **captura y ___** / uptake and ___.

almanaque *m.* calendar, almanac.

almeja *f.* clam.

almendra *f.* almond.

almidón *m.* starch, main form of storage of carbohydrates.

almohada *f.* pillow.

almohadilla *f.* pad.

almorzar *vi.* to have lunch.

almuerzo *m.* lunch.

alógeno-a *a.* allogenic, having a different genetic constitution from others belonging to the same species; **sistema ___** / ___ system; **células ___-as** / ___ cells.

aloinjerto *m.* allograft, V. homoinjerto.

alojamiento *m.* lodging.

alojar *v.* to lodge, to accommodate.

alopecia *f.* alopecia, loss of hair.

alquilar *v.* to rent.

alrededor *adv.* around, about.

alteración *f.* alteration, change, modification.

alterar *v.* to alter, to change.

alternar *v.* to alternate.

alternativa *f.* alternative, option.

alto-a *a.* tall. *alta — discharge (from hospital)*

altura *f.* height.

alucinación, alucinamiento *f., m.* hallucination, subjective feeling not related to a real stimulus; **___ auditiva** / auditory ___, imaginary perception of sound; **___ gustativa** / gustatory ___, imaginary perception of taste; **___ motor** / motor ___, imaginary perception of body movements; **___ olfativa** / olfactory ___, imaginary perception of odors; **___ táctil** / haptic ___, imaginary perception of pain, temperature or other skin sensations.

alucinar *v.* to hallucinate.

alucinógeno *m.* hallucinogen, drug that produces hallucinations, such as LSD, peyote or mescaline.

alucinosis *f.* hallucinosis, state of persistent hallucinations; **___ alcohólica** / alcoholic ___, extreme fear accompanied by auditory hallucinations.

alumbramiento *m.* parturition, the act of giving birth.

alveolar *a.* alveolar, rel. to an alveolus.

alvéolo *m.* alveolus, cavity; ___ **pulmonar** / air sac.

alzar *vt.* to raise, to lift; *vr.* **alzarse** to raise oneself, to get up.

Alzheimer, enfermedad de *f.* Alzheimer's disease, presenile dementia.

allí *adv.* there.

amable *a.* kind, nice.

amalgamar *v.* to amalgamate, to mix.

amamantar *v.* to nurse, to suckle, to breast-feed.

amar *v.* to love.

amargado-a *m., f.* a bitter person; *a.* [*persona*] bitter.

amargar *vi.* to make bitter; **amargarse** *vr., vi.* to become bitter.

amargo-a *a.* bitter.

amargura *f.* bitterness.

amarillento-a *a.* yellowish.

amarillo-a *a.* yellow.

amarrar *v.* to tie, to fasten, to secure.

amasadura, amasamiento *f., m.* kneading, methodical rubbing and pressing of muscles.

amastia *f.* amastia, absence of breasts.

ambarino-a *a.* amber-colored.

ambición *f.* ambition.

ambicionar *v.* to aspire.

ambidextro *a.* ambidextrous.

ambiente *m.* environment, ambiance, setting.

ambivalencia *f.* ambivalence.

ambliopía *f.* amblyopia, diminished vision.

ambos-as *a.* both.

ambulancia *f.* ambulance.

ambulante, ambulatorio-a *a.* ambulant, ambulatory. Canbe[as an outpatient]

ameba *m.* amoeba, ameba, one-celled organism.

amebiano-a *a.* amebid, rel. to amebae.

amebiasis *f.* amebiasis, infection by amebae.

amenaza *f.* threat; menace.

amenazar *vi.* to threaten.

ameno-a *a.* pleasant, affable.

amenorrea *f.* amenorrhoea, absence of menstrual period.

americano-a *a.* American.

ametropía *f.* ametropia, poor vision due to an anomaly or disturbance in the refractive powers of the eye.

amígdalas *f. pl.* amygdalae, tonsils.

amigdalitis *f.* tonsillitis, infl. of the tonsils.

amigdalotomía *f. surg.* tonsillectomy, removal of the tonsils.

amigo-a *m., f.* friend.

amiloide *a.* amyloid, starch-like protein.

amiloidosis *m.* amyloidosis, accumulation of amyloid in different tissues of the body.

amina *f.* amine, one of the basic compounds derived from ammonia.

aminoácido *m.* amino acid, an organic metabolic compound that is the end product of protein and necessary for the growth and development of the human body.

amistad *f.* friendship.

amnesia *f.* amnesia, loss of memory.

amniocentesis *m.* amniocentesis, puncture of the uterus to obtain amniotic fluid.

amnios *m.* amnion, membranous sac surrounding the embryo in the womb.

amniótico-a *a.* amniotic, rel. to the amnion; **fluido** ___ / ___ fluid; **saco** ___ / ___ sac.

amoldamiento *m.* molding, adjustment of the head of the fetus to the shape and size of the birth canal.

amoníaco *m.* ammonia.

amor *m.* love.

amoratado-a *a.* black and blue.

amorfo-a *a.* amorphous, without shape.

amparar *v.* to protect; to shelter.

ampicilina *f.* ampicillin, semisynthetic penicillin.

ampliación *f.* amplification.

ampliar *v.* to amplify, to magnify, to enlarge.

amplio-a *a.* wide, large, ample.

ampolla *f.* blister, bulla.

ámpula *f.* ampule, vial, small glass container.

amputación *f.* amputation.

amputar *v.* to amputate.

anabólico-a *a.* anabolic, rel. to anabolism; **esteroides** ___-s / ___ steroids.

anabolismo *m.* anabolism, cellular process by which simple substances are converted into complex compounds; constructive metabolism.

anacidez *f.* anacidity, state of being without acid.

anaeróbico-a *a.* anaerobic, rel. to anaerobes.

anaerobio *m.* anaerobe, germ that multiplies in the absence of air or oxygen.

anafase *f.* anaphase, a stage in cell division.

anafiláctico-a *a.* anaphylactic, rel. to anaphylaxis.

anafilaxis *f.* anaphylaxis, extreme allergic reaction; hypersensitivity.

anal *a.* anal; **fístula** ___ / *f.* ___ fistula.

analfabeto-a *m., f. a.* illiterate.

analgésico *m.* analgesic, pain reliever.

análisis *m.* analysis, test, assay.

analizar *vi.* to analyze, to examine.

analogía *f.* analogy, similarity.

anaplasia *f.* anaplasia, lack or loss of differentiation of cells.

anaplástico-a *a.* anaplastic, rel. to anaplasia.

anaquel *m.* shelf; shelf-like structure.

anaranjado-a *a.* orange.

anasarca *f.* anasarca, generalized edema; dropsy.

anastomosis *f. surg.* anastomosis, creation of a passage or communication between two or more organs; inosculating.

anatomía *f.* anatomy, science that studies the structure of the human body and its organs; ___ **macroscópica** / gross ___, rel. to structures that can be seen with the naked eye; ___ **topográfica** / topographic ___, rel. to a specific area of the body.

anatómico-a *a.* anatomic, anatomical, rel. to anatomy.

anciandad *f.* old age.

anciano-a *m., f.* old man, old woman.

andador *m.* walker, device used to help a person walk.

andar *vi.* to walk; to go; ___ **con cuidado** / to be careful.

andrógeno *m.* androgen, masculine hormone; *a.* androgenic, rel. to the male sexual characteristics.

androginoide *a.* androgynous, having both male and female characteristics.

androtomía *f.* androtomy, dissection of a cadaver.

anejos, anexos *m. pl.* adnexa, appendages such as found in the uterine tubes.

anemia *f.* anemia, insufficiency of blood cells either in quality, quantity or in hemoglobin content; ___ **aplástica** / aplastic ___, highly deficient production of blood cells; ___ **de glóbulos falciformes** / sickle cell ___; ___ **hemorrágica o hemolítica** / hemorrhagic, hemolytic ___, progressive destruction of red blood cells; ___ **hipercrómica** / hyperchromic ___, abnormal increase in the hemoglobin content; ___ **hipocrómica y microcítica** / hypochromic and microcytic ___, small-sized blood cells and insufficient amount of hemoglobin; ___ **macrocítica** / macrocytic ___, large-sized blood cells, pernicious anemia; ___ **por deficiencia de hierro** / iron deficiency ___.

anergia *f.* anergy, 1. asthenia, lack of energy; 2. reduction or lack of response to a specific antigen.

anestesia *f.* anesthesia; ___ **en silla de montar** / saddle block ___; ___ **epidural** / epidural ___; ___ **general** / general ___; ___ **general intravenosa** / general intravenous ___; ___ **general por inhalación** / general ___ by inhalation; ___ **general por intubación** / general ___ by intubation; ___ **local** / local ___; ___ **raquídea** / spinal ___; ___ **regional** / regional ___.

Anestesia	*Anesthesia*
con hipotensión controlada	hypotensive
en silla de montar	saddle block
endotraqueal	endotracheal
epidural	epidural
general intravenosa	general intravenous
general por inhalación	general by inhalation
general por intubación	general by intubation
intercostal	intercostal
local	local
por hipnosis	hypnosis
tópica	topical
térmica	thermic
raquídea	spinal
regional	regional

anestesiar *v.* to anesthetize.

anestésico *m.* anesthetic.

anestesiólogo-a *m., f.* anesthesiologist.

aneurisma *m.* aneurysm, dilation of a portion of the wall of the artery; ___ **aórtico** / aortic ___; ___ **cerebral** / cerebral ___; ___ **saculado** / berry ___; ___ **desecante** / dissecting ___; ___ **falso** / false ___; ___ **fusiforme** / fusiform ___; ___ **verdadero** / true ___.

aneurismal *a.* aneurysmal, rel. to an aneurysm.

aneurismectomía *f. surg.* aneurysmectomy, excision of an aneurysm.

anexo-a *a.* contiguous, annexive. **anfetamina** *f.* amphetamine, type of drug used as a stimulant of the nervous system.

anfetamina *f.* amphetamine, type of drug used as a stimulant of the nervous system.

angiitis *f.* angiitis, infl. of a blood or lymph vessel.

angina *f.* angina, painful constrictive sensation; ___ **intestinal** / intestinal ___, acute abdominal pain caused by insufficient blood supply to the intestines; ___ **laríngea** / laryngeal ___, infl. of the throat; ___ **pectoris** / ___ pectoris, chest pain caused by insufficient blood supply to the heart muscle.

angiocardiografía *f.* angiocardiography, x-ray of the heart chambers.

angioedema *f.* angioedema, angioneurotic edema, allergic infl., gen. of the face.

angioespasmo *m.* angiospasm, prolonged contraction of a blood vessel.

angiogénesis *f.* angiogenesis, the development of the vascular system.

angiografía *f.* angiography, x-ray of the blood vessels after injection of a substance to show their outline.

angiograma *m.* angiogram; visualization of a blood vessel obtained after injecting a radiopaque substance.

angioma *m.* angioma, benign vascular tumor.

angioplastia *f. surg.* angioplasty, plastic surgery of the blood vessels; ___ **coronaria percutánea** / percutaneous coronary ___; ___ **periférica percutánea** / percutaneous peripheral ___.

angioplastia transluminal percutánea *f.* percutaneous transluminal angioplasty, process of dilating an artery or vessel by using a balloon that is inflated by pressure.

angloparlante *m., f.* English speaker.

angosto-a *a.* narrow; tapered.

ángulo *m.* angle.

angustia *f.* anguish, distress.

angustiado-a *a.* distraught, distressed.

anhidrasa *f.* anhydrase, enzyme that catalyzes the removal of water from a compound; **inhibidores de** ___ **carbónica** / carbonic ___ inhibitors.

anhidrosis *f.* anhidrosis, diminished secretion of sweat.

anillo *m.* ring, margin, verge; ___ **anal** / anal verge.

animal *m.* animal.

animar *v.* to animate, to cheer up; **animarse** *vr.* to become more lively.

ánimo *m.* spirit; **estado de** ___ / mood; **no tener** ___ / to be without spirit.

animosidad *f.* animosity, rancor.

aniquilación *f.* annihilation, total destruction.

anisocitosis *f.* anisocytosis, unequal size of red blood cells.

ano *m.* anus.

anoche *adv.* last night.

anodino *m.* anodyne, pain reliever; **-a** *a.* insipid.

anomalía, anormalidad *f.* anomaly, abnormality, irregularity.

anorexia *f.* anorexia, disorder characterized by total lack of appetite.

anoréxico-a *a.* 1. lacking appetite; 2. *n.* person affected with anorexia nervosa.

anormal *a.* abnormal, irregular.

anosmia *f.* anosmia, lack of the sense of smell.

anotar *v.* to make or take note.

anovulación *f.* anovulation, cessation of ovulation.

anoxemia *f.* anoxemia, insufficient oxygen in the blood.

anoxia *f.* anoxia, lack of oxygen in body tissues.

anquilosado-a *a.* ankylosed, immobilized.

anquilosis *f.* ankylosis, immobility of an articulation.

ansiedad *f.* anxiety, anguish, state of apprehension or excessive worry; **estados de** ___ / ___ disorders; **neurosis de** ___ / ___ neurosis.

ansioso-a *a.* anxious, apprehensive.

anteayer *adv.* the day before yesterday.

antebrazo *f.* forearm.

antecubital *a.* antecubital, preceding the elbow.

anteflexión *f.* anteflexion, bending forward.

antemano *adv.* beforehand.

anteojos *m. pl.* eyeglasses; binoculars. *V.* **espejuelos.**

antepasados *m. pl.* ancestors.

antepié *m.* ball of the foot.

anterior *a.* preceding, previous; [*tiempo*] before, pre-existing; [*posición*] ___ **ventral** / ventral ___.

anteroposterior *a.* anteroposterior, from front to back.

antes *adv.* before, sooner; **lo** ___ **posible** / as soon as possible; ___ **de** / before, prior to; ___ **de las comidas** / ___ meals.

anteversión *f.* anteversion, turn toward the front.

antiácido *m.* antacid, acidity neutralizer.

antialérgico *m.* antiallergic, drug used to treat allergies.

antiarrítmico-a *a.* antiarrhythmic, that can prevent or be effective in the treatment of arrhythmia; **agentes** ___**-s** / cardiac depressants.

antiartrítico-a *a.* antiarthritic, rel. to medication used in the treatment of arthritis.

antibiótico *m.* antibiotic, antibacterial drug.

anticarcinógeno *m.* anticarcinogen, drug used

in the treatment of cancer.

anticipar *v.* to anticipate.

anticoagulante *m.* anticoagulant, substance used in the prevention of blood clotting.

anticolinérgico-a *a.* anticholinergic, that rel. to the blockage of the impulses of the parasympathetic nerves.

anticonceptivo *m.* contraceptive; **-a** *a.* that acts as a contraceptive; **drogas** ___**-s** / anovulatory drugs; **injerto** ___ / ___ implant; ___ **oral** / oral ___.

anticonvulsante, anticonvulsivo *m.* anticonvulsant, medication used to prevent fits or convulsions.

anticuerpo *m.* antibody, protein substance produced by lymph tissue in response to the presence of an antigen; ___**-s de reacción cruzada** / cross reacting ___**-s**; ___ **monoclónico** / monoclonal ___, derived from hybridoma cells.

antidepresivo *m.* antidepressant, medication or process used in the treatment of depression.

antidiurético *m.* antidiuretic, drug that decreases urine secretion.

antídoto *m.* antidote, substance used to neutralize a poison; ___ **universal** / universal ___.

antiemético *m.* antiemetic, medication used to treat nausea.

antiespasmódico *m.* antispasmodic, drug used in the treatment of spasms.

antígeno *m.* antigen, toxic substance which stimulates formation of antibodies; ___ **carcinoembriogénico** / carcinoembryogenic ___.

antihipertensivo *m.* antihypertensive, medication to lower elevated blood pressure.

antihistamínico *m.* antihistamine, medication used in the treatment of some allergies.

antiinflamatorio *m.* anti-inflammatory, agent used to treat inflammations.

antineoplástico *m.* antineoplastic, drug that controls or destroys cancer cells.

antipatía *f.* antipathy, aversion.

antipirético *m.* antipyretic, agent that reduces fever.

antiprurítico *m.* antipruritic, medication used to reduce itching.

antiséptico *m.* antiseptic, agent that destroys bacteria.

antitóxico *m.* antitoxin, neutralizer of the effects of toxins.

antitoxina *f.* antitoxin, antibody that has a neutralizing effect on a given poison introduced in the body by a microorganism.

antivirósico *m.* antiviral, agent that stops the action of a virus.

antracosis *f.* anthracosis, lung condition due to prolonged inhalation of coal dust.

antrectomía *f. surg.* antrectomy, removal of the wall or walls of an antrum.

antro *m.* antrum, cavity.

antropoide *a.* anthropoid, of human resemblance.

anular *a.* annular, circular, ring-shaped; **erupción** ___ / ___ rash; *v.* to cancel, to make void, to annul.

anuria *f.* anuria, lack of urine production due to kidney malfunction.

año *m.* year.

aorta *f.* aorta, major artery originating from the left ventricle; ___ **ascendente** / ascending ___; **cayado de la** ___ / aortic arch; **coartación o compresión de la** ___ / coarctation of the ___; **descendente** / descending ___.

aórtico-a *a.* aortic, rel. to the aorta; **válvula semilunar** ___ / ___ semilunar valve.

aortocoronaria *a.* aortocoronary, rel. to the aorta and coronary arteries.

aortografía *f.* aortography, outline of the aorta on an x-ray.

aortoilíaca *a.* aortoiliac, rel. to the aorta and the iliac arteries.

apagado-a *a.* turned off; dim, unlit.

apagar *vi.* [*luces*] to turn off; [*fuego*] to put out.

aparato digestivo *m.* digestive system.

aparato eléctrico *m.* electrical appliance.

aparente *a.* apparent, manifest, patent, visible.

apariencia *f.* appearance.

apasionado-a *a.* passionate.

apatía *f.* apathy, lack of interest.

apático-a *a.* apathetic, listless, languid.

apelar *v.* to appeal.

apellido *m.* surname, family name.

apenado-a *a.* grieved.

apenas *adv.* barely; no sooner than; as soon as.

apendectomía *f. surg.* appendectomy, removal of the appendix.

apéndice *m.* appendix.

apendicitis *f.* appendicitis, infl. of the appendix.

apendicular *a.* appendicular, rel. to the appendix.

apepsia *f.* apepsia, poor digestion.

aperitivo *m.* aperitive, aperient. 1. mild laxative, physic; 2. aperitif, agent that stimulates the appetite.

apesadumbrado-a *a.* mournful, grieved.

apetito *m.* appetite.

ápice *m.* apex, the upper or base point of an organ.

apio *m.* celery.

aplanar *v.* to flatten.

aplasia *f.* aplasia, failure of organ development.

aplazar *vi.* to postpone, to put off.

aplicación *f.* application; ___ **de hielo** / ice treatment, icing.

aplicador *m.* applicator; ___ **de algodón** / cotton ___.

aplicar *vi.* to apply.

apnea *f.* apnea, shortness of breath; ___ **del sueño** / sleep ___, intermittent apnea that occurs during sleep.

apófisis *f.* apophysis, bony outgrowth.

aponeurosis *f.* aponeurosis, connective tissue that attaches the muscles to the bones and to other tissue.

apoplejía *f.* apoplexy, stroke, cerebrovascular accident.

apoyar *v.* to back, to support; **apoyarse** *vr.* to lean on.

apoyo *m.* backing, support.

apraxia *f.* apraxia, lack of muscular coordination and movement.

apreciar *v.* to appreciate, to value; to be grateful.

aprender *v.* to learn.

apretado-a *a.* tight.

apretar *vi.* to tighten, to squeeze, to press down.

aprisa *adv.* fast.

aprobación *f.* approval, consent, acceptance.

aprobar *v.* to approve; to accept.

apropiado-a *a.* appropriate, adequate.

aprovechar *v.* to make use of; to take advantage of.

aproximado-a *a.* approximate; **-mente** *adv.* approximately.

aptitud *f.* aptitude, capacity, ability; **prueba de** ___ / ___ test.

apto-a *a.* competent, apt.

apurado-a *a.* in a hurry; in difficulty.

apurarse *vr.* to hurry.

apuro *m.* need; hurry; **estar en un** ___ / to be in trouble.

aquí *adv.* here; **por** ___ / this way.

aquietar *v.* to calm down.

Aquiles, tendón de *m.* Achilles tendon, the tendon that originates in the muscles of the calf and attaches to the heel.

aracnoide *m.* arachnoid, weblike membrane that covers the brain and spinal cord.

araña *f.* spider; ___ **viuda negra** / black widow ___.

arañar *v.* to scratch.

arañazo *m.* scratch.

árbol *m.* 1. anatomical structure resembling a tree; 2. tree.

arcadas *f. pl.* retching, spasmodic abdominal contractions that precede vomiting.

arco *m.* arch.

arder *v.* to have a burning feeling.

ardor *m.* ardor, burning feeling; ___ **en el estómago** / heartburn.

arena *f.* sand.

arenilla *f.* minute, sandlike particles.

arenoso-a *a.* sandy.

aréola *f.* areola, circular area of a different color around a central point.

Argyll Robertson, pupila de *f.* Argyll Robertson's pupil, a pupil of the eye that accommodates to distance but does not react to the refraction of light.

arma de fuego *m.* firearm.

armazón *f.* frame, supportive structure.

aroma *m.* aroma, pleasant smell.

aromático-a *a.* aromatic, rel. to an aroma.

arquetipo *m.* archetype, original type from which modified versions evolve.

arraigado-a *a.* deep-rooted.

arrancar *vi.* to tear off; to pull out.

arrebato *m.* fit; temporary insanity.
arreglado-a *a.* in order; neat; fixed.
arreglar *v.* to fix, to arrange.
arreglo *m.* settlement, agreement.
arrepentido-a *a.* repentant, regretful.
arrepentirse *vr., vi.* to regret; to repent.
arriba *adv.* above, upstairs; **de ___ a abajo** / from top to bottom.
arriesgado-a *a.* risky.
arriesgar *vi.* to risk, to imperil; **arriesgarse** *vr.* to take a risk.
arritmia *f.* arrhythmia, irregular heartbeats.
arrodillarse *vr.* to kneel.
arrojar *v.* to throw up, to vomit.
arroz *m.* rice.
arruga *f.* wrinkle.
arrugado-a *a.* wrinkled.
arrugar *vi.* to wrinkle; **arrugarse** *vr.* to become wrinkled.
arsénico *m.* arsenic; **envenenamiento por ___ / ___ poisoning.**
arteria *f.* artery; vessel carrying blood from the heart to tissues throughout the body; **___ innominada** / innominate **___.**
arterial *a.* arterial, rel. to the arteries; **enfermedades ___-es oclusivas** / **___ occlusive diseases; sistema ___ / ___ system.**
arterioesclerosis *f.* arteriosclerosis, hardening of the walls of the arteries.
arteriografía *f.* arteriography, x-ray of the arteries.
arteriograma *m.* arteriogram, angiogram of the arteries; **___ cerebral o carótico** / cerebral or carotid **___; ___ mesentérico** / mesenteric **___; ___ periférico** / peripheral **___ / ___ renal** / renal **___.**
arteriola *f.* arteriole, minute artery ending in a capillary.
arteriotomía *f. surg.* arteriotomy, opening of an artery.
arteriovenoso-a *a.* arteriovenous; rel. to an artery and a vein; **anastomosis ___ quirúrgica / ___ shunt, surgical; fístula ___ / ___ fistula; malformaciones ___-s / ___ malformations.**
arteritis *f.* arteritis, infl. of an artery.
articulación *f.* joint, articulation. 1. joint between two or more bones; **___ de la cadera** / hip **___; ___ esferoidea** / ball and socket **___; ___ del hombro** / shoulder **___; ___ de la rodilla** / knee **___; ___ sacroilíaca** / sacroiliac **___;** 2. articulation, distinctive and clear pronunciation of words in speech.
articular *a.* articular, rel. to the articulations; *v.* to articulate, to pronounce words clearly.
artículo *m.* article.
artificial *a.* artificial.
artrítico-a *a.* arthritic, rel. to or suffering from arthritis.
artritis *f.* arthritis, infl. of an articulation or joint; **___ aguda** / acute **___; ___ crónica** / chronic **___; ___ degenerativa** / degenerative **___; ___ hemofílica** / hemophilic **___; ___ reumatoidea**

/ rheumatoid **___; ___ traumática** / traumatic **___.**
artrodesis *f. surg.* arthrodesis. 1. fusion of the bones of a joint; 2. artificial ankylosis.
artrograma *m.* arthogram, x-ray of a joint.
artropatía *f.* arthropathy, any disease of the joints.
artroplastia *f. surg.* arthroplasty, reparation of a joint or building of an artificial one.
artroscopía *f.* arthroscopy, examination of the inside of a joint with an arthroscope.
artroscopio *m.* arthroscope, device used to examine the inside of a joint.
artrotomía *f. surg.* arthrotomy, incision of a joint for therapeutic purposes.
asa *f.* loop.
asado-a *a.* roasted.
asbesto *m.* asbestos.
asbestosis *f.* asbestosis, chronic infection of the lungs caused by asbestos.
ascariasis *f.* ascariasis, intestinal infection caused by a worm of the genus *Ascaris.*
ascárido *m.* ascaris, type of worm commonly found in the intestinal tract.
ascendencia *f.* ancestry, genealogy.
ascendiente *m.* ascendent, ancestor.
ascitis *f.* ascites, accumulation of fluid in the peritoneal cavity.
asco *m.* nausea; disgust, loathing; **dar ___ / to** produce nausea.
aseado-a *a.* clean, tidy.
asear *v.* to clean; **asearse** *vr.* to clean oneself.
asegurar *v.* to assure; **asegurarse** *vr.* to make sure.
asentaderas *f. pl.* buttocks.
asepsia *f.* asepsia, total absence of germs.
aséptico-a *a.* aseptic, sterile.
asexual *a.* asexual, having no gender; **reproducción ___ / ___ reproduction.**
asfixia *f.* asphyxia, suffocation; **___ fetal / ___ fetalis.**
asfixiarse *vr.* to asphyxiate, to suffocate.
así *adv.* like this; **___ que** / therefore.
asiento *m.* seat, space upon which a structure rests.
asignación *f.* assignment, task, mission.
asignar *v.* to assign.
asilo *m.* nursing home, shelter; **___ para ancianos / ___ for the aged.**
asimilación *f.* assimilation, absorption, and transformation of digested food by the body.
asimilar *v.* to assimilate.
asinergia *f.* asynergia, lack of coordination among normally harmonious organs.
asintomático-a *a.* asymptomatic, without symptoms.
asistencia *f.* 1. assistance, care, help; **___ social** / welfare; **___ social a la infancia** / child welfare; **recibir ___ / to be on relief;** 2. attendance.
asistente *m., f.* attendant, assistant.
asistir *v.* to attend; to help.

asistolia *f.* asystole, asystolia, absence of heart contractions.

asma *m.* asthma, allergic condition that causes bouts of short breath, wheezing, and edema of the mucosa.

asmático-a *a.* asthmatic, rel. to or suffering from asthma.

asociación *f.* association.

asociado-a *m., f.* associate.

asombrar *v.* to amaze; **asombrarse** *vr.* to be amazed.

aspecto *m.* appearance, aspect.

aspereza *f.* roughness, harshness.

aspermia *f.* aspermia, failure to form or emit semen.

áspero-a *a.* rough, harsh; **piel __ / __ skin.**

aspersión nasal *f.* the act of using nasal spray.

aspiración *f.* aspiration, inhalation.

aspirar *v.* to breathe in, to inhale; **__ por la mucosa nasal** / to snort.

aspirina *f.* aspirin, a derivative of salicylic acid.

astigmatismo *m.* astigmatism, defective curvature of the refractive surfaces of the eye.

astilla *f.* splinter.

astrágalo *m.* astragalus, ankle bone.

astringente *m.* astringent, agent that has the power to constrict tissues and mucous membranes.

astrocitoma *f.* astrocytoma, brain tumor.

asunto *m.* subject, matter; business.

asustado-a *a.* frightened, startled.

asustar *v.* to frighten, to scare; **asustarse** *vr.* to become frightened.

ataque *m.* attack, fit, stroke, bout, seizure; **__ cardíaco / heart __.**

ataraxia *f.* ataraxia, impassiveness.

atareado-a *a.* busy.

ataúd *m.* coffin, casket.

atavismo *m.* atavism, inherited trait from remote ancestors.

ataxia *f.* ataxia, deficiency in muscular coordination; **__ sifilítica** / tabes dorsal.

atelectasia *f.* atelectasis, partial or total collapse of a lung.

atención *f.* attention; care; courtesy; **__ médica** / medical care; **falta de __** / lack of __; **prestar __** / to pay attention.

atender *v.* to attend, to look after; to pay attention.

atento-a *a.* attentive; polite; **estar __ / to be __.**

atenuación *f.* attenuation, rendering less virulent.

ateo-a *m., f.* atheist.

atérmico-a *a.* athermic, without fever.

ateroma *f.* atheroma, fatty deposits in the intima of an artery.

atetosis *f.* athetosis, infantile spasmodic paraplegia.

atleta *m.* athlete.

atlético-a *a.* athletic.

atmósfera *f.* atmosphere.

atmósferico-a *a.* atmospheric.

atolondrado-a *a.* confused, bewildered.

atolondramiento *m.* confusion, bewilderment.

atomizador *m.* atomizer.

átomo *m.* atom.

atonía *f.* atony, lack of normal tone, esp. in the muscles.

atontado-a *a.* stunned, stupefied.

atopía *f.* atopy, type of allergy considered as having a hereditary tendency.

atópico-a *a.* rel. to atopia.

atorarse *vr.* to gag, to choke.

atormentar *v.* to torment.

atrás *adv.* behind; **ir hacia __ / to go backwards.**

atrasado-a *a.* backward, late, behind; **__ mental** / mentally retarded.

atravesar *v.* to cross; to go through; **__ la calle** / to cross the street.

atresia *f.* atresia, congenital absence or closure of a body passage.

atreverse *vr.* to dare, to take a chance.

atrevido-a *a.* daring; insolent.

atrial *a.* atrial, rel. to an atrium; **defecto septal __** / atrial septal defect.

atribuir *vi.* to attribute; to confer.

atrio *m.* atrium. 1. cavity that is connected to another structure; 2. upper chamber of the heart that receives the blood from the veins.

atrioventricular, auriculoventricular *a.* atrioventricular, auriculoventricular, rel. to an atrium and a ventricle of the heart, **nudo __ / __ node; orificio __ / __ orifice.**

atrofia *f.* atrophy, deterioration of cells, tissue, and organs of the body.

atropellar *v.* to run over, to trample.

atropina *f.* atropine sulphate, agent used as a muscle relaxer, esp. applied to the eyes to dilate the pupil and paralyze the ciliary muscle during eye examination.

atún *m.* tuna fish.

aturdido-a *a.* confused, stunned.

aturdimiento *m.* confusion, bewilderment.

aturdir *v.* to stun; to confuse.

audición *f.* audition, sense of hearing; **pérdida de la __** / hearing loss.

audífono *m.* hearing aid.

audiograma *m.* audiogram, instrument that records the degree of hearing.

audiovisual *a.* audiovisual, rel. to hearing and vision.

auditivo-a, auditorio-a *a.* auditory, rel. to hearing; **conducto __ / __ canal; nervio __ / __ nerve; tapón __ / ear plug.**

aumentar *v.* to increase, to augment, to magnify; **__ de peso** / to gain weight.

aumento *m.* increase.

aún *adv.* still, yet; **__ cuando** / even though.

aunque *conj.* although.

aura *f.* aura, sensation preceding an epileptic attack.

aurícula *f.* auricle. 1. the outer visible part of the ear; 2. either of the two upper chambers of the heart.

auricular *m.* earphone; *a.* 1. rel. to the sense of hearing; 2. rel. to an auricle of the heart.

auscultación *f.* auscultation, the act of listening to sounds arising from organs such as the lungs and the heart for diagnostic purposes.

auscultar *v.* to auscultate, to examine by auscultation.

ausencia *f.* absence.

ausente *a.* absent.

autismo *m.* autism, behavioral disorder manifested by extreme self-centeredness; ___ **infantil** / infantile ___.

autístico-a *a.* autistic, suffering from or rel. to autism.

autoclave *f.* autoclave, an instrument for sterilizing by steam pressure.

autóctono-a *a.* native, autoctonous, indigenous.

autodigestión *f.* autodigestion, digestion of tissues by their own enzymes and juices.

autógeno-a *a.* autogenous, produced within the individual.

autohipnosis *f.* autohypnosis, self-hypnosis.

autoinfección *f.* autoinfection, infection by an agent from the same body.

autoinjerto *m.* autograft, autogenous implant taken from another part of the patient's body.

autoinmunización *f.* autoimmunization, immunity resulting from a substance developed within the affected person's own body.

autoinoculable *a.* autoinoculable, susceptible to a germ from within.

autólogo-a *a.* autologous, derived from the same individual.

automatismo *m.* automatism, behavior not under voluntary control.

automedicación *f.* self-medication.

automóvil *m.* automobile.

autonomía *f.* autonomy.

autónomo-a *a.* autonomic, autonomous, that functions independently; **sistema nervioso** ___ / ___ nervous system.

autoplastia *f. surg.* autoplasty, implantation of an autograft.

autoplástico-a *a.* autoplastic, rel. to autoplasty.

autopsia *f.* autopsy, postmortem examination of the body.

autorización *f.* authorization.

autorizar *vi.* to authorize.

autosugestión *f.* autosuggestion, self-suggested thought.

auxilio *m.* aid, help; **primeros** ___-**s** / first ___.

avanzar *vi.* to advance.

avena *f.* oats; **harina de** ___ / oatmeal.

aventado-a *a.* bloated.

aventarse *vr.* to become bloated.

aversión *f.* aversion, dislike.

aviso *m.* notice; **dar** ___ / to notify.

avispa *f.* wasp; **picadura de** ___ / ___ sting.

avispón *m.* hornet.

avitaminosis *f.* avitaminosis, disorder caused by a lack of vitamins.

avivar *v.* to liven up; to strengthen.

avulsión *f. surg.* avulsion, removal or extraction of part of a structure.

axénico-a *a.* axenic, germ-free.

axial *a.* axial, rel. to the axis.

axila *f.* axilla, armpit.

axilar *a.* axillary, rel. to the axilla.

axis *m.* axis, imaginary central line passing through the body or through an organ.

ayer *adv.* yesterday.

Ayerza, síndrome de *m.* Ayerza's syndrome, syndrome manifested by multiple symptoms, esp. dyspnea and cyanosis, gen. as a result of pulmonary deficiency.

ayuda *f.* help; **sin** ___ / unassisted.

ayudante *m., f.* helper.

ayudar *v.* to help, to assist.

ayunar *v.* to fast.

ayuno *m.* fast.

azoospermia *f.* azoospermia, lack of spermatozoa in the semen.

azotemia *f.* azotemia, excess urea in the blood.

azúcar *m.* sugar, carbohydrate consisting essentially of sucrose; ___ **de la uva** / grape ___, dextrose.

azufre *m.* sulfur.

azul *a.* blue; **mal** ___ / ___ baby.

b *abr.* bacilo / bacillus; bucal / buccal.

baba *f.* spittle.

babear *v.* to slobber.

babero *m.* bib.

Babinski, reflejo de *m.* Babinski's reflex, dorsiflexion of the big toe when the sole of the foot is stimulated.

bacalao *m.* codfish.

bacilar *a.* bacillary, rel. to bacillus.

bacilemia *f.* bacillemia, presence of bacilli in the blood.

bacilo *m.* bacillus (*pl.* bacilli), rod-shaped bacteria; ___ **de Calmette-Guérin** / Calmette-Guérin bacillus, bacile bilié; ___ **de Koch** / Koch's ___, Mycobacterium tuberculosis; ___ **de la fiebre tifoidea** / typhoid ___, Salmonella typhi; **portador de** ___**-s** / bacilli carrier.

bacilosis *f.* bacillosis, infection caused by bacilli.

baciluria *f.* bacilluria, presence of bacilli in the urine.

bacín *m.* basin, large bowl; bedpan.

bacitracina *f.* bacitracin, antibiotic effective against some staphylococci.

bacteremia *f.* bacteremia, presence of bacteria in the blood.

bacteria *f.* bacterium; germ.

bacteriano-a *a.* bacterial; **infecciones** ___**-s** / ___ infections; **endocarditis** ___ / ___ endocarditis; **pruebas de sensibilidad** ___ / ___ sensitivity tests.

bactericida *m.* bactericide, agent that kills bacteria.

bacteriógeno *a.* bacteriogenic. 1. of bacterial origin; 2. that produces bacteria.

bacteriolisina *f.* bacteriolysin, antibody that destroys bacterial cells.

bacteriólisis *f.* bacteriolysis, the destruction of bacteria.

bacteriología *f.* bacteriology, the study of bacteria.

bacteriológico-a *a.* bacteriologic, bacteriological, rel. to bacteria.

bacteriólogo-a *m., f.* bacteriologist, specialist in bacteriology.

bacteriosis *f.* bacteriosis, an infection caused by bacteria.

bacteriostático-a *a.* bacteriostatic, that inhibits the growth or multiplication of bacteria.

bacteriuria *f.* bacteriuria, presence of bacteria in the urine.

baipás *m. (bypass) surg.* bypass, surgically created alternate channel or route. *V.* **derivación.**

bajar *v.* [*escaleras*] to go down; [*movimiento*] to lower; ___ **el brazo** / to lower the arm; ___ **de peso** / to lose weight.

bajo-a *a.* low, short; **presión** ___ / ___ blood pressure; **bajo** *prep.* under; ___ **observación** / ___ observation; ___ **tratamiento** / ___ treatment.

bala *f.* bullet; **herida de** ___ / ___ wound.

balance *m.* balance, equilibrium; ___ **acidobásico** / acid-base ___; ___ **hídrico** / fluid ___.

balanceado-a *a.* balanced; in a state of equilibrium.

balanitis *f.* balanitis, an infl. of the glans penis, gen. accompanied by infl. of the prepuce.

balanopostitis *f.* balanoposthitis, infl. of the glans penis and prepuce.

balanza *f.* balance, scale.

balbucear *v.* to babble.

baldado-a *a.* maimed, crippled.

balón *m.* balloon; ___ **insuflable** / ___ tamponade.

balsámico-a *a.* balmy.

bálsamo *m.* balsam, soothing agent.

banana *f.* banana.

banco *m.* bank; bench.

bandeja *f.* tray.

bañar *v.* to bathe; **bañarse** *vr.* to take a bath.

bañadera, bañera *f.* bathtub.

baño *m.* bath; bathroom; ___ **antipirético** / antipyretic ___, to reduce fever; ___ **aromático** / aromatic ___; ___ **con esponja** / sponge ___; ___ **de agua caliente** / hot ___; ___ **de agua fría** / cold ___; ___ **de agua tibia** / warm ___; ___ **de asiento caliente** / Sitz ___, from the waist down; ___ **de remolino** / whirlpool ___; **cuarto de** ___ / bathroom; **papel de** ___ / toilet tissue.

baragnosis *f.* baragnosis, inability to recognize weight and pressure.

barato-a *a.* inexpensive.

barba *f.* beard.

barbilla *f.* chin, the tip of the chin.

barbituratos *m.* barbiturates, derivatives of barbituric acid.

barbitúrico *m.* barbiturate, hypnotic and sedative agent.

barestesia *f.* baresthesia, the sensation of pressure or weight.

barifonia *f.* baryphonia, thick, heavy voice.

bario *m.* barium.

barorreceptor *m.* baroreceptor, a sensory nerve ending that reacts to changes in pressure.

barrer *v.* to sweep.

barrera *f.* barrier, obstacle.

barriga *f.* belly; **dolor de** ___ / ___ ache.

barrigón-a *a. pop.* pot-bellied.

barrio *m.* neighborhood.

barro *m.* blackhead, pimple; mud.

bartolinitis *f.* bartholinitis, infl. of Bartholin's vulvovaginal gland.

Bartolino, glándula de *f.* Bartholin's vulvovaginal gland.

basal *a.* basal, pertaining or close to a base; **enfermedad de los ganglios** ___**-es** / ___ ganglia disease; **metabolismo** ___ / ___ metabolic rate.

basca *f.* nausea. *V.* **arcadas.**

base *f.* base, foundation.

basial, basilar *a.* basal, basilar, rel. to a base.

básico-a *a.* basic.

basofobia *f.* basophobia, fear of walking.

bastante *a.* sufficient, enough.

bastar *v.* to be enough; **bastarse** *vr.* to be self-sufficient.

bastardo-a *m., f.* bastard; *a.* bastard, illegitimate.

bastón *m.* cane.

bastoncillo *m.* rod; ___-s y conos / ___-s and cones, sensitive receptors of the retina.

basura *f.* garbage, trash, refuse; **cesto de** ___ / wastebasket.

bata *f.* gown, housecoat.

batalla *f.* battle, struggle.

batallar *v.* to struggle.

batir *v.* to whip; beat; pound.

bazo *m.* spleen, vascular lymphatic organ situated in the abdominal cavity; ___ **accesorio** / accessory ___.

bebé *m.* baby, infant.

bebedero *m.* drinking fountain.

beber *v.* to drink.

bebida *f.* beverage; **dado a la** ___ / heavy drinker.

beca *a.* scholarship, grant.

bel *m.* bel, a unit of sound intensity.

beligerante *a.* belligerent.

Bell, parálisis de *f.* Bell's palsy, paralysis of one side of the face caused by an affliction of the facial nerve.

belladona *f.* belladona, medicinal herb whose leaves and roots contain atropine and related alkaloids.

bello-a *a.* beautiful.

Bencedrina *f.* Benzedrine, trade name for amphetamine sulfate.

Benedict, prueba de *f.* Benedict's test, chemical analysis to determine the presence of sugar in the urine.

benefactor-a *m., f.* benefactor.

beneficiado-a *a.* beneficiary.

beneficiar *v.* to do good; **beneficiarse** *vr.* to benefit, to profit.

beneficio *m.* benefit; **asignación de** ___ / allocation of ___; ___-s **de asistencia social** / welfare ___-s.

benigno-a *a.* benign.

benjuí *m.* benzoin, resin used as an expectorant.

béquico *m.* cough medicine.

beriberi *m.* beriberi, endemic neuritis caused by a deficiency of thiamine in the diet.

berrinche *m.* tantrum, fit of anger.

berro *m.* watercress.

besar *v.* to kiss.

beso *m.* kiss.

bestialidad *f.* bestiality, sexual relations with an animal.

bezoar *m.* bezoar, concretion found in the stomach or the intestines constituted by elements such as hair or vegetable fibers.

biaxial *a.* biaxial, having two axes.

biberón *m.* baby bottle; **suplemento con** ___ / bottle propping.

bibliografía *f.* bibliography.

biblioteca *f.* library.

bicarbonato *m.* bicarbonate, a salt of carbonic acid.

bíceps *m.* biceps muscle.

bicicleta *f.* bicycle: ___ **estacionaria** / stationary ___.

bicipital *a.* bicipital. 1. rel. to the biceps muscle; 2. having two heads.

bicóncavo-a *a.* biconcave, having two concave surfaces as in a lens.

biconvexo-a *a.* biconvex, with two convex surfaces as in a lens.

bicúspide *a.* bicuspid, having two points.

bicho *m.* bug, insect.

bien *adv.* well; **todo va o está** ___ / all is well.

bienestar *m.* well-being, welfare, solace.

bienvenida *f.* welcome.

bienvenido-a *a.* welcome, pleasant, well received.

bífido-a *a.* bifid, split in two.

bifocal *a.* bifocal, having two foci.

bifurcación *f.* bifurcation, division into two branches or parts.

bigeminia *f.* bigeminy, two pulse beats occurring in rapid succession.

bigote *m.* moustache.

bilabial *a.* bilabial, having two lips.

bilateral *a.* bilateral, having or rel. to two sides.

bilharziasis *f.* bilharziasis. *V.* **esquistosomiasis.**

biliar *a.* biliary, rel. to the bile, to the bile ducts, or to the gallbladder; **ácidos y sales** ___-es / ___ acids and salts; **conductos** ___-es / bile ducts; **cálculo** ___ / gallstone; **enfermedades de los conductos** ___-es / ___ tract diseases; **obstrucción del conducto** ___ / ___ duct obstruction; **pigmentos** ___-es / ___ pigments.

bilingüe *a.* bilingual.

biliosidad *f.* biliousness, disorder manifested by constipation, headache, and indigestion due to excess secretion of bile.

bilioso-a *a.* bilious, excess bile.

bilirrubina *f.* bilirubin, a red pigment of the bile.

bilirrubinemia *f.* bilirubinemia, presence of bilirubin in the blood.

bilirrubinuria *f.* bilirubinuria, presence of bilirubin in the urine.

bilis *f.* bile, gall, bitter secretion stored in the gallbladder.

bimanual *a.* bimanual, performed with both hands.

binario-a *a.* binary, consisting of two of the same.

bioensayo *m.* bioassay, sampling the effect of a drug on an animal to determine its potency.

biología *f.* biology, the study of live organisms; ___ **celular** / cellular ___; ___ **molecular** /

molecular ___ .

biólogo-a *m., f.* biologist.

biopsia *f.* biopsy, procedure to remove sample tissue for diagnostic examination; ___ **de la mama** / ___ of the breast; ___ **de la médula ósea** / bone marrow ___ ; ___ **del nodulo linfático** / ___ of lymph nodes; ___ **del cuello uterino** / ___ of the cervix; ___ **endoscópica** / endoscopic ___ ; ___ **por ablación** / ___ by ablation; ___ **por aspiración** / needle ___ ; ___ **por excisión** / excision ___ .

bioquímica *f.* biochemistry, the chemistry of living organisms.

biosíntesis *f.* biosynthesis, formation of chemical substances in the physiological processes of living organisms.

biotipo *m.* biotype, group of individuals with the same genotype.

bípedo *m.* biped, two-legged animal.

birrefringente *a.* birefringent, refracting twice.

bisabuelo-a *m., f.* great-grandfather; great-grandmother.

bisagra *f.* hinge; **movimiento de** ___ / ___ movement.

bisexual *a.* bisexual. 1. having gonads of both sexes, hermaphrodite; 2. having sexual relations with both sexes.

bisturí *m.* scalpel, surgical knife.

bizco-a *a.* cross-eyed.

biznieto-a *m., f.* great-grandson; great-granddaughter.

bizquera *f.* squint, the condition of being cross-eyed. *V.* **estrabismo.**

blanco *m.* target. 1. an object or area at which something is directed; 2. a cell or organ that is affected by a particular agent such as a drug or a hormone; 3. the color white; **-a** *a.* white.

blancura *f.* whiteness.

blancuzco-a *a.* whitish.

blando-a *a.* soft, bland.

blastema *f.* blastema, primitive mass substance from which cells are formed.

blastomicosis *f.* blastomycosis, infectious fungus disease.

blástula *f.* blastula, an early stage of the embryo.

blefarectomía *f. surg.* blepharectomy, excision of a lesion of the eyelid.

blefaritis *f.* blepharitis, infl. of the eyelid.

blefarocalasis *f.* blepharochalasis, relaxation of the skin of the upper eyelid due to loss of interstitial elasticity.

blefaroplastia *f. surg.* blepharoplasty, plastic surgery of the eyelids.

blefaroplejía *f.* blepharoplegia, paralysis of the eyelid.

blenorragia *f.* blennorrhagia. 1. discharge of mucus; 2. gonorrhea.

bloqueado-a *a.* blocked, obstructed.

bloqueador *m.* blocker, ___ **de canal cálcico, antagonista cálcico** / calcium channel ___ .

bloqueo *m.* block, stoppage, obstruction; ___

atrioventricular / heart ___ , atrioventricular, interruption in the A-V node; ___ **de rama** / heart ___ , bundle-branch; ___ **interventricular** / heart ___ , interventricular; ___ **senoatrial** / heart ___ , sinoatrial.

blusa *f.* blouse.

bobería *f.* foolishness.

bobo-a *m., f.* fool, simpleton; *a.* silly, foolish.

boca *f.* mouth; ___ **abajo** / face-down; ___ **arriba** / face-up; **por la** ___ / by mouth, orally.

boca de trinchera *f.* trench mouth, infection with ulceration of the mucous membranes of the mouth and the pharynx.

bocado *m.* mouthful, bite.

bocio *m.* goiter, enlargement of the thyroid gland; ___ **coloide endémico** / endemic, colloid ___ ; ___ **congénito** / congenital ___ ; ___ **exoftálmico** / exophthalmic ___ ; ___ **móvil** / wandering ___ ; ___ **tóxico** / toxic ___ .

bochorno *m.* embarrassment.

bofetada *f.* slap.

bofetón *m.* hard blow, forceful slap.

bola *f.* ball; ___ **adiposa** / fat pad; ___ **de pelo** / hair ___ , a type of bezoar.

bolo *m.* bolus, 1. a specific amount of a given substance administered intravenously; 2. dose in a rounded mass given to obtain an immediate response; 3. mass of soft consistency ready to be ingested; ___ **alimenticio** / alimentary ___ ; **infusión en** ___ / bolus ___ .

bolsa *f.* sac; bag; handbag, pouch, pocket; ___ **amniótica (de agua)** / amniotic ___ (water bag); ___ **de agua cliente** / hot water bottle; ___ **de hielo** / icepack; ___ **de papel** / paper bag; ___ **eléctrica** / heating pad.

bolsillo *m.* pocket.

bomba *f.* pump.

bombear *v.* to pump; ___ **hacia afuera** / to ___ out.

bombeo *m.* pumping; ___ **del corazón** / heart ___ ; ___ **estomacal** / stomach ___ .

bombero-a *m., f.* firefighter.

bombilla *f.* light bulb.

bondadoso-a *a.* kind.

boniato *m.* sweet potato.

bonito-a *a.* pretty.

bonito *m.* tuna fish.

boquiabierto-a *a.* open-mouthed.

borato de sodio *m.* borax.

borde *m.* border, edge; ___ **bermellón** / vermillion ___ , the exposed pink margin of a lip.

bordeando *a.* bordering.

borrachera *f.* drunken spree.

borracho-a *a.* drunk.

borradura, borramiento *f., m.* effacement, obliteration of an organ, such as the cervix during labor.

borrar *v.* to erase, scrape; wipe out.

bosquejo *m.* profile.

bostezar *vi.* to yawn.

bostezo *m.* yawn; yawning.

bota *f.* boot; ___ **enyesada** / short-leg cast.

botar *v.* to throw away; to hurl.
botella *f.* bottle.
botica *f.* drugstore, pharmacy.
boticario-a *m., f.* druggist, pharmacist.
botiquín *m.* medicine cabinet; ___ **de primeros auxilios** / first aid kit.
botón *m.* button; ___ **para llamar** / push ___.
botulismo *m.* botulism, food poisoning caused by a toxin that grows in improperly canned or preserved foods.
bóveda *f.* vault, dome-shaped anatomical structure.
bovino *a.* bovine, rel. to cattle.
bracero *m.* farmhand; laborer.
bradicardia *f.* bradycardia, abnormally slow heart beat.
bradipnea *f.* bradypnea, abnormally slow respiration.
braguero *m.* truss, binding device used to keep a reduced hernia in place; brace; ___ **de cuello** / neck ___.
braquidactilia *f.* brachydactyly, abnormally short fingers and toes.
braquiocefálico-a *a.* brachiocephalic, rel. to the arm and the head.
bravo-a *a.* angry; brave.
brazalete de identificación *m.* identification bracelet.
brazo *m.* arm.
brea *f.* tar.
bregma *m.* bregma, the point in the skull at the junction of the sagittal and coronal sutures.
breve *a.* brief; short; **en** ___ / in short, briefly.
Bright, enfermedad de *f.* Bright's disease. *V.* **glomerulonefritis.**
brillante *a.* bright.
brincar *vi.* to hop, to skip.
brindar *v.* to offer.
brisa *f.* breeze.
broma *f.* joke; **en** ___ / jokingly, kidding.
bromidrosis *f.* bromhidrosis, fetid perspiration.
broncoconstricción *f.* bronchoconstriction, diminution in the caliber of a bronchus.
broncodilatación *f.* bronchodilation, dilation of a bronchus.
broncodilatador *m.* bronchodilator, agent that dilates the caliber of a bronchus; **-a** *a.* **agentes** ___-**es** / ___ agents.
broncoesofagoscopía *f.* bronchoesophagoscopy, examination of the bronchi and esophagus with an instrument.
broncoespasmo *m.* bronchospasm, spasmodic contraction of the bronchi and bronchioles.
broncógeno-a *a.* bronchogenic, rel. to or originating in the bronchus.
broncografía *f.* bronchography, x-ray of the tracheobronchial tree using an opaque medium in the bronchi.
broncolito *m.* broncholith, a bronchial calculus.
bronconeumonía *f.* bronchopneumonia, acute infl. of the bronchi and the alveoli of the lungs.

broncopulmonar *a.* bronchopulmonary, rel. to the bronchi and the lungs.
broncoscopía *f.* bronchoscopy, inspection of the bronchi with a bronchoscope.
broncoscopio *m.* bronchoscope, instrument to examine the interior of the bronchi.
bronquial *a.* bronchial, rel. to the bronchi; **árbol** ___ / ___ tree; **espasmo** ___ / ___ spasm; **lavado** ___ / ___ washing.
bronquiectasia *f.* bronchiectasis, chronic dilation of the bronchi due to an inflammatory disease or obstruction.
bronquio *m.* bronchus, one of the larger tubes through which air enters the lungs.
bronquiocele *m.* bronchiocele, a localized dilation of a bronchus.
bronquiolitis *f.* bronchiolitis, infl. of the bronchioles.
bronquiolo *m.* bronchiole, one of the small branches of the bronquial tree.
bronquitis *f.* bronchitis, infl. of the bronchial tubes.
brotar *v.* to flare up.
brote *m.* flare-up, outburst, outbreak, reddening of the skin due to a lesion, infection, or allergic reaction.
brucelosis *f.* brucellosis, Mediterranean fever, undulant fever, disease caused by bacteria obtained through contact with infected animals or their by-products.
brusco-a *a.* abrupt, rude.
brutal *a.* brutal.
bruto-a *a.* stupid; rough.
bubón *m.* bubo, swelling of one or more lymph nodes, esp. in the axilla or groin.
bucal *a.* buccal, rel. to the mouth; **antiséptico** ___ / mouthwash; **higiene** ___ / oral hygiene; **por vía** ___ / by mouth.
buche *m.* mouthful; **un** ___ **de agua** / a ___ of water.
bueno-a *a.* good, kind; **buenos días** / good morning, **buenas tardes** / good afternoon; **buenas noches** / [*saludo*] good evening, [*despedida*] good night; **de buena fé** / in good faith.
bulbo *m.* bulb, circular or oval expansion of a tube or cylinder; ___ **piloso** / hair ___.
bulbouretral *a.* bulbourethral, rel. to the bulb of the urethra and the penis.
bulimia *f.* bulimia, hiperorexia, exaggerated appetite.
bulto *m.* lump; swelling; bundle, package.
bunio *m.* bunion, swelling of the bursa on the first joint of the big toe.
bunionectomía *f.* *surg.* bunionectomy, excision of a bunion.
burbuja *f.* bubble.
burdo-a *a.* coarse; rough.
buril *m.* burr, type of drill used to make openings in bones or teeth.
bursa *L.* bursa, saclike cavity containing

synovial fluid, situated in tissue areas where friction would otherwise occur; ___ **del tendón calcáneo** / Achille's ___; ___ **popliteal** / popiteal ___.

bursitis *f.* bursitis, infl. of a bursa.

buscar *vi.* to look for, to search.

búsqueda *f.* search; pursuit.

búster *m.* booster shot, reactivation of an original immunizing agent.

busto *m.* bust.

buzo *m.* diver.

buzón *m.* mailbox.

C *abr.* **caloría** / kilocalorie; **centígrado** / centigrade; **carbono** / carbon; **Celsius** / Celsius.

c *abr.* **caloría** / calorie; **cobalto** / cobalt; **cocaína** / cocaine; **contracción** / contraction.

cabalgamiento *m.* [*fracturas*] overriding, the slipping of one part of the bone over the other.

caballero *m.* gentleman.

caballo *m.* horse.

caballo de fuerza *m.* horsepower, a unit of power.

cabecear *v.* to nod; to drop one's head as when snoozing; *pop.* to nod off.

cabecera *f.* head of a bed or table.

cabellera *f.* head of hair.

cabello *m.* hair.

caber *vi.* to fit into something; to have enough room.

cabestrillo *m.* sling, bandage-like support.

cabeza *f.* head; **caída de la** ___ / ___ drop; **traumatismo del cráneo, golpe en la** ___ / ___ injury; **apoyo de** ___ / ___rest; **asentir con la** ___ / to nod one's head.

cabezón-a *a.* big-headed; stubborn.

cabizbajo-a *a.* crestfallen, downcast.

cabra *f.* goat; **leche de** ___ / ___ milk.

caca *f.* excrement, stool of a child.

cacao *m.* cacao. 1. plant from which chocolate is derived; 2. diuretic alkaloid.

cacosmia *f.* cacosmia, perception of imaginary disagreeable odors.

cachetada *f.* slap in the face.

cachete *m.* cheek.

cada *a.* each; ___ **día** / every day; ___ **dos, tres horas** / every two, three hours; ___ **uno-a** / ___ one; ___ **vez** / ___ time.

cadáver *m.* cadaver, corpse.

cadavérico-a / *a.* cadaverous, rel. to or having the appearance of a cadaver.

cadena *f.* chain; **reacción en** ___ / ___ reaction; **sutura en** ___ / ___ suture.

cadera *f.* hip; **articulación de la** ___ / ___ joint; ___ **de resorte** / ___ snapping; **dislocación congénita de la** ___ / congenital ___ dislocation; **restitución total de la** ___ / total ___ replacement.

cadmio *m.* cadmium, a bivalent metal similar to tin.

caducidad *f.* 1. expiration date; 2. old age.

caer *vi.* to fall; **caerse** *vr.* to fall down; ___ **muerto** / to drop dead.

café *m.* coffee.

cafeína *f.* caffeine, alkaloid present chiefly in coffee and tea used as a stimulant and diuretic.

cafetería *f.* cafeteria.

caída *f.* fall.

caído-a *a. pp.* of **caer**, fallen.

cajero-a *m., f.* cashier.

calabaza *f.* pumpkin, squash.

calambre *m.* cramp, painful contraction of a muscle; ___ **muscular localizado** / Charley horse.

calamina *f.* calamine, astringent and antiseptic used for skin disorders.

calavera *f.* skull.

calcáneo *m.* calcaneus, heel bone.

calcáreo-a *a.* calcareous, rel. to lime or calcium.

calcemia *f.* calcemia, presence of calcium in the blood.

calcetines *m.* socks.

cálcico *a.* calcic, rel. to lime.

calciferol *m.* calciferol, derivative of ergosterol, vitamin D_2.

calcificación *f.* calcification, hardening of organic tissue by deposits of calcium salts.

calcificado-a *a.* calcified.

calcinosis *f.* calcinosis, presence of calcium salts in the skin, subcutaneous tissues, or other organs.

calcio *m.* calcium; **antagonista del** ___ / ___ antagonist.

calcitonina *f.* calcitonin, a hormone secreted by the thyroid gland.

calciuria *f.* calciuria, presence of calcium in the urine.

cálculo *m.* calculus (*pl.* calculi), stone; ___ **biliar** / biliary ___, gallstone; ___ **de cistina** / cystine ___; ___ **de fibrina** / fibrin ___; ___ **de oxalato de calcio** / calcium oxalate ___; ___ **urinario** / urinary ___.

caldo *m.* broth, stock; ___ **de pollo** / chicken ___.

calefacción *f.* heating system; heat.

calendario *m.* calendar.

calentador *m.* heater.

calentamiento *m.* [*acondicionamiento físico*] warm-up.

calentar *vi.* to heat; **calentarse** *vr.* to warm oneself up.

calentura *f.* fever, temperature.

calenturiento-a *a.* feverish.

calibrador *m.* calibrator, gauge, measuring device.

calibrar *v.* to calibrate; to gauge, to measure the diameter of a canal or tube.

calibre *m.* caliber, the diameter of a tube or canal.

caliceal *a.* caliceal, rel. to the calix.

calicreína *f.* kallicrein, an inactive enzyme present in blood, plasma, and urine, that when activated acts as a powerful vasodilator.

calidad *f.* quality, property.

caliente *a.* hot, warm.

calificar *vi.* to qualify; to correct.

caliuresis *f.* kaliuresis, kaluresis, increased urinary excretion of potassium.

cáliz *m.* calyx, a cup-shaped organ, such as the renal calyx.

calma *f.* calm; calmness; **tener** ___ / to be calm.

calmado-a *a.* calm, serene.

calmante *m.* sedative, tranquilizer; *a.* soothing, mitigating.

calmar *v.* to calm down, to soothe; **calmarse** *vr.* to become calm.

calomel *m.* calomel, mercurous chloride used primarily as a local antibacterial element.

calor *m.* heat; warmth; ___ **de conducción** / ___, conductive; ___ **de convección** / ___, convective; **pérdida de** ___ / ___ loss; ___ **seco** / dry ___; **hace** ___ / it is hot; **tener** ___ / to be hot.

caloría *f.* calorie, a heat unit, commonly referred to as the energy value of a particular food; **gran** ___ / large ___; ___ **pequeña** / small ___.

calórico-a *a.* caloric, rel. to the energy value of food; **ingestión** ___ / ___ intake.

calostro *m.* colostrum, fluid secreted by the mammary glands before the secretion of milk.

calva *f.* bald crown of the head.

calvaria *f.* calvaria, superior portion of the cranium.

calvicie *f.* calvities, baldness.

calvo-a *a.* bald, without hair.

calzoncillos *m. pl.* men's underpants; shorts.

callado-a *a.* quiet, low-key.

callar *v.* to hush, to silence; **callarse** *vr.* to become quiet.

calle *f.* street.

callo, callosidad *m., f.* callus, corn.

calloso-a *a.* callous, rel. to a callus.

cama *f.* bed; **orinarse en la** ___ / bedwetting; **al lado de la** ___ / at bedside; **estar en** ___ / to be bedridden; **guardar** ___ / to stay in ___, bedrest; **ocupación de** ___-s / ___ occupancy; **recluido en** ___ / bed-confined; **ropa de** ___ / bedclothes.

cámara *f.* 1. chamber, cavity; ___ **anterior** / anterior ___; ___ **acuosa** / aqueous ___; ___ **hiperbárica** / hyperbaric ___; ___-s **oculares** / ___-s of the eye; 2. photographic camera.

camarón *m.* shrimp.

cambiar *v.* to change; **cambiarse** *vr.* to change clothes.

cambio *m.* change; [*posición*] shift.

camilla *f.* stretcher.

caminar *v.* to walk; to hike.

caminata *f.* a walk; a hike.

camino *m.* road; course, way.

camión *m.* truck; *Mex.* bus.

camisa *f.* shirt; ___ **de fuerza** / straightjacket.

camiseta *f.* men's undershirt; T-shirt.

camisón *m.* nightgown.

campanilla *f.* uvula, epiglottis.

campo *m.* field. 1. area or open space; 2. specialization.

cana *f.* gray hair.

canal *m.* canal, channel, trough, groove, tubular structure; ___ **femoral** / femoral ___; ___ **del parto** / birth ___; ___ **inguinal** / inguinal ___; ___ **radicular** / root ___.

canalículo *m.* canaliculus, small channel; ___ **biliar** / biliary ___, between liver cells; ___ **lacrimal, lagrimal** / lacrimal ___.

canasta *f.* basket.

cancelación *f.* cancellation.

cancelar *v.* to cancel, to annul.

canceloso-a *a.* cancellous, spongy, resembling a lattice.

cáncer *m.* cancer, tumor; **fases o etapas en relación a la extensión del** ___ / ___ staging; **grado de malignidad del** ___ / ___ grading; ___ **incipiente** / early ___.

cancerofobia *f.* cancerophobia, morbid fear of cancer.

canceroso-a *a.* cancerous, rel. to or afflicted by cancer.

candela *f.* fire; flame.

candente *a.* red-hot, burning.

candidiasis *f.* candidiasis, skin infection caused by a yeastlike fungus.

canela *f.* cinnamon.

cangrejo *m.* crab.

canilla *f.* shinbone; tibia.

canino *m.* cuspid tooth; **-a** *a.* rel. to dogs.

cannabis *L.* cannabis, marihuana, plant whose leaves have a narcotic or hallucinatory effect when smoked.

canoso-a *a.* gray-haired.

cansado-a *a.* tired, weary.

cansancio *m.* tiredness, fatigue.

cansar *v.* to tire; **cansarse** *vr.* to get tired.

cantidad *f.* quantity.

canto *m.* canthus. 1. angles at the corner of the eyes formed by the joining of the external and internal eyelids on both sides of the eye; 2. edge, rim.

cánula *f.* cannula, tube through which fluid and gas are put into the body.

canulación *f.* cannulation, the act of introducing a cannula through a vessel or duct; ___ **aórtica** / aortic ___.

caolín *m.* kaolin, natural hydrated aluminum silicate having absorbing qualities.

caos *m.* chaos.

capa *f.* layer.

capacidad *f.* capacity. 1. ability to contain; ___ **vital** / vital ___; 2. qualification, competence.

capaz *a.* able, capable.

capilar *m.* capillary, small blood vessel; ___ **arterial** / arterial ___, tiny channels carrying arterial blood; ___ **linfático** / lymph ___, minute vessels of the lymphatic system; ___ **venoso** / venous ___, small channels carrying venous blood; *a.* resembling hair.

capitélum *L.* capitellum. 1. bulb of a hair; 2. part of the humerus.

capítulo *m.* chapter.

caprichoso-a *a.* capricious; stubborn.

cápsula *f.* capsule, membranous enclosure.

cápsula articular *n.* capsular ligament, fibrous structure lined with synovial membrane surrounding the articulations.

capsulación *f.* capsulation, enclosure in a capsule or sheath.

caquéctico-a *a.* cachectic, rel. to cachexia.

caquexia *f.* cachexia, a grave condition marked by great loss of weight and general weakness.

cara *f.* face; __ **de luna** / moon __, round, puffy face usu. characteristic of someone who has been under steroid treatment for a long period of time; **peladura de** __ / __ peeling; *coloq.* **estiramiento de** __ / facelift.

caracol *m.* snail.

carácter *m.* character; quality; **tener buen** __ / to be good-natured; **tener mal** __ / to be ill-tempered.

característico-a *a.* characteristic.

caramba *int.* good gracious!

caramelo *m.* hard candy.

carbohidrato *m.* carbohydrate, organic substance composed of carbon, hydrogen, and oxygen such as starch, sugar, and cellulose.

carbólico *a.* carbolic, rel. to phenylic acid.

carbón *m.* coal.

carbonatado-a *a.* carbonated.

carbonización *f.* carbonization.

carbonizado-a *a.* charred.

carbono *m.* carbon; **dióxido de** __ / __ dioxide; **monóxido de** __ / __ monoxide.

carboxihemoglobina *f.* carboxyhemoglobin, a combination of carbon monoxide and hemoglobin that impairs the transportation of oxygen in the blood.

carbunco *m.* carbuncle, large boil of the skin that discharges pus.

cárcel *f.* jail.

carcinogénesis *f.* carcinogenesis, production of cancer.

carcinógeno *m.* carcinogen, cancer producing substance; **-a** *a.* carcinogenic.

carcinoma *m.* carcinoma, cancer derived from living cells of organs; __ **basocelular** / basal cell __; __ **broncogénico** / __ of the bronchi; __ **del cerebro** / cerebral __; __ **cervical** / cervical __; __ **de células escamosas epiteliales** / squamous cell __; __ **de células transicionales** / transitional cell __; __ **de la mama** / breast __; __ **endometrial** / endometrial __; __ **invasivo** / invasive __; __ **mucinoso** / mucinous __; __ **ovárico** / ovarian __; __ **papilar** / papillary __; __ **testicular** / testicular __.

carcinoma in situ *m.* carcinoma in situ, localized tumor cells that have not invaded adjacent structures.

carcinomatosis *f.* carcinomatosis, cancer that has spread throughout the body.

cardíaco-a *a.* cardiac, rel. to the heart; **asma** __ / __ asthma; **aurícula** __ / __ heart atrium; **ataque** __ / heart attack; **cateterización** __ / __ catheterization; **estimulación** __ **artificial** / __ pacing, artificial; **frecuencia** __ / heart rate; **gasto o rendimiento** __ / heart output; **generador del impulso** __ / __ impulse generator; **insuficiencia o fallo** __ **congestivo** / heart failure, congestive; **insuficiencia** __, **ventricular derecha** / heart failure, right-sided; **insuficiencia** __, **ventricular izquierda** / heart failure, left-sided; **masaje** __ / __

massage; **paro** __ / heart arrest, standstill; **reanimación** __ / __ resuscitation; **reflejo** __ / heart reflex; **taponamiento** __ / __ tamponade.

cardias *m.* cardia, esophageal orifice of the stomach.

cardioangiograma *m.* cardioangiogram, image by x-rays of the blood vessels and the chambers of the heart taken after injecting a dye.

cardiocentesis, cardiopuntura *f.* cardiocentesis, puncture or incision of a heart chamber.

cardioespasmo *m.* cardiospasm, contraction or spasm of the cardia.

cardiografía *f.* cardiography, recording of the movements of the heart by a cardiograph.

cardiógrafo *m.* cardiograph, instrument that traces the movements of the heart.

cardiograma *m.* cardiogram, electrical tracing of the impulses of the heart.

cardiología *f.* cardiology, the study of the heart.

cardiólogo-a *m., f.* cardiologist, specialist in cardiology.

cardiomegalia *f.* cardiomegaly, enlarged heart.

cardiomiopatía *f.* cardomyopathy, a disorder of the heart muscle; __ **alcohólica** / alcoholic __; __ **congestiva** / congestive __; __ **hipertrófica** / hypertrophic __.

cardiopatía *f.* heart disease; __ **por hipertensión** / hypertensive heart disease.

cardioplegia *f.* cardioplegia, heart paralysis.

cardiopulmonar *a* cardiopulmonary, rel. to the heart and the lungs; **máquina** __ / heart-lung machine; **puente** __ / __ bypass; **resucitación, reanimación** __ / __ resuscitation.

cardiotomía *f. surg.* cardiotomy 1. incision in the cardiac end of the stomach; 2. incision of the heart.

cardiotónico-a *a.* cardiotonic, having a tonic or favorable effect on the heart; **agente** __ / cardiac stimulant.

cardiovascular *a.* cardiovascular, rel. to the heart and blood vessels.

cardioversión *f.* cardioversion, the act of restoring the heart to a normal sinus rhythm by electrical countershock.

carditis *f.* carditis, infl. of the heart.

carecer *vi.* to lack.

carga *f.* load, burden.

cargar *vi.* to load; to carry.

caridad *f.* charity.

caries *f.* caries, dental cavity.

cariñoso-a *a.* affectionate.

cariólisis *f.* karyolysis, breakdown of the nucleus of a cell.

cariolítico-a *a.* karyolytic, rel. to or that produces karyolysis.

carión *m.* karyon, cellular nucleus.

cariotipo *m.* karyotype, chromosome characteristics of an individual species.

caritativo-a *a.* charitable.

carmesí, carmín *m.* carmine.

carne *f.* 1. meat; __ **asada** / roast beef; __ **de**

carnero / lamb; ___ **de puerco** / pork; ___ **de ternera** / veal; 2. flesh, muscular tissue of the body.

carnívoro-a *a.* carnivorous, that eats meat.

carnosidad *f.* carnosity, fleshy excrescence.

caro-a *a.* expensive, costly.

carótida *f.* carotid, main artery of the neck; **arterias ___-s** / ___ arteries.

carotina *f.* carotene, yellow-red pigment found in some vegetables that converts into vitamin A in the body.

carpo *m.* carpus, portion of the upper extremity between the hand and the forearm.

carraspera *f.* hoarseness; sore, itchy throat.

carretera *f.* highway.

carro *m.* automobile, car; cart.

carta *f.* letter.

cartera *f.* lady's handbag; wallet.

cartílago *m.* cartilage, elastic, semihard tissue that covers the bones.

carúncula *f.* caruncle, small, irritated piece of flesh; ___ **uretral** / urethral ___.

casa *f.* house, home; ___ **de socorro** / first aid station.

casado-a *a.* married.

casarse *vr.* to get married.

cáscara *f.* peel, shell.

cáscara sagrada *f.* cascara sagrada, the bark of *Rhamus Purshiana* shrub, commonly used to treat chronic constipation.

caseína *f.* casein, the main protein found in milk.

caseoso-a *a.* caseous, resembling curd or cheese.

casi *adv.* almost.

caso *m.* case, a specific instant of disease; ___ **ambulatorio** / ambulatory ___; **presentación de un** ___ / ___ reporting; **en** ___ **de** / in of; **hacer** ___ / to pay attention; **no viene al** ___ / it is irrelevant.

caspa *f.* dandruff; dander.

castaño-a *a.* brown, chestnut colored.

castigar *vi.* to punish.

castigo *m.* punishment.

castrar *v.* to castrate, to remove the gonads; [*animales hembras*] to spay.

casual *a.* casual, accidental.

casualidad *f.* chance; **de** ___ / by ___; **por** ___ / by ___.

catabolismo *m.* catabolism, cellular process by which complex substances are converted into simpler compounds; destructive metabolism.

catalepsia *f.* catalepsy, a condition characterized by loss of voluntary muscular movement and irresponsiveness to any outside stimuli, gen. associated with psychological disorders.

catálisis *f.* catalysis, alteration of the velocity of a chemical reaction by the presence of a catalyst.

catalítico-a *a.* catalytic.

catalizador *m.* catalyst, an agent that stimulates a chemical reaction.

cataplasma *f.* poultice.

cataplexia *f.* cataplexy, sudden loss of muscular tone caused by an exaggerated emotional state.

catarata *f.* cataract, opacity of the lens of the eye; ___ **blanda** / soft ___; ___ **madura** / mature ___; ___ **senil** / senile ___; ___ **verde** / green ___.

catarral *a.* rel. to catarrh.

catarro *m.* catarrh, cold, sniffle; ___ **de pecho, bronquial** / chest cold.

catarsis *f.* catharsis, purification. 1. purging the body of chemical or other material; 2. therapeutic liberation of anxiety and tension.

catártico *m.* cathartic, laxative; **-a** *a.* cathartic, rel. to catharsis.

catatonía *f.* catatony, a phase of extreme negativism in schizophrenia in which the patient does not speak, remains in a fixed position, and resists any attempts to activate his or her movement or speech. The same symptoms are present in other mental conditions.

catatónico-a *a.* catatonic, rel. to or affected by catatony.

catecolaminas *f., pl.* catecholamines, amines such as norepinephrine, epinephrine, and dopamine that are produced in the adrenal glands and have a sympathomimetic action.

categoría *f.* category; quality.

catéter *m.* catheter, a rubber or plastic tube used to drain fluid from a body cavity such as urine from the bladder, or to inject fluid, as in cardiac catheterization.

cateterización *f.* catheterization, insertion of a catheter.

cateterizar *vi.* to catheterize, to insert a catheter.

catgut *f.* catgut, type of surgical suture made from the gut of some animals.

cauda *f.* cauda, taillike structure.

caudal *a.* caudal, rel. to the tail.

causa *f.* cause, reason; **sin** ___ / unreasonable.

causalgia *f.* causalgia, burning pain in the skin.

causar *v.* to cause.

cáustico *m.* caustic, substance used to destroy tissue.

cautela *f.* caution.

cauterización *f.* cauterization, burning by application of a caustic, heat, or electric current.

cauterizar *vi.* to cauterize, to burn by application of heat or electric current.

cava *f.* cava, hollow organ, cavity. V. **vena cava.**

caverna *f.* cavern, cave, pathological cavity or depression.

cavernoso-a *a.* cavernous, having hollow spaces.

cavidad *f.* cavity, hole; ___ **abdominal** / abdominal ___; ___**-es cardíacas: auricular y ventricular** / heart chambers; ___**-es craneales** / cranial cavities; ___ **pelviana** / pelvic ___; ___ **torácica** / thoracic ___.

cebada *f.* barley.

cebolla *f.* onion.

cecostomía *f. surg.* cecostomy, surgical opening

into the cecum.

cefalea, cefalalgia *f.* cephalea, cephalalgia, headache.

cefálico-a *a.* cephalic, rel. to the head.

cefalorraquídeo-a *a.* V. **cerebroespinal.**

cefalosporina *f.* cephalosporin, wide spectrum antibiotic.

ceguera, ceguedad *f.* blindness; ___ **al color** / color ___; ___ **nocturna** / night ___; ___ **verde** / green ___; ___ **roja** / red ___.

ceja *f.* eyebrow.

celíaco-a *a.* celiac, rel. to the abdomen.

celiotomía *f. surg.* celiotomy. V. **laparotomía**

celoso-a *a.* jealous.

célula *f.* cell, structural unit of all living organisms; ___ **adiposa** / adipose ___; ___ **anaplástica** / anaplastic ___; ___ **basal** / basal ___; ___ **basurera** / scavenger ___; ___ **caliciforme** / goblet ___; ___ **columnar** / columnar ___; ___ **en diana** / target ___; ___ **ependimaria** / ependymal ___; ___ **epidérmica** / epidermal ___; ___ **errante** / wandering ___; **fagocítica** / phagocytic ___; ___ **falciforme** / sickle ___; ___ **gigante** / giant ___; ___ **madre** / stem ___; ___ **piramidal** / pyramidal ___.

celular *a.* cellular, rel. to the cell; **agua** ___ / ___ water; **compartimentos** ___-es / ___ compartments; **crecimiento** ___ / ___ growth; **tejido** ___ / ___ tissue.

celularidad *f.* cellularity, the condition of cells present in a tissue or mass.

celulitis *f.* cellulitis, infl. of connective tissue.

celulosa *a.* cellulose.

cementerio *m.* cemetery.

cemento *m.* cement.

cena *f.* evening meal, supper.

cenar *v.* to have dinner or supper.

cenizas *f. pl.* ashes; ___ **radioactivas** / fallout.

censo *m.* census.

centeno *m.* rye.

centígrado *a.* centigrade.

central, céntrico-a *a.* central; **sistema nervioso** ___ / ___ nervous system.

centrífugo-a *a.* centrifugal, going from the center outward.

centrípeto-a *a.* centripetal, going from the outside towards the center.

centro *m.* 1. center; ___ **de servicio de la salud** / community health ___; 2. middle, core.

ceño *m.* brow; **fruncir el** ___ / to frown.

cepa *f.* strain, group of microorganisms within a species or variety characterized by some particular quality.

cepillo *m.* brush; ___ **de dientes** / toothbrush.

cera *f.* wax. 1. beeswax; 2. waxy secretion of the body; ___ **depilatoria** / depilatory ___.

cerca *f. adv.* near; ___ **de aquí** / close by.

cercanía *f.* vicinity.

cercano-a *a.* close; neighboring, proximate.

cerclaje *m.* cerclage, procedure that consists of encircling a part with a wire loop or catgut, such as in binding together parts of a frac-

tured bone.

cereal *m.* cereal.

cerebelo *m.* cerebellum, posterior brain mass; **enfermedades del** ___ / cerebellar diseases.

cerebral *a.* cerebral, rel. to the brain; **apoplejía** ___ / cerebrovascular accident; **concusión o conmoción** ___ / ___ concussion; **edema** ___ / ___ edema; **embolismo y trombosis** ___ / ___ embolism and thrombosis; **hemorragia o infarto** ___ / ___ hemorrhage or infarct; **muerte** ___ / brain death; **trauma** ___ / brain injury; **tronco** ___ / brain stem; **tumor** ___ / brain tumor.

cerebro *m.* brain, cerebrum, portion of the central nervous system contained within the cranium that is the chief regulator of body functions; ___ **medio** / midbrain; **escán del** ___ **(gammagrama)** / ___ scan.

cerebroespinal, cefalorraquídeo-a *a.* cerebrospinal, rel. to the brain and the spinal cord.

cerebrovascular *a.* cerebrovascular, rel. to the blood vessels of the brain.

cereza *f.* cherry.

cero *m.* zero.

ceroso-a *a.* waxy.

cerrado-a *a.* closed.

cerradura *f.* lock.

cerrar *vi.* to close; ___ **con llave** / to lock.

certero-a *a.* accurate.

certeza *f.* certainty; accuracy.

certificado *m.* certificate; ___ **de defunción** / death ___.

cerumen *m.* cerumen, wax that builds up in the ear.

cerveza *f.* beer.

cervical *a.* cervical. 1. rel. to the cervix; 2. rel. to the area of the neck; **displasia** ___ / ___ dysplasia; **erosión** ___ / ___ erosion; **pólipo** ___ / ___ polyp.

cerviz *f.* nape of the neck.

cesar *v.* to cease, to stop.

cesárea *f.* cesarean section.

cese *m.* stoppage.

cetoacidosis *f.* ketoacidosis, acidosis caused by the increase of ketone bodies in the blood.

cetogénesis *f.* ketogenesis, production of acetone.

cetosa *f.* ketose.

cetosis *f.* ketosis, excessive production of acetone as a result of incomplete metabolism of fatty acids; acidosis.

cianocobalamina *f.* cyanocobalamin, vitamin B_{12}, complex of cyanide and cobalamin used in the treatment of pernicious anemia.

cianosis *f.* cyanosis, purplish blue discoloration of the skin, often as a result of cardiac, anatomic or functional abnormalities.

cianótico-a *a.* cyanotic, rel. to or afflicted by cyanosis.

cianuro *m.* cyanide.

ciática *f.* sciatica, neuralgia along the course of the sciatic nerve.

cibernética *f.* cybernetics, the study of biological systems such as the brain and the nervous system by electronic means.

cicatriz *f.* scar.

cicatrización *f.* cicatrization, scarring.

cicatrizante *m.* cicatrizant, agent that aids the healing process of a wound.

cicatrizar *v.* to scar, the healing process of a wound.

ciclamato *m.* cyclamate, artificial sweetening agent.

ciclectomía *f. surg.* cyclectomy, excision of a portion of the ciliary muscle.

ciclitis *f.* cyclitis, infl. of the ciliary body.

ciclo *m.* cycle, recurring period of time; ___ gravídico / pregnancy ___.

cicloforia *f.* cyclophoria, rotation of the eye due to muscle weakness.

ciclofosfamida *f.* cyclophosphamide, antineoplastic drug also used as an immunosuppressive in organ transplants.

ciclofotocoagulación *f.* cyclophotocoagulation, photocoagulation through the pupil with a laser, gen. used in glaucoma.

cicloplejía *f.* cycloplegia, paralysis of the ciliary muscle.

ciclosporina *f.* cyclosporine, immunosuppressive agent used in organ transplant.

ciclotimia *f. psych.* cyclothymia, disorder manifested by alternate states of agitation and depression.

ciclotímico-a *m., f.* cyclothymic, person afflicted with extreme changes of mood.

ciclotomía *f. surg.* cyclotomy, incision through the ciliary body of the eye.

ciclotropía *f.* cyclotropia, deviation of the eye around the anteroposterior axis.

ciego-a *m., f.* blind person; *a.* blind.

ciego *m.* cecum. 1. cul-de-sac lying below the terminal ileum forming the first part of the large intestine; 2. any cul-de-sac structure.

cielo *m.* sky.

cien, ciento *a., m.* a hundred.

ciencia *f.* science; ___ médica / medical ___; a ___ cierta / for sure.

científico-a *m., f.* scientist; *a.* scientific.

cierto-a *a.* certain, true; por ___ / as a matter of fact.

cifosis *f.* kyphosis, exaggerated posterior curvature of the thoracic spine.

cifótico-a *a.* kyphotic, suffering from or rel. to kyphosis.

cigarrillo, cigarro *m.* cigarette.

cigoma, zigoma *m.* zygoma, osseous prominence at the point where the temporal and malar bones join.

cigoto *m.* zygote, the fertilized ovum, cell resulting from the union of two gametes.

ciliar *a.* ciliary, rel. to or resembling the eyelash or eyelid.

cilíndrico-a *a.* cylindrical.

cilindro *m.* cylinder. 1. barrel of a syringe; 2. geo-

metrical form resembling a column.

cilindro granuloso *m.* [*renal*] granular cast, [*ortopedia*] urinary cylinder seen in degenerative or inflammatory nephropathies.

cilindroma *m.* cylindroma, frequently malignant tumor, usu. found in the face or in the orbit of the eye.

cilindruria *f.* cylindruria, presence of cylinders in the urine.

cilio *m.* cilium, eyelid.

cima *f.* summit, top.

cimetidina *f.* cimetidine, antacid used in the treatment of gastric and duodenal ulcers.

cimiento *m.* foundation, base.

cinc *m.* zinc.

cinconismo *m.* cinchonism. V. quinismo.

cinéreo *m.* cinerea, the gray substance of the nervous system.

cinerradiografía *f.* cineradiography, x-ray of an organ in motion.

cinesioterapia *f.* kinesiotherapy, treatment involving physical exercises or specific movements.

cinesis *f.* kinesis, term used to designate physical movements in general, including those that result as a response to a stimulus such as light.

cinestesia *f.* kinesthesia, sensorial experience, sense and perception of a movement.

cinética *f.* kinesics, the study of the body and its static and dynamic positions as a means of communication.

cinético-a *a.* kinetic, rel. to movement or what causes it.

cínico-a *m., f.* cynic; *a.* cynical.

cinta magnética *f.* audiotape.

cinto *m.* belt; waistband.

cintura *f.* waist; waistline.

cinturón *m.* girdle; wide belt; ___ escapular o torácico / thoracic ___.

circinado-a *a.* circinate, ring-shaped.

circuito *m.* circuit.

circulación *f.* circulation; mala ___ / poor ___; ___ periférica / peripheral ___.

círculo *m.* circle, a round figure or structure.

circuncidar *v.* to circumcise.

circuncisión *f. surg.* circumcision, removing part or all of the prepuce.

circundar *v.* to encircle, to surround.

circunducción *f.* circumduction, circular movement of the distal end of a limb or part such as the eye, while keeping a proximal end fixed.

circunferencia *f.* circumference.

circunstancia *f.* circumstance; ___-s atenuantes / mitigating ___-s.

circunvolución *f.* gyrus, elevated portion of the cerebral cortex; ___-es de Broca / ___, Broca's, third, frontal or inferior; ___ frontal, superior / ___, frontal, superior; ___-es occipitales / ___, occipital first, superior.

cirrosis *f.* cirrhosis, progressive disease of the liver characterized by interstitial infl. and associated with failure in the function of hepatocytes and resistance to the flow of blood through the liver; ___ **alcohólica** / alcoholic ___; ___ **biliar** / biliary ___.

ciruela *f.* plum; ___ **pasa** / prune.

cirugía *f.* surgery; the branch of medicine that treats diseases, malformations, and injuries and restores or reconstructs body structures through operative procedures; ___ **ambulatoria** / ambulatory ___; ___ **artroscópica** / arthroscopic ___; ___ **cardiotorácica** / cardio-thoracic ___; ___ **conservadora** / conservative ___; ___ **correctiva** / corrective ___; ___ **cosmética** / cosmetic ___; ___ **endoscópica** / endoscopic ___; ___ **mayor** / major ___; ___ **menor** / minor ___; ___ **oral** / oral ___; ___ **ortopédica** / orthopedic ___; ___ **plástica** / plastic ___; ___ **radical** / radical ___; ___ **reconstructiva** / reconstructive ___; ___ **torácica** / chest or thoracic ___.

cirujano-a *m., f.* surgeon, specialist in surgery.

cistadenocarcinoma *m.* cystadenocarcinoma, carcinoma and cystadenoma.

cistadenoma *m.* cystadenoma, adenoma that has one or more cysts.

cistectomía *f. surg.* cystectomy, total or partial resection of the urinary bladder.

cisteína *f.* cysteine, amino acid derived from cystine and found in most proteins.

cisterna *f.* cistern, a closed space that serves as a reservoir or receptacle.

cístico-a *a.* cystic, rel. to the gallbladder or the bladder.

cistina *f.* cystine, amino acid that is produced by the digestion of proteins, at times found in the urine.

cistinuria *f.* cystinuria, excessive cystine in the urine.

cistitis *f.* cystitis, infl. of the urinary bladder characterized by frequent urination accompanied by pain and burning.

cistocele *m.* cystocele, hernia of the bladder.

cistografía *f.* cystography, x-ray of the bladder using a radiopaque substance.

cistograma *m.* cystogram, x-ray of the bladder using air or a contrasting medium.

cistolitotomía *f. surg.* cystolithotomy, removal of a stone by cutting into the bladder.

cistometría *f.* cystometry, cystometrography, study of the bladder functions through the use of a cystometer.

cistómetro *m.* cystometer, device used to study the pathophysiological functions of the urinary bladder by measuring its capacity and pressure reactions.

cistopexia *f. surg.* cystopexy, fixation of the urinary bladder to the abdominal wall.

cistoscopía *f. surg.* cystoscopy, inspection of the bladder through a cystoscope.

cistoscopio *m.* cystoscope, tube-shaped instrument used to examine the bladder and the urethra.

cistostomía *f. surg.* cystostomy, creation of an opening into the bladder for drainage.

cistotomía *f. surg.* cystotomy, incision in the bladder.

cistouretrografía *f.* cystourethrography, x-ray of the urinary bladder and the urethra.

cistouretroscopio *m.* cystourethroscope, instrument for endoscopic visualization of the bladder and urethra.

cisura *f.* cleft, elongated opening; fissure.

cita *f.* appointment, engagement; **hacer una** ___ / to make an ___; **tener una** ___ / to have an ___.

citocromo *m.* cytochrome, hemochromogen that plays an important part in the oxidation processes.

citolítico-a *a.* cytolytic, having the power to dissolve or destroy a cell.

citología *f.* cytology, the science that deals with the nature of cells.

citomegálico-a *a.* cytomegalic, characterized by abnormally enlarged cells.

citomegalovirus *m.* cytomegalovirus, any of a group of herpes viruses that causes cellular enlargement and is the causative agent of cytomegalic inclusion disease.

citómetro *m.* cytometer, a device used for counting and measuring blood cells.

citopenia *f.* cytopenia, deficiency of cellular elements in the blood.

citoplasma *m.* cytoplasm, protoplasm of a cell with exception of the nucleus.

citotoxicidad *f.* cytotoxicity, the capacity of an agent to destroy certain cells.

citotoxina *f.* cytotoxin, toxic agent that damages or destroys cells of certain organs.

citrato *m.* citrate, salt of citric acid.

cítrico-a *a.* citric, citrous.

ciudad *f.* city.

ciudadanía *f.* citizenship.

ciudadano-a *m., f.* citizen.

clara *f.* the white of the egg.

claridad *f.* clarity, brightness.

clarificación *f.* clarification.

clarificar *vi.* to clarify.

claro-a *a.* clear.

clase *f.* class, sort, kind.

clasificación *f.* classification.

clasificar *vi.* to classify, to sort out.

claudicación *f.* claudication, limping; ___ **intermitente** / intermittent ___.

clavícula *f.* clavicle, collarbone.

clavo *m.* nail, slender rod of metal or bone used to fasten together parts of a broken bone; ___ **ortopédico** / orthopedic pin.

cleidocostal *a.* cleidocostal, rel. to the ribs and the clavicle.

cleptomanía *f. psych.* kleptomania, morbid compulsion to steal.

cleptómano-a *m., f.* kleptomaniac, person afflicted with kleptomania.

clérigo *m.* clergyman.

clima *m.* climate.

climaterio *m.* climacteric, termination of the reproductive period in women.

clímax *m.* climax. 1. crisis in an illness; 2. sexual orgasm.

clínica *f.* clinic, a health-care facility; ___ de consulta **externa** / outpatient ___.

clínico-a *a.* clinical. 1. rel. to a clinic; 2. rel. to direct observation of patients; **cuadro** ___ / ___ picture; **curso** ___ / ___ progress; **ensayos** ___-s / ___ trials; **historia** ___, **expediente médico** / ___ history; **procedimiento** ___ / ___ procedure.

clisis *f.* clysis, the act of supplying fluid to the body by other means than orally.

clitoridectomía *f. surg.* clitoridectomy, excision of the clitoris.

clítoris *m.* clitoris, small protruding body situated in the most anterior part of the vulva.

cloaca *f.* cloaca. 1. common opening for the intestinal and urinary tracts in the early development of the embryo; 2. sewage.

cloasma *f.* chloasma, skin discoloration seen during pregnancy.

clónico-a *a.* clonic, rel. to clonus.

clono *m.* 1. clonus, a series of rapid and rhythmic contractions of a muscle; 2. clone, an individual derived from a single organism through asexual reproduction.

clonorquiasis *f.* chlonorchiasis, parasitic infection that affects the distal bile ducts.

clorambucil *m.* chlorambucil, a form of nitrogen mustard used to combat some forms of cancer.

cloranfenicol *m.* chloramphenicol, chloromycetin, antibiotic esp. effective in the treatment of typhoid fever.

clorhidria *f.* chlorhydria, excess acidity in the stomach.

cloro *m.* chlorine, gaseous element used as a disinfectant and bleaching agent.

clorofila *f.* chlorophyll, green pigment in plants by which photosynthesis takes place.

cloroformo *m.* chloroform, anesthetic.

cloroma *m.* chloroma, green-colored tumor that can occur in different parts of the body.

cloroquina *f.* chloroquine, a compound used in the treatment of malaria.

clorosis *f.* chlorosis, type of anemia usu. seen in women and gen. associated with iron deficiency.

clorotetraciclina *f.* chlortetracycline, antibiotic agent.

clorpromacina *f.* chlorpromazine, tranquilizing and antiemetic agent.

cloruro *m.* chloride, a compound of chlorine.

coaglutinación *f.* coagglutination, group agglutination.

coaglutinina *f.* coagglutinin, agglutinate that affects two or more organisms.

coagulación *f.* coagulation, clot; ___ **diseminada intravascular** / disseminated intravascular ___; **propiedad de** ___ / blood clotting ability;

tiempo de ___ / blood ___ time.

coagulante *m.* coagulant, that which causes or precipitates coagulation.

coagular *v.* to coagulate, to clot.

coágulo *m.* coagulation, clot.

coagulopatía *f.* coagulopathy, a disease or condition that affects the coagulation mechanism of the blood.

coalescencia *f.* coalescence, the fusion of parts or elements.

coartación *f.* coarctation, stricture; compression.

cobalto *m.* cobalt.

cobarde *a.* coward.

cobija *f.* cover, blanket.

cobrar *v.* to charge; to collect.

cobre *m.* copper.

coca *f.* coca, bush from whose leaves cocaine is extracted.

cocaína *f.* cocaine, addictive narcotic alkaloid derived from coca leaves.

coccidioidina *f.* coccidioidin, a sterile solution used intracutaneously as a test for coccidioidomycosis.

coccidioidomicosis *f.* coccidioidomycosis, valley fever, endemic respiratory infection in the Southwestern United States, Mexico, and parts of South America.

coccigodinia *f.* coccygodynia, pain in the region of the coccyx.

cóccix *m.* coccyx, last bone at the bottom of the vertebral column.

cocer *vi.* to cook; to stew; ___ **a fuego lento** / to simmer.

cociente *m.* quotient; ___ **de inteligencia** / intelligence ___.

cocimiento *m.* concoction made of medicinal herbs.

cocina *f.* kitchen, stove.

cocinado-a *a.* cooked; **bien** ___ / well-done.

cocinar *v.* to cook.

cóclea *f.* cochlea, spiral tube that forms part of the inner ear.

coco *m.* 1. coccus, bacteria; 2. coconut; **agua de** ___ / ___ milk.

cocoa *f.* cocoa.

coche *m.* automobile.

cochinada *f.* filthy act; dirty trick; filth.

cochino-a *m., f.* pig; *a.* filthy.

codeína *f.* codeine, narcotic analgesic.

codo *m.* elbow; ___ **de tenista** / tennis ___; **coyuntura del** ___ / ___ joint.

coenzima *f.* coenzyme, a substance that enhances the action of an enzyme.

coerción *f.* duress, coercion; **bajo** ___ / under ___.

coger *vi.* to take, to grasp; to get; ___ **un resfriado** / to catch a cold.

cognado *m.* cognate. 1. that which is of the same nature; 2. *gr.* word that derives from the same root.

cogote *m.* nape, back of neck.

cohabitar *v.* to live together.
coherente *a.* coherent.
cohesión *f.* cohesion, the force that holds molecules together.
cohibido *a.* inhibited; uneasy.
coincidencia *f.* coincidence.
coincidir *v.* to coincide.
coito *m.* coitus, sexual intercourse.
cojear *v.* to limp.
cojera *f.* lameness.
cojinete *m.* cushion.
cojo-a *a.* lame, crippled.
col *f.* cabbage.
cola *f.* 1. glue; **inhalar** ___ / ___ sniffing; 2. tail.
colaborar *v.* to collaborate.
colador *m.* sieve, strainer.
colágeno *m.* collagen, the main supportive protein of skin, bone, tendon, and cartilage.
colangiectasia *f.* cholangiectasis, dilation of the biliary ducts.
colangiografía *f.* cholangiography, x-ray of the biliary ducts.
colangiograma *m.* cholangiogram, x-ray of the biliary ducts using a contrast medium.
colangitis *f.* cholangitis, infl. of the biliary ducts.
colapso *m.* collapse; ___ **circulatorio** / circulatory failure; ___ **nervioso** / nervous breakdown.
colar *vi.* to strain; to sift.
colateral *a.* collateral, accessory, or secondary.
colcha *f.* cover, coverlet.
colchón *m.* mattress.
colecistectomía *f. surg.* cholecystectomy, removal of the gallbladder.
colecistitis *f.* cholecystitis, infl. of the gallbladder.
colecistoduodenostomía *f. surg.* cholecystoduodenostomy, anastomosis of the gallbladder and the duodenum.
colecistogastrostomía *f. surg.* cholecystogastrostomy, anastomosis of the gallbladder and the stomach.
colecistografía *f.* cholecystography, x-ray of the gallbladder by administration of a dye, orally or by injection.
colectar, coleccionar *v.* to collect.
colectomía *f. surg.* colectomy, excision of part or all of the colon.
colédoco *m.* choledochus, common bile duct, formed by the union of the hepatic and cystic ducts.
coledocoduodenostomía *f. surg.* choledochoduodenostomy, anastomosis of the choledochus and the duodenum.
coledocolitiasis *f.* choledocholithiasis, presence of calculi in the common bile duct.
coledocoyeyunostomía *f. surg.* choledochojejunostomy, anastomosis of the common bile duct and the jejunum.
colega *m., f.* colleague.
colegio *m.* school.
colelitiasis *f.* cholelithiasis, presence of stones

in the gallbladder or in the common bile duct.
colemia *f.* cholemia, presence of bile in the blood.
cólera *f.* cholera. 1. acute infectious disease characterized by severe diarrhea and vomiting; 2. anger, rage.
colestasis *f.* cholestasis, biliary stasis.
colesteatoma *m.* cholesteatoma, a tumor containing cholesterol, found most commonly in the middle ear.
colesteremia, colesterolemia *f.* cholesteremia, cholesterolemia, excessive cholesterol in the blood.
colesterol *m.* cholesterol, component of animal oils, fats, and nerve tissue, a precursor of sex hormones and adrenal corticoids; ___ **alto** / high ___; **reductor de** ___ / ___ reducer.
colesteroluria *f.* cholesteroluria, presence of cholesterol in the urine.
colgajo *m. surg.* flap, detached tissue.
colgar *vi.* to hang.
cólico *m.* colic, acute spasmodic abdominal pain.
coliflor *f.* cauliflower.
colinesterasa *f.* cholinesterase, a family of enzymes.
colirio *m.* colyrium, liquid medicinal preparation for the eye.
colitis *f.* colitis, infl. of the colon; ___ **crónica** / chronic ___; ___ **espasmódica** / spasmodic ___; ___ **mucomembranosa** / pseudomembranous ___; ___ **mucosa** / mucous ___; ___ **ulcerativa** / ulcerative ___.
colmena *f.* beehive.
colmillo *m.* canine tooth; tusk, fang.
colocar *vi.* to place, to set; **colocarse** *vr.* to position oneself.
colodión *m.* collodion, liquid substance used to cover or protect skin cuts.
coloide *m.* colloid, gelatinlike substance produced by some forms of tissue decay.
colon *m.* colon, the portion of the intestine extending from the cecum to the rectum; ___ **ascendente** / ascending ___; ___ **descendente** / descending ___; **neoplasma del** ___ / colonic neoplasm.
colonia *f.* colony, a group of bacteria in a culture, all derived from the same organism.
colónico-a *a.* colonic, rel. to the colon.
colonoscopía *f.* colonoscopy, examination of the inner surface of the colon through a colonoscope.
colonoscopio *m.* colonoscope, instrument used to examine the colon.
color *m.* color.
coloración *f.* coloration, staining.
colorado-a *a.* red; **ponerse** ___ / to blush.
colorante *m.* dye, stain.
colorimétrico-a *a.* rel. to color; **guía** ___ / color index.
colostomía *f. surg.* colostomy, creation of an artificial anus; **bolsa de** ___ / ___ bag.
colpitis *f.* colpitis, infl. of the vaginal membrane.

Colores	*Colors*
amarillo	yellow
ámbar	amber
anaranjado	orange
azul	blue
blanco	white
carmelita	brown
cenizo	ashen
cetrino	greenish yellow
gris	gray
morado	purple, black and blue
pardo	brown
negro	black
rojizo	reddish
rojo	red
rosáceo	pinkish
verde	green

colpocele *m.* colpocele, a hernia into the vagina.

colporrafia *f. surg.* colporrhaphy, suture of the vagina.

colporragia *f.* colporrhagia, vaginal hemorrhage.

colposcopía *f.* colposcopy, examination of the vagina and the cervix through a colposcope.

colposcopio *m.* colposcope, endoscopic instrument that allows direct observation of the vagina and the cervix.

colpotomía *f. surg.* colpotomy, incision in the vagina.

columna *f.* column, pillar-like structure.

columna, espina vertebral *f.* spinal column, osseous structure formed by thirty-three vertebrae that surround and contain the spinal cord.

coluria *f.* choluria, presence of bile in the urine.

colutorio *m.* mouthwash, antiseptic solution for rinsing the mouth.

coma *m.* coma, state of unconsciousness.

comadre *f.* godmother; woman friend.

comadrona *f.* midwife.

comatoso-a *a.* comatose, rel. to or in a state of coma; **estado** ___ / ___ state.

combatir *v.* to combat, to fight.

combinación *f.* combination.

combinar *v.* to combine.

comedón *m.* blackhead, comedo.

comedor *m.* dining room.

comensal *m.* commensal, host, organism that benefits from living within or on another living organism without either benefiting or harming it.

comentar *v.* to comment.

comentario *m.* commentary, remark.

comenzar *vi.* to commence, to begin.

comer *v.* to eat; **dar de** ___ / to feed.

comestible *m.* food; *a.* edible.

cometer *v.* to commit.

comezón *f.* itch.

comida *f.* food; meal; **hora de** ___ / meal time.

comienzo *m.* beginning; start.

comilón-a *a.* big eater.

comisión *f.* commission, assignment.

comisura *f.* commissure, coming together of two parts, such as the labial angles.

comisurotomía *f.* commissurotomy, incision of the fibrous bands of a commissure, such as the labial angles or the commissure of a cardiac valve.

como *adv.* how, as; ___ **quiera** / as you wish; *conj.* like, as; ___ **no** / of course; *prep.* about; **está** ___ **a (una milla)** / it is about (a mile) away; ___ **a (las ocho)** / about (eight o'clock).

cómodo-a *a.* comfortable.

compacto-a *a.* compact.

compadecer *vi.* to pity; **compadecerse** *vr.* to feel sorry for; ___ **a sí mismo** / self-pity.

compadre *m.* godfather; close friend.

compañero *m.* companion, mate.

compañía *f.* company; ___ **de seguros** / insurance ___.

comparación *f.* comparison.

comparar *v.* to compare.

compartir *v.* to share.

compasión *f.* compassion.

compatible *a.* compatible.

compensación *f.* compensation. 1. that which makes up for a defect or counterbalances some deficiency; 2. defense mechanism; 3. remuneration.

compensar *v.* to compensate.

competente *a.* competent, qualified, able to perform well.

complejo *m. psych.* complex, a series of related mental processes that affect behavior and personality; ___ **de castración** / castration ___; ___ **de culpa** / guilt ___; ___ **de Edipo** / Oedipus ___, morbid love of a son for the mother; ___ **de Electra** / Electra's ___, morbid love of a daughter for the father; ___ **de inferioridad** / inferiority ___; **-a** *a.* complicated; intricate.

complementar *v.* to supplement.

complemento *m.* complement, a serum protein substance that destroys bacteria and other cells with which it comes into contact.

completar *v.* to complete.

completo-a *a.* complete.

complexión *f.* complexion, appearance of the facial skin.

complicación *f.* complication.

complicar *vi.* to complicate; **complicarse** *vr.*, to become difficult; to become involved, to get entangled.

componente *m.* component.

componer *vi.* [*una fractura*] to set; to put together; to heal, to restore.

composición *f.* composition.

compostura *f.* composure; serenity.

compota *f.* compote, fruit stew.

comprar *v.* to buy, to purchase.

comprender *v.* to understand.

compresa *f.* compress, pack; ___ **fría** / cold ___ . ~~sanitaria = san. towel~~
compresión *f.* compression, exertion of pressure on a point of the body.
comprimidos *m. pl.* pills.
comprobar *v.* to prove, to verify.
comprometer *v.* to compromise; **comprometerse** *vr.* to commit oneself; to compromise, to become involved.
compromiso *m.* commitment, obligation.
compuesto *m.* compound.
compulsivo-a *a.* compulsive.
computadora *f.* computer.
común *a.* common; **lugar** ___ / ___ place; **nombre** ___ / ___ name; **no** ___ / uncommon; **por lo** ___ / gen.; **sentido** ___ / ___ sense.
comunicación *f.* communication.
comunicación privilegiada privileged communication, such as that between a doctor or psychotherapist and a patient; it is the patient's privilege to keep this information confidential.
comunicar *v.* to communicate, to inform; **comunicarse** *vr.* to communicate with.
comunidad *f.* community.
con *prep.* with, by; ___ **frecuencia** / frequently; ___ **mucho gusto** / gladly; ___ **permiso** / excuse me; ___ **regularidad** / regularly.
cóncavo-a *a.* concave, hollowed.
concebir *vi.* to conceive.
concentración *f.* concentration. 1. increased strength of a fluid by evaporation; 2. the act of concentrating.
concentrado-a *a.* concentrated; ___ **en sí mismo-a** / self-conscious.
concentrar *v.* to concentrate; **concentrarse** *vr.* to concentrate oneself.
concepción *f.* conception.
concepto *m.* concept, idea.
concha *f.* shell; that which resembles a shell.
conciencia *f.* consciousness; conscience, state of awareness.
conciso-a *a.* concise.
concluir *vi.* to conclude; to infer.
conclusión *f.* conclusion.
concreción *f.* concretion, hardening, solidification.
concretio cordis *L.* concretio cordis, partial or complete obliteration of the pericardial cavity due to chronic constrictive pericarditis.
concreto-a *a.* concrete.
concusión *f.* concussion, trauma gen. caused by a head injury and manifested at times by dizziness and nausea; ___ **cerebral** / cerebral ___ ; ___ **de la médula espinal** / spinal ___ .
condensar *v.* to condense, to make something more dense.
condición *f.* condition, quality; ___ **anterior** / preexisting ___ .
condicionar *v.* to condition, to train.
cóndilo *m.* condyle, rounded portion of the bone usu. present at the joint.
condiloma *f.* condyloma, warty growth usu.

found around the genitalia and the perineum.
condimentado-a *a.* spicy.
condón *m.* condom, contraceptive device.
condral *a.* chondral, of a cartilaginous nature.
condritis *f.* chondritis, infl. of a cartilage.
condrocalcinosis *f.* chondrocalcinosis, condition that resembles gout, characterized by calcification and degenerative alterations in cartilage.
condrocostal *a.* chondrocostal, rel. to the ribs and the costal cartilages.
condromalacia *f.* chondromalacia, abnormal softening of cartilage.
condrosarcoma *m.* chondrosarcoma, malignant tumor of a cartilage.
conducir *vi.* to conduct; to drive.
conducta *f.* conduct, behavior.
conducto *m.* duct, conduit; ___ **biliar** / biliary ___ ; ___ **endolinfático** / endolymphatic ___ ; ___ **eyaculatorio** / ejaculatory ___ ; ___ **hepático** / hepatic ___ ; ___ **lacrimal** / lacrimal ___ ; ___ **lactífero** / lactiferous ___ ; ___ **mamario** / mammary ___ ; ___ **seminal** / seminal ___ ; **seminífero** / seminiferous tubule.
conectar *v.* to connect; to switch on.
conejillo de Indias *m.* guinea pig.
conejo *m.* rabbit; **fiebre de** ___ / ___ fever, tularemia; **la prueba del** ___ / ___ test, pregnancy test.
conexión *f.* connection.
confabulación *f.* confabulation, condition by which the individual fabricates imaginary situations soon to be forgotten.
conferencia *f.* conference, lecture, meeting.
confianza *f.* confidence, trust; ___ **en uno, en sí mismo-a** / self-___ ; **falta de** ___ **en sí mismo-a** / lack of self-esteem.
confiar *v.* to entrust, to trust.
confidencial *a.* confidential; **comunicación o información** ___ / privileged communication or information.

Conducto	Duct
biliar	biliary
cístico	cystic
colédoco	common bile
de Müeller	mullerian
de Wolff	wolffian
deferente	deferent
excretorio	excretory
eyaculatorio	ejaculatory
hepático	hepatic
lacrimal, lagrimal	lacrimal
linfático	lymphatic
nasolagrimal	nasolacrimal
seminal	seminal
seminífero	seminiferous tubule

confinación, confinamiento *f., m.* confinement, restraint.
confirmación *f.* confirmation.
confirmar *v.* to confirm.
conflicto *m.* conflict.
confluencia *f.* confluence, meeting point of several channels.
conformar *v.* to conform, to adapt; **conformarse** *vr.* to resign oneself.
confortar *v.* to comfort.
confrontar *v.* to confront.
confundido-a, confuso-a *a.* confused, at a loss; **estar __ /** to be at a loss.
confundir *v.* to confuse, to mix up; **confundirse** *vr.* to be or to become confused.
confusión *f.* confusion.
congelación *m.* freezing; **corte por __ /** frozen cut; **punto de __ /** point; **secar por __ /** freeze-dry; **sección por __ /** frozen section, thin specimen of tissue that is frozen quickly and aids in diagnosing malignancies.
congelado-a *a.* frozen; **__ al instante /** quick-frozen.
congelar *v.* to freeze; **congelarse** *vr.* to become frozen.
congénito-a *a.* congenital, existing since birth; ingrown.
congestión *f.* congestion, excessive accumulation of blood in a given body part or organ.
congestionado-a *a.* congested.
conización *f.* conization, removal of a cone shaped tissue such as the mucosa of the cervix.
conjugar *vi. gr.* to conjugate.
conjuntiva *f.* conjunctiva, delicate mucous membrane covering the eyelids and the anterior surface of the eyeball.
conjuntivitis *f.* conjunctivitis, infl. of the conjunctiva; **__ aguda contagiosa /** acute contagious __; **__ alérgica /** allergic __; **__ catarral /** catarrhal __; **__ folicular /** follicular __; **__ vernal /** vernal __.
conjunto *m.* whole, sum of parts; a set; **en __ /** as a whole.
conminuto-a *a.* comminuted, broken in many small fragments as in a fracture.
conmoción *f.* commotion.
cono *m.* cone, sensory organ that together with the rods of the retina receives color stimuli.
conocer *vi.* to know; to know about; **conocerse** *vr.* to know each other; to know oneself.
conocimiento *m.* 1. consciousness; **perder el __ /** to lose __; 2. knowledge; **no tener __ de /** to be unaware of.
conque *conj.* so, so then.
consanguíneos *m.* blood relatives.
consciencia, conciencia *f.* conscience.
consciente *a.* conscious, aware.
consecuencia *f.* consequence; aftermath; **a __ de /** as a result of.
conseguir *vi.* to obtain, to get.
consejero-a *m., f.* counselor.
consejo *m.* counsel, advice.

consenso *m.* consensus.
consentimiento *m.* consent, permission; **__ informado** informed consent, voluntary permission given by the patient or guardian to perform a medical procedure or study after understanding all the different aspects involved in the procedure.
consentir *vi.* to consent, to permit; to pamper.
conservación *f.* conservation, preservation.
conservar *v.* to keep, to preserve.
consideración *f.* consideration; regard.
considerado-a *a.* considerate.
considerar *v.* to consider.
consistencia *f.* consistency.
consistente *a.* consistent, stable.
consistir *v.* to consist of, to be comprised by.
consolar *v.* to console, to comfort.
consomé *m.* consommé, broth.
constante *a.* constant, invariable.
constitución *f.* constitution, physical makeup.
constituir *vi.* to constitute.
constituyente *a.* constituent.
constricción *f.* constriction, narrowing, contraction.
consulta *f.* consultation; consulting room; **__ particular /** private practice; **horas de __ /** office hours.
consultar *v.* to consult, to confer.
consultor-a *m., f.* consultant, person who acts in an advisory capacity.
consultorio *m.* doctor's office; consulting room.
consumación *f.* consummation, completion.
consumir *v.* to consume; **consumirse** *vr.* to waste away.
consunción *f.* consumption, wasting, general emaciation of the body, as seen in patients with tuberculosis.
contacto *m.* contact; **__ inicial /** initial __; **lentes de __ /** __ lenses.
contado-a *a.* numbered; scarce; **al __ /** in cash.
contagiar *v.* to transmit, to pass on, to infect.
contagio *m.* contagion, communication of disease.
contagioso-a *a.* contagious, communicable.
contaminación *f.* contamination.
contaminar *v.* to contaminate.
contar *vi.* to count; to tell; **__ con /** to rely on.
contener *vi.* to contain; **contenerse** *vr.* to restrain oneself, to hold back.
contenido *m.* content.
contento-a *a.* happy, content, pleased.
conteo *m.* count; **__ globular o de células sanguíneas /** blood cell __.
contestación *f.* answer.
contestar *v.* to answer.
contiguo-a *a.* contiguous, adjacent, next to.
continencia *f.* continence, abstinence, or moderation.
continuación *f.* continuation.
continuar *v.* to continue.
continuidad *f.* continuity.
contorno *m.* contour, outline.

contra *prep.* against.
contracción *f.* contraction, temporary shortening, as of a muscle fiber; ___ **de fondo** / deep ___; ___ **de hambre** / hunger ___; ___ **espasmódica** / twitching; ___ **ulterior** / after-___.
contracepción *f.* contraception, birth control.
contraceptivo *m.* contraceptive; **métodos ___-s** / methods of contraception.
contráctil *a.* contractile, having the capacity to contract.
contractilidad *f.* contractility, capacity to contract.
contractura *f.* contracture, prolonged or permanent involuntary contraction.
contradecir *vi.* to contradict, to negate.
contradicción *f.* contradiction.
contraer *vi.* to contract, [*una enfermedad*] to catch a sickness; **contraerse** *vr.* to be reduced in size, to shrink up, to crumple up.
contragolpe *m.* countercoup, lesion that occurs as a result of a blow to the opposite point.
contraindicación *f.* contraindication.
contraindicado-a *a.* contraindicated.
contralateral *a.* contralateral, rel. to the opposite side.
contrariado-a *a.* upset.
contrariar *v.* to disappoint, to upset.
contrario-a *a.* contrary; **al ___** / on the ___; **de lo ___** / otherwise.
contrarrestar *v.* to counter, to oppose.
contrastar *v.* to contrast.
contraste *m.* contrast; **medio de ___** / ___ medium.
contraveneno *m.* counterpoison, antidote.
contribución *f.* contribution.
contribuir *vi.* to contribute.
control *m.* control.
controlar *v.* to control, to regulate; **controlarse** *vr.* to control oneself.
contusión *f.* contusion, bruise.
convalecencia *f.* convalescence, period of time between an illness and the return to health.
convaleciente *a.* convalescent.
convencer *vi.* to convince.
conveniente *a.* convenient, handy.
convergencia *f.* convergence, inclination of two elements toward a common point.
conversación *f.* conversation.
conversión *f.* conversion, 1. change, transformation; 2. *psych.* transformation of an emotion into a physical manifestation.
convertir *vi.* to convert; **convertirse** *vr.* to become.
convexo-a *a.* convex.
convulsión *f.* convulsion, violent involuntary muscular contraction of the muscles; ___ **febril** / febrile ___; ___**jacksoniana** / Jacksonian ___; ___ **tónico-clónica** / tonic-clonic ___.
convulsivo-a *a.* convulsive, rel. to convulsions; **actividad ___** / seizure activity.
cooperación *f.* cooperation.
cooperar *v.* to cooperate.

cooperativo-a *a.* cooperative.
coordinación *f.* coordination; **falta de ___** / lack of ___.
coordinar *v.* to coordinate.
copa *f.* cup.
copia *f.* copy, imitation.
copiar *v.* to copy; to imitate.
coproemoliente *m.* stool softener.
coprofagia *f.* *psych.* coprophagy, disorder that drives a person to eat feces.
coprolito *m.* coprolith, small mass of fecal concretion.
cópula *f.* copulation, sexual intercourse.
coqueluche *m.* whooping cough.
cor *L.* cor, heart; ___ **errante** / ___ mobile; ___ **juvenil** / ___ juvenum; ___ **pulmonar** / ___ pulmonale.
coracoclavicular *a.* coracoclavicular, rel. to the scapula and the clavicle.
coraje *m.* courage; anger.
corazón *m.* heart; hollow, muscular organ situated in the thorax that maintains the circulation of blood; **anormalidades congénitas del ___** / congenital ___ diseases; **bloqueo del ___** / ___ block; **bulbo del ___** / bulbus cordis; **hipertrofia del ___** / ___, hypertrophy; **latido del ___** / heartbeat; **operación a ___ abierto** / open ___ surgery; **ruido del ___** / ___ sound; **trasplante del ___** / ___ transplant; **válvula del ___** / ___ valve.
corazón artificial *m.* artificial heart, instrument or device that pumps blood with the same capacity as a normal heart.
cordal *a.* **muela ___** / wisdom tooth.
cordectomía *f.* *surg.* cordectomy, excision of a vocal cord.
cordel *m.* string, cord.
cordero *m.* lamb; **chuleta de ___** / ___ chop; **lana de ___** / ___'s wool.
cordón *m.* any elongated, rounded structure; cord.
cordón umbilical *m.* umbilical cord, structure that connects the fetus with the placenta during the gestation period.
cordotomía *f.* *surg.* cordotomy, an operation to cut certain sensory fibers in the spinal cord.
cordura *f.* sanity.
corea *f.* chorea, Huntington's disease, St. Vitus' dance, nervous disorder manifested by involuntary, rapid, and jerky, but well-coordinated movements of the limbs or facial muscles.
coriocarcinoma *m.* choriocarcinoma, malignant tumor found primarily in the testicle and the uterus.
corion *m.* 1. chorion, one of the two membranes that surround the fetus; 2. corium, dermis or true skin.
coriza *f.* coryza, acute or chronic rhinitis; runny nose.
córnea *f.* cornea, transparent membrane on the anterior surface of the eyeball.
córneo-a *a.* corneous, callous.

cornetes nasales *m. pl.* nasal concha.

cornezuelo de centeno *m.* ergot, fungus used in dry form or as an extract to induce uterine contractions or stop hemorrhaging after delivery.

coroides *f.* choroid membrane, membrane that supplies blood to the eye.

coroiditis *f.* choroiditis, infl. of the choroid.

corona *f.* corona, circular structure; crown.

coronario-a *a.* coronary, encircling in the manner of a crown; **arteria** ___ / ___ artery; **desviación** ___ / ___ bypass; **trombosis** ___ / ___ thrombosis; **vasoespasmo** ___ / ___ vasospasm.

corporal *a.* corporeal, rel. to the body; **líquido** ___ / body fluid; **peso** ___ / body weight; **temperatura** ___ / body temperature.

corpulento-a *a.* corpulent, stout, robust.

corpus *m.* corpus, the human body.

corpus callosum *L.* corpus callosum, the great commissure of the brain.

corpúsculo *m.* corpuscle, bud, small mass.

corpus luteum *L.* corpus luteum, yellow body, yellow glandular mass in the ovary that is formed by a ruptured follicle and produces progesterone.

correa *f.* strap, belt.

correctivo-a *m., f.* corrective; antidote.

correcto-a *a.* correct; accurate.

corregir *vi.* to correct, to rectify.

correo *m.* mail.

correr *v.* to run, to jog.

correspondencia *f.* correspondence; reciprocity.

corriente *f.* current, stream, flow of fluid, air, or electricity along a conductor; **al** ___ / current, up-to-date; *a.* current.

corroído-a *a.* corroded.

corromperse *vr.* to be affected with putrefaction, to taint.

corrosión *f.* corrosion, deterioration by chemical reaction.

corsé *m.* corset, jacket.

cortado-a *a.* cut, incised.

cortadura *f.* cut, slit.

cortar *v.* to cut, to incise; **cortarse** *vr.* to cut oneself.

corte *m.* cut, slit; ___ **transversal** / transection.

corteza *f.* cortex, the outer layer of an organ; ___ **suprarrenal** / adrenal ___; ___ **cerebral** / cerebral ___.

Corti, órgano de *m.* Corti's organ, the end organ of hearing by which sound is directly perceived.

cortical *a.* cortical, rel. to the cortex.

corticoide, corticosteroide *m.* corticoid, corticosteroid, a steroid produced by the adrenal cortex.

corticotropina *f.* corticotropin, hormonal substance of adrenocorticotropic activity.

cortina *f.* curtain; blinds.

cortisol *m.* cortisol, hormone secreted by the adrenal cortex.

cortisona *f.* cortisone, glycogenic steroid derived from cortisol or produced synthetically.

corto-a *a.* short; ___ **de vista** / nearsighted.

cosa *f.* thing.

coser *v.* to sew.

cosmético *m.* cosmetic; **-a** *a.* cosmetic.

cosquillas *f. pl.* tickle, tickling; **hacer** ___ / to tickle; **tener** ___ / to be ticklish.

cosquilleo *m.* tingling or prickling sensation.

costado *m.* side, flank; **al** ___ / to the ___.

costal *a.* costal, rel. to the ribs.

costalgia *f.* costalgia, neuralgia, pain in the ribs.

costar *vi.* to cost; ___ **trabajo** / to be difficult.

costilla *f.* rib. 1. one of the bones of twelve pairs that form the thoracic cage; 2. chop, a cut of meat.

costo *m.* cost; ___ **de vida** / ___ of living.

costoclavicular *a.* costoclavicular, rel. to the ribs and the clavicle.

costocondritis *f.* costochondritis, infl. of one or more costal cartilages.

costoso-a *a.* costly, expensive.

costovertebral *a.* costovertebral, rel. to the angle of the ribs and the thoracic vertebrae.

costra *f.* crust, scab; ___ **láctea** / cradle cap.

costumbre *f.* custom, habit; **tener la** ___ / to be in the habit of.

costura *f.* seam.

cowperitis *f.* cowperitis, infl. of Cowper's gland.

coyuntura *f.* joint; articulation.

coxa *f.* coxa, hip; ___ **magna,** abnormal widening of the head of the femur; ___ **valga,** hip deformity resulting in abnormal angulation of the femoral shaft away from the midline of the body; ___ **vara,** hip deformity resulting in abnormal angulation of the femoral shaft toward the midline of the body.

coxalgia *f.* coxalgia, pain in the hip.

coxitis *f.* coxitis, infl. of the hip joint.

craneal *a.* cranial, rel. to the cranium; **fractura** ___ / skull fracture.

craneales, nervios *m. pl.* cranial nerves, each of the twelve pairs of nerves connected to the brain; **I. olfatorio** / olfactory; **II. óptico** / optic; **III. motor ocular común** / oculomotor; **IV. troclear** / trochlear; **V. trigémino** / trigeminal; **VI. motor ocular externo, abducente** / abducent; **VII. facial** / facial; **VIII. auditivo** / auditory; **IX. glosofaríngeo** / glossopharyngeal; **X. neumogástrico, vago** / vagus; **XI. espinal** / accessory; **XII. hipogloso** / hypoglossal.

cráneo *m.* cranium, skull, braincase, the bony structure of the head that covers the brain; **base del** ___ / base of the ___.

craneofaringioma *m.* craniopharyngioma, malignant brain tumor seen esp. in children.

creaneoplastia *f. surg.* cranioplasty, reparation of a cranial bone.

craneotomía *f. surg.* craniotomy, trepanation of the cranium.

cráter *m.* crater, cavity.
creación *f.* creation.
crear *v.* to create.
creatina *f.* creatine, component of muscular tissue important in the anaerobic phase of muscular contraction.
creatinina *f.* creatinine, end product of the metabolism of creatine present in urine; **depuración de la** ___ / ___ clearance, volume of plasma that is clear of creatinine.
crecer *vi.* to grow; ___ **hacia adentro** / to grow inward.
crecido-a *a.* grown; large.
crecimiento *m.* growth.
crecimiento cero de población (CCP) *m.* zero population growth (ZPG), a demographic condition during a certain period of time, in which a population is stable, neither increasing nor diminishing.
crédito *m.* credit.
creer *vi.* to believe; to think.
crema *f.* cream, ointment.
cremastérico *a.* cremasteric, rel. to the cremaster muscle of the scrotal wall.
creosota *f.* creosote, antiseptic, oily liquid used as an expectorant.
crepitación *f.* crepitation, crackling; ___ **pleural** / pleural ___.
cresta *f.* crest. 1. a bony ridge; 2. the peak of a graph.
cretinismo *m.* cretinism, congenital hypothyroidism due to severe deficiency of the thyroid hormone.
cretino-a *m., f.* cretin, person afflicted with cretinism.
cretinoide *a.* cretinoid, having characteristics similar to cretinism.
cribiforme *a.* cribiform, perforated.
cricoides *a.* cricoid, shaped like a ring.
crimen *m.* crime.
criminal *m.* criminal; felon.
crioanestesia *f.* cryanesthesia. 1. anesthesia applied by means of localized refrigeration; 2. loss of ability to perceive cold.
criocirugía *f.* cryosurgery, destruction of tissue through the application of intense cold.
criógeno *a.* cryogenic, that which produces low temperatures.
crioglobulina *f.* cryoglobulin, a serum globulin that crystallizes spontaneously at low temperatures.
crioterapia *f.* cryotherapy, therapeutic treatment using a cold medium.
cripta *f.* crypt, small tubular recess.
críptico *m.* cryptic, hidden.
criptococosis *f.* cryptococcosis, a systemic fungus that may affect different organs of the body, esp. the brain.
criptogénico-a *a.* cryptogenic, of an unknown cause.
criptorquidia *f.*, **criptorquismo** *m.* cryptorchism, failure of a testis to descend into the scrotum.

crisis *f.* crisis, turning point in a disease; ___ **de identidad** / identity ___; ___ **nerviosa** / nervous breakdown.
crisoterapia *f.* chrysotherapy, treatment with gold salts.
crista *f.* crista, a projecting structure or ridge gen. surmounting a bone.
cristal *m.* crystal.
cristalino *m.* crystalline lense, lense of the eye behind the pupil; **-a** *a.* crystalline, transparent.
cristaloideo-a *a.* crystalloid, resembling crystal.
cromático-a *a.* chromatic, rel. to colors.
cromatina *f.* chromatin, portion of the cell nucleus that stains more readily.
cromocito *m.* chromocyte, a colored or pigmented cell.
cromófobo *m.* chromophobe, a cell or tissue that resists stain.
cromógeno *m.* chromogen, a substance that produces color.
cromosoma *m.* chromosome, part of the nucleus of the cell that contains the genes.
cromosoma X *m.* X-chromosome, differential chromosome that determines the female sex characteristics.
cromosoma Y *m.* Y-chromosome, differential chromosome that determines the male sex characteristics.
cromosómico-a *a.* chromosomic, rel. to the chromosome; **aberraciones** ___-s / chromosome aberrations.
crónico-a *a.* chronic.
cronológico-a *a.* chronological, rel. to the sequence of time.
cronotropismo *m.* chronotropism, modification of the rate of a regular pace or beat such as the heartbeat.
crudo-a *a.* raw; crude; **carne** ___ / ___ meat.
cruel *a.* cruel.
cruento-a *a.* bloody.
crup *m.* croup, infl. of the larynx in children, usu. accompanied by hoarse coughing, fever, and difficulty in breathing; ___ **espasmódico** / spasmodic ___.
crus *L.* crus, leg or a structure resembling one; ___ **del cerebro** / ___ cereberi; ___ **pene** / ___ of the penis.
Cruz Roja Internacional *f.* International Red Cross, international organization for medical assistance.
cruzar *vi.* to cross.
cuadra *f.* city block.
cuadrado-a *a.* square.
cuadrángulo *m.* quadrangle.
cuadrante *m.* quadrant, 90°, one-fourth of a circle.
cuadrar *v.* to square; to fit.
cuadriceps *m.* quadriceps, four-headed muscle, extensor of the leg.
cuadriplegia *f.* quadriplegia, paralysis of the four extremities.
cuajado-a *a.* curdled; **leche** ___ / ___ milk.

63

cuajar *v.* to curdle; **cuajarse** *vr.* to congeal, to thicken.

cuajo *m.* curd.

cualidad *f.* quality.

cualitativo-a *a.* qualitative, rel. to quality; **prueba** ___ / ___ test.

cualquier-a *a.* any.

cuando, cuándo *adv.* when, whenever; **de** ___ **en** ___ / from time to time; ___ **usted quiera** / whenever you want; ¿ ___ **empezó?** / ___ did it start?

cuantitativo-a *a.* quantitative, rel. to amount.

cuanto, cúanto-a *a., adv.* how much, how many; ¿ ___ **tiempo?** / how long?; ___ **antes** / as soon as possible; **en** ___ / as soon as; **en** ___ **a** / in regard to; **unos** ___**-s** / a few.

cuarentena *f.* quarantine, period of forty days during which a restraint is put on the activities of persons or animals to prevent the spread of a disease.

cuarto *m.* 1. room; ___ **de baño** / bathroom; ___ **de dormir** / bedroom; ___ **de niños** / nursery room; 2. quart, one-fourth of a whole; **-a** *a.* fourth.

cubeta *f.* basin.

cubierta *f.* covering, sheath, shield.

cubierto-a *a. pp.* of **cubrir,** covered.

cubital *a.* cubital, rel. to the cubital bone or elbow.

cúbito *m.* cubitus, ulna, the inner, long bone of the forearm.

cubreboca *m.* surgical mask.

cubrir *v.* to cover, to drape as with a sterilized cloth.

cucaracha *f.* cockroach.

cuclillas (en) *adv.* in a squatting position.

cuchara *f.* spoon; tablespoon.

cucharada *f.* spoonful; scoop; ___ **de postre** / *L.* cochleare medium; ___ **de sopa** / *L.* cochleare magnum.

cucharita *f.* teaspoon; **de café** / cochleare parvum.

cuchichear *v.* to whisper.

cuchillita *f.* small knife; razor blade.

cuchillo *m.* knife.

cuello *m.* neck; collar. 1. part that joins the head and the trunk of the body; 2. area between the crown and the root of a tooth.

cuello uterino *m.* uterine neck; cervix uteri; **dilatación del** ___ / dilation of the cervix; **incompetencia del** ___ / cervical incompetence.

cuenta *f.* account, bill; **arreglar la** ___ / to settle the ___; ___ **bancaria** / bank ___; **darse** ___ / to realize; **pagar la** ___ / to pay the ___; **tener en** ___ / to take into ___.

cuentacélulas *m.* cell counting device.

cuerda *f.* cord, cordon.

cuerdas vocales *f. pl.* vocal chords, main organ of the voice; ___ **superiores o falsas** / false ___; ___ **inferiores o verdaderas** / true ___.

cuerdo-a *a.* sane; wise.

cuerno *m.* horn.

cuero *m.* skin, hide; ___ **cabelludo** / scalp; **en** ___**-s** / naked.

cuerpo *m.* body; ___**-s extraños** / foreign bodies.

cuerpo amarillo *m.* yellow body. *V.* **corpus luteum.**

cuerpos cetónicos, acetónicos *m. pl.* ketone bodies, known as acetones.

cuestión *f.* question; issue, matter.

cuidado *m.* care, attention; ___ **intensivo** / intensive ___; **negación de** ___ / refusal of ___; ___ **postnatal** / postnatal ___; ___ **prenatal** / prenatal ___; ___ **primario** / primary ___; **nivel de** ___ **satisfactorio** / reasonable ___; **estar al** ___ **de** / to be under the ___ of; **tratar con** ___ / to handle with care.

cuidadoso-a *a.* careful, mindful.

cuidar *v.* to take care, to look after.

cul-de-sac *Fr.* cul-de-sac. 1. blind pouch, cavity closed on one end; 2. rectouterine pouch.

culdoscopía *f.* culdoscopy, viewing of the pelvic and abdominal cavity with a culdoscope.

culdoscopio *m.* culdoscope, an endoscopic instrument inserted through the vagina to do a visual examination of the pelvis and the abdominal cavity.

culebra *f.* snake.

culebrilla *f.* the shingles, herpes zoster, herpes-like cutaneous disease.

culero *m.* diaper.

culpa *f.* guilt; fault, blame; **tener la** ___ / to be at fault.

culpar *v.* to blame.

cultivar *v.* to cultivate.

cultivo *m.* culture, artificial growth of microorganisms or living tissue cells in the laboratory; ___ **de orina** / urine ___; ___ **de sangre** / blood ___; ___ **de tejido** / tissue ___; **medio de** ___ / ___ medium.

cuna *f.* crib, cradle, bassinet.

cunilinguo-a *a.* cunnilingus, rel. to the practice of oral stimulation or manipulation of the penis or clitoris.

cuña *f.* wedge; bedpan.

cuñado-a *m., f.* brother-in-law; sister-in-law.

cúpula *f.* dome.

cura *f.* 1. cure; 2. *m.* priest.

curable *a.* curable, healable.

curación *f.* cure; healing process.

curanderismo *m.* faith healing.

curandero *m.* faith healer, medicine man, shaman.

curar *v.* to cure, to heal.

curare *m.* curare, venom extracted from various plants used to provide muscle relaxation during anesthesia.

curativo-a *a.* curative, having healing properties.

cureta *f.* curette, scoop-like instrument with sharp edges used for curettage.

curetaje *m.* curettage, scraping of a surface or cavity with a sharp-edged instrument; ___

uterino / D&C, dilation and curettage of the uterine cavity.

curioso-a *a.* curious.

curita *f.* bandaid.

curso *m.* course; direction.

curva *f.* curve, bend.

curvatura *f.* curvature, deviation from a straight line.

Cushing, síndrome de *m.* Cushing's syndrome, adrenogenital syndrome manifested by obesity and muscular weakness gen. associated with an excessive production of cortisol.

cuspídeo-a *a.* cuspidal, pointed.

cúspide *f.* cuspid, point.

custodia *f.* custody; **bajo ___ del estado** / ward of the state.

cutáneo-a *a.* cutaneous, rel. to the skin; **absorción ___ / ___** absorption; **glándulas ___-s o sebáceas / ___** glands; **manifestaciones ___-s /** skin manifestations; **pruebas ___-s /** skin tests; **úlcera ___ /** skin ulcer.

cutícula *f.* cuticle, outer layer of the skin.

cutis *m.* cutis, complexion, skin.

cutis colgante *m.* sagging facial skin.

ch *f.* fourth letter of the Spanish alphabet.

chalación *f.* chalazion, meibomian cyst, a cyst of the eyelid.

chancro *m.* chancre, the primary lesion of syphilis.

chancroide *m.* chancroid, a nonsyphilitic venereal ulcer.

chaparro-a *a. Mex.* short person.

chaqueta *f.* jacket.

charlatán-a *m., f.* charlatan, a quack, someone claiming knowledge and skills he or she does not have.

chasquido *m.* snap, sharp brief sound related to the abrupt opening of the cardiac valve, gen. the mitral valve; ___ **de apertura** / opening ___.

chata *f.* bedpan.

cheque *m.* check.

chequear *v.* to check, to verify.

chequeo *m.* checkup, complete medical examination.

Cheyne-Stokes, respiración de *f.* Cheyne-Stokes respiration, respiration manifested by alternating periods of apnea of increased rapidity and depth, gen. associated with dis-

orders of the neurologic respiration center.

chicano-a *a. pop.* (U.S.) Mexican-American.

chico-a *m., f.* young boy; young girl; *a.* small.

chícharo *n.* green pea.

chichón *m.* bump in the head.

chiflado-a *a. pop.* crazy, nuts.

chile *m.* hot pepper.

chillar *v.* to screech, to scream.

chinche *f.* bedbug.

chiquito-a *a.* small.

chocolate *m.* chocolate.

chochera *f.* senility.

chocho-a *a.* senile.

choque *m.* 1. shock; an abnormal state, gen. following trauma, in which insufficient flow of blood through the body can cause reduced cardiac output, subnormal temperature, descending blood pressure and rapid pulse; ___ **alérgico** / allergic ___; ___ **anafiláctico** / anaphylactic ___; ___ **eléctrico** / electric ___; ___ **séptico** / septic ___; 2. collision.

chorizo *m.* sausage.

chorrear *v.* to drip; to spout.

chorro *n.* jet, spurt; stream.

chueco-a *a.* crooked, bent.

chupar *v.* to suck; to absorb; **chuparse el dedo** / thumb sucking.

chupete *n.* pacifier.

churre *m.* dirt, grime.

d *abr.* **densidad** / density; **difunto** / deceased; **dosis** / dose.

dacriadenitis *f.* dacryadenitis, infl. of the lacrimal gland.

dacriagogo *m.* dacryagogue, an agent that stimulates tear formation.

dacricistalgia *f.* dacrycystalgia, pain in the lacrimal sac.

dacrioadenectomía *f. surg.* dacryoadenectomy, removal of a lacrimal gland.

dacriocistitis *f.* dacryocystitis, infl. of the lacrimal sac.

dacriocistotomía *f. surg.* dacryocystotomy, incision of the lacrimal sac.

dacriolitiasis *f.* dacryolithiasis, stones in the lacrimal apparatus.

dactilitis *f.* dactylitis, infl. of a finger or toe.

dáctilo *m.* dactyl, finger or toe.

dactilocopista *m., f.* fingerprint expert.

dactilografía *f.* dactylography, study of fingerprints.

dactilograma *f.* dactylogram, fingerprint.

dactilología *f.* dactylology, sign language.

dactilomegalia *f.* dactylomegaly, excessive growth of fingers and toes.

dactiloscopia *f.* dactyloscopy, study of fingerprints for the purpose of identification.

dado-a *a. pp.* of **dar,** given; ___ **a** / ___ to; ___ **que** / ___ that.

Dakin, solución de *f.* Dakin's solution, solution used for cleansing wounds.

daltonismo *m.* daltonism, defective perception of the colors red and green.

damiana *f.* damiana, native plant from Mexico the leaves of which are used as a diuretic.

danazol *m.* danazol, Deprancol, Danocrine, synthetic hormone that suppresses the action of the anterior pituitary.

dañado-a *a.* hurt; [*comida*] spoiled; tainted.

dañar *v.* to harm; to hurt; to injure.

dañino-a *a.* harmful; noxious.

daño *m.* harm, damage, hurt; *v.* **hacer** ___ / to harm, to hurt.

dapsona *f.* dapsone, sulfone drug used in the treatment of leprosy.

dar *vi.* to give; to minister; ___ **a luz** / to give birth; ___ **de comer** / to feed; ___ **el pecho** / to breast-feed; ___ **de alta** / to discharge; ___ **lugar a** / to cause; **darse** *vr.* to give oneself; ___ **por vencido** / to give up; ___ **prisa** / to hurry.

dartos *m.* dartos, a layer of smooth muscle fibers found beneath the skin of the scrotum.

Darvon *m.* Darvon, trade name for dextro propoxyphene hydrochloride, an oral analgesic.

dátil *m.* date.

dato *m.* fact, piece of information.

de *prep.* of, from; [*posesión*], **los rayos X** ___ **la paciente** / the patient's x-rays; [*contenido*]

bicarbonato ___ **sodio** / sodium bicarbonate; [*procedencia*] **vengo** ___ **la consulta** / I am coming from the doctor's office.

debajo *adv.* underneath; ___ **de** / under; **por** ___ / beneath.

deber *v.* to be obligated; to owe.

débil *a.* debilitated, weak, feeble.

debilidad *f.* debility, weakness.

debilitarse *vr.* to become weak.

decaer *vi.* to weaken; [*en ánimo*] to decline.

decaído-a *a.* dispirited, dejected.

decaimiento *m.* dejection.

decalcificación *f.* decalcification, loss or reduction of lime salts from bones or teeth.

deceleración *f.* deceleration, diminished velocity, such as of heart frequency.

decidido-a *a.* decided; determined.

decidir *v.* to decide; **decidirse** *vr.* to make up one's mind.

decidua *f.* decidua, mucous membrane of the uterus that develops during pregnancy and is discharged after delivery.

deciduo-a *a.* deciduous, of a temporal nature.

decir *vi.* to say; to tell; **querer** ___ / to mean.

decisión *f.* decision, resolution.

declinación *f.* declination, rotation of the eye.

decorticación *f. surg.* decortication, removal of part of the cortical surface of an organ such as the brain.

decrépito-a *a.* decrepit, worn with age.

decúbito *m.* decubitus, lying down position; ___ **dorsal** / dorsal ___, on the back; ___ **lateral** / lateral ___, on the side; ___ **ventral** / ventral ___, on the stomach.

decusación *f.* decussation, crossing of structures in the form of an X; ___ **de las pirámides** / ___ of pyramids, crossing of nervous fibers from one pyramid to the other in the medulla oblongata; ___ **óptica** / optic ___, crossing of the fibers of the optic nerves.

dedalera *f.* foxglove, common name for *Digitalis purpurea.*

dedo *m.* finger; toe; **caída de los** ___-**s del pie** / toe drop; ___ **del pie** / toe; ___ **en garra, en martillo** / hammer, mallet finger or toe; ___ **en palillo de tambor** / clubbing; ___ **gordo** / hallux; ___ **índice** / index ___, forefinger; ___ **meñique** / little ___; ___ **pulgar** / thumb; **desviación de un** ___ / valgus; **separación de un** ___ / varus.

deducción *f.* deduction, to reason from the general to the particular.

deducible *a.* deductible.

deducir *vi.* to deduce, to infer.

defecación *f.* defecation, bowel movement.

defecar *vi.* to defecate.

defectivo-a *a.* defective.

defecto *m.* defect; blemish; ___ **congénito** / congenital ___.

defectuoso-a *a.* defective, faulty.

defender *vi.* to defend.

defensa *f.* defense, resistance to a disease;

mecanismo de ___ / ___ mechanism; ___ propia / self-___.

defensa por demencia *f.* the concept that a defendant who is declared insane cannot be found guilty of the crime committed.

deferente *a.* deferent, conveying away from.

defibrilación *f.* defibrillation, the act of changing an irregular heart beat to a normal rhythm.

deficiencia *f.* deficiency; ___ **mental** / mental ___, **enfermedad por** ___ / ___ disease.

deficiente *a.* deficient, wanting.

déficit *m.* deficit, deficiency.

definición *f.* definition.

deflexión *f.* deflection, diversion; *psych.* unconscious diversion of ideas.

deformación *f.* deformation, distortion.

deforme *a.* deformed.

deformidad *f.* deformity, irregularity, a congenital or acquired malformation.

defunción *f.* demise, death.

defurfuración *f.* defurfuration, shedding fine, branlike scales from the skin.

degeneración *f.* degeneration, deterioration.

degenerado-a *a.* degenerate.

degenerar *v.* to degenerate.

deglución *f.* deglutition, the act of swallowing.

deglutir *v.* to swallow.

degradación *f.* degradation, reducing a chemical compound to a simpler one.

dehidroandrosterona *f.* dehydroandrosterone, previously known as dehydroepiandrosterone, androgenic steroid found in the urine.

dehidrocolesterol *m.* dehydrocholesterol, skin substance that becomes vitamin B complex by the action of the sun's rays.

dehidrocorticosterona *f.* dehydrocorticosterone, steroid found in the adrenal cortex.

dehiscencia *f.* dehiscence, splitting open of a wound.

déjà vu *Fr.* déjà vu, an illusory impression of having seen or experienced a new situation before.

dejadez *f.* lassitude, neglect, carelessness.

dejar *v.* to leave; to let, to allow; ___ **dicho** / ___ word; ___ **órdenes** / ___ orders; ___ **de** / to stop from, to quit.

del *gr.* contraction of the *prep.* **de** and the *art.* **el.**

delante *adv.* in front; before.

deletéreo-a *a.* deleterious, harmful, noxious.

delgado-a *a.* thin, slender, slim.

delgaducho-a *a.* thin; delicate.

delicado-a *a.* delicate, tender.

delicioso-a *a.* delicious.

delicuescencia *f.* deliquescence, condition of a substance when it becomes liquified by absorption of water from the air.

deligación *f.* deligation, art of applying ligatures or binders.

delimitación *f.* delimitation, process of marking the limits or circumscribing.

delincuencia *f.* delinquency; ___ **juvenil** / juve-

nile ___.

delincuente *a.* delinquent.

delirante *a.* delirious, raving.

delirar *v.* to be delirious, to rave.

delirio *m.* delirium, temporary mental disturbance marked by hallucinations and distorted perceptions; ___ **agudo** / acute ___; ___ **crónico** / chronic ___; ___ **de persecución** / persecution complex; ___ **tremens** / ___ tremens, a form of alcoholic psychosis.

deltoideo-a *a.* deltoid. 1. rel. to the deltoid muscle that covers the shoulder; 2. shaped like a triangle.

delusión *f.* delusion, false beliefs.

demacrado-a *a.* gaunt, wasted.

demanda *f.* demand; **alimentación por** ___ / ___ feeding.

demandar *v.* to demand; to sue.

demás *adv.* besides; that which is beyond a certain measure; **lo** ___ / the rest.

demasiado-a *a.* excessive; *adv.* too much.

demencia *f.* dementia, dementia praecox, insanity. *V.* **esquizofrenia;** ___ **alcohólica** / alcoholic ___; ___ **orgánica** / organic ___; ___ **senil** / senile ___.

demente *a.* demented, one suffering from dementia.

Demerol *m.* Demerol, meperidine hydrochloride, trade name for an analgesic drug with properties similar to morphine.

demora *f.* delay.

demorar *v.* to delay; **demorarse** *vr.* to be delayed, to take too long.

demostración *f.* demonstration.

demostrar *vi.* to demonstrate; to prove.

demulcente *m.* demulcent, agent that soothes and softens the skin or mucosa.

dendrita *f.* dendrite, protoplasmic prolongation of the nerve cell that receives the nervous impulses.

dengue *m.* dengue fever, acute febrile and infectious disease caused by a virus and transmitted by the *Aedes* mosquito.

denominación *f.* denomination, name.

densidad *f.* density.

denso-a *a.* dense; thick.

dentado-a *a.* dentiform, toothed. 1. having projections like teeth on the edge; 2. shaped like a tooth.

dentadura *f.* teeth; ___ **postiza** / denture.

dental, dentario-a *a.* dental, rel. to the teeth; **cuidado** ___ / ___ care; **esmalte** ___ / ___ enamel; **hilo** ___ / ___ floss; [*mordisco*] **impresión** ___ / ___ impression; **placa dentaria** / ___ plaque; **sarro** ___ / ___ tartar; **servicios de salud** ___ / ___ health services; **técnico** ___ / ___ technician; **técnico en profiláctica** ___ / ___ hygienist.

dentición *f.* dentition, time when children's teeth are cut; ___ **primaria** / primary ___, first teeth; ___ **secundaria o dientes permanentes** / secondary ___, permanent teeth.

dentilabial *a.* dentilabial, rel. to the teeth and the lips.

dentina *f.* dentin, calcified tissue that constitutes the larger portion of the tooth.

dentinogénesis *f.* dentinogenesis, formation of dentin.

dentinoma *m.* dentinoma, tumor consisting mainly of dentin.

dentista *m., f.* dentist; ___ **de niños** / pedodontist.

dentoide *a.* dentoid, tooth-shaped.

dentro *adv.* within; **por** ___ / inside.

denudación *f.* denudation, deprival of a protecting surface by surgery, trauma, or pathologic change.

dependencia *f.* dependence, subordination.

depender *v.* to depend; to rely.

depilación *f.* depilation, removal of hair by the roots.

depilar *v.* to depilate, to remove hair.

depilatorio *m.* depilatory, hair remover.

depleción *f.* depletion.

deporte *m.* sports; athletics.

deposición *f.* bowel movement; ___-**es blandas o acuosas** / loose bowels.

depositar *v.* to deposit.

depósito *m.* deposit; precipitate.

depravación *f.* depravation, perversion.

depravado-a *a.* depraved, corrupt; perverted.

depresión *f.* depression. 1. *psych.* state of sadness and melancholia accompanied by apathy; 2. cavity.

depresor *m.* depressor. 1. agent used to lower an established level of function or activity of the organism; ___ **de lengua** / tongue ___; 2. tranquilizer; **-a** *a.* producing or rel. to depression.

deprimente *n.* depressing.

deprimido-a *a.* depressed, downcast.

deprimir *v.* to depress; **deprimirse** *vr.* to become depressed.

depuración *f.* depuration, purification.

depurar *v.* to depurate, to purify.

derecha *f.* right hand side; **a la** ___ / to the right.

derecho-a *a.* straight, erect; *adv.* straight, straight ahead.

derecho *m.* right; the study of law; **los** ___-**s del paciente** / the patient's ___-s; **tener** ___ / to have the right.

derecho a rehusar tratamiento *m.* the patient's right to refuse treatment.

derecho a tratamiento *m.* right to treatment, the patient's right to receive adequate treatment by a medical facility that has assumed responsibility for the patient's care.

derivación *f.* derivation, bypass; 1. shunt, alternate or lateral course that occurs through anastomosis or through a natural anatomical characteristic; ___ **aortocoronaria** / aortocoronary bypass; ___ **aortoilíaca** / aortoiliac bypass; ___ **portacava** / portacaval shunt; 2. origin or source of a substance.

derivar *v.* to derive; to infer, to deduce.

dermabrasión *f. surg.* dermabrasion, procedure to remove acne scars, nevi or fine wrinkles of the skin.

dermalgia, dermatalgia *f.* dermalgia, dermatalgia, pain in the skin.

dermático-a *a.* dermal, dermatic, rel. to the skin.

dermatitis *f.* dermatitis, infl. of the skin; ___ **actínica** / actinic ___, produced by sunlight or ultraviolet light; ___ **alérgica** / allergic ___; ___ **atópica** / atopic ___; ___ **por contacto** / contact ___.

dermatofito *m.* dermatophyte, fungus that attacks the skin.

dermatofitosis *f.* dermatophytosis, athlete's foot, fungal infection of the skin caused by a dermatophyte.

dermatología *f.* dermatology, the study of skin diseases.

dermatológico-a *a.* dermatological, rel. to the skin.

dermatólogo *m.* dermatologist, specialist in dermatology.

dermatomicosis *f.* dermatomycosis, infl. of the skin by fungi.

dermatomiositis *f.* dermatomyositis, disease of the connective tissue manifested by edema, dermatitis, and infl. of the muscles.

dermátomo, dermatótomo *m.* dermatome, dermatotome, instrument used for cutting skin in thin slices.

dermatosífilis *f.* dermatosyphilis, skin manifestation of syphilis.

dermatosis, dermatopatía *f.* dermatosis, dermatopathy, general term used for skin disease; ___ **eritematosa de los pañales** / diaper rash.

dérmico-a *a.* dermic, rel. to the skin.

dermis *f.* dermis, skin.

dermitis *f.* dermitis, infl. of the skin.

dermoflebitis *f.* dermophlebitis, infl. of superficial veins.

dermoideo-a *a.* dermoid, resembling skin; **quiste** ___ / ___ cyst, congenital, usu. benign.

derramar *v.* to spill.

derrame *m.* spill, overflow, outflow. *effusion (lung)*

derretir *vi.* to melt; **derretirse** *vr.* to become liquified by heat.

desabrido-a *a.* tasteless; insipid.

desabrigado-a *a.* underclothed; too exposed to the elements.

desacostumbrado-a *a.* unaccustomed.

desacuerdo *m.* disagreement.

desadvertidamente *adv.* inadvertently; unintentionally.

desafortunado-a *a.* unfortunate, unlucky.

desagradable *a.* disagreeable, unpleasant.

desagradecido-a *a.* ungrateful.

desahogarse *vr., vi.* to release one's grief; *pop.* to let out steam.

desalentar *v. vi.* to discourage; **desalentarse** *vr.* to become discouraged.

desangramiento *m.* excessive bleeding.

desangrarse *vr.* to bleed excessively.
desanimado-a *a.* downhearted, discouraged.
desaparecer *vi.* to disappear.
desaprobar *vi.* to disprove; to refute.
desarrollado-a *a.* developed.
desarrollar *v.* [*síntomas*] to develop; to grow.
desarrollo *m.* development; growth.
desarrollo motor *n.* motor development.
desarticulación *f.* disarticulation, separation or amputation of two or more bones from one joint.
desarticulado-a *a.* disarticulated, rel. to a bone that has been separated from its joint.
desaseo *m.* uncleanliness.
desasosiego *m.* uneasiness, unrest.
desastre *m.* disaster.
desatendido-a *a.* unattended.
desatinado-a *a.* lacking good judgment, wild.
desayunar *v.* to have breakfast.
desayuno *m.* breakfast.
desbridamiento *m. surg.* debridement, removal of foreign bodies or dead or damaged tissue, esp. from a wound.
descafeinado-a *a.* decaffeinated.
descalcificación *f.* decalcification, 1. loss of calcium salts from a bone; 2. removal of calcareous matter.
descalzo-a *a.* barefooted.
descamación *f.* desquamation, the act of shedding scales from the epidermis.
descansado-a *a.* rested, refreshed.
descanso *m.* rest, tranquility.
descarado-a *a.* impudent, shameless.
descarga *f.* discharge, excretion.
descarnado-a *a.* without skin, fleshless; very thin person.
descartar *v.* to reject, to dismiss.
descendente *a.* descending.
descendiente *m.* descendant, offspring.
descentrado-a *a.* decentered, not centered.
descoloramiento *m.* discoloration.
descolorido-a *a.* discolored, washed out.
descompensación *f.* decompensation, inability of the heart to maintain adequate circulation.
descomponerse *vr., vi.* to decompose.
descomposición *f.* decomposition, decay; **índice de ___ / ___** rate.
descompresión *f.* decompression, lack of air or gas pressure as in deep-sea diving; **cámara de ___ / ___** chamber; **___ quirúrgica** / surgical **___**; **enfermedad por ___ / ___** sickness; *pop.* the bends.
desconcierto *m.* uncertainty, confusion.
desconectar *v.* to disconnect; to switch off.
desconfiar *v.* to distrust; to lack confidence.
descongelación *f.* thawing.
descongelar *v.* to defrost; to thaw.
descongestionante *m.* decongestant.
descongestionar *v.* to decongest.
descontaminación *f.* decontamination, the process of freeing the environment, objects, or persons from contaminated or harmful agents

such as radioactive substances.
descontaminar *v.* to decontaminate, to free from contamination.
descontento-a *a.* unhappy.
descontinuado-a *a.* discontinued, suspended.
descontinuar *v.* to discontinue.
descoyuntamiento *m.* luxation, dislocation.
descremar *v.* [*leche*] to skim.
describir *v.* to describe.
descripción *f.* description.
descrito-a *a. pp.* of **describir**, described.
descubierto-a *a. pp.* of **descubrir**, uncovered.
descubrir *vi.* to discover; to uncover.
descuento *m.* discount.
descuidado-a *a.* careless, negligent.
descuido *m.* carelessness.
desde *prep.* since, from; **___ ahora en adelante** / from now on; **___ hace (una semana, un mes)** / it has been (a week, a month) since; **___ luego** / of course.
desdentado-a *a.* edentulous, toothless.
desdoblamiento *m.* splitting.
desear *v.* to wish, to desire.
desecado-a *a.* desiccated, dried up.
desecante *m.* desiccant, substance that causes dryness.
desecar *vi.* to desiccate, to dry up.
desechable *a.* disposable.
desechar *v.* to discard, to cast aside.
desempeñar *v.* to perform a given task or role.
desencadenamiento *m.* trigger, impulse that initiates other events; **puntos de ___ / ___** points.
desencadenar *v.* to trigger, to initiate a succession of events.
desencajado-a *a.* disengaged; disjointed; gaunt.
desencajar *v.* to disengage.
desenlace *m.* outcome, conclusion.
desensibilizar *v.* to desensitize, to reduce or eliminate sensitivity, physically or emotionally.
deseo *m.* wish, desire.
deseoso-a *a.* desirous, eager.
desequilibrio *m.* imbalance.
desesperación *f.* desperation, despair, despondency; hopelessness.
desesperado-a *a.* desperate, despairing, despondent.
desesperarse *vr.* to despair, to despond.
desfallecer *vi.* to faint; to become weak.
desfervescencia *f.* defervescence, period of fever decline.
desfibrilación *f.* defibrillation, action of returning an irregular heart beat to its normal rhythm.
desfibrilador *m.* defibrillator, electrical device used to restore the heart to a normal rhythm.
desfiguración, desfiguramiento *f., m.* defacement; disfigurement.
desfigurar *v.* to disfigure, to distort.
desganarse *vr.* to lose appetite.
desgarradura, desgarro *f., m.* tear, laceration.
desgarrar *v.* to tear, to pull apart; to rip.

desgastado-a *a.* worn; eroded; [*persona*] wasted.

desgastar *v.* to erode; **desgastarse** *vr.* to wear down or away.

desgaste *m.* wearing down.

desgracia *f.* adversity, mishap.

desgraciadamente *adv.* unfortunately.

desgrasar *v.* to degrease, to remove the fat.

deshacer *vi.* to undo.

deshecho *m.* waste.

deshidratado-a *a.* dehydrated, free of water.

deshidratar *v.* to dehydrate, eliminate water from a substance.

deshidratarse *vr.* to dehydrate, to lose liquid from the body or tissues.

deshumanización *f.* dehumanization, loss of human qualities.

deshumectante *m.* dehumidifier, device to diminish humidity.

desierto *m.* desert.

desigual *a.* uneven; unlike, unequal.

desilusión *f.* disillusion, disenchantment.

desilusionar *v.* to disillusion; **desilusionarse** *vr.* to become disenchanted.

desinfectante *m.* disinfectant, agent that kills bacteria.

desinfectar *v.* to disinfect.

desinflamar *v.* to reduce or remove an inflammation.

desintegración *f.* disintegration; decomposition.

desintoxicar *v.* to detoxicate, to eliminate toxic matter.

deslizarse *vr., vi.* to glide.

deslumbramiento *m.* glare. 1. blurring of the vision with possible permanent damage to the retina; 2. intense light.

desmayarse *vr.* to faint, to pass out; to swoon.

desmayo *m.* fainting.

desmembración, desmembradura *f.* dismemberment.

desmembrar *v.* to dismember, to amputate.

desmielinación, desmielinización *f.* demyelination, demyelinization, loss or destruction of the myelin layer of the nerve.

desmineralización *f.* demineralization, loss of minerals from the body, esp. the bones.

desmoma *f.* desmoma, tumor of the connective tissue.

desmosis *f.* desmosis, disease of the connective tissue.

desnaturalización *f.* denaturation, change of the usual nature of a substance as by adding methanol or acetone to alcohol.

desnervado-a *a.* denervated, deprived of nerve supply.

desnivel *m.* unevenness.

desnudarse *vr.* to undress.

desnudo-a *a.* naked, bare.

desnutrición *f.* malnutrition, undernutrition; ___ **proteinocalórica** / protein caloric ___.

desnutrido-a *a.* undernourished, malnourished, underfed.

desobedecer *vi.* to disobey.

desobediencia *f.* disobedience.

desobediente *a.* disobedient.

desodorante *m.* deodorant.

desodorizar *vi.* to deodorize, to remove fetid or unpleasant odors.

desorden *m.* disorder, abnormal condition of the body or mind.

desordenado-a *a.* disorderly, unorganized.

desorganización *f.* disorganization.

desorganizado-a *a.* disorganized, unstructured.

desorientado-a *a.* disoriented, confused.

desosificación *f.* deossification, loss or removal of minerals from the bones.

desoxicorticosterona *f.* deoxycorticosterone, desoxycorticosterone, steroid hormone produced in the cortex of the adrenal glands that has a marked effect on the metabolism of water and electrolytes.

desoxigenación *f.* deoxygenation, process of removing oxygen.

desoxigenado-a *a.* deoxygenated, lacking oxygen.

despacio *adv.* slow, slowly.

despejado-a *a.* clear, cloudless; [*persona*] smart, vivacious.

despellejarse *vr.* to peel; to shed skin.

desperdiciar *v.* to waste, to squander.

desperdicio *m.* waste.

despersonalización *f. psych.* depersonalization, loss of identity.

despertarse *vr., vi.* to wake up.

despierto-a *a. pp.* of **despertar,** awake; diligent.

despigmentación *f.* depigmentation, abnormal change in the color of skin and hair.

despiojamiento *m.* delousing, freeing the body from lice.

desplazamiento *m.* 1. displacement; 2. *psych.* transfer of emotion from the original idea or situation to a different one.

desplazar *vi.* to displace.

despliegue *m.* display, exhibition.

desprender *v.* to loosen, to unfasten; **desprenderse** *vr.* to become loose.

desprendimiento *m.* detachment, separation.

despreocupado-a *a.* unconcerned, carefree.

despreocuparse *vr.* to be unconcerned.

desproporción *f.* disproportion.

desproporcionado-a *a.* disproportionate.

después *adv.* after, afterward.

despuntado-a *a.* [*instrumento*] blunt.

destapar *v.* to uncover.

desteñir *vi.* to fade; **desteñirse** *vr.* to become faded.

destetado-a *m., f.* weanling.

destetar *v.* to wean, to adjust an infant to a form of nourishment other than breast or bottle feeding.

destete *m.* delactation, discontinued breast-feeding; weaning.

destilado-a *a.* distilled; **agua** __ / __ water.

destilar *v.* to distil, to create vapor by heat.

destino *m.* fate.

destorsión *f.* detorsion, detortion. 1. surgical correction of a testicular or intestinal torsion; 2. correction of the curvature or malformation of a structure.

destoxicación, destoxificación *f.* detoxification, reduction of the toxic quality.

destreza *f.* skill.

destruido-a *a.* destroyed; exhausted, physically or emotionally.

destruir *vi.* to destroy.

destupir *v.* to unclog.

desunión *f.* disengagement. 1. emergence of the fetal head from the vulva; 2. separation.

desvalido-a *a.* destitute, helpless, handicapped.

desvanecerse *vr., vi.* to black out; to swoon.

desvelado-a *a.* unable to sleep, wakeful.

desvelarse *vr.* to stay awake at night.

desvelo *m.* insomnia.

desventaja *f.* disadvantage; diminished capacity.

desvestir *vi.* to strip; **desvestirse** *vr.* to undress.

desviación, desvío *f., m.* deviation, shunt. 1. departure from the established path; 2. *psych.* mental aberration.

desviar *v.* to shunt, to change course; **desviarse** *vr.* to deviate.

detalle *m.* detail.

detectado-a *a.* detected; **no** __ / undetected.

detectar *v.* to detect.

detector *m.* detector.

detener *vi.* to detain, to stop.

detergente *m.* detergent, cleaning agent.

deterioración, deterioro *f., m.* deterioration, wear, decay.

deteriorarse *vr.* to deteriorate.

determinación *f.* determination; decision; resolution; __ **propia** / self- __ .

determinado-a *a.* determined, strong-minded; [*una prueba*] proven.

determinante *m.* determinant, prevailing element; *a.* rel. to a prevailing element or cause.

determinar *v.* to determine.

determinismo *m.* determinism, theory by which all physical or psychic phenomena are predetermined and therefore uninfluenced by the will of the individual.

detestar *v.* to hate, to abhor.

detrás (de) *adv.* behind, in back of.

detrito *m.* detritus, residue of disintegrating matter.

detrusor *m.* detrusor, muscle that expels or projects outward.

deuteranopía *f.* deuteranopia, blindness to the color green.

devitalizar *v.* to devitalize, to debilitate; to deprive from vital force.

devolución *f.* devolution. *V.* **catabolismo.**

devolver *vi.* to return, to give back.

Dexedrina *f.* Dexedrine, amphetamine type

drug that stimulates the nervous system.

dextrocardia *f.* dextrocardia, dislocation of the heart to the right.

dextrómano-a *m.* dextromanual, person who gives preference to the use of the right hand.

dextroposición *f.* dextroposition, displacement to the right.

dextrosa *f.* dextrose, form of glucose in the blood popularly called grape sugar.

dextroversión *f.* dextroversion, turn to the right.

deyección *f.* 1. *psych.* dejection, state of depression; 2. the act of defecating.

día *m.* day; **de** __ / daytime, daylight; **(dos, tres) veces al** __ / (two, three) times a __ ; **todo el** __ / all day.

diabetes *f.* diabetes, a disease manifested by excessive urination. This term is often used in reference to diabetes mellitus.

diabetes insípida *f.* diabetes insipidus, type of diabetes caused by a deficiency in antidiuretic hormone.

diabetes mellitus *f.* diabetes mellitus, diabetes caused by insufficient production or use of insulin and resulting in hyperglycemia and glycosuria; __ **con dependencia de insulina** / insulin-dependent ; __ **sin dependencia de insulina** / noninsulin-dependent __ .

diabético-a *a.* diabetic, rel. to or suffering from diabetes; **angiopatías** __-s / __ angiopathies; **coma** __ /__ coma; __ **inestable** / brittle __ ; **dieta** __ / __ diet; **neuropatía** __ / __ neuropathy; **retinopatía** __ / __ retinopathy.

diabetogénico-a *a.* diabetogenic, that produces diabetes.

diabetógrafo *m.* diabetograph, instrument used to determine the proportion of glucose in the urine.

diacetemia *f.* diacetemia, presence of diacetic acid in the blood.

diacetilmorfina *f.* diacetylmorphine, heroin.

diadococinesis *f.* diadochokinesia, ability to make opposing movements in rapid succession.

diáfisis *f.* diaphysis, shaft or middle part of a long, cylindrical bone such as the humerus.

diaforesis *f.* diaphoresis, profuse perspiration.

diaforético *m.* diaphoretic, agent that stimulates perspiration; **-a** *a.* sweating profusely.

diafragma *m.* diaphragm. 1. muscle that separates the thorax and the abdomen; 2. contraceptive device.

diagnosticar *vi.* to diagnose.

diagnóstico, diagnosis *m., f.* diagnosis, determination of the patient's ailment; __ **computado** / computer __ ; __ **de imágenes por medios radioactivos** / __ imaging; __ **diferencial** / differential __ ; __ **equivocado o erróneo** / misdiagnosis; __ **físico** / physical __ ; __ **propio** / autodiagnosis; **errores de** __ / diagnostic errors.

diagonal *a.* diagonal.

diálisis *f.* dialysis, procedure used to filter and eliminate waste products from the blood of patients with renal insufficiency; **aparato de** ___ [*riñón artificial*] / ___ machine; ___ **peritoneal** / peritoneal ___.

dializado *m.* dialysate, the part of the liquid that goes through the dialyzing membrane in dialysis; **-a** *a.* dialyzed. having been separated by dialysis.

dializador *m.* dialyzer, device used in dialysis.

dializar *vi.* to dialyze.

diámetro *m.* diameter.

diapasón *m.* diapason, U-shaped metal device used to determine the degree of deafness.

diapédesis *f.* diapedesis, passage of blood cells, esp. leukocytes, through the intact walls of a capillary vessel.

diaplasis *f.* diaplasis, reduction of a dislocation or fracture.

diapositiva *f.* slide.

diario-a *a.* daily; **-mente** *adv.* daily.

diarrea *f.* diarrhea; ___ **del recién nacido** / ___ of the newborn; ___ **del viajero** / traveler's ___; ___ **infantil** / infant ___; ___ **nerviosa** / nervous ___; ___ **pancreática** / pancreatic ___.

diartrosis *f.* diarthrosis, articulation that allows ample movement, such as the hip articulation.

diastasa *f.* diastase, enzyme that acts in the digestion of starches and sugars.

diastasis *f.* diastasis. 1. separation of normally attached bones; 2. the rest period of the cardiac cycle, just before systole.

diástole *f.* diastole, dilation period of the heart during which the cardiac chambers are filled with blood.

diastólico-a *a.* diastolic, rel. to the diastole; **presión** ___ / ___ pressure, the lowest pressure point in the cardiovascular system.

diatermia *f.* diathermy, application of heat to body tissues through an electric current.

diátesis *f.* diathesis, organic disposition to contract certain diseases; ___ **hemorrágica** / hemorrhagic ___; ___ **reumática** / rheumatic ___.

diatrizoato de meglumina *m.* diatrizoate meglumine, radiopaque substance used to visualize arteries and veins of the heart and the brain as well as the gallbladder, kidneys, and urinary bladder.

diazepam *m.* diazepam, Valium, drug used as a tranquilizer and muscle relaxer.

diccionario *m.* dictionary.

dicigótico-a *a.* dizygotic, rel. to twins derived from two separate fertilized ova.

dicloxacilina *f.* dicloxacillim sodium, semisynthetic penicillin used against gram-positive organisms.

dicoriónico-a *a.* dichorionic, having two chorions.

dicotomía *f.* dichotomy, dichotomization, process of dividing into two parts.

dicroísmo *m.* dichroism, property of some solutions or crystals to present more than one color in reflected or transmitted light.

dicromatismo *m.* dichromatism, the property of presenting two different colors.

dicrómico-a *a.* dichromic, rel. to two colors.

dicromófilo-a *a.* dichromophil, stainable by both acid and basic dyes.

dicroto-a *a.* dicrotic, having two pulse beats for each heartbeat.

dictioma *m.* dictyoma, diktyoma, tumor of the ciliary epithelium.

Dicumarol *m.* Dicumarol, Dicoumarin, anticoagulant drug used in the treatment of embolism and thrombosis.

dicho *a. pp.* of **decir,** said.

didáctico-a *a.* didactic, rel. to teaching through textbooks and lectures as opposed to a clinical or physical approach.

didelfo-a *a.* didelphic, rel. to a double uterus.

didimitis *f. V.* **orquitis.**

diembrionismo *m.* diembryony, production of two embryos from a single egg.

diencéfalo *m.* diencephalon, part of the brain.

dienestrol *m.* dienestrol, synthetic nonsteroid estrogen.

diente *m.* tooth (*pl.* teeth); ___**-s deciduos, de leche** / deciduous teeth, baby teeth; ___ **desviado** / wandering ___; ___ **impactado** / impacted ___; ___ **incisivo** / incisor; ___ **molar** / wall ___; ___ **no erupcionado** / unerupted ___; ___**-s permanentes** / permanent teeth; ___**-s postizos** / denture; ___**-s secundarios** / second teeth.

diestro-a *a.* dexter, rel. to the right side; right-handed.

dieta *f.* diet; ___ **alta en residuos** (*fibras celulosas*) / high-residue ___; ___ **balanceada** / balanced ___; ___ **blanda** / bland ___; ___ **diabética** / diabetic ___; ___ **hospitalaria** / ward ___; ___ **libre de gluten** / gluten-free ___; ___ **líquida** / liquid ___; **macrocítica** / macrocytic ___; ___ **para bajar de peso** / weight reduction ___; ___ **rica en calorías** / high-calorie ___; ___ **sin sal** / salt-free ___.

dietética *f.* dietetics, the science of regulating diets to preserve or recuperate health.

dietético-a *a.* dietetic, rel. to diets.

dietilamida de ácido lisérgico *f.* lysergic acid

Diarrea	*Diarrhea*
del viajero	traveler's
disentérica	dysenteric
emocional	emotional
estival	summer
infantil	infantile
lientírica	lienteric
mucosa	mucous
nerviosa	nervous
pancreática	pancreatic
purulenta	purulent

73

diethylamide, LSD.

dietilestilbestrol *m.* diethylstilbestrol, synthetic estrogen compound.

dietista *m., f.* dietitian, nutrition specialist.

diezma *f.* decimation, high mortality rate.

difalo *a.* diphallus, partial or complete duplication of the penis.

difásico-a *a.* diphasic, that occurs in two different stages.

difenhidramina *f.* diphenhydramine, Benadryl, antihistamine.

diferencia *f.* difference.

diferenciación *f.* differentiation, distinction of one substance, disease, or entity from another.

diferencial *a.* differential, rel. to differentiation.

diferente *a.* different.

diferido-a *a.* deferred, postponed.

diferir *vi.* to disagree.

difícil *a.* difficult.

dificultad *f.* difficulty.

difonía *f.* diphonia, double voice.

difracción *f.* diffraction, the breaking up of a ray of light into its component parts when it passes through a glass or a prism; **patrón de** ___ / ___ pattern.

difteria *f.* diphtheria, acute infectious and contagious disease caused by the bacillus *Corynebacterium diphtheriae* (Klebs-Loffler bacillus) characterized by the formation of false membranes esp. in the throat; **antitoxina contra la** ___ / ___ antitoxin.

difterotoxina *f.* diphtherotoxin, toxin derived from cultures of diphtheria bacillus.

difundir *v.* to diffuse.

difunto-a *a.* deceased.

difusión *f.* diffusion. 1. the process of becoming widely spread; 2. dialysis through a membrane.

digerible, digestible *a.* digestible.

digerido-a *a.* digested; **no** ___ / undigested.

digerir *vi.* to digest.

digestión *f.* digestion, transformation of liquids and solids into simpler substances that can be absorbed easily by the body; ___ **gástrica** / gastric ___ ; ___ **intestinal** / intestinal ___ ; ___ **pancreática** / pancreatic ___ .

digestivo *m.* digestant, digestive, an agent that assists in the digestive process.

digitación *f.* digitation, finger-shaped protrusion as in a muscle.

digitalis *f.* digitalis, cardiotonic agent obtained from the dried leaves of *Digitalis purpurea;* **intoxicación por** ___ / ___ toxicity, poisoning.

digitalización *f.* digitalization, therapeutic use of digitalis.

digitiforme *a.* finger-shaped.

dígito *m.* digit, digitus, finger or toe.

digitoxina *f.* digitoxin, cardiotonic glycoside obtained from *Digitalis purpurea* used in the treatment of congestive heart failure.

digoxina *f.* digoxin, cardiotonic glycoside obtained from *Digitalis purpurea* used in the treatment of cardiac arrhythmia.

dihidroestreptomicina *f.* dihydrostreptomycin, antibiotic derived from and used more commonly than streptomycin as it causes less neurotoxicity.

Dilantina *f.* Dilantin, antispasmodic drug.

dilatación *f.* dilation, stretching; normal or abnormal enlargement of an organ or orifice; ___ **de la pupila** / ___ of the pupil.

dilatador *m.* dilator, stretcher. 1. muscle that on contraction dilates an organ; 2. device used to enlarge cavities or an opening; ___ **de Hegar** / Hegar's ___ , used to enlarge the cervical canal.

dilatar *v.* to dilate, to expand.

dilaudid *m.* dilaudid, opium-derived drug that can produce dependence.

diluente *m.* diluent, agent that has the property of diluting.

diluir *vi.* to dilute; ___ **con agua** / to water down; **sin** ___ / undiluted.

dimercaprol *m.* dimercaprol, antidote used in cases of poisoning from heavy metals such as gold and mercury.

dimetilsulfóxido *m.* dimethyl sulfoxide, analgesic and anti-inflammatory agent.

dimetría *f.* dimetria, double uterus.

diminuir, disminuir *vi.* to diminish.

diminuto-a *a.* minute, very small.

dimorfismo *m.* dimorphism, occurring in two different forms; ___ **sexual, hermafroditismo** / sexual ___ , hermaphrodism.

dina *f.* dyne, unit of force needed to accelerate one gram of mass one centimeter per second.

dinámica *f.* dynamics, the study of organs or parts of the body in movement.

dinámico-a *a.* dynamic.

dinamómetro *m.* dynamometer. 1. instrument to measure muscular strength; 2. device that determines the magnifying power of a lens.

dinero *m.* money.

dioptómetro *m.* dioptometer, instrument used to measure ocular refraction.

dioptría *f.* diopter, dioptre, unit of the refracting power of a lens.

dióptrica *f.* dioptrics, the science that studies the refraction of light.

dióptrico-a *a.* dioptric, rel. to the refraction of light.

Dios *m.* God.

dióxido de carbono *m.* carbon dioxide.

diplacusia *f.* diplacusis, hearing disorder characterized by the perception of two tones for every sound produced.

diplejía *f.* diplegia, bilateral paralysis; ___ **facial** / facial ___ ; ___ **espástica** / spastic ___ .

diplocoria *f.* diplocoria, double pupil.

diploe *m.* diploe, spongy layer that lies between the two flat compact plates of the cranial bones.

diploide *a.* diploid, having two sets of chromosomes.

diplópagos *m.* diplopagus, conjoined twins, each with fairly complete bodies but sharing

diplopía f. diplopia, double vision.

dipsógeno m. dipsogen, thirst-causing agent.

dipsomanía f. dipsomania, recurring, uncontrollable urge to drink alcohol.

dipsosis f. dipsosis, abnormal thirst.

dirección f. direction; address.

directo-a a. direct, in a straight line; uninterrupted; -mente adv. directly.

directrices f. guidelines.

dirigir vi. to direct; to guide.

disacusia, disacusis f. dysacusia, dysacousis, difficulty in hearing.

disafea f. dysaphia, impaired sense of touch.

disartria f. dysarthria, unclear speech due to impairment of the tongue or any other muscle related to speech.

disautonomía f. dysautonomy, hereditary disorder of the autonomic nervous system.

disbarismo m. dysbarism, condition caused by decompression.

disbasia f. dysbasia, difficulty in walking gen. caused by nervous lesions.

disbulia f. dysbulia, inability to concentrate.

discalculia f. dyscalculia, inability to solve mathematical problems due to brain disease or damage.

discefalia f. dyscephalia, malformation of the head and the facial bones.

discinesia f. dyskinesia, inability to perform voluntary movements.

disciplina f. discipline, strict behavior.

disco m. disk; ___ desplazado / slipped ___; ___ óptico / optic ___; ruptura de ___ / ___ rupture.

discógeno-a a. discogenic, rel. to an intervertebral disk.

discografía f. x-ray of a vertebral disk following injection of a radiopaque substance.

discoide a. discoid, shaped like a disk.

discordancia f. discordance, the absence of a genetic trait in one of a pair of twins.

discoria f. dyscoria, abnormal shape of the pupil.

discrasia f. dyscrasia, synonym of disease.

discrepancia f. discrepancy.

discreto-a a. discrete, moderate, subtle; noncontinuous.

discriminación f. discrimination, differentiation of race or quality.

discriminar v. to discriminate.

discrinismo, disendocrinismo m. dyscrinism, abnormal function in the production of secretions, esp. the endocrine glands.

discusión f. discussion, argument, debate.

discutir v. to discuss; to argue.

disdiadocoquinesia f. dysdiadochokinesia, inability to reverse immediately a motor impulse.

disecar vi. surg. to dissect, to separate and cut parts and tissues of a body.

disección f. dissection, the act of dissecting.

diseminación f. dissemination, spreading.

diseminado-a a. disseminated, spread out over a large area.

disentería f. dysentery, painful infl. of the intestines, esp. of the colon, gen. caused by bacteria or parasites and accompanied by diarrhea; ___ amebiana / amebic ___; ___ bacilar / bacillary ___.

disentir vi. to disagree, to have an opposite view.

disergia f. dysergia, lack of coordination in muscular voluntary movement.

disestesia f. dysesthesia, impaired sense of touch.

disfagia f. dysphagia, difficulty in swallowing; ___ esofágica / esophageal ___; ___ orofaríngea / oropharyngeal ___.

disfasia f. dysphasia, speech impairment caused by a brain lesion.

disfonía f. dysphonia, hoarseness.

disforia f. dysphoria, severe depression.

disfrutar v. to enjoy.

disfunción f. dysfunction, malfunction, defective function.

disfuncional a. dysfunctional.

disgenesia f. dysgenesis, malformation.

disgerminoma m. dysgerminoma, malignant tumor in the ovary.

disgnosia f. dysgnosia, impairment of the intellectual function.

dishidrosis f. dyshidrosis, anomaly of the sweating function.

dislalia f. dyslalia, speech impairment due to functional anomalies of the speech organ.

dislexia f. dyslexia, reading disorder, sometimes hereditary or caused by a brain lesion.

dislocación, dislocadura f. dislocation, displacement; ___ cerrada / closed ___, simple; ___ complicada / complicated ___; ___ congénita / congenital ___.

dismenorrea, dismenia f. dysmenorrhea, painful and difficult menstruation.

dismetría f. dysmetria, impaired ability to control range of movement in a coordinated fashion.

dismetropsia f. dysmetropsia, disorder that impairs the visual appreciation of size and shape of objects.

disminución f. diminution, reducing process.

disminuir vi. to diminish, to reduce, to lessen.

dismiotonía f. dysmyotonia, abnormal muscular tonicity.

dismnesia f. dysmnesia, impaired memory.

dismorfismo m. dysmorphism, capacity of a parasite or agent to change its shape.

disnea, dispnea f. dispnoea, dyspnea, shortness of breath.

disneico-a a. dyspneic, rel. to or suffering from dyspnea.

disoluble a. dissoluble.

disolución f. dissolution, decomposition; death.

disolvente m. dissolvent; a. capable of being dissolved.

disolver vi. to dissolve, to liquify.

disonancia *f.* dissonance, combination of tones that produces an unpleasant sound.

disosmia *f.* dysosmia, impaired smell.

disostosis *f.* dysostosis, abnormal bone growth.

dispareunia *f.* dispareunia, painful coitus.

disparidad *f.* disparity, inequality.

dispensar *v.* to dispense, to distribute.

dispensario *m.* dispensary, a place that provides medical assistance and dispenses medicines and drugs.

dispepsia *f.* dyspepsia, indigestion characterized by irregularities in the digestive process such as eructation, nausea, acidity, flatulence, and loss of appetite.

dispermia *f.* dyspermia, pain on ejaculation.

dispersar *v.* to disperse, to scatter.

dispigmentación *f.* dyspigmentation, abnormal change in the color of the skin and hair.

displasia *f.* dysplasia, abnormal development of the tissues; ___ **cervical** / cervical ___.

disponer *vi.* to arrange, to prepare.

disponibilidad *f.* availability.

disponible *a.* available.

disposición *f.* disposition, tendency to acquire certain disease.

dispositivo *m.* device, mechanism; ___ **intrauterino** / intrauterine ___.

dispraxia *f.* dyspraxia, pain or difficulty in performing coordinated movements.

disquiria *f.* dyschiria, inability of a person to distinguish if he or she is being touched on the right or the left side of the body.

disrritmia *f.* dysrhythmia, any alteration of a rhythm.

distal *a.* distal, farthermost away from the beginning or center of a structure.

distancia *f.* distance.

distasia *f.* dystasia, difficulty in maintaining a standing position.

distensibilidad *f.* distensibility.

distensión *f.* distension, distention, dilation; ___ **gaseosa** / gas ___, resulting from accumulation of gas in the abdominal cavity.

distinguido-a *a.* [*persona o característica*] distinguished.

distinguir *vi.* to distinguish, to differentiate.

distinto-a *a.* different.

distobucal *a.* distobuccal, rel. to the distal and buccal surfaces of a tooth.

distocia *f.* dystocia, difficult labor.

distoclusión *f.* distoclusion, defective closure, irregular bite.

distonía *f.* dystonia, defective tonicity, esp. muscular.

distorsión *f.* distorsion, bending or twisting out of shape.

distracción *f.* distraction. 1. separation of the surfaces of a joint without dislocation; 2. *psych.* inability to concentrate or fix the mind on a given experience.

distraído-a *a.* absentminded.

distribución *f.* breakdown, distribution; ___

detallada / detailed ___.

distribuir *vi.* to distribute.

distrofia *f.* dystrophy, degenerative disorder caused by defective nutrition or metabolism.

distrofia muscular *f.* muscular dystrophy, slow, progressive muscular degeneration.

disturbio *m.* disturbance, confusion.

disuelto-a *a. pp.* of **disolver**, dissolved.

disulfiram *m.* disulfiram, Antabuse, drug used in the treatment of alcoholism.

disuria *f.* dysuria, difficult urination.

disyunción *f.* disjunction, chromosome separation at the anaphase state of cell division.

diuresis *f.* diuresis, increased excretion of urine.

diurético *m.* diuretic, agent that causes increased urination; *pop.* water pill.

divergencia *f.* divergence, spreading apart, separation from a common center.

divergente *a.* divergent, moving in different directions.

diverticulectomía *f. surg.* diverticulectomy, removal of a diverticulum.

diverticulitis *f.* diverticulitis, infl. of a diverticulum.

divertículo *m.* diverticulum (*pl.* diverticula), pouch or sac that originates from a hollow organ or structure.

diverticulosis *f.* diverticulosis, presence of diverticula in the colon.

divertirse *vr., vi.* to have fun.

dividido-a *a.* divided.

dividir *v.* to divide, to disunite; to split.

división *f.* division, separation; split.

divorciado-a *a.* divorced.

divulsión *f.* divulsion, separation or detachment.

doblarse *vr.* to bend; ___ **hacia adelante** / ___ forward; ___ **hacia atrás** / ___ backward.

doble *m.* double; *a.* double; ___ **útero** / ___ uterus.

docena *f.* dozen.

doctor-a *m., f.* doctor.

doler *vi.* to be in pain; to ache.

dolicocefálico-a *a.* dolichocephalic, having a narrow, long head.

dolor *m.* pain; ___ **errático** / wandering ___; ___ **localizado** / localized ___; ___ **referido** / referred ___, perceived in a different area from where it originates; **sin** ___ / painless; ___ **subjetivo** / subjective ___, of no apparent physical cause.

doloroso-a *a.* painful.

doméstico-a *a.* domestic.

domiciliario-a *a.* domiciliary, taking place in the home.

dominancia *f.* dominance, predominance; ___ **cerebral** / cerebral ___; ___ **ocular** / ocular ___.

dominante *a.* dominant, predominant; **características** ___**-s** / ___ characteristics.

donación *f.* donation.

donante *m.* donor; **tarjeta de** ___ / ___'s card.

donante universal *m.* universal donor, individ-

distermia – cold

Dolor	Pain
cólico	colicky
constante	constant
fuerte	strong
lancinante	pressing
leve	mild
localizado	localized
opresivo	oppressive
penetrante	piercing
profundo	deep
quemante	burning
referido	referred
sordo	dull
subjetivo	subjective

ual belonging to blood group O or whose blood can be given to persons belonging to any other of the AB blood groups with minimal risk of complication.

donde *adv.* where.

dondequiera *adv.* anywhere; everywhere.

Donovanía granulomatosis *f.* Donovania granulomatosis, Donovan's body, bacterial infection that affects the skin and the mucous membranes of the genitalia and the anal area.

dopamina *f.* dopamine, substance synthesized by the adrenal glands that increases blood pressure and is gen. used in shock treatment.

dormido-a *a.* asleep; **profundamente ___ / sound ___.**

dormir *vi.* to sleep; **dormirse** *vr.* to fall asleep.

dorsal *a.* dorsal, rel. to the back; **fisura o corte ___ / ___ slit.**

dorsalgia *f.* dorsalgia, backache.

dorsiflexión *f.* dorsiflexion, bending backward.

dorso *m.* dorsum, posterior part, such as the back of the hand or the body.

dorsocefálico-a *a.* dorsocephalic, rel. to the back of the head.

dorsodinia *f.* dorsodynia, pain in the muscles of the upper part of the back.

dorsoespinal *a.* dorsospinal, rel. to the back and the spine.

dorsolateral *a.* dorsolateral, rel. to the back and the side.

dorsolumbar *a.* dorsolumbar, rel. to the lower thoracic and upper lumbar vertebrae area of the back.

dosimetría *f.* dosimetry, precise and systematic determination of doses.

dosímetro *m.* dosimeter, instrument used to detect and measure exposure to radiation; **___ de película / film badge, a badge carrying a film sensitive to x-rays and used to measure the cumulative exposure to the rays.**

dosis, dosificación *f.* dose, dosage; **___ de bolo, intravenosa / bolus ___, intravenous; ___ de refuerzo / booster ___; ___ diaria / daily**

___; ___ dividida / divided ___; ___ individual / unit ___; ___ subletal / sublethal ___, of insufficient amount to cause death; ___ terapéutica / therapeutic ___; ___ umbral / threshold ___, minimal dose needed to produce an effect.

Douglas, placa (saco) de *m.* Douglas cul de sac, peritoneal pouch between the uterus and the rectum.

Down, síndrome de *m.* Down syndrome, chromosomal abnormality that causes physical deformity and moderate to severe mental retardation.

dramamina *f.* dramamine, antihistaminic used in the prevention and treatment of motion sickness.

dramatismo *m. psych.* dramatism, pompous behavior and language, gen. seen in mental disorders.

drapetomanía, dromomanía *f.* drapetomania, dromomania, abnormal impulse to wander.

drástico *m.* drastic, strong cathartic; **-a** *a.* extreme, very strong.

drenaje *m.* drainage, outlet; **___ abierto / open ___; ___ postural / postural ___, that allows drainage by gravity; tubo de ___ / ___ tube.**

drenar *v.* to drain, to draw off fluid or pus from a cavity or an infected wound.

drepanocito *m.* drepanocyte, sickle cell.

droga *f.* drug; medication; **abuso de la ___ / ___ abuse; anomalías causadas por la ___ / ___ anomalies; ___ adictiva / dependence producing ___; ___ neuroléptica / neuroleptic ___, causing symptoms similar to those manifested by nervous diseases; ___ de acción prolongada / long-acting ___; entregarse a la ___ / to become ___ addicted; resistencia microbiana a la ___ / ___ resistance, microbial.**

drogadicción *f.* drug addiction.

drogadicto-a *m., f.* drug addict.

ductus *m.* ductus, duct.

ducha *f.* douche, jet of water applied to the body for medicinal or cleansing effects; shower; *vr.* **darse una ___, ducharse / to shower.**

duda *f.* doubt.

dudar *v.* to doubt, to question.

dudoso-a *a.* doubtful.

duela *f.* fluke, parasitic worm of the *Trematoda* family; **___ hepática / liver ___; ___ intestinal / intestinal ___; ___ pulmonar / lung ___; ___ sanguínea / blood ___.**

dulce *a.* sweet.

dulces *m. pl.* [*golosinas*] sweets.

dulcificante *m.* sweetener.

duodenal *a.* duodenal, rel. to the duodenum.

duodenectomía *f. surg.* duodenectomy, partial or total excision of the duodenum.

duodenitis *f.* duodenitis, infl. of the duodenum.

duodeno *m.* duodenum, essential part of the alimentary tract situated between the pylorus and the jejunum.

duodenoenterostomía *f. surg.* duodenoen-

terostomy, anastomosis between the duodenum and the small intestine.

duodenoscopía *f.* duodenoscopy, endoscopic
examination of the duodenum.

duodenostomía *f. surg.* duodenostomy, opening into the duodenum through the abdominal wall to alleviate stenosis of the pylorus.

duodenotomía *f. surg.* duodenotomy, incision of
the duodenum.

duodenoyeyunostomía *f. surg.* duodenojejunostomy, creation of a communication between the duodenum and the jejunum.

duplicar *vi.* to duplicate; to double.

durabilidad *f.* durability; duration.

durable *a.* durable, lasting.

duración *f.* duration; continuation.

duramadre, duramáter *f.* dura mater, the outer
membrane that covers the encephalum and
the spinal cord.

durante *prep.* during; lasting; ___ los días de invierno / ___ winter days.

durar *v.* to last; to endure.

durazno *m.* peach.

dureza *f.* hardness.

duro-a *a.* hard, firm.

E *abr.* emetropía / emmetropia; **enema** / enema; **enzima** / enzyme.

e *conj.* and.

ebrio-a *a.* drunk.

ebullición *f.* ebullition, boiling; **punto de ___** / boiling point.

eclampsia *f.* eclampsia, toxic, convulsive disorder that usu. occurs near the end of pregnancy or right after delivery.

eclámptico-a *a.* eclamptic, rel. to eclampsia.

eco *m.* echo, repercussion of sound.

ecocardiografía *f.* echocardiography, diagnostic procedure that uses sound waves (ultrasound) to visualize the internal structures of the heart; **___ transesofágica** / transesophageal ___.

ecocardiograma *m.* echocardiogram, ultrasonic record obtained by an echocardiography.

ecoencefalografía *f.* echoencephalography, diagnostic procedure that sends sound waves (ultrasound) to the brain structure and records the returning echoes.

ecografía *f.* echography. *V.* **ultrasonografía.**

ecograma *m.* echogram, graphic representation of an echography.

ecolalia *f.* echolalia, disorder manifested by involuntary repetition of words spoken by another person.

ecología *f.* ecology, the study of plants and animals and their relationship to the environment.

ecológico-a *a.* ecological; **sistema ___** / ___ system.

económico-a *a.* economical, economic.

ecosistema *f.* ecosystem, ecologic microcosm.

ectopia *f.* ectopia, ectopy, displacement of an organ, usu. congenital. *ectasia —*

ectópico-a *a.* ectopic, rel. to ectopia.

ectoplasma *m.* ectoplasm, external membrane surrounding the cell cytoplasm.

ectropión *m.* ectropion, eversion of the margin of a body part, such as the eyelid.

ecuador *m.* equator, imaginary line that divides a body in two equal parts.

ecuanimidad *f.* equanimity; steadfastness.

eczema, eccema *m.* eczema, inflammatory, noncontagious skin disease.

echar *v.* to throw, to cast; [*líquido*] to pour; **___ a perder** / to spoil.

Echinococcus *L.* Echinococcus. *V.* **equinococo.**

Echo, virus *m.* echovirus, any of a group of viruses found in the gastrointestinal tract, associated with meningitis and enteritis.

edad *f.* age; **___ cronológica** / chronological ___; **de ___ avanzada** / elderly; **mayor de ___** / ___ of consent; **menor de ___** / under___, a minor.

edad gestacional *f.* gestational age, estimated age of a fetus counted by weeks of gestation.

edema *m.* edema, abnormal amount of fluid in the intercellular tissue; **___ angioneurótico** / angioneurotic ___; **___ cardíaco** / cardiac ___; **___ cerebral** / cerebral ___; **___ dependiente** / dependent ___; **___ de fóvea** / pitting ___; **___ pulmonar** / pulmonary ___.

edematoso-a *a.* edematous, rel. to or affected by edema.

edetato *m.* edetate, calcium disodium, agent used in diagnosing and treating lead poisoning.

edificio *m.* building.

educación *f.* education.

educar *vi.* to educate.

efectivo-a *a.* effective; **en ___** / cash; **-mente** *adv.* in effect, actually.

efecto *m.* effect, impression; result; **___ secundario** / side ___.

efector *m.* effector, nerve ending that produces an efferent action on muscles and glands.

efedrina *f.* ephedrine, adrenalinelike drug used chiefly as a bronchodilator.

eferente *a.* efferent, centrifugal, that pulls away from the center.

efervescente *a.* effervescent, that produces gas bubbles.

eficaz, eficiente *a.* efficacious, efficient.

eficientemente *adv.* efficiently.

efímero-a *a.* ephemeral, of brief duration.

efluente *a.* effluent, flowing out.

efusión *f.* effusion, escape of fluid into a cavity or tissue.

ego *m. psych.* ego, the self, human consciousness.

egocéntrico-a *a.* egocentric, self-centered.

egoísmo *m.* selfishness, self-centeredness.

egoísta *m., f.* selfish person; *a.* selfish.

egomanía *f.* egomania, excessive self-esteem.

egosintónico-a *a. psych.* ego-syntonic, in harmony with the ego.

egreso *m.* output; [*dar de alta*] discharge; **sumario de ___** / discharge summary.

eje *m.* axis.

ejemplo *m.* example.

ejercer *vi.* [*una profesión*] to practice; [*autoridad*] to exercise.

ejercicio *m.* exercise; **___ físico** / physical ___; **___ para adelgazar** / reducing ___.

elación *f.* elation, state of jubilation and exaltation characterized by mental and physical excitement.

elastasa *f.* elastase, enzyme that catalyzes the digestion of elastic fibers, esp. of the pancreatic juice.

elasticidad *f.* elasticity, ability to expand easily and resume normal shape.

elástico *m.* elastic; **-a** *a.* elastic, that can be returned to its original shape after being extended or distorted; **tejido ___** / ___ tissue.

elastinasa *f.* elastinase. *V.* **elastasa.**

electivo-a *a.* elective, optional; **terapia ___** / ___ therapy; **cirugía ___** / ___ surgery.

renal ectasia? ¿qué es? **79**

electricidad *f.* electricity.

eléctrico-a *a.* electric, electrical; **corriente** ___ / ___ current.

electrocardiógrafo *m.* electrocardiograph, instrument for recording the electrical variations of the heart muscle in action.

electrocardiograma *m.* electrocardiogram, graphic record of the changes in the electric currents produced by the contractions of the heart muscle; ___ **de esfuerzo** / exercise ___.

electrocauterización *m.* electrocauterization, destruction of tissues by an electric current.

electrocirugía *f.* electrosurgery, use of electric current in surgical procedures.

electrocución *f.* electrocution, termination of life by electric current.

electrochoque *m.* electroshock, electroconvulsive therapy, treatment of some mental disorders by applying an electric current to the brain.

electrodo *m.* electrode, a medium between the electric current and the object to which the current is applied.

electroencefalografía *f.* electroencephalography, registering of the electrical currents produced in the brain.

electroencefalograma *m.* electroencephalogram, graphic record obtained during an electroencephalography.

electrofisiología *f.* electrophysiology, the study of the relationship between physiological processes and electrical phenomena.

electroforesis *f.* electrophoresis, movement of coloidal particles suspended in a medium charged with an electric current that separates them, such as occurs in the separation of proteins in plasma.

electrólisis *f.* electrolysis, destruction or disintegration by means of an electric current.

electrólito *m.* electrolyte, ion that carries an electrical charge.

electromagnético-a *a.* electromagnetic.

electromiografía *f.* electromyography, use of electrical stimulation to record the strength of muscle contraction.

electromiograma *m.* electromyogram, graphic report obtained by electromyography.

electrónico-a *a.* electronic.

electroquirúrgico-a *a.* electrosurgical; **destrucción** ___ **de lesiones** / ___ destruction of lesions.

electroversión *f.* cardioversion, termination of a cardiac dysrhythmia by electric means.

elefantiasis *f.* elephantiasis, chronic disease produced by obstruction of the lymphatic vessels and hypertrophy of the skin and subcutaneous cellular tissue, that affects most frequently the legs and scrotum.

elegible *a.* eligible, qualified for selection.

elegir *vi.* to elect, to choose.

elemental *a.* elemental; rudimentary.

elemento *m.* element.

elevación *f.* elevation.

elevado-a *a.* elevated, raised.

elevador *m.* elevator. 1. surgical device used for lifting a sunken part or for elevating tissues; 2. elevator.

elevar *v.* to raise, to elevate.

elminación *f.* elimination, exclusion.

eliminar *v.* to eliminate; to discard waste from the body.

eliptocito *m.* elliptocyte, oval red cell.

eliptocitosis *f.* elliptocytosis, condition of increased number of elliptocytes occurring in certain types of anemia.

elixir *m.* elixir, aromatic, sweet liquor containing an active medicinal ingredient.

emaciación *f.* emaciation, an extreme loss of weight.

embalsamamiento *m.* embalming, treatment of a dead body to retard its decay.

embarazada *a.* pregnant.

embarazo *m.* pregnancy; ___ **de probeta** / test-tube ___; ___ **ectópico** / ectopic ___, extra-uterine; ___ **falso** / false ___, enlargement of the abdomen simulating pregnancy; ___ **intersticial** / interstitial ___, located in the part of the uterine tube within the wall of the uterus; ___ **múltiple** / multiple ___, more than one fetus in the uterus at the same time; ___ **prolongado** / prolonged ___, beyond full term; **prueba del** ___ / ___ test; ___ **subrogado** / surrogate ___; ___ **tubárico** / tubal ___, when the egg develops in the Fallopian tube; ___ **tuboabdominal** / tuboabdominal ___.

embolia, embolismo *f., m.* embolism, sudden obstruction of a cerebral artery by a loose piece of clot, plaque, fat, or air bubble; ___ **cerebral** / cerebral ___, stroke; ___ **gaseosa** / air ___; **embolismo pulmonar** / pulmonary ___.

émbolo *m.* embolus, clot of blood or other material that when traveling through the bloodstream becomes lodged in a vessel of lesser diameter.

emborrachamiento, embriaguez *m., f.* intoxication, drunkenness.

emborracharse *vr.* to get drunk.

embotamiento *m.* torpor, sluggishness.

embriología *f.* embryology, study of the embryo and its development up to the moment of birth.

embrión *m.* embryo, primitive phase of an organism from the moment of fertilization to about the second month.

embriónico-a *a.* embryonal, embryonic, rel. to the embryo.

embudo *m.* funnel.

emergencia *f.* emergency, urgency; **línea telefónica de** ___ / hotline; **servicios de** ___ / ___ medicine.

emético *m.* emetic, agent that stimulates vomiting.

emetina *f.* emetine, emetic and antiamebic.

embolisación: intro. of substances to occlude vessels and stop hemorraging.

emigración, migración *f.* emigration, escape, such as of leucocytes, through the walls of capillaries and small veins.

eminencia *f.* eminence, prominence or elevation such as on the surface of a bone.

emisión *f.* emission, discharge; ___ **seminal nocturna** / wet dream, involuntary emission of semen during sleep.

emitir *v.* to emit, to expel; to issue.

emoción *f.* emotion, intense feeling.

emocional, emocionante *a.* emotional, rel. to emotion.

emoliente *a.* emollient, soothing to the skin or mucous membrane.

empachado-a *a.* suffering from indigestion.

empacho *m.* indigestion.

empapar *v.* to soak, to drench; **empaparse** *vr.* to get soaked.

empaste *m.* [*dientes*] filling.

empatía *f.* empathy, understanding and appreciation of the feelings of another person.

empeine *m.* instep, arched medial portion of the foot.

empeorar *v.* to worsen; **empeorarse** *vr.* to get worse.

empezar *vi.* to begin, to start.

empiema *f.* empyema, presence of pus in a cavity, esp. the pleural cavity.

empírico-a *a.* empiric, empirical, based on practical observations.

empleado-a *m., f.* employee.

emplear *v.* to employ, to use.

empleo *m.* employment, job.

emprender *v.* to undertake.

empujar *v.* to push, to press forward.

empuje *m.* impulse; driving force.

empujón *m.* push, shove.

emulsión *f.* emulsion, distribution of a liquid in small globules throughout another liquid.

emulsionar *v.* to emulsify, to convert into an emulsion.

en *prep.* in, on, at; ___ **el hospital** / in the hospital; ___ **la mesa** / on the table; ___ **casa** / at home.

enajenación mental *m.* derangement, mental disorder.

enajenamiento *m.* conversion disorder, the process by which repressed emotions are translated into physical manifestations.

enamorarse *vr.* to fall in love; ___ **de** / ___ with.

enanismo *m.* dwarfism, impaired growth of the body caused by hereditary or physical deficiencies.

enano-a *m., f.* dwarf, individual who is undersized in relation to the group to which he or she belongs; ___ **acondroplástico-a** / achondroplastic ___; ___ **asexual** / asexual ___; ___ **infantil** / infantile ___; **micromélico-a** / micromelic ___.

encadenamiento *m.* linkage.

encadenar *v.* to link; to chain.

encajamiento *m.* engagement. *V.* **aligeramiento.**

encajar *v.* to fit one thing into another; to insert in; to engage; **encajarse** *vr.* to fit in; to become inserted.

encajonamiento *m.* encasement, the act of becoming enclosed in another structure .

encaminar *v.* to put someone or something on the right path.

encapricharse *vr.* to become obstinate or stubborn about something.

encapsulado-a *a.* enclosed in a capsule; walled-off.

encarcelado-a *a.* incarcerated; constricted.

encefalalgia *f.* encephalalgia, intense headache.

encefálico-a *a.* encephalic, rel. to the encephalon.

encefalinas *f.* enkephalins, chemical substances produced in the brain.

encefalitis *f.* encephalitis, infl. of the brain; ___ **equina del este** / eastern equine ___; ___ **equina del oeste** / western equine ___; ___ **infantil** / infantile ___.

encéfalo *m.* encephalon, portion of the nervous system contained in the cranium.

encefalocele *m.* encephalocele, protrusion of brain matter through a congenital or traumatic defect in the skull.

encefalografía *f.* encephalography, x-ray examination of the brain.

encefaloma *m.* encephaloma, brain tumor.

encefalomalacia *f.* encephalomalacia, softening of the brain.

encefalomielitis *f.* encephalomyelitis, infl. of the brain and the spinal cord.

encefalopatía *f.* encephalopathy, any disease or malfunction of the brain.

encender *vi.* [*una bombilla*] to switch on; [*un fuego*] to kindle.

encerrar *vi.* to enclose; **encerrarse** *vr.* to lock oneself up.

encía *f.* gum.

encigótico-a, enzigótico-a *a.* enzygotic, rel. to twins developed from the same fertilized ovum.

encima *adv.* on, upon, on top of.

encinta *a.* pregnant.

enclenque *a.* emaciated; feeble.

encogerse *vr., vi.* to shrink.

enconarse *vr.* to fester, to become ulcerated.

encondroma *f.* enchondroma, tumor that develops within a bone.

encontrar *vi.* to encounter, to find; **encontrarse** *vr.* to meet with someone; to find.

encopresis *f.* encopresis, incontinence of feces.

encuesta *f.* inquest, official investigation.

endarterectomía *f. surg.* endarterectomy, excision of the thickened inner lining of an artery.

endarteritis *f.* endarteritis, infl. of the lining of an artery.

endémico-a *a.* endemic, endemical, rel. to a disease that remains for an indefinite length of time in a given community or region.

endentado-a *a.* serrated, teethlike projection.

enderezar *vi.* to straighten out.

endocardio *m.* endocardium, the serous inner lining membrane of the heart.

endocarditis *f.* endocarditis, acute or chronic infl. of the endocardium; ___ **aguda bacteriana** / ___, acute bacterial; ___ **crónica** / ___, chronic; ___ **no bacteriana** / ___, nonbacterial; ___ **reumática** / ___, rheumatic; ___ **subaguda bacteriana** / ___, subacute bacterial; ___ **valvular** / ___, valvular; ___ **vegetativa** / ___ vegetative.

endocervix *m.* endocervix, mucous membrane of the cervix.

endocrino-a *a.* endocrine, rel. to internal secretions and the glands that secrete them; **glándulas** ___-s / endocrine glands, glands that secrete hormones directly into the bloodstream.

endocrinología *f.* endocrinology, the study of the endocrine glands and the hormones secreted by them.

endodermo *m.* endoderm, the innermost of the three layers of the embryo.

endógeno-a *a.* caused by internal factors.

endolinfa *f.* endolymph, fluid contained in the membranous labyrinth of the ear.

endometrial *a.* endometrial, rel. to the endometrium; **biopsia** ___ / ___ biopsy.

endometrio *m.* endometrium, inner mucous membrane of the uterus.

endometrioma *f.* endometrioma, mass containing endometrial tissue.

endometriosis *f.* endometriosis, disorder by which endometrial-like tissue is found in areas outside the uterus.

endometritis *f.* endometritis, infl. of the mucous membrane.

endomorfo *m.* endomorph, person whose body is more heavily developed in the torso than in the limbs.

endorfinas *f.* endorphins, chemical substances produced in the brain that have the property of easing pain.

endoscopía *f.* endoscopy, examination of a cavity or conduit using an endoscope.

endoscópico-a *a.* endoscopic, rel. to endoscopy.

endoscopio *m.* endoscope, instrument used to examine a hollow organ or cavity.

endostio *m.* endosteum, tissue that covers the medullar cavity of the bone.

endotelial *a.* endothelial, rel. to the endothelium.

endotelio *m.* endothelium, thin layer of cells that form the inner lining of the blood vessels, the lymph channels, the heart, and other cavities.

endotérmico-a *a.* endothermic, that absorbs heat.

endotraqueal *a.* endotracheal, within or through the trachea; **tubo** ___ **con manguito** / ___ tube, cuffed.

endulzar *vi.* to sweeten.

endurecer *vi.* to harden; **endurecerse** *vr.* to become hardened.

endurecimiento *m.* hardening.

enema *f.* enema; ___ **de bario** / barium ___; ___ **de contraste doble** / double-contrast ___.

energía *f.* energy, vigor.

enérgico-a *a.* energetic, vigorous.

enfadar *v.* to make angry, to upset; **enfadarse** *vr.* to become angry.

énfasis *m.* emphasis; **hacer** ___ / to emphasize.

enfermar *v.* to cause disease; **enfermarse** *vr.* to become ill, to get sick.

enfermedad *f.* disease, illness, malady; **control de** ___-**es contagiosas** / communicable ___ control; ___ **ambulante** / walking ___; ___ **concomitante** / companion ___; ___ **de la altura** / high altitude sickness, caused by diminished oxygen; ___ **de los mineros** / coal miner's ___; ___ **de red o cadena** / heavy chain ___; ___ **funcional** / functional ___, of unknown origin; ___ **renal** / renal ___; ___ **respiratoria crónica** / chronic respiratory ___; ___ **venérea** / venereal ___; **licencia por** ___ / sick leave.

enfermería *f.* infirmary, a place used for treatment of the sick.

enfermero-a *m., f.* nurse; ___ **anestesista** / ___ anesthetist; **asistente de** ___ / orderly; ___ **de cirugía** / scrub ___, surgical ___; ___ **de salud pública** / community or public health ___; ___ **graduado-a** / trained ___; ___ **práctico-a** / practical ___; ___ **privado-a** / private duty ___; ___ **registrado-a** / registered ___; **jefe-a de** ___-**s** / chief or head ___.

enfermizo-a *a.* sickly; predisposed to become ill.

enfermo-a *m., f.* sick person; **cuidado de** ___-**s** / nursing.

enfisema *m.* emphysema, chronic lung condition that causes distension of the small air sacs (alveoli) in the lungs and atrophy of the tissue between them, impairing the respiratory process.

enfisematoso-a *a.* emphysematous, affected by emphysema.

enfocar *vi.* to focus.

enfrente *adv.* across from; in front of.

enfriamiento *m.* cold, chill; [*acondicionamiento físico*] cool-down.

enfriar *v.* to cool down.

engañar *v.* to deceive; to fool; **engañarse** *vr.* to deceive oneself.

engordar *v.* to gain weight; to get fat.

engorroso-a *a.* cumbersome, troublesome.

engrama *f.* engram. 1. permanent mark or trace left in the protoplasm by a passing stimulus; 2. *psych.* a latent permanent picture produced by a sensorial experience.

engrasar *v.* to grease; to oil.

engurgitado-a *a.* engorged, distended by excess of liquid.

enjabonar *v.* to soap; **enjabonarse** *vr.* to soap oneself.

enjambrazón *f.* swarming, the act of multiplying or spreading, such as bacteria over a culture.

enjuagar *v.* to rinse; **enjuagarse** *vr.* to rinse oneself out.

enjuague *m.* rinse, mouthwash.

enoftalmia *f.* enophthalmos, receded eyeball.

enojado-a *a.* angry, fretful.

enojar *v.* to anger; **enojarse** *vr.* to get angry.

enorme *a.* enormous, huge.

enquistado-a *a.* encysted, enclosed in a sac or cyst.

enredadera *f.* vine.

enredado-a *a.* tangled; [*situación médica*] complicated.

enredar *v.* to tangle; to make things more difficult; **enredarse** *vr.* to become tangled up or complicated.

enriquecer *vi.* to enrich; **enriquecerse** *vr.* to be enriched; to become rich.

enriquecido-a *a.* enriched; of increased value.

enriquecimiento *m.* enrichment.

enrojecer *vi.* to redden.

enrojecimiento *m.* redness.

ensalada *f.* salad.

ensanchar *v.* to widen.

ensangrentado-a *a.* bloody, stained with blood.

ensartar *v.* to thread.

ensayo *m.* assay.

enseñado-a *a.* taught.

enseñar *v.* to teach; to show; to instruct.

ensimismado-a *a.* absorbed in thought, pensive.

ensordecedor-a *a.* deafening; **ruido** ___ / ___ noise.

ensuciar *v.* to dirty; to defecate.

entablillar *v.* to splint.

entamebiasis *f.* entamebiasis, infestation by an ameba.

ente *m.* entity, being.

entender *vi.* to understand, to comprehend.

entendido-a *a.* understood; agreed; informed; wise, learned.

enteralgia *f.* enteralgia, neuralgia of the intestine.

entérico-a. enteral *a.* enteral, rel. to the intestine; **cubierta** ___ / ___ coated.

enteritis *f.* enteritis, infl. of the intestine, esp. the small intestine.

entero-a *a.* whole; undiminished.

enteroclisis *f.* enteroclysis, irrigation of the colon.

enterococo *m.* enterococcus, a streptococcus that inhabits the intestinal tract.

enterocolecistostomía *f. surg.* enterocholecystostomy, opening between the gallbladder and the small intestine.

enterocolitis *f.* enterocolitis, infl. of both the large and small intestine.

enterocutáneo-a *a.* enterocutaneous, that communicates between the intestines and the cutaneous surface.

enteropatía *f.* enteropathy, any anomaly or disease of the intestines.

enteropatógeno-a *a.* enteropathogenic, rel. to a microorganism causing an intestinal disease.

enterostomía *f. surg.* enterostomy, opening or communication between the intestine and the abdominal wall skin; **revisión de una** ___ / ___ revision.

enterotoxina *f.* enterotoxin, a toxin produced by or originating in the intestines.

enterovirus *m.* enterovirus, a group of viruses that infect the human gastrointestinal tract, and can cause respiratory diseases and neurological anomalies.

enterrar *vi.* to bury.

entibiar *v.* to make lukewarm.

entidad *f.* entity, that which constitutes the essence of something.

entierro *m.* burial.

entonces *adv.* then, at that time.

entorno *m.* environment, setting, ambiance.

entrada *f.* entrance; entry; inlet; access to a cavity.

entrañas *f.* entrails, bowels; insides.

entrar *v.* to go in; to come in.

entre *prep.* between.

entrenamiento *m.* training.

entrenar *v.* to train; **entrenarse** *vr.* to receive training.

entrevista *f.* interview.

entropía *f.* entropy, in thermodynamics, diminished capacity to convert internal energy into work.

entropión *m.* entropion, inversion or turning inward such as that of the eyelid.

entuerto *m.* afterbirth pains.

entumecido-a *a.* numb.

entumecimiento *m.* numbness; torpor.

entusiasmo *m.* enthusiasm.

enucleación *f. surg.* enucleation, removal of a tumor or a structure.

enuclear *v. surg.* to enucleate. 1. to remove a tumor without causing it to rupture; 2. to destroy or take out the nucleus of a cell; 3. to remove the eyeball.

enuresis, enuresia *f.* enuresis, incontinence; bed-wetting; ___ **nocturna** / nocturnal ___ .

envejecer *vi.* to grow old.

envejecido-a *a.* grown old, looking old.

envenenado-a *a.* poisoned.

envenenamiento *m.* poisoning.

envenenar *v.* to poison; **envenenarse** *vr.* to poison oneself.

enviar *v.* to send.

envidia *f.* envy.

enviudar *v.* to become a widow or a widower.

envoltura *f.* pack, cold or hot wrapping.

envolver *vi.* to wrap; to wrap around.

enyesar *v.* to make a cast using plaster of Paris; to plaster.

enzima *f.* enzyme, protein that acts as a catalyst in vital chemical reactions.

enzimología *f.* enzymology, the study of enzymes.

eosina *f.* eosin, insoluble substance used as a red dye for coloring tissue in microscopic studies.

eosinofilia *f.* eosinophilia, presence of a large number of eosinophilic leukocytes in the blood.

eosinófilo-a *a.* eosinophilic, that stains readily with eosin.

eosinopenia *f.* eosinopenia, deficiency of eosinophilic cells in the blood.

eosinopénico-a *a.* eosinopenic, rel. to eosinopenia.

ependimario-a *a.* ependymal, rel. to the ependyma; **membrana** ___ / ___ layer, one of the interior membranes of the neural tube of the embryo.

ependimitis *f.* ependymitis, infl. of the ependyma.

epéndimo *m.* ependyma, membrane that lines the ventricles of the brain and the central canal of the spinal cord.

ependimoma *f.* ependymoma, a tumor of the central nervous system that contains fetal ependymal cells.

epicardio *m.* epicardium, visceral surface of the pericardium.

epicóndilo *m.* epicondyle, a projection or eminence above the condyle of a bone.

epidemia *f.* epidemic, disease that affects a large number of people in a region or community at the same time.

epidémico-a *a.* epidemic; **brote** ___ / ___ outbreak.

epidemiología *f.* epidemiology, the study of epidemic diseases.

epidérmico-a *a.* epidermal, epidermic, rel. to the epidermis.

epidermis *f.* epidermis, external epithelial covering of the skin.

epidermoide *m.* epidermoid, tumor that contains epidermal cells; *a.* 1. resembling the dermis; 2. rel. to a tumor that has epidermal cells.

epidermólisis *f.* epidermolysis, loosening of the epidermis.

epididimitis *f.* epididymitis, infection and infl. of the epididymis.

epidídimo *m.* epididymis, a tube along the back side of the testes that collects the sperm from the testicle to be transported by the vas deferens to the seminal vesicle.

epidural *a.* epidural, situated above or outside of the dura mater.

epifisario-a *a.* epiphysial, epiphyseal, rel. to the epiphysis.

epífisis *f.* epiphysis, the end of a long bone, usu. wider than the diaphysis.

epifisitis *f.* epiphysitis, infl. of an epiphysis.

epifora *f.* epiphora, watering of the eye.

epigástrico-a *a.* epigastric, rel. to the epigastrium; **reflejo** ___ / ___ reflex.

epigastrio *m.* epigastrium, upper back portion of the abdomen.

epiglotis *f.* epiglottis, cartilage that covers the entrance to the larynx and prevents food or liquid from entering it during swallowing.

epiglotitis *f.* epiglottitis, infl. of the epiglottis and adjacent tissues.

epilación *f.* epilation, removal of hair by electrolysis.

epilepsia *f.* epilepsy, grand mal, neurological disorder, gen. chronic and in some cases hereditary, manifested by periodic convulsions and sometimes by loss of consciousness.

epilepsia jacksoniana *f.* Jacksonian epilepsy, partial epilepsy without loss of consciousness.

epiléptico-a *m., f.* person affected with epilepsy; *a.* epileptic, rel. to or suffering from epilepsy; **ataque o crisis** ___ / ___ seizure; **ausencia** ___ / absentia epileptica, momentary loss of consciousness during an epileptic seizure.

epileptógeno *m.* epileptogenic, epileptogenous, agent that causes epileptic seizures.

epinefrina *f.* epinephrine. *V.* **adrenalina.**

epiploico-a *a.* epiploic, rel. to the epiploon; **foramen** ___ / ___ foramen, opening that connects the greater and the lesser peritoneal cavities.

epiplón *m.* epiploon, pad of fat that covers the intestines.

episiotomía *f. surg.* episiotomy, incision of the perineum to avoid tearing during parturition.

epispadias *m.* epispadias, abnormal congenital opening of the male urethra on the upper surface of the penis.

epistaxis *f.* epistaxis, nosebleed.

epitálamo *m.* epithalamus, the uppermost portion of the diencephalon.

epitelial *a.* epithelial, rel. to the epithelium.

epitelio *m.* epithelium, the outer layer of mucous membranes; ___ **ciliado** / ciliated ___; ___ **columnar** / columnar ___; ___ **cuboidal** / cuboidal ___; ___ **de transición** / transitional ___; ___ **escamoso** / squamous ___; ___ **estratificado** / stratified ___.

epitelioma *f.* epithelioma, carcinoma consisting mainly of epithelial cells.

epitelización *f.* epithelization, growth of epithelium over an exposed surface, such as a wound.

epitímpano *m.* epitympanum, upper back portion of the eardrum.

epónimo *m.* eponym, a noun that names a medical disorder or device after the name of its discoverer or inventor, such as Down syndrome.

epoxia *f.* epoxy, compound characterized by its adhesiveness.

Epsom, sales de *f.* Epsom salts, magnesium sulfate used as laxative.

Epstein-Barr, virus de *m.* Epstein-Barr virus, virus thought to be the causative agent of infectious mononucleosis.

equilibrado-a *a.* balanced.

equilibrar *v.* to equilibrate, to balance.

equilibrio *m.* equilibrium, balance.

equimosis *f.* ecchymosis, bruise, gradual blue-black discoloration of the skin due to blood filtering into the cellular subcutaneous tissue.

equinococo *m.* echinococcus, a genus of tapeworm.

equinococosis *f.* echinococcosis, infestation by echinococcus; ___ **hepática** / hepatic ___; ___ **pulmonar** / pulmonary ___.

equinovaro *m.* equinovarus, congenital deformity of the foot.

equitativo-a *a.* equitable.

equivalencia *f.* equivalence.

equivalente *a.* equivalent.

equivocación *f.* mistake, error.

equivocado-a *a.* mistaken, in error.

equivocarse *vr., vi.* to make a mistake; to be in error; to miscalculate.

erección *f.* erection, state of rigidity or hardening of erectile tissue when it is filled with blood, such as the penis.

eréctil *a.* erectile, capable of erection or dilation.

erector *m.* erector, a structure that erects, such as a muscle.

ergonomía *f.* ergonomics, branch of ecology that studies design and operations of machines and the physical environment as related to humans.

ergotamina *f.* ergotamine, alkaloid used chiefly in the treatment of migraine headaches.

ergotismo *m.* ergotism, chronic poisoning due to excessive intake of ergot.

erina *f.* dissecting hook.

erisipela *f.* erysipelas, acute infection of the skin.

eritema *f.* erythema, redness of the skin due to congestion of the capillaries; ___ **de los pañales** / diaper rash; ___ **solar** / sunburn.

eritematoso-a *a.* erythematic, erythematous, rel. to erythema.

eritremia *f.* erythremia, increase of red blood cells due to an excessive production of erythroblasts by the bone marrow.

eritroblasto *m.* erythroblast, primitive red blood cell.

eritroblastosis *f.* erythroblastosis, excessive number of erythroblasts in the blood.

eritrocito *m.* erythrocyte, red blood cell made in the bone marrow that serves to transport oxygen to tissues; **índice de sedimentación de ___-s** / sedimentation rate.

eritrocitopenia *f.* erythrocytopenia, deficiency in the number of erythrocytes present in the blood.

eritrocitosis *f.* erythrocytosis, increase in the number of erythrocytes in the blood.

eritroide *a.* erythroid, reddish.

eritroleucemia *f.* erythroleukemia, malignant blood disease caused by abnormal growth of both red and white blood cells.

eritromicina *f.* erythromycin, antibiotic used chiefly in infections caused by gram-positive bacteria.

eritrón *m.* erythron, system formed by erythrocytes circulating in the blood and the organ from which they arise.

eritropoyesis *f.* erythropoiesis, red blood cell production.

eritropoyetina *f.* erythropoietin, a non-dialyzable protein that stimulates red blood cell production.

erógeno-a *a.* erogenous, that which produces erotic sensations; **zona ___** / ___ zone.

erosión *f.* erosion, the act of wearing out or away.

erosivo-a *a.* erosive, that causes erosion.

erótico-a *a.* erotic, rel. to eroticism or having the power to arouse sexual impulses.

erotismo *m.* eroticism, erotism, lustful sexual impulses.

erradicar *vi.* to eradicate, to remove, to extirpate.

errante, errático-a *a.* wandering, deviating from the normal course.

error *m.* error, mistake.

eructación *f.* eructation, belching.

eructar, erutar *v.* to eructate, to belch.

eructo, eruto *m.* eructation, belch.

erupción *f.* eruption, rash, skin outbreak; ___ **escamosa** / squamous ___; ___ **maculopapular** / maculopapular ___.

escafoide *a.* scaphoid, shaped like a boat, esp. in reference to the bone of the carpus or the tarsus.

escala *f.* scale; ___ **de diferenciación** / range.

escaldadura *f.* scald, skin burn caused by boiling liquid or vapor.

escaldar *v.* to scald; to burn.

escalera *f.* staircase; ladder; ___ **de escape** / fire escape.

escalofrío *m.* chill, a cold, shivering sensation.

escalonar *v.* to stagger; to distribute in sequence.

escalpelo, escarpelo *m.* scalpel, surgical blade, dissecting knife.

escama *f.* scale, a thin, small lamina shed from the epidermis.

escamoso-a *a.* squamous, scaly.

escán *m.* scan, the process of producing an image of a specific organ or tissue by means of a radioactive substance that is injected as a contrasting element; ___ **cardíaco** / heart ___; ___ **de la tiroides** / thyroid ___; ___ **de los huesos** / bone ___; ___ **del cerebro** / brain ___; ___ **pulmonar** / lung ___.

escáner *m.* scanner, exploratory device.

escápula *f.* scapula, shoulder blade.

escara *f.* eschar, dark-colored scab or crust that forms in the skin after a burn.

escarificación *f.* scarification, the act of producing a number of small superficial scratches or punctures on the skin.

escarlatina *f.* scarlatina, scarlet fever, an acute contagious disease characterized by fever and a bright red rash on the skin and tongue.

escasez *f.* scarcity, shortage, lack.

escaso-a *a.* scarce, scanty, in short supply.

escatología *f.* scatology; 1. the study of feces; 2. a morbid preoccupation with feces and filth.

escenario *m.* scenario; scene.

escindir *v.* to excise, to cut, to divide.

escintigrama *f.* scintigram, radionucleid imaging, procedure that uses radioisotopes to obtain a two-dimensional image of the distribution of bodily radiation, previously administered as a radiopharmaceutical agent.

escintilador *m.* escintillator.

escintiscan *m.* scintiscan.

escirro *m.* scirrhus, hard cancerous tumor.

escirroso-a *a.* scirrhous, hard, rel. to a scirrhus.

escleritis *f.* scleritis, infl. of the sclera.

esclerosis *f.* sclerosis, progressive hardening of organs or tissues; ___ **arterial** / arterial ___; ___ **de Alzheimer** / Alzheimer's ___; ___ **lateral amiotrófica** / amyotrophic lateral ___.

esclerosis múltiple *f.* multiple sclerosis, slow, progressive disease of the central nervous system caused by a loss of the protective myelin covering of the nerve fibers of the brain and spinal cord.

esclerosis tuberosa *f.* tuberous sclerosis, familial disease manifested by convulsive seizures, progressive mental deficiency, and multiple tumor formations in the skin and the brain.

escleroterapia *f.* sclerotherapy, the process of injecting chemical solutions to treat varices in order to produce sclerosis.

esclerótica *f.* sclera, sclerotica, the hard, white exterior part of the eye made of fibrous tissue.

esclerótico-a *a.* sclerotic, rel. to or afflicted by sclerosis.

escobillón *m.* swab.

escoger *vi.* to choose, to elect.

escoliosis *f.* scoliosis, pronounced lateral curvature of the spine.

esconder *v.* to hide, to conceal.

escorbuto *m.* scurvy, disease caused by lack of vitamin C and manifested by anemia, bleeding gums, and a general state of inanition.

escorpión *m.* scorpion; **picadura de** ___ / ___ sting.

escotadura *f.* notch; ___ **supraesternal** / suprasternal ___.

escotoma *m.* scotoma, area of lost or diminished vision within the visual field.

escotopía *f.* scotopia, adjustment to nocturnal vision.

escotópico-a *a.* scotopic, rel. to scotopia; **visión** ___ / ___ vision.

escribir *v.* to write.

escrito-a *a. pp.* of **escribir,** written.

escrófula *f.* scrofula, tuberculosis of the lymphatic glands.

escrofuloderma *m.* scrofuloderma, a type of scrofula with skin lesions.

escrotal *a.* scrotal, rel. to the scrotum.

escroto *m.* scrotum, the sac surrounding and enclosing the testes.

escrúpulo *m.* scruple.

escrupuloso-a *a.* scrupulous.

escrutinio *m.* scrutiny; screening.

escudo *m.* shield, a protective covering.

escupir *v.* to spit.

esencial *a.* essential, indispensable.

esfacelo *m.* slough, mass of dead tissue that has been shed or fallen off from live tissue.

esfenoidal *a.* sphenoidal, rel. to the sphenoid bone.

esfenoides *m.* sphenoid bone, large bone at the base of the skull.

esfera *f.* sphere. 1. a structure shaped like a globe or ball; 2. sociological environment.

esférico-a *a.* spherical, rel. to a sphere.

esferocito *m.* spherocyte, sphere-shaped erythrocyte.

esferocitosis *f.* spherocytosis, presence of spherocytes in the blood.

esferoide *a.* spheroid, shaped like a sphere.

esférula *f.* spherule, minute sphere.

esfigmomanómetro *m.* sphygmomanometer, instrument for determining blood pressure.

esfínter *m.* sphincter, circular muscle that opens and closes an orifice.

esfinteroplastia *f. surg.* sphincteroplasty, plastic surgery of a sphincter muscle.

esfinterotomía *f. surg.* sphincterotomy, cutting of a sphincter muscle.

esfuerzo *m.* effort; ___ **coordinado** / teamwork; ___ **excesivo** / overexertion, strain; **prueba de** ___ / stress test; **sin** ___ / effortless.

esguince *m.* sprain. *V.* **torcedura.**

eslabón *m.* link.

esmalte *m.* enamel, hard substance that covers and protects the dentin of a tooth.

esmegma *m.* smegma, thick cheesy substance secreted by sebaceous glands, esp. seen in the external genitalia.

esofagectomía *f. surg.* esophagectomy, excision of a portion of the esophagus.

esofágico-a *a.* esophageal, rel. to the esophagus; **dilatación** ___ / ___ dilatation.

esofagitis *f.* esophagitis, infl. of the esophagus.

esófago *m.* esophagus, portion of the alimentary tract between the pharynx and the stomach.

esofagodinia *f.* esophagodynia, pain in the esophagus.

esofagogastritis *f.* esophagogastritis, infl. of the stomach and the esophagus.

esofagogastroduodenoscopía *f.* esophagogastroduodenoscopy, examination of the esophagus, the stomach, and the duodenum by means of an endoscope.

esofagogastroscopía *f.* esophagogastroscopy, endoscopic examination of the esophagus and the stomach.

esoforia *f.* esophoria, crossed eyes, inward deviation of the eyes.

esotropía *f.* esotropia. *V.* **esoforia.**
espacial *a.* spatial, rel. to space.
espacio *m.* space, area.
espalda *f.* back; **dolor de** ___ / backache.
espanto *m.* fright, excessive fear.
español *m.* [*idioma*] Spanish; [*nativo-a*] Spanish; **-a** *a.* Spanish.
esparadrapo *m.* adhesive tape.
esparcido-a *a.* spread out; scattered.
esparcir *vi.* to scatter, to spread.
espárrago *m.* asparagus.
espasmo *m.* spasm, twitch, involuntary muscular contraction.
espasmódico-a *a.* spasmodic, rel. to spasms; **crup** ___ / ___ croup.
espasticidad *f.* spasticity, increase in the normal tension of a muscle resulting in stiffness and difficult movement.
espástico-a *a.* spastic. 1. resembling, or of the nature of spasms; 2. afflicted with spasms.
espátula *f.* spatula, palette-knife.
especia *f.* spice.
especial *a.* special, especial, unique; **-mente** *adv.* specially.
especialidad *f.* specialty.
especialista *m., f.* specialist.
especialización *f.* specialization.
especializarse *vr., vi.* to specialize.

Especialidades	Specialties
anestesiología	anesthesiology
cirugía cardiotorácica	cardiothoracic surgery
cirugía general	general surgery
cirugía plástica	plastic surgery
dermatología	dermatology
medicina de emergencia o de urgencia	emergency medicine
medicina general	family practice
medicina interna	internal medicine
medicina nuclear	nuclear medicine
nefrología	nephrology
neurología	neurology
neurocirugía	neurosurgery
obstetricia y ginecología	obstetrics and gynecology
oftalmología	ophthalmology
oncología	oncology
ortopedia	orthopedics
otolaringología	otolaringology
patología	pathology
pediatría	pediatrics
perinatología	perinatology
psiquiatría	psychiatry
radiología	radiology
urología	urology

especie *f.* species, kind, class of organisms belonging to a biological category.
especificar *vi.* to specify.
específico-a *a.* specific; determined; precise; **no** ___ / nonspecific.
espécimen *m.* specimen, sample.
espectro *m.* spectrum. 1. range of activity of an antibiotic against a variety of microorganisms; 2. series of images resulting from the refraction of electromagnetic radiation; 3. series of colors of refracted sunlight that can be seen with the naked eye or with the help of a sensitive instrument.
especular *v.* to speculate.
espéculo *m.* speculum, instrument used for dilating a conduit or cavity; ___ **rectal** / proctoscope.
espejo *m.* mirror.
espejuelos *m. pl.* eyeglasses, spectacles; ___ **bifocales** / bifocal ___; ___ **para leer** / reading ___; ___ **trifocales** / trifocal ___.
espera *f.* wait; **salón de** ___ / waiting room.
esperanza *f.* hope; **perder la** ___ / to give up ___; **tener** ___ / to have ___.
esperar *v.* to wait; to hope; to expect.
esperma *f.* sperm. *V.* **semen.**
espermaticida, espermicida *m.* spermatocide, spermicidal, agent that destroys spermatozoa; *a.* spermatocidal, that kills spermatozoa.
espermático-a *a.* spermatic; rel. to sperm or semen.
espermatocele *m.* spermatocele, a cystic tumor of the epididymis containing spermatozoa.
espermatogénesis *f.* spermatogenesis, the process of formation and development of spermatozoa.
espermatoide *a.* spermatoid, resembling spermatozoa.
espermatorrea *f.* spermatorrhea, involuntary loss of semen.
espermatozoide *m.* spermatozoid, spermatozoon, male reproductive cell that fertilizes the ovum.
espermiograma *m.* spermiogram, evaluation of spermatozoa as an aid to determine sterility.
espesar *v.* to thicken; to condense; **espesarse** *vr.* to become thicker; to become condensed.
espeso-a *a.* thick, condensed.
espesor *m.* thickness, consistency.
espica *f.* spica, a type of bandage.
espícula *f.* spicule, a body shaped like a small needle.
espicular *a.* spicular, needle-shaped.
espiga *f.* spike, sharp rise in a curve, such as in the tracing of brain waves.
espina *f.* 1. the spine or vertebral column; 2. spina; thorn; fishbone.
espina bífida *f.* spina bifida, congenital anomaly of the spine with a gap; ___ **oculta** / ___ occulta, without protrusion, gen. at the lumbar level.
espinaca *f.* spinach.

espinal *a.* spinal, rel. to the spine or the spinal cord; **canal** ___ / ___ canal; **choque** ___ / ___ shock; **fusión** ___ / ___ fusion; **médula** ___ / ___ cord; **nervio accesorio** ___ / ___ accessory nerve; **nervios** ___-**es** / ___ nerves; **punción** ___ / ___ puncture.

espinazo *m.* spine, *pop.* backbone.

espinilla *f.* 1. blackhead; 2. shinbone, anterior edge of the tibia.

espinoso-a *a.* spinous, acanthoid, spine-shaped.

espiral *f.* spiral. 1. sphere-like arrangement of cardiac muscular fibers; 2. a type of finger-print; *a.* winding around a center or axis.

espirar *v.* to exhale.

espíritu *m.* spirit. 1. alcoholic solution of a vola-tile substance; 2. soul; **tranquilidad de** ___ / peace of mind.

espiritual *a.* spiritual, rel. to the soul; **cura** ___ / ___ healing.

espirometría *f.* spirometry, the act of measuring the breathing capacity through the use of a spirometer.

espirómetro *m.* spirometer, device used to meas-ure the amount of inhaled and exhaled air.

espiroqueta *f.* spirochete, spinal microorgan-ism that belongs to the order *Spirochaetales* that includes the syphilis causing agent.

espiroquetósico-a *a.* spirocheta, rel. to spiro-chetes.

esplácnico-a *a.* splanchnic, rel. to or that reaches the viscera; **nervios** ___-**s** / ___ nerves.

esplenectomía *f. surg.* splenectomy, excision of the spleen.

esplénico-a *a.* splenic, rel. to the spleen.

esplenoportografía *f.* splenoportography, x-ray of the splenic and portal veins following injec-tion of a radiopaque dye into the spleen.

esplenorrenal *a.* splenorenal, rel. to the spleen and the kidneys; **derivación** ___ / ___ shunt, anastomosis of the splenic veins or artery to the renal vein, esp. used in the treatment of portal hypertension.

espolón *m.* spur, pointed projection, as of a bone; ___ **calcáneo** / calcaneal ___ .

espondilitis *f.* spondylitis, infl. of one or more vertebrae; ___ **anquilosante** / ankylosing ___ , rheumatoid.

espondilólisis *f.* spondylolysis, dissolution or destruction of a vertebra.

espondilolistesis *f.* spondylolisthesis, forward displacement of one vertebra over another, usu. the fourth lumbar over the fifth or the fifth over the sacrum.

espondilopatiá *f.* spondylopathy, any disease or disorder of a vertebra.

espondilosis *f.* spondylosis. 1. vertebral anky-losis; 2. any degenerative condition affecting the vertebrae.

esponja *f.* sponge.

esponjar *v.* to sponge, to soak with a sponge.

esponjoso-a *a.* spongy, porous.

espontáneo-a *a.* spontaneous.

espora *f.* spore, unicellular reproductive cell.

esporádico-a *a.* sporadic, occurring irregularly.

esporicida *m.* sporicide, agent that destroys spores.

esposo-a *m., f.* husband; wife.

esprue *m.* sprue, chronic disease that affects the ability to absorb dietary gluten.

espulgar *vi.* to cleanse of lice or fleas.

espuma *f.* froth, foam; scum.

espurio-a *a.* spurious, false.

esputo *m.* sputum, spittle; ___ **sanguinolento** / bloody ___ .

esquelético-a *a.* skeletal, rel. to the skeleton.

esqueleto *m.* skeleton, the bony structure of the body.

esquema *f.* schema; outline, plan.

esquemático-a *a.* schematic, rel. to a schema.

esquina *f.* corner.

esquirla *f.* bone splinter.

esquistosoma *m. Schistosoma*, blood fluke, a tre-matode larva that enters the blood through the digestive tract or through the skin by con-tact with contaminated water.

esquistosomiasis *f.* schistosomiasis, infesta-tion with blood flukes.

esquizofrenia *f.* schizophrenia, a breaking down of the mental functions with different psy-chotic manifestations such as delusion, with-drawal, and distorted perception of reality.

esquizofrénico-a *a. psych.* schizophrenic, rel. to or suffering from schizophrenia.

esquizoide *a.* schizoid, resembling schizophre-nia.

estabilidad *f.* stability, permanence.

estabilización *f.* stabilization, the act of making stable.

estabilizar *vi.* to stabilize, to eliminate fluctua-tions.

estable *a.* stable, nonfluctuating.

establecer *vi.* to establish.

estación *f.* station. 1. status of condition; 2. stop-ping place such as a nurse's station; 3. season of the year.

estacionario-a *a.* stationary, in a fixed position.

estadificación *f.* staging, classification in the process of the degree of an illness.

estadío *m.* stage or transition period during the evolution of an illness.

estadística *f.* statistics; statistic, figure.

estado *m.* state, condition; ___ **asmaticus** / status asthmaticus; ___ **crepuscular** / twilight ___ ; ___ **de gestación** / pregnancy; ___ **nutricional** / nutritional ___ .

estafilococemia *f.* staphylococcemia, presence of staphylococci in the blood.

estafilocócico-a *a.* staphylococcal, staphylococ-cic, rel. to or caused by staphylococci.

estafilococo *m.* staphylococcus, any pathologi-cal microcci. **intoxicación alimentaria por** ___-**s** / staphylococcal food poisoning.

estafilotoxina *f.* staphylotoxin, toxin produced by staphylococci.

estancación, estancamiento *f., m.* stagnation, lack of movement or circulation in fluids.

estándar *a.* standard, normal established way; **atención o cuidado** ___ / ___ of care; **desviación** ___ / ___ deviation; **error** ___ / ___ error; **procedimiento** ___ / ___ procedure.

estandarización *f.* standardization, uniformity; normalcy.

estanolona *f.* stanolone, anabolic steroid drug.

estapedectomía *f. surg.* stapedectomy, excision of the stapes of the ear to improve hearing.

estar *vi.* to be; ___ **de guardia** / to be on call.

estasis *f.* stasis, stagnation of a body fluid such as blood or urine.

estático-a *a.* static, without movement.

estatura *f.* stature, height.

este *m.* [*punto cardinal*] east; **al** ___ **de** / to the ___ of; **-a** *a.* this; **estos-as** *pl.* these; **éste-a** *dem. pron.* this, this one; **éstos-as** *pl.* these; **esto** *neut.* this, this one.

estearina *f.* stearine, white crystalline component of fats.

esteatorrea *f.* steatorrhea, excess fat in the stool.

estenia *f.* sthenia, normal strength and vigor.

estenosado-a *a.* stenosed, rel. to stenosis.

estenósico-a *a.* stenotic, produced or characterized by stenosis.

estenosis *f.* stenosis, constriction or abnormal narrowing of a passageway; ___ **aórtica** / aortic ___; ___ **espinal** / spinal ___; ___ **pilórica** / pyloric ___; ___ **traqueal** / tracheal ___.

éster *m.* ester, compound formed by the combination of an organic acid and alcohol.

estereorradiografía *a.* stereoradiography, a three-dimensional x-ray.

estereotaxia *f.* stereotaxis, technique used in neurological procedures to locate with precision an area in the brain.

estereotipia *f.* stereotype, a type that represents a whole group.

estereotípico-a *a.* stereotypic, rel. to a stereotype.

esterificación *f.* esterification, transformation of an acid into ester.

estéril *a.* sterile. 1. aseptic, free of germs; 2. incapable of producing offspring.

esterilidad *f.* sterility, the condition of being sterile.

esterilización *f.* sterilization. 1. procedure to prevent reproduction; 2. total destruction of microorganisms; ___ **por calor** / thermosterilization; ___ **por gas** / gas ___; ___ **por vapor** / steam ___.

esterilizador *m.* sterilizer.

esterilizar *vi.* to sterilize.

esternal *a.* sternal, rel. to the sternum; **punción** ___ / ___ puncture.

esternocostal *a.* sternocostal, rel. to the sternum and the ribs.

esternón *m.* sternum, breastbone.

esternotomía *f. surg.* sternotomy, cutting through the sternum.

esteroide *a.* steroid, rel. to steroids.

esteroides *m.* steroids, complex organic compounds that resemble cholesterol and of which many hormones such as estrogen, testosterone, and cortisone are made.

estertor *m.* rale, stertor, an abnormal rattle-like sound heard on auscultation; ___ **agónico** / death rattle; ___ **áspero** / coarse ___; ___ **crepitante** / crepitant ___; ___ **crujiente** / crackling ___; ___ **húmedo** / moist ___; ___ **roncus** / rhonchus ___, rattling in the throat; ___ **seco** / dry ___.

estesia *f.* esthesia, perception or sensation, or any anomaly affecting them.

estetoscopio *m.* stethoscope, instrument used for auscultation.

estigma *m.* stigma. 1. a specific sign of a disease; 2. a mark or sign on the body.

estilete *m.* style, stylet, stylus; *surg.* flexible probe.

estiloide *a.* styloid, long and pointed.

estimado *m.* estimate, evaluation.

estimulación *f.* stimulation; motivation.

estimulador cardíaco *m.* pacemaker.

estimulante *m.* stimulant, agent that incites a reaction; *pop.* upper.

estimular *v.* to stimulate; to motivate, to animate to action, to boost, to prompt.

estímulo *m.* stimulus, agent or factor that produces a reaction; ___ **condicionado** / conditioned ___; ___ **subliminal** / subliminal ___.

estíptico *a.* styptic, agent with astringent power.

estirado-a *a.* extended, elongated.

estirar *v.* to stretch, to extend.

estirón *m.* stretch, forceful pull.

estoma *m.* stoma, artificial permanent opening, esp. in the abdominal wall.

estomacal *a.* stomachic, rel. to the stomach.

estómago *m.* stomach, sac-like organ of the alimentary canal; ___ **en cascada** / cascade ___; ___ **en bota de vino** / leather bottle ___; **lavado de** ___ / ___ pumping.

estomal *a.* stomal, rel. to a stoma.

estomatitis *f.* stomatitis, infl. of the mucosa of the mouth; ___ **aftosa** / aphthous ___.

estornudar *v.* to sneeze.

estornudo *m.* sneeze.

estrabismo *m.* strabismus, squint, abnormal alignment of the eyes due to muscular deficiency.

estradiol *m.* estradiol, steroid produced by the ovaries.

estrangulación *f.* strangulation. 1. asphyxia or suffocation gen. caused by obstruction of the air passages; 2. constriction of an organ or structure due to compression.

estrangulado-a *a.* strangulated; constricted.

estrangular *v.* to strangle.

estratificación *f.* stratification; arrangement in layers.

estratificado-a *a.* stratified, arranged in layers; **epitelio** ___ / ___ epithelium.

estrato *m.* stratum, layer.

[handwritten: × eupneic(o) – breathing easily]

estrechamiento *m.* narrowing; tightness.

estrechar *v.* to make narrower.

estrechez, estrechura *f.* stricture, narrowness, closeness.

estrecho-a *a.* narrow.

estrella *f.* star; star-shaped body.

estrellado-a *a.* stellate, shaped like a star.

estremecerse *vr., vi.* to shudder, to tremble.

estreñido-a *a.* constipated; hard bound.

estreñimiento *m.* constipation; infrequent or incomplete bowel movements.

estreptococcemia *f.* streptococcemia, blood infection caused by the presence of streptococci.

estreptocócico-a *a.* streptococcal, rel. to or caused by streptococci; **infecciones ___ -s / ___** infections.

estreptococo *m.* streptococcus, organism of the genus *Streptococcus.*

estreptomicina *f.* streptomycin, antibiotic drug used against bacterial infections.

estrés *m.* stress.

estría *f.* stria, streak.

estriado-a *a.* striated, striate, marked by streaks; **músculo ___ / ___** muscle.

estribo *m.* stapes, the innermost of the auditory ossicles shaped like a stirrup.

estricnina *f.* strychnine, highly poisonous alkaloid.

estricto-a *a.* strict; exact.

estricturotomía *f. surg.* stricturotomy, the cutting of strictures.

estridor *m.* stridor, whoop, harsh sound during respiration such as following an attack of whooping cough.

estrinización *m.* estrinization, epithelial changes of the vagina due to stimulation by estrogen.

estrogénico-a *a.* estrogenic, rel. to estrogen.

estrógeno *m.* estrogen, female sex hormone produced by the ovaries; **receptor de ___ / ___** receptor.

estroma *m.* stroma, the supporting tissue of an organ.

estrona *f.* estrone, oestrone, estrogenic hormone.

estropear *v.* to spoil; to maim; to cripple.

estructura *f.* structure; order.

estudiante *m., f.* student.

estudiar *v.* to study.

estudio *m.* study.   *[handwritten: en estudio : investigation under]*

estudios cruzados *m. pl.* cross studies.

estupefaciente *m.* stupefacient, agent causing stupor.

estupidez *f.* stupidity, foolishness.

estúpido-a *a.* stupid, foolish.

estupor *m.* stupor, daze, state of lethargy.

éter *m.* ether, chemical liquid used as a general anesthetic through inhalation of its vapor.

eternal, eterno-a *a.* eternal.

ética *f.* ethics, norms and principles that rule professional conduct.

etileno *m.* ethylene, anesthetic.

etiología *f.* etiology, branch of medicine that studies the cause of diseases.

etiológico-a *a.* etiologic, rel. to etiology.

etiqueta *f.* label, tag.

etmoidectomía *f. surg.* ethmoidectomy, removal of ethmoid cells or part of the ethmoid bone.

etmoideo-a *a.* ethmoid, sievelike; **seno ___ / ___** sinus, air cavity within the ethmoid bone.

etmoides *m.* ethmoid bone, spongy bone located at the base of the cranium.

eubolismo *m.* eubolism, normal metabolism.

eucalipto *m.* eucalyptus tree.

euforia *f. psych.* euphoria, an abnormal or exaggerated state of well-being.

eugenesia *f.* eugenics, the science that deals with improving and controling procreation to achieve more desirable hereditary characteristics.

eunuco *m.* eunuch, castrated male. *[handwritten: eupneic]*

euploidia *f.* euploidy, complete set of chromosomes.

Eustaquio, trompa de *m.* Eustachian tube, part of the auditory conduit.

eutanasia *f.* euthanasia, mercy killing.

eutiroideo-a *a.* euthyroid, rel. to the normal function of the thyroid gland.

evacuación *f.* evacuation. 1. act of emptying or evacuating esp. the bowels; 2. the act of making a vacuum.

evacuante *m.* evacuant, an agent that stimulates bowel movement.

evacuar *v.* to evacuate, to empty; to void.

evaginación *f.* evagination, protrusion of some part or organ from its normal position.

evaluación *f.* evaluation, assessment, rating, score; weighing the physical and mental state and capabilities of an individual; **___ clínica /** clinical assessment; **___ del estado de salud /** health assessment; **___ del proceso evolutivo /** follow-up assessment.

evaluar *v.* to evaluate.

evanescente *a.* evanescent, of brief duration.

evaporación *f.* evaporation, conversion of a liquid or a solid into vapor.

eversión *f.* eversion, outward turning, esp. of the mucosa surrounding a natural orifice.

evidencia *f.* evidence, manifestation; [*legal*] evidence; testimony.

evisceración *f. surg.* evisceration, removal of the viscera or contents of a cavity; disembowelment.

evitar *v.* to avoid.

evocar *vi.* to evoke.

evolución *f.* evolution, gradual change.

evulsión *f.* evulsion, tearing away, pulling out.

exacerbación *f.* exacerbation, increase in the severity of a symptom or disease.

exacto-a *a.* exact; **-mente** *adv.* exactly.

exageración *f.* exaggeration.

exagerar *v.* to exaggerate.

exaltación *f.* exaltation, state of jubilation.

examen *m.* exam, examination; evaluation; investigation; ___ **físico completo** / complete physical checkup.

examinar *v.* to examine, to view and study the human body to determine a person's state of health; to look into, to investigate.

exantema *f.* exanthem, exanthema, cutaneous eruption.

exasperado-a *a.* exasperated.

exasperar *v.* to exasperate, to aggravate.

exceder *v.* to exceed; to outweigh; to surpass; **excederse** *vr.* to go too far, *pop.* to go overboard.

excéntrico-a *a.* eccentric, odd, different from the norm.

excepción *f.* exception, outside of the rule; **a ___ de** / with the ___ of.

excesivo-a *a.* excessive, too much.

exceso *m.* excess; **en ___** / excessively.

excisión *f.* excision, removal, ablation.

excitación *f.* excitation, reaction to a stimulus.

excitado-a *a.* excited, worked up.

excitante *m.* stimulant, *pop.* upper; *a.* stimulating, exciting.

excitar *v.* to stimulate; to provoke.

excluir *vi.* to exclude, to leave out.

excoriación *f.* excoriation, abrasion of the skin.

excrecencia *f.* excrescence, tumor protruding from the surface of a part or organ.

excreción *f.* excretion, elimination of waste matter.

excremento *m.* excrement, feces.

excreta *f.* excreta, all waste matter of the body.

excretar *v.* to excrete, to eliminate waste from the body.

excusa *f.* excuse.

excusado *m.* outside toilet; privy.

excusar *v.* to excuse.

exenteración *f. surg.* exenteration. *V.* **evisceración.**

exfoliación *f.* exfoliation, shedding or peeling of tissue.

exhalación *f.* exhalation, the act of breathing out.

exhalar *v.* to exhale.

exhausto-a *a.* exhausted, fatigued.

exhibicionismo *m.* exhibitionism, obsessive drive to expose one's body, esp. the genitals.

exhibicionista *m., f.* exhibitionist, one who practices exhibitionism.

exhumación *f.* exhumation, disinterment.

exigir *vi.* to demand; to require.

existente *a.* existent, on hand.

existir *v.* to exist, to be.

éxito *m.* success; good result.

exocrino-a *a.* exocrine, rel. to the external secretion of a gland.

exoftalmía *f.* exophthalmia, exophthalmos, exophthalmus, abnormal protrusion of the eyeball.

exoftálmico-a *a.* exophthalmic, rel. to or suffering from exophthalmia.

exógeno-a *a.* exogenous, originating outside the organism.

exostosis *f.* exostosis, cartilaginous osseus hypertrophy that projects outward from a bone, or the root of a tooth.

exótico-a *a.* exotic.

exotoxina *f.* exotoxin, toxic substance secreted by bacteria.

exotropía *f.* exotropia, a type of strabismus, outward turning of the eyes due to muscular imbalance.

expandir *v.* to expand, to dilate; **expandirse** *vr.* to become expanded.

expansión *f.* expansion, extension.

expansivo-a *a.* expansive; [*persona*] outgoing.

expectoración *f.* expectoration, the expulsion of mucus or phlegm from the lungs, trachea or bronchi.

expectorante *m.* expectorant, an agent that stimulates expectoration.

expediente *m.* medical record; file; **sumario del ___** / summary of hospital records.

experiencia *f.* experience, knowledge gained by practice.

experimental *a.* experimental, rel. to or known by experiment.

experimentar *v.* to experiment.

experimento *m.* experiment.

experto-a *m., f.* expert.

expiración *f.* expiration, termination; death.

expirar *v.* to expire, to die.

explicación *f.* explanation; interpretation.

exploración *f.* exploration, search, investigation.

exploratorio-a *a.* exploratory, rel. to exploration.

exponer *vi.* to expose.

expresión *f.* expression, facial appearance.

expresividad *f.* expressivity, degree of manifestation of a given hereditary trait in the individual that carries the conditioning gene.

exprimir *v.* to squeeze; to extrude.

expuesto-a *a. pp.* of **exponer,** exposed.

expulsar *v.* to expel, to eject forcefully.

exsanguinación *f.* exsanguination, severe blood loss.

exsanguinotransfusión *f.* exsanguino-transfusion, exchange transfusion, gradual and simultaneous withdrawal of a recipient's blood with transfusion of a donor's blood.

éxtasis *m. psych.* ecstasy, trance accompanied by a pleasurable feeling.

extendedor *m.* stretcher.

extender *vi.* to extend, to stretch out; **extenderse** *vr.* to spread out.

extendido-a *a.* extended; widespread.

extensión *f.* extension, prolongation, straightening of a contracted finger or limb or aligning a dislocated or fractured bone.

extensor-a *a.* extensor, having the property of extending.

extenuado-a *a.* extenuated, exhausted.

exterior *a.* exterior.

91

exteriorizar *v. surg.* to exteriorize, to temporarily expose a part or organ.

extinción *f.* extinction, cessation.

extinguir *vi.* to extinguish, to put out.

extirpación *f. surg.* extirpation, removal of a part or organ.

extirpar *v.* to eradicate, to remove.

extracción *f.* extraction, the process of removing, pulling, or drawing out.

extracelular *a.* extracellular, occurring outside a cell.

extracorporal *a.* extracorporeal, occurring outside the body.

extracto *m.* extract, a concentrated product.

extradural *a.* extradural. *V.* **epidural.**

extraer *vi.* to extract, to remove; to dig out.

extrañarse *vr.* to wonder, to question.

extraño-a *a.* extraneous. 1. unrelated to or outside an organism; 2. strange, rare; 3. foreign.

extraocular *a.* extraocular, outside the eye.

extrasístole *f.* extrasystole, arrhythmic beat of the heart, *pop.* skipped beat.

extravasado-a *a.* extravasated, rel. to the escape of fluid from a vessel or organ into the surrounding tissue.

extravascular *a.* extravascular, outside a vessel.

extremidad *f.* extremity. 1. the end portion; 2. a limb of the body; **amputación de una** ___ / limb amputation; **rigidez de una** ___ / limb rigidity.

extremo-a *a.* extreme, excessive.

extrínseco-a *a.* extrinsic, that comes from without.

extrofia *f.* extrophy, *V.* **eversión.**

extrovertido-a *a. psych.* extroverted, excessive manifestation and attention outside the self.

extubación *f. surg.* extubation, removal of a tube, as the laryngeal tube.

exuberante *a.* exuberant, excessive proliferation; overabundant.

exudación *f.* exudation. *V.* **exudado.**

exudado *m.* exudate, inflammatory fluid such as pus or serum.

exudar *v.* to exude, to ooze out gradually through the tissues.

eyaculación *f.* ejaculation, sudden and rapid expulsion, such as the emission of semen.

eyacular *v.* to ejaculate, to expel fluid secretions such as semen.

eyección *f.* ejection, throwing out with force.

F *abr.* **Fahrenheit** / Fahrenheit.

f *abr.* **fallo** / failure; **femenino** / feminine; **fórmula** / formula; **función** / function.

fabela *f.* fabella, sesamoid fibrocartilage that can develop in the head of the gastrocnemius muscle.

fabricación *f.* fabrication. *V.* confabulación.

faceta *f.* facet, facette *Fr.* small, smooth area on the surface of a hard structure such as a bone.

facetectomía *f. surg.* facetectomy, removal of the auricular facet of a vertebra.

facial *a.* facial, rel. to the face; **huesos __-es** / __ bones; **nervios __-es** / __ nerves; **parálisis** __ / __ paralysis; **reflejo** __ / __ reflex; **espasmo** __ / __ spasm.

facies *f.* (*pl.* **facies**) facies, expression or appearance of the face; __ **inexpresiva** / masklike __; __ **leontina** / __ leontina.

fácil *a.* easy; **-mente** *adv.* easily.

facilitar *v.* to facilitate, to make easier.

facticio-a *a.* factitious, not natural, artificial.

factor *m.* factor, element that contributes to produce an action; __ **angiogenético tumoral** / tumor angiogenetic __; __ **antihemofílico** / antihemophilic __; __ **de coagulación de la sangre** / clotting __; __ **dominante** / dominant __; __ **liberador** / releasing __; __ **Rh** [*erre-ache*] / Rh __; __ **reumatoideo** / rheumatoid __.

facultad *f.* faculty. 1. capability to perform a normal function; 2. professional staff.

facultativo-a *a.* facultative. 1. not obligatory, voluntary; 2. of a professional nature; **asistencia** __ **médica** / professional medical help; **cuidado** __ / professional care.

fagocitario-a, fagocítico-a *a.* phagocytic, rel. to phagocytes.

fagocito *m.* phagocyte, cell that ingests and destroys microorganisms or other cells and foreign particles.

fagocitosis *f.* phagocytosis, the process of ingestion and digestion by phagocytes.

Fahrenheit, escala de *f.* Fahrenheit scale, a temperature scale with a freezing point of water at 32° and a normal boiling point at 212°.

faja *f.* girdle; band.

fajero *m.* swaddling band, strip of cloth used to restrain an infant's movements.

falange *f.* phalanx, any of the long bones of the fingers or toes.

falciforme *a.* falciform, shaped like a sickle; **ligamento** __ **del hígado** / __ ligament of the liver.

falda *f.* skirt.

fálico-a *a.* phallic, rel. to or resembling the penis.

falo *m.* phallus, the penis.

Falopio, trompas de *f.* Fallopian tubes, tubes leading from the uterus to the ovaries.

falsificación *f.* falsification, distortion or alteration of an event or object.

falsificador-a *m., f.* forger.

falsificar *vi.* to forge; to simulate.

falso-a *a.* false, untrue; __ **negativo** / __ negative; __ **positivo** / __ positive.

falta *f.* fault, error; __ **de alimentos** / __ of food; __ **de orientación** / __ of orientation; **sin** __ / without fail; for sure.

faltar *v.* to be lacking or wanting; to be absent.

falla *f.* defect, deficiency.

fallar *v.* to miss, to fail.

fallecer *vi.* to die.

fallecimiento *m.* death.

fallo *m.* failure; insufficiency; __ **cardíaco** / heart __; __ **renal** / renal __; __ **respiratorio** / respiratory __.

Fallot, tetralogía de *f.* tetralogy of Fallot, congenital deformity of the heart involving defects in the great blood vessels and the walls of the heart chambers.

famélico-a *a.* famished.

familia *f.* family.

familiar *m.* family member; *a.* familiar, familial; **descendencia** __ / kinship.

fanático-a *m., f.* fanatic; *a.* fanatic, fanatical.

Fanconi, síndrome de *m.* Fanconi's syndrome, congenital hypoplastic anemia.

fantasear *v.* to fantasize, to fancy, to imagine.

fantasía *f.* fantasy, the use of the imagination to transform an unpleasant reality into an imaginary, satisfying experience.

fantasma *f.* phantasm, optical illusion, apparition.

fantoma *m.* phantom. 1. mental image; 2. a transparent model of the human body or any of its parts.

farina *f.* farina, corn flour.

faringe *f.* pharynx, part of the alimentary canal extending from the base of the skull to the esophagus.

faríngeo-a *a.* pharyngeal, rel. to the pharynx.

faringitis *f.* pharyngitis, infl. of the pharynx.

farmacéutico-a *m., f.* pharmacist, specialist in pharmacy; *a.* pharmaceutical, rel. to pharmacy.

farmacia *f.* pharmacy. 1. the study of drugs and their preparation and dispensation; 2. drugstore.

farmacocinética *f.* pharmacokinetics, the study *in vivo* of the metabolism and action of drugs.

farmacodependencia *f.* drug dependence.

farmacodinamia *f.* pharmacodynamics, the study of the effects of medication.

farmacogenética *f.* pharmacogenetics, the study of genetic factors as related to drug metabolism.

farmacología *f.* pharmacology, the study of drugs and their effect on living organisms.

farmacólogo-a *m., f.* pharmacologist, pharmacist, specialist in pharmacology.

farmacopea *f.* pharmacopeia, a publication containing a listing of drugs and formulas as well as information providing standards for their preparation and dispensation.

farmacoterapia *f.* pharmacotherapy, treatment of a disease with the use of medications.

fascia *L.* fascia, fibrous connective tissue that envelops the body beneath the skin and encloses muscles, nerves, and blood vessels; ___ aponeurótica / aponeurotic ___, provides muscle protection; ___ de Buck / Buck's ___, covers the penis; ___ de Colles / Colle's ___, inner layer of the perineal fascia; ___ lata / lata ___, protects the muscles of the thigh; ___ transversalis / transversalis ___, between the transversalis muscle of the abdomen and the peritoneum.

fasciculación *f.* fasciculation. 1. formation of fascicles; 2. involuntary contraction of muscle fibers.

fascículo *m.* fascicle, fasciculus, a bundle of muscular and nervous fibers.

fasciectomía *f. surg.* fasciectomy, partial or total removal of a fascia.

fasciotomía *f. surg.* fasciotomy, incision or partition of a fascia.

fascitis *f.* fascitis, infl. of a fascia.

fase *f.* phase, stage.

fásico-a *a.* phasic, rel. to a phase.

fatal *a.* fatal, deadly, mortal.

fatalidad *f.* fatality.

fatiga *f.* fatigue, extreme tiredness.

fatigarse *vr., vi.* to become fatigued, to get tired.

fauces *f. pl.* fauces, the passage from the mouth to the pharynx.

favor *m.* favor, good deed.

favorable *a.* favorable, advantageous.

faz *f.* face.

fe *f.* faith, **de buena** ___ / in good ___.

fealdad *f.* ugliness.

febril *a.* febrile, having a body temperature above normal; **convulsiones ___-es** / ___ convulsions.

fecal *a.* fecal, containing or rel. to feces.

fecalito *m.* fecalith, intestinal concretion of fecal material.

fecaloma *m.* fecaloma, tumor-like accumulation of feces in the colon or rectum.

fecaluria *f.* fecaluria, presence of fecal material in the urine.

fécula *f.* starch.

feculento-a *a.* starchy; **alimentos ___-s, almidones** / ___ foods.

fecundación *f.* fecundation; fertilization.

fecundidad *f.* fecundity, fertility.

fecundo-a *a.* fruitful; fertile; abundant.

fecha *f.* [*día, mes o año*] date; ___ **de defunción** / ___ of death; ___ **de nacimiento** / birth date; ___ **de vigencia** / effective ___; ___ **del espécimen** / specimen ___ or sample ___.

felación *f.* fellatio. *V.* **cunilinguo.**

felino-a *a.* feline, rel. to or resembling a cat.

feliz *a.* happy; felicitous.

femenino-a *a.* feminine.

feminismo *m.* feminism.

feminista *m., f.* feminist, one who fosters feminism.

feminización *f.* feminization, development of feminine characteristics.

femoral *a.* femoral, rel. to the femur; **arco ___ profundo** / deep ___ arch; **arteria ___** / ___ artery; **vena ___** / ___ vein.

fémur *m.* femur, the thighbone.

fenestración *f. surg.* fenestration. 1. creation of an opening in the inner ear to restore lost hearing; 2. the act of perforating.

fenestrado-a *a.* fenestrated, having openings.

fénico, fenol *a.* phenic, carbolic.

fenobarbital *m.* phenobarbital, barbiturate used as a hypnotic or sedative.

fenómeno *m.* phenomenon. 1. objective symptom of a disease; 2. event or manifestation; 3. *pop.* freak.

fenotipo *m.* phenotype, characteristics of a species produced by the environment and heredity.

feo-a *a.* ugly.

fermentación *f.* fermentation, splitting a complex compound into simpler ones by the action of enzymes or ferments.

fermentar *v.* to ferment, to produce fermentation.

fermento *m.* ferment, the product of fermentation.

ferritina *f.* ferritin, an iron complex that provides a way to store iron in the body.

ferroproteína *f.* ferroprotein, protein combined with a radical containing iron.

ferruginoso-a *a.* ferruginous, rel. to or containing iron.

fértil *a.* fertile, fruitful.

fertilidad *f.* fertility, fruitfulness.

fertilización *f.* fertilization.

fertilizante *m.* fertilizer.

férula *f.* splint, device made of any material such as wood, metal, or plaster, used to immobilize or support a fractured bone or a joint.

fetal *a.* fetal, rel. to the fetus; **circulación ___** / ___ circulation; **latido del corazón ___** / ___ heart tone; **membranas ___-es** / ___ membranes; **monitorización ___** / ___ monitoring; **retardo del crecimiento ___** / ___ growth retardation; **viabilidad ___** / ___ viability.

feticidio *m.* feticide, destruction of the fetus in the uterus.

fetiche *m.* fetish.

fetidez, fetor *f., m.* stench, offensive odor.

fétido-a *a.* fetid, having a very bad odor.

feto *m.* fetus, phase of gestation between three months and the moment of birth.

fetoproteína *f.* fetoprotein, an antigen present in the human fetus.

fetoscopio *m.* fetoscope, instrument used to visualize the fetus *in utero* to facilitate prenatal diagnosis.

fiasco *m.* fiasco; gross failure.

fibra *f.* fiber, filament; **___-s ópticas** / fiberoptics.

fibrilación *f.* fibrillation. 1. involuntary or abnormal muscular contraction; **___ auricular** / atrial, auricular **___**, irregular movement of the atria; **___ ventricular** / ventricular **___**; 2. formation of fibrils.

fibrilación-aleteo *f.* flutter-fibrillation, auricular activity that shows signs of flutter and fibrillation.

fibrilar *a.* fibrillar, fibrillary, rel. to a fibril.

fibrilla *f.* fibril, a very small fiber.

fibrina *f.* fibrin, insoluble protein that is essential to the coagulation of blood.

fibrinógeno *m.* fibrinogen, protein present in blood plasma that converts into fibrin during blood clotting.

fibrinogenólisis *f.* fibrinogenolysis, the dissolution of fibrinogen in the circulating blood.

fibrinólisis *f.* fibrinolysis, the dissolution of fibrinogen by the action of enzymes.

fibrinoso-a *a.* fibrous, fibrinous, of the nature of fibers.

fibroadenoma *f.* fibroadenoma, a benign tumor composed of fibrous and glandular tissue.

fibroblasto *m.* fibroblast, a cell from which connective tissue develops.

fibrocartílago *m.* fibrocartilage, a type of cartilage in which the matrix contains a large amount of fibrous tissue.

fibrocístico-a, fibroquístico-a *a.* fibrocystic, cystic and fibrous in nature; **enfermedad ___ de la mama** / **___** disease of the breast.

fibroide *a.* fibroid, rel. to or of a fibrinous nature.

fibrolipoma *m.* fibrolipoma, tumor that contains fibrous and adipose tissue.

fibroma *m.* fibroma, a benign tumor composed of fibrous tissue.

fibromioma *m.* fibromyoma, tumor that contains muscular and fibrous tissue.

fibromuscular *a.* fibromuscular, of a fibrous and muscular nature.

fibroplasia *f.* fibroplasia, formation of fibrous tissue as seen in the healing of a wound: **___ retrolental** / retrolental **___**.

fibrosis *f.* fibrosis, abnormal formation of fibrous tissue; **___ cística** / cystic **___**; **___ intersticial del pulmón** / diffuse interstitial pulmonary **___**; **___ proliferativa** / proliferative **___**; **___ pulmonar** / pulmonary **___**; **___ retroperitoneal** / retroperitoneal **___**.

fibroso-a, fibrinoso-a *a.* fibrous, fibrinous; 1. rel. to or of the nature of fibrin; 2. threadlike.

fibrótico-a *a.* fibrotic, rel. to fibrosis.

ficticio *a.* fictitious, false.

fidelidad *f.* fidelity; loyalty.

fideo *m.* noodle.

fiebre *f.* fever; **ampollas de ___** / **___** blisters; **___ de conejo** / rabbit **___**, tularemia; **___ de origen desconocido** / **___** of unknown origin;

___ del heno / hay **___**; **___ entérica** / enteric **___**, intestinal; **___ familiar del Mediterráneo** / familiar Mediterranean **___**; **___ intermitente** / intermittent **___**; **___ ondulante** / undulant **___**, brucellosis; **___ recurrente** / relapsing **___**; **___ remitente** / remittent **___**; **___ reumatoidea** / rheumatoid **___**; **___ tifoidea** / typhoid **___**; **___ de trinchera** / trench **___**; **tener ___** / to run a temperature.

fiebre amarilla *f.* yellow fever, endemic disease of tropical areas, transmitted by the bite of a female mosquito, *Aedes aegypti,* and manifested by fever, jaundice, and albuminuria.

fiebre del valle *f.* valley fever. *V.* **coccidiomicosis.**

fiebre manchada de las Montañas Rocosas *f.* Rocky Mountain spotted fever, acute febrile disease caused by a germ transmitted by infected ticks.

figura *f.* form, shape; figure.

fijación *f.* fixation. 1. immobilization; 2. the act of focusing the eyes directly upon an object; 3. the act of being strongly attached to a particular person or object; 4. *psych.* interruption of the development of the personality before reaching maturity.

fijador *m.* fixative, a substance used to harden and preserve pathological specimens.

fijar *v.* to fix, to affix, [*una fractura*] to set.

filamento *m.* filament, strand, delicate fiber or fine thread.

film *m.* film; thin layer.

filtración *f.* filtration, the act of straining through a filter impeding passage of certain molecules.

filtrar *v.* to strain; **filtrarse** *vr.* to filter through, to filtrate.

filtro *m.* filter, any device used to strain liquids.

fimbria *f.* fimbria. 1. fingerlike structure; 2. appendage of certain bacteria.

fimosis *f.* phimosis, narrowness of the orifice of the prepuce that prevents its being drawn back over the glans penis.

fin *m.* end, conclusion; **¿con qué ___?** / for what purpose?; **a ___ de** / in order to.

fin de semana *m.* weekend.

final *m.* end; **al ___** / at the end; *a.* final, conclusive.

financiero-a *a.* financial, monetary; **gastos ___-s** / **___** expenses.

fingir *vi.* to fake, to malinger.

finito-a *a.* finite, having limits.

fino-a *a.* fine, as opposed to thick or coarse.

firma *f.* signature.

firmar *v.* to sign, to subscribe.

firme *a.* firm, secure.

física *f.* physics, the study of matter and its changes.

físicamente *adv.* physically, referring to the body as opposed to the mind.

físico *m.* 1. physique, appearance, figure; 2. **-a** *m., f.* physicist, specialist in physics; *a.* physical, rel.

to the body and its condition; **examen** ___ /
___ examination; **terapia** ___ / ___ therapy.

fisicoquímico-a *a.* physicochemical, rel. to
physics and to chemistry.

fisiología *f.* physiology, the study of the physical
and chemical processes affecting organisms.

fisiológico-a *a.* physiologic, physiological, rel. to
physiology; **no** ___ / unphysiological.

fisiólogo-a *m., f.* physiologist, a specialist in
physiology.

fisión *f.* fission, a breaking up into parts; ___ **nuclear** / nuclear ___.

fisioterapia *f.* physiotherapy, treatment by
means of physical manipulation and agents
such as heat, light, and water.

fisonomía *f.* physiognomy, facial features.

fístula *f.* fistula, abnormal passage from a hollow
organ to the skin or from one organ to another; ___ **arteriovenosa** / arteriovenous ___;
___ **biliar** / biliary ___; ___ **del ano** / anal ___.

fistular, fistuloso-a *a.* fistular, fistulous, rel. to
or resembling a fistula.

fistulización *f.* fistulization, pathological or surgical formation of a fistula.

fisura *f.* fissure, cleft, a longitudinal opening.

fitobezoar *m.* phytobezoar, a concretion of undigested vegetable fiber that forms in the stomach or intestine.

fláccido-a *a.* flaccid, limber, lax.

flaco-a *a.* very thin, lanky.

flagelado-a *a.* flagellated, provided with flagella.

flageliforme *a.* flagelliform, shaped like a whip.

flagelo *m.* flagellum, prolongation or tail in the
cells of some protozoa or bacteria.

flanco *m.* flank, loin, part of the body situated
between the ribs and the upper border of the
ilium.

flato *m.* flatus, gas or air in the stomach or intestines.

flatulencia *f.* flatulence, condition marked by
distention and abdominal discomfort due to
excessive gas in the gastrointestinal tract.

flebitis *f.* phlebitis, infl. of a vein.

flebograma *m.* phlebogram, venogram, a tracing of the venous pulse.

flebolito *m.* phlebolith, phlebolite, a calcareous
deposit in a vein.

flebotomía *f. surg.* phlebotomy, venotomy, incision into a vein for the purpose of drawing
blood.

flegmasia *f.* phlegmasia, inflammation.

flema *f.* phlegm. 1. thick mucus; 2. one of the
four humors of the body.

flemático-a *a.* phlegmatic. 1. that produces
phlegm; 2. apathetic.

flemón *m.* phlegmon, an infl. of the cellular
tissue.

flexibilidad *f.* flexibility, pliability, the capability
to flex.

flexible *a.* flexible, bendable, able to change.

flexión *f.* flexion, flexure, the act of bending.

flexionar *v.* to flex, to bend.

flexor *m.* flexor, a muscle that can flex a joint.

flexura *f.* flexure, fold, curvature, bend; ___
hepática / hepatic ___, right curvature of the
colon; ___ **esplénica** / splenic ___, left curvature of the colon; ___ **sigmoidea** / sigmoid ___,
curved part of the colon that precedes the
rectum.

floculación *f.* flocculation, precipitation and agglomeration of very small invisible particles
into large visible flakes.

flogosis *f.* phlogosis. *V.* **flegmasia.**

flojera *f.* weakness.

flojo-a *a.* weak, flaccid; sluggish.

flor *f.* flower.

flora *f.* flora, group of bacteria within a given
organ; ___ **intestinal** / intestinal ___.

florido-a *a.* florid, showing a bright red coloring
of the skin.

flotador *m.* floater, macule, specks in the vision.

flotante *a.* floating, free, not adhered.

flotar *v.* to float.

fluctuación *f.* fluctuation, wavering, wavelike
movements produced by vibrations of body
fluids on palpation.

fluctuar *v.* to fluctuate, to waver, to go back and
forth.

fluidez *f.* fluidity, liquidity.

fluído *m.* fluid, liquid.

fluir *vi.* to flow.

flujo *m.* afflux, flow, flux. 1. large amount of fluid
discharge from a cavity or surface of the body;
___ **laminar** / laminar ___; ___ **turbulento** /
turbulent ___; **medidor de** ___ / flowmeter; 2.
the rush of blood or liquid; 3. menstruation.

flúor *m.* fluorine, gaseous chemical element.

fluoresceína *f.* fluorescein, red dye.

fluorescencia *f.* fluorescence, the property of a
substance to emit light when exposed to certain types of radiation such as x-rays.

fluorescente *a.* fluorescent, rel. to fluorescence;
anticuerpo ___ / ___ antibody; **técnica del anticuerpo** ___ / ___ treponemal antibody absorption test.

fluoridación *f.* fluoridation, fluoridization, addition of fluorides to water.

fluoroscopía *f.* fluoroscopy, examination of tissues and structures of the body using the
fluoroscope.

fluoroscopio *m.* fluoroscope, instrument that
makes x-rays visible on a fluorescent screen.

fluorosis *f.* fluorosis, excess fluoride content.

fluoruro *m.* fluoride, combination of fluorine
with a metal or a metalloid.

fobia *f.* phobia, abnormal irrational fear.

fóbico-a *a.* phobic, rel. to phobia.

focal *a.* focal, rel. to focus.

foco *m.* focus, the main point or principal spot.

fofo-a *a.* flabby, soft.

fogaje *m.* hot flash.

folicular *a.* follicular, rel. to a follicle; **fase** ___ /
___ phase.

foliculitis *f.* folliculitis, infl. of a follicle, usu. in reference to a hair follicle.

folículo *m.* follicle, sac or pouchlike secretory depression or cavity; __ **atrésico** / atretic __; __ **de Graaf, ovárico** / Graafian, ovaric __; __ **gástrico** / gastric __; __ **piloso** / hair __; __ **tiroideo** / thyroid __.

folleto *m.* pamphlet, brochure.

fomento *m.* hot compress.

fomes *L.* (*pl.* **fomites**) fomes, an element that can absorb and transmit infectious agents.

fonación *f.* phonation, emission of the voice.

fondillo *m.* buttocks.

fondo *m.* bottom; __ **del ojo** / eyeground.

fonética *f.* phonetics, the study of speech and pronunciation.

fonético-a *a.* phonetic, rel. to the voice and articulated sounds.

foniatra *m.*, *f.* phoniatrist, specialist in voice treatment.

foniatría *f.* phoniatrics, treatment and study of voice defects.

fonograma *m.* phonogram, a graphic that indicates the intensity of a sound.

fonoscopio *m.* phonoscope, a device that registers heart sounds.

fontanela *f.* fontanel, fontanelle, soft spot in the skull of a newborn that closes as the cranial bones develop; **caída de la** __ / fallen __.

foramen *m.* foramen, orifice, passage, opening; __ **intervertebral** / intervertebral __; __ **óptico** / optic __; __ **oval** / oval __; __ **sacro-ciático mayor** / sciatic, greater __; __ **yugular** / jugular __.

fórceps *m.* forceps, a surgical, tonglike instrument used to grasp, pull, or manipulate tissues or body parts.

forense *a.* forensic, rel. to the courts; **laboratorio** __ / __ laboratory; **médico** __ / __ physician.

forma *f.* form, shape; established manner of doing something; __ **frustrada** / forme fruste, *Fr.*, an aborted or atypical form of a disease.

formación *f.* formation, the manner in which something is arranged.

formaldehído *m.* formaldehyde, antiseptic.

formalina *f.* formalin, formaldehyde compound.

formar *v.* to form, to shape.

formicación *f.* formication, skin sensation comparable to one produced by crawling insects.

fórmula *f.* formula, a prescribed way or model.

formulario *m.* 1. form, [*planilla*] blank; 2. formulary, prescription tablet, a book of formulas.

fórnix *m.* fornix, vaultlike structure such as the vagina.

fortalecer *vi.* to fortify, to strengthen.

fortificar *vi. V.* **fortalecer.**

forúnculo *m.* boil.

fosa *f.* fossa, cavity, depression, hole; __ **etmoidal** / ethmoid __; __ **glenoidea** / glenoid __; __ **interpenduncular** / interpenduncular __; __ **mandibular** / mandibular __; __ **nasal** / nasal __; __ **navicular** / navicular

__; __ **supraclavicular** / supraclavicular __; __ **yugular** / jugular __.

fósforo *m.* phosphorus.

fotocoagulación *f.* photocoagulation, localized tissue coagulation by an intense controlled ray of light or laser beam, esp. used in surgery of the eye.

fotofobia *f.* photophobia, fear of light.

fotólisis *f.* photolysis, disintegration by rays of light.

fototerapia *f.* phototherapy, light therapy, exposure to sun rays or to an artificial light for therapeutic purposes.

fóvea *f.* fovea, small depression, esp. used in reference to the central fossa of the retina.

fracaso *m.* failure; **neurosis del** __ / __ neurosis.

fracción *f.* fraction, separable part of a unit.

fractura *f.* fracture, breaking or separation of a bone; __ **abierta** / open __; __ **cerrada** / closed __; __ **conminuta** / comminuted __; __ **completa** / complete __; __ **con hundimiento** / depressed __; __ **de línea fina** / hairline __; __ **en caña o tallo verde** / greenstick __; __ **espiral** / spiral __; __ **impactada** / impacted __; __ **con luxación** / dislocation __; __ **patológica** / pathologic __; __ **por avulsión** / avulsion __; __ **por compresión** / compression __; __ **por estallamiento** / blow-out __; __ **por herida de bala** / gunshot __; __ **por sobrecarga** / stress __.

fracturar *v.* to fracture, to break a bone.

frágil *a.* fragile, brittle; breakable.

fragilidad *f.* fragility, disposition to tear or break easily.

fragmentación *f.* fragmentation, splitting.

fragmento *m.* fragment, small piece of a whole.

frambesia *f.* frambesia, yaws, pian, infectious tropical disease caused by a spirochete of the genus *Treponema pertenue* and manifested by a primary cutaneous lesion followed by raspberry-like ulcers that spread to different areas of the body.

francés *m.* [*idioma*] French; [*nativo-a*] French; **francés, francesa** *a.* French.

frasco *m.* flask, bottle.

frase *f.* phrase.

frazada *f.* blanket.

frecuencia *f.* frequency; rate; __ **intrínseca** / intrinsic rate; **con** __ / frequently.

frecuente *a.* frequent; **-mente** *adv.* frequently.

freír *vi.* to fry.

frémito *m.* fremitus, a vibration that can be detected during auscultation or on palpation, such as the chest vibrations during coughing.

frenectomía *f. surg.* frenectomy, removal of the frenum.

frenesí *m.* frenzy; madness.

frenético-a *a.* phrenetic, frantic, raving, maniacal.

frenillo *m.* frenum of the tongue; **con** __ /

tongue-tied.

frente *f.* forehead, brow; *prep.* in front; **en** ___ **de** / in ___ of; ___ **a** ___ / face to face; ___ **a** across from.

frenulum *f.* frenulum, frenum, small membranous fold that limits the movement of an organ or part.

fresa *f.* bur, burr. 1. [*dental*] dental drill; ___ **de fisura** / fissure ___; 2. strawberry; **marca en** ___ / strawberry mark.

fresco *m.* refreshing air; **hace** ___ / it is cool.

freudiano-a *a. psych.* Freudian, rel. to the doctrines of Sigmund Freud, Viennese neurologist, father of psychoanalysis, (1856–1939).

friable *a.* friable, that pulverizes easily.

fricción *f.* friction, rub; ___ **de alcohol** / alcohol rub; **roce de** ___ / ___ rub.

frigidez *f.* frigidity, coldness, inability to respond to sexual arousement.

frígido-a *a.* frigid, cold.

frijol *m.* bean.

frío-a *a.* cold; [*persona*] without warmth or affection; **hace** ___ / it is cold.

friolento-a *a.* chilly; too sensitive to cold.

frito-a *a. pp.* of **freír**, fried.

Frohlich, síndrome de *m.* Frohlich's syndrome, adiposogenital dystrophy, manifested by obesity and sexual infantilism.

frontal *a.* frontal, rel. to the forehead; **hueso** ___ / ___ bone; **músculo** ___ / ___ muscle; **senos** ___**-es** / ___ sinuses.

frotar *v.* to rub; ___ **suavemente** / to stroke.

frote *m.* rub. 1. friction; massage; 2. sound heard on auscultation, produced by two dry surfaces rubbing against each other.

frotis *m.* smear, sample of blood or a secretion for the purpose of microscopic study.

fructosa *f.* fructose, sugar of fruits; levulose.

fruta *f.* fruit.

ftiriasis *f.* phthiriasis. *V.* **pediculosis.**

fuego *m.* fire.

fuente *f.* source, origin; fountain.

fuera *adv.* out, outside; **estar** ___ / to be ___ or away; ___ **de sí** / beside oneself; **hacia** ___ / outward.

fuerte *a.* strong, vigorous; hard.

fuerza *f.* force, strength; power; ___ **catabólica** / catabolic ___; ___ **de gravedad** / ___ of gravity; **no tengo** ___ / I feel weak.

fuga *f.* flight; *psych.* ___ **de ideas** / ___ of ideas, interrupted line of thought and talk.

fulguración *f.* fulguration, use of electric current to destroy or coagulate tissue.

fulminante *a.* fulminant, appearing suddenly and with great intensity, esp. in reference to a disease or pain.

fumador-a *m., f.* person who smokes heavily.

fumante *a.* fuming, that gives forth a visible vapor.

fumar *v.* to smoke.

fumigación *f.* fumigation, extermination; or disinfection through the use of vapors.

fumigante *m.* fumigant, agent used in fumigation.

función *f.* function.

funcional *a.* functional, having practical use or value.

funcionamiento *m.* performance; functioning, working.

funcionar *v.* to function, to work.

funda *f.* pillowcase; covering.

fundir *v.* to fuse, to liquefy with heat.

funeral *m.* funeral.

funeraria *f.* funeral parlor, mortuary; **empresario de** ___ / mortician.

fungemia *f.* fungemia, presence of fungi in the blood.

fungicida *m.* fungicide, agent that destroys fungi.

fungistasis *f.* fungistasis, the action of thwarting the growth of fungi.

fungoso-a *a.* fungous, fungal, rel. to fungi.

furioso-a *a.* furious, frantic.

furor *m.* furor, extreme anger.

furosemida *f.* furosemide, diuretic agent.

fusiforme *a.* fusiform, spindle shaped.

fusión *f.* fusion, the act of melting; ___ **nuclear** / nuclear ___.

futuro *m.* future; **-a** *a.* future.

g *abr.* **género** / gender; **glucosa** / glucose **gramo** / gram; **grano** / grain.

gabinete *m.* cabinet.

gafas *f.* spectacles, eyeglasses.

gago-a *m., f.* stutterer.

gaguear *v.* to stutter.

galactagogo, galactógeno *m.* galactagogue, agent that stimulates the flow of milk.

galactasa *f.* galactase, enzyme present in milk.

galactocele *m.* galactocele, breast cyst containing milk.

galactosa *f.* galactose, monosaccharide derived from lactose by the action of an enzyme or mineral acid.

galactosemia *f.* galactosemia, congenital absence of the enzyme necessary to convert galactose to glucose and its derivatives.

galactosuria *f.* galactosuria, milklike urine due to the presence of galactose.

galactoterapia *f.* galactotherapy. 1. the treatment of breast-fed infants by the administration of medication to the nursing mother; 2. therapeutic use of milk in the diet.

galio *m.* gallium, metallic element.

galvánico-a *a.* galvanic, rel. to galvanism; **batería** ___ / ___ battery; **célula** ___ / ___ cell; **corriente** ___ / ___ current.

galvanismo *m.* galvanism, therapeutic use of a direct electrical current.

galvanocauterización *f.* galvanocautery. *V.* **electrocauterización.**

galvanómetro *m.* galvanometer, instrument that measures currents by electromagnetic action.

galleta *f.* cracker.

gallina *f.* hen.

gallo *m.* cock, rooster.

gameto *m.* gamete, sexual cell, masculine or feminine.

gametocida *m.* gametocide, agent that kills gametes.

gametocito *m.* gametocyte, a cell that divides to produce gametes, such as the malarial parasite when taken into the mosquito host.

gametogénesis *f.* gametogenesis, development of gametes.

gamma globulina *f.* gamma globulin, a class of antibodies produced in the lymph tissue or synthetically.

gammagrama *m.* scintiscan, a two-dimensional image representation of the interior distribution of a radiopharmaceutical in a previously selected area for diagnostic purposes.

gamopatía *f.* gammopathy, disorder manifested by an excessive amount of immunoglobulins due to an abnormal proliferation of lymphoid cells.

gana *f.* desire, inclination; **tener** ___-s **de** / to desire, to want to; **de buena** ___ / willingly; **de mala** ___ / unwillingly.

ganancia *f.* gain; advantage.

ganar *v.* to win; to earn.

gancho *m.* hook; clasp; **-s** [*dental*] braces.

gangliectomía, ganglionectomía *f. surg.* gangliectomy, ganglionectomy, excision of a ganglion.

ganglio *m.* ganglion, collection of nerve cells resembling a knot; ___ **basal** / basal ___; ___ **carotídeo** / carotid ___; ___ **celíaco** / celiac ___.

gangliocito *m.* gangliocyte, a ganglion cell.

ganglioctomía *f. surg.* ganglioctomy, excision of a ganglion.

ganglioglioma *m.* ganglioglioma, tumor with a large number of ganglionic cells.

ganglioma *m.* ganglioma, tumor of a ganglion, esp. a lymphatic ganglion.

ganglión *m.* ganglion, a cystic tumor that develops in a tendon or an aponeurosis, often seen in the wrist, the heel or the knee.

ganglionar *a.* ganglionic, rel. to a ganglion; **bloqueo** ___ / ___ blockade.

gangrena *f.* gangrene, local death, destruction and putrefaction of body tissue due to interrupted blood supply.

Gantrisin *f.* Gantrisin, trade name for sulfisoxazole, an antibacterial agent used in the treatment of urinary infections.

garabato *m.* scribble.

garantía *f.* guarantee, warranty.

garantizar *vi.* to guarantee, to warrant.

garbanzo *m.* chickpea.

garganta *f.* throat, the area of the larynx and the pharynx; anterior part of the neck; **dolor de** ___ / sore ___.

gárgara, gargarismo *f., m.* gargarism, gargle, gargling, rinsing of the throat and the mouth; **hacer** ___-s / to gargle.

gargolismo *m.* gargoylism, hereditary condition characterized by skeletal abnormalities and sometimes mental retardation.

garra *f.* claw; **mano en** ___ / ___ hand; **pie en** ___ / ___ foot.

garrapata *f.* tick, bloodsucking acarid that transmits specific diseases; **picadura de** ___ / ___ bite.

garrotillo *m.* croup.

gas *m.* gas; ___ **lacrimógeno** / tear ___; ___ **mostaza** / mustard ___; ___ **neurotóxico** / nerve ___; ___-**es arteriales** / arterial blood ___-es; ___-**es en la sangre** / blood ___-es.

gasa *f.* gauze; ___ **antiséptica** / antiseptic ___; **compresa de** ___ / ___ compress.

gaseoso-a *a.* gaseous, of the nature of gas.

gasolina *f.* gasoline; **envenenamiento por** ___ / ___ poisoning.

gastado-a *a.* worn out.

gastar *v.* [*dinero*] to spend; **gastarse** *vr.* to wear out.

gasto *m.* [*cardíaco*] output; costs, expense(s); expenditure; ___ **cubiertos** / covered ___.

gastralgia *f.* gastralgia, stomachache.

gastrectomía *f. surg.* gastrectomy, removal of part or all of the stomach.

gástrico-a *a.* gastric, rel. to the stomach; **digestión** ___ / ___ digestion; **jugo** ___ / ___ juice; **lavado** ___ / ___ lavage; **vaciamiento** ___ / ___ emptying.

gastrina *f.* gastrin, hormone secreted by the stomach.

gastritis *f.* gastritis, infl. of the stomach; ___ **aguda** / acute ___; ___ **crónica** / chronic ___.

gastroanálisis *m.* gastric analysis, analysis of the stomach contents.

gastrocnemio *m.* gastrocnemius, large calf muscle.

gastrocolostomía *f. surg.* gastrocolostomy, anastomosis of the stomach and the colon.

gastroduodenal *a.* gastroduodenal, rel. to the stomach and the duodenum.

gastroduodenoscopía *f.* gastroduodenoscopy, visual examination of the stomach and the duodenum with an endoscope.

gastroenteroanastomosis *f. surg.* gastroenteroanastomosis, anastomosis of the stomach and the small intestine.

gastroenterocolitis *f.* gastroenterocolitis, infl. of the stomach and the small intestine.

gastroenterostomía *f. surg.* gastroenterostomy, anastomosis of the stomach and the small bowel.

gastroepiploico-a *a.* gastroepiploic, rel. to the stomach and the epiploon.

gastroesofagitis *f.* gastroesophagitis. *V.* **esofagogastritis.**

gastrogavage *m.* gastrogavage, artificial feeding into the stomach through a tube.

gastroileostomía *f. surg.* gastroileostomy, anastomosis of the stomach and the ileum.

gastrointestinal *a.* gastrointestinal, rel. to the stomach and the intestine; **decompresión** ___ / ___ decompression; **examen** ___ **superior** / upper ___ examination; **sangramiento** ___ / ___ bleeding.

gastrorragia *f.* gastrorrhagia, hemorrhaging from the stomach.

gastroscopía *f.* gastroscopy, examination of the stomach and the abdominal cavity with a gastroscope.

gastroscopio *m.* gastroscope, endoscope for visualizing the inside of the stomach.

gastrostomía *f. surg.* gastrostomy, creation of a gastric fistula through the abdominal wall.

gastroyeyunostomía *f. surg.* gastrojejunostomy, anastomosis of the stomach and the jejunum.

gástrula *f.* gastrula, an early stage in embryonic development.

gatear *v.* to crawl on all fours, such as babies.

gato-a *m., f.* cat.

gelatina *f.* gelatin.

gelatinoso-a *a.* gelatinous, having the consistency of or rel. to gelatin.

gemelo-a *m., f.* twin, either of two offspring born

of the same pregnancy; ___ **dicigótico-a** / dizygotic ___; ___ **encigótico-a** / enzygotic ___; ___ **fraternal** / fraternal ___; ___ **idéntico-a** / identical ___; ___ **monocigótico-a** / monozygotic ___; ___ **siamés-a** / Siamese ___; ___ **verdadero-a** / true ___.

gemido *m.* groan, moan.

gemir *vi.* to groan, to moan.

gen, gene *m.* gene, basic unit of hereditary traits; ___ **dominante** / dominant ___; ___ **letal** / lethal ___; ___ **ligado al sexo** / sex-linked ___; ___ **recesivo** / recessive ___.

generación *f.* generation, procreation. 1. the act of creating a new organism; 2. the whole body of individuals born within a time span of approximately thirty years.

generador *m.* generator.

general *a.* general; **estado** ___ / ___ condition; **tratamiento** ___ / ___ treatment; *adv.* **-mente** generally.

generalización *f.* generalization.

generalizar *v.* to generalize.

genérico-a *a.* generic, rel. to the gender; **nombre** ___ / ___ name, not protected by a trademark.

género *m.* 1. gender, sex of an individual; 2. genus, a category of biological classification.

generoso-a *a.* generous.

génesis *f.* genesis, origin, beginning; reproduction.

genética *f.* genetics, branch of biology that studies heredity and the laws that govern it; ___ **médica** / medical ___.

genético-a *a.* genetic, rel. to heredity or genetics; **asesoramiento** ___ / ___ counseling; **ingeniería o construcción** ___ / ___ engineering; **marcador** ___ / ___ marker; **patrón** ___ / ___ code; **sustrato** ___ / ___ substratum.

genio *m.* genius, extraordinary mental power or faculties.

geniplastia *f. surg.* genyplasty, reconstructive surgery of the jaw.

genital *a.* genital, rel. to the genitals.

genitales *m. pl.* genitals, genitalia, reproductive organs; *pop.* privates; ___ **externos** / ___ externalia.

genocidio *m.* genocide, systematic extermination of an ethnic or social group of people.

genoma *m.* genome, the complete basic haploid set of chromosomes of an organism.

genotipo *m.* genotype, the basic genetic constitution of an individual.

gentamicina *f.* gentamicin, antibiotic that acts effectively against many gram-negative bacteria.

gente *f.* people, persons in general.

genuflexión *f.* genuflexion, bending of the knee.

genuino-a *a.* genuine, authentic, real.

genu valgum *L.* genu valgum, abnormal inward curvature of the knees that begins at infancy as a result of osseus deficiency, *pop.*

knock-knee.

genu varum *L.* genu varum, abnormal outward curvature of the knees, *pop.* bowleg.

geofagia, geofagismo *f., m.* geophagia, geophagism, geophagy, propensity to eat soil or similar substances.

geriatra *m., f.* geriatrician, specialist in geriatrics.

geriatría *f.* geriatrics, a branch of medicine that deals with the problems of aging and the treatment of diseases and ills of old age.

germen *m.* germ. 1. microorganism or bacteria, esp. one that causes disease; 2. a substance that can develop and form an organism.

germicida *m.* germicide, germicidal, agent that destroys germs.

germinal *a.* germinal, rel. to or of the nature of germs.

germinoma *m.* germinoma, neoplasm of germinal cells in the testis or ovaries.

geromorfismo *m.* geromorphism, premature senility.

gerontología *f.* gerontology. *V.* **geriatría.**

gerundio *m. gr.* gerund, the present participle of the verb.

gestación *f.* gestation, childbearing, pregnancy.

gestacional *a.* rel. to gestation; **edad ___** / fetal maturity, chronologic.

Gestalt *m.* Gestalt, *psych,* a school of thought that explains behavior as an integrated response to a situation as a whole.

gesticular *v.* to gesticulate, to communicate or express by means of gestures or signs.

gesto *m.* gesture.

Ghon, foco, lesión, tubérculo de *m.* Ghon's primary lesion, tubercule, first tubercular lesion in children.

giardiasis *f.* giardiasis, common intestinal infection with *Giardia lamblia* that spreads by contaminated food or water or through direct contact.

gibosidad *f.* gibbosity, the condition of having a hump.

giboso-a *a.* gibbous, humpbacked.

Giemsa, coloración de *f.* Giemsa's stain, stain used for blood smears in lab tests.

gigante *m.* giant; *a.* giant, unnaturally large.

gigantismo *m.* gigantism, excessive development of the body or some of its parts; **___ acromegálico** / acromegalic ___; **___ eunocoide** / eunochoid ___; **___ normal** / normal ___.

Gilles de la Tourette, síndrome de *m.* Gilles de la Tourette syndrome, a childhood disease affecting boys more frequently than girls, thought to be of a neurological nature and manifested by muscular anomalies; sometimes accompanied at puberty by involuntary uttering of obscenities and swearing.

Gimbernat, ligamento de *m.* Gimbernat's ligament, membrane attached to the inguinal ligament on one end and the pubis on the other.

gimnasia, gimnástica *f.* gymnastics.

ginandroide *a.* gynandroid, having enough hermaphroditic characteristics to give the appearance of the opposite sex.

ginecología *f.* gynecology, the study of the female reproductive organs.

ginecológico-a *a.* gynecologic, gynecological, rel. to gynecology.

ginecólogo-a *m., f.* gynecologist, specialist in gynecology.

ginecomastia *f.* gynecomastia, excessive development of the mammary glands in the male.

gingiva *L.* gingiva, gum, tissue around the neck of the teeth.

gingivitis *f.* gingivitis, infl. of the gums.

girar *v.* to rotate, to revolve.

glacial *a.* glacial, resembling or rel. to ice.

glande *m.* glans, gland-like mass located at the distal end of the penis (glans penis), or clitoris (glans clitoridis).

glándula *f.* gland, an organ that secretes or excretes substances that have specific functions or that eliminate products from the organism; **___ inflamada** / swollen ___.

glándulas endocrinas *f. pl.* endocrine glands, glands that secrete hormones directly absorbed into the blood or lymph such as the gonads and the pituitary and adrenal glands.

glándulas exocrinas *f. pl.* exocrine glands, glands that discharge their secretion through a duct, such as the mammary and sweat glands.

Glanzmann, trombastenia de *f.* Glanzmann's thrombasthenia, rare congenital disease caused by platelet abnormality.

Glasgow, escala de *f.* Glasgow's scale, instrument used to evaluate the degree of coma.

glaucoma *m.* glaucoma, eye disease caused by intraocular hypertension that results in hardening of the eye, atrophia of the retina, and sometimes blindness; **___ absoluto** / absolutum ___, final stage of acute glaucoma; **___ infantil** / infantile ___, between birth and three years of age; **___ juvenil** / juvenile ___, in older children and young adults without enlargement of the eyeball.

glenohumeral *a.* glenohumeral, rel. to the humerus and the glenoid cavity.

glenoideo-a *a.* glenoid, socket-like cavity; **cavidad ___** / ___ cavity; **fosa ___** / ___ fossa.

glía *f.* glia. *V.* **neuroglia.**

gliacito *m.* gliacyte, neuroglia cell.

glicemia, glucemia *f.* glycemia, concentration of glucose in the blood.

glicerina, glicerol *f.* glycerine, glycerol, an alcohol found in fats.

glicina *f.* glycine, a nonessential amino acid.

glicógeno, glucógeno *m.* glycogen, polysaccharide usu. stored in the liver that converts into glucose as needed.

glicogenólisis, glucogenólisis *f.* glycogenolysis, the breakdown of glycogen into glucose.

glicólisis *f.* glycolysis, breakdown of sugar into

simpler compounds.

glicosuria *f.* glycosuria. *V.* **glucosuria.**

glioblastoma *f.* glioblastoma, a type of brain tumor.

glioma *m.* glioma, malignant brain tumor composed of neuroglia cells.

glioneuroma *f.* glioneuroma, a glioma combined with a neuroma.

globina *f.* globin, protein that is a part of hemoglobin.

globo *m.* globe, spherical body.

globular *a.* globular, spherical.

globulina *f.* globulin, one of a class of simple proteins that is insoluble in water but soluble in moderately concentrated salt solutions; ___ **antilinfocítica** / antilymphocyte ___, immunosuppressant; **gamma** ___ / gamma ___, a family of proteins capable of carrying antibodies.

globulinuria *f.* globulinuria, presence of globulin in the urine.

glóbulo *m.* globule, small spherical mass; ___ **blanco** / white blood cell, leukocyte; ___ **rojo** / red blood cell, erythrocyte.

globus *L.* globus, spheric body; ___ **histérico** / ___ hystericus, sensation of having a lump in the throat.

glomerular *a.* glomerular, rel. or resembling a glomerulus; cluster-like.

glomerulitis *f.* glomerulitis, infl. of the glomeruli, esp. the renal glomeruli.

glomérulo *m.* glomerulus, collection of capillaries in the shape of a tiny ball, present in the kidney.

glomeruloesclerosis *f.* glomerulosclerosis, degenerative process within the renal glomeruli that occurs in renal arteriosclerosis and diabetes.

glomerulonefritis *f.* glomerulonephritis, Bright's disease, infl. of the kidney glomeruli.

glomo *m.* glomus, small mass of arterioles rich in nerve supply and connected directly to veins.

glosa *f.* glossa, tongue.

glosalgia *f.* glossalgia, pain in the tongue.

glosectomía *f. surg.* glossectomy, partial or total excision of the tongue.

glositis *f.* glossitis, infl. of the tongue; ___ **aguda** / acute ___, associated with stomatitis.

glosodinia *f.* glossodynia. *V.* **glosalgia.**

glosoplejía *f.* glossoplegia, partial or total paralysis of the tongue.

glosotomía *f.* glossotomy, incision in the tongue.

glotis *f.* glottis, opening in the upper part of the larynx between the vocal cords; vocal apparatus of the larynx.

glotitis *f.* glottitis, infl. of the glottis.

glucagón *m.* glucagon, one of the two hormones produced by the islets of Langerhans that increase the concentration of glucose in the blood and also have an anti-inflammatory effect.

glucagonoma *a.* glucagonoma, malignant glucagon secreting tumor.

glucocorticoide *a.* glucocorticoid, adrenal cortical hormones active in protecting against stress and affecting carbohydrate and protein metabolism.

glucofosfato deshidrogenasa *m.* glucose-6-phosphate dehydrogenase, enzyme found in the liver and kidney, important in the conversion of glyceryl to glucose.

glucogénesis *f.* glucogenesis, formation of glucose from glycogen.

gluconeogénesis *f.* gluconeogenesis, glyconeogenesis, formation of glycogen in the liver from noncarbohydrate sources.

glucopenia *f.* glycopenia. *V.* **hipoglicemia.**

glucopéxico-a *a.* glycopexic, that stores sugar.

glucosa *f.* glucose, dextrose, grape sugar, the main source of energy for living organisms; **nivel de** ___ **en la sangre** / blood level of ___; **prueba de tolerancia a la** ___ / ___ tolerance test.

glucósido *m.* glucoside, glycoside, natural or synthetic compound that liberates sugar upon hydrolysis.

glucosuria *f.* glucosuria, glycosuria, abnormal amount of sugar in the urine; ___ **diabética** / diabetic ___; ___ **pituitaria** / pituitary ___; ___ **renal** / renal ___.

glutamato *m.* glutamate, salt of glutamic acid.

gluten *m.* gluten, albuminoid vegetable matter.

glúteo-a *a.* gluteal, rel. to the buttocks; **pliegue** ___ / ___ fold; **reflejo** ___ / ___ reflex.

gnosia *f.* gnosia, ability to perceive and recognize people and things.

gola *f.* throat; *pop.* gullet.

goloso-a *m., f.* person very fond of sweets and snacks; *a.* fond of snacking; sweet tooth.

golpe *m.* blow; bruise; bang; ___ **en la cabeza** / ___ to the head.

golpear *v.* to beat, to hit.

goma *f.* 1. gumma, syphilitic tumor; 2. gum rubber; [*de borrar*] eraser; glue.

gónada *f.* gonad, a gland that produces sex cells (gametes). In males the gonads are the testes, in females, the ovaries.

gonadal *a.* gonadal, rel. to a gonad gland; **disgenesia** ___ / ___ dysgenesis, malformation.

gonadotropina *f.* gonadotropin, gonad stimulating hormone; ___ **coriónica** / chorionic ___, present in the blood and the urine of the female during pregnancy and used in the pregnancy test; ___ **hipofisaria** / anterior pituitary ___; **hormona que estimula la secreción de** ___ / ___ releasing hormone.

gonión *m.* gonion, the most inferior, posterior, and lateral point on the external angle of the mandible.

goniopuntura *f. surg.* goniopuncture, puncture of the anterior chamber of the eye as a means to treat glaucoma.

goniotomía *f. surg.* goniotomy, procedure to relieve congenital glaucoma.

102

gonococo m. gonococcus, microorganism of the species *Neisseria gonorrhoeae* that causes gonorrhea.

gonorrea f. gonorrhea, highly contagious catarrhal bacterial infection of the genital mucosa, sexually transmitted.

gonorreico-a a. gonorrheal, rel. to gonorrhea; **artritis** ___ / ___ arthritis.

gordiflón-a m., f. fat, flabby person.

gordo-a a. fat, overweight.

gordura f. fatness, corpulence.

gorra f. cap, head covering.

gota f. gout. 1. a hereditary disease caused by a defect in uric acid metabolism; 2. drop, a very small portion of a liquid.

gotear v. to drip; to leak.

goteo m. drip, dripping.

gotero m. dropper; ___ **para los ojos** / eye ___ .

gotica f. droplet.

gozar vi. to enjoy, to rejoice.

grabadora f. tape recorder.

grabar v. to record.

gracias f. pl. thanks; **muchas** ___ / thank you very much.

gracilis m. gracilis, long internal muscle of the thigh.

gradiente a. gradient, index or curve representing the increase or decrease of a variable.

grado m. [*temperatura*] degree; [*evaluación*] grade.

gradual a. gradual; **-mente** adv. gradually.

gráfica, gráfico f., m. graph, chart, diagram.

grafología f. graphology, the study of handwriting as an indication of an individual's character, also used as an aid in diagnosis.

Gram, método de m. Gram's method, a system of coloring bacteria for the purpose of identifying them on analysis.

gramática f. grammar.

gramicidina f. gramicidin, antibacterial substance produced by *Bacillis brevis*, active locally against gram-positive bacteria.

gramnegativo m. gram-negative, bacteria or tissue that loses coloration when subjected to Gram's method.

gramo m. gram, unit of weight in the metric system.

grampositivo m. gram-positive, bacteria or tissue that retains coloration when subjected to Gram's method.

gran, grande a. big, large.

grano m. grain, granum, a small spherical mass; bead.

granulación f. granulation, round, small, fleshy masses that form in a wound.

granular, granuloso-a a. granular, made up or marked by grains; **cilindro granuloso** / ___ cast, urinary cast seen in degenerative and inflammatory nephropathy.

gránulo m. granule, small grain or particle; ___ **acidófilo** / acidophil ___, a stain with acid dyes; ___ **basófilo** / basophil ___, a stain with basic dyes.

granulocito m. granulocyte, leukocyte containing granules.

granulocitopenia f. granulocytopenia, deficiency in the number of granulocytes in the blood.

granuloma m. granuloma, tumor or neoplasm of granular tissue; ___ **de cuerpo extraño** / foreign body ___; ___ **infeccioso** / infectious ___; ___ **inguinal** / inguinale ___; ___ **ulcerativo de los genitales** / venereum ___ .

granulomatosis f. granulomatosis, multiple granuloma.

granulopenia f. granulopenia. V. **granulocitopenia.**

granulosa f. granulosa, ovarian membrane of epithelial cells; **tumor de células de la** ___ / ___ cell tumor; **tumor de la** ___ **teca** / ___ teca cell tumor.

grapar v. to staple; surgical procedure.

grasa f. fat, adipose tissue.

grasiento-a, grasoso-a a. fatty, greasy; **degeneración** ___ / ___ degeneration.

gratificación f. gratification, reward.

gratificar vi. to gratify, to reward.

gratis adv. gratis, free.

grave a. critically ill; of a serious nature.

Grave, enfermedad de f. Grave's disease, exophthalmic goiter.

gravedad f. gravity. 1. seriousness; **estado de** ___ / critical condition; 2. force of gravity.

grávida f. gravida, pregnant woman.

grieta f. crevice, cleft, fissure; ___ **-s en las manos** / chapped hands.

gripe f. grippe, flu; ___ **asiática** / Asiatic flu.

griposis f. gryposis, abnormal curvature, esp. as seen in nails.

gris a. gray.

gris, materia o sustancia f. gray matter, highly vascularized gray tissue of the central nervous system made up primarily of nerve cells and unmyelinated nerve fibers.

griseofulvina f. griseofulvin, antibiotic used in fungus skin diseases.

gritar v. to scream, to cry out.

grito m. scream, cry; **estar en un** ___ / to be in great pain.

grosero-a a. gross, coarse.

grosor m. thickness; density.

grueso-a a. heavy; thick.

grumoso-a a. grumose, grumous, lumpy, clotted.

grupo m. group, cluster; team, an associated group; ___ **de soporte, de apoyo** / support ___ .

grupo sanguíneo m. blood group, the different types of human erythrocytes, genetically determined and differentiated immunologically; ___ **RH** / Rh ___ .

guanetidina f. guanethidine, agent used in the treatment of hypertension.

guante m. glove; ___ **-s de goma** / rubber ___ -s.

guardar *v.* to put away; to keep.
guardería infantil *f.* nursery; children's day care center.
guardián *m.* guardian; custodian.
guayaco *m.* guaiac, substance used in tests as a reagent to detect the presence of blood.
guayacol *m.* guaiacol, antiseptic; expectorant.
gubernaculum *L.* gubernaculum, direction, guidance.
guerra *f.* war.
guía *m., f.* guide, director; ___ **de teléfono** / telephone directory.
guiar *v.* to guide, to direct.
guillotina *f.* guillotine, surgical instrument.

guiñar *v.* to wink.
guisado *m.* stew.
guisar *v.* to stew.
gusano *m.* earthworm, maggot, caterpillar; ___ **plano** / flatworm, intestinal worm; ___ **nematodo que infesta los pulmones** / lungworm.
gustar *v.* to like, to enjoy.
gusto *m.* the sense of taste; taste; **buen** ___ / good taste; **mal gusto** / bad taste.
gutapercha *f.* gutta-percha, dried and purified latex of some trees that is used in medical and dental treatments.
gutta *L.* (*pl.* **guttae**) gutta, drop.
gutural *a.* guttural, pronounced in the throat.

H *abr.* **heroína** / heroin; **hidrógeno** / hydrogen; **hipermetropía** / hypermetropia; **hipodérmico-a** / hypodermic.

h *abr.* **hora** / hour; **horizontal** / horizontal.

haba *f.* lima bean.

haber *vi. aux.* to have.

habichuela *f.* string bean.

hábil, habilidoso-a *a.* able, skillful.

habilidad *f.* ability, aptitude.

habilitar *v.* to habilitate; to equip.

habitación *f.* room.

hábito *m.* habit.

habitual *a.* habitual, customary; **-mente** *adv.* habitually.

habla *m.* [*locución*] speech; **defecto del ___** / **___** defect; **patología del ___** / **___** pathology; **trastorno del ___** / **___** disorder.

hablar *v.* to speak.

hacer *vi.* to do, to make; **___ caso** / to mind, to pay attention; **___ daño** / to harm or hurt; **___ hincapié** / to emphasize; **___ lo mejor posible** / to do one's best.

hacia *prep.* towards; **___ acá** / this way; **___ allá** / that way; **___ adelante** / forward; **___ atrás** / backwards.

hachís *m.* hashish, euphoria producing narcotic extracted from marihuana.

halar *v.* to pull.

hálito *m.* halitus, breath.

halitosis *f.* halitosis, bad breath.

hallar *v.* to find; **hallarse** *vr.* [*en un lugar o condición*] to find oneself.

hallazgos *m. pl.* findings, results of an investigation or inquiry.

hallux valgus *L.* hallux valgus, inward turning of the big toe.

hallux varus *L.* hallux varus, separation of the big toe from the others.

haloide *m.* haloid, salt resulting from the combination of a halogen element and a metal.

halótano *m.* halothane, Fluothane, anesthetic administered by inhalation.

hamartoma *m.* hamartoma, nodule simulating a tumor, usu. benign.

hambre *m.* hunger; **tener ___** / to be hungry.

hambriento-a *a.* hungry, starved, famished.

Hanot, enfermedad de *f.* Hanot's disease, hypertrophic cirrhosis of the liver accompanied by jaundice; biliary cirrhosis.

Hansen, enfermedad de *f.* Hansen's disease. *V.* **leprosy.**

haploide *a.* haploid, a sex cell that has half the number of chromosomes characteristic of the species.

haptoglobina *f.* haptoglobin, mucoprotein that links itself to the released hemoglobin in the plasma.

haptómetro *m.* haptometer, device used to measure the acuteness of the sense of touch.

haragán-a *m., f.* lazy person; *a.* lazy.

harina *f.* flour, cornmeal.

harmonía, armonía *f.* harmony, congenial communication.

harmonizar, armonizar *v.* to harmonize.

hartarse *vr.* to overeat, to stuff oneself.

hasta *prep.* until; up to; as far as; **___ ahora** heretofore, so far; **___ aquí** / up to this point; **___ luego** / goodbye, see you later.

haustrum *L.* haustrum, cavity or pouch, esp. in the colon.

Havers, sistema de *m.* Haversian system, concentric formation of small conduits that constitute the base of the compact bone.

hay *v.* there is, there are; **___ que** / it is necessary; **no ___ remedio** / it can't be helped.

haz *m.* bundle; **___ ascendente** / ascending tract.

heces *f. pl.* feces.

hecho-a *a. pp.* of hacer, done, made; **bien ___** well ___; **mal ___** / badly ___; **de ___** as a matter of fact.

Heimlich, maniobra de *f.* Heimlich maneuver, technique applied to force the expulsion of a foreign body that is blocking the passage of air from the trachea or pharynx.

helado *m.* ice cream; **-a** *a.* frozen.

helicoideo-a *a.* helical, in the shape of a helix or a spiral.

helicóptero *m.* helicopter.

helio *m.* helium, gaseous inert chemical element mixed with air or oxygen to be used in the treatment of some respiratory disorders.

heliofobia *f.* heliophobia, excessive fear of the sun.

helioterapia *f.* heliotherapy, sunbathing as therapy.

helmintiasis *f.* helminthiasis, intestinal infection with worms.

helminticida *m.* helminthicide, agent that kills parasites; vermicide.

helminto *m.* helminth, worm found in the human intestines.

hemaglutinación, hemoaglutinación *f.* hemagglutination, agglutination of red cells.

hemaglutinina, hemoaglutinina *f.* hemagglutinin, antibody that causes agglutination of red cells.

hemangioma *m.* hemangioma, benign tumor formed by clustered blood vessels that produce a reddish birth mark.

hemangiosarcoma *m.* hemangiosarcoma, malignant tumor of the vascular tissue.

hemartrosis *f.* hemarthrosis, extravasation into a joint cavity.

hematemesis *f.* hematemesis, vomiting of blood.

hematerapia, hemoterapia *f.* hematherapy, hemotherapy, therapeutic use of blood.

hemático *m.* drug used in the treatment of anemia; **-a** *a.* rel. to blood; **biometría ___** / complete blood count (CBC).

hematocolpos *m.* hematocolpos, retention of menstrual blood in the vagina due to an imperforated hymen.

hematócrito *m.* hematocrit. 1. centrifuge that is used for separating cells and particles in the blood from the plasma; 2. the volume percentage of erythrocytes in the blood.

hematogénesis *f.* hematogenesis. *V.* **hematopoyesis.**

hematógeno-a *a.* hematogenous. 1. rel. to the production of blood and to its constituents; 2. originating in the blood.

hematología *f.* hematology, the study of the blood and the organs that intervene in its formation.

hematológico-a *a.* hematologic, hematological, rel. to blood; **estudios** ___-s / ___ studies.

hematólogo-a *m., f.* hematologist, specialist in hematology.

hematoma *m.* hematoma, localized collection of blood that has escaped from a blood vessel into an organ, space, or tissue; ___ **pélvico** / pelvic ___.; ___ **subdural** / subdural, under the dura mater.

hematomielia *f.* hematomyelia, bleeding into the spinal cord.

hematopoyesis, hemopoyesis *f.* hematopoiesis, hemopoiesis, formation of blood.

hematoquezia *f.* hematochezia, presence of blood in the stool.

hembra *f.* the female of a species.

hemianalgesia *f.* hemianalgesia, insensitivity to pain in one side of the body.

hemianopia, hemanopsia *f.* hemianopia, hemanopsia, loss of vision in one half of the visual field of the left or right eye, or of both.

hemiataxia *f.* hemiataxia, lack of muscular coordination in one side of the body.

hemiatrofia *f.* hemiatrophy, atrophy of half of an organ or half of the body.

hemibalismo *m.* hemiballism, hemiballismus, brain lesion that causes involuntary and rapid movements in half of the body.

hemicolectomía *f. surg.* hemicolectomy, removal of one half of the colon.

hemihipertrofia *f.* hemihypertrophy, hypertrophy of one half of the body.

hemilaminectomía *f. surg.* hemilaminectomy, removal of the vertebral lamina on one side.

hemiparálisis *f.* hemiparalysis, paralysis of one side of the body.

hemiparesia, hemiparesis *f.* hemiparesia, hemiparesis, paralysis affecting one side of the body.

hemiparético-a *a.* hemiparetic, rel. to hemiparesia.

hemiplejía *f.* hemiplegia, paralysis of the side of the body opposite to the affected cerebral hemisphere.

hemipléjico-a *a.* hemiplegic, affected or rel. to hemiplegia.

hemisferio *m.* hemisphere, half of a spherical structure or organ.

hemitórax *m.* hemithorax, each side of the thorax.

hemobilia *f.* hemobilia, bleeding in the bile ducts.

hemoblastosis *f.* hemoblastosis, proliferative disorders of the blood tissues.

hemocitoblasto *m.* hemocytoblast, primordial blood cell from which all others are derived.

hemoconcentración *f.* hemoconcentration, concentration of red blood cells due to a decrease of liquid elements in the blood.

hemoconcentrar *v.* hemoconcentrate, to concentrate red blood cells.

hemocromatosis *f.* hemochromatosis, iron storage disease, bronze diabetes, disorder of iron metabolism due to excess deposition of iron in the tissues accompanied by anomalies such as bronze skin pigmentation, cirrhosis of the liver, diabetes mellitus, and malfunction of the pancreas.

hemocultivo *m.* blood culture.

hemodiálisis *f.* hemodialysis, dialysis process used to eliminate toxic substances from the blood in cases of acute renal disorders.

hemodializador *m.* hemodyalizer, artificial kidney machine used in the dialysis process.

hemodilución *f.* hemodilution, increase in the proportion of plasma to red cells in the blood.

hemodinamia *f.* hemodynamics, the study of the dynamics of blood circulation.

hemofilia *f.* hemophilia, inherited disease characterized by abnormal clotting of the blood and propensity to bleed.

hemofílico-a *m., f.* hemophiliac, person who suffers from hemophilia; *a.* hemophiliac, rel. to or suffering from hemophilia.

hemófilo *m.* hemophilus, haemophilus, one of a group of gram-negative aerobic bacteria.

hemofobia *f.* hemophobia, pathologic fear of blood.

hemoglobina *f.* hemoglobin, important protein element of the blood that gives it its red color and participates in the transportation of oxygen; **índice corpuscular de** ___ / mean corpuscular ___.

hemoglobinemia *f.* hemoglobinemia, presence of freed hemoglobin in the plasma.

hemoglobinuria *f.* hemoglobinuria, presence of hemoglobin in the urine.

hemograma *m.* hemogram, graphic representation of the differential blood count.

hemólisis *f.* hemolysis, rupture of erythrocytes with release of hemoglobin into the plasma; ___ **del recién nacido** / hemolytic disease of the newborn, gen. caused by incompatibility of the Rh factor.

hemolítico-a *a.* hemolytic, rel. to or that causes hemolysis; **anemia** ___ / ___ anemia, red cells that rupture easily due to a congenital condition caused by toxic agents; **trastorno** ___ / ___ disorder.

hemolito *m.* hemolith, concretion in a blood vessel.

hemopneumotórax *m.* hemopneumothorax, accumulation of blood and air in the pleural cavity.

hemoptisis *f.* hemoptysis, bloody expectoration.

hemorragia *f.* hemorrhage, profuse bleeding; ___ **cerebral** / cerebrovascular accident; ___ **intracraneana** / intracranial ___; ___ **petequial** / petechial ___; ___ **puerperal** / postpartum ___.

hemorrágico-a *a.* hemorrhagic, rel. to hemorrhage.

hemorroide(s) *f.* hemorrhoid, pile, a mass of dilated veins in the inferior anal or rectal wall; ___ **de prolapso** / prolapsed ___, that protrudes outside the anus; ___ **externa** / external ___, outside the anal sphincter; ___ **interna** / internal ___, hidden, proximal to the anorectal line.

hemorroidectomía *f. surg.* hemorrhoidectomy, removal of hemorrhoids.

hemosálpinx *m.* hemosalpinx, accumulation of blood in the fallopian tubes.

hemosiderina *f.* hemosiderin, insoluble iron compound stored in the body for use in the formation of hemoglobin as needed.

hemosiderosis *f.* hemosiderosis, hemosiderin deposit in the liver and the spleen.

hemostasia, hemostasis *f.* hemostasis, cessation of bleeding, natural or otherwise.

hemóstato *m.* hemostat, a surgical clamp or a medication used to suppress bleeding.

hendidura *f.* fissure, crack, cleavage.

heparina *f.* heparin, anticoagulant.

heparinización *f.* heparinization, process of administering heparin.

heparinizar *vi.* heparinize, to avoid coagulation by the use of heparin.

hepatectomía *f. surg.* hepatectomy, removal of a part or all of the liver.

hepático-a *a.* hepatic, rel. to the liver; **circulación** ___ / liver circulation; **cirrosis** ___ / liver cirrhosis; **coma** ___ / ___ coma; **conducto** ___ / ___ duct; **fallo** ___ / liver failure; **lesión** ___ / liver damage; **lóbulos o subdivisiones** ___-s / ___ lobes; **manchas** ___-s / liver spots; **pruebas funcionales** ___-s / liver function tests; **venas** ___-s / ___ veins.

hepatitis *f.* hepatitis, infl. of the liver; ___ **tipo A, viral** / type A, viral; ___ **tipo B, viral** / type B ___, viral; ___ **no A–no B** / non A–non B ___, linked to blood transfusion; ___ **amébica** / amebic ___; ___ **crónica activa** / chronic active; ___ **crónica persistente** / chronic persistent ___; ___ **fulminante** / fulminant ___; ___ **sérica** / serum ___.

hepatocito *m.* hepatocyte, liver cell.

hepatoentérico-a *a.* hepatoenteric, rel. to the liver and the intestines.

hepatoesplenomegalia *f.* hepatosplenomegaly, enlargement of the liver and the spleen.

hepatolenticular *a.* hepatolenticular, rel. to the lenticular nucleus of the eye and the liver; **degeneración** ___ / ___ degeneration.

hepatología *f.* hepatology, the study of the liver.

hepatólogo-a *m., f.* hepatologist, specialist in liver diseases.

hepatomegalia *f.* hepatomegaly, enlargement of the liver.

hepatorrenal *a.* hepatorenal, rel. to the liver and the kidneys.

hepatotoxina *f.* hepatotoxin, toxin that destroys liver cells.

heredado-a *a.* inherited.

heredar *v.* to inherit

hereditario-a *a.* hereditary, inherited.

herencia *f.* heredity, inheritance, transmission of genetic traits from parents to children; ___ **familiar** / heredofamilial, rel. to a disease or condition that is inherited.

herida *f.* wound, injury; ___ **contusa** / contused ___, subcutaneous lesion; ___ **de perforación** / puncture ___; ___ **de bala** / gunshot ___; ___ **penetrante** / penetrating ___.

herido-a *a.* wounded; hurt.

herir *vi.* to injure, to hurt.

hermafrodita *f.* hermaphrodite, an individual that has both ovaric and testicular tissue combined in the same organ or separately.

hermafroditismo *m.* hermaphroditism, condition of being a hermaphrodite.

hermano-a *m., f.* brother; sister.

hermético-a *a.* hermetic, airtight.

hernia *f.* hernia, abnormal protrusion of an organ or viscera through the cavity wall that encloses it; ___ **del núcleo pulposo** / herniation nucleus pulposus, prolapse or rupture of the intervertebral disk; ___ **escrotal** / scrotal ___, that descends into the scrotum; ___ **estrangulada** / strangulated ___, obstructing the intestines; ___ **femoral** / femoral ___, protruding into the femoral canal; ___ **hiatal** / hiatus ___, protruding through the esophagic hiatus of the diaphragm; ___ **incarcerada** / incarcerated ___, frequently caused by adherences; ___ **inguinal** / inguinal ___, protruding from the viscera into the inguinal canal; ___ **lumbar** / lumbar ___, in the loin; ___ **por deslizamiento** / sliding ___, of the colon; ___ **reducible** / reducible ___, that can be treated by manipulation; **saco de la** ___ / hernial sac, peritoneal sac into which the hernia descends; ___ **umbilical** / umbilical ___, occurring at the navel; ___ **ventral** / ventral ___, protrusion through the abdominal wall.

herniación *f.* herniation, development of a hernia.

herniado-a *a.* herniated, hernial, rel. to or having a hernia.

herniografía *f.* herniography, x-ray of a hernia with the use of a contrasting medium.

herniorrafía *f. surg.* herniorrhaphy, reparation or reconstruction of a hernia.

Hernia	*Hernia*
del núcleo pulposo	herniation nucleus pulposus
escrotal	scrotal
estrangulada	strangulated
femoral	femoral
hiatal	hiatus
incarcerada	incarcerated
inguinal	inguinal
lumbar	lumbar
por deslizamiento	sliding
reducible	reducible
umbilical	umbilical
ventral	ventral

heroico-a *a.* heroic, rel. to very strong medication or extreme medical procedures.

heroína *f.* heroin, diacetylmorphine, addictive narcotic derived from morphine; **adicto-a a la ___, heroinómano-a /** ___ addict.

heroinismo, heroinomanía *m.* heroinism, addiction to heroin.

herpangina *f.* herpangina, infectious disease (epidemic in the summer) that affects the mucous membranes of the throat.

herpes *m.* herpes, inflammatory, painful viral disease of the skin manifested by the formation of small, clustered, blisterlike eruptions; ___ **genital /** ___ genitalis; ___ **ocular /** ocular ___; ___ **simple /** ___ simplex, simple vesicles that keep recurring in the same area of the skin; ___ **zóster** [*culebrilla*] / ___ zoster, *pop.* shingles, painful eruption along the course of a nerve.

herpético-a *a.* herpetic, rel. to herpes or similar in nature.

hervido-a *a.* boiled.

hervir *vi.* to boil.

heterogéneo-a *a.* heterogeneous, dissimilar, not alike.

heteroinjerto *m.* heterograft, graft that comes from a donor of a different species or type than that of the recipient.

heterólogo-a *a.* heterologous. 1. formed by foreign cell tissue; 2. derived or obtained from a different species.

heteroplasia *f.* heteroplasia, presence of tissue in areas foreign to its normal location.

heteroplastia *f. surg.* heteroplasty, transplant of tissue from an individual of a different species.

heteroplástico-a *a.* heteroplastic, rel. to heteroplasia.

heterosexual *a.* heterosexual, attracted to the opposite sex.

heterosexualidad *f.* heterosexuality.

heterotaxia *f.* heterotaxis, abnormal or irregular position of some organs or parts of the body.

heterotopia *f.* heterotopia, displacement or deviation of an organ or part of the body from its normal position.

heterotópico-a *a.* heterotopic, rel. to heterotopia.

hético-a *a.* hectic, febrile.

heurístico-a *a.* heuristic, rel. to empirical discoveries or investigations.

hexacloruro de gamma-benceno *m.* gammabenzene hexachloride, powerful insecticide used in the treatment of scabies.

hialina *f.* hyalin, protein that results from the degeneration of amyloids, colloids, and hyaloids.

hialinización *f.* hyalinization, degenerative process by which functioning tissue is replaced by a firm, glasslike material.

hialino-a *a.* hyaline, glasslike, or almost transparent; **cilindro** ___ / ___ cast, found in the urine; **enfermedad de la membrana** ___ / ___ membrane disease, respiratory disorder of the newborn.

hialoide, hialoideo-a *a.* hyaloid, resembling glass.

hiatus *m.* hiatus, opening, orifice, fissure.

hibernoma *m.* hibernoma, benign tumor localized in the hip or the back.

híbrido-a *a.* hybrid, resulting from the crossing of different species of animals or plants.

hibridoma *m.* hybridoma, hybrid cell capable of producing a continuous supply of antibodies.

hidátide *m.* hydatid, cyst found in tissues, esp. in the liver.

hidatídico-a *a.* hydatid, rel. to a hydatid; **enfermedad** ___ / ___ disease, echinococcosis; **quiste** ___ / ___ mole, uterine cyst that produces hemorrhaging.

hidradenitis *f.* hidradenitis, infl. of the sweat glands.

hidramnios *m.* hydramnion, excess of amniotic fluid.

hidratar *v.* to hydrate, to combine a body with water.

hídrico-a *a.* hydric, rel. to water.

hidrocefalia *f.* hydrocephaly, hydrocephalus, abnormal accumulation of cerebrospinal fluid within the ventricles of the brain.

hidrocefálico-a *a.* hydrocephalic, rel. to hydrocephaly.

hidrocele *m.* hydrocele, an accumulation of serous fluid esp. in the vaginal tunic of the testes.

hidrocelectomía *f. surg.* hydrocelectomy, removal of a hydrocele.

hidrocortisona *f.* hydrocortisone, corticosteroid hormone produced by the adrenal cortex.

hidroeléctrico-a *a.* hydroelectric, rel. to water and electricity; **equilibrio** ___ / water-electrolyte balance; **desequilibrio** ___ / water-electrolyte imbalance.

hidrofílico-a *a.* hydrophilic, having a propensity to attract and retain water.

hidrofobia *f.* hydrophobia. 1. fear of water; 2. rabies, nervous disorder transmitted by an infected animal.

hidrógeno *m.* hydrogen; **concentración de ___ / ___** concentration.

hidrólisis *f.* hydrolysis, dissolution of a compound by the action of water.

hidrolizar *vi.* to hydrolyze.

hidromielia *f.* hydromyelia, increase of fluid in the central canal of the spinal cord.

hidronefrosis *f.* hydronephrosis, distension of the renal pelvis and calices due to obstruction.

hidroneumotórax *m.* hydropneumothorax, presence of gas and fluids in the pleural cavity.

hidropesía, hidropsia *f.* hydropsy, dropsy, accumulation of serous fluid in a cavity or cellular tissue.

hidrópico-a *a.* hydropic, rel. to hydropsy.

hidrosálpinx *m.* hydrosalpinx, accumulation of watery fluid in the fallopian tubes.

hidrosis *f.* hidrosis, hydrosis, abnormal sweating.

hidrostático-a *a.* hydrostatic, rel. to the equilibrium of liquids.

hidroterapia *f.* hydrotherapy, therapeutic use of applied external water in the treatment of diseases.

hidrotórax *m.* hydrothorax, collection of fluid in the pleural cavity without inflammation.

hidrouréter *m.* hydroureter, abnormal distension of the ureter due to obstruction.

hidroxiapatita *f.* hydroxyapatite, calcium phosphate, inorganic compound found in teeth and bones.

hiel *f.* bile; gall.

hielo *m.* ice.

hierro *m.* iron.

hifema *f.* hyphema, bleeding in the anterior chamber of the eye.

hígado *m.* liver, largest gland of the body, located in the upper right part of the abdominal cavity. It secretes bile, stabilizes and produces sugar, enzymes, and cholesterol, and eliminates toxins from the body.

higiene *f.* hygiene, the study and practice of health standards; **___ mental** / mental **___**; **___ oral** / oral **___**; **___ pública** / public **___**.

higiénico-a *a.* hygienic, sanitary; rel. to hygiene; **absorbente ___** / sanitary napkin.

higienista *m., f.* hygienist, specialist in hygiene; **___ dental** / dental **___**, technician in dental profilaxis.

higroma *m.* hygroma, liquid containing sac.

hijastro-a *m., f.* stepson; stepdaughter.

hijo-a *m., f.* son; daughter.

hilio *m.* hilum, hilus, depression or opening in an organ from which blood vessels and nerves enter or leave.

hilo *m.* thread. 1. material used in sutures; 2. filament-like structure.

himen *m.* hymen, membranous fold that covers partially the entrance of the vagina.

himenectomía *f. surg.* hymenectomy, excision of the hymen.

himenotomía *f.* hymenotomy, incision in the hymen.

hinchado-a *a.* swollen, bloated.

hinchar *v.* to swell, to inflate; **hincharse** *vr.* to become swollen or bloated.

hinchazón *f.* swelling.

hioides *m.* hyoid bone, horseshoe-shaped bone situated at the base of the tongue.

hipalgesia, hipalgia *f.* hypalgia, diminished sensitivity to pain.

hiperacidez *f.* hyperacidity, excessive acidity.

hiperactividad *f.* hyperactivity, excessive activity; *psych.*, excessive activity manifested in children and adolescents, usu. accompanied by irritability and inability to concentrate for any length of time.

hiperalbuminosis *f.* hyperalbuminosis, excess albumin in the blood.

hiperalimentación *f.* hyperalimentation, supplemental intravenous feeding; **___ intravenosa** / parenteral **___**.

hiperbilirrubinemia *f.* hyperbilirubinemia, excessive bilirubin in the blood.

hipercalcemia *f.* hypercalcemia, excessive amount of calcium in the blood.

hipercalemia, hiperpotasemia *f.* hyperkalemia, hyperpotasemia, abnormal elevation of potassium in the blood.

hipercapnia *f.* hypercapnia, excessive amount of carbon dioxide in the blood.

hipercinesia *f.* hyperkinesia, abnormal increase of muscular activity.

hipercloremia *f.* hyperchloremia, excess of chlorides in the blood.

hipercoagulabilidad *f.* hypercoagulability, abnormal increase in the coagulability of the blood.

hipercolesterolemia *f.* hypercholesterolemia, *V.* **colesteremia.**

hipercromático-a *a.* hyperchromatic, having excessive pigmentation.

hiperemesis *f.* hyperemesis, excessive vomiting.

hiperemia *f.* hyperemia, excessive blood in an organ or part.

hiperesplenismo *m.* hypersplenism, exacerbation of spleen function.

hiperestesia *f.* hyperesthesia, abnormal increased sensitivity to sensorial stimuli.

hiperflexión *f.* hyperflexion, exaggerated flexion of a limb, gen. caused by traumatism.

hiperfunción *f.* hyperfunction, excessive function.

hipergammaglobulinemia *f.* hypergammaglobulinemia, excess gamma globulin in the blood.

hiperglucemia *f.* hyperglycemia, excessive amount of sugar in the blood, such as in diabetes.

hiperglucémico-a *a.* hyperglycemic, rel. to or suffering from hyperglycemia.

hiperglucosuria *f.* hyperglycosuria, excessive

amount of sugar in the urine.

hiperhidratación *f.* hyperhydration, abnormal increase of water content in the body.

hiperhidrosis *f.* hyperhidrosis, excessive perspiration.

hiperinsulinismo *m.* hyperinsulinism, excessive secretion of insulin in the blood resulting in hypoglycemia.

hiperlipemia *f.* hyperlipemia, excessive amount of fat in the blood.

hiperlipidemia *f.* hyperlipidemia, excess of lipids in the blood.

hipermetropía *f.* hypermetropia, farsightedness, visual defect in which the rays of light come to focus behind the retina making distant objects better seen than closer ones.

hipermovilidad *f.* hypermobility, excessive mobility.

hipernatremia *f.* hypernatremia, excessive amount of sodium in the blood.

hipernefroma *m.* hypernephroma, Grawitz tumor, neoplasm of the renal parenchyma.

hiperopía *f.* hyperopia. *V.* **hipermetropía.**

hiperópico-a *a.* farsighted.

hiperorexia *f.* hyperorexia, excessive appetite.

hiperosmia *f.* hyperosmia, increased sensitivity of smell.

hiperostosis *f.* hyperostosis, excessive growth of a bony tissue.

hiperpirexia *f.* hyperpyrexia, abnormally high body temperature.

hiperpituitarismo *m.* hyperpituitarism, excessive activity of the pituitary gland.

hiperplasia *f.* hyperplasia, excessive proliferation of normal cells of tissues.

hiperpnea *f.* hyperpnea, increase in the depth and rapidity of breathing.

hiperreflexia *f.* hyperreflexia, exaggerated reflexes.

hipersalivación *f.* hypersalivation, excessive secretion of saliva.

hipersecreción *f.* hypersecretion, excessive secretion.

hipersensibilidad *f.* hypersensibility, excessive sensitivity to the effect of a stimulus or antigen.

hipertelorismo *m.* hypertelorism, excessive distance between two parts or organs.

hipertensión *f.* hypertension, high blood pressure; ___ **benigna** / benign ___ ; ___ **esencial** / essential ___ ; ___ **maligna** / malignant ___ ; ___ **portal** / portal ___ ; ___ **renal** / renal ___ .

hipertenso-a *a.* hypertensive, rel. to or suffering from hypertension.

hipertermia *f.* hyperthermia. *V.* **hiperpirexia.**

hipertiroidismo *m.* hyperthyroidism, excessive activity of the thyroid gland.

hipertónico-a *a.* hypertonic, rel. to increased tonicity or tension.

hipertrofia *f.* hypertrophy, abnormal growth or development of an organ or structure; ___ **cardíaca** / cardiac ___ , enlarged heart; ___ **compensadora** / compensatory ___ , resulting

from a physical defect.

hipertropía *f.* hypertropia, a form of strabismus.

hiperuricemia *f.* hyperuricemia, excessive amount of uric acid in the blood.

hiperventilación *f.* hyperventilation, extremely rapid and deep inspiration and expiration of air.

hiperviscosidad *f.* hyperviscosity, excessive viscosity.

hipnagógico-a *a.* hypnagogic. 1. that induces sleep; **estado** ___ / ___ state, between wakefulness and sleep; 2. *psych.* rel. to an hallucination or daydream as sleep begins.

hipnosis *f.* hypnosis, an artificially induced passive state during which the subject is responsive to suggestion.

hipnotismo *m.* hypnotism, the practice of hypnosis.

hipnotizar *vi.* to hypnotize, to put a subject under hypnosis.

hipo *m.* hiccups, involuntary contraction of the diaphragm and the glottis.

hipoadrenalismo *m.* hypoadrenalism, condition caused by diminished activity of the adrenal gland.

hipoalbuminemia *f.* hypoalbuminemia, low level of albumin in the blood.

hipocalcemia *f.* hypocalcemia, low amount of calcium in the blood.

hipocalemia, hipopotasemia *f.* hypokalemia, hypopotasemia, deficiency of potassium in the blood.

hipocampo *m.* hippocampus, curved elevation localized in the inferior horn of the lateral ventricle of the brain.

hipocapnia *f.* hypocapnia, deficiency of carbon dioxide in the blood.

hipociclosis *f.* hypocyclosis, deficiency in eye accommodation; ___ **ciliar** / ciliary ___ , weakness of the ciliary muscle; ___ **lenticular** / lenticular ___ , rigidity of the crystalline lens.

hipocinesia *f.* hypokinesia, diminished motor movement.

hipoclorhidria *f.* hypochlorhydria, deficiency of hydrochloric acid in the stomach, which can be a manifestation of cancer or anemia.

hipocolesteremia *f.* hypocholesteremia, diminished presence of cholesterol in the blood.

hipocondría *f.* hypochondria, obsessive concern over one's mental and physical health.

hipocondríaco-a *a.* hypochondriac, rel. to or suffering from hypochondria.

hipocondrio *m.* hypochondrium, upper abdominal region on either side of the thorax.

hipocromatismo *m.* hypochromatism, lack of pigmentation, esp. in the cell nucleus.

hipocromía *f.* hypochromia, abnormally pale erythrocytes.

hipocrómico-a *a.* hypochromic, rel. to hypochromia.

hipodérmico-a *a.* hypodermic, beneath the skin.

hipofaringe *f.* hypopharynx, portion of the pharynx situated under the upper edge of the epiglottis.

hipofibrinogenemia *f.* hypofibrinogenemia, low content of fibrinogen in the blood.

hipofisectomía *f. surg.* hypophysectomy, removal of the pituitary gland.

hipófisis *f.* hypophysis, pituitary gland, epithelial body situated at the base of the sella turcica.

hipofunción *f.* hypofunction, deficiency in the function of an organ.

hipogammaglobulinemia *f.* hypogammaglobulinemia, low level of gamma globulin in the blood; ___ **adquirida** / acquired ___, manifested after infancy.

hipogastrio *m.* hypogastrium, anterior, middle and inferior portion of the abdomen.

hipoglicemia, hipoglucemia *f.* hypoglycemia, abnormally low level of glucose in the blood.

hipoglicémico-a, hipoglucémico-a *a.* hypoglycemic, rel. to or that produces hypoglycemia.

hipoglosal *a.* hypoglossal, rel. to the hyoid bone and the tongue.

hipogloso *m.* hypoglossus, muscle of the tongue that has retractive and lateral action; hypoglossal nerve; **-a** *a.* hypoglossal, beneath the tongue.

hipoinsulinismo *m.* hypoinsulinism, deficient insulin secretion in the blood. *V.* **diabetes mellitus.**

hipomanía *f.* hypomania, moderate form of manic-depressive illness.

hiponatremia *f.* hyponatremia, sodium deficiency in the blood.

hipopituitarismo *m.* hypopituitarism, pathological condition due to diminished secretion of the pituitary gland.

hipoplasia *f.* hypoplasia, defective, or incomplete development of an organ or tissue.

hipoplástico-a *a.* hypoplastic, rel. to or suffering from hypoplasia.

hiporreflexia *f.* hyporeflexia, weak reflexes.

hipospadias *m., f.* hypospadias, congenital anomaly by which the wall of the urethra remains open in different degrees in the undersurface of the penis. In the female the urethra opens into the vagina.

hipotálamo *m.* hypothalamus, portion of the diencephalon situated beneath the thalamus at the base of the cerebrum.

hipotensión *f.* hypotension, low blood pressure.

hipotenso-a *a.* hypotensive, rel. to or suffering from low blood pressure.

hipotermia *f.* hypothermia, low body temperature.

hipótesis *f.* hypothesis, a proposition to be proven by experimentation; ___ **nula** / null ___.

hipotiroideo-a *a.* hypothyroid, rel. to or suffering from hypothyroidism.

hipotiroidismo *m.* hypothyroidism, condition due to a deficiency in the production of thyroxin.

hipotónico-a *a.* hypotonic. 1. rel. to a deficiency in muscular tonicity; 2. having a lower osmotic pressure as compared to another element.

hipotrombinemia *f.* hypothrombinemia, deficiency of thrombin in the blood, which can cause a propensity to bleed.

hipoventilación *f.* hypoventilation, reduction of air entering the alveoli.

hipovolemia *f.* hypovolemia, decreased volume of blood in the body.

hipoxemia, hipoxia *f.* hypoxemia, hypoxia, diminished availability of oxygen to the blood.

hirviente *a.* boiling; **agua** ___ / ___ water.

hispano-a *m., f.* Hispanic person; *a.* Hispanic.

hispanoamericano-a *m., f.* Spanish-American person; *a.* Hispanic.

histamina *f.* histamine, substance that acts as a dilator of blood vessels and stimulates gastric secretion.

histerectomía *f. surg.* hysterectomy, partial or total removal of the uterus; ___ **abdominal** / abdominal ___, through the abdomen; ___ **total** / total ___, removal of the uterus and the cervix; ___ **vaginal** / vaginal ___, through the vagina.

histeria *f.* hysteria, extreme neurosis.

histérico-a *a.* hysteric, hysterical, rel. to or suffering from hysteria.

histerismo *m.* hysterics, hysteria.

histerosalpingografía *f.* hysterosalpingography, x-ray of the uterus and fallopian tubes after injecting a radiopaque substance.

histerosalpingooforectomía *f. surg.* hysterosalpingoophorectomy, excision of the uterus, ovaries, and oviducts.

histeroscopía *f.* hysteroscopy, endoscopic examination of the uterine cavity.

histeroscopio *m.* hysteroscope, endoscope used in the examination of the uterine cavity.

histerotomía *f.* hysterotomy, incision of the uterus.

histidina *f.* histidine, amino acid essential in the growth and restoration of tissue.

histiocito *m.* histiocyte, large interstitial phagocytic cell of the reticuloendothelial system.

histocompatibilidad *f.* histocompatibility, state in which the tissues of a donor are accepted by the receiver; **complejo de** ___ **mayor** / major ___ complex.

histología *f.* histology, study of organic tissues.

histólogo-a *m., f.* histologist, specialist in histology.

histoplasmina *f.* histoplasmin, substance used in the cutaneous test for histoplasmosis.

histoplasmosis *f.* histoplasmosis, respiratory disease caused by the fungus *Histoplasma capsulatum.*

histriónico-a *a.* histrionic, dramatic.

Hodgkin, enfermedad de *f.* Hodgkin's disease, malignant tumors in the lymph nodes and the spleen.

hoja *f.* leaf; [*de papel o metal*] sheet; ___ **clínica** / medical chart.

hola *int.* hi, hello.

holgazán-a *m., f.* lazy person, loafer; *a.* lazy.

holístico-a *a.* holistic, rel. to a whole or unit.

holocrino-a *a.* holocrine, rel. to the sweat glands.

holodiastólico-a *a.* holodiastolic, rel. to a complete diastole.

holografía *f.* holography, tridimensional representation of a figure by means of a photographic image.

holograma *m.* hologram, production of a holography.

holosistólico-a *a.* holosystolic, rel. to a complete systole.

hombre *m.* man, male.

hombro *m.* shoulder, the union of the clavicle, the scapula, and the humerus.

homeopatía *f.* homeopathy, cure by means of administering medication diluted in minute doses that are capable of producing symptoms of the disease being treated.

homeopático-a *a.* homeopathic, rel. to homeopathy.

homicidio *m.* homicide; ___ **sin premeditación** / manslaughter.

homocigótico-a *a.* homozygotic, homozygous, rel. to twins that develop from gametes with similar alleles in regard to one or all characters.

homofobia *f.* homophobia, fear of or revulsion regarding homosexuals.

homofóbico-a *a.* fearful of or having an aversion to homosexuals.

homogéneo-a *a.* homogeneous, similar in nature.

homoinjerto *m.* homograft, transplant from a subject of the same species or type.

homólogo-a *a.* homologous, similar in structure and origin but not in function.

homosexual *a.* homosexual, sexually attracted to persons of the same sex.

homotónico-a *a.* homotonic, having the same tension.

homotópico-a *a.* homotopic, rel. to or occurring in the same corresponding parts.

homúnculo-a *m., f.* homunculus, dwarf with no deformities and with proportionate parts of the body.

hondo-a *a.* deep.

honesto-a, honrado-a *a.* honest.

hongo *m.* fungus; mushroom; ___ **venenoso** / toadstool.

honorario *m.* fee, charges; ___-**s razonables** / reasonable charges.

hora *f.* hour, time; **a cada** ___ / hourly; ___ **de acostarse** / bedtime; **¿qué** ___ **es?** what time is it?

horario *m.* schedule; timetable.

horizontal *a.* horizontal, parallel to the floor.

hormiga *f.* ant.

hormigueo *m.* tingling sensation.

hormona *f.* hormone, natural chemical substance in the body that produces or stimulates the activity of an organ; ___ **del crecimiento** / growth ___; ___ **estimulante** / stimulating ___.

hormona luteinizante *f.* luteinizing hormone produced by the anterior pituitary gland. It stimulates the secretion of sex hormones by the testis (testosterone) and the ovaries (progesterone) and also acts in the formation of sperm and ova.

hormona paratiroidea *f.* parathormona, parathyroid hormone, a hormone that regulates calcium in the body.

hormonal *a.* hormonal, rel. to or acting like a hormone; **receptor** ___ / hormone ___; **terapia** ___ / hormone therapy.

hornear *v.* to bake.

Horner, síndrome de *m.* Horner's syndrome, sinking of the eyeball with accompanying eye and facial disorders due to paralysis of the cervical sympathetic nerve.

horno *m.* oven.

horquilla *f.* fourchette, posterior junction of the vulva.

horrible *a.* horrible; abominable, hideous.

hospedar *v.* to host; to lodge.

hospicio *m.* hospice, nursing facility.

hospital *m.* hospital.

hospitalización *f.* hospitalization.

hospitalizar *vi.* to hospitalize.

hostil *a.* hostile, unfriendly.

hostilidad *f.* hostility, animosity.

hotel *m.* hotel.

hoy *adv.* today; **de** ___ **en adelante** / from now on; ___ **en día** / nowadays.

hoyo *m.* pit, hole.

hoyuelo *m.* dimple, dimple sign; small hole.

hueco *m.* depression, socket; hole; -**a** *a.* hollow.

huella *f.* impression; print; ___-**s dactilares** / fingerprints; ___ **del pie** / footprint.

huérfano-a *m., f.* orphan.

huesecillo *m.* bonelet.

hueso *m.* bone; ___ **compacto** / hard ___; ___ **esponjoso** / spongy ___; ___ **quebrado** / fractured ___.

huésped *m.* [*parásito*] host; **defensas del** ___ / ___ defenses.

huesudo-a *a.* bony.

huevo *m.* egg, ovum, female sexual cell; **cáscara de** ___ / eggshell; **clara de** ___ / ___ white; **frito** / fried ___; ___ **pasado por agua** / soft-boiled ___; **yema de** ___ / ___ yolk.

humanidad *f.* humanity.

humano-a *a.* human; humane; rel. to humanity.

humear *v.* to fume; to emit vapor or gas.

humectante *m.* humidifier, device that controls and maintains humidity in the air within a given area.

humedad *f.* humidity.

homolateral - ipsilateral

humedecer *v.* to moisten, to dampen.

húmedo-a *a.* humid, damp.

húmero *m.* humerus, long bone of the upper arm.

humo *m.* smoke.

humor *m.* humor. 1. any liquid form in the body; ___ **acuoso** / aqueous ___, clear fluid in the eye chambers; ___ **cristalino** / crystalline ___, substance that constitutes the lens of the eye; ___ **vítreo** / vitreous ___, clear, semifluid substance between the lens and the retina; 2. secretion. 3. disposition, mood; **buen** ___ / good ___; **estar de buen** ___ / to be in a good ___;

estar de mal ___ / to be in a bad mood; **mal** ___ / bad ___.

humoral *a.* humoral, rel. to the body fluids.

hundido-a *a.* sunken.

Hunt, neuralgia de *f.* Hunt's neuralgia or syndrome. *V.* **neuralgia.**

Huntington, corea de *f.* Huntington's chorea. *V.* **corea.**

huso *m.* spindle. 1. structure or cell shaped like a round pin with tapered ends; 2. achromatic arrangements of chromosomes in the nuclear cell during mitosis and meiosis.

¡huy! *int.* ouch!

I *abr.* **iodo, yodo** / iodine.

iátrico-a *a.* iatric, rel. to medicine, the medical profession, or physicians.

iatrogénico-a, iatrógeno-a *a.* iatrogenic. *V.* **yatrógeno.**

ibuprofén *m.* ibuprofen, anti-inflammatory, pyrectic, and analgesic agent used in the treatment of rheumatoid arthritis.

ictericia *f.* jaundice, disorder caused by excessive bilirubin in the blood and manifested by a yellow-orange coloring of the skin and other tissues and fluids of the body; ___ **del neonato** / icterus gravis neonatorum.

ictérico-a *a.* icteric, jaundiced, or rel. to jaundice.

icterogénico-a *a.* icterogenic, agent that causes jaundice.

icterohepatitis *f.* icterohepatitis, hepatitis associated with jaundice.

icterus *L.* icterus. *V.* **ictericia.**

ictiosis *f.* ichthyosis, dry and scaly skin.

ictus *L.* ictus, sudden attack.

idea *f.* idea, concept, thought; ___ **fija** / fixed ___, idée fixe.

ideación *f.* ideation, process by which ideas are formed.

ideal *a.* ideal.

idem *L.* idem, the same.

idéntico-a *a.* 1. identical, same; 2. rel. to twins that result from the fertilization of only one ovum.

identidad *f.* identity, self-recognition.

identificación *f. psych.* identification, unconscious process of identifying oneself with another person or group and assuming its characteristics.

identificar *vi.* to identify.

ideocracia *f.* ideocracy, tendency to submit oneself to certain habits and drugs.

ideología *f.* ideology, a set of concepts and ideas.

ideomoción *f.* ideomotion, muscular activity directed by a prevailing idea.

idiograma *f.* idiogram, graphic representation of the chromosomes of a given cell.

idioma *m.* language.

idiopatía *f.* idiopathy, disease or morbid state of unknown origin.

idiopático-a *a.* idiopathic. 1. rel. to idiopathy; 2. of a spontaneous nature.

idiosincracia *f.* idiosyncrasy. 1. set of individual characteristics; 2. an individual's own reaction to a given action, idea, medication, treatment or food.

idiota *m., f.* idiot, fool.

idiotez *f.* idiocy, mental deficiency.

idiotrópico-a *a.* idiotropic. *V.* **egocéntrico.**

idioventricular *a.* idioventricular, rel. to that which affects ventricles only.

ido-a *a.* absentminded, distracted.

ignorante *a.* ignorant.

ignorar *v.* to ignore.

igual *a.* equal, even, same; **-mente** *adv.* equally.

igualar *v.* to equate.

ileal *a.* ileal, rel. to the ileum.

ilegal *a.* illegal, illicit.

ilegítimo-a *a.* illegitimate, bastard.

ileítis *f.* ileitis, infl. of the ileum; ___ **regional** / regional ___.

ileocecal *a.* ileocecal, rel. to the ileum and the cecum; **válvula** ___ / ___ valve.

ileocistoplastia *f. surg.* ileocystoplasty, anastomosis of a segment of the ileum to the bladder in order to increase the bladder's capacity.

ileocolitis *f.* ileocolitis, infl. of the mucous membrane of the ileum and the colon.

íleon *m.* ileum, distal portion of the small intestine extending from the jejunum to the cecum; **desviación quirúrgica del** ___ / ileal bypass.

ileoproctostomía *f. surg.* ileoproctostomy, anastomosis of the ileum and the rectum.

ileosigmoidostomía *f. surg.* ileosigmoidostomy, anastomosis of the ileum and the sigmoid colon.

ileostomía *f. surg.* ileostomy, anastomosis of the ileum and the anterior abdominal wall.

ileotransversostomía *f. surg.* ileotransversostomy, anastomosis of the ileum and the transverse colon.

ilíaco-a *a.* iliac, rel. to the ilium.

ilimitado-a *a.* unlimited, boundless.

iliofemoral *a.* iliofemoral, rel. to the ilium and the femur.

iliohipogástrico-a *a.* iliohypogastric, rel. to the ilium and the hypogastrium.

ilioinguinal *a.* ilioinguinal, rel. to the iliac and inguinal regions.

iliolumbar *a.* iliolumbar, rel. to the iliac and lumbar regions.

ilión *m.* ilium, hip bone.

iluminación *f.* illumination; ___ **lateral o indirecta del campo oscuro** / lateral or indirect dark field ___.

ilusión *f.* illusion, false interpretation of sensory impressions.

iluso-a *a.* deluded.

ilusorio-a *a.* illusory, illusional or rel. to an illusion.

ilustración *f.* illustration, graph.

imagen *f.* image.

imagenelogia *f.* imaging.

imágenes por resonancia magnética *f. pl.* magnetic resonance imaging, procedure based in the quantitative analysis of the chemical and biological structure of a tissue.

imágenes por ultrasonido *f. pl.* ultrasound imaging, creation of images of organs or tissues through the use of reflex techniques (echogram).

imaginar *v.* to imagine.

114

imaginario-a *a.* imaginary, illusory; unreal.

imán *m.* magnet, a body that has the property of attracting iron.

imbécil *m., f.* imbecile, stupid person; *a.* imbecilic, stupid.

imbibición *f.* imbibition, absorption of a liquid.

imbricado-a *a.* imbricate, imbricated, in layers.

imitación *f.* imitation.

imitar *v.* to imitate.

impacción *f.* impaction. 1. the condition of being lodged or wedged within a given space; 2. impediment of an organ or part.

impacientarse *vr.* to become impatient.

impaciente *a.* impatient.

impactado-a *a.* impacted; **diente** ___ / ___ tooth.

impalpable *a.* impalpable, incorporeal, intangible.

impedimento *m.* impediment; handicap; obstacle.

impedir *vi.* to impede, to prevent; to impair.

impenetrable *a.* impenetrable.

imperativo *m. gr.* imperative mood; **-a** *a.* imperative.

imperdible *m.* safety pin.

imperfección *f.* imperfection; defect.

imperfecto-a *m. gr.* past tense; *a.* imperfect; defective.

imperforado-a *a.* imperforate, abnormally closed; **himen** ___ / ___ hymen.

impermeable *a.* impermeable, not allowing passage, such as fluids; waterproof.

impersonal *a.* impersonal.

impétigo *m.* impetigo, bacterial skin infection marked by vesicles that become pustular and form a yellow crust on rupturing.

ímpetu *m.* impetus, impulse.

impetuoso-a *a.* impetuous, violent.

implacable *a.* implacable, not able to be appeased.

implantación *f.* implantation, insertion and fixation of a part or tissue in an area of the body.

implantar *v.* to implant; to insert.

implante *m.* implant, any material inserted or grafted into the body.

implicación *f.* implication.

implicar *vi.* to imply.

imponer *vi.* to impose; to tax; **imponerse** *vr.* to prevail.

importancia *n.* importance, significance; **sin** ___ / of no significance.

importante *a.* important.

importar *v.* to matter.

imposible *a.* impossible.

impotencia *f.* impotence, inability to have or maintain an erection.

impotente *a.* impotent, rel. to or suffering from impotence.

impráctico-a *a.* impractical.

impregnar *v.* to impregnate; to saturate.

imprescindible *a.* indispensable.

impresión *f.* impression, print; image; ___ **digital** / fingerprint.

impresionante *a.* impressive.

imprevisto-a *a.* unexpected, unforeseen.

improbable *a.* improbable, unlikely.

improvisado-a *a.* improvised.

improvisar *v.* to improvise.

impúbero-a *a.* below the age of puberty.

impuesto *m.* tax; **exempto de** ___ / ___ exempt, free of ___ .

impular *v.* to impel; to accelerate.

impulsivo-a *a.* impulsive; driven.

impulso *m.* drive, thrust; sudden pushing force; ___ **cardíaco** / cardiac ___ ; ___ **excitante** / excitatory ___ ; ___ **inhibitorio** / inhibitory ___ ; ___ **nervioso** / nervous ___ ; ___ **vital** / élan vital.

impuro-a *a.* impure, contaminated, adulterated.

inaccesible *a.* inaccessible.

inacción *f.* inaction, failure to respond to a stimulus.

inaceptable *a.* unacceptable.

inactividad *f.* inactivity; ___ **física** / physical ___ .

inactivo-a *a.* inactive, passive; in a state of rest.

inadaptado-a *a.* maladjusted, unable to adjust to the environment or to endure stress.

inadecuado-a *a.* inadequate.

inanición *f.* inanition, starvation, hunger.

inarticulado-a *a.* inarticulate, 1. unable to articulate words or syllables; 2. disjointed.

in articulo mortis *L.* in articulo mortis, at the moment of death.

incandescente *a.* incandescent, glowing with light.

incansable *a.* tireless, untiring.

incapacitado-a *a.* disabled; unable.

incapaz *a.* incapable, unable.

incendio *m.* fire.

incentivo *m.* incentive.

incertidumbre *f.* uncertainty.

incesante *a.* incessant; continuous.

incesto *m.* incest.

incestuoso-a *a.* incestuous.

incidencia *f.* incidence.

incidental *a.* incidental.

incinerar *v.* to incinerate; to cremate.

incipiente *a.* incipient, just coming into existence.

incisión *f.* incision; surgical cut.

incisura *f.* slit; notch.

inclinación *f.* slant, slope, tilt; inclination, predisposition.

inclinado-a *a.* inclined.

incluido *a.* included; enclosed.

incluir *vi.* to include; to embed, to surround a tissue specimen in a firm medium to keep intact in preparation for cutting sections for examination.

inclusión *f.* inclusion, the act of enclosing one thing in another; **cuerpos de** ___ / ___ bodies, present in the cytoplasm of some cells in cases of infection.

incoherencia *f.* incoherence, lack of coordination of ideas.

incoherente *a.* incoherent.

incoloro-a *a.* colorless; achromatic.

incomodar *v.* to disturb, to annoy.

incómodo-a *a.* uncomfortable; annoyed.

incompatibilidad *f.* incompatibility

incompatible *a.* incompatible.

incompetente *a.* incompetent.

incompleto-a *a.* incomplete, unfinished.

inconsciencia *f.* unconsciousness, impaired consciousness or the loss of it; unawareness.

inconsciente *a.* unconscious. 1. that has lost consciousness; 2. that does not respond to sensorial stimuli.

inconsistencia *f.* inconsistency.

inconsistente *a.* inconsistent.

incontinencia *f.* incontinence, inability to control the emission or expulsion of urine or feces; ___ **por rebozamiento** / ___, overflow; ___ **urinaria de esfuerzo** / ___, urinary stress.

incontinente *a.* incontinent, rel. to incontinence.

inconveniencia *f.* inconvenience, hardship.

inconveniente *m.* difficulty, obstacle; *a.* inconvenient.

incorporar *v.* to incorporate, to include.

incorrecto-a *a.* incorrect, inaccurate; **acción** ___ / improper action.

incredulidad *f.* disbelief, skepticism.

incrustación *f.* inlay.

incubación *f.* incubation; 1. latent period of a disease before its manifestation; **período de** ___ / ___ period; 2. the care of a premature infant in an incubator.

incubadora *f.* incubator, device used to keep optimal conditions of temperature and humidity, esp. in the care of premature infants.

incurable *a.* incurable, not subject to healing.

incus *L.* incus, small bone of the middle ear.

indeciso-a *a.* undecided, undecisive, hesitant.

indefinido-a *a.* indefinite, undefined.

independiente *a.* independent, self-sufficient.

indeseable *a.* undesirable.

indeterminado-a *a.* undetermined; undefined.

indicación *f.* indication; suggestion; hint.

indicado-a *a.* indicated; appropriate.

indicador *m.* marker, indicator.

indicar *vi.* to indicate; to point out.

índice *m.* rate, index; mean; ___ **de mortalidad, de mortandad** / death ___; ___ **de natalidad** / birthrate; ___ **de natalidad cero** / zero population growth.

indiferenciación *f.* undifferentiation. *V.* **anaphasia.**

indiferente *a.* indifferent.

indígena *m., f.* native, aboriginal; *a.* indigenous.

indigestarse *vr.* to suffer from indigestion.

indigestión *f.* indigestion, maldigestion.

indirecto-a *a.* indirect.

indispensable *a.* indispensable, necessary.

indisponer *vi.* to indispose; to make ill.

indispuesto-a *a. pp.* of **indisponer**, indisposed,

ill; upset.

individual *a.* individual.

individualidad *f.* individuality.

individuo *m.* individual, person; fellow.

inducido-a *a.* induced.

inducir *vi.* to induce; to force; to provoke.

ineficiente *a.* inefficient, ineffective.

inercia *f.* inertia, stillness; lack of activity.

inerte *a.* inert, rel. to inertia.

inervación *f.* innervation, distribution of nerves or nervous energy in an organ or area.

inervar *v.* to innervate, to stimulate a nerve.

inesperado-a *a.* unexpected, occurring without warning.

inestable *a.* unstable, fluctuating.

inevitable *a.* inevitable, unavoidable.

inexperiencia *f.* inexperience.

infancia *f.* infancy, period of time from birth to one or two years of age; early age.

infantil *a.* infantile. 1. rel. to infancy; 2. childish.

infantilismo *m.* infantilism, infantile characteristics carried into adult life.

infarto *m.* infarct, infarction, necrosis of a tissue area due to a lack of blood supply; ___ **blando** / bland ___; ___ **cardíaco** / myocardial ___; ___ **cerebral** / cerebral ___; ___ **hemorrágico** / hemorrhagic ___; ___ **pulmonar** / pulmonary ___.

infección *f.* infection, invasion of the body by pathogenic microorganisms and the reaction of tissue to their presence and effect; ___ **aerógena** / airborne ___; ___ **aguda** / acute ___; ___ **contagiosa** / contagious ___; ___ **crónica** / chronic ___; ___ **de hongos** / fungus ___; ___ **hídrica** / waterborne ___; ___ **hospitalaria** / cross ___; ___ **masiva** / massive ___; ___ **piógena** / pyogenic ___; ___ **secundaria** / secondary ___; ___ **sistémica** / systemic ___; ___ **subclínica** / subclinical ___.

infección oportunista *f.* opportunistic infection, caused by an organism, gen. harmless, that can become pathogenic when resistance to disease is impaired, such as occurs in AIDS.

infeccioso-a *a.* infectious, rel. to an infection; **agente** ___ / ___ agent; **enfermedad** ___ / ___

Infección	*Infection*
aerógena	airborne
aguda	acute
contagiosa	contagious
crónica	chronic
de hongos	fungus
hidrica	waterborne
hospitalaria	cross
masiva	massive
piógena	pyogenic
secundaria	secondary
sistémica	systemic
subclínica	subclinica

disease.

infectado-a *a*. infected.

infectar *v*. to infect; **infectarse** *vr*. to become infected.

infectivo-a *a*. infectious.

infecundarse *vr*. to become sterile.

infecundidad *f*. infecundity, sterility.

infecundo-a *a*. sterile; barren.

infeliz *a*. unhappy.

inferior *a*. inferior, lower.

inferir *vi*. to infer, to surmise.

infertilidad *f*. infertility, inability to conceive or procreate.

infestación *f*. infestation, invasion of the body by parasites.

infiltración *f*. infiltration, the accumulation of foreign substances in a tissue, organ, or cell.

infiltrar *v*. to infiltrate, to penetrate.

inflación *f*. inflation, distension.

inflamación *f*. inflammation, reaction of a tissue to injury.

inflamarse *vr*. to become inflamed.

inflamatorio-a *a*. inflammatory, rel. to inflammation.

inflexible *a*. inflexible.

inflexión *f*. inflection, inflexion, the act of bending inward.

influencia *f*. influence.

influenza *f*. influenza, acute contagious viral infection of the respiratory tract.

influjo *m*. influx.

información *f*. information.

informar *v*. to inform; **informarse** *vr*. to become informed.

informe *m*. report; account.

infraclavicular *a*. infraclavicular, under the clavicle.

infradiafragmático-a *a*. infradiaphragmatic, under the diaphragm.

infraescapular *a*. infrascapular, situated below the scapula.

infraorbitario *a*. infraorbital, situated under the floor of the orbit.

infrarrojo-a *a*. infrared; **rayos** ___-s / ___ rays.

infrecuente *a*. infrequent.

infundíbulo *m*. infundibulum, funnel-like structure.

infusión *f*. infusion. 1. slow gravitational introduction of fluid into a vein; 2. the steeping of an element in water to obtain its soluble active principles.

ingerir *vi*. to ingest, to take in.

ingesta *f*. ingesta, ingestant; oral feeding.

ingestión *f*. ingestion, the amount of liquids and substances taken into the body by mouth or parenterally; ___ **calórica** / caloric ___.

ingle *f*. groin.

inglés *m*. [*idioma*] English; [*nativo*] **inglés** *m*., **inglesa** *f*. English; *a*. English.

ingravidez *f*. weightlessness.

ingrávido-a *a*. weightless.

ingrediente *m*. ingredient, component.

ingresar *v*. [*en un hospital*] to be admitted.

ingreso *m*. income; *v*. **dar** ___ / to admit.

inguinal *a*. inguinal, rel. to the groin; **anillo** ___ / ___ ring; **canal** ___ / ___ canal; **hernia** ___ / ___ hernia; **ligamento** ___ / ___ ligament.

ingurgitado-a *a*. engorged, distended by excess fluid.

inhábil *a*. unfit.

inhabilidad *f*. inability, incapacity.

inhalación *f*. inhalation, aspiration; the act of drawing air or other vapor into the lungs; ___ **de humo** / smoke ___ .

inhalante *m*. inhalant, medication administered by inhalation.

inhalar *v*. to inhale, to draw in air or vapor.

inherente *a*. inherent, innate, natural to an individual or thing.

inhibición *f*. inhibition, interruption or restriction of a process.

inhibidor *m*. inhibitor, agent that causes inhibition.

inhibir *v*. to inhibit; **inhibirse** *vr*. to restrain from.

inicial *a*. initial.

iniciar *v*. to initiate, to start.

inicio *m*. beginning, start.

injertable *a*. graftable.

injertar *v*. to graft, to implant.

injerto *m*. graft, implant, inlay, any tissue or organ used for transplantation or implantation; ___ **alogénico** / allogenic ___, taken from a genetically nonidentical donor; ___ **autógeno, autoinjerto** / autogenous ___, taken from the same patient; ___ **cutáneo** / skin ___, as in burns; ___ **cutáneo de capa gruesa partida** / thick-split ___, thick layer of skin used to cover a bare area; ___ **de derivación** / bypass ___ ; ___ **dermoepidérmico** / full thickness ___, entire layer of the skin without the subcutaneous fat; ___ **óseo** / bone ___ ; **rechazo de** ___ / ___ rejection.

inmaduro-a *a*. immature.

inmediato-a *a*. immediate, close; **-mente** *adv*. immediately.

inmersión *f*. immersion, submersion of a body in a liquid.

inmigrante *m*., *f*. immigrant.

inminente *a*. imminent, about to happen.

inmoderado-a *a*. immoderate, without moderation.

inmoral *a*. immoral, corrupt.

inmóvil *a*. immobile, motionless.

inmovilización *f*. immobilization.

inmovilizar *vi*. to immobilize.

inmundicia *f*. filth, dirt; garbage.

inmune *a*. immune, resistant to contracting a specific disease.

inmunidad *f*. immunity. 1. condition of the organism to resist a particular antigen by activating specific antibodies; 2. resistance to contracting a specific disease; ___ **activa** / active ___, own production of antibodies; ___

adquirida / acquired ___, as by vaccination; **artificial** / artificial ___, as from vaccination; ___ **natural** / natural ___, genetic type; ___ **pasiva** / passive ___, acquired from a donor.

inmunización *f.* immunization, making the organism immune to a given disease.

inmunizar *vi.* to immunize.

inmunocompetencia *f.* immunocompetency, the process of becoming immune following exposure to an antigen.

inmunodeficiencia *f.* immunodeficiency, inadequate cellular immunity reaction that diminishes the ability to respond to antigenic stimuli; **enfermedad grave de ___ combinada** / severe combined ___ disease.

inmunoelectroforesis *f.* immunoelectrophoresis, the use of electrophoresis as a technique of finding the amount and type of proteins and antibodies in body fluids.

inmunoensayo *m.* immunoassay, the process of identifying a substance by its capacity to act as an antigen and antibody in a tissue; ___ **enzimático** / enzyme ___.

inmunoestimulante *m.* immunostimulant, agent that can stimulate an immune response.

inmunofluorescencia *f.* immunofluorescence, method that uses antibodies labeled with fluorescein to locate antigen in tissues.

inmunógeno *m.* immunogen, stimulator that produces an antibody; *a.* immunogenic; that produces immunity; ___ **específico** / targeted ___.

inmunoglobulina *f.* immunoglobulin. 1. one of a group of proteins of animal origin that participates in the immune reaction; 2. one of the five types of gamma globulin capable of acting as an antibody.

inmunología *f.* immunology, the study of the body's response to bacteria, virus, or any other foreign invasion, such as transplanted tissue or organ.

inmunológico-a *a.* immunologic, rel. to immunology; **respuesta o reacción ___** / immune response.

inmunólogo-a *m.* immunologist, specialist in immunology.

inmunoproteína *f.* immunoprotein, protein that acts as an antibody.

inmunoquimoterapia *f.* immunochemotherapy, combined process of immunotherapy and chemotherapy used in the treatment of some malignant tumors.

inmunosupresivo *m.* immunosuppressant, agent capable of suppressing an immune response.

inmunoterapia *f.* immunotherapy, prevention or treatment of a disease using passive immunization of agents such as serum or gamma globulin.

innato-a *a.* inborn; congenital; ingrown.

innecesario-a *a.* unnecessary.

inocente *a.* innocent.

inoculable *a.* inoculable, that can be transmitted by inoculation.

inoculación *f.* inoculation, immunization, administration of a serum, vaccine, or some other substance to increase immunization to a given disease.

inocular *v.* to inoculate, to administer an inoculation.

inóculo *m.* inoculum, substance that is inoculated.

inodoro *m.* toilet, commode; **-a** *a.* odorless.

inofensivo-a *a.* harmless.

inoperable *a.* inoperable, lacking potential for surgical treatment.

inoportuno-a *a.* untimely, inopportune.

inorgánico-a *a.* inorganic, independent of living organisms.

inotrópico-a *a.* inotropic, affecting the intensity or energy of muscular contractions.

inquieto-a *a.* uneasy, restless, jumpy.

inquietud *f.* unrest, restlessness.

insalubre *a.* insalubrious, unsanitary.

inscribirse *v.* to register.

insecticida *m.* insecticide.

insecto *m.* insect.

inseguridad *f.* insecurity.

inseminación *f.* insemination, fertilization of an ovum.

insensible *a.* insensible, without sensibility.

inseparable *a.* inseparable.

inserción *f.* insertion. 1. the act of inserting; 2. the place where a muscle attaches to the bone.

insertar *v.* to insert.

inservible *a.* useless, unserviceable.

insidioso-a *a.* insidious, rel. to a disease that develops gradually and subtly without warning or early symptoms.

insignificante *a.* insignificant.

insípido-a *a.* insipid, tasteless.

insistir *v.* to insist.

in situ *L.* in situ. 1. in its normal place; 2. that does not extend beyond the place of origin.

insolación *f.* insolation, sunstroke, heat exhaustion, disorder caused by the effect of prolonged exposure to the rays of the sun; ___ **con colapso** / heat prostration.

insoluble *a.* insoluble, that does not dissolve.

insomne *a.* insomniac, insomnious, rel. to or suffering from insomnia.

insomnio *m.* insomnia, inability to sleep.

insoportable *a.* unbearable.

inspección *f.* inspection.

instalación *f.* installation; facility.

instalar *v.* to install.

instante *m.* instant; **en este ___** / right now.

instilación *f.* instillation, dripping of a liquid into a cavity or onto a surface.

instintivo-a *a.* instinctive.

instinto *m.* instinct.

institución *f.* institution, establishment.

instrumento *m.* instrument.

insuficiencia *f.* insufficiency, lacking; ___

cardíaca / heart failure; ___ **coronaria** / coronary ___; ___ **hepática** / hepatic ___; ___ **mitral** / mitral ___; ___ **pulmonar-valvular** / pulmonary valvular ___; ___ **renal** / renal ___; ___ **respiratoria** / respiratory ___; ___ **suprarrenal** / adrenal ___; ___ **valvular** / valvular ___; ___ **venosa** / venous ___.

insuficiente *a.* insufficient.

insuflar *v.* to insufflate, to blow into a tube, cavity, or organ of the body.

insufrible *a.* insufferable, unbearable.

ínsula *f.* insula, central lobe of the cerebral hemisphere.

insulina *f.* insulin, hormone secreted by the pancreas.

insulinemia *f.* insulinemia, excess amount of insulin in the blood.

insulinodependiente *a.* insulin-dependent.

inteligente *a.* intelligent; smart.

intención *f.* intention. 1. goal, purpose; **con** ___ / purposely; 2. natural healing process of a wound.

intensidad *f.* intensity.

intensificar *vi.* to intensify.

intensivo-a *a.* intensive.

intenso-a *a.* intense.

intentar *v.* to attempt, to try.

interacción *f.* interaction; ___ **de medicamentos** / drug ___.

intercalado-a *a.* intercalated, situated or placed between two parts or elements.

intercostal *a.* intercostal, between two ribs.

intercurrente *a.* intercurrent, that appears during the course of another disease modifying it in some way.

interdigitación *f.* interdigitation, interlocking of parts like the fingers of folded hands.

interés *m.* interest.

interferencia *f.* interference, mutual annulment of, or collision between two parts.

interferir *vi.* to interfere.

interferona *f.* interferon, a natural protein released by cells exposed to viruses that can be used in the treatment of infections and neoplasms.

interfibrilar *a.* interfibrillar, between fibrils.

ínterin *m.* interim, meantime.

interior *a.* interior.

interlobular *a.* interlobular, occurring between lobules of an organ.

intermediario-a *a.* intermediary, situated between two bodies.

intermedio-a *a.* intermediate, situated between two extremes.

interminable *a.* endless.

intermitente *a.* intermittent, not continuous; **pulso** ___ / ___ pulse; **ventilación** ___ **bajo presión positiva** / ___ positive-pressure ventilation.

internacional *a.* international; **unidad** ___ / ___ unit, accepted measured amount of a substance as defined by the international confer-

ence of unification of formulae.

internado *m.* internship.

internalización *f. psych.* internalization, unconscious process by which an individual adopts the beliefs, values, and attitudes of another person or of the society in which she or he lives.

internista *m., f.* physician specializing in internal medicine.

interno-a *m., f.* intern; *a.* internal, inside the body; **hemorragia** ___ / ___ bleeding.

interpretación *f.* interpretation.

interpretar *v.* to interpret.

interrogatorio *m.* questioning.

interrumpir *v.* to interrupt.

intersticial *a.* interstitial, rel. to spaces within an organ, cell, or tissue.

intervalo *m.* interval, period of time.

intervención *f.* surgical intervention, operation.

intervenir *vi.* to intervene; to assist; to supervise.

interventricular *a.* interventricular, between the ventricles; **defecto del tabique** ___ / ___ septal defect; **tabique** ___ **del corazón** / ___ septum.

intervertebral *a.* intervertebral, between the vertebrae; **disco** ___ / ___ disk.

intestinal *a.* intestinal, rel. to the intestines; **desviación quirúrgica** ___ / ___ bypass surgery; **flora** ___ / ___ flora; **obstrucción** ___ / ___ obstruction; **perforación** ___ / ___ perforation.

intestino *m.* intestine, the alimentary canal extending from the pylorus to the anus; ___ **delgado** / small ___; ___ **grueso** / large ___; ___ **medio del embrión** / midgut.

íntima *f.* intima. 1. the innermost of the three layers of a blood vessel; 2. the innermost layer of several organs or parts.

intimal *a.* intimal, rel. to the intima.

intolerancia *f.* intolerance, inability to withstand pain or the effects of drugs.

intoxicación *f.* intoxication; poisoning, food poisoning, toxic state produced by the intake of a drug or toxic substance; ___ **de pescado** / fish poisoning.

intoxicar *vi.* to intoxicate, to poison; **intoxicarse** *vr.* to become intoxicated; to become poisoned.

intra-abdominal *a.* intra-abdominal, within the abdominal cavity.

intra-aórtico-a *a.* intra-aortic, within the aorta.

intra-arterial *a.* intra-arterial, within an artery.

intra-articular *a.* intra-articular, within an articulation or joint.

intracapsular *a.* intracapsular, within a capsule.

intracelular *a.* intracellular, within a cell.

intracraneal *a.* intracranial, within the cranium.

intracutáneo-a *a.* intracutaneous, within the dermis.

intrahepático-a *a.* intrahepatic, within the liver.

intralobular *a.* intralobular, within a lobule.

intraluminal *a.* intraluminal, within the lumen of a tube.

intramuscular *a.* intramuscular, within a muscle.

intranquilidad *f.* restlessness, uneasiness.

intranquilo-a *a.* restless, uneasy.

intraocular *a.* intraocular, within the eye; **presión** ___ / ___ pressure.

intraoperatorio-a *a.* intraoperative, within the time frame of a surgical procedure.

intraóseo-a *a.* intraosseous, within the bone substance.

intrarrenal *a.* intrarenal, within the kidney; **fallo** ___ / ___ failure.

intrauterino-a *a.* intrauterine, within the uterus; **dispositivo** ___ / ___ device, coil.

intravenoso-a *a.* intravenous, within a vein; **infusión** ___ / ___ infusion; **inyección** ___ / ___ injection.

intraventricular *a.* intraventricular, within a ventricle.

intrínseco-a *a.* intrinsic, inherent; **factor** ___ / ___ factor, protein normally present in the gastric juice of humans.

introducir *vi.* to introduce.

introductor, intubador *m.* introducer, intubator, device used to intubate.

introitus *L.* introitus, an entrance or opening to a canal or cavity.

introspección *f.* introspection, self-analysis.

introversión *f. psych.* introversion, the act of turning one's interests inward with diminished interest in the outside world.

introvertido-a *m., f.* introvert; *a.* rel. to introversion.

intubación *f.* intubation, insertion of a tube into a conduit or cavity of the body.

intuición *f.* intuition.

intususcepción *f.* intussusception, invagination of one part of the intestine into the lumen of the adjoining part causing obstruction.

in utero *L.* in utero, within the uterus.

inútil *a.* useless; ineffective.

invadir *v.* to invade, to take over.

invaginación *f.* invagination, process of inclusion of one part into another.

invaginar *v.* invaginate, to introduce one part of a structure into another part of the same structure.

inválido-a *m., f.* invalid; *a.* crippled; void.

invariable *a.* invariable.

invasión *f.* invasion, the act of invading.

invasivo-a, invasor-a *a.* invasive, rel. to a germ or substance that invades adjacent tissues; **procedimiento no** ___ / non___ procedure.

inverso-a, invertido-a *a.* inverse, inverted.

investigación *f.* research; ___ **clínica** / clinical ___; ___ **de laboratorio** / laboratory ___.

investigar *vi.* to investigate, to research.

invisible *a.* invisible, that cannot be seen with the naked eye.

in vitro *L.* in vitro, rel. to laboratory tests or biological experimentation occurring outside the living body esp. in a test-tube; **fertilización** ___ / ___ fertilization.

in vivo *L.* in vivo, within the body of living organisms.

involución *f.* involution, a retrogressive change.

involucrado-a *a.* involved; **estar** ___ / to be ___; to become ___.

involuntario-a *a.* involuntary.

inyección *f.* injection, shot.

inyectar *v.* to inject, to introduce fluid in a tissue, cavity, or blood vessel with an injector.

inyector *m.* injector, device used to inject; syringe.

iodo, yodo *m.* iodine, nonmetallic element used as a germicide and as an aid in the development and function of the thyroid gland.

ión *m.* ion, an atom or group of atoms carrying a charge of electricity.

ionización *f.* ionization, dissociation of compounds into their constituent ions; **radiación por** ___ / ionizing radiation.

ipeca, jarabe de, *m.* syrup of ipecac, an emetic and expectorant agent.

ipsolateral *a.* ipsolateral, on the same side.

ir *vi.* to go; **irse** *vr.* to go away, to leave.

irascible *a.* irascible, easily angered.

iridectomía *f. surg.* iridectomy, removal of a part of the iris.

iridología *f.* iridology, study of the changes suffered by the iris during the course of an illness.

iris *m.* iris, contractile membrane situated between the lens and the cornea in the aqueous humor of the eye which regulates the entrance of light.

iritis *f.* iritis, infl. of the iris.

irracional *a.* irrational.

irradiación *f.* irradiation, therapeutic use of radiation.

irradiar *v.* to irradiate, to expose to or treat by radiation; to emit rays.

irreducible *a.* irreducible, that cannot be reduced.

irregular *a.* irregular.

irrigación *f.* irrigation, the act of washing out; flushing.

irrigar *vi.* to irrigate, to wash out.

irritabilidad *f.* irritability, property of an organism or tissue to react to its environment.

irritable *a.* irritable, that reacts to a stimulus.

irritación *f.* irritation, intense reaction to a pain or pathological condition.

isla *f.* island, isolated piece of tissue or group of cells.

islote *m.* islet, group of isolated cells of a different structure from the one of surrounding cells.

isométrico-a *a.* isometric, of equal dimensions.

isoniacida *f.* isoniazid, antibacterial medication used in the treatment of tuberculosis.

isotónico-a *a.* isotonic, having equal tension.

isótopo *m.* isotope, one of a group of chemical elements that present almost identical qualities but differ in atomic weight.

isquemia *f.* ischemia, lack of blood supply to a given part of the body; ___ **silenciosa** / silent ___.

isquémico-a *a.* ischemic, rel. to or suffering from ischemia; **ataque** ___ **transitorio** / transient ___ attack, temporary stoppage of blood supply to the brain.

isquión *m.* ischium, posterior part of the pelvis.

izquierda *f.* left; left hand; **a la** ___ / to the ___.

izquierdo-a *a.* left.

jabón *m.* soap.
jadear *v.* to pant.
jadeo *m.* panting, gasping, shortness of breath; wheeze.
jalea *f.* jelly; ___ **anticonceptiva** / contraceptive ___; ___ **vaginal** / vaginal ___.
jamais vu *Fr.* jamais vu, the perception of familiar surroundings as a new experience.
jamás *adv.* never, ever.
jamón *m.* ham.
jaqueca *f.* severe headache.
jarabe *m.* cough syrup; ___ **de ipecacuanca** / ipecac syrup.
jarra *f.* jar, pitcher; ___ **de agua** / pitcher of water.
jazmín *m.* jasmine; **té de** ___ / ___ tea.
jején *m.* gnat.
jengibre *m.* ginger.
jeringa, jeringuilla *f.* syringe; ___ **de aguja hueca** / hollow needle ___; ___ **con tubo de cristal** / glass cylinder ___; ___ **desechable** / disposable ___; ___ **hipodérmica** / hypodermic ___.
jimaguas *m. pl., Cuba* twins.
joroba *f.* hump.
jorobado-a *a.* hunchbacked; crooked.
joven *a.* young.
jovencito-a *a.* youngster.

juanete *m.* bunion *V.* **hallux valgus.**
jubilado-a *m., f.* retiree; *a.* retired.
juez-a *m., f.* judge.
jugar *vi.* to play.
jugo *m.* juice; ___ **gástrico** / gastric ___; ___ **intestinal** / intestinal ___; ___ **pancreático** / pancreatic ___; ___ **de ciruela** / prune ___; ___ **de manzana** / apple ___; ___ **de naranja** / orange ___; ___ **de piña** / pineapple ___; ___ **de tomate** / tomato ___; ___ **de toronja** / grapefruit ___; ___ **de uva** / grape ___; ___ **de zanahoria** / carrot ___.
jugoso-a *a.* juicy.
juguete *m.* toy.
junta *f.* meeting, gathering.
juntar *v.* to join, to gather together.
junto-a *a.* together.
juntura *f.* joint, juncture.
jurado *m.* jury.
juramento *m.* oath; ___ **hipocrático** / Hippocratic ___, medical oath.
jurisprudencia médica *f.* medical jurisprudence, the law as applied to the practice of medicine.
justicia *f.* justice.
justificar *vi.* to justify.
justo-a *a.* just, fair; **-mente** *adv.* justly.
juvenil *a.* juvenile; **delincuencia** ___ / ___ delinquency.
juventud *f.* youth.
juzgar *vi.* to judge; **a** ___ **por** / judging by.

K *abr.* **potasio** / kalium, potassium.

k *abr.* **kilogramo** / kilogram.

kala-azar *m.* kala-azar, *Hindi* black fever, visceral infestation by a protozoa.

Kaposi, enfermedad de *f.* Kaposi's disease, malignant neoplasm found on the skin of the lower extremities of adult males, very prevalent among individuals suffering from AIDS.

kernicterus *m.* kernicterus, type of jaundice found in the newborn.

kerosén, kerosene *m., f.* kerosene.

kilómetro *m.* kilometer.

Klebsiella *m.* Klebsiella, gram-negative bacilli associated with respiratory and urinary tract infections.

Klebs-Löffler, bacilo de *m.* Klebs-Löffler bacillus, the diphtheria bacillus.

Koch, bacilo de *m.* Koch's bacillus, *Mycobacterium tuberculosis,* the cause of tuberculosis in mammals.

Kussmaul, respiración de *f.* Kussmaul's breathing, deep and gasping respiration seen in cases of diabetic acidosis.

kwashiorkor *m.* kwashiorkor, severe protein deficiency seen in infants after weaning, esp. in tropical and subtropical areas.

l *abr.* **letal** / lethal; **ligero** / light.
L *abr.* **litro** / liter.
laberintitis *f.* labyrinthitis. 1. acute or chronic infl. of the labyrinth; 2. internal otitis.
laberinto *m.* labyrinth, maze. 1. communicating channels of the internal ear that function in rel. to hearing and to body balance; 2. channels and cavities that communicate forming a system.
labial *a.* labial, rel. to the lips; **glándulas ___-es** / ___ glands, situated between the labial mucosa and the orbicular muscle of the mouth.
labihendido-a *a.* harelipped.
lábil *a.* labile, unstable, fragile, changeable or easily altered.
labilidad *f.* lability, instability.
labio *m.* lip. 1. fleshy border; 2. liplike structure.
labio leporino *m.* harelip, cleft lip, congenital anomaly at the level of the upper lip, caused by faulty fusion of the upper jaw and the nasal processes; **cirugía del ___** / ___ suture.
laboratorio *m.* laboratory; ___ **de trabajo** / workshop.
laboratorista *m., f.* medical laboratory technician.
laborioso-a *a.* labored, laborious; difficult.
laceración *f.* laceration; tear.
lacerar *v.* to lacerate.
lacrimal, lagrimal *a.* lacrimal, lachrymal, rel. to tears or to tear ducts; **conducto ___** / ___ duct; **hueso ___** / ___ bone; **saco ___** / ___ sac.
lacrimógeno-a *a.* lachrymogenous, that produces tears.
lactacidemia *f.* lactacidemia, excessive lactic acid in the blood.
lactancia, lactación *f.* lactation, secretion of milk; ___ **materna** / breast-feeding.
lactar *v.* to nurse; to suckle.
lactasa *f.* lactase, intestinal enzyme that hydrolizes lactose producing dextrose and galactose.
lácteo-a *a.* lacteal, rel. to milk; **productos ___-s** / dairy products.
lactífero-a *a.* lactiferous, that secretes and conducts milk.
lactocele *m.* lactocele. V. **galactocele.**
lacto-ovovegetariano-a *m., f.* lacto-ovovegetarian, person whose diet consists of vegetables, eggs, and dairy products.
lactosa, lactina *f.* lactose, lactin, milk sugar; **intolerancia a la ___** / ___ intolerance, characterized by gastrointestinal disorders.
lado *m.* side; **al ___** / alongside; **al ___ de** / next to; **de ___** / sideways.
lagaña, legaña *f.* lema, gummy secretion of the eye.
lágrima *f.* tear.
lagrimear *v.* to shed tears.
lagrimeo *m.* lacrimation, tearing.

lagrimoso-a *a.* tearful.
laguna *f.* lacuna, small cavity or depression such as those found in the brain.
lalación, lambdacismo *f., m.* lallation. 1. phonetic disorder by which the letter *r* is pronounced as *l;* 2. infantile babbling.
Lamaze, método de *m.* Lamaze technique or method, method of natural childbirth by which the mother is trained in techniques of breathing and relaxation that facilitate the process of delivery.
lamentable *a.* regrettable.
lamentar *v.* to regret; **lamentarse** *vr.* to lament, to complain.
lamento *m.* lament, complaint.
lámina *f.* lamina, thin sheath or layer.
laminado-a *a.* laminated, formed by one or more laminae.
laminar *a.* laminar, rel. to a lamina; *v.* to laminate, to roll.
laminectomía *f. surg.* laminectomy, removal of one or more vertebral laminae.
laminilla *f.* lamella. 1. thin layer; 2. disk that is inserted in the eye to apply a medication.
lámpara *f.* lamp; ___ **de hendidura** / slit ___; ___ **infrarroja** / infrared ___; **luz de una ___** / lamplight.
lana *f.* wool.
lanceta *f.* lancet, lance, surgical instrument.
Landsteiner, clasificación de *f.* Landsteiner's classification, differentiation of blood types: O-A-B-AB.
langosta *f.* lobster.
languidez *f.* languor, languidness, exhaustion, lack of energy.
lánguido-a *a.* languid, weak.
lanolina *f.* lanolin, purified substance obtained from lamb's wool and used in ointments.
lanugo *m.* lanugo, soft fine hair that covers the body of the human fetus.
laparoscopía *f.* laparoscopy, examination of the peritoneal cavity with a laparoscope.
laparoscopio *m.* laparoscope, instrument used to visualize the peritoneal cavity.
laparotomía *f. surg.* laparotomy, incision and opening of the abdomen.
lápiz *m.* pencil.
lapso *m.* lapse, span, time interval.
largo-a *a.* long.
laringe *f.* larynx. 1. part of the respiratory tract situated in the upper part of the trachea; 2. voice organ.
laringectomía *f. surg.* laryngectomy, removal of the larynx.
laríngeo-a *a.* laryngeal, rel. to the larynx; **reflejo ___** / ___ reflex, cough produced by irritation of the larynx.
laringitis *f.* laryngitis, infl. of the larynx.
laringoespasmo *m.* laryngospasm, spasm of the laryngeal muscles.
laringofaringe *f.* laryngopharynx, inferior portion of the larynx.

laringofaringitis *f.* infl. of the larynx and the pharynx.

laringoplastia *f. surg.* laryngoplasty, plastic reconstruction of the larynx.

laringoscopia *f.* laryngoscopy, examination of the larynx; ___ **directa** / direct ___, by means of a laryngoscope; ___ **indirecta** / indirect ___, by means of a mirror.

laringoscopio *m.* laryngoscope, instrument used to examine the larynx.

larva *f.* larva, maggot, early stage of some organisms such as insects.

larvado-a *a.* larvate, rel. to an insidious or atypical symptom.

larval *a.* larval, rel. to larvae.

larvicida *m.* larvicide, agent that exterminates larvae.

lascivo-a *a.* lascivious, salacious, lustful.

laser *m.* laser. 1. acronym for Light Amplification by Stimulated Emission of Radiation; 2. microsurgical scalpel used in the cauterization of tumors.

laser, rayos de *m. pl.* laser beams, radiation rays applied for the purpose of destroying tissue or separating parts.

lasitud *f.* lassitude, languor.

lástima *f.* pity, compassion; *v.* **tener** ___ / to feel sorry, to pity; **¡qué** ___! / what a ___!

lastimado-a *a.* injured, hurt.

lastimadura *f.* injury, hurt.

lastimar *v.* to hurt, to injure; **lastimarse** *vr.* to get hurt.

lata *f.* [*metal*] tin; [*de alimento*] can.

latencia *f.* latency, the condition of being latent; **período de** ___ / ___ period.

latente *a.* latent, present but not active; with no apparent symptoms or manifestations.

lateral *a.* lateral, rel. to a side.

lateroflexión *f.* lateroflexion, lateral flexion.

latido *m.* beat; throb; ___ **del corazón** / heart ___; ___ **ectópico** / ectopic ___.

latir *v.* to beat, to throb.

lavabo *m.* washstand, basin.

lavado *m.* lavage, enema, irrigation of a cavity.

lavado de cerebro *m.* brain washing.

lavadora *f.* washing machine.

lavamanos *m.* washstand, washbowl.

lavaojos *m.* eyecup.

lavar *v.* to wash; **lavarse** *vr.* to wash oneself.

lavativa *f.* enema.

laxante *m.* laxative, mild physic.

laxitud *f.* laxity, relaxation; weakness.

laxo-a *a.* lax, relaxed, loose.

lección *f.* lesson.

lecitina *f.* lecithin, essential substance in the metabolism of fats found in animal tissue, esp. in the nervous tissue.

lectura *f.* reading; **impedimentos de la** ___ / ___ disorders; ___ **labial** / lip ___.

leche *f.* milk; ___ **condensada** / condensed ___; ___ **descremada** / skim ___; ___ **evaporada** / evaporated ___; ___ **materna** / mother's ___.

lechoso-a *a.* milky.

lechuga *f.* lettuce.

leer *vi.* to read.

legal *a.* legal, legitimate, according to the law; **pleito** ___ / lawsuit.

legaña *f.* lema, gummy secretion of the eye.

legislación médica *f.* medical legislation.

legitimidad *f.* legitimacy.

legítimo-a *a.* legitimate, that goes by the law; authentic.

lego-a *a.* lay, secular.

legumbre *f.* legume, vegetable.

leiomiofibroma *m.* leiomyofibroma, benign tumor of essentially connective fibrous and smooth muscular tissue.

leiomioma *m.* leiomyoma, benign tumor of essentially smooth muscular tissue.

leiomiosarcoma *f.* leiomyosarcoma, combined tumor of leiomyoma and sarcoma.

lejía *f.* lye, bleach; **envenenamiento por** ___ / ___ poisoning.

lejos *adv.* far, afar; **de** ___ / ___ away; **desde** ___ / from afar.

lengua *f.* 1. tongue, lingua; **depresor de** ___ / ___ depressor; 2. language; ___ **materna** / native ___.

lengua geográfica *f.* geographic tongue, tongue characterized by bare patches surrounded by thick epithelium, resembling a geographic map.

lenguaje *m.* language; ___ **hablado** / spoken ___.

lente *m.* lens; ___ **acromático** / achromatic ___; ___ **bicóncavo** / biconcave ___; ___**-s bifocales** / bifocal ___; ___ **de aumento** / magnifying glass; ___**-s de contacto** / contact lens; ___**-s intraoculares** / ___ implantation, intraocular; ___**-s trifocales** / trifocal ___.

lenteja *f.* lentil.

lenticular *a.* lenticular. 1. rel. to a lens; 2. rel. to the lens of the eye.

lento-a *a.* slow; sluggish, inactive; **-mente** *adv.* slowly.

lepra *f.* leprosy, Hansen's disease, infectious disease caused by the *Mycobacterium leprae* and characterized by more or less severe skin lesions.

leproso-a *m., f.* leper, person suffering from leprosy.

leptomeninges *f.* leptomeninges, the thinnest of the cerebral membranes: the pia madre and the arachnoid.

lesbiana *f.* lesbian, homosexual female.

lesbianismo *m.* lesbianism, feminine homosexuality.

lesión *f.* injury, lesion, contusion, wound; ___ **de latigazo** / whiplash ___; ___ **por una explosión próxima** / airblast ___; **sin** ___ **alguna** / injury-free.

letal *a.* lethal, mortal, that causes death; **dosis** ___ / ___ dose.

letárgico-a *a.* lethargic, lethargical.

Lesión	Lesion
de latigazo	whiplash
degenerativa	degenerative
depresiva	depressive
difusa	diffuse
funcional	functional
grosera	gross
periférica	peripheral
precancerosa	precancerous
sistemática	systemic
tóxica	toxic
traumática	traumatic
vascular	vascular

letargo *m.* lethargy, torpor.

letra *f.* [*del alfabeto*] letter; [*escritura*] handwriting.

leucaferesis *f.* leukapheresis, separation of leukocytes from a patient's blood and transfusion of the treated blood back into the patient.

leucemia *f.* leukemia, blood cancer; ___ **crónica** / chronic ___; ___ **linfocítica** / lymphocytic ___.

leucémico-a *a.* leukemic, rel. to or suffering from leukemia.

leucemoide *a.* leukemoid, with leukemia-like signs and symptoms.

leucina *f.* leucine, amino acid that is essential to the growth and metabolism of humans.

leucocito *m.* leukocyte, white blood cell, element of the blood important in the defensive and reparative functions of the body; ___ **acidófilo** / acidophil ___, that changes color with acid dye; ___ **basófilo** / basophil ___, that changes color with basic dye; ___ **eosinofílico** / eosinophilic ___, that stains readily with eosin; ___ **linfoide** / nongranular lymphoid ___; ___ **neutrófilo** / neutrophil ___, that has an affinity for neutral stains; ___ **polimorfonucleado** / polymorphonuclear ___, having multilobed nuclei.

leucopenia *f.* leukopenia, below normal number of leukocytes in the blood.

leucoplasia *f.* leukoplakia, opalescent, precancerous patches of the mucous membrane of the mouth or tongue.

leucorrea *f.* leukorrhea, whitish vaginal discharge.

levadura *f.* yeast, leaven, minute fungi capable of producing fermentation; used in nutrition as a source of protein and vitamin.

levantar *v.* to raise, to lift, to pull up; **levantarse** *vr.* to get up.

leve *a.* light, slight.

levocardia *f.* levocardia, transposition of the abdominal viscera with normal position of the heart on the left side of the thorax.

levodopa *f.* levodopa, *L.* dopa, chemical substance used in the treatment of Parkinson's disease.

levulosa *f.* levulose. *V.* **fructosa.**

ley *f.* law; ___ **del buen Samaritano** / good Samaritan ___, legal protection to a professional who gives aid in an emergency.

liberación *f.* liberation.

liberado-a *a.* freed.

liberar, librar *v.* to liberate, to free, to release.

libertad *f.* liberty; *v.* **tener** ___ **para** / to be free to.

libre *a.* free; **asociación** ___ / ___ association.

librería *f.* bookstore.

libreta *f.* notebook.

libro *m.* book.

licencia *f.* license, permit, licensure, authorization; ___ **para ejercer la medicina** / medical ___.

licenciado-a *m., f.* attorney, licentiate.

licor *m.* liquor. *V.* **liquor.**

licuar *v.* to liquify, to dissolve.

lidocaína *f.* lidocaine, anesthetic.

Liga de la Leche, La *f.* La Leche League, an organization that promotes breast-feeding.

ligadura *f.* ligature, tie, affixture; linkage.

ligamento *m.* ligament. 1. bands of connective tissue fibers that protect the joints; ___ **acromioclavicular** / acromioclavicular ___, extending from the clavicle to the acromion; ___ **ancho uterino** / broad uterine ___, peritoneal fold that extends laterally from the uterus to the pelvic wall; 2. protective band of fascia and muscles that connect or support viscerae.

ligar *vi.* to tie, to apply a ligature; ___ **las trompas** / ___ the tubes.

ligazón *f.* binding, bandage.

ligero-a *a.* light, slight; **-mente** *adv.* lightly, slightly.

lima *f.* [*fruta*] lime; **jugo de** ___ / ___ juice; [*instrumento*] file.

limar *v.* to file; to smooth.

límbico-a *a.* limbic, marginal; **sistema** ___ / ___ system, group of cerebral structures.

limbo *m.* limbus, the edge or border of a part; ___ **de la córnea** / ___ cornea.

liminal *a. psych.* liminal, almost imperceptible.

limitación *f.* limitation; restriction.

limitado-a *a.* limited, restricted; **movimiento** ___ / restricted motion.

limitar *v.* to limit, to restrict.

límite *m.* limit; ___ **de asimilación** / assimilation ___; ___ **de percepción** / ___ of perception; ___ **de saturación** / saturation ___.

limón *m.* lemon.

limonada *f.* lemonade.

limpiar *v.* to clean.

limpieza *f.* cleaning; cleanliness.

limpio-a *a.* clean.

linaje *m.* pedigree, ancestral line of descent.

lindo-a *a.* pretty.

línea *f.* line; wrinkle; guide.

linear *a.* lineal, resembling a line.

linfa *f.* lymph, clear fluid found in lymphatic vessels.

linfadenectomía *f. surg.* lymphadenectomy, removal of lymphatic channels and nodes.

linfadenitis *f.* lymphadenitis, infl. of the lymphatic ganglia.

linfadenopatía *f.* lymphadenopathy, any disease affecting the lymph nodes; ___ **axilar** / axillary ___; ___ **biliar** / portal ___ /; ___ ´cervical / cervical ___; ___ **generalizada** / generalized ___; ___ **mediastínica** / mediastinal ___; ___ **supraclavicular** / supraclavicular ___.

linfangiectasis *f.* lymphangiectasis, dilation of the lymphatic vessels.

linfangiograma *m.* lymphangiogram, x-ray of the lymph nodes and vessels obtained with the use of a contrasting medium.

linfangitis *f.* lymphangitis, infl. of the lymphatic vessels.

linfático-a *a.* lymphatic, rel. to lymph; **ganglios** ___-s / lymph nodes; **sistema** ___ / ___ system.

linfedema *m.* lymphedema, edema caused by blockage of the lymph vessels.

linfoblasto *m.* lymphoblast, early stage of a lymphocyte.

linfocito *m.* lymphocyte, lymphatic cell; ___ **B** / B cell, important in the production of antibodies.

linfocitopenia, linfopenia *f.* lymphocytopenia, lymphopenia, diminished number of lymphocytes in the blood.

linfocitos T *m. pl.* T cells, lymphocytes differentiated in the thymus that direct the immunological response and alert the B cells to respond to antigens; ___ **inductor, (ayudante)** / helper ___, enhance production of antibody forming cells from B cells; ___ **citotóxico** / cytotoxic ___, kill foreign cells (as in rejection of transplanted organs); ___ **supresor** / suppressor ___, suppress production of antibody forming cells from B cells.

linfocitosis *f.* lymphocytosis, excessive number of lymphocytes in the blood.

linfogranuloma venéreo *f.* lymphogranuloma venereum, viral disorder that may lead to elephantiasis of the genitalia and rectal stricture.

linfogranulomatosis *f.* lymphogranulomatosis. *V.* **Hodgkin, enfermedad de.**

linfoide *a.* lymphoid, that resembles the lymphatic tissue.

linfoma *m.* lymphoma, any neoplasm of the lymphatic tissue.

linfomatoide *a.* lymphomatoid, rel. to or resembling a lymphoma.

linfopenia, linfocitopenia *f.* lymphopenia, lymphocytopenia, diminished number of lymphocytes in the blood.

linforreticular *a.* lymphoreticular, rel. to reticuloendothelial cells of the lymph nodes.

linfosarcoma *m.* lymphosarcoma, malignant neoplasm of the lymphoid tissue.

lingual *a.* lingual, rel. to the tongue.

língula *f.* lingula, tonguelike projection or structure.

linimento *m.* liniment, liquid substance for external use.

linitis *f.* linitis. *V.* **gastritis.**

lino *m.* linen.

linterna *f.* flashlight.

lío *m.* mess, confusion.

liodermia *f.* glossy skin, a sign of atrophy or traumatism of the nerves.

liofilización *f.* freeze-drying.

lipectomía *f. surg.* lipectomy, removal of fat tissue; ___ **submental** / submental ___, under the chin.

lipemia *f.* lipemia, abnormal presence of fat in the blood.

lipidemia *f.* lipidemia, excess lipids in the blood.

lípido *m.* lipid, lipide, organic substance that does not dissolve in water but is soluble in alcohol, ether, or chloroform.

lipodistrofia *f.* lipodystrophy, metabolic disorder of fats.

lipoma *m.* lipoma, adipose tissue tumor.

lipomatosis *f.* lipomatosis. 1. condition caused by excessive accumulation of fat in a given area; 2. multiple lipomas.

lipoproteínas *f. pl.* lipoproteins, proteins combined with lipid compounds that contain a high concentration of cholesterol; ___ **de densidad baja** / low-density ___.

liposarcoma *m.* liposarcoma, malignant tumor containing fatty elements.

liposis *f.* liposis, obesity, excessive accumulation of fat in the body.

liposoluble *a.* liposoluble, that dissolves in fatty substances.

liposucción *f.* liposuction, process of extracting fat by high vacuum pressure.

liquen *m.* lichen, noncontagious papular skin lesion; ___ **plano** / ___ planus.

líquido *m.* fluid, liquid; **balance de** ___ / ___ balance; ___ **amniótico** / amniotic ___; ___ **cefalorraquídeo** / cerebrospinal ___; ___ **extracelular** / extracellular ___; ___ **extravascular** / extravascular ___; ___. **intercelular, intersticial** / intercellular, interstitial ___; **retención de** ___ / ___ retention; *v.* **tomar** ___-s / to take ___-s; **-a** *a.* liquid.

liquor *L.* liquor. 1. a liquid, esp. an aqueous solution containing a medicinal substance; 2. general term used for certain fluids of the body.

lisiado-a *a.* crippled.

lisina *f.* lysin, antibody that dissolves or destroys cells or bacteria.

lisis *f.* lysis. 1. destruction or dissolution of red cells, bacteria, or any antigen by lysin; 2. gradual cessation of the symptoms of a disease.

lista *f.* list; ___ **de accidentados** / casualty ___.

listo-a *a.* ready; clever.

litiasis *f.* lithiasis, formation of calculi, esp. in the biliary and urinary tracts.

litio *m.* lithium, metallic element used as a tranquilizer in severe cases of psychosis.

litotomía *f. surg.* lithotomy, incision in an organ

or conduit to remove stones.

litotripsia *f.* lithotripsy, crushing of calculi present in the kidney, ureter, bladder, or gallbladder.

litotriturador *m.* lithotriptor, machine or device used to crush calculi; ___ **extracorporal con ondas de choque** / extracorporeal shock wave ___.

lividez *f.* lividity, discoloration resulting from the gravitation of blood; ___ **cadavérica** / postmortem lividity.

lívido-a *a.* livid, [una persona] ash blue.

lobar *a.* lobar, rel. to a lobe; **pulmonía** ___ / ___ pneumonia.

lobectomía *f. surg.* lobectomy, excision of a lobe.

lobotomía *f. surg.* lobotomy, incision of a cerebral lobe to correct certain mental disorders; ___ **completa** / complete ___; ___ **izquierda anterior** / left lower ___; ___ **parcial** / partial ___.

lobular *a.* lobular, rel. to a lobule.

lobulillo *m.* lobule, small lobe.

lóbulo *m.* lobe, rounded, well-defined portion of an organ.

local *a.* local, rel. to an isolated area, such as local anesthesia; **aplicación** ___ / ___ application; **reaparición** ___ / ___ recurrence.

localización *f.* localization, location. 1. reference to the point of origin of a sensation; 2. determination of the origin of an infection or lesion.

localizar *vi.* to localize; to locate.

loción *f.* lotion.

loco-a *m., f.* insane person; *a.* mad, insane.

locomoción *f.* locomotion.

locular *a.* locular, loculated, rel. to loculi.

lóculo *m.* loculus, small cavity.

locura *f.* madness, insanity, lunacy.

locus *L.* locus, localization of a gene in a chromosome.

logafasia *f.* logaphasia, motor aphasia gen. caused by a cerebral lesion.

logagrafia *f.* logagraphia, inability to express thoughts in writing.

logamnesia *f.* logamnesia, sensorial aphasia, inability to recognize written or spoken words.

lógico-a *a.* logic, logical; reasonable.

logopedia *f.* logopedics, study and treatment of speech defects.

lograr *v.* to achieve; to reach.

lombriz *f.* earthworm; ___ **intestinal** / pinworm, belly worm; ___ **solitaria** / tapeworm.

lonche *m. H.A.* lunch, midday meal.

longevidad *f.* longevity. 1. long duration of life; 2. life span.

longitudinal *a.* longitudinal, lengthwise.

loquios *m.* lochia, bloody, serosanguineous discharge from the uterus and the vagina during the first few weeks after delivery.

lordosis *f.* lordosis, abnormally increased curvature of the lumbar spine; saddle back.

lubricación *f.* lubrication.

lubricante *m.* lubricant, oily agent that when applied diminishes friction between two surfaces; ___ **oleaginoso** / oil-based ___.

lubricar *vi.* to lubricate, to apply a lubricant to a surface.

lúcido-a *a.* lucid, clear of mind.

lucha *f.* struggle; fight.

luchar *v.* to struggle; to fight.

luego *adv.* in a while; then; **conj.** therefore; **desde** ___ / of course; **hasta** ___ / so long, good-bye.

luético-a *a.* luetic, syphilitic, rel. to or suffering from syphilis.

lugar *m.* place, space; **en** ___ **de** / in ___ of; *v.* **poner en su** ___ / to put in ___; **tener** ___ / to take ___.

lujuria *f.* lust, lewdness, lasciviousness.

lujurioso-a *a.* lustful, lewd, libidinous.

lumbago *m.* lumbago, pain in the lower portion of the back.

lumbalgia *f.* low backache.

lumbar *a.* lumbar, rel. to the part of the back between the thorax and the pelvis; back; **punción** ___ / ___ puncture, spinal tap; **vértebras** ___-es / ___ vertebrae.

lumbricosis *f.* lumbricosis, infestation by earthworms.

lumen *m.* lumen. 1. space in a cavity, conduit, or organ; 2. unit of light.

Luminal *m.* Luminal, trade name for a compound containing phenobarbital and used as a sedative.

luminal *a.* luminal, rel. to light in a conduit or canal.

luminiscencia, luminosidad *f.* luminescence, luminosity, emission of light without production of heat.

luminoso-a *a.* luminous, rel. to luminosity.

luna *f.* moon.

lunar *m.* mole; blemish; *a.* rel. to the moon.

lunático-a *m., f.* lunatic, crazy person.

lupa *f.* magnifying glass.

lupa binocular *f.* loupe, convex magnifying lens used esp. by surgeons and ophthalmologists.

lupus *L.* lupus, chronic skin disease of unknown origin that causes degenerative local lesions; ___ **eritematoso discoide** / ___ erythematosus, discoid, disease that causes irritation of the skin and is characterized by squamous plaques with reddish borders; ___ **eritematoso sistémico** / ___ erythematosus, systemic, characterized by febrile episodes affecting the viscera and the nervous system.

lúteo-a, luteínico-a *a.* luteal, rel. to the corpus luteum.

luto *m.* mourning; **estar de** ___ / to mourn.

luxación *f.* dislocation, luxation; ___ **cerrada** / closed ___; ___ **complicada** / complicated ___; ___ **congénita** / congenital ___.

luz *f.* light; *v.* **dar a** ___ / to give birth.

128

LL fourteenth letter of the Spanish alphabet.
llaga *f.* sore, ulcer, blain.
llamada *f.* call; ___ **de teléfono** / telephone ___.
llave *f.* key.
llegada *f.* arrival; coming.
llegar *vi.* to arrive; to reach; to attain; ___ **a ser** / to become; **llegarse** *vr.* to approach.
llenar *v.* to fill; to complete.
lleno-a *a.* full, complete.

llenura *f.* fullness, plenty, abundance; **tener** ___ / to be very full.
llevar *v.* to carry; to take; to transport; ___ **puesto** / to be wearing; ___ **a cabo** / to carry out; **llevarse** *vr.* to take away; ___ **a cabo** / to take place; ___ **bien** / to get along well; ___ **mal** / not to get along.
llorar *v.* to cry.
lloradera *f.* weeping.
llover *vi.* to rain.
lluvia *f.* rain.
lluvioso-a *a.* rainy.

M *abr.* **maduro** / mature; **maligno-a** / malignant; **minuto** / minute; **morfina** / morphine.

macerar *v.* to macerate, to soften by soaking.

macizo-a *a.* compact, solid.

macrocefalia *f.* macrocephalia, abnormally large head.

macrocefálico-a *a.* macrocephalic, having an abnormally large head.

macrocitemia, macrocitosis *f.* macrocythemia, macrocytosis, larger than normal erythrocytes in the blood.

macrocosmo *m.* macrocosm. 1. the universe considered as a whole; 2. the total or entire structure of something.

Macrodantina *f.* Macrodantin, trade name for furantoin, bactericide used in the treatment of urinary infections.

macrófago *m.* macrophage, macrophages, mononuclear phagocytic cell; **migración de ___-s** / ___ migration.

macroglosia *f.* macroglossia, enlargement of the tongue.

macrognatia *f.* macrognathia, enlargement of the jaw.

macromolécula *f.* macromolecule, a large molecule such as a protein.

macroscópico-a *a.* macroscopic, visible to the naked eye.

macrospora *f.* macrospore, large spore.

mácula *f.* macula, macule, speck, small discolored spot in the skin; **___ lútea** / ___ lutea, small yellowish area next to the center of the retina.

maculado-a *a.* maculate.

macular *a.* macular, rel. to macules.

maculopapular *a.* maculopapular, rel. to macules and papules.

macho *m.* male; *a.* male; manly.

madera *f.* wood.

madrastra *f.* stepmother.

madre *f.* mother, **___ soltera** / unwed ___.

madrugada *f.* daybreak; **de ___** / at dawn.

madrugar *vi.* to rise early.

madurar *v.* to mature; to ripen.

madurez *f.* maturity; ripeness, stage of full development.

maduro-a *a.* mature, ripened.

magistral *a.* magistral, rel. to medication that is prepared according to the physician's indications.

magma *f.* magma. 1. suspension of particles in a small amount of water; 2. viscous mass composed of organic material.

magnesia *f.* magnesia, magnesium oxide; **leche de ___** / milk of ___.

magnesio *m.* magnesium; **sulfato de ___** / ___ sulfate.

magnético-a *a.* magnetic, magnetical, rel. to or that has the property of a magnet; **campo ___** / ___ field.

magnetismo *m.* magnetism, the property of attracting or repelling.

magnetoelectricidad *f.* magnetoelectricity, electricity induced by a magnet.

magnífico-a *a.* superb, wonderful.

magnitud *f.* magnitude.

magulladura *f.* bruise, contusion.

majadero-a *a.* spoiled, cranky.

mal *m.* malady, illness, disease.

mal, malo-a *a.* bad; evil; **mal genio** / ill temper; **mal** *adv.* badly; wrongly; **de ___ en peor** / from bad to worse; *v.* **hacer ___** / to harm, to hurt.

malacia *f.* malacia, softening or loss of consistency of organs or tissues.

malacoplaquia *f.* malacoplakia, formation of soft patches in the mucous membrane of a hollow organ.

malagradecido-a *a.* ungrateful.

malar *a.* malar, rel. to the cheek or the cheekbone.

malaria *f.* malaria. *V.* **paludismo.**

malaricida *a.* malariacidal, that kills the parasites of malaria.

malcriado-a *a.* ill-bred, spoiled.

maleable *a.* malleable.

maléolo *m.* malleolus, hammerlike protuberance, such as the ones on either side of the ankle.

malestar *m.* malaise, discomfort, uneasiness.

maleta *f.* valise, suitcase.

malformación *f.* malformation, anomaly, or deformity, esp. congenital.

malfuncionamiento *m.* malfunction, disorder.

malhumor *m.* bad temper.

malhumorado-a *a.* sullen, bad-tempered.

malignidad *f.* malignancy. 1. quality of being malignant; 2. cancerous tumor.

maligno-a *a.* malignant, virulent, pernicious, having a destructive effect.

malnutrición *f.* malnutrition, deficient nutrition.

maloclusión *f.* malocclusion, defective bite.

malpresentación *f.* malpresentation, abnormal presentation of the fetus at the time of delivery.

malrotación *f.* malrotation, abnormal or defective rotation of an organ or part.

malta *f.* malt.

maltosa *f.* maltose, a type of sugar.

maltratar *v.* to abuse, to mistreat, to manhandle; **___ de palabra** / verbal abuse.

malunión *f.* malunion, imperfect union of a fracture.

malleus *L.* (*pl.* **mallei**) malleus, one of the three ossicles of the middle ear.

mama *f.* mamma, breast, milk-secreting gland in the female; **enfermedad benigna de la ___** / benign breast disease.

mamá *f.* mom, endearing term for mother.

mamalgia *f.* mammalgia, pain in the mamma.

mamaplastia, mamoplastia *f. surg.* mammaplasty, mammoplasty, plastic surgery of the breasts; **___ de aumento** / augmentation **___**; **___ de reconstrucción** / reconstructive **___**; **___ de reducción** / reduction **___**.

mamar *v.* to suckle, to draw milk from the breast; **dar de ___** / to breast-feed.

mamario-a *a.* mammary, rel. to the mamma; **glándulas ___-s** / **___ glands.**

mamectomía *f.* mammectomy. *V.* **mastectomía.**

mamífero *m.* mammal.

mamilado-a *a.* mammillated, presenting small protuberances that resemble nipples.

mamilar *a.* mammillary, resembling a nipple.

mamiliplastia *f. surg.* mammilliplasty, plastic surgery of the nipple.

mamilitis *f.* mammillitis, infl. of the nipple.

mamitis, mastitis *f.* mammitis, mastitis, infl. of the mammary gland.

mamograma *m.* mammogram, x-ray of the breast.

manco-a *m., f.* one-handed person.

mancha *f.* spot, blemish, macula, stain.

manchado-a *a.* spotted, soiled.

manchar *v.* to soil, to spot; to stain; **mancharse** *vr.* to become stained or spotted.

mandar *v.* to order, to command; to send.

mandato *m.* order, command.

mandíbula *f.* mandible, mandibula, horseshoe-shaped bone that constitutes the lower jaw; **___ inferior** / lower **___**; **___ superior** / upper **___**.

mandibular *a.* mandibular, rel. to the mandible.

manejable *a.* manageable.

manejar *v.* to conduct, to drive.

manera *f.* manner, method, way.

manerismo *m.* mannerism, peculiar manifestation in dress, speech, or action.

manga *f.* sleeve.

mango *m.* mango. 1. tropical fruit; 2. handle.

manguito *m.* cuff, bandlike fibrous tissue surrounding a joint; **___ rotador** / rotator **___**, musculotendinous; **ruptura del ___ rotador** / rotator tear.

maní *m.* peanut; **mantequilla de ___** / **___ butter.**

manía *f. psych.* mania, emotional disorder characterized by extreme excitement, exalted emotions, rapid succession of ideas, and fluctuating moods.

maníaco-a, maniático-a *a.* maniac, maniacal, afflicted by mania; **maníacodepresivo** / manic-depressive.

manicomio *m.* insane asylum, madhouse.

manifestación *f.* manifestation, revelation.

manifestar *vi.* to manifest, to express; **manifestarse** *vr.* to appear, [*enfermedad*] to reveal itself.

maniobra *f.* maneuver, skillful manual procedure such as executed by the obstetrician in the delivery of a baby.

manipulación *f.* manipulation, professional treatment involving the use of hands.

manipular *v.* to manipulate, to handle.

maniquí *m.* manikin, representative figure of the human body.

mano *f.* hand; **deformidades adquiridas de la ___** / acquired **___** deformities; **apoyo de la ___** / **___** rest; **hecho a ___** / handmade.

manómetro *m.* manometer, device used to measure the pressure of liquids or gases.

manteca *f.* lard, animal fat.

mantener *vi.* to sustain, to support; **mantenerse** *vr.* to hold or keep up; to support oneself.

mantenimiento *m.* maintenance, sustenance.

mantequilla *f.* butter.

manto *m.* mantle, covering.

manual *a.* manual.

manubrium *L.* manubrium, handle-shaped structure.

manutención *f.* maintenance, support; child care.

manzana *f.* apple.

manzanilla *f.* camomile, sedative tea used to alleviate gastrointestinal discomfort.

maña *f.* bad habit.

mañana *f.* morning; tomorrow; **por la ___** / in the morning; **muy de ___** / very early in the morning.

máquina *f.* machine, apparatus.

mar *m.* sea.

marasmo *m.* marasmus, extreme malnutrition, emaciation, esp. in young children.

maravilloso-a *a.* marvelous, wonderful.

marca *f.* mark, sign; **___ de la viruela** / pockmark; **___ de nacimiento** / birthmark; **___ en fresa** / strawberry **___**; **___ registrada** trademark.

marcador *m.* marker, indicator.

marcapaso *m.* pacemaker, electronic cardiac pacer; pacer, regulator of cardiac rhythm; **___ interno** / internal **___**; **___ temporal** / temporary **___**.

marcar *vi.* to mark; to brand; to point out.

marcha *f.* gait, walk; **___ anserina** / waddling **___**, widespread walk; **___ atáxica** / ataxic **___**, staggering; **___ cerebelosa** / cerebellar **___**; **___ espástica** / spastic **___**; **___ hemipléjica** / hemiplegic **___**, circular movement of one of the lower extremities.

mareado-a *a.* dizzy, light-headed.

marearse *vr.* to get motion sickness; to become dizzy.

mareo *m.* dizziness; motion sickness; **___ de altura** / altitude sickness.

margarina *f.* margarine.

margen *m.* margin, border.

marginación *f.* margination, accumulation and adhesion of leukocytes to the epithelial cells of the blood vessel walls at the beginning of an inflammatory process.

marginal *a.* marginal, rel. to a margin; **caso ___** / **___** case.

marido *m.* husband.

mariguana, marihuana *f.* marihuana, marijuana. *V.* **cannabis.**

marisco *m.* shellfish.

marital *a.* marital, rel. to marriage.

marsupialización *f. surg.* marsupialization, conversion of a closed cavity into an open pouch.

martillo *m.* hammer. 1. common name for malleus, small bone of the middle ear; 2. instrument used in physical examination.

más *adv.* more, to a greater degree; **a ___ tardar** / at the latest; **por ___ que** / however much; **___ allá** / beyond; **___ que** / more than; **___ vale** / better to.

masa *f.* mass, body formed by coherent particles.

masaje *m.* massage, process of manipulation of different parts of the body by rubbing or kneading; **___ cardíaco** / cardiac **___**, resuscitation.

masajista *m., f.* masseur, masseuse, person who performs massage.

mascar, masticar *vi.* to chew.

máscara *f.* mask. 1. covering of the face; 2. appearance of the face, esp. as a pathological manifestation.

mascarilla *f.* death mask.

masculinización *f.* masculinization. *V.* **virilización.**

masculino-a *a.* masculine, rel. to the male sex.

masetero *m.* masseter, principal muscle in mastication.

masivo-a *a.* massive.

masoquismo *m. psych.* masochism, abnormal condition by which sexual gratification is obtained from self-inflicted pain or pain inflicted by others.

massa *L.* massa, middle commissure of the brain.

mastadenitis *f.* mastadenitis. *V.* **mamitis.**

mastalgia *f.* mastalgia. *V.* **mamalgia.**

mastectomía *f. surg.* mastectomy, plastic surgery of the breasts.

masticación *f.* mastication, the act of chewing.

mastitis *f.* mastitis. *V.* **mamitis; ___ cística** / cystic **___**, fibrocystic disease of the mamma; **___ por estasis** / caked breast.

mastoideo-a *a.* mastoid. 1. rel. to the mastoid process; **antro ___** / **___ antrum; células ___-s** / cells, air spaces in the mastoid process; 2. that resembles a breast or nipple.

mastoides *m.* mastoid process, rounded apophysis of the temporal bone.

mastoiditis *f.* mastoiditis, infl. of the air cells of the mastoid process.

mastopatía *f.* mastopathy, any disorder of the mammary glands.

mastopexia *f. surg.* correction of a pendulous breast.

masturbación *f.* masturbation, autostimulation and manipulation of the genitals to achieve sexual pleasure.

matar *v.* to kill.

materia *f.* matter, substance.

material *m.* material; *a.* material.

maternidad *f.* maternity; **hospital de ___** / **___** hospital.

materno-a *a.* maternal, rel. to the mother; **línea ___** / matrilineal, tracing descent on the female side.

matidez *f.* dullness, diminished resonance to palpation.

matriz *f.* matrix, basic material; cast.

matutino-a *a.* of the morning, rel. to the early hours of the day; **enfermedad ___ del embarazo** / morning sickness; **rigidez ___ muscular y de las articulaciones** / morning stiffness.

maxilar *a.* maxillary, rel. to the maxilla; **hueso ___ de la mandíbula** / jawbone.

maxilla *L.* maxilla, bone of the upper jaw.

mayonesa *f.* mayonnaise.

mayor *a.* greater, [*edad*] older; **-mente** *adv.* mostly, mainly.

mayoría *f.* majority.

máximo-a *a.* maximum, the most.

meatal *a.* meatal, rel. to a meatus.

meato *m.* meatus, passage or channel in the body.

mecánico-a *m., f.* mechanic; *a.* mechanical.

mecanismo *m.* mechanism. 1. involuntary response to a stimulus; **___ de defensa** / defense **___**; 2. machine-like structure.

meconio *m.* meconium. 1. first feces of the newborn; 2. opium.

media *f.* mean. 1. average; 2. middle coat of a blood vessel or artery.

mediador-a *m., f.* mediator, entity or person that mediates.

medial *a.* medial, rel. to or situated towards the middle.

medianoche *f.* midnight.

mediante *adv.* by means of.

mediar *v.* to mediate.

medias *f. pl.* socks, stockings; **___ elásticas** / elastic stockings.

mediastinitis *f.* mediastinitis, infl. of the tissues of the mediastinum.

mediastino *m.* mediastinum. 1. mass of tissues and organs separating the lungs; 2. cavity between two organs.

mediastinoscopía *f.* mediastinoscopy, endoscopic examination of the mediastinum.

medicación, medicamento *f., m.* medication, medicament; **medicamento de patente** / patent medicine.

Medicaid *m.* Medicaid, U.S. government program to provide health care for the poor.

Medicare *m.* Medicare, U.S. government program that subsidizes health care esp. for the elderly and the disabled.

medicina *f.* 1. medicine, the healing arts; **___ clínica** / clinical **___**; **___ comunal, al servicio de la comunidad** / community **___**; **___ deportiva** / sports **___**; **___ ecológica** / environmental **___**; **___ del espacio** / aerospace **___**; **___ familiar** / family practice; **___ forense** / forensic **___**; **___ industrial** / industrial **___**; **___ interna** / internal **___**; **___ legal** / legal

___; ___ **nuclear** / nuclear ___; ___ **ocupacional** / occupational ___; ___ **preventiva** / preventive ___; ___ **socializada** / socialized ___; ___ **tropical** / tropical ___; ___ **veterinaria** / veterinary ___; 2. medication, medicine, drug; **estudiante de** ___ / medical student.

medicina holística *f.* holistic medicine, an approach to medicine that considers the human being as an integral functional unit.

medicinal *a.* medicinal, rel. to medicine or with medical properties.

médico-a *m., f.* physician, doctor; **cuerpo** ___ / medical staff; ___ **consultante, asesor** / consulting ___; ___ **de asistencia primaria** / primary ___; ___ **de cabecera o primario** / primary ___; ___ **de familia** / family ___; ___ **de guardia** / doctor on call; ___ **forense** / coroner; ___ **interno** / intern; ___ **recomendante** / referring ___; ___ **residente** / resident, physician serving a residency; *a.* medical, medicinal, rel. to medicine or that cures; **asistencia** ___ / ___ assistance; **atención** ___ / ___ care.

medicolegal *a.* medicolegal, the practice of medicine as related to law.

medida *f.* measure; measurement; **con** ___ / moderately.

medio *m.* medium; 1. means to attain an effect; 2. substance that transmits impulses; 3. substance used in the culture of bacteria; **en** ___ **de** / in the middle of; **por** ___ **de** / by means of; **-a** half; in part; **línea** ___ / medial line; **punto** ___ / medium.

medioambiental *a.* environmental, rel. to the environment.

medio ambiente *m.* environment; **peligros del** ___ / environmental hazards.

mediodía *m.* noon.

medir *vi.* to measure; **cinta de** ___ / measuring tape; **taza de** ___ / measuring cup.

médula espinal *f.* spinal cord, a column of nervous tissue that extends from the medulla oblongata to the first or second lumbar vertebrae, and from which arise all the nerves that go to the trunk of the body and to the extremities.

médula oblongata *f.* medulla oblongata, portion of the medulla located at the base of the brain.

médula ósea *f.* bone marrow, spongelike tissue present in the cavities of bones; **punción y aspiración de la** ___ / ___ puncture and aspiration; **fallo de la** ___ / ___ failure; **transplante de la** ___ / ___ transplant.

medular *a.* medullary, rel. to the medulla; **celularidad** ___ / ___ cellularity; **infiltración** ___ / ___ infiltration; **insuficiencia** ___ / ___ failure; **lesión** ___ / ___ injury.

megacéfalo-a *a.* megacephalic. *V.* **macrocéfalo.**

megacolon *m.* megacolon, abnormally large colon.

megaesófago *m.* megaesophagus, abnormally large dilation of the inferior portion of the esophagus.

megalomanía *f. psych.* megalomania, delusions of grandeur.

megalómano-a *a. psych.* megalomaniac, suffering from megalomania.

megavitamina *f.* megavitamin, a dose of vitamin that exceeds the daily requirement.

meiosis *f.* meiosis, process of cell division that results in the production of gametes.

mejilla *f.* cheek.

mejor *a.* [*comp. of* bueno] better; best; **la** ___ **medicina** / the best medication; *sup.* es el, la ___ / it is the best; *adv.* better; *v.* **estar** ___ / to be ___; *vr.* **ponerse** ___ / to get ___; **tanto** ___ / so much the ___.

mejoramiento, mejoría *m., f.* improvement, amelioration.

mejorana *f.* marjoram.

mejorar *v.* to improve; **mejorarse** *vr.* to get better.

mejoría *f.* improvement, amelioration.

melancolía *f.* melancholia, marked depression.

melancólico-a *a.* rel. to or suffering from melancholia.

melanina *f.* melanin, dark pigmentation of the skin, hair, and parts of the eye.

melanocito *m.* melanocyte, melanine-producing cell.

melanoma *m.* melanoma, malignant tumor made of melanocytes.

melanosis *f.* melanosis, condition characterized by an unusual deposit of dark pigmentation in various tissues or organs.

melanuria *f.* melanuria, presence of dark pigmentation in the urine.

melena *f.* melena, abnormally dark and pasty stool containing digested blood.

melocotón *m.* peach.

mellizos-as *m., f., pl.* twins. *V.* **gemelos.**

membrana *f.* membrane, web, thin layer of tissue that covers or protects an organ or structure; ___-s **arteriopulmonares** / pulmonary arterial webs; ___ **de la placenta** / placental ___; ___ **mucosa** / mucous ___; ___ **nuclear** / nuclear ___; ___ **permeable** / permeable ___; ___ **semipermeable** / semipermeable ___; ___ **sinovial** / synovial ___; ___ **timpánica** / tympanic ___.

membranoso-a *a.* membranous, rel. to or of the nature of a membrane.

memorando *m.* memorandum.

memoria *f.* memory, faculty that allows the registration and recall of experiences; ___ **inmediata** / short-term ___.

memorizar *vi.* to memorize.

menarca *m.* menarche, beginning of menstruation.

mendelismo *m.* Mendelism, set of principles that explains the transmission of certain genetic traits.

menguar *v.* to subside, to diminish.

meníngeo-a *a.* meningeal, rel. to the meninges.

meninges *f.* meninges, three layers of connective tissue that surround the brain and the spinal cord.

meningioma *m.* meningioma, a slow-growing vascular neoplasm arising from the meninges.

meningismo *m.* meningism, meningismus, congestive irritation of the meninges, gen. of a toxic nature, that presents symptoms similar to those of meningitis but without infl., seen esp. in children.

meningitis *f.* (*pl.* **meningitis**) infl. of the meninges ; ___ **criptocóccica** / cryptoccocal ___; ___ **viral** / viral ___.

meningocele *m.* meningocele, protrusion of the meninges through a defect in the skull or the vertebral column.

meningococo *m.* meningococcus, microorganism that causes epidemic cerebral meningitis.

meningoencefalitis *f.* meningoencephalitis, cerebromeningitis, infl. of the encephalum and the meninges.

meningoencefalocele *m.* meningoencephalocele, protrusion of the encephalum and the meninges through a defect in the cranium.

meningomielitis *f.* meningomyelitis, infl. of the spinal cord and the membranes that cover it.

meningomieiocele *m.* meningomyelocele, protrusion of the spinal cord and meninges through a defect of the vertebral column.

meniscectomía *f. surg.* meniscectomy, excision of a meniscus.

menisco *m.* meniscus, crescent-shaped, cartilaginous, interarticular structure.

menometrorragia *f.* menometrorrhagia, excessive or irregular menstruation.

menopausia *f.* menopause, cessation of the fertility stage of adult women and decrease in their hormone production.

menor *a.* smaller, less, lesser, [*comp. of pequeño*] younger; smallest, [*sup. of pequeño*] youngest; **el hijo** ___ / the youngest son.

menorragia *f.* menorrhagia, excessive bleeding in menstruation.

menorralgia *f.* menorrhalgia, painful menstruation.

menorrea *f.* menorrhea, normal menstrual flow without obstruction.

menos *adv.* less; **poco más o** ___ / more or less; **por lo** ___ / at least; **a** ___ **que** / unless.

menospreciar *v.* to underestimate; to hold in low esteem.

mensaje *m.* message.

menstruación *f.* menstruation, periodic flow of bloody fluid from the uterus; **trastornos de la** ___ / menstrual disorders.

menstrual *a.* menstrual, rel. to menstruation; **ciclo** ___ / ___ cycle.

menstruar *v.* to menstruate.

menstruo *m.* menses, menstruation, period.

mensual *a.* monthly; **-mente** *adv.* monthly.

menta *f.* mint.

mental *a.* mental, rel. to the mind; **actividad** ___

/ ___ activity, mentation; **edad** ___ / ___ age; **deficiencia** ___ / ___ deficiency; **enfermedad** ___ / ___ illness; **higiene** ___ / ___ hygiene; **retraso** ___ / ___ retardation; **trastorno** ___ / ___ disorder; **-mente** *adv.* mentally.

mentalidad *f.* mentality, mental capacity.

mente *f.* mind, intellectual power.

mentecato-a *m., f.* numbskull.

mentir *vi.* to lie.

mentira *f.* lie, falsehood.

mentol *m.* menthol, an alcohol obtained from peppermint oil and used for its soothing effects.

mentón *m.* mentus, chin.

meñique *m.* small finger.

merbromina *f.* merbromin, odorless red powder, soluble in water, used to kill germs.

mercurial *a.* mercurial, rel. to mercury.

mercurio *m.* mercury, volatile liquid metal.

Mercurocromo *m.* Mercurochrome, trade name for merbromin.

merecer *vi.* to deserve.

meridiano *m.* meridian, an imaginary circular line through the poles of a spherical body which connects the opposite ends of its axis.

mermelada *f.* marmalade.

mes *m.* month.

mesa *f.* table; ___ **de operaciones** / operating ___; ___ **de reconocimiento** / examination ___.

mescalina *f.* mescaline, poisonous alkaloid with hallucinatory properties.

mesectodermo *m.* mesectoderm, mass of cells that combine with others to form the meninges.

mesencéfalo *m.* mesencephalon, the midbrain of the embrionary stage.

mesénquima *m.* mesenchyme, embryonic tissue from which the connective tissue and the lymph and blood vessels arise in the adult.

mesentérico-a *a.* mesenteric, rel. to the mesentery.

mesenterio *m.* mesentery, peritoneal folds that fix parts of the intestine to the posterior abdominal wall.

mesial *a.* mesial. V. **medial.**

mesión *f.* mesion, imaginary midlongitudinal plane that divides the body in two symmetric parts.

mesmerismo *m.* mesmerism, therapy by hypnotism.

mesocardia *f.* mesocardia, displacement of the heart toward the center of the thorax.

mesocolon *m.* mesocolon, mesentery that fixes the colon to the posterior abdominal wall.

mesodermo *m.* mesoderm, middle germ layer of the embryo, between the ectoderm and the endoderm, from which bone, connective tissue, muscle, blood, blood vessels, and lymph tissue, as well as the membranes of the heart and abdomen, arise.

mesotelio *m.* mesothelium, cell layer of the embryonic mesoderm that forms the epithelium covering the serous membranes in the adult.

mestizaje *m.* crossbreeding of different races.

mestizo-a *m.*, *f.*, *a.* mestizo, half-breed; crossbred, hybrid.

meta *f.* goal, objective.

metabólico-a *a.* metabolic, rel. to metabolism; índice ___ / ___ rate.

metabolismo *m.* metabolism, physiochemical changes that take place following the digestive process; ___ **basal** / basal ___, lowest level of energy waste; ___ **de proteína** / metabolic protein, digestion of proteins as amino acids.

metabolito *m.* metabolite, substance produced during metabolism or essential to the metabolic process.

metacarpiano-a *a.* metacarpal, rel. to the metacarpus.

metacarpo *m.* metacarpus, the five small metacarpal bones of the hand.

metadona *f.* methadone, highly potent habitforming synthetic drug with narcotic action weaker than that of morphine.

metafase *f.* metaphase, one of the phases of cell division.

metáfisis *f.* metaphysis, the growing portion of a bone.

metal *m.* metal.

metálico-a *a.* metallic, rel. to or composed of metal.

metamorfosis *f.* metamorphosis. 1. change of form or structure; 2. degenerative process.

metanol *m.* methanol, methyl alcohol, wood alcohol.

metástasis *f.* metastasis, extension of a pathological process from a primary focus to another part of the body through blood or lymph vessels, as occurs in some types of cancer.

metastatizar *vi.* to metastasize, to spread by metastasis.

metatálamo *m.* metathalamus, part of the diencephalon.

metatarsiano-a *a.* metatarsal, rel. to the metatarsus.

metatarso *m.* metatarsus, the five small metatarsal bones located between the tarsus and the toes.

meteorismo *m.* meteorism, bloated abdomen due to gas in the stomach or the intestines.

meter *v.* to put in; to put one thing into another.

meticuloso-a *a.* meticulous, scrupulous.

método *m.* method, procedure, process, treatment.

metópico-a *a.* metopic, frontal, rel. to the forehead.

metria *f.* metria, puerperal infl. of the uterus.

métrico-a *a.* metric, rel. to meter or the metric system; **sistema** ___ / ___ system.

metritis *f.* metritis, infl. of the walls of the uterus.

metro *m.* meter.

metrorragia *f.* metrorrhagia, uterine bleeding other than menstruation.

mezcla *f.* mixture, compound.

mezclar *v.* to mix, to blend.

mialgia *f.* myalgia, muscle pain.

miastenia *f.* myasthenia, muscle weakness; ___ **grave** / ___ gravis.

miatonía *f.* myatonia, deficiency or loss of muscle tone.

micetoma *m.* mycetoma, severe infection caused by fungi that affects the skin, the connective tissue, and the bone.

micobacteria *f. V.* **Mycobacterium.**

micología *f.* mycology, the study of fungi and the diseases caused by them.

micoplasmas *m. pl.* mycoplasmas, the smallest free-living organisms, some of which produce diseases such as a type of viral pneumonia and pharyngitis.

micosis *f.* mycosis, general term used for any disease caused by fungi.

micótico-a *a.* mycotic, rel. to or affected by mycosis.

micotoxina *f.* mycotoxin, a fungal toxin.

micrencefalia *f.* micrencephaly, abnormal smallness of the encephalon.

microabsceso *m.* microabscess, very small abscess.

microanatomía *f.* microanatomy, histology.

microbacterium *L.* microbacterium, gram-positive bacteria resistant to high temperatures.

microbiano-a *a.* microbic, microbial, rel. to microbes.

microbicida *m.* microbicide, agent that destroys microbes.

microbio *m.* microbe, minute living organism.

microbiología *f.* microbiology, science that studies microorganisms.

microcefalia *f.* microcephalia, microcephaly, congenital abnormally small head.

microcirugía *f.* microsurgery, surgery performed with the aid of special operating microscopes and very small precision instruments.

micrococo *m.* micrococcus, microorganism.

microcolon *m.* microcolon, abnormally small colon.

microcosmo *m.* microcosm, a world in miniature.

microcurie *m.* microcurie, measure of radiation.

microfalo *m.* microphallus, abnormally small penis.

microficha *f.* microfiche, small film capable of storing a large amount of data.

microfilm, microfilme *m.* microfilm, film that contains information reduced to a minimal size.

micrognatia *f.* micrognathia, congenital abnormally small lower jaw.

micrografía *f.* micrography, microscopic study.

microinvasión *f.* microinvasion, invasion of the cellular tissue adjacent to a localized carcinoma that cannot be seen with the naked eye.

micromelia *f.* micromelia, abnormally small

limbs.

micromélico-a *a.* micromelic, rel. to micromelia.

microonda *f.* microwave, electromagnetic short wave with a very high frequency.

microorganismo *m.* microorganism, an organism that cannot be seen with the naked eye.

microscopía *f.* microscopy, microscopic examination.

microscópico-a *a.* microscopic, rel. to microscopy.

microscopio *m.* microscope, optical instrument used to amplify objects that cannot be seen with the naked eye; ___ **de luz** / light ___; ___ **electrónico** / electron ___.

microsoma *m.* microsome, a fine granular element of the protoplasm.

microsomía *f.* microsomia, condition of having an abnormally small body with otherwise normal structure.

microtomía *f.* microtomy, cutting thin sections of tissue.

micrótomo *m.* microtome, instrument used to prepare thin sections of tissue for microscopic study.

midriasis *f.* mydriasis, dilation of the pupil of the eye.

midriático *m.* mydriatic, agent used to dilate the pupil of the eye; **-a** *a.* causing dilation of the pupil of the eye.

miectomía *f. surg.* myectomy, excision of a portion of a muscle.

miedo *m.* fear, apprehension.

miel *f.* honey.

mielina *f.* myelin, the fat-like substance that forms a covering around certain nerve fibers.

mielinación, mielinización *f.* myelination, myelinization, growth of a myelin sheath around a nerve fiber.

mielinolisis *f.* myelinolysis, disease that destroys the myelin cover; ___ **aguda** / acute ___.

mielitis *f.* myelitis, infl. of the spinal cord.

mielocele *m.* myelocele, hernia of the spinal cord through a defect in the vertebral column.

mielocítico-a *a.* myelocytic, rel. to myelocytes; **leucemia** ___ / ___ leukemia.

mielocito *m.* myelocyte, a large, granular leukocyte in the bone marrow that is present in the blood in certain diseases.

mielodisplasia *f.* myelodysplasia abnormal formation of the spinal cord.

mielofibrosis *f.* myelofibrosis, fibrosis of the bone marrow.

mielógeno-a *a.* myelogenic, myelogenous, produced in the bone marrow.

mielografía *f.* myelography, x-ray of the spine after injection of a contrast medium.

mielograma *m.* myelogram, x-ray of the spinal cord with the use of a contrasting medium.

mieloide *a.* myeloid, rel. to or resembling the spinal cord or the bone marrow; **médula** ___ / ___ tissue.

mieloma *m.* myeloma, tumor formed by a type of cells usu. found in the bone marrow; ___ **múltiple** / multiple ___.

mielomeningocele *m.* myelomeningocele, hernia of the spinal cord and its meninges through a defect in the vertebral canal.

mielopatía *f.* myelopathy, pathological condition of the spinal cord.

mieloproliferativo-a *a.* myeloproliferative, characterized by proliferation of bone marrow inside or outside of the medulla.

mielosupresión *f.* myelosuppression, failure of the bone marrow to produce red blood cells and platelets.

miembro *m.* member. 1. organ or limb of the body; 2. person affiliated with an organization; *vr.* **hacerse** ___ / to become a ___.

mientras *adv.* meanwhile; ___ **que** / while.

migración *f.* migration, movement of cells from one place to another.

migraña *f.* migraine, severe headache usu. unilateral, accompanied by disturbed vision and in some cases by nausea and vomiting.

migratorio-a *a.* migratory, rel. to migration.

milagro *m.* miracle.

milagroso-a *a.* miraculous.

miliar *a.* miliary, characterized by the presence of small tumors.

miliaria *f.* miliaria, prickly heat, noncontagious cutaneous eruption caused by the obstruction of sweat glands and characterized by small red vesicles and papules accompanied by itching and prickling.

milieu *Fr.* milieu, environment, surroundings.

milla *f.* mile.

mimado-a *a.* pampered.

mimar *v.* to pamper.

mimético-a *a.* mimetic, mimic, that imitates.

minar *v.* to undermine.

mineral *m.* mineral, inorganic element; *a.* rel. to a mineral; **agua** ___ **efervescente** / carbonated ___ water.

mineralización *f.* mineralization, abnormally large deposition of mineral in tissues.

mineralocorticoide *m.* mineralocorticoid, hormone released by the adrenal cortex involved in the regulation of fluids and electrolytes.

minero-a *m., f.* miner.

mínimo-a *a.* minimal, least, smallest; **dosis letal** ___ / ___ lethal dose, smallest amount needed to cause death; **dosis** ___ / ___ dose, smallest amount needed to produce an effect.

ministro-a *m., f.* minister, pastor.

minoría *f.* minority.

minucioso-a *a.* thorough, detailed; **examen** ___ / ___ exam; **-mente** *adv.* very carefully; thoroughly.

minuto *m.* minute, fraction of time.

miocárdico-a *a.* myocardial, myocardiac, rel. to the myocardium.

miocardio *m.* myocardium, the middle and thickest muscular layer of the heart wall;

contracción del ___ / myocardial contraction.
miocardiopatías *f. pl.* myocardial diseases.
miocarditis *f.* myocarditis, infl. of the myocardium.
miocito *m.* myocyte, cell of the muscular tissue.
mioclonus *m.* myoclonus, muscular spasm or contraction as seen in epilepsy.
miodistrofia *f.* myodystrophy, muscular dystrophy.
miofibrilla *f.* myofibril, myofibrilla; minute, slender fiber of the muscle tissue.
miofibroma *m.* myofibroma, tumor containing muscular elements.
miofilamento *m.* myofilament, microscopic element that makes up myofibrils in muscles.
miogénico-a *a.* myogenic, originating in or starting from the muscle.
mioglobina *f.* myoglobin, muscle tissue pigment that participates in the transport of oxygen.
miografía *f.* myography, a recording of muscular activity.
miolisis *f.* myolysis, destruction of muscle tissue.
mioma *m.* myoma, benign tumor of muscular tissue.
miomectomía *f. surg.* myomectomy. 1. excision of a portion of a muscle or of muscular tissue; 2. excision of a myoma, esp. one localized in the uterus.
miometrio *m.* myometrium, muscle wall of the uterus.
miometritis *f.* myometritis, infl. of the muscular wall of the uterus.
mionecrosis *f.* myonecrosis, necrosis of muscle tissue.
mioneural *a.* myoneural, rel. to muscles and nerves; **unión** ___ / ___ junction, a nerve ending in a muscle.
miopatía *f.* myopathy, muscle disease.
miope *a.* myopic. 1. nearsighted; 2. rel. to myopia.
miopía *f.* myopia, nearsightedness, a defect in the eyeball that causes parallel rays to be focused in front of the retina.
miosina *f.* myosin, the most abundant protein in muscle tissue.
miosis *f.* miosis, excessive contraction of the pupil.
miositis *f.* myositis, infl. of a muscle or group of muscles.
miotomía *f.* myotomy, dissection of muscles.
miotonía *f.* myotonia, increased rigidity of a muscle following muscle contraction, with diminished power of relaxation.
mirar *v.* to look, to view; ___ **fijamente** / to stare; **mirarse** *vr.* to look at oneself.
miringectomía *f. surg.* myringectomy, myringodectomy, excision of part or all of the tympanic membrane.
miringitis *f.* myringitis, infl. of the eardrum.
miringoplastia *f. surg.* myringoplasty, plastic surgery of the tympanic membrane.
miringotomía *f.* myringotomy, incision of the tympanic membrane.

misantropía *f.* misanthropy, abhorrence of mankind.
miscegenación *f.* miscegenation, sexual relations between individuals of different races.
miscible *a.* miscible, capable of mixing or dissolving.
mismo-a *a.* same; **sí** ___ / oneself; **dominio de** ___ / self-control.
misogamia *f.* misogamy, aversion to marriage.
misoginia *f.* misogyny, hatred of women.
mitad *f.* moiety, half, each of the two halves in which a whole is divided; **a la** ___ / in half.
mitigado-a *a.* mitigated, diminished, moderated.
mitigar *vi.* to mitigate, to alleviate.
mitocondria *f.* mitochondria, microscopic filaments of the cytoplasm that constitute the main source of energy in cells.
mitogenesia, mitogénesis *f.* mitogenesia, mitogenesis, the cause of cell mitosis.
mitógeno *m.* mitogen, substance that induces cell mitosis.
mitosis *f.* mitosis, cell division process that results in new cells and replacement of injured tissue.
mitral *a.* mitral, rel. to the mitral valve; **estenosis** ___ / ___ stenosis, a narrowing of the left atrioventricular orifice; **incompetencia** ___ / ___ insufficiency; **regurgitación** ___ / ___ regurgitation, the flow of blood back from the left ventricle into the left atrium due to a lesion of the mitral valve; **soplo** ___ / ___ murmur.
mittelschmerz *m.* mittelschmerz, lower abdominal pain related to ovulation and occurring midway in the menstrual cycle.
mixedema *m.* myxedema, condition caused by deficient thyroid gland function.
mixoma *m.* myxoma, a tumor of the connective tissue.
mixto-a *a.* mixed.
mixtura *f.* mixture.
mnemónica *f.* mnemonics, recall of memory through free association of ideas and other techniques.
moción *f.* motion, movement.
moco *m.* mucus, viscid matter secreted by the mucous membranes and glands.
modalidad *f.* modality, any form of therapeutic application.
moderación *f.* moderation.
moderado-a *a.* moderate, temperate; **-mente** *adv.* moderately.
modesto-a *a.* modest.
modificación *f.* modification, change.
modificar *vi.* to modify, to change.
modo *m.* mode. 1. manner, way; 2. in a series, the value that is repeated most frequently; **de cualquier** ___ / in any way; anyway; **de ningún** ___ / in no way.
modulación *f.* modulation, the action of adjust-

ing or adapting, such as occurs with the inflection of the voice.

moho *m.* mildew, mold caused by a fungus.

mojado-a *a.* wet.

mojar *v.* to wet, to dampen; **mojarse** *vr.* to get wet.

molar *m.* molar, any of the twelve molar teeth.

molde *m.* 1. cast, hardened bandage made stiff when pouring a hardening material; 2. template, pattern, mold.

moldear *v.* to cast.

molécula *f.* molecule, the smallest unit of a substance above the atomic level.

molécula gramo *m.* gram molecule, weight in grams equal to the molecular weight.

molecular *a.* molecular, rel. to molecules.

moler *vi.* to grind.

molestar *v.* to annoy, to bother.

molestia *f.* discomfort, annoyance.

molesto-a *a.* annoyed, grievous.

momentáneo-a *a.* momentary, of short duration.

momento *m.* moment, fraction of time.

momentum *L.* momentum, impetus, a force of motion.

momificación *f.* mummification, conversion into a state that resembles that of a mummy, as occurs in dry gangrene or in a dead fetus that dries up in the uterus.

mongolismo *m.* mongolism. *V.* **Down, síndrome de.**

mongoloide *a.* mongoloid, rel. to or suffering from mongolism.

moniliasis *f.* moniliasis. *V.* **candidiasis.**

monitor *m.* monitor. 1. electronic device used to monitor a function; 2. person who oversees an activity or function.

monitorear *v.* to monitor, to check systematically with an electronic device an organic function such as the heartbeat.

monitoreo, monitorización *m., f.* monitoring; ___ **cardíaco** / cardiac ___; ___ **de presión arterial** / blood pressure ___; ___ **fetal** / fetal ___.

monitoreo de Holter *m.* Holter monitoring, ambulatory electrocardiography.

monja *f.* nun.

monoarticular *a.* monoarticular, rel. to only one joint.

monocigótico-a *a.* monozygotic, rel. to twins that have identical genetic characteristics.

monocito *m.* monocyte, large, granular, mononuclear leukocyte.

monoclonal *a.* monoclonal, rel. to a single group of cells; **anticuerpos** ___**-es** / ___ antibodies.

monocromático-a *a.* monochromatic, having only one color.

monocular *a.* monocular, rel. to only one eye.

monogamia *f.* monogamy, legal marriage to only one person.

mononuclear *a.* mononuclear, having one nucleus; **célula** ___ / ___ cell.

mononucleosis *f.* mononucleosis, presence of an abnormally large number of monocytes in the blood; ___ **infecciosa** / infectious ___, acute febrile infectious disease.

monosacárido *m.* monosaccharide, simple sugar.

monotonía *f.* monotony; monotone.

monótono-a *a.* monotonous.

monstruo *m.* monster.

montar *v.* to ride; ___ **en bicicleta** / ___ a bycicle; to set up; ___ **una consulta** / ___ a doctor's office; to assemble, to fit, to adjust.

montón *m.* heap, pile.

morado *m.* bruise, black and blue spot; the color purple; **-a** *a.* purple.

mórbido-a, morboso-a *a.* morbid, rel. to disease.

morbilidad *f.* morbidity. 1. an illness or disorder; 2. the rate of a disease in a given population or locality.

morbo *m.* illness.

mordedura *f.* 1. bite; 2. a wound caused by a bite.

morder *vi.* to bite.

mordida *f.* 1. bite; 2. the mark left in the skin by the teeth of an animal; 3. forced occlusion of the inferior jaw on the upper teeth; **cruzada** / cross-bite; ___ **de perro** / dog bite.

mordido-a *pp.* of **morder,** bitten; *a.* bitten.

moretón *m.* bruise, black and blue.

morfina *f.* morphine, the main alkaloid of opium, used as a narcotic analgesic.

morfinismo *m.* morphinism, condition caused by addiction to morphine.

morgue *Fr.* morgue, place for temporarily holding dead bodies.

moribundo-a *a.* moribund, dying, on the verge of death.

morir *vi.* to die.

morón, morona *m., f.* moron, a mentally retarded person with an IQ of 50 to 70.

mortal *m.* mortal, a human being; *a.* deadly, mortal; **herida** ___ / fatal wound; **veneno** ___ / deadly poison.

mortalidad, mortandad *f.* mortality, death rate; **índice de** ___ / death rate.

mortífero-a *a.* deadly, that can cause death.

mortinatalidad *f.* natimortality, index of stillbirths.

mortinato-a *m., f.* stillborn.

morula *f.* morula, solid, spheric mass of cells that results from cell division of a fertilized ovum.

mosaico *m.* mosaic, the presence in one individual of different cell populations derived from the same cell as a result of mutation.

mosca *f.* fly.

moscardón *m.* gadfly.

mosquito *m.* mosquito.

mostaza *f.* mustard.

mostrar *vi.* to show, to point out.

moteado-a *a.* mottling, mottled, discolored.

motivación *f.* motivation, driving force.

motivar *v.* to motivate, to animate.

motivo *m.* motive, cause, driving force.

motocicleta *f.* motorcycle.

motor *m.* motor, agent that causes or induces movement; **-a** *a.* that causes movement.

mover *vi.* to move, to put in motion; **moverse** *vr.* to move oneself.

movible, móvil *a.* mobile, able to move or be moved.

movilidad *f.* mobility, motility.

movilización *f.* mobilization.

movimiento *m.* movement, move, motion; **alcance de** ___ / range of motion.

mucina *f.* mucin, glycoprotein that is the chief ingredient of mucus.

mucocele *m.* mucocele, dilation of a cavity due to accumulated mucous secretion.

mucocutáneo-a *a.* mucocutaneous, rel. to the mucous membrane and the skin.

mucoide *m.* mucoid, glycoprotein similar to mucin; *a.* having the consistency of mucus.

mucomembranoso-a *a.* mucomembranous, rel. to the mucous membrane.

mucosa *f.* mucosa, mucous membrane, thin sheets of tissue cells that line openings or canals that communicate to the outside.

mucoso-a *a.* mucous, mucosal, rel. to or of the nature of the mucosa; **membrana** ___ / ___ membrane, mucosa.

muchacho-a *m., f.* boy; girl.

mudar *v.* to move; ___ **los dientes** / to get one's second teeth; ___ **la piel** / to shed skin.

mudo-a *m., f.* mute.

mueca *f.* grimace.

muela *f.* molar tooth, grinder; **dolor de** ___**-s** / toothache; ___**-s del juicio** / wisdom teeth.

muerte *f.* death; ___ **aparente** / apparent ___.

muerte de cuna *f.* crib-death; sudden infant death syndrome (SIDS).

muerto-a *m., f.* a dead person; *a.* dead.

muestra *f.* sample; **tomar** ___**-s** / sampling; **tomar** ___**-s al azar** / random sampling.

muestreo *m.* sampling; ___ **al azar** / random ___.

mugre *f.* grime.

muguet *Fr.* thrush, fungus infection of the oral mucosa, manifested by white patches in the lips, tongue, and the interior surface of the cheek.

mujer *f.* woman.

muletas *f. pl.* crutches.

multicelular *a.* multicellular, having many cells.

multifactorial *a.* multifactorial, rel. to many factors.

multifocal *a.* multifocal, rel. to many foci.

multilocular *a.* multilocular. *V.* **multicelular.**

multiparidad *f.* multiparity. 1. condition of having borne more than one living child; 2. multiple birth.

múltiple *a.* multiple, more than one; **fallo** ___ **de órganos** / ___ organ failure; **personalidad** ___ / ___ personality.

mundo *m.* world.

muñeca *f.* 1. wrist; ___ **caída** / drop ___; *V.* **carpus;** 2. doll.

muñón *m.* stump of an amputated arm or leg.

mural *a.* mural, rel. to the walls of an organ or part.

muriático-a *a.* muriatic, derived from common salt; **ácido** ___ / ___ acid.

murino-a *a.* murine, rel. to rodents, esp. mice and rats.

murmullo *m.* murmur, bruit, gen. in reference to an abnormal heart sound.

muscular, musculoso-a *a.* muscular, rel. to the muscles; **atrofia** ___ / ___ atrophy; **contracción** ___ **brusca** / jerk; **desarrollo** ___ / muscle building; **distensión** ___ / muscle strain; **pérdida de la tonicidad** ___ / loss of muscle tone; **relajador** ___ / muscle relaxer; **rigidez** ___ / ___ rigidity; **tonicidad** ___ / muscle toning.

muscularis *L.* muscularis, muscular layer of an organ or tubule.

musculatura *f.* musculature, the total muscular system.

músculo *m.* muscle, a type of fibrous tissue that has the property to contract allowing movement of the parts and organs of the body; ___ **estriado voluntario** / striated voluntary ___; ___ **flexor** / flexor ___; ___ **visceral involuntario** / visceral involuntary ___.

musculoesquelético-a *a.* musculoskeletal, rel. to the muscles and the skeleton.

musculotendinoso-a *a.* musculotendinous, having both muscle and tendons.

muslo *m.* thigh, the portion of the lower extremity between the hip and the knee.

mutación *f.* mutation, spontaneous or induced change in genetic structure.

mutágeno *m.* mutagen, substance or agent that causes mutation.

mutante *a.* mutant, rel. to an individual or organism with a genetic structure that has undergone mutation.

mutilación *f.* mutilation, castration.

mutilado-a *a.* mutilated.

mutilar *v.* to mutilate, to maim; to cut in pieces.

mutismo *m.* mutism.

mutuo-a *a.* mutual, reciprocal.

muy *adv.* very.

Mycobacterium *L.* Mycobacterium, gram-positive, rod-shaped bacteria, including species that cause leprosy and tuberculosis.

N *abr.* **nasal** / nasal; **nervio** / nerve; **nitrógeno** / nitrogen; **normal** / normal; **número** / number.

Naboth, quistes de *m.* nabothian cysts, small, usu. benign cysts that form in one of many small mucus-secreting glands of the neck of the uterus due to obstruction.

nacer *vi.* to be born.

nacido-a *a., pp del verbo* nacer, born; **recién** __ / newly __; __ **vivo** / __ alive.

naciente *a.* nascent, incipient. 1. just born; 2. liberated from a chemical compound.

nacimiento *m.* birth; __ **prematuro** / premature __; __ **tardío** / post-term __; **certificado de** __ / __ certificate; __ **sin vida** / stillbirth.

nacionalidad *f.* nationality.

nada *f.* nothing, nothingness; *indef. pron.* (after thanks) **de** __ / Don't mention it!; not at all; by no means.

nadie *pron.* nobody, no one.

nalgas *f. pl.* buttocks.

nanismo *m.* nanism. *V.* **enanismo.**

naranja *f.* orange.

narcisismo *m.* narcissism. 1. excessive love of self; 2. sexual pleasure derived from contemplation and admiration of one's own body.

narcolepsia *f.* narcolepsy, chronic uncontrollable disposition to sleep.

narcoléptico-a *a.* narcoleptic, rel. to or suffering from narcolepsia.

narcosis *f.* narcosis, unconsciousness caused by a narcotic.

narcótico *m.* narcotic, substance with potent analgesic effects that can become addictive.

narcotismo *m.* narcotism, the stuporous state caused by narcotics.

naris *L.* (*pl.* **nares**) naris, nostril.

nariz *f.* nose; **sangramiento por la** __ / nosebleed; *vr.* **sonarse la** __ / to blow one's nose.

nasal *a.* nasal, rel. to the nose; **cavidad** __ / cavity; **congestión** __ / __ congestion; **fosa** __ / nostril; **goteo** __ / __ drip; **instilación** __ / __ instillation; **tabique** __ / __ septum.

nasofaringe *f.* nasopharynx, portion of the pharynx that lies above the soft palate.

nasogástrico-a *a.* nasogastric, rel. to the nose and the stomach; **tubo** __ / __ tube.

nasolabial *a.* nasolabial, rel. to the nose and the lip.

nata *f.* cream.

natal *a.* natal, rel. to birth.

natalidad *f.* natality; **control de la** __ / birth control; **índice de la** __ / birth rate.

natilla *f.* custard.

natimortalidad *f. V.* **mortinatalidad.**

nativo-a *a.* native. 1. in its natural state; 2. indigenous.

natriurético *m.* natriuretic. *V.* **diurético.**

natural *a.* natural; **derechos** __-es / birth rights; *v.* **ser** __ **de** / to be from; **-mente** *adv.* naturally.

naturaleza *f.* nature.

naturópata *m.* naturopath, practitioner of naturopathy.

naturopatía *f.* naturopathy, therapeutic treatment by natural means.

náusea *f.* nausea, nauseousness; seasickness; *v.* **dar, provocar** __ / to nauseate; **tener** __-s / to be nauseated.

nauseabundo-a *a.* nauseous, that causes nausea.

nauseado-a *a.* nauseated.

nauseoso-a *a.* nauseous, that causes nausea.

navicular *a.* navicular, boat-shaped.

nebulización *f.* nebulization, conversion of liquid into spray or mist.

nebulizador *m.* nebulizer, device used to produce spray or mist from liquid.

nebuloso-a *a.* nebulous.

necesario-a *a.* necessary; **lo** __ / what is __; *v.* **ser** __ / to be __.

necesidad *f.* necessity, need; *v.* **tener** __ / to need.

necesitado-a *a.* needy; **los** __-s / the needy.

necesitar *v.* to need.

necrocomio *m.* morgue, place to store dead bodies temporarily.

necrofilia *f.* necrophilia. 1. morbid attraction to corpses; 2. sexual intercourse with a corpse.

necrofobia *f.* necrophobia, morbid fear of death and corpses.

necrógeno-a *a.* necrogenic. 1. rel. to death; 2. formed or composed of dead matter.

necrología *f.* necrology, the study of statistics in mortality.

necropsia, necroscopia *f.* necropsy. *V.* **autopsia.**

necrosar *v.* to necrose, necrotizing, to cause or undergo necrosis.

necrosis *f.* necrosis, death of some or all of the cells in a tissue such as occurs in gangrene.

necrótico-a *a.* necrotic, rel. to necrosis.

nefrectomía *f. surg.* nephrectomy, removal of a kidney.

néfrico-a *a.* nephric, renal.

nefrítico-a *a.* nephritic, rel. to or affected by nephritis.

nefritis *f.* nephritis, infl. of a kidney.

nefrocalcinosis *f.* nephrocalcinosis, renal calcium deposits in the tubules of the kidney that may cause renal insufficiency.

nefroesclerosis *f.* nephrosclerosis, hardening of the arterial system and the interstitial tissue of the kidney.

nefrograma *m.* nephrogram, kidney x-ray.

nefrolitiasis *f.* nephrolithiasis, kidney stones.

nefrolitotomía *f.* nephrolithotomy, incision in the kidney to remove kidney stones.

nefrología *f.* nephrology, the study of the kidney and the diseases affecting it.

nefroma *m.* nephroma, kidney tumor.

nefrona *f.* nephron, the functional and anatomical unit of a kidney.

nefropatía *f.* nephropathy, disease of the kidney.

nefropexia *f. surg.* nephropexy, fixation of a floating kidney.

nefrosis *f.* nephrosis, degenerative renal disorder associated with large amounts of protein in the urine, low levels of albumin in the blood, and marked edema.

nefrostomía *f. surg.* nephrostomy, creation of a fistula in the kidney or renal pelvis.

nefrotomía *f. surg.* nephrotomy, surgical incision into the kidney.

nefrotomografía *f.* nephrotomography, tomography of the kidney.

nefrotóxico-a *a.* nephrotoxic, that destroys kidney cells.

nefrotoxina *f.* nephrotoxin, agent that destroys kidney cells.

negación *f.* negation, denial.

negar *vi.* to deny.

negativismo *m. psych.* negativism, behavior characterized by acting in a manner opposite to the one suggested.

negativo-a *a.* negative; **cultivo** ___ / ___ culture; **-mente** *adv.* negatively.

negligencia *f.* negligence; ___ **profesional** / malpractice.

negligente *a.* negligent.

negro-a *m., f.* 1. a black person; 2. the color black; *a.* black.

nematelminto *m.* nemathelminth, roundworm, intestinal worm of the phylum *Nemathelminthes.*

nematocida *m.* nematocide, agent that kills nematodes.

Nematoda *Gr.* Nematoda, class of worms of the phylum *Nemathelminthes.*

nemátodo *m.* nematode, worm of the class *Nematoda.*

nematología *f.* nematology, the study of worms of the class *Nematoda.*

nene-a *m., f.* baby.

neoartrosis *f.* nearthrosis, neoarthrosis, false or artificial joint.

neologismo *m.* neologism. 1. *psych.* word or phrase to which a mentally disturbed individual attributes a meaning unrelated to its real meaning; 2. new word or phrase or an old one to which a new meaning has been attributed.

neomicina *f.* neomycin, broad-spectrum antibiotic.

neonatal *a.* neonatal, rel. to the first four to six weeks after birth.

neonato-a *a.* neonate, newborn.

neonatología *f.* neonatology, specialty that studies the care and treatment of newborns.

neonatólogo-a *m., f.* neonathologist, specialist in neonatology.

neoplasia *f.* neoplasia, formation of neoplasms.

neoplasma *m.* neoplasm, abnormal growth of new tissue such as a tumor.

neoplástico-a *a.* neoplastic, rel. to a neoplasm.

nervio *m.* nerve, one or more bundles of fibers that connect the brain and spinal cord with other parts and organs of the body; **bloqueo del** ___ / ___ block; **degeneración del** ___ / ___ degeneration; ___ **pellizcado** / pinched ___; **terminación del** ___ / ___ ending.

nervio ciático *m.* sciatic nerve, nerve that extends from the base of the spine down to the thigh with branches throughout the lower leg and the foot.

nerviosismo *m.* nervousness; *pop.* jitters.

nervioso-a *a.* nervous, rel. to the nerves; **crisis** ___ / ___ breakdown, collapse; **fibra** ___ / nerve fiber; **impulso** ___ / nerve impulse; **tejido** ___ / nerve tissue.

nestiatría *f.* nestiatria, fasting therapy.

neumático-a *a.* pneumatic, rel. to air or respiration.

neumatización *f.* pneumatization, formation of air cavities in a bone, esp. the temporal bone.

neumatocele *m.* pneumatocele. 1. hernial protuberance of lung tissue; 2. a tumor or sac containing gas.

neumococal, neumocócico-a *a.* pneumococcal, rel. to or caused by pneumococci.

neumococo *m.* pneumococcus, one of a group of gram-positive bacteria that cause acute pneumonia and other infections of the upper respiratory tract.

neumoencefalografía *f.* pneumoencephalography, x-ray of the brain by previous injection of air or gas allowing visualization of the cerebral cortex and ventricles.

neumonía *f.* pneumonia, infectious disease of the upper respiratory tract caused by bacteria or virus that affect the lungs; ___ **doble** / double ___; ___ **estafilocócica** / staphylococcal ___; ___ **lobar** / lobar ___.

neumonía neumocística carinii *f.* pneumocystis pneumonia carinii, a type of acute pneumonia caused by the bacillus *Pneumocystis carinii* and one of the opportunistic diseases seen in cases of AIDS.

neumónico-a *a.* pneumonic, rel. to the lungs or to pneumonia.

neumonitis *f.* pneumonitis. *V.* **neumonía.**

neumopatía *f.* lung disease.

neumotórax *m.* pneumothorax, accumulation of gas or air in the pleural cavity that results in the collapse of the affected lung; ___ **espontáneo** / spontaneous ___; ___ **por tensión** / tension ___.

neural *a.* neural, rel. to the nervous system.

neuralgia *f.* neuralgia, pain along a nerve.

neurálgico-a *a.* neuralgic, rel. to neuralgia; **puntos** ___-s / tender points.

neurapraxia *f.* neurapraxia, temporary paralysis of a nerve without degeneration.

neurastenia *f.* neurasthenia, term usu. associated with increased irritability, tension, and anxiety, accompanied by physical exhaustion.

neurasténico-a *a.* neurasthenic, rel. to or afflicted by neurasthenia.

neurilema *f.* neurilemma, thin membranous covering that encloses a nerve fiber.

neurinoma *m.* neurinoma, benign neoplasm of the sheath surrounding a nerve.

neuritis *f.* neuritis, infl. of a nerve.

neuroanatomía *f.* neuroanatomy, the study and practice of the anatomy of the nervous system.

neuroblasto *m.* neuroblast, the immature nerve cell.

neuroblastoma *m.* neuroblastoma, malignant tumor of the nervous system formed mostly of neuroblasts.

neurocirugía *f.* neurosurgery, the study and practice of surgery of the nervous system.

neurocirujano-a *m., f.* neurosurgeon, specialist in neurosurgery.

neurodermatitis *f.* neurodermatitis, chronic skin disease of unknown origin manifested by intense itching in localized areas.

neuroectodermo *m.* neuroectoderm, embryonary tissue from which the nerve tissue derives.

neuroendocrinología *f.* neuroendocrinology, the study of the nervous system as it relates to hormones.

neurofarmacología *f.* neuropharmacology, the study of drugs and medications as they affect the nervous system.

neurofibroma *m.* neurofibroma, tumor of the fibrous tissue of a peripheral nerve.

neurofibromatosis *f.* neurofibromatosis, disease characterized by the presence of multiple neurofibromas along the peripheral nerves.

neurofisiología *f.* neurophysiology, the study of the physiology of the nervous system.

neuroglia *f.* neuroglia, connective, supportive cells that constitute the interstitial tissue of the nervous system.

neurohipófisis *f.* neurohypophysis, posterior and nervous portion of the pituitary gland.

neuroléptico *m.* neuroleptic, tranquilizer; **-a** *a.* **anestesia ___ / ___** anesthesia.

neurología *f.* neurology, the study of the nervous system.

neurólogo-a *m., f.* neurologist, specialist in neurology.

neuroma *f.* neuroma, tumor composed mainly of nerve cells and fibers.

neuromarcapaso *m.* neuropacemaker, instrument used to stimulate electrically the spinal cord.

neuromuscular *a.* neuromuscular, rel. to the nerves and the muscles.

neurona *f.* neuron, nerve cell, the basic functional and structural unit of the nervous system; **___ motor /** motor **___,** carries the impulses that initiate muscle contraction.

neuro-oftalmología *f.* neuro-ophthalmology, the study of the relationship between the nervous and visual systems.

neuropatía *f.* neuropathy, a disorder or pathological change in the peripheral nerves.

neurópilo *m.* neuropil, network of nervous fibers (neurites, dendrites, and glia cells) that concentrate in different parts of the nervous system.

neurorradiología *f.* neuroradiology, x-ray study of the nervous system.

neurorregulador *m.* neurotransmitter, a chemical substance that affects the transmission of impulses across a synapse between nerves or between a nerve and a muscle.

neurosicofarmacología *f.* neuropsychopharmacology, the study of drugs as they affect the treatment of mental disorders.

neurosífilis *f.* neurosyphilis, syphilis that affects the nervous system.

neurosis *f.* neurosis, condition manifested primarily by anxiety and the use of defense mechanisms.

neurótico-a *a.* neurotic, rel. to or suffering from neurosis.

neurotoxicidad *f.* neurotoxicity, toxic or harmful effect on the nervous system tissue.

neurovascular *a.* neurovascular, rel. to the nervous and vascular systems.

neutral, neutro-a *a.* neutral.

neutralización *f.* neutralization, process that annuls or counteracts the action of an agent.

neutralizar *vi.* to neutralize, to counteract.

neutrofilia *f.* neutrophilia, increase in number of neutrophils in the blood.

neutropenia *f.* neutropenia. *V.* **agranulocitosis.**

neutrotaxis *f.* neutrotaxis, stimulation of neutrophils by a substance that either attracts or repels them.

nevar *vi.* to snow.

nevo *m.* nevus, mole, birthmark.

nexo *m.* nexus, connection.

ni *conj.* neither, nor; **___ bueno ___** malo / neither good nor bad; **___ siquiera** / not even.

niacina *f.* niacin, nicotinic acid.

nicotina *f.* nicotine, toxic alkaloid that is the main ingredient of tobacco.

nictalopía *f.* nyctalopia, night blindness.

nicturia, nocturia *f.* nocturia, nycturia, frequent urination during the night.

nicho *m.* niche, small defect or depression esp. in the wall of a hollow organ.

nido *m.* nest, small cellular mass resembling a bird's nest.

niebla *f.* fog.

nieto-a *m., f.* grandson, granddaughter.

nieve *f.* snow; *Mex.* ice cream.

nigua *f.* chigger, chigoe.

ninfa *f.* nympha, inner lip of the vulva.

ninfomanía *f.* nymphomania, excessive sexual desire in the female.

ninfomaníaca *f.* nymphomaniac, rel. to or suffering from nymphomania.

ningún, ninguno-a *a.* not one, not any; **de __ modo, de ninguna manera** / in no way; *pron.* nobody; none, no one; neither.

niña del ojo *f.* pupil of the eye.

niñez *f.* childhood.

niño-a *m., f.* child; **__ maltratado-a** / battered __.

nistagmo *m.* nystagmus, involuntary spasm of the eyeball.

nitrato *m.* nitrate, chemical agent.

nitrógeno *m.* nitrogen.

nitroglicerina *f.* nitroglycerine, a nitrate of glycerin used in medicine as a vasodilator, esp. in angina pectoris.

nivel *m.* level.

nivelación *f.* levelling.

no *adv.* no, not; **__ importa** / it doesn't matter; **__ obstante** / nevertheless.

Nocardia *f.* Nocardia, gram-positive microorganism, cause of nocardiasis.

nocardiasis *f.* nocardiasis, infection caused by the species *Nocardia* that gen. affects the lungs but can also expand to other parts of the body.

nocivo-a *a.* noxious, harmful, pernicious.

nocturno-a *a.* nocturnal.

noche *f.* night; **de __** / at __; **buenas __-s** good evening, good night; **por la __** / in the evening.

nodal *a.* nodal, rel. to a node.

nodular *a.* nodular, rel. to or resembling a nodule.

nódulo *m.* nodule, small node; **__ linfático** / lymphatic __.

nómada *a.* nomadic, free, wandering.

nombre *m.* name; **__ genérico** / generic __, common name of a drug or medication that is not registered commercially; **__ de pila** / given __.

nomenclatura *f.* nomenclature, terminology.

nonato-a *m., f.* 1. unborn; 2. born by Cesarean section.

non compos mentis *L.* non compos mentis, mentally incompetent.

norepinefrina *f.* norepinephrine, vasoconstrictor agent produced in the adrenal gland.

norma *f.* norm, model, standard.

normal *a.* normal.

normalización *f.* normalization, return to a normal state.

normocalcemia *f.* normocalcemia, normal level of calcium in the blood.

normoglicemia *f.* normoglycemia, normal concentration of glucose in the blood.

normopotasemia *f.* normokalemia, normal level of potassium in the blood.

normotenso-a *a.* normotensive, having a normal blood pressure.

normotermia *f.* normothermia, normal temperature.

norte *m.* north; **al __** / to the __.

nosocomial *a.* nosocomial, rel. to a hospital or infirmary; **infección __** / __ infection, acquired in a hospital.

nostalgia *f.* nostalgia, homesickness.

nota *f.* note; remark.

notable *a.* remarkable.

notar *v.* to note; to become aware of something.

noticias *f. pl.* news.

notificar *vi.* to notify, to make known.

notocordio *m.* notochord, the axial fibrocellular cord in the embryo that is replaced by the vertebral column.

novocaína *f.* novocaine, anesthetic.

núbil *a.* nubile, rel. to female sexual maturity.

nublado-a *a.* bleary; cloudy; **vista __** / __ eyed.

nuca *f.* nucha, nape, posterior part of the neck.

nucal *a.* nuchal, rel. to the nape.

nuclear *a.* nuclear. 1. rel. to the nucleus; **envoltura __** / __ envelope, the two parallel membranes surrounding the nucleus, as seen under an electron microscope; 2. rel. to atomic power; **desecho __** / __ waste.

núcleo *m.* nucleus, the essential part of the cell; **__ pulposo** / __ pulpous, central gelatinous mass within an intervertebral disk.

nucléolo *m.* nucleolus, small spherical structure found in the nucleus of cells.

nucleótido *m.* nucleotide, the structural unit of nucleic acid.

nudillo *m.* knuckle.

nudo *m.* node, knotlike mass of tissue; knot.

nudoso-a *a.* nodose, that has nodules or protuberances.

nuevo-a *a.* new.

nuez *f.* walnut; nut.

nuez de Adán *f.* Adam's apple.

nuligrávida *f.* nulligravida, a woman who has never conceived.

nulípara *f.* nullipara, nulliparous, nonparous, a woman who has never borne a living child.

nulo-a *a.* null, void.

número *m.* number; figure.

numeroso-a *a.* numerous.

nunca *adv.* never; at no time; **casi __** / hardly ever.

nutrición *f.* nutrition, nourishment.

nutriente *m.* nutrient, nutritious substance; *a.* nourishing.

nutritivo-a *a.* nutritious, providing nourishment.

Ñ seventeenth letter of the Spanish alphabet.
ñame *m.* yam.
ñoñería *f.* childishness; simpleness.
ñoño-a *-a.* childlike; simple-minded.

144

O *abr.* oral, oralmente / oral, orally; ojo / oculus; oxígeno / oxygen.

o *conj.* either, or; ___ **bien** ___ **mal** / one way or another, anyway.

obedecer *vi.* to obey.

obediente *a.* obedient, compliant.

obesidad *f.* obesity, excess fat.

obeso-a *a.* obese, excessively fat.

objetivo *m.* objective, goal; target; **-a** *a.* rel. to the perception of any happening or phenomenon as it is manifested in real life; **-mente** *adv.* objectively.

oblicuo-a *a.* oblique, diagonal; skewed.

obligación *f.* obligation, duty.

obligar *vi.* to obligate, to force.

obliteración *f.* obliteration, destruction, occlusion by degeneration or by surgery.

obliterar *v.* to obliterate, to annul, to destroy.

obrar *v.* to act, to work; *Mex.* to have a bowel movement.

obscuridad, oscuridad *f.* darkness.

obscuro-a, oscuro-a *a.* dark.

observación *f.* observation; remark.

observar *v.* to observe.

obsesión *f.* obsession, abnormal preoccupation with a single idea or emotion; *pop.* hang-up.

obsesivo-compulsivo-a *a. psych.* obsessive-compulsive, rel. to an individual that is driven to repeat actions excessively as a relief of tension and anxiety.

obseso-a *a.* possessed, dominated by an idea or passion.

obsoleto-a *a.* obsolete, outdated; inactive.

obstáculo *m.* obstacle, hurdle.

obstetra *m., f.* obstetrician.

obstetricia *f.* obstetrics, the study of the care of women during pregnancy and delivery.

obstétrico-a *a.* obstetric, rel. to obstetrics.

obstinado-a *a.* obstinate, headstrong, opinionated, stubborn.

obstipación *f.* obstipation, severe constipation.

obstrucción *f.* obstruction, blockage; ___ **crónica del pulmón** / obstructive lung disease, chronic condition caused by the physical or functional narrowing of the bronchial tree; ___ **en el conducto aéreo superior** / upper airway ___; ___ **intestinal** / ___ intestinal blockage.

obstruido-a *a.* obstructed, blocked; **no** ___ / unobstructed.

obstruir *vi.* to obstruct, to block, to impede.

obtener *vi.* to obtain, to attain, to achieve.

obturación *f.* obturation, occlusion.

obturador-a *a.* obturator, that obstructs an opening.

obtuso-a *a.* obtuse. 1. lacking mental acuity; 2. [*filo*] blunt, dull.

obvio-a *a.* obvious, evident.

ocasión *f.* occasion.

ocasionar *v.* to cause.

occipital *a.* occipital, rel. to the back part of the head; **hueso** ___ / ___ bone; **lóbulo** ___ / ___ lobe.

occipitofrontal *a.* occipitofrontal, rel. to the occiput and the forehead.

occipitoparietal *a.* occipitoparietal, rel. to the occipital and parietal bones and lobes.

occipitotemporal *a.* occipitotemporal, rel. to the occipital and temporal bones.

occipucio *m.* occiput, posteroinferior part of the skull.

oclusión *f.* occlusion, obstruction.

octogenario-a *m., f.* octogenarian, individual that is about eighty years old.

ocular *a.* ocular, visual, rel. to the eyes; **globo** ___ / eyeball; ___ [*de un aparato óptico*] / eyepiece; **órbita** ___ / eyesocket; **traumatismo** ___ / eye injury.

oculista *m., f.* oculist. *V.* **oftalmólogo.**

oculógiro-a *a.* oculogyric, rel. to the rotation of the eyeball.

oculomotor *a.* oculomotor, rel. to the movement of the eyeball.

ocultar *v.* to conceal, to hide.

oculto-a *a.* occult, concealed, not visible.

oculus *L.* oculus, eye.

ocupación *f.* occupation.

ocupacional *a.* occupational, rel. to an occupation.

ocupado-a *a.* busy; occupied.

odiar *v.* to hate.

odinofobia *f. psych.* odynophobia, morbid fear of pain.

odio *m.* hate, hatred.

odontalgia *f.* odontalgia, toothache.

odontectomía *f. surg.* odontectomy, tooth extraction.

odontogénesis *f.* odontogenesis, tooth development.

odontoideo-a *a.* odontoid, dentiform, resembling a tooth.

odontología *f.* odontology, the study of dentistry.

odontólogo-a *m., f.* odontologist, dentist or oral surgeon.

oeste *m.* west; **al** ___ / to the ___.

oficial *a.* official, authorized; **no** ___ / unofficial, rel. to medication not listed in the Pharmacopeia or standard formulary.

oficina *f.* office.

oftalmia *f.* ophthalmia. 1. severe conjunctivitis; 2. internal infl. of the eye.

oftálmico-a *a.* ophthalmic, rel. to the eye; **nervio** ___ / ___ nerve; **solución** ___ / ___ solution.

oftalmitis *f.* ophthalmitis, infl. of the eye.

oftalmología *f.* ophthalmology, the study of the eye and its disorders.

oftalmólogo-a *m., f.* ophthalmologist, oculist, specialist in eye disorders.

oftalmopatía *f.* ophthalmopathy, eye disorder.

oftalmoplastia *f. surg.* ophthalmoplasty, plastic surgery of the eye.

oftalmoplejía *f.* ophthalmoplegia, paralysis of an eye muscle.

oftalmoscopía *f.* ophthalmoscopy, examination of the eye with an ophthalmoscope.

oftalmoscopio *m.* ophthalmoscope, instrument for viewing the interior of the eye.

oído *m.* ear. 1. hearing organ formed by the inner, middle, and external ear; **dolor de ___** / earache; **___ tapado con cerumen** / glue ___; **zumbido en los ___-s** / ringing ___-s; 2. the sense of hearing.

oír *vi.* to hear.

ojeada *f.* glance; **dar una ___** / to glance.

ojeras *f. pl.* dark circles under the eyes.

ojeroso-a *a.* haggard, referring to someone with dark circles under their eyes.

ojo *m.* eye; **banco de ___-s** / ___ bank; **cuenca del ___** / ___ socket; **fondo del ___** / eyeground; **gotas para los ___-s** / ___ drops; **___ de vidrio** / glass ___; **___-s inyectados** / bloodshot ___-s; **___-s llorosos** / watery ___-s; **___-s saltones** / goggle-eyed.

oleada *f.* tide, a space of time; rise and fall.

oleaginoso-a *a.* oleaginous, oily, unctuous.

oleomargarina *f.* oleomargarine.

oler *vi.* to smell, to scent.

olfatear *v.* to sniff.

olfato *m.* 1. the sense of smell; 2. odor.

olfatorio-a *a.* olfactory, rel. to smell.

oligohemia *f.* oligemia, hyphemia. *V.* **hipovolemia.**

oligohidramnios *m.* oligohydramnios, low level of amniotic fluid.

oligomenorrea *f.* oligomenorrhea, deficient or infrequent menstruation.

oligospermia *f.* oligospermia, diminished number of spermatozoa in the semen.

oliguria *f.* oliguria, diminished formation of urine.

oliva *f.* olive. 1. gray body behind the medulla oblongata; 2. green olive color.

olor *m.* odor, smell, scent; **___ penetrante** / penetrating smell.

oloroso-a *a.* odorous.

olvidadizo-a *a.* forgetful.

olvidar *v.* to forget.

ombligo *m.* umbilicus, navel, a depression in the center of the abdomen at the point of insertion of the uterine canal at the time of birth; *pop.* belly button.

omental *a.* omental, rel. to or formed from omentum.

omentectomía *f. surg.* omentectomy, partial or total removal of the omentum.

omentitis *f.* omentitis, infl. of the omentum.

omento *m.* omentum, a fold of the peritoneum that connects the stomach with some abdominal viscera.

omisión *f.* omission.

omitir *v.* to omit.

onanismo *m.* onanism, coitus interruptus, interrupted coitus.

oncogénesis *f.* oncogenesis, formation and development of tumors.

oncogénico-a *a.* oncogenic, rel. to oncogenesis.

oncólisis *f.* oncolysis, destruction of tumor cells.

oncología *f.* oncology, the study of tumors.

oncótico-a *a.* oncotic, rel. to or caused by swelling.

onda *f.* wave. 1. ondulant movement or vibration that travels along a fixed direction; 2. ondulant graphic representation of an activity, such as seen in an electroencephalogram; **guía de ___-s** / waveguide; **longitud de ___** / wavelength; **___-s cerebrales** / brain ___-s; **___-s de excitación** / excitation ___-s; **___ sonora** / sound ___; **___-s ultrasónicas** / ultrasound ___-s.

onda T *f.* T wave, part of the electrocardiogram that represents the repolarization of the ventricles.

onda V *f.* V wave, positive wave that follows the T wave in an electrocardiogram.

ondulado-a *a.* ondulant, having an irregular or wavy border.

onfalectomía *f. surg.* omphalectomy, removal of the umbilicus.

onfálico-a *a.* omphalic, rel. to the umbilicus.

onfalitis *f.* omphalitis, infl. of the umbilicus.

onfalocele *m.* omphalocele, umbilical hernia.

onicosis *f.* onychosis, deformity or sickness of a nail.

oniomanía *f. psych.* oniomania, pathological urge to spend money.

oniquectomía *f. surg.* onychectomy, excision of a nail.

oniquia *f.* onychia, infl. of a nailbed.

onírico-a *a.* oneiric, rel. to dreams.

onirismo *m.* oneirism, dreamlike state while awake.

onomatonamía *f. psych.* onomatonamia, obsessive urge to repeat words.

oocito, ovocito *m.* oocyte, female ovum before maturation.

ooforectomía *f. surg.* oophorectomy, partial or total excision of an ovary.

ooforitis *f.* oophoritis, infl. of an ovary.

oogénesis, ovogénesis *f.* oogenesis, ovogenesis, formation and development of an ovum.

oospermo *m.* oosperm, a fertilized ovum.

opacidad *f.* opacity, dimness, lack of transparency.

opacificación *f.* opacification, process of rendering something opaque.

opaco-a *a.* opaque, that does not filter light.

operable *a.* operable, that can be treated by surgery.

operación *f.* operation, surgical procedure.

operar *v.* to operate, to intervene surgically.

opérculo *m.* operculum. 1. covering or lid; 2. any of the several parts of the cerebrum covering the insula.

operón *m.* operon, a system of linked genes in which the operator gene regulates the remaining structural genes.

opiáceo *m.* opiate, opium-derived drug.

opinar *v.* to express an opinion.

opinión *f.* opinion, judgment.

opio *m.* opium, *Papaver somniferum,* narcotic, analgesic.

opistótonos *m.* opisthotonos, tetanic spasm of the muscles of the back in which the heels and head bend backward and the trunk projects forward.

oponer *vi.* to oppose; **oponerse** *vr.* to be against, to oppose.

oportunidad *f.* opportunity, chance.

oportunista *a.* opportunistic; opportune.

oportuno-a *a.* timely, opportune.

oposición *f.* opposition; objection.

opresión *f.* oppression; heaviness; ___ **en el pecho** / an ___ in the chest.

opresivo-a *a.* oppressive; overwhelming.

oprimir *v.* to oppress.

opsoclono *m.* opsoclonus, irregular movement of the eyes, esp. seen in some cases of brain lesion.

opsonina *f.* opsonin, antibody that combines with a specific antigen and makes it more susceptible to phagocytes.

óptica *f.* optics, the study of light and its relation to vision; **óptico-a** *a.* optic, optical, rel. to vision; **disco** ___ / ___ disk, blind spot of the retina; **ilusión** ___ / ___ illusion; **nervio** ___ / ___ nerve.

óptimo-a *a.* optimum, the best, the ideal.

optómetra, optometrista *m., f.* optometrist, professional who practices optometry.

optometría *f.* optometry, the practice of examining the eyes for visual acuity and prescribing corrective lenses and other optical aids.

optómetro *m.* optometer, instrument used to measure eye refraction.

opuesto-a *a.* opposite; opposed.

oral *a.* oral, delivered or taken by mouth.

orbicular *a.* orbicular, circular; **músculo** ___ / ___ muscle, that surrounds a small opening such as the orbicular muscle of the mouth.

órbita *f.* orbit, bony cavity that contains the eyeball and associated structures.

orbital *a.* orbital, rel. to the orbit.

orden *m.* order, arrangement; regulation.

ordenar *v.* to order; to arrange.

ordeño *m.* milking, maneuver to force material out of a tube.

ordinario-a *a.* ordinary, usual, common.

oreja *f.* external ear; **lóbulo de la** ___ / ear lobe.

orejera *f.* ear protector.

organelo, organito *m.* organelle, minute organ of unicellular organisms.

orgánico-a *a.* organic. 1. rel. to an organ; 2. rel. to organisms of vegetable or animal origin; **enfermedad** ___ / ___ disease.

organismo *m.* organism, a living being.

organización *f.* organization, association.

organizar *vi.* to organize, to arrange.

órgano *m.* organ, part of the body with a specific function; **desplazamiento de** ___ / ___ displacement; ___ **terminal** / end ___; **transplante de un** ___ / ___ transplant.

organogénesis *f.* organogenesis, growth and development of an organ.

orgasmo *m.* orgasm, sexual climax.

orgulloso-a *a.* proud.

orientación *f.* orientation, direction.

orificio *m.* orifice, aperture, opening.

origen *m.* origin, source, beginning.

original *a.* original.

orín, orina *m., f.* urine, the clear fluid secreted by the kidneys, stored in the urinary bladder, and discharged by the urethra, ___ **claro-a** / clear ___; **cultivo de** ___ / ___ culture; **especimen de** ___ **a mitad de chorro** / midstream ___ specimen; ___ **lechoso-a** / milky ___; **muestra de** ___ sample; **sedimento de** ___ / ___ sediment; ___ **turbio-a** / hazy ___.

orinal *m.* urinal, chamber pot, container or receptacle for urine.

orinar *v.* to urinate, to micturate; **ardor al** ___ / burning on urination; ___ **a menudo** / frequent urination; ___ **con dificultad** / difficult urination; ___ **con dolor** / painful urination; **orinarse** *vr.* to wet oneself; ___ **en la cama** / bedwetting.

orofaringe *m.* oropharynx, central part of the pharynx.

orquidectomía, orquiectomía *f. surg.* orchidectomy, orchiectomy, removal of a testicle.

orquiditis, orquitis *f.* orchiditis, orchitis, infl. of a testicle.

orquidopexia, orquiopexia *f. surg.* orchidopexy, orchiopexy, procedure by which an undescended testicle is lowered into the scrotum and fixed to it.

orquiotomía *f.* orchiotomy, incision in a testicle.

ortocromático-a *a.* orthochromatic, of natural color or that accepts coloration.

ortodoncia *f.* orthodontics, the study of irregularities and corrective procedures of teeth.

ortodoncista *m., f.* orthodontist, specialist in orthodontics.

ortógrado-a *a.* orthograde, that walks in an erect position.

ortopedia *f.* orthopedics, the study of bones, joints, muscles, ligaments, and cartilages and the preventive and corrective procedures that deal with their related disorders.

ortopédico-a, ortopedista *m., f.* orthopedist, specialist in orthopedics; *a.* orthopedic, rel. to orthopedia; **calzado** ___ / ___ shoes.

ortopnea *f.* orthopnea, difficulty in breathing except when in an upright position.

ortostático-a *a.* orthostatic, rel. to an erect position.

ortotópico-a *a.* orthotopic, in the normal or correct position.

orzuelo *m.* sty, stye, infl. of the sebaceous glands of the eyelid.

os *L.* os, bone.

oscilación *f.* oscillation, a pendulum-like motion.

óseo-a *a.* osseous, rel. to bone; **desarrollo ___** / bone development; **lesiones ___-s** / bone lesions; **placa ___** / bone plate.

osículo *m.* ossicle, small bone.

osificación *f.* ossification. 1. conversion of a substance into bone; 2. bone development.

osificar *vi.* to ossify, to turn into bone.

osífico-a *a.* ossific, rel. to the formation of bone tissue.

osmolar, osmótico-a *a.* osmolar, osmotic, rel. to or of the nature of osmosis.

osmología *f.* osmology, the study of odors.

osmorreceptor *m.* osmoreceptor. 1. a group of cells in the brain that receive olfactory stimuli; 2. a group of cells in the hypothalamus that respond to changes in the osmotic pressure of the blood.

osmosis *f.* osmosis, diffusion of a solvent through a semipermeable membrane separating two solutions of different concentration.

osmótico-a *a.* osmotic, rel. to or of the nature of osmosis.

osteítis, ostitis *f.* osteitis, ostitis, infl. of a bone; **___ fibrosa quistica** / **___** fibrosa cystica, with cystic and nodular manifestations.

osteoartritis *f.* osteoarthritis, degenerative hypertrophy of the bones and joints.

osteoartropatía *f.* osteoarthropathy, disease of a joint and a bone, gen. accompanied by pain.

osteoblasto *m.* osteoblast, a cell that forms bone tissue.

osteocarcinoma *m.* osteocarcinoma, bone cancer.

osteocartilaginoso-a *a.* osteocartilaginous, rel. to or formed by bone and cartilage.

osteocito *m.* osteocyte, a mature osteoblast that has become isolated in a lacuna of the bone substance.

osteoclasto *m.* osteoclast, giant multinuclear cell that participates in the formation of bone tissue and replaces cartilage during ossification.

osteocondral *a.* osteochondral, rel. to or made of bone and cartilage.

osteocondritis *f.* osteochondritis, infl. of bone and cartilage.

osteodistrofia *f.* osteodystrophia, osteodystrophy, defective bone formation.

osteófito *m.* osteophyte, bony outgrowth.

osteogénesis *f.* osteogenesis. *V.* **osificación.**

osteoide *a.* osteoid, rel. to or resembling bone.

osteología *f.* osteology, the study of bones.

osteoma *m.* osteoma, a tumor of bone tissue.

osteomalacia *f.* osteomalacia, softening of the bones due to loss of calcium in the bone matrix.

osteomielitis *f.* osteomyelitis, infection of bone and bone marrow.

osteonecrosis *f.* osteonecrosis, destruction and death of bone tissue.

osteópata *m., f.* osteopath, specialist in osteopathy.

osteopatía *f.* osteopathy. 1. an approach to medicine that places emphasis on a favorable environment and on normal structural relationships of the musculoskeletal system, using extensive manipulation as a corrective tool; 2. any sickness of the bones.

osteopenia *f.* osteopenia, diminished calcification of the bones.

osteoporosis *f.* osteoporosis, loss of bone density.

osteotomía *f. surg.* osteotomy, the cutting or sawing of a bone.

ostial *a.* ostial, rel. to an opening or orifice.

ostium *L.* (*pl.* **ostia**) ostium, small opening.

ostomía *f. surg.* ostomy, creation of an artificial opening between the bowel or intestine and the skin, as in ileostomy and colostomy.

ostra *f.* oyster.

otalgia, otodinia *f.* otalgia, otodynia, earache.

otectomía *f. surg.* otectomy, excision of the structural contents of the middle ear.

ótico-a *a.* otic, rel. to the ear.

oticodinia *f.* oticodinia, vertigo caused by an ear disorder.

otitis *f.* otitis, infl. of the external, middle, or inner ear; **___ del nadador** / swimmer's ear.

otolaringología *f.* otolaryngology, the study of the ear, nose and throat.

otolaringólogo-a *m., f.* otolaryngologist, specialist in otolaryngology.

otología *f.* otology, the study of the ear and its disorders.

otoneurología *f.* otoneurology, the study of the inner ear as related to the nervous system.

otoplastia *f. surg.* otoplasty, plastic surgery of the ear.

otorragia *f.* otorrhagia, bleeding from the ear.

otorrea *f.* otorrhea, purulent discharge from the ear.

otosclerosis *f.* otosclerosis, progressive deafness due to formation of spongy tissue in the labyrinth of the ear.

otoscopia *f.* otoscopy, examination of the ear with an otoscope.

otoscopio *m.* otoscope, instrument to examine the ear.

ototóxico-a *a.* ototoxic, having toxic effects on the eighth pair of cranial nerves or on the hearing organs.

otro-a *a.* other; *pron.* another; **el ___, la ___** / the **___** one; **los ___-s, las ___-s** / the others.

oval *a.* oval. 1. rel. to an ovum; 2. in the shape of an egg; **ventana ___** / **___** window, membrane that separates the middle and the inner ear.

ovárico-a *a.* ovarian, rel. to the ovaries.

ovariectomía *f. surg.* ovariectomy. *V.* **ooforectomía.**

ovario *m.* ovary, female reproductive organ that produces the ova.

oviducto *m.* oviduct, uterine conduit.

ovoide *a.* ovoid, egg-shaped.

ovotestis *f.* ovotestis, hermaphroditic gland that contains both ovarian and testicular tissue.

ovulación *f.* ovulation, periodic release of the ovum from the ovary.

óvlo *m.* ovum, egg cell.

oxidación *f.* oxidation, the chemical change resulting from the combination of oxygen with another substance.

oxidado-a *a.* rusty.

oxidante *m.* oxidant, agent that causes oxidation.

oxigenación *f.* oxygenation, saturation with oxygen.

oxigenado-a *a.* oxygenated.

oxigenador *m.* oxygenator, device that oxygenates blood, gen. used during surgery.

oxígeno *m.* oxygen, free element found in the atmosphere as a colorless, tasteless, and odorless gas; **cámara de** ___ / ___ tent; **distribución de** ___ / ___ distribution; **falta de** ___ / ___ deficiency; **tratamiento de** ___ / ___ treatment.

oxímetro *m.* oximeter, instrument used to measure the amount of oxygen in the blood.

oxitocina *f.* oxytocin, pituitary hormone that stimulates uterine contraction.

P *abr.* **plasma** plasma; **positivo-a** / positive; **posterior** / posterior; **presión** / pressure; **psiquiatría** / psychiatry; **pulso** / pulse.

pábulum *L.* pabulum, nutrient.

paciencia *f.* patience; **con** ___ / patiently.

paciente *m., f.* patient; **alta del** ___ / patient's discharge; **cuidado del** ___ / ___'s care; ___ **externo, no hospitalizado** / outpatient; ___ **privado** / private ___; ___ **solvente** / self-paying ___; *a.* patient.

padecer *vi.* to be afflicted by a sickness or injury; ___ **de** / to suffer from.

padecimiento *m.* suffering; affliction.

padrastro *m.* stepfather.

padre *m.* father; **-s** the parents, mother and father.

pagado-a *a.* paid.

pagar *vi.* to pay; ___ **al contado** / ___ in cash.

pago *m.* payment; ___ **compartido** / copayment; ___ **de una vez de la suma total** / lump sum ___.

palabra *f.* word.

paladar *m.* palate, the roof of the mouth; ___ **blando** / soft ___; ___ **duro** / hard ___; ___ **hendido** / cleft ___, congenital fissure; ___ **óseo** / bony ___.

palatino-a *a.* palatine, rel. to the palate.

paliativo-a *a.* palliative, that mitigates.

palidecer *vi.* to become pale.

palidez *f.* pallor.

pálido-a *a.* pallid, pale, sallow.

paliza *f.* beating.

palma *f.* 1. palm, palm of the hand; 2. palm tree; **aceite de** ___ / ___ oil.

palmacristi *f.* castor oil.

palmar *a.* palmar, rel. to the palm of the hand.

palpable *a.* palpable, that can be touched.

palpación *f.* palpation, examination with the hands.

palpar *v.* to palpate, to feel, to touch.

palpitación *f.* palpitation, rapid pulsation or throbbing.

palpitante *a.* throbbing.

palpitar *v.* to palpitate; to pant.

palúdico-a *a.* rel. to or afflicted by malaria.

paludismo *m.* malaria, paludism, highly infectious, febrile, and often chronic disease caused by the bite of an infected *Anopheles* mosquito.

pampiniforme *a.* pampiniform, simulating the structure of a vine.

pan *m.* bread; ___ **y mantequilla** / ___ and butter.

panacea *f.* panacea, a remedy to cure all ills.

panadizo *m.* felon, painful abscess of the distal phalanx of a finger.

panarteritis *f.* panarteritis, infl. of the layers of an artery.

panartritis *f.* panarthritis. 1. infl. of some joints of the body; 2. infl. of all the tissues of a joint.

pancitopenia *f.* pancytopenia, abnormal decrease in the number of blood cells.

páncreas *m.* pancreas, gland of the digestive system that externally secretes the pancreatic juice, and internally secretes insulin and glucagon.

pancreatectomía *f. surg.* pancreatectomy, partial or total removal of the pancreas.

pancreático-a *a.* pancreatic, rel. to the pancreas; **conducto** ___ / ___ duct; **jugo** ___ / ___ juice; **quiste** ___ / ___ cyst.

pancreaticoenterostomía *f. surg.* pancreaticoenterostomy, creation of a passage between the pancreatic duct and the intestines.

pancreatina *f.* pancreatin, digestive enzyme obtained from the pancreas.

pancreatitis *f.* pancreatitis, infl. of the pancreas; ___ **aguda** / acute ___; ___ **hemorrágica aguda** / acute hemorrhagic ___.

pandémico-a *a.* pandemic, that occurs over a wide geographical area.

panendoscopio *m.* panendoscope, optical instrument used to examine the urethra and the bladder.

panfleto *m.* pamphlet.

panglosia *f.* panglossia, excessive talking.

panhidrosis *f.* panhidrosis, generalized sweating.

panhipopituitarismo *m.* panhypopituitarism, deficiency of the anterior pituitary gland.

panhisterectomía *f. surg.* panhysterectomy, total excision of the uterus.

pánico *m.* panic, excessive fear; *v.* **tener** ___ / to panic.

paniculitis *f.* paniculitis, infl. of the panniculus adiposus.

panículo *m.* panniculus, layer of tissue; ___ **adiposo** / ___ adiposus; ___ **carnoso** / ___ carnosus.

pannus *L.* pannus, a membrane of granulation tissue covering a normal surface.

pansinusitis *f.* pansinusitis, infl. of all the paranasal sinuses in one or both sides.

pantalones *m.* pants, slacks.

pantalla *f.* screen.

pantorrilla *f.* calf of the leg.

panza *f.* belly.

panzudo-a *a. pop.* potbellied.

pañal *m.* diaper; ___**-es desechables** / disposable ___**-s**.

papa, patata *m.* potato.

papá *m.* dad.

papada *f.* double chin.

Papanicolau, prueba de *f.* Papanicolau's test, Pap smear, sample of mucus from the vagina and the cervix for the purpose of early detection of cancer cells.

papaya *f.* papaya.

papel *m.* paper; ___ **higiénico** / toilet ___; role; *v.* **hacer el** ___ **de** / to play the ___ of.

paperas *f.* mumps, acute, febrile, highly contagious disease characterized by swelling of the salivary glands.

papila *f.* papilla, bud, small, nipple-like eminence of the skin, esp. seen in the mouth; ___ **gustativa** / taste bud.

papilar *m.* papillary, rel. to a papilla.

papiledema *m.* papilledema, edema of the optic disk.

papiliforme *a.* papilliform, resembling a papilla.

papilitis *f.* papillitis, infl. of the optic disk.

papiloma *m.* papilloma, benign epithelial tumor.

papilomatosis *f.* papillomatosis, presence of multiple papillomas.

papovavirus *m.* papovavirus, type of virus used in the study of cancer.

pápula *f.* papule, small, hard eminence of the skin.

papular *a.* papular, rel. to papules.

papuloescamoso-a *a.* papulosquamous, rel. to papules and scales.

paquete celular *m.* packed cells, red blood cells that have been separated from the plasma.

paquidermia *f.* pachydermia. *V.* **elefantiasis.**

paquigiria *f.* pachygyria, thick convolutions of the cerebral cortex.

par *m.* pair, couple.

para *prep.* to, for; for the purpose of; in order to; ___ **siempre** / forever; ¿ ___ **qué?** / what for?

paracentesis *f.* paracentesis, puncture to obtain or remove fluid from a cavity.

parado-a *a.* in a standing position.

paraesternal *a.* parasternal, adjacent to the sternum.

parafasia *f.* paraphasia, type of aphasia manifested by inability to use words coherently.

parafimosis *f.* paraphimosis. 1. retraction or constriction of the prepuce behind the glans penis; 2. retraction of the eyelid behind the eyeball.

parafina *f.* paraffin.

parainfluenza, virus de *m.* parainfluenza virus, any of several viruses associated with some respiratory infections, esp. in children.

paralaje *m.* parallax, the apparent displacement of an object according to the position of the viewer.

parálisis *f.* palsy, paralysis, partial or total loss of function of a part of the body; ___ **cerebral** / cerebral ___, partial paralysis and lack of muscular coordination due to a congenital brain lesion; ___ **de los buzos** / diver's paralysis, decompression sickness (bends); ___ **infantil** / infantile paralysis.

paralítico-a *a.* paralytic, invalid, rel. to or suffering from paralysis; **íleo** ___ / ___ ileus, paralysis of the intestines.

paralizar *vi.* to paralyze.

paramagnético-a *a.* paramagnetic, rel. to substances that are susceptible to magnetism.

paramédico-a *m., f.* paramedic, individual trained and certified to offer emergency medical assistance.

parametrio *m.* parametrium, loose cellular tissue around the uterus.

paranasal *a.* paranasal, adjacent to the nasal cavity.

paraneumonía *f.* parapneumonia, illness with clinical characteristics resembling pneumonia.

paranoia *f. psych.* paranoia, mental disorder characterized by delusions of persecution and grandeur.

paranoico-a *a. psych.* paranoid, rel. to or afflicted with paranoia.

parapancreático-a *a.* parapancreatic, adjacent to the pancreas.

paraparesia *f.* paraparesis, partial paralysis esp. of the lower limbs.

paraplejía *f.* paraplegia, paralysis of the legs and the lower half of the body.

parapléjico-a *a.* paraplegic, rel. to or affected with paraplegia.

parapsicología *f.* parapsychology, the study of psychic phenomena such as mental telepathy and extrasensory perception.

parar *v.* to stop, to halt; **pararse** *vr.* to stand up; ___ **de puntillas** / to stand on tiptoe.

pararrectal *a.* pararectal, adjacent to the rectum.

parasimpático-a *a.* parasympathetic, rel. to one of two branches of the autonomic nervous system.

parasístole *f.* parasystole, an irregularity in cardiac rhythm.

parasítico-a *a.* parasitic.

parasitismo *m.* parasitism, infestation with parasites.

parásito *m.* parasite, organism that lives upon another one.

parasitología *f.* parasitology, the study of parasites.

paratífica, fiebre *f.* paratyphoid fever, a fever that simulates typhoid fever.

paratiroidectomía *f. surg.* parathyroidectomy, removal of one or more of the parathyroid glands.

paratiroideo-a *a.* parathyroid, located close to the thyroid gland.

paratiroides *f.* parathyroid, group of small endocrine glands situated behind the thyroid gland.

paraumbilical *a.* parumbilical, close to the navel.

paravertebral *a.* paravertebral, adjacent to the vertebral column.

parcial *a.* partial; **-mente** *adv.* partially.

parco-a *a.* sparing, scanty, moderate.

parche *m.* patch, piece of cloth or adhesive used to protect wounds; **prueba del** ___ / ___ **test,** for allergies.

parecer *vi.* to seem, to appear; **parecerse** *vr.* to look alike, to resemble.

parecido-a *a.* resembling.

pared *f.* wall; partition.

paregórico *m.* paregoric, sedative derived from

opium.

pareja *f.* pair, couple.

parejo-a *a.* even, equal.

parénquima *m.* parenchyma, the functional elements of an organ.

parenteral *a.* parenteral, that is introduced in the body in a way other than the gastrointestinal route.

parentesco *m.* kindred, family relationship.

paresia *f.* paresis, slight or partial paralysis.

parestesia *f.* paresthesia, sensation of pricking, tingling, or tickling, gen. associated with partial damage to a peripheral nerve.

parético-a *a.* paretic, rel. to or afflicted by paresis.

pariente-a *m.*, *f.* family relative; ___ consanguíneo / blood relation.

parietal *m.* parietal bone; *a.* parietal. 1. rel. to the parietal bone; 2. rel. to the wall of a cavity.

parir *v.* to give birth.

Parkinson, enfermedad de *f.* Parkinson's disease, degenerative process of the brain nerves characterized by tremor, progressive muscular weakness, blurred speech, and shuffling gait.

paro *m.* standstill, arrest.

parodinia *f.* parodynia, difficult or abnormal delivery.

paroniquia *f.* paronychia, infl. of the area adjacent to a fingernail.

parótida *f.* parotid, gland that secretes saliva, situated near the ear.

parotiditis, parotitis *f.* parotiditis, parotitis. *V.* **paperas.**

paroxismal, paroxístico-a *a.* paroxysmal, rel. to paroxysm.

paroxismo *m.* paroxysm. 1. attack, spasm, or convulsion; 2. recurring intensified symptoms.

parpadear *v.* to blink.

parpadeo *m.* blinking; flicker.

párpado *m.* eyelid; cilium.

parrilla *f.* grill; **a la** ___ / grilled.

pars *L.* part, portion.

parte *f.* part, portion; **por todas** ___-s / everywhere.

partenogénesis *f.* parthenogenesis, unusual reproductive process in which the ovum develops without being fertilized by a spermatozoon; ___ **artificial** / artificial ___.

partición *f.* partition, sectioning, division.

participar *v.* to participate.

partícula *f.* particle, one of the minute parts that form matter.

particular *a.* particular; **-mente** *adv.* particularly.

particularidad *f.* peculiarity.

partir *v.* to sever, to break; to divide.

parto *m.* labor, delivery, parturition; **antes del, después del** ___ / before, after delivery; **canal del** ___ / birth canal; **dolor de** ___ / ___ pains; **estar de** ___ / to be close to delivery; **etapas del** ___ / stages of ___; ___ **activo** / active ___; ___ **de un feto sin vida** / stillbirth; ___ **falso** / false ___; ___ **inducido** / induced ___; ___ **laborioso**

/ hard, difficult ___; ___ **natural** / natural childbirth; ___ **normal** / normal delivery; ___ **prematuro** / premature delivery; ___ **prolongado, tardío** / prolonged ___; ___ **seco** / dry ___.

parturienta *f.* parturient, a woman in the act of delivering or who has just delivered.

parturifaciente *m.* parturifacient, an agent that induces parturition.

párulis *f.* gumboil, an abscess of the gums.

parvovirus *m.* parvovirus, any of a group of viruses that cause diseases in animals but not in humans.

pasa *f.* raisin.

pasado *m.* the past tense; **-a** *a.* past; ___ **mañana** / the day after tomorrow; **la semana** ___ / last week.

pasaje *m.* passage. 1. conduit or meatus; 2. evacuation of the bowels.

pasar *v.* to pass, to pass by; to happen.

pasear *v.* to go for a stroll or an outing.

paseo *m.* a stroll; an outing.

pasillo *m.* hall, hallway, corridor; covered way.

pasión *f.* passion, intense emotion.

pasividad *f.* passivity, abnormal dependency on others.

pasivo-a *a.* passive, not spontaneous or active; **ejercicio** ___ / ___ exercise.

paso *m.* step, pace.

pasta *f.* pasta; paste; ___ **de dientes** / toothpaste.

pasteurización *f.* pasteurization, the process of destroying microorganisms by applying regulated heat.

pasteurizar *vi.* to pasteurize, to perform pasteurization.

pastilla *f.* pill, tablet; lozenge; ___ **para dormir** / sleeping ___; ___ **para el dolor** / pain ___.

pastoso-a *a.* clammy; doughy.

patada *f.* hard kick.

patear *v.* to kick.

patelectomía *f. surg.* patellectomy, excision of the patella.

patelofemoral *a.* patellofemoral, rel. to the patella and the femur.

patella *L.* patella, kneecap.

patente *m.* patent, exclusive right or privilege; **medicina de** ___ / ___ medicine; *a.* patulous; open, not obstructed; evident.

paternidad *f.* paternity; **prueba de** ___ / ___ test.

paterno-a *a.* paternal, rel. to the father.

patético-a *a.* pathetic.

patizambo-a *a.* pigeon-toed, feet turned inward.

patofisiología *f.* pathophysiology, the study of the effects of a disease on the physiological processes.

patogénesis *f.* pathogenesis, origin and development of a sickness.

patógeno *m.* pathogen, agent that causes disease; **-a** *a.* pathogenic, that can cause a disease.

patognomónico-a *a.* pathognomonic, rel. to a sign or symptom characteristic of a given disease.

patología *f.* pathology, the study of the origin and nature of disease.

patológico-a *a.* pathologic, pathological, rel. to disease.

patólogo-a *m., f.* pathologist, specialist in pathology.

patrón *m.* pattern, model, type.

pausa *f.* pause, rest; interruption; __ **compensadora** / compensatory __, long interval of the heart, following a heartbeat.

pausado-a *a.* slow, deliberate.

pavo *m.* turkey.

paz *f.* peace; *v.* **dejar en** __ / to leave alone; **en** __ / at __.

peau d'orange *Fr.* peau d'orange, skin condition resembling that of the peel of an orange, an important sign in breast cancer.

peca *f.* freckle, spot, small discoloration of the skin.

pecoso-a *a.* freckled.

pectina *f.* pectin, carbohydrate obtained from the peel of citrus fruits or apples.

pectoral *a.* pectoral, rel. to the chest.

pectus *L.* (*pl.* **pectora**) pectus, breast, chest.

peculiar *a.* peculiar.

pecho *m.* chest; __ **de paloma** / pigeon breast; *v.* **dar el** __ / to breast-feed.

pechuga *a.* breast or white meat of a fowl.

pedal *a.* pedal, rel. to the foot.

pedazo *m.* piece, part of a whole.

pederastia *f.* pederasty, anal intercourse between males, esp. between an adult and a young boy.

pediatra *m., f.* pediatrician, specialist in pediatrics.

pediatría *f.* pediatrics, the study of the care and development of children and the treatment of diseases affecting them.

pediátrico-a *a.* pediatric, rel. to pediatrics.

pedículo *m.* pedicle, narrow, stemlike part of a tumor that connects it with its base.

pediculosis *f.* pediculosis, infestation with lice.

pedir *vi.* to ask for something, to request.

pedofilia *f.* pedophilia, morbid sexual attraction to children.

pedunculado-a *a.* pedunculate, pedunculated, rel. to, or having peduncles.

pedúnculo *m.* peduncle, stemlike connection.

pedunculus *L.* pedunculus. *V.* **pedúnculo.**

pegajoso-a *a.* sticky, gummy.

pegar *vi.* to stick together, to glue, to adhere.

peinar *v.* to comb; **peinarse** *vr.* to comb one's hair.

peine *m.* comb.

peladura *f.* peeling, scaling. *V.* **exfoliación;** __ **química** / chemical __.

pelagra *f.* pellagra, illness caused by deficiency of niacin and characterized by dermatitis, gastrointestinal, and mental disorders.

pelar *v.* to peel; to give a haircut; **pelarse** *vr.* to get a haircut.

pelea *f.* fight, quarrel.

pelear *v.* to fight, to quarrel.

película *f.* 1. film, movie; 2. thin layer or membrane.

peligro *m.* danger, risk; hazard; peril; *v.* **estar en** __ / to be in __; **poner en** __ / to endanger, to jeopardize.

peligroso-a *a.* dangerous, risky, hazardous.

pelo *m.* hair; **raíz del** __ / __ root; **bola de** __ / __ ball, type of bezoar; **trasplante de** __ / __ transplant.

pelota *f.* ball.

peloteo *m.* ballottement, maneuver used during examination of the abdomen and pelvis to determine the presence of tumors or enlargement of organs.

peluca *f.* wig.

peludo-a *a.* hairy.

pélvico-a, pelviano-a *a.* pelvic, rel. to the pelvis.

pelvis *f.* pelvis. 1. cavity in the lower end of the trunk formed by the hip bone, the sacrum, and the coccyx; **enfermedad inflamatoria de la** __ / inflammatory pelvic disease; 2. basin-shaped cavity.

pelvis menor, verdadera *f.* true pelvis, the inferior and contractile part of the pelvis.

pellejo *m.* peel, hide; *pop.* skin.

pellizcar *vi.* to pinch.

pellizco *m.* pinch.

pena *f.* sorrow, affliction.

penacho *m.* tuft, a small cluster or mass.

pendiente *a.* pending, unfinished.

pendular *a.* pendulous, oscillating or hanging.

pene *m.* penis, the external part of the male reproductive organ that contains the urethral orifice through which urine and semen pass.

peneal, peneano-a *a.* penile, rel. to the penis.

penetración *f.* penetration. 1. the act of penetrating; 2. the ability of radiation to go through a substance.

penetrante *a.* penetrating; piercing.

penetrar *v.* to penetrate, to go through.

pénfigo *m.* pemphigus, a variety of dermatosis characterized by the presence of blisters that can become infected on rupturing.

penfigoideo-a *a.* pemphigoid, similar to pemphigus but having clinical differences.

penicilina *f.* penicillin, antibiotic derived directly or indirectly from cultures of the fungus *Penicillum.*

pensar *vi.* to think.

peor *a. comp.* worse; *sup.* worst; *adv.* worse.

pepino *m.* cucumber.

pepsina *f.* pepsin, the main enzyme of the gastric juice.

péptico-a *a.* peptic, rel. to the action or the digestion of gastric juices.

pequeño-a *a.* small in size.

pera *f.* pear; __ **de goma** / bulb syringe.

percepción *f.* perception. 1. the conscious mental recognition of a sensory stimulus; __ **extrasensorial** / extrasensory __; 2. understanding or comprehension of an idea.

percibir *v.* to perceive, to realize.

percusión *f.* percussion, procedure that consists in tapping the surface of the body with the fingers or a small tool, in order to produce sounds or vibrations that indicate the condition of a given part of the body; ___ **ausculta-toria** / auscultatory ___.

percutáneo-a *a.* percutaneous, applied through the skin.

percutir *v.* to percuss, to use percussion.

perder *vi.* to lose, to forfeit; ___ **sangre** / to bleed; ___ **la oportunidad** / to miss, to lose an opportunity; ___ **tiempo** / to waste time; ___ **un turno** / to miss an appointment.

pérdida *f.* loss; ___ **de sangre** / ___ of blood; ___ **del conocimiento** / ___ of consciousness; ___ **del contacto con la realidad** / ___ of contact with reality; ___ **del equilibrio** / ___ of balance; ___ **del movimiento** / ___ of motion; ___ **de la audición** / ___ of hearing; ___ **de la memoria** / ___ of memory; ___ **de la tonicidad muscular** / ___ of muscle tone; ___ **de la visión** / ___ of vision.

perdido-a *a.* lost.

perfeccionismo *m. psych.* perfectionism, excessive drive to attain perfection, regardless of the importance of the task.

perfeccionista *m., f.* perfectionist.

perfecto-a *a.* perfect; **-mente** *adv.* perfectly.

perfil *m.* profile, side view; outline; ___ **bio-químico** / biochemical ___; ___ **físico** / physical ___.

perforación *f.* perforation, hole.

perforar *v.* to perforate; to pierce.

perfusión *f.* perfusion, passage of a liquid through a conduit.

periamigdalino-a *a.* peritonsillar, close to the tonsils.

perianal *a.* perianal, located around the anus.

pericardial, pericárdico-a *a.* pericardiac, pericardial, rel. to the pericardium; **derrame** ___ / ___ effusion; **efusión** ___ / ___ effusion; **resec-ción** ___ / ___ window.

pericardiectomía *f. surg.* pericardiectomy, partial or total excision of the pericardium.

pericardio *m.* pericardium, saclike, double-layered membrane that surrounds the heart and the origins of the large blood vessels.

pericarditis *f.* pericarditis, infl. of the pericardium; ___ **constrictiva** / constrictive ___; ___ **localizada** / localized ___; ___ **reumática** / rheumatic ___.

periferia *f.* periphery, part of a body or organ away from the center.

periférico-a *a.* peripheral, rel. to or occurring in the periphery; **sistema nervioso** ___ / ___ nervous system, the group of nerves situated outside the central nervous system.

perilla *f.* rubber bulb.

perinatal *a.* perinatal, rel. to or occurring before, during, or right after birth.

perinatología *f.* perinatology, study of the fetus and newborn during the perinatal period.

perinatólogo-a *m., f.* perinatologist, specialist in perinatology.

perineal *a.* perineal, rel. to the perineum.

perinéfrico-a *a.* perinephric, close to the kidney.

perineo *m.* perineum, the pelvic outlet bounded anteriorly by the scrotum in the man and the vulva in the woman, and posteriorly by the anus.

perineural *a.* perineural, around the nerve.

periódico *m.* newspaper; **-a** *a.* periodical; **-mente** *adv.* periodically.

período *m.* period. 1. interval of time, epoch; ___ **de tiempo** / time span.

periodo *m.* menstruation.

periodoncia *f.* periodontics, branch of odontology dealing with areas surrounding the teeth.

periodoncio *m.* periodontium, support tissue surrounding a tooth.

periodoncista *m., f.* periodontist, specialist in periodontics.

periodontal *a.* periodontal, surrounding the tooth.

periodontitis *f.* periodontitis, infl. of the periodontium.

periostio *m.* periosteum, thick fibrous membrane that covers all the surface of the bone except the articular surface.

peristalsis *f.* peristalsis, wavelike contractions that occur in a tubular structure such as the alimentary canal, by which the contents are forced onward.

peristáltico-a *a.* peristaltic, rel. to peristalsis.

peritoneal *a.* peritoneal, rel. to the peritoneum.

peritoneo *m.* peritoneum, serous membrane that lines the abdominopelvic walls and the viscera.

peritoneoscopía *f.* peritoneoscopy. *V.* **laparo-scopía.**

peritonitis *f.* peritonitis, infl. of the peritoneum.

periungual *a.* periungual, around the nail.

periuretral *a.* periurethral, around the urethra.

perjudicial *a.* detrimental, damaging.

perleche *Fr.* perleche, disorder manifested by fissures at the corner of the mouth, seen esp. in children and gen. as a result of malnutrition.

permanecer *vi.* to remain; to last.

permanente *a.* permanent, lasting; **-mente** *adv.* permanently.

permeabilidad *f.* permeability, patency, the quality of being permeable, not obstructed; ___ **capilar** / capillary ___.

permeable *a.* permeable, allowing passage through structures such as a membrane.

permiso *m.* permit; consent.

permitido-a *a.* permissible; permitted.

permitir *v.* to allow, to consent, to agree.

pernicioso-a *a.* pernicious, noxious, harmful.

pero *conj.* but.

peroné *m.* perone, fibula, calf bone, the outer and thinner of the two lower leg bones.

perpendicular *a.* perpendicular.
per rectum *L.* per rectum, by the rectum.
perro *m.* dog.
persecución *f.* persecution.
perseveración *f. psych.* perseveration, mental disorder manifested by the abnormal repetition of an idea or action.
persistir *v.* to persist, to persevere.
persona *f.* person. 1. individual; 2. *psych.* outward personality that conceals the real one.
personal *m.* personnel; ___ **médico** / medical ___; *a.* personal, rel. to a person.
personalidad *f.* personality, traits, characteristics, and individual behavior that distinguish one person from another; ___ **antisocial** / antisocial ___; ___ **compulsiva** / compulsive ___; ___ **esquizoide** / schizoid, split ___; ___ **extrovertida** / extroverted ___; ___ **introvertida** / introverted ___; ___ **neurótica** / neurotic ___; ___ **paranoica** / paranoid ___; ___ **psicopática** / psychopathic ___.
perspectiva *f.* perspective.
perspiración *f.* perspiration, exudation.
persuadir *v.* to persuade.
persuasión *f.* persuasion, therapeutic treatment that tries to deal with the patient through the use of reason.
pertenecer *vi.* to belong.
perteneciente *a.* pertaining or rel. to.
pertinente *a.* pertinent, relevant.
perturbación *f.* perturbation. 1. feeling of uneasiness; 2. abnormal variation from a regular state.
perturbar *v.* to perturb, to disrupt, to disturb.
pertussis *L.* pertussis. V. **tos ferina.**
perversión *f.* perversion, deviation from socially accepted behavior; ___ **sexual** / sexual ___.
pervertido-a *m., f.* pervert, individual given to sexual perversion.
pervio-a *a.* pervious. V. **permeable.**
pes *L.* pes, the foot or a structure resembling it.
pesa *f.* weighing scale.
pesadez *f.* heaviness.
pesadilla *f.* nightmare.
pesado-a *m., f.* a boring person; *a.* heavy; [*conducta*] boring; **sueño** ___ / deep sleep.
pésame *m.* condolences.
pesar *m.* grief, sorrow; *v.* to weigh; **a** ___ **de** / in spite of.
pesario *m.* pessary, uterus-supporting device inserted in the vagina.
pescado *m.* fish.
pescuezo *m.* neck.
pesimismo *m.* pessimism, an inclination to see and judge situations in their most unfavorable light.
pesimista *m., f.* pessimist; *a.* pessimist, rel. to, or that manifests pessimism.
peso *m.* weight; **aumento de** ___ / ___ gain; **falto de, bajo de** ___ / underweight; **pérdida de** ___ / ___ loss; ___ **al nacer** / birth ___.
pestañas *f. pl.* eyelashes.

pestañear *v.* to blink, to wink.
pestañeo *m.* blink; blinking.
peste *f.* 1. bubonic plague, an epidemic infectious disease transmitted by the bite of infected rats or fleas; 2. plague, any epidemic contagious disease with a high rate of mortality; 3. foul smell.
pesticida *m.* pesticide, chemical agent that kills insects and rodents.
petequia *f.* petechiae, minute hemorrhagic spots in the skin and the mucosa that appear in connection with some severe fevers such as typhoid.
petición *f.* petition, request; claim; **proceso para revisión de** ___**-es** / claim review procedure.
petit mal *Fr.* petit mal, benign epileptic attack with loss of consciousness at times, but with no convulsions.
petrificado-a *a.* petrified. 1. made rigid like stone; 2. terrified.
peyote *m.* peyote, plant from which the hallucinatory drug mescaline is obtained.
pezón *m.* nipple; ___ **agrietado** / cracked ___; ___ **enlechado** / engorged ___.
piamadre *f.* pia mater, thin vascular membrane, the innermost of the three cerebral meninges.
pica *f.* pica, a craving for inedible substances.
picada, picadura *f.* sting, bite.
picante *a.* piquant, highly seasoned.
picar *vi.* to bite; to pierce, to prick.
picazón *f.* itching.
pie *m.* foot; ___ **de atleta** / athlete's ___, dermatofitosis; ___ **en extensión** / footdrop; ___ **plano** / flatfoot; **planta del** ___ / sole; *v.* **estar de** ___ / to be standing; *vr.* **ponerse de** ___ / to stand up; *v.* **ir a** ___ / to go on foot.
pie de trinchera *m.* trench foot, infectious condition of the feet resembling from long exposure to cold.
piedra *f.* stone, calculus.
piel *f.* skin; hide, epidermis; **cáncer de la** ___ / ___ cancer; **injerto de** ___ / ___ graft.
pielografía *f.* pyelography. V. **pielograma.**
pielograma *m.* pyelogram, x-ray of the renal pelvis and the ureter using a contrasting medium.
pielolitotomía *f. surg.* pyelolithotomy, incision to remove a calculus from the renal pelvis.
pielonefritis *f.* pyelonephritis, infl. of the kidney and the renal pelvis.
pieloplastia *f. surg.* pyeloplasty, plastic surgery of the renal pelvis.
pielostomía *f.* pyelostomy, creation of an opening in the renal pelvis to divert the urine to the exterior.
pielotomía *f. surg.* pyelotomy, incision of the renal pelvis.
pierna *f.* leg, lower extremity that extends from the knee to the ankle; ___ **arqueada** / bowleg, genu varum; **traumatismo de la** ___ / ___ injury.
pigmentación *f.* pigmentation.
pigmento *m.* pigment, coloring element.

pijama, piyamas *f.* pajamas.

pila *f.* faucet; battery.

píldora *f.* pill; ___ **de control del embarazo** / birth control ___ .

piliación *f.* piliation, formation and development of hair.

pilórico-a *a.* pyloric, rel. to the pylorus.

píloro *m.* pylorus, the lower aperture of the stomach that opens into the duodenum.

piloroplastia *f. surg.* pyloroplasty, plastic surgery to repair the pylorus.

pilus *L.* (*pl.* **pili**) pilus, hair.

pimienta *f.* pepper.

pincelación *f.* penciling, pencilling, application of a medical solution to an area of the skin or to a cavity with a medicated pencil, brush, or cotton swab.

pinchar *v.* to prick.

pinchazo *m.* prick, jab; cut.

pinna *L.* pinna, ear lap.

pinocitosis *f.* pinocytosis, absorption of liquids by cells.

pintar *v.* to paint; to apply a medication to the skin.

pinzas *f. pl.* clip, forceps, pincers, tweezers, devices used to assist in the extraction process; ___ **de secuestro** / sequestrum forceps.

piocito *m.* pyocite, a pus corpuscle.

piógeno-a *a.* pyogenic, that produces pus.

piojo *m.* louse, parasite that is the primary transmitter of some diseases such as typhus.

piorrea *f.* pyorrhea. *V.* **periodontitis.**

pipeta *f.* pipet, pipette, glass tube.

pirámide *f.* pyramid, a cone-shaped structure such as the medulla oblongata.

pirético *m.* pyretic, rel. to fever.

pirexia *f.* pyrexia, high temperature; fever.

pirógeno *m.* pyrogen, agent that elevates a fever.

piromanía *f.* pyromania, obsession with fire.

piscina *f.* swimming pool.

piso *m.* floor; ground.

pistola *f.* pistol, handgun.

pituitaria, glándula *f.* pituitary gland. *V.* **hipófisis.**

piuria *f.* pyuria, presence of pyocites in the urine.

pivote *m.* pivot, part used to support the artificial crown of a tooth.

placa *f.* 1. plate, flat structure such as a thin layer of bone; 2. plate, thin layer of metal used to support a structure; 3. plaque, a patch on the skin or mucous membrane; 4. x-ray.

placebo *m.* placebo, harmless substance of no medical value, gen. used for experimental purposes.

placenta *f.* placenta, vascular organ that develops in the wall of the uterus through which the fetus derives its nourishment; ___ **previa** / ___ previa, placenta situated before the fetus in relation to the cervical opening causing at times severe hemorrhaging.

placentario-a *a.* placental, rel. to the placenta; **insuficiencia** ___ / ___ insufficiency.

plaga *f.* plague, epidemic infectious disease.

plan *m.* plan; design.

planeamiento *m.* planning.

planear *v.* to plan.

planificación familiar *f.* planned parenthood; family planning.

planilla *f.* [*formulario*] form.

plano *m.* plane. 1. flat surface; 2. a relatively smooth surface formed by making an imaginary or real cut through a part of the body; ___ **axial** / axial ___ ; ___ **coronal** / coronal ___ ; ___ **frontal** / frontal ___ ; ___ **horizontal** / horizontal ___ ; ___ **medio** / midplane; ___ **sagital** / sagittal ___ .

planta *f.* plant; ___ **del pie** / sole; ___ **-s medicinales** [*hierbas*] / medicinal ___ -s or herbs.

plantar *a.* plantar, rel. to the sole of the foot; **reflejo** ___ / ___ reflex, Babinski's reflex.

plaqueta *f.* platelet, thrombocyte, an element of the blood in the form of minute disks, essential to coagulation; **conteo de** ___ **-s** / ___ count.   plaquetocrito - plateletcrit

plasma *m.* plasma, liquid component of the blood and lymph made of 91 percent water and 9 percent of a combination of elements such as proteins, salts, nutrients, and vitamins.

plasticidad *f.* plasticity, the capacity to be molded.

plástico *m.* plastic; **-a** *a.* plastic.

plata *f.* silver; **nitrato de** ___ / ___ nitrate.

plátano *m.* banana.

Platelmintos *m. pl.* Platyhelminthes, a phylum of flatworms that includes the *Cestoda* and *Trematoda*, among others.

platicar *vi.* to converse, to talk.

plegado-a *a.* plicate, folded.

pleomorfismo *m.* pleomorphism, the quality of assuming various forms.

pletismografía *f.* plethysmography, the recording of the changes in size of a part of the body as affected by circulation.

plétora *f.* plethora, an excess of any one of the body fluids.

pleura *f.* pleura, doublefold membrane that covers each lung; ___ **parietal** / parietal ___ ; ___ **visceral** / visceral ___ .

pleural *a.* pleural, rel. to the pleura; **cavidad** ___ / ___ cavity, space between the folds of the pleura; **derrame** ___ / ___ effusion.

pleuresía *f.* pleurisy, infl. of the pleura.

pleurítico-a *a.* pleuritic, rel. to pleurisy.

pleuritis *f. V.* **pleuresía.**

pleuroscopía *f.* pleuroscopy, inspection of the pleural cavity through an incision into the thorax.

plexiforme *a.* plexiform, in the shape of a plexus or net.

plexo *m.* plexus, an interlacing of nerves, blood, or lymphatic vessels.

plica *f.* plica, fold, crease.

pliegue *m.* fold.

plomo *m.* lead; **delantal de** ___ / ___ apron; **en-**

venenamiento por ___ / ___ poisoning; **sonda de** ___ / ___ probe.

pluma *f.* pen.

plumbismo *m.* plumbism, chronic lead poisoning.

plural *m.* plural, indicator of the presence of more than one.

pluripotencial *a.* pluripotent, pluripotential, able to take more than one course of action.

población *f.* population.

pobre *a.* poor.

pobreza *f.* poverty.

poción *f.* draft, potion, a single dose of liquid medicine.

poco-a *a.* little, in small quantity; *adv.* little, small; **dentro de** ___ / in a short while; ___ **a** ___ / little by little; **por** ___ / almost.

poder *m.* power, strength; *vi.* to be able to; to have the power to.

podíatra *m., f.* podiatrist, specialist in podiatry.

podiatría *f.* podiatry, the diagnosis and treatment of conditions affecting the feet.

podrido-a *a.* rotten, decomposed.

polar *a.* polar, rel. to a pole.

polaridad *f.* polarity. 1. the quality of having poles; 2. the quality of presenting opposite effects at the two extremities.

polen *m.* pollen.

poli *m.* poly, polymorphonuclear leukocyte.

poliarticular *a.* polyarticular, affecting more than one joint.

poliartritis *f.* polyarthritis, infl. of more than one joint.

policitemia *f.* polycythemia, excess of red blood cells; ___ **primaria** / primary ___, **vera**; ___ **rubra** / rubra ___, vera; ___ **secundaria** / secondary ___, erythrocythemia; ___ **vera** / vera ___, erythremia.

policlínica *f.* polyclinic, a general hospital.

polidactilia *f.* polydactylia, polydactyly, the presence of more than five fingers or toes.

polidipsia *f.* polydipsia, excessive thirst.

poligamia *f.* polygamy, the practice of having more than one spouse at the same time.

polígrafo *m.* polygraph, device that registers simultaneously the arterial and venous pulsations.

polihidramnios *m.* polyhydramnios, an excess of amniotic fluid.

poli-insaturado-a *a.* polyunsaturated, denoting a fatty acid.

polimialgia *f.* polymyalgia, condition characterized by pain affecting several muscles.

polimiositis *f.* polymyositis, V. **dermatomiositis.**

polimorfonucleado-a, polimorfonuclear *a.* polymorphonuclear, having a deeply lobed nucleus; **granulocito** ___ / ___ granulocyte, having a nucleus with multiple lobes.

polineuropatía *f.* polyneuropathy, any disease that affects several nerves at one time.

polio, poliomielitis *f.* polio, poliomyelitis, contagious disease that attacks the central nervous system and causes paralysis of the muscles, esp. of the legs.

poliomiopatía *f.* polymyopathy, any disease that affects several muscles at the same time.

poliovirus *m.* poliovirus, causative agent of poliomyelitis.

polipectomía *f. surg.* polypectomy, excision of a polyp.

pólipo *m.* polyp, tag, mass, or growth protruding from a mucous membrane.

poliposis *f.* polyposis, formation of multiple polyps.

poliquístico-a *a.* polycystic, having many cysts.

polisacárido *m.* polysaccharide, a carbohydrate capable of hydrolysis.

polivalente *a.* polyvalent, having an effect against more than one agent.

póliza de seguro *f.* insurance policy.

polo *m.* pole, each of the two opposite extremes of a body, organ, or spherical or oval part.

polución *f.* pollution, contamination.

polvo *m.* dust; powder; **en** ___ / powdered.

pollo *m.* chicken.

pomada *f.* ointment, pomade, salve, semisolid medicinal substance for external use; ___ **contraceptiva** / contraceptive jelly; ___ **facial** / cold cream; ___ **vaginal** / vaginal jelly.

pomo *m.* jar; bottle.

pómulo *m.* molar bone, cheekbone.

poner *vi.* to put, to set, to lay down; **ponerse** *vr.* [*vestimenta*] to put on; to become; ___ **viejo** / to grow or become old.

pons *L.* pons, tissue formation that connects two separate parts of an organ.

poplíteo-a *a.* popliteal, rel. to the area behind the knee.

por *prep.* for, by, through, from; ___ **ahora** / for the time being; ___ **atrás** / from or through the back; ___ **delante** / from or through the front; ___ **eso** / because of that; ___ **lo tanto** / therefore.

porcentaje *m.* percentage, percent.

porcino-a *a.* porcine, rel. to swine.

porción *f.* portion.

porfiria *f.* porphyria, congenital defect in metabolism manifested by the presence of great amounts of porphyrin in the blood, urine, and stools causing physical and psychiatric disorders.

porfirina *f.* porphyrin, compound occurring in the protoplasm, basis of the respiratory pigments.

poro, porus *m.* pore, porus, minute opening of the skin such as the duct of a sweat gland.

poroso-a *a.* porous, permeable.

porque *conj.* because, for the reason that; *interr.* ¿**por qué?** / why?, for what reason?

porta *L.* porta, opening, or entry, esp. one through which blood vessels and nerves penetrate into an organ.

porta, vena *f.* portal vein, short, thick trunk formed by branches of many veins leading from abdominal organs.

portacatéter *m.* catheter holder.

portacava *a.* portacaval, rel. to the porta and the inferior vena cava.

portador *m.* carrier, a disease causing agent that can be transmitted to other individuals; ___ **de bacilos** / bacillicarrier.

portal *m.* portal, entryway; *a.* rel. to the portal system.

portal, circulación *f.* portal circulation, flow of blood into the liver by the portal vein and out by the hepatic vein.

portal, hipertensión *f.* portal hypertension, increase in pressure in the portal vein due to an obstruction in blood circulation in the liver.

portaobjeto *m.* slide, specimen holder for microscopic examination.

poseer *vi.* to possess.

poseído-a *a. pp.* of **poseer**, possessed, dominated by an idea or passion.

posesivo *m. gr.* possessive; **-a** *a.* possessive.

posibilidad *f.* possibility.

posible *a.* possible; **-mente** *adv.* possibly.

posición *f.* position; ___ **anatómica** / anatomic ___; ___ **de litotomía** / lithotomy ___; ___ **distal** / distal ___; ___ **dorsal recumbente** / dorsal recumbent ___; ___ **erecta** / upright ___; ___ **genucubital** / genocubital ___, knee-elbow; ___ **genupectoral** / knee-chest ___; ___ **inadecuada** / malposition; ___ **lateral** / lateral ___; ___ **prona** / prone ___, face down; ___ **supina, yacente** / supine ___, face up.

positividad *f.* positivity, manifestation of a positive reaction.

positivo-a *a.* positive; certain, without doubt.

posponer *vi.* to postpone, to delay.

posterior *a.* posterior. 1. rel. to the back or the back part of a structure; 2. following in sequence.

posthipnótico-a *a.* posthypnotic, following the hypnotic state.

postictal *a.* postictal, following a seizure or attack.

postmaduro *a.* postmature, rel. to an infant born after the forty-first week of gestation.

post mortem *L.* postmortem, occurring after death; autopsy.

postnasal *a.* postnasal, behind the nose.

postparto *m.* postpartum, period of time following childbirth; **depresión del** ___ / ___ depression; **psicosis del** ___ / ___ psychosis.

postoperatorio-a *a.* postoperative, following surgery; **complicación** ___ / ___ complication; **cuidado** ___ / ___ care.

postprandial *a.* postprandial, after a meal.

postración *f.* prostration, exhaustion, extreme fatigue.

postrado-a *a.* prostrate. 1. in prone position; 2. exhausted, debilitated.

postre *m.* dessert.

póstumo-a *a.* posthumous, occurring after death; **examen** ___ / postmortem examina-

tion.

postura *f.* posture, position of the body.

postural *a.* postural, rel. to position or posture; **hipotensión** ___ / ___ hypotension, decrease in blood pressure in an erect position.

potable *a.* potable, drinkable, that can be drunk without harm.

potasemia *f.* kalemia, presence of potassium in the blood.

potasio *m.* potassium, mineral which, combined with others in the body, is essential in the transmission of nerve impulses and in muscular activity.

potencia *f.* potency, strength.

potencial *m.* potential, electric pressure or tension; *a.* having a ready disposition or capacity.

potente *a.* potent, strong.

práctica *f.* practice.

practicar *vi.* to practice.

práctico-a *a.* practical.

prandial *a.* prandial, rel. to meals.

preagónico-a *a.* preagonal, rel. to a condition preceding death.

preanestésico *m.* preanesthetic, preliminary agent given to ease the administration of general anesthesia.

precanceroso-a *a.* precancerous, tending to become malignant.

precario-a *a.* precarious, uncertain.

precaución *f.* precaution.

precavido-a *a.* cautious, on guard.

preceder *v.* to precede.

precio *m.* price, cost.

precipitado *m.* precipitate, deposit of solid particles that settles out of a solution; **-a** *a.* that occurs suddenly.

precisión *f.* precision, exactness.

precocidad *f.* precocity, early development of physical or mental adult traits.

precoz *a.* precocious.

precursor *m.* precursor, something that precedes, such as a symptom or sign of a disease; **-a** *a.* introductory, preliminary.

predecir *vi.* to predict.

predisposición *f.* predisposition, propensity to develop a condition or illness caused by environmental, genetic, or psychological factors.

predispuesto-a *a.* predisposed, prone or susceptible to contract a disease.

predominante *a.* predominant.

predominio *m.* predominance.

preeclampsia *f.* preeclampsia, a toxic condition of late pregnancy, manifested by hypertension, albuminuria, and edema.

preferencia *f.* preference.

preferible *a.* preferable.

preferir *vi.* to prefer, to favor one thing, person, or condition over another.

prefijo *m. gr.* prefix.

pregunta *f.* question; *v.* **hacer una** ___ / to ask a ___ .

preguntar *v.* to ask, to inquire.

prejuicio *m.* prejudice, bias.

preliminar *a.* preliminary.

premadurez *f.* prematurity, the condition of a viable infant born prior to completion of the thirty-seventh week of gestation.

prematuro-a *m., f.* premature baby; *a.* born prior to the thirty-seventh week of gestation.

premedicación *f.* premedication. *V.* **preanestésico.**

premenstrual *a.* premenstrual; **tensión ___** / **___ tension.**

premonición *f.* premonition, forewarning.

premonitorio-a *a.* premonitory, **advertencia o señal ___** / **___ signal; síntoma ___** / **___ symptom.**

premunición *f.* premunition, immunity to a given infection established by the previous presence of the causative agent.

prenatal *a.* prenatal, prior to birth; **cuidado ___** / **___ care.**

prensil *a.* prehensile, adapted or shaped for grasping or lifting.

preñada *a.* pregnant.

preocupación *f.* preoccupation, concern.

preocupado-a *a.* concerned, worried.

preocuparse *vr.* to worry, to be preoccupied; **no se preocupe, no te preocupes** / don't worry.

preoperativo-a *a.* preoperative; **cuidado ___** / **___ care.**

preparación *f.* preparation. 1. the act of making something ready; 2. a medication ready for use.

preparar *v.* to prepare, to make ready.

preposición *f. gr.* preposition.

prepubescente *a.* prepubescent, before puberty.

prepucio *m.* prepuce, foreskin, loose fold of skin that covers the glans penis.

prerrenal *a.* prerenal. 1. in front of the kidney; 2. that occurs in the circulatory system before reaching the kidney.

presacro-a *a.* presacral, in front of the sacrum.

presbiopía *f.* presbyopia, farsightedness that occurs with increasing age due to the loss of elasticity of the lens of the eye.

prescribir *vi.* to prescribe.

prescripción *f.* prescription.

prescrito-a *a. pp.* of **prescribir,** prescribed, ordered.

presencia *f.* presence.

presentación *f.* presentation. 1. position of the fetus in the uterus as detected upon examination; 2. position of the fetus in reference to the birth canal at the time of delivery; **___ cefálica** / cephalic **___**; **___ de cara** / face **___**; **___ de nalgas** / breech **___**; **___ transversa** / transverse **___**; 3. oral report.

presente *a.* present, manifest.

preservación *f.* preservation, conservation.

preservar *v.* to preserve.

preservativo *m.* preservative, agent that is added to food or medication to destroy or

impede multiplication of bacteria.

presilla *f.* staple.

presión *f.* pressure, stress, strain, tension; **___ arterial** / arterial **___**, pressure of the blood in the arteries; **___ atmosférica** / atmospheric **___**, pressure exerted by the mass of air surrounding the earth; **___ central venosa** / central venous **___**, blood pressure of the right atrium of the heart; **___ del pulso** / pulse **___**, the difference between sistolic and diastolic pressure; **___ diastólica** / diastolic **___**, lowest arterial blood pressure during diastole of the heart; **___ intracraneana** / intracranial **___**, pressure exerted within the cranium; **___ parcial** / partial **___**, exerted by a single gas component in a single, mixed composition; **___ osmótica** / osmotic **___** *V.* **osmosis; ___ sistólica** / systolic **___**, arterial pressure during contraction of the ventricles; **___ venosa** / venous **___**, exerted by the blood in the walls of the veins. *v.* **hacer ___** / to exert pressure.

presión sanguínea *f.* blood pressure, pressure of the blood in the arteries, produced by the action of the left ventricle, the resistance of the arterioles and capillaries, the elasticity of the arterial walls, and the viscosity and volume of the blood expressed in relation to the atmospheric pressure; **___ alta** / high **___**; **___ baja** / low **___**; **___ normal** / normal **___**.

presionar *v.* to exert pressure.

presor *a.* pressor, that tends to raise the blood pressure.

pretender *v.* to pretend.

pretérito *m. gr.* preterite.

pretérmino *m.* preterm, occurring during the period of time prior to the thirty-seventh week in a pregnancy.

prevaleciente *a.* prevailing.

prevalencia *f.* prevalence, the total number of cases of a specific disease present in a given population at a certain time.

prevención *f.* prevention.

prevenir *vi.* to prevent, to forestall.

preventivo-a *a.* preventive; **servicios de salud ___** / **___ health services.**

prever *vi.* to foresee.

prevertebral *a.* prevertebral, in front of a vertebra.

previo-a *a.* previous, prior.

previsto-a *a. pp.* of **prever,** foreseen.

priapismo *m.* priapism, painful and continued erection of the penis as a result of disease.

primario-a *a.* primary, initial; chief, principal.

primavera *f.* springtime.

primer, primero-a *a.* first, prime.

primeriza *f.* woman who gives birth to a child for the first time.

primeros auxilios *m. pl.* first aid.

primitivo-a *a.* primitive; embryonic.

primo-a *m., f.* cousin.

primogénito-a *a.* first-born.

primordial *a.* primordial, essential.

principal *a.* principal, foremost; **-mente** *adv.* primarily, mainly.

principiante *m.* beginner, novice.

principio *m.* 1. beginning, start; 2. principle, chief ingredient of a medication or chemical compound; 3. principle, rule.

principio del placer *m. psych.* pleasure principle, behavior directed at obtaining immediate gratification and avoiding pain.

principio de la realidad *m. psych.* reality principle, orientation to reality and self-gratification through awareness of the outside world.

prioridad *f.* priority, precedence.

prisa *f.* haste, rush; **a toda** ___ / right away; *vr.* **darse** ___ / to hurry; *v.* **tener** ___ / to be in a hurry.

privación *f.* privation, hardship; withdrawal.

privado-a *a.* private; **cuarto** ___ / private room; **-mente** *adv.* privately.

privilegio *m.* privilege.

probabilidad *f.* probability.

probable *a.* probable; **-mente** *adv.* probably.

probador *m.* tester.

probar *vi.* [*esfuerzo*] to try; [*gusto*] to taste; [*comprobar*] to prove; to sample.

probeta *f.* pipet, pipette, glass tube.

problema *m.* problem; trouble.

problemático-a *a.* problematic, disputable.

procedente *a.* originating.

proceder *v.* to proceed, to continue.

procedimiento *m.* procedure; ___ **clínico** / clinical ___; ___ **quirúrgico** / surgical ___; ___ **terapéutico** / therapeutic ___.

proceso *m.* process, method, system.

procrear *v.* to procreate, to beget.

proctalgia *f.* proctalgia, pain in the rectum and anus.

proctitis *f.* proctitis, infl. of the rectum and the anus.

proctología *f.* proctology, the branch of medicine that studies the colon, rectum, and anus, and the treatment of the diseases affecting them.

proctólogo-a *m., f.* proctologist, specialist in proctology.

proctoscopio *m.* proctoscope, endoscope used to examine the rectum.

procurar *v.* to procure; to try.

prodrómico-a *a.* prodromal, rel. to the initial stages of a disease.

pródromo *m.* prodrome, a premonitory symptom.

producción *f.* production, rendering.

producir *vi.* to produce.

productivo-a *a.* productive.

producto *m.* product; result or effect.

profase *f.* prophase, first stage of cell division.

profesión *f.* profession.

profesional *m., f.* professional; *a.* professional.

profiláctico-a *a.* prophylactic. 1. agent or method used to prevent infection; 2. condom.

profilaxis *f.* prophylaxis, preventive treatment.

profunda *L.* profunda, deep, esp. in reference to the location of some arteries.

profundidad *f.* depth.

profundo-a *a.* deep.

profuso-a *a.* profuse, plentiful; **-mente** *adv.* profusely.

progesterona *f.* progesterone, steroid hormone secreted by the ovaries.

prognato-a *a.* prognathous, having a pronounced jaw.

programar *v.* to schedule; to program.

progresar *v.* to advance; to improve; to thrive.

progresivo-a *a.* progressive, advancing.

progreso *m.* progress.

prohibir *v.* to forbid, to prohibit, to ban.

prolapso *m.* prolapse, the falling down or slipping of a body part from its usual position.

proliferación *f.* proliferation, multiplication, esp. of similar cells; ___ **excesiva** / overgrowth.

prolífico-a *a.* prolific, that multiplies readily.

prólogo *m.* preface.

prolongación *f.* prolongation, extension.

prolongar *vi.* to prolong, to delay.

promedio *m.* average.

promesa *f.* promise.

prometer *v.* to promise, to give one's word.

prominencia *f.* prominence, elevation of a part; projection.

promontorio *m.* promontory, elevation; projection.

pronar *v.* to pronate, to put the body or a body part in a prone position.

prono-a *a.* prone, lying in a face down position.

pronombre *m. gr.* pronoun.

pronosticar *vi.* to prognosticate, to predict.

pronóstico *m.* prognosis, evaluation of the probable course of an illness.

pronto *adv.* soon, fast, quickly; **por lo** ___ / for the time being.

pronunciar *v.* to pronounce, to articulate sounds.

propagación *f.* propagation, reproduction.

propagar *vi.* to propagate.

propenso-a *a.* having a disposition for; ___ **a** / inclined to.

propiedad *f.* property. 1. possessions; 2. quality that distinguishes a person, specie, or object from another.

propio-a *a.* proper, naturally suiting, complying with, relevant to.

propioceptivo-a *a.* proprioceptive, receiving stimulations within the tissues of the body.

propioceptor *m.* proprioceptor, sensory nerve ending that reacts to stimuli and gives information concerning movements and position of the body.

proporción *f.* proportion.

proporcionado-a *a.* proportionate.

próposito *m.* purpose; **a** ___ / on purpose, by the way.

propranolol, clorhidrato de *m.* propranolol hydrochloride, Inderal, blocking agent used

Propiedades	Properties
abundante	abundant
ácido	acid
afilado	[instrumento] sharp
agrio	sour
agudo, penetrante	[dolor] sharp
alto	tall
amargo	bitter
bajo	[estatura] short
caliente	hot
claro	clear
deficiente	deficient
desabrido	tasteless
dulce	sweet
esbelto	slender, svelte
espeso	thick
fresco	cool
frío	cold
fuerte	strong
grasoso	fatty
grueso, gordo	heavy, fat
húmedo	humid, moist
insípido	tasteless
largo	long
ligero	light
líquido	liquid
mojado	wet
pesado	[peso] heavy
pobre	poor
rico	rich
seco	dry
sólido	solid
sucio	dirty
tibio	lukewarm

in the treatment of high blood pressure and of certain arrhythmias.

proptosis *f.* proptosis, forward displacement of a part, such as the eyeball.

prosencéfalo *m.* prosencephalon, anterior portion of the primary cerebral vesicle from which the diencephalon and the telencephalon develop.

próstata *f.* prostate, male gland that surrounds the bladder and the urethra; **hipertrofia de la** ___ / prostatic hypertrophy, benign enlargement of the prostate.

prostatectomía *f. surg.* prostatectomy, partial or total excision of the prostate.

prostático-a *a.* prostatic, rel. to the prostate.

prostatismo *m.* prostatism, disorder resulting from obstruction of the bladder neck by an enlarged prostate.

prostatitis *f.* prostatitis, infl. of the prostate.

prostitución *f.* prostitution.

protección *f.* protection.

protector-a *a.* protective.

proteger *vi.* to protect.

proteico-a *a.* protean, that has various forms of manifestation.

proteína *f.* protein, nitrogen compound essential in the development and preservation of body tissues.

proteináceo-a *a.* proteinaceous, of the nature of or resembling protein.

proteinemia *f.* proteinemia, concentration of proteins in the blood.

proteínico-a *a.* proteinic, rel. to protein; **balance** ___ / protein balance.

proteinosis *f.* proteinosis, excess protein in the tissues.

proteinuria *f.* proteimuria, the presence of protein in the urine.

prótesis *f.* prosthesis, artificial replacement of a missing part of the body such as a limb.

protética *f.* prosthetics, branch of *surg.* concerned with the replacement of parts of the body.

protocolo *m.* protocol. 1. a record taken from notes; 2. a written proposal of a procedure to be performed; ___ **toxicológico** / toxicology screen.

protoplasma *m.* protoplasm, essential part of the cell that includes the cytoplasm and the nucleus.

prototipo *m.* prototype, role-model, example.

protozoario-a *a.* protozoan, rel. to protozoa.

protozoo *m.* protozoan, unicellular organism.

protracción *f.* protraction, extension of teeth or other structures of the jaw into a position anterior to their normal position.

protrombina *f.* prothrombin, one of the four major plasma proteins along with albumin, globulin, and fibrinogen.

protuberancia *f.* protuberance, prominence.

provechoso-a *a.* beneficial.

proveer *vi.* to provide, to administer.

provisional *a.* provisional, temporary.

provisiones *f. pl.* provisions, supplies.

proximal *a.* proximal, closest to the point of reference.

próximo-a *a.* next to, close by.

proyección *f.* projection. 1. protuberance; 2. *psych.* a mechanism by which one's own unacceptable ideas or traits are attributed to others.

prueba *f.* test, proof, trial; indication; ___ **antinuclear de anticuerpo** / antibody ___ ; ___ **controlada por placebo** / placebo controlled ___ ; ___ **cutánea** / skin ___ ; ___ **de aclaramiento de creatinina** / creatinine clearance ___ ; ___ **de ciego simple** / single-blind trial; ___ **de coagulación sanguínea** / blood coagulation ___ ; ___ **de control sin método** / random controlled trial; ___ **de doble incógnita** / double-blind trial; ___ **de esfuerzo** / stress ___ , treadmill; ___ **de función hepática** / liver function ___ ; ___ **de función respiratoria** / respiratory function ___ ; ___ **de función tiroidea** / thyroid function ___; ___ **de grasa fecal** / stool fat ___; ___ **de rasguño** / scratch ___, allergy ___; ___ **de tolerancia** / tolerance ___; ___ **eliminatoria** / screening ___; ___**-s sanguíneas cruzadas** / crossmatching ___-s; ___ **serológica** / serology ___; ___ **sin pronóstico o tratamiento cierto** / double-blind technique; ___ **subsecuente, de seguimiento** / follow-up ___; ___ **visual de campimetría** / visual field ___; ___ **visual de letras** / visual ___; a ___ **de agua** / waterproof; a ___ **de fuego** / fireproof; **hay** ___ / there is an indication.

pruriginoso-a *a.* pruriginous, rel. to prurigo.

prurigo *m.* prurigo, chronic inflammatory condition characterized by small papules and severe itching.

prurito *m.* pruritus, severe itching.

pseudoaneurismo *m.* pseudoaneurysm, an aneurysm-like dilation in a vessel.

pseudociesis *f.* pseudocyesis, V. **pseudoembarazo.**

pseudoembarazo *m.* pseudopregnancy, false or imaginary pregnancy.

pseudoquiste *m.* pseudocyst, cystlike formation.

psicoactivo-a *a.* psychoactive, affecting the mind.

psicoanálisis *m.* psychoanalysis, branch of psychiatry founded by Sigmund Freud that endeavors to make the patient conscious of repressed conflicts through techniques such as interpretation of dreams and free association of ideas.

psicoanalista *m., f.* psychoanalyst, one who practices psychoanalysis.

psicobiología *f.* psychobiology, the study of the mind in relation to biological processes.

psicodélico-a *a.* psychedelic, rel. to a substance that can induce pathological states of altered perception such as hallucinations and delusions.

psicodrama *m.* psychodrama, the psychiatric method of diagnosis and therapy by which the patient acts out conflicting situations of his or her real life.

psicofarmacología *f.* psychopharmacology, the study of the effect of drugs on the mind and behavior.

psicofisiológico-a *a.* psychophysiologic, rel. to the mind's influence on bodily processes, as manifested in some disorders or diseases.

psicofisiológicos, desórdenes *m. pl.* psychophysiologic disorders, disorders that result from the relation between psychological and physiological processes.

psicología *f.* psychology, the study of mental processes, esp. as related to the individual's environment.

psicológico-a *a.* psychological, rel. to psychology.

psicólogo-a *m., f.* psychologist, person who practices psychology.

psicomotor-a *a.* psychomotor, rel. to motor actions that result from mental activity.

psicópata *m., f.* psychopath, person suffering from mental illness.

psicopatología *f.* psychopathology, the branch of medicine that deals with the causes and nature of mental illness.

psicosis *f.* psychosis, severe mental disorder of organic or emotional origin in which the patient loses touch with reality and suffers hallucinations and mental aberrations; ___ **alcohólica** / alcoholic ___; ___ **depresiva** / depressive ___; ___ **maniacodepresiva** / manic-depressive ___; ___ **orgánica** / organic ___; ___ **por droga** / drug-related ___; ___ **senil** / senile ___; ___ **situacional** / situational ___; ___ **tóxica** / toxic ___; ___ **traumática** / traumatic ___.

psicosocial *a.* psychosocial, rel. to both psychological and social factors.

psicosomático-a *a.* psychosomatic, rel. to both mind and body; **síntoma** ___ / ___ symptom. V. **psicofisiológico-a.**

psicoterapia *f.* psychotherapy, the treatment of mental or emotional disorders through psychological means, such as psychoanalysis.

psicótico-a *a.* psychotic, rel. to or suffering from psychosis.

psicotrópicas, drogas *f.* psychotropic drugs, drugs that affect mental stability.

psique *f.* psyche, conscious and unconscious mental life.

psiquiatra *m., f.* psychiatrist, specialist in psychiatry.

psiquiatría *f.* psychiatry, the study of the psyche and its disorders.

psiquiátrico-a *a.* psychiatric, rel. to psychiatry.

psíquico-a *a.* psychic, rel. to the psyche.

psoas *Gr.* psoas, one of the two muscles of the loin.

psoriasis *f.* psoriasis, chronic dermatitis manifested chiefly by red patches covered with white scales.

ptosis *Gr.* ptosis, prolapse of an organ or part, such as the upper eyelid.

púbero-a *a.* pubescent, having reached puberty.

pubertad *f.* puberty, the period of adolescence that marks the development of the secondary sexual characteristics and the beginning of reproductive capacity.

pubescencia *f.* pubescence. 1. beginning of puberty; 2. covering of soft, fine hair, lanugo.

púbico-a *a.* pubic, rel. to the pubis; **pelo** ___ / ___ hair.

público-a *a.* public.

pudendum *L.* (*pl.* **pudenda**) pudendum, external sexual organs, esp. the female.

pudrirse *vr.* to rot; to decay.

puente *m.* bridge, [*dental*] **pilar de** ___ / ___ abutment.

puerco *m.* pig, pork.

pueril *a.* puerile. 1. rel. to a child; 2. childish.

puerperal *a.* puerperal, rel. to the puerperium.

puerperio *m.* puerperium, the period of approximately six weeks following childbirth during which the organs of the mother return to normalcy.

puerta *f.* door.

pues *conj.* therefore; then; so.

puesto-a *a. pp.* of **poner,** placed, put.

pujar *v.* to bear down.

pulga *f.* flea, blood-sucking insect.

pulgada *f.* inch.

pulgar *m.* the thumb.

pulmón *m.* lung, respiratory organ situated inside the pleural cavity of the thorax, connected to the pharynx through the trachea and the larynx; **cáncer del** ___ / ___ cancer; **colapso del** ___ / collapse of the ___ .

pulmón de granjero *m.* farmer's lung, hypersensitivity of the pulmonary alveoli caused by exposure to fermented hay.

pulmón de hierro *m.* iron lung, machine used to produce artificial respiration.

pulmonar *a.* pulmonary, pulmonic, rel. to the lungs or to the pulmonary artery; **absceso** ___ / lung abscess; **arteria** ___ / ___ artery; **elasticidad** ___ / lung elasticity; **embolismo** ___ / ___ embolism; **enfisema** ___ / ___ emphysema; **estenosis** ___ / ___ stenosis; **hemorragia** ___ / ___ hemorrhage; **insuficiencia** ___ / ___ insufficiency; **presión diferencial de la arteria** ___ / ___ artery wedge pressure; **proteinosis alveolar** ___ / ___ alveolar proteinosis; **válvula** ___ / ___ valve; **vena** ___ / ___ vein; **volumen** ___ / lung capacity.

pulmonía *f.* pneumonia. *V.* **neumonía.**

pulpa *f.* pulp. 1. soft part on an organ; 2. chyme; 3. soft inner part of a tooth.

pulsación *f.* pulsation, throbbing, rhythmic beat such as that of the heart.

pulsátil *a.* pulsatile, having a rhythmic pulsation.

pulsímetro *m.* pulsimeter, instrument for measuring the force of the pulse.

pulso *m.* pulse, rhythmic arterial dilation gen. coinciding with the heartbeat; ___ **alternante** / alternating ___ ; ___ **bigeminado** / bigeminal

Pulso	*Pulse*
alternante	alternating
bigeminado	bigeminal
de la arteria dorsal del pie	dorsalis pedis
femoral	femoral
filiforme	filiform
irregular	irregular
lleno	full
periférico	peripheral
rápido	rapid
regular	regular
saltón	bounding

___ ; ___ **de la arteria dorsal del pie** / dorsalis pedis ___ ; ___ **en martillo de agua** / water hammer ___ ; ___ **femoral** / femoral ___ ; ___ **filiforme** / filiform ___ ; ___ **irregular** / irregular ___ ; ___ **lleno** / full ___ ; ___ **periférico** / peripheral ___ ; ___ **radial** / radial ___ ; ___ **rápido** / rapid ___ ; ___ **regular** / regular ___ ; ___ **saltón** / bounding ___ .

pulverizar *vi.* to pulverize, to reduce a substance to powder.

punción *f.* puncture, perforation, the act of perforating a tissue with a sharp instrument.

pungente *a.* pungent, sharp.

punta *f.* tip, point, sharp end of an instrument.

punteado *m.* stippling, the condition of being spotted such as seen in red corpuscles.

puntiagudo-a *a.* sharp, pointed.

punto *m.* 1. stitch; 2. point, a position in time and space; *v.* **estar a** ___ **de** / to be on the verge of; 3. spot; ___ **ciego** / blind ___ ; 4. *gr.* period.

puntos de presión *m. pl.* pressure points, points in an artery where the pulse can be felt or where pressure can be exerted to control bleeding.

puntual *a.* punctual, prompt, in time.

punzada *f.* twinge; sharp, sudden pain; jab.

punzante *a.* piercing, sharp.

punzar *vi.* to puncture; to tap, to perforate.

puñalada *f.* stab.

puño *m.* fist; **cerrar el** ___ / to make a fist.

pupila *f.* pupil, contractile opening of the iris of the eye that allows the passage of light; ___ **saltona** / bounding ___ ; ___ **fija** / fixed ___ .

pupilar *a.* pupillary, rel. to the pupil.

puré *m.* puree; ___ **de papas** / mashed potatoes.

purgante *m.* purgative, laxative, agent used to cause evacuation of the intestines; ___ **de sal** / saline cathartic.

purificar *vi.* to purify.

puro-a *a.* pure, uncontaminated.

purpura *L.* purpura, condition characterized by reddish or purple spots that result from escape of blood into tissues; ___ **trombocitopénica** / thrombocytopenic ___ .

purulencia *f.* purulence, the condition of being purulent.

purulento-a *a.* purulent, containing pus.

pus *f.* pus, thick, yellowish fluid that results from inflammation.

pústula *f.* pustule, sore, small elevation of the skin filled with pus.

putrefacción *f.* putrefaction, the condition of being putrid.

putrefacto-a, pútrido-a *a.* putrid, rotten, foul.

q *abr.* **quaque (cada)** / quaque (every).
quadratus *L.* quadratus. 1. four-sided muscle; 2. four-sided figure.
quantum *L.* quantum, a unit of energy.
quaque *L..* quaque, each; every.
quebradizo-a *a.* brittle, that breaks easily.
quebradura *f.* split; break.
quebrar *vi.* to break, to crack.
quedarse *vr.* to stay, to remain in one place; ___ **atrás** / to lag behind.
queilectomía *f. surg.* cheilectomy, partial excision of the lip.
queilitis *f.* cheilitis, infl. of the lips.
queiloplastia *f. surg.* cheiloplasty, plastic surgery of the lip.
queilosis *f.* cheilosis, disorder caused by a deficiency of vitamin B₂ complex (riboflavin) and marked by fissures at the angles of the lips.
queilosquisis *f.* cheiloschisis. *V.* **labio leporino.**
queirología *f.* cheirology. 1. the study of the hand; 2. sign language.
queja *f.* complaint, grievance; ___ **principal** / chief ___.
quejarse *vr.* to complain; to whine.
quejido *m.* groan, moan, whimper, whine.
quelis *m.* kelis, keloid.
queloide *m.* keloid, thick, reddish scar formation following a wound or surgical incision.
quemadura *f.* burn; ___ **de primer, segundo, tercer grado** / first-, second-, third-degree ___; ___ **por frío** / frostbite; ___ **por radiación** / radiation ___; ___ **de sol** / sunburn; ___ **por viento** / windburn.
quemar *v.* to burn, to scorch; **quemarse** *vr.* to burn oneself.
quemazón *m.* burning.
queratina *f.* keratin, organic, insoluble protein component of nails, skin, and hair.
queratinización *f.* keratinization, process by which cells become horny due to a deposit of keratin.
queratinoso-a *a.* keratinous, rel. to or of the nature of keratin.
queratitis *f.* keratitis, infl. of the cornea; ___ **intersticial** / interstitial ___; ___ **micótica** / mycotic ___, caused by fungus; ___ **trófica** / trophic ___, caused by the herpes virus.
queratocele *m.* keratocele, hernia of the innermost layer of the cornea.
queratoconjuntivitis *f.* keratoconjunctivitis, simultaneous infl. of the cornea and the conjunctiva.
queratoideo-a *a.* keratose, resembling the cornea.
queratólisis *f.* keratolysis. 1. exfoliation of the skin; 2. congenital anomaly that causes the skin to shed periodically; ___ **neonatal** / ___ neonatorum.

queratolítico-a *a.* keratolytic, agent that causes exfoliation of the skin.
queratomalacia *f.* keratomalacia, degeneration of the cornea due to a deficiency of vitamin A.
queratoplastia *f. surg.* keratoplasty, plastic surgery of the cornea.
queratosis *f.* keratosis, horny condition of the skin; ___ **actínica** / actinic ___, precancerous lesion; ___ **blenorrágica** / blenorrhagica, manifested by a scaly rash, esp. in the palms of the hands and the soles of the feet.
queratotomía *f. surg.* keratotomy, surgical incision of the cornea.
querer *vi.* to want, to desire; to love.
querido-a *a.* dear, beloved.
querubismo *m.* cherubism, fibro-osseous disease in children that causes an enlargement of the jaw bones.
queso *m.* cheese.
quiasma *m.* chiasm, chiasma, the crossing of two elements or structures; ___ **óptico** / optic ___, the point at which the fibers of the optic nerve cross.
quiescente *a.* quiescent, inactive; latent.
quieto-a *a.* quiet, still; *v.* **estar** ___ / to be still.
quijada *f.* jaw, osseous structure of the mouth.
quilemia *f.* chylemia, presence of chyle in the blood.
quilo *m.* chyle, milky fluid that results in the absorption and emulsification of fats in the small intestine.
quilocele *m.* chylocele, presence of chyle within the tunica vaginalis of the testis.
quilomicrón *m.* chylomicron, microscopic particle of fat found in the blood.
quilorrea *f.* chylorrhea, discharge of chyle due to a rupture of the thoracic duct.
quiloso-a *a.* chylous, rel. to or that contains chyle.
quilotórax *m.* chylothorax, accumulation of chyle in the thoracic cavity.
quiluria *f.* chyluria, passage of chyle in the urine.
quimera *f.* chimera, an organism containing cells derived from different zygotes as in the case of twins.
química *f.* chemistry, the science that studies the composition, structure, and properties of matter, and the transformations that they may undergo.
químico-a *m., f.* chemist; *a.* chemical, rel. to chemistry.
quimiocirugía *f. surg.* chemosurgery, removal of diseased tissue through the use of chemicals.
quimiocoagulación *f.* chemocoagulation, coagulation that results from the use of chemicals.
quimionucleólisis *f.* chemonucleolysis, dissolution of the nucleus pulposus of a hernia by injection of a proteolytic enzyme.
quimioprofilaxis *f.* chemoprophylaxis, drug used as a preventive agent.
quimiorreceptor *m.* chemoreceptor, a cell or a

receptor that can be excited by chemical change.

quimiotaxis *m.* chemotaxis, movement by a cell or an organism as a reaction to a chemical stimulus.

quimioterapia *f.* chemotherapy, treatment of a disease by chemical agents.

quimo *m.* chyme, semiliquid substance that results from the gastric digestion of food.

quimografía *f.* kymography, technique or method used to register involuntary movement of an organ or structure, esp. the heart and the diaphragm.

quimotripsina *f.* chymotrypsin, pancreatic enzyme.

quimotripsinógeno *m.* chymotrypsinogen, pancreatic enzyme, precursor of chymotrypsin.

Quincke, edema de *m.* Quincke's edema. *V.* **angioedema.**

quinidina *f.* quinidine, alkaloid derived from the cortex of the cinchona, used in the treatment of cardiac arrhythmia.

quinina *f.* quinine, the most important alkaloid obtained from the cortex of the cinchona, used as an antipyretic in the treatment of malaria and typhoid fever.

quininismo *m.* quininism, cinchonism, quinine poisoning.

quintana *f.* quintan, fever occurring every fifth day.

quíntuple *m., f.* quintuplet, any of a set of five children born at one birth.

quiropráctica *f.* chiropractic, therapeutic treatment that consists of manipulation and adjustment of body structures, esp. of the spinal column in relation to the nervous system.

quirúrgico-a *a.* surgical, rel. to surgery; **colgajo** ___ / ___ flap; **equipo** ___ / ___ equipment; **instrumento** ___ / ___ instrument; **malla** ___ / ___ mesh.

quiste *m.* cyst, sac, or pouch containing a fluid or semifluid substance; ___ **pilonidal** / pilonidal ___, containing hair and gen. occurring in the dermis of the sacroccygeal area; ___ **sebáceo** / sebaceous ___, gen. localized in the scalp.

quitar *v.* to take away, to remove.

quizás *adv.* perhaps.

R *abr.* **radioactivo-a** / radioactive; **resistencia** / resistance; **respiración** / respiration; **respuesta, reacción** / response.

rabadilla *f.* coccyx, the extremity of the backbone.

rábano *m.* radish.

rabdomioma *m.* rhabdomyoma, benign tumor composed of muscle-striated fiber.

rabdomiosarcoma *m.* rhabdomyosarcoma, malignant tumor of muscle-striated fibers affecting primarily the skeletal muscles.

rabdosarcoma *m.* rhabdosarcoma. *V.* **rabdomiosarcoma.**

rabia *f.* rabies. 1. *V.* **hidrofobia;** 2. rage, anger; *v.* **tener ___** / to be enraged.

rabieta *f.* tantrum.

rabino *m.* rabbi.

rabioso-a *a.* rabid. 1. rel. to or afflicted by rabies; 2. enraged.

rabo *m.* tail.

racemoso-a, racimoso-a *a.* racemose, resembling a cluster of grapes.

racial *a.* racial, ethnic, rel. to race; **inmunidad ___** / **___** immunity, natural immunity of the members of a race; **prejuicio ___** / **___** prejudice.

ración *f.* ration, food portion.

racional *a.* rational, reasonable, based on reason.

racionalización *f. psych.* rationalization, defense mechanism by which behavior or actions are justified by explanations that may seem reasonable but are not necessarily based on reality.

racionar *v.* to ration.

rad *L.* rad. 1. unit of absorbed radiation; 2. *abr.* radix, root.

radiación *f.* radiation. 1. emission of particles of radioactive material; 2. propagation of energy; 3. emission of rays from a common center; **enfermedad por ___** / **___** sickness, radiation syndrome, illness caused by overexposure to x-rays or radioactive materials; **___ electromagnética** / electromagnetic **___;** **___ ionizante** / ionizing **___;** **___ por rayos infrarrojos** / infrared **___;** **___ por rayos ultravioletas** / ultraviolet **___.**

radiactividad, radioactividad *f.* radioactivity, property of some elements to produce radiation.

radiactivo-a *a.* radioactive, rel. to or having radioactivity.

radial *a.* radial. 1. rel. to the radius; 2. that radiates from a center in all directions.

radiante *a.* radiant, that emits rays.

radical *a.* radical. 1. aimed at eradicating the root of a disease or all the diseased tissue; 2. rel. to the root; **-mente** *adv.* radically.

radicular *a.* radicular, rel. to the root or source.

radiculectomía *f. surg.* radiculectomy, excision of the root of a nerve, esp. a spinal nerve.

radiculitis *f.* radiculitis, infl. of a nerve root.

radiculomielopatía *f.* radiculomyelopathy, a disease affecting the spinal cord and the roots of the spinal nerves.

radiculoneuritis *f.* radiculoneuritis, Guillain-Barré syndrome, infl. of the roots of a spinal nerve.

radiculoneuropatía *f.* radiculoneuropathy, disease of the nerves and nerve roots.

radiculopatía *f.* radiculopathy, disease of the roots of the spinal nerves.

radio *m.* 1. radium, metallic, radioactive, fluorescent element used in some of its variations in the treatment of malignant tumors; **agujas de ___** / **___** needles, needle-shaped, radium containing device used in radiotherapy; 2. radius, the outer bone of the forearm; 3. radio.

radiobiología *f.* radiobiology, the study of the effect of radiation on living tissue.

radiocardiografía *f.* radiocardiography, graphic recording of a radioactive substances as it travels through the heart.

radiocurable *a.* radiocurable, curable using radiotherapy.

radiofármaco *m.* radiopharmaceutical, radioactive drug used for diagnosis and treatment of diseases.

radiografía *f.* radiography. *V.* **roentgenograma.**

radioisótopo *m.* radioisotope, radioactive isotope.

radiología *f.* radiology, the study of x-rays and rays emanating from radioactive substances, esp. for medical use.

radiológico-a *a.* radiologic, rel. to radiology.

radiólogo-a *m., f.* radiologist, specialist in radiology.

radiolúcido-a *a.* radiolucent, that allows the passage of most x-rays.

radionecrosis *f.* radionecrosis, disintegration of tissue by radiation.

radiopaco-a *a.* radiopaque, that does not allow the passage of x-rays or any other form of radiation; **colorante ___** / **___** dye.

radiorresistente *a.* radioresistant, having the quality of being resistant to the effects of radiation.

radiosensitivo-a *a.* radiosensitive, that is affected by or responds to radiation treatment.

radioterapia *f.* radiotherapy, radiation therapy.

radón *m.* radon, colorless, gaseous radioactive element.

rafe *m.* raphe, joining line of two symmetrical halves of a structure such as the tongue.

raíz *f.* root.

rajadura *f.* crack, slit.

rama *f.* ramus, branch.

ramificación *f.* ramification, separation into branches.

ramificarse *vr., vi.* to ramify.

rancio-a *a.* rancid, stale, having an unpleasant smell, gen. due to decomposition.

ránula *f.* ranula, cystic tumor under the tongue caused by an obstruction of a gland duct.

ranura *f.* groove, slit.

rapidez *f.* speed, velocity.

rápido-a *a.* quick, fast; swift; **-mente** *adv.* quickly.

raptus *L. psych.* raptus, sudden violent attack such as of a maniacal or nervous nature.

raquídeo-a *a.* rachial, rel. to the rachis or the spine.

raquis *m.* rachis, the vertebral column, backbone.

raquítico-a *a.* rachitic. 1. rel. to rachitism; 2. stunted, feeble.

raquitis *f.* rickets. *V.* **raquitismo.**

raquitismo *m.* rachitism, rachitis, a deficiency disease that affects the skeletal growth in the young usu. caused by lack of calcium, phosphorus, and vitamin D; *pop.* rickets.

raro-a *a.* rare, different, unusual; **-mente** *adv.* rarely, seldom.

rascar *vi.* to scratch; **rascarse** *vr.* to scratch oneself.

rasgo *m.* trait, feature, strain; ___ **adquirido** / acquired ___; ___ **heredado** / inherited ___.

rasguño, rascuño *m.* scratch.

rash, rasche *Fr.* rash, any eruption of the skin; ___ **hemorrágico** / hemorrhagic ___; ___ **medicamentoso** / drug ___.

raspado *m.* curettage, scraping of the interior of a cavity; ___ **uterino** / D&C, dilation and curettage.

raspador *m.* scraper.

raspadura, rasponazo *f., m.* scrape.

raspante *a.* abrasive.

raspar *v.* to scrape.

rastrear *v.* scanning, tracing, and recording with a sensitive detecting device.

rastreo *m.* scan. *V.* **escán.**

rastro *m.* trace. 1. small quantity; 2. a visible sign or mark.

rasura *f.* rasura, scrapings or filings.

rata *f.* rat.

ratio *L.* ratio, quantity of one substance in relation to another.

rato *m.* while, a short time.

Rauwolfia serpentina *f. Rauwolfia serpentina,* a plant species that is the source of reserpine, an extract used in the treatment of hypertension and some mental disorders.

raya *f.* streak.

Raynaud, enfermedad de *f.* Raynaud's disease. *V.* **acrocianosis.**

Raynaud, fenómeno de *m.* Raynaud's phenomenon, the symptoms associated with Raynaud's disease.

rayo *m.* ray.

rayos gamma *m. pl.* gamma rays, high-energy rays emitted by radioactive substances.

rayos X *m. pl.* 1. x-rays, high-energy electromagnetic short waves used to penetrate tissues and record densities on film; 2. films obtained through the use of x-rays.

raza *f.* race, a distinctive ethnic group with common inherited characteristics.

razón *f.* the faculty of reason; **a** ___ **de** / at the rate of; *v.* **tener** ___ / to be right.

razonable *a.* reasonable.

razonar *v.* to reason.

reabsorber *v.* to reabsorb.

reacción *f.* reaction, response; ___ **alérgica** / allergic ___; ___ **anafiláctica** / anaphylactic ___; ___ **de ansiedad** / anxiety ___; ___ **de conversión** / conversion ___; ___ **depresiva psicótica** / psychotic depressive ___; ___ **en cadena** / chain ___; ___ **inmune** / immune ___.

reaccionar *v.* to react, to respond to a stimulus.

reactivación *f.* reactivation; the act of activating again; ___ **de una vacuna** / booster shot.

reactivar *v.* to stimulate or activate again.

reactividad *f.* reactivity, manifestation of a reaction.

reactivo *m.* reagent, agent that stimulates a reaction; **-a** *a.* reactive, that has the property of reacting or causing a reaction.

reagina *f.* reagin, antibody used in the treatment of allergies that causes the production of histamine.

real *a.* real, actual; **-mente** *adv.* really.

realidad *f.* reality.

realimentación, retroalimentación *f.* feedback, regeneration of energy, action of taking the energy or the effects of the process back to its original source.

realzar *vi.* to enhance, to intensify, to increase; to highlight.

reanimar *v.* to reanimate, to bring back to life.

rebelde *a.* rebellious.

reblandecimiento *m.* ripening, softening, dilation, such as of the cervix during childbirth.

reborde *m.* ridge, elongated elevation.

rebote *m.* rebound, a return to a previous condition after the removal of a stimulus; **fenómeno de** ___ / ___ phenomenon, intensified onward movement of a part when the initial resistance is removed.

rebuscado-a *a.* farfetched.

recado *m.* message.

recaer *vi.* to relapse.

recaída *f.* relapse, setback, the recurrence of a disease after a period of recovery.

recalcificación *f.* recalcification, restoration of calcium compounds to tissues.

recámara *f. Mex.* bedroom.

recapacitar *v.* to reconsider.

receptáculo *m.* receptacle, vessel for liquids.

receptaculum *L.* (*pl.* **receptacula**) receptaculum, container, receptacle.

receptivo-a *a.* receptive.

receptor *m.* receptor, a nerve end that receives a nervous stimulus and passes it on to other nerves; ___ **auditivo** / auditory ___; ___ **de contacto** / contact ___; ___ **de estiramiento** /

stretch ___; ___ **de temperature** / temperature ___; ___ **gustativo** / taste ___; ___ **propioceptivo** / proprioceptive ___; ___ **sensorial** / sensory ___.

recesión *f.* recession, pathological withdrawal of tissue such as retraction of the gums.

recesivo-a *a.* recessive. 1. tending to withdraw; 2. in genetics, rel. to nondominant genes.

receta *f.* prescription; recipe.

recetar *v.* to medicate, to prescribe medication.

recibir *v.* to receive.

recibo *m.* receipt.

recidiva *f.* recidivation, recidivism, the recurrence of a disease or symptom.

recién *adv.* recently.

recién nacido-a *m., f.* newborn; **sala de** ___-**s** / nursery.

reciente *a.* recent; **-mente** *adv.* recently.

recipiente *m.* 1. recipient, individual who receives blood, or an implant of tissue or organ from a donor; 2. container.

recipiente universal *m.* universal recipient, person belonging to blood group AB.

reciprocidad *f.* reciprocity.

recíproco-a *a.* reciprocal.

reclamación *f.* claim.

reclinado-a *a.* reclined, reclining, recumbent.

reclinarse *vr.* to recline, to lean back.

recluido-a *a.* confined.

recluir *vi.* to confine.

reclutamiento *m.* recruitment, gradual intensification of a reflex by an unaltered but prolonged stimulus.

recobrar *v.* to regain; ___ **el conocimiento** / ___ consciousness; to retrieve.

recoger *vi.* to gather; to pick up.

recomendable *a.* advisable.

recomendación *f.* recommendation; referral.

recomendar *vi.* to recommend, to advise.

recompresión *f.* recompression, the return to normal environmental pressure.

reconocer *vi.* 1. to examine physically; 2. to recognize; to admit; to acknowledge.

reconocimiento *m.* 1. physical examination; 2. recognition.

reconstitución *f.* reconstitution, restitution of tissue to its initial form.

reconstituir *vi.* to reconstitute; ___ **la salud** / to build up one's health.

reconstituyente *m.* tonic.

reconstruir *vi.* to reconstruct.

récord *m.* record, chart.

recordar *vi.* to recall; to recollect; to remind; **recordarse** *vr.* to remember.

recostado-a *a.* lying down, recumbent.

recostarse *vr., vi.* to lie down.

recreo *f.* recreation.

recrudescencia *f.* recrudescence, relapse, return of symptoms.

rectal *a.* rectal, rel. to the rectum.

rectificación *f.* rectification, correction.

rectificar *vi.* to rectify, to correct.

recto *m.* rectum, the distal portion of the long intestine that connects the sigmoid and the anus; **-a** *a.* straight.

rectocele *m.* rectocele, herniation of part of the rectum into the vagina.

rectosigmoide *a.* rectosigmoid, rel. to the sigmoid and the rectum.

rectovaginal *a.* rectovaginal, rel. to the rectum and the vagina.

rectovesical *a.* rectovesical, rel. to the rectum and the bladder.

rectus *L.* rectus. 1. straight; 2. rel. to any of a group of straight muscles such as the ones in the eye and the abdominal wall.

recuento sanguíneo completo *m.* complete blood count.

recumbente *a.* recumbent, in a lying down position.

recuperación *f.* recuperation, recovery, restoration to health.

recuperado-a *a. pp.* of **recuperar**, recovered; improved.

recuperar *v.* to recover; ___ **el conocimiento** / to regain consciousness; **recuperarse** *vr.* to get well, *pop.* to pull through, to recoup.

recurrencia *f.* recurrence. 1. the return of symptoms after a period of remission; 2. relapse; repetition.

recurrente *a.* recurrent, intermittent.

recurso *m.* recourse; resource; ___-**s económicos** / source of income.

rechazar *vi.* to reject, to drive back.

rechazo *m.* rejection. 1. immune reaction of incompatibility to transplanted tissue cells; ___ **agudo** / acute ___; ___ **crónico** / chronic ___; ___ **hiperagudo** / hyperacute ___; 2. denial, refusal.

rechinamiento *m.* [*los dientes*] gnashing.

rechinar *v.* [*los dientes*] to chatter; to squeak.

red *f.* web, network, netlike arrangement of nerve fibers and blood vessels; ___ **de membranas arteriopulmonares** / pulmonary arterial ___.

redondo-a *a.* round, circular.

reducción *f.* reduction, the act of reducing.

reducible *a.* reducible, able to be reduced.

reducido-a *a.* reduced, diminished.

reducir *vi.* to reduce, to cut down. 1. to restore to its normal position, such as a fragmented or dislocated bone; 2. to weaken the potency of a compound by adding hydrogen or suppressing oxygen; 3. to lose weight.

reductasa *f.* reductase, enzyme that acts as a catalyst in reduction.

reductor *m.* reducer, agent that causes reduction.

reeducación *f.* reeducation, training to regain motor and mental functions.

reemplazar *vi.* to replace, to substitute; to supplant.

reemplazo *m.* replacement, substitution.

reevaluación *f.* reevaluation; reassessment.

referencia *f.* reference; **valores de** ___ / ___ values.

referir *vi.* to refer; to direct; **referirse** *vr.* to refer to, to cite.

refinar *v.* to refine, to purify.

reflejar *v.* to reflect.

reflejo *m.* reflex, a conscious or unconscious motor response to a stimulus; **acto, acción** ___ / ___ action; ___ **adquirido** / behavior ___; **arco** ___ / ___ arc; ___ **condicionado** / conditioned ___; ___ **de estiramiento** / stretch ___; ___ **del tendón de Aquiles** / Achilles tendon ___; ___ **en cadena** / chain ___; ___ **instintivo** / instinctive ___; ___ **no condicionado, natural** / unconditioned ___; ___ **patelar o rotuliano** / patellar ___; ___ **radial** / radial ___; ___ **rectal** / rectal ___; ___ **vagal** / vagal ___.

reflejo hepatoyugular *a.* hepatojugular reflex, ingurgitation of the jugular veins, produced by pressure over the liver in cases of right cardiac failure.

reflexión *f.* reflection. 1. the rejection of light or another form of radiant energy from a surface; 2. the turning or bending back, as of the folds of a membrane when it passes over the surface of an organ returning later to the body walls that it lines; 3 introspection.

reflexógeno-a *a.* reflexogenic, that causes a reflex action.

reflujo *m.* reflux, backflow of a fluid substance.

reforzar *vi.* to reinforce, to strengthen.

refracción *f.* refraction, the act of refracting; ___ **ocular** / ocular ___.

refractar *v.* to refract. 1. to change the direction from a straight path, such as of a ray of light when it passes from one medium to another one of different density; 2. to detect abnormalities of refraction in the eyes and correct them.

refractario-a *a.* refractory. 1. resistant to treatment; 2. nonresponsive to a stimulus.

refractividad *f.* refractivity, the ability to refract.

refrescante *a.* refreshing, cooling.

refrescar *vi.* to refresh, to revive; **refrescarse** *vr.* to cool off.

refresco *m.* refreshment, soft drink.

refrigeración *f.* refrigeration, reduction of heat by external means.

refrigerante *m.* refrigerant; antipyretic.

refrigerar *v.* to refrigerate.

refringente *a.* refringent, rel. to or that causes refraction.

refugiado-a *m., f.* refugee.

refugiar *v.* to shelter; **refugiarse** *vr.* to seek refuge, to seek shelter.

refugio *m.* shelter, refuge; asylum.

regalo *m.* present, gift.

regazo *m.* lap.

regeneración *f.* regeneration, restoration, renewal; feedback.

regenerar *v.* to regenerate.

régimen *m.* regimen, structured plan, such as a regulated diet.

región *f.* region, a part of the body with more or less definite boundaries.

regional *a.* regional.

registrar *v.* to register, to record.

registro *m.* registry, record; registration.

regla *f.* 1. menstruation; 2. rule; 3. ruler, device for measuring.

reglamento *m.* set of rules, policy.

regresar *v.* to return to a place.

regresión *f.* regression. 1. return to an earlier condition; 2. abatement of the symptoms or process of a disease.

regüeldo *m.* belch.

regulación *f.* regulation.

regular *a.* regular, normal; *v.* to regulate; **-mente** *adv.* regularly.

regurgitación *f.* regurgitation. 1. the act of expelling swallowed food; 2. the backflow of blood through a defective valve of the heart; ___ **aórtica** / aortic ___; ___ **mitral** / mitral ___.

regurgitante *a.* regurgitant, rel. to regurgitation.

regurgitar *v.* to regurgitate.

rehabilitación *f.* rehabilitation, the act of rehabilitating.

rehabilitado-a *a.* rehabilitated.

rehabilitar *v.* to rehabilitate, to help regain normal functions through therapy.

rehén *m., f.* hostage.

rehidratación *f.* rehydration, establishment of normal liquid balance in the body.

rehuir *vi.* to evade, to shun.

reimplantación *f.* reimplantation. 1. restoration of a tissue or part; 2. restitution into the uterus of an ovum removed from the body and fertilized *in vitro*.

reinervación *f.* reinnervation, grafting of a nerve to restore the function of a muscle.

reinfección *f.* reinfection, subsequent infestation caused by the same microorganism.

reinfusión *f.* reinfusion, reinjection of blood serum or cerebrospinal fluid.

reinoculación *f.* reinoculation, subsequent in-

Reflejo	*Reflex*
adquirido	behavior
condicionado	conditioned
de estiramiento	stretch
del tendón de Aquiles	Achilles tendon
en cadena	chain
instintivo	instinctive
no condicionado, natural	unconditioned
patelar o rotuliano	patellar
radial	radial
rectal	rectal

169

oculation with the same microorganisms.

reírse *vr., vi.* to laugh.

rejuvenecer *vi.* to rejuvenate; **rejuvenecerse** *vr.* to become rejuvenated.

rejuvenecimiento *m.* rejuvenescence.

relación *f.* relation; relationship; ___ **armoniosa** / rapport.

relacionado-a *a.* rel. to, related.

relacionar *v.* to relate, to establish a relationship; **relacionarse** *vr.* to become acquainted.

relajación *f.* relaxation, act of relaxing or becoming relaxed.

relajado-a *a.* relaxed.

relajante *m.* relaxant, agent that reduces tension.

relajar *v.* to relax, to reduce tension; **relajarse** *vr.* to become less tense, *pop.* to loosen up.

relativo-a *a.* relative; **-mente** *adv.* relatively.

religión *f.* religion.

religioso-a *a.* religious.

reloj *m.* watch; clock.

rellenar *v.* to refill.

relleno *m.* padding; stuffing.

remediador-a *a.* remedial, rel. to remedy.

remediar *v.* to remedy, to help, to alleviate.

remedio *m.* remedy, relief.

remineralización *f.* remineralization, replacement of lost minerals from the body.

remisión *f.* remission. 1. diminution or cessation of the symptoms of a disease; 2. period of time during which the symptoms of a disease diminish.

remitente *a.* remittent, occurring at intervals.

remojar *v.* to soak; to wet again.

remolacha *f.* beet.

remordimiento *m.* remorse.

remoto-a *a.* remote, distant.

removible *a.* removable; that can be removed surgically.

renal *a.* renal, rel. to or resembling the kidney; **fallo, insuficiencia** ___ / ___ failure, insufficiency; **pelvis** ___ / ___ pelvis; **prueba de aclaramiento o depuración** ___ / ___ clearance test.

rendido-a *a.* tired out, exhausted.

rendimiento *m.* output, yield; **fallo en el** ___ / ___ failure.

renina *f.* renin, an enzyme released by the kidney that is a factor in the regulation of blood pressure.

renograma *m.* renogram, monitoring of the rate at which the kidney eliminates from the blood a radioactive substance previously injected intravenously.

renovar *vi.* to renew, to renovate.

renuente *a.* reluctant.

reñir *vi.* to quarrel, to fight.

reparación *f.* repair, restoration.

reparar *v.* to repair, to restore.

repartir *v.* to distribute, to divide.

repasar *v.* to review, to look over.

repaso *m.* review; ___ **por sistemas, aparatos** / ___ of systems.

repelente *m.* repellent.

repentino-a *a.* sudden; **-mente** *adv.* suddenly.

repercusión *f.* repercussion. 1. penetration or spreading of a swelling, tumor, or eruption; 2. ballottement.

repetir *vi.* to repeat, to reiterate.

repleto-a *a.* replete, full.

repliegue *m.* replication, reproduction, duplication.

reporte *m.* report, account.

reposar *v.* to repose, to rest.

reposo *m.* rest, repose; **cura de** ___ / ___ cure; **en** ___ / resting.

represión *f.* repression. 1. inhibition of an action; 2. *psych.* exclusion from consciousness of unacceptable desires or impulses.

reprimir *v.* to repress, to hold back.

reproducción *f.* reproduction.

reproducir *vi.* to reproduce.

reproductivo-a *a.* reproductive, rel. to reproduction.

reprovisión *f.* feedback. 1. [*información*] regeneration of information; 2. *V.* **realimentación.**

repugnante *a.* repugnant, disgusting.

repulsión *f.* repulsion, the act of driving back or away; aversion.

repulsivo-a *a.* repulsive, repugnant.

reputación *f.* reputation.

requerido-a *a.* required, mandatory, necessary.

requerimiento *m.* requirement.

requerir *vi.* to require.

requisito *m.* requisite.

resbaladizo-a, resbaloso-a *a.* slippery.

resbalar *v.* to slip; to slide.

rescatar *v.* to rescue, to save.

rescate *m.* rescue; **método de** ___, **método de salvamento** / ___ method.

resecar *v.* to resect. 1. to perform a resection; 2. to cut a portion of tissue or organ; 3. to dry thoroughly.

resección *f.* resection, the act of cutting a portion of tissue or organ; ___ **en cuña** / wedge ___; ___ **gástrica** / gastric ___; ___ **transuretral** / transurethral ___.

reseco-a *a.* dried up; parched.

resectoscopía *f.* resectoscopy, resection of the prostate with a resectoscope.

resectoscopio *m.* resectoscope, instrument provided with a cutting electrode used in surgery within cavities, such as the one used for the resection of the prostate through the urethra.

resentimiento *m.* resentment, rancor, hard feelings.

reserpina *f.* reserpine, derivative of *Rauwolfia serpentina* used primarily in the treatment of hypertension and emotional disorders.

reserva *f.* reserve, that which is kept in store for future use.

reservar *v.* to reserve.

resfriado *m.* a cold.

170

resfriarse *vr.* to catch a cold.

residencia *f.* residency, period of specialized training in a hospital following completion of medical school.

residente *m.* resident, physician completing a residency.

residir *v.* to reside, to live.

residual *a.* residual, remainder; **función** ___ / ___ function; **orina** ___ / ___ urine.

residuo *m.* residue; **dieta de** ___ **alto** / high-___ diet; **dieta de bajo** ___ / low-___ diet.

resiliente *a.* resilient, elastic.

resina *f.* resin, resina, organic substance of vegetable origin, insoluble in water but readily soluble in alcohol and ether, that has a variety of uses in medicine and dentistry.

res ipsa loquitor *L.* res ipsa loquitor, evident, that which speaks for itself.

resistencia *f.* resistance, endurance, capacity of an organism to resist harmful effects; ___ **adquirida** / acquired ___; ___ **a un colorante** / fast resistant; ___ **inicial** / initial ___; ___ **periférica** / peripheral ___.

resistente *a.* resistant.

resolución *f.* resolution. 1. termination of an inflammatory process; 2. the ability to distinguish fine and subtle details as through a microscope.

resolver *vi.* to resolve. 1. to cause resolution; 2. to become separated into components.

resonancia *f.* resonance, capacity to increase the intensity of a sound; ___ **normal** / normal ___; ___ **vesicular** / vesicular ___; ___ **vocal** / vocal ___.

resonante *a.* resonant, ringing, that gives out a vibrant sound on percussion.

resorcinol *m.* resorcinol, agent used in the treatment of acne and other forms of dermatosis.

resorción *f.* resorption, partial or total loss of a process, tissue, or exudate by biochemical reactions such as lysis and absorption.

respetar *v.* to respect.

respeto *m.* respect.

respiración *f.* breathing, respiration; **aguantar o sostener la** ___ / to hold one's breath; ___ **abdominal** / abdominal ___; ___ **acelerada** / accelerated ___; ___ **aeróbica** / aerobic ___; ___ **anaeróbica** / anaerobic ___; ___ **diafragmática** / diaphragmatic ___; ___ **gruesa** / coarse ___; ___ **laboriosa** / labored ___; ___ **profunda** / deep ___.

respiración sibilante *f.* wheezing.

respirador *m.* respirator, breather, device used to purify the air reaching the lungs or to administer artificial respiration; ___ **torácico** / chest ___.

respirar *v.* to breathe; ___ **por la boca** / ___ through the mouth; ___ **por la nariz** / ___ through the nose.

respiratorio-a *a.* respiratory, rel. to respiration; **aparato** ___ **superior** / upper ___ tract; **cociente** ___ / ___ quotient; **ejercicios** ___ **-s** / breathing exercises; **infección del tracto** ___ **superior** / upper ___ tract infection; **infecciones y enfermedades de las vías** ___ **-s** / tract infections and diseases; **insuficiencia o fallo** ___ / ___ failure, insufficiency; **pruebas de función** ___ / ___ function tests; **unidad de cuidado** ___ / ___ care unit.

respiratorio, centro *m.* respiratory center, region in the medulla oblongata that regulates respiratory movements.

responsabilidad *f.* responsibility.

responsable *a.* responsible; **persona** ___ / reliable person.

respuesta *f.* response; answer. 1. reaction of an organ or tissue to a stimulus; 2. reaction of a patient to a treatment; ___ **evocada** / evoked ___, sensorial test; ___ **no condicionada** / unconditioned ___, nonrestricted reaction.

restablecer *vi.* to restore; **restablecerse** *vr.* to recover.

restablecido-a *a.* [*de una enfermedad*] recovered.

restablecimiento *m.* V. **restauración**.

restauración *f.* restoration, the act of returning to the original state.

restaurativo-a *a.* restorative, that stimulates restoration.

restenosis *f.* restenosis, recurrence of stenosis after corrective surgery.

restitutio ad integrum *L.* restitutio ad integrum, total restitution of health.

resto *m.* rest, remainder.

restricción *f.* restraint, confinement; ___ **de movimiento** / limitation of motion; ___ **en cama** / bed confinement.

restringido-a *a.* restricted.

restringir *vi.* to restrict, to confine.

resucitación *f.* resuscitation. 1. return to life; 2. artificial respiration.

resucitador *m.* resuscitator, an apparatus to provide artificial respiration.

resucitar *v.* to resuscitate, to revive.

resultado *m.* result, outcome.

resumen *m.* resumé; summary.

resurgencia *f.* resurgency.

retardo *m.* V. **retraso**.

rete *L.* (*pl.* **retia**). rete; V. **red**.

retención *f.* retention; ___ **de líquido** / fluid ___; **enema de** ___ / ___ enema; ___ **gástrica** / gastric ___; ___ **urinaria** / urinary ___; [*dental*] *m.* **freno de** ___ / retainer.

retener *vi.* to retain; to keep.

reticulación *f.* reticulation, reticular formation.

reticular, retiforme *a.* reticular, resembling a network.

retículo *m.* reticulum, a network, esp. of nerve fibers and blood vessels.

retículo endoplásmico *m.* endoplasmic reticulum, a network of canals in the cells in which the functions of anabolism and catabolism take place.

reticulocito *m.* reticulocyte, an immature red blood cell with a network of threads and granules that appears primarily during blood regeneration.

reticulocitopenia *f.* reticulocytopenia, an abnormal decrease in the number of reticulocytes in the blood.

reticulocitosis, reticulosis *f.* reticulocytosis, reticulosis, increase in the number of reticulocytes in the blood.

reticuloendotelial, sistema *m.* reticuloendothelial system, network of phagocytic cells (except circulating leukocytes) throughout the body, involving processes such as blood cell formation, elimination of worn-out cells, and immune responses to infection.

reticuloendotelio *m.* reticuloendothelium, tissue of the reticuloendothelial system.

reticuloendotelioma *m.* reticuloendothelioma, tumor of the reticuloendothelial system.

reticulohistiocitoma *m.* reticulohistiocytoma, a large aggregate of granular and giant cells.

reticulopenia *f.* reticulopenia. *V.* **reticulocitopenia.**

Retin-A *f.* Retin-A, trade name for retinoic acid, esp. used in the treatment of acne.

retina *f.* retina, the innermost layer of the eyeball that receives images and transmits visual impulses to the brain; **conmoción de la ___** / commotio retinae, traumatic condition of the retina that produces temporary blindness; **desprendimiento de la ___** / retinal detachment, separation of all or part of the retina from the choroid; **deterioración de la ___** / retinal degeneration.

retiniano-a *a.* retinal, rel. to the retina; **perforación ___** / ___ perforation.

retinitis *f.* retinitis, infl. of the retina.

retinoblastoma *m.* retinoblastoma, gen. inherited malignant tumor of the retina.

retinol *m.* retinol, vitamin A$_1$.

retinopatía *f.* retinopathy, any abnormal condition of the retina.

retinoscopía *f.* retinoscopy, determination and evaluation of refractive errors of the eye.

retirado-a *a.* retired; isolated.

retoque *m.* touch-up.

retorno *m.* return.

retortijón *m.* brief and acute intestinal cramp.

retracción *f.* retraction, the act of drawing or pulling back; **___ del coágulo** / clot **___**.

retractable, retráctil *a.* retractile, capable of being retracted.

retractar *v.* to retract, to draw back, to withdraw.

retractor *m.* retractor. 1. instrument for holding back the edges of a wound; 2. retractile muscle.

retraído-a *a.* withdrawn, introverted, that keeps to himself or herself.

retrasado-a, retardado-a *a.* retarded; **___ mental** / mentally **___**.

retraso *m.* retardation, abnormal slowness of a motor or a mental process.

retroacción *f.* retroaction, retroactive action.

retroactivo-a *a.* retroactive, that acts upon or affects a past event.

retroauricular *a.* retroauricular, rel. to or situated behind the ear or auricle.

retrocecal *a.* retrocecal, rel. to or situated behind the cecum.

retroceso *m.* retrocession, throwback.

retrofaríngeo-a *a.* retropharyngeal, rel. to or situated behind the pharynx.

retroflexión *f.* retroflexion, the flexing back of an organ.

retrógrado-a *a.* retrograde, that moves backward or returns to the past; **amnesia ___** / ___ amnesia; **aortografía ___** / ___ aortography; **pielografía ___** / ___ pyelography.

retrogresión *f.* 1. retrogression, return to a simpler level of development; 2. *psych.* flashback, retrospection and retroversion of past images.

retrolental *a.* retrolental, rel. to or situated behind the lens of the eye; **fibroplasia ___** / ___ fibroplasia.

retroperitoneal *a.* retroperitoneal, rel. to or situated behind the peritoneum.

retroplasia *f. V.* **anaplasia.**

retroprovisión *f.* feedback.

retrospectivo-a *a.* retrospective; **estudio ___** / ___ study.

retroversión *f.* retroversion, turning backward, such as an organ.

retrovirus *m.* retrovirus, a virus belonging to a group of RNA viruses, some of which are oncogenic; **___ endógeno humano** / human endogenous **___**.

Retzius, espacio de *m.* Retzius' space, space between the bladder and the pubic bones.

reuma *f.* rheum. 1. aqueous secretion; 2. rheumatism.

reumática, fiebre *f.* rheumatic fever, a fever that gen. follows a streptococcal infection manifested by acute generalized pain of the joints, showing cardiac arrythmia and renal disorders as residual effects.

reumático-a *a.* rheumatic, rel. to or afflicted by rheumatism.

reumátide *f.* rheumatid, any dermatosis associated with rheumatic fever.

reumatismo *m.* rheumatism, painful chronic or acute disease marked by infl. and pain in the joints.

reumatoide *a.* rheumatoid, rel. to or resembling rheumatism; **artritis ___** / ___ arthritis.

reunión *f.* 1. reunion; 2. meeting of parts, such as those of a fractured bone or the edges of a wound.

revacunación *f.* booster shot.

revascularización *f.* revascularization. 1. restoration of blood supply to a part following a lesion or a bypass; 2. bypass.

reventar *vi.* to burst; **reventarse** *vr.* to burst open.

reversión *f.* reversal, restitution to a previously existing condition.

revestimiento *m.* covering; investment.

revisar *v.* to review; to revise.
revisión *f.* revision, review.
revista *f.* magazine.
revivir *v.* to revive, to bring back to life.
revólver *m.* revolver, handgun.
revulsión *f.* revulsion. *V.* **contrairritación.**
revulsivo-a *a.* revulsive, rel. to or causing revulsion.
Reye, síndrome de *m.* Reye's syndrome, acute disease in children and adolescents manifested by severe edema that can affect the brain and other major organs of the body such as the liver.
rezar *vi.* to pray.
riboflavina *f.* riboflavin, component of vitamin B₂ complex, essential to nutrition.
ribonucleasa *f.* ribonuclease, enzyme that catalyzes the hydrolysis of ribonucleic acid.
ribonucleoproteína *f.* ribonucleoprotein, a substance containing both protein and ribonucleic acid.
ricino *m.* castor oil plant; **aceite de ___** / castor oil.
rickettsia *f.* Rickettsia, any of the gram-negative microorganisms of the group *Rickettsiaceae* that multiply only in host cells of fleas, lice, ticks, and mice, and are transmitted to humans by their bites.
rico-a *a.* rich; affluent; *pop.* very tasty.
riego *m.* flow; **___ sanguíneo** / blood ___.
riesgo *m.* risk; hazard; **grupos de alto ___** / high-___ groups; **posible ___** / potential ___; **___ de contaminación** / ___ of contamination; **-s / ___** factors.
riesgoso-a *a.* risky.
rifampicina *f.* rifampicin, a semisynthetic antibacterial substance used primarily in the treatment of pulmonary tuberculosis.
rigidez *f.* rigidity, stiffness, inflexibility; **___ cadavérica** / cadaveric ___, rigor mortis.
rígido-a *a.* rigid, stiff.
rigor *m.* rigor. 1. inflexibility of a muscle; 2. chill with high temperature; **___ mortis** / ___ mortis.
rinal *a.* rhinal, rel. to the nose.
rinitis *f.* rhinitis, infl. of the nasal mucosa.
rinofaringitis *f.* rhinopharyngitis, infl. of the nasopharynx.
rinofima *f.* rhinophyma, severe form of acne rosacea in the area of the nose.
rinolaringitis *f.* rhinolaryngitis, simultaneous infl. of the mucous membrane of the nose and the larynx.
rinoplastia *f.* rhinoplasty, plastic surgery of the nose.
rinorrea *f.* rhinorrhea, liquid mucous discharge from the nose.
rinoscopia *f.* rhinoscopy, examination of the nasal cavities.
riñón *m.* kidney, organ situated in the back of each side of the abdominal cavity; **___ artificial** / hemodyalizer; **fallo del ___** / ___ failure;

necrosis papilar del ___ / renal papillary necrosis; **piedras en el ___** / ___ stones; ___ **poliquístico** / polycystic ___; **trasplante del ___** / renal transplant.
risa *f.* laugh, laughter; **___ histérica** / hysteric ___; **sardónica** / sardonic ___, contraction of facial muscles that gives the appearance of a smile.
risorio *m.* risorius, muscle inserted at the corners of the mouth.
ristocetina *f.* ristocetin, antibiotic substance used in the treatment of infections by gram-positive cocci.
risueño-a *a.* smiling, affable.
Ritalin, clorhidrato de *m.* Ritalin hydrochloride, stimulant and antidepressant.
ritidectomía *f. surg.* rhytidectomy, face-lift, removal of wrinkles through plastic surgery.
rítmico-a *a.* rhythmical.
ritmo *m.* rhythm, regularity in the action or function of an organ of the body such as the heart; **___ acoplado** / coupled ___; **___ atrioventricular** / atrioventricular ___; **___ de galope** / gallop ___; **___ ectópico** / ectopic ___; **___ idioventricular** / idioventricular ___; **___ nodal** / nodal ___; **___ sinusal** / sinus ___.
ritmo circadiano *m.* circadian rhythm, rhythmic biological variations in a 24-hour cycle.
ritual *m.* ritual.
rizotomía *f. surg.* rhizotomy, transection of the root of a nerve.
Robitussin *m.* Robitussin, expectorant.
robustecer *vi.* to strengthen.
robusto-a *a.* robust, stout.
rociar *v.* to spray.
rodar *vi.* to roll; to wheel.
rodeado-a *a.* surrounded.
rodenticida *m.* rodenticide, agent that destroys rodents.
rodilla *f.* knee; **dislocación de la ___** / ___ dislocation.
rodillera *f.* knee protector.
rodopsina *f.* rhodopsin, purple-red pigment found in the retinal rods that enhances vision in dim light.
roedor *m.* rodent.
roentgen *m.* roentgen, the international unit of x- or gamma radiation; **rayos de ___** / ___ rays, x-rays.
roentgenograma *m.* roentgenogram, radiograph, photograph made with x-rays on a fluorescent surface.
rojizo-a *a.* reddish.
rojo-a *a.* red; **___ Congo** / Congo ___; **___ escarlata** / scarlet ___.
Romberg, signo de *m.* Romberg's sign, swaying of the body when in an erect position with eyes closed and feet close together as a sign of an inability to maintain balance.
romero *m.* rosemary.
romper *v.* to break; **romperse** *vr.* to break into pieces.

roncar *vi.* to snore.

ronco-a *a.* hoarse, with a husky voice.

roncha *f.* blotch; wheal; **-s** hives.

rongeur *Fr.* rongeur, forceps to remove minute bone chips.

ronquera *f.* hoarseness.

ronquido *m.* snore.

ropa *f.* clothing; __ **de cama** / bed clothes, bed linens; __ **interior** / underclothing.

Rorschach, prueba de *f.* Rorschach test, psychological test by which personality traits are revealed through the subject's interpretation of a series of ink blots.

rosáceo-a *a.* pinkish, rosy.

rosado-a *a.* pink.

rosario *m.* rosary, structure that resembles a string of beads.

rosbif *m.* roast beef.

roséola *f.* roseola, rose-colored skin eruption.

rosette *Fr.* rosette, a rose-shaped cluster of cells.

rostral *a.* rostral, rel. to or resembling a rostrum.

rostro *m.* rostrum. 1. human face; 2. beak or projection.

rotación *f.* rotation.

rotador-a *a.* rotator.

rotar *v.* to rotate, to turn around.

rotatorio-a *a.* rotatory, that rotates.

roto-a *a. pp.* of **romper**, broken.

rótula *f.* patella, kneecap; ball-and-socket joint.

rotura *f.* breakage; fracture.

rubefaciente *a.* rubefacient, that causes redness of the skin.

rubeola *f.* rubella, German measles, highly contagious benign viral infection manifested by fever, rose-colored eruption, and sore throat. It can have serious effects on the development of the fetus if acquired by the mother during early pregnancy.

rubio-a *a.* fair, blond, of light coloring.

rubor *m.* rubor, redness of the skin; blush.

ruborizado-a *a.* rubescent, that blushes.

ruborizarse *vr., vi.* to blush.

rudimento *m.* rudiment. 1. a partially developed organ; 2. an organ or part with a partial or total loss of function.

rueda de andar *f.* [*acondicionamiento físico*] treadmill.

ruga *L.* (*pl.* **rugae**) ruga, wrinkle or fold.

ruido *m.* noise; bruit, murmur; [*corazón*] sound; __ **sordo** / rumble.

ruptura *f.* rupture.

ruta *f.* route, direction.

rutina *f.* routine.

rutinario-a *a.* routine, done habitually.

S *abr.* **sulfuro** / sulfur.
s *abr.* **sacral** / sacral; **sección** / section; **segundo** / second.
sábana *f.* sheet.
sabañón *m.* chilblain, a hand or foot sore produced by cold.
saber *vi.* to know; **hacer ___** / to make known; **___ cómo** / ___ how; **___ de** / ___ of, about.
Sabin, vacuna de *f.* Sabin vaccine, oral poliomyelitis vaccine.
sabor *m.* taste; flavor, aftertaste; *v.* **tener ___ a, de** / to taste like.
sabroso-a *a.* tasteful, pleasurable to the taste.
sacabocados *m.* punch, surgical instrument used to perforate or cut a resistant tissue.
sacar *vi.* to take out; to draw out.
sacárido *m.* saccharide, chemical compound, one of a series of carbohydrates that includes sugars.
sacarina *f.* saccharin, crystalline substance used as an artificial sweetener; **-o** *a.* saccharine, overly sweet.
sacerdote *m.* priest, clergyman.
saciado-a *a.* satiated.
saciar *v.* to quench; to satiate; **___ la sed** / ___ the thirst.
saciedad *f.* satiety, the state of being fully satisfied.
saco *m.* sac, pocket, pouchlike structure; jacket.
sacral *a.* sacral, rel. to or near the sacrum; **nervios ___-es** / ___ nerves; **plexo ___** / ___ plexus.
sacralización *f.* sacralization, fusion of the fifth lumbar vertebra and the sacrum.
sacrificar *vi.* to sacrifice.
sacro *m.* sacrum, the large triangular bone formed by five fused vertebrae that lies at the base of the spine between the two hip bones.
sacroilitis *f.* sacroilitis, infl. of the sacroiliac joint.
sacrolumbar *a.* sacrolumbar, rel. to the sacral and the lumbar regions.
sacudida *f.* jerk, jolt.
sacudir *v.* to shake; to jerk.
sáculo *m.* saccule, small sac.
sádico-a *a.* sadistic, rel. to sadism.
sadismo *m.* sadism, perverted sexual pleasure derived from inflicting physical or psychological pain on others.
sadista *m., f.* sadist, person who practices sadism.
sadomasoquismo *m.* sadomasochism, perverted sexual pleasure derived from inflicting pain on oneself or on others.
sadomasoquista *m., f.* person who practices sadomasochism; *a.* sadomasochistic, rel. to the practice of sadomasochism.
safeno-a *a.* saphenous, rel. to or associated with

the saphenous veins; **venas ___-s** / ___ veins, the veins of the leg.
safismo *m.* sapphism, lesbianism.
sagital *a.* sagittal, resembling an arrow; **plano ___** / ___ plane, parallel to the long axis of the body.
sal *f.* salt, sodium chloride; **___-es aromáticas** / smelling ___-s; **___ corriente** / noniodized ___; **___ yodada** / iodized ___; *v.* **echar o poner ___** / to salt or add salt; **sin ___** / unsalted.
sala *f.* room; living room; [hospital] ward; **___ de aislamiento** / isolation ward; **___ de cuidado cardíaco** / cardiac care unit; **___ de cuidados intensivos** / intensive care unit; **___ de emergencia** / emergency ___; **___ de espera** / waiting ___; **___ de operaciones** / operating ___; **___ de parto** / delivery ___; **___ de recuperación** / recovery ___.
salado-a *a.* salty.
salario *m.* salary, wages.
salcochar, sancochar *v.* to parboil.
salchicha *f.* sausage.
salicilato *m.* salicylate, any salt of salicylic acid.
salicilismo *m.* salicylism, toxic condition produced by excess intake of salicylic acid.
salida *f.* outlet; exit, way out.
saliente *m.* protrusion; *a.* salient, projecting, protruding.
salino-a *a.* saline; **solución ___** / ___ solution, distilled water and salt.
salir *vi.* to go out; to leave; to come out.
saliva *f.* saliva, spit, secretion of the salivary glands that moistens and softens foods in the mouth.
salivación *f.* salivation, excessive discharge of saliva.
salival *a.* salivary, rel. to saliva.
Salk, vacuna de *f.* Salk vaccine, poliomyelitis vaccine.
salmón *m.* salmon.
Salmonela *f.* Salmonella, a genus of gram-negative bacteria of the *Enterobacteriaceae* family that causes enteric fever, gastrointestinal disorders, and septicemia.
salmonelosis *f.* salmonellosis, infectious condition caused by ingestion of food contaminated by bacteria of the genus *Salmonella*.
salón *m.* large hall or room.
salpingectomía *f. surg.* salpingectomy, removal of one or both fallopian tubes.
salpingitis *f.* salpingitis, infl. of a fallopian tube.
salpingooforectomía *f. surg.* salpingo-oophorectomy, removal of a fallopian tube and an ovary.
salpingoplastia *f. surg.* salpingoplasty, plastic surgery of the fallopian tubes.
salpinx *Gr.* (*pl.* **salpinges**) salpinx, a tube, such as the fallopian tube.
salpullido, sarpullido *m.* heat rash.
salsa *f.* sauce; gravy.
saltar *v.* to jump; to skip; **___ un turno** / to skip an appointment or turn.

saltear *v.* to stagger; to alternate.

salto *m.* jump; skip; omission, [*del corazón*] palpitation.

saltón, saltona *a.* jumpy.

salubre *a.* salubrious, healthy.

salubridad *f.* the state of public health.

salud *f.* health; **atención a la ___ / ___** care; **certificado de ___ / ___** certificate; **cuidado de la ___ / ___** care; **cuidado de ___ en el hogar /** home ___ care; **estado de ___ / ___** status; **instituciones de ___ pública /** public ___ facilities; **servicios de ___ / ___** services; **servicios de ___ para los ancianos /** ___ services for the aged; **___ pública /** public ___; **___ urbana /** urban ___.

saludar *v.* to greet.

saludo *m.* greeting.

salvado *m.* bran, a by-product of the milling of grain.

salvamento *m.* salvage, rescue.

salvar *v.* to save.

sanar *v.* to cure, to heal.

sanatorio *m.* sanatorium, sanitarium, health establishment for physical and mental rehabilitation.

saneamiento *m.* sanitation.

sangramiento *m.* bleeding; **___ por la nariz /** nosebleed.

sangrar *v.* to bleed.

sangre *f.* blood; **___ autóloga /** autologous ___; **coágulo de ___ / ___** clot; **conteo de ___ / ___** count; **donante de ___ / ___** donor; **periférica /** peripheral ___; **prueba selecta de ___ / ___** screening; **transfusión de ___ / ___** transfusion; **___ vital /** lifeblood; **a ___ fría /** in cold ___; **banco de ___ / ___** bank.

sangre oculta *f.* occult blood, blood that is present in such a minute amount that it cannot be seen with the naked eye.

sangría *f.* bloodletting.

sangriento-a *a.* bloody.

sanguíneo-a *a.* 1. sanguineous, rel. to blood or that contains it; **derivados ___-s, hemoderivados /** blood derivatives; **determinación de grupos ___-s /** blood grouping; **gases ___-s /** blood gases; **plasma ___ /** blood plasma; **producto ___ /** blood product; **proteína ___ /** blood protein; **sustitutos ___-s /** blood substitutes; **tipo ___ /** blood group; **tiempo de coagulación ___ /** blood coagulation time; 2. sanguine, of a cheerful nature.

sanguinolento-a *a.* sanguinolent, containing blood; **esputo ___ /** blood sputum.

sanitario-a *m., f.* sanitarian, person trained in matters of sanitation and public health; *a.* sanitary, hygienic; **toalla, servilleta ___ / ___** napkin.

sano-a *a.* healthy; sound; wholesome.

saprófito *m.* saprophyte, vegetable organism that lives on decaying or dead organic matter.

sarampión *m.* measles, highly contagious disease esp. in school age children, caused by the rubeola virus; **suero de globulina preventivo al ___ / ___** immune serum globulin administered within five days after exposure to the disease.

sarcoidosis *f.* sarcoidosis. *V.* **Schaumann, enfermedad de.**

sarcoma *m.* sarcoma, malignant neoplasm of the connective tissue.

sardina *f.* sardine.

sarna *f.* scabies, mange, parasitic cutaneous infection that produces itching.

satélite *m.* satellite, a small structure accompanying a larger one.

satisfacer *vi.* to satisfy.

satisfecho-a *a. pp.* of **satisfacer,** satisfied.

saturación *f.* saturation.

saturado-a *a.* saturated, unable to absorb or receive any given substance beyond a given limit; **no ___ /** unsaturated.

saturar *v.* to saturate.

savia *f.* sap, natural juice.

saya *f.* skirt.

sazonado-a *a.* seasoned.

sazonar *v.* to season.

Schaumann, enfermedad de *f.* Schaumann's disease, chronic disease of unknown cause manifested by the presence of small tubercles, esp. in the lymph nodes, lungs, bones, and skin.

Schilling, prueba de *f.* Schilling test, use of radioactive Vitamin B_{12} for the purpose of diagnosing primary pernicious anemia.

sebáceo-a *a.* sebaceous, rel. to or containing sebum; **glándulas ___-s /** glands, glands of the skin; **quiste ___ / ___** cyst.

sebo *m.* sebum, fatty thick substance secreted by the sebaceous glands.

secar *vi.* to dry; **secarse** *vr.* to dry out.

sección *f.* section, portion, part; **___ media /** midsection.

seccionar *v.* to section; to cut.

seco-a *a.* dry.

secreción *f.* secretion. 1. the production of a given substance as a result of glandular activity; 2. substance produced by secretion; **___ apocrina /** apocrine ___; **___ externa /** external ___; **___ interna /** internal ___; **___ purulenta /** purulent ___.

secretagogo *m.* secretagogue, secretogogue, agent that stimulates glandular secretion.

secretar *v.* to secrete.

secretario-a *m., f.* secretary.

secretorio-a *a.* secretory, that has the property of secreting.

secuela *f.* sequela, aftereffects, condition following or resulting from a disease or treatment.

secuencia *f.* sequence, succession, order.

secuestración *f.* sequestration. 1. the act of isolating; 2. the formation of sequestrum.

secuestrar *v.* to sequester, to isolate.

secuestro *m.* sequestrum, fragment of dead bone that has become separated from adjoining bone.

secundario-a *a.* secondary.

secundinas *f. pl.* afterbirth, placenta and membranes expelled at the time of delivery.

sed *f.* thirst; *v.* **tener** ___ / to be thirsty.

seda *f.* silk.

sedación *f.* sedation, the act and effect of inducing calm through medication.

sedante, sedativo *m.* sedative, agent with a quieting and tranquilizing effect.

sedentario-a *a.* sedentary. 1. having little or no physical activity; 2. rel. to a sitting position.

sediento-a *a.* thirsty.

sedimentación *f.* sedimentation, the process of depositing sediment; **índice de** ___ / ___ rate.

sedimento *m.* sediment, matter that settles at the bottom of a solution.

segmentación *f.* segmentation, the act of dividing into parts.

segmento *m.* segment, section or part.

seguido-a *a.* continuous, unbroken; following.

seguimiento *m.* follow-up.

seguir *vi.* to follow; to continue.

según *prep.* according to; in accordance with.

segundo *m.* second of time; **-a** *a.* second.

seguridad *f.* safety, security; assurance; **medidas de** ___ / ___ measures.

seguro *m.* insurance; ___ **de incapacidad** / disability ___; ___ **de vida** / life ___; ___ **médico** / health ___; ___ **social** / social security; **-a** *a.* safe; certain; **-mente** *adv.* surely.

selección *f.* selection, choice; sampling.

selenio *m.* selenium, a nonmetallic chemical element resembling sulfur, used in electronic devices.

sellar *v.* to seal, to close tightly.

semana *f.* week; **la** ___ **pasada** / last ___; **la** ___ **próxima, la** ___ **que viene** / next ___.

semanal *a.* weekly; **-mente** *adv.* weekly.

semántica *f.* semantics, the study of the meaning of words.

semblante *m.* appearance of the face.

semejante *a.* resembling, similar.

semejar *v.* to resemble.

semen *m.* semen, sperm, thick whitish secretion of the male reproductive organs.

semicoma *m.* semicoma, slight comatose state.

semilla *f.* seed; pit.

seminal *a.* seminal, rel. to or consisting of seed.

seminífero-a *a.* seminiferous, that produces or bears seeds or semen; **conductos** ___-s / ___ tubules.

semiótica *f.* semiotics, the branch of medicine concerned with signs and symptoms of diseases.

semiótico-a *a.* semiotic, rel. to the signs and symptoms of a disease.

sencillo-a *a.* simple, plain.

senescencia *f.* senescence, the process of becoming old.

senil *a.* senile, rel. to old age esp. as it affects mental and physical functions.

senilidad *f.* senility, the state of being senile.

seno *m.* breast, bust, bosom; **autoexamen de los** ___-s / ___ self-examination.

senos paranasales *m. pl.* paranasal sinuses, any of the air cavities in the adjacent bones of the nasal cavity.

sensación *f.* sensation, feeling, perception through the senses.

sensato-a *a.* sensible, reasonable.

sensibilidad *f.* sensitivity, the condition of being sensitive to touch or palpation; tenderness; **entrenamiento de la** ___ / ___ training; ___ **profunda** / deep ___.

sensibilización *f.* sensitization, the act of making sensible.

sensibilizar *vi.* to sensitize, to make sensitive.

sensible *a.* sensitive, sensible.

sensitivo-a *a.* 1. sensorial, that is perceived through the senses; 2. tender, sensitive to touch or palpation.

sensitivomotor *a.* sensorimotor, rel. to sensory and motor activities of the body.

sensorial, sensorio-a *a.* sensory, rel. to sensation or to the senses; **afasia** ___ / ___ aphasia; **nervio** ___ / ___ nerve; **privación** ___ / ___ deprivation; **umbral** ___ / ___ threshold.

sensual *a.* sensual, sensuous; carnal.

sentado-a *a.* seated.

sentarse *vr., vi.* to sit down.

sentido *m.* sense; a perception or impression received through the senses; ___ **de la vista** / of sight; ___ **del oído** / ___ of hearing; ___ **del olfato** / ___ of smell; ___ **del sabor** / ___ of taste; ___ **del tacto** / ___ of touch; ___ **común** / common ___; ___ **del humor** / ___ of humor.

sentimiento *m.* feeling; sentiment.

sentir *vi.* to feel, to perceive through the senses; **sentirse** *vr.* [*estado corporal*] to feel, general state of the body or mind; ___ **bien** / to ___ good; ___ **mal** / to ___ sick.

señal *f.* sign, indication.

señalado-a *a.* conspicuous, pronounced.

señalar *v.* to point out, to indicate; to mark.

señor *m.* mister; *abr.* Mr.

señora *f.* married woman; *abr.* Mrs.

señorita *f.* miss, young lady; *abr.* Miss.

separación *f.* separation; in obstetrics, disengagement.

separado-a *a.* separate; **-mente** *adv.* separately.

separar *v.* to separate, to sever.

sepsis *L.* sepsis, toxic condition caused by bacterial contamination.

septal *a.* septal, rel. to a septum; **desviación** ___ / ___ deviation.

septicemia *f.* septicemia, blood poisoning, invasion of the blood by virulent microorganisms.

séptico-a *a.* septic, rel. to sepsis; **choque** ___ / ___ shock.

septum *L.* (*pl.* **septa**) septum, partition between two cavities.

sequedad *f.* dryness.

sequía *f.* drought.

ser *vi.* to be.

sereno-a *a.* serene, calm; *pop.* cool.

serie *f.* distribution, set, succession; series, a group of specimens or types arranged in sequence; **en** ___ / serial; ___ **selectiva bioquímica** / biochemical screening.

serio-a *a.* serious; [*caso médico*] complicated; **en** ___ / seriously; **-mente** *adv.* seriously.

seroconversión *f.* seroconversion, development of antibodies as a response to an infection or to the administration of a vaccine.

serología *f.* serology, the science that studies sera.

serológico-a *a.* serologic, serological, rel. to serum.

seroma *m.* seroma, accumulation of blood serum that produces a tumorlike swelling, gen. subcutaneous.

seronegativo-a *a.* seronegative, presenting a negative reaction in serological tests.

seropositivo-a *a.* seropositive, presenting a positive reaction in serological tests.

serosa *f.* serosa, serous membrane.

serosanguíneo-a *a.* serosanguineous, of the nature of serum and blood.

seroso-a *a.* serous. 1. of the nature of serum; 2. producing or containing serum.

serotipo *m.* serotype, type of microorganism determined by the class and combination of antigens present in the cell; **determinación del** ___ / serotyping.

serpiente *f.* snake, serpent; ___ **de cascabel** / rattlesnake; **mordida de** ___ / ___ bite; ___ **venenosa** / poisonous ___ .

serpiginoso-a *a.* serpiginous, that crawls from one place to another.

servible *a.* usable.

servicio *m.* service; ___-s **de cuidado exterior** / extended care facility; ___-s **de emergencia** / emergency ___ ; ___-s **de salud preventiva** / preventive health ___ .

servilleta *f.* napkin.

servir *vi.* to serve; to be of help or service.

sesamoideo-a *a.* sesamoid, rel. to or resembling a small mass in a joint or cartilage.

sésil *a.* sessile, attached by a broad base with no peduncle.

sesión *f.* session.

seso *m.* brain.

seudogota *f.* pseudogout, recurrent arthritic condition with symptoms similar to gout.

severo-a *a.* severe.

sexo *m.* sex; **relacionado con el** ___ / ___-linked, transmitted by genes located in the sex chromosome.

sexual *a.* sexual, rel. to sex; **características** ___-es / ___ characteristics; **conducta** ___ / ___ behavior; **desarrollo** ___ / ___ development; **educación** ___ / ___ education; **madurez** ___ / ___ maturity; **relaciones** ___-es / ___ intercourse; **trastorno** ___ / ___ disorder; **vida** ___ / ___ life; **-mente** *adv.* sexually; **enfermedad** ___

transmitida / ___ transmitted disease.

sexualidad *f.* sexuality, collective characteristics of each sex.

shigelosis *f.* shigellosis, bacillary dysentery.

shock *m.* shock, abnormal state generated by insufficient blood circulation that can cause disorders such as low blood pressure, rapid pulse, pallor, abnormally low body temperature, and general weakness; ___ **anafiláctico** / anaphylactic ___ ; ___ **endotóxico** / endotoxic ___ ; ___ **insulínico** / insulin ___ ; ___ **séptico** / septic ___ .

si *conj.* if, in case.

sí *adv.* yes; **diga** ___ o **no, di** ___ o **no** / say ___ or no.

sialadenitis *f.* sialadenitis, sialoadenitis, infl. of a salivary gland.

sialogogo *m.* sialogogue, agent that stimulates secretion of saliva.

sialograma *m.* sialogram, x-ray of the salivary tract.

SIDA *abr.* AIDS, acquired immunodeficiency syndrome, characterized by immunodeficiency, infections (such as pneumonia, tuberculosis, and chronic diarrhea), and tumors (esp. lymphoma and Kaposi's sarcoma).

siempre *adv.* always; **para** ___ / forever.

sien *f.* temple, the flattened lateral region on either side of the head.

siesta *f.* nap; break of activities at midday.

sietemesino-a *a.* born after seven months of gestation.

sífilis *f.* syphilis, contagious venereal disease usu. transmitted by direct contact and manifested by structural and cutaneous lesions; ___ **terciaria** / tertiary ___ , the third and most advanced stage of syphilis.

sifilítico-a *m.*, *f.* syphylitic, person infected with syphilis; *a.* rel. to or caused by syphilis.

sifilología *f.* syphilology, branch of medicine that studies the diagnosis and treatment of syphilis.

sifón *m.* syphon.

sigmoide, sigmoideo-a *a.* sigmoid. 1. shaped like the letter *s;* 2. rel. to the sigmoid colon.

sigmoidoscopía *f.* sigmoidoscopy, examination of the sigmoid flexure with a sigmoidoscope.

sigmoidoscopio *m.* sigmoidoscope, long hollow tubular instrument used for the examination of the sigmoid flexure.

significado *m.* meaning, significance.

significar *vi.* to signify, to mean.

significativo-a *a.* significant; meaningful, important.

signo *m.* sign; mark, objective manifestation of a disease; ___-s **vitales** / vital ___-s.

siguiente *a.* following, next.

sílaba *f. gr.* syllable.

silbar *v.* to whistle.

silbido *m.* whistle.

silencio *m.* silence.

silencioso-a *a.* silent.

silicio *m.* silicon, nonmetallic element found in the soil.

silicón *m.* silicone, organic silicon compound used in lubricants, synthetics and also in plastic surgery and prostheses.

silicosis *f.* silicosis, dust inhalation.

Silvio, acueducto de *m.* aqueduct of Silvius, narrow channel connecting the third and fourth ventricles of the brain.

silla *f.* chair; ___ **de ruedas** / wheelchair.

silla turca *f.* sella turcica, depression on the superior surface of the sphenoid bone that contains the hypophysis.

sillón *m.* armchair; *Cuba* rocking chair.

simbiosis *f.* symbiosis, close association of two dissimilar organisms.

simbiótico-a *a.* symbiotic, rel. to symbiosis.

simbolismo *m.* symbolism. 1. *psych.* mental abnormality by which the patient conceives occurrences as symbols of his or her own thoughts; 2. in psychoanalysis, symbolic representation of repressed thoughts and emotions.

símbolo *m.* symbol.

simetría *f.* symmetry, perfect correspondence of parts situated on opposite sides of an axis or plane of a body.

simétrico-a *a.* symmetrical.

similar *a.* similar.

simpatectomía *f. surg.* sympathectomy, interruption of the sympathetic nerve pathways.

simpatía *f.* sympathy, relationship, affinity. 1. affinity between mind and body whereby one is affected by the other; 2. relationship between two organs in which an anomaly in one affects the other.

simpático-a *a.* sympathetic, rel. to the sympathetic nervous system.

simpatolítico-a *a.* sympatholytic, resistant to the activity produced by the stimulation of the sympathetic nervous system.

simpatomimético-a *a.* sympathomimetic, having the capacity to cause physiological changes similar to those produced by the action of the sympathetic nervous system.

simple *a.* simple; **-mente** *adv.* merely.

simplificar *vi.* to simplify.

simulación *f.* simulation, imitation; feigning an illness or symptom.

simulador-a *m., f.* malingerer, person who deliberately feigns or exaggerates the symptoms of an illness.

sin *prep.* without; ___ **embargo** / nevertheless.

sinapsis *f.* 1. synapse, the point of contact between two neurons, where the impulse traveling through the first neuron originates an impulse in the second one; 2. synapsis, the pairing of homologous chromosomes at the start of meiosis.

sináptico-a *a.* synaptic, rel. to synapse or synapsis.

sinartrosis *f.* synarthrosis, an immovable joint in which the bony elements are fused.

sincitial *a.* syncytial, rel. to or constituting syncytium.

sincitio *m.* syncytium, mass of protoplasm resulting from cell fusion.

sincondrosis *f.* synchondrosis, an immovable joint in which the surfaces are joined by cartilaginous tissue.

sincopal *a.* syncopal, rel. to a syncope.

síncope *m.* syncope, temporary loss of consciousness due to inadequate supply of blood to the brain.

sincrónico-a *a.* synchronous, occurring at the same time.

sindactilia *f.* syndactylism, syndactyly, congenital anomaly consisting in the fusion of two or more fingers or toes.

síndrome *m.* syndrome, the totality of the symptoms and signs of a disease; ___ **adiposo** / adipose ___; ___ **de choque tóxico** / toxic shock ___, blood poisoning due to *Staphylococci;* ___ **de dificultad respiratoria** / respiratory distress ___; ___ **de escaldadura** / scalded skin ___, burns in the epidermis that gen. do not harm the underlying dermis; ___ **de malabsorción** / malabsorption ___, gastrointestinal disorder caused by poor absorption of food; ___ **de muerte infantil súbita** / sudden infant death ___; ___ **de niños maltratados** / battered children ___; ___ **de privación** / withdrawal ___, resulting from discontinued use of alcohol or a drug; ___ **de transfusión múltiple** / transfusion ___, multiple; ___ **de vaciamiento gástrico rápido** / dumping ___, rapid dumping of the stomach contents into the small intestine; ___ **del lóbulo medio del pulmón** / middle lobe ___ of the lung; ___ **del secuestro subclavicular** / subclavian steal ___; ___ **nefrótico** / nephrotic ___, excessive loss of protein; ___ **suprarrenogenital** / adrenogenital ___.

síndrome de inmunodeficiencia adquirida *m.* acquired immunodeficiency syndrome. *V.* **SIDA.**

sinequia *f.* synechia, union or abnormal adherence of tissue or organs, esp. in reference to the iris, the lens, and the cornea.

sinérgico-a *a.* synergistic, synergic, the capacity to act together.

sinergismo *m.* synergism, correlated or harmonious action between two or more structures or drugs.

sínfisis *f.* symphysis, a joint in which adjacent bony surfaces are united by a fibrocartilage.

singular *m. gr.* singular, only one; *a.* singular, not common, unique.

singulto *m.* singultus, hiccup, hiccough.

sinoauricular o sinusal, nódulo *m.* sinoauricular, sinoatrial node located at the meeting point of the vena cava and the right cardiac atrium, point of origin of the impulses that stimulate the heartbeat.

sinograma *m.* sinogram, x-ray of a sinus by

means of a contrasting dye.

sinovia *f.* synovia, synovial fluid, transparent and viscid liquid secreted by synovial membranes that lubricates joints and connective tissue.

sinovial *a.* synovial, rel. to or producing synovia; **bursa, saco** ___ / ___ bursa; **membrana** ___ / ___ membrane; **quiste** ___ / ___ cyst.

sinovitis *f.* synovitis, an infl. of the synovial membrane; ___ **purulenta** / purulent ___; ___ **seca** / dry ___; ___ **serosa** / serous ___.

síntesis *f.* synthesis, the composition of a whole by a union of the parts.

sintético-a *a.* synthetic, rel. to or produced by synthesis.

sintetizar *vi.* to synthesize, to produce synthesis.

síntoma *m.* symptom, any manifestation of a disease as perceived by the patient; ___ **constitucional** / constitutional ___; ___ **demorado** / delayed ___; ___ **de supresión** / withdrawal ___; ___ **objetivo** / objective ___; ___ **patognomónico** / pathognomonic ___; ___ **presente** / presenting ___; ___ **prodrómico** / prodromal ___; ___ **-s premonitorios** / warning ___ -s.

sintomático-a *a.* symptomatic; **-mente** *adv.* symptomatically.

sintomatología *f.* symptomatology, symptoms pertaining to a given condition or case.

sintónico-a *m., f.* syntonic, a type of personality that responds and adjusts normally to his or her environment.

sinuoso-a *a.* sinuous, winding, wavy.

sinus *L.* sinus, cavity or hollow passage.

sinusitis *f.* sinusitis, infl. of a sinus, esp. a paranasal sinus.

sinusoide *m.* sinusoid, a minute passage that carries blood to the tissues of an organ, such as the liver; *a.* resembling a sinus.

siringobulbia *f.* syringobulbia, the presence of abnormal cavities in the medulla oblongata.

siringocele *m.* syringocele. 1. the central canal of the spinal cord; 2. a meningomyelocele containing a cavity in the ectopic spinal cord.

siringomielia *f.* syringomyelia, chronic, progressive disease of the spinal cord manifested by formation of liquid-filled cavities, gen. in the cervical region and sometimes extending into the medulla oblongata.

sirope *m.* syrup, concentrated solution of sugar.

sistema *m.* system, a group of correlated parts or organs constituting a whole that performs one or more vital functions; ___ **cardiovascular** / cardiovascular ___; ___ **digestivo** / digestive ___; ___ **endocrino** / endocrine ___; ___ **genitourinario** / genitourinary ___; ___ **inmunológico** / immune ___; ___ **hematopoyético** / hematopoietic ___; ___ **linfático** / lymphatic ___; ___ **nervioso** / nervous ___; ___ **óseo** / osseous ___; ___ **portal** / portal ___; ___ **reproductivo** / reproductive ___; ___ **respiratorio** / respiratory ___; ___ **reticuloendotelial** / reticuloendothelial ___; ___ **amortiguador** / buffer ___.

Sistemas	Systems
cardiovascular	cardiovascular
digestivo	digestive
endocrino	endocrine
genitourinario	genitourinary
hematopoyético	hematopoietic
inmunológico	immune
linfático	lymphatic
nervioso	nervous
óseo	osseous
portal	portal
reproductivo	reproductive
respiratorio	respiratory
reticuloendotelial	reticuloendothelial

sistemático-a *a.* systematic, that follows a system; **-mente** *adv.* systematically.

sistematización *f.* systematization, the act of following a system.

sistémico-a *a.* systemic, that affects the body as a whole; **circulación** ___ / ___ circulation.

sístole *f.* systole, the contractive cycle of the heartbeat, esp. of the ventricles; ___ **auricular** / atrial ___; ___ **prematura** / premature ___; ___ **ventricular** / ventricular ___.

sistólico-a *a.* systolic, rel. to the systole; **murmullo** ___ / ___ murmur; **presión** ___ / ___ pressure.

situación *f.* situation.

situado-a *a.* situated, placed, located.

situs *L.* situs, position or place.

Snellen, prueba de ojo de *f.* Snellen's eye test, a chart of black letters that gradually diminish in size used in testing visual acuity.

sobra *f.* excess, surplus; **hay de** ___ / there is more than enough.

sobrante *m.* surplus, leftover, excess.

sobrar *v.* to be or have in excess.

sobre *prep.* above, over; ___ **todo** / above all.

sobrealimentación *f.* hyperalimentation; ___ **intravenosa** / parenteral ___.

sobrecierre *m.* overclosure, condition caused when the mandible closes before the upper and lower teeth meet.

sobrecompensación *f.* overcompensation; *psych.* an exaggerated attempt to conceal feelings of guilt or inferiority.

sobrecorrección *f.* overcorrection, use of too powerful a lens to correct an eye defect.

sobredosis *f.* overdose, excessive dose of a drug.

sobreextensión *f.* overextension.

sobrellevar *v.* to endure.

sobremordida *f.* overbite.

sobrenombre *m.* surname, family name.

sobrepeso *m.* overweight.

sobreponerse *vr., vi.* to overcome.

sobreproducción *f.* overproduction.

sobrerrespuesta *f.* overresponse, excessive reaction to a stimulus.

sobresalir *vi.* to protrude; to be conspicuous.

sobresaltado-a *a.* frightened, startled.

sobretodo *m.* coat.

sobrevivir *v.* to survive.

sobrino-a *m., f.* nephew; niece.

sobrio-a *a.* sober.

socavar *v.* to undermine.

sociable *a.* sociable.

social *a.* social; **seguro** ___ / ___ security; **asistencia** ___ / ___ work; **trabajador-a** ___ / ___ worker.

socialización *f.* socialization, social adaptation.

socializado-a *a.* socialized; **medicina** ___ / ___ medicine.

sociedad *f.* society; corporation; fellowship.

socio-a *m., f.* member; partner; fellow.

sociobiología *f.* sociobiology, the science that studies genetic factors as determinants of social behavior.

sociología *f.* sociology, the science that studies social relations and phenomena.

sociólogo-a *m., f.* sociologist, specialist in sociology.

sociópata *m., f.* sociopath, an individual that manifests antisocial behavior.

socorrer *v.* to help, to assist, to aid.

soda *f.* soda, sodium carbonate.

sodio *m.* sodium, soft alkaline metallic element found in the fluids of the body; **bicarbonato de** ___ / baking soda; **carbonato de** ___ / soda.

sodomía *f.* sodomy, term used in reference to sexual relations between males.

sodomita *m., f.* sodomite, one who commits sodomy.

sofisticación *f.* sophistication; the adulteration of a substance.

sofocación *f.* suffocation, asphyxia, shortness of breath.

sofocar *vi.* to suffocate, to smother; to choke.

sofoco *m.* hot flash; suffocation.

soja, soya *f.* soy, soybean.

sol *m.* sun; **baño de** ___ / sunbathing; **mancha del** ___ / sunspot; **quemadura de** ___ / sunburn; **tomar** ___ / to sunbathe.

solar *a.* solar, rel. to the sun; **bloqueador** ___ / sunscreen.

solaz *m.* solace, comfort, rest from work.

sólido-a *a.* solid; firm; sound.

solo-a *a.* alone, only; **-mente** *adv.* only.

soltar *vi.* to release; to loosen.

soltero-a *a.* single, unmarried.

soluble *a.* soluble.

solución *f.* solution.

solvente *m.* solvent, liquid that dissolves or is capable of producing a solution; thinner; *a.* financially responsible.

sollozar *vi.* to sob; to cry.

somático-a *a.* somatic, rel. to the body.

somatización *f. psych.* somatization; the process of converting mental experiences into bodily manifestations.

sombra *f.* shadow; opacity; shade; **a la** ___ / in the shade.

sombrero *m.* hat.

someter *v.* to submit; **someterse** *vr.* to undergo; to submit oneself.

somnífero *m.* sleeping pill.

somnolencia *f.* sleepiness, drowsiness.

sonambulismo *m.* somnambulance, somnambulism, sleepwalking.

sonámbulo-a *m., f.* somnambule, person who walks in his or her sleep.

sonar *vi.* to sound, to ring.

sonda *f.* probe, thin, smooth, and flexible instrument used to explore cavities and body passages or to measure the depth and direction of a wound; ___ **acanalada** / hollow ___; ___ **intestinal** / intestinal decompression tube; ___ **uretral** / urethral catheter.

sonido *m.* sound.

sonografía *f.* sonography. *V.* **ultrasonografía.**

sonograma *m.* sonogram, image obtained by ultrasonography.

sonoluciente *a.* sonolucent, in ultrasonography, having the quality of permitting the passage of ultrasound waves without remitting them back to their source.

sonoro-a *a.* sonorous, resonant, having a radiant sound.

sonreír *vi.* to smile.

sonrisa *f.* smile.

soñar *vi.* to dream; ___ **despierto** / to daydream.

sopa *f.* soup.

soplar *v.* to blow.

soplo *m.* murmur, bruit, flutter; short, raspy, or fluttering sound, esp. an abnormal beat of the heart; ___ **aórtico, regurgitante** / aortic ___, regurgitant; ___ **cardíaco** / cardiac ___; ___ **continuo** / continuous ___; ___ **creciente, en crescendo** / crescendo ___; ___ **diastólico** / diastolic ___; ___ **en vaivén** / to-and-fro ___; ___ **funcional** / functional ___; ___ **inocente** / innocent ___; ___ **mitral** / mitral ___; ___ **pansistólico** / pansystolic ___; ___ **presistólico** / presystolic ___; ___ **sistólico** / systolic ___.

sopor *m.* drowsiness, sleepiness.

soporífero, soporífico *m.* soporific, agent that produces sleep.

soportable *a.* bearable, tolerable.

soportar *v.* to endure, to bear, to sustain.

soporte *m.* support.

sorber *v.* to sip; to suck; to absorb.

sorbo *m.* sip.

sordera *f.* deafness.

sordo-a *m., f.* a deaf person; *a.* deaf.

sordomudo-a *m., f.* deaf-mute person.

soso-a *a.* tasteless.

sostén *m.* support, backing; buttress.

sostener *vi.* to sustain; to maintain.

sostenido-a *a.* sustained; maintained.

spina *L.* spina. 1. thornlike projection; 2. the spinal column.

Staphylococcus *Gr. Staphylococcus,* genus of

gram-positive bacteria of which several pathogenic species include parasites that are present in the skin and mucous membrane.

status *L.* status, state or condition; ___ **asmaticus** / ___ asthmaticus, severe asthma condition; ___ **epilepticus** / ___ epilepticus, series of seizures with loss of consciousness throughout.

Still, enfermedad de *f.* Still's disease, juvenile rheumatoid arthritis.

stratum *L.* (*pl.* **strata**) stratum, layer.

Streptococcus *Gr.* Streptococcus, a genus of gram-positive bacteria of the tribe *Streptococceae* that occur in pairs or chains, many of which are causal agents of serious infection.

stress *m.* stress, physical, chemical, or emotional factor that provokes an immediate or delayed response on the functions of the body or any of its parts.

struma *L.* struma, enlargement of the thyroid gland, goiter.

suave *a.* soft, smooth; **-mente** *adv.* softly.

suavizar *vi.* to soften.

subacromial *a.* subacromial, below the acromion.

subagudo-a *a.* subacute, rel. to a condition that is neither acute nor chronic.

subaracnoideo-a *a.* subarachnoid, situated or occurring below the arachnoid membrane; **espacio** ___ / ___ space.

subatómico-a *a.* subatomic, smaller than an atom.

subcapsular *a.* subcapsular, located below a capsule.

subclavicular *a.* subclavian, subclavicular, located beneath the clavicle; **arteria** ___ / ___ artery; **vena** ___ / ___ vein.

subclínico-a *a.* subclinical, without clinical manifestations.

subconsciencia, subconsciente *f., m. psych.* subconscious, state during which mental processes affecting thought, feeling, and behavior occur without the individual's awareness.

subconsciente *a. psych.* subconscious, partially conscious.

subcostal *a.* subcostal, below the ribs.

subcultivo *m.* subculture, a culture of bacteria derived from another culture.

subcutáneo-a *a.* subcutaneous, under the skin.

subdesarrollado-a *a.* underdeveloped.

subdesarrollo *m.* underdevelopment.

subdural *a.* subdural, under the dura mater. **espacio** ___ / ___ space.

subependimario-a *a.* subependymal, situated under the ependyma.

subescapular *a.* subscapular, below the scapula.

subesternal *a.* substernal, below the sternum.

subestructura *f.* substructure, supporting structure.

subfrénico-a *a.* subphrenic, situated below the diaphragm; **absceso** ___ / ___ abscess.

subhepático-a *a.* subhepatic, situated under the liver.

subintimal *a.* subintimal, situated below the intima.

subir *v.* to go up; to lift up; to climb; ___ **las escaleras** / to climb the stairs.

súbito-a *a.* sudden; **muerte** ___ / ___ death; **-mente** *adv.* suddenly.

subjetivo-a *a.* subjective; **síntomas** ___-s / ___ symptoms.

sublimación *f.* sublimation. 1. the change from a solid state to vapor; 2. *psych.* a Freudian term indicating a process by which instinctual drives and impulses are modified into socially acceptable behavior.

sublimado *m.* sublimate, substance obtained by sublimation.

sublingual *a.* sublingual, under the tongue; **glándula** ___ / ___ gland.

subluxación *f.* subluxation, an incomplete dislocation.

submandibular *a.* submandibular, under the mandible.

submental *a.* submental, under the chin.

submucosa *f.* submucosa, layer of cellular tissue situated under a mucous membrane.

subnormal *a.* subnormal, below normal or below average.

subóptimo-a *a.* suboptimal, less than optimum.

subproducto *m.* by-product.

subrogado-a *a.* surrogate, that takes the place of someone or something.

subscripción *f.* subscription, part of the prescription that contains instructions for its preparation.

subsistir *v.* to subsist, to survive.

substantivo, sustantivo *m. gr.* substantive, noun.

subtotal *m.* subtotal.

subungueal *a.* subungual, beneath a nail.

succión *f.* suction; **dispositivo de** ___ / ___ device.

suceder *v.* to happen.

sucesivo-a *a.* successive, consecutive.

suceso *m.* happening, event.

suciedad *f.* filth.

sucio-a *a.* dirty, filthy.

suco *m.* succus, juice; sap.

sucrosa *f.* sucrose, natural saccharose obtained mostly from sugarcane and sugar beets.

sudado-a *a.* sweaty, moist with perspiration; perspiring.

sudar *v.* to sweat, to perspire.

sudatorio, sudorífico *m.* sudorific, an agent promoting sweat.

sudor *m.* sweat, perspiration, secretion of the sweat glands; ___**-es nocturnos** / night ___-s.

sudores fríos *m. pl.* cold sweat.

sudoriento-a *a.* sweated, covered with sweat.

sudorífico-a *a.* sudorific, that produces sweat.

sudoroso-a *a.* perspiring, sweaty.

suegro-a *m., f.* father-in-law; mother-in-law.

sueldo *m.* salary, wages.

suelo *m.* ground; floor.

suelto-a *a. pp.* of **soltar,** loose, unattached.

sueño *m.* sleep; dream; **ciclos del __ / __** cycles; **__ crepuscular** / twilight **__; estadíos del __ / __** stages; **__ profundo** / deep **__; __ reparador** / balmy **__; trastornos del __** / sleep disorders; *v.* **tener __** / to be sleepy.

sueño, enfermedad del *f.* sleeping sickness, endemic, acute disease of Africa caused by a protozoon transmitted by the tsetse fly and characterized by a state of lethargy, chills, loss of weight, and general weakness.

suero *m.* serum. 1. clear, watery portion of the plasma that remains fluid after clotting of blood; 2. any serous fluid; 3. immune serum of an animal that is inoculated to produce passive immunization; **__ antitóxico** / immune **__; __ de globulina** / globulin **__; __ de la verdad** / truth **__**.

suerte *f.* luck; *v.* **tener __** / to be lucky.

suficiente *a.* sufficient, enough; **-mente** *adv.* sufficiently.

sufijo *m. gr.* suffix.

sufrible *a.* sufferable, bearable.

sufrimiento *m.* suffering.

sufrir *v.* to suffer; [*herida*] to sustain; [*operación*] to undergo.

sufusión *f.* suffusion, infiltration of a bodily fluid into the surrounding tissues.

sugerencia, sugestión *f.* suggestion, intimation, indication.

sugerir *vi.* to suggest, to indicate, to hint.

sugestivo-a *a.* suggestive, rel. to suggestion or that suggests.

suicida *a.* suicidal, prone to commit suicide.

suicidarse *vr.* to commit suicide.

suicidio *m.* suicide; **intento de __** / attempted **__**.

sujeto *m.* subject. 1. term used in reference to the patient; 2. topic; 3. *gr.* subject of the verb.

sulcus *L. (pl.* **sulci**) sulcus, slight depression, fissure.

sulfa, medicamentos de *m. pl.* sulfa drugs, *sulfonamides,* antibacterial drugs of the sulfonamide group.

sulfato *m.* sulfate, a salt of sulfuric acid.

sulfonamidas *f. pl.* sulfonamides, a group of bacteriostatic sulfur organic compounds.

sulfúrico-a *a.* sulfuric, rel. to sulfur.

sulfuro *m.* sulfur.

suma *f.* summation, total amount.

sumamente *adv.* extremely, very.

sumar *v.* to add.

sumario *m.* summary, clinical history of the patient.

sumergir *vi.* to submerge, to immerse.

superar *v.* to overcome.

superfecundación *f.* superfecundation, successive fertilization of two or more ova from the same menstrual cycle in two separate instances of sexual intercourse.

superficial *a.* superficial, rel. to a surface; **tensión __** / surface tension; shallow; **-mente** *adv.* superficially, shallowly.

superficie *f.* surface, outer portion or limit of a structure.

superhembra *f.* superfemale, a female organism that contains more than the normal number of sex-determining chromosomes.

superinfección *f.* superinfection, new infection that occurs while a previous one is still present, gen. caused by a different organism.

superior *a.* superior; upper; higher; greater.

supernumerario-a *a.* supernumerary, that exceeds the normal number.

superolateral *a.* superolateral, situated above and to the side.

supersaturado-a *a.* supersaturated, beyond saturation.

supersaturar *v.* to supersaturate, to add a substance in an amount greater than that which can be dissolved normally by a liquid.

supersensibilidad *f.* supersensitiveness, hypersensibility.

supersónico-a *a.* supersonic, rel. to vibrations of sound waves at speeds above the capacity of human hearing.

superstición *f.* superstition.

supersticioso-a *a.* superstitious.

supervisar *v.* to supervise.

supervisor-a *m., f.* supervisor.

supervivencia *f.* survivorship; annuity.

superyó *m.* superego, in psychoanalysis the part of the psyche concerned with social standards, ethics, and conscience.

supinación *f.* supination, turning the hand with the palm facing forward and upward.

supino-a *a.* supine, rel. to the position of lying on the back, face up, with palms of the hands turned upward.

suplemental *a.* supplemental, additional.

suplemento *m.* supplement, supply.

suplicio *m.* torture, punishment, extreme suffering.

suponer *vi.* to suppose, to surmise.

suposición *f.* supposition, guess.

supositorio *m.* suppository, a semisolid, soluble, medicated mass that is introduced in a body passage such as the vagina or the rectum.

supraclavicular *a.* supraclavicular, situated above the clavicle.

supraglótico-a *a.* supraglottic, situated above the glottis.

suprapúbico-a *a.* suprapubic, above the pubis; **catéter __ / __** catheter; **cistotomía __ / __** cystotomy.

suprarrenal *a.* suprarenal, above the kidney; **glándula __ / __** gland.

suprasillar *a.* suprasellar, above the sella turcica.

supratentorial *a.* supratentorial, above the dura mater.

supresión *f.* suppression; withdrawal; 1. arrest in the production of a secretion, excretion, or any normal discharge; 2. in psychoanalysis, inhibition of an idea or desire.

suprimir *v.* to discontinue, to withdraw.

supuración *f.* suppuration, formation or discharge of pus.

supurar *v.* to suppurate, to fester, to ooze.

supurativo-a *a.* suppurative, rel. to suppuration.

sur *m.* south.

sural *a.* sural, rel. to the calf of the leg.

surco *m.* line, wrinkle; groove, track; ___ **bicipital** / bicipital ___; ___ **costal** / costal ___.

surfactante *m.* surfactant, active agent that modifies the surface tension of a liquid.

susceptibilidad *f.* susceptibility.

susceptible *a.* susceptible.

suscitar *v.* to rouse, to stir up.

suspender *v.* to suspend, to cancel, to halt.

suspensión *f.* suspension. 1. temporary stoppage of a vital process; 2. treatment that consists of immobilizing and suspending a patient in a desired position; 3. the state of a substance when its particles are not dissolved in a fluid or solid; 4. detention, stoppage.

suspenso-a *a.* pending.

suspensorio-a *a.* suspensory, sustaining or providing support; **ligamento** ___ / ___ ligament.

sustancia *f.* substance, matter; ___ **blanca** / white matter, neural tissue formed mainly by myelinated fibers that constitutes the conducting portion of the brain and the spinal cord; ___ **fundamental** / ground ___, gelatinous matter of connective tissue, cartilage, and bone that fills the space between cells and fibers.

sustancioso-a *a.* nutritious.

sustantivo *m. gr.* substantive, noun.

sustentacular *a.* sustentacular, sustaining or supporting.

sustentaculum *L.* sustentaculum, support.

sustitución *f.* substitution, the act of replacing one thing for another; **terapéutica por** ___ / ___ therapy.

sustituir *vi.* to substitute.

sustituto *m.* substitute.

susto *m.* fright, sudden fear.

sustrato *m.* 1. substrate, a substance acted upon by an enzyme; 2. substratum, an underlying foundation.

susurro *m.* whisper, murmur.

sutil *a.* subtile, subtle, fine, delicate; inadvertent.

sutura *f.* suture, line of union; ___ **absorbible** / absorbable surgical ___; ___ **de catgut** / catgut ___; ___ **compuesta** / bolster ___; ___ **continua, de peletero** / continuous, uninterrupted ___; ___ **de colchonero** / vertical mattress ___; ___ **en bolsa de tabaco** / purse-string ___; ___ **no absorbible** / nonabsorbable ___; ___ **de seda** / silk ___.

Swan-Ganz, catéter de *m.* Swan-Ganz catheter, soft, flexible catheter with a balloon near the tip used to measure the blood pressure in the pulmonary artery.

T *abr.* **temperatura absoluta** / absolute temperature; **T+, tensión aumentada** / T+, increased tension; **T−, tensión disminuida** / T−, diminished tension.

tabaco *m.* 1. tobacco, the dried and prepared leaves of *Nicotiana tabacum* that contain nicotine; 2. cigar; **contaminación por humo de ___** / ___ smoke pollution.

tabaquismo *m.* tabacism, tabacosis, acute or chronic intoxication due to excessive intake of tobacco dust.

tabes *L.* tabes, progressive deterioration of the body or any part of it caused by a chronic illness.

tabético-a *a.* tabetic, rel. to or suffering from tabes.

tabicado-a *a.* septate, that has a dividing wall.

tabique *m.* thin wall; **___ nasal, o de la nariz** / nose ridge.

tabla *f.* table. 1. a flat osseous plate or lamina; 2. an arranged collection of many particulars that have a common standard.

tableta *f.* tablet, a solid dosage of medication; **___ de capa entérica** / enteric-coated ___.

tabú *m.* taboo, tabu, a forbidden thing or behavior; *a.* forbidden.

tabular *a.* tabular, resembling a table or square; *v.* to tabulate, to make lists or tables.

tacón *m.* heel of a shoe.

táctica *f.* tactic.

táctil *a.* tactile, rel. to touch or to the sense of touch; **discriminación ___** / **___ discrimination; sistema ___** / **___ system.

tacto *m.* the sense of touch.

tacha *f.* defect, blemish, imperfection.

taenia *L.* taenia. *V.* **tenia.**

tajada *f.* slice, cut.

tal, tales *a.* such, as, so, so much; **¿qué ___?** / how goes it?; **___ cual, ___ como** / ___ as; *adv.* thus, in such a way, in such manner.

talámico-a *a.* thalamic, rel. to the thalamus.

tálamo *m.* thalamus, one of the two large, oval-shaped masses of gray matter situated at the base of the cerebrum that are the main relay centers of sensory impulses to the cerebral cortex.

talar *a.* talar, rel. to the ankle.

talasemia *f.*, thalassemia, a group of inherited hypochromic anemias caused by genetic factors that produce failure or reduction in the total synthesis of hemoglobin; **___ mayor** / major ___; **___ menor** / minor ___.

talasoterapia *f.* thalassotherapy, the treatment of disease by sea bathing or by exposure to the sea.

talco *m.* talc, talcum powder.

talidomida *f.* thalidomide, hypnotic sedative known to cause severe malformation in devel-

oping fetuses.

talon *m.* talon, posterior part of a molar tooth.

talón *m.* talus, astragalus, heel, ankle bone.

talotibial *a.* talotibial, rel. to the talus and the tibia.

taller *m.* workshop.

tallo *m.* stalk; stem, an elongated, slender structure resembling the stalk or stem of a plant.

tamaño *m.* size.

tambalearse *vr.* to stagger, to waver.

también *adv.* also, as well, too.

tampoco *adv.* neither, not either.

tan *adv.* so, as well, as much.

tanatología *f.* thanatology, branch of medicine that deals with death in all its aspects.

tangible *a* tangible.

tanto-a *a.* so much, as much, so many, as many; *adv.* so much, as much; **___ mejor** / **___ the better; ___ peor** / **___ the worse; estar al ___ de** / to be alerted to; **por lo ___** / therefore.

tapa *f.* cover; lid.

tapado-a *a.* covered; clogged.

tapar *v.* to cover.

tapón *m.* 1. pledget, pack of absorbent material applied to a part of the body or inserted in a cavity to stop hemorrhage or absorb secretions; 2. plug, tampon, buffer.

taponamiento *m.* tamponade, packing. 1. the process of filling a cavity with cotton, gauze or some other material; 2. wrapping.

taponamiento cardíaco *m.* cardiac tamponade, acute compression of the heart due to excess fluid in the pericardium.

taquiarritmia *f.* tachyarrhythmia, arrhythmia combined with a rapid pulse.

taquicardia *f.* tachycardia, acceleration of the heart activity, gen. at a frequency of more than one hundred beats per minute in adults; **___ auricular** / atrial ___; **___ auricular paroxística** / paroxysmal atrial ___; **___ ectópica** / ectopic ___; **___ supraventricular** / supraventricular ___; **___ ventricular** / ventricular ___.

taquipnea *f.* tachypnea, abnormally rapid respiration.

tarántula *f.* tarantula, large, black, venomous spider.

tardar *v.* to delay; **a más ___** / at the latest; **tardarse** *vr.* to be delayed.

tarde *f.* afternoon; *adv.* late; **más ___ o más temprano** / sooner or later.

tardío-a *a.* late; delayed.

tardive *Fr.* tardive, late in appearing.

tarea *f.* task.

tarjeta *f.* card; **___ de crédito** / credit ___; **___ de visita** / calling ___.

tarsal, tarsiano-a *a.* tarsal, rel. to the connective tissue that supports the eyelid or the tarsus.

tarso *m.* tarsus, posterior part of the foot located between the bones of the lower leg and the metatarsus; **huesos del ___** / tarsal bones.

tarsometatarsiano-a *a.* tarsometatarsal, rel. to

the tarsus and the metatarsus.

tartamudear *v.* to stammer, to stutter.

tartamudeo, tartamudez *m., f.* stammering, stuttering.

tatuaje *m.* tattooing, the act of puncturing the skin for the purpose of creating designs with permanent colors.

taxis *L.* taxis. 1. manipulation or reduction of a part or an organ to restore it to its normal position; 2. directional reaction of an organism to a stimulus.

taza *f.* cup.

té *m.* tea; ___ de jazmín / jasmine ___.

tebaína *f.* thebaine, toxic alkaloid obtained from opium.

teca *f.* theca, covering or sheath of an organ.

tecnecio 99m *m.* technetium 99m, a radioisotope that emits gamma rays and that is the most frequently used radioisotope in nuclear medicine.

técnica *f.* technic, technique, method, or procedure.

técnico-a *m., f.* technician, an individual who has the necessary knowledge and skill to carry out specialized procedures and treatments, gen. under the supervision of a health care professional; ___ de rayos X / x-ray ___; dental / dental ___; ___ de terapia respiratoria / respiratory therapy ___.

tecnología *f.* technology, the science of applying technical knowledge for practical purposes.

tecnólogo-a *m., f.* technologist, an expert in technology.

tecoma *m.* thecoma, tumor of an ovary, gen. benign.

tectorium *L.* tectorium, membrane that covers Corti's organ.

tectum *L.* tectum, rooflike structure.

techo *m.* roof; ceiling.

tedioso-a *a.* tedious; tiresome.

tegumento *m.* tegument, the skin.

tejido *m.* tissue, a group of similar cells and their intercellular substance that act together in the performance of a particular function; ___ adiposo / adipose ___; ___ cartilaginoso / cartilaginous ___; ___ cicatricial / scar ___; ___ conectivo / connective ___; ___ de granulación / granulation ___; ___ elastico / elastic ___; ___ endotelial / endothelial ___; ___ epitelial / epithelial; ___ eréctil / erectile ___; ___ fibroso / fibrous ___; ___ glandular / glandular ___; ___ linfoide / lymphoid ___; ___ mesenquimatoso / mesenchymal ___; ___ mucoso / mucous ___; ___ muscular / muscular ___; ___ nervioso / nerve, nervous ___; ___ óseo / bony, bone ___; ___ subcutáneo / subcutaneous ___.

tela *f.* fabric, cloth.

telangiectasia *f.* telangiectasia, telangiectasis, condition caused by an abnormal dilation of the capillary vessels and arterioles that sometimes can produce angioma.

teléfono *m.* telephone; llamar por ___, telefonear / to telephone.

telemetría *f.* telemetry, electronically transmitted data.

telencéfalo *m.* telencephalon, anterior portion of the prosencephalon.

telepatia *f.* telepathy, apparent communication of thought by extrasensory means.

telerradiografía *f.* teleradiography, x-ray taken with the radiation source at a distance of about two meters or more from the subject to minimize distortion.

televisión *f.* television.

televisor *m.* television set.

telofase *f.* telophase, last phase of a process.

tembladera *f. pop.* the shakes.

temblar *v.* to quiver, to shiver.

temblor *m.* tremor, an involuntary quivering or trembling; ___ alcohólico / alcoholic ___; ___ continuo / continuous ___; ___ de aleteo / flapping ___; ___ de reposo / rest ___; ___ de variaciones rápidas / fine ___; ___ esencial / essential ___; ___ fisiológico / physiologic ___; ___ intencional / intentional ___; ___ intermitente / intermittent ___; ___ lento y acentuado / coarse ___; ___ muscular / muscular ___.

temblores *m. pl. pop.* the shakes.

temer *v.* to fear, to dread.

temor *m.* fear, dread.

temperamento *m.* temperament, the combined physical, emotional, and mental constitution of an individual that distinguishes him or her from others.

temperatura *f.* temperature. 1. degree of heat or cold as measured on a specific scale; ___ absoluta / absolute ___; ___ ambiente / room ___; ___ axilar / axillary ___; ___ crítica / critical ___; ___ del cuerpo / body ___; ___ máxima / maximum ___; ___ mínima / minimum ___; ___ normal / normal ___; ___ oral / oral ___; ___ rectal / rectal ___; ___ subnormal / subnormal ___; 2. the natural degree of heat of a living body.

temple *m.* temper; character.

temporal *a.* 1. temporal, rel. to the temple; huesos ___-es / ___ bones; lóbulo ___ / ___ lobe; músculo ___ / ___ muscle; 2. temporary, limited in time.

temporomandibular *a.* temporomandibular, rel. to or affecting the joint between the temporal bone and the mandible; articulaciones ___-es / ___ joints.

temprano-a *a.* early.

tenáculo *m.* tenaculum, type of hook used in *surg.* to grasp or hold a part.

tenar *a.* thenar, rel. to the palm of the hand; eminencia ___ / ___ eminence; músculos ___-es / ___ muscles.

tenaz *a.* tenacious, persistent, determined.

tenaza *f.* clamp, pincers.

tendencia *f.* tendency, propensity; trend.

tendinitis _f._ tendinitis, tendonitis, infl. of a tendon.

tendinoso-a _a._ tendinous, rel. to or resembling a tendon; **reflejo** ___ / tendon reflex; **reflejo** ___ **profundo** / deep tendon reflex; **tirón** ___ / tendon jerk.

tendón _m._ tendon, sinew, highly resistant, fibrous tissue that attaches the muscles to the bones or to other parts; ___**-es de la corva** / hamstring; ___ **de Aquiles** / Achilles ___.

tenedor _m._ fork.

tener _vi._ to have, to possess; ___ **diez años** / to be ten years old; ___ **dolor** / to be in pain; ___ **ganas de** / to want to; ___ **hambre** / to be hungry; ___ **miedo** / to be afraid; ___ **que** / to have to; ___ **razón** / to be right; ___ **sed** / to be thirsty.

tenesmo _m._ tenesmus, continuously painful, ineffectual, and straining efforts to urinate or defecate.

tenia _f._ flatworm of the class _Cestoda_ that in the adult stage lives in the intestines of vertebrates; _pop._ tapeworm.

teniasis _f._ taeniasis, infestation by taenia.

tenosinovitis _f._ tenosynovitis, infl. of a tendon sheath.

tensión _f._ tension, tenseness; 1. the act or effect of stretching or being extended; 2. the degree of stretching; 3. physical, emotional, or mental stress; ___ **premenstrual** / premenstrual ___; ___ **superficial** / surface ___; 4. the expansive pressure of a gas or vapor.

tenso-a _a._ tense, in a state of tension; rigid, stiff.

tensoactivo _m._ surfactant, an agent that modifies the surface tension of a liquid.

tensor _a._ tensor, term applied to any muscle that stretches or produces tension.

tentativo-a _a._ tentative, experimental, or subject to change.

tentorial _a._ tentorial, rel. to a tentorium.

tentorium _L._ tentorium, tentlike structure.

tenue _a._ tenuous, slight.

teñir _vi._ to dye; to color.

teoría _f._ theory. 1. an exposition of the principles of any science; 2. hypothesis that lacks scientific proof.

teórico-a _a._ theoretical, rel. to a theory.

terapeuta, terapista _m., f._ therapist, person skilled in giving or applying therapy in a given health field; ___ **patólogo-a del habla y del lenguage** / speech ___; ___ **fisico** / physical ___.

terapéutica _f._ therapeutics, the branch of medicine that deals with treatments and remedies.

terapéutica, terapia _f._ therapy, the treatment of a disease; ___ **adjutora** / adjuvant ___; ___ **anticoagulante** / anticoagulant ___; ___ **de apoyo** / supportive ___; ___ **de conducta** / behavioral ___; ___ **de grupo** / group ___; ___ **del habla y del lenguage** / speech ___; ___ **de oxígeno** / oxygen ___; ___ **de sostén** / maintenance ___; ___ **hormonal** / hormone ___; ___

Terapéutica, terapia	Therapy
anticoagulante	anticoagulant
biológica	biological
de conducta	behavioral
de grupo	group
de oxigeno	oxygen
diatérmica	diathermic
inespecífica	nonspecific
inmunosupresiva	immunosuppressive
ocupacional	occupational
por choque	shock
por inhalación	inhalation
por radiación	radiation
por sugestión	suggestion
respiratoria	respiratory
sustitutiva	substitutive

inmunosupresiva / immunosuppressive ___; ___ **ocupacional** / occupational ___; ___ **paliativa** / palliative ___; ___ **por choque** / shock ___; ___ **por inhalación** / inhalation ___; ___ **por radiación externa** / external beam ___; ___ **respiratoria** / respiratory ___; ___ **sistémica** / systemic ___.

terapéutica por realidad _f._ reality therapy, method by which the patient is confronted with his or her real-life situation and helped to accept it as such.

terapéutico-a _a._ therapeutic. 1. rel. to therapy; **indicaciones** ___**-s** / therapeutic ___-s. 2. that has healing properties.

teratogénesis _f._ teratogenesis, the production of gross fetal abnormalities.

teratógeno _m._ teratogen, agent that causes teratogenesis.

teratoide _a._ teratoid, resembling a monster; **tumor** ___ / ___ tumor.

teratología _f._ teratology, the study of malformations in fetuses.

teratoma _m._ teratoma, neoplasm derived from more than one embryonic layer and therefore constituted by different types of tissues.

terciano-a _a._ tertian, that repeats itself every three days.

terco-a _a._ stubborn, obstinate; _pop._ hardheaded.

teres _L._ teres, term applied to describe some elongated, cylindrical muscles and ligaments.

termal _a._ thermal, thermic, rel. to heat or produced by it.

terminación _f._ ending; [_de un nervio_] twig.

terminal _a._ terminal, final.

terminar _v._ to terminate, to rescind.

término _m._ term. 1. a definite period of time or its completion, such as a pregnancy; 2. word.

terminología _f._ terminology, nomenclature.

termistor _m._ thermistor, a type of thermometer used for measuring minute changes of temperature.

termo *m.* thermos.

termocoagulación *f.* thermocoagulation, co-agulation of tissue with high-frequency currents.

termodinámica *f.* thermodynamics, the science that studies the relationship between heat and other forms of energy.

termoesterilización *f.* thermosterilization, sterilization by heat.

termografía *f.* thermography, recording obtained by the use of a thermograph.

termógrafo *m.* thermograph, infrared detector that registers variations in temperature by reaction to the blood flow.

termómetro *m.* thermometer; device that measures heat or cold; ___ **clínico** / clinical ___; ___ **de Celsius** / Celsius ___, centigrade; ___ **de Fahrenheit** / Fahrenheit ___; ___ **de registro automático** / self-recording ___; ___ **rectal** / rectal ___.

termonuclear *a.* thermonuclear.

termorregulación *f.* thermoregulation, regulation by heat and temperature.

termostato *m.* thermostat, instrument used for regulating temperature.

termotaxis *f.* thermotaxis. 1. regulation of the temperature of the body; 2. the reaction of an organism to heat.

termoterapia *f.* thermotherapy, therapeutic use of heat.

ternario-a *a.* ternary, triple, made up of three elements.

ternura *f.* tenderness, sensitivity.

Terramicina *f.* Terramycin, trade name for a tetracycline antibiotic.

terremoto *m.* earthquake.

terrible *a.* terrible.

terror *m.* terror; panic.

tesis *f.* thesis.

testamento *m.* testament, last will.

testarudo-a *a.* hardheaded, stubborn, headstrong.

testicular *m.* testicular, rel. to a testicle; **tumores** ___-**es** / ___ tumors.

testículo *m.* testicle, the male gonad, one of the two male reproductive glands that produce spermatozoa and the hormone testosterone; ___ **ectópico** / ectopic ___; ___ **no descendido** / undescended testis.

testificar *vi.* to testify.

testigo *m., f.* to witness; ___ **experto especializado** / expert witness.

testis *L.* (*pl.* **testes**) testis, testicle.

testosterona *f.* testosterone, male hormone produced chiefly by the testicle and responsible for the development of male secondary characteristics such as facial hair and a deep voice; **implante de** ___ / ___ implant.

teta *f.* teat. 1. mammary gland; 2. nipple.

tetania *f.* tetany, a neuromuscular affliction associated with parathyroid deficiencies and di-minished mineral balance, esp. calcium, and manifested by intermittent tonic spasms of the voluntary muscles.

tetánico-a *a.* tetanic, rel. to tetanus; **antitoxina** ___ / tetanus antitoxin; **convulsión** ___ / ___ convulsion; **toxoide** ___ / ___ toxoid.

tétano *m.* tetanus, an acute infectious disease caused by the toxin of the tetanus bacillus, gen. introduced in the body through a wound and manifested by muscular spasms and rigidity of the jaw, neck, and abdomen; *pop.* lockjaw; **globulina inmune para el** ___ / ___ immune globulin.

tetera, teto *f., m.* pacifier; nipple of a nursing bottle.

tetilla *f.* male nipple.

tetraciclina *f.* tetracycline, a type of broad-spectrum antibiotic effective against gram-positive and gram-negative bacteria, rickettsia, and a variety of viruses.

tétrada *f.* tetrad, a group of four similar elements.

tetralogía *f.* tetralogy, term applied to the combination of four factors or elements.

tetraplejía *f.* tetraplegia, paralysis of the four extremities.

tetraploide *a.* tetraploid, having four sets of chromosomes.

tetravalente *m.* tetravalent, element that has a chemical valance of four.

textura *f.* texture, the composition of a tissue or structure.

tez *f.* complexion.

thrill *m.* thrill, a vibration felt on palpation; ___ **aneurismal** / aneurysmal ___; ___ **aórtico** / aortic ___; ___ **arterial** / arterial ___; ___ **diastólico** / diastolic ___.

tibia *f.* tibia, the inner and larger bone of the leg below the knee.

tibial *a.* tibial, rel. to or situated close to the tibia.

tibio-a *a.* tepid, lukewarm.

tic *Fr.* tic, spasmodic, involuntary movement or twitching of a muscle; ___ **convulsivo** / convulsive ___; ___ **coordinado** / coordinated ___; ___ **doloroso** / douleureux ___; ___ **facial** / facial ___.

tiempo *m.* 1. time, the duration of an event; ___ **de coagulación** / coagulation ___; ___ **de exposición** / exposure ___; ___ **de latencia** / ___ lag; ___ **de percepción** / perception ___; ___ **de protrombina** / prothrombin ___; ___ **de sangramiento** / bleeding ___; **a** ___ / in time; **a su debido** ___ / in due ___; **¿cuánto** ___? / how long?; **espacio de** ___ / time frame; ___ **limitado** / a limited time; ___ **medido** / timed; **medir el** ___ / to time, to set the time; **pérdida de** ___ / waste of ___; **por algún** ___ / for some ___; **regulador de** ___ / timer; ___ **suplementario** / overtime; 2. weather; **pronóstico del** ___ / ___ forecasting; **hace buen** ___ / the ___ is good; **hace mal** ___ / the ___ is bad.

tienda *f.* tent, a cover or shelter made of fabric,

gen. used to enclose the patient within a given area; ___ **de oxígeno** / oxygen ___ .

tierno-a *a.* tender, sensitive.

tierra *f.* soil; earth.

tieso-a *a.* stiff, rigid.

tífico-a *a.* typhoid, rel. to typhus.

tiflitis *f.* typhlitis, infl. of the cecum.

tifoidea, fiebre *f.* typhoid fever, acute intestinal infection caused by a bacterium of the genus *Salmonella,* characterized by fever, prostration, headache, and abdominal pain.

tifus *m.* typhus, acute infectious disease caused by *rickettsia* with manifestations of high fever, delirium, prostration, and severe headache, gen. transmitted by lice, fleas, ticks, and mites.

tijeras *f. pl.* scissors.

tila, tilo *m.* tea made with linden flowers.

timectomía *f. surg.* thymectomy, excision of the thymus.

tímico-a *a.* thymic, rel. to the thymus gland.

tímido-a *a.* timid, bashful, shy.

timo *m.* thymus, glandular organ situated in the inferior portion of the neck and the antero-superior portion of the thoracic cavity. It plays an important part in the immunological process of the body.

timocito *m.* thymocyte, a lymphocyte arising in the thymus.

timoma *m.* thymoma, tumor derived from the thymus.

timpanectomía *f. surg.* tympanectomy, excision of the tympanic membrane.

timpánico-a *a.* tympanic, resonant or rel. to the tympanum; **membrana** ___ / ___ membrane.

timpanismo *m.* tympanites, distension of the abdomen caused by accumulation of gas in the intestine.

timpanítico-a *a.* tympanitic, rel. to or affected with tympanites; **resonancia** ___ / ___ resonance.

timpanitis *f.* tympanitis, infl. of the middle ear.

tímpano *m.* tympanum, the eardrum, middle ear.

timpanoplastia *f. surg.* tympanoplasty, reconstruction of the middle ear.

timpanotomía *f. surg.* tympanotomy, incision of the tympanic membrane.

tina *f.* tub.

tinea *L.* tinea, cutaneous fungal infection in the form of a ring; ___ **capitis** / ___ capitis; ___ **corporis** / ___ corporis; ___ **pedis** / ___ pedis, athlete's foot; ___ **versicolor** ___ / versicolor.

tinnitus *L.* tinnitus, buzzing or ringing sound in the ears.

tinta *f.* ink.

tinte *m.* dye.

tintura *f.* tincture, an alcoholic extract of animal or vegetable origin.

tiña *f.* tinea, ringworm. *V.* **tinea.**

tío-a *m., f.* uncle; aunt.

típico-a *a.* typical; characteristic.

tipificación *f.* typing, determination by types;

___ **de tejido** / tissue ___ ; ___ **inmunológica** / immunotyping.

tipo *m.* type; kind, the general character of a given entity.

tira *f.* strap.

tirante *a.* tense, extended; pulling; stretched; [*relación*] strained.

tirar *v.* 1. to throw, to toss; to throw out; 2. to pull, to tug, as in tracheal tugging.

tiritar *v.* to shiver.

tiro *m.* shot from a firearm.

tiroadenitis *f.* thyroadenitis, inf. of the thyroid gland.

tiroglobulina *f.* thyroglobulin. 1. a glycoprotein secreted by the thyroid gland; 2. a substance obtained by the fractioning of the thyroid gland of the hog, used in the treatment of hyperthyroidism.

tirogloso-a *a.* thyroglossal, rel. to the thyroid and the tongue; **conducto** ___ / ___ duct.

tiroidectomía *f. surg.* thyroidectomy, excision of the thyroid gland.

tiroideo-a *a.* thyroid, rel. to the thyroid gland; **cartílago** ___ / ___ cartilage; **crisis** ___ / ___ storm; **hormonas** ___-s / ___ hormones.

tiroides, glándula *f.* thyroid gland, one of the endocrine glands situated in the front part of the trachea and made up of two lateral lobules that connect in the middle; **prueba del funcionamiento de la** ___ / thyroid function test.

tiroiditis *f.* thyroiditis, infl. of the thyroid gland.

tiromegalia *f.* thyromegaly, enlargement of the thyroid gland.

tirón *m.* forceful pull; tugging.

tiroparatiroidectomía *f. surg.* thyroparathyroidectomy, excision of the thyroid and parathyroid glands.

tirotóxico-a *a.* thyrotoxic, rel. to or affected by toxic activity of the thyroid gland.

tirotoxicosis *f.* thyrotoxicosis, disorder caused by hyperthyroidism and marked by an enlargement of the thyroid gland, increased metabolic rate, tachycardia, rapid pulse, and hypertension.

tirotropina *f.* thyrotropin, thyroid-stimulating hormone produced in the anterior lobe of the pituitary gland; **hormona estimulante de la** ___ / ___-releasing hormone.

tiroxina *f.* thyroxine, iodine containing hormone produced by the thyroid gland, also obtained synthetically for use in the treatment of hypothyroidism.

titulación *f.* titration, determination of volume using standard solutions of known strength.

titular *v.* to titrate, to determine by titration.

título *m.* titer, titre, the required amount of a substance to produce a reaction with a given volume of another substance.

toalla *f.* towel.

tobillera *f.* ankle brace.

tobillo *m.* ankle.

tocar *vi.* to touch, to palpate.

tocino *m.* bacon.

tocógrafo *m.* tocograph, device used to estimate and record the force of uterine contractions.

tocómetro *m.* tocometer. *V.* **tocógrafo.**

todavía *adv.* still, yet.

todo-a *a.* all, entire; **ante** ___ / above all; ___ **el día** / the whole day; ___-**s los días** / every day; ___-**s los meses** / every month.

tofáceo-a *a.* tophaceous, rel. to a tophus or of a gritty nature.

tofo *m.* tophus. 1. deposits of urates in tissues as seen in gout; 2. dental calculus.

toilette *Fr.* toilette, cleansing, as related to a medical procedure.

tolerable *a.* tolerable, bearable.

tolerancia *f.* tolerance, the ability to endure the use of a medication or performance of a given amount of physical activity without ill effects.

tolerante *a.* tolerant.

tolerar *v.* to tolerate, to endure.

tomar *v.* to take; to eat or drink.

tomate *m.* tomato.

tomografía *f.* tomography, scan, diagnostic technique by which a series of x-ray pictures taken at different depths of an organ are obtained; ___ **axial computada** / computerized axial ___; ___ **computada dinámica auricular** / atrial bolus dynamic computerized ___; ___ **de emisión por positrón** / positron emission ___.

tomógrafo *m.* tomograph, x-ray machine used in tomography.

tomograma *m.* tomogram, sectional x-ray of a part of the body.

tonicidad *f.* tonicity, normal quality of tone or tension.

tónico *m.* tonic, medication for restoring tone and vitality; **-a** *a.* 1. that restores the normal tone; 2. characterized by continuous tension.

tono *m.* tone; pitch. 1. the quality of the body with its organs and parts in a normal and balanced state; ___ **muscular** / muscle ___; 2. a particular quality of sound or voice.

tonoclónico-a *a.* tonoclonic, rel. to muscular spasms that are both tonic and clonic.

tonometría *f.* tonometry, the measurement of tension or pressure.

tonómetro *m.* tonometer, instrument that measures tone, esp. intraocular tension.

tonsila *f.* tonsil. *V.* **amígdala;** ___ **cerebelosa** / cerebellar ___; ___ **faríngea** / pharyngeal ___; ___ **lingual** / lingual ___; ___ **palatina** / palatine ___.

tonsilar *a.* tonsillar, rel. to a tonsil; **cripta** ___ **o amigdalina** / crypt; **fosa** ___ / ___ fossa.

tonsilectomía *f. surg.* tonsillectomy. *V.* **amigdalotomía.**

tonsilitis *f.* tonsillitis. *V.* **amigdalitis.**

tonsiloadenoidectomía *f. surg.* tonsilloadenoidectomy, excision of the tonsils and adenoids.

tonto-a *a.* foolish, fatuous.

tonus *L.* tonus, tone.

tópico-a *a.* topical, rel. to a specific area.

toracentesis *f.* thoracentesis, surgical puncture and drainage of the thoracic cavity.

torácico-a *a.* thoracic, rel. to the thorax; **cavidad** ___ / ___ cavity; **conducto** ___ / ___ duct; **pared** ___ / ___ cage, chest wall, osseous structure enclosing the thorax; **traumatismos** ___-**s** / ___ injuries.

toracicoabdominal *a.* thoracicoabdominal, rel. to the thorax and the abdomen.

Toracina *f.* Thorazine, antiemetic sedative.

toracolumbar *a.* thoracolumbar, rel. to the thoracic and lumbar vertebrae.

toracoplastia *f. surg.* thoracoplasty, plastic surgery of the thorax that consists in removing a portion of the ribs to allow the collapse of a diseased lung.

toracostomía *f. surg.* thoracostomy, incision of the chest wall to allow for drainage.

toracotomía *f. surg.* thoracotomy, incision of the thoracic wall.

tórax *m.* thorax, the chest; ___ **inestable** / flail chest, condition of the wall of the thorax caused by multiple fracture of the ribs.

torcedura *f.* strain, sprain, warp, twisting of a joint with distension and laceration of its ligaments, usu. accompanied by pain and swelling.

torcer *vi.* to twist, to strain, to curve, to warp; **torcerse** *vr.* to sprain.

torcido-a *a.* twisted, sprained.

tormenta *f.* storm, abrupt and temporary intensification of the symptoms of a disease.

tormento *a.* torment.

tornillo *m.* screw.

torniquete *m.* tourniquet, tourniquette, device used to apply pressure over an artery to stop the flow of blood.

toronja *f.* grapefruit.

torpe *a.* dull, clumsy, slow.

torpeza *f.* dullness; clumsiness.

tórpido-a *a.* torpid, sluggish, slow.

torpor *m.* sluggishness, cloudiness; ___ **mental** / clouding of consciousness.

torque *m.* torque, a force that produces rotation.

torsión *f.* torsion, twisting or rotating of a part on its long axis; ___ **ovárica** / ovarian ___; ___ **testicular** / testicular ___.

torso *m.* torso, trunk of the body.

tortícolis *f.* torticollis, toniclonic spasm of the muscles of the neck that causes cervical torsion and immobility of the head.

tortuoso-a *a.* tortuous, twisted.

tortura *f.* torture.

torus *L.* (*pl.* **tori**) torus, prominence, swelling.

tos *f.* cough; **ataque de** ___ / coughing spell; **calmante para la** ___ / suppressant; **jarabe para la** ___ / ___ syrup; **pastillas para la** ___ / lozenges; ___ **metálica, bronca** / brassy ___; ___ **seca recurrente** / hacking ___.

tos ferina *f.* pertussis, whooping cough, infectious children's disease that gen. begins with a cold followed by a persistent dry cough.

tosecilla *f.* slight cough.

toser *v.* to cough.

tostada *f.* toast.

tostado-a *a.* toasted; **pan ___** / toast.

total *a.* total, whole; **-mente** *adv.* totally.

totipotencia *f.* totipotency, ability of a cell to regenerate or develop into another type of cell.

totipotente *a.* totipotent, that can generate totipotency.

toxemia *f.* toxemia, generalized intoxication due to absorption of toxins formed at a local source of infection.

toxicidad *f.* toxicity, the quality of being poisonous.

tóxico-a *a.* toxic, rel. to a poison or of a poisonous nature.

toxicología *f.* toxicology, the study of poisons and their effects and treatment.

toxicológico-a *a.* toxicological, rel. to toxicology; **protocolo ___** / toxicology screen.

toxicólogo-a *m., f.* toxicologist, a specialist in toxicology.

toxicosis *f.* toxicosis, morbid state caused by a poison.

toxina *f.* toxin, a noxious substance produced by a plant or animal microorganism; **___ bacteriana** / bacterial **___**.

toxina antitoxina *f.* toxin-antitoxin, a nearly neutral mixture of a toxin and its antitoxin used for immunization against the specific disease caused by the toxin.

toxoide *m.* toxoid, a toxin void of toxicity that causes antibody formation and produces immunity to the specific disease caused by the toxin; **___ diftérico** / diphtheria **___**; **___ tetánico** / tetanus **___**.

Toxoplasma *m. Toxoplasma,* a genus of parasitic protozoa.

toxoplasmosis *f.* toxoplasmosis, infection with organisms of the genus *Toxoplasma* that can cause minimal symptoms of malaise or swelling of the lymph glands, or serious damage to the central nervous system.

trabajador-a *m., f.* worker; **___ social** / social **___**.

trabajar *v.* to work, to labor.

trabajo *m.* work, job, occupation; **___ de beneficencia social** / welfare **___**; **___ de casa** / housework; **___ excesivo** / overwork.

trabajoso-a *a.* laborious, hard.

trabécula *f.* trabecula, term used to designate a supporting structure of connective tissue that divides or secures an organ.

trabeculado-a *a.* trabeculate, having trabeculae.

tracción *f.* traction. 1. the action of drawing or pulling; 2. a pulling force; **___ cervical** / cervical **___**; **___ lumbar** / lumbar **___**.

tracoma *f.* trachoma, a viral contagious disease of the conjunctiva and the cornea, manifested by photophobia, pain, tearing, and, in severe cases, blindness.

tracto *m.* tract, an elongated system of tissue or organs that acts to carry out a common function; **___ alimenticio** / alimentary **___**; **___ dorsolateral** / dorsolateral **___**; **___ genitourinario** / genitourinary; **___ intestinal** / intestinal **___**; **___ respiratorio** / respiratory **___**.

tractor *m.* tractor, any instrument or machine used to apply traction.

traducción *f.* translation.

traer *vi.* to bring; to fetch.

tragar *vi.* to swallow; **___ apresuradamente** / to gulp down.

trago *m.* tragus, triangular cartilaginous eminence in the outer part of the ear.

traicionero-a *a.* deceitful, treacherous; **enfermedad ___** / **___** disease.

trance *m. psych.* trance, hypnotic-like state characterized by detachment from the surroundings and diminished motor activity.

tranquilidad *f.* tranquility, rest; **___ de espíritu** / peace of mind.

tranquilizante *m.* tranquilizer, sedative.

tranquilizar *vi.* to tranquilize, to calm; **tranquilizarse** *vr.* to quiet down; to ease one's mind.

tranquilo-a *a.* tranquil, calm, restful.

transabdominal *a.* transabdominal, through or across the abdominal wall.

transaminasa glutámica oxalacética *f.* glutamic-oxaloacetic transaminase, enzyme present in several tissues, such as the heart, liver, and brain, that presents a high concentration of serum when there is cardiac or hepatic damage.

transaminasa glutámica pirúvica *f.* glutamic-pyruvic transaminase, enzyme that presents an elevated serum content when there is an injury or acute damage to liver cells.

transaxial *a.* transaxial, through or across the long axis of a structure.

transcapilar *a.* transcapillary, existing or taking place across the capillary walls.

transcurrir *v.* to elapse; [*tiempo*] to go by.

transcutáneo-a *a.* transcutaneous, through the skin; **neuroestimulación eléctrica ___** / **___** electrical nerve stimulation.

transductor *a.* transducer, device that transforms one form of energy to another.

transección *f.* transection, cross section, cutting across the long axis of an organ.

transexual *a.* transexual. 1. individual with a psychological urge to be of the opposite sex; 2. person who has undergone a surgical sex change.

transferencia *f.* transfer, transference. 1. in psychoanalysis, shifting feelings and behavior towards a new object, gen. the psychoanalyst; 2. transmission of symptoms from one part of the body to another.

transferir *vi.* to transfer.

transferrina *f.* transferrin, a type of beta globulin in blood plasma that fixes and transports iron.

transfixión *f. surg.* transfixion, the act of cutting through soft tissues from the inside outwards, such as in amputations and excision of tumors.

transformación *f.* transformation, change of form or appearance.

transformar *v.* to transform, to change the appearance, character, or structure of something or someone.

transfusión *f.* transfusion, the process of transferring fluid into a vein or artery; ___ **directa** / direct ___; ___ **indirecta** / indirect ___.

transición *f.* transition.

transicional *a.* transitional, rel. to or subject to change.

transiluminación *f.* transillumination, passage of light through a body part.

transitorio-a *a.* transitory, of a temporal nature.

translocación *f.* translocation, displacement of all or part of a chromosome to another chromosome.

translúcido-a *a.* translucent.

transmigración *f.* transmigration, the passing from one place to another such as of blood cells in diapedesis.

transmisible *a.* transmissible, that can be transmitted.

transmisión *f.* transmission, the act of transmitting, such as an infectious disease or a hereditary condition; ___ **patógena** / pathogen ___; ___ **placentaria** / placental ___; ___ **por contacto** / ___ by contact; ___ **por instilación** / droplet ___.

transmural *a.* transmural, that occurs or is administered through a wall.

transmutación *f.* transmutation. 1. transformation, evolutionary change; 2. change of one chemical into another.

transocular *a.* transocular, occurring or passing through the orbit of the eye.

transonancia *f.* transonance, transmitted resonance.

transorbitorio-a *a.* transorbital, occurring or passing through the orbit of the eye.

transparencia *f.* transparency; [*diapositiva*] slide.

transparente *a.* transparent, clear.

transplacentario-a *a.* transplacental, occurring through the placenta.

transpleural *a.* transpleural, occurring or administered through the pleura.

transporte *m.* transport, the movement of materials within the body, esp. across the cellular membrane.

transposición *f.* transposition. 1. displacement of an organ to the opposite side; 2. displacement of genetic material from one chromosome to another resulting at times in congenital defects.

transposición de los grandes vasos *f.* transposition of great vessels, congenital defect by which the aorta rises from the right ventricle and the pulmonary artery from the left ventricle.

transuretral *a.* transurethral, occurring or administered through the urethra.

• **transvaginal** *a.* transvaginal, occurring or done through the vagina.

transversal *a.* transverse, across; **plano** ___ / ___ plane.

transvestido-a, transvestita *m., f.* transvestite, person who practices transvestism.

transvestismo *m.* transvestism, adoption of modalities of the opposite sex, esp. dress; cross-dressing.

trapecio *m.* trapezius, flat, triangular muscle essential in the rotation of the scapula.

tráquea *f.* trachea, respiratory conduit between the inferior extremity of the larynx and the beginning of the bronchi; *pop.* windpipe.

traqueal *a.* tracheal, rel. to the trachea.

traqueítis *f.* tracheitis, infl. of the trachea.

traqueoesofágico-a *a.* tracheoesophageal, rel. to the trachea and the esophagus.

traqueomalacia *f.* tracheomalacia, softening of the cartilages of the trachea.

traqueostenosis *f.* tracheostenosis, narrowing of the trachea.

traqueostomía *f. surg.* tracheostomy, incision into the trachea through the neck to allow the passage of air in cases of obstruction.

traqueotomía *f. surg.* tracheotomy, incision into the trachea through the skin and muscles of the neck.

tras *prep.* after, behind.

trasero *m. pop.* buttocks, rear.

trasmitir *v.* to transmit.

trasplantación *f.* transplantation, the act of transplanting; ___ **autoplástica** / autoplastic ___; ___ **heteroplástica** / heteroplastic ___; ___ **homotópica** / homotopic ___.

trasplantar *v.* to transplant.

trasplante *m.* transplant, the transfer of an organ or tissue from a donor to a recipient, or from one part of the body to another in order to replace a diseased organ or to restitute impaired function.

trastornado-a *a.* deranged, mentally disturbed.

trastorno *m.* disturbance, disorder, derangement; ___ **del procesor metabólico** / deranged metabolic process; ___ **mental** / mental disorder.

trasudado *m.* transudate, fluid that has passed through a membrane or that has been forced out from a tissue as a result of infl.

tratado-a *a.* treated; **no** ___ / untreated.

tratamiento *m.* treatment, method, or procedure used in curing illnesses, lesions, or malformations; **método o plan de** ___ / ___ plan; ___ **de desintoxicación** / withdrawal ___; **sujeto a** ___ / under ___.

tratar *v.* [*a un paciente*] to treat; to try.

trato *m.* care; treatment; **buen** ___ / good ___; **mal** ___ / bad ___.

trauma, traumatismo *m.* trauma. 1. physical injury caused by an external agent; 2. *psych.* severe emotional shock.

traumático-a *a.* traumatic, rel. to, resulting from, or causing trauma.

traumatizado-a *a.* traumatized.

traumatizar *vi.* to traumatize, to injure.

traumatología *f.* traumatology, the branch of *surg.* that deals with injuries and wounds and their treatment.

trazador *m.* tracer, a radioisotope that when introduced into the body leaves a trace that can be detected and followed.

trazar *vi.* to trace.

trazo *m.* tracing, the graphic record of movement or change made by an instrument.

trefinación *f. surg.* trephination, the act of removing a circular disk of bone, gen. from the skull, or of removing tissue from the cornea or sclera.

Trematoda *Gr. Trematoda,* a class of parasitic worms that includes the flatworms and the flukes, both pathogenic to humans.

tremendo-a *a.* tremendous.

tremor *m.* tremor, trembling.

trémulo-a *a.* tremulous, rel. to or affected by a tremor.

Trendelenburg, posición de *f.* Trendelenburg position, slanted position used in abdominal surgery in which the body and lower extremities are placed higher than the head.

trepanación *f. surg.* trepanation, perforation of the skull with a special instrument to relieve increased pressure caused by fracture or accumulation of intracranial blood or pus.

trepanar *v.* to trepan, to perforate with a trepan.

trépano *m.* trepan, bur, burr, type of drill used for trepanation.

Treponema *Gr. Treponema,* microorganisms of the genus *Spirochaetales,* some which are pathogenic to humans and other animals; ___ **pallidum** / ___ pallidum, causing agent of syphilis.

treponema *m.* treponema, any organism of the genus *Treponema.*

treponemiasis *f.* treponemiasis, infection with organisms of the genus *Treponema.*

tríada *f.* triad, a group of three related elements, objects, or symptoms.

triage *Fr.* triage, screening and classification of injured persons during a battle or disaster for the purpose of establishing priority of treatment in order to maximize the number who will survive.

triangular *a.* triangular.

triángulo *m.* triangle.

tribu *f.* tribe.

tríceps *m.* triceps, a three-headed muscle; **reflejo del** ___ / ___ reflex.

tricobezoar *m.* trichobezoar, concretion or bezoar of hair found in the intestine or stomach.

tricomonas *m. V.* **Trichomonas.**

tricomoniasis *f.* trichomoniasis, infestation with *Trichomonas.*

tricromático-a *a.* trichromatic, rel. to or consisting of three colors.

tricúspide *a.* tricuspid. 1. having three points; 2. rel. to the tricuspid valve of the heart; **atresia** ___ / ___ atresia; **soplo** ___ / ___ murmur; **válvula** ___ / ___ valve.

Trichinella *Gr. Trichinella,* a genus of nematode worms parasitic in carnivorous mammals.

Trichomonas *Gr.* **tricomonas** *m. Trichomonas,* a genus of parasitic protozoa that lodge in the alimentary and genitourinary tracts of vertebrates; ___ **vaginal** / ___ vaginalis.

trifásico-a *a.* triphasic, occurring in three stages, esp. in relation to electric currents.

trifocal *a.* trifocal.

trigémino-a *a.* trigeminal, rel. to the trigeminus nerve; **neuralgia** ___ / ___ neuralgia.

trigeminus *L.* trigeminus, trigeminus nerve. *V.* **craneales, nervios.**

triglicéridos *m. pl.* triglycerides, combination resulting from one molecule of glycerol and three molecules of fatty acids; elevated triglycerides are considered an important factor in heart disease.

trigo *m.* wheat; **germen de** ___ / ___ germ.

trigonitis *f.* trigonitis, infl. of the trigone of the urinary bladder.

trígono *m.* trigone, space or area in a triangular shape.

trigueño-a *a.* dark-complexioned, brunet, brunette.

trimestre *m.* trimester, three-month period.

trinchera *f.* trench, ditch, moat; **fiebre de** ___ / ___ fever; **pie de** ___ / ___ foot, infection caused by exposure to severe cold.

tripa *f.* tripe, gut.

Tripanosoma *m. V.* **Trypanosoma.**

tripanosomiasis *f.* trypanosomiasis, infection caused by a flagellated organism of the genus *Trypanosoma.*

tripanosómico-a *a.* trypanosomal, caused by or belonging to the genus *Trypanosoma.*

triple *a.* triple, consisting of three components.

triplopía *f.* triplopia, eye disorder in which three images of the same object are seen at one time.

tripsina *f.* trypsin, an enzyme present in the pancreatic juice formed by trypsinogen.

tripsinógeno *m.* trypsinogen, inactive substance released by the pancreas into the duodenum to form trypsin.

triptófano *m.* tryptophan, crystalline amino acid present in proteins essential to animal life.

triquina *f.* trichina, a worm that lives as a parasite in the muscles in the larval stage, and in the intestines when mature.

triquinosis *f.* trichinosis, disease acquired by ingestion of raw or inadequately cooked meat, esp. pork, that contains the larvae of *Trichinella spiralis.*

triquitis *f.* trichitis, infl. of hair bulbs.

trismo *m.* trismus, a spasm of the mastication muscles.

trisomía *f.* trisomy, genetic disorder in which there are three homologous chromosomes per cell instead of the usual two (diploid), causing severe fetal malformation.

triste *a.* sad, sorrowful.

tristeza *f.* sadness; sorrow.

trituración *f.* trituration; pulverization.

triturar *v.* to triturate, to crush, to grind; to shatter in many small fragments.

triunfar *v.* to succeed.

triunfo *m.* success, triumph.

trocánter *m.* trochanter, each of the two outer prominences below the neck of the femur; ___ **mayor** / major ___; ___ **menor** / lesser ___.

tróclea *f.* trochlea, structure that functions as a pulley.

trófico-a *a.* trophic, rel. to nutrition.

trombectomía *f. surg.* thrombectomy, removal of a thrombus.

trombina *f.* thrombin, an enzyme present in extravasated blood which catalyzes the conversion of fibrinogen to fibrin.

trombinógeno *m.* thrombinogen. *V.* **protrombina.**

trombo *m.* thrombus, a blood clot that causes a total or partial vascular obstruction; ___ **blanco** / white ___, pale; ___ **estratificado** / stratified ___, layered; ___ **mural** / mural ___, attached to the wall of the endocardium; ___ **oclusivo** / occluding ___, that closes the vessel completely.

tromboangiítis *f.* thromboangiitis, thrombosis of a blood vessel.

trombocito *m.* thrombocyte, platelet.

trombocitopenia *f.* thrombocytopenia, abnormal decrease in the number of blood platelets.

trombocitopénico-a *a.* thrombocytopenic, rel. to thrombocytopenia.

trombocitosis *f.* thrombocytosis, abnormal increase in the number of blood platelets.

tromboembolia *f.* thromboembolism, obstruction of a blood vessel by a blood clot that has broken away from its site of origin.

tromboflebitis *f.* thrombophlebitis, dilation of a vein wall associated with thrombosis.

trombogénesis *f.* thrombogenesis, formation of blood clots.

trombólisis *f.* thrombolysis, dissolution of a thrombus.

trombolítico-a *a.* thrombolytic, rel. to or causing the dissolution of a thrombus.

trombosado-a *a.* thrombosed, rel. to a blood vessel containing a thrombus.

trombosis *f.* thrombosis, formation, development, or presence of a thrombus; ___ **biliar** / biliary ___; ___ **cardíaca** / cardiac ___; ___ **coronaria** / coronary ___; ___ **embólica** / embolic ___; ___ **traumática** / traumatic ___; ___ **venosa** / venous ___.

trombótico-a *a.* thrombotic, rel. to or affected by thrombosis.

trompa *f.* tube, conduit; **ligadura de las ___-s** / tubal ligation.

troncal *a.* truncal, rel. to the trunk of the body.

tronco *m.* trunk, the human body exclusive of the head and the extremities.

tropezar *vi.* to bump or stumble into something or somebody.

tropical *a.* tropical, rel. to the tropics.

tropismo *m.* tropism, the reaction of a cell or living organism toward or away from the source of an external stimulus.

truncado-a *a.* truncate, having the end squarely cut off; amputated.

truncar *vi.* to truncate, to cut off, to shorten; to amputate.

truncus *L.* truncus, trunk.

Trypanosoma *m. Trypanosoma*, a genus of parasitic protozoa found in the blood of many vertebrates, transmitted to them by insect vectors.

tsetsé *m.* tsetse fly, bloodsucking fly of southern Africa that transmits sleeping sickness.

tuba *L.* tuba, tube; ___ **acústica** / eustachian tube.

tubario-a *a.* tubal, rel. to a tube; **embarazo ___** / ___ pregnancy occurring in the fallopian tube.

tuber *L.* (*pl.* **tubera**) tuber, enlargement.

tubercular *a.* tubercular, rel. to or marked by tubercles.

tuberculicida *a.* tuberculocidal, that destroys the tubercle bacilli.

tuberculina *f.* tuberculin, compound prepared from the tubercle bacillus and used in the diagnosis of tuberculosis infection; **prueba de la ___** / ___ test.

tubérculo *m.* tubercle. 1. small nodule; 2. small knobby prominence of a bone; 3. the characteristic lesion produced by the tuberculosis bacilli.

tuberculosis *f.* tuberculosis, an acute or chronic bacterial infection caused by the germ *Mycobacterium tuberculosis* that gen. affects the lungs, although it can affect other organs as well; ___ **espinal** / spinal ___; ___ **infantil** / childhood ___; ___ **meníngea** / meningeal ___; ___ **pulmonar** / pulmonary ___; ___ **urogenital** / urogenital ___.

tuberculosis miliar *f.* miliary tuberculosis, disease that invades the organism through the bloodstream and is characterized by the formation of minute tubercles in the different organs affected by it.

tuberculoso-a *a.* tuberculous, rel. to or affected by tuberculosis.

tubérculum *L.* tuberculum, tubercle.

tuberosidad *f.* tuber, a swelling or enlargement.

tuberoso-a *a.* tuberous, rel. to or resembling a tuber.

tubo *m.* tube, elongated, cylindrical, hollow structure; ___ **colector** / collecting tubule; ___ **contorneado del riñón** / convoluted tubule of the kidney; ___ **de drenaje** / drainage ___; ___

de ensayo / test ___; ___ de inhalación / inhalation ___; ___ de toracostomía / thoracostomy ___; ___ de traqueotomía / tracheotomy ___; ___ en T / T-___; ___ endotraqueal / endotracheal ___; ___ nasogástrico / nasogastric ___; ___ urinífero / uriniferous tubule.

tuboovárico-a *a.* tubo-ovarian, rel. to the fallopian tube and the ovary; **absceso** ___ / ___ abscess.

tuboplastia *f. surg.* tuboplasty, plastic surgery of a tube, esp. the fallopian tube.

túbulo *m.* tubule, a small anatomical tube; ___ **colector** / collecting ___; ___ **renal** / renal ___.

tuerto-a *a.* one-eyed or blind in one eye.

tularemia *f.* tularemia, rabbit fever, infection transmitted to humans by the bite of a vector insect or by handling of infected meat.

tumefacción, tumescencia *f.* tumefaction, the process of swelling.

tumor *m.* tumor, swelling, new spontaneous growth of mass or tissue of no physiological use; ___ **desdiferenciado** / undifferentiated ___; ___ **difundido o difuso** / diffuse ___; ___ **escirroso** / scirrhous ___; ___ **inflamatorio** / inflammatory ___; ___ **medular** / medullary ___; ___ **necrótico** / necrotic ___; ___ **no sólido** / nonsolid ___; ___ **radiocurable** / radiocurable ___; ___ **radiorresistente** / radioresistant ___; ___ **radiosensitivo** / radiosensitive ___; ___ **sin diferenciación** / undifferentiated ___.

tumoral *a.* tumorous, rel. to a tumor.

tumorectomía *f.* lumpectomy, excision of a breast tumor excluding lymph nodes and adjacent tissue.

tumoricida *a.* tumoricidal, that destroys tumorous cells.

tumorigénesis *f.* tumorigenesis, production of tumors.

túnel *m.* tunnel, a bodily channel; ___ **del carpo** / carpal ___; ___ **flexor** / flexor ___; ___ **torsal, tarsiano** / torsal ___.

tunica *L.* tunica, tunic, protective membrane; ___ **adventicia** / ___ adventitia; ___ **albugínea** / ___ albuginea; ___ **dartos** / ___ dartos; ___ **mucosa** / ___ mucosa; ___ **muscular** / ___ muscularis; ___ **serosa** / ___ serosa; ___ **vaginal** / ___ vaginalis.

túnica *f.* tunic, covering, outer layer of an organ or part.

tupido-a *a.* plugged, obstructed; **oídos** ___ / ___ ears.

turbinado-a *a.* turbinate. 1. rel. to the nasal concha; 2. shaped like a dome.

turbio-a *a.* turbid, cloudy, not translucent.

túrgido-a *a.* turgid, distended, swollen.

turgor *m.* turgor. 1. swelling, distension; 2. normal cellular tension.

Turner, síndrome de *m.* Turner's syndrome, congenital endocrine abnormality manifested by amenorrhea, failure of sexual maturation, short stature and neck, and the presence of only forty-five chromosomes.

turno *m.* turn; [*cita*] appointment; shift.

tusivo-a *a.* tussive, rel. to cough or caused by it.

tussis *L.* tussis, cough.

tympanum *L.* tympanum, the middle ear. *V.* **tímpano.**

U *abr.* **unidad** / unit; **uranio** / uranium; **urología** / urology.

u *conj.* or, used instead of *o* before words beginning with *o* or *ho.*

ubre *f.* udder, mammary gland of female animals, such as cows.

úlcera *f.* ulcer, sore, or lesion of the skin or mucous membrane with gradual disintegration of tissue; ___ **duodenal** / duodenal ___; ___ **gástrica** / gastric ___; ___ **perforante** / perforating ___; ___ **por decúbito** / decubitus ___, bedsore; ___ **roedora** / rodent ___, that destroys gradually; ___ **varicosa crónica de la pierna** / chronic varicose leg ___; ___ **vesical** / vesical ___.

úlcera péptica *f.* peptic ulcer, ulceration of the mucous membranes of the esophagus, stomach, or duodenum caused by excessive acidity of the gastric juice, gen. produced by acute or chronic stress.

ulceración *f.* ulceration, the formation process of an ulcer.

ulcerado-a *a.* ulcerated, rel. to or of the nature of an ulcer.

ulcerar *v.* to ulcerate.

ulcerativo *a.* ulcerative, rel. to or causing an ulcer.

ulceroso-a *a.* ulcerous, rel. to or affected by an ulcer.

uleritema *m.* ulerythema, erythematous dermatitis characterized by formation of scars.

ulnar *a.* ulnar, rel. to the ulna or to the arteries and nerves related to it.

ulocarcinoma *m.* ulocarcinoma, cancer of the gums.

último-a *a.* last, ultimate, final; **-mente** *adv.* lately; **por** ___ / finally.

ultracentrífuga *f.* ultracentrifuge, machine with a centrifugal force capable of separating and sedimenting the molecules of a substance.

ultraestructura *f.* ultrastructure, structure of the smallest elements of a body, visible only through an electron microscope.

ultrafiltración *f.* ultrafiltration, a filtration process that allows the passage of small molecules, holding back larger ones.

ultramicroscopio *m.* ultramicroscope, a microscope that makes visible objects that cannot be seen under a common light microscope.

ultrasónico-a *a.* ultrasonic. *V.* **supersónico.**

ultrasonido *m.* ultrasound, a sound wave with a frequency above the range of human hearing used in ultrasonography for diagnostic and therapeutic purposes; **diagnóstico por** ___ / ultrasonic diagnosis.

ultrasonografía *f.* ultrasonography, diagnostic technique that uses ultrasound waves to develop the image of a structure or tissue of the body.

ultrasonograma *m.* ultrasonogram, the image produced by ultrasonography.

ultravioleta *a.* ultraviolet, beyond the visible, violet end of the spectrum; **rayos** ___ / ___ rays; **terapia de radiación** ___ / ___ therapy.

ululación *f.* ululation, the act of screaming hysterically as seen in mental patients.

umbilical *a.* umbilical, rel. to the umbilicus.

umbral *m.* threshold, the minimum degree of stimulus needed to produce an effect or response; ___ **absoluto** / absolute ___; ___ **auditivo** / auditory ___; ___ **de la conciencia** / ___ of consciousness; ___ **renal** / renal ___; ___ **sensorio** / sensory ___.

unánime *a.* unanimous.

unción *f.* unction; ointment.

ungueal *a.* ungual, rel. to the nails.

ungüento *m.* unguent, liniment, salve, medicated preparation for external use.

uniarticular *a.* uniarticular, rel. to a single joint.

unibásico-a *a.* unibasal, rel. to a single base.

unicelular *a.* unicellular, having only one cell.

único-a *a.* only, sole; **-mente** *adv.* only, solely.

unidad *f.* unit. 1. one of a kind; ___ **motora** / motor ___, that provides motor activity; 2. standard of measurement; 3. unity.

unidad internacional *f.* international unit, standard measurement of a given substance as adopted by the International Conference for Unification of Formulae.

unido-a *a.* joined; close.

uniforme *m.* uniform; *a.* uniform, even.

unigrávida *f.* unigravida, woman who is pregnant for the first time.

unilateral *a.* unilateral, rel. to one side only.

unión *f.* union. 1. the action or effect of joining two things into one; 2. the growing together of severed parts of a bone or of the lips of a wound.

unípara *f.* uniparous, woman who gives birth to only one child.

unipolar *a.* unipolar, having one pole, such as the nerve cells.

unir *v.* to join; to unite, to merge.

unitario-a *a.* unitary, rel. to a single unit.

universal *a.* universal, general.

universidad *f.* university.

universo *m.* universe.

Unna, bota de pasta de *f.* Unna's paste boot, compression dressing applied to the lower part of the leg in the treatment of varicose ulcers consisting of layers of gauze applied with and covered with Unna's paste.

unsinaria *f.* hookworm, intestinal parasite; **enfermedad de la** ___ / ___ disease.

untadura *f.* application; ointment.

untar *v.* to apply ointment; to rub, to smear.

untuoso-a *a.* unctuous, greasy, oily.

uña *f.* nail; ___ **del dedo del pie** / toenail; ___ **encarnada** / ingrown ___; *vr.* **comerse las** ___-**s** / to bite one's ___-s.

uñero *m.* ingrown nail.

uranio *m.* uranium, heavy metallic element.

urato *m.* urate, uric acid salt.

urea *f.* urea, crystalline substance found in the blood, lymph, and urine that is the final product of the metabolism of proteins and is excreted through the urine as nitrogen.

ureico-a *a.* ureal, rel. to urea.

uremia *f.* uremia, toxic condition caused by renal insufficiency that produces retention of nitrogen substances, phosphates, and sulphates in the blood.

urémico-a *a.* uremic, rel. to or affected by uremia.

uréter *m.* ureter, one of the ducts by which urine passes from the kidney to the urinary bladder.

ureteral, uretérico-a *a.* ureteral, rel. to a ureter; **obstrucción** ___ / ___ obstruction.

ureterectasis *f.* ureterectasis, abnormal dilation of the ureter.

ureterectomía *f. surg.* ureterectomy, partial or total excision of the ureter.

ureteritis *f.* ureteritis, infl. of the ureter.

ureterocele *m.* ureterocele, cystic dilation of the distal intravesical portion of the ureter due to stenosis of the ureteral orifice.

ureterocistoneostomía *f. surg.* uretercystoneostomy. *V.* **ureteroneocistostomía.**

ureterocistostomía *f. surg.* ureterocystostomy. *V.* **ureteroneocistostomía**

ureterografía *f.* ureterography, x-ray of the ureter with the use of a radiopaque substance.

ureteroheminefrectomía *f. surg.* ureteroheminephrectomy, resection of a portion of the kidney and its ureter in cases of duplication of the upper urinary tract.

ureterohidronefrosis *f.* ureterohydronephrosis, distension of the ureter and the kidney due to obstruction.

ureteroileostomía *f. surg.* ureteroileostomy, anastomosis of a ureter to an isolated segment of the ileum.

ureterolitiasis *f.* ureterolithiasis, formation of a ureteral calculus.

ureterolitotomía *f. surg.* ureterolithotomy, incision into a ureter for removal of a calculus.

ureteronefrectomía *f. surg.* ureteronephrectomy, excision of the kidney and its ureter.

ureteroneocistostomía *f. surg.* ureteroneocystostomy, reimplantation of the ureter into the bladder.

ureteropieloplastia *f. surg.* ureteropyeloplasty, plastic surgery of a ureter and the renal pelvis.

ureteroplastia *f. surg.* ureteroplasty, plastic surgery of the ureter.

ureterosigmoidostomía *f. surg.* ureterosigmoidostomy, implantation of a ureter in the sigmoid colon.

ureterostomía *f. surg.* ureterostomy, formation of a permanent fistula for drainage of a ureter.

ureterotomía *f.* ureterotomy, incision into a ureter.

ureteroureterostomía *f. surg.* ureteroureterostomy, anastomosis of two ureters or of extreme parts of the same ureter.

ureterovesical *a.* ureterovesical, rel. to the ureter and the urinary bladder.

uretra *f.* urethra, urinary canal.

uretral *a.* urethral, rel. to the urethra; **estrechez** ___ / ___ stricture.

uretralgia *f.* urethralgia, pain in the urethra.

uretrectomía *f. surg.* urethrectomy, partial or total excision of the urethra.

uretritis *f.* urethritis, chronic or acute infl. of the urethra.

uretrografía *f.* urethrography, x-ray of the urethra after injection of a radiopaque substance.

uretroscopio *m.* urethroscope, instrument for viewing the interior of the urethra.

uretrotomía *f. surg.* urethrotomy, incision of the urethra, usu. to alleviate a stricture.

uretrótomo *m.* urethrotome, instrument used in urethrotomy.

urgente *a.* urgent, pressing; **-mente** *adv.* urgently.

uricemia *f.* uricemia, excess uric acid in the blood.

úrico-a *a.* uric, rel. to the urine.

uricosuria *f.* uricosuria, presence of an excessive amount of uric acid in the urine.

urinación *f.* urination, the act of urinating.

urinálisis *m.* urinalysis, analysis of the urine.

urinario-a *a.* urinary, rel. to the urine; **infección** ___ / ___ infection; **órganos** ___-s / ___ organs; **sedimento** ___ / ___ sediment.

urinario, sistema *m.* urinary system, the group of organs and conduits that participate in the production and excretion of urine.

urinífero-a *a.* uriniferous, containing or carrying urine.

urinogenital, urogenital *a.* urinogenital, urogenital, rel. to the urinary and the genital tracts.

urinoma *m.* urinoma, urine containing cyst or tumor.

urobilinógeno *m.* urobilinogen, pigment derived from the reduction of bilirubin by action of intestinal bacteria.

urocinasa *f.* urokinase, enzyme present in human urine used to dissolve blood clots.

urodinámica *f.* urodynamics, the study of the active process and pathophysiology of urination.

urodinia *f.* urodynia, painful urination.

urogenital *a.* urogenital, rel. to the urinary and the genital tracts; **diafragma** ___ / ___ diaphragm.

urografía *f.* urography, x-ray of a part of the urinary tract by injection of a radiopaque substance; ___ **descendente o excretora** / descending or excretory ___ ; ___ **retrógrada** / retrograde ___ .

urograma *m.* urogram, x-ray record of a urography.

urolitiasis *f.* urolithiasis, formation of urinary

calculi and disorders associated with their presence.

urolítico-a *a.* urolithic, rel. to urinary calculi.

urología *f.* urology, the branch of medicine that studies the diagnosis and treatment of diseases of the genitourinary tract in men and the urinary tract in women.

urológico-a *a.* urologic, rel. to urology.

úrologo-a *m., f.* specialist in urology.

uropatía *f.* uropathy, any disease that affects the urinary tract.

urticaria *f.* urticaria, hives, eruptive skin disease characterized by pink patches accompanied by intense itching, gen. allergic in nature and caused by an internal or external agent.

usado-a *a.* used.

usar *v.* to use; [*ropa*] to wear.

uso *m.* use; function; usage; ___ **no aprobado** / off-label ___; **de poco** ___ / under___.

usual *a.* usual, customary; **-mente** *adv.* usually.

uterino-a *a.* uterine, rel. to the uterus; **prolapso** ___ / ___ prolapse; **ruptura** ___ / ___ rupture; **sangramiento** ___ / ___ bleeding unrelated to menstruation.

útero *m.* uterus, womb, hollow, muscular organ of the female reproductive system that contains and nourishes the embryo and fetus during the period of gestation; **cáncer del** ___ **o de la matriz** / uterine cancer; ___ **didelfo** / didelphys ___, double uterus.

uterosalpingografía *f.* uterosalpingography, x-ray examination of the uterus and the fallopian tubes following injection of a radiopaque substance.

uterovaginal *a.* uterovaginal, rel. to the uterus and the vagina.

uterovesical *a.* uterovesical, rel. to the uterus and the urinary bladder.

útil *a.* useful, practical.

uva *f.* grape.

úvea *f.* uvea, the vascular layer of the eye formed by the iris and the ciliary body together with the choroid coat.

uveítis *f.* uveitis, infl. of the uvea.

úvula *f.* uvula, small, fleshy structure hanging in the middle of the posterior border of the soft palate.

V abr. **válvula** / valve; **vena** / vein; **visión** / vision; **volumen** / volume.

vaca f. cow.

vacaciones f. pl. vacation.

vaccinia L. vaccinia, cowpox, a virus that causes disease in cattle and that when inoculated in humans gives a degree of immunity against smallpox.

vaciar v. to empty; to flush out, to void; **vaciarse** vr. to become empty.

vacilante a. vacillating, fluctuating; shaky.

vacilar v. to vacillate; to fluctuate; to hesitate.

vacío-a a. empty; **envasado al ___** / vacuum packed. ~~abdomen~~ — side flank ribs

vacuna f. vaccine, a preparation of attenuated or killed microorganisms that when introduced in the body establishes immunity to the specific disease caused by the microorganisms; **___ antipolio oral, trivalente atenuada de Sabin** / poliovirus, live oral trivalent ___, Sabin; **___ antirrábica** / rabies ___; **___ antisarampión de virus vivo** / measles virus ___, live; **___ antisarampión, inactivada** / measles virus ___, inactivated; **___ antitífica** / typhoid fever ___; **___ antivariólica, antivariolosa** / smallpox ___; **___ BCG, contra la tuberculosis** / BCG ___ against tuberculosis; **___ contra la influenza** / influenza ___; **___ de Salk, contra la poliomielitis** / Salk ___, antipolio; **___ neumocócica polivalente** / pneumococcal polyvalent virus ___; **___ de virus vivo contra la rubéola** / rubella virus ___, live; **___ triple contra la difteria, el tétano y la tos ferina** / DPT ___, against diphtheria, pertussis, and tetanus.

vacunación f. vaccination, inoculation of vaccine.

vacunar v. to vaccinate.

vacuola f. vacuole, small cavity or space filled with fluid or air in the cellular protoplasm.

vacuolización f. vacuolization, formation of vacuoles.

vacuum L. vacuum, emptiness, a space devoid of air or matter.

vagal a. vagal, rel. to the pneumogastric or vagus nerve.

vagante a. vagrant, wandering; loose, free.

vagar vi. to wander.

vagina f. vagina. 1. female canal extending from the uterus to the vulva; 2. structure resembling a sheath.

vaginal a. vaginal, rel. to the vagina or to a sheathlike structure.

vaginismus L. vaginismus, sudden and painful spasm of the vagina.

vaginitis f. vaginitis, infl. of the vagina; **___ bacteriana** / bacterial ___.

vago-a a. vague, indistinct; **-mente** adv. vaguely.

vago, nervio m. vagus nerve. **V. nervios craneales.**

vagolítico-a a. vagolytic, inhibiting the function of the vagus nerve.

vagotomía f. surg. vagotomy, interruption of the vagus nerve.

vahído m. dizziness, fainting spell.

vaina f. sheath, a protective covering structure.

vainilla f. vanilla.

vaivén m. swaying; pop. to and fro.

valencia f. valence, valency.

valer vi. to cost; to be worth; to be valid, good, or acceptable; vr. **valerse por sí mismo** / to be self-sufficient.

valgus L. valgus, bent or twisted outward.

validez f. validity.

válido-a a. valid, acceptable.

valiente a. valiant, brave, courageous.

valioso-a a. valuable, of worth.

valor m. value, worth.

valorización f. valorization, evaluation.

Valsalva, maniobra de f. Valsalva's maneuver, procedure to test the patency of the eustachian tubes or to adjust the pressure of the middle ear by forcibly exhaling while holding the nostrils and mouth closed.

válvula f. valve, a membranous structure in a canal or orifice that closes temporarily to prevent the backward flow of the contents passing through it; **___ aórtica** / aortic ___, between the left ventricle and the aorta; **___ atrioventricular derecha, tricúspide** / atrioventricular ___ right, tricuspid; **___ atrioventricular izquierda, bicúspide, mitral** / atrioventricular ___ left, bicuspid, mitral; **___ ileocecal** / ileocecal ___; **___ pilórica** / pyloric ___; **___ pulmonar** / pulmonary.

válvula mitral f. mitral valve, the left atrioventricular valve of the heart, **insuficiencia de la ___** / insufficiency of the ___; **prolapso de la ___** / prolapse of the ___.

válvulas conniventes f. pl. valvulae conniventes, circular membranous folds found in the small intestine that slow the passage of food along the bowels.

valvuloplastia f. surg. valvuloplasty, plastic surgery of a heart valve.

valvulótomo m. valvulotome, instrument to incise a valve.

vano-a a. vain; **en ___** / in vain, needlessly.

vapor m. vapor, gas, fume.

vaporización f. vaporization. 1. action and effect of vaporizing; 2. therapeutic use of vapors.

vaporizador m. vaporizer, device used to convert a substance into a vapor for therapeutic purposes.

vaporizar vi. to vaporize, to change a substance into vapor.

variabilidad f. variability.

variable f. variable, a changing factor; a. that can change.

variación f. variation, diversity in the charac-

Collins dictionary

teristic of related elements.

variado-a *a.* varied.

variante *f.* variant, that which is essentially the same as another but different in form; *a.* different, changing.

variar *v.* to change, to vary.

várice *f.* varix, an enlarged and tortuous vein, artery or lymphatic vessel.

varicella *L.* varicella, chicken pox, viral contagious disease, gen. manifested during childhood, characterized by an eruption that evolves into small vesicles.

varicocele *m.* varicocele, varicose condition of the veins of the spermatic cord that produces a soft mass in the scrotum.

varicoide *a.* varicoid, resembling a varix.

varicoso-a *a.* varicose, resembling or related to varices; **venas ___-s / ___ veins.**

varicotomía *f. surg.* varicotomy, excision of a varicose vein.

variedad *f.* variety.

varilla *f.* thin, short rod; wand; **___ de aceite /** dipstick.

variola *L.* variola. *V.* **viruela.**

variólico-a, varioloso-a *a.* variolous, rel. to smallpox or affected by it.

varioliforme *a.* varioliform, resembling smallpox.

varios-as *a.* several.

varón *m.* male.

varonil *a.* manly.

varus *L.* varus, twisted or turned inward.

vas *L.* (*pl.* **vasa**) vas, vessel; **___ recta / ___ recta; ___ vasorum / ___ vasorum.**

vas deferens *L.* vas deferens, the excretory duct of the spermatozoa.

vascular *a.* vascular, rel. to the blood vessels; **sistema ___ / ___** system, all the vessels of the body, esp. the blood vessels.

vascularización *f.* vascularization, formation of new blood vessels.

vascularizar *vi.* to vascularize, to develop new blood vessels.

vasculatura *f.* vasculature, arrangement of blood vessels in an organ or part.

vasculitis *f.* vasculitis. *V.* **angitis.**

vasculopatía *f.* vasculopathy, any disease of a blood vessel.

vasectomía *f. surg.* vasectomy, partial excision and ligation of the vas deferens to prevent the passage of spermatozoa into the semen, usu. done as a means of birth control.

vaselina *f.* vaseline, petroleum jelly.

vasija *f.* receptacle, vessel.

vaso *m.* vessel; conduit. 1. any channel or tube that carries fluid such as blood or lymph; **___ colateral / collateral ___; ___ linfático / lymphatic ___; grandes ___-s ___-s / great ___-s; sanguíneo / blood ___;** 2. a drinking glass.

vasoactivo *m.* vasoactive, agent that affects the blood vessels.

vasoconstricción *f.* vasoconstriction, decrease

in the caliber of the blood vessels.

vasoconstrictor *m.* vasoconstrictor, that which causes vasoconstriction; **-a** *a.* vasoconstrictive, rel. to constriction of the blood vessels.

vasodilatación *f.* vasodilation, increase in the caliber of the blood vessels.

vasodilatador *m.* vasodilator, that which causes vasodilation; **-a** *a.* that causes vasodilation.

vasoespasmo *m.* vasospasm. *V.* **angioespasmo; ___ coronario /** coronary **___.**

vasomotor *m.* vasomotor, that which regulates the contraction and dilation of blood vessels; **-a** *a.* rel. to dilation or contraction of blood vessels.

vasopresina *f.* vasopressin, hormone secreted by the posterior pituitary gland that increases the reabsorption of water by the kidneys, raising the blood pressure.

vasopresor *m.* vasopressor, that which has a vasoconstrictive effect; **-a** *a.* having a vasoconstrictive effect.

vasotónico-a *a.* vasotonic, rel. to a vessel tone.

vasovagal *a.* vasovagal, rel. to the vessels and the vagus nerve; **síncope ___ / ___** syncope, brief fainting spell caused by vascular and vagal disturbances.

vasto-a *a.* *V.* **vastus.**

vastus *L.* vastus, dilated, large, extensive.

Vater, ámpula de *f.* Vater's ampulla or papilla, the point where the biliar and pancreatic excretory systems enter the duodenum.

vecino-a *m., f.* neighbor.

vector *m.* vector, a carrier that transmits infectious agents.

vegetación *f.* vegetation, a wartlike, abnormal growth on a body part as seen in endocarditis.

vegetal *m.* vegetable; *a.* vegetal, rel. to plants.

vegetarianismo *m.* vegetarianism, the practice of eating only vegetables and fruits. Dairy products may not be excluded.

vegetariano-a *m., f.* individual who eats mainly vegetables; *a.* rel. to vegetables.

vegetativo-a *a.* vegetative. 1. rel. to functions of growth and nutrition; 2. rel. to involuntary or unconscious bodily movements; 3. pertaining to plants.

vehículo *m.* vehicle. 1. agent without therapeutic action that carries the active ingredient of a medication; 2. an agent of transmission.

vejez *f.* old age.

vejiga *f.* bladder; **cálculos de la ___ / ___** calculi; **irrigación de la ___ / ___** irrigation; **___ llena de aire / air ___; ___ neurogénica /** neurogenic **___.**

vejiga urinaria *f.* urinary bladder, sac-shaped organ that serves as a receptacle to urine secreted by the kidneys.

vela *f.* candle.

velar *v.* to watch over, to take care of someone.

velo *m.* veil. 1. thin membrane or covering of a body part; 2. a piece of amniotic sac seen sometimes covering the face of a newborn; 3.

slight alteration in the voice.

velocidad *f.* speed, velocity.

vello *m.* body hair; ___ **axilar** / axillary ___; ___ **púbico** / pubic hair.

vellosidad *f.* villus, short, filiform projection from a membranous surface; ___ **aracnoidea** / arachnoid ___; ___ **coriónica** / chorionic ___; ___-**es intestinales (villi intestinales)** / intestinal ___; ___-**es sinoviales** / synovial ___.

velloso-a, velludo-a *a.* villous, hairy.

vena *f.* vein, fibromuscular vessel that carries blood from the capillaries toward the heart.

vena cava *f.* vena cava, either of two large veins returning deoxygenated blood to the right atrium of the heart; ___ **inferior** / inferior ___; ___ **superior** / superior ___.

vencimiento *m.* expiration; **fecha de** ___ / ___ date.

venda *f.* bandage.

vendaje *m.* bandage, dressing, curative, protective covering; ___ **abdominal** / abdominal binder; ___ **de yeso** / plaster cast; ___ **protector** / surgical dressing.

vendar *v.* to bandage.

vender *v.* to sell.

veneno *m.* poison, venum, toxic substance; **centro de control de** ___-s / ___ control center.

venenoso-a *a.* poisonous, venenous, toxic; **hiedra** ___ / poison ivy.

venéreo-a *a.* venereal, resulting from or transmitted by sexual intercourse; **enfermedad** ___ / ___ disease.

venina *f.* venene, toxic substance present in snake venom.

veninantivenina *f.* venin-antivenin, vaccine to counteract the effect of snake poison.

venipuntura *a.* venepuncture, venipuncture, surgical puncture of a vein.

venir *vi.* to come; ___ **al caso** / to be relevant.

venisección *f.* venisection. *V.* **flebotomía.**

venoclusivo-a *a.* veno-occlusive, rel. to the obstruction of veins. *envenoclisis*

venoconstricción *f.* venoconstriction, constriction of the muscular walls of the veins.

venografía *f.* venography, recording of a venogram.

venografía radionuclear *f.* radionuclear tomography, study of the veins by means of gamma rays.

venograma *m.* venogram, x-ray of a vein with the use of a contrasting medium.

venoso-a *a.* venous, rel. to the veins; **congestión** ___ / ___ congestion; **retorno** ___ / ___ return; **sangre** ___ / ___ blood; **seno** ___ / ___ sinus; **trombosis** ___ / ___ thrombosis.

venotomía *f. surg.* venotomy. *V.* **flebotomía.**

vent *Fr.* vent, opening.

ventaja *f.* advantage.

ventajoso-a *a.* advantageous.

ventana *f.* window; ___ **oval** / oval ___, aperture in the middle ear.

ventilación *f.* ventilation. 1. the act of circulating

fresh air in a given area; 2. oxygenation of blood; 3. *psych.*, open discussion and airing of grievances.

ventilador *m.* ventilator, artificial respirator; fan.

ventilar *v.* to ventilate, to air.

ventolera *f.* strong gust of wind.

ventral *a.* ventral, abdominal, rel. to the belly or to the front side of the body; **hernia** ___ / ___ hernia.

ventricular *a.* ventricular, rel. to a ventricle; **defecto del tabique** ___ / ___ septal defect.

ventriculitis *f.* ventriculitis, infl. of a ventricle.

ventrículo *m.* ventricle, a small cavity, esp. in reference to such structures as seen in the heart, the brain, or the larynx; **cuarto** ___ **del cerebro** / fourth ___ of the brain; **tercer** ___ **del cerebro** / third ___ of the brain; ___ **de la laringe** / ___ of the larynx; ___ **derecho del corazón** / right ___ of the heart; ___ **izquierdo del corazón** / left ___ of the heart; ___ **lateral del cerebro** / lateral ___ of the brain.

ventriculografía *f.* ventriculography. *V.* **neumoencefalografía.**

ventriculotomía *f. surg.* ventriculotomy, incision of a ventricle.

ventrodorsal *a.* ventrodorsal, rel. to the ventral and the dorsal surfaces.

vénula *f.* venule, minute vein that connects the capillaries with larger veins.

ver *vi.* to see; **está por** ___ / it remains to be seen; **tener que** ___ **con** / to have to do with; **verse** *vr.* to see oneself; to see each other.

verano *m.* summer

verbatim *L.* verbatim, exactly as stated.

verbo *m. gr.* verb.

verdad *f.* truth; **decir la** ___ / to tell the ___; **de** ___ / truly, really; **¿no es** ___? / isn't it so?

verdadero-a *a.* true, real; **pelvis** ___ / ___ pelvis; -**mente** *adv.* truly.

verde *a.* green; not ripe.

verdugón *m.* welt.

verdura *f.* [*vegetales*] greens.

veredicto *m.* verdict.

vergonzoso-a *a.* shameful.

vergüenza *f.* shame; bashfulness; *v.* **tener** ___ / to be ashamed.

verificación *f.* verification, proof.

verificar *vi.* to verify, to prove true.

vermicida, vermífugo *m.* vermicide, agent that destroys worms.

vermiforme *a.* vermiform, wormlike, resembling worm; **apéndice** ___ / ___ appendix.

vermis *L.* vermis. 1. parasitic worm; 2. wormlike structure.

vernix *L.* vernix, varnish; ___ **caseosa** / ___ caseosa, sebaceous secretion protecting the skin of a fetus.

verruca *L.* (*pl.* **verrucae**) verruca, wart; ___ **filiformis** / ___ filiformis; ___ **plantaris** / ___ plantaris; ___ **vulgaris** / ___ vulgaris.

verruga *f. V.* **verruca.**

verrugoso-a *a.* verrucose, warty, or rel. to warts.

intravenously

versátil *a.* versatile, having multiple applications.

versión *f.* version. 1. change of direction of an organ, such as the uterus; 2. change of position of the fetus in utero to facilitate delivery; ___ **bimanual** / bimanual ___; ___ **bipolar** / bipolar ___; ___ **cefálica** / cephalic ___; ___ **combinada** / combined ___; ___ **externa** / external ___; ___ **espontánea** / spontaneous ___.

vértebra *f.* vertebra, any of the thirty-three bones of the vertebral column; ___ **cervical** / cervical ___; ___ **coccígea** / coccygeal ___; ___ **lumbar** / lumbar ___; ___ **sacra** / sacral ___; ___ **torácica** / thoracic ___.

vertebrado-a *a.* vertebrate, having or resembling a vertebral column.

vertebral *a.* vertebral, rel. to the vertebrae; **arteria** ___ / ___ artery; **conducto** ___ / ___ canal; **costillas** ___-es / ___ ribs.

vertebrobasilar *a.* vertebrobasilar, rel. to the basilar and vertebral arteries.

verter *vi.* to spill; to pour.

vertex *L.* (*pl.* **vértices**) vertex. 1. the highest point of a structure, such as the top of the head; 2. convergence point of the two sides of an angle.

vertical *a.* vertical. 1. upright; 2. rel. to the vertex.

vértice *m. V.* **vertex.**

vertiginoso-a *a.* vertiginous, rel. to, affected by, or producing vertigo.

vértigo *m.* vertigo, sensation of whirling motion either of oneself (subjective vertigo), or of surrounding objects (objective vertigo) gen. caused by a disease of the inner ear or by gastric or cardiac disorders; ___ **laberíntico** / labyrinthine ___.

verumontanitis *f.* verumontanitis, infl. of the verumontanum.

verumontanum *L.* verumontanum, an elevation in the urethra at the point of entry of the seminal ducts.

vesicación *f.* vesication. 1. the formation of blisters; 2. a blister.

vesical *a.* vesical, rel. to or resembling a bladder.

vesicouretral *a.* vesicoureteral, rel. to the urinary bladder and the ureters.

vesicovaginal *a.* vesicovaginal, rel. to the urinary bladder and the vagina.

vesícula *f.* vesicle, vesicula, small sac or elevation of the skin containing serous fluid.

vesícula biliar *f.* gallbladder, pear-shaped receptacle on the lower part of the liver that stores bile.

vesicular *a.* vesicular, rel. to a vesicle.

vesiculoso-a *a.* vesiculate, of the nature of a vesicle.

vestibular *a.* vestibular, rel. to a vestibule; **nervio** ___ / ___ nerve.

vestíbulo *m.* vestibule. 1. space or cavity that gives access to a duct or canal; 2. lobby, waiting room.

vestigial *a.* vestigial, rudimentary, rel. to a vestige.

vestigio *m.* vestige, remains of a structure that was fully developed in a previous stage of the species or of the individual.

vestimenta *f.* clothing; garment.

vestir *vi.* to dress; **vestirse** *vr.* to dress oneself.

veterano-a *m., f.* veteran.

veterinaria *f.* veterinary medicine, the science that deals with prevention and cure of animal diseases, esp. domestic animals.

veterinario-a *m., f.* veterinarian, specialist in veterinary medicine; *a.* rel. to veterinary medicine.

vez *f.* time, occasion; **a la** ___ / at the same ___; **alguna** ___ / sometime; **cada** ___ / each ___; **de una** ___ / all at once; **de** ___ **en cuando** / once in a while; **en** ___ **de** / instead of; **otra** ___ / again; **rara** ___ / rarely; **tal** ___ / perhaps; **una** ___ / once.

vía *f.* tract, via, passage, conduit; ___-s **biliares** / biliary ___; ___-s **digestivas** / gastrointestinal ___; ___ **olfatoria** / olfactory ___; ___ **piramidal** / pyramidal ___; ___-s **respiratorias** / respiratory ___; ___-s **urinarias** / urinary ___.

viabilidad *f.* viability, the quality of being viable.

viable *a.* viable, capable of surviving, gen. in reference to a newborn; **no** ___ / nonviable.

viajar *v.* to travel.

viaje *m.* trip.

vianda *f.* starchy vegetables such as potatoes.

víbora *f.* viper.

vibración *f.* vibration, oscillation.

vibrante *a.* vibrant.

vibrar *v.* to vibrate.

vibratorio-a *a.* vibratory, vibratile, vibrating or producing vibration; **sentido** ___ / ___ sense.

vicario-a *a.* vicarious, acting or assuming the place of another.

vicio *m.* vice, bad habit.

vicioso-a *a.* given to vice.

víctima *f.* victim; ___ **de accidente** / casualty.

vida *f.* life; vitality; **medidas para el sostenimiento de la** ___ / ___-saving measures; **promedio de duración de** ___ / ___ expectancy; **que pone la** ___ **en peligro** / ___-threatening; ___ **cotidiana** / daily ___.

vida media *f.* half-life. 1. the time required for half the nuclei of a radioactive substance to disintegrate; 2. the time required for half the amount of a substance taken in by the body to dissolve by natural means.

video *m.* video.

videocinta *f.* videotape.

vidrio *m.* glass; ___ **de fibra** / fiberglass.

viejo-a *a.* old, aged; stale.

viento *m.* wind; **hace** ___ / it is windy.

vientre *m.* belly; abdomen.

vigente *a.* in force, in effect.

vigilancia *f.* 1. vigilance, state of alertness or responsiveness; 2. surveillance.

vigilar *v.* to watch, to guard; to survey.

vigilia *f.* vigil. 1. the state of being consciously responsive to a stimulus; 2. insomnia.

vigor *m.* vigor, strength; fortitude; stamina.

vigorizar *vi.* to invigorate, to strengthen, to energize.

vigoroso-a *a.* vigorous, strong; having fortitude; **-mente** *adv.* vigorously.

VIH *m.* HIV, human immunodeficiency virus-1, a retrovirus considered to be the cause of AIDS that can be transmitted by sexual relations or by blood transfusion from someone who is infected with HIV. The virus can be transmitted to children of mothers with HIV in utero, at birth, or, likely, through breast-feeding.

vinagre *m.* vinegar, solution of acetic acid.

vínculo *m.* link.

vino *m.* wine.

violáceo-a *a.* purplish.

violación *f.* rape; violation; ___ **estatutaria** / statutory ___.

violar *a.* to rape; to harm or injure.

violencia *f.* violence; ___ **doméstica** / domestic ___.

violento-a *a.* violent.

violeta *a.* [*color*] violet.

viral *a.* viral, rel. to a virus.

virar *a.* to turn; **virarse** *vr.* to turn oneself around.

viremia *f.* viremia, the presence of virus in the blood.

virgen *f.* virgin. 1. uncontaminated, pure; 2. having had no sexual intercourse.

virginal *a.* virginal, pure.

virginidad *f.* virginity.

viril *a.* virile, rel. to the male.

virilidad *f.* virility. 1. sexual potency; 2. the quality of being virile.

virilización *f.* virilization, the process by which secondary male characteristics develop in the female, gen. due to adrenal malfunction or to intake of hormones.

virión *m.* virion, mature viral particle that constitutes the extracellular, infectious form of a virus.

virolento-a *a.* 1. rel. to or afflicted with smallpox; 2. pockmarked.

virología *f.* virology, the study of viruses.

virtual *a.* virtual, existing in appearance and effect, but not in reality.

viruela *f.* smallpox, highly contagious viral disease characterized by high temperature and generalized blisters and pustules; ___-s **locas** / chickenpox.

virulencia *f.* virulence. 1. the power of an organism to produce disease in the host; 2. the quality of being virulent.

virulento-a *a.* virulent, highly poisonous or infectious.

virus *m.* virus, ultramicroscopic microorganisms capable of causing infectious diseases; ___ **atenuado** / attenuated ___; ___ **citomegálico** / cytomegalic ___; ___ **Coxsackie** / Coxsackie

___; ___ **de la parainfluenza** / parainfluenza ___; ___ **ECHO** / ECHO ___; ___ **entérico** / enteric ___; ___ **herpético** / herpes ___; ___ **oncogénico, tumoral** / tumor ___; ___ **sincitial respiratorio** / respiratory syncytial ___; ___ **variólico** / pox ___.

visceral *a.* visceral, rel. to viscera.

vísceras *f. pl.* viscera, large internal organs of the body, esp. the abdomen.

visceromegalia *f.* visceromegaly, abnormal enlargement of a viscus.

viscosidad *f.* viscosity, the quality of being viscous, esp. the property of fluids to offer resistance due to molecular friction.

viscoso-a *a.* viscous, gummy, sticky; slimy.

visibilidad *f.* visibility.

visible *a.* visible; evident; **-mente** *adv.* visibly.

visión *f.* vision, the sense of sight. 1. the ability to see, to perceive things through the action of light on the eyes and on related centers in the brain; ___ **acromática** / achromatic ___; ___ **binocular** / binocular ___; ___ **central** / central ___; ___ **cromática** / chromatic ___; ___ **diurna** / day ___; ___ **doble** / double ___, diplopia; ___ **nocturna** / night ___; ___ **periférica** / peripheral ___; 2. imaginary apparition.

visión en túnel *f.* tunnel vision, eye anomaly manifested by a great reduction in the visual field, as if looking through a tunnel, such as occurs in cases of glaucoma.

visita *f.* visit; call; **horas de** ___ / visiting hours; ___ **médica** / house call.

visitar *v.* to visit.

vista *f.* sight; eyesight; view; **corto de** ___ / near-sighted; ___ **cansada** / eyestrain; **enfermedades de la** ___ / eye diseases; ___ **nublada** / bleary-eyed; *v.* **tener buena** ___ / to have good eyesight; **a primera** ___ / at first ___; **en** ___ **de** / in view of.

vistazo *m.* glance, glimpse; *v.* **dar un** ___ / to take a look.

visto-a *a. pp.* of **ver**, seen.

visual *a.* visual, rel. to vision; **campo** ___ / ___ field, field of vision; **contacto** ___ / eye contact; **memoria** ___ / eye memory.

visualización *f.* visualization. 1. the act of viewing an image or picture, as in the study of an x-ray, when a body part is examined in detail; 2. mental conception of health created for the purpose of aiding the healing process.

visualizar *vi.* to visualize. 1. to form a mental image; 2. to make visible, such as through x-rays.

vital *a.* vital, rel. to life or essential to maintaining it; **capacidad** ___ / ___ capacity; **signos** ___-es / ___ signs.

vitalicio-a *a.* for life.

vitalidad *f.* vitality. 1. the quality of having life; 2. physical or mental vigor.

vitalizar *vi.* to vitalize, to give life; to reanimate.

vitamina *f.* vitamin, any one of a group of organic compounds found in small amounts in foods and essential to the growth and development of the body and its functions; **pérdida de** ___-s / loss of ___-s.

vitamínico-a *a.* vitaminic, rel. to vitamins.

vitíligo *m.* vitiligo, benign skin disease characterized by smooth white spots, gen. in exposed areas.

vítreo-a *a.* vitreous, glassy, hyaline; **cámara** ___ / ___ chamber; **cuerpo** ___ / ___ body; **humor** ___ / ___ humor.

viudo-a *m., f.* widower; widow.

vivificante *a.* vivifying.

vivir *v.* to live.

vivisección *f.* vivisection, the cutting or operating upon living animals for research purposes.

vivo-a *a.* alive; living; *pop.* ingenuous.

vocabulario *m.* vocabulary.

vocación *f.* vocation, profession.

vocal *f. gr.* vowel; *a.* rel. to the voice or produced by it; **ligamentos** ___-es / ___ ligaments.

vocalización *f.* vocalization.

volar *vi.* to fly; to travel by airplane.

volátil *a.* volatile, readily vaporized.

volición *f.* volition, will, the power to determine.

volumen *m.* volume, space occupied by a body or substance; ___ **cardíaco** / heart ___; ___ **de reserva espiratoria o aire de reserva** / expiratory air reserve ___; ___ **de ventilación pulmonar** / tidal ___; ___ **residual** / residual ___; ___ **sanguíneo** / blood ___; ___ **sistólico** / stroke ___.

volumétrico-a *a.* volumetric, rel. to the measurement of volume.

voluntad *f.* will, determination; **fuerza de** ___ / ___ power.

voluntario-a *m., f.* volunteer; *a.* voluntary; **músculo** ___ / ___ muscle.

voluptuoso-a *a.* voluptuous, sensually provocative.

volver *vi.* to return; to turn; ___ **en sí** / to come to; **volverse** *vr.* to turn over; to return to.

vólvulo *m.* volvulus, intestinal obstruction caused by torsion of the intestine on its mesentery.

vómer *m.* vomer, the impaired flat bone that forms part of the nasal septum.

vomitar *v.* to vomit.

vomitivo *m.* vomitive, emetic.

vómito *m.* vomit, vomiting.

von Recklinghausen, enfermedad de *f.* von Recklinghausen's disease. *V.* **neurofibromatosis.**

voraz *a.* voracious, having an excessive appetite.

vórtice *m.* vortex, spiral-shaped structure.

voyeur *Fr.* voyeur, one who practices voyeurism.

voyeurismo *m.* voyeurism, sexual perversion by which erotic gratification is derived from watching sexual organs or activity.

voz *f.* voice.

vozarrón *m.* strong, deep voice.

vuelo *m.* flight; trajectory.

vuelta *f.* turning; turn; rotation; **media** ___ / about-face; *v.* **dar una** ___ / to take a stroll, ride, or walk; *v.* **estar de** ___ / to be back.

vulnerable *a.* vulnerable, prone to injury or disease.

vulva *f.* vulva, external female organ.

vulvar *a.* vulval, vulvar, rel. to the vulva.

vulvectomía *f. surg.* vulvectomy, excision of the vulva.

vulvitis *f.* vulvitis, infl. of the vulva.

vulvovaginal *a.* vulvovaginal, rel. to the vulva and the vagina.

Waldeyer, anillo de *m.* Waldeyer's ring, the ring of lymphatic tissue that consists of the palatine, lingual, and pharyngeal tonsils.

Waller, degeneración de *f.* Wallerian degeneration, degeneration of nerve fibers that have been separated from their center of nutrition.

warfarina *f.* warfarin, generic name for Coumadine, anticoagulant used in the prevention of thrombosis and infarcts.

Wasserman, reacción de *f.* Wasserman reaction, serological test for syphilis.

Western Blot *m.* Western Blot, immunoblot, test to confirm HIV infection in patients with evidence of exposure to HIV by a previous enzyme-linked immunosorbent assay (ELISA).

Wharton, conducto de *m.* Wharton's duct, excretory duct of the submandibular gland.

Whipple, enfermedad de *f.* Whipple's disease, rare disease caused by deposit of lipids in the lymphatic and intestinal tissues.

Wilms, tumor de *m.* Wilms tumor, rapidly developing neoplasm of the kidney, seen esp. in children.

Wilson, enfermedad de *f.* Wilson's disease, hereditary disease manifested by severe hepatic and cerebral disorders.

xantina *f.* xanthin, one of a group of stimulants of the central nervous system and the heart, such as caffeine.

xantocromía *f.* xanthochromia, yellowish discoloration as seen in skin patches or in the cerebrospinal fluid.

xantocrómico-a *a.* xanthochromic, having a yellowish appearance or rel. to xanthochromia.

xantoderma *m.* xanthoderma, yellowish coloration of the skin.

xantoma *m.* xanthoma, condition characterized by the presence of yellowish plaques or nodules in the skin, gen. due to deposit of lipids.

xantosis *f.* xanthosis, yellowing of the skin due to excessive ingestion of foods such as carrots and egg yolks.

xenofobia *f.* xenophobia, morbid fear or aversion to anything foreign.

xenoinjerto *m.* xenograft; **rechazo de __ / __** rejection. *V.* **heteroinjerto.**

xenón *m.* xenon, a dense, colorless element found in small amounts in the atmosphere.

xenotransplante *m.* xenotransplant, the act of transplanting an organ, tissue, or part from one species to another.

xerodermia *f.* xeroderma, xerosis, excessively dry skin.

xeroftalmía *f.* xerophthalmia, dryness of the conjunctiva due to lack of vitamin A.

xerografía *f.* xerography. *V.* **xerorradiografía.**

xeromamografía *f.* xeromammography, xerodiography of the breast.

xerorradiografía *f.* xeroradiography, dry process of registering electrostatic images by the use of metal plates covered with a substance such as selenium.

xerosis *f.* xerosis, abnormal dryness as seen in the skin, eyes, and mucous membranes.

xerostomía *f.* xerostomia, abnormal dryness of the mouth due to deficiency of salivary secretion.

xifoide, xifoideo-a *a.* xiphoid, shaped like a sword, as the xiphoid process.

xifoides, apéndice *m.* xiphoid process, cartilaginous, sword-shaped formation joined to the lowest portion of the sternum.

y *conj.* and.

ya *adv.* already; ___ **que** / as long as.

yarda *f.* yard.

yatrogénico-a, yatrógeno-a *a.* iatrogenic, rel. to the adverse condition of a patient resulting from an erroneous medical treatment or procedure.

yaws *m.* yaws. V. **frambesia.**

yema *f.* yolk. 1. the yolk of the egg of a bird; 2. contents of the ovum that supply the embryo.

yerbabuena, hierbabuena *f.* peppermint.

yerno *m.* son-in-law.

yeso *m.* plaster, plaster cast.

yeyunal *a.* jejunal, rel. to the jejunum.

yeyunectomía *f. surg.* jejunectomy, excision of part or all of the jejunum.

yeyuno *m.* jejunum, portion of the small intestine that extends from the duodenum to the ileum.

yeyunostomía *f. surg.* jejunostomy, permanent opening in the jejunum through the abdominal wall.

yo *m.* self, [*el yo*] the ego, Freudian term that refers to the part of the psyche that mediates between the person and reality; *gr. pron.* I.

yodismo *m.* iodism, poisoning by iodine.

yodo *m.* iodine, nonmetallic element used in medications, esp. those that stimulate the function and development of the thyroid gland and the prevention of goiter; **prueba radiactiva del** ___ / radioactive ___ excretion test, used for evaluating the function of the thyroid gland.

yodurar *v.* to iodize, to treat with iodine.

yoga *m.* yoga, Hindu system of beliefs and practices by which the individual tries to reach the union of self with a universal self through contemplation, meditation, and self-control.

yogurt *m.* yogurt, milk that is fermented by the action of *Lactobacillus bulgaricus* and to which nutritive and therapeutic value is attributed.

yugular *a.* jugular, rel. to the throat; **venas** ___**-es** / ___ veins, veins that carry blood from the cranium, the face, and the neck to the heart.

yuxtaglomerular *a.* juxtaglomerular, close to a glomerulus; **aparato** ___ / ___ apparatus; group of cells that participate in the production of renin and in the metabolism of sodium situated around arterioles leading to a glomerulus of the kidney.

yuxtaponer *vi.* to juxtapose, to put next to.

yuxtaposición *f.* juxtaposition, a position that is adjacent or side by side to another.

z *abr.* **zona** / zone.

zambo-a *a.* bandy-legged; bow-legged.

zanahoria *f.* carrot.

zinc, cinc *m.* zinc, crystalline metallic chemical element with astringent properties; **pomada de ___** / **___** ointment.

Zollinger-Ellison, síndrome de *m.* Zollinger-Ellison syndrome, manifested by gastric hypersecretion and hyperacidity and by peptic ulceration of the stomach and small intestine.

zona *f.* 1. zona, a specific area or layer; 2. zoster; 3. zone, a belt-like anatomical structure.

zona desencadenante *f.* trigger zone, a sensitive area of the body that triggers a reaction in a different part of the body on stimulation.

zooinjerto *m.* zoograft, graft from an animal.

zoster *f.* zoster, *pop.* shingles. *V.* **herpes zoster.**

zumbar *v.* to hum, to buzz, to ring.

zumbido *m.* hum, buzz.

Gramática inglesa simplificada

Simplified English Grammar

El alfabeto / The Alphabet

A diferencia del español, en el que cada letra tiene un sonido más o menos definido, en inglés una misma letra puede tener más de una pronunciación de acuerdo con su posición en la sílaba. Esa variación establece la diferencia fundamental en la pronunciación de los dos idiomas y la mayor dificultad que la persona hispanoparlante confronta al tratar de aprender la pronunciación de la lengua inglesa. La mayoría de los textos lingüísticos recurren al uso de algún alfabeto fonético que sirve de clave para la pronunciación del inglés y cuyo uso recomendamos al estudiante que quiera perfeccionar la pronunciación. Para los efectos de este diccionario nos hemos limitado a dar una sencilla orientación que ayude al lector a pronunciar aquellas letras y sonidos que más difieren de la correspondiente pronunciación en español y que, por lo tanto, presentan mayor dificultad al hispanoparlante. Debemos señalar que esta presentación simplificada de las letras en inglés no abarca todas las posibilidades; las excepciones a las reglas generales son muy numerosas.

El alfabeto inglés tiene veintiséis letras: cinco vocales y veintiuna consonantes. La letra **y**, como en español, puede ser vocal (se pronuncia como la **i** en español) o consonante (se pronuncia como la **y** en *ya*).

El alfabeto

Letra	Pronunciación aproximada
A	ei
B	bi
C	si
D	di
E	i
F	ef
G	yi (*sonido africado como la* **j** *de Jean en francés*)
H	eich
I	ai
J	yei (*sonido africado*)
K	quei
L	el
M	em
N	en
O	ou
P	pi
Q	quiu
R	ar
S	es
T	ti
U	iu
V	vi
W	doblyu
X	ecs
Y	uai
Z	zi (*sonido parecido a la* **s** *en mismo o desde*)

La pronunciación del inglés / English Pronunciation

Vocales

Las vocales en inglés tienen generalmente dos sonidos, uno breve o corto y otro largo. La **e** puede además ser muda al final de la palabra.

Sonido breve o corto: Ocurre generalmente cuando la vocal es seguida por una consonante en la misma sílaba.

211

Letra	Palabra en inglés	Sonido aproximado en español
a	nap / siesta	sonido intermedio entre la a de mano y la e de pesa.
	call / llamada	boca (gen. en palabras que terminan en ll).
e	bed / cama	frente.
	late / tarde	muda (gen. ocurre al final de la palabra).
i	chill / enfriamiento	sonido intermedio entre la i y la e en español.
o	compare / comparar	comparar
	hot / caliente	sonido intermedio entre la a y la o en español.
	move / mover	cura
u	drug / droga	sonido intermedio entre la o y la u en español.
	full / lleno	tú

Sonido largo: Ocurre generalmente cuando la vocal es la vocal final de una sílaba o cuando va seguida de una e muda o de una e muda y una consonante. Es un sonido vocálico demorado en el cual algunas veces una vocal sencilla tiene un sonido diptongado.

a	basic / básico	ley
e	he / él	sí
i	bite / picadura	hay
o	dose / dosis	sonido equivalente al sonido del diptongo ou en español.
oo	blood / sangre	poro
	book / libro	cura
u	putrid / pútrido	ciudad, la combinación

Diptongos

ew: Sonido en inglés corresponde al sonido iu:

few / varios.   ciudad

ou: Sonido semejante al diptongo au en español o sonido breve semejante a la o en español:

mouth / boca   causa
bought / compró   dosis

Consonantes

El alfabeto en inglés tiene dos consonantes que casi no se usan en español, la k y la w; la ñ, en cambio, no existe en el alfabeto inglés y las letras ch, ll, y rr no se consideran caracteres propios, sino combinación de dos letras (letra dígrafa). En general, la pronunciación de la mayoría de las consonantes es semejante en ambos idiomas, aunque en inglés la pronunciación de las mismas es más explosiva.

Consonantes y letras dígrafas que más difieren de la pronunciación española

b Sonido semejante a la b inicial en español; es muda en algunas palabras cuando precede a la letra t.

Sonido aproximado en español
bacillus / bacilo   bacilo
doubt / duda   (muda)

ch Presenta varios sonidos según su posición en la palabra.

child / niño   chico
cholera / cólera   cólera
machine / máquina   shshsh! (*semejante al sonido que se emplea para indicar silencio*)

g Cuando le sigue una e o una i tiene un sonido semejante a la y en español (*sonido suave*). Esta regla tiene por excepción las palabras monosílabas:

general / general   yeso (*sonido africado*)
giant / gigante   yeso (*sonido africado*)
girl / muchacha   gota

212

En casi todas las otras situaciones, tiene el mismo sonido que la **g** fuerte en español.

gastric / gástrico   gástrico
gram / gramo   gramo
guide / guía   guía

gh   En medio de la palabra, esta combinación de letras es generalmente muda.

daughter / hija

h   Sonido aproximado al de la **j** en español, pero algo más suave.

hemorrhage / hemorragia   jarabe

j   Sonido semejante a la **y** en español.

jejunum / yeyuno   yeyuno (*con africación*)

ll   Sonido igual al de la **l** sencilla.

generally / generalmente   generalmente

kn   La **k** es muda.

knee / rodilla   nuez

mm   Sonido igual a la **m** simple.

immunology / inmunología   ameba

ph   Sonido de **f**.

pharmacy / farmacia   farmacia

r   Sonido articulado en inglés sin trino y con la lengua situada más hacia atrás de la boca y la parte anterior curvada hacia el paladar sin tocarlo.

surgery / cirugía   cirugía

rr   Sonido igual al del la **r** sencilla.

hemorrhage / hemorragia   cirugía

s   Sonido semejante a la **s** sorda en español en la mayoría de los vocablos.

consult / consultar   consulta
sperm / esperma   esperma

Sonido semejante a la **s** sonora de mismo o desde cuando está entre vocales o antes de la consonante **m**.

disease / enfermedad   mismo
metabolism / metabolismo desde

Al final de la palabra, puede tener sonido de **s** o de **z** en inglés.

yes / sí   sí
is / es   (*sonido de z en inglés*)

Cuando está seguida del diptongo **io**, tiene sonido semejante al de la **y** (*sonido de consonante*), muy exagerado, o al de la **j** en francés como en Jean.

213

lesion / lesión   leyó

Cuando está seguida de la vocal **u,** tiene un sonido semejante a la **sh** en inglés.

sure / seguro   **sh**shsh (*como cuando se está silenciando a alguien*)

ss   Sonido igual al de la **s** en español.

class / clase   cla**s**e

th   Tiene dos sonidos: (1) parecido a la **d;** (2) parecido a la **z** castellana.

this / este   **d**e**d**o
therapy / terapia   **z**apato (*con ceceo castellano*)

w   Sonido semejante al de la **u** en español como en la palabra h**u**eso.

weight / peso   h**u**eso

z   Sonido semejante al que se hace para imitar el zumbido de una abeja.

zero / cero   **zz**zz . . .

Acentuación de las palabras en inglés

El acento gráfico no existe en inglés. Las reglas a seguir son pocas, pero tienen muchas excepciones.

   1. Las palabras de dos sílabas se acentúan generalmente en la penúltima sílaba:

swollen / hinchado
abscess / abceso

   2. Palabras a las que se le hayan añadido sufijos o prefijos retienen el acento en la misma sílaba acentuada de la raíz o palabra básica:

normal: abnormal / anormal

coloration: discoloration / descoloración

   3. Palabras de tres o más sílabas generalmente tienen una sílaba que se acentúa más enfáticamente y otra sílaba que lleva un acento menos pronunciado:

cartilaginous / cartilaginoso

El nombre o sustantivo / The Noun

Género / Gender

Los nombres o sustantivos en inglés se clasifican en masculinos, femeninos y neutros. El género de cosas inanimadas es generalmente neutro.

Femenino   nombre de mujer o animal hembra
               la mujer / **the woman**
Masculino   nombre de hombre o animal varón
               el hombre / **the man**
Neutro   nombres de cosas, concretas o abstractas
               la inyección / **the shot**   el dolor / **the pain**

   En ciertos nombres se distingue el género por medio de las palabras: hembra / **female,** varón / **male,** o por niño / **boy** y niña / **girl.**

214

enfermera / **female nurse**   enfermero / **male nurse**
bebita / **baby girl**   bebito / **baby boy**

Note: En este diccionario se ha incorporado la palabra **person** / persona a palabras como **chairman**, cambiada a **chairperson**, para evitar el uso exclusivo del masculino en nombres que pueden referirse al sexo masculino o femenino.

Número / Number

El plural de los nombres

Añada **-s** para formar el plural de la mayor parte de los nombres.

síntoma / **symptom**   síntomas / **symptoms**

Añada **-es** si la palabra termina en **ch, h, sh, ss, x,** u **o.**

punto quirúrgico / **stitch**   puntos quirúrgicos / **stitches**
fogaje / **hot flash**   fogajes / **hot flashes**
absceso / **abscess**   abscesos / **abscesses**
reflejo / **reflex**   reflejos / **reflexes**
mosquito / **mosquito**   mosquitos / **mosquitoes**

Añada **-es** si la palabra termina en **y;** cambie la **y** por **i.**

deformidad / **deformity**   deformidades / **deformities**

Añada **-es** si la palabra termina en **f** o **fe;** cambie la **f** por **v.**

vida / **life**   vidas / **lives**
hoja / **leaf**   hojas / **leaves**

Plurales irregulares más comunes en inglés / Most Common Irregular Plurals in English

Singular	*Plural*	*Singular*	*Plural*
diente / **tooth**	dientes / **teeth**	hombre / **man**	hombres / **men**
mujer / **woman**	mujeres / **women**	niño / **child**	niños / **children**
pie / **foot**	pies / **feet**	piojo / **louse**	piojos / **lice**
ratón / **mouse**	ratones / **mice**		

El caso posesivo de los nombres

El caso posesivo de los nombres en inglés se forma invirtiendo el orden del caso posesivo en español.

Poseedor + ' (apóstrofe) + **s** + nombre de lo que posee

la enfermedad de la mujer / **the woman's illness**

Los nombres que terminan en **-s** y los nombres plurales añaden solamente un apóstrofe al final de la palabra.

215

> Poseedor + ' (apóstrofe) + nombre de lo que posee

la opinión de los doctores / **the doctors' opinion**

Comparativo de igualdad de los nombres

> Singular: **as much** + nombre + **as**

Ella tiene tanta fiebre hoy como ayer. / **She has as much fever today as yesterday.**

> Plural: **as many** + nombre + **as**

Ella tiene tantos síntomas hoy como ayer. / **She has as many symptoms today as yesterday.**

El artículo / The Article

Los articulos en inglés son invariables en género y número.

El artículo definido / The Definite Article

| el, la, los, las / **the** | el hospital / **the hospital**
la medicina / **the medicine**
los riñones / **the kidneys**
las recetas / **the prescriptions** |

El artículo definido se omite en inglés cuando:

1. el sustantivo es un nombre común que expresa una idea general.

    una vacuna contra la difteria / a vaccine against diptheria

2. precede a los títulos de Sr., Sra. y Srta., o a cargos dignatarios o profesionales.

    el Sr. Jones / **Mr. Jones**   el Dr. Jones / **Dr. Jones**

El artículo indefinido / The Indefinite Article

| un, una / **a** | una píldora / **a pill**
un laboratorio / **a laboratory**
una unión / **a union**
un eufemismo / **a euphemism** |

| un, una / **an** | una hora / **an hour**
un accidente / **an accident** |

1. **a:** Se emplea delante de las palabras que empiezan con consonante o con la vocal **u**, o el diptongo **eu** cuando éste se pronuncia como la letra **y.**
2. **an:** Se emplea delante de palabras que empiezan con una vocal o una **h** muda.

Usos del artículo indefinido

1. Con nombres que designan el empleo o la profesión después del verbo **to be.**

Ella es enfermera. / **She is a nurse.**

2. En generalizaciones sobre especies o clases precediendo a un nombre en singular; si el nombre está en plural el artículo se omite.

El mosquito puede transmitir enfermedades. / **A mosquito can transmit disease.**
Los antibióticos son indispensables. / **Antibiotics are indispensable.**

Nota: El plural del artículo indefinido **unos, unas,** se traduce al inglés **some:**

unas indicaciones preventivas / **some preventive indications**
unos procedimientos quirúrgicos / **some surgical procedures**

El adjetivo y el adverbio / The Adjective and the Adverb

Los adjetivos en inglés generalmente preceden al nombre y son invariables en género y número. Los adjetivos demostrativos son una excepcion a esta regla, ya que cambian del singular al plural de acuerdo con el nombre que modifican.

Formación del adverbio / How Adverbs Are Formed

1. Los adverbios de modo que en español terminan generalmente en **-mente,** se forman en inglés añadiendo la terminación **-ly** al adjetivo.

   frecuente / **frequent**   frecuentemente / **frequently**

2. Si el adjetivo en inglés termina en **-ble,** la **e** se convierte en **y.**

   posible / **possible**   posiblemente / **possibly**

3. Si el adjetivo en inglés termina en **-ic,** el adverbio se forma añadiendo la terminación **-ally:**

   crónico / **chronic**   crónicamente / **chronically**

Comparación de los adjetivos y adverbios / Comparative Forms of Adjectives and Adverbs

Tanto los adjetivos como los adverbios admiten grados de comparación.

1. Los monosílabos y algunos bisílabos cortos añaden la terminación **-er** y **-est** a la forma positiva:

a. frío / **cold** más frío / **colder** (el) (la) más frío-a / **the coldest**
adv. despacio / **slow** más despacio / **slower** más despacio / **slowest**

2. Palabras que terminan en **-y** cambian la **-y** en **i** y añaden **-er** y **-est** para formar el comparativo y el superlativo, respectivamente:

a. contento-a / **happy** más contento-a / **happier** (el) (la) más contento-a / **the happiest**
adv. temprano / **early** más temprano / **earlier** más temprano / **earliest**

3. El resto de los adjetivos y adverbios forman el comparativo de superioridad y el superlativo anteponiendo las palabras **more** y **most.**

a. doloroso-a / **painful** más doloroso-a / **more painful** (el) (la) más doloroso-a / **the most painful**
adv. frecuentemente / **frequently** más frecuentemente / **more frequently** más frecuentemente / **most frequently**

4. El comparativo y el superlativo de inferioridad se forma anteponiendo las palabras **less** y **least.**

a. contagioso-a / **contagious**   menos contagioso-a / **less contagious**   (el) (la) menos contagioso-a / **the least contagious**

adv. frecuentemente / **frequently**   menos frecuentemente / **less frequently**   menos frecuentemente / **least frequently**

5. El comparativo de igualdad se forma usando la palabra **as** antes y después del adjetivo y del adverbio.

as + adjetivo + **as**	tan infeccioso como / **as infectious as**
as + adverbio + **as**	tan temprano como / **as early as**

Adjetivos comunes con comparativos y superlativos irregulares

malo / **bad**	peor / **worse**	(el) (la) peor / **the worst**
bueno / **good**	mejor / **better**	(el) (la) mejor / **the best**
poco / **little**	menos / **less**	(el) (la) menos / **the least**
mucho / **much, many**	más / **more**	(el) (la) más / **the most**

Adverbios comunes con comparativos y superlativos irregulares

lejos / **far**	más lejos / **farther**	más lejos / **farthest**
poco / **little**	menos / **less**	menos / **least**
much / **mucho**	más / **more**	más / **most**
bien / **well**	mejor / **better**	mejor / **best**

Pronombres y adjetivos / Pronouns and Adjectives

Pronombres personales / Subject Pronouns

1. Los pronombres personales nominativos, es decir, los que sirven de sujeto, nunca se omiten en inglés:

(Yo) Tengo dolor / **I have a pain; I am in pain.**

El pronombre **I** (yo) siempre se escribe con mayúscula en inglés.

Pronombres personales / Subject Pronouns		
Persona	*Singular*	*Plural*
1a.	I	we
2a.	you	you
3a. (*m.*)	he	they
3a. (*f.*)	she	they
3a. (*neut.*)	it	they

2. El pronombre (objeto directo) siempre precede al pronombre (objeto indirecto). El pronombre que actúa de objeto indirecto va precedido por la preposición (**to, from, for, of**).

Me las dio. / She gave **them to me.**

Cuando el objeto directo es un nombre y el objeto indirecto es un pronombre, el pronombre precede al objeto directo.

La enfermera me dio las instrucciones / The nurse gave **me the instructions.**

218

Pronombres como complemento		
Persona	*Singular*	*Plural*
1a.	me	us
2a.	you	you
3a. (*m.*)	him	them
3a. (*f.*)	her	them
3a. (*neut.*)	it	them

3. Además de actuar como sujeto o complemento, el pronombre personal en inglés puede también ser reflexivo cuando el complemento es la misma persona que el sujeto:

Él **se** curó a **sí** mismo. / He cured **himself.**

Pronombres reflexivos		
Persona	*Singular*	*Plural*
1a.	myself	ourselves
2a.	yourself	yourselves
3a. (*m.*)	himself	themselves
3a. (*f.*)	herself	themselves
3a. (*neut.*)	itself	themselves

Pronombres y adjetivos demostrativos / Demonstrative Pronouns and Adjectives

Los demostrativos son los únicos adjetivos que cambian del singular al plural de acuerdo con el número del nombre que modifican.

Adjetivos demostrativos	
este, esta	**this**
estos, estas	**these**
ese, esa	**that**
aquel, aquella	
esos, esas	**those**
aquellos, aquellas	

esta enfermedad / **this disease**
estas enfermedades / **these diseases**
esa pastilla / **that pill**
aquellos casos / **those cases**

Pronombres demostrativos	
éste, ésta, esto	**this one, this**
éstos, éstas	**these**
ése, ésa, eso	**that one, that**
aquél, aquélla, aquello	
ésos, ésas	**those**
aquéllos, aquéllas	

Tome ésta. / **Take this one.**
Tome éstas. / **Take these.**

219

Ese es mejor. / **That one is better.**
Es aquélla. / **It is that one.**

Pronombres y adjetivos posesivos / Possessive Adjectives and Pronouns

Persona		Adjetivo	Pronombre
Sing.	1a.	my	mine
	2a.	your	yours
	3a. (*m.*)	his	his
	3a. (*f.*)	her	hers
	3a. (*neut.*)	its	its
Plur.	1a.	our	ours
	2a.	your	yours
	3a.	their	theirs

mi paciente / **my patient**
sus síntomas / **her symptoms**
La medicina es mía. / **The medicine is mine.**
El problema es nuestro. / **The problem is ours.**

Nota: En inglés el adjetivo posesivo se emplea con las partes del cuerpo:

Me lastimé el brazo. / **I hurt my arm.**

Pronombres y adjetivos interrogativos / Interrogative Adjectives and Pronouns

Interrogativos / Interrogatives	
¿quién?, ¿quiénes?	**who?**
¿de quién?, ¿de quiénes?	**whose?**
¿a quién?, ¿a quiénes?	**whom?**
¿qué?, ¿cuál?, ¿cuáles?	**which, what?**

¿Quién está enfermo? / **Who is ill?**
¿De quién es la receta? / **Whose is the prescription?**
¿A quién vio ella? / **Whom did she see?**
¿Qué medicina prefiere? / **Which medicine do you prefer?**
¿Qué recomendó el doctor? / **What did the doctor recommend?**
¿Cuál recomendó el doctor? / **Which did the doctor recommend?**
De esos antibióticos, ¿cuáles prefiere? / **Of those antibiotics, which do you prefer?**

Pronombres relativos / Relative Pronouns

que, el cual, la cual, el que, la que, lo que, los que, las que	**that**
que, quien, el cual, la cual, el que, etc.	**which**
quien, que, el cual, la cual, etc.	**who**
que, quien, el cual, la cual, etc.	**whom**
de quien, cuyo, del cual, de la cual, etc.	**whose**

el jarabe que (ella) tomó / **the cough syrup that she took**
la medicina que se recetó / **the medicine which was prescribed**

el paciente que está esperando / **the patient who is waiting**
el paciente que (a quien) la enfermera atiende / **the patient whom the nurse is helping**
el paciente cuya radiografía necesita el doctor / **the patient whose x-rays the doctor needs**

Nota: Las terminaciones **-ever** y **-soever** se añaden a **who, which,** y **what** para formar los pronombres relativos compuestos **whoever** / quienquiera, **whichever** / cualquiera y **whatever** / quienquiera o cualquiera.

Pronombres y adjetivos indefinidos más comunes / Most Common Indefinite Adjectives and Pronouns

all	todo	**many**	muchos
another	otro	**nobody**	nadie
any	cualquiera	**none**	ninguno
anybody	cualquiera	**no one**	nadie
anyone	cualquiera	**nothing**	nada
anything	cualquier cosa, algo	**one**	uno-a
both	ambos, ambas	**other**	otro-a
each (one)	cada (uno), cada cual	**some**	algunos
everybody	todos	**somebody**	alguien
everyone	todos	**someone**	alguien
everything	todo	**something**	algo
few	pocos		
a few	unos pocos		

El verbo / The Verb

Formas del verbo / Forms of the Verb

Infinitivo	*Pasado*	*Participio*	*Gerundio*
curar / to heal	healed	healed	healing
comer / to eat	ate	ate	eating

Infinitivo / Infinitive El verbo precedido de la preposición **to:**

examiner / **to examine**

Presente / Present La misma forma verbal del infinitivo sin la preposición **to** precedida del pronombre correspondiente:

yo examino / **I examine** nosotros examinamos / **we examine**

Pasado / Past El infinitivo + la terminación **-d** o **-ed**

yo examiné / **I examined** nosotros examinamos / **we examined**

Participio pasado / Past Participle La misma forma verbal que el pasado:

examinado / **examined**

Participio de presente / Present Participle El infinitivo + **-ing**

examinando / **examining**

Nota: Para formar el pasado o el participio de verbos regulares se añade la terminación **-ed** al infinitivo. Las variaciones a esta regla son las siguientes.

a. Si el infinitivo termina en **e,** se añade **-d** (die, die**d**).
b. Si el infinitivo termina en la letra **y** precedida de una consónante, se cambia la **y** por **i** antes de añadir **-ed** (try, tri**ed**).

221

c. Si el infinitivo termina en consonante precedida de una vocal y la sílaba final lleva el énfasis, se dobla la consonante antes de añadir -ed (permit, permitted).

Nota: Para formar el gerundio se añade la terminación **-ing** al infinitivo. Las variaciones a esta regla son las siguientes.

a. Si el infinitivo termina en **-e** precedida de una consonante, la **e** se pierde antes de añadir la terminación **-ing** (arise, arising).
b. Si el infinitivo termina en **ie**, la **ie** se sustituye por la letra **y** antes de añadir **-ing** (lie, lying).
c. En algunos verbos se dobla la consonante antes de añadir **-ing** si la sílaba final del infinitivo lleva el énfasis (spit, spitting), excepto en verbos terminados en **h, w**, e **y**, los cuales no doblan la consonante al formar el gerundio.

Tiempos del verbo / Tenses of the Verb

Tiempos simples / Simple Tenses

To cough / Toser

Presente / Present	yo toso / **I cough**
Pasado (pretérito e imperfecto) / Past	yo tosí, tosía / **I coughed**
Futuro / Future	yo toseré / **I will, shall cough**

El imperfecto se traduce al inglés con las formas **used to** o **would** para indicar una acción repetida indefinidamente o habitualmente en el pasado.

Yo tomaba la medicina todos los días. / **I used to take the medicine every day.**

El futuro de todas las personas se forma con el verbo auxiliar **will** o **shall,** que precede a la forma del verbo en todos los tiempos.

Tomaré la medicina. / **I will take the medicine.**

Tiempos compuestos / Compound Tenses

Los tiempos compuestos se forman con el verbo auxiliar haber / **to have.** (Véase la conjugación del verbo **to have** al final de la explicación del verbo.)

Perfecto / Present perfect	yo he tosido / **I have coughed**
Pluscuamperfecto / Past perfect	yo había, hube tosido / **I had coughed**
Futuro anterior / Future perfect	yo habré tosido / **I will, I shall have coughed**

Nota: Además de los seis tiempos indicados, todos los verbos tienen una forma progresiva que indica una acción continuada dentro de la configuración del tiempo a que se refieren. Se forma con el verbo auxiliar estar / **to be** seguido del participio presente (gerundio). (Véase la conjugación del verbo **to be** al final de la explicación del verbo.)

Presente	yo estoy tosiendo / **I am coughing**
Pasado	yo estaba, estuve tosiendo / **I was coughing**
Futuro	yo estaré tosiendo / **I will, shall be coughing**
Perfecto	yo he estado tosiendo / **I have been coughing**
Pluscuamperfecto	yo había, hube estado tosiendo / **I had been coughing**
Futuro anterior	yo habré estado tosiendo / **I will, shall have been coughing**

Modos del verbo / Moods of the Verb

Indicativo / Indicative

Yo toso / **I cough.**

La oración interrogativa, negativa y enfática se forma con el verbo auxiliar **to do.** (Véase la conjugación del verbo al final de la explicación del verbo.)

Interrogación	¿Tose usted por las mañanas? / **Do** you cough in the morning?
Negación	No toso durante el día. / I **do** not cough during the day.
Énfasis	Toso mucho por las noches. / I **do** cough a lot at night.

Nota: El verbo **to do** también se emplea para dar énfasis a la respuesta de sí o no a una pregunta:

¿Tose mucho? / **Do you cough much?**   **Yes, I do.**
                                           No, I do not.

Imperativo / Imperative

Tosa, por favor. / **Cough please.**

Conjugación de un verbo regular

preparar / **to prepare**

| *Infinitivo* | *Participio* | *Gerundio* |
| preparar / **to prepare** | preparado / **prepared** | preparando / **preparing** |

Indicativo

Presente / Present
yo preparo / **I prepare**
Ud. prepara, tú preparas / **you prepare**
él, ella prepara / **he, she, it prepares**

nosotros preparamos / **we prepare**
vosotros preparáis, ustedes preparan / **you prepare**
ellos, ellas preparan / **they prepare**

Pretérito e Imperfecto / Past
preparé, preparaba / **I prepared**
preparó, preparaba, preparaste,
  preparabas / **you prepared**
preparó, preparaba / **he, she, it, prepared**

preparamos, preparábamos / **we prepared**
prepararon, preparaban, preparasteis,
  preparabais / **you prepared**
prepararon, preparaban / **they prepared**

Futuro / Future
prepararé / **I will, shall prepare**
preparará, prepararás / **you will prepare**
preparará / **he, she, it will prepare**

prepararemos / **we will, shall prepare**
prepararéis, prepararán / **you will prepare**
prepararán / **they will prepare**

Perfecto / Perfect
he preparado / **I have prepared**
ha preparado, has preparado / **you have
  prepared**
ha preparado / **he, she, it has prepared**

hemos preparado / **we have prepared**
habéis, han preparado / **you have prepared**
han preparado / **they have prepared**

Pluscuamperfecto / Past perfect
había preparado / **I had prepared**
había, habías preparado / **you had
  prepared**
había preparado / **he, she, it had prepared**

habíamos preparado / **we had prepared**
habíais, habían preparado / **you had prepared**
habían preparado / **they had prepared**

Futuro anterior / Future perfect
habré preparado / **I will, shall have
  prepared**
habrá, habrás preparado / **you will have
  prepared**
habrá preparado / **he, she, it will have
  prepared**

habremos preparado / **we will, shall have prepared**
habréis, habrán preparado / **you will have
  prepared**
habrán preparado / **they will have prepared**

Imperativo

prepara (tú), prepare (usted), preparad
  (vosotros), preparen (ustedes, ellos)
preparemos (nosotros)

prepare

let's prepare

223

En inglés no existe la distinción entre el **tú** familiar y el **usted** formal. La segunda persona del singular es siempre **you.** La segunda persona del plural (**vosotros** y **ustedes**) tiene igualmente una sola forma, que se traduce también como **you.**

La tercera persona singular del presente es la única forma verbal que difiere de las demás al tomar la terminación **-s.** Las excepciones a esta regla son las siguientes:

a. Si el verbo en el infinitivo termina en **-s, -x, -z, -ch,** o **-sh,** se añade **-es.**
   alcanzar / **to reach;** he, she, it **reaches.**
b. Si el verbo termina en **-z** precedida por una sola vocal, la **z** se dobla y se añade **-es.**
   preguntar / **to quiz;** he, she, it **quizzes.**
c. Si el verbo termina en **y** precedida de consonante, la **y** cambia a **i** y se añade **-es.**
   llevar / **to carry;** he, she, it **carries.**

Conjugación de los verbos auxiliares / Conjugation of Auxiliary Verbs

haber / **to have**

Infinitivo	Participio	Gerundio
haber / **to have**	habido / **had**	habiendo / **having**

Indicativo

Presente / Present
yo he / **I have**   nosotros hemos / **we have**
Ud. ha, tú has / **you have**   vosotros habéis, ustedes han / **you have**
él, ella ha / **he, she, it has**   ellos han / **they have**

Pretérito e Imperfecto / Past
hube, había / **I had**   hubimos, habíamos / **we had**
hubo, había, hubiste, habías / **you had**   hubisteis, habíais, hubieron, habían / **you had**
hubo, había / **he, she, it had**   hubieron, habían / **they had**

Futuro / Future
habré / **I will, shall have**   habremos / **we will, shall have**
habrá, habrás / **you will, have**   habréis, habrán / **you will, have**
habrá / **he, she, it will, have**   habrán / **they will, have**

Nota: Para formar los tiempos compuestos se añade el participio de pasado **had** a las formas simples: **I have had, I had had, I will, shall have had.**

ser, estar / **to be**

Infinitivo	Participio	Gerundio
ser / **to be**	sido / **been**	siendo / **being**

Presente / Present
yo soy / **I am**   nosotros somos / **we are**
Ud. es, tú eres / **you are**   vosotros sois, ustedes son / **you are**
él, ella es / **he, she, it is**   ellos, ellas son / **they are**

Pretérito e Imperfecto / Past
fui, era / **I was**   fuimos, éramos / **we were**
fue, era, fuiste, eras / **you were**   fuisteis, erais, fueron, eran / **you were**
fue, era / **he, she, it was**   fueron, eran / **they were**

Futuro / Future
seré / **I will, shall be**   seremos / **we will, shall be**
será, serás / **you will be**   seréis, serán / **you will, be**
será / **he, she, it will, be**   serán / **they will, be**

Nota Para formar los tiempos compuestos se usan las formas simples del verbo auxiliar **to have** y el participio de **to be: been. I have been; I had been; I will, shall have been.**

hacer / **to do**

El verbo **to do** no existe como verbo auxiliar en español; por lo tanto, las formas **do, does** y **did** en oraciones interrogativas, negativas y enfáticas no tienen traducción al español.

Infinitivo	*Participio*	*Gerundio*
hacer / **to do**	hecho / **done**	haciendo / **doing**

Presente / Present

yo hago / **I do**	nosotros hacemos / **we do**
Ud. hace, tú haces / **you do**	vosotros hacéis, ustedes hacen / **you do**
él, ella hace / **he, she, it does**	ellos, ellas hacen / **they do**

Pretérito e Imperfecto / Past

hice, hacía / **I did**	hicimos, hacíamos / **we did**
hiciste, hacías / **you did**	hicisteis, hacíais, hicieron, hacían / **you did**
hizo, hacía / **he, she, it did**	hicieron, hacían / **they did**

Futuro / Future

haré / **I will, shall do**	haremos / **we will, shall do**
hará, harás / **you will do**	haréis, harán / **you will do**
hará / **he, she, it will do**	harán / **they will do**

Nota: Para formar los tiempos compuestos se usan las formas simples del verbo auxiliar **to have** y el participio de **to do, done: I have done, I had done, I will, shall have done.**

Imperativo / Imperative

haz (tú), haga (usted), haced (vosotros), hagan (ustedes, ellos)	**do**
hagamos (nosotros)	**let us do**

Subjuntivo / Subjunctive

El modo subjuntivo se emplea en inglés con mucha menos frecuencia que en español, y para los efectos de este diccionario, no lo hemos incluido.

Verbos de participio y pretínte irregulares / Verbs with an Irregular Preterit and/or Past Participle

Infinitivo / Infinitive	*Pretérito / Preterit*	*Participio pasado / Past Participle*
to arise / levantarse, surgir	arose	arisen
to awake / despertarse	awoke	awoke, awoken
to be / ser, estar	was, were	been
to become / volverse, hacerse	became	become
to begin / empezar	began	begun
to bend / inclinarse, doblarse	bent	bent
to bite / morder	bit	bit, bitten
to bleed / sangrar	bled	bled
to blow / soplar	blew	blown
to break / romper; quebrar	broke	broken
to bring / traer	brought	brought
to build / construir	built	built
to burn / quemar	burnt, burned	burnt, burned
to burst / reventar	burst	burst
to buy / comprar	bought	bought
can (*defectivo, aux.*) / poder	could	—
to catch / agarrar, coger	caught	caught
to choose / escoger, elegir	chose	chosen

225

Infinitivo / Infinitive	Pretérito / Preterit	Participio pasado / Past Participle
to come / venir	came	come
to cost / costar	cost	cost
to cut / cortar	cut	cut
to deal / tratar	dealt	dealt
to dig / cavar, extraer	dug	dug
to draw / dibujar	drew	drawn
to dream / soñar	dreamt, dreamed	dreamt, dreamed
to drink / beber, tomar	drank	drunk
to drive / manejar, conducir	drove	driven
to eat / comer	ate	eaten
to fall / caerse; desprenderse	fell	fallen
to feed / alimentar, dar de comer	fed	fed
to feel / sentir; palpar	felt	felt
to fight / pelear	fought	fought
to find / encontrar, hallar	found	found
to fly / volar	flew	flown
to foresee / prever	foresaw	foreseen
to forget / olvidar	forgot	forgot, forgotten
to forgive / perdonar	forgave	forgiven
to freeze / congelar	froze	frozen
to get / conseguir, obtener	got	got, gotten
to give / dar	gave	given
to grind / moler; pulverizar	ground	ground
to grow / crecer; madurar	grew	grown
to hang / colgar; suspender	hung	hung
to have / tener, haber	had	had
to hear / oír, escuchar	heard	heard
to hide / esconder (se)	hid	hid, hidden
to hit / pegar	hit	hit
to hold / aguantar	held	held
to hurt / lastimar, doler	hurt	hurt
to keep / guardar	kept	kept
to kneel / arrodillarse	knelt	knelt
to knit / tejer	knit, knitted	knit, knitted
to know / saber, conocer	knew	known
to lay / poner, colocar	laid	laid
to lead / dirigir	led	led
to leap / saltar	leapt, leaped	leapt, leaped
to leave / irse, dejar	left	left
to lend / prestar	lent	lent
to let / permitir, dejar	let	let
to lie / echarse, acostarse	lay	lain
to light / encender	lit, lighted	lit, lighted
to lose / perder	lost	lost
to make / hacer	made	made
may / poder	might	—
to meet / conocer	met	met
to melt / derretir	melted	melted, molten
to mistake / equivocarse	mistook	mistaken
must (defectivo; aux.) / deber de; tener que	—	—
ought (defectivo; aux.) / deber de	—	—
to pay / pagar	paid	paid
to put / poner	put	put
to quit / renunciar, dejar	quit	quit
to read / leer	read	read
to rid / librar, deshacerse	rid, ridded	rid, ridded
to ride / montar, pasear	rode	ridden

226

Infinitivo / Infinitive	Pretérito / Preterit	Participio pasado / Past Participle
to ring / sonar	rang, rung	rung
to rise / alzarse, levantarse	rose	risen
to run / correr	ran	run
to say / decir	said	said
to see / ver	saw	seen
to seek / buscar	sought	sought
to sell / vender	sold	sold
to send / enviar	sent	sent
to set / colocar, poner	set	set
to sew / coser	sewed	sewn
to shake / batir, temblar	shook	shaken
to shine / brillar	shone	shone
to shoot / disparar	shot	shot
to show / mostrar	showed	shown, showed
to shrink / encogerse	shrank, shrunk	shrunk, shrunken
to shut / cerrar	shut	shut
to sit / sentarse	sat	sat
to sleep / dormir (se)	slept	slept
to slide / deslizar (se)	slid	slid
to slit / rajar	slit	slit
to speak / hablar	spoke	spoken
to speed / acelerar	sped	sped
to spend / gastar	spent	spent
to spill / botar, derramar	spilled, spilt	spilled, spilt
to spin / dar vueltas	spun	spun
to spit / escupir	spit, spat	spit, spat
to split / partir	split	split
to spread / regar, esparcir	spread	spread
to stand / pararse	stood	stood
to steal / robar	stole	stolen
to stick / punzar, picar	stuck	stuck
to sting / picar, pinchar	stung	stung
to stink / apestar	stank, stunk	stunk
to strike / golpear, herir	struck	struck
to swear / jurar	swore	sworn
to sweep / barrer	swept	swept
to swell / hincharse	swelled	swollen, swelled
to swim / nadar	swam	swum
to swing / mecer (se)	swung	swung
to take / tomar	took	taken
to teach / enseñar	taught	taught
to tear / rasgar, desgarrar	tore	torn
to tell / decir, contar	told	told
to think / pensar	thought	thought
to throw / tirar	threw	thrown
to understand / comprender, entender	understood	understood
to undo / deshacer	undid	undone
to upset / indisponer (se)	upset	upset
to wake / despertar	woke, waked	waked, woken
to wear / usar, llevar	wore	worn
to weep / llorar	wept	wept
to wet / mojar, humedecer	wet, wetted	wet, wetted
will / (v. aux.)	would	—
to win / ganar	won	won
to withstand / soportar, resistir	withstood	withstood
to write / escribir	wrote	written

English-Spanish Vocabulary

Vocabulario inglés-español

a *abbr.* **absolute** / absoluto; **acidity** / acidez; **accommodation** / acomodación; **allergy** / alergia; **anterior** / anterior; **aqua** / agua; **artery** / arteria.

a *art. indef.* un, una; **a contagious disease** / una enfermedad contagiosa; **a good doctor** / un buen médico; (antes de vocal o *h* muda) **an; an abdominal pain** / un dolor abdominal; *a.* algún, alguna; **Is there a doctor on duty?** / ¿Hay algún médico de guardia?; *prep.* a; **three times a day** / tres veces al (a + el) día.

abandon *v.* abandonar, dejar; desamparar.

abandoned *a.* abandonado-a; irresponsable.

abasia *n.* abasia, movimiento incierto.

abbreviate *v.* abreviar, acortar, reducir, resumir.

abbreviation *n.* abreviación, abreviatura.

abdomen *n.* abdomen, vientre. *pop.* barriga, panza; **pendulous** ___ / ___ colgante, pendular; **scaphoid** ___ / ___ escafoideo.

abdominal *a.* abdominal, rel. al abdomen; ___ **bandage** / vendaje ___; ___ **breathing** / respiración ___; ___ **cavity** / cavidad ___; ___ **cramps** / retortijón, torzón; ___ **distention** / distensión ___; ___ **injuries** / traumatismos ___-es; ___ **rigidity** / rigidez ___; ___ **tumor** / tumor ___.

abdominocentesis *n.* abdominocentesis, punción abdominal.

abdominohysterectomy *n. cirg.* abdominohisterectomía, excisión del útero por medio de una incisión abdominal.

abdominoplasty *n. cirg.* abdominoplastia, reparación de la pared abdominal.

abdominovaginal *a.* abdominovaginal, rel. al abdomen y la vagina.

abduce *v.* abducir, desviar, separar.

abducent *a.* abducente; abductor.

abduction *n.* abducción, separación.

aberrant *a.* aberrante, desviado del curso normal; anómalo.

aberration *n.* aberración. 1. visión defectuosa o imperfecta; **chromatic** ___ / ___ cromática; 2. desviación de lo normal; 3. trastorno mental; **mental** ___ / ___ mental.

abhor *v.* aborrecer; tener aversión a algo o a alguien.

ability *n.* habilidad, aptitud; talento, capacidad.

abiotrophy *n.* abiotrofia, pérdida prematura de la vitalidad.

ablatio *n.* ablación, separación, desprendimiento; ___ **placentae** / desprendimiento de la placenta; ___ **retinae** / desprendimiento de la retina.

ablation *n.* ablación.

able *a.* hábil, capaz, apto-a; *v.* **to be** ___ / [*to be or do something*] ser capaz de; poder.

abnormal *a.* anormal, anómalo-a; disforme, irregular.

abnormality *n.* anormalidad, anomalía; irregularidad; deformidad.

abort *v.* abortar; hacer abortar, interrumpir el curso de una gestación o de una enfermedad antes del término natural.

abortifacient *n.* abortivo, estimulante para inducir un aborto.

abortion *n.* aborto, expulsión prematura; **caused** ___ / ___ provocado; **criminal** ___ / ___ criminal; **elective** ___ / ___ electivo, por elección; **imminent** ___ / ___ inevitable; **induced** ___ / ___ inducido; **incomplete** ___ / ___ incompleto; **spontaneous** ___ / ___ espontáneo; **suction** ___ / ___ por succión; **therapeutic** ___ / ___ terapéutico.

about *prep.* cerca de; junto a; alrededor de; a eso de, sobre; **it is** ___ **a block from here** / está cerca de una cuadra de aquí; *adv.* [*time*] **it is** ___ **one thirty** / es alrededor de la una y media; *v.* **to speak** ___ / hablar de.

above *n.* antecedente, precedente; *a.* antedicho-a, anterior; *prep.* sobre, por encima de; ___ **the heart** / encima del corazón; *adv.* arriba; la parte alta; más de o más que; ___ **all** / sobre todo; **from** ___ / desde lo alto, desde arriba.

abrasion *n.* abrasión, excoriación, irritación o raspadura de las mucosas o de una superficie a causa de una fricción o de un trauma; ___ **collar** / círculo de ___, marca circular de pólvora que deja en la piel el disparo de un arma de fuego.

abrasive *a.* abrasivo-a, irritante, raspante, rel. a una abrasión o que la causa.

abreast *adv.* de frente; en frente.

abrupt *a.* abrupto-a, precipitado-a, repentino-a.

abruptio *L.* abruptio, abrupción, acción violenta de separación, desprendimiento; ___ **placentae, placental abruption** / desprendimiento

Abortion	Aborto
accidental	accidental
afebrile	afebril
ampullar	ampollar
cervical	cervical
complete	completo
contagious	contagioso
criminal	criminal
epizootic	epizoótico
incomplete	incompleto
induced	provocado o inducido
infectious	infeccioso
in progress	en curso
natural	natural
septic	séptico
spontaneous	espontáneo
therapeutic	terapéutico
tubal	tubárico

prematuro de la placenta.

abruption n. abrupción.

abscess n. absceso, acumulación de pus gen. debido a una desintegración del tejido; **acute** ___ / ___ agudo; **alveolar** ___ / ___ alveolar; **chronic** ___ / ___ crónico; **drainage** ___ / ___ de drenaje; **encysted** ___ / ___ enquistado; **gingival** ___ / ___ de las encías; **hepatic** ___ / ___ hepático; **mammary** ___ / ___ mamario; **pelvic** ___ / ___ de la pelvis; **pulmonary** ___ / ___ pulmonar o en un pulmón.

absence n. ausencia, falta; pérdida momentánea del conocimiento.

absent a. ausente; distraído-a, absorto-a;

absentia epileptica n. absencia epiléptica, (epilepsia menor) pérdida momentánea del conocimiento en ciertos casos de ataques epilépticos.

absentminded a. distraído-a; absorto-a.

absolute a. absoluto-a, incondicional; ___ **alcohol (ethyl)** / alcohol ___ (alcohol etílico).

absorb v. absorber, sorber, chupar.

absorbency n. absorbencia.

absorbent a. absorbente; que puede absorber.

absorption n. absorción. 1. acto de ingerir o introducir líquidos u otras sustancias en el organismo; **cutaneous** ___ / ___ cutánea; **mouth** ___ / ___ bucal; **parenteral** ___ / ___ parenteral; **intestinal** ___ / ___ entérica; **stomach** ___ / ___ estomacal; 2. psic. ensimismación.

abstain v. abstenerse, privarse de; ___ **from sexual intercourse** / ___ de relaciones sexuales; Mex. cuidarse.

abstainer, abstemious a. abstemio-a; persona sobria.

abstention n. abstinencia, abstención, privación.

abstinence n. abstinencia, privación voluntaria, templanza, moderación.

abstract n. extracto, cantidad pequeña; resumen; a. abstracto-a; v. separar, alejar; extractar; resumir.

abstracted a. pensativo-a, abstraído-a; puro-a, sin mezcla alguna.

absurd a. absurdo-a, ridículo-a.

abulia n. abulia, pérdida de la voluntad; **cyclic** ___ / ___ cíclica.

abundance n. abundancia.

abundant a. abundante, copioso-a.

abuse n. abuso, uso exagerado; maltrato; ___ **of medication** / uso exagerado de medicamentos o drogas; **verbal** ___ / maltrato de palabra, insulto; v. [to take advantage of] abusar de; maltratar; seducir.

abutment n. refuerzo, remate; [dentistry] soporte.

acanthoid n. acantoide, espinoso-a, en forma de espina.

acanthosis n. acantosis, enfermedad que causa una condición áspera y verrugosa en la piel.

acapnia n. acapnia, estado producido por una disminución de ácido carbónico en la sangre.

acariasis n. acariasis, infección causada por ácaros; comezón, sarna.

acarid n. ácaro, parásito; a. acárido-a.

accelerate v. acelerar, apresurar, aumentar la velocidad; **to** ___ **the healing process** / ___ la cura.

acceleration n. aceleración, aceleramiento.

accelerator n. acelerador, sustancia o agente que tiene la propiedad de acelerar un proceso.

accent n. acento, énfasis, intensificación; v. acentuar, hacer énfasis; recalcar.

accented a. acentuado-a.

accept v. aceptar, admitir, acoger, aprobar.

acceptable a. aceptable, permitido-a; admitido-a.

access n. 1. ataque, acceso; paroxismo; 2. [entrance] entrada.

accessible a. accesivo-a, asequible, accesible.

accessory a. accesorio-a, adicional, adjunto-a.

accident n. accidente; **by** ___ / por casualidad, sin querer; **car** ___ / ___ automovilístico; **occupational** ___ / ___ del trabajo, ocupacional; **traffic** ___ / ___ de tráfico.

accidental a. accidental, inesperado-a, casual.

acclimate v. aclimatar.

acclimatization n. aclimatación.

accommodate v. acomodar, ajustar, cuadrar; [to lodge] alojar, hospedar.

accommodation n. acomodación, ajustamiento; [lodging] alojamiento.

accompany v. acompañar.

accomplish v. acabar, realizar, lograr, cumplir, finalizar.

accomplishment n. realización, éxito, logro.

accord n. acuerdo, convenio, arreglo, transacción; v. acordar, poner de acuerdo; **of one's own** ___ / espontáneamente, voluntariamente; **of mutual** ___ / de acuerdo mutuo.

accordingly adv. de acuerdo con, por consiguiente; conformemente, en conformidad.

account n. cuenta, cálculo; nota, relación; **bank** ___ / ___ bancaria; **current** ___ / ___ corriente; **on** ___ **of** / por motivo de; v. **to pay the** ___ / pagar la ___; **to settle the** ___ / arreglar la ___; **to take into** ___ / tener en ___, tener en consideración.

accountable a. responsable, contable.

accredit v. dar crédito, acreditar; certificar; dar credenciales.

accreditation n. crédito; credencial; capacitación.

accredited a. acreditado-a.

accretion n. aumento, acrecentamiento; acumulación.

accumulate v. acumular, añadir, aumentar.

accumulation n. acumulación, amontonamiento; hacinamiento.

accuracy n. exactitud, precisión, cuidado.

accurate a. exacto-a, preciso-a, correcto-a.

accurateness n. precisión, exactitud, esmero.

accusation n. acusación, imputación.

accuse v. acusar, denunciar, culpar.

accustom *v.* acostumbrar, hacer algo de costumbre.

accustomed *a.* acostumbrado-a; *v.* **to be** ___ **to** / estar acostumbrado-a a.

acentric *a.* acéntrico, fuera del centro.

acerbic *a.* agrio-a, ácido-a, áspero-a.

acetabulum *n.* acetábulo, hueso cóncavo de la cadera.

acetic *a.* acético, agrio, relacionado con el vinagre; ___ **acid** / ácido ___.

acetone *n.* acetona, sustancia fragante que se usa como solvente y se observa en cantidad excesiva en casos de diabetes.

acetonemia *n.* acetonemia, exceso de acetona en la sangre.

acetonuria *n.* acetonuria, exceso de acetona en la orina, característico de la diabetes.

acetylsalicylic acid *n.* ácido acetilsalicílico, aspirina.

achalasia *n.* acalasia, falta de capacidad de relajación esp. de una abertura o esfínter.

ache *n.* dolor constante, padecimiento, *pop.* achaque.

achieve *v.* llevar a cabo, realizar, lograr un éxito.

achievement quotient (A.Q.) *n.* cociente de inteligencia.

Achilles tendon *n.* tendón de Aquiles, tendón mayor que se une a los músculos posteriores de la pierna y se inserta en el talón del pie.

achillobursitis *n.* aquilobursitis, infl. de la bursa situada en la parte anterior del tendón de Aquiles.

achillodynia *n.* aquilodinia, dolor en la región del tendón de Aquiles.

aching *a.* doloroso-a, doliente; mortificante.

achlorhydria *n.* aclorhidria, ausencia de ácido hipoclorhídrico en las secreciones estomacales.

achloropsia *n.* acloropsia, inhabilidad de distinguir el color verde.

acholia *n.* acolia, ausencia de bilis.

achondroplasia *n.* acondroplasia, deformidad ósea de nacimiento; enanismo.

achromasia *n.* acromasia, falta o pérdida de la pigmentación de la piel, característica de los albinos.

achromatic *a.* acromático-a, sin color.

achromatopsia *n.* acromatopsia, ceguera cromática.

achylia *n.* aquilia, deficiencia de jugos estomacales.

acid *n.* ácido; ___-**fast** / acidorresistente; ___-**proof** / a prueba de ___; **acetic** ___ / ___ acético; **aminoacetic** ___ / ___ aminoacético (suplemento dietético); **ascorbic** ___ / ___ ascórbico; **boric** ___ / ___ bórico; **butyric** ___ / ___ butírico; **chlorogenic** ___ / ___ clorogénico; **cholic** ___ / ___ cólico o coleico; **citric** ___ / ___ cítrico; **deoxyribonucleic** ___ / ___ desoxirribonucleico; **fatty** ___ / ___ graso; **folic** ___ / ___ fólico; **gastric** ___ / ___ gástrico; **glucuramic** ___ / ___ glucurámico; **glutamic** ___ / ___ glutámico; **lactic** ___ / ___ láctico; **nicotinic** ___ / ___ nicotínico; **nitric** ___ / ___ nítrico; **nucleic** ___ / ___ nucleico; **phenic** ___ / ___ fenílico; **ribonucleic** ___ / ___ ribonucleico; **salicylic** ___ / ___ salicílico; **sulfonic** ___ / ___ sulfónico; **sulfuric** ___ / ___ sulfúrico; **uric** ___ / ___ úrico.

acidemia *n.* acidemia, exceso de ácido en la sangre.

acidify *v.* acedar, agriar, acidular.

acidity *n.* acidez, exceso de ácido, acedia, agrura.

acidosis *n.* acidosis, exceso de acidez en la sangre y los tejidos del cuerpo; **diabetic** ___ / ___ diabética; **metabolic** ___ / ___ metabólica.

acknowledge *v.* reconocer, agradecer; [*correspondence*] acusar recibo.

acne *n.* acné, condición inflamatoria de la piel; ___ **rosacea** / ___ rosácea; ___ **vulgaris** / ___ vulgar o común.

acoustic *a.* acústico-a, rel. al sonido o la audición.

acquaint *v.* dar a conocer, enterar, informar.

acquaintance *n.* conocimiento; trato; [*person*] un conocido, una conocida.

acquainted *a.* conocido-a, informado-a; **to be** ___ **with a case** / tener conocimiento del caso.

acquire *v.* adquirir, obtener, conseguir.

acquired *a.* adquirido-a; contraído-a.

acquired immunodeficiency syndrome (AIDS) *n.* síndrome de inmunodeficiencia adquirida (SIDA), colapso del sistema inmune del organismo que lo incapacita a responder a la invasión de infecciones.

acquisition *n.* adquisición.

acrid *a.* amargo-a, agrio-a, acre, irritante.

acridity *n.* acritud, amargura.

acroarthritis *n.* acroartritis, infl. de las articulaciones de las extremidades.

acrocyanosis, Raynaud's disease *n.* acrocianosis, Raynaud, enfermedad de, cianosis y frialdad en las extremidades a causa de un trastorno circulatorio asociado con tensión emocional o por exposición al frío.

acrodermatitis *n.* acrodermatitis, infl. de la piel de las manos y los pies; **chronic** ___ / ___ crónica atrófica.

acromegaly *n.* acromegalia, enfermedad crónica de la edad madura manifestada por un agrandamiento progresivo de las extremidades óseas y los huesos de la cabeza debido a un malfuncionamiento de la pituitaria.

acromion *n.* acromión, parte del hueso escapular del hombro.

acrophobia *n.* acrofobia, temor excesivo a la altitud.

across *adv.* a través, de una parte a otra, al otro lado de; *prep.* a través de, por, sobre, contra; *v.* **to come** ___ / encontrarse con.

act *n.* acto; ___ **of God** / fuerza mayor; *v.* actuar, obrar, ejecutar, hacer algo; portarse; **do not** ___ **like that** / no se porte así, no te portes así.

actine *n.* actina, proteína del tejido muscular

que, unida a la miosina, hace posible la contracción muscular.

action *n.* acción, actuación.

activate *v.* activar.

active *a.* activo-a; diligente, hábil, enérgico-a.

activity *n.* actividad, ejercicio, ocupación.

actual *a.* actual, real, verdadero-a; **-ly** *adv.* en realidad, actualmente; **the __ symptom** / el síntoma verdadero.

acuity *n.* agudeza; precisión; **visual __** / __ visual.

acupuncture *n.* acupuntura, método de cura por inserción de agujas en áreas determinadas del cuerpo con el propósito de reducir o suprimir un dolor.

acute *a.* agudo-a, punzante; **an __ pain** / un dolor __; **__ care facility** / centro de cuidado crítico; **__ care center** / centro de emergencia.

Adam's apple *n.* nuez de Adán.

adapt *v.* adaptar; *vr.* adaptarse, ajustarse.

adaptation *n.* adaptación, ajuste.

add *v.* añadir, sumar, agregar.

addict *n.* adicto-a; vicioso-a; *a.* adicto-a, entregado-a, dependiente física o psicológicamente de una sustancia, esp. referente a una persona alcohólica o narcómana.

addicted *a.* enviciado-a; entregado-a, habituado-a a una sustancia, esp. alcohol o narcóticos; *v.* **to become __** / enviciarse, entregarse a una droga.

addiction *n.* adicción, propensión, dependencia.

Addison's disease *n.* enfermedad de Addison, hipofunción de las glándulas suprarrenales.

additive *n.* aditivo, sustancia que se agrega.

address *n.* dirección, señas; *v.* [*to speak or write to*] dirigirse a; hablar con; [*to write*] escribir a; [*to speak to an audience*] hablar en público.

adduct *v.* aducir, mover hacia la línea media.

adduction *n.* aducción. 1. movimiento hacia la línea media del cuerpo o hacia adentro de un miembro o parte del cuerpo; 2. movimiento hacia un centro común.

adductor *n.* músculo aductor, músculo que tira hacia una línea media o el centro.

adenectomy *n. cirg.* adenectomía, extirpación de una glándula.

adenitis *n.* adenitis, infl. de una glándula.

adenoacanthoma *n.* adenoacantoma, cáncer en el útero que crece lentamente.

adenocarcinoma *n.* adenocarcinoma, cáncer maligno que se origina en una glándula.

adenocystoma *n.* adenocistoma, tumor benigno de una glándula formado por quistes.

adenofibroma *n.* adenofibroma, tumor benigno formado por tejido fibroso y glandular, visto en el útero y en los pechos.

adenoid *a.* adenoideo, semejante a una glándula.

adenoidectomy *n. cirg.* adenoidectomía, extirpación de la adenoide.

adenoiditis *n.* adenoiditis, infl. de la adenoide.

adenoids *n. pl.* adenoides, acumulación de tejido linfático en la nasofaringe en la niñez.

adenoma *n.* adenoma, tumor de una consistencia parecida a la del tijido glandular; **basophil __** / __ basófilo; **sebaceous __** / __ sebáceo; **toxic __** / __ tóxico.

adenomyoma *n.* adenomioma, tumór benigno visto con frecuencia en el útero.

adenopathy, adenopalia *n.* adenopatía, adenopalia, enfermedad de una glándula linfática.

adenosarcoma *n.* adenosarcoma, tumor maligno.

adenosis *n.* adenosis, engrosamiento de una glándula.

adequate *a.* adecuado-a, proporcionado-a.

adherent lens *n.* lente de contacto.

adhesion *n.* adhesión, adherencia.

adhesive *n.* adhesivo, tela adhesiva; **__ strips** / esparadrapo.

adipose tissue *n.* tejido adiposo, grasa.

adiposogenital *a.* adiposogenital. *V.* **syndrome.**

adjacent *a.* adyacente, contiguo, al lado de.

adjective *n. gr.* adjetivo.

adjoin *v.* juntar, asociar, unir.

adjunct *a.* adjunto-a, unido-a, asociado-a, arrimado-a.

adjust *v.* ajustar, arreglar, acomodar.

adjuvant *n.* adjutor, agente o sustancia que acentúa la potencia de un medicamento.

administer *v.* administrar, proveer, dar algo necesario.

administration *n.* administración.

admirable *a.* admirable, digno-a.

admission *n.* admisión, internación, ingreso.

admit *v.* admitir, dar entrada o ingreso a una institución.

admittance *n.* entrada, admisión.

admix *v.* mezclar, juntar.

admonish *v.* advertir, amonestar.

admonition *n.* advertencia, admonición, consejo.

adnexa *n. pl.* anejos, anexos, apéndices tales como los tubos uterinos.

adolescence *n.* adolescencia, pubertad.

adolescent *n.* adolescente; pubescente.

adopt *v.* adoptar, prohijar.

adoption *n.* adopción.

adoptive *a.* adoptivo-a.

adrenal *a.* suprarrenal, adrenal; **__ cortex hormones** / corticosteroides; **__ gland diseases** / enfermedades de la glándula __; **__ glands** / glándulas __-es; **__ gland neoplasms** / neoplasmas de las glándulas __-es.

adrenalectomy *n.* adrenalectomía, *cirg.* extirpación de las glándulas suprarrenales.

adrenaline *n.* adrenalina, marca registrada de la epinefrina, hormona usada como vasoconstrictor secretada por la médula suprarrenal.

adrenalism *n.* adrenalismo, disfunción de la glándula suprarrenal que ocasiona síntomas de debilidad y decaimiento.

adrenocorticotropin (ACTH) *n.* adrenocorticotropina, hormona secretada por la pituitaria, estimulante de la corteza suprarrenal.

adrenogenic *a.* adrenogénico, que proviene de las glándulas suprarrenales.

adsorbent *a.* adsorbente.

adult *n., a.* adulto-a.

adulterate *v.* adulterar, cambiar el original, viciar; falsificar.

adultery *n.* adulterio.

advance *v.* avanzar, adelantar, pasar adelante; **in** ___ / por adelantado.

advancement *n.* [*improvement*] mejora, mejoría, progreso; promoción, ascenso.

advantage *n.* ventaja, ganancia, beneficio; *v.* **to take** ___ / aprovecharse, valerse de.

advantageous *a.* provechoso-a, ventajoso-a, favorable, propicio-a.

adverb *n. gr.* adverbio.

adverbial *a.* adverbial.

adverse *a.* desfavorable, adverso-a, contrario-a, opuesto-a.

advisable *a.* recomendable, conveniente.

advise *n.* advertencia, consejo; opinión, parecer; *v.* advertir; aconsejar, recomendar.

aerate *v.* airear, ventilar. 1. saturar un líquido de aire; 2. cambiar la sangre venosa en sangre arterial en los pulmones.

aerobe *n.* aerobio, organismo que requiere oxígeno para vivir.

aerobic *a.* aeróbico-a. 1. rel. a un aerobio; 2. rel. a un ejercicio coordinado como una actividad física; ___ **dance** / baile ___; ___ **exercises** / ejercicios ___s; 3. que ocurre o vive en la presencia de oxígeno.

aerobics *n.* aeróbic, técnica gimnástica que consiste en ejercicios y calistenia combinados con una rutina de baile.

aerocele *n.* aerocele, hernia de la tráquea.

aeroembolism *n.* aeroembolismo, "enfermedad de los buzos", condición causada por burbujas de nitrógeno liberadas en la sangre debido a un cambio brusco de presión atmosférica; *pop.* **the bends.**

aeroemphysema *n.* aeroenfisema, "enfermedad de los aviadores", condición causada por un ascenso súbito en el espacio sin decompresión adecuada; *pop.* **the chokes.**

aerogenic *a.* aerógeno-a, que produce gas.

aerophagia *n.* aerofagia, tragar aire en exceso.

afebrile *a.* afebril, sin fiebre, sin calentura.

affair *n.* asunto, cuestión.

affect *v.* afectar, causar un cambio en la salud; conmover, excitar.

affectation *n.* artificio, afectación.

affected *a.* afectado-a, que padece de una enfermedad física o de un sufrimiento emocional; ___ **by** / por.

affection *n.* [*sickness*] afección, dolencia, enfermedad; [*feeling*] expresión de cariño, afecto o afección.

affectionate *a.* afectuoso-a, cariñoso-a.

affective *a.* afectivo-a; ___ **disorders** / trastornos ___-s; ___ **symptoms** / síntomas ___-s.

afferent *a.* aferente, que se dirige hacia el centro, hacia adentro.

affinity *n.* afinidad, conformidad; conexión.

affirm *v.* afirmar, asegurar.

affirmation *n.* afirmación, confirmación, ratificación de una medida.

affirmed *a.* afirmado-a, confirmado-a, ratificado-a.

affix *v.* aplicar, colocar, adaptar; ligar, unir.

affixture *n.* ligadura, adición.

afflict *v.* afligir, causar dolor o sufrimiento; [*lament*] afligirse, inquietarse.

afflicted *a.* afligido-a, sufrido-a.

affliction *n.* aflicción, padecimiento, sufrimiento.

afflux *n.* flujo.

afford *v.* poder costear, tener solvencia; soportar.

affront *v.* hacer frente, confrontar; encararse.

afibrinogenemia *n.* afibrinogenemia, deficiencia de fibrinógeno en la sangre.

afire *a.* encendido-a; *adv.* en llamas.

afraid *a.* temeroso-a, miedoso-a, intimidado-a, *v.* **to be** ___ / tener miedo.

after *prep.* después; *adv.* después, más tarde; ___-**effects** / consecuencias, secuelas; acción retardada de una droga; ___-**treatment** / tratamiento de recuperación.

afterbirth *n.* secundinas, placenta y membranas que se expelen en el parto.

aftercare *n.* convalescencia, restablecimiento; *cirg.* tratamiento post-operatorio.

afterimage *n.* impresión mantenida por la retina.

aftermath *n.* secuela, consecuencias de una enfermedad.

afterpains *n. pl.* entuertos, dolores de parto.

aftersleep *n.* sueño secundario.

aftersound *n.* impresión auditiva que persiste después de cesar el estímulo.

aftertaste *n.* permanencia de la sensación del gusto.

afterwards *adv.* después, luego, más tarde.

again *adv.* otra vez; ___ **and** ___ / una y otra vez, muchas veces; **do it** ___ / hágalo, hazlo ___.

against *prep.* contra, enfrente; *v.* **to be** ___ / oponerse; enfrentarse a, con.

agalorrhea *n.* agalorrea, cesación o falta de leche en los pechos.

agamic *a.* agámico-a, rel. a la reproducción sin unión sexual.

agammaglobulinemia *n.* agammaglobulinemia, deficiencia de gamma globulina en la sangre.

age *n.* edad; generación; **full** ___ / mayor de edad; **tender** ___ / infancia, primera edad; ___ **of consent** / mayor de ___, mayoría de ___; **legal** ___ / ___ legal.

agenesis, agenesia *n.* agénesis, agenesia. 1. defecto congénito en el desarrollo de un órgano o parte del cuerpo; 2. esterilidad;

impotencia.

agent *n.* agente, factor.

agglomeration *n.* aglomeración, acumulación.

agglutinants *n. pl.* aglutinantes, agentes o factores que unen partes separadas en un proceso de curación.

agglutinate *v.* aglutinar; causar unión.

agglutination *n.* aglutinación, acción de aglutinar o causar unión.

aggravate *v.* agravar, empeorar, irritar.

aggression *n.* agresión, actitud y acción hostil.

aggressive *a.* agresivo-a, hostil.

agile *a.* ágil, ligero-a, expedito-a.

aging *n.* envejecimiento.

agitate *v.* [*to shake*] agitar, sacudir; [*to upset*] inquietar, perturbar.

agitation *n.* agitación, perturbación; alboroto.

ago *adv.* atrás; [*with time*] hace; **ten years ___** / [*hace + length of time*] hace diez años.

agonize *v.* agonizar, estar en agonía; sufrir en extremo.

agony *n.* agonía. 1. sufrimiento extremo; 2. estado que precede a la muerte.

agoraphobia *n.* agorafobia, temor excesivo a los espacios abiertos.

agranulocytosis *n.* agranulocitosis, condición aguda causada por la disminución excesiva de leucocitos en la sangre.

agraphia *n.* agrafia, pérdida de la habilidad de escribir causada por un trastorno cerebral.

agree *v.* acordar; estar de acuerdo; sentar bien, caer bien; **we ___** / estamos de acuerdo; **coffee does not ___** with me / el café no me sienta bien; el café no me cae bien.

agreeable *a.* agradable, ameno-a, placentero-a, grato-a.

agreement *n.* acuerdo, pacto, consolidación, ajustamiento; **to come to an ___** / llegar a un acuerdo; acordar.

ahead *adv.* adelante, enfrente, hacia adelante; *v.* **look ___** / mire, mira ___.

aid *n.* ayuda, asistencia; **government ___** / subsidio del gobierno; **nurse ___** / enfermero, enfermera asistente.

AIDS *abbr.* **acquired immunodeficiency syndrome** *n.* SIDA *abr.* síndrome de inmunodeficiencia adquirida, estado avanzado de infección por el virus VIH, caracterizado por inmunodeficiencia, infecciones (tales como neumonía, tuberculosis y diarrea crónica) y tumores (esp. linfoma y sarcoma de Kaposi).

ailing *a.* achacoso-a, enfermizo-a.

ailment *n.* dolencia, achaque, indisposición.

air *n.* aire; **___ bladder** / vejiga llena de ___; **___ blast injury** / lesión por una explosión; **___ bubbles** / burbujas de ___; **___ chamber** / cámara de ___; **___-conditioned** / ___ acondicionado; **___ contamination** / ___ contaminado; contaminación del aire, polución; **cool ___** / ___ fresco; **___ dressing** / vendaje; **___ embolism** / embolia gaseosa; **___ hole** / respiradero; **air hunger** falta de aire; **___ mattress** /

colchón neumático; **___ passages** / conductos de ___; **___ pocket** / bolsa de ___; **___ pollution** / polución atmosférica; **___ sac** [*lung*] / alvéolo pulmonar; **tidal ___** / respiratorio; **ventilated ___** / ___ de ventilación; *v.* [*to ventilate*] airear, ventilar.

airborne *a.* en vuelo; [*transported*] llevado-a por el aire.

airing *n.* aireo, ventilación.

airless *a.* falto de respiración, sin aire.

airmail *n.* correo aéreo.

airplane *n.* avión, aeroplano.

airsickness *n.* mareo de altura.

airtight *a.* hermético-a.

airway *n.* conducto de aire.

akin *a.* consanguíneo, de cualidades uniformes.

akinesthesia *n.* aquinestesia, falta del sentido de movimiento.

alalia *n.* pérdida del habla.

alarm *n.* alarma, peligro; **fire ___** / ___ de fuego.

alarm *v.* alarmar, inquietar, inpacientar; turbar.

alarming *a.* alarmante, inquietante, desesperante; sorprendente.

albinism *n.* albinismo, falta de pigmentación en la piel, el cabello y los ojos.

albino *n.* albino-a, persona afectada por albinismo.

albumin *n.* albúmina, componente proteínico.

albuminuria *n.* albuminuria, presencia de proteína en la orina, esp. albúmina o globulina.

alcohol *n.* alcohol.

alcoholic *n., a.* alcohólico-a.

alcoholism *n.* alcoholismo, uso excesivo de bebidas alcohólicas.

aldosterone *n.* aldosterona, hormona producida por la corteza suprarrenal.

aldosteronism *n.* aldosteronismo, trastorno causado por una secreción excesiva de aldosterona.

alert *a.* alerta, dispuesto-a.

aleukemia *n.* aleucemia, falta o deficiencia de leucocitos en la sangre.

alexia *n.* alexia, inhabilidad de comprender la palabra escrita.

algesia *n.* algesia, hipertesia.

algid *a.* álgido-a, frío-a.

algor *n.* escalofrío, algor.

algorithm *n.* algoritmo, método aritmético y algebraico que se usa en el diagnóstico y tratamiento de una enfermedad.

alien *a.* incompatible; extranjero-a, forastero-a.

alienation *n.* separación; *psic.* ofuscación.

alimentary *a.* alimenticio-a, rel. a los alimentos; **___ tract** / tubo digestivo, tracto ___.

alimentation *n.* alimentación, nutrición; **forced ___** / ___ forzada; **rectal ___** / ___ por el recto.

alimony *n.* manutención, pensión alimenticia, apoyo monetario.

alive *a.* vivo-a, con vida; *v.* **to be ___** / estar ___.

alkaloid *n.* alcaloide, grupo de sustancias orgánicas básicas de origen vegetal.

alkalosis *n.* alcalosis, trastorno patológico en el

balance acidobásico del organismo.

all *n.* el todo, compuesto de partes iguales; *a.* todo-a, todos-as; [*everyone*] todo el mundo; **before** ___ / ante todo; ___ **day** / todo el día; ___ **night** / todo la noche; **at** ___ **risks** / a todo riesgo; *adv.* todo, del todo, completamente; enteramente; ___ **along** / todo el tiempo; ___ **the better** / tanto mejor; **by** ___ **means** / sin duda, por supuesto; ___ **right** / está bien; ___ **of a sudden** / de pronto, de golpe, de repente; ___ **the worse** / tanto peor.

allele *n.* alelo, alelomorfo, uno de dos o más genes de una serie que ocupan la misma posición en cromosomas homólogos y que determinan características alternantes en los descendientes.

allergens *n. pl.* alérgenos, agentes causantes de alergias; **environmental** ___ / ___ ambientales.

allergic *a.* alérgico-a; ___ **reaction** / reacción alérgica; ___ **rhinitis** / rinitis ___ .

allergist *n.* alergista, especialista en alergias.

allergy *n.* alergia.

alleviate *v.* aliviar, calmar, mejorar, atenuar.

alliance *n.* alianza, unión; acuerdo.

allogeneic, allogenic *a.* alogénico-a, de constitución genética distinta dentro de una misma especie; ___ **cells** / células ___s; ___ **system** / sistema ___ .

allograft *n.* aloinjerto. V. **homograft.**

allow *v.* admitir, aceptar, consentir.

allowance *n.* asignación, regalía, dieta alimenticia.

almanac *n.* almanaque, calendario.

Almighty *n.* Dios; **almighty** *a.* todopoderoso-a, omnipotente.

almond *n.* almendra.

almost *adv.* casi, cerca de, alrededor de.

alone *a.* solo-a, solitario-a.

along *adv.* a lo largo de, próximo a, junto a; *v.* **to get** ___ / llevarse bien; **come** ___ / venga; ven.

alongside *adv.* al costado de, junto a.

aloof *a.* apartado-a, aislado-a, lejos de todo o de todos.

alopecia *n.* alopecia, pérdida del cabello.

aloud *adv.* en voz alta; **to speak** ___ / hablar recio.

already *adv.* ya.

also *adv.* del mismo modo, también.

alter *v.* cambiar, variar; reformar.

alteration *n.* alteración, modificación, reforma, cambio.

alternate *v.* alternar, turnar.

alternative *n.* alternativa, opción.

although *conj.* aunque, si bien, bien que.

altitude *n.* altitud, altura, elevación.

alveolar *a.* alveolar, rel. a un alvéolo.

alveolus *n.* alvéolo, cavidad.

always *adv.* siempre, para siempre.

Alzheimer's disease *n.* enfermedad de Alzheimer, deteriorización cerebral progresiva con características de demencia senil.

am *v.* soy, estoy, *primera persona pres. ind. v.* **to be** /

ser; estar.

amalgamate *v.* amalgamar, mezclar, juntar.

amastia *n.* amastia, ausencia de los pechos.

amateur *a.* aficionado-a; principiante.

amaze *v.* asombrar, maravillar, pasmar.

amazement *n.* asombro, pasmo, admiración.

amber *n.* ámbar; *a.* ambarino-a.

ambiance *n.* ambiente.

ambidextrous *a.* ambidextro-a.

ambisexual *a.* ambisexual, bisexual.

ambition *n.* ambición, aspiración; *v.* ambicionar, aspirar.

ambivalence *n.* ambivalencia.

amblyopia *n.* ambliopía, visión reducida.

ambulance *n.* ambulancia.

ambulant *a.* ambulante.

ambulatory *a.* ambulatorio-a; ambulante.

amebiasis *n.* amebiasis, amibiasis, estado infeccioso causado por amebas.

amebic *a.* amebiano-a, rel. a la ameba o causado por ésta.

ameliorate *v.* mejorar; adelantar; mejorarse.

amend *v.* enmendar, corregir.

amenorrhea *n.* amenorrea, ausencia del período menstrual.

American *n., a.* americano-a.

ametropia *n.* ametropía, falta de visión causada por una anomalía de los poderes refractores del ojo.

amine *n.* amina, uno de los compuestos básicos derivados del amoníaco.

amino acid *n.* aminoácido, compuesto orgánico metabólico necesario en el desarrollo y crecimiento humano esencial en la digestión e hidrólisis de proteínas.

ammonia *n.* amoníaco, gas alcalino que se forma por la descomposición de sustancias nitrogenadas y por aminoácidos.

amnesia *n.* amnesia, pérdida de la memoria.

amniocentesis *n.* amniocentesis, punción del útero para obtener líquido amniótico.

amnion *n.* amnios, saco membranoso que envuelve el embrión.

amniotic *a.* amniótico, en relación con el amnios; ___ **sac** / saco ___ ; ___ **fluid** / fluido ___ .

amoeba, ameba *n.* ameba, organismo de una sola célula.

amorphous *a.* amorfo-a, sin forma.

amphetamine *n.* anfetamina, tipo de droga usada como estimulante del sistema nervioso.

ampicillin *n.* ampicilina, penicilina semisintética.

ample *a.* amplio-a, ancho-a; abundante, copioso-a.

amplification *n.* amplificación, ampliación, extensión.

amplify *v.* ampliar, extender, dilatar.

ampoule, ampule *n.* ámpula, ampolla, tubo de jeringuilla.

amputate *v.* amputar, desmembrar.

amputation *n.* amputación, desmembración.

amygdala *n.* amígdala. V. **tonsil.**

amyloid *n.* amiloide, proteína que se asemeja a los almidones.

amyloidosis *n.* amiloidosis, acumulación de amiloide en los tejidos.

anabolic *a.* anabólico-a, rel. al anabolismo; ___ **steroid** / esteroide ___.

anabolism *n.* anabolismo, proceso celular por el cual sustancias simples se convierten en complejas, fase constructiva del metabolismo.

anacidity *n.* anacidez, sin ácido.

anaerobe *n.* anaerobio, microorganismo que se multiplica en ausencia de aire u oxígeno.

anaerobic *a.* anaeróbico, rel. a los anaerobios o de la naturaleza de éstos.

anal *a.* anal, rel. al ano; ___ **fistula** / fístula ___.

analgesic *n.* analgésico, calmante.

analogy *n.* analogía, semejanza.

analphabet *n.* analfabeto-a.

analysis *n.* análisis, prueba.

analyze *v.* analizar, hacer análisis.

anaphase *n.* anafase, etapa de la división celular.

anaphylactic *a.* anafiláctico-a, rel. a la anafilaxis.

anaphylaxis *n.* anafilaxis, hipersensibilidad, reacción alérgica extrema.

anaplasia *n.* anaplasia, falta de diferenciación en las células.

anaplastic *a.* anaplástico-a, rel. a la anaplasia.

anasarca *n.* anasarca, edema generalizado, hidropesía.

anastomosis *n. cirg.* anastomosis, pasaje o comunicación entre dos o más órganos.

anatomic, anatomical *a.* anatómico-a, rel. a la anatomía.

anatomy *n.* anatomía, ciencia que estudia la estructura del cuerpo humano y de sus órganos; **macroscopic** ___ / ___ macroscópica, estudio de estructuras que se distinguen a simple vista; **topographic** ___ / ___ topográfica, estudio de estructuras y partes de las mismas en las distintas regiones del cuerpo.

ancestors *n. pl.* antepasados, padres o abuelos, *pop.* los mayores.

ancestry *n.* ascendencia; extracción étnica, raza; alcurnia.

anconal *a.* anconal, referente al codo.

and *conj.* y; e (*gr. used instead of y before words beginning with i or hi*); **two thirty** / las dos y media; **father and son** / padre e hijo.

androgen *n.* andrógeno, hormona masculina.

androgenic *a.* androgénico-a, rel. a las características sexuales masculinas.

androgynous *a.* androginoide, que tiene las características de ambos sexos.

androtomy *n.* androtomía, disección de un cadáver.

anemia *n.* anemia, insuficiencia hemática o de glóbulos rojos en calidad, cantidad o en hemoglobina; **aplastic** ___ / ___ aplástica, falta anormal de producción de glóbulos rojos; **hemorrhagic, hemolytic** ___ / ___ hemorrágica, hemolítica, destrucción progresiva de glóbulos rojos; **hyperchromic** ___ / ___ hiper-

crómica, aumento anormal en la hemoglobina; **hypochromic microcytic** ___ / ___ hipocrómica microcítica, [*células pequeñas*], deficiencia de glóbulos rojos en menor cantidad que de hemoglobina; **macrocytic** ___ / ___ macrocítica, glóbulos rojos de un tamaño exagerado [*anemia perniciosa*]; **sickle cell** ___ / ___ de glóbulos falciformes; **iron deficiency** ___ / ___ por deficiencia de hierro.

anergy *n.* anergia. 1. astenia, falta de energía; 2. reducción o falta de respuesta a un antígeno específico.

anesthesia *n.* anestesia; **epidural** ___ / ___ epidural; **general** ___ / ___ general; **general** ___ **by inhalation** / ___ general por inhalación; **general** ___ **by intubation** / ___ general por intubación; **intravenous general** ___ / ___ general intravenosa; **local** ___ / ___ local; **regional** ___ / ___ regional; **saddle block** ___ / ___ en silla de montar; **spinal** ___ / ___ raquídea.

anesthesiologist *n.* anestesista, anestesiólogo-a.

anesthesiology *n.* anestesiología.

anesthetic *n.* anestésico.

anesthetize *v.* anestesiar.

aneurysm *n.* aneurisma, dilatación de una porción de la pared de una arteria; **aortic** ___ / ___ aórtico; **berry** ___ / ___ cerebral saculado; **cerebral** ___ / ___ cerebral; **dissecting** ___ / ___ disecante; **false** ___ / ___ falso; **fusiform** ___ / ___ fusiforme; **true** ___ / ___ verdadero.

aneurysmal *a.* aneurismal, rel. a un aneurisma.

aneurysmectomy *n. cirg.* aneurismectomía, extirpación de un aneurisma.

anger *n.* ira, cólera.

angiitis *n.* angiitis, infl. de un vaso linfático o de un vaso sanguíneo.

angina *n.* angina, sensación de dolor constrictivo o ahogo; **intestinal** ___ / ___ intestinal, dolor abdominal agudo debido a insuficiencia de flujo sanguíneo a los intestinos; **laryngeal** ___ / ___ laríngea, infl. de la garganta; ___ **pectoris, angor pectoris** / angina de pecho, dolor en el pecho causado por insuficiencia de flujo sanguíneo al músculo cardíaco.

angiocardiography *n.* angiocardiografía, visión radiográfica de las aurículas y los ventrículos del corazón.

angioedema *n.* edema angioneurótico, infl. alérgica localizada gen. en la cara.

angiogenesis *n.* angiogénesis, desarrollo del sistema vascular.

angiogram *n.* angiograma, visualización radiográfica de un vaso sanguíneo mediante inyección de una sustancia radioopaca; **coronary** ___ / ___ coronario; **lymph** ___ / ___ linfático.

angiography *n.* angiografía, proceso de obtener una radiografía de los vasos sanguíneos haciendo resaltar su contorno.

angioma *n.* angioma, tumor vascular benigno.

angioplasty *n. cirg.* angioplastia, intervención quirúrgica para la reconstrucción de vasos sanguíneos enfermos o traumatizados; **percuta-**

neous coronary ___ / ___ coronaria percutánea; **peripheral percutaneous** ___ / ___ periférica percutánea.

angiospasm *n.* angioespasmo, contracción prolongada y fuerte de un vaso sanguíneo.

angiotensin *n.* angiotensina, agente presor en los trastornos hipotensivos, estimulante de la aldosterona.

angle *n.* ángulo, abertura formada por dos líneas que salen separadamente de un mismo punto.

anguish *n.* agonía, angustia.

anhidrosis *n.* anhidrosis, deficiencia o falta de secreción sudoral.

animal *n.* animal.

animate *v.* animar, dar vida.

animosity *n.* animosidad, rencor, aversión, mala voluntad; *v.* **to have** ___ / tener ___.

anisocytosis *n.* anisocitosis, tamaño desigual de los glóbulos rojos.

ankle *n.* tobillo; ___-bone / hueso del ___.

ankylosis *n.* anquilosis, inflexibilidad o falta de movimiento de una articulación.

ankylotic *a.* anquiloso-a, anquilosado-a.

annexive *a.* anexo, contiguo.

annihilation *n.* aniquilación, destrucción total.

annotate *v.* anotar, hacer un comentario.

annotation *n.* anotación, nota.

announce *v.* anunciar, publicar.

announcement *n.* anuncio, aviso, declaración pública.

annoy *v.* importunar, fastidiar, molestar.

annual *a.* anual; **-ly** *adv.* anualmente, cada año.

annul *v.* anular, cancelar, revocar.

annular *a.* anular, en forma de anillo; ___ **eruption** / erupción ___.

anodyne *n.* anodino, agente mitigador del dolor; *a.* insípido-a.

anoint *v.* untar, administrar la extremaunción.

anomalous *a.* anómalo-a, irregular, disforme.

anomaly *n.* trastorno, anomalía, irregularidad contraída o congénita.

anorexia *n.* anorexia, trastorno causado por falta de apetito; ___ **nervosa** / ___ nerviosa, aversión histérica a la comida.

anosmia *n.* anosmia, falta de olfato.

another *a.* otro-a, otros-as; *pron.* el otro, la otra.

anovulation *n.* anovulación, cese de ovulación.

anovulatory drugs *n. pl.* drogas anticonceptivas, drogas para evitar la ovulación.

anoxemia *n.* anoxemia, insuficiencia de oxígeno en la sangre.

anoxia *n.* anoxia, ausencia de oxígeno en los tejidos.

answer *n.* contestación, respuesta.

ant *n.* hormiga.

antacid *n.* antiácido, neutralizador de acidez.

antagonist *a.* antagonista, droga que neutraliza los efectos de otra.

antecubital *a.* antecubital, en posición anterior al codo.

anteflexion *n.* anteflexión, acto de doblarse hacia adelante.

antemetic *n.* antiemético, medicamento para controlar las naúseas.

anterior *a.* anterior, precedente; [*body position*] anterior o ventral; [*time*] previo-a.

anteversion *n.* anteversión, vuelta hacia el frente.

anthracosis *n.* antracosis, condición pulmonar causada por la inhalación prolongada de polvo de carbón.

anthropomorphic *a.* antropomórfico-a, de forma humana.

antiallergic *a.* antialérgico-a, rel. a los medicamentos que se usan para combatir alergias.

antiarrythmic *a.* antiarrítmico-a, que previene la arritmia cardíaca o es efectivo en tratamientos contra ésta; ___ **agents** / agentes ___-s.

antiarthritics *n. pl.* antiartríticos, medicamentos para combatir la artritis o aliviarla.

antibiotic drugs *n. pl.* antibióticos, drogas antibacterianas.

antibody *n.* anticuerpo, sustancia de proteína que actúa como respuesta a la presencia de antígenos; ___ **formation** / formación de ___-s; **cross-reacting** ___ / ___ de reacción cruzada; **monoclonal** ___ / ___ monoclónico, derivado de células de hibridoma.

anticancer drug, anticarcinogen *n.* anticarcinógeno, droga usada en el tratamiento del cáncer.

anticholinergic *a.* anticolinérgico-a, rel. al bloqueo de los impulsos transmitidos a través de los nervios parasimpáticos.

anticipate *v.* anticipar, prevenir.

anticoagulant *n.* anticoagulante, medicamento usado para evitar coágulos.

anticonvulsant *n.* anticonvulsivo, medicamento usado en la prevención de convulsiones o ataques.

antidepressant *n.* antidepresivo, medicamento o proceso curativo usado para evitar estados de depresión.

antidiabetic *n.* antidiabético, medicamento usado en el tratamiento de la diabetes.

antidiuretic *n.* antidiurético, sustancia que evita la emisión excesiva de orina.

antidote *n.* antídoto, contraveneno.

antiemetic *n.* antiemético, medicamento usado en el tratamiento de la naúsea.

antigen *n.* antígeno, sustancia tóxica que estimula la formación de anticuerpos; **carcinoembriogenic** ___ **(CEA)** / ___ carcinoembriogénico.

antiglobulin test *n.* prueba de la antiglobulina.

antihistamine *n.* antihistamina, medicamento usado en el tratamiento de reacciones alérgicas.

antihypertensive *n.* antihipertensivo, medicamento para bajar la presión arterial.

anti-inflammatory agents *n. pl.* agentes anti-inflamatorios.

antineoplastic *a.* antineoplástico, droga que controla o mata células cancerosas.

antioncotic *n.* antioncótico, agente reductor de la tumefacción.

antipathy *n.* antipatía, adversión.

antipruritic *a.* antipruriginoso-a, sustancia que trata o alivia la picazón.

antipyretic *n.* antipirético-a, agente reductor de la fiebre.

antiseptic *n.* antiséptico, agente desinfectante que destruye bacterias.

antispasmodic *n.* antiespasmódico, medicamento usado para aliviar o prevenir espasmos.

antitoxic *n.* antitóxico, neutralizador de los efectos de las toxinas.

antitoxin *n.* antitoxina, anticuerpo que actúa como neutralizante de la sustancia tóxica introducida por un microorganismo.

antiviral *a.* antivirósico-a, antiviral, que detiene la acción de un virus.

antrectomy *n. cirg.* antrectomía, excisión de la pared de un antro.

antrum *n.* antro, cavidad o cámara casi cerrada; **mastoid** ___ / ___ mastoideo.

anuria *n.* anuria, escasez o ausencia de orina.

anus *n.* ano, orificio del recto.

anxiety *n.* ansiedad, angustia; estado de preocupación excesiva; aprehensión, abatimiento de ánimo, desasosiego; ___ **disorders** / estados de ___; ___ **neurosis** / neurosis de ___.

anxious *a.* ansioso-a, anheloso-a, abatido-a, perturbado-a.

any *a.* algún, alguna, cualquier, cualquiera; **are you taking any medicine?** / ¿toma, tomas **alguna** medicina?; ¿toma, tomas **algún** medicamento?; ___ **further** / más lejos; **don't go** ___ **further** / no vaya, no vayas más lejos; ___ **more** / más; **you don't need** ___ **more pills** / no necesita, no necesitas **más** pastillas; [*after negation*] ningún, ninguno-a; **don't take** ___ **of those pills** / no tome, no tomes ninguna de esas pastillas.

anybody *pron.* alguien, alguno-a; cualquiera; **did** ___ **call?** / ¿llamó alguien?; [*negative*] nada, nadie, ninguno-a; **no one called** / no llamó nadie.

anything *pron.* algo, alguna cosa, cualquier cosa; [*negative*] nada; **do you feel** ___? / ¿siente, sientes algo?; **don't you feel** ___? / ¿no siente, sientes nada?

anyway *adv.* de todas maneras, de cualquier modo, sea lo que fuera.

anywhere *adv.* dondequiera, en cualquier parte.

aorta *n.* aorta, arteria mayor que se origina en el ventrículo izquierdo del corazón; **ascending** ___ / ___ ascendiente; **arch of the** ___ / cayado de la ___; **coarctation of the** ___ / coartación o compresión de la ___; **descending** ___ / ___ descendiente, descendente.

aortic *a.* aórtico-a, rel. a la aorta; ___ **murmur** / soplo, ruido ___; ___ **stenosis** / estenosis o estrechamiento ___.

aortocoronary *n.* aortocoronaria, rel. a las arterias aorta y coronaria.

aortogram *n.* aortograma, rayos X de la aorta.

aortography *n.* aortografía, técnica empleada con rayos X para ver el contorno de la aorta.

aortoiliac *a.* aortoilíaca, rel. a las arterias aorta e ilíaca.

apart *adv.* aparte, separadamente; hacia un lado.

apathetic *a.* apático-a, indolente, insensible.

apathy *n.* apatía, insensibilidad.

apepsia *n.* apepsia, mala digestión.

aperitive *n.* aperitivo. 1. purgante suave; 2. estimulante del apetito.

aperture *n.* apertura, abertura, paso, boquete.

apex *n.* apex. 1. ápice, extremo superior o punta de un órgano; 2. extremidad puntiaguda de una estructura.

aphasia *n.* afasia, incapacidad de coordinar el pensamiento y la palabra.

aphemia *n.* afemia, pérdida del habla, gen. debido a una hemorragia cerebral, coágulo o tumor.

aphonia *n.* afonía, pérdida de la voz debido a una afección localizada en la laringe.

aphonic *a.* afónico-a, sin sonido, sin voz.

aphrodisiac *a.* afrodisíaco-a, que estimula deseos sexuales.

aphtha *n.* afta, úlcera pequeña que aparece como señal de infección en la mucosa oral.

aphthous stomatitis *n.* estomatitis aftosa, dolor de garganta acompañado de pequeñas aftas en la boca.

aplasia *n.* aplasia, falta de desarrollo normal en un órgano.

apnea *n.* apnea, falta de respiración.

aponeurosis *n.* aponeurosis, membrana que cubre los músculos.

apophysis *n.* apófisis, parte saliente de un hueso.

apoplexy *n.* apoplejía, hemorragia cerebral.

appalling *a.* espantoso-a, aterrador-a, atemorizante.

apparent *a.* aparente, evidente, preciso-a; claro-a; patente; **-ly** *adv.* aparentemente, evidentemente, precisamente.

appeal *n.* apelación, recurso, súplica; *v.* apelar, recurrir, suplicar.

appear *v.* aparecer, parecer, responder; manifestarse.

appearance *n.* apariencia, aspecto.

appendage *n.* apéndice; dependencia; accesorio.

appendectomy *n. cirg.* apendectomía, extirpación del apéndice.

appendicitis *n.* apendicitis, infl. del apéndice.

appendicular *a.* apendicular, rel. al apéndice.

appendix *n.* apéndice.

appetite *n.* apetito, deseos de, ganas de comer; **altered** ___ / ___ alterado; **excessive** ___ / ___ excesivo; **poor** ___, **loss of** ___ / falta de ___, pérdida del ___.

appetizing *a.* grato-a, gustoso-a.

apple *n.* manzana.

appliance *n.* aplicación; accesorio, instrumento,

aparato eléctico.

applicable *a.* aplicable, adecuado-a, apropiado-a para utilizarse.

application *n.* aplicación, solicitud; ___ **blank** / formulario; [*ointment*] untadura.

applicator *n.* aplicador; **cotton** ___ / ___ de algodón.

apply *u.* aplicar, solicitar, requerir.

appointment *n.* cita, consulta, turno; [*job related*] nombramiento, cargo.

appraise *u.* apreciar, estimar, evaluar, ponderar.

appreciate *u.* apreciar, agradecer, reconocer.

approach *n.* [*avenue*] acceso, entrada; [*words*] las palabras acertadas; método; [*decision*] las medidas necesarias; *u.* abordar; *vr.* acercarse, aproximarse.

appropriate *a.* apropiado-a, adecuado-a, apto-a.

approval *n.* aprobación, aceptación, consentimiento, admisión.

approve *u.* aprobar, aceptar, dar estimación.

approximate *a.* aproximado-a.

apraxia *n.* apraxia, falta de coordinación muscular en los movimientos causada por una afección cerebral.

apricot *n.* albaricoque; *Mex.* chabacano.

apron *n.* delantal.

aptitude *n.* aptitud, capacidad, destreza para hacer algo; ___ **test** / prueba de ___.

aqua *n. L.* agua; **aq.** *abbr.* / aq. *abr.;* **aq. bull, aqua bulliens** / ___ hirviendo; **aq. dest.**, ___ **destillata** / ___ destilada; **aq. pur.**, ___ **pura** / ___ pura; **aq. tep.**, ___ **tepid** / ___ tépida, tibia. *V.* **water.**

aqueous *a.* acuoso-a, aguado-a; ___ **humor** / humor ___.

aquiline *a.* aquilino-a; ___ **nose** / nariz aguileña.

arachnoid *n.* aracnoides, membrana media cerebral que cubre el cerebro y la médula espinal.

arch *n.* arco, estructura de forma circular o en curva.

archetype *n.* arquetipo, tipo original ideal del que se derivan versiones modificadas.

ardor *n.* ardor, sensación quemante.

areola *n.* aréola, areola, área circular alrededor de un centro.

argue *u.* razonar, discutir, sostener.

Argyll Robertson symptom *n.* signo de Argyll Robertson, condición de la pupila de acomodarse a una distancia, pero no a refracciones de la luz.

arise *vi.* subir, levantarse, surgir.

arm *n.* brazo, una de las extremidades superiores; ___ **sling** / cabestrillo; ___ **span** / de mano a mano, distancia de la mano derecha a la izquierda con los ___-s extendidos; **open arms** / ___-s abiertos.

armless *a.* sin brazos.

armpit *n.* axila, *pop.* sobaco.

aroma *n.* aroma, olor agradable.

aromatic *a.* aromático-a, rel. al aroma.

around *prep.* en, cerca de; *adv.* alrededor, cerca,

a la vuelta; más o menos; ___ **here** / por aquí, en los alrededores; *u.* **to look** ___ / buscar; *u.* **to turn** ___ / voltear, dar la vuelta; virarse.

arrange *u.* arreglar, colocar, poner en su sitio.

arrest *n.* paro, arresto; detención; **cardiac** ___ / ___ del corazón, ___ cardíaco.

arrhythmia *n.* arritmia, falta de ritmo, esp. latidos irregulares del corazón.

arrival *n.* arribo, llegada; **dead on** ___ / paciente que llega sin vida, que llega muerto-a; [*newborn*] **new** ___ / neonato-a, recién nacido-a.

arsenic *n.* arsénico; ___ **poisoning** / envenenamiento por arsénico.

arterial *a.* arterial, referente a las arterias; ___ **blood gases** / gases ___; ___ **occlusive diseases** / enfermedades oclusivas ___-es; ___ **system** / sistema ___.

arteriogram *n.* arteriograma, angiograma de las arterias; **cerebral or carotid** / ___ cerebral o carotinoide; **mesenteric** ___ / ___ mesentérico; **peripheral** ___ / ___ periférico; **renal** ___ / ___ renal.

arteriography *n.* arteriografía, proceso de obtener una radiografía de las arterias.

arteriole *n.* arteriola, arteria diminuta que termina en un capilar.

arteriosclerosis *n.* arterioesclerosis, endurecimiento de las paredes de las arterias.

arteriotomy *n.* arteriotomía, *cirg.* apertura de una arteria.

arteriovenous *a.* arteriovenoso-a, relacionado con una arteria y una vena; ___ **fistula** / fístula ___; ___ **malformations** / malformaciones ___-s; ___ **shunt, surgical** / anastomosis ___ quirúrgica.

arteritis *n.* arteritis, infl. de una arteria.

artery *n.* arteria, uno de los vasos mayores que llevan la sangre del corazón a otras partes del cuerpo; **innominate** ___ / ___ innominada.

arthritic *a.* artrítico-a, que padece de artritis.

arthritis *n.* artritis, infl. de una articulación o coyuntura; **acute** ___ / ___ aguda; **chronic** ___ / ___ crónica; **degenerative** ___ / ___ degenerativa; **hemophilic** ___ / ___ hemofílica; **rheumatoid** ___ / ___ reumatoidea; **juvenile rheumatoid** ___ / ___ reumatoidea juvenil; **traumatic** ___ / ___ traumática.

arthrodesis *n.* artrodesis. 1. *cirg.* fusión de los huesos que hacen una articulación; 2. anquilosis artificial.

arthrogram *n.* artrograma, radiografía de una articulación por medio de un tinte opaco.

arthropathy *n.* artropatía, enfermedad de las articulaciones.

arthroplasty *n.* artroplastia, *cirg.* reparación quirúrgica plástica de una articulación.

arthroscope *n.* artroscopio, instrumento que se usa para el diagnóstico y tratamiento de ciertas condiciones en las articulaciones.

arthroscopy *n.* artroscopia, examen del interior de una articulación.

arthrotomy *n.* artrotomía, *cirg.* incisión en una

articulación con fines terapéuticos.

articular *a.* articular, rel. a las articulaciones.

articulate *a.* articulado-a, que se pronuncia con precisión; ___ **person** / persona que tiene facilidad de palabra, que puede expresarse bien; *v.* articular, pronunciar las palabras claramente.

articulation *n.* articulación. 1. unión de dos o más huesos; 2. pronunciación clara y distinta de los sonidos de las palabras; ___ **disorders** / trastornos de la ___.

artificial *a.* artificial, artificioso-a; ___ **limb** / extremidad o parte ___.

artificial heart *n.* corazón artificial, aparato que bombea la sangre con la capacidad funcional de un corazón normal.

as *conj.* como, del mismo modo; ___ **a child** / de niño; *comp.* ___ **much** / tanto; ___ **much** ___ **possible** / lo más posible; ___ **you please** / como Ud. quiera, tú quieras; ___ **soon** ___ **you can** / tan pronto como pueda, puedas; ___ **usual** / como de costumbre; **not** ___ **yet** / todavía no.

asbestos *n.* asbesto, amianto.

asbestosis *n.* asbestosis, infección crónica de los pulmones causada por el polvo del asbesto.

ascariasis *n.* ascariasis, infección causada por parásitos del género *Ascaris*.

ascaris *n. Ascaris*, género de parásitos que se aloja en el intestino de animales vertebrados.

ascend *v.* ascender, subir, escalar.

ascendent *a.* ascendiente, ascendente.

ascites *n.* ascitis, acumulación de líquido en la cavidad abdominal.

ascorbic acid *n.* ácido ascórbico, vitamina C.

asepsia *n.* asepsia, ausencia total de gérmenes.

aseptic *a.* aséptico-a, estéril.

asexual *a.* asexual, sin género; ___ **reproduction** / reproducción sin unión sexual.

ash *n.* ceniza; ___-**colored** / ceniciento-a.

ashamed *a.* avergonzado-a, apenado-a; *v.* **to be** ___ / tener vergüenza, tener pena.

Asiatic flu *n.* gripe asiática.

aside *adv.* aparte, a un lado; *v.* **to lay** ___ / dejar de lado.

ask *v.* preguntar, interrogar, hacer preguntas; [*about someone*] preguntar por; **to** ___ **for;** [*to request*] pedir.

asking *n.* súplica, petición, demanda.

asleep *a.* dormido-a; *v.* **to fall** ___ / dormirse, quedarse ___.

aspect *n.* aspecto, apariencia.

aspermia *n.* aspermia, fallo en la emisión de semen.

asphyxia *n.* asfixia, sofocación, falta de respiración; ___ **fetalis** / ___ del feto.

asphyxiate *v.* asfixiarse.

aspirate *v.* aspirar.

aspiration *n.* aspiración, inhalación, succión, extracción de un líquido sin dejar entrar el aire; ___ **biopsy** / biopsia con aguja.

aspirin *n.* aspirina, ácido acetilsalicílico.

assay *n.* ensayo; análisis.

assert *v.* afirmar, sostener.

assessment *n.* evaluación; **clinical** ___ / ___ clínica; **health** ___ / ___ del estado de salud.

assets *n.* capital existente, fondos.

assign *v.* asignar, indicar, señalar.

assignment *n.* asignación, tarea, misión.

assimilate *v.* asimilar, convertir los alimentos en sustancias.

assimilation *n.* asimilación, transformación y absorción por el organismo de los alimentos digeridos.

assist *v.* ayudar, asistir, socorrer.

assistance *n.* asistencia, ayuda.

assistant *n., a.* asistente, ayudante.

associate *a.* asociado-a, socio-a.

association *n.* asociación, sociedad, unión.

assurance *n.* seguridad, confianza, certeza.

assure *v.* asegurar, dar confianza.

astasia *n.* astasia, condición histérica.

asthenia *n.* astenia, pérdida de vigor.

asthma *n.* asma, condición alérgica con ataques de coriza y falta de la respiración a causa de la infl. de las membranas mucosas.

asthmatic *a.* asmático-a, rel. al asma.

astigmatism *n.* astigmatismo, defecto de la visión a causa de una irregularidad en la curvatura del ojo.

astragalus *n.* astrágalo, calus, hueso del tobillo.

astringent *a.* astringente, agente con poder de constricción de los tejidos y las membranas mucosas.

astrocytoma *n.* astrocitoma, tumor cerebral.

asylum *n.* asilo.

asymmetry *n.* asimetría, falta de simetría.

asymptomatic *a.* asintomático-a, sin síntoma alguno.

asynergy *n.* asinergia, falta de coordinación entre órganos gen. armónicos.

asystole, asystolia *n.* asístole, asistolia, paro del corazón, ausencia de contracciones cardíacas.

ataraxia *n.* ataraxia; *psic.* impasividad.

atavism *n.* atavismo, reproducción de rasgos y características ancestrales.

ataxia *n.* ataxia, deficiencia de coordinación muscular.

atelectasis *n.* atelectasis, colapso parcial o total de un pulmón.

athermic *a.* atérmico-a, sin fiebre.

atheroma *n.* ateroma, depósito graso o lípido en la capa íntima de una arteria que causa endurecimiento de la misma.

atherosclerosis *n.* aterosclerosis, condición causada por la deposición de grasa en las capas interiores de las arterias y fibrosis de las mismas.

athetosis *n.* atetosis, condición con síntomas de contracciones involuntarias en las manos y los dedos y movimientos sin coordinación de las extremidades, esp. los brazos.

athlete's foot *n.* pie de atleta. *V.* **dermatophy-**

tosis.

atmosphere *n.* atmósfera.

atmospheric *a.* atmosférico-a.

atom *n.* átomo.

atomic *a.* atómico-a.

atomizer *n.* atomizador.

atonia, atony *n.* atonía, falta de tono, esp. en los músculos.

atopic *a.* atópico-a, rel. a la atopía.

atopy *n.* atopía, tipo de alergia considerada de carácter hereditario.

atresia *n.* atresia, cierre congénito anormal de una abertura o conducto del cuerpo.

atrial *a.* auricular, atrial, rel. al atrio o la aurícula; ___ **septal defect** / defecto septal ___.

atrioventricular *a.* atrioventricular, rel. a la aurícula y ventrículo del corazón; ___ **node** / nudo aurículoventricular; ___ **orifice** / orificio ___.

atrium *n.* (*pl.* **atria**) atrio. 1. cavidad que tiene comunicación con otra estructura; 2. cavidad superior del corazón.

atrophy *n.* atrofia, deteriorización de las células, tejidos y órganos del cuerpo.

atropine sulfate *n.* atropina, agente usado como relajador muscular, esp. aplicado para dilatar la pupila y paralizar el músculo ciliar durante un examen de la vista.

attach *v.* añadir, juntar, pegar, unir.

attached *a.* añadido-a, pegado-a, unido-a.

attack *n.* ataque, acceso; **heart** ___ / ataque al corazón; *v.* atacar, combatir.

attempt *v.* intentar, tratar de obtener algo; hacer un esfuerzo; esforzarse, arriesgarse.

attend *v.* atender, asistir, cuidar, tener cuidado; **to** ___ **the sick** / asistir, cuidar a los enfermos.

attendant *n.* auxiliar, asistente.

attending physician *n.* médico-a de cabecera.

attention *n.* atención, cuidado; **lack of** ___ / falta de ___; *v.* **to pay** ___ / atender, prestar atención.

attentive *a.* atento-a; **-ly** *adv.* atentamente, con cuidado.

attenuation *n.* atenuación, acto de disminución, esp. de una virulencia.

attitude *n.* actitud; ___ **of health personnel** / ___ del personal de salud; ___ **toward death** / ___ frente a la muerte.

attorney *n.* abogado-a, agente legal.

attract *v.* atraer.

attraction *n.* atracción.

attribute *n.* atributo, característica.

atypical *a.* atípico-a, que no es común; fuera de lo corriente.

audiogram *n.* audiograma, instrumento para anotar la agudeza de la audición.

audiovisual *a.* audiovisual, rel. a la vista y a la audición.

auditory *a.* auditivo-a, rel. a la audición; ___ **canal** / conducto ___; ___ **nerve** / nervio ___.

augment *n.* aumento, crecimiento; *v.* aumentar, crecer; agrandarse.

aunt *n.* tía.

aura *n.* aura, síntoma premonitorio de un ataque epiléptico.

aural, auricular *a.* aural, auricular. 1. rel. al sentido del oído; 2. rel. a una aurícula del corazón.

auricle, auricula *n.* aurícula. 1. oreja, la parte externa del oído. 2. cavidad superior del corazón: aurícula derecha e izquierda.

auscultate *v.* auscultar, examinar, detectar sonidos de órganos tales como el corazón y los pulmones con el propósito de hacer un diagnóstico.

auscultation *n.* auscultación, acto de auscultar, detección de sonidos en un examen directo o por medio del estetoscopio.

authority *n.* autoridad, facultad.

authorization *n.* autorización.

authorize *v.* autorizar, permitir.

autism *n.* autismo, trastorno de la conducta que se manifiesta en un egocentrismo extremo; **infantile** ___ / ___ infantil.

autistic *a.* autístico-a, rel. al autismo o que padece de éste.

autoclave *n.* autoclave, aparato de esterilización al vapor.

autodiagnosis *n.* autodiagnosis, diagnóstico propio, de sí mismo-a.

autodigestion *n.* autodigestión, digestión de tejidos por las mismas sustancias que los producen.

autogenous *n.* autógeno-a, que se produce en el mismo organismo.

autogenous vaccine *n.* vacuna autógena, inoculación que proviene del cultivo de bacterias del mismo paciente y se hace para crear anticuerpos.

autograft *n.* autoinjerto, injerto que se transfiere de una parte a otra del cuerpo del mismo paciente.

autohypnosis *n.* autohipnosis, hipnotismo propio, de sí mismo-a.

autoimmunization *n.* autoinmunización, inmunidad producida por una sustancia desarrollada dentro del organismo de la persona afectada.

autoinfection *n.* autoinfección, infección causada por un agente del propio organismo.

autoinoculable *a.* autoinoculable, susceptible a organismos que provienen del propio cuerpo.

autologous *a.* autólogo-a, que indica algo que proviene del propio individuo.

automatic *a.* automático, de movimiento propio.

automatism *n.* automatismo, conducta que no está bajo control voluntario.

automobile *n.* automóvil, carro, *Cuba* máquina, *Spain* coche.

autonomic, autonomous *a.* autonómico-a, autónomo-a, que funciona independientemente; ___ **nervous system** / sistema nervioso ___.

autonomy *n.* autonomía, de funcionamiento propio.

autoplastic *a.* autoplástico-a, rel. a la autoplastia.

autoplasty *n.* autoplastia, *cirg.* cirugía plástica con el uso de un injerto que se obtiene de la misma persona que lo recibe.

autopsy *n.* autopsia, examen de un cadáver.

autosuggestion *n.* autosugestión, acto de sugestionarse.

auxiliary *a.* auxiliar; ayudante.

availability *n.* disponibilidad, facilidad.

available *a.* disponible, servicial; a la mano; **to be ___** / estar a la disposición, estar ___.

avaricious *a.* avaricioso-a, ruin, miserable.

average *n.* promedio, término medio; de mediana proporción.

aversion *n.* aversión, aborrecimiento, odio.

avitaminosis *n.* avitaminosis, trastorno o enfermedad causada por una deficiencia vitamínica.

avoid *v.* evitar.

avulsion *n. cirg.* avulsión, extracción o remoción de una estructura o parte de ésta.

awake *a.* despierto-a.

aware *a.* enterado-a; conocedor-a; *v.* **to be ___** / estar al tanto.

away *adv.* lejos; *a.* distante, ausente; *v.* **to go ___** / irse, ausentarse; *interj.* **get ___!** / quítese, quítate; váyase, vete.

awful *a.* terrible, desagradable; tremendo-a.

awhile *adv.* por un rato, por algún tiempo.

awkward *a.* [*movement*] torpe; desmañado-a; [*appearance*] extraño-a; **___ feeling** / sentimiento extraño.

axial *a.* axil, axial, rel. al axis o a un eje.

axilla *n.* (*pl.* **axillae**) axila, *pop.* sobaco.

axillary *a.* axilar, rel. a la axila.

axis *n.* axis, eje, línea central imaginaria que pasa a través del cuerpo o de un órgano.

ay, aye *adv.* sí, claro, desde luego, seguramente.

Ayerza's syndrome *n.* síndrome de Ayersa, síndrome caracterizado por multiples síntomas, esp. dispnea y cianosis, gen. como resultado de insuficiencia pulmonar.

azoospermia *n.* azoospermia, falta de espermatozoos en el esperma.

azotemia *n.* azotemia, exceso de urea en la sangre.

azure *n.* azul celeste.

244

b *abbr.* **bacillus** / bacilo; **behavior** / conducta; **buccal** / bucal.

babble *n.* balbuceo; *v.* balbucear.

Babinski sign *n.* reflejo de Babinski, dorsiflexión del dedo gordo al estimularse la planta del pie.

baby, babe *n.* bebé, *dim.* bebito-a; nene-a.

bachelor *n.* soltero-a, célibe; [*degree*] bachiller.

bacillar, bacillary *a.* bacilar, rel. a un bacilo.

bacillemia *n.* bacilemia, presencia de bacilos en la sangre.

bacillicarrier *n.* portador de bacilos.

bacillosis *n.* bacilosis, infección provocada por bacilos.

bacilluria *n.* baciluria, presencia de bacilos en la orina.

bacillus *n.* (*pl.* **bacilli**) bacilo, microbio, bacteria en forma de bastoncillo; **Calmette-Guérin, bacille bilié (BCG)** ___ / ___ de Calmette Guérin, bacille bilié; **Koch's** ___, **Mycobacterium tuberculosis** / ___ de Koch, micobacteria de la tuberculosis; **typhoid** ___, **Salmonella typhi** / ___ de la fiebre tifoidea, Salmonela tifoidea.

bacitracin *n.* bacitracin, antibiótico efectivo en contra de ciertos estafilococos.

back *n.* espalda; ___ **tooth** / muela; **low** ___ **pain** / lumbalgia. *adv.* atrás, detrás.

backache *n.* dolor de espalda.

backboard *n.* respaldar.

backbone *n.* columna vertebral, espina dorsal.

background *n.* fondo; [*knowledge*] preparación, experiencia.

backing *n.* apoyo, sostén.

backlash *n.* contragolpe.

backside *n.* nalgas, *pop.* sentaderas, posaderas, trasero.

backslide *v.* resbalar o caer hacia atrás.

backward *a.* atrasado-a, tardío-a, lento-a, retraído-a; *adv.* atrás, hacia atrás, al revés; [*direction*] en sentido contrario.

backwardness *n.* atraso, retraso, ignorancia, torpeza.

bacon *n.* tocino.

bactermia *n.* bacteremia, presencia de bacterias en la sangre.

bacteria *n. pl.* bacterias, gérmenes.

bacterial *a.* bacteriano-a; ___ **infections** / infecciones ___-s; ___ **endocarditis** / endocarditis ___; ___ **sensitivity tests** / pruebas de sensibilidad ___.

bactericidal *n.* bactericida, exterminador de bacterias.

bacteriogenic *a.* bacteriogénico-a. 1. de origen bacteriano; 2. que produce bacterias.

bacteriological *a.* bacteriológico-a, rel. a las bacterias.

bacteriologist *n.* bacteriólogo-a, especialista en bacteriología.

bacteriology *n.* bacteriología, ciencia que estudia las bacterias.

bacteriolysin *n.* bacteriolisina, anticuerpo antibacteriano que destruye bacterias.

bacteriolysis *n.* bacteriolisis, destrucción de bacterias.

bacteriosis *n.* bacteriosis, toda infección causada por gérmenes o bacterias.

bacteriostatic *a.* bacteriostático-a, que detiene el desarrollo o multiplicación de bacterias.

bacterium *n.* (*pl.* **bacteria**) bacteria, germen.

bacteriuria *n.* bacteriuria, presencia de bacterias en la orina.

bad *a.* malo-a, nocivo-a, [*harmful*] dañino-a; **it is** ___ **for your health** / es dañino a la salud; **from** ___ **to worse** / de mal en peor; *v.* **to look** ___ / tener mal aspecto, tener mala cara; ___ **breath** / mal aliento; ___ **looking** / mal parecido; ___ **mood** / mal humor; ___ **taste in the mouth** / mal sabor en la boca; *slang* ___ **trip** / mala experiencia con una droga; *adv.* mal; *v.* **to feel** ___ / sentirse mal; **-ly** *adv.* mal, malamente; *v.* **to need** ___ / necesitar con urgencia.

bag *n.* bolsa, bolso; saco; **colostomy** ___ / bolso de colostomía; ___ **of waters** / saco amniótico, *pop.* ___ de aguas; **ice** ___ / ___ de hielo.

baked *a.* asado-a, guisado-a al horno, horneado-a.

balance *n.* balance. 1. estado de equilibrio; **acid-base** ___ / ___ acidobásico; **fluid** ___ / ___ hídrico; 2. *psic.* estabilidad mental o emocional; 3. balanza, pesa.

balanced *a.* balanceado-a; en control; ___ **diet** / dieta ___.

balanitis *n.* balanitis, infl. del glande gen. acompañada de infl. del prepucio.

balanoposthitis *n.* balanopostitis, infl. del glande y del prepucio.

bald *a.* calvo-a, sin pelo; franco-a, espontáneo-a, escueto-a.

baldness *n.* calvicie.

ball *n.* bola; asiento del pie; ___ **forceps** / pinzas sacabalas; ___ **of the foot** / antepié; ___-**and-socket joint** / articulación esférica.

ballistocardiogram *n.* balistocardiograma, registro fotográfico del volumen sistólico para calcular el volumen por minuto.

balloon *n.* balón; *slang* [*heroin*] globo.

ballottement *Fr.* peloteo, movimiento manual de rebote por palpación usado en el examen abdominal y pélvico para determinar la presencia de un tumor o el agrandamiento de un órgano.

balm *n.* bálsamo, ungüento, calmante de uso externo.

balmy *a.* balsámico; suave, reparador; ___ **sleep** / sueño reparador.

balsam *n.* bálsamo, agente suavizante.

ban *v.* prohibir, suspender, suprimir.

banana *n.* banana, plátano.

bandage *n.* venda, vendaje, faja; *v.* vendar, ligar, atar.

Band-Aid *n. pop.* curita; parche.

bandy-legged *n.* zambo-a, patizambo-a.

bane *n.* veneno; ruina.

baneful *a.* venenoso-a, dañino-a, destructivo-a.

bang *n.* golpe; detonación.

bank *n.* banco; **blood** ___ / ___ de sangre.

baragnosis *n.* baragnosis, pérdida de la capacidad de reconocer pesos y presiones.

barbiturate *n.* barbitúrico, hipnótico, sedante.

bare *a.* desnudo-a, descubierto-a; ___-**legged** / sin medias; **-ly** *adv.* apenas.

barefoot *a.* descalzo-a, sin zapatos.

baresthesia *n.* barestesia, sensación de presión o peso.

barium *n.* bario; ___ **enema** / enema de ___.

barley *n.* cebada.

barometer *n.* barómetro, instrumento para medir la presión atmosférica.

baroreceptor *n.* barorreceptor, terminación nerviosa sensorial que reacciona a los cambios de presión.

barrel *n.* [*part of a syringe*] cilindro; barril.

barren *a.* estéril, infecundo-a.

barrier *n.* obstrucción, barrera.

bartholinitis *n.* bartolinitis, infl. de la glándula de Bartolino o glándula vulvovaginal.

baryphonia *n.* barifonía, tipo de voz gruesa.

basal, basilar *a.* basal, basilar, rel. a una base; ___ **ganglia diseases** / enfermedades de los ganglios ___-es; ___ **metabolic rate** / índice del metabolismo ___.

base, basis *n.* base.

bashful *a.* tímido-a, *pop.* corto-a.

basic *a.* básico-a, fundamental.

basil *n.* albahaca.

basilar *a.* basilar, rel. a la base o parte basal.

basin *n.* 1. vasija redonda tal como una palangana; 2. cavidad de la pelvis.

basophobia *n. psic.* basofobia, temor excesivo de caminar.

bassinet *n.* bacinete, cuna.

bastard *n.* bastardo-a; hijo o hija ilegítimo-a.

bath *n.* baño; **aromatic** ___ / ___ aromático; **alcohol** ___ / fricción de alcohol; **antipyretic** ___ / ___ antipirético, para reducir la fiebre; **cold** ___ / ___ de agua fría; **Sitz** ___ / ___ de asiento caliente; **sponge** ___ / ___ con esponja; **warm** ___ / ___ tibio.

bathe *v.* bañar, lavar; bañarse, lavarse.

bathrobe *n.* bata de baño.

bathroom *n.* baño, cuarto de baño.

bathtub *n.* tina, bañadera.

battered *a.* abatido-a, maltratado-a.

battle *n.* batalla, lucha; *v.* batallar, combatir, luchar.

bay leaves *n. pl.* hojas de laurel.

bay-salt *n.* sal marina.

be *vi.* ser, estar; **there is, there are** / hay; **there was** / hubo, había; **there will be** / será, estará; habrá; *pp.* **been** / sido, estado; *p.p.* **being** / siendo, estando; **to** ___ **afraid** / tener miedo; **to** ___ **calm** / calmarse; **to** ___ **careful** / tener cuidado; **to** ___ **cold** / tener frío; **to** ___ **hot** / tener calor; **to** ___ **hungry** / tener hambre; **to be at a loss** ___ / estar confundido-a; **to** ___ **quiet** / callarse; estar tranquilo-a; **to** ___ **right** / tener razón; **to** ___ **all right** / estar bien; **to** ___ . . . **years old** / tener . . . años; **to** ___ **sick** / estar enfermo-a; **to** ___ **sleepy** / tener sueño; **to** ___ **successful** / tener éxito; **to** ___ **thirsty** / tener sed; **to** ___ **warm** [*with a temperature*] / tener fiebre, tener calentura; tener calor; **to want to** ___ / querer ser; **to want to** ___ [*somewhere*] / querer estar.

bean *n.* frijol; ___-**shaped** / en forma de riñon o frijol.

bear *vi.* soportar; aguantar; ___ **down** / pujar, empujar hacia afuera con fuerza.

bearable *a.* soportable, tolerable.

beard *n.* barba.

bearded *a.* barbudo.

bearer *n.* soporte, apoyo.

bearing *n.* gestación; conexión; [*in obstetrics*] ___ **down** / [*second stage of labor*] pujo, expulsión hacia afuera.

beat *n.* [*heart*] latido, pulsación; **heart** ___ / ___ del corazón; *vi.* pulsar; [*heart*] palpitar; pegar, golpear.

beaten *a. pp.* de **to beat,** maltratado-a; golpeado-a; vencido-a, derrotado-a.

beating *n.* pulsación, latido; paliza, zurra.

beautiful *a.* hermoso-a, bello-a.

beauty *n.* belleza, hermosura, beldad.

become *vi.* hacerse, convertirse; ___ **a doctor** / hacerse médico-a; [*conversion*] ___ **a** / convertirse en; ___ **accustomed** / acostumbrarse; ___ **crazy** / volverse loco-a; ___ **frightened** / asustarse; ___ **ill** / ponerse enfermo-a; enfermarse; ___ **inflamed** / inflamarse; ___ **swollen** / hincharse.

becoming *a.* apropiado-a, conveniente, que sienta o cae bien.

bed *n.* cama, lecho; ___ **occupancy** / ocupación de ___-s; ___ **rest** / reclusión en ___.

bedbug *n.* chinche.

bedclothes *n. pl.* ropa de cama.

bedding *n.* ropa de cama; colchón y almohada.

bedfast *a.* recluido-a en cama.

bedpan *n.* bacín, chata, cuña.

bedridden *a.* postrado-a en cama.

bedroom *n.* cuarto de dormir, alcoba, dormitorio; *Mex.* recámara.

bedside *a.* al lado de la cama.

bedsore *n.* úlcera por decúbito.

bedspread *n.* colcha, sobrecama, cubrecama.

bedtime *n.* hora de acostarse.

bed-wetting *n.* enuresis; orinarse en la cama, mojar la cama.

bee *n.* abeja; ___ **venom** / veneno de ___.

beef *n.* carne de res, carne de vaca; ___ **broth** / caldo de carne; **roast** ___ / carne asada, rosbif; ___ **steak** / biftec.

beer n. cerveza.

beet n. remolacha.

before adv. delante; enfrente de; antes de; anterior a; conj. antes que; antes de que.

beforehand adv. con anterioridad, con anticipación; de antemano.

beg v. pedir, rogar, mendigar.

begin vi. comenzar, empezar, principiar.

beginner n. principiante, novicio-a; autor-a, iniciador-a.

beginning n. principio, origen, génesis.

behalf n. en beneficio, a favor; **on your** ___ / a su favor, por usted.

behavior n. conducta, comportamiento; ___ **reflex** / reflejo adquirido; ___ **therapy** / terapia de la ___; **high-risk** ___ / comportamiento arriesgado.

behind adv., prep., detras, trás, atrás, hacia atrás.

bel n. bel, belio, unidad que expresa la intensidad relativa de un sonido.

belch n. eructo, regüeldo; v. eructar.

belief n. creencia, opinión.

belittle n. dar poca importancia, humillar.

belladonna n. belladona, yerba medicinal cuyas hojas y raíces contienen atropina y alcaloides.

bellied a. panzudo-a, barrigón-a, con barriga.

belligerent a. beligerante.

Bell's palsy n. parálisis de Bell, parálisis de un lado de la cara causada por una afección del nervio facial.

belly n. abdomen, barriga, vientre, pop. panza; ___ **button** / ombligo; ___ **worm** / lombriz intestinal.

bellyache n. dolor de estómago, de barriga.

below prep. después de, debajo de; adv. abajo, bajo, debajo; **down** ___ / en la parte baja; más abajo.

belt n. cinturón, cinto.

bend vi. doblarse, inclinarse; ___ **back** / ___ hacia atrás; ___ **forward** / ___ hacia adelante.

beneath prep., adv. abajo, debajo, bajo.

Benedict test n. prueba de Benedict, análisis químico para encontrar la presencia de azúcar en la orina.

beneficial a. beneficioso-a, favorable, provechoso-a.

beneficiary n., a. beneficiado-a, favorecido-a.

benefit n. beneficio, favor; servicio, provecho; **allocation of** ___-s / asignación de ___-s.

benign a. benigno-a, que no es de naturaleza maligna.

bent n. inclinación, curvatura; a. encorvado-a; inclinado-a.

Benzedrine n. Bencedrina, nombre comercial del sulfato de anfetamina.

benzoin n. benjuí, resina usada como expectorante.

beriberi n. beriberi, tipo de neuritis múltiple causada por deficiencia de vitamina B_1 (tiamina).

beside adv. además, prep. al lado de, cerca de, junto a; ___ **oneself** / fuera de sí, loco-a.

best a. sup. mejor, superior, óptimo; v. **to do one's** ___ hacer lo ___ posible.

bestial a. bestial, irracional, brutal.

bestiality n. bestialidad, relaciones sexuales con animales.

beta blocker n. beta bloqueador, agente que bloquea la acción de la epinefrina.

better a. comp. mejor, superior; [better than] mejor que; v. **to be** ___ / estar mejor, ponerse mejor; **to make** ___ / mejorar, aliviar; **so much the** ___ / tanto major; v. **to change for the** ___ / recuperarse, restablecerse; **to be** ___ **than** / ser mejor que; **to be** ___ **than before** / estar, ser mejor que antes; **to like** ___ / preferir.

between adv. en medio; prep. entre, en medio de.

beverage n. bebida; **alcoholic** ___-s / bebidas alcoholicas; **nonalcoholic** ___ / refresco, soda.

beware of vi. cuidarse de.

bewilder v. confundir, perturbar, turbar.

bewildered a. perplejo-a, confundido-a; atolondrado-a.

beyond adv. más allá, más lejos.

bezoar n. bezoar, concreción formada de distintas materias como fibras vegetales y pelo, presente en el estómago y en el intestino humano y en el de los animales.

bias n. parcialidad, prejuicio, tendencia.

biaxial a. biaxial, que tiene dos ejes.

bib n. babero; pechera.

bibliography n. bilbiografía.

bicarbonate n. bicarbonato, sal de ácido carbónico.

biceps n. músculo bíceps.

bicipital a. bicipital. 1. rel. al músculo bíceps; 2. bicípite, que tiene dos cabezas.

biconcave a. bicóncavo-a, de dos superficies cóncavas.

biconvex a. biconvexo-a, de dos caras convexas, tal como los lentes para la presbicia.

bicuspid a. bicúspide, que presenta dos puntas.

bicycle n. bicicleta; **stationary** ___ / ___ estacionaria.

bicycling n. ciclismo.

bifid a. bífido-a, partido en dos.

bifocal a. bifocal, referente a dos focos o enfoques.

bifurcation n. bifurcación, división en dos ramas o bifurcaciones.

big a. grande, enorme; mayor; ___ **bellied** / barrigón-a, panzudo-a; ___ **head** / cabezón-a; ___ **sister, brother** / hermana mayor, hermano mayor; ___ **toe** / dedo gordo; ___ **with child** / encinta, en estado.

bigeminy n. bigeminia, pulsación duplicada en sucesión rápida.

bigger a. comp. mayor, más grande.

bilabial a. bilabial.

bilateral a. bilateral, de dos lados.

bile n. bilis, hiel, producto de la secreción del hígado; ___ **acids and salts** / ácidos y sales biliares; ___ **ducts** / conductos biliares; ___

pigments / pigmentos biliares.
bilharziasis *n.* bilharziasis. *V.* **schistosomiasis.**
biliary *a.* biliar, rel. a la bilis, los conductos biliares o la vesícula ___; ___ **duct obstruction** / obstrucción del conducto ___; ___ **stasis** / colestasis; ___ **tract diseases** / enfermedades de las vías ___-es; ___ **tract hemorrhage** / hemobilia.
bilingual *a.* bilingüe.
bilious *a.* bilioso-a, con exceso de bilis.
biliousness *n.* biliosidad, trastorno con síntomas de estreñimiento, dolor de cabeza e indigestión atribuidos a un exceso de secreción biliar.
bilirubin *n.* bilirrubina, pigmento rojo de la bilis.
bilirubinemia *n.* bilirrubinemia, presencia de bilirrubina en la sangre.
bilirubinuria *n.* bilirrubinuria, presencia de bilirrubina en la orina.
bill *n.* [*statement*] cuenta; [*currency*] billete.
bimanual *a.* bimanual, rel. a las dos manos.
binary *a.* binario, doble.
bind *vi.* unir, ligar, vendar.
binding *n.* enlace; ligazón; venda; vendaje.
binocular *n.* binocular, lentes, gemelos.
bioassay *n.* bioensayo, prueba de determinación de la potencia de una droga en animales.
biochemical *a.* bioquímico-a, rel. a la bioquímica.
biochemistry *n.* bioquímica, ciencia que estudia los organismos vivos.
biologist *n.* biólogo-a.
biology *n.* biología, ciencia que estudia los organismos vivos; **cellular** ___ / ___ celular; **molecular** ___ / ___ molecular.
biopsy *n.* biopsia, proceso para obtener un espécimen de tejido con fines de diagnóstico; ___ **by ablation** / ___ por ablación; ___ **by frozen section** / ___ en frío; ___ **of the bone marrow** / ___ de la medula ósea; ___ **of the breast** / ___ de la mama, del seno; ___ **of the cervix** / ___ del cuello uterino; ___ **of the lymph nodes** / ___ de los ganglios linfáticos; **needle** ___ / ___ por aspiración: **endoscopic** ___ / ___ endoscópica; **excision** ___ / ___ por excisión.
biosynthesis *n.* biosíntesis, formación de sustancias químicas en los procesos fisiológicos de los organismos.
biotype *n.* biotipo, grupo de individuos con igual genotipo.
biped *n.* bípedo, animal de dos pies.
birefringent *a.* birrefringente, de refracción doble.
birth *n.* nacimiento, parto, alumbramiento; ___ **canal** / canal del parto; ___ **certificate** / certificado de ___; ___ **control** / control de la natalidad, planeamiento familiar; ___-**death ratio** / índice de mortalidad; **post-term** ___ / ___ tardío; **premature** ___ / ___ prematuro; ___ **rate** / natalidad; ___ **right** / derechos naturales; ___ **weight** / peso al nacer; *v.* **to give** ___ / dar a luz, estar de parto.
birth date *n.* fecha de nacimiento.
birthday *n.* cumpleaños, natalicio.
birthplace *n.* lugar de nacimiento.
bisect *v.* bisecar, dividir en dos partes.
bisexual *a.* bisexual, con gónadas de los dos sexos.
bite *n.* mordida, picadura; [*snake*] mordida de serpiente; [*insect*] picadura; ___ **block** / bloque de ___; ___ **rim** / reborde de la ___; *vi.* morder, picar.
biting *a.* penetrante, picante.
bitter *a.* agrio-a, amargo-a; [*person*] amargado-a.
black *a.* negro-a; ___ **and blue** / amoratado; ___ **eye** / ojo amoratado; ___ **death** / peste bubónica; ___ **urine** / melanuria.
blackhead *n.* barro, espinilla, comedón.
blackout *n.* desmayo, vértigo, condición caracterizada por la falta de visión y pérdida momentánea del conocimiento.
bladder *n.* vejiga; saco musculomembranoso situado en la cavidad pélvica; ___ **calculi** / cálculos, piedras de la ___; ___ **infection** / infección de la ___; ___ **irrigation** / irrigación de la ___; ___, **neurogenic** / ___ neurogénica.
blain *n.* llaga, ampolla, pústula.
bland *a.* blando-a, suave; ___ **diet** / dieta ___.
blanket *n.* manta, frazada, cobija.
blastema *n.* blastema, sustancia primaria de la que se originan las células.
blastomycosis *n.* blastomicosis, infección causada por hongos que se inicia gen. en los pulmones.
blastula *n.* blástula, etapa primitiva del óvulo.
bleach *n.* lejía.
bleariness *n.* lagaña, secreción pegajosa del ojo; vista nublada.
bleary-eyed *a.* [*eye*] legañoso; [*sight*] vista nublada; vista cansada.
bleed *vi.* sangrar, derramar, perder sangre; [*profusely*] desangrarse.
bleeding *n.* sangramiento.
blemish *n.* mancha, imperfección, defecto.
blend *n.* mezcla; *v.* mezclar, combinar.
blennorrhagia *n.* blenorragia, flujo de mucus.
blepharectomy *n.* blefarectomía, *cirg.* excisión de una parte o de todo el párpado.
blepharitis *n.* blefaritis, infl. de los párpados.
blepharochalasis *n.* blefarocalasis, relajación o caída del párpado superior por pérdida de elasticidad del tejido intersticial.
blepharoplasty *n.* *cirg.* blefaroplastia, operación plástica de los párpados.
blepharoplegia *n.* blefaroplejía, parálisis del párpado.
blind *a.* ciego-a, sin vista, ofuscado-a; *v.* cegar, deslumbrar; ___ **in one eye** / tuerto-a; ___ **spot** / punto ___.
blindness *n.* ceguera; **color** ___ / acromatopsia, ___ al color; **night** ___ / nictalopía, ___ nocturna; **red** ___ / ___ roja; **total** ___ / pérdida

completa de la visión.

blinds *n. pl.* cortinas.

blink *v.* parpadear.

blinking *n.* parpadeo.

blister *n.* ampolla, vesícula, flictena.

bloat *n.* aventación. *V.* **tympanites;** *v.* entumecerse, hincharse.

bloated *a.* aventado-a, abotagado-a.

block *n.* bloqueo, obstrucción; *v.* obstruir, bloquear.

blocked *a.* bloqueado-a, obstruído-a; ___ **bowel** / obstrucción intestinal; ___ **ureter** / obstrucción ureteral.

blocker *n.* bloqueador; **calcium channel** ___ / ___ del canal cálcico.

blond *a.* rubio-a, *Mex.* güero-a.

blood *n.* sangre; **autologous** ___ / ___ autóloga; ___ **bank** / banco de ___ ; ___ **cell count** / conteo globular, conteo de células sanguíneas; ___ **clotting ability** / propiedad de coagulación; ___ **count** / conteo sanguíneo; ___ **culture** / hemocultivo; ___ **clot** / coágulo de ___ ; ___ **coagulation time** / tiempo de coagulación sanguínea; ___ **derivatives** / derivados sanguíneos, hemoderivados; ___ **donor** / donante de ___; ___ **gases** / gases sanguíneos; ___ **groups** / grupos sanguíneos; ___ **grouping** / determinación de grupos sanguíneos; ___ **oxygen analysis** / análisis del oxígeno contenido en la ___; **packed** ___ **cells** / células paquete, células sanguíneas compactadas; **peripheral** ___ / ___ periférica; ___ **plasma** / plasma sanguíneo; ___ **pressure** / presión arterial; ___ **products** / productos sanguíneos; ___ **proteins** / proteínas sanguíneas; ___ **relation** / consanguíneo-a; ___ **screening** / prueba selecta de ___; ___ **sputum** / esputo sanguinolento; ___ **substitutes** / substitutos sanguíneos; ___ **sugar** / glucemia; ___ **transfusion** / transfusión sanguínea; ___ **type** / grupo sanguíneo; ___ **typing** / determinación del grupo sanguíneo; ___ **vessel** / vaso sanguíneo.

bloodless *a.* exangüe, debilitado-a.

bloodletting *n.* efusión de sangre; *pop.* sangría.

blood pressure *n.* presión sanguínea, tensión de la sangre en las arterias producida por la contracción del ventrículo izquierdo, la resistencia de las arteriolas y capilares, la elasticidad de las paredes arteriales y la viscosidad y volumen de la sangre, expresada en relación con la presión atmosférica; **high** ___ / ___ alta; **low** ___ / ___ baja; **normal** ___ / ___ normal.

bloodshot *a.* [*eye*] inyectado de sangre.

bloody *a.* ensangrentado-a, con sangre, sanguinolento-a, cruento-a.

blotch *n.* marca, roncha.

blouse *n.* blusa, corpiño.

blow *n.* golpe; *vi.* soplar, **to give a** ___ / golpear; **to** ___ **one's nose** / soplarse, sonarse la nariz.

blown *a., pp.* de **to blow,** soplado-a; ___ **up** / hinchado-a.

blue *n.* color azul; triste, malancólico-a; ___ **baby**

syndrome / cianosis congénita, *pop.* mal azul.

blunder *n.* disparate, desatino.

blunt *a.* despuntado-a; embotado-a; ___ **injuries** / heridas contusas.

blur *v.* empañar, nublar los ojos.

blurred *a., pp.* de **to blur,** borroso-a, nublado-a, empañado-a.

blush *vr.* sonrojarse, ruborizarse.

blushing *n.* rubor.

board *n.* tabla.

body *n.* cuerpo; [*dead*] cadáver; tronco; materia, sustancia; ___ **fluid** / líquido corporal; ___ **height** / estatura; ___ **temperature** / temperatura corporal; ___ **weight** / peso corporal; ___ **wall** / tronco.

bogus *a.* falso-a; podrido-a.

boil *n.* forúnculo, *Cuba* nacido; *Mex.* elacote; *v.* hervir, cocer.

boiled *a.* hervido-a; ___ **water** / agua ___ .

boiling point *n.* punto de ebullición.

bolster *n.* cabezal; sostén, refuerzo; ___ **suture** / sutura compuesta.

bolus *n.* bolo. 1. cantidad de una sustancia que se administra en determinado tiempo por vía oral o intravenosa para obtener una respuesta inmediata; 2. masa de consistencia suave lista para ser ingerida; **alimentary** ___ / ___ alimenticio.

bond *n.* vínculo, unión.

bone *n.* hueso; ___ **cell** / osteoblasto; ___ **development** / desarrollo óseo; ___ **fracture** / fractura, ___ quebrado; ___ **fragility** / fragilidad ósea; ___ **graft** / injerto oseo; ___ **hook** / gancho óseo; ___ **lesions** / lesiones en los ___-s; ___ **marrow** / médula ósea, *pop.* tuétano; **marrow failure** / fallo de la médula ósea; ___ **plate** / placa ósea; ___ **splinter** / esquirla, astilla ósea; **hard** ___ / ___ compacto; **spongy** ___ / ___ esponjoso *v.* **to make no** ___**-s about it** / hablar sin rodeos; **skin and** ___**-s** / piel y ___**-s,** muy delgado *pop.* estar en el hueso; *v.* deshuesar; sacar los ___**-s.**

bonelet *n. dim.* huesecillo.

bonesetter *n.* componedor de huesos; curandero-a.

book *n.* libro.

boost *v.* estimular, aumentar, [*electricity*] elevar.

booster shot *n.* búster, inyección de refuerzo; dosis suplementaria; reactivación de una vacuna o agente inmunizador.

boot *n.* bota.

booze *n.* bebida alcohólica.

borax *n.* bórax, borato de sodio.

border *n.* borde, margen; frontera; ___ **line case** / caso incierto.

bordering *a.* cercano-a, fronterizo-a, adyacente.

bored *a.* aburrido-a.

boredom *n.* fastidio, aburrimiento.

boric acid *n.* ácido bórico.

born *a.* nacido-a; ___ **alive** / ___ vivo; **new** ___ / recién nacido-a; *v.* **to be** ___ / nacer.

borne *a.* acarreado-a, transmitido-a; llevado-a.

bosom *n.* seno, pecho.

both *a., pron.* ambos, los dos.

bothersome *a.* incómodo-a, molesto-a.

bottle *n.* botella, frasco, [*infant*] biberón, mamadera; *Mex. A.* pote, tele; ___ **feeding** / alimentación por biberón; ___ **propping** / suplemento con biberón.

bottom *n.* fondo, parte inferior; asiento; *pop.* posaderas, asentaderas; *Cuba* fondillo.

botulin *n.* botulina, toxina causante del botulismo.

botulism *n.* botulismo, intoxicación ocasionada por la ingestión de alimentos contaminados por *Clostridium botulinum* que se desarrolla en alimentos que no han sido propiamente conservados.

bougie *n.* bujía; candelilla, instrumento usado en la dilatación de la uretra.

bouillon *n.* caldo, líquido alimentacio.

bounding pulse *n.* pulso saltón.

bounding pupil *n.* pupila saltona.

bout *n.* acceso, ataque, episodio.

bovine *n.* bovino, referente al ganado.

bowel *n.* intestino. ___ **movement** / evacuación, deposición; ___ **obstruction** / obstrucción intestinal.

bowels *n. pl.* intestinos.

bowl *n.* bacín, taza.

bowleg *n.* V. **genu-varum.**

box *n.* caja, estuche.

boy *n.* niño, muchacho.

boyfriend *n.* amigo, novio.

brace *n.* braguero, corsé, vendaje; abrazadera; **ankle** ___ / tobillera; **neck** ___ / ___ de cuello; **braces** *n. pl.* [*dentistry*] ganchos, aros.

brachiocephalic *a.* braquiocefálico, rel. a la cabeza y al brazo.

brachydactyly *n.* braquidactilia, condición de manos y pies anormalmente pequeños.

bracing *n.* aplicación de una abrazadera.

bradycardia *n.* bradicardia, espanocardia, lentitud anormal en los latidos del corazón.

bradypnea *n.* bradipnea, movimientos respiratorios lentos.

brain *n.* cerebro, parte del sistema nervioso central que se localiza en el cráneo y actúa como regulador principal de las funciones del cuerpo; ___ **death** / muerte cerebral; ___ **edema** / edema cerbral; ___ **injuries** / traumatismo cerebral; ___ **or cerebral concussion** / concusión o conmoción cerebral; ___ **scan** / escán del ___; ___ **stem** / tronco cerebral; ___ **tumor** / tumor cerebral.

braincase *n.* cráneo, parte que encierra el cerebro.

brainless *a.* tonto-a, insensato-a.

brainwashing *n.* lavado de cerebro.

brainy *a.* inteligente, listo-a, talentoso-a.

braise *v.* asar al fuego; a la brasa.

bran *n.* salvado, producto procesado del trigo.

branch *n.* rama, bifurcación; sección, dependencia.

brassiere *n.* sostén, ajustador, corpiño.

brassy cough *n.* tos metálica, tos bronca.

bread *n.* pan; ___ **and butter** / pan y mantequilla.

break *n.* fractura, rotura; quebradura; *vi.* romper, quebrar, fracturar; *v.* fracturarse, romperse, quebrarse; **to** ___ **down** / [*health*] perder la salud; **to** ___ **in** / forzar, abrir; **to** ___ **loose** / separarse, desprenderse; **to** ___ **through** / avanzar; **to** ___ **up** / fraccionar.

breakable *a.* frágil, quebradizo.

breakage *n.* rotura, quebradura.

breakdown *n.* distribución detallada; descomposición; colapso; **nervous** ___ / crisis nerviosa.

breakfast *n.* desayuno.

breakout *n.* erupción.

breast *n.* pecho, seno, busto, mama; *slang* teta; **benign** ___ **disease** / enfermedad benigna de la ___; **caked** ___ / mastitis por estasis; *v.* **to** ___ **-feed** / dar el pecho, dar de mamar, dar la teta, *Mex. A.* criar con pecho; ___ **pump** / sacaleche, mamadera; ___ **self-examination** / autoexamen de los senos.

breastbone *n.* esternón.

breastfeeding *n.* lactancia materna.

breath *n.* respiración, aliento, soplo; *pop.* resuello; **coarse** ___ / ___ gruesa; **short of** ___ / corto de resuello, falto de aliento; **out of** ___ / falto de ___, sin aliento; *v.* **to be out of** ___ / faltar la ___, estar sofocado-a; **to gasp for** ___ / jadear, resollar; **to take a deep** ___ / respirar profundamente; **to hold one's** ___ / sostener, aguantar la ___.

breathanalyzer *n.* instrumento que analiza el aliento de una persona para indicar el grado de consunción de alcohol.

breathe *v.* respirar; [*to exhale*] exhalar; [*to inhale*] aspirar; *pop.* resollar; **to** ___ **through the mouth** / ___ por la boca; **to** ___ **through the nose** / ___ por la nariz.

breather *n.* respirador; tregua, reposo.

breathing *n.* respiración, aliento, respiro; *pop.* resuello; inhalación, aspiración; ___ **exercises** / ejercicios respiratorios; ___ **space,** ___ **time** / descanso, parada, reposo.

breathless *a.* sofocado-a, sin aliento; falto de respiración.

breathlessness *n.* sofocación.

breech *n.* trasero, posaderas, nalgas; [*in obstetrics*] ___ **birth** / presentación de nalgas, presentación trasera.

breed *vi.* criar, producir, engendrar.

breeding *n.* cria, crianza.

breeze *n.* brisa, aire suave.

bregma *Gr.* bregma, intersección de las suturas coronal y sagital del cráneo.

bridge *n.* puente; [*dental*] ___ **abutment** / pilar de ___, anclaje.

brief *n.* sumario, resumen; *a.* breve, corto-a, conciso-a; **-ly** *adv.* brevemente, concisamente; en pocas palabras.

bright *a.* brillante, lustroso-a, luminoso-a.

Bright's disease *n.* enfermedad de Bright. *V.* **glomerulonephritis.**

brim *n.* borde.

bring *vi.* traer; inducir; **to ___ down** / bajar; **to ___ down the fever** / bajar la fiebre; [*raise children*] **to ___ up** / educar, criar.

brochure *n.* folleto, panfleto.

bromhidrosis *n.* bromhidrosis, perspiración fétida; sudor fétido.

bronchial *a.* bronquial, rel. a los bronquios; **___ spasm** / espasmo **___;** **___ tree** / árbol **___;** **___ washing** / lavado **___.**

bronchiectasis *n.* bronquiectasia, dilatación crónica de los bronquios debida a una obstrucción o a una condición inflamatoria.

bronchiocele *n.* bronquiocele, dilatación localizada de un bronquiolo.

bronchiole *n.* bronquiolo, una de las ramas menores del árbol bronquial.

bronchiolitis *n.* bronquiolitis, infl. de los bronquiolos.

bronchitis *n.* bronquitis, infl. de los tubos bronquiales.

bronchoconstriction *n.* broncoconstricción, reducción del calibre bronquial.

bronchodilation *n.* broncodilatación, dilatación bronquial.

bronchodilator *n.* broncodilatador, medicamento que dilata el calibre de un bronquio; **___ agents** / agentes **___-es.**

bronchogenic *a.* broncogénico-a, broncógeno-a, que se origina en los bronquios.

bronchography *n.* broncografía, radiografía del árbol bronquial usando un medio de contraste.

broncholith *n.* broncolito, cálculo bronquial.

bronchopneumonia *n.* bronconeumonía, infl. aguda de los bronquiolos y de los lóbulos pulmonares que afecta gen. ambos pulmones.

bronchopulmonary *a.* broncopulmonar, rel. a los bronquios y los pulmones.

bronchoscopy *n.* broncoscopía, examen del árbol bronquial por medio del broncoscopio.

bronchospasm *n.* broncoespasmo, contracción espasmódica de los bronquios y los bronquiolos.

bronchus *n.* (*pl.* **bronchia**) bronquio, uno de los tubos por los cuales el aire pasa a los pulmones.

brother *n.* hermano; **___-in-law** / cuñado; **half-___** / medio **___.**

brow *n.* ceño; frente.

brown *n.* castaño, café, carmelita; [*skin*] moreno-a.

Brown-Séquard syndrome *n.* síndrome de Brown Séquard, hemisección de la médula espinal que causa hiperestesia en el lado lesionado y pérdida de la sensibilidad en el lado opuesto.

brucellosis *n.* brucelosis, fiebre ondulante o fiebre mediterránea, condición infecciosa bacteriana que se contrae por contacto con ganado vacuno o sus productos.

bruise *n.* magulladura, morado.

brunet, brunette *a.* trigueño-a, de piel oscura.

brush *n.* cepillo; *v.* cepillar; cepillarse.

brutal *a.* brutal, bruto-a.

bubble *n.* burbuja, ampolla; **to ___ over with joy** / rebozar de gozo.

bubo *n.* bubón, infl. linfática de la ingle.

bubonic plague *n.* peste bubónica.

bucca *n.* boca.

buccal *a.* bucal.

bucket *n.* cubeta, cubo, balde.

buckle *n.* hebilla; *v.* **to ___ together** / unir, atar, juntar.

bud *n.* brote, retoño.

budget *n.* presupuesto.

buffer *n.* tampón, tope; *v.* neutralizar, tamponar; **___ system** / sistema amortiguador.

build *vi.* construir; **to ___ up one's health** / reconstituir la salud; **___-up phase** / fase de ascenso.

bulb *n.* bulbo, pera; bombillo; 1. [*syringe*] pera de goma; 2. expansión oval o circular de un conducto o cilindro.

bulbourethral *a.* bulbouretral, uretrobulbar, rel. al bulbo del pene y la uretra.

bulbus cordis *n. L.* bulbo del corazón.

bulge *n.* hinchazón, protuberancia.

bulging *n.* protuberancia; **___ abdomen** / abdomen prominente, vientre abombado; **___ eyes** / ojos saltones.

bulimia *n.* bulimia, apetito exagerado.

bulla *n.* ampolla.

bullet *n.* bala; **___ wound** / balazo, herida de **___.**

bump *n.* golpe, [*on the head*] chichón; *v.* tropezar; golpearse, darse un golpe.

bundle *n.* manojo, haz; bulto; **___-branch block** / bloque de rama.

bunion *n.* bunio, juanete, infl. de la bursa en la primera coyuntura del dedo pulgar del pie. *V.* **Hallux valgus.**

bunionectomy *n. cirg.* extirpación de un juanete.

burden *v.* agobiar.

burn *n.* quemadura; **___-s, chemical** / **___-s** por sustancias químicas; **___, dry heat** / **___** por calor seco; **sun___** / insolación, eritema solar; **first-, second- and third-degree ___-s** / **___-s** de primer, segundo y tercer grado; *vi.* arder, quemar, incendiar.

burning *n.* ardor, quemadura; irritación; **a ___ feeling** / sensación de **___**, quemazón; **___ on urination** / **___** al orinar.

burp *n.* eructo, eructación; *v.* eructar, sacar el aire.

burr *n.* taladro; [*dentistry*] fresa; **fissure ___** / **___** de fisura; **diamond point ___** / **___** diamantada.

bursa *L.* bursa, bolsa o saco en forma de cavidad que contiene líquido sinovial en áreas de los tejidos donde puede ocurrir una fricción.

bursitis *n.* bursitis, infl. de una bursa.

burst *v.* reventar, reventarse, abrirse; **to ___ out** / brotar, reventar; **to ___ open** / abrirse, reventarse; **to ___ into tears** / deshacerse en lágrimas.

butter *n.* mantequilla.

buttocks *n. pl.* nalgas, *pop. Mex.* asentaderas, *Cuba* fondillo.

button *n.* botón.

buttress *n.* contrafuerte, resfuerzo, sostén.

buy *vi.* comprar.

buzz *n.* murmullo, zumbido.

by *prep.* por, cerca de, al lado de, según; **___ day** / de día, por el día; **___ night** / de noche, por la noche.

bypass *n.* 1. baipás, derivación, puente externo; 2. creación de una nueva vía o derivación; **___ graft** / injerto de derivación; **aortocoronary ___** / derivación aortocoronaria; *v.* desviar; esquivar.

by-product *n.* subproducto.

C *abbr.* **Kilocalorie** / kilocaloría; **carbon** / carbono; **centigrade** / centígrado; **celsius** / Celsius.

c *abbr.* **cobalt** / cobalto; **cocaine** / cocaína; **contraction** / contracción; **calorie** / caloría

cabbage *n.* col, repollo.

cacao *n.* cacao, planta de la cual se deriva el chocolate, alcaloide diurético.

cachexia *n.* caquexia, condición grave que se caracteriza por pérdida excesiva de peso y debilidad general progresiva.

cacosmia *n.* cacosmia, percepción de olores imaginarios, esp. olores fétidos.

cadaver *n.* cadáver.

cadaverous *a.* cadavérico-a.

cafeteria *n.* cafetería.

caffeine *n.* cafeína, alcaloide presente esp. en el café y el té, estimulante y diurético.

calamine *n.* calamina, antiséptico astringente secante que se usa en afecciones de la piel.

calcaneus *n.* calcáneo, hueso del talón; *pop.* calcañal, calcañar.

calcareous *n.* calcáreo, que contiene calcio o cal.

calcemia *n* calcemia, presencia de calcio en la sangre.

calcic *a.* cálcico, rel. a la cal.

calciferol *n.* calciferol, producto derivado de ergosterol, vitamina D_2.

calcification *n.* calcificación, endurecimiento de tejidos orgánicos por depósitos de sales de calcio.

calcified *a.* calcificado-a.

calcinosis *n.* calcinosis, presencia de sales cálcicas en la piel, los tejidos subcutáneos y los órganos.

calcitonin *n.* calcitonina, hormona segregada por la tiroides que estimula el transporte del calcio de la sangre a los huesos.

calcium *n.* calcio, sustancia mineral necesaria en el desarrollo de los huesos y tejidos.

calciuria *n.* calciuria, presencia de calcio en la orina.

calculate *v.* calcular.

calculation *n.* calculación.

calculus *n.* (*pl.* **calculi**) cálculo, concreción o pequeña piedra que puede formarse en las secreciones y fluidos del organismo; **biliary** ___ / ___ biliar; **calcium oxalate** ___ / ___ de oxalato de calcio; **cystine** ___ / ___ de cistina; **fibrin** ___ / ___ de fibrina; **urinary** ___ / ___ urinario.

calendar *n.* calendario, almanaque.

calf *n.* pantorrilla; [*animal*] ternero-a.

caliber *n.* calibre, diámetro de un conducto o canal.

calibrator *n.* calibrador, instrumento para medir el diámetro de un conducto o canal.

caliceal *n.* caliceal, rel. a un cáliz.

call *n.* llamada; *v.* llamar; **to** ___ **for** / pedir; **to be on** ___ / estar de guardia.

callosity *n.* callosidad.

callous *a.* calloso-a.

callus *n.* callo, callosidad.

calm *n.* calma, serenidad; *v.* calmar, tranquilizar; calmarse, serenarse, tranquilizarse.

calmative *a.* calmante, sedante.

calomel *n.* calomel, cloruro mercurioso, usado como agente local antibacteriano.

caloric *n.* calórico-a, rel. al calor o las calorías; ___ **intake** / ingestión ___ .

calorie *n.* caloría, unidad de calor a la que se refiere al evaluar la energía alimenticia; **kilocalorie, large** ___ / gran ___ ; **small** ___ / pequeña ___ .

calorific *n.* calorífico.

calvaria, skullcap *n.* calvaria, bóveda craneal.

calyx *n.* cáliz, colector en forma de copa.

camera *n.* cámara. 1. espacio abierto o ventrículo; 2. cámara fotográfica.

camphor *n.* alcanfor; ___ **julep** / aqua alcanforada.

can *n.* lata, bote, envase; *vi.* poder.

canal *n.* canal, pasaje, estructura tubular; **birth** ___ / ___ del parto; **femoral** ___ / ___ femoral; **inguinalis** ___ / ___ inguinal, **root** ___ / ___ radicular.

canaliculus *n.* canalículo, canal o pasaje diminuto; **bilary** ___ / ___ biliar, entre las células del hígado; **lacrimal** ___ / ___ lacrimal, lagrimal.

cancel *v.* cancelar, suprimir.

cancellation *n.* cancelación.

cancellous *a.* canceloso-a, esponjoso-a, reticulado-a; ___ **bone** / hueso ___ .

cancer *n.* cáncer, tumor maligno; **early** ___ / ___ incipiente; ___ **grading** / determinacíon del grado patológico del ___ ; ___ **staging** / estadío o extensión del tumor canceroso.

cancerophobia *n.* cancerofobia, fobia a contraer cáncer.

cancerous *a.* canceroso-a.

candid *a.* cándido-a; sincero-a.

candidiasis *n.* candidiasis, infección de la piel producida por un hongo semejante a la levadura.

candy *n.* dulce, confite, caramelo.

cane *n.* bastón; caña; ___ **sugar** / azúcar de caña, sucrosa, sacarosa.

canine *n.* canino; cúspide; diente; *a.* rel. a los perros.

canker *n.* ulceración de la boca o los labios; ___ **sore** / afta, llaga ulcerosa.

cannabis, marijuana *n.* canabis, marijuana, mariguana, marihuana, planta de hojas que producen un efecto narcótico y halucinógeno al fumarse; *slang* **grass; bomber** / cigarrillo de marijuana; *v. slang* **to blast, to blow weed** / fumar marijuana.

cannula *n.* (*pl.* **cannulae**) cánula, sonda, tubo

que insertado en el cuerpo conduce o saca líquidos.

cannulation *n.* canulación, acto de introducir una cánula a través de un vaso o conducto; **aortic** ___ / ___ aórtica.

canthus *n.* 1. canto, borde; 2. ángulo formado por el párpado externo y el interno al unirse en ambas partes del ojo.

cap *n.* gorra; tapa.

capable *a.* capaz.

capacity *n.* a capacidad; **vital** ___ / ___ vital.

capillary *n.* capilar; vaso capilar; *a.* semejante a un cabello; **arterial** ___ / ___ arterial; **lymph** ___ / ___ linfático; **venous** ___ / ___ venoso.

capitellum *n.* capitelum. 1. bulbo de un pelo; 2. parte del húmero.

capsula, capsule *n.* cápsula. 1. envoltura membranosa. 2. pastilla; **articular** ___ / ___ articular, que envuelve una articulación sinovial; **enclosed in a** ___ / encapsulado.

capsulation *n.* encapsulación, acto de envolver en una cápsula o envoltura.

car *n.* automóvil, carro; *Sp.* coche; ___ **accident** / accidente automovilístico.

carbohydrase *n.* carbohidrasa.

carbohydrate *n.* carbohidrato, grupo de compuestos de carbono, hidrógeno y oxígeno entre los que se encuentran los almidones, azúcares y celulosas.

carbolic *a.* carbólico-a, rel. al fenol o ácido fenílico.

carbon *n.* carbono; ___ **dioxide** / dióxido de ___; ___ **monoxide** / monóxido de ___.

carbonated *a.* carbonatado-a.

carbonic *a.* carbónico-a.

carbonization *n.* carbonización.

carboxyhemoglobin *n.* carboxihemoglobina, combinación de monóxido de carbono y hemoglobina que desplaza el oxígeno e interrumpe la función oxidante de la sangre.

carbuncle *n.* carbunco, furúnculo, infl. con pus, *pop.* avispero.

carcinogen *n.* carcinógeno, cualquier sustancia que puede producir cáncer.

carcinogenesis *n.* carcinogénesis, origen del cáncer.

carcinogenic *n.* carcinógeno-a, de origen canceroso.

carcinoma *n.* carcinoma, tumor canceroso; **alveolar** ___ / ___ alveolar; **basal cell** ___ / ___ basocelular; **breast** ___ / ___ de la mama; **bronchial or bronchogenic** ___ / ___ broncogénico; **cervical** ___ / ___ cervical; **endometrial** ___ / ___ endometrial; **invasive** ___ / ___ invasor; **mucinous** ___ / ___ mucinoso; **ovarian** ___ / ___ ovárico; **papillary** ___ / ___ papilar; **squamous cell** ___ / ___ de células escamosas epiteliales; **testicular** ___ / ___ testicular; **transitional cell** ___ / ___ de células transicionales.

carcinoma in situ *L.* carcinoma in situ, células tumorales localizadas en estado de desarrollo

Cardiac	*Cardiaco*
arrest, standstill	paro
catheterization	cateterización
depressants	agentes antiarrítmicos
chambers	cavidades
failure	insuficiencia
output	gasto, rendimiento
pacing, artificial	estimulación c. artificial
stimulants	agentes cardiotónicos
tamponade	taponamiento

que no han invadido aún estructuras adyacentes.

carcinomatosis *n.* carcinomatosis, invasión de cáncer diseminado en varias partes del cuerpo.

cardiac *a.* cardíaco-a, referente al corazón; ___ **arrest, standstill** / paro ___; ___ **asthma** / asma ___; ___ **catheterization** / cateterización ___; ___ **depressants** / agentes antiarrítmicos; **chambers** / cavidades ___-s; ___ **failure** / insuficiencia ___; ___ **massage** / masaje ___; ___ **output** / gasto, rendimiento ___; ___ **pacing, artificial** / estimulación ___ artificial; ___ **pulse generator** / generador del impulso ___; **rupture** / ruptura ___; ___ **stimulants** / agentes cardiotónicos; ___ **tamponade** / taponamiento ___.

cardias *n.* cardias, desembocadura del esófago en el estómago.

cardiataxia *n.* cardiataxia, falta de coordinación de los movimientos cardíacos.

cardiectomy *n. cirg.* cardiectomía, extirpación de la región superior extrema del estómago.

cardioangiogram *n.* cardioangiograma, imagen por rayos X de los vasos sanguíneos y las cámaras del corazón usando un medio de contraste.

cardiocentesis *n. cirg.* cardiocentesis, cardiopuntura, punción de una cavidad del corazón.

cardiogram *n.* cardiograma, trazado que representa los impulsos del corazón.

cardiograph *n.* cardiógrafo, instrumento que traza gráficamente los movimientos del corazón.

cardiography *n.* cardiografía, uso del cardiógrafo para registrar los movimientos del corazón.

cardiologist *n.* cardiólogo-a, especialista del corazón.

cardiology *n.* cardiología, ciencia que estudia el corazón, sus funciones y enfermedades.

cardiomegaly *n.* cardiomegalia, hipertrofia cardíaca.

cardiomyopathy *n.* cardiomiopatía, alteración del músculo del corazón; **alcoholic** ___ / ___ alcohólica; **congestive** ___ / ___ congestiva; **hypertrophic** ___ / ___ hipertrófica.

cardiopathy *n.* cardiopatía, enfermedad cardíaca.

cardioplegia *n.* cardioplegia, paro o traumatismo cardíaco.

cardiopulmonary *a.* cardiopulmonar, rel. al corazón y los pulmones; ___ **bypass** / puente cardiopulmonar; ___ **resuscitation** / resucitación ___; ___ **resuscitator** / resucitador, reanimador ___.

cardiospasm *n.* cardiospasmo, espasmo o contracción del cardias.

cardiotomy *n. cirg.* cardiotomía, incisión en el corazón.

cardiotonic *a.* cardiotónico-a, de efecto tónico o favorable al corazón.

cardiovascular *a.* cardiovascular, rel. al corazón y los vasos sanguíneos.

cardioversion *n.* cardioversión, restauración del ritmo sinusal normal del corazón por medio de una corriente directa.

carditis *n.* carditis, infl. del pericardio, miocardio y endocardio; **rheumatic** ___ / ___ reumática.

care *n.* cuidado, asistencia, atención; **cardiac** ___ **unit (CCU)** / sala de ___ cardíaco; **free of** ___ / libre de ___; **intensive** ___ **unit (ICU)** / sala de ___ intensivo; **prenatal** ___ / ___ y atención prenatal; **postnatal** ___ / ___ después del parto; **primary** ___ / ___ primario; **proper** ___ / ___ apropiado; **refusal of** ___ / negación de ___; *v.* **to be under the** ___ **of** / estar bajo el ___ de.

career *n.* profesión.

careful *a.* cuidadoso-a; esmerado-a; atento-a.

careless *a.* descuidado-a; desatento-a.

carelessness *n.* descuido; negligencia.

caries *n. pl.* caries. 1. destrucción progresiva de tejido óseo; 2. caries dentales, *pop.* dientes picados.

carmine *n.* carmín, carmesí.

carnivorous *a.* carnívoro-a.

carnosity *n.* carnosidad, excrecencia carnosa.

carotene *n.* caroteno, pigmento amarillo rojizo presente en vegetales que se convierte en vitamina A en el cuerpo.

carotid *n.* carótida, arteria principal del cuello; ___ **arteries** / arterias ___-s.

carpal *a.* carpal, rel. al carpo.

carpus *n.* (*pl.* **carpi**) carpo, muñeca de la mano, porción de la extremidad superior situada entre el antebrazo y la mano.

carrier *n.* portador, agente transmisor; ___ **state** / estado portador.

carrot *n.* zanahoria.

carry *v.* llevar; cargar; **to** ___ **out** / llevar a cabo.

cartilage *n.* cartílago, tejido semiduro que cubre los huesos.

caruncle *n.* carúncula, pequeña irritación de la piel; **urethral** ___ / ___ uretral.

cascara sagrada *n.* cáscara sagrada, corteza de la planta *Rhamnus purshiana*, comúnmente usada como medicamento en casos de estreñimiento crónico.

case *n.* caso; ___ **fatality rate** / índice de mortalidad por ___; ___ **history** / historia clínica; ___ **reporting** / presentación del ___; ___ **control study** / estudio comparativo de ___-s; **in** ___ **of** / en ___ de; **just in** ___ / por si ___.

casein *n.* caseína, proteína principal de la leche.

caseous *a.* caseoso, de queso o parecido al queso.

cash *n.* dinero al contado; ___ **payment** / ___, pago al contado; *v.* **to pay** ___ / pagar al contado.

casket *n.* ataúd, caja.

cast *n.* molde; yeso; [*orthopedics*] férula; [*kidney*] cilindro; *v.* **to put in a** ___ / enyesar, moldear; **to** ___ **aside** / desechar / *V.* **granular cast.**

castor oil *n.* aceite de ricino, palmacristi.

castrate *v.* castrar.

casual *a.* casual, accidental.

casualty *n.* víctima; accidentado-a; [*wounded*] herido-a; ___ **list** / lista de accidentados.

cat *n.* gato-a.

catabolism *n.* catabolismo, proceso por el cual sustancias complejas se reducen a compuestos más simples.

catalepsy *n.* catalepsia, condición caracterizada por la pérdida de la capacidad de movimiento muscular voluntario y disminución acentuada de la habilidad de reaccionar a estímulos, gen. asociada con transtornos psicológicos.

catalysis *n.* catálisis, alteración de la velocidad de una reacción química por la presencia de un catalítico.

catalyst, catalytic *a.* catalítico-a, agente estimulante de una reacción química sin afectarla.

cataplexy *n.* cataplejía, pérdida repentina del tono muscular causada por un estado emocional intenso.

cataract *n.* catarata, opacidad del cristalino; **green** ___ / ___ verde; **mature** ___ / ___ madura; **senile** ___ / ___ senil; **soft** ___ / ___ blanda.

catarrh *n.* catarro, resfriado, constipado.

catarrhal *a.* catarral, referente a un catarro.

catatonia *n.* catatonía, esquizofrenia caracterizada por mutismo, postura rígida y resistencia a cooperar para activar los movimientos o el habla. Los mismos síntomas se asocian con otras enfermedades mentales.

catch *vi.* contraer; agarrar; coger; ___ **an illness** / una enfermedad.

catecholamines *n. pl.* catecolaminas, aminas de acción simpatomimética producidas en las glándulas suprarrenales (incluyen la dopamina, la epinefrina y la norepinefrina).

category *n.* categoría, clase.

catgut *n.* catgut, tipo de ligadura que se hace con la tripa del intestino de algunos animales.

catharsis *n.* catarsis. 1. acción purgativa; 2. *psic.* análisis con el fin terapéutico de liberar al paciente de un estado de ansiedad.

cathartic *n.* catártico, medicamento con efectos laxativos o purgativos; *a.* catártico-a, rel. a la catarsis.

catheter *n.* catéter, sonda, tubo usado para drenar o introducir líquidos; ___ **holder** / portacatéter.

catheterization *n.* cateterización, inserción de un catéter.

catheterize *v.* cateterizar, insertar un catéter.

cauda *n.* cauda, apéndice similar a una cola.

caudal *a.* caudal, rel. a la cola.

cauliflower *n.* coliflor.

causal *a.* causal.

causalgia *n.* causalgia, dolor con ardor en la piel.

cause *n.* causa, principio. origen; **without** ___ / sin ___ .

cause *v.* causar, ocasionar.

caustic *a.* cáustico-a.

cauterization *n.* cauterización, quemadura producida por medio de un agente cauterizante tal como el calor, la corriente eléctrica, o un cáustico.

cauterize *v.* cauterizar, quemar por medio de un agente cauterizante.

caution *n.* advertencia, precaución, cautela.

cautious *a.* precavido-a, cuidadoso-a.

cava *n. pl.* de **cavum,** cavidad, hueco. *V.* **vein, cava.**

cave *n.* depresión.

cavern *n.* caverna, cavidad patológica.

cavernous *a.* cavernoso-a, que contiene espacios huecos.

cavity *n.* cavidad, lugar hueco; **abdominal** ___ / ___ abdominal; **cranial** ___ / ___ craneal; **pelvic** ___ / ___ pelviana; **thoracic** ___ / ___ torácica.

cease *v.* cesar, parar, detener.

cecostomy *n. cirg.* cecostomía, creación de una apertura artificial en el ciego.

cecum *n.* ciego, bolsa que forma la primera parte del intestino grueso.

celery *n.* apio.

celiac *a.* celíaco, abdominal, rel. al abdomen.

celiotomy *n. cirg.* celiotomía. *V.* **laparotomía.**

cell *n.* célula, unidad estructural de todo organismo viviente; **adipose** ___ / ___ adiposa; **anaplastic** ___ / ___ anaplástica; **B** ___ / linfocito B, tipo de linfocito importante en la producción de anticuerpos; **basal** ___ / ___ basal; **columnar** ___ / ___ columnar; **giant** ___ / ___ gigante; **goblet** ___ / ___ calciforme; **ependymal** ___ / ___ ependimaria; **epidermal** ___ / ___ epidérmica; **interstitial** ___ / ___ intersticial; **mononuclear** ___ / ___ mononuclear; **phagocyte** ___ / ___ fagocitaria; **pyramidal** ___ / ___ piramidal; **red blood** ___-s / ___-s sanguíneas (eritocitos y leucocitos); **reproductive** ___ / ___ reproductiva; **scavenger** ___ / ___ basurera; **sickle** ___ / ___ falciforme.

cellular *a.* celular, de naturaleza semejante o referente a la célula; ___ **compartmentation** / compartimentos ___-es; ___ **counting device** / cuenta células; ___ **growth** / crecimiento ___; ___-**like** / en forma ___; ___ **tissue** / tejido ___;

___ **water** / agua ___ .

cellularity *n.* celularidad, condición y calidad de las células presentes en un tejido o masa.

cellulitis *n.* celulitis, infl. del tejido conectivo celular.

cellulose *n.* celulosa.

cement *n.* cemento.

cemetery *n.* cementerio, camposanto.

census *n.* censo.

center *n.* centro.

Center for Disease Control *n.* Centro para Control de Enfermedades.

centigrade *n* centígrado.

centimeter *n.* centímetro.

central *a.* central; céntrico-a; ___ **nervous system** / sistema nervioso ___ .

centrifugal *a.* centrífugo-a, rel. al movimiento de repulsión, del centro hacia afuera.

centripetal *a.* centrípeto-a, con movimiento de atracción hacia el centro.

cephalalgia *n.* cefalalgia, dolor de cabeza, *pop.* jaqueca.

cephalic *a.* cefálico-a, rel. a la cabeza.

cephalosporin *n.* cefalosporina, antibiótico de espectro amplio.

cerclage *n.* cerclaje, en ortopedia procedimiento usado en ciertas fracturas por el cual se unen partes rodeándolas con un hilo metálico o con catgut.

cereal *n.* cereal.

cerebellum *n.* cerebelo, parte posterior del cerebro, centro de coordinación de los movimientos musculares voluntarios.

cerebral *a.* cerebral, rel. al cerebro; ___ **edema** / edema ___; ___ **embolism and thrombosis** / embolia y trombosis ___; ___ **hemorrhage** / hemorragia ___; ___ **palsy** / parálisis ___; ___ **tumor** / tumor ___ .

cerebrospinal *a.* cefalorraquídeo, cerebroespinal; ___ **fluid** / líquido ___ .

cerebrovascular *a.* cerebrovascular; ___ **accident (CVA)** / apoplegía, hemorragia cerebral.

cerebrum *n.* cerebro, encéfalo, centro de coordinación de actividades sensoriales e intelectuales.

certain *a.* cierto-a; seguro-a; *v.* **to be** ___ / estar seguro-a; **-ly** *adv.* ciertamente, seguramente.

certainty *n.* certeza.

certificate *n.* certificado; **death** ___ / ___ de defunción.

cerumen *n.* cerumen, segregación cerosa que lubrica y protege el oído.

cervical *a.* cervical. 1. referente al área del cuello; 2. rel. al cuello uterino; ___ **dysplasia** / displasia ___; ___ **incompetence** / incompetencia del cuello uterino; ___ **erosion** / erosión ___; ___ **polyp** / pólipo ___ .

cervicovesical *a.* cervicovesical, rel. al cuello uterino y a la vejiga.

cervix *n.* cuello uterino, parte baja del útero en forma de cuello; **dilation of the** ___ / dilatación del ___ .

cesarean *n.* cesárea; ___ **section** / cirugía de parto.

chain *n.* cadena; ___ **reaction** / reacción en ___; ___ **suture** / sutura en ___.

chair *n.* silla.

chalazion *n.* chalazión, quiste del párpado, quiste meiboniano.

chalk *n.* yeso.

chamber *n.* cámara, cavidad; **anterior** ___ / ___ anterior, situada entre la córnea y el iris; **aqueous** ___ / ___ acuosa; ___**-s of the eye** / ___-s oculares; **hyperbaric** ___ / ___ hiperbárica; ___**-s of the heart** / cavidades del corazón: aurículas y ventrículos del corazón.

chamomile *n.* manzanilla, té sedante gastrointestinal.

chancre *n.* chancro; lesión primaria de la sífilis.

chancroid *n.* chancroide, úlcera venérea no sifilítica.

change *n.* cambio, alteración; ___ **of life** / menopausia; *v.* cambiar, mudar.

changeless *a.* invariable, inmutable.

channel *n.* canal; estructura tubular; **birth** ___ / ___ del parto.

chaos *n.* caos, desorden.

chaotic *n.* caótico-a, desordenado-a.

chap *n.* hendidura, raja, grieta.

chapel *n.* capilla.

chapped *a.* agrietado-a, cuarteado-a; rajado-a; ___ **hands** / manos ___-s; ___ **lips** / labios ___-s.

chapter *n.* capítulo.

character *n.* carácter; personalidad; personaje.

characteristic *n.* característica, peculiaridad; *a.* característico-a; peculiar.

charcoal *n.* carbón vegetal.

charge *n.* costo; *v.* cobrar.

charitable *a.* caritativo-a.

charity *n.* caridad; beneficencia.

charlatan *n.* charlatán-a; dícese de una persona que pretende tener cualidades o conocimientos para curar enfermedades.

charley horse *n.* dolor y sensibilidad en un músculo; *pop.* calambre.

charred *a.* carbonizado-a.

chart *n.* plano, gráfico; **medical** ___ / hoja clínica.

chat *n.* charla, plática; *v.* charlar, platicar.

chatter *v.* [*teeth*] rechinar los dientes.

cheap *a.* barato-a.

check *n.* control; acción o efecto de regular; [*bank*] cheque; *v.* controlar; chequear, verificar.

checkbook *n.* chequera; talonario.

checkup *n.* *Am.* chequeo, examen físico completo.

cheek *n.* mejilla.

cheekbone *n.* carrillo, pómulo, hueso malar.

cheer up *v.* animarse, alegrarse.

cheese *n.* queso.

cheilectomy *n.* *cir.* queilectomía, excisión parcial del labio.

cheilitis, chilitis *n.* queilitis, infl. de los labios.

cheiloplasty *n.* *cir.* queiloplastia, reparación del labio.

cheiloschisis *n.* queilosquisis. *V.* **harelip**.

cheilosis *n.* queilosis, manifestación con marcas y fisuras en la comisura de los labios debida a deficiencia de vitamina B_2 (riboflavina).

cheirology *n.* quirología. 1. estudio de la mano; 2. uso del lenguaje por señas como medio de comunicación con los sordomudos.

chemical *a.* químico-a; ___ **peel** / peladura ___.

chemist *n.* químico-a; farmacéutico-a, boticario-a.

chemistry *n.* química, ciencia que estudia los elementos, estructura y propiedades de las sustancias y las transformaciones que éstas sufren.

chemocoagulation *n.* quimiocoagulación, coagulación por medio de agentes químicos.

chemonucleolysis *n.* quimionucleólisis, disolución por inyección de una enzima proteolítica del núcleo pulposo de una hernia.

chemoprophylaxis *n.* quimioprofilaxis, uso de una droga o de una sustancia química con fines preventivos.

chemoreceptor *n.* quimiorreceptor-a, célula suceptible a cambios químicos o que puede ser afectada por éstos.

chemosurgery *n.* quimiocirugía, extirpación o remoción de tejidos por medio de sustancias químicas.

chemotaxis *n.* quimiotaxis, movimiento de un organismo o célula como reacción a un estímulo químico.

chemotherapy *n.* quimioterapia, tratamiento de una enfermedad por medio de agentes químicos.

cherubism *n.* querubismo, condición fibroósea infantil que causa agrandamiento de los huesos de la mandíbula.

chest *n.* tórax, pecho; ___ **cold** / catarro bronquial, *pop.* catarro al pecho; ___ **respirator** / respirador torácico; ___ **surgery** / cirugía torácica; ___ **wall** / pared torácica.

chew *v.* masticar, mascar.

Cheyne-Stokes respiration syndrome *n.* síndrome de respiración de Cheyne-Stokes, respiración cíclica con períodos de apnea y aumento rápido y profundo de la respiración gen. asociada con trastornos del centro neurológico respiratorio.

chiasm, chiasma *n.* quiasma. 1. cruzamiento de dos vías o conductos; 2. punto de cruzamiento de las fibras de los nervios ópticos.

chiasma opticum *n.* quiasma óptico.

chicken *n.* pollo; ___ **breast** / pechuga.

chickenpox, varicella *n.* varicela, enfermedad viral contagiosa que se manifiesta gen. en la infancia y se caracteriza por una erupción que se convierte en pequeñas vesículas; *pop.* viruelas locas.

chief *n.* jefe-a; ___ **complaint** / queja principal.

chilblain *n.* sabañón, eritema debido a frío intenso que gen. se manifiesta en las manos y los pies.

child *n.* niño-a; ___ **nurse** / niñera; ___ **nursery** / guardería infantil, jardín de la infancia; ___ **support** / manutención, pensión alimenticia; ___ **welfare** / asistencia social a la infancia.

childbearing *n.* gestación, embarazo.

childbirth *n.* parto, nacimiento, alumbramiento.

childhood *n.* infancia, niñez.

chill *n.* enfriamiento, escalofrío.

chin *n.* barba, mentón, barbilla.

chiropodist *n.* quiropodista. *V.* **podiatrist.**

chiropractic *n.* quiropráctica, sistema terapéutico que recurre a la manipulación y ajustamiento de las estructuras del cuerpo esp. la columna vertebral en relación con el sistema nervioso.

chisel *n.* cincel.

chloasma *n.* cloasma, hiperpigmentación facial que puede ocurrir en algunas mujeres durante el embarazo.

chlorambucil *n.* clorambucil, forma de mostaza nitrogenada usada para combatir algunas formas de cáncer.

chloramphenicol, chloromycetin *n.* cloranfenicol, cloromicetina, antibiótico esp. efectivo en el tratamiento de la fiebre tifoidea.

chlorhydria *n.* clorhidria, exceso de ácido clorhídrico en el estómago.

chloride *n.* cloruro.

chlorine *n.* cloro, agente desinfectante y blanqueador.

chloroform *n.* cloroformo, anestésico.

chloroma *n.* cloroma, tumor de color verde que puede manifestarse en distintas partes del cuerpo.

chlorophyll *n.* clorofila, pigmento verde de las plantas esencial en la producción de carbohidratos por fotosíntesis.

chloroquine *n.* cloroquina, compuesto usado en el tratamiento de la malaria.

chlorosis *n.* clorosis, tipo de anemia vista esp. en la mujer y usu. relacionada con deficiencia de hierro.

chlorpromazine *n.* cloropromacina, antiemético y tranquilizante.

chlortetracycline *n.* clorotetraciclina, antibiótico antimicrobiano de espectro amplio.

chocolate *n.* chocolate.

choice *n.* opción, alternative; elección.

choke *v.* ahogar, sofocar, estrangular; [*choke on something*] atragantarse.

cholangiectasis *n.* colangiectasis, dilatación de los conductos biliares.

cholangiogram *n.* colangiograma, radiografía de las vías biliares usando un medio de contraste.

cholangiography *n.* colangiografía, rayos X de las vías biliares.

cholangitis *n.* colangitis, infl. de los conductos biliares.

cholecystectomy *n. cirg.* colecistectomía, extir-

pación de la vesícula biliar.

cholecystitis *n.* colecistitis, infl. de la vesícula biliar.

cholecystoduodenostomy *n. cirg.* colecistoduodenostomía, anastomosis de la vesícula y el duodeno.

cholecystogastrostomy *n. cirg.* colecistogastrostomía, anastomosis de la vesícula y el estómago.

cholecystogram *n.* colecistograma, radiografía de la vesícula biliar.

cholecystography *n.* colecistografía, rayos X de la vesícula biliar usando un medio radioopaco.

choledochojejunostomy *n. cirg.* coledocoyeyunostomía, anastomosis del colédoco y el yeyuno.

choledocholithiasis *n.* coledocolitiasis, cálculos en el colédoco.

choledochus *n.* colédoco, conducto biliar formado por la unión de los conductos hepático y cístico.

cholelithiasis *n.* colelitiasis, litiasis biliar, presencia de cálculos en la vesícula biliar o en un conducto biliar.

cholemia *n.* colemia, presencia de bilis en la sangre.

cholera *n.* cólera, enfermedad infecciosa grave caracterizada por diarrea severa y vómitos; ___ **fulminans** / ___ fulminante.

choleric *a.* colérico-a.

cholestasis *n.* colestasis, estasis biliar.

cholesteatoma *n.* colesteatoma, tumor que contiene colesterol, situado comúnmente en el oído medio.

cholesteremia, cholesterolemia *n.* colesteremia, colesterolemia, exceso de colesterol en la sangre.

cholesterol *n.* colesterol, lípido precursor de las hormonas sexuales y corticoides adrenales, componente de las grasas y aceites animales, del tejido nervioso y de la sangre; **high** ___ / ___ alto; ___ **reducer** / ___ reductor de ___ .

cholic acid *n.* ácido cólico, uno de los ácidos no conjugados de la bilis.

cholinesterase *n.* colinesterasa, familia de enzimas.

choluria *n.* coluria, presencia de bilis en la orina.

chondritis *n.* condritis, infl. de un cartílago.

chondrocalcinosis *n.* condrocalcinosis, condición semejante a la gota, con manifestaciones de cicatrización por calcificación y deteriorización o alteraciones degenerativas de los cartílagos.

chondrocostal *a.* condrocostal, rel. a los cartílagos costales y las costillas.

chondrodynia *n.* condrodinia, dolor en un cartílago.

chondromalacia *n.* condromalacia, reblandecimiento anormal de los cartílagos.

choose *vi.* escoger, elegir.

chord *n.* cuerda; **vocal** ___ / ___ vocal.

chorea, Huntington's disease *n.* corea; enfermedad de Huntington, padecimiento nervioso que se manifiesta en movimientos abruptos coordinados aunque involuntarios de las extremidades y los músculos faciales; *pop.* baile se San Vito.

choriocarcinoma *n.* coriocarcinoma, tumor maligno visto gen. en el útero y en los testículos.

chorion *n.* corión, una de las dos membranas que rodean al feto.

chorionic *a.* coriónico-a, rel. al corión.

choroid *n.* coroides, membrana situada en el ojo al que nutre con la sangre.

choroiditis *n.* coroiditis, infl. de la coroides.

chromatic *a.* cromático-a, rel. al color.

chromatin *n.* cromatina, parte del núcleo de la célula más propensa a absorber color.

chromocyte *n.* cromocito, célula pigmentada.

chromogen *n.* cromógeno, sustancia que produce color.

chromophobe *n.* cromófobo, tipo de célula que ofrece resistencia al color.

chromophobia *n.* cromofobia, aversión anormal a ciertos colores.

chromosomal *a.* cromosómico-a, rel. al cromosoma; __ **aberrations** / aberraciones __-s.

chromosome *n.* cromosoma, la parte dentro del núcleo de la célula que contiene los genes.

chronic *a.* crónico-a, de larga duración.

chronological *a.* cronológico-a, rel. a la secuencia del tiempo.

chronotropism *n.* cronotropismo, modificación de funciones regulares tales como los latidos del corazón.

chubby *a.* regordete-a, macizo-a.

chyle *n.* quilo, sustancia lechosa que resulta de la absorción y emulsión de las grasas, presente en el intestino delgado.

chylemia *n.* quilemia, presencia de quilo en la sangre.

chylomicron *n.* quilomicrón, pequeña partícula de lípido visto en la sangre después de la ingestión de grasas.

chylorrhea *n.* quilorrea, derrame de quilo debido a una ruptura del conducto torácico.

chylous *a.* quiloso-a, que contiene quilo o de la naturaleza de éste.

chyluria *n.* quiluria. *V.* **galacturia.**

chyme *n.* quimo, sustancia o materia semilíquida que proviene de la digestión gástrica.

chymotrypsin *n.* quimotripsina, tripsina, enzima de la secreción pancreática.

chymotrypsinogen *n.* quimotripsinógeno, enzima pancreática precursora de la quimotripsina.

cicatrix *L.* (*pl.* **cicatrices**) cicatriz.

cicatrizant *n.* cicatrizante, agente que contribuye a la cicatrización.

cicatrization *n.* cicatrización.

cigar *n.* puro, *H.A.* tabaco.

cigarette *n.* cigarro, cigarrillo.

ciliary *n.* ciliar, rel. a las pestañas o al párpado.

cilium *L.* (*pl.* **cilia**) párpado.

Cimetidine *n.* Cimetidina, nombre comercial de un antiácido usado en el tratamiento de úlceras gástricas y duodenales.

cineradiography *n.* cinerradiografía, película radiográfica de un órgano en movimiento.

cinerea *n.* cinérea, la sustancia gris del sistema nervioso.

cinnamon *n.* canela.

circadian rhythm *n.* ritmo circadiano, ref. a variaciones rítmicas biológicas en un ciclo de 24 horas.

circinate *a.* circinado-a, semejante a un anillo o círculo.

circle *n.* círculo, circunferencia.

circuit *n.* circuito, vuelta, rotación.

circulation *n.* circulación; **peripheral** __ /__ periférica; **poor** __ / mala __; __ **rate** / volumen circulatorio por minuto.

circulatory *a.* circulatorio-a.

circumcise *v.* circuncidar.

circumcision *n.* circuncisión, excisión del prepucio.

circumduction *n.* circunducción, movimiento circular de una parte del cuerpo tal como el ojo o alguna extremidad.

circumference *n.* circunferencia; círculo.

cirrhosis *n.* cirrosis, enfermedad asociada con infl. intersticial, fallo en la función de hepatocitos y trastornos en la circulación de la sangre en el hígado; **alcoholic** __ / __ alcohólica; **biliary** __ / __ biliar.

cistern *n.* cisterna, receptáculo de agua, aljibe.

cite *v.* citar, referirse a.

citizen *n.* ciudadano-a.

citizenship *n.* ciudadanía.

citric, citrous *a.* cítrico-a; __ **acid** / ácido __.

city *n.* ciudad.

claim *n.* reclamación; petición; __ **review procedure** / proceso para revisión de peticiones (reclamaciones); *v.* reclamar, demandar.

clam *n.* almeja.

clammy *a.* frío y húmedo.

clamp *n.* pinza; presilla.

clamping *n.* pinzado.

clap *n. pop.* gonorrea, blenorragia; [*hand*] palmada.

clarification *n.* aclaración, clarificación.

clarify *v.* aclarar, clarificar.

clarity *n.* claridad.

clasp *n.* gancho.

class *n.* clase; tipo.

classification *n.* clasificación; distribución.

classify *v.* clasificar, distribuir.

claudication *n.* claudicación; **intermittent** __ / __ intermitente.

claustrophobia *n.* claustrofobia, miedo o fobia a espacios cerrados.

clavicle *n.* clavícula, hueso de la faja pectoral que conecta al esternón con la escápula.

clavicular *a.* clavicular, rel. a las clavículas.

claw n. garra; ___ **foot** / pie en ___; ___ **hand** / mano en ___.
clean a. limpio-a, aseado-a; v. limpiar, asear.
clear a. claro-a.
clearance n. aclaramiento, eliminación renal de una sustancia en el plasma sanguíneo.
cleft n. fisura, abertura alargada.
cleft lip n. labio leporino. V. **harelip**.
cleft palate n. paladar hendido, defecto congénito del velo del paladar por falta de fusión en la línea media.
cleidocostal a. cleidocostal, rel. a la clavícula y las costillas.
clergyman n. clérigo.
climacteric a. climatérico-a.
climacterium L. climaterio, menopausia, cese de actividad reproductiva.
climate n. clima.
climax L. climax. 1. crisis de una enfermedad; 2. orgasmo sexual.
climb v. subir; trepar; subirse, treparse.
clinic n. clínica; **small** ___ / dispensario.
clinical a. clínico-a. 1. rel. a una clínica; 2. rel. a la observacíon directa de pacientes; ___ **history** / historia ___, expediente; ___ **picture** / cuadro ___; ___ **procedure** / procedimiento ___; ___ **trials** / ensayos ___-s.
clip n. pinza; v. sujetar con pinzas.
clitoridectomy n. cirg. clitoridectomía, excisión del clítoris.
clitoris n. clítoris, pequeña protuberancia situada en la parte anterior de la vulva.
cloaca n. cloaca, abertura común del intestino y de las vías urinarias en la fase de desarrollo primario del embrión.
clock n. reloj; **around the** ___ / durante las veinticuatro horas, de día y de noche.
clone n. clono, derivación de un organismo simple por reproducción asexual.
clonic a. clónico-a, rel. a un clono.
clonorchiasis n. clonorquiasis, infección parasitaria que afecta los conductos biliares distales.
clonus Gr. clono, serie de contracciones rápidas y rítmicas de un músculo.
close v. cerrar.
closed a. cerrado-a; ___ **ecological system** / sistema ecológico ___; ___-**circuit television** / televisión en circuito ___.
closure n. acto de cerrar o sellar; encierro.
clot n. cóagulo, cuajo, grumo, pop. cuajarón.
clothes, clothing n. ropa.
clotting n. coagulación; ___ **time** / tiempo de ___; ___ **factor** / factor de ___.
cloudiness n. nebulosidad, enturbamiento.
cloudy a. turbio-a, nebuloso-a, oscuro-a.
clove n. clavo de especia.
club foot n. pie torcido, pop. patizambo, slang chueco.
club hand n. mano zamba, pop. mano de gancho.
clubbing n. dedo en palillo de tambor.
cluster n. racimo, grupo.

cluster headache, Horton's syndrome n. cefalalgia de Horton, dolor de cabeza producido por histaminas.
clysis n. clisis, administración de líquidos por cualquier vía excepto la oral.
coagglutination n. coaglutinación, aglutinación de grupos.
coagglutinine n. coaglutinina, aglutinante que afecta dos o más organismos.
coagulant a. coagulante, que produce coagulación.
coagulate v. coagular, coagularse.
coagulation n. coagulación, coágulo; **disseminated intravascular** ___ (**DIC**) / ___ intravascular diseminada.
coagulopathy n. coagulopatía, enfermedad o condición que afecta el mecanismo de la coagulación de la sangre.
coalescense n. coalescencia, fusión de dos o más partes.
coal miners' disease n. enfermedad de los mineros. V. **anthracosis**.
coarctation n. coartación, estrechez.
coarse a. grueso-a; rudo-a, tosco-a, burdo-a, ordinario-a.
coat n. membrana, cubierta; [clothing] abrigo.
cobalt n. cobalto.
coca n. coca, planta de cuyas hojas se extrae la cocaína.
cocaine n. cocaína, narcótico alcaloide adictivo complejo obtenido de las hojas de coca; slang nieve.
coccidioidin n. coccidioidina, solución estéril suministrada por medio intercutáneo en la prueba de la coccidioidomicosis (fiebre del valle).
coccidioidomycosis, valley fever n. coccidioidomicosis, fiebre del valle, infección respiratoria endémica en el suroeste de los Estados Unidos, México y algunas partes de América del Sur.
coccus L. (pl. **cocci**) coco, bacteria de forma esférica.
coccygeal a. coccígeo, rel. al cóccix.
coccygodynia n. coccigodinia, dolor en la región coccígea.
coccyx Gr. cóccix; último hueso de la columna vertebral; pop. rabadilla.
cochlea n. coclea, parte del oído interior en forma de caracol.
cochleare L. cucharada; ___ **magnum** / ___ de sopa; ___ **medium** / ___ de postre; ___ **parvum** / cucharita de café.
cockroach n. cucaracha.
cod n. bacalao; ___ **liver oil** / aceite de hígado de ___.
codeine n. codeína, narcótico analgésico.
coefficient n. coeficiente, indicación de cambios físicos o químicos producidos por variantes de ciertos factores.
coenzyme n. coenzima, sustancia que activa la acción de una enzima.

coffee *n.* café.

coffin *n.* ataúd, caja.

cognac *n.* coñac, aguardiente.

cognate *n.* cognado, palabra que proviene del mismo tronco o raíz; *a.* cognado-a, de la misma naturaleza o calidad.

cohabit *v.* cohabitar, vivir en unión sin matrimonio legal.

coherence *n.* coherencia, cohesión.

coherent *a.* coherente.

cohesion *n.* cohesión, unión, fuerza que une a las moléculas.

coil *n.* espiral, serpentina, dispositivo intrauterino.

coincide *v.* coincidir.

coincidence *n.* coincidencia; **by** ___ / por casualidad.

coitus *L.* coito, acto sexual.

cold *n.* catarro; resfriado; [*weather*] frío; *a* [*temperature*] frío-a; ___-**blooded** / de sangre fría o de temperatura muy baja; ___ **sore** / úlcera de herpes simple; ___ **sweat** / sudor frío; ___ **cream** / crema, pomada facial; ___ **pack** / compresa fría; *v.* **to be** ___ / tener frío; **it is** ___ / hace frío.

coldness *n.* frialdad.

colectomy *n.* *cirg.* colectomía, extirpación de una parte o de todo el colon.

colic *n.* cólico, dolor espasmódico abdominal agudo.

colicky *a.* rel. al cólico.

colitis *n.* colitis, infl. del colon; **chronic** ___ / ___ crónica; **spasmodic** ___ / ___ espasmódica; **pseudomembranous** ___ / ___ mucomembranosa; **ulcerative** ___ / ___ ulcerativa.

collaborate *v.* colaborar, cooperar.

collagen *n.* colágeno, principal proteína de sostén del tejido conectivo de la piel, huesos, tendones y cartílagos.

collapse *n.* colapso; postración; desplome; **circulatory** ___ / ___ circulatorio; ___ **therapy** / terapia de ___ ; *v.* sufrir un ___ .

collapsed *a.* desplomado-a; derrumbado-a; estado de vacuidad.

collar *n.* cuello.

collarbone *n.* clavícula.

collateral *a.* colateral, al lado; accesorio-a.

colleague *n.* colega; compañero-a.

collect *v.* coleccionar, recoger, juntar; acumular.

collodion *n.* colodión, sustancia usada para proteger heridas en la piel.

colloid *n.* coloide, sustancia gelatinosa producida por ciertas formas de degeneración de los tejidos.

collyrium *n.* colirio, medicamento aplicado a los ojos.

colon *n.* colon, porción del intestino grueso entre el ciego y el recto; **ascending** ___ / ___ ascendente; **descending** ___ / ___ descendente.

colonic *a.* colónico, referente al colon; ___ **neoplasms** / neoplasmas del colon.

colonoscopy *n.* colonoscopía, examen de la superficie interna del colon a través del colonoscopio.

colony *n.* colonia, cultivo de bacterias derivadas del mismo organismo.

color *n.* color; ___ **index** / guía colorimétrica; *v.* colorar; teñir o dar color.

coloration *n.* coloración.

colostomy *n.* *cirg.* colostomía, creación de un ano artificial.

colostrum *n.* colostro, secreción de la glándula mamaria anterior a la leche.

colpitis *n.* colpitis, vaginitis, infl. de la vagina.

colpocele *n.* colpocele, hernia vaginal.

colporrhagia *n.* colporragia, hemorragia vaginal.

colporrhaphy *n.* *cirg.* colporrafia, sutura de la vagina.

colposcope *n.* colposcopio, instrumento que se usa para examinar visualmente la vagina y el cuello uterino.

colposcopy *n.* colposcopía, examen de la vagina y del cuello uterino a través de un colposcopio.

colpotomy *n.* *cirg.* colpotomía, incisión de la vagina.

column *n.* columna.

coma *n.* coma, en estado de coma; sueño profundo o estado inconsciente.

comatose *a.* comatoso-a; **in a** ___ **state** / en estado de coma.

comb *n.* peine; *v.* peinar, peinarse.

combat *v.* combatir; *n.* combate, lucha.

combatting *p. p.* de **to combat**, combatiendo.

combine *v.* combinar, unir.

come *vi* venir; **to** ___ **to terms** / ponerse de acuerdo; ___ **in!** / pase, pasa; entre, entra.

comfort *n.* comodidad, alivio, bienestar; *v.* confortar, alentar.

comfortable *a.* cómodo-a; a gusto.

comfortless *a.* incómodo-a.

command *n.* orden; *gr.* mandato.

commensal *n.* comensal, organismo que vive a expensas de otro sin beneficiarlo ni perjudicarlo.

comment *n.* comentario; *v.* comentar; hacer un comentario.

comminute *v.* pulverizar, triturar.

comminuted *a.* conminuto-a, roto-a en fragmentos tal como en una fractura.

commiserate *v.* tener compasión, tener lástima; apiadarse, compadecerse; tenerse lástima.

commission *n.* comisión, encargo.

commissure *n.* comisura, punto de unión de estructuras tal como la unión de los labios.

commisurotomy *n.* *cirg.* comisurotomía, incisión de las bandas fibrosas de una comisura tal como la de los labios o la de los bordes de válvulas cardíacas.

commit *v.* cometer; [*intern*] internar, encerrar.

commitment *n.* obligación, compromiso.

commode *n.* inodoro, servicio.

common *a.* común, corriente; ___ **name** / nombre ___; ___ **place** / lugar ___; ___ **sense** / sentido ___.

commotion *n.* conmoción; agitación.

commotio retinae *L.* conmoción retinal, condición traumática que produce ceguera momentánea.

communicable *a.* contagioso-a; comunicable; ___ **disease control** / control de enfermedades ___.

communicate *v.* comunicar; *vr.* comunicarse con.

communication *n.* comunicación; acceso; entrada.

community *n.* comunidad, sociedad, barrio; ___ **health center** / centro de servicio de la salud; ___ **medicine** medicina comunitaria.

companion *n.* compañero-a; acompañante; ___ **disease** / enfermedad concomitante.

company *n.* compañía, establecimiento.

comparative *a.* comparativo-a.

compare *v.* comparar.

compassion *n.* compasión, lástima.

compatible *a.* compatible.

compensate *v.* compensar, recompensar.

compensation *n.* compensación. 1. cualidad de compensar o equilibrar un defecto; 2. mecanismo de defensa; 3. remuneración.

competent *a.* competente, capaz.

complain *v.* quejarse, lamentarse.

complainer *a.* quejoso-a.

complaint *n.* queja, síntoma; trastorno, molestia; **chief** ___ / ___ principal.

complement *n.* complemento, sustancia proteínica presente en el plasma que destruye las bacterias y las células con que se pone en contacto.

complex *n.* complejo, serie de procesos mentales interrelacionados que afectan la conducta y la personalidad; **castration** ___ / ___ de castración; **guilt** ___ / ___ de culpa; **inferiority** ___ / ___ de inferioridad; **Electra's** ___ / ___ de Electra; **Oedipus** ___ / ___ de Edipo; *a.* complejo-a; complicado-a.

complexion *n.* cutis, complexión, tez.

compliance *n.* adaptabilidad, conformidad, grado de elasticidad de un órgano para distenderse o de una estructura para perder la forma; ___ **with standards** / ___ con las normas.

complicate *v.* complicar.

complication *n.* complicación.

component *n.* componente.

composition *n.* composición, mezcla, compuesto.

composure *n.* compostura, serenidad.

compote *n.* compota.

compound *n.* compuesto.

comprehension *n.* comprensión.

compress *n.* compresa, apósito; **cold** ___ / ___ fría; **hot** ___ / fomento; *v.* comprimir, apretar.

compromise *v.* comprometerse, obligarse.

compulsion *n.* compulsión.

compulsive *a.* compulsorio-a, compulsivo-a; obsesivo-a.

computer diagnosis *n.* diagnóstico computado.

concave *a.* cóncavo-a.

conceive *v.* concebir.

concentrate *v.* concentrar.

concentration *n.* concentración.

concept *n.* concepto, opinión, noción, idea.

conception *n.* concepción, acto de concebir.

concern *n.* preocupación, cuidado.

concise *a.* conciso-a; definido-a.

conclusion *n.* conclusión.

concoction *n.* cocimiento, mezcla, concocción.

concrete *a.* concreto-a; definido-a.

concretio cordis *L.* concretio cordis, obliteración parcial o total de la cavidad del pericardio debido a una pericarditis constrictiva.

concretion *n.* concreción, bezoar o masa inorgánica que se acumula en partes del cuerpo.

concubitus *L.* concúbito.

concussion *n.* concusión, conmoción, traumatismo esp. del cerebro causado por una lesión en la cabeza que puede presentar síntomas de náusea y mareos; **cerebral** ___ / ___ cerebral.

condemn *v.* condenar.

condense *v.* condensar, hacer más denso o compacto.

condition *n.* condición, cualidad; **guarded** ___ / en estado de gravedad; **preexisting** ___ / ___ preexistente.

conditioning *n.* acondicionamiento, condicionamiento.

condole *v.* condolerse; dar el pésame.

condolence *n.* condolencia, pésame.

condom *n.* condón, contraceptivo masculino.

conduct *v.* dirigir, conducir.

conduit *n.* conducto; **airway** ___ / ___ para aire; **tear** ___ / ___ lagrimal.

condyle *n.* cóndilo, porción redondeada de un hueso, usu. en la articulación.

condyloma *n.* condiloma, tipo de verruga vista alrededor de los genitales y el perineo.

cone *n.* cono, uno de los órganos sensoriales que, con los bastoncillos de la retina, facilitan la visión del color; ___ **cells** / ___-s de la retina.

confabulation *n. psic.* confabulación, condición en la que el individuo imagina situaciones que olvida fácilmente.

confer *v.* consultar; conferenciar.

confess *v.* admitir, reconocer; confesar.

confidential *a.* confidencial; en secreto.

confine *v.* recluir, internar, confinar; **to** ___ **in bed** / ___ en la cama.

confined *a.* recluido-a, confinado-a.

confinement *n.* confinación, reclusión, internación.

confirm *v.* confirmar.

conflict *n.* conflicto, problema.

confluence *n.* confluencia, punto de reunión de varios canales.

confront *v.* confrontar.

confuse *v.* confundir, trastornar, aturdir.

confused *a.* confuso-a, confundido-a, distraído-a; *v.* to be ___ / estar ___, confundirse.

confusion *n.* confusión; atolondramiento; aturdimiento.

congenital *a.* congénito-a; engendrado-a, rel. a una característica que se hereda y existe desde el nacimiento.

congested *a.* congestionado-a; en estado de congestión.

congestion *n.* congestión, aglomeración; acumulación excesiva de sangre en un órgano.

congestive *a.* congestivo-a, rel. a la congestión; ___ **heart failure** / insuficiencia cardíaca ___.

conical, conic *a.* cónico-a, semejante a un cono.

conization *n.* conización, extirpación de tejido que tiene forma cónica, semejante al de la mucosa del cuello uterino.

conjunctiva *n.* conjuntiva, membrana mucosa protectora del ojo.

conjunctival *a.* conjuntivo-a, rel. a la conjuntiva; ___ **diseases** / enfermedades de la conjuntiva.

conjunctivitis *n.* conjuntivitis, infl. de la conjuntiva; ___ **acute, contagious** / ___ aguda contagiosa; **allergic** ___ / ___ alérgica; **catarrhal** ___ / ___ catarral; **follicular** ___ / ___ folicular; **vernal** ___ / ___ vernal.

consanguineous *a.* consanguíneo-a, de la misma sangre u origen.

conscious *a.* consciente, en posesión de las facultades mentales.

consciousness *n.* consciencia, conocimiento, sentido; estado consciente; *v.* to lose ___ / perder el conocimiento; perder el sentido; **clouding of** ___ / torpor, confusión, entorpecimiento mental.

consensus *n.* consenso.

consent *n.* consentimiento, autorización; *v.* permitir, consentir; **informed** ___ / ___ autorizado.

consequences *n. pl.* consecuencias, secuelas.

conservation *n.* conservación, preservación.

conservative *a.* conservador-a; preservativo-a.

conserve *v.* conservar, mantener.

consider *v.* considerar, ponderar.

considerate *a.* considerado-a; moderado-a.

consideration *n.* consideración.

consist *v.* consistir; estar formado de; componerse.

consistency *n.* consistencia; solidez.

consistent *a.* consistente, firme, estable.

console *v.* consolar, confortar; dar aliento.

consomme *n.* consomé, caldo.

conspicuous *a.* sobresaliente, señalado-a, conspicuo-a.

constant *a.* constante, persistente.

constipate *v.* estreñir, constipar.

constipated *a.* estreñido-a; constipado-a; *v.* to be ___ / estar ___.

constipation *n.* estreñimiento, trastorno intestinal caracterizado por la imposibilidad de evacuar con facilidad.

constituent *n.* constituyente.

constitute *v.* constituir, componer, formar.

constitution *n.* constitución, fortaleza.

constrain *v.* restringir; impedir.

constrict *v.* apretar, estrangular.

constriction *n.* constricción.

consult *v.* consultar.

consultant *n.* consultor-a, consejero-a.

consultation *n.* consulta.

consulting room *n.* consultorio médico.

consume *v.* consumir.

consummation *n.* consumación.

consumption *n.* consunción; desgaste progresivo; tisis, tuberculosis.

contact *n.* contacto; **close** ___ / ___ íntimo; ___ **lenses** / lentes de ___; **initial** ___ / ___ inicial.

contagion *n.* contagio, transmisión de una enfermedad por contacto.

contagious *a.* contagioso-a; infeccioso-a; que se comunica por contagio.

contain *v.* contener; reprimir.

container *n.* recipiente, envase.

contaminate *v.* contaminar, infectar.

contamination *n.* contaminación; infección.

content *n.* contenido.

contented *a.* satisfecho-a.

contiguous *a.* contiguo-a, adyacente.

continence *n.* continencia, control o automoderación en relación con actividades sexuales o físicas.

continuation *n.* continuación.

continue *v.* continuar.

continuity *n.* continuidad.

continuous *a.* continuo-a, seguido-a.

contour *n.* contorno.

contraception *n.* contracepción, anticoncepción.

contraceptive *n.* contraceptivo, anticonceptivo, agente o método para impedir la concepción; ___ **agents** / agentes anticonceptivos; ___ **implant** / implante de ___; ___ **methods** / métodos ___-s, métodos anticonceptivos; **oral** ___ / ___ oral.

contract *v.* [*a disease*] contraer.

contracted *n.* contraído-a; retenido-a.

contractile *a.* contráctil, que tiene la capacidad de contraerse.

contractility *n.* contractilidad, capacidad de contraerse.

contraction *n.* contracción; **after-** ___ / ___ ulterior; **deep** ___ / ___ de fondo; **hunger** ___ / ___ de hambre; **muscular** ___ / ___ muscular; **spasmodic** ___ / ___ espasmódica.

contracture *n.* contractura, contracción prolongada involuntaria.

contradict *v.* contradecir, negar.

contradiction *n.* contradicción, oposición.

contraindicated *a.* contraindicado-a.

contraindication *n.* contraindicación.

contralateral *a.* contralateral, rel. al lado opuesto.

contrary *a.* contrario-a, adverso-a, opuesto-a.

contrast *n.* contraste; ___ **medium** / medio de ___; *v.* contrastar, resaltar.

contribute *v.* contribuir.

control *n.* control, regulación; *v.* controlar, regular, dominar; **to** ___ **oneself** / controlarse, dominarse.

contuse *v.* magullar.

contusion *n.* contusión, magulladura.

convalesce *v.* convalecer, reponerse.

convalescence *n.* convalecencia, proceso de restablecimiento, estado de recuperación.

convalescent *a.* convaleciente.

convergence *n.* convergencia, inclinación de dos o más elementos hacia un punto común.

conversion *n.* conversión. 1. cambio, transformación; 2. *psic.* transformación de una emoción en una manifestación física; ___ **disorder** / enajenamiento.

convex *a.* convexo-a.

convict *n.* preso-a, detenido-a, presidiario-a.

convulsion *n.* convulsión, contracción involuntaria de un músculo; **febrile** ___ / ___ febril; **Jacksonian** ___ / ___ Jacksoniana; **tonic-clonic** ___ / ___ tonicoclónica.

convulsive, convulsant *a.* convulsivo-a, rel. a la convulsión; ___ **activity** / actividad ___.

cook *n.* cocinero-a; *v.* cocinar.

cooked *a.* cocinado-a; guisado-a; **well** ___ / bien ___.

cool *a.* fresco-a; refrescado-a; [*weather*] **it is** ___ / hace fresco; [*body temperature*] **he, she, it is** ___ / está fresco-a; ___ **headed** / sereno-a, calmado-a.

cool-down *n.* [*physical fitness*] enfriamiento.

cooler *n.* refrigerante, refresco.

coolness *n.* frialdad; serenidad.

cooperate *v.* cooperar, ayudar.

coordinate *v.* coordinar.

coordination *n.* coordinación; **lack of** ___ / falta de ___.

copayment *n.* pago compartido.

copious *a.* abundante, copioso-a.

coprolith *n.* coprolito, pequeña masa fecal de consistencia dura.

coprophagy *n.* coprofagia, trastorno mental manifestado en la ingestión de heces fecales.

copulation *n.* copulación, relaciones sexuales.

copy *n.* copia; imitación; *v.* copiar; imitar.

cor *L.* cor, corazón.

coracoclavicular *a.* coracoclavicular, referente a la escápula y la clavícula.

coracoid *n.* coracoides, apófisis del omóplato.

Coramine *n.* Coramina, nombre comercial de la niquetamida.

cord *n.* cordón, cuerda, cordel; **umbilical** ___ / ___ umbilical.

cordectomy *n.* *cirg.* cordectomía, excisión de una cuerda vocal o parte de ésta.

core *n.* centro, corazón, núcleo.

corium *L.* corion, dermis o piel.

corn *n.* callo, callosidad; [*grain*] maíz.

cornea *n.* córnea, parte anterior transparente del globo del ojo.

corneous *a.* córneo, rel. a la córnea; calloso-a.

coronary *a.* coronario-a, que circunda tal como una corona; ___ **artery** / arteria ___; ___ **bypass** / desviación ___; ___ **care unit** / unidad de cuidado ___; ___ **thrombosis** / trombosis ___; ___ **vasospasm** / vasoepasmo ___.

coroner *n.* médico-a forense.

corporeal *a.* corporal, físico-a, rel. al cuerpo.

corpse *n.* cadáver, muerto-a.

corpus *L.* (*pl.* **corpora**) corpus, el cuerpo humano.

corpus callosum *L.* corpus callosum, comisura mayor del cerebro.

corpuscle *n.* corpúsculo, cuerpo diminuto.

corpuscular *a.* corpuscular, diminuto-a.

corpus luteum *L.* corpus luteum, cuerpo lúteo, cuerpo amarillo, masa glandular amarillenta que se forma en el ovario por la ruptura de un folículo y produce progesterona.

correct *a.* correcto-a, exacto-a; *v.* corregir, enmendar.

correction *n.* corrección.

corrective *a.* correctivo-a.

correspondence *n.* correspondencia; reciprocidad.

corroded *a.* corroído-a, desgastado-a.

corrosion *n.* corrosión, desgaste.

corset *n.* corsé.

cortex *n.* corteza, córtex, la capa más exterior de un órgano; **adrenal** ___ / ___ suprarrenal; **cerebral** ___ / ___ cerebral.

cortical *a.* cortical, rel. a la corteza.

corticoid, corticosteroid *n.* corticoide, corticoesteroide, esteroide producido por la corteza suprarrenal.

corticotropin *n.* corticotropina, sustancia hormonal de actividad adrenocorticotrópica.

cortisol *n.* cortisol, hormona secretada por la corteza suprarrenal.

cortisone *n.* cortisona, esteroide glucogénico derivado del cortisol o sintéticamente.

Corti's organ *n.* órgano de Corti, órgano terminal de la audición a través del cual se perciben directamente los sonidos.

cosmetic *n.* cosmético; *a.* cósmetico-a.

cosmetic surgery *n.* cirugía plástica con fines estéticos.

cost *n.* coste, costo, precio; *v.* costar.

costal *a.* costal, rel. a las costillas.

costalgia *n.* costalgia, neuralgia, dolor en las costillas.

costly *a.* costoso-a, caro-a; *adv.* costosamente.

costochondritis *n.* costocondritis, infl. de uno o más cartílagos costales.

costoclavicular *a.* costoclavicular, rel. a las costillas y la clavícula.

costovertebral *a.* costovertebral, rel. a las costillas y vértebras torácicas.

cotton *n.* algodón.

cough *n.* tos; **hacking** ___ / ___ seca recurrente;

___ **lozenges** / pastillas para la ___; ___ **suppressant** / calmante para la ___; ___ **syrup** / jarabe para la ___; *v.* toser; **to** ___ **up phlegm** / expectorar la flema; **coughing spell** / ataque de ___.

count *v.* contar.

counter *n.* contador.

counteract *v.* contrarrestar, oponerse a; contraatacar.

counterattack *n.* contraataque.

countercoup *n.* contragolpe.

counterpoison *n.* antídoto, contraveneno.

counterreaction *n.* reacción opuesta; reacción en contra de.

countershock *n.* contrachoque, corriente eléctrica aplicada al corazón para normalizar el ritmo cardíaco.

courage *n.* coraje, valor, firmeza.

courageous *a.* valiente, valeroso-a.

course *n.* curso, dirección.

cousin *n.* primo-a.

cover *n.* cobertor, manta, cobija; *v.* cubrir, proteger; tapar; abrigar.

covered *a.* cubierto-a; protegido-a.

cow *n.* vaca.

coward *a.* cobarde.

cowperitis *n.* cowperitis, infl. de las glándulas de Cowper (bulbouretrales).

Cowper's glands *n.* glándulas de Cowper (bulbouretrales), pequeñas glándulas adyacentes al bulbo de la uretra masculina en la que vacían una secreción mucosa.

cowpox *n.* vacuna, cowpox.

coxa *L.* (*pl.* **coxae**) coxa, cadera; ___ **magna** / ___ magna, ensanchamiento anormal de la cabeza y del cuello del fémur; ___ **valga** / ___ valga, deformidad de la cadera por desplazamiento lateral y angular del fémur; ___ **vara** / ___ vara, deformidad de la cadera por desplazamiento angular interno del fémur.

coxalgia *n.* coxalgia, dolor en la cadera.

coxitis *n.* coxitis, infl. de la articulación coxofemoral, (articulación de la cadera).

crab *n.* cangrejo, cámbaro.

crack *n.* rajadura, quebradura; *v.* rajar, quebrar.

cracker *n.* galleta.

cradle *n.* cuna; ___ **cap** / costra láctea.

cramp *n.* calambre, entumecimiento; contracción dolorosa de un músculo.

cranial *a.* craneal, craneano-a, del cráneo o rel. al mismo.

cranial nerves *n.* nervios craneales, cada uno de los doce pares de nervios que salen de la región inferior del cerebro; **I. olfactory** / olfatorio; **II. optic** / óptico; **III. oculomotor** / motor ocular común; **IV. trochlear** / patético; **V. trigeminal** / trigémino; **VI. abducens** / motor ocular externo abducente; **VII. facial** / facial; **VIII. auditory** / auditivo; **IX. glossopharyngeal** / glosofaríngeo; **X. vagus** / neumogástrico; **XI. spinal accessory** / espinal; **XII. hypoglossal** / hipoglosal.

Cranial Nerves	*Nervios craneales*
olfactory	olfatorio
optic	óptico
oculomotor	motor ocular común
trochlear	patético
trigeminal	trigémino
abducens	motor ocular externo abducente
facial	facial
auditory	auditivo
glossopharyngeal	glosofaríngeo
vagus	neumogástrico
spinal accesory	espinal
hypoglossal	hipoglosal

craniopharingioma *n.* craneofaringioma, tipo de tumor cerebral maligno visto esp. en los niños.

cranioplasty *n. cirg.* craneoplastia, reparación de defectos en los huesos del cráneo.

craniotomy *n. cirg.* craneotomía. trepanación del cráneo.

cranium *n.* cráneo, parte ósea de la cabeza que cubre el cerebro.

cranky *a.* majadero-a; inquieto-a.

crash *n.* choque violento; accidente de tráfico.

crater *n.* cráter. *V.* **niche**.

crave *v.* apetecer; ansiar; desear algo excesivamente.

craving *n.* deseo exagerado.

crawl *v.* arrastrarse; andar a gatas, gatear.

craze *n.* manía, locura.

crazy *a.* loco-a, demente.

cream *n.* crema, nata.

create *v.* crear.

creatine *n.* creatina, componente del tejido muscular, esencial en la fase anaeróbica de la contracción muscular.

creatinine *n.* creatinina, sustancia presente en la orina que representa el producto final del metabolismo de la creatina; ___ **clearance** / depuración de ___, volumen de plasma libre de ___.

creation *n.* creación, obra; universo.

credit *n.* crédito; *v.* acreditar, dar crédito.

cremasteric *a.* cremastérico, referente al músculo cremastérico del escroto.

cremate *v.* incinerar.

cremation *n.* incineración.

creosote *n.* creosota, líquido aceitoso gen. usado como desinfectante y como expectorante catarral.

crepitation *n.* crepitación, chasquido, crujido; **pleural** ___ / ___ **pleural**.

crest *n.* cresta, prominencia; copete. 1. reborde o prominencia de un hueso; 2. la elevación máxima de una línea en un gráfico.

crestfallen *a.* decaído-a, alicaído-a; acobardado-a.

cretin *n.* cretino-a, persona con manifestaciones de cretinismo.

cretinism *n.* cretinismo, hipotiroidismo congénito debido a una deficiencia acentuada de la hormona tiroidea.

cretinoid *a.* cretinoide, con características similares a un cretino.

crib *n.* cuna, camita.

crib death *n.* muerte de cuna, síndrome de muerte infantil súbita.

cribriform *a.* cribriforme, perforado-a.

cricoid *a.* cricoide, de forma anular.

crime *n.* crimen, delito.

criminal *n.* criminal.

cripple *a.* lisiado-a, paralítico-a, inválido-a, tullido-a; *v.* lisiar, baldar, paralizar; tullir.

crisis *n.* crisis; **identity** ___ / ___ de identidad.

crisscross *a.* cruzado-a, entrelazado-a; *adv.* en cruz.

crista *n.* cresta, proyección.

critical *a.* crítico-a; ___ **condition** / estado ___, gravedad extrema.

crossed eyes, strabismus *n.* estrabismo, *pop.* bizquera, debilidad de los músculos que controlan la posición del ojo impidiendo la coordinación visual.

cross-eyed *a.* bizco-a.

cross-legged *a.* patizambo-a; cruzado-a de piernas.

cross matching *n.* pruebas sanguíneas cruzadas que comprueban la compatibilidad de la sangre antes de una tranfusión.

cross studies *n. pl.* estudios cruzados.

crotch *n.* bifurcación, horquilla.

croup *n.* crup, *pop.* garrotillo, síndrome respiratorio visto en los niños, causado gen. por una infección o una reacción alérgica; **spasmodic** ___ / ___ espasmódico.

crown *n.* corona.

crucial *a.* crucial, definitivo-a.

crude *a.* rudo-a, crudo-a.

cruel *a.* cruel, inhumano-a.

crus *L.* crus, 1. pierna o parte semejante a una pierna; 2. parte de la pierna entre la rodilla y el tobillo.

crush *v.* triturar, moler, aplastar.

crust *n.* costra.

crutches *n. pl.* muletas.

cry *v.* llorar; lamentarse.

cryoanesthesia *n.* crioanestesia, 1. anestesia producida por aplicación de frío localizado; 2. pérdida de la sensibilidad al frío.

cryogenic *n.* criogénico, que produce temperaturas bajas.

cryoglobulin *n.* crioglobulina, globulina que se precipita del suero por acción del frío.

cryoprecipitate *n.* crioprecipitado, precipitado producido por enfriamiento.

cryosurgery *n.* criocirugía, destrucción de tejidos por aplicación de temperatura fría local o general.

cryotherapy *n.* crioterapia, tratamiento terapéutico por aplicación de frío local o general.

crypt *n.* cripta, pequeño receso tubular.

cryptic *a.* críptico-a, escondido-a.

cryptococcosis *n.* criptococosis, infección que afecta distintos órganos del cuerpo, esp. el cerebro y sus meninges.

cryptogenic *a.* criptogénico, de causa desconocida.

cryptorchism *n.* criptorquismo, falta de descenso testicular al escroto.

crystal *n.* cristal, vidrio.

crystalline *a.* cristalino-a, transparente.

crystalline lens *n.* cristalino, lente del ojo.

cubiform *a.* cúbico-a, rel. a la forma cúbica.

cubital *a.* cubital, codal.

cubitus, ulna *L.* cubitus, cúbito, hueso interno del antebrazo.

cucumber *n.* pepino, pepinillo.

cuff *n.* manguito, tejido fibroso que rodea una articulación; **rotator** ___ / ___ rotador, músculo tendinoso; **rotator** ___ **tear** / ruptura del ___ rotador.

cul-de-sac *Fr.* 1. cul-de-sac, fondo de saco, bolsa sin boquete de salida; 2. saco rectouterino.

culdoscope *n.* culdoscopio, instrumento endoscópico que se inserta en la vagina para examinar visualmente la pelvis y la cavidad abdominal.

culdoscopy *n.* culdoscopía, examen de la pelvis y la cavidad abdominal por medio del culdoscopio.

cultivate *v.* cultivar; estudiar.

culture *n.* cultivo, crecimiento artificial de microorganismos o células de tejido vivo en el laboratorio; **blood** ___ / ___ de sangre; ___ **medium** / medio de ___; **tissue** ___ / ___ de tejido.

cunnilingus *a.* cunilinguo-a, rel. a la práctica de estimulación oral del pene o del clítoris.

cup *n.* copa; ventosa; **optic** ___ / ___ de ojo, ___ ocular; **measuring** ___ / taza de medir.

cupful *n.* una taza llena.

curable *a.* curable, sanable.

curare *n.* curare, veneno extraído de varios tipos de plantas y usado como relajante muscular y anestésico.

curative *n.* curativo, remedio, agente que tiene propiedades curativas.

curd *n.* cuajo, cuajarón, coágulo sanguíneo grande; [*milk*] leche cuajada.

curdle *v.* cuajarse, coagularse, engrumecerse.

cure *n.* curación, remedio; *v.* curar, sanar, remediar.

cureless *a.* incurable.

curettage *n. cirg.* curetaje, raspado de una superficie o cavidad con uso de la cureta.

curette *n.* cureta, instrumento quirúrgico en forma de cuchara o pala usado para raspar los tejidos de una superficie o cavidad.

curious *a.* curioso-a, extraño-a.

current *n.* corriente, trasmisión de fluido o electricidad que pasa por un conductor; *a.* corriente, actual; **-ly** *adv.* actualmente.

curvature *n.* curvatura.

curve *n.* curva; *v.* torcer, encorvar.

Cushing's syndrome *n.* síndrome de Cushing, síndrome adrenogenital asociado con una producción excesiva de cortisol, caracterizado por obesidad y debilitamiento muscular.

cushion *n.* cojinete, cojín.

cusp *n.* cúspide, punta.

cuspid *n.* [*tooth*] colmillo.

cuspidal *a.* cuspídeo, puntiagudo.

custard *n.* flan, natilla.

custom *n.* costumbre, hábito.

cut *n.* cortada, cortadura; *v.* cortar; **to** ___ **down** / rebajar, reducir; **to** ___ **off** / extirpar, amputar; [*oneself*] cortarse.

cutaneous *a.* cutáneo-a; ___ **absorption** / absorción ___; ___ **glands** / glándulas ___-s o sebáceas.

cuticle *n.* cutícula, capa exterior de la piel.

cutis *n.* cutis; piel de la cara.

cyanide *n.* cianuro, compuesto extremadamente venenoso.

cyanocobalamin *n.* cianocobalamina, vitamina B_{12} usada en el tratamiento de la anemia perniciosa.

cyanosis *n.* cianosis, condición azulada o amoratada de la piel y las mucosas a causa de anomalías cardíacas o funcionales.

cyanotic *a.* cianótico-a, rel. a la cianosis o causado por ésta.

cybernetics *n.* cibernética, estudio del uso de medios electrónicos y mecanismos de comunicación aplicados a sistemas biológicos tales como los sistemas nervioso y cerebral.

cyclamate *n.* ciclamato, agente artificial dulcificante.

cycle *n.* ciclo, período; **pregnancy** ___ / ___ gravídico.

cyclectomy *n. cirg.* cicletomía, excisión de una parte del músculo ciliar.

cyclic *a.* cíclico-a, que ocurre en períodos o ciclos.

cyclitis *n.* ciclitis, infl. del músculo ciliar.

cyclophoria *n.* cicloforia, rotación del globo ocular debido a debilidad muscular.

cyclophosphamide *n.* ciclofosfamida, droga antineoplástica usada también como inmunosupresor en trasplantes.

cyclophotocoagulation *n.* ciclofotocoagulación, fotocoagulación a través de la pupila con un laser, procedimiento usado en el tratamiento de glaucoma.

cycloplegia *n.* cicloplejía, parálisis del músculo ciliar.

cyclosporine *n.* ciclosporina, agente inmunosupresivo usado en trasplantes de órganos.

cyclothymia *n. psic.* ciclotimia, personalidad cíclica con trastornos de agitación y depresión.

cyclotomy *n. cirg.* ciclotomía, incisión a través del músculo ciliar.

cyclotropia *n.* ciclotropia, desviación del ojo alrededor del eje anteroposterior.

cylinder *n.* cilindro. 1. émbolo de una jeringa; 2. forma geométrica semejante a una columna.

cylindrical *a.* cilíndrico-a.

cylindroma *n.* cilindroma, tumor generalmente maligno visto en la cara o en la órbita del ojo.

cylindruria *n.* cilindruria, presencia de cilindros en la orina.

cynic *a.* cínico-a.

cyst *n.* quiste, saco o bolsa que contiene líquido o materia semilíquida; **pilonidal** ___ / ___ pilonidal, que contiene pelo, gen. localizado en el área sacrococcígea; **sebaceous** ___ / ___ sebáceo, gen. localizado en el cuero cabelludo.

cystadenocarcinoma *n.* cistadenocarcinoma, carcinoma y cistadenoma combinados.

cystadenoma *n.* cistadenoma, adenoma que contiene uno o varios quistes.

cystectomy *n. cirg.* cistectomía, extirpación o resección de la vejiga.

cysteine *n.* cisteína, aminoácido derivado de la cistina, presente en la mayor parte de las proteínas.

cystic *a.* cístico-a, rel. a la vesícula biliar o la vejiga urinaria; ___ **duct** / conducto ___.

cystic fibrosis *n.* fibrosis cística del páncreas, fibroquiste.

cystine *n.* cistina, aminoácido producido durante la digestión de las proteínas, presente a veces en la orina.

cystinuria *n.* cistinuria, exceso de cistina en la orina.

cystitis *n.* cistitis, infl. de la vejiga urinaria caracterizada por ardor, dolor y micción frecuente.

cystocele *n.* cistocele, hernia de la vejiga.

cystogram *n.* cistograma, rayos X de la vejiga.

cystography *n.* cistografía, rayos X de la vejiga urinaria usando un medio de contraste.

cystolithotomy *n.* cistolitotomía, extracción de una piedra o cálculo por medio de una incisión en la vejiga.

cystometer *n.* cistómetro, instrumento usado para estudiar la patofisiología de la vejiga que mide la capacidad y las reacciones de ésta a presiones aplicadas.

cystometry *n.* cistometría, estudio de las funciones de la vejiga con uso del cistómetro.

cystopexy *n. cirg.* cistopexia, fijación de la vejiga urinaria a la pared abdominal.

cystoscope *n.* cistoscopio, instrumento en forma de tubo usado para examinar y tratar trastornos de la vejiga, los uréteres y los riñones.

cystoscopy *n.* cistoscopía, examen por medio del cistoscopio.

cystostomy *n. cirg.* cistostomía, creación de un boquete o fístula en la vejiga para permitir el drenaje urinario.

cystotomy *n. cirg.* cistotomía, incisión en la

vejiga.

cystourethrography *n.* cistouretrografía, radiografía de la vejiga y la uretra.

cystourethroscope *n.* cistouretroscopio, instrumento usado en la exploración de la vejiga y la uretra.

cytochrome *n.* citocromo, hemocromógeno importante en el proceso de oxidación.

cytology *n.* citología, ciencia que estudia la estructura, forma y función de las células.

cytolytic *a.* citolítico-a, que tiene la cualidad de disolver o destruir células.

cytomegalic *a.* citomegálico-a, caracterizado-a por células agrandadas.

cytomegalovirus *n.* citomegalovirus, virus herpético que infecta al hombre y a otros animales, causante de la enfermedad de inclusión citomegálica.

cytometer *n.* citómetro, dispositivo usado en el conteo y medida de los hematíes.

cytopenia *n.* citopenia, deficiencia de elementos celulares en la sangre.

cytoplasm *n.* citoplasma, protoplasma de una célula con exclusión del núcleo.

cytotoxicity *n.* citotoxicidad, la capacidad de un agente de destruir ciertas células.

cytotoxin *n.* citotoxina, agente tóxico que afecta a las células de ciertos órganos.

d *abbr.* **death** / muerte; **deceased** / difunto-a; **degree** / grado; **density** / densidad; **dose** / dosis.

dacryadenitis *n.* dacriadenitis, infl. de una glándula lagrimal.

dacryagogue *n.* dacriagogo, agente estimulante de las glándulas lagrimales.

dacrycystalgia *n.* dacricistalgia, dolor en el saco lagrimal.

dacryoadenectomy *n. cirg.* dacrioadenectomía, extirpación de una glándula lagrimal.

dacryocystitis *n.* dacriocistitis, infl. del saco lagrimal.

dacryocystotomy *n. cirg.* dacriocistotomía, incisión del saco lagrimal.

dacryolithiasis *n.* dacriolitiasis, formación de cálculos lacrimales.

dactyl *n.* dáctilo, dedo de la mano o del pie.

dactylogram *n.* dactilograma, proceso de determinación de las huellas digitales.

dactylography *n.* dactilografía, estudio de las huellas digitales.

dactylology *n.* dactilología, lenguaje mímico o por señas.

dactylomegaly *n.* dactilomegalia, dedos de los pies o las manos de tamaño demasiado grande.

dad *n.* papá; **daddy** / *H.A.* papi, papacito, tata.

daily *a.* diario-a, cotidiano-a; ___ **life** / vida cotidiana; *adv.* diariamente, todos los días, cada día, cotidianamente.

dairy products *n. pl.* productos lácteos.

daltonism *n.* daltonismo, dificultad para percibir colores.

dam *v.* acción de detener, estancar, tapar.

damage *n.* daño, deterioro, lesión; *v.* dañar, perjudicar; dañarse, perjudicarse.

damaging *a.* perjudicial.

damiana *n.* damiana, planta originaria de *Mex.* cuyas hojas tienen acción diurética.

damp *a.* húmedo-a.

dampen *v.* humedecer, mojar.

danazol *n.* danazol, nombre comercial Danocrina, hormona sintética que suprime la acción de la pituitaria anterior.

dance *n.* baile; **St. Vitus'** ___ / ___ de San Vito. *V.* **chorea;** *v.* bailar, danzar.

dandruff *n.* caspa.

danger *n.* peligro, riesgo; *v.* **to be in** ___ / correr ___.

dangerous *a.* peligroso-a, arriesgado-a.

dapsone *n.* dapsona, sulfonildianilina, droga usada en el tratamiento de la lepra.

dare *v.* atreverse, arriesgarse.

dark *a.* oscuro-a; ___ **adaptation** / adaptación a la oscuridad; ___ **field illumination** / iluminación del campo ___, iluminación lateral u oblicua.

darken *v.* oscurecer.

darkness *n.* oscuridad.

Darvon *n.* Darvón, Deprancol, nombre comercial de dextropropoxifeno hidroclórico, analgésico oral.

data *n. pl.* datos.

date *n.* fecha; **effective** ___ / ___ de vigencia; **specimen** ___ / ___ del espécimen o muestra; **up-to-**___ / hasta la fecha; [*current*] al corriente; ___ **de vencimiento** / expiration ___.

daughter *n.* hija; ___**-in-law** / nuera.

dawn *n.* amanecer.

day *n.* día, **all** ___ / todo el ___; **by** ___ / por el ___, de ___; ___ **after tomorrow** / pasado mañana; ___ **before yesterday** / anteayer; ___ **in** ___ **out** / ___ tras ___; **each** ___ / cada ___; **every** ___ / todos los ___-s; **every other** ___ / un ___ sí y un ___ no; **three times a** ___ / tres veces al ___; **twice a** ___ / dos veces al ___.

daybreak *n.* amanecer, alba.

daydream *n.* ilusión, ensueño; *v.* **to** ___ / soñar despierto-a.

daylight *n.* luz del día.

daytime *a.* de día.

daze *n.* ofuscación, desorientación.

deacidify *v.* neutralizar un ácido.

deactivation *n.* desactivación, proceso de transformar lo activo en inactivo.

dead *a.* difunto-a; muerto-a.

deaden *v.* [*sound*] amortiguar; [*nerve*] adormecer; anestesiar.

deadly *a* mortífero-a, mortal, que puede causar la muerte; ___ **poison** / veneno ___; ___ **wound** / herida ___.

deaf *n., a.* sordo-a.

deafen *v.* ensordecer.

deaf-mute *n.* sordomudo-a.

deaf-muteness, deafmutism *n.* sordomudez.

deafness *n.* sordera.

deal *n.* cantidad, porción; **a good** ___ / bastante; **a great** ___ **of time** / mucho tiempo; *v.* repartir, distribuir; **to** ___ **with** / tratar con.

deambulatory *a.* ambulatorio-a; móvil.

dear *a.* querido-a; estimado-a.

death *n.* muerte, fallecimiento; **apparent** ___ / ___ aparente; ___ **certificate** / certificado de defunción; **fetal** ___ / ___ del feto; ___ **instinct** / instinto mortal; ___ **rate** / mortalidad; ___ **rattle** / estertor agónico.

debilitate *v.* debilitar; debilitarse.

debilitated *a.* debilitado-a.

debility *n.* debilidad; atonía.

debridement *n.* desbridamiento, proceso quirúrgico de limpieza de una herida o quemadura para prevenir una infección.

debt *n.* deuda.

decalcification *n.* descalcificación, pérdida o disminución de sales de calcio en los huesos o dientes.

decay *n.* deterioración, deterioro, descomposición gradual; [*teeth*] caries; **dental** ___ / carie dental, *pop.* dientes picados; ___ **rate** / índice de descomposición gradual; *v.* deteriorar, descomponer, decaer, declinar; deteriorarse, descomponerse, [*teeth*] cariarse; [*wood*] carcomerse; [*matter*] podrirse, pudrirse.

decayed *a.* deteriorado-a, decaído-a; empeorado-a; cariado-a; carcomido-a; podrido-a; putrefacto-a.

deceased *n.* difunto-a, persona muerta.

deceit *n.* engaño, fraude.

deceitful *a.* traicionero-a, engañador-a; ___ sickness / enfermedad ___.

deceive *v.* engañar, defraudar, embaucar.

deceleration *n.* desaceleración, disminución de la velocidad tal como en la frecuencia cardíaca.

decency *n.* decencia.

decent *a.* decente.

decentered *a.* descentrado-a, fuera del centro.

decide *v.* decidir, determinar.

decided *a.* decidido-a.

decidua *n.* decidua, tejido membranoso formado por la mucosa uterina durante la gestación y expulsado después del parto.

deciduous *a.* deciduo-a, de permanencia temporal; ___ dentition / primera dentición; ___ teeth / dientes ___-s, dientes de leche.

decimate *v.* diezmar.

decimation *n.* gran mortalidad, diezma.

decipher *v.* descifrar, resolver un problema.

decision *n.* decisión, resolución.

decisive *a.* decisivo-a, terminante.

declination *n.* declinación. 1. rotación del ojo; 2. declive, descenso.

decline *n.* declinación; decadencia, decaimiento; [*invitation*] excusa; *v.* declinar, decaer; [*invitation, offer*] declinar, rehusar, rechazar; [*health*] desmejorarse.

decoction *n.* cocimiento, té de yerbas medicinales.

decompensation *n.* descompensación, inhabilidad del corazón para mantener una circulación adecuada.

decompose *v.* descomponerse, corromperse; [*food*] podrirse, pudrirse.

decomposed *a.* descompuesto-a; [*food*] podrido-a, putrefacto-a.

decompression *n.* descompresión, reducción de presión; ___ chamber / cámara de ___; surgical ___ / ___ quirúrgica; ___ sickness / condición por ___, *pop.* the bends.

decongest *v.* descongestionar.

decongestant *n.* descongestionador, descongestionante.

decontaminate *v.* descontaminar, librar de contaminación.

decontamination *n.* descontaminación, proceso de librar el ambiente, objetos o personas de sustancias o agentes contaminados o nocivos tales como sustancias radioactivas.

decrepit *a.* decrépito-a, senil.

decrepitude *n.* decrepitud.

decubitus *n.* decúbito, posición acostada; ___

dorsal / dorsal, de espalda o boca arriba; ___ lateral / lateral, ___ de lado; ___ ventral / ___ de vientre o boca abajo; ___ ulcer / úlcera o escara por ___.

decussation *n.* decusación, cruzamiento de estructuras en forma de X; ___ of pyramids / ___ de las pirámides, cruzamiento de fibras nerviosas de una pirámide a otra en la médula oblongata; optic ___ / ___ óptica, cruzamiento de las fibras del nervio óptico.

dedicate *v.* dedicar.

deduce *v.* deducir, inferir.

deduct *v.* descontar; rebajar.

deductible *a.* deducible.

deep *a.* profundo-a, hondo-a; ___ breathing / respiración ___; ___ contractions / contracciones ___-s, de fondo; ___-chested / ancho-a de pecho; ___ dredging / dragado; ___-rooted / arraigado-a; ___ sensibility / sensibilidad ___; ___ sleep / sueño ___, sopor; ___ x-ray therapy / terapia ___; ___ tendon reflex / reflejos tendónicos ___-s.

deface *v.* mutilar, deformar, desfigurar.

defacement *n.* deformación; deterioro; mutilación.

defecate *v.* defecar, evacuar; *Mex.* obrar.

defecation *n.* defecación, evacuación intestinal

defect *n.* defecto; insuficiencia; fallo.

defective *a.* defectuoso-a; incompleto-a.

defend *v.* defender.

defense *n.* defensa; protección; resistencia; ___ mechanism / mecanismo de ___; [*organic*] antitoxina; *psic.* autoprotección.

defenseless *a.* indefenso-a, inerme.

defer *v.* diferir, aplazar.

deferent *a.* deferente, hacia afuera.

deferred *a.* aplazado-a, diferido-a.

defibrillation *n.* desfibrilación, acción de cambiar latidos irregulares del corazón a su ritmo normal.

defibrillator *n.* desfibrilador, dispositivo eléctrico usado para restaurar el ritmo normal del corazón.

deficiency *n.* deficiencia, falta de algún elemento esencial al organismo; ___ disease / enfermedad por deficiencia; mental ___ / ___ mental; oxygen ___ / falta de oxígeno.

deficient *a.* deficiente, careciente.

deficit *n.* déficit, deuda; falta; deficiencia.

definition *n.* definición.

deflate *v.* desinflar, deshinchar.

deflect *v.* desviar, apartar.

deflection, deflexion *n.* desviación, desvío; *psic.* diversión inconsciente de ideas.

deform *v.* deformar.

deformed *a.* deformado-a, irregular.

deformity *n.* deformidad, irregularidad, defecto congénito o adquirido.

defurfuration *n.* defurfuración, acto de soltar escamas de la piel semejantes a hojuelas.

degenerate *a.* degenerado-a; anómalo-a.

degeneration *n.* degeneración, deteriorización.

deglutition *n.* deglución, acto de ingerir.

degree *n.* grado. 1. unidad de medida de la temperatura; 2. intensidad.

dehiscence *n.* dehiscencia, abertura espontánea de una herida.

dehumidifier *n.* deshumectante, aparato para disminuir la humedad.

dehydrate *v.* deshidratar, eliminar el agua de una sustancia; deshidratarse, perder líquido del cuerpo o de los tejidos.

dehydrated *a.* deshidratado-a.

dehydrocholesterol *n.* dehidrocolesterol, esterol presente en la piel que se convierte en vitamina D por la acción de rayos solares.

déjà fu *Fr.* déjà vu, impresión ilusoria de haber experimentado antes una situación que es totalmente nueva.

dejection *n.* deyección. 1. estado de abatimiento, depresión; 2. expulsión de excremento.

delay *n.* demora; *v.* demorar, atrasar; postergar.

delayed *a.* tardío-a, demorado-a; ___ **delivery** / parto ___.

deleterious *a.* deletéreo-a, nocivo-a, dañino-a.

delicate *a.* delicado-a.

delicious *a.* delicioso-a; exquisito-a.

delight *n.* deleite; delicia; *v.* agradar, deleitar.

delighted *a.* encantado-a; *v.* **to be** ___ / tener mucho gusto.

delinquency *n.* delincuencia; **juvenile** ___ / ___ juvenil.

delirious *a.* delirante, en estado de delirio.

delirium *n.* delirium, estado de confusión mental acompañado gen. de alucinaciones y sensaciones distorsionadas; ___ **tremens** / ___ tremens, tipo de psicosis alcohólica.

deliver *v.* extraer; partear; [*in childbirth*] **to be delivered** / dar a luz, estar de parto, *Mex.A.* aliviarse.

delivery *n.* parto, alumbramiento; **after** ___ / después del ___; **before** ___ / antes del ___; **false** ___ / ___ falso; **hard** ___ / ___ laborioso; **induction of** ___ / ___ inducido; **normal** ___ / ___ normal; ___ **of the placenta** / expulsión de la placenta; **premature** ___ / ___ prematuro; **prolonged** ___ / ___ prolongado; ___ **room** / sala de ___-s; **stages of** ___ / etapas del ___.

deltoid *a.* deltoideo-a. 1. en forma de delta; 2. rel. al músculo deltoides.

delusion *n.* decepción, engaño; creencias falsas; ___ **of persecution** / delirio de persecución.

demand *n.* petición, demanda; ___ **feeding** / alimentación por demanda.

demented *a.* demente, enajenado-a; que sufre de demencia.

dementia *n.* demencia, locura; declinación de las funciones mentales; **organic** ___ / ___ orgánica; ___ **paralytica** / ___ paralítica; **praecox** / ___ precoz, esquizofrenia; **senile** ___ / ___ senil.

Demerol *n.* Demerol, hidrocloruro de meperidina, nombre comercial de un analgésico con efecto similar al de la morfina.

demineralization *n.* desmineralización, pérdida de sales minerales del organismo.

demulcent *n.* emoliente, demulcente, aceite u otro agente que suaviza y alivia molestias de la piel.

demyelination *n.* desmielinización, pérdida de la capa de mielina de un nervio.

dendrite *n.* dendrita, prolongación protoplasmática de la célula de un nervio que recibe los impulsos nerviosos.

dengue fever *n.* dengue, fiebre endémica producida por un virus, transmitida por el mosquito *Aedes.*

denomination *n.* denominación, nombre.

dense *a.* denso-a, espeso-a.

density *n.* densidad.

dental *a.* dental, dentario-a, rel. a los dientes; ___ **care** / cuidado ___; ___ **caries** / caries ___-es; ___ **drill** / taladro, torno; ___ **enamel** / esmalte dentario; ___ **floss** / hilo ___, hilo de seda encerada; ___ **health services** / servicios de salud ___; ___ **hygienist** / técnico-a en profiláctica ___; ___ **impression** / impresión, mordisco; ___ **plaque** / placa dentaria; ___ **surgeon** / odontólogo; ___ **tartar** / sarro ___; ___ **technician** / mecánico ___.

dentiform *a.* odontoide, dentado-a, de proyección similar a un diente.

dentifrice *n.* dentífrico, pasta dental.

dentilabial *a.* dentilabial, rel. a los dientes y los labios.

dentin *n.* dentina, marfil dentario, tejido calcificado de un diente.

dentinogenesis *n.* dentinogénesis, formación de la dentina.

dentinoma *n.* dentinoma, tumor benigno que consiste mayormente de dentina.

dentist *n.* dentista.

dentistry *n.* arte o profesión de dentistas.

dentition *n.* dentición, brote de los dientes; ___, **primary** / ___ primaria [*first teeth*] o dientes de leche; ___, **secondary** / ___ secundaria o dientes permanentes.

denture *n.* dentadura, prótesis; [*artificial*] dentadura postiza; ___ **plates** / ___ parcial, *pop.* plancha dental.

denudation *n.* denudación, privación de la cubierta de una superficie de una manera traumática, sea por cirugía, trauma, o por un cambio patológico.

denutrition *n.* desnutrición, malnutrición, deficiencia alimenticia; **protein-calorie** ___ / ___ proteinocalórica.

deny *v.* negar, rehusar.

deodorant *n.* desodorante.

deodorize *v.* desodorizar, destruir olores fétidos o desagradables.

deoxycorticosterone *n.* desoxicorticosterona, hormona producida en la corteza de las glándulas suprarrenales de efecto marcado en el metabolismo del agua y los electrólitos.

deoxygenated *a.* desoxigenado-a.

depart *v.* partir, salir.

departed *a.* difunto-a; ausente.

depend *v.* depender.

dependence, dependency *n.* dependencia, subordinación; ___ **producing drugs** / drogas adictivas, de dependencia.

dependent *a.* dependiente.

depersonalization *n.* despersonalización, pérdida de la personalidad.

depilate *v.* depilar, acción de quitar o extirpar pelo.

depilation *n.* depilación, procedimiento de extirpación del pelo y la raíz.

depilatory *n.* depilatorio.

deplete *v.* agotar, vaciar; depauperarse.

depleted *a.* agotado-a, vaciado-a, depauperado-a.

depletion *n.* deplección. 1. acción de vaciar; 2. pérdida o remoción de los líquidos del cuerpo.

deposit *n.* depósito; *v.* depositar.

depravation *n.* depravación.

depress *v.* deprimir; desalentar, desanimar.

depressant *n.* depresor; tranquilizante; ___ **drug** / medicamento tranquilizante.

depressed *a.* deprimido-a, abatido-a; *v.* **to become** ___ / deprimirse.

depression *n.* depresión. 1. *psic.* sensación de tristeza o melancolía acompañada de apatía y estados de abatimiento; 2. cavidad.

depressive *a.* depresivo-a, deprimente; ___ **disorder** / trastorno ___ .

depressor *n.* depresor. 1. agente usado para reducir un nivel establecido de una función o actividad del organismo; 2. tranquilizante que produce depresión.

depurate *v.* depurar.

depurated *a.* depurado-a.

depuration *n.* depuración, purificación.

derange *v.* perturbar, desordenar, causar trastorno.

deranged *a.* perturbado-a; trastornado-a; ___ **metabolic process** / trastorno del proceso metabólico.

derangement *Fr.* trastorno, desequilibrio, irregularidad de una función del cuerpo.

derivation *n.* derivación. 1. desviación, curso alterado o lateral que tiene lugar por anastomosis o por una característica anatómica natural; 2. descendencia.

derive *v.* derivar, inferir, deducir; descender, proceder.

dermabrasion *n.* dermabrasión, abrasión cutánea, proceso empleado para eliminar los nevos y cicatrices de la acné.

dermatitis *n.* dermatitis, dermitis, cualquier infl. de la piel.

dermatological *a.* dermatológico-a, rel. a la dermis.

dermatologist *n.* dermatólogo-a, especialista en dermatología.

dermatology *n.* dermatología, parte de la medicina que estudia la piel, su estructura, sus funciones y el tratamiento de la misma.

dermatoma *n.* dermatoma, neoplasma de la piel.

dermatome *n.* dermátomo, instrumento quirúrgico empleado para cortar capas o tejidos finos de la piel.

dermatomere *n.* dermatomera, segmento del tegumento embrionario.

dermatomycosis *n.* dermatomicosis, infl. de la piel producida por hongos.

dermatomyositis *n.* dermatomiositis, enfermedad del tejido conectivo con manifestaciones de dermatitis, edema e infl. de los músculos.

dermatopathy, dermatosis *n.* dermatopatía, dermatosis, cualquier enfermedad de la piel.

dermatophiliasis *n.* dermatofiliasis, infección de la piel producida por pulgas o niguas.

dermatophyte *n.* dermatófito, hongo parásito que ataca la piel.

dermatophytosis *n.* dermatofitosis, pie de atleta, infección fungosa producida por dermatófilos.

dermatosyphilis *n.* dermatosífilis, manifestación sifilítica en la piel.

dermic *a.* dermal, dermático-a, cutáneo-a.

dermis, derma *n.* dermis, piel.

dermoid *a.* dermoideo-a, semejante o rel. a la piel; ___ **cyst** / quiste ___ , de origen congénito, gen. benigno.

descend *v.* descender, bajar; derivarse.

descendant *n., a.* descendiente.

descending *a.* descendente, descendiente; ___ **aorta** / aorta ___ , parte mayor de la aorta; ___ **colon** / colon ___ .

descent *n.* descenso, bajada; descendencia, sucesión.

describe *v.* describir.

described *a.* descrito-a, narrado-a.

desensitize *v.* desensibilizar, reducir o eliminar una sensibilidad de origen físico o emocional.

desert *n.* desierto, yermo, páramo.

deserve *v.* merecer.

desexualizing *n.* desexualización. 1. eliminación de un impulso sexual; 2. castración.

desiccant *a.* desecante, que tiene la propiedad de secar.

desiccate *v.* desecar, secar, quitar la humedad.

desiccated *a. pp.* de **to desiccate**, desecado-a.

desirable *a.* deseado-a; conveniente.

desire *n.* deseo, ansia; *v.* desear, ansiar.

desk *n.* enscritorio; **front** ___ / mesa de admisión.

desmoid *a.* desmoide, en forma de ligamento.

desmoma *n.* desmoma, tumor del tejido conjuntivo.

despair *n.* desesperación; *v.* [*to lose hope*] perder la esperanza; desesperarse.

despondency *n.* desaliento; desesperación.

despondent *a.* desesperado-a, desalentado-a; *v.* to be ___ / estar ___.

desquamation *n.* descamación, exfoliación, desprendimiento de la piel en forma de escamas.

destroy *v.* destruir, aniquilar; arruinar.

detach *v.* separar, desprender, despegar; desprenderse; soltarse.

detachment *n.* desprendimiento, separación; ___ of the retina / ___ de la retina.

detail *n.* detalle; **in** ___ / con detalle, detalladamente; *v.* detallar, destacar; **to go into** ___ / explicar todo detalladamente.

detain *v.* detener, parar.

detect *v.* detectar, descubrir.

detector *n.* detector, revelador, descubridor.

detergent *n.* detergente, agente limpiador, *a.* detergente, limpiador-a.

deteriorate *v.* deteriorar, desmejorar; deteriorarse; desmejorarse.

deterioration *n.* deterioración, deterioro, desmejoramiento.

determinant *n.* determinante, elemento que predomina o causa una determinación.

determination *n.* determinación, decisión, resolución.

determine *v.* determinar, decidir; resolver; concluir.

determined *a.* decidido-a; [*in tests*] comprobado-a.

determinism *n.* determinismo, teoría que establece que todo fenómeno físico o psíquico está predeterminado y no es influido por la voluntad individual.

detorsion *n.* destorsión. 1. corrección de la curvatura o malformación de una estructura; 2. corrección quirúrgica de la torsión de un testículo o del intestino.

detoxicate *v.* desintoxicar.

detoxification *n.* destoxificación, reducción de las propiedades tóxicas de una sustancia.

detoxify *v.* destoxificar, desintoxicar, extraer sustancias tóxicas.

detrimental *a.* perjudicial, nocivo-a.

detritus *n. pl.* desechos.

detrusor *n.* detrusor, músculo que expulsa o echa hacia afuera.

deuteranopia *n.* deuteranopía, ceguera al color verde.

develop *v.* [*to expand, to grow*] desarrollar, crecer, progresar; evolucionar; avanzar; [*film*] revelar; [*symptom*] surgir; manifestarse.

developed *a.* desarrollado-a; revelado-a, manifestado-a.

development *n.* desarrollo; adelanto; progreso, crecimiento; [*germs*] proliferación.

deviation *n.* desviación, desvío. 1. alejamiento de una pauta establecida; 2. *psic.* aberración mental; mala conducta, mal comportamiento.

device *n.* dispositivo; mecanismo.

devious *a.* desviado-a; descaminado-a; extra-viado-a.

devise *v.* idear, inventar, considerar.

devitalize *v.* devitalizar, debilitar, privar de la fuerza vital.

devolution *n.* devolución. V. **catabolism.**

Dexedrine *n.* Dexedrina, tipo de anfetamina, estimulante del sistema nervioso.

dexter *a.* diestro-a; a la derecha.

dextrocardia *n.* dextrocardia, dislocación del corazón hacia la derecha.

dextromanual *a.* dextromanual, preferencia por el uso de la mano derecha.

dextroposition *n.* dextroposición, desplazamiento hacia la derecha.

dextrose *n.* dextrosa, glucosa, forma de azúcar simple, *pop.* azúcar de uva.

diabetes *n.* diabetes, enfermedad que se manifiesta por excesiva emisión de orina.

diabetes insipidus *n.* diabetes insípida nefrógena, causada por una deficiencia en el gasto de hormona antidiurética.

diabetes mellitus *n.* diabetes mellitus, diabetes causada por una deficiencia en la producción de insulina que resulta en hiperglucemia y glucosuria; ___ **noninsulin-dependent** / ___ sin dependencia de insulina.

diabetic *a.* diabético-a; rel. a la diabetes o que padece de ella; ___ **angiopathies** / angiopatías ___-s; **brittle** ___ / ___ inestable; ___ **coma** / coma ___, por falta de insulina; ___ **diet** / dieta ___; ___ **neuropathy** / neuropatía ___; ___ **retinopathy** / retinopatía ___-a.

diabetogenic *a.* diabetogénico-a, que produce diabetes.

diabetograph *n.* diabetógrafo, aparato para medir la proporción de glucosa en la orina.

diacetemia *n.* diacetemia, presencia de ácido diacético en la sangre.

diacetic acid *n.* ácido diacético.

diacetylmorphine *n.* diacetilmorfina, heroína.

diagnose *v.* diagnosticar, dar un diagnóstico, hacer un diagnóstico o diagnosis.

diagnosis *n.* diagnóstico, diagnosis, determinación de la enfermedad del paciente; **computer** ___ / ___ por computadora; **differential** ___ / ___ diferencial, por comparación; ___ **error** / errores de ___; **physical** ___ / ___ físico, por medio de un examen físico completo.

diagnostic *n.* diagnóstico; ___ **chart** / ficha de ___; ___ **imaging** / ___ de imágenes por medios radioactivos.

diagonal *a.* diagonal, sección transversal.

diagram *n.* diagrama.

dialysate *n.* dializado, líquido que pasa por la membrana separadora o dializadora.

dialysis *n.* diálisis, procedimiento para filtrar y eliminar toxinas presentes en la sangre de pacientes con insuficiencia renal; ___ **machine** / aparato de ___ (riñón artificial); **peritoneal** ___ / ___ peritoneal; **renal** ___ / ___ renal.

dialyze v. dializar, hacer una diálisis.

dialyzer n. dializador, instrumento usado en el proceso de diálisis.

diameter n. diámetro.

diapedesis n. diapédesis, paso de células sanguíneas, esp. leucocitos, a través de la pared intacta de un vaso capilar.

diaper n. pañal; culero; *Mex. A.* pavico; *Mex.* zapeta; ___ **rash** / eritema de los pañales, erupción.

diaphoretic n. diaforético, agente que estimula la transpiración.

diaphragm n. diafragma. 1. músculo que separa el tórax del abdomen; 2. anticonceptivo uterino.

diaphragmatic a. diafragmático-a, rel. al diafragma.

diaphysis n. diáfisis, porción media de un hueso largo tal como se presenta en el húmero.

diaplasis n. diaplasis, reducción de una luxación o fractura.

diarrhea n. diarrea; **acute** ___ / ___ severa; **dysenteric** ___ / ___ disentérica; ___ **of the newborn** / ___ epidémica del recién nacido; ___ **infantile** / ___ infantil; **lienteric** ___ / ___ lientérica; **nervous** ___ / ___ nerviosa; **pancreatic** ___ / ___ pancreática; **summer** ___ / ___ estival o de verano; **travelers'** ___ / ___ del viajero.

diarrheal a. diarreico-a, rel. a la diarrea.

diarthrosis n. diartrosis, tipo de articulación que permite movimiento amplio, tal como la de la cadera.

diastase n. diastasa, enzima que actúa en la digestión de almidones y azúcares.

diastasis n. diastasis. 1. separación anormal de partes unidas esp. huesos; 2. tiempo de descanso del ciclo cardíaco inmediatamente anterior a la sístole.

diastole n. diástole, fase de dilatación del corazón durante la cual se llenan de sangre las cavidades cardíacas.

diastolic a. diastólico-a, rel. a la diástole del corazón; ___ **pressure** / presión ___.

diathermy n. diatermia, aplicación de calor a los tejidos del cuerpo por medio de una corriente eléctrica.

diathesis n. diátesis, propensión constitucional u orgánica a contraer ciertas enfermedades; **hemorrhagic** ___ / ___ hemorrágica; **rheumatic** ___ / ___ reumática.

diatrizoate meglumine n. diatrizoate de meglumina, sustancia radiopaca que se usa para hacer visibles las arterias y venas del corazón y del cerebro así como la vesícula, los riñones y la vejiga.

diazepam n. diazepam, nombre comercial Valium, sedante y relajador muscular.

dichorionic n. dicoriónico, que tiene dos coriones.

dichotomy, dichotomization n. dicotomía, dicotomización, división en dos partes; bifurcación.

dichroism n. dicroísmo, propiedad de algunas soluciones o cristales de diferenciar colores a través de la luz reflejada o transmitida.

dichromic a. dicrómico-a, rel. a dos colores.

dichromophil a. dicromófilo-a, que permite la coloración básica y ácida.

dictate v. dictar, ordenar.

Dicumarol n. Dicumarol, Dicoumarin, anticoagulante usado en el tratamiento de embolismo y trombosis.

didactic a. didáctico-a, instructivo-a, que se enseña por medio de libros de texto y conferencias a diferencia de un planteamiento clínico.

didelphic a. didélfico-a, rel. a un útero doble.

didymitis n. didimitis. V. **orchitis.**

die n. molde, troquel; v. morir, fallecer, dejar de existir; morirse.

diembryony n. diembrionismo, producción de dos embriones de un solo óvulo.

diencephalon n. diencéfalo, parte del cerebro.

dienestrol n. dienestrol, estrógeno sintético.

diet n. dieta, régimen; **balanced** ___ / ___ balanceada, equilibrada; **bland** ___ / ___ blanda; **diabetic** ___ / ___ diabética; **gluten-free** ___ / ___ libre de gluten; **low-salt** ___ / ___ baja de sal; **liquid** ___ / ___ líquida; **salt-free** ___ / ___ sin sal; **weight reduction** ___ / ___ para bajar de peso.

dietary a. dietético-a; alimenticio-a; ___ **vitamins** / vitaminas ___-s.

dietetic a. dietético-a, rel. a la dieta o aplicado a ésta.

dietetics n. dietética, ciencia que regula el régimen alimenticio para preservar o recuperar la salud.

dietitian n. dietista, especialista en nutrición.

different a. diferente, distinto-a.

differential a. diferencial, rel. a la diferenciación; ___ **diagnosis** / diagnóstico ___.

differentiate v. diferenciar.

differentiation n. diferenciación, comparación y distinción de una sustancia, enfermedad o entidad con otra o de otra.

difficult a. difícil.

difficulty n. dificultad; penalidad; obstáculo.

diffraction n. difracción. 1. desviación de dirección; 2. la descomposición de un rayo de luz y sus componentes al atravesar un cristal o prisma; ___ **pattern** / patrón de ___.

diffusion n. difusión. 1. proceso de difundir; 2. diálisis a través de una membrana.

dig vi. excavar, extraer.

digest v. digerir.

digestant n. digestivo, agente que facilita la digestión.

digestion n. digestión, transformación de líquidos y sólidos en sustancias más simples para ser asimiladas por el organismo; **gastric** ___ / ___ gástrica; **intestinal** ___ / ___ intestinal, del intestino; **pancreatic** ___ / ___ pancreática.

digestive a. digestivo-a; rel. a la digestión; ___

system / sistema ___.

digit *n.* dedo.

digital *a.* digital, rel. a los dedos.

digitalis *n.* digitalis, agente cardiotónico que se obtiene de las hojas secas de la *Digitalis purpurea;* ___ **intoxication** / intoxicación por ___.

digitalization *n.* digitalización, uso terapéutico de digitalis.

digitation *n.* digitación, proceso en forma de dedos.

digitoxin *n.* digitoxina, glucósido cardiotónico obtenido de digitalis y usado en el tratamiento de la congestión pasiva del corazón.

digitus *n.* dígito, dedo; ___ **malleus, mallet finger** / dedo en martillo; ___ **valgus, varus** / desviación de un dedo.

digoxin *n.* digoxina, un derivado de digitalis que se emplea en el tratamiento de arritmias cardíacas.

dihydrostreptomycin *n.* dihidroestreptomicina, antibiótico derivado de la estreptomicina más usado que ésta por causar menos neurotoxicidad.

Dilantin *n.* Dilantin, droga antiespasmódica.

dilatation, dilation *n.* dilatación, aumento o expansión anormal de un órgano u orificio.

dilate *v.* dilatar, expandir.

dilation and curettage (D&C) *n.* dilatación y curetaje, *pop.* raspado.

dilator *n.* dilatador. 1. músculo que dilata un órgano al contraerse. 2. instrumento quirúrgico para expandir o dilatar un orificio o paredes; **Hegar's** ___ / ___ de Hegar, instrumento usado para dilatar el canal uterino.

diluent *a.* diluente, diluyente, agente o medicamento que tiene la propiedad de diluir.

dim *a.* débil, mortecino-a; confuso-a; opaco-a.

dimension *n.* dimensión, medida de un cuerpo.

dimercaprol *n.* dimercaprol, antídoto usado en el envenenamiento producido por metales tales como oro y mercurio.

dimethylsulfoxide *n.* dimetilsulfóxido, medicamento antiinflamatorio y analgésico.

dimetria *n.* dimetría, útero o matriz doble.

diminish *v.* disminuir, reducir; amortiguar.

diminution *n.* disminución, proceso de disminuir o reducir.

diminutive *n. gr.* diminutivo; *a.* diminuto-a, pequeño-a.

dimness *n.* opacidad; obscurecimiento de la vista.

dimorphism *n.* dimorfismo, caracterización de dos formas diferentes; **sexual** ___ / ___ sexual, hermafrodismo.

dimple *n.* hoyuelo o hendidura en la piel, esp. en la mejilla o la barbilla.

dinner *n.* cena.

diopter, dioptre *n.* dioptría, unidad de medida de refracción de un lente.

dioptometer *n.* dioptómetro, instrumento usado para medir la refracción ocular.

dioptric *a.* dióptrico, referente a la refración de la luz.

dioptrics *n.* dióptrica, ciencia que trata de la formación de imágenes y lentes.

diphallus *n.* difalo, duplicación parcial o completa del pene.

diphasic *a.* difásico-a, que tiene lugar en dos etapas diferentes.

diphenhydramine *n.* difenhidramina, nombre comercial Benadryl, antihistamínico.

diphonia *n.* difonía, producción de dos tonos diferentes.

diphtheria *n.* difteria, enfermedad contagiosa e infecciosa aguda, causada por el bacilo. *Corynebacterium diphtheriae* (Klebs-Löffler), caracterizada por la formación de membranas falsas esp. en la garganta; ___ **antitoxin** / antitoxina contra la ___.

diphtherotoxin *n.* difterotoxina, toxina derivada del cultivo de bacilos de la difteria.

diplacusis *n.* diplacusia, desorden auditivo caracterizado por la percepción de dos tonos por cada sonido producido.

diplegia *n.* diplejía, parálisis bilateral; **facial** ___ / ___ facial, parálisis de ambos lados de la cara; **spastic** ___ / ___ espástica.

diplocoria *n.* diplocoria, pupila doble.

diploe *n.* diploe, tejido esponjoso localizado entre las dos capas compactas de los huesos craneales.

diploid *a.* diploide, que posee dos combinaciones de cromosomas.

diplopagus *n.* diplópagos, mellizos unidos, cada uno de cuerpo casi completo, pero que comparten algunos órganos.

diplopia *n.* diplopía, visión doble.

dipsesis, dipsosis *n.* dipsesis, dipsosis, sed insaciable.

dipsomania *n.* dipsomanía, tipo de alcoholismo en el cual el paciente sufre una urgencia incontrolable por consumir sustancias alcohólicas.

direct *a.* directo-a; *v.* dirigir, ordenar; instruir.

direction *n.* dirección; instrucción.

directory *n.* directorio; junta; **telephone** ___ / guía telefónica.

dirty *a.* sucio-a, mugriento-a; *pop.* cochino-a.

disability *n.* incapacidad, inhabilidad; invalidez, impedimento; disminución de una capacidad física o mental.

disabled *a.* inválido-a; impedido-a; incapacitado-a.

disadvantage *n.* desventaja; alguna capacidad disminuida.

disagree *v.* no estar de acuerdo; disentir; altercar, argumentar.

disagreeable *a.* desagradable; ofensivo-a.

disappoint *v.* contrariar, desengañar.

disappointment *n.* contrariedad; desengaño, desilusión.

disarticulated *a.* desarticulado-a, dislocado-a, rel. a un hueso separado de la articulación.

disarticulation *n.* desarticulación, separación o amputación de dos o más huesos articulados entre sí.

disaster *n.* desastre; desdicha, infortunio.

disbelief *n.* incredulidad, escepticismo.

disbelieve *v.* desconfiar, dudar.

discard *n.* desecho, descarte; *v.* descartar, desechar.

discharge *n.* flujo; supuración; excreción; descarga; derrame; ___ **summary** / sumario o nota de egreso; *v.* [*fluid, pus*] secretar, supurar; [*from the hospital*] dar de alta; librar; soltar; [*electricity*] descargar.

discipline *n.* disciplina, comportamiento estricto.

discitis *n.* discitis, infl. de un disco.

disclose *v.* revelar, descubrir; destapar, abrir.

discogenic *a.* discogénico, rel. a un disco intervertebral.

discography *n.* discografía, radiografía de un disco vertebral usando un medio de contraste.

discolor *v.* cambiar de color, quitar el color.

discolored *a.* descolorido-a, [*skin*] ensombrecido-a, sin color, empañado-a.

discomfort *n.* incomodidad, malestar, aflicción.

discomposed *a.* descompuesto-a; desordenado-a.

disconnect *v.* desconectar, desunir, quitar la conexión; separar.

disconnected *a.* desconectado-a, separado-a, sin conexión, desunido-a.

discontented *a.* descontento-a; insatisfecho-a; disgustado-a.

discontinue *v.* suspender, interrumpir, descontinuar; **to ___ the medication** / ___ la medicina.

discontinued *a.* suspendido-a, interrumpido-a, descontinuado-a.

discourage *v.* desanimar, desalentar; **to ___ from** / disuadir.

discouraged *a.* desanimado-a, desalentado-a.

discredit *v.* desacreditar.

discreet *a.* discreto-a, prudente.

discrepancy *n.* desacuerdo, discrepancia, diferencia.

discretion *n.* discreción, prudencia; acuerdo.

discriminate *v.* discriminar; mostrar prejuicio; hacer notar diferencias.

discrimination *n.* discriminación; diferenciación de raza o cualidad.

discuss *v.* discutir, argumentar.

discussion *n.* discusión, debate, argumento.

disease *n.* enfermedad, dolencia, anomalía; indisposición; **a crippling ___** / ___ que causa invalidez; *v.* causar una enfermedad, contagiar, enfermar, dañar, hacer daño.

disengage *v.* librar, separar, desplazar.

disengagement *n.* desencajamiento, separación, desunión; [*in obstetrics*] desplazamiento de la cabeza del feto de la vulva.

disfiguration *n.* desfiguración, desfigura-miento.

disfigure *v.* desfigurar, afear.

disillusion *n.* desencanto, desilusión; *v.* perder la ilusión; desilusionarse.

disinfect *v.* desinfectar, esterilizar.

disinfectant *n.* desinfectante, antiséptico, esterilizante.

disintegrate *v.* desintegrar, reducir a fragmentos o partículas; desintegrarse; separarse.

disintegration *n.* desintegración, descomposición, separación.

disjoint *v.* desunir, separar, desarticular.

disjointed *a.* desarticulado-a, descoyuntado-a, dislocado-a.

disjunction *n.* disyunción, desunión, separación de cromosomas en la anafase de la división celular.

disk, disc *n.* disco; **herniated ___** / ___ herniado; **ruptured ___** / ruptura del ___.

dislike *n.* aversión, antipatía; *v.* aborrecer, desagradar, repugnar; **I ___ this medicine** / no me gusta, me desagrada, me repugna esta medicina.

dislocate *v.* dislocar, descoyuntar, desencajar.

dislocation *n.* luxación, desviación, desplazamiento de una articulación; **closed ___** / ___ cerrada; **complicated ___** / ___ complicada; **congenital ___** / ___ congénita.

dismember *v.* desmembrar, amputar; [*to break apart*] despedazar.

dismemberment *n.* desmembración, amputación.

dismiss *v.* rechazar; descartar; [*an employee*] despedir.

disobedience *n.* desobediencia.

disobedient *a.* desobediente.

disorder *n.* desorden, desarreglo, trastorno; **mental ___** / desarreglo emocional, trastorno mental.

disorganized *a.* desorganizado-a.

disorient *v.* desorientar.

disorientation *n.* desorientación, incapacidad de encontrar una dirección o local, de reconocer a otras personas, y de establecer una relación temporal lógica.

disoriented *a.* desorientado-a; confundido-a, confuso-a.

dispensary *n.* dispensario, clínica, establecimiento que proporciona asistencia médica y dispensa medicamentos.

dispense *v.* dispensar; distribuir.

disperse *v.* dispersar, disipar.

dispirited *a.* descorazonado-a, desalentado-a.

displace *v.* desplazar; poner fuera de lugar.

displaced *a.* desplazado-a; dislocado-a; *v.* **to be ___** / estar fuera de lugar, estar ___; [*bone, joint*] estar dislocado-a.

displacement *n.* desplazamiento; dislocación; *psic.* transferencia de una emoción a otra distinta de la inicial.

display *n.* muestra, exhibición, *v.* mostrar, exhibir, extender.

displease v. desagradar; incomodar.
displeased a. descontento-a; insatisfecho-a.
disposable a. desechable.
dispose v. disponer; desechar; **to __ of** / deshacerse de.
disposition n. disposición; tendencia.
disproportion n. desproporción; desproporcionamiento.
disproportionate a. desproporcionado-a, desigual, sin simetria.
disprove v. refutar.
disregard v. ignorar; no prestar atención, descuidar.
disrespect n. falta de respeto, irreverencia; v. desatender; dejar de respetar, faltar el respeto.
dissect v. cirg. disecar, acto de dividir y cortar; hacer una disección.
dissecting hook n. erina.
dissecting knife n. escalpelo, bisturí.
dissection n. disección.
disseminated a. diseminado-a, difundido-a; **__ intravascular coagulation** / coagulación intravascular __.
dissemination n. diseminación, esparcimiento.
dissipation n. disipación, vida disipada; dispersión.
dissociation n. disociación, separación.
dissolution n. disolución; descomposición; muerte.
dissolve v. disolver, diluir, deshacer; destruir.
dissolved a. pp. de **to dissolve,** disuelto-a, diluido-a.
dissolvent a. disolvente, capaz de disolver.
distal a. distal, distante, rel. a la parte más lejana; **__ end** / extremo __.
distance n. distancia, lejanía; **at a __** / a lo lejos; v. **to keep at a __** / mantener a __.
distaste n. aversión, disgusto.
distend v. distender, dilatar; distenderse, dilatarse.
distensibility n. distensibilidad.
distension, distention n. distensión, condición de dilatación o expansión.
distill v. destilar, crear vapor por medio de calor.
distillation n. destilación.
distinct a. diferente; definido-a; **-ly** adv. definidamente; con diferencia, con precisión.
distinguish v. distinguir; diferenciar, clasificar.
distinguished a. [person] distinguido-a; [characteristics] señalado-a, marcado-a.
distobuccal a. distobucal, rel. a la superficie distal y bucal de un diente.
distoclusion n. distoclusión, mordida irregular.
distort v. torcer, deformar, desfigurar.
distorted a. torcido-a; deformado-a; desfigurado-a.
distortion n. distorsión, deformación, desfiguración.
distract v. distraer, interrumpir.
distracted a. distraído-a, [madness] trastornado-a.
distraction n. distracción. 1. psic. inhabilidad

para concentrarse en una experiencia determinada; 2. separación de articulaciones sin dislocación.
distraught a. atolondrado-a, confundido-a, desconcertado-a; [irrational] demente.
distress n. angustia, apuro, preocupación, aflicción; v. **to be in __** / estar angustiado-a, estar afligido-a.
distressed a. adolorido-a, angustiado-a, afligido-a.
distribute v. distribuir, dispensar, repartir.
distribution n. distribución.
distrust n. desconfianza, falta de confianza; v. desconfiar.
disturb v. perturbar, incomodar, molestar, inquietar.
disturbance n. confusión, disturbio.
diuresis n. diuresis, aumento en la secreción de orina.
diuretic a. diurético, rel. a agentes que provocan aumento en la secreción de orina.
diuria n. diuria, frecuencia de excreción de orina durante el día.
diver n. buzo-a; **__ 's paralysis** / parálisis de los __-s.
divergence n. divergencia, separación de un centro común.
divergent a. divergente, movimiento en sentido opuesto; **__ reactor** / reactor de potencia __ .
diverticulitis n. diverticulosis, diverticulitis, infl. de un divertículo, esp. de pequeños sacos que se forman en el colon.
diverticulum n. (pl. **diverticula**) divertículo, saco o bolsa que se origina en la cavidad de un órgano o estructura.
divide v. dividir, repartir.
divided a. dividido-a, separado-a.
division n. división, desunión; separación.
divorce n. divorcio, disolución.
divulsion n. divulsión, separación o desprendimiento.
dizygotic twins n. pl. gemelos dicigóticos, mellizos de embriones producidos por dos óvulos.
dizziness n. mareo, sensación de desvanecimiento, vahído.
dizzy a. mareado-a.
do vi. aux. hacer; **How do you __?** / ¿cómo está usted?, ¿cómo estás tú? [introduction] mucho gusto; **What do you __?** / ¿Qué hace usted?, ¿qué haces tú?; **whatever you __** / cualquier cosa que haga; hagas; **__ it!** / ¡hágalo!,¡hazlo!; **__ not __ it!** / ¡No lo haga!, ¡no lo hagas!, **to __ one's best** / hacer lo mejor posible; **to __ harm** / hacer daño; **to __ without** / pasar sin, prescindir de; **that will __** / eso es suficiente; **__ you cough a lot?** / ¿Tose mucho?, ¿toses mucho?; **he, she does** / él, ella hace. (**Do** is not translated in Spanish when used as an auxiliary verb.)
doctor n. doctor-a, médico-a; **__'s discretion** / al

criterio del ___; según opinión facultativa.

document *n.* documento.

documentation *n.* documentación.

doer *n.* hacedor-a, agente, ejecutor-a.

dog *n.* perro-a; ___ **bite** / mordida de ___.

dolichocephalic *a.* dolicocefálico-a, de cráneo alargado y estrecho.

domestic *a.* doméstico-a.

domiciliary *a.* domiciliario-a, rel. a lo que se trata en el domicilio.

dominance *n.* dominancia, predominio.

dominant *a.* dominante, característica primordial; ___ **characteristics** / características ___-s, con tendencia a heredarse; ___ **factor** / factor ___.

donate *v.* donar, regalar.

donation *n.* donativo, donación.

donor *n.* donante, donador; persona contribuyente; ___ **card** / tarjeta de ___.

Donovania granulomatosis, Donovan's body *n.* Donovania granulomatosis, cuerpos de Donovan, infección bacteriana que afecta la piel y las membranas mucosas de los genitales y el ano.

door *n.* puerta; [*entrance*] ___ de entrada; **back** ___ / ___ de atrás.

dopamine *n.* dopamina, neurotransmisor, sustancia sintetizada por la glándula suprarrenal que aumenta la presión arterial; gen. usada en el tratamiento de choque.

dope *n.* narcótico; ___ **fiend** / narcómano-a; ___ **addict** / drogadicto-a.

dormancy *n.* sueño pesado, estupor, letargo.

dorsal *a.* dorsal, situado-a en la parte posterior del cuerpo o rel. a ésta; ___ **recumbent position** / posición recumbente; ___ **slit** / fisura o corte ___.

dorsalgia *n.* dorsalgia, dolor de espalda.

dorsiflexion *n.* dorsiflexión, movimiento de doblar o de doblarse hacia atrás.

dorsocephalad *a.* dorsocefálico-a, situado-a en la parte posterior de la cabeza.

dorsodynia *n.* dorsodinia, dolor en los músculos de la parte superior de la espalda.

dorsolateral *a.* dorsolateral, rel. a la espalda y un costado.

dorsolumbar *a.* dorsolumbar, lumbodorsal, rel. a la espalda y la región lumbar de la columna.

dorsospinal *a.* dorsoespinal, rel. a la espalda y la espina dorsal.

dorsum *n.* (*pl.* **dorsa**) dorso. 1. proción posterior, tal como el dorso de la mano o el pie; 2. espalda.

dose, dosage *n.* dosis, dosificación; **average** ___ / ___ promedio, media; **booster** ___ / ___ de refuerzo; **daily** ___ / ___ diaria; **divided** ___ / ___ dividida; **lethal** ___ / ___ letal; **radiation** ___ / ___ de radiación; **therapeutic** ___ / ___ terapéutica; **unit** ___ / ___ individual; **volume** ___ / ___ volumen.

dosimeter *n.* dosímetro, instrumento usado para detectar y medir la exposición a radiaciones.

dosimetry *n.* dosimetría, determinación precisa y sistemática de las dosis de radiación.

dossier *n.* expediente.

dot *n.* cúmulo, mancha.

dotage *n.* senilidad, chochera, chochez.

double *a.* doble; ___-**edged** / con dos bordes; ___ **personality** / desdoblamiento de la personalidad; ___ **uterus** / útero didelfo, útero o matriz doble; *v.* duplicar.

doubt *n.* duda, incertidumbre.

douche *n.* 1. ducha, regadera; 2. lavado vaginal; irrigación; *v.* tomar una ducha; ducharse.

Douglas cul-de-sac *n.* saco de Douglas, pliegue del peritoneo que se introduce entre el recto y el útero.

down *adv.* abajo, hacia abajo; ___ **below** / más abajo; *v.* **to cut** ___ / recortar; reducir; **to lie** ___ / acostarse, recostarse.

downcast *a.* deprimido-a, alicaído-a, abatido-a.

downstairs *adv.* abajo; *v.* **to go** ___ / bajar las escaleras.

Down syndrome *n.* síndrome de Down, anormalidad citogenética del cromosoma 21 caracterizada por retraso mental y facciones mongoloides.

downtown *n.* centro (de la ciudad).

doze *v.* dormitar, quedarse medio dormido.

dozen *n.* docena.

draft *n.* 1. líquido prescrito para ser tomado en una sola dosis; 2. [*air*] corriente de aire; 3. [*art design*] diseño, bosquejo.

drain *n.* desagüe, escurridor; *v.* drenar, desaguar, eliminar una secreción o pus de una parte infectada.

drainage *n.* drenaje; **open** ___ / ___ abierto; **continuous** ___ / ___ continuo; **postural** ___ / ___ postural, por gravedad; ___ **tube** / tubo de ___; **tidal** ___ / ___ periódico.

Dramamine, dimenhydrinate *n.* Dramamina, dimenhidrinato, anthistamínico usado en el tratamiento de náusea.

dramatism *n.* *psic.* dramatismo, conducta espectacular y lenguaje dramatizado manifestados en ciertos trastornos mentales.

drape *v.* *cirg.* cubrir el campo operatorio con paños esterilizados.

drastic *a.* drástico-a; ___ **therapy** / tratamiento ___.

draw *vi.* extraer, sacar; [*air*] aspirar; [*art*] dibujar, trazar; **to** ___ **back** / retroceder; **to** ___ **in** / atraer; incitar; **to** ___ **near** / acercarse, arrimarse.

drawer *n.* gaveta, cajón.

dream *n.* sueño, ilusión; *v.* soñar, imaginar, hacerse ilusiones.

dreary *a.* monótono-a, escabroso-a, pesado-a.

drenched *a.* empapado-a, mojado-a.

drepanocyte *n.* drepanocito, glóbulo rojo de células falciformes.

dress *n.* vestido; *v.* [*a wound*] vendar, curar; [*a* corpse] amortajar; [*put on clothes*] vestirse.

dressing *n.* venda de gasa u otro material para cubrir una herida.

dribble *n.* goteo.

drill *n.* taladro; [*dentistry*] fresa.

drink *n.* bebida, trago; *v.* beber, tomar.

drinker *a.* bebedor, tomador.

drip *n.* gota, goteo; gotera; *v.* gotear.

drive *n.* paseo, vuelta; *v.* **to go for a** ___ / dar un paseo; *psic.* impulso; [*haste*] exigencia; [*energy*] energía, vigor; *vi.* [*vehicles*] conducir, manejar, guiar; **to** ___ **someone crazy** / enloquecer, volver loco-a.

drivel *n.* baba o saliva que sale por los extremos de la boca.

drop *n.* gota; caída; ___ **by** ___ / gota a gota; *v.* dejar caer; [*from school*] dejar la escuela; caerse.

droplet *n.* partícula, gotica; ___ **infection** / infección trasmitida por goticas o partículas.

dropper *n.* gotero.

dropsy *n.* hidropesía, acumulación excesiva de fluido seroso en una cavidad o tejido celular.

drought *n.* sequía.

drown *v.* ahogar; anegar; sumergir; sofocar; ahogarse.

drowning *n.* ahogamiento, acción de ahogar o ahogarse.

drowse *v.* adormecerse, adormitarse.

drowsiness *n.* sopor, somnolencia, abotagamiento, pesadez.

drug *n.* droga, medicamento, narcótico, barbitúrico; ___ **abuse** / uso excesivo de una ___ por adicción; ___ **addict** / narcómano-a, drogadicto-a; ___**-induced abnormality** / anomalía causada por el uso de ___-s; ___ **interactions** / interacciones de medicamentos; / **long acting** ___ / ___ de acción prolongada; ___ **resistance, microbial** / resistencia microbiana a las ___.

drugged *a.* endrogado-a, drogado-a.

drunk *n.* borracho-a, ebrio-a.

drunkenness *n.* borrachera, embriaguez.

dry *a.* seco-a; árido-a; *v.* secar; **to** ___ **out** / secarse.

dryness *n.* sequedad; aridez.

duct *n.* conducto, canal; **biliary** ___ / ___ biliar; **ejaculatory** ___ / ___ eyaculatorio; **lymphatic** ___ / ___ endolinfático; **hepatic** ___ / ___ hepático; **lacrimal** ___ / ___ lacrimal; **lactiferous** ___ / ___ lactífero; **mammary** ___ / ___ mamario; **seminal** ___ / ___ seminal.

ductal *a.* rel. a un conducto o canal.

dues *n. pl.* deuda; obligación.

dull *a.* aburrido-a; [*pain*] dolor sordo; [*blade*] mellado-a.

dullness *n.* 1. matidez, resonancia disminuida en la palpación; 2. estado de aburrimiento, torpeza, estupidez; 3. [*instrument's edge*] melladura.

dumb *a.* mudo-a; torpe, estúpido-a.

dumping syndrome *n.* síndrome de vaciamiento gástrico demasiado rápido del contenido estomacal en el intestino delgado.

duodenal *a.* duodenal, rel. al duodeno.

duodenal ulcer *n.* úlcera duodenal.

duodenectomy *n. cirg.* duodenectomía, excisión del duodeno o una parte de éste.

duodenitis *n.* duodenitis, infl. del duodeno.

duodenoenterostomy *n. cirg.* duodenoenterostomía, anastomosis entre el duodeno y el intestino delgado.

duodenography *n.* duodenografía, radiografía del duodeno.

duodenojejunostomy *n. cirg.* duodenoyeyunostomía, operación para construir un pasaje artificial entre el yeyuno y el duodeno.

duodenoplasty *n. cirg.* duodenoplastia, operación para reparar el duodeno.

duodenostomy *n. cirg.* duodenostomía, creación de una salida en el duodeno, para aliviar la estenosis del píloro.

duodenum *n.* duodeno, parte esencial del canal alimenticio y del intestino delgado situado entre el píloro y el yeyuno.

duplication *n.* doblez, pliegue; duplicación.

durability *n.* durabilidad, duración.

durable *a.* durable, duradero-a; estable.

dura mater *n.* duramadre, membrana externa que cubre el encéfalo y la médula espinal.

duration *n.* duración, continuación.

duress *n.* coerción; coacción, **under** ___ / bajo ___.

during *prep.* durante; mientras, entre tanto.

dust *n.* polvo [*mortal remains*] cenizas, restos mortales; ___ **count** / conteo de partículas de ___ en el aire.

duty *n.* deber, obligación; [*tax*] impuesto; **on** ___ / de guardia.

dwarf *n.* enano-a, persona de estatura inferior a la normal; **achondroplastic** ___ / ___ acondroplástico-a; **asexual** ___ / ___ asexual; **infantile** ___ / ___ infantil; **micrometic** ___ / ___ micromético-a.

dwarfism *n.* enanismo, insuficiencia del desarrollo en el crecimiento de una persona.

dye *n.* tinte, color saturado; colorante.

dying *a.* moribundo-a, agonizante, mortal.

dynamics *n.* dinámica, estudio de órganos o partes del cuerpo en movimiento.

dyne *n.* unidad de fuerza necesaria para acelerar un gramo de masa un centímetro por segundo.

dysacousia, dysacusia *n.* disacusis, disacusia, trastorno o dificultad para oír.

dysaphia *n.* disafia, entorpecimiento del sentido del tacto.

dysarthria *n.* disartria, dificultad del habla a causa de una afección de la lengua u otro músculo esencial al lenguaje.

dysautonomia *n.* disautonomía, trastorno del sistema nervioso autónomo.

dysbarism *n.* disbarismo, condición causada por descompresión.

dyscalculia *n.* discalculia, incapacidad de resolver problemas matemáticos debido a una anomalía cerebral.

dyscephalia *n.* discefalia, malformación de la cabeza y los huesos de la cara.

dyschiria *n.* disquiria, incapacidad de percibir sensaciones táctiles en ciertas áreas.

dyscoria *n.* discoria, pupila deformada.

dyscrasia *n.* discrasia, sinónimo de enfermedad.

dyscrinism *n.* discrinismo, funcionamiento anormal en la producción de secreciones, esp. de las glándulas endocrinas.

dysdiadochokinesia *n.* disdiadocoquinesia, alteración de la función de detener un impulso motor y substituirlo por otro diametralmente opuesto.

dysentery *n.* disentería, condición inflamatoria del intestino grueso causada por bacilos o parásitos con síntomas de diarrea y dolor abdominal; **amebic** ___ / ___ amebiana; **bacillar** ___ / ___ bacilar.

dysergia *n.* disergia, falta de coordinación en los movimientos musculares voluntarios.

dysesthesia *n.* disestesia, reacción excesiva de molestia a algunas sensaciones que por lo común no producen dolor.

dysfunction *n.* desorden, trastorno, malfuncionamiento de un órgano o parte.

dysgenesis *n.* disgénesis, defecto, malformación hereditaria.

dysgerminoma *n.* disgerminoma, tumor maligno del ovario.

dysgnosia *n.* disgnosia, cualquier impedimento relacionado con el intelecto.

dyshidrosis *n.* dishidrosis. 1. trastorno transpiratorio; 2. erupción recurrente de vesículas y picazón tal como en el pie de atleta.

dyskinesia *n.* discinesia, disquinesia, inhabilidad de realizar movimientos voluntarios tal como sucede en la enfermedad de Parkinson.

dyslalia *n.* dislalia, impedimento en el habla debido a trastornos vocálicos funcionales.

dyslexia *n.* dislexia, impedimento en la lectura, dificultad que puede ser una condición hereditaria o causada por una lesión cerebral.

dysmenorrhea, dysmenorrhoea *n.* dismenorrea, menstruación difícil, acompañada de dolor y trastornos.

dysmetria *n.* dismetría, afección del cerebelo que incapacita el control de la distancia en movimientos musculares.

dysmetropsia *n.* dismetropsia, defecto en la apreciación visual del tamaño y forma de objetos.

dysmnesia *n.* dismnesia, trastorno de la memoria.

dysmorphism *n.* dismorfismo, malformación anatómica.

dysmyotonia *n.* dismiotonía, distonía muscular con tonicidad muscular anormal.

dysosmia *n.* disosmia, malfuncionamiento de la función olfatoria.

dysostosis *n.* disostosis, desarrollo deficiente de los huesos y dientes.

dyspareunia *n.* dispareunia, relaciones sexuales dolorosas.

dyspepsia *n.* dispepsia, indigestión caracterizada por irregularidades digestivas tales como eructos, náuseas, acidez, flatulencia y pérdida del apetito.

dyspermia *n.* dispermia, dolor durante la eyaculación.

dysphagia *n.* disfagia, dificultad al tragar a causa de una obstrucción; **esophageal** ___ / ___ esofágica; **oropharyngeal** ___ / ___ orofaríngea.

dysphasia *n.* disfasia, defecto del habla causado por una lesión cerebral.

dysphonia *n.* disfonía, ronquera.

dysphoria *n.* disforia, excesiva depresión o angustia.

dyspigmentation *n.* despigmentación, decoloración anormal de la piel y del pelo.

dysplasia *n.* displasia, cambio o desarrollo anormal de los tejidos.

dyspnea, dyspnoea *n.* disnea, dificultad en la respiración.

dyspneic *a.* disneico-a, rel. a o que padece de disnea.

dyspraxia *n.* dispraxia, impedimento o dolor al realizar cualquier movimiento coordinado.

dysrhythmia *n.* disritmia, sin coordinación o ritmo.

dysstasia *n.* distasia, dificultad de mantenerse en pie.

dyssynergia *n.* disinergia. V. **ataxia.**

dystocia *n.* distocia, parto difícil, laborioso.

dystonia *n.* distonía, tonicidad alterada, esp. muscular.

dystrophy *n.* distrofia. 1. anomalía causada por desnutrición; 2. desarrolo defectuoso o de malformación.

dysuria *n.* disuria, dificultad o dolor al orinar.

E *abbr.* **emmetropia** / emetropía; **enema** / enema; **enzyme** / enzima; **eye** / ojo.

each *a.* cada; todo; cualquier-a; *pron.* cada uno, cada una; cada cual.

eager *a.* ansioso-a, deseoso-a; impaciente.

ear *n.* oreja; oído, órgano de la audición formado por el oído interior, el medio, y el externo; ___ **cup** / audífono; ___ **lap** / pabellón de la oreja; ___ **lobe** / lóbulo de la oreja; ___ **plug** / tapón auditivo; ___ **protector** / orejera; *a.* ___ **deafening** / ensordecedor-a.

earache *n.* dolor de oído.

eardrum *n.* tímpano del oído.

early *adv.* temprano, pronto; **at the earliest** / lo más ___; **as** ___ **as possible** / lo más ___ posible; ___ **age** / infancia; ___ **cancer** / cáncer incipiente; ___ **death** / muerte prematura; ___ **stage of** / la primera fase de, al principio de.

earn *v.* ganar, merecer.

earphone *n.* auricular, audífono.

earthquake *n.* terremoto, temblor de tierra, sismo.

earthworm *n.* lombriz de tierra; gusano.

ease *n.* alivio; descanso; facilidad; *v.* aliviar, facilitar; **to** ___ **one's mind** / tranquilizarse.

easily *adv.* fácilmente, sin dificultad.

east *n.* este, oriente; **to the** ___ / al ___.

easy *a.* fácil; **within** ___ **reach** / al alcance de la mano.

easygoing *a.* sereno-a, tranquilo-a, de buena disposición.

eat *vi.* comer, sustentarse, ingerir alimentos; **to** ___ **breakfast** / desayunarse, tomar el desayuno; **to** ___ **lunch** / almorzar; tomar el almuerzo; **to** ___ **supper** / cenar.

eating *n.* acto de comer; *a.* rel. a comer o para comer.

ebullient *a.* hirviente; ___ **water** / agua ___.

ebullition *n.* ebullición, acto de hervir.

eccentric *a.* excéntrico-a; extravagante.

ecchymosis *n.* equimosis, *pop.* morado, moratón. 1. cambio de color de la piel de azulado a verde debido a extravasación de sangre en el tejido subcutáneo celular; 2. contusión.

eccrine sweat glands *n.* glándulas sudoríparas ecrinas, secretoras de la transpiración.

echinococcosis *n.* equinococosis, infestación de equinococos; **hepatic** ___ / ___ hepática.

Echinococcus *n.* Equinococo, especie de tenia o trematodo.

echo *n.* eco, repercusión del sonido; *v.* **to** ___ / hacer eco.

echocardiogram *n.* ecocardiograma, gráfico producido por una ecocardiografía.

echocardiography *n.* ecocardiografía, método de diagnóstico por sonido ultrasónico para hacer visuales estructuras internas del corazón.

echoencephalography *n.* ecoencefalografía, técnica de diagnóstico por medio de ultrasonido para examinar estructuras intracraneales.

echogram *n.* ecograma, registro de una ecografía.

echography *n.* ecografía. *V.* **ultrasonography**.

echolalia *n.* ecolalia, trastorno de repetición involuntaria de sonidos y palabras después de oírlas.

Echo virus *n.* Echo virus, virus presente en el tracto gastrointestinal asociado con la meningitis, enteritis e infecciones respiratorias agudas.

eclampsia *n.* eclampsia, desorden convulsivo tóxico que se presenta gen. al final del embarazo o pocos días después del parto.

eclamptic *a.* eclámptico-a, rel. a la eclampsia.

ecology *n.* ecología, estudio de plantas y animales en relación con el ambiente.

economic *a.* económico-a; módico-a, moderado-a.

ecosystem *n.* ecosistema, microcosmo ecológico.

ecstasy *n. psic.* éxtasis, trance acompañado de un sentimiento de placer.

ectopic pregnancy *n.* embarazo ectópico, gestación fuera del útero.

ectoplasm *n.* ectoplasma, capa externa del citoplasma en una célula viva.

ectopy *n.* ectopia, desplazamiento de un órgano, condición gen. congénita.

ectropion *n.* ectropión, anomalía de eversión congénita o adquirida, gen. vista en la comisura del párpado.

eczema *n.* eczema, infección cutánea inflamatoria no contagiosa.

edema *n.* edema, acumulación anormal de líquido en los tejidos intracelulares; **angioneurotic** ___ / ___ angioneurótico; **brain** ___ / ___ cerebral; **cardiac** ___ / ___ cardíaco; **dependent** ___ / ___ dependiente; **pitting** ___ / ___ de fóvea; **pulmonary** ___ / ___ pulmonar.

edematous *a.* edematoso-a, rel. a un edema o afectado por éste.

edentulous *n.* desdentado, sin dientes.

edetate, calcium disodium *n.* disodio de calcio, agente usado en el tratamiento de envenenamiento por plomo.

edge *n.* borde, orilla, canto; [*of cutting instruments*] filo; **on** ___ / irritable, impaciente, nervioso-a.

edible *a.* comestible; edible.

educate *v.* educar, enseñar, instruir.

education *n.* educación, enseñanza; **medical** ___ / ___ médica.

effacement *n.* borradura, deformación de las características de un órgano tal como la del cuello uterino durante el parto.

effect *n.* efecto, impresión, resultado; *v.* **to carry into** ___ / llevar a cabo; **to this** ___ / en este sentido; **in** ___ / en ___, en realidad; **no** ___

/ sin ___.

effective *a.* efectivo-a.

effector *n.* efector, terminación nerviosa que produce un efecto eferente en una glándula de secreción o en una célula muscular.

effeminate *a.* afeminado, *pop.* invertido-a.

efferent *a.* eferente, de fuerza centrífuga.

effervescence *n.* efervescencia, producción de burbujas.

effervescent *a.* efervescente, que produce efervescencia.

efficacious, efficient *a.* eficaz, eficiente, competente.

efficiency *n.* eficiencia, competencia.

efficient *a.* eficiente; **-ly** *adv.* eficientemente.

effluent *a.* efluente, que tiene salida de dentro hacia afuera.

effort *n.* esfuerzo, empeño; *v.* **to make every ___ to** / hacer todo lo posible por.

effortless *a.* fácil, sin esfuerzo.

effusion *n.* efusión, derrame, escape de líquido a una cavidad o tejido.

egg *n.* heuvo; *Mex.* blanquillos; **___ cell** / óvulo; **fried ___** / huevo frito; **hard-boiled ___** / huevo duro; **___-shaped** / ovoide; **soft-boiled ___** / **___** pasado por agua; **___ white** / clara de **___**; **___ yolk** / yema de **___**.

eggplant *n.* berenjena.

eggshell *n.* cáscara de huevo.

ego *n. psic.* ego, el yo; la conciencia humana; término freudiano que se refiere a la parte de la psique mediadora entre la persona y la realidad.

egocentric *a.* egocéntrico-a, concentrado-a en sí mismo-a.

egoism *n.* egoísmo.

egomania *n.* egomanía, concentración excesiva en sí mismo-a.

ego-syntonic *a. psic.* egosintónico-a, en armonía o correspondencia con el ego.

either *a., pron.* uno-a u otro-a; *conj.* o; *adv.* también; [*after negation*] tampoco.

ejaculate *v.* eyacular, expeler.

ejaculation *n.* eyaculación, expulsión rápida y súbita tal como la emisión del semen.

ejaculatory duct *n.* conducto eyaculatorio.

ejection *n.* eyección, acto de expulsar con fuerza.

elaborate *v.* elaborar, tratar o explicar con detalle.

elastase *n.* elastasa, enzima que cataliza la digestión de las fibras elásticas, esp. en el jugo pancreático.

elastic *n.* elástico, cinta de goma; *a.* elástico-a, capaz de extenderse y de volver luego a la forma inicial; **___ tissue** / tejido **___**.

elasticity *n.* elasticidad, habilidad de expandirse.

elastinase *n.* elastinasa; *V.* **elastase.**

elation *n.* estado de exaltación o euforia, caracterizado por excitación física y mental.

elbow *n.* codo; **___ joint** / coyuntura del **___**; **___**

room / espacio suficiente; **tennis ___** / **___** de tenista.

elder *a.* mayor, de más edad; anciano-a; **elders** *pl.* antepasados, los mayores.

elderly *adv.* de avanzada edad.

eldest *a. sup.* el mayor, la mayor.

elect *v.* elegir, escoger.

elective *a.* electivo-a, elegido-a; **___ surgery** / cirugía **___**, planeada; **___ therapy** / terapia **___**.

electric *a.* eléctrico-a; **___ current** / corriente **___**; **___ eye** / ojo mágico, ojo **___**.

electrical *a.* eléctrico-a.

electricity *n.* electricidad.

electrocardiogram (ECG) *n.* electrocardiograma, gráfico de cambios eléctricos que se producen durante las contracciones del músculo cardíaco.

electrocardiograph *n.* electrocardiógrafo, instrumento para registrar las variaciones eléctricas del músculo cardíaco en acción.

electrocauterization *n.* electrocauterización, destrucción de tejidos por medio de una corriente eléctrica.

electroconvulsive therapy *n.* terapéutica de choque, electrochoque, tratamiento de ciertos desórdenes mentales con aplicación de corriente eléctrica al cerebro.

electroencephalogram *n.* electroencefalograma, registro obtenido de una encefalografía.

electroencephalography *n.* electroencefalografía, gráfico descriptivo de la actividad eléctrica desarrollada en el cerebro.

electrolysis *n.* electrólisis, descomposición de una sustancia por medio de una corriente eléctrica.

electrolyte *n.* electrólito, ion que conduce una carga eléctrica.

electrolyzation *n.* electrolización, descomposición por electricidad.

electromagnetic *a.* electromagnético-a.

electromyogram *n.* electromiograma, reporte gráfico por medio de una electromiografía.

electromyography *n.* electromiografía, uso de estimulación eléctrica para registrar la fuerza de contracción muscular.

electronic *a.* electrónico-a.

electrophoresis *n.* electroforesis, movimiento de partículas coloidales en un medio que, al someterse a una corriente eléctrica, las separa, tal como ocurre con la separación de proteínas en el plasma.

electrophysiology *n.* electrofisiología, estudio de la relación entre procesos fisiológicos afectados por fenómenos eléctricos.

electrosurgery *n.* electrocirugía, uso de electricidad en procesos quirúrgicos.

electrosurgical *a.* electroquirúrgico-a; **___ destruction of lesions** / destrucción **___** de lesiones.

electroversion *n.* electroversión, cesación de

una disrritmia cardíaca por un medio eléctrico.

element n. elemento, componente.

elementary a. elemental; rudimentario-a.

elephantiasis n. elefantiasis, enfermedad crónica caracterizada por obstrucción de los vasos linfáticos e hipertrofia de la piel y tejido celular subcutáneo que afecta gen. las extremidades inferiores y los órganos genitales externos.

elevate v. elevar, levantar, alzar.

elevation n. elevación; altura.

elevator n. elevador. 1. instrumento quirúrgico que se usa para levantar partes hendidas o para extirpar tejido óseo; 2. ascensor.

eligible a. elegible, electivo-a.

eliminate v. eliminar, expeler del organismo; suprimir.

elimination n. eliminación; exclusión.

elixir n. elixir, licor dulce y aromático que contiene un ingrediente medicinal activo.

elliptocyte n. eliptocito, eritrocito, célula roja ovalada.

elongated a. alargado-a, estirado-a, como el sistema de las vías digestivas.

else a. otro-a; más; **Who ___ needs help?** / ¿Quién más necesita ayuda?; **anyone ___** / alguien más; **anything ___** / algo más; **nothing ___** / nada más.

elsewhere adv. en otra parte, a otra parte.

emaciated a. enflaquecido-a; excesivamente delgado-a.

emasculation n. emasculación; castración; mutilación.

embalm v. embalsamar.

embalming n. embalsamamiento, preservación del cuerpo después de la muerte por medio de sustancias químicas.

embarrass v. avergonzar, trastornar, turbar, interferir, desconcertar.

embolism n. embolismo, embolia, oclusión súbita de un vaso por un coágulo, placa o aire; **cerebral ___** / ___ cerebral; **pulmonary ___** / ___ pulmonar.

embolus n. émbolo, coágulo u otro tipo de materia que, al circular a través de la corriente sanguínea, se aloja en un vaso de menor diámetro.

embrace n. abrazo; v. abrazar; [each other] abrazarse.

embryo n. embrión; 1. fase primitiva de desarrollo del ser humano desde la concepción hasta la séptima semana; 2. organismo en la fase primitiva de desarrollo.

embryology n. embriología, estudio del embrión y su desarrollo hasta el momento del nacimiento.

embryonic a. embriónico-a, embrional.

emerge v. brotar, emerger, surgir.

emergency n. emergencia, urgencia; **___ room** / sala de ___; **___ care** / servicio de ___.

emetic a. emético-a, que estimula el vómito.

emetine n. emetina, droga emética y antiamébica.

emigration n. emigración o migración, escape tal como el de leucocitos a través de las paredes de los capilares y las venas.

eminence n. eminencia o prominencia, forma de elevación semejante a la de la superficie de un hueso.

emission n. emisión, salida de líquido; derrame; **nocturnal ___** / ___ nocturna, escape involuntario de semen durante el sueño.

emit v. emitir, descargar; manifestar una opinión.

emollient a. emoliente, que suaviza la piel o mucosas interiores.

emotion n. emoción, sentimiento intenso.

emotional a. emocional, rel. a las emociones; **___ disturbances** / síntomas afectivos; **___ life** / vida afectiva.

emotive a. emotivo-a.

empathy n. empatía, comprensión y apreciación de los sentimientos de otra persona.

emphasis n. énfasis; acentuación.

emphatic a. enfático-a, acentuado-a, marcado-a.

emphysema n. enfisema, enfermedad crónica pulmonar en la cual los alvéolos pulmonares se distienden y los tejidos localizados entre los mismos se atrofian y dificultan el proceso respiratorio.

emphysematous a. enfisematoso-a, rel. al enfisema.

empiric a. empírico-a, que se basa en observaciones prácticas.

emplacement n. colocación, ubicación.

employ v. emplear, ocupar.

employee n. empleado-a.

employment n. empleo, ocupación.

empty a. vacío-a, desocupado-a.

empty v. vaciar, desocupar; **to ___ itself** / vaciarse, desocuparse.

empyema n. (pl. empyemata) empiema, acumulación de pus en una cavidad, esp. la cavidad torácica.

emulsify v. emulsionar, convertir en emulsión.

emulsion n. emulsión, mezcla de dos líquidos, uno de los cuales permanece suspendido.

enamel n. esmalte, sustancia dura que protege la dentina del diente.

encephalalgia n. encefalalgia, dolor de cabeza intenso.

encephalic a. encefálico-a, rel. al encéfalo o cerebro.

encephalitis n. encefalitis, infl. del encéfalo; **equine ___, eastern** / ___ equina, del este, viral aguda; **equine ___, western** / ___ equina, del oeste, viral benigna.

encephalocele n. encefalocele, hernia del encéfalo, protrusión del encéfalo a través de una abertura congénita o traumática en el cráneo.

encephalography n. encefalografía, examen radiográfico del cerebro.

encephaloma n. encefaloma, tumor del encéfalo.

encephalomalacia *n.* encefalomalacia, reblandecimiento del encéfalo.

encephalomyelitis *n.* encefalomielitis, infl. del encéfalo y de la médula espinal.

encephalon *n.* encéfalo, porción del sistema nervioso contenido en el cráneo.

encephalopathy *n.* encefalopatía, cualquier enfermedad cerebral.

enchondroma *n.* encondroma, tumor que se desarrolla en un hueso.

encircle *v.* rodear, circundar.

enclose *v.* encerrar, cercar; [*in a letter*] incluir, adjuntar.

enclosed *a. pp.* de **to enclose,** [*in a letter*] incluido-a, adjunto-a.

encopresis *n.* encopresis, incontinencia de heces fecales.

encounter *n.* encuentro; *v.* encontrar, salir al encuentro.

encourage *v.* alentar, animar.

encouragement *n.* aliento, incentivo.

encysted *a.* enquistado-a, que se encuentra envuelto en un saco o quiste.

end *n.* fin, término, extremidad; extremo; **at the ___ of** / al extremo de; [*date*] a fines de; **To what ___?** / ¿Con qué ___?; *a.* terminal, final; **___ artery** / arteria ___; **___ organ** / órgano ___.

endanger *v.* poner en peligro; *vr.* arriesgarse.

endarterectomy *n. cirg.* endarterectomía, extirpación de la túnica interna (intima) engrosada de una arteria.

endarteritis *n.* endarteritis, infl. de la túnica (intima) de una arteria.

endeavor *n.* empeño, esfuerzo.

endemic *a.* endémico-a, rel. a una enfermedad que permanece por un tiempo indefinido en una comunidad o región.

ending *n.* final; terminación, conclusión.

endless *a.* interminable, inacabable, sin fin.

endocarditis *n.* endocarditis, infl. aguda o crónica del endocardio; **acute bacterial ___** / **___ aguda bacteriana; chronic ___** / **___ crónica; rheumatic ___** / **___ reumática; subacute bacterial ___** / **___ subaguda bacteriana; valvular ___** / **___ valvular; vegetative ___** / **___ vegetativa.**

endocardium (pl. endocardia) *n.* endocardio, membrana serosa interior del corazón.

endocervix *n.* endocérvix, mucosa glandular del cuello uterino.

endocrine *a.* endocrino-a, rel. a secreciones internas y a las glándulas que las producen.

endocrine glands *n.* glándulas endocrinas, glándulas que segregan hormonas directamente en la corriente sanguínea (gónadas, pituitaria y suprarrenales).

endocrinology *n.* endocrinología, estudio de las glándulas endocrinas y las hormonas segregadas por éstas.

endoderm *n.* endodermo, la más interna de las tres membranas del embrión.

endogenous *a.* endógeno-a, que ocurre debido a factores internos del organismo.

endolymph *n.* endolinfa, fluido contenido en el laberinto membranoso del oído.

endolymphatic duct *n.* conducto endolinfático localizado en el oído.

endometrial *a.* endometrial, rel. al endometrio; **___ biopsy** / biopsia ___.

endometrioma *n.* endometrioma, tumor constituido por tejido endometrial.

endometriosis *n.* endometriosis, trastorno por el cual tejido similar al del endometrio se manifiesta en otras partes fuera del útero.

endometritis *n.* endometritis, infl. de la mucosa uterina.

endometrium *n.* endometrio, membrana mucosa interior del útero.

endomorph *a.* endomorfo-a, de torso más pronunciado que las extremidades.

endoplasmic reticulum *n.* retículo endoplásmico, sistema de canales en los cuales se llevan a cabo las funciones de anabolismo y catabolismo de la célula.

endorphins *n. pl.* endorfinas, sustancias químicas naturales del cerebro a las que se le atribuye la propiedad de aliviar el dolor.

endoscope *n.* endoscopio, instrumento usado para examinar un órgano o una cavidad interior hueca.

endoscopic *a.* endoscópico-a, rel. a la endoscopía.

endoscopy *n.* endoscopía, examen interior hecho con el endoscopio.

endosteum *n.* (*pl.* **endostea**) endostio, capa de tejido conectivo que protege la cavidad medular de un hueso.

endothelial *a.* endotelial, rel. al endotelio.

endothelium *n.* (*pl.* **endothelia**) endotelio, capa celular interna que reviste los vasos sanguíneos, los canales linfáticos, el corazón y otras cavidades.

endothermic *a.* endotérmico-a, rel. a la absorción de calor.

endotracheal *a.* endotraqueal, dentro de la tráquea; **___ tube, cuffed** / tubo ___ con manguito.

end-stage *n.* fase final.

endurable *a.* soportable, aguantable, tolerable.

endurance *n.* resistencia; tolerancia; **beyond ___** / más allá de lo que puede soportarse, intolerable.

endure *v.* soportar, sobrellevar, resistir, aguantar.

enema *n.* enema, lavado, lavativa; **barium ___** / **___ de bario; cleansing ___** / lavativa, lavado; **double contrast ___** / **___ de contraste doble; retention ___** / **___ de retención.**

energetic *a.* enérgico-a, vigoroso-a, lleno-a de energía.

energize *v.* desplegar energía; vigorizar.

energy *n.* energía, vigor.

engage *v.* encajar, ajustar, conectar; [*in a relationship*] comprometerse.

engaged *a.* encajado-a, ajustado-a, conectado-a; [*undertaken*] comprometido-a.

engender *v.* engendrar, procrear.

English *n.* [*language*] inglés; [*native*] *a.* inglés, inglesa.

engorged *a.* ingurgitado-a. 1. distendido por exceso de líquidos; 2. congestionado de sangre.

engram *n.* engrama. 1. marca permanente hecha en el protoplasma por un estímulo pasajero; 2. vestigio o visión imborrable producida por una experiencia sensorial.

enhance *v.* aumentar el valor, intensificar; [*beautify*] realzar.

enhancement *n.* aumento de un efecto tal como el de radiaciones por oxígeno u otro elemento químico.

enjoy *v.* disfrutar, gozar de.

enkephalins *n. pl.* encefalinas, sustancias químicas (polipéptidos) producidas en el cerebro.

enlarge *v.* ampliar, expandir, agrandar; ensanchar.

enlargement *n.* agrandamiento; ampliación, expansión, ensanchamiento.

enophthalmos *n.* enoftalmia, hundimiento del globo ocular.

enormous *a.* enorme, muy grande.

enough *a., adv.* bastante, suficiente; *int.* ¡basta!; ¡no más!

enrich *v.* enriquecer.

enriched *a.* [*added qualities*] enriquecido-a, de valor aumentado.

enrichment *n.* enriquecimento.

enter *v.* entrar, introducir, penetrar.

enteral, enteric *a.* entérico-a, rel. al intestino.

enteric coated *n.* cubierta entérica, revestimiento de ciertas tabletas y cápsulas para evitar que se disuelvan antes de llegar al intestino.

enteritis *n.* enteritis, infl. del intestino delgado.

enterocholecystostomy *n. cirg.* enterocolecistotomía, abertura entre la vesícula biliar y el intestino delgado.

enteroclysis *n.* enteroclisis. 1. irrigación del colon; 2. enema intenso.

enterococcus *n.* (*pl.* **enterococci**) enterococo, clase de estreptococo que se aloja en el intestino humano.

enterocolitis *n.* enterocolitis, infl. del intestino grueso y delgado.

enterocutaneous *a.* enterocutáneo-a, que comunica la piel y el intestino.

enteropathogen *n.* enteropatógeno, microorganismo causante de una enfermedad intestinal.

enteropathy *n.* enteropatía, cualquier anomalía o enfermedad del intestino.

enterostomy *n. cirg.* enterostomía, apertura o comunicación entre el intestino y la piel de la pared abdominal.

enterotoxin *n.* enterotoxina, toxina producida en el intestino.

enterovirus *n.* enterovirus, grupo de virus que infecta el tubo digestivo y que puede ocasionar enfermedades respiratorias y trastornos neurológicos.

enthusiasm *n.* entusiasmo.

entire *a.* entero-a, completo-a, íntegro-a; **-ly** *adv.* completamente, del todo, totalmente.

entity *n.* entidad, integridad, esencia o cualidad de algo.

entrance *n.* [*local*] entrada; [*acceptance*] ingreso; acceso a una cavidad.

entropion *n.* entropión, inversión del párpado.

entropy *n.* entropía, disminución de la capacidad de convertir la energía en trabajo.

entry *n.* entrada, acceso.

enucleate *v. cirg.* enuclear. 1. extirpar un tumor sin causar ruptura; 2. destruir o separar el núcleo de una célula; 3. extirpar el globo ocular.

enucleation *n.* enucleación, extirpación de un tumor o estructura.

enumerate *v.* enumerar, contar.

enuresis *n.* enuresis, incontinencia de orina; **nocturnal ___ / ___** nocturna.

environment *n.* ambiente, medio ambiente, entorno.

environmental *a.* rel. al medio ambiente; **___ hazards /** peligros del medio ambiente.

envy *v.* envidia.

enzygotic *a.* encigótico-a, que se deriva del mismo óvulo fecundado.

enzyme *n.* enzima, proteína que actúa como catalítico en reacciones químicas vitales.

enzymology *n.* enzimología, estudio de las enzimas.

eosin *n.* eosina, sustancia insoluble usada como colorante rojo en algunos tejidos que se estudian bajo el microscopio.

eosinopenia *n.* eosinopenia, número reducido de células eosinófilas en la sangre.

eosinopenic *a.* eosinopénico-a, rel. a la eosinopenia.

eosinophil *n.* eosinófilo, célula granulocítica que acepta fácilmente la acción colorante de la eosina.

eosinophilia *n.* eosinofilia, aumento en exceso de eosinófilos en la sangre por unidad de volumen.

eosinophilic *a.* eosinófilo-a, que tiene afinidad con o por la eosina.

eosinophilic leukocytes *n.* leucocitos eosinófilos, leucocitos con abundante granulación ácida que con los colorantes básicos se tiñen de color violeta.

ependyma *n.* epéndimo, membrana que cubre los ventrículos del cerebro y el canal central de la médula espinal.

ependymal *a.* ependimario-a, rel. al epéndimo: **___ cells /** células **___**-s; **___ layer /** membrana **___**.

ependymitis *n.* ependimitis, infl. del epéndimo.

ependymoma *n.* ependimoma, tumor del sistema nervioso central que se origina de inclusiones fetales ependimarias.

ephedrine *n.* efedrina, alcaloide, tipo de adrenalina de efecto broncodilatador.

ephemeral *a.* efímero-a, pasajero-a.

epicardium *n.* (*pl.* **epicardia**) epicardio, cara visceral del pericardio.

epicondyle *n.* epicóndilo, eminencia sobre el cóndilo de un hueso.

epidemic *n.* epidemia, enfermedad que se manifiesta con alta frecuencia y que afecta a un número considerable de personas en una región o comunidad; *a.* epidémico-a; ___ outbreak / brote ___.

epidemiologist *n.* epidemiólogo-a, especialista en el estudio de enfermedades epidémicas.

epidemiology *n.* epidemiología, estudio de las enfermedades epidémicas.

epidermic *a.* epidérmico-a, rel. a la epidermis.

epidermis *n.* epidermis, cubierta externa epitelial de la piel.

epidermoid *a.* epidermoide. 1. semejante a la piel; 2. rel. a un tumor que contiene células epidérmicas.

epidermolysis *n.* epidermólisis, descamación de la piel.

epididymis *n.* epidídimo, conducto situado en la parte posterior del testículo que recoge el esperma que es transportado por el conducto deferente a la vesícula seminal.

epididymitis *n.* epididimitis, infección e infl. del epidídimo.

epidural *a.* epidural, situado-a sobre o fuera de la duramadre.

epigastric *a.* epigástrico-a, rel. al epigastrio; ___ reflex / reflejo ___.

epigastrium *n.* (*pl.* **epigastria**) epigastrio, región superior media del abdomen.

epiglottis *n.* epiglotis, cartílago que cubre la laringe e impide la entrada de alimentos en la misma durante la deglución.

epiglottitis *n.* epiglotitis, infl. de la epiglotis.

epilation *n.* epilación, depilación por medio de electrólisis.

epilepsy, grand mal *n.* epilepsia, desorden neurológico gen. crónico y con frecuencia hereditario que se manifiesta con ataques o convulsiones y a veces con pérdida del conocimiento.

epileptic *n.* epiléptico-a, persona que padece de epilepsia; *a.* epiléptico-a, rel. a la epilepsia o que sufre de ella; ___ seizure / ataque ___, crisis ___.

epileptogenic, epileptogenous *a.* epileptógeno-a, causante de crisis epilépticas.

epinephrine *n.* epinefrina. *V.* **adrenaline.**

epiphora *n.* epifora, lagrimeo.

epiphysial *a.* epifisiario-a, rel. a la epífisis.

epiphysis *n.* epífisis, extremo de un hueso largo, gen. parte más ancha que la diáfisis.

epiphysitis *n.* epifisitis, infl. de una epífisis.

epiploic *a.* epiploico-a, rel. al epiplón.

epiploic foramen *n.* foramen epiploico, abertura que comunica la cavidad mayor peritoneal con la menor.

epiploon *n.* epiplón, repliegue de grasa que cubre el intestino.

episiotomy *n.* *cirg.* episiotomía, incisión del perineo durante el parto para evitar desgarros.

epispadias *n.* epispadias, abertura congénita anormal de la uretra en la parte superior del pene.

epistaxis *n.* epistaxis, sangramiento por la nariz.

epithalamus *n.* epitálamo, porción extrema superior del diencéfalo.

epithelial *a.* epitelial, rel. al epitelio.

epithelial casts *n.* cilindro epitelial, cilindro urinario constituido por células epiteliales renales y células redondas.

epithelialization *n.* epitelialización, crecimiento de epitelio sobre una superficie expuesta tal como en la cicatrización de una herida.

epithelioma *n.* epitelioma, carcinoma compuesto mayormente de células epiteliales.

epithelium *L.* (*pl.* **epithelia**) epitelio, tejido que cubre las superficies expuestas e interiores del cuerpo; **ciliated** ___ / ___ ciliado; **columnar** ___ / ___ columnar; **cuboidal** ___ / ___ cuboidal; **squamous** ___ / ___ escamoso; **stratified** ___ / ___ estratificado; **transitional** ___ / ___ de transición, transicional.

epitympanum *n.* epitímpano, porción superior del tímpano.

eponym *n.* epónimo, uso del nombre propio de una persona para nombrar instrumentos médicos, anomalías o síndromes tal como el síndrome de Down.

epoxy *n.* epoxia, adhesivo.

epsilon-amino caproic acid *n.* ácido epsilón-amino caproico; ácido sulfúrico.

Epsom salt *n.* sal de Epsom; sal de higuera; sulfato de magnesio; medicamento usado como catártico.

Epstein-Barr virus *n.* virus de Epstein-Barr, posible causa de la mononucleosis.

equal *a.* igual; parejo-a; uniforme; ___ rights / ___ de derechos; **-ly** *adv.* igualmente.

equality *n.* igualdad, uniformidad.

equalize *v.* igualar, emparejar, uniformar.

equanimity *n.* ecuanimidad; entereza.

equator *n.* ecuador, línea imaginaria que divide un cuerpo en dos partes iguales.

equilibrate *v.* equilibrar, balancear.

equilibration *n.* equilibración, mantenimiento del equilibrio.

equilibrium *n.* equilibrio, balance.

equinovarus *n.* equinovarus, deformidad congénita del pie.

equipment *n.* equipo, provisión; accesorios.

equitable *a.* equitativo-a; justo-a.

equivalence *n.* equivalencia.

equivalent *a.* equivalente, del mismo valor.

eradicate *v.* erradicar, extirpar; desarraigar.

erase *v.* borrar; raspar.

erectile *a.* eréctil, capaz de ponerse en erección

o de dilatarse; ___ **tissue** / tejido ___ .

erection *n.* erección, estado de rigidez, endurecimiento o dilatación de un tejido eréctil cuando se llena de sangre, tal como el pene.

erector *n.* erector, con propiedad de erección.

ergonomics *n.* ergonomía, rama de la ecología que estudia la creación y diseño de maquinarias en su ambiente físico y la relación de las mismas con el bienestar humano.

ergot *n.* cornezuelo de centeno, hongo que en forma seca o en extracto se usa como medicamento para detener hemorragias o para inducir contracciones uterinas.

ergotamine *n.* ergotamina, alcaloide usado en el tratamiento de migraña.

ergotism *n.* ergotismo, intoxicación crónica producida por el uso excesivo de alcaloides del cornezuelo de centeno.

erode *v.* desgastar.

erogenous *a.* erógeno-a, que produce sensaciones eróticas; ___ **zone** / zona erótica.

erosion *n.* erosión, desgaste

erosive *a.* erosivo-a, que causa erosión.

erotic *a.* erótico-a, rel. al erotismo o capaz de despertar impulsos sexuales.

eroticism, erotism *n.* erotismo, exaltación sexual.

erratic *a.* errático-a, que no sigue un curso o ritmo estable.

error *n.* error, falta, equivocación.

eructation *n.* eructación, eructo.

erupt *v.* brotar, salir con fuerza, hacer erupción.

eruption *n.* erupción, brote; salpullido.

erysipelas *n.* erisipela, enfermedad infecciosa de la piel.

erythema *n.* eritema, enrojecimiento de la piel debido a una congestión de los capilares.

erythematic, erithematous *a.* eritematoso-a, rel. al eritema.

erythremia *n.* eritremia. V. **polycythemia.**

erythroblast *n.* eritroblasto, hematíe, glóbulo rojo primitivo.

erythroblastosis *n.* eritroblastosis, número excesivo de eritoblastos en la sangre.

erythrocyte *n.* eritrocito, célula roja producida en la médula ósea que actúa como transportadora de oxígeno a los tejidos; ___ **sedimentation rate** / índice de sedimentación de ___-s.

erythrocytopenia *n.* eritrocitopenia, deficiencia en la cantidad de glóbulos rojos circulantes.

erythrocytosis *n.* eritrocitosis, aumento de eritrocitos en la sangre.

erythroid *n.* eritroide, de color semejante al rojo.

erythroleukemia *n.* eritroleucemia, enfermedad sanguínea maligna caracterizada por el crecimiento anormal de glóbulos rojos y blancos.

erythromycin *n.* eritromicina, antibiótico usado en el tratamiento de bacterias gram-positivas.

erythron *n.* eritrón, concepto de la sangre como un sistema compuesto por los eritrocitos y sus precursores, así como también los órganos de los que provienen.

erythropoiesis *n.* eritropoyesis, producción de eritrocitos.

erythropoietin *n.* eritropoyetina, proteína no dializable que estimula la producción de eritrocitos.

eschar *n.* escara, costra de color oscuro que se forma en la piel después de una quemadura.

esophageal *a.* esofágico-a, rel. al esófago: ___ **dilatation** / dilatación ___ .

esophagectomy *n. cirg.* esofagectomía, excisión de una porción del esófago.

esophagitis *n.* esofagitis, infl. del esófago.

esophagodynia *n.* esofagodinia, dolor en el esófago.

esophagogastritis *n.* esofagogastritis, infl. del estómago y del esófago.

esophagogastroduodenoscopy *n.* esofagogastroduodenoscopía, examen del estómago, esófago y duodeno por medio de un endoscopio.

esophagogastroscopy *n.* esofagogastroscopía, examen del esófago y del estómago por medio de un endoscopio.

esophagus *n.* esófago, porción del tubo digestivo situado entre la faringe y el estómago.

esophoria *n.* esoforia, movimiento del ojo hacia adentro; *pop.* bizquera.

esotropia *n.* esotropia. V. **esophoria.**

essence *n.* esencia, cualidad indispensable.

essential *a.* esencial, indispensable.

establish *v.* establecer, determinar.

estate *n.* estado, condición de una persona, animal o cosa.

ester *n.* éster, compuesto formado por la combinación de un ácido órganico con alcohol.

esterification *n.* esterificación, transformación de un ácido en un éster.

esthesia *n.* estesia. 1. percepción, sensación; 2. cualquier anomalía que afecte las sensaciones.

esthetics *n.* estética, rama de la filosofía que se refiere a la belleza y el arte.

estradiol *n.* estradiol, esteroide producido por los ovarios.

estrinization *n.* estrinización, cambios epiteliales de la vagina producidos por estimulación de estrógeno.

estrogen *n.* estrógeno, hormona sexual femenina producida por los ovarios; ___ **receptor** / receptor de ___ .

estrogenic *a.* estrogénico-a, rel. al estrógeno.

estrone *n.* estrona, hormona estrogénica.

eternal *a.* eterno-a.

ethanol *n.* alcohol etílico.

ether *n.* éter, fluido químico cuyo vapor es usado en anestesia general.

ethics *n.* ética, normas y principios que gobiernan la conducta profesional.

ethmoid *n.* etmoides, hueso esponjoso situado en la base del cráneo.

ethmoidectomy *n. cirg.* etmoidectomía, extirpación de las células etmoideas o de parte del hueso etmoide.

ethmoid sinus *n.* seno etmoideo, cavidad aérea situada dentro del etmoide.

ethylene *n.* etileno, anestésico.

etiologic *a.* etiológico-a, rel. a la etiología.

etiology *n.* etiología, rama de la medicina que estudia la causa de las enfermedades.

eubolism *n.* eubolismo, metabolismo normal.

eucalyptus *n.* eucalipto.

eugenics *n.* eugenesia, ciencia que estudia el mejoramiento de la especie humana de acuerdo con las leyes biológicas de la herencia.

eunuch *n.* eunuco, hombre castrado.

euphoria *n. psic.* estado exagerado de sensación de bienestar.

euploidy *n.* euploidia, grupos completos de cromosomas.

Eustachian tube *n.* trompa de Eustaquio, parte del conducto auditivo.

euthanasia *n.* eutanasia, muerte infringida sin sufrimiento en casos de una enfermedad incurable.

euthyroid *a.* eutiroideo-a, rel. a la función normal de la glándula tiroides.

evacuant *a.* evacuante, catártico, estimulante de la evacuación.

evacuate *v.* evacuar, eliminar; defecar; vaciar, *Mex.* obrar.

evacuation *n.* evacuación. 1. acción de vaciar esp. los intestinos; 2. acción de hacer un vacío.

evagination *n.* evaginación, salida o protuberancia de un órgano o parte de éste de su propia localización.

evaluate *v.* evaluar, estimar.

evaluation *n.* evaluación, consideración del estado de salud mental y físico de una persona enferma o sana.

evanescent *a.* evanescente, que se desvanece, efímero-a.

evaporation *n.* evaporación, conversión de un estado líquido a vapor.

even *a.* igual, uniforme; [*same*] mismo-a, parejo-a; *adv.* ___ **so** / aun cuando; ___ **though** / aun cuando.

evening *n.* tardecita, anochecer, por la noche; **last** ___ / ayer por la noche; **this** ___ / esta noche.

ever *adv.* siempre; **for** ___ **and** ___ / por ___ jamás; **hardly** ___ / casi nunca; ___ **since** / desde entonces, desde que.

eversion *n.* eversión, versión hacia afuera, esp. la de una mucosa que rodea un orificio natural.

every *a.* todo; cada; ___ **day** / ___-s los días; ___ **once in a while** / a veces, de vez en cuando; ___ **other day** / día por medio, cada dos días, un día sí y otro no.

everybody *pron.* todos, todo el mundo.

everything *pron.* todo.

evidence *n.* evidencia, manifestación; [*legal*] evidencia, testimonio.

evil *n.* mal; *a.* malo-a, maligno-a; **-ness** *n.* maldad.

evisceration *n. cirg.* evisceración, extirpación del contenido de una víscera o de una cavidad.

evoke *v.* evocar.

evoked response *n.* respuesta evocada.

evolution *n.* evolución, cambio gradual.

evulsion *n.* evulsión, acción de sacar hacia afuera, arranque.

exacerbation *n.* exacerbación, agravamiento de un síntoma o enfermedad.

exact *a.* exacto-a; **-ly** *adv.* exactamente.

exaggerate *v.* exagerar.

exaggeration *n.* exageración, alarde.

exam *n.* examen, evaluación, investigación.

examination *n.* examen; **medical** ___ / ___ médico, examen físico completo, reconocimiento o inspección del cuerpo para establecer el estado de salud de una persona.

examine *v.* examinar, evaluar, investigar, indagar.

example *n.* ejemplo, muestra.

exanthem, exanthema *Gr.* exantema, erupción cutánea, salpullido.

exasperate *v.* exasperar, agravar.

exasperated *a.* exasperado-a.

excellent *a.* excelente, óptimo-a.

except *prep.* excepto, menos.

exception *n.* excepción; **with the** ___ **of** / a ___ de.

excess *n.* exceso, sobrante.

excessive *a.* excesivo-a.

exchange *v.* cambiar, trocar.

exchange transfusion *n.* ex-sanguinotransfusión, transfusión gradual y simultánea de sangre al recipiente mientras se saca la sangre del donante.

excise *v.* extirpar, cortar, dividir.

excision *n.* excisión, extirpación, ablación.

excitation *n.* excitación, reacción a un estímulo.

excite *v.* excitar, estimular; provocar.

excited *a.* excitado-a; acalorado-a.

exclude *v.* excluir, suprimir.

exclusive *a.* exclusivo-a.

excoriation *n.* excoriación, abrasión de la epidermis.

excrement *n.* excremento, heces fecales, *pop.* [*infant's*] caca.

excrescence *n.* excrecencia, tumor saliente en la superficie de un órgano o parte.

excreta *n.* excreta, todo lo excretado por el cuerpo.

excrete *v.* excretar, eliminar desechos del cuerpo.

excretion *n.* excreción, expulsión de lo secretado.

excretory *a.* excretorio-a, rel. a la excreción.

excuse *v.* excusar, perdonar, dispensar; ___ **me** / con permiso.

exenteration *n. cirg.* exenteración. V. **evisceration**.

exercise *n.* ejercicio; ___ **electrocardiogram, stress test** / prueba de esfuerzo máximo;

physical ___ / ___ físico; ___ **tolerance test** / prueba física de ___ tolerado.

exfoliation *n.* exfoliación, descamación del tejido.

exhalation *n.* exhalación, proceso de salida del aire hacia afuera.

exhale *v.* espirar, exhalar.

exhaust *v.* agotar; extraer; vaciar; **to ___ all means** / agotar todos los recursos.

exhausted *a.* agotado-a, exhausto-a, extenuado-a.

exhaustion *n.* agotamiento, postración, fatiga extrema.

exhibition *n.* exhibición, exposición.

exhibitionism *n.* exhibicionismo, deseo obsesivo de exhibir partes del cuerpo esp. los genitales.

exhibitionist *n.* exhibicionista, persona que practica el exhibicionismo.

exhumation *n.* exhumación, desenterramiento.

exist *v.* existir, ser, vivir.

existent *a.* existente.

exit *n.* salida.

exocrine *a.* exocrino-a, rel. a la secreción externa de una glándula.

exocrine glands *n.* glándulas exocrinas, glándulas que secretan hormonas a través de un conducto o tubo tal como las mamarias y las sudoríparas.

exogenous *a.* exógeno-a, externo-a, que se origina fuera del organismo.

exomphalos *n.* exónfalo. *V.* **omphalocele.**

exophthalmia, exophthalmos *n.* exoftalmia, protrusión anormal del globo del ojo.

exophthalmic *a.* exoftálmico-a, rel. a la exoftalmia.

exophthalmic goiter *n.* bocio exoftálmico.

exostosis *n.* exóstosis, hipertrofia ósea cartilaginosa que sobresale hacia afuera de un hueso o de la raíz de un diente.

exotic *a.* exótico-a, raro-a, extraño-a.

exotoxin *n.* exotoxina, toxina secretada por bacterias.

exotropia *n.* exotropía, tipo de estrabismo divergente, rotación anormal de un ojo o de ambos hacia afuera por falta de balance muscular.

expand *v.* ensanchar, expandir, dilatar; expandirse.

expansion *n.* expansión, extensión.

expect *v.* esperar; suponer.

expectorant *n.* expectorante, agente que estimula la expectoración.

expectoration *n.* expectoración, esputo, expulsión de mucosidades o flema de los pulmones, tráquea y bronquios.

expel *v.* expulsar.

expense, expenditure *n.* gasto; **covered ___-s /** ___-s cubiertos.

experience *n.* experiencia, práctica.

experiment *n.* experimento; *v.* experimentar.

expert *a.* experto-a, perito-a.

expiration *n.* expiración, terminación; espira-

ción. 1. acto de dar salida al aire aspirado por los pulmones; 2. acto de fallecer o morir.

expire *v.* 1. espirar, expeler el aire aspirado; 2. expirar, morir, dejar de existir.

explain *v.* explicar, aclarar.

explanation *n.* explicación, interpretación.

exploration *n.* exploración, investigación, búsqueda.

exploratory *a.* exploratorio-a, rel. a una exploración.

expose *v.* exponer, mostrar; expulsar bajo presión.

expression *n.* expresión, aspecto o apariencia que se registra en la cara; medio de expresar algo.

expressivity *n.* expresividad, apreciación de un rasgo heredado según se manifiesta en el descendiente portador del gene.

extended care facility *n.* centro de atención médica externa.

extension *n.* 1. prolongación, extensión; 2. acto de enderezar un dedo o alinear un miembro o hueso dislocado.

extensor *a.* extensor-a, que tiene la propiedad de extender.

exterior *a.* exterior, externo-a; visible.

exteriorize *v. cirg.* exteriorizar, exponer un órgano o una parte temporalmente.

externalia *n. pl.* genitales externos.

externalize *v.* externalizar, *V.* **exteriorize.**

extinction *n.* extinción; supresión; cesación.

extinguish *v.* extinguir, apagar.

extirpation *n.* extirpación, ablación de una parte u órgano.

extra *a.* extraordinario-a; adicional.

extracellular *a.* extracelular, fuera de la célula.

extracorporeal *a.* extracorporal, fuera del cuerpo.

extract *n.* extracto, producto concentrado.

extraction *n. cirg.* extracción, proceso de extraer, separar o sacar afuera.

extradural *a.* extradural, *V.* **epidural.**

extraneous *a.* extraño-a, sin relación con un organismo o fuera del mismo.

extraocular *a.* extraocular, fuera del ojo.

extrasensory perception (ESP) *n.* percepción extrasensorial, percepción o conocimiento de las acciones o pensamientos de otras personas adquirido sin participación sensorial.

extrasystole *n.* extrasístole, latido arrítmico del corazón.

extravasated *a.* extravasado-a, rel. al escape de fluido de un vaso a tejidos circundantes.

extravascular *a.* extravascular, que ocurre fuera de un vaso o vasos.

extreme *a.* extremo-a, excesivo-a; último-a; **-ly** *adv.* extremadamente, excesivamente; sumamente.

extremity *n.* extremidad, la parte terminal de algo.

extrinsic *a.* extrínseco-a, que proviene de

afuera.

extrophy *n.* extrofia. *V.* **eversion.**

extrovert *a.* extrovertido-a, tipo de personalidad que dirige la atención a sucesos u objetos fuera de sí mismo-a.

extrude *v.* exprimir, forzar hacia afuera.

extrusion *n.* extrusión, expulsión.

extubation *n. cirg.* extubación, extracción de un tubo.

exuberant *a.* exuberante, de proliferación excesiva.

exudate *n.* exudado, fluido inflamatorio tal como el de secreciones y supuraciones.

exudation *n.* exudación.

exude *v.* exudar, sudar, supurar a través de los tejidos.

eye *n.* ojo; ___ **bank** / banco de ojos; **bloodshot** ___ / ___ inyectado; ___ **contact** / contacto visual; ___ **diseases** / enfermedades de los ojos, enfermedades de la vista; ___ **drops** / gotas para los ojos; **glass** ___ / ___ de vidrio;

___ **injuries** / traumatismos oculares; *v.* **to keep an** ___ **on** / cuidar, vigilar.

eyeball *n.* globo del ojo, globo ocular.

eyeband *n.* venda para los ojos.

eyebrow *n.* ceja.

eyecup *n.* copita para los ojos.

eyeglasses *n. pl.* espejuelos, gafas, lentes, anteojos; **bifocal** ___ / ___ bifocales; **trifocal** ___ / ___ trifocales.

eyeground *n.* fondo del ojo.

eyelash *n.* pestaña.

eyelid *n.* párpado.

eye memory *n.* memoria visual.

eyepiece *n.* ocular.

eyesight *n.* vista; *v.* **to have good** ___ / tener buena ___.

eye socket *n.* órbita ocular; cuenca del ojo.

eyestrain *n.* vista cansada.

eyewash *n.* solución ocular, colirio, solución para los ojos.

eyewitness *n.* testigo ocular o visual.

F *abbr.* **Fahrenheit** / Fahrenheit.

f *abbr.* **failure** / fallo; **feminine** / femenino; **formula** / fórmula; **function** / función.

fabella *n.* fabela, fibrocartílago sesamoideo que puede desarrollarse en la cabeza del músculo gastronecmio.

face *n.* cara, rostro, faz; ___-**down** / boca abajo; ___-**lift** / estire de la cara, *cirg.* ritidectomía; ___ **peeling** / peladura de la ___; ___ **to face** / frente a frente; ___-**up** / boca arriba.

facet *n.* faceta, pequeña parte lisa en la superficie de una estructura dura semejante a la de los huesos.

facetectomy *n. cirg.* extirpación de la faceta auricular.

facial *a.* facial, rel. a la cara; ___ **bones** / huesos de la cara, huesos ___-es; ___ **injuries** / traumatismos ___-es; ___ **nerves** / nervios ___-es; ___ **paralysis** / parálisis ___ .

facies *n.* (*pl.* **facies**) facies, expresión o apariencia de la cara; **leontina** ___ / ___ leontina; **masklike** ___ / ___ inexpresiva.

facilitate *v.* facilitar; proporcionar.

facility *n.* facilidad; instalación; [*conveniences*] *pl.* comodidades; servicios en general.

facing *n.* [*dental*] revestimiento.

fact *n.* hecho, realidad; **in** ___ / en efecto, en realidad.

factitious *a.* facticio-a, artificial, no natural.

factor *n.* factor, elemento que contribuye a producir una acción; **antihemophilic** ___ / ___ antihemofílico; **clotting, coagulation** ___ / ___ de coagulación; **releasing** ___ / ___ liberador; **rheumatoid** ___ / ___ reumatoideo; **Rh** ___ / ___ Rh [*erre ache*]; **tumor angiogenesis** ___ / ___ angiogenético tumoral.

factual *a.* objetivo-a, real.

facultative *a.* facultativo-a. 1. voluntario, no obligatorio; 2. de naturaleza profesional.

faculty *n.* facultad. 1. cuerpo facultativo; 2. aptitud o habilidad para llevar a cabo funciones normales.

fade *v.* descolorar; perder el color, atenuar la imagen o el color, desteñirse.

Fahrenheit scale *n.* escala de Fahrenheit, escala de temperatura que usa el punto de congelación a 32° y el de ebullición a 212°.

fail *v.* [*to be deficient*] fallar, faltar; dejar de; **without** ___ / sin falta.

failing *n.* debilidad; deterioro; flaqueza; falla, falta.

failure *n.* insuficiencia, fallo; omisión; fracaso; **heart** ___ / ___ cardíaca, fallo cardíaco; ___ **neurosis** / neurosis de fracaso; **renal** ___ / ___ renal; **respiratory** ___ / ___ respiratoria; **gross** ___ / fiasco.

faint *n.* desmayo, desvanecimiento, vahído; *v.* dar un vahído; desmayarse, desvanecerse; **-ly** *adv.*

débilmente, lánguidamente; escasamente.

fainting *n.* desmayo; desfallecimiento; ___ **spell** / desmayo.

faintness *n.* desaliento, [*weakness*] debilidad.

fair *a.* [*blonde*] rubio-a; [*light skin*] de tez blanca; [*average*] regular; ___ **complexion** / rubio-a, de tez clara; [*weather*] claro, despejado, favorable; [*decision*] imparcial, razonable, justa.

faith *n.* fe; **in good** ___ / de buena ___ .

faithful *a.* exacto-a, veraz; **-ly** *adv.* fielmente, exactamente.

faith healer *n.* curandero-a.

faith healing *n.* curanderismo.

fake *v.* fingir; falsificar, simular.

falciform *a.* falciforme, en forma de hoz; ___ **ligament of liver** / ligamento ___ del hígado.

fall *n.* caída; [*season*] otoño; *vi.* caer; caerse; **to** ___ **asleep** / quedarse dormido-a; **to** ___ **back** / echarse atrás; **to** ___ **behind** / atrasarse, quedarse atrás; **to** ___ **short** / faltar, ser deficiente.

fallen *a. pp.* de **to fall**, caído-a.

falling *n.* caída; [*temperature*] descenso.

Fallopian tubes *n.* trompas de Falopio, conductos que se extienden del útero a los ovarios.

Fallot, tetralogy of *n.* tetralogía de Fallot, deformación cardíaca congénita que comprende cuatro defectos de los grandes vasos sanguíneos y de las paredes de las aurículas y ventrículos.

fallout *n.* cenizas radioactivas.

false *a.* falso-a, incorrecto-a. no real; ___ **negative** / ___ negativo; ___ **positive** / ___ positivo.

falsification *n.* falsificación, distorsión o alteración de un suceso u objeto.

fame *n.* fama, nombre.

familial, familiar *a.* familiar, rel. a la familia; frecuente; ___ **Mediterranean fever** / fiebre ___ del Mediterráneo; ___ **periodic paralysis** / parálisis periódica ___ .

family *n.* familia; ___ **man** / padre de familia; ___ **name** / apellido.

family planning *n.* planificación familiar, planeamiento de la concepción de los hijos gen. con el uso de métodos contraceptivos.

family practice *n.* medicina familiar, atención médica especial de la familia como unidad.

famine *n.* hambre, carestía.

famished *a.* famélico-a, hambriento-a.

fanatic, fanatical *a.* fanático-a.

Fanconi's syndrome *n.* síndrome de Fanconi, anemia hipoplástica congénita.

fancy *v.* imaginar, fantasear.

fantasy, phantasy *n.* fantasía, uso de la imaginación para transformar una realidad desagradable en una experiencia satisfactoria.

far *adv.* lejos; distante; ___ **apart** / infrecuente; **from** ___ **away** / de lejos, a lo lejos; ___ **better** / mucho mejor; ___ **cry** / gran diferencia; ___ **off** / a lo lejos, distante; **so** ___ / hasta ahora, hasta aquí.

farfetched *a.* rebuscado-a; inconcebible.

farina *n.* farina, harina, combinación de harina de trigo con otro cereal.

farmer *n.* campesino-a, granjero-a.

farmer's lung *n.* pulmón de granjero, hipersensibilidad de los alvéolos pulmonares causada por exposición a heno fermentado.

farsighted *a.* hiperópico-a, que sufre de hipermetropía.

farsightedness *n.* presbiopía, hiperopía, hipermetropía, defecto visual en el cual los rayos de luz hacen foco detrás de la retina y los objetos lejanos se ven mejor que los que están a corta distancia.

fascia *n.* fascia, tejido fibroso conectivo que envuelve el cuerpo bajo la piel y protege los músculos, los nervios y los vasos sanguíneos; ___, **aponeurotic** / ___ aponeurótica, tejido fibroso que sirve de soporte a los músculos; ___, **Buck's** / ___ de Buck, tejido fibroso que cubre el pene; ___, **Colles'** / ___ de Colles, cubierta interna de la fascia perineal; ___, **lata** / ___ lata, protectora de los músculos del muslo; ___, **tranversalis** / ___ tranversal, localizada entre el peritoneo y el músculo transverso del abdomen.

fascicle, fasciculum *n.* (*pl.* **fascicula**) fascículo, haz de fibras musculares y nerviosas.

fasciculation *n.* fasciculación. 1. formación de fascículos; 2. contracción involuntaria breve de fibras musculares.

fascietomy *n. cirg.* fascietomía, excisión parcial o total de una fascia.

fasciitis *n.* fascitis, infl. de una fascia.

fasciotomy *n. cirg.* fasciotomía, incisión de una fascia.

fast *n.* ayuno; *a.* [*speed*] rápido-a, ligero-a; [*of a color*] que tiene resistencia a un colorante: ___ **asleep** / profundamente dormido-a; ___ **day** / día de ayuno; *v.* ayunar, estar en ayunas.

fasten *v.* sujetar; amarrar; abrochar; abotonar.

fasting *n.* ayuno.

fastness *n.* resistencia.

fat *n.* [*grease*] grasa; *a.* gordo-a, grueso-a, obeso-a; [*greasy*] grasoso-a; *v.* **to get** ___ / engordar.

fatal *a.* fatal.

fatality *n.* fatalidad, desgracia; muerte.

fate *n.* destino.

father *n.* padre; papá; tata.

father-in-law *n.* suegro.

fatherless *n.* huérfano-a de padre.

fatigability *n.* fatigabilidad, predisposición a la fatiga.

fatigue *n.* cansancio; sensación de agotamiento; *v.* fatigarse, cansarse.

fatness *n.* gordura.

fatty *a.* adiposo-a, grasoso-a; ___ **acids** / ácidos grasos; ___ **degeneration** / degeneración ___; ___ **tumor** / lipoma; ___ **tissue** / tejido ___.

fauces *L.* fauces, región intermedia entre la boca y la faringe.

faucet *n.* pila, llave de agua.

fault *n.* falta, defecto, culpa; *v.* **to be at** ___ / ser culpable.

faultless *a.* perfecto-a; intachable.

faulty *a.* defectuoso-a, imperfecto-a.

favor *n.* favor.

favorable *a.* favorable; propicio-a.

fear *n.* temor, miedo, aprehensión.

fearful *a.* temeroso-a, miedoso-a.

fearless *a.* sin temor, intrépido-a.

feasible *a.* posible, factible.

feast *n.* banquete.

feather *n.* pluma.

feature *n.* rasgo, característica.

febrile *a.* febril, calenturiento-a; ___ **convulsion** / convulsión ___.

fecal *a.* fecal, que contiene heces fecales.

fecalith *n.* fecalito, concreción intestinal formada alrededor de materia fecal.

fecaloma *n.* fecaloma, acumulación de heces fecales en el recto con apariencia de tumor abdominal.

fecaluria *n.* presencia de materia fecal en la orina.

feces *n. pl.* heces, excremento.

fecund *a.* fecundo-a; fértil.

fecundity *n.* fecundidad, fertilidad.

fed *a. pp.* de **to feed; to be** ___ **up** / estar harto-a, *pop.* estar hasta la coronilla.

fee *n.* honorario, cuota.

feeble *a.* débil, endeble.

feed *vi.* alimentar, dar de comer; proveer materiales o asistencia.

feedback *n.* 1. [*information*] reprovisión de material informativo distribuido; 2. retroalimentación, retorno parcial del rendimiento o efectos de un proceso a su fuente de origen o a una fase anterior; *v.* proveer de nuevo material informativo; regenerar la energía.

feeding *n.* alimentación; **breast-** ___ / lactancia materna; **enteral** ___ / ___ enteral; **forced** ___ / ___ forzada; **intravenous** ___ / ___ intravenosa; **rectal** ___ / ___ por el recto; ___ **time** / horario de ___; **tube** ___ / ___ por sonda.

feel *vi.* sentir, percibir; **to** ___ **hungry** / tener hambre; **to** ___ **the effects of** / sentir los efectos de; **Do you** ___ **the effects of the medication?** / ¿Siente, sientes los efectos de la medicina?; **to** ___ **like** / tener ganas de; **to** ___ **sleepy** / tener sueño; **to** ___ **sorry for** / compadecerse de; tener lástima de; **to** ___ **the pulse** / tomar el pulso; **to** ___ **thirsty** / tener sed; sentirse; **to** ___ **bad** / ___ mal; **to** ___ **better** / ___ mejor; **to** ___ **good, fine** / ___ bien; **to** ___ **uncomfortable** / ___ incómodo-a.

feeling *n.* sensación; [*emotion*] sentimiento, emoción, sensibilidad.

feet *n. pl.* de **foot** pies.

feline *a.* felino-a, rel. a la familia de los gatos o con características semejantes a éstos.

fellatio *n.* felación. *V.* **cunnilingus.**

felon *n.* 1. panadizo, absceso doloroso de la falange distal de un dedo; 2. felón, criminal.

female *n.* hembra; *a.* femenino-a, rel. a la mujer.

feminine *a.* femenino-a; afeminado.

feminist *a.* feminista.

feminization *n.* feminización, desarrollo de características femeninas.

femoral *a.* femoral, rel. al fémur; ___ **artery** / arteria ___; **deep** ___ **arch** / arco ___ profundo; ___ **vein** / vena ___.

femur *n.* fémur, hueso del muslo.

fenestrated *a.* fenestrado-a; que tiene orificios o aperturas.

fenestration *n. cirg.* fenestración. 1. creación de una abertura en el laberinto del oído para restaurar la audición; 2. acto de perforar.

ferment *n.* fermento. 1. sustancia o agente que activa la fermentación; 2. producto de fermentación; *v.* fermentar, hacer fermentar.

fermentation *n.* fermentación, descomposición de sustancias complejas por la acción de enzimas o fermentos.

ferritin *n.* ferritina, una de las formas en que el hierro se almacena en el organismo.

ferroprotein *n.* ferroproteína, proteína compuesta de un radical ferruginoso.

ferruginous *a.* ferruginoso-a, rel. al hierro o que lo contiene.

fertile *a.* fértil, fecundo-a, productivo-a.

fertility *n.* fertilidad.

fertilization *n.* fertilización, fecundación.

fertilize *v.* fecundar, hacer fértil.

fertilizer *n.* fertilizante.

fester *v.* enconarse; supurar superficialmente.

fetal *a.* fetal, rel. al feto; ___ **alcohol syndrome** / síndrome alcohólico ___; ___ **circulation** / circulación ___; ___ **drug syndrome** / síndrome ___ del abuso de droga; ___ **heart tone** / latido del corazón ___; ___ **growth retardation** / retardo del crecimiento ___; ___ **maturity, chronologic** / edad gestacional; ___ **monitoring** / monitorización ___; ___ **transfusion** / transfusión de sangre *in utero;* ___ **viability** / viabilidad ___.

feticide *n.* feticidio, destrucción del feto en el útero.

fetid *a.* fétido-a, hediondo-a, de mal olor.

fetish *n.* fetiche.

fetoprotein *n.* fetoproteína, antígeno presente en el feto humano.

fetor *n.* fetor, mal olor, hedor.

fetoscope *n.* fetoscopio, instrumento usado para visualizar al feto y facilitar diagnosis prenatales.

fetus *n.* feto, embrión en desarrollo, fase de la gestación desde los tres meses hasta el parto.

fever *n.* fiebre, calentura; ___ **blister** / herpes febril; **enteric** ___ / ___ entérica, intestinal; ___ **of unknown origin** (FUO) / ___ de origen desconocido; **intermittent** ___ / ___ intermitente; **rabbit** ___ / ___ de conejo, tularemia; **rheumatoid** ___ / ___ reumatoidea; **remittent** ___ / ___ remitente; **Rocky Mountain** ___ / ___ manchada de las Montañas Rocosas; **scarlet** ___ / escarlatina; **yellow** ___ / ___ amarilla,

paludismo, malaria; **typhoid** ___ / ___ tifoidea; **undulant** ___ / brucelosis.

fiber *n.* fibra, filamento en forma de hilo.

fiberoptic *a.* fibróptico, rel. a las fibras ópticas.

fiberoptics *n. pl.* fibras ópticas, filamentos flexibles de cristal o plástico que conducen una imagen transmitida.

fibril *n.* filamento, fibrilla, fibra pequeña.

fibrillar, fibrillary *a.* fibrilar, rel. a una fibra.

fibrillation *n.* fibrilación. 1. contracción muscular involuntaria que afecta fibras musculares individuales; 2. formación de fibrillas; **atrial** ___ / ___ auricular; **flutter** ___ / ___ de aleteo; **ventricular** ___ / ___ ventricular.

fibrin *n.* fibrina, proteína insoluble indispensable en la coagulación de la sangre.

fibrinogen *n.* fibrinógeno. 1. proteína presente en el plasma sanguíneo que se convierte en fibrina en el proceso de coagulación; 2. el Factor I.

fibrinogenolysis *n.* fibrinogenólisis, disolución o inactivación del fibrinógeno en la corriente sanguínea.

fibrinolysis *n.* fibrinólisis, disolución de fibrina por la acción de enzimas.

fibrinolytic *a.* fibrinolítico-a, rel. a la desintegración de fibrina.

fibrinous, fibrous *a.* fibrinoso-a, fibroso-a. 1. rel. a la naturaleza de una fibra; 2. semejante a un hilo.

fibroadenoma *n.* fibroadenoma, tumor benigno formado por tejido fibroso y glandular.

fibroblast *n.* fibroblasto, células de soporte de las que proviene el tejido conectivo.

fibrocartilage *n.* fibrocartílago, tipo de cartílago en el que la matriz contiene abundante tejido fibroso.

fibrocyst *n.* fibroquiste. 1. fibroma formado por quistes; 2. neoplasma de degeneración cística.

fibrocystic *a.* fibrocístico-a, fibroquístico-a, de naturaleza fibrosa con degeneración cística; ___ **disease of the breast** / enfermedad ___ de la mama.

fibrocystoma *n.* fibrocistoma, tumor benigno con elementos císticos.

fibroid *a.* fibroide, de naturaleza fibrosa.

fibrolipoma *n.* fibrolipoma, tumor que contiene tejido fibroso y adiposo en exceso.

fibroma *n.* fibroma, tumor benigno compuesto de tejido fibroso.

fibromuscular *a.* fibromuscular, de naturaleza muscular y fibrosa; ___ **dysplasia** / displasia

fibromyoma *n.* fibromioma, tumor benigno formado por tejido muscular y fibroso.

fibroplasia *n.* fibroplasia, producción de tejido fibroso tal como en la cicatrización de una herida.

fibrosis *n.* fibrosis, formación anormal de tejido fibroso; **diffuse interstitial pulmonary** ___ / ___ intersticial del pulmón; **proliferative** ___ / ___ proliferativa; **retroperineal** ___ / ___

retroperineal.

fibrositis n. fibrositis, infl. de tejido blanco conjuntivo esp. en el área de las articulaciones.

fibrotic a. fibrótico-a, rel. a la fibrosis.

fibula a. peroné, el hueso más externo y más delgado de la pierna.

fictitious a. ficticio-a, falso-a.

fidelity n. fidelidad, lealtad; precisión.

field n. campo. 1. área o espacio abierto; ___ of vision / ___ visual; 2. área de especialización.

fight n. pelea, lucha; vi. pelear, combatir, luchar con.

figure n. figura; cifra, número.

filament n. filamento, fibra o hilo fino.

file n. [instrument] lima; [record] expediente, ficha; v. limar, suavizar; clasificar.

fill v. llenar; rellenar; llenarse.

filling n. [dental] empaste; obturación; restauración.

film n. 1. película; radiografía; 2. telilla, membrana o capa fina.

filter n. filtro; v. filtrar; **to ___ through** / filtrarse.

filth n. suciedad, immundicias, mugre; H. A. cochinada.

filthy a. sucio-a, mugriento-a, mugroso-a.

filtration n. filtración, colación, acción de pasar a través de un filtro.

fimbria n. (pl. **fimbriae**) fimbria, borde o canto; apéndice de ciertas bacterias.

final a. final, último-a; conclusivo-a; definitivo-a.

financial a. financiero-a, monetario-a; ___ **expenses** / gastos ___-s; ___ **income** / ingresos, honorarios; ___ **responsibility** / solvencia, capacidad ___; **-ly** adv. ___ **responsible** / persona solvente, persona responsable de los gastos.

find vi. hallar, encontrar, descubrir.

findings n. pl. hallazgos, resultados de una investigación o indagación.

fine a. fino-a, delicado-a; v. **to feel ___** / sentirse bien.

finger n. dedo de la mano; **first ___** / dedo índice; **little ___** / dedo meñique; **mallet ___** / dedo en martillo; ___**-shaped** / digitiforme.

fingernail n. uña.

fingerprint n. impresión, huella digital; v. tomar las impresiones digitales; ___ **expert** / dactiloscopista.

finish n. final, terminación; v. acabar, terminar.

finished a. acabado-a, terminado-a.

finite a. finito-a, que tiene límites.

fire n. fuego; [conflagration] incendio; ___ **alarm** / alarma de ___; ___ **department** / cuerpo de bomberos; ___ **escape** / escalera de ___; v. **to catch ___** / encenderse, prenderse; **to set ___ to** / encender, quemar.

firearm n. arma de fuego.

firm a. firme, fijo-a, consistente.

first n. primero-a; a. primero-a, primer (before a m. singular n.) ___ **degree** / de primer grado; ___ **name** / nombre de pila.

first aid n. primeros auxilios; ___ **kit** / botiquín de ___.

firstborn n. primogénito-a.

fish n. (pl. **fish**) pez; [fish caught] pescado.

fish poisoning n. intoxicación de pescado.

fission n. fisión. 1. división en partes. 2. división de un átomo para ser descompuesto y desplazar energía y neutrones.

fissure n. fisura. V. **cleft**.

fist n. puño; v. **to make a ___** / cerrar el ___.

fistula n. fístula, canal o pasaje anormal que permite el paso de secreciones de una cavidad a otra o a la superficie exterior; **anal ___** / ___ anal; **arteriovenous ___** / ___ arteriovenosa; **biliary ___** / ___ biliar.

fistulization n. fistulización, formación de una fístula por un medio quirúrgico o patológico súbito.

fistulous a. fistuloso-a, rel. a una fístula.

fit n. ataque súbito; convulsión; a. [suitable] adecuado-a: vi. [glasses] ajustar, encajar, montar.

fitness n. aptitud, vigor físico, acondicionamiento físico; **physical ___** / ___ física.

fix v. [fasten] fijar, asegurar; **to fix up** / arreglar; convenir.

fixation n. fijación. 1. inmovilización de una parte; 2. acción de fijar la vista en un objeto; 3. psic. interrupción del desarrollo de la personalidad antes de alcanzar la madurez.

fixative n. fijador, sustancia usada para endurecer muestras de exámenes patológicos.

fixed a. fijo-a; decidido-a [resolved] resuelto; arreglado-a, determinado-a; compuesto-a; ___ **fee** / honorario ___ o definido; ___ **term** / plazo ___.

flabby a. blando-a, flojo-a; pop. fofo-a.

flaccid a. flácido-a; débil, flojo-a; ___ **paralysis** / parálisis ___.

flagellated a. flagelado-a, provisto de flagelo o flagelos.

flagelliform n. flageliforme, en forma de látigo.

flagellum n. (pl. **flagella**) flagelo, prolongación o cola en la célula de algunos protozoos.

flail chest n. tórax inestable, condición de la pared del tórax causada por la fractura múltiple de costillas.

flake n. escama; copo; **snow ___-s** / copos de nieve.

flaky a. escamoso-a.

flank n. flanco, parte del cuerpo entre las costillas y el borde superior del íleo.

flap n. [sound of wings] aleteo; sonido de alas; cubierta; colgajo.

flare n. brote, irritación rosácea o área difundida; destello, fulgor; ___**-up** / ___ con irritación; v. brotar, irritar.

flash n. fulguración, destello; **hot ___** / fogaje, rubor.

flashback n. retrogresión; retroversión; psic. retrospección y actualización de imágenes pasadas.

flashlight n. linterna eléctrica.

flask n. frasco, pomo.

flat a. plano-a, llano-a; extendido-a.

flatfoot *n.* pie plano.

flatulence *n.* flatulencia, distensión y molestias abdominales por exceso de gas en el tracto gastrointestinal.

flatus *n.* flato, *pop.* aventación, gas o aire en los intestinos.

flatworm *n.* gusano plano que se aloja en los intestinos.

flavor *n.* sabor, gusto.

flaw *n.* falta, defecto, falla.

flea *n.* pulga, insecto chupador de sangre; ___ **bite** / picadura de ___.

flesh *n.* carne, tejido muscular suave del cuerpo; ___ **wound** / herida superficial.

fleshless *a.* descarnado-a.

flex *v.* flexionar, doblar.

flexibility *n.* flexibilidad, propiedad de flexionar.

flexion *n.* flexión, acto de flexionar o de ser flexionado.

flexor *n.* flexor, músculo que hace flexionar una articulación.

flexure *n.* flexura, pliegue o doblez de una estructura u órgano; **hepatic** ___ / ___ hepática, ángulo derecho del colon; **sigmoid** ___ / sigmoidea, curvatura del colon que antecede al recto; **splenic** ___ / ___ esplénica, ángulo izquierdo del colon.

flicker *v.* fluctuar, vacilar; [*to quiver*] oscilar; causar una sensación visual de contraste con interrupción de la luz.

flight *n.* escape, fuga; vuelo; trayectoria; viaje aéreo.

flight of ideas *n. psic.* fuga de ideas, interrupciones en el pensamiento y la expresión de palabras.

float *n.* flotador; *v.* flotar.

floaters *n. pl.* flotadores, manchas visuales, máculas.

floating *a.* flotante, libre, sin adhesión; ___ **ribs** / costillas ___-s.

flocculation *n.* floculación, precipitación o aglomeración en forma de copos de partículas usu. invisibles.

floor *n.* piso, suelo.

flora *n.* flora, grupo de bacterias que se alojan en un órgano; **intestinal** ___ / ___ intestinal.

florid *a.* florido-a; encarnado-a; de color rojo vivo.

floss *n.* seda floja; **dental** ___ / hilo dental.

flour *n.* harina.

flow *n.* flujo, salida; riego; [*menstrual*] *pop.* pérdida; *v.* fluir; correr; derramar; **blood** ___ / riego sanguíneo; **laminar** ___ / ___ laminar; **turbulent** ___ / ___ turbulento.

flower *n.* flor, órgano reproductor de la planta.

flowmeter *n.* medidor de flujo.

fluctuate *v.* fluctuar, cambiar.

fluctuation *n.* fluctuación. 1. acto de fluctuar, variación de un curso a otro; 2. sensación de movimiento ondulante producido por líquidos en el cuerpo que se percibe en un examen de palpación.

Fluids	*Líquido, fluido*
amniotic	amniótico
cerebrospinal	cerebroespinal
extracellular	extracelular
extravascular	extravascular
interstitial	intersticial
intracellular	intracelular
seminal	seminal
serous	seroso
synovial	sinovial

fluid *n.* líquido, fluido; secreción; **amniotic** ___ / ___ amniótico; **cerebrospinal** ___ / ___ cerebroespinal; **extracellular** ___ / ___ extracelular; **extravascular** ___ / ___ extravascular; **interstitial** ___ / ___ intersticial; **intracellular** ___ / ___ intracelular; **seminal** ___ / ___ seminal; **serous** ___ / ___ seroso; **synovial** ___ / ___ sinovial.

fluid balance *n.* balance hídrico.

fluid retention *n.* retención de líquido.

fluke *n.* duela, gusano de la orden *Trematoda*; **blood** ___ / ___ sanguínea; **intestinal** ___ / ___ intestinal; **liver** ___ / ___ hepática; **lung** ___ / ___ pulmonar.

fluorescence *n.* fluorescencia, propiedad de emisión de luminosidad de ciertas sustancias cuando son expuestas a cierto tipo de radiación, tal como los rayos X.

fluorescent *a.* fluorescente, rel. a la fluorescencia; ___ **antibody** / anticuerpo ___; ___ **troponemal antibody absorption test** / técnica del anticuerpo ___.

fluoridation *n.* fluoridización, adición de fluoruro al agua.

fluoride *n.* fluoruro, combinación de flúor con un metal o metaloide.

fluorine *n.* flúor, elemento químico gaseoso.

fluoroscope *n.* fluoroscopio, instrumento que hace visibles los rayos X en una pantalla fluorescente.

fluoroscopy *n.* fluoroscopía, uso del fluoroscopio para examinar los tejidos y otras estructuras internas del cuerpo.

fluorosis *n.* fluorosis, exceso de absorción de flúor.

flush *n.* rubor; [*cleansing*] irrigación; [*to empty out*] vaciar; irrigar; ruborizarse, sonrojarse.

flutter *n.* aleteo, acción similar al movimiento de las alas de los pájaros; **atrial** ___ / ___ auricular; **ventricular** ___ / ___ ventricular; ___ **and fibrillation** / fibrilación y ___; *v.* aletear, sacudir; agitarse.

flux *n.* flujo excesivo proveniente de una cavidad u órgano del cuerpo.

fly *n.* mosca; *vi.* volar.

foam *n.* espuma.

focal *a.* focal, rel. a un foco.

focus *n.* (*pl.* **foci**) foco; *v.* enfocar.

fold *n.* pliegue de un margen; **aryepiglottic** ___ /

___ ariepiglótico; **gastric** ___ / ___ gástrico; **gluteal** ___ / ___ glúteo.

folic acid *n.* ácido fólico, miembro del complejo de vitaminas B.

follicle *n.* folículo, saco, bolsa, depresión o cavidad excretora; **atretic** ___ / ___ atrésico; **gastric** ___ / ___ gástrico; **hair** ___ / ___ piloso; **ovarian** ___ / ___ ovárico; **thyroid** ___ / ___ tiroideo.

follicular *a.* folicular, rel. a un folículo; ___ **phase** / fase ___.

folliculitis *n.* foliculitis, infl. de un folículo, gen. un folículo piloso.

follow *v.* seguir, continuar; ___-up / acción continuada, seguimiento, (estudio, procedimiento del caso); ___-up evaluation / evaluación del proceso evolutivo; **to** ___ **through** / continuar el procedimiento; llevar hasta el final; continuar la observación de un caso.

fomes *L.* (*pl.* **fomites**) fomes, cualquier sustancia que puede absorber y luego transmitir agentes infecciosos.

fontanel, fontanella *n.* fontanela, *pop.* mollera, parte suave en el cráneo del recién nacido que normalmente se cierra al desarrollarse los huesos craneales.

food *n.* alimento; comida; ___ **additives** / aditivos alimenticios; ___ **contamination** / contaminación de ___-s; ___ **handling** / manipulación de ___-s; ___ **poisoning** / intoxicación alimenticia; ___ **requirements** / requisitos alimenticios; ___ **supplements** / alimentos enriquecidos.

foolishness *n.* tontería, bobería.

foot *n.* (*pl.* **feet**) pie; **athlete's** ___ / ___ de atleta; **flat** ___ / ___ plano.

foot-drop *n.* pie caído.

footprint *n.* impresión o huella del pie, pisada.

footsore *a.* que presenta molestia o dolor en el pie.

footstep *n.* paso, pisada; [*print*] huella del pie.

for *prep.* [*intended for the use of*] para, **the medicine is** ___ **the patient** / la medicina es ___ el paciente; [*for the purpose of*] para; **a thermometer** ___ **taking the temperature** / un termómetro ___ tomar la temperatura; [*for the benefit of*] para; **an antibiotic** ___ **the infection** / un antibiótico ___ la infección; [*in exchange for*] por; **you pay a dollar** ___ **each pill** / paga un dólar ___ cada pastilla; [*for the sake of*] por; **do it** ___ **her** / hágalo, hazlo ___ ella; ___ **the time being** / ___ ahora, ___ el momento.

foramen *n.* foramen, orificio, pasaje, abertura; **intervertebral** ___ / ___ intervertebral; **jugular** ___ / ___ yugular; **optic** ___ / ___ óptico; **ovale** ___ / ___ oval; **sciatic, greater** ___ / ___ sacrociático mayor; **sciatic, lesser** ___ / ___ sacrociático menor.

forbid *vi* prohibir, impedir; **God** ___! / ¡no lo permita Dios!

force *n.* fuerza, vigor, energía; *v.* forzar, violentar, obligar; *v.* **to** ___ **out** / echar a la fuerza; **to** ___ **through** / hacer penetrar a la fuerza.

forceps *n. pl.* fórceps, pinza en forma de tenaza que se emplea para sujetar y manipular tejidos o partes del cuerpo.

forearm *n.* antebrazo.

forebrain *n.* prosencéfalo, porción anterior de la vesícula primaria cerebral de donde se desarrollan el diencéfalo y el telencéfalo.

forecast *n.* pronóstico, predicción; *v.* predecir, pronosticar.

forefinger *n.* dedo índice.

forefoot *n.* antepié, parte anterior del pie.

foregut *n.* intestino anterior, porción cefálica del tubo digestivo primitivo en el embrión.

forehead *n.* frente.

foreign *a.* extranjero-a; extraño-a.

foreign bodies *n. pl.* cuerpos extraños, máculas, materia o pequeños objetos ajenos al lugar en que se alojan.

forensic *a.* forense, rel. a asuntos legales; ___ **laboratory** / laboratorio ___; ___ **medicine** / medicina legal; ___ **physician** / médico ___.

foreplay *n.* estímulo erótico que precede al acto sexual.

foresee *vi.* prever; prevenir

foreseen *a. pp.* de **to foresee,** previsto-a.

foresight *n.* precaución, previsión.

foreskin *n.* prepucio. *V.* **prepuce.**

forever *adv.* siempre, para siempre, por siempre.

forge *v.* falsificar, falsear

forger *n.* falsificador, -a, falsario-a.

forget *vi.* olvidar; olvidarse de; ___ **it** / olvídese, olvídate de eso; no se preocupe, no te preocupes.

forgetful *a.* olvidadizo-a; negligente.

forgive *vi.* perdonar.

fork *n.* tenedor; bifurcación.

forked *a.* bifurcado-a.

form *n.* forma; [*document*] formulario; *v.* formar, dar forma; establecer.

formaldehyde *n.* formaldehído, antiséptico.

formalin *n.* formalina, solución compuesta de formaldehído.

formation *n.* formación; composición; conjunto.

forme fruste *Fr.* forma frustrada, enfermedad abortada o manifestada de manera atípica.

formication *n.* formicación, sensación de hormigueo en la piel.

formula *n.* fórmula, forma prescrita o modelo a seguir.

fornix *L.* (*pl.* **fornices**) fornix. 1. estructura en forma de arco; 2. concavidad en forma de bóveda semejante a la vagina.

forth *adv.* [*forward*] hacia adelante; [*out, away*] afuera, hacia afuera.

forthcoming *a.* venidero-a; disponible.

fortify *v.* fortalecer, fortificar.

fossa *n.* (*pl.* **fossae**) fosa, cavidad, hueco, depresión; ___, **glenoid** / ___ glenoidea; ___, **interpeduncular** / ___ interpeduncular; ___, **jugular** / ___ yugular; ___, **mandibular** / ___ mandibular; ___, **nasal** / ___ nasal; ___, **navicular** / ___ navicular.

fourchette *Fr.* horquilla, comisura posterior de la vulva.

fovea *n.* fóvea, fosa o depresión pequeña, esp. en referencia a la fosa central de la retina.

foxglove *n.* dedalera, nombre común de *Digitalis purpurea*.

fraction *n.* fracción, parte separable de una unidad.

fracture *n.* fractura, rotura; *pop.* quebradura; **avulsion** ___ / ___ por avulsión; **blow-out** ___ / ___ por estallamiento; **closed** ___ / ___ cerrada; **comminuted** ___ / ___ conminuta; **complete** ___ / ___ completa; **compression** ___ / ___ por compresión; **depressed** ___ / ___ con hundimiento; **dislocation** ___ / ___ por luxación; **greenstick** ___ / ___ en tallo verde o ___ de caña; **hairline** ___ / ___ de raya fina; **impacted** ___ / ___ impactada; **open** ___ / ___ expuesta; **pathologic** ___ / ___ patológica; **spiral** ___ / ___ en espiral; **stress** ___ / ___ por sobrecarga.

fracture *v.* fracturar, quebrar.

fragility *n.* fragilidad, con disposición a romperse o quebrarse con facilidad.

fragment *n.* fragmento, parte; *v.* fragmentar, romper, dividir en pedazos.

frambesia, yaws *n.* frambesia, enfermedad cutánea tropical infecciosa que se manifiesta con lesiones aframbuesadas ulcerosas.

frame *n.* armazón. estructura de soporte; [*eyeglasses*] armazón.

frank *a.* obvio-a, rel. a una condición física presente.

frantic *a.* frenético-a.

fraternal twins *n. pl.* mellizos fraternales, desarrollados de dos óvulos fecundados separadamente.

freckle *n.* peca, mácula pigmentada que se manifiesta en el exterior de la piel esp. en la cara.

freckled *a.* pecoso-a.

free *a.* libre, suelto-a; [*of charge*] gratis; ___ **asso-ciation** / ___ asociación; **-ly** *adv.* libremente.

freedom *n.* libertad, independencia; *v.* **to have** ___ **to** / tener ___ para.

freeze *n.* helada; congelación; ___ **drying** / secar por congelación; *vi.* congelar, helar; congelarse, helarse; **to** ___ **to death** / morirse de frío.

freezing *n.* congelación; ___ **point** / punto de ___.

fremitus *n.* fremitus, frémito, vibración detectable por palpación o auscultación tal como las vibraciones del pecho al toser.

French *n.* [*language*] francés; [*native*] francés, francesa; *a.* francés, francesa.

frenectomy *n. cirg.* frenectomía, excisión de un frenillo.

frenulum, frenum *L.* (*pl.* **frenulla**) frenulum, pliegue membranoso que impide los movimientos de un órgano o parte; ___ **of the tongue** / frenillo de la lengua.

frenzy *n.* locura, frenesí, extravío, arrebato.

frequency *n.* frecuencia.

frequent *a.* frecuente, habitual, regular; **-ly** *adv.* frecuentemente, con frecuencia.

fresh *a.* fresco-a, reciente.

freshen *v.* refrescar; renovar; refrescarse; renovarse.

Freudian *a.* freudiano, *psic.* rel. a las doctrinas de Sigmund Freud, neurólogo vienés (1856–1939).

friable *a.* friable, que se pulveriza o rompe fácilmente.

friction *n.* fricción, rozamiento; ___ **rub** / roce de ___.

fried *a. pp.* de **to fry**, frito-a.

fright *n.* espanto, temor excesivo.

frightened *a.* asustado-a, atemorizado-a.

frigid *a.* frígido-a.

frigidity *n.* frígidez, frialdad, esp. de la mujer incapaz de responder a estímulos sexuales.

frivolous *a.* frívolo-a; tonto-a; vano-a.

Frohlich's syndrome *n.* síndrome de Frolich, distrofia adipogenital manifestada en infantilismo sexual con cambios en las características sexuales secundarias.

front *n.* frente; **in** ___ **of** / en ___ de, delante de.

frontal *a.* frontal, rel. a la frente; ___ **bone** / hueso ___; ___ **muscle** / músculo ___; ___ **sinuses** / senos ___-es.

frost *n.* escarcha, helada.

frostbite *n.* quemadura por frío.

froth *n.* espuma; *v.* echar espuma, espumar; **to** ___ **at the mouth** / echar ___ por la boca.

frozen *a. pp.* de **to freeze**, congelado-a; *v.* **to become** ___ / congelarse, helarse.

frozen section *n. cirg.* corte por congelación, espécimen de tejido fino que se toma y congela inmediatamente para ser usado en el diagnóstico de tumores.

fructose *n.* fructosa, azúcar de frutas; lebulosa.

fruit *n.* fruta; *v.* **to eat** ___ **-s** / comer ___-s.

fruitful *a.* productivo-a; provechoso-a.

Bone Fractures	Fracturas óseas
avulsion	por avulsión
blow-out	por estallamiento
closed	cerrada
comminuted	conminuta
complete	completa
compressed	por compresión
depressed	con hundimiento
greenstick	de tallo verde
hairline	de raya fina
impacted	impactada
open	expuesta
pathologic	patológica
spiral	espiral
stress	de sobrecarga

fry *v.* freír.

fulfill *v.* cumplir; llevar a cabo; realizar.

fulguration *n.* fulgaración, uso de corriente eléctrica para destruir tejido vivo.

full *a.* completo-a; lleno-a, pleno-a; **in full** / completamente, por completo; ___ **answer** / respuesta ___; ___ **payment** / pago total.

full-grown *a.* completamente desarrollado-a; crecido-a.

full term *n.* a término, [*in obstetrics*] embarazo a término, de 38 a 41 semanas de duración incluyendo el nacimiento.

fulminant *a.* fulminante, que aparece súbitamente con extrema intensidad tal como un dolor o enfermedad.

fume *v.* humear, emitir vapores o gases.

fumes *n. pl.* vapores.

fumigant *n.* fumigante, agente usado en la fumigación.

fumigation *n.* fumigación, exterminación por medio de vapores.

fuming *a.* fumante, que desprende vapores visibles.

fun *n.* diversión, entretenimiento; *v.* **to have** ___ / divertirse, entretenerse.

function *n.* función; facultad; *v.* funcionar, desempeñar un trabajo.

functional *a.* funcional, de utilidad o valor práctico.

functional disease *n.* enfermedad funcional, desorden o trastorno que no tiene una causa orgánica conocida.

functioning *n.* funcionamiento.

fundus *n.* fondo, la parte más distante al orificio de entrada de un órgano; ___ **of stomach** / ___ del estómago; ___ **uteri** / ___ del útero.

funeral *n.* funeral, entierro; ___ **parlor** / funeraria.

fungal, fungous *a.* fungoso-a, rel. a hongos o causado por éstos.

fungate *v.* reproducirse rápidamente como los hongos.

fungemia *n.* fungemia, presencia de hongos en la sangre.

fungicide *n.* fungicida, exterminador de hongos.

fungistasis *n.* fungistasis, acto de impedir o arrestar el desarrollo de hongos.

fungus *n.* (*pl.* **fungi**) hongo.

funnel *n.* embudo.

furious *a.* furioso-a; enfurecido-a.

furor *n.* furor, ira extrema.

furosemide *n.* furosemida, diurético.

furuncle *n.* furúnculo; *pop.* grano enterrado.

furunculous *a.* foruncular, rel. a un forúnculo.

fuse *v.* fundir, fusionar, derretir un metal por medio de calor.

fusiform *a.* fusiforme, en forma de huso.

fusion *n.* fusión. 1. reacción termonuclear en la cual núcleos atómicos de luz se unen para formar átomos más potentes; 2. acto de fusionar o fundir; **nuclear** ___ / ___ nuclear.

future *n.* futuro, porvenir.

fuzzy *a.* 1. nublado-a, que no es claramente visible; 2. velloso-a; cubierto de pelusa.

G *abbr.* **constant of gravitation** / constante de gravitación.

g *abbr.* **gender** / género; **glucose** / glucosa; **grain** / grano.

gadfly *n.* tábano, moscardón; moscón.

gag *n.* abrebocas, instrumento para mantener la boca abierta durante ciertas intervenciones quirúrgicas; ___ **reflex** / reflejo de **arqueada.**

gage *v.* medir, calibrar.

gain *n.* ganancia, ventaja; provecho; *v.* ganar; **to** ___ **weight** / aumentar de peso.

gainful *a.* ventajoso-a, provechoso-a.

gait *n.* marcha, andar; **abnormal** ___ / porte, paso irregular; ___, **ataxic** / ___ atáxica, tambaleante; ___, **cerebellar** / ___ cerebelosa, andar tambaleante, relacionado con trastornos cerebrales; ___, **hemiplegic** / ___ hemiplégica, movimiento semicircular de una de las extremidades inferiores al andar; ___, **spastic** / ___ espasmódica, andar rígido; ___, **waddling** / ___ anserina, de pies excesivamente separados al andar, *pop.* andar de pato.

galactagogue *n.* galactagogo, galactógeno, agente que promueve la secreción de leche.

galactase *n.* galactasa, enzima presente en la leche.

galactocele *n.* galactocele, quiste de la mama que contiene leche.

galactose *n.* galactosa, monosacárido derivado de la lactosa por acción de una enzima o un ácido mineral.

galactosemia *n.* galactosemia, ausencia congénita de la enzima necesaria para la conversión de galactosa a glucosa o sus derivados.

galactosuria *n.* galactosuria, orina con apariencia lechosa.

galactotherapy *n.* galactoterapia. 1. tratamiento dirigido a un lactante mediante administración de medicamentos a la madre; 2. uso terapéutico de la leche en una dieta especial.

gall *n.* bilis, hiel; ___ **ducts** / conductos biliares.

gallbladder *n.* vesícula biliar; ___ **attack** / ataque de la vesícula.

gallium *n.* galio, metal.

gallop rhythm *n.* ritmo de galope, sonido anormal del corazón percibido en casos de taquicardia.

gallstone *n.* cálculo biliar.

galvanic *a.* galvánico-a, rel. al galvanismo; ___ **battery** / batería; ___ **cell** / célula ___; ___ **current** / corriente ___.

galvanism *n.* galvanismo, uso terapéutico de corriente eléctrica directa.

galvanocautery *n.* galvanocauterización. *V.* **electrocautery.**

galvanometer *n.* galvanómetro, instrumento que mide la corriente por acción electro-magnética.

gamete *n.* gameto, célula sexual masculina o femenina.

gametocide *n.* gametocida, agente que destruye gametos.

gametocyte *n.* gametocito, célula que al dividirse produce gametos tal como el parásito de la malaria cuando se divide y pasa al mosquito portador.

gametogenesis *n.* gametogénesis, desarrollo de gametos.

gamma benzene hexachloride *n.* hexacloruro de gamma-benceno, insecticida poderoso utilizado contra la sarna.

gamma globulin *n.* gamma globulina, tipo de anticuerpo producido en el tejido linfático o sintéticamente.

gammagraphy *n.* gammagrafía, registro de rayos gamma después de la administración de isótopos radioactivos.

gamma rays *n. pl.* rayos gamma, rayos emitidos por sustancias radioactivas.

gammopathy *n.* gammopatía, trastorno manifestado por un exceso de inmunoglobulinas como resultado de una proliferación anormal de células linfoides.

gangliectomy *n. cirg.* gangliectomía, ganglionectomía, excisión de un ganglio.

gangliocyte *n.* gangliocito, célula ganglionar.

ganglioglioma *n.* ganglioglioma, ganglioneuroma, tumor caracterizado por un gran número de células ganglionares.

ganglioma *n.* ganglioma, tumor de un ganglio, esp. linfático.

ganglion *n.* (*pl.* **ganglia**) ganglio. 1. masa de tejido nervioso en forma de nudo; 2. quiste de un tendón o en una aponeurosis, que se observa a veces en la muñeca, en el talón o en la rodilla; ___, **celiac** / ___ celíaco; ___**-a, basal** / ___**-s basales**; ___ **carotid** / ___ carotídeo.

ganglionic blockade *n.* bloqueo ganglionar.

gangrene *n.* gangrena, destrucción de un tejido debido a riego sanguíneo interrumpido gen. por infección bacteriana y putrefacción.

Gantrisin *n.* Gantricin, nombre comercial de sulfisoxazol, agente antibacteriano usado en el tratamiento de infecciones urinarias.

gap *n.* laguna, vacío; intervalo, abertura.

gargle *n.* gargarización; *v.* hacer gárgaras.

gargoylism *n.* gargolismo, condición hereditaria caracterizada por anormalidades físicas, en algunos casos con retraso mental.

garlic *n.* ajo.

gas *n.* gas, sustancia con propiedades de expansión indefinida; **mustard** ___ / ___ de mostaza; **nerve** ___ / ___ neurotóxico; **tear** ___ / ___ lacrimógeno.

gaseous *a.* gaseoso-a, rel. a o de la naturaleza del gas.

gasoline *n.* gasolina; ___ **poisoning** / envenenamiento por ___.

gastralgia *n.* gastralgia, dolor de estómago.

gastrectomy *n. cirg.* gastrectomía, extirpación de una parte o de todo el estómago.

gastric *a.* gástrico-a, rel. o concerniente al estómago; ___ **acid** / ácido ___; ___ **analysis** / gastroanálisis; ___ **digestion** / digestión ___; ___ **emptying** / vaciamiento ___; ___ **juice** / jugo ___; ___ **lavage** / lavado ___; ___ **ulcer** / úlcera ___.

gastrin *n.* gastrina, hormona segregada por el estómago.

gastritis *n.* gastritis, infl. del estómago; **acute** ___ / ___ aguda; **chronic** ___ / ___ crónica.

gastrocolostomy *n. cirg.* gastrocolostomía, anastomosis del estómago y el colon.

gastroduodenal *a.* gastroduodenal, rel. al estómago y el duodeno.

gastroduodenoscopy *n.* gastroduodenoscopía, uso del endoscopio para examinar visualmente el estómago y el duodeno.

gastroenteroanastomosis *n. cirg.* gastroenteroanastomosis, unión quirúrgica del estómago al intestino delgado.

gastroenterocolitis *n.* gastroenterocolitis, infl. del estómago y el intestino delgado.

gastroepiploic *a.* gastroepiploico-a, rel. al estómago y el epiplón.

gastroesophagitis *n.* gastroesofagitis. *V.* **esophagogastritis.**

gastrogavage *n.* gastrogavaje, alimentación artificial al estómago por tubo o a través de una abertura.

gastroileostomy *n. cirg.* gastroileostomía, anastomosis entre el estómago y el íleo.

gastrointestinal *a.* gastrointestinal, rel. al estómago y el intestino; ___ **barrier** / barrera ___; ___ **bleeding** / sangramiento ___; ___ **decompression** / descompresión ___.

gastrojejunostomy *n. cirg.* gastroyeyunostomía, anastomosis del estómago y el yeyuno.

gastrorrhagia *n.* gastrorragia, hemorragia estomacal.

gastrostomy *n. cirg.* gastrostomía, creación de una fístula gástrica.

gastrula *n.* gástrula, etapa primitiva del desarrollo embriónico.

gauze *n.* gasa: **absorbable** ___ / ___ absorbible; **absorbent** ___ / ___ absorbente; **antiseptic** ___ / ___ antiséptica; ___ **compress** / compresa de ___.

gel *n.* jalea.

gelatin *n.* gelatina.

gelatinous *a.* gelatinoso-a, de consistencia semejante a la gelatina o que la contiene.

gender *n.* género, denominación del sexo masculino o femenino.

gene *n.* gen, gene, unidad básica de rasgos hereditarios; **dominant** ___ / ___ dominante; ___ **frequency** / frecuencia del ___; **lethal** ___ / ___ letal; **recessive** ___ / ___ recesivo; **sex-linked** ___ / ___ ligado al sexo.

general *a.* general; ___ **appearance** / aspecto ___; ___ **condition** / estado ___; ___ **treatment** / tratamiento ___; ___ **practitioners** / médicos de familia.

generalization *n.* generalización.

generalize *v.* generalizar.

generation *n.* generación. 1. acción de crear un nuevo organismo; 2. producción por proceso natural o artificial; 3. conjunto de personas nacidas dentro de un período de unos treinta años aproximadamente.

generator *n.* generador, máquina que convierte energía mecánica en eléctrica.

generic *n.* nombre común de un producto o medicamento no patentado; *a.* genérico-a, rel. al género; ___ **name** / nombre genérico.

genesis *n.* génesis, acto de creación, reproducción y desarrollo.

genetic *a.* genético-a, rel. a la génesis y a la genética; ___ **code** / patrón ___; ___ **counseling** / asesoramiento ___; ___ **engineering** / construcción ___; ___ **marker** / marcador ___; ___ **substrate** / substrato ___.

genetics *n.* genética, rama de la biología que estudia la herencia y las leyes que la gobiernan; **medical** ___ / ___ médica.

genioplasty *n. cirg.* genioplastia, reconstrucción plástica de la mandíbula.

genital *a.* genital, rel. a los genitales; ___ **herpes** / herpes ___.

genitals, genitalia *n. pl.* genitales, órganos de la reproducción.

genocide *n.* genocidio, exterminación sistemática de un grupo étnico.

genom, genome *n.* genoma, el conjunto básico completo de cromosomas haploides en un organismo.

genotype *n.* genotipo, constitución genética de un organismo.

gentamicin *n.* gentamicina, antibiótico efectivo en varios tipos de bacterias gram-negativas.

gentle *a.* suave, sutil, tierno-a; moderado-a; **-ly** *adv.* suavemente, sutilmente, tiernamente; moderadamente.

genucubital *a.* genucubital, rel. a los codos, las rodillas y su posición; ___ **position** / posición ___.

genuine *a.* auténtico-a, genuino-a; legítimo-a.

genupectoral *a.* genupectoral, rel. a las rodillas y el tórax y su posición; ___ **position** / posición ___.

genu valgum, knock knee *n.* genu valgum, curvatura anormal hacia adentro de las rodillas y separación de los tobillos al caminar que comienza en la infancia a causa de una deficiencia ósea.

genu varum, bow-leg *n.* piernas arqueadas, *pop.* zambo-a, curvatura anormal de las rodillas hacia afuera.

genus *n.* (*pl.* **genera**) género, categoría perteneciente a una clasificación biológica.

geographic tongue *n.* lengua geográfica, lengua caracterizada por áreas desnudas rodeadas de epitelio grueso que simulan áreas terrestres.

geophagia, geophagism, geophagy *n.* geofagia, geofagismo, propensión a comer sustancias terrosas tales como tierra o barro.

geriatrics *n.* geriatría, rama de la medicina que trata de las enfermedades y de los problemas que se manifiestan en la vejez.

germ *n.* germen, microorganismo o bacteria esp. causante de enfermedades.

German measles *n.* rubela, rubéola, *pop.* sarampión de tres días, infección viral benigna muy contagiosa en los niños de 3 a 10 años. Puede causar trastornos serios en el desarrollo del feto al contraerla la madre; ___ **vaccination** / vacunación antirubeólica.

germ-free *n.* axénico.

germinal *a.* germinal, rel. a o de la naturaleza de un germen o gérmenes; ___ **vesicle** / vesícula o núcleo ___.

germination *n.* germinación, brote de una planta o desarrollo de una persona o animal.

germinoma *n.* germinoma, neoplasma de tejido o células germinales usu. localizado en los testículos u ovarios.

geromorphism *n.* geromorfismo, senilidad prematura.

gerontology *n.* gerontología. *V.* **geriatrics.**

gestalt *n.* gestalt, *psic.* teoría que mantiene que la conducta responde a la percepción íntegra de una situación y no es posible analizarla atendiendo sólo a las partes componentes de la misma.

gestation *n.* embarazo, gestación, estado de gravidez. *V.* **pregnancy.**

gesticulate *v.* gesticular, expresar por medio de gestos o señas.

gesticulation *n.* gesticulación, seña, gesto, ademán.

gesture *n.* gesto, ademán.

get *vi.* obtener, adquirir, conseguir; [*communication*] **to** ___ **across** / lograr comunicarse, hacer comprender; **to** ___ **ahead** / prosperar; **to** ___ **back something** / recobrar; [*to return*] **to** ___ **back** / volver; [*to swallow*] **to** ___ **down** / tragar; [*steps*] **to** ___ **down** / bajar; **to** ___ **into** / meterse; **to** ___ **it over** / acabar de una vez; **to** ___ [*someone, something*] **out of the way** / sacar de, quitar de, apartar de; **to** ___ **sick** / enfermarse; **to** ___ **underway** / empezar, comenzar; **to** ___ **up** / levantarse; **to** ___ **well** / curarse, sanarse.

giant *a.* gigante, de un tamaño grande anormal; ___ **cell** / célula ___; ___ **cell tumor** / tumor de células ___-s.

giardiasis *n.* giardiasis, infección intestinal común causada por la *Giardia lamblia* que se trasmite por contaminación de alimentos, de agua o por contacto directo.

gibbosity *n.* gibosidad, corcova, condición de joroba.

Giemsa stain *n.* coloración de Giemsa, usada en frotis de sangre en análisis microscópicos.

gigantism *n.* gigantismo, desarrollo en exceso del cuerpo o de una parte de éste; ___, **acromegalic** / ___ acromegálico; ___, **eunuchoid** / ___ eunucoide, gigantismo acompañado de características e insuficiencia sexual propias del eunuco; ___, **normal** / ___ normal, desarrollo normal de los órganos sexuales y proporción normal de los órganos y partes del cuerpo, gen. causado por secreción excesiva de la glándula pituitaria.

Gimbernat's ligament *n.* ligamento de Gimbernat, membrana que se adhiere por un extremo al ligamento inguinal y por otro al pubis.

ginger *n.* jengibre.

gingiva *n.* (*pl.* **gingivae**) gingiva, encía, porción de tejido que rodea el cuello de los dientes.

gingivitis *n.* gingivitis, infl. de las encías.

girdle *n.* faja, cinturón; **pelvic** ___ / cinturón pélvico; **scapular or shoulder** ___ / cinturón torácico.

gitalin *n.* gitalina, glucósido extraído de la digitalis.

give *vi.* dar; ___ **birth** / dar a luz, estar de parto; **to** ___ **and take** / hacer concesiones mutuas; **to** ___ **out** / repartir; **to** ___ **up** / renunciar a, perder la esperanza; darse por vencido.

given *a., pp.* de **to give,** dado-a; ___ **name** / nombre de pila.

glacial *a.* glacial, rel. al. hielo o semejante al mismo.

glad *a.* alegre, contento-a; *v.* **to be** ___ **of** / alegrarse de; **to be** ___ **to** / tener mucho gusto en; **-ly** *adv.* con mucho gusto; con satisfacción; alegremente.

glance *n.* mirada, ojeada, vistazo; *v.* dar un vistazo, dar una ojeada; **at first** ___ / a primera vista.

gland *n.* glándula, órgano que segrega o secreta sustancias que realizan funciones fisiológicas específicas o que eliminan productos del organismo; **eccrine** ___ / ___ ecrina; **endocrine** ___ / ___ endocrina; **swollen** ___ / ___ inflamada.

glans *n.* glande, masa redonda de estructura similar a una glándula situada en la extremidad del pene (glans penis) y del clítoris (glans clitorides).

glare *n.* resplandor, deslumbramiento, relumbrón; resol., excesiva exposición a un objeto luminoso que puede resultar en daño permanente a la retina.

glaring *a.* deslumbrante, intenso-a; brillante.

Glasgow coma scale *n.* escala de coma de Glasgow, método para evaluar el grado de un estado de coma.

glass *n.* vidrio, cristal; **magnifying** ___ / lente de aumento.

glasses *n. pl.* lentes, espejuelos, gafas; **bifocal** ___ / ___ bifocales; **trifocal** ___ / ___ trifocales.

glaucoma *n.* glaucoma, enfermedad de los ojos producida por hipertensión del globo ocular, atrofia de la retina y ceguera; **absolutum** ___ / ___ absoluto, etapa final del glaucoma agudo que resulta en ceguera; **chronic** ___ / ___ crónico; **congential** ___ / ___ congénito; **juvenile** ___ / ___ juvenil, se manifiesta en niños mayores y jóvenes sin agrandamiento del globo ocular; **infantile** ___ / ___ infantil, se manifiesta a partir del nacimiento o desde los tres años.

glenohumeral *a.* glenohumeral, rel. al húmero y la cavidad glenoide.

glenoid *a.* glenoideo-a, con apariencia de fosa o cuenca; ___ **cavity** / cavidad ___; ___ **fossa** / fosa ___.

glia *n.* glía *V.* **neuroglia.**

gliacyte *n.* gliacito, célula de una neuroglía.

glide *v.* resbalar; deslizarse.

glimpse *n.* mirada fugaz.

glioblastoma *n.* glioblastoma, tipo de tumor cerebral.

gliocytoma *n.* gliocitoma, tumor de células de neuroglia.

glioma *n.* glioma, neoplasma del cerebro compuesto de células de neuroglia.

gliomyoma *n.* gliomioma, combinación de glioma y mioma.

glioneuroma *n.* glioneuroma, glioma combinado con neuroma.

globin *n.* globina, proteína que constituye la hemoglobina.

globule *n.* glóbulo, pequeña masa esférica.

globulin *n.* globulina, una de las cuatro proteínas más importantes que componen el plasma; **antilymphocyte** ___ / ___ antilinfocítica; **gamma** ___ / gamma ___.

globulinuria *n.* globulinuria, presencia de globulina en la orina.

globus *n.* globo, esfera; ___ **hystericus** / ___ histérico, sensación subjetiva de tener una bola en la garganta.

glomerular *a.* glomerular, rel. a un glomérulo; en forma de racimo.

glomerulonephritis *n.* glomerulonefritis, enfermedad de Bright, infl. del glomérulo renal.

glomerulosclerosis *n.* glomeruloesclerosis, proceso degenerativo del glomérulo renal que se asocia con arterioesclerosis y diabetes.

glomerulus *n.* (*pl.* **glomeruli**) glomérulo, colección de capilares en forma de bola pequeña localizados en el riñón.

glomus *n.* (*pl.* **glomera**) glomo, bola, grupo de arteriolas conectadas directamente a las venas, ricas en inervación.

gloom *n.* tristeza, desaliento.

gloomy *a.* triste, abatido-a.

glossa *n.* glosa, lengua.

glossalgia *n.* glosalgia, dolor en la lengua.

glossectomy *n.* *cirg.* glosectomía, excisión parcial o completa de la lengua.

glossitis *n.* glositis, infl. de la lengua; **acute** ___ / ___ aguda, asociada con estomatitis.

glossodynia *n.* glosodinia, *V.* **glosalgia.**

glossopathy *n.* glosopatía, enfermedad de la lengua.

glossoplegia *n.* glosoplejía, parálisis total o parcial de la lengua.

glossorrhaphy *n.* *cirg.* glosorrafía, sutura de la lengua.

glossotomy *n.* glosotomía, *cirg.* incisión de la lengua.

glossy skin *n.* liodermia, apariencia brillante de la piel. síntoma de atrofia o traumatismo de los nervios.

glottal *a.* glótico-a; ___ **stop** / oclusión ___.

glottis *n.* glotis, hendidura en la parte superior de la laringe entre las cuerdas vocales verdaderas; aparato vocal de la laringe.

glottitis *n.* glotitis, *V.* **glossitis.**

glove *n.* guante; *v.* **to handle with kid** ___-s / tratar con mucho cuidado, tratar delicadamente; *v.* **to fit like a** ___ / ajustar.

glucagon *n.* glucagón, una de dos hormonas producidas por los islotes de Langerhans cuya función consiste en aumentar la concentración de glucosa en la sangre y que tiene un efecto antiinflamatorio.

glucagonoma *n.* glucagonoma, tumor que secreta glucagón.

glucocorticoid *n.* glucocorticoide, grupo de hormonas segregadas por la corteza suprarrenal que intervienen en el proceso metabólico del organismo y tienen un efecto antiinflamatorio.

glucogenesis *n.* glucogénesis, proceso de desdoblamiento del glucógeno.

gluconeogenesis *n.* gluconeogénesis. 1. formación hepática de glucógeno a partir de fuentes distintas de los carbohidratos; 2. formación de azúcar por desdoblamiento de glucógeno.

glucose *n.* glucosa, dextrosa, azúcar de fruta, fuente principal de energía en organismos vivos; **blood level of** ___ / nivel de ___ en la sangre; ___, **tolerance test** / prueba de tolerancia a la ___.

glucose-6-phosphate dehydrogenase *n.* glucofosfato de deshidrogenasa, enzima presente en el hígado y los riñones necesaria en la conversión de glicerol a glucosa.

glucoside, glycoside *n.* glucósido, compuesto natural o sintético que al hidrolizarse libera azúcar.

glucosuria, glycosuria *n.* glucosuria, presencia excesiva de glucosa en la orina; **diabetic** ___ / ___ diabética; **pituitary** ___ / ___ pituitaria; **renal** ___ / ___ renal.

glucuronic acid, glycuronic acid *n.* ácido glucurónico, ácido de efecto desintoxicante en el metabolismo humano.

glue *n.* cola, goma de pegar; ___ **ear** / oído tupido o tapado con cerumen; ___**-sniffing** / adicción a inhalar ___.

gluey *a.* gomoso-a, viscoso-a, glutinoso-a.

glutamate *n.* glutamato, sal de ácido glutámico.

glutamic-oxaloacetic transaminase *n.* transaminasa glutámica oxaloacética (GOT o SGOT), enzima presente en varios tejidos y líquidos del organismo cuya concentración elevada en el suero indica daño cardíaco o hepático.

glutamic-pyruvic transaminase *n.* transaminasa glutámica pirúvica (GPT o SGPT), enzima cuyo aumento en la sangre es indicio de daño cardíaco o hepático.

gluteal *a.* glúteo-a, rel. a las nalgas; ___ **fold** / pliegue ___; ___ **reflex** / reflejo ___.

gluten *n.* gluten, materia vegetal albuminoidea; ___-**free diet** / dieta libre de ___.

glycemia *n.* glicemia, glucemia, concentración de glucosa en la sangre.

glycerin *n.* glicerina, glicerol, alcohol que se encuentra en las grasas.

glycine *n.* glicina, ácido aminoacético, aminoácido no esencial.

glycocholic acid *n.* ácido glicocólico, combinación de glicina y ácido cólico.

glycogen *n.* glucógeno, polisacárido usu. almacenado en el hígado que se convierte en glucosa según lo necesite el organismo; ___ **storage disease** / hepatina, almacenamiento de glucógeno en el hígado.

glycolysis *n.* glicólisis, subdivisión de azúcar en compuestos más simples.

glycopenia *n.* glucopenia. *V.* **hypoglicemia.**

glycopexic *n.* glucopéxico, que fija o acumula azúcar.

gnashing *n.* rechinamiento de los dientes.

gnat *n.* [*insect*] jején.

gnosia *n.* gnosia, facultad de reconocer y distinguir objetos y personas.

go *vi.* ir; irse; to ___ **after** / seguir; to ___ **about** / andar, caminar; [*to accompany*] **to** ___ **along with** / acompañar; **to** ___ **against** / ir en contra de; **to** ___ **ahead** / adelantar; emprender; **to** ___ **along with a decision** / aceptar, aprobar una decisión; **to** ___ **bad** / echarse a perder; **to** ___ **back** / volver, retroceder; **to** ___ **crazy** / enloquecer; **to** ___ **in or into** / entrar; **to** ___ **deep into** / ahondar; **to** ___ **down with** / enfermarse, caer enfermo-a; [*distance*] **to** ___ **far** / ir lejos; [*to succeed*] tener éxito, progresar; **to** ___ **on** / continuar; **to let** ___ / soltar, dejar; **to** ___ **over** / examinar, estudiar; **to** ___ **through** / examinar o estudiar con cuidado; **to let oneself** ___ / soltarse; dejarse; relajarse.

goat *n.* cabra; ___ **milk** / leche de ___.

goblet cell *n.* célula caliciforme secretora que se localiza en el epitelio del tubo digestivo y del tubo respiratorio.

godchild *n.* ahijado-a.

godfather *n.* padrino.

godless *n.* ateo-a; incrédulo-a.

godmother *n.* madrina.

goggle-eyed *a.* de ojos saltones.

goiter *n.* bocio, engrosamiento de la glándula tiroides; **congenital** ___ / ___ congénito; **endemic, colloid** ___ / ___ endémico, coloide;

exophtalmic ___ / ___ exoftálmico; **toxic** ___ / ___ tóxico (de síntomas similares a la tirotoxicosis); **wandering** ___ / ___ móvil.

gold *n.* oro.

gonad *n.* gónada, glándula productora de gametos: los ovarios en la mujer y los testículos en el hombre.

gonadal *a.* gonadal, rel. a una glándula gónada; ___ **dysgenesis** / distenesia, malformación ___.

gonadotropin *n.* gonadotropina, hormona estimulante de las gónadas; ___ **of the anterior pituitary** / ___ hipofisaria; **chorionic** ___ / ___ coriónica, presente en la sangre y orina de la mujer durante el embarazo, base de la prueba del embarazo.

gonadotropin-releasing hormone *n.* hormona que estimula la secreción de gonadotropina.

gonion *n.* gonión, punto extremo inferior, posterior y lateral del ángulo de la mandíbula.

goniopuncture *n.* *cirg.* goniopuntura, tratamiento de glaucoma por punción en la cámara anterior del ojo.

goniotomy *n.* *cirg.* goniotomía, procedimiento para tratar el glaucoma congénito.

gonococcal *a.* gonocócico, rel. a los gonococos.

gonococcus *n.* (*pl.* **gonococci**) gonococo, microorganismo de la especie *Neisseria gonorrhoeae,* causante de la gonorrea.

gonorrhea *n.* gonorrea, enfermedad infecciosa catarral contagiosa de la mucosa genital.

gonorrheal *a.* gonorreico-a, rel. a la gonorrea; ___ **arthritis** / artritis ___.

good *a.* bueno-a; **all in** ___ **time** / todo a su debido tiempo; **in** ___ **time** / a buen tiempo, puntual, *v.* **to be** ___ **at** / tener talento para; **to put in a** ___ **word** / recomendar; **to do someone** ___ / hacer bien a alguien; **good!** / ¡muy bien! ___ **afternoon** / buenas tardes; ___ **behavior** / ___ conducta, buen comportamiento; ___ **cause** / causa justificada; **in** ___ **faith** / de fe; ___ **luck** / buena suerte; ___ **morning** / buenos días, buen día; ___ **night** / buenas noches; ___-**bye** / adiós.

Good Samaritan Law *n.* Ley del buen samaritano, protección legal al facultativo o a otras personas que prestan ayuda médica en casos de emergencia.

gooseflesh *n.* *pop.* carne de gallina.

gout *n.* gota, enfermedad hereditaria causada por defecto del metabolismo de ácido úrico.

gracilis *n.* gracilis, músculo largo interno del muslo.

gradient *a.* gradiente, línea que indica aumento o disminución en una variable.

graft *n.* injerto, tejido u órgano usado en un trasplante o implante; **allogenic** ___, **allograft** / ___ alogénco, de un donante genéticamente disigual al paciente; **autogenous** ___ / ___ autógeno, injerto que se toma del propio paciente; **bone** ___ / ___ óseo; **bypass** ___ / ___

de derivación; **full thickness** ___ / ___ de capa gruesa completa, dermoepidérmico; **skin** ___ / ___ cutáneo, esp. en quemaduras; **thick-split** ___ / ___ de capa gruesa partida, que se injerta en un área descarnada; *v.* injertar.

graftable *a.* injertable.

graftage *n.* práctica de hacer injertos.

grain *n.* grano, cereal.

gram *n.* gramo, unidad de medida métrica.

gramicidin *n.* gramicidina, antibiótico producido por *Bacillus brevis,* localmente activo contra bacterias gram-positivas.

grammar *n. gr.* gramática.

gram-molecule *n.* molécula gramo, el peso en gramos de una sustancia igual a su peso molecular.

gram-negative *n.* gram-negativo, resultado de la aplicacion del método de Gram de decoloración de una bacteria o tejido por medio de alcohol.

gram-positive *n.* gram-positivo, retención del color o resistencia a la decoloración en la aplicación del método de Gram.

Gram's method *n.* método de Gram, proceso de coloración de bacterias para identificarlas en un análisis.

granular *a.* granuloso-a, granulado-a, hecho o formado de gránulos.

granular cast *n.* cilindro granuloso, cilindro urinario visto en nefropatías degenerativas o de tipo inflamatorio.

granulation *n.* granulación, masa redonda y carnosa que se forma en la superficie de un tejido, membrana u órgano; ___ **tissue** / tejido de ___ .

granule *n.* gránulo, partícula pequeña formada de gránulos; **acidophil** ___ / ___ acidófilo, que acepta colorantes ácidos; **basophil** ___ / ___ basófilo, que acepta colorantes básicos.

granulocyte *n.* granulocito, leucocito que contiene gránulos.

granulocytopenia *n.* granulocitopenia, deficiencia de granulocitos en la sangre.

granuloma *n.* granuloma, tumor o neoplasma de tejido granular; **foreign body** ___ / ___ de cuerpo extraño; **infectious** ___ / ___ infeccioso; **inguinal** ___ / ___ inguinal; **venereum** ___ / ___ ulcerativo de los genitales.

granulomatosis *n.* granulomatosis, granuloma múltiple.

granulopenia *n.* granulopenia. *V.* **granulocytopenia.**

granulosa *n.* granulosa, membrana ovárica de células epiteliales que rodea el folículo ovárico.

granulosa cell tumor *n.* tumor de la granulosa.

granulosa-teca cell tumor *n.* tumor de células de la granulosa-teca, tumor ovárico de células que provienen del folículo de Graaf.

grape *n.* uva.

grape sugar *n.* dextrosa, azúcar de uva y de otras frutas.

graphology *n.* grafología, estudio de la escritura como indicación de la personalidad del paciente y como ayuda en el diagnóstico de enfermedades nerviosas.

grass *n.* hierba, yerba.

grateful *a.* agradecido-a.

gratefulness *n.* gratitud.

gravamen *n.* agravio, motivo de queja.

grave *a.* severo-a, serio-a, peligroso-a.

Graves' disease *n.* enfermedad de Graves, hipertiroidismo. *V.* **exophthalmic goiter.**

graveyard *n.* cementerio, camposanto.

gravida *n.* mujer embarazada, preñada, encinta, en estado.

gravidity *n.* gravidez, embarazo.

gravity *n.* fuerza de gravedad.

gravy *n.* salsa, jugo de carne.

gray *n.* color gris; *a.* gris.

gray matter *n.* materia o sustancia gris, tejido nervioso muy vascularizado de color gris pardo compuesto de células nerviosas y fibras nerviosas amielínicas.

great *a.* grande, grandioso-a; **in** ___ **detail** / muy minucioso; **it is going** ___ / todo va muy bien.

green *n.* verde.

green blindness *n.* ceguera al color verde.

green pepper *n.* pimiento verde.

greet *v.* saludar; recibir.

greeting *n.* saludo.

grid *n.* rejilla.

grief *n.* pesar, aflicción.

grief reaction *n.* reacción de aflicción.

grief-stricken *a.* desconsolado-a; afligido-a; acongojado-a; lleno-a de pesar.

grievance *n.* queja; agravio.

grieve *v.* afligirse, apenarse.

grievous *a.* penoso-a, doloroso-a.

grilled *a.* asado-a a la parrilla.

grime *n.* mugre, tizne.

grind *vi.* moler; triturar; picar.

grinder *n.* [*dental*] molar, *pop.* muela; pulverizador.

grinder's disease *n.* enfermedad de los pulmones producida por inhalación de polvo.

grinding wheel *n.* [*dental*] disco de esmeril.

grip *n.* apretón de la mano; *v.* agarrar, apretar.

grip, grippe *n.* gripe, *Mex. A.* gripa; influenza.

griseofulvin *n.* griseofulvina, antibiótico usado en el tratamiento de algunas enfermedades de la piel.

gristle *n.* cartílago.

groan *v.* gemir; quejarse.

groggy *a.* atontado-a, vacilante, tambaleante.

groin *n.* ingle.

groove *n.* surco, ranura; **bicipital** ___ / ___ bicipital; **costal** ___ / ___ costal.

gross *a.* grave; grueso-a, denso-a; grotesco-a; ___ **negligence** / imprudencia o negligencia ___ .

gross anatomy *n.* anatomía macroscópica, estudio de los órganos y partes del cuerpo que se ven a simple vista.

ground *n.* base; suelo; terreno; *a. pp.* de **to grind,**

molido-a.

ground substance *n.* sustancia fundamental que llena los espacios intercelulares de los huesos, cartílagos y tejido fibroso.

group *n.* grupo, conglomerado; **support** ___ / ___ de soporte.

group therapy *n. psic.* terapia de grupo.

grow *vi.* crecer, desarrollar; **to** ___ **old** / envejecer.

growth *n.* desarrollo, crecimiento.

growth hormone *n.* hormona del crecimiento, secreción de la glándula pituitaria que estimula el crecimiento.

grumous *a.* grumoso-a, coagulado-a.

gryposis *n.* griposis, curvatura anormal esp. rel. a una uña.

guaiacol *n.* guayacol, antiséptico y anestésico.

guanethidine *n.* guanetidina, agente usado en el tratamiento de la hipertensión.

guarantee *n.* garantía; *u.* garantizar; acreditar.

guard *v.* [*protect*] guardar, proteger, cuidar; guardarse, cuidarse; **to** ___ **against** / tomar precauciones, cuidarse de, guardarse de.

guarded *a.* de cuidado; guardado-a; vigilado-a; protegido-a; **in** ___ **condition** / en estado de cuidado; en estado grave.

guardian *n.* guardián-a, custodio-a; tutor-a.

gubernaculum *n.* gubernaculum, dirección o guía.

guess *n.* suposición. *u.* adivinar, suponer; acertar.

guest *n.* invitado-a, huésped, comensal; parásito.

guidance *n.* guía, consejo, dirección.

guide *n.* guía; *u.* guiar, dirigir.

guideline *n.* pauta, guía, directriz.

guillotine *n.* guillotina, instrumento quirúrgico.

guinea pig *n.* conejillo de Indias.

gullet *n.* esófago; *pop.* garguero, gaznate.

gulp down *u.* engullir, tragar apresuradamente.

gum *n.* encía. *V.* **gingiva;** goma; **chewing** ___ / goma de mascar, *pop.* chicle.

gumboil *n.* absceso en la encía, flemón.

gumma *n.* (*pl.* **gummata**) goma, tumor sifilítico.

gummy *a.* pegajoso-a, gomoso-a, viscoso-a.

gun *n.* escopeta; revólver; pistola.

gunshot wound *n.* herida de bala.

gush *u.* salir a borbotones, derramar, verter.

gustation *n.* gustación, sentido del gusto.

gut *n.* intestino, *pop.* tripas.

gutta *n.* (*pl.* **guttae**) gutta, gota.

gutta-percha *n.* gutapercha, látex vegetal seco y purificado, que se usa en tratamientos dentales y médicos.

guttural *a.* gutural.

gymnastics *n.* gimnasia, calistenia.

gynandroid *n.* ginandroide, persona de características hermafroditas que muestra la apariencia del sexo opuesto.

gynecologic, gynecological *a.* ginecológico-a, rel. al estudio de enfermedades del tracto reproductivo femenino.

gynecologic operative procedures *n.* procedimientos quirúrgicos ginecológicos.

gynecologist *n.* ginecólogo-a, especialista en ginecología.

gynecology *n.* ginecología, estudio de los trastornos que afectan los órganos reproductivos femeninos.

gynecomastia *n.* ginecomastia, desarrollo excesivo de las glándulas mamarias en el hombre.

gyrus *n.* circunvolución, porción elevada de la corteza cerebral; **Broca's** ___ / ___ de Broca, tercera, frontal inferior; **frontal, superior** ___ / ___ frontal superior; **inferior, lateral occipital** ___ / ___ occipital inferior lateral; **superior occipital** ___ / ___ occipital superior.

H *abbr.* **hydrogen** / hidrógeno; **heroin** / heroína; **hypermetropia** / hipermetropía; **hypodermic** / hipodérmico.

h *abbr.* **height** / altura; **hour** / hora; **horizontal** / horizontal.

habilitate *v.* habilitar, equipar.

habit *n.* hábito, uso, costumbre; adicción al uso de una droga o bebida; *v.* **to be in the ___ of** / tener la costumbre de; acostumbrarse a; habituarse; [*drugs*] *pop.* **to kick the ___** / dejar la adicción; curarse.

habit-forming *a.* adictivo-a, rel. a una sustancia que envicia, que crea una adicción.

habit training *n.* entrenamiento de hábitos, enseñanza impartida a los niños para realizar actividades básicas tales como comer, dormir, vestirse, asearse y usar el servicio sanitario.

habitual *a.* habitual, usual, acostumbrado-a; **-ly** *adv.* habitualmente.

hacking cough *n.* tos seca recurrente.

had *prep., pp.* de **to have.**

haggard *a.* ojeroso-a; desfigurado-a; desaliñado-a.

hair *n.* pelo, cabello, vello; **axillary ___** / ___ axilar; **curly ___** / ___ rizado; **gray ___** / cana; **pubic ___** / vello púbico; **straight ___** / ___ lacio, liso; **wavy ___** / ___ ondeado.

hairball *n.* bola de pelo, tipo de bezoar.

hairbrush *n.* cepillo para el cabello.

hair bulb *n.* bulbo piloso.

hair follicle *n.* folículo piloso.

hairless *a.* pelón -ona, pelado-a, calvo-a.

hairline *n.* raya del pelo; línea fina; trazo fino; **___ fracture** / fractura de línea fina.

hair remover *n.* depilatorio.

hair root *n.* raíz del pelo.

hair transplantation *n. cirg.* trasplante de pelo, trasplante de epidermis que contiene folículos pilosos de una parte del cuerpo a otra.

hairy *a.* peludo-a, velludo-a; **___ tongue** / lengua velluda, lengua infectada de hongos parásitos.

half *n.* mitad, medio; **in ___** / en dos mitades; **___ as much** / la mitad; **___ and ___** / a mitades, en igual proporción; **___ brother** / medio hermano; **___ sister** / media hermana; **___-hour** / media hora; **___-starved** / medio muerto de hambre.

half-life *n.* 1. vida media, tiempo requerido para que la mitad de una sustancia ingerida o inyectada en el organismo se elimine por medios naturales; 2. semidesintegración, tiempo requerido por una sustancia radioactiva para perder la mitad de su radioactividad por desintegración.

halide *n.* haloide, haluro, sales producidas por la combinación de un elemento halógeno y un metal.

halitosis *n.* halitosis, mal aliento.

halitus *n.* hálito, aire aspirado.

hall *n.* vestíbulo; recepción; pasillo.

hallucinate *v.* alucinar, desvariar.

hallucination *n.* alucinación, alucinamiento, sensación subjetiva que no tiene precedencia o estímulo real; **auditory ___, imaginary perception of sounds** / ___ auditiva, percepción imaginaria de sonidos; **gustatory ___, imaginary sensation of taste** / ___ gustativa, sensación imaginaria del gusto; **haptic ___, imaginary perception of pain, temperature, or skin sensations** / ___ táctil, percepción imaginaria de dolor, de temperatura o de sensaciones en la piel; **motor ___, imaginary movement of the body** / ___ de movimiento, percepción imaginaria de movimiento del cuerpo; **olfactory ___, imaginary smells** / ___ olfativa, de olores imaginarios.

hallucinatory *a.* alucinante, alucinador-a.

hallucinogen *n.* alucinógeno, droga que produce alucinaciones o desvaríos tal como LSD, peyote, mescalina y otras.

hallucinosis *n.* alucinosis, delirio alucinatorio crónico; **acute alcoholic ___** / ___ alcohólica, manifestación de temor patológico acompañado de alucinaciones auditivas.

hallux *n.* (*pl.* **halluces**) dedo gordo del pie; **___ valgus** / ___ valgus, desviación del dedo gordo hacia los otros dedos; **___ varus** / varus, separación del dedo gordo de los demás dedos.

halo *n.* aréola. 1. área del seno de tono más oscuro que rodea el pezón; 2. círculo de luz.

halothane *n.* halótano, anestésico administrado por inhalación, nombre comercial Fluotane.

ham *n.* 1. corva de la pierna, región poplítea detrás de la rodilla; 2. jamón.

hamartoma *n.* hamartoma, nódulo de tejido superfluo semejante a un tumor usualmente benigno.

hamate bone *n.* hueso medio del carpo de la muñeca.

hammer *n.* martillo. 1. huesecillo del oído medio; 2. instrumento empleado en exámenes físicos; **___ finger or toe** / dedo en garra; **percussion ___** / ___ de percusión; **reflex ___** / ___ de reflejo.

hamstring *n.* 1. tendones de la corva; 2. músculos flexores y aductores de la parte posterior del muslo.

hand *n.* mano; **give me a ___** / ayúdeme, ayúdame; **close at ___** / muy de cerca; **in good ___-s** / en buenas manos; *v.* **to have a free ___** / tener libertad para, tener carta blanca; **to have one's ___-s tied** / tener atadas las manos, sin poder hacer nada; **to keep one's ___-s off** / no meterse; **to shake ___-s** / dar la ___; **on the other ___** / por otra parte; **___ deformities, acquired** / deformidades adquiridas de la ___; **___ rest** / apoyo de la ___; *v.* **to ___ in a report** / presentar un informe; **to ___ out news** / facilitar noticias; **to ___ out information** /

facilitar información.

handful n. puñado, manojo.

handicap n. impedimento; obstáculo, desventaja; **handicapped person** / persona desvalida, inválida, baldada, impedida.

handle n. asa, mango; v. tratar, manejar, manipular; ___ **with care** / trátese con cuidado.

handling n. manejo, manipulación.

handmade a. hecho a mano.

handpiece n. [*dental*] pieza de mano.

handsome a. guapo-a, hermoso-a, distinguido-a.

handwriting n. escritura a mano.

handy a. a la mano; conveniente; cercano-a.

hang vi. colgar, suspender, ahorcar; ahorcarse.

hanging n. suspensión, colgajo; ejecución en la horca.

hangnail n. uñero, uña encarnada.

hangover n. malestar después de una borrachera.

hang-up n. obsesión o problema que irrita.

Hanot's disease n. enfermedad de Hanot, cirrosis biliar, cirrosis hipertrófica del hígado acompañada de ictericia.

Hansen's disease n. enfermedad de Hansen. *V.* **leprosy**.

haploid n. haploide, célula sexual que contiene en el cromosoma la mitad de las características somáticas de la especie.

happen v. suceder, acontecer, ocurrir.

happening n. suceso, hecho, acontecimiento; **What is** ___? / ¿Qué sucede?, ¿qué pasa?

happiness n. alegría, felicidad.

happy a. contento-a, alegre, feliz.

haptoglobin n. haptoglobina, mucoproteína que se une a la hemoglobina libre en el plasma.

haptometer n. haptómetro, instrumento para medir la agudeza del sentido del tacto.

harass v. acosar, perturbar, hostigar, hostilizar.

harassment n. acosamiento, perturbación, vejamen.

hard a. duro-a, endurecido-a, sólido; trabajoso-a, difícil; [*bone*] osificado; ___ **of hearing** / medio sordo; v. **to grow** ___ / endurecerse; [*parturition*] ___ **labor** / parto laborioso; **-ly** adv. a duras penas, difícilmente, escasamente.

hard bone n. hueso compacto.

hardbound a. estreñido-a.

hard contact lens (HCL) n. lentes duros de contacto.

harden v. endurecer, solidificar.

hardening n. endurecimiento, solidez.

hard feelings n. pl. resentimiento.

hardheaded a. obstinado-a, terco-a, testarudo-a.

hard palate n. paladar óseo.

hard pressed a. acosado-a, apremiado-a.

hardship n. sufrimiento, privación, penalidad.

harelip n. labio leporino, deformidad congénita a nivel del labio superior causada por falta de fusión del proceso nasal interno y el lateral maxilar; ___ **suture** / sutura del ___.

harelipped a. labihendido-a, que tiene labio leporino.

harm n. daño, mal, perjuicio; v. dañar, perjudicar.

harmful a. perjudicial, dañino-a.

harmless a. inofensivo-a, inocuo-a.

harmonize v. armonizar; [*relations*] llevarse bien.

harmony n. armonía, reunión o comunicación agradable.

harness n. cinturón corrector.

harvest n. recolección, obtención o separación de bacterias u otros microorganismos de un cultivo; cosecha.

hashish n. hachís, *pop.* yerba, narcótico de efecto eufórico extraído de la marihuana.

hate, hatred n. odio, aversión; v. odiar, repudiar.

haustrum L. haustrum, cavidad o saco, esp. el del colon.

have vi. aux. haber; tener; **to** ___ **to** / tener que.

haversian system n. sistema de Havers, serie de canículos o pequeños conductos y láminas en formación concéntrica que forman la base estructural del hueso compacto.

hay fever n. fiebre del heno, asma del heno, catarro del heno, catarro primaveral, alergia causada por un agente irritante externo, gen. polen.

hazard n. riesgo, peligro; **a** ___ **to your health** / un ___ para su salud.

hazardous a. arriesgado-a, peligroso-a.

head n. 1. cabeza; 2. parte principal de una estructura; ___ **birth** / presentación cefálica; ___ **drop** / caída de la ___; **from** ___ **to toe** / de la ___ a los pies; ___ **injury** / traumatismo del cráneo, golpe en la ___; ___ **of the family** / ___ de familia; v. **to nod one's** ___ / asentir con la ___.

headache n. cefalalgia, dolor de cabeza, jaqueca.

headrest n. apoyo para la cabeza, cabezal.

headshrinker n. psiquiatra.

headstrong a. voluntarioso-a, testarudo-a.

heal v. curar, sanar, recobrar la salud; [*a wound*] cicatrizar; curarse, sanarse; recobrarse.

healer n. curador-a; curandero-a.

healing n. 1. curación, recuperación de la salud; ___ **process** / proceso de ___; 2. curanderismo.

health n. salud; [*government*] ___ **authorities** / autoridades de Sanidad; **Department of** ___ / Ministerio de Salud o Salubridad; ___ **assessment** / evaluación del estado de salud; ___ **care** / atención o cuidado de la ___; ___ **care reform** / reforma al sistema de ___; ___ **certificate** / certificado de ___; ___ **education** / educación de la ___; ___ **facilities** / instituciones de ___; **home** ___ **care** / cuidado de salud en el hogar; ___ **laws** / estatutos sanitarios; ___ **personnel** / profesionales médicos y de asistencia pública; ___ **planning** / planeamiento de métodos de ___; **rural** ___ / ___ rural; ___ **services** / servicios o atención de la ___; ___ **services for the aged** / servicios de salud a los ancianos; ___ **status** / estado de ___; **urban** ___

/ ___ urbana.

healthy *a.* sano-a, saludable, fornido-a.

hear *vi.* oír, escuchar.

hearing *n.* audición, oído; ___ **aid** / audífono, dispositivo para aumentar la audición; ___ **loss** / pérdida de la audición.

heart *n.* corazón, órgano muscular cóncavo cuya función es mantener la circulación de la sangre; ___ **atrium** / aurícula cardíaca; ___ **attack** / ataque al ___; ___ **block** / bloqueo del ___; ___ **block, atrioventricular** / bloqueo auriculoventricular, interrupción en el nódulo A-V; ___ **block, bundle-branch** / bloqueo de rama; ___ **block, interventricular** / bloqueo interventricular; ___ **block, partial** / bloqueo parcial; ___ **block, sinoatrial** / bloqueo senoauricular, interferencia completa o parcial del paso de impulsos del nódulo senoauricular; ___ **catherization** / cateterización o cateterismo cardíaco; **congenital disease** / anomalías congénitas del ___; ___ **disease** / cardiopatías; ___ **failure, congestive** / insuficiencia cardíaca congestiva, colapso o fallo cardíaco; ___ **failure, low output** / deficiencia en mantener un flujo sanguíneo adecuado; ___ **failure, left** / insuficiencia ventricular izquierda, deficiencia en mantener un gasto normal del ventrículo izquierdo; ___ **failure, right-sided** / insuficiencia del ventrículo derecho; **hypertensive** ___ **disease** / cardiopatía por hipertensión; ___ **hypertrophy** / hipertrofia del ___; **low** ___ **output** / gasto bajo; ___ **murmur** / soplo cardíaco; ___ **output** / gasto cardíaco; ___ **pacemaker** / estimulador cardíaco, marcapasos; ___ **palpitation** / palpitación cardíaca; ___ **pump, nuclear powered** / bomba del ___ de fuerza nuclear; ___ **rate** / frecuencia cardíaca; ___ **reflex** / reflejo cardíaco; ___ **scan** / escán cardíaco; ___ **sound** / ruido del ___; ___ **transplant** / trasplante del ___; ___ **valve** / válvula del ___.

heartbeat *n.* latido del corazón, [*rapid*] palpitación; **ectopic** ___ / ___ ectópico.

heartburn *n.* acedía, acidez, *pop.* ardor en el estómago; agruras.

heart-lung machine *n.* máquina corazón-pulmón, máquina cardiopulmonar que se usa para mantener artificialmente las funciones del corazón y de los pulmones.

heat *n.* calor; **conductive** ___ / ___ de conducción; ___ **cramps** / espasmo muscular (debido a trabajos realizados en altas temperaturas); **dry** ___ / ___ seco; ___ **exhaustion** / colapso por calor; ___ **loss** / pérdida de ___; ___ **prostration** / insolación con colapso; ___ **stroke** / insolación; ___ **unit** / caloría; ___ **therapy** / termoterapia; *v.* calentar; dar calor.

heater *n.* calentador; aparato de calefacción; **electric** ___ / ___ eléctrico.

heating pad, electric *n.* almohadilla eléctrica.

heavier *a.* muy pesado; *comp.* más pesado que.

heaviness *n.* pesadez, pesantez, peso; [*sleep*] sueño pesado, modorra; [*feelings*] abatimiento, decaimiento.

heavy *a.* pesado-a, grueso-a, fornido-a; ___ **chain disease** / enfermedad de red o cadena.

hectic *a.* hético-a, febril; agitado-a; consumido-a, tísico-a.

heel *n.* talón, calcañal, parte posterior redondeada del pie.

hefty *a.* fuerte, macizo-a.

height *n.* altura, alto; estatura.

Heimlich maneuver *n.* maniobra de Heimlich, técnica que se usa para sacar o forzar la expulsión de un cuerpo extraño que impide el paso del aire de la tráquea o la faringe.

helical *a.* helicoideo-a, en forma de hélice o espiral.

heliophobia *n.* heliofobia, temor exagerado al sol de personas que han sufrido de insolación.

heliotherapy *n.* helioterapia, exposición o baños de sol con propósito terapéutico

helium *n.* helio, elemento gaseoso inerte empleado en tratamientos respiratorios y en cámaras de descompresión para facilitar el aumento o disminución de la presión del aire.

helminth *n.* helminto, gusano que se localiza en el intestino humano.

helminthiasis *n.* helmintiasis, condición parasítica intestinal.

helminthicide *n.* helminticida, vermicida, medicamento que extermina parásitos.

help *n.* ayuda, asistencia, socorro, auxilio; *v.* ayudar, asistir, auxiliar; remediar.

helpful *a.* útil, provechoso-a.

helpless *a.* desamparado-a, indefenso-a; desvalido-a, abandonado-a.

hemacytometer *n.* hemacitómetro, instrumento contador de las células sanguíneas.

hemagglutination *n.* hemoaglutinación, aglutinación de células rojas sanguíneas.

hemagglutinin *n.* hemoaglutinina, anticuerpo de células rojas o hematíes que causa aglutinación.

hemangioblastoma *n.* hemangioblastoma, hemangioma localizado generalmente en el cerebelo.

hemangioma *n.* hemangioma, tumor benigno formado por vasos capilares en racimo que producen una marca de nacimiento de color rojo púrpura en la piel.

hemangiosarcoma *n.* hemangiosarcoma, tumor maligno del tejido vascular.

hemarthrosis *n.* hemartrosis, derrame de sangre en la cavidad de una articulación.

hematemesis *n.* hematemesis, vómito de sangre.

hematherapy, hemotherapy *n.* hematerapia, hemoterapia, uso terapéutico de la sangre.

hematic *n.* hemático, droga usada en el tratamiento de anemia; *a.* hemático-a, relacionado con la sangre.

hematochezia *n.* hematoquezia, presencia de

sangre en el excremento.

hematocolpos *n.* hematocolpos, retención del flujo menstrual en la vagina debido a imperforación del himen.

hematocrit *n.* hematócrito, 1. aparato centrifugador que se usa en la separación de células y partículas del plasma; 2. promedio de eritrocitos en la sangre.

hematocyst *n.* hematoquiste. 1. quiste sanguinolento; 2. hemorragia dentro de un quiste.

hematogenesis *n.* hematogénesis. *V.* **hematopoiesis.**

hematologic, hematological *a.* hematológico-a, rel. a la sangre.

hematologist *n.* hematólogo-a, especialista en hematología.

hematology *n.* hematología, ciencia que estudia la sangre y los órganos que intervienen en la formación de ésta.

hematoma *n.* hematoma, hinchazón por sangre coleccionada fuera de un vaso; *pop.* chichón; **pelvic** __ / __ pélvico; **subdural** __ / derrame subdural.

hematomyelia *n.* hematomielia, derrame de sangre dentro de la médula espinal.

hematopoiesis, hemopoiesis *n.* hematopoyesis, hemopoyesis, formación de sangre.

hemianalgesia *n.* hemianalgesia, insensibilidad al dolor en un lado del cuerpo.

hemianopia, hemianopsia *n.* hemianopia, hemianopsia, pérdida de la visión en la mitad del campo visual de uno o ambos ojos.

hemiataxia *n.* hemiataxia, falta de coordinación muscular que afecta un lado del cuerpo.

hemiatrophy *n.* hemiatrofia, atrofia de la mitad de un órgano o de la mitad del cuerpo.

hemiballism *n.* hemibalismo, lesión en el cerebro que afecta a la mitad del cuerpo con movimientos involuntarios rápidos sin coordinación, esp. en las extremidades superiores.

Hematologic Values	*Valores hematológicos*
bleeding time	tiempo de sangrameinto
coagulation time	tiempo de coagulación
erythrocyte sedimentation	sedimentación de eritrocitos
hematocrit	promedio de eritrocitos
hemoglobin	hemoglobina
partial thromboplastin time	tiempo parcial de tromboplastina
arterial blood pH	pH de la sangre arterial
prothrombin time	tiempo de protrombina

hemicolectomy *n. cirg.* hemicolectomía, extirpación de una mitad del colon.

hemihypertrophy *n.* hemihipertrofia unilateral con desarrollo excesivo de la mitad del cuerpo.

hemilaminectomy *n. cirg.* hemilaminectomía, extirpación de un lado de la lámina vertebral.

hemiparalysis *n.* hemiparálisis, parálisis de un lado del cuerpo.

hemiparesis *n.* hemiparesis, debilidad muscular que afecta un lado del cuerpo.

hemiparetic *a.* hemiparético-a, rel. a la hemiparesis o de la naturaleza de la misma.

hemiplegia *n.* hemiplejía, parálisis gen. ocasionada por una lesión cerebral que afecta la parte del cuerpo opuesta al hemisferio cerebral afectado.

hemiplegic *a.* hemipléjico-a, que sufre de hemiplejía.

hemisphere *n.* hemisferio, mitad de una estructura u órgano de forma esférica.

hemithorax *n.* hemitórax, cada mitad del tórax.

hemobilia *n.* hemobilia, sangramiento en los conductos biliares.

hemoblastosis *n.* hemoblastosis, desórdenes proliferativos de los tejidos que forman la sangre.

hemochromatosis, iron storage disease *n.* hemocromatosis, trastorno del metabolismo férrico acompañado por exceso de depósitos de hierro en los tejidos que causa anomalías de pigmentación de la piel, cirrosis hepática y diabetes.

hemoconcentrate *v.* hemoconcentrar, concentrar hematíes.

hemoconcentration *n.* hemoconcentración, concentración de hematíes a causa de una disminución del volumen líquido sanguíneo.

hemocytoblast *n.* hemocitoblasto, célula sanguínea primitiva de la cual se derivan las demás.

hemodialysis *n.* hemodiálisis, proceso de diálisis usado para eliminar sustancias tóxicas de la sangre.

hemodialyzer *n.* hemodializador, riñón artificial, aparato que se usa en el proceso de diálisis.

hemodilution *n.* hemodilución, aumento del plasma sanguíneo en relación al de los glóbulos rojos.

hemodynamics *n.* hemodinamia, el estudio de la dinámica de la circulación de la sangre.

hemoglobin *n.* hemoglobina, la proteína de mayor importancia en la sangre a la que da color y por la que se transporta el oxígeno.

hemoglobinemia *n.* hemoglobinemia, presencia de hemoglobina libre en el plasma sanguíneo.

hemoglobinuria *n.* hemoglobinuria, presencia de hemoglobina en la orina.

hemogram *n.* hemograma, representación gráfica de un conteo sanguíneo diferencial.

hemolith *n.* hemolito, concreción en un vaso sanguíneo.

hemolysis *n.* hemólisis, ruptura de eritrocitos con liberación de hemoglobina en el plasma.

hemolytic *a.* hemolítico-a, rel. a hemólisis o que la produce; ___ **disorder** / trastorno ___.

hemolytic anemia *n.* anemia hemolítica, anemia congénita causada por agentes tóxicos de eritrocitos frágiles de forma esferoidal.

hemolytic disease of the newborn *n.* hemólisis en el recién nacido, trastorno gen. causado por la incompatibilidad del factor Rh. V. **Rh factor.**

hemophilia *n.* hemofilia, condición hereditaria caracterizada por deficiencia de coagulación y tendencia a sangrar.

hemophiliac *a.* hemofílico-a, persona afectada por hemofilia.

hemophilus, haemophilus *n.* hemófilo, bacteria anaeróbica gram-negativa del género *Haemophilus.*

hemophobia *n.* hemofobia, temor patológico a la sangre.

hemopneumothorax *n.* hemoneumotórax, acumulación de sangre y de aire en la cavidad pleural.

hemoptysis *n.* hemoptisis, expectoración sanguinolenta de color rojo vivo.

hemorrhage *n.* hemorragia, derrame profuso de sangre; **internal** ___ / ___ interna; **cerebral** ___ / ___ cerebral, accidente cerebrovascular; **intracranial** ___ / ___ intracraneana; **petechial** ___ / ___ petequial; **postpartum** ___ / ___ puerperal.

hemorrhagic *a.* hemorrágico-a.

hemorrhoid *n.* hemorroide, *pop.* almorrana, masa de venas dilatadas en la pared rectal; **external** ___ / ___-s externas, fuera del esfínter anal; **internal** ___ / ___ interna; **prolapsed** ___ / ___ de prolapso, protrusión de almorranas internas por el ano.

hemorrhoidectomy *n. cirg.* hemorroidectomía, extirpación de hemorroides.

hemosalpinx *n.* hemosálpinx, acumulación de sangre en las trompas de Falopio.

hemosiderin *n.* hemosiderina, compuesto insoluble de hierro derivado de la hemoglobina que se almacena para ser usado en la formación de hemoglobina en el momento necesario.

hemosiderosis *n.* hemosiderosis, depósitos de hemosiderina en el hígado y el vaso.

hemospermia *n.* hemospermia, presencia de sangre en el semen.

hemostasis *n.* hemostasis, hemostasia, detención o contención (artificial o natural) de sangramiento.

hemostat *n.* hemóstato, instrumento o medicamento que se emplea para contener un sangramiento.

hen *n.* gallina; [*broth*] caldo de ___.

heparin *n.* heparina, sustancia que actúa como anticoagulante.

heparinization *n.* heparinización, proceso de administrar heparina.

heparinize *n.* heparinizar, evitar la coagulación por medio del uso de heparina.

hepatectomy *n. cirg.* hepatectomía, extirpación de una parte o de todo el hígado.

hepatic *a.* hepático-a, rel. al hígado; ___ **coma** / coma ___ ; ___ **duct** / conducto ___ ; ___ **lobes** / lóbulos o subdivisiones ___-s; ___ **veins** / venas ___-as.

hepatitis *n.* hepatitis, infl. del hígado; **fulminant** ___ / ___ aguda fulminante; **infectious** ___ / ___ infecciosa o viral; **non-A, non-B** ___ / ___ no A, no B, asociada con transfusiones de sangre; ___ **A(HAV)** / ___ A, viral, afecta primordialmente a los niños; ___ **B(HBV)** / ___ B, causada por un virus y trasmitida en líquidos del organismo; saliva, lágrimas, semen; **serum** ___ / ___ sérica.

hepatocholangiogastrostomy *n. cirg.* hepatocolangiogastrostomía, establecimiento de drenaje de las vías biliares hacia el estómago.

hepatocyte *n.* hepatocito, célula del hígado.

hepatojugular reflex *n.* reflejo hepatoyugular, ingurgitación de las venas yugulares producida por el hígado en casos de insuficiencia cardíaca derecha.

hepatolenticular degeneration *n.* degeneración hepatolenticular.

hepatologist *n.* hepatólogo-a, especialista en trastornos hepáticos.

hepatology *n.* hepatología, estudio del hígado.

hepatomegaly *n.* hepatomegalia, agrandamiento del hígado.

hepatorenal *a.* hepatorrenal, rel. a los riñones y el hígado.

hepatosplenomegaly *n.* hepatosplenomegalia, agrandamiento del hígado y del bazo.

hepatotoxin *n.* hepatotoxina, toxina destructora de células hepáticas.

herb *n.* yerba, hierba, planta clasificada como medicinal o usada como condimento; ___ **tea** / infusión.

here *adv.* aquí; ___ **and now** / ahora mismo; ___ **and there** / aquí y allá.

hereditary *a.* hereditario-a; que se trasmite por herencia.

heredity *n.* herencia, trasmisión de características o rasgos genéticos de padres a hijos.

heredofamilial *a.* herencia familiar, rel. a cualquier enfermedad o condición cuya manifestación indica un proceso heredado.

hermaphrodite *n.* hermafrodita, persona cuyo cuerpo presenta los tejidos ovárico y testicular combinados en un mismo órgano o separadamente.

hermaphroditism *n.* hermafroditismo, condición de hermafrodita.

hermetic *a.* hermético-a, que no deja pasar el aire.

hernia *n.* hernia, protrusión anormal de un órgano o víscera a través de la cavidad que la contiene; **cystic** ___ / ___ cística; **hiatus** ___ / ___ hiatal, a través del hiato esofágico del diafragma; **incarcerated** ___ / ___ incarcerada, gen. causada por adherencias; **inguinal** ___ / ___ inguinal, de una víscera con protrusión en la ingle o el escroto; **lumbar** ___ / ___ lumbar, protrusión en la región lumbar; **reducible** ___ / ___ reducible, que puede tratarse por manipulación; **scrotal** ___ / ___ escrotal; **sliding** ___ / ___ por deslizamiento, de una víscera intestinal; **strangulated** ___ / ___ estrangulada, que obstruye los intestinos; **umbilical** ___ / ___ umbilical; **ventral** ___ / ___ ventral, protrusión a través de la pared abdominal.

hernial, herniated *a.* herniado-a, rel. a una hernia o que padece de ella; ___ **sac** / saco de la hernia, bolsa peritoneal en la cual desciende la hernia.

herniation *n.* herniación, desarrollo de una hernia; ___ **of nucleus pulposus** / ___ del núcleo pulposo, prolapso o ruptura del disco intervertebral.

herniography *n.* herniografía, radiografía de una hernia usando un medio de contraste.

herniorrhaphy *n. cirg.* herniorrafía, reconstrucción o reparación quirúrgica de una hernia.

heroic *a.* heroico-a, rel. a medicamentos de acción muy intensa.

heroin, diacetylomorphine *n.* heroína, diacetilomorfina, narcótico adictivo derivado de la morfina; ___ **addict** / heroinómano-a.

heroinism *n.* heroinismo, heroinomanía, adicción a la heroína.

herpangina *n.* herpangina, enfermedad infecciosa, epidémica en el verano, que afecta las membranas mucosas de la garganta.

herpes *n.* herpes, enfermedad inflamatoria viral dolorosa de la piel que se manifiesta con erupción y ampollas; ___ **genitales** / ___ de los genitales; ___ **ocular** / ___ ocular; ___ **simplex** / ___ simple, de simples vesículas que recurren una y otra vez en la misma área de la piel; ___ **zoster,** *pop.* **shingles** / ___ zóster, erupción dolorosa a lo largo de un nervio, *pop.* culebrilla.

herpetic *a.* herpético-a, rel. al herpes o de naturaleza similar; ___ **gingivostomatitis** / gingivostomatitis ___, infl. de la boca y las encías causada por herpes simple.

hesitant *a.* indeciso-a, vacilante.

hesitate *v.* vacilar, mostrarse indeciso-a; **Don't** ___ **to call us** / No deje, no dejes de llamarnos; no vacile, no vaciles en llamarnos.

heterogeneous *a.* heterogéneo-a, de naturaleza diferente.

heterograft *n.* heteroinjerto, injerto de un donante de especie o tipo diferente al del receptor.

heterologous *a.* heterólogo-a; derivado de un organismo o especie diferente.

heteroplasia *n.* heteroplasia, presencia anormal de tejido en un área diferente a la que le corresponde según su origen.

heteroplastia *n.* heteroplastia, trasplante de tejido obtenido de un donante que pertenece a una especie diferente.

heterosexual *n.* heterosexual, inclinación sexual hacia el sexo opuesto.

heterosexuality *n.* heterosexualidad.

heterotaxia *n.* heterotaxia, posición anormal o irregular de vísceras o partes del cuerpo.

heterotopia *n.* heterotopia, desplazamiento de un órgano o parte de la posición normal.

heterotopic *a.* heterotópico-a, rel. a la heterotopía.

heuristic *a.* heurístico-a, que descubre una investigación o la estimula.

hiatus *n.* hiatus, abertura, orificio, fisura.

hibernoma *n.* hibernoma, tumor benigno localizado en la cadera o en la espalda.

hiccough, hiccups *n.* hipo, contracción involuntaria del diafragma y la glotis.

hidden *a. pp.* de **to hide,** oculto-a, escondido-a, latente.

hide *vi.* esconder; ocultar; esconderse.

hideous *a.* horrible; abominable.

hidradenitis *n.* hidradenitis, infl. de las glándulas sudoríparas.

hidrosis *n.* hidrosis, sudor excesivo.

high *a.* alto-a, elevado-a; ___ **blood pressure** / presión alta; ___ **-calorie diet** / dieta rica en calorías; ___ **color** / de color subido; ___ **cholesterol** / ___ nivel de colesterol; ___ **-risk** / ___ peligro o riesgo; ___ **-risk behavior** / conducta o actividades de ___ riesgo; ___ **-residue diet** / dieta ___ en residuous (fibras, celulosas); ___ **nuclear waste** / desechos nucleares de alta radiactividad; **-ly** *adv.* altamente, sumamente, excesivamente.

high altitude sickness *n.* enfermedad de la altura, trastorno por altura excesiva manifestado en dificultades respiratorias por imposibilidad de adaptarse a la disminución de la presión del oxígeno.

highlight *v.* destacar, realzar, subrayar.

high-risk groups *n. pl.* pacientes o personas con alto riesgo de contraer una determinada enfermedad debido a factores genéticos o conductales; ___ ___ **in HIV** / personas de actividades sexuales múltiples sin adecuada protección; drogadictos que intercambian agujas y jeringuillas; feto *in utero* o infante lactante de madre drogadicta o infectada por el virus.

hike *n.* caminata; *v.* **to go on a** ___ / ir a caminar, ir andando.

hilum, hilus *n.* (*pl.* **hila**) hilio, depresión o apertura en un órgano que sirve de entrada o salida a nervios, vasos y conductos.

hindwater *n.* aguas posteriores, líquido amniótico.

hinge *n.* bisagra; ___ **joint** / coyuntura; ___ **movement** / movimiento de bisagra; ___ **position** /

posición de gozne.

hint *n.* insinuación; indicación.

hip *n.* cadera, región lateral de la pelvis; ___ **dislocation** / dislocación de la ___; ___ **dislocation, congenital** / dislocación congénita de la ___; ___ **joint** / articulación de la ___; **snapping** ___ / ___ de resorte; **total** ___ **replacement** / restitución total de la ___.

hippocampus *n.* (*pl.* **hippocampi**) hipocampo, circunvolución de materia gris que forma la mayor parte de la corteza cerebral olfatoria.

hippocratic facies *n.* facies hipocrática, máscara facial que precede a la muerte.

hippocratic oath *n.* juramento hipocrático, juramento ético de la medicina.

hirsute *a.* hirsuto-a, peludo-a.

hirsutism *n.* hirsutismo, desarrollo excesivo del pelo en áreas no comunes, esp. en la mujer.

histamine *n.* histamina, sustancia que produce efecto dilatador en los vasos capilares y estimula la secreción gástrica.

histidine *n.* histidina, aminoácido esencial en el crecimiento y en la restauración de los tejidos.

histocompatibility *n.* histocompatibilidad, estado en el cual los tejidos de un donante son aceptados por el receptor; **major** ___ **complex (MHC)** / complejo de ___ mayor.

histologist *n.* histólogo-a, especialista en histología.

histology *n.* histología, estudio de los tejidos orgánicos.

histoplasmin *n.* histoplasmina, sustancia que se usa en la prueba cutánea de histoplasmosis.

histoplasmosis *n.* histoplasmosis, enfermedad de las vías respiratorias causada por el hongo *Histoplasma capsulatum.*

histrionic *a.* histriónico-a, dramático-a.

HIV *n. abbr.* **human immunodeficiency virus** / VIH *abr.* virus de inmunodeficiencia humano, retrovirus del SIDA. Se transmite a través de relaciones sexuales o por intercambio de agujas y jeringuillas con una persona infectada. Puede transmitirse también a través de una transfusión de sangre obtenida de donantes infectados. El virus puede ser transmitido igualmente al feto *in utero,* durante el parto o al recién nacido en la lactancia a través de la leche materna de una madre afectada.

hives *n. pl.* ronchas, erupción alérgica.

hoarse *a.* ronco-a; áspero-a.

hoarseness *n.* ronquera, manifestación en la voz de una afección de la laringe.

Hodgkin's disease *n.* enfermedad de Hodgkin, presencia de tumores malignos en los nódulos linfáticos y el bazo.

hold *vi.* aguantar, sujetar; detener, mantener; sostener; contener; **to get** ___ **of** / agarrar; **to** ___ **off** / mantener a distancia; **to** ___ **an interview** / tener una entrevista; **to** ___ **responsible** / hacer responsable.

hole *n.* hueco, agujero.

holistic *a.* holístico-a, rel. a un todo o unidad.

holistic medicine *n.* medicina holística, sistema médico que considera al ser humano integrado como una unidad funcional.

hollow *a.* hueco-a, cóncavo-a.

holocrine *a.* holocrino-a, rel. a las glándulas secretorias.

holodiastolic *a.* holodiastólico-a, rel. a una diástole completa.

hologram *n.* holograma, producción de una holografía.

holography *n.* holografía, figura tridimensional de un objeto por medio de una imagen fotográfica.

holosystolic *a.* holosistólico-a, rel. a una sístole completa.

Holter monitoring *n.* monitoreo de Holter (de funda al hombro), electrocardiografía ambulatoria.

homeopathic *a.* homeopático-a, rel. a la homeopatía.

homeopathy *n.* homeopatía, curación por medio de medicamentos diluidos en cantidades ínfimas que producen efectos semejantes a los síntomas producidos por la enfermedad.

homogeneous *a.* homogéneo-a, semejante, de la misma naturaleza.

homograft *n.* homoinjerto, transplante tomado de la misma especie o tipo.

homologous *a.* homólogo-a, similar en estructura y origen pero no en funcionamiento.

homophobia *n.* homofobia, temor o repulsión a los homosexuales.

homophobic *a.* homofóbico-a, que tiene repulsión o temor a homosexuales.

homosexual *n.* homosexual, invertido-a, atracción sexual por las personas del mismo sexo.

homotonic *a.* homotónico-a, de la misma tensión.

homotopic *a.* homotópico-a, que ocurre en o corresponde al mismo lugar o parte.

homozygote *n.* homocigoto-a, que presenta alelos idénticos en una característica o en varias.

homozygous *a.* homocigótico-a, rel. a un homocigoto.

homunculus *n.* homúnculo-a, enano-a sin deformidades y proporcionado-a en todas las partes del cuerpo.

honest *a.* honesto-a, honrado-a.

honey *n.* miel de abeja.

hook *n.* gancho.

hookworm *n.* uncinaria, lombriz de gancho, nematodo del intestino; ___ **disease** / enfermedad de la ___.

hope *n.* esperanza; *v.* esperar, tener esperanzas.

hopelessness *n.* estado de desesperanza; desesperación.

hordeolum *n.* hordeolo, orzuelo. *V.* **sty.**

horizontal *n., a.* horizontal; ___ **position** / posición acostada.

hormonal *a.* hormonal, rel. a una hormona o

que actúa como tal.

hormone *n.* hormona, sustancia química natural del cuerpo que produce o estimula la actividad de un órgano; **growth** ___ / ___ del crecimiento ___ **receptor** / receptor hormonal; ___ **therapy** / terapia hormonal.

hornet *n.* avispa, avispón.

hospice *n.* hospicio.

hospital *n.* hospital.

hospitalization *n.* hospitalización.

hospitalize *v.* hospitalizar, ingresar en un hospital; dar ingreso en un hospital.

host *n.* [*parasite*] huésped, organismo que sostiene o alberga a otro llamado parásito; ___ **defenses** / defensas del ___.

hostage *n.* rehén.

hostile *a.* hostil; enemigo-a.

hostility *n.* hostilidad, agravio, animosidad.

hot *a.* caliente, de temperatura alta; contaminado-a por material radioactivo; ___ **flashes** / fogaje, sofoco; rubores, bochorno.

hot line *n.* línea telefónica de emergencia.

hour *n.* hora; **by the** ___ / por hora; **-ly** *adv.* a cada hora.

house *n.* casa, vivienda, domicilio; ___ **call** / visita médica.

household *n.* familia.

housewife *n.* ama de casa, madre de familia.

housework *n.* tareas domésticas, trabajo de la casa.

how *adv.* cómo, cuánto; ___ **are you?** / ¿Cómo está?, ¿Cómo estás?; ___ **many?** / ¿Cuántos-as?; ___ **late?** / ¿Hasta qué hora?; ___ **often?** / ¿Cuántas veces?, ¿Con qué frecuencia?

however *adv.* sin embargo, no obstante.

huge *a.* inmenso-a; enorme.

hum *n.* susurro; tarareo; zumbido; *v.* [*music*] tararear; zumbar; murmurar, susurrar.

human *a.* humano-a, rel. a la humanidad.

human immunodeficiency virus, HIV *n.* virus de inmunodeficiencia humana, VIH, retrovirus del SIDA. *V.* **HIV.**

humanity *n.* humanidad.

humeral *a.* humeral, rel. al húmero.

humerus *n.* (*pl.* **humeri**) húmero, hueso largo del brazo.

humid *a.* húmedo-a, que contiene humedad.

humidifier *n.* humectante, humedecedor, aparato que controla y mantiene la humedad en el aire de una habitación.

humidity *n.* humedad.

humor *n.* humor. 1. cualquier forma líquida en el cuerpo; **aqueous** ___ / ___ acuoso, líquido claro en las cámaras del ojo; **crystalline** ___ / ___ cristalino, sustancia que forma el cristalino; **vitreus** ___ / ___ vítreo, sustancia transparente semilíquida localizada entre el cristalino y la retina; 2. secreción; 3. disposición de carácter; *v.* **to be in good** ___ / estar de buen ___; **to be in bad** ___ / estar de mal ___.

humoral *a.* humoral, rel. a los fluidos del cuerpo.

hump *n.* joroba, corcova, jiba.

hunchback *n.* corcova, joroba, deformación con curvatura de la espina dorsal.

hunger *n.* hambre.

hungry *a.* hambriento-a; **to be** ___ / tener hambre; **to go** ___ / pasar hambre.

Huntington's chorea *n.* corea de Huntington, *V.* **chorea.**

Hunt's neuralgia, syndrome *n.* neuralgia de Hunt. *V.* **neuralgia.**

hurdle *n.* obstáculo.

hurry *n.* prisa, apuro; **Are you in a** ___? / ¿Tiene prisa?, ¿tienes prisa?; *v.* apresurar; **to** ___ **him, her in** / traerlo, traerla inmediatamente.

hurt *vi.* lastimar, herir, hacer daño, dañar.

husband *n.* esposo, marido.

hyalin *n.* hialina, sustancia proteínica producto de la degeneración de amiloides, hialoides y coloides.

hyaline *a.* hialino-a, vítreo-a o casi transparente; ___ **cast** / cilindro ___, que se observa en la orina; ___ **membrane disease** / enfermedad de la membrana hialina, trastorno respiratorio que se manifiesta en recién nacidos.

hyalinization *n.* hialinización, conversión a una sustancia semejante al vidrio.

hyalinosis *n.* hialinosis, degeneración hialina.

hyalitis *n.* hialitis, infl. del humor vítreo.

hyaloid *a.* hialoide, hialoideo-a, semejante al vidrio.

hyaluronic acid *n.* ácido hialurónico, presente en la sustancia del tejido conjuntivo, actúa como lubricante y agente conector.

hybrid *a.* híbrido-a, rel. al producto de un cruzamiento de diferentes especies en animales y plantas.

hybridization *n.* hibridación, cruzamiento de especies.

hybridoma *n.* hibridoma, célula somática híbrida capaz de producir anticuerpos.

hydatid *n.* hidátide, quiste que se manifiesta en los tejidos esp. en el hígado; *a.* hidatídico, rel. a un tumor enquistado; ___ **disease** / equinococcosis; ___ **mole** / quiste ___ en el útero que produce hemorragia.

hydramnion *n.* hidramnios, exceso de líquido amniótico.

hydrate *v.* hidratar, combinar un cuerpo con el agua.

hydrocele *n.* hidrocele, acumulación de líquido esp. en la túnica vaginal del testículo.

hydrocelectomy *n.* *cirg.* hidrocelectomía, extirpación de un hidrocele.

hydrocephalus *Gr.* hidrocéfalo, acumulación de líquido cefalorraquídeo en los ventrículos del cerebro.

hydrochloric acid *n.* ácido clorhídrico o hidroclórico, constituyente del jugo gástrico.

hydrocortisone *n.* hidrocortisona, hormona corticosteroide producida por la corteza suprarrenal.

hydroelectric *a.* hidroeléctrico-a, rel. a la electricidad y el agua.

313

hydrogen *n.* hidrógeno; ___ **concentration** / concentración de ___.

hydrogen peroxide *n.* peróxido de hidrógeno, agua oxigenada, limpiador y desinfectante.

hydrolysis *n.* hidrólisis, disolución química de un compuesto por acción del agua.

hydrolyze *v.* hidrolizar.

hydromyelia *n.* hidromielia, aumento de líquido cefalorraquídeo en el canal central de la médula espinal.

hydronephrosis *n.* hidronefrosis, distensión en la pelvis renal y cálices a causa de una obstrucción.

hydrophilic *a.* hidrofílico-a, que tiene tendencia a retener agua.

hydrophobia *n.* hidrofobia, 1. temor excesivo al agua; 2. *pop.* rabia.

hydropic *a.* hidrópico-a, rel. a la hidropesía.

hydropneumothorax *n.* hidroneumotórax, acumulación de líquido y de gas en la cavidad pleural.

hydrops, hydropsy *n.* hidropesía, hidropsia o edema.

hydrosalpinx *n.* hidrosálpinx, acumulación de fluido seroso en la trompa de Falopio.

hydrostatic *a.* hidrostático-a, rel al equilibrio de líquidos, o a la presión ejercida por un líquido estacionario.

hydrotherapy *n.* hidroterapia, uso terapéutico del agua con aplicaciones externas en el tratamiento de enfermedades.

hydrothorax *n.* hidrotórax, colección de fluido en la cavidad pleural sin producir inflamación.

hydroureter *n.* hidrouréter, distensión por obstrucción del uréter.

hydroxyapatite *n.* hidroxiapatita, forma de fosfato de calcio, compuesto inorgánico presente en los dientes y los huesos.

hygiene *n.* higiene, estudio de la salud y la conservación de un cuerpo sano; **mental** ___ / ___ mental; **oral** ___ / ___ oral; **public** ___ / ___ pública.

hygienic *a.* higiénico-a, sanitario-a, rel. a la higiene.

hygienist *n.* higienista, especialista en higiene; **dental** ___ / ___ dental, técnico en profiláctica dental.

hygroma *n.* hidroma, saco o bursa que contiene líquido.

hymen *n.* himen, repliegue membranoso que cubre parcialmente la entrada de la vagina.

hymenectomy *n. cirg.* himenectomía, excisión del himen.

hymenotomía *n. cirg.* himenotomía, incisión del himen.

hyoglossal *a.* hioglosal, rel. al hioides y a la lengua.

hyoglossus *n.* hiogloso, músculo de la lengua de acción retractora y lateral.

hyoid *a.* hioideo-a, rel. al hueso hioides.

hyoid bone *n.* hioides, hueso en forma de herradura situado en la base de la lengua.

hypalgesia, hypalgia *n.* hipalgesia, hipalgia, disminución en la sensibilidad del dolor.

hyperacidity *n.* hiperacidez, acidez excesiva.

hyperactive *a.* hiperactivo-a, excesivamente activo-a.

hyperactivity *n.* actividad excesiva; *psic.* desorden caracterizado por actividad excesiva que se manifiesta en niños y adolescentes acompañado de irritabilidad e incapacidad de mantener la atención.

hyperacuity *n.* desarrollo anormal de uno de los sentidos esp. la vista o el olfato.

hyperacute *a.* sobreagudo-a, extremadamente agudo-a.

hyperalbuminosis *n.* hiperalbuminosis, exceso de albúmina en la sangre.

hyperalimentation *n.* hiperalimentación, sobrealimentación por vía intravenosa.

hyperbilirubinemia *n.* hiperbilirrubinemia, exceso de bilirrubina en la sangre.

hypercalcemia *n.* hipercalcemia, cantidad excesiva de calcio en la sangre.

hypercapnia *n.* hipercapnia, cantidad excesiva de dióxido de carbono en la sangre.

hyperchloremia *n.* hipercloremia, exceso de cloruros en la sangre.

hypercholesterolemia *n.* hipercolesterolemia, *V.* **cholesteremia.**

hyperchromatic *a.* hipercromático-a, con exceso de colorante o pigmentación.

hypercoagulability *n.* hipercoagulabilidad, aumento anormal de la coagulabilidad.

hyperemesis *n.* hiperemesis, vómitos excesivos.

hyperemia *n.* hiperemia, exceso de sangre en un órgano, tejido o parte.

hyperesthesia *n.* hiperestesia, aumento exagerado de la sensibilidad sensorial.

hyperflexion *n.* hiperflexión, flexión excesiva de una articulación, gen. causada por un traumatismo.

hyperfunction *n.* hiperfunción, funcionamiento excesivo.

hypergammaglobulinemia *n.* hipergammaglobulinemia, exceso de gamma globulina en la sangre.

hyperglycemia *n.* hiperglucemia, aumento excesivo de azúcar en la sangre.

hyperglycemic *a.* hiperglucémico-a, que sufre de hiperglucemia, o rel. a la misma.

hyperglycosuria *n.* hiperglucosuria, exceso de azúcar en la orina.

hyperhidrosis *n.* hiperhidrosis, sudor excesivo.

hyperhydration *n.* hiperhidratación, aumento excesivo del contenido de agua en el cuerpo.

hyperinsulinism *n.* hiperinsulinismo, exceso de secreción de insulina en la sangre causando hipoglicemia.

hyperkalemia *n.* hipercalemia, hiperpotasemia, aumento excesivo de potasio en la sangre.

hyperkinesia *n.* hipercinesia, aumento en exceso de actividad muscular.

hyperlipemia *n.* hiperlipemia, cantidad excesiva

de grasa en la sangre.

hyperlipidemia *n.* hiperlipidemia, exceso de lípidos en la sangre.

hypermobility *n.* hipermobilidad, movilidad excesiva.

hypernatremia *n.* hipernatremia, cantidad excesiva de sodio en la sangre.

hypernephroma *n.* hipernefroma, tumor de Grawitz, neoplasma del parénquima renal.

hyperopia *n.* hiperopia, hipermetropía, *V.* **farsightedness.**

hyperorexia *n.* hiperorexia, apetito excesivo.

hyperosmia *n.* hiperosmia, sensibilidad olfativa exagerada.

hyperostosis *n.* hiperostosis, desarrollo excesivo del tejido óseo.

hyperpituitarism *n.* hiperpituitarismo, actividad excesiva de la glándula pituitaria.

hyperplasia *n.* hiperplasia, proliferación excesiva de células normales en un tejido.

hyperpnea *n.* hiperpnea, aumento de la respiración en rapidez y profundidad.

hyperpyrexia *n.* hiperpirexia, temperatura del cuerpo excesivamente alta.

hyperreflexia *n.* hiperreflexia, reflejos exagerados.

hypersalivation *n.* hipersalivación, excesiva secreción de las glándulas salivales.

hypersecretion *n.* hipersecreción, secreción excesiva.

hypersensibility *n.* hipersensibilidad, sensibilidad excesiva al efecto de un antígeno o a un estímulo.

hypersensitive *a.* hipersensible, hiperestésico-a.

hypersplenism *n.* hiperesplenismo, funcionamiento exagerado del bazo.

hypertelorism *n.* hipertelorismo, distancia exagerada en la localización de dos órganos o partes.

hypertension *n.* hipertensión, presión arterial alta; **benign** ___ / ___ benigna; **essential** ___ / ___ esencial; **malignant** ___ / ___ maligna; **portal** ___ / ___ portal; **primary** ___ / ___ primaria; **renal** ___ / ___ renal.

hypertensive *a.* hipertensivo-a, hipertenso-a. 1. que causa elevación en la presión; 2. rel. a la hipertensión o que padece de ella.

hyperthermia *n.* hipertermia. *V.* **hyperpyrexia.**

hyperthyroidism *n.* hipertiroidismo, actividad excesiva de la tiroides.

hypertonic *a.* hipertónico-a, rel. a, o caracterizado por aumento de tonicidad o tensión.

hypertrophy *n.* hipertrofia, desarrollo excesivo o agrandamiento anormal de un órgano o parte; **cardiac** ___ / ___ cardíaca, corazón agrandado; **compensatory** ___ / ___ compensatoria, como resultado de un defecto físico.

hypertropia *n.* hipertropia, tipo de estrabismo.

hyperuricemia *n.* hiperuricemia, exceso de ácido úrico en la sangre.

hyperventilation *n.* hiperventilación, respiración excesivamente rápida y profunda con expiración del aire igualmente rápida.

hyperviscosity *n.* hiperviscosidad, viscosidad excesiva.

hyphema *n.* hifema. 1. ojo inyectado; 2. sangramiento en la cámara anterior del ojo.

hypnagogic *a.* hipnagógico-a. 1. adormecedor-a, que induce al sueño; 2. *psic.* que experimenta alucinaciones o sueños antes de perder el conocimiento o de pasar a un sueño profundo.

hypnosis *n.* hipnosis, estado sugestivo durante el cual la persona sometida responde a mandatos siempre que éstos no contradigan convicciones arraigadas.

hypnotherapy *n.* hipnoterapia, tratamiento terapéutico con práctica de hipnosis.

hypnotism *n.* hipnotismo, práctica de la hipnosis.

hypnotize *v.* hipnotizar, producir hipnosis.

hypoadrenalism *n.* hipoadrenalismo, desorden causado por deficiencia de la glándula suprarrenal.

hypoalbuminemia *n.* hipoalbuminemia, deficiencia de albúmina en la sangre.

hypocalcemia *n.* hipocalcemia, nivel de calcio en la sangre anormalmente bajo.

hypocapnia *n.* hipocapnia, disminución del dióxido de carbono en la sangre.

hypochlorhydria *n.* hipocloridria, deficiencia en la secreción de ácido clorhídrico en el estómago, condición que puede indicar una fase primaria de cáncer.

hypocholesteremia *n.* hipocolesteremia, disminución de colesterol en la sangre.

hypochondria *n.* hipocondría, excesiva preocupación por la salud propia, con síntomas imaginarios de enfermedades.

hypochondriac *n. a.* hipocondríaco-a, hipocóndrico-a, que cree haber contraído alguna enfermedad cuando goza de salud y se preocupa por ello.

hypochondrium *n.* hipocondrio, parte del abdomen a cada lado del epigastrio.

hypochromatism *n.* hipocromatismo, falta o disminución de color o pigmentación, esp. en el núcleo de la célula.

hypochromia *n.* hipocromía, deficiencia de hemoglobina en la sangre.

hypochromic *a.* hipocrómico-a rel. a la hipocromía.

hypocyclosis *n.* hipociclosis, deficiencia en la acomodación visual; **lenticular** ___ / ___ por deficiencia muscular o rigidez del cristalino.

hypodermic *a.* hipodérmico-a, que se aplica por debajo de la piel.

hypofibrinogenemia *n.* hipofibrinogenemia, contenido bajo de fibrinógeno en la sangre.

hypofunction *n.* hipofunción, deficiencia en el funcionamiento de un órgano.

hypogammaglobulinemia *n.* hipogammaglobulinemia, nivel anormalmente bajo de gamma globulina en la sangre; **acquired** ___ / ___ adquirida, que se manifesta después de la infancia.

hypogastrium *n.* hipogastrio, área inferior media y anterior del abdomen.

hypoglossal *a.* hipoglosal, rel. a una posición debajo de la lengua.

hypoglossal nerve *n.* nervio hipogloso.

hypoglycemia *n.* hipoglicemia, hipoglucemia, disminución anormal del contenido de glucosa en la sangre.

hypoglycemic *a.* hipoglicémico-a, hipoglucémico-a, que produce o tiene relación con la hipoglicemia; ___ **agents** / agentes ___-s; ___ **shock** / choque ___ .

hypoinsulinism *n.* hipoinsulinismo, deficiencia en la secreción de insulina.

hypokalemia *n.* hipocalemia, deficiencia en el contenido de potasio en la sangre.

hypokinesia *n.* hipocinesia, disminución de la actividad motora.

hypomania *n.* hipomanía, manía moderada.

hyponatremia *n.* hiponatremia, deficiencia en el contenido de sodio en la sangre.

hypopharynx *n.* hipofaringe, parte de la faringe situada bajo el borde superior de la epiglotis.

hypophysectomy *n. cirg.* hipofisectomía, extirpación de la glándula pituitaria.

hypophysis *n.* hipófisis, glándula pituitaria, cuerpo epitelial localizado en la base de la silla turca.

hypopituitarism *n.* hipopituitarismo, condición patológica debida a disminución de la secreción de la glándula pituitaria.

hypoplasia *n.* hipoplasia, desarrollo incompleto de un órgano o parte.

hypoplastic *a.* hipoplástico-a, rel. a la hipoplasia.

hypoprothrombinemia *n.* hipoprotrombinemia, deficiencia en la cantidad de protrombina en la sangre.

hyporeflexia *n.* hiporreflexia, reflejos débiles.

hypospadias *n.* hipospadias, anomalía congénita de la uretra masculina que consiste en el cierre incompleto de la cara ventral de la uretra en distintos grados de longitud. (En la mujer la uretra tiene salida a la vagina.)

hypotelorism *n.* hipotelorismo, disminución anormal de la distancia entre dos órganos o partes.

hypotension *n.* hipotensión, presión arterial baja.

hypotensive *a.* hipotensivo-a, hipotenso-a, rel. a la presión baja o que sufre de ella.

hypothalamus *n.* hipotálamo, parte del diencéfalo.

hypothermia *n.* hipotermia, temperatura baja.

hypothesis *n.* (*pl.* **hypotheses**) hipótesis, suposición asumida en el desarrollo de una teoría.

hypothrombinemia *n.* hipotrombinemia, deficiencia de trombina en la sangre que causa una tendencia a sangrar.

hypothyroid *a.* hipotiroideo-a, rel. al hipotiroidismo.

hypothyroidism *n.* hipotiroidismo, deficiencia en el funcionamiento de la tiroides.

hypotonic *a.* hipotónico-a. 1. rel. a la deficiencia en tonicidad muscular; 2. de presión osmótica más baja en comparación con otros elementos.

hypoventilation *n.* hipoventilación, reducción en la entrada de aire a los pulmones.

hypovolemia *n.* hipovolemia, disminución del volumen de la sangre en el organismo.

hypoxemia *n.* hipoxemia, insuficiencia de oxígeno en la sangre.

hysterectomy *n. cirg.* histerectomía, extirpación del útero; **abdominal** ___ / ___ abdominal, a través del abdomen; **total** ___ / ___ total, del útero y del cuello uterino; **vaginal** ___ / ___ vaginal, a través de la vagina.

hysteria *n.* histeria, neurosis extrema.

hysteric, hysterical *a.* histérico-a, rel. a la histeria o que padece de ella; ___ **laughter** / risa ___ ; *v.* **to get** ___ / ponerse ___ ; **-ly** *adv.* histéricamente.

hysterics *n.* histerismo, histeria.

hysteroid *n.* histeroide, semejante a la histeria.

hysteromania *n.* histeromanía, ninfomanía.

hysterosalpingography *n.* histerosalpingografía, radiografía del útero y de los oviductos por medio de material de contraste.

hysterosalpingo-oophorectomy *n. cirg.* histerosalpingo-ooforectomía, excisión del útero, de los tubos uterinos y de los ovarios.

hysteroscopy *n.* histeroscopía, examen endoscópico de la cavidad uterina.

hysterotomy *n. cirg.* histerotomía, incisión del útero.

I *abbr.* símbolo químico del iodo.

i *abbr.* **iatric** / iátrico; **immune** / inmune; **implant** / implante; **impotence** / impotencia; **incomplete** / incompleto.

I *pron.* yo, primera persona del singular.

iatric *a.* iátrico-a, rel. a la medicina, a la profesión médica, o a los que la ejercen.

iatrogenic *a.* yatrógeno-a, iatrogénico-a, rel. a un trastorno o lesión producido por un tratamiento o por una instrucción errónea del facultativo.

ibuprofen *n.* ibuprofén, agente antiinflamatorio, antipirético y analgésico usado en el tratamiento de artritis reumatoidea.

ice *n.* hielo; __ **cap,** __ **bag** / bolsa de __; __ **cream** / helado; __ **water** / agua helada, agua con hielo; __ **treatment** / aplicación de hielo; **My hands are like** __. / Tengo las manos heladas.

ichthyosis *n.* ictiosis, dermatosis congénita caracterizada por sequedad y peladura escamosa esp. de las extremidades.

icing *n.* aplicación de hielo.

icteric *a.* ictérico-a, rel. a la ictericia.

icterogenic *a.* icterogénico-a, causante de ictericia.

icterohepatitis *n.* icterohepatitis, hepatitis asociada con ictericia.

icterus *n.* icterus, ictericia. *V.* **jaundice.**

icterus gravis *n.* atrofia amarilla aguda del hígado.

icterus neonatorum *n.* ictericia del recién nacido.

ictus *n.* ictus, ataque súbito.

idea *n.* idea, concepto; **fixed** __ / __ fija.

ideal *n., a.* ideal; perfecto-a.

ideation *n.* ideación, proceso de formación de ideas.

idée fixe *Fr.* idea fija.

identical *a.* idéntico-a, igual, mismo-a.

identical twins *n. pl.* gemelos idénticos formados por la fertilización de un solo óvulo.

identification *n.* identificación; *psic.* proceso en el cual una persona adopta inconscientemente características semejantes a otra persona o grupo; __ **papers** / documento oficial de identidad.

identify *v.* identificar; reconocer.

identity *n.* identidad, reconocimiento propio; __ **crisis** / crisis de __.

ideology *n.* ideología, formación de conceptos e ideas.

ideomotion *n.* ideomoción, actividad muscular dirigida por una idea predominante.

idiocracy *n.* idiocracia, tendencia a someterse a ciertos hábitos o drogas.

idiocy *n.* idiotez, deficiencia mental.

idiogram *n.* idiograma, gráfico repesentativo de los cromosomas de una célula en particular.

idiopathic *a.* idiopático-a. 1. rel. a la idiopatía; 2. que tiene origen espontáneo.

idiopathy *n.* idiopatía, enfermedad espontánea o de origen desconocido.

idiosyncrasy *n.* idiosincrasia. 1. características individuales; 2. reacción peculiar de cada persona a una acción, idea, medicamento, tratamiento o alimento.

idiot *a.* idiota, imbécil.

idiotropic *a.* idiotrópico-a. *V.* **egocentric.**

idioventricular *a.* idioventricular, rel. a los ventrículos o que afecta exclusivamente a éstos.

ignorance *n.* ignorancia.

ignorant *a.* ignorante.

ignore *v.* desatender, ignorar, desconocer, no hacer caso.

ileal *a.* ileal, rel. al íleon.

ileal bypass *n.* desviación quirúrgica del íleon.

ileitis *n.* ileítis, infl. del íleon; **regional** __ / __ regional.

ileocecal *a.* ileocecal, rel. al íleon y al ciego; __ **valve** / válvula __.

ileocolitis *n.* ileocolitis, infl. de la mucosa del íleon y el colon.

ileocystoplasty *n. cirg.* ileocistoplastia, sutura de un segmento del íleon a la vejiga para aumentar la capacidad de ésta.

ileoproctostomy *n. cirg.* ileoproctostomía, anastomosis entre el íleon y el recto.

ileosigmoidostomy *n.* ileosigmoidostomía, anastomosis del íleon al colon sigmoide.

ileostomy *n. cirg.* ileostomía, anastomosis del íleon y la pared abdominal anterior.

ileotransversostomy *n. cirg.* ileotransversostomía, anastomosis del íleon y el colon transverso.

ileum *n.* (*pl.* **ílea**) íleon, porción distal del intestino delgado que se extiende desde el yeyuno al ciego.

iliac *a.* ilíaco-a, rel. al ilion.

iliofemoral *a.* iliofemoral, rel. al ilion y el fémur.

iliohypogastric *a.* iliohipogástrico, rel. al ilion y el hipogastrio.

ilioinguinal *n.* ilioinguinal, rel. a las regiones inguinal e ilíaca.

iliolumbar *a.* iliolumbar, rel. a las regiones ilíaca y lumbar.

ilium *n.* (*pl.* **ilia**) ilion, porción del ilíaco.

ill *a.* enfermo-a, insano-a; *v.* **to be** __ / estar enfermo-a; **to become** __ / enfermarse; **to feel** __ / sentirse indispuesto-a; sentirse mal.

ill-advised *a.* mal aconsejado; mal informado-a; desacertado; imprudente.

ill-behaved *a.* de mala conducta.

illegal *a.* ilegal.

illegible *a.* ilegible.

illegitimate *a.* ilegítimo-a.

ill health *n.* mala salud; *v.* **to be in** __ / no estar bien de salud.

illicit *a.* ilícito, ilegal.

illiterate *a.* analfabeto-a.

ill-mannered *a.* descortés.
illness *n.* enfermedad, dolencia.
ill-tempered *a.* de mal carácter, de mal genio.
illumination *n.* iluminación; **dark field** ___ / iluminación lateral u oblicua del campo oscuro.
illusion *n.* ilusión, interpretación imaginaria de impresiones sensoriales.
illusory *a.* ilusorio-a, rel. a la ilusión.
illustration *n.* ilustración, gráfico.
image *n.* imagen, figura; representación.
imaginary *a.* imaginario-a, ilusorio-a.
imagination *n.* imaginación.
imaging *n.* creación de imágenes.
imbalance *n.* desequilibrio.
imbecile *a.* imbécil.
imbed *v. V.* **embed.**
imbibition *n.* imbibición, absorción de un líquido.
imbricated *a.* imbricado-a, en forma de capas.
imitable *a.* imitable.
imitate *v.* imitar, copiar.
imitation *n.* imitación, copia.
immature *a.* inmaturo-a, inmaduro-a; prematuro-a; sin madurez.
immediate *a.* inmediato-a, cercano-a.
immediately *adv.* inmediatamente, en seguida.
immerse *v.* sumergir, hundir.
immersion *n.* inmersión, sumersión de un cuerpo o materia en un líquido.
immigrant *n.* inmigrante.
imminent *a.* inminente; irremediable.
immobile *a.* inmóvil, estable, fijo-a; que no se puede mover.
immobility *n.* inmovilidad, sin movimiento.
immobilization *n.* inmovilización.
immobilize *v.* inmovilizar.
immoderate *a.* inmoderado-a, sin moderación.
immoral *a.* inmoral, corrompido-a, vicioso-a.
immorality *n.* inmoralidad.
immortal *a.* inmortal, imperecedero-a.
immune *a.* inmune, resistente a contraer una enfermedad; ___ **response** / respuesta ___; ___ **reaction** / reacción ___.
immune system *n.* sistema inmunológico.
immunity *n.* inmunidad. 1. condición del organismo de resistir a un determinado antígeno por activación de anticuerpos específicos; 2. resistencia creada por el organismo en contra de una enfermedad específica; **active** ___ / ___ activa, producción propia de anticuerpos; **acquired** ___ / ___ adquirida, presencia de anticuerpos y reactivación de células que forman anticuerpos; **natural** ___ / ___ natural, de tipo genético; **passive** ___ / ___ pasiva, adquirida de un donante; **artificial** ___ / ___ artificial, tal como la inmunidad adquirida en una vacunación.
immunization *n.* inmunización, proceso para activar la producción de inmunidad en el organismo en contra de una determinada enfermedad.
immunize *v.* inmunizar, hacer inmune.
immunoassay *n.* inmunoensayo, proceso para determinar la capacidad de una sustancia para

Immunizations/Inmunizaciones

Age	Vaccine	Method	Edad	Vacuna	Método
2 months	DTP (diphteria, tetanus, pertussis) OPV (oral poliovirus)	vaccination by mouth	2 meses	DTP (difteria, tétano, pertusis o tosferina); VOP (virus oral de la polio)	vacuna por vía oral
4 months	DTP OPV	vaccination by mouth	4 meses	DTP VOP	vacuna por vía oral
6 months	DTP	vaccination	6 meses	DTP	vacuna
15 months	MMR (measles, mumps, rubella)	vaccination	15 meses	SPR (sarampión, paperas, rubéola)	vacuna
18 months	DTP OPV	vaccination by mouth	18 meses	DTP VOP	vacuna por vía oral
2 years	Hib (Haemophilus Influenzae b)	vaccination	2 años	Hib (hemófilo, influenza b)	vacuna
4–6 years	DTP OPV	vaccination by mouth	4–6 años	DTP VOP	vacuna por vía oral

actuar como antígeno y anticuerpo en un tejido; **enzyme** ___ / ___ enzimático.

immunochemotherapy *n.* inmunoquimioterapia, proceso combinado de inmunoterapia y quimioterapia aplicado en el tratamiento de ciertos tumores malignos.

immunocompetency *n.* inmunocompetencia, proceso de alcanzar inmunidad después de la exposición a un antígeno.

immunodeficiency *n.* inmunodeficiencia, reacción inmune celular inadecuada que limita la habilidad de responder a estímulos antigénicos; **severe combined ___ disease** / enfermedad grave de ___ combinada.

immunoelectrophoresis *n.* inmunoelectroforesis, uso de electroforesis como técnica para investigar el número y tipo de proteínas y anticuerpos presentes en los líquidos del organismo.

immunofluorescence *n.* inmunofluorescencia, método que usa anticuerpos marcados con fluorescina para localizar antígenos en los tejidos.

immunogen *n.* inmunógeno, sustancia que produce inmunidad; **targeted ___** / ___ específico.

immunoglobuline *n.* inmunoglobulina. 1. proteína de origen animal que pertenece al grupo del sistema de respuesta inmune; 2. uno de los cinco tipos de gamma globulina capaz de actuar como anticuerpo.

immunologic *a.* inmunológico-a, rel. a la inmunología.

immunologist *n.* inmunólogo-a, especialista en inmunología.

immunology *n.* inmunología, rama de la medicina que estudia las reacciones del cuerpo a cualquier invasión extraña, tal como la de bacterias, virus o trasplantes.

immunoprotein *n.* inmunoproteína, proteína que actúa como anticuerpo.

immunostimulant *n.* inmunoestimulante, agente capaz de inducir o estimular una respuesta inmune.

immunosuppressant *n.* inmunosupresor, agente capaz de suprimir una respuesta inmune.

immunotherapy *n.* inmunoterapia, inmunización pasiva del paciente por medio de anticuerpos preformados (suero o gamma globulina).

immunotyping *n.* tipificación inmunológica.

impact *n.* colisión, impacto; efecto; golpe; *v.* impactar, fijar, rellenar, asegurar; incrustar.

impacted tooth *n.* diente impactado.

impaction *n.* impacción. 1. condición de estar alojado o metido con firmeza en un espacio limitado; 2. impedimento de un órgano o parte.

impair *v.* dañar; debilitar, desmejorar.

impaired *a.* impedido-a, baldado-a; desmejorado-a, debilitado-a.

impalpable *n.* impalpable.

impartial *a.* imparcial.

impatient *a.* impaciente; *v.* **to get, to become ___** / impacientarse, perder la paciencia.

impede *v.* impedir, obstruir.

impediment *n.* impedimento, obstáculo, obstrucción.

impenetrable *a.* impenetrable, que no puede ser penetrado.

imperative *n. gr.* inperativo; *a.* imperativo-a; requerido-a.

imperfect *n. gr.* tiempo imperfecto; *a.* imperfecto-a; defectuoso-a.

imperfection *n.* imperfección, deformidad, defecto.

imperforate *a.* imperforado-a; **___ hymen** / himen ___.

imperil *v.* poner en peligro, arriesgar, hacer daño.

impermeable *a.* impermeable, impenetrable, que no deja pasar líquidos.

impersonal *a.* impersonal.

impetigo *n.* impétigo, infección bacteriana de la piel que se caracteriza por pústulas dolorosas de tamaño diferente que al desecarse forman costras amarillentas.

impetuous *a.* impetuoso-a.

implant *n.* implante, cualquier material insertado o injertado en el cuerpo; *v.* implantar, injertar, insertar.

implantation *n.* implantación, inserción o fijación de una parte o tejido en un área del cuerpo.

implanted *a. pp.* de **to implant**, implantado-a.

implication *n.* implicación.

imply *v.* implicar, insinuar.

importance *n.* importancia.

important *a.* importante.

impose *v.* imponer.

impossible *a.* imposible.

impotence *n.* impotencia, incapacidad de tener o mantener una erección.

impotent *a.* impotente.

impractical *a.* poco práctico-a.

impregnate *n.* impregnar; saturar.

impression *n.* impresión; imagen.

impressive *a.* impresionante.

improbable *a.* improbable.

improper action *n.* acción incorrecta.

improve *v.* mejorar; adelantar; mejorarse, recuperarse; restablecerse.

improved *a. pp.* de **to improve**, mejorado-a, recuperado-a.

improvement *n.* mejoría, restablecimiento, recuperación.

improvise *v.* improvisar.

improvised *a.* improvisado-a.

impulse *n.* impulso; fuerza súbita impulsiva; **cardiac ___** / ___ cardíaco; **excitatory ___** / ___ excitante; **inhibitory ___** / ___ inhibitorio; **nervous ___** / ___ nervioso; *v.* **to act on ___** / dejarse llevar por un ___.

impulsive *a.* impulsivo-a; irreflexivo-a.
impure *a.* impuro-a; contaminado-a, adulterado-a.
in *prep.* [*inside of*] dentro de; [*in time*] con; [*in the night, day, etc.*] durante, por; [*in place*] en; *adv.* dentro; adentro; ___ **the meantime** / mientras tanto; ___ **the care of** / al cuidado de.
inability *n.* inhabilidad, incapacidad.
inaccurate *a.* inexacto-a, incorrecto-a.
inaction *n.* inacción, fallo en responder a un estímulo.
inactive *a.* inactivo-a, pasivo-a.
inactivity *n.* inactividad; **physical** ___ / ___ física.
inadequate *a.* inadecuado-a, impropio-a.
inanition *n.* inanición; debilidad; desnutrición.
inarticulate *a.* inarticulado-a, incapaz de articular palabras o sílabas.
in articulo mortis *L.* in articulo mortis, a la hora de la muerte, al instante de morir.
inborn *a.* innato-a, cualidad congénita.
incandescent *a.* incandescente, con brillo de luz.
incapable *a.* incapaz.
incapacitate *v.* incapacitar, imposibilitar, inhabilitar.
incapacitated *a.* incapacitado-a.
incarcerated *a.* constricto-a; encarcelado-a; limitado-a.
incase *v.* encajar, encajonar.
incasement *n.* encajonamiento, encerramiento.
incentive *n.* incentivo, estímulo; incitante, estimulante.
incessant *a.* incesante, constante.
incest *n.* incesto.
incestuous *a.* incestuoso-a.
inch *n.* pulgada.
incidence *n.* incidencia; frecuencia.
incidental *a.* incidental, casual.
incinerate *v.* incinerar.
incipient *a.* incipiente, principiante, que comienza a existir.
incise *v.* cortar, hacer un corte.
incised *a.* cortado-a, inciso-a.
incision *n.* incisión, corte, cortadura.
incisor *n.* diente incisivo.
incisura *n. L.* incisura, corte, raja.
inclination *n.* inclinación.
inclusion *n.* inclusión, acto de contener una cosa dentro de otra; ___ **bodies** / cuerpos de ___, presentes en el citoplasma de ciertas células en casos de infección.
incoherence *n.* incoherencia, falta de coordinación de las ideas.
incoherent *a.* incoherente, que no coordina las ideas.
income *n.* ingreso, entrada; ___ **tax** / impuestos.
incompatibility *n.* incompatibilidad.
incompatible *a.* incompatible.
incompetent *a.* incompetente, incapacitado-a.
incomplete *a.* incompleto-a.
inconsiderate *a.* desconsiderado-a.
inconsistency *n.* inconsistencia.

inconsistent *a.* inconsistente.
incontinence *n.* incontinencia, emisión involuntaria, inhabilidad de controlar la orina o las heces fecales; **overflow** ___ / ___ por rebosamiento; **urinary stress** ___ / ___ urinaria de esfuerzo.
incontinent *a.* incontinente, rel. a la incontinencia.
inconvenience *n.* inconveniencia.
inconvenient *a.* inconveniente.
incoordinate *a.* incoordinado, sin coordinación.
incoordination *n.* falta de coordinación.
incorporate *v.* incorporar, añadir.
incorrect *a.* incorrecto-a.
increase *v.* aumentar, agrandar.
incubation *n.* incubación. 1. período de latencia de una enfermedad antes de manifestarse; 2. mantenimiento de un ambiente especial ajustado a las necesidades de recién nacidos, esp. prematuros; ___ **period** / período de ___.
incubator *n.* incubadora, receptáculo usado para asegurar las condiciones óptimas en el cuidado de prematuros.
incurable *a.* incurable, que no tiene cura.
incus *L.* incus, huesecillo del oído medio.
indecision *n.* indecisión; irresolución.
indecisive *a.* indeciso-a; irresoluto-a.
indefinite *a.* indefinido-a; indeterminado-a.
indemnity *n.* indemnización, resarcimiento; ___ **benefits** / beneficios de ___; ___ **insurance** / seguro de ___.
independent *a.* independiente.
indeterminate *a.* indeterminado-a, desconocido-a.
index *n.* índice; sumario.
indicate *v.* indicar, señalar.
indicated *a.* indicado-a; apropiado-a.
indication *n.* indicación; señal.
indicator *n.* indicador, señalador.
indifferent *a.* indiferente.
indigenous *a.* autóctono-a, indígena.
indigestion *n.* indigestión.
indirect *a.* indirecto-a.
indispensable *a.* indispensable, necesario-a.
indispose *v.* indisponer, enfermar.
indisposed *a.* maldispuesto-a; indispuesto-a; **to become** ___ / enfermarse.
indisposition *n.* indisposición, desorden o enfermedad pasajera.
indissoluble *a.* indisoluble.
individual *n.* individuo; *a.* individual.
individuality *n.* individualidad.
indivisible *a.* indivisible.
indolent *a.* indolente, perezoso-a; inactivo-a, lento-a en desarrollarse, tal como sucede en ciertas úlceras.
induce *v.* inducir, provocar, suscitar, ocasionar.
induced *a. pp.* de **to induce,** inducido-a, provocado-a.
induction *a.* inducción, acción o efecto de in-

ducir.

ineffective *a.* inefectivo-a; inútil.

inefficient *a.* deficiente; ineficaz.

inert *a.* inerte, rel. a la inercia.

inertia *n.* incercia, falta de actividad.

inexperience *n.* inexperiencia, sin experiencia.

infancy *n.* infancia, menor edad, primera edad, período desde el nacimiento hasta los primeros dos años.

infant *n.* infante, lactante.

infanticide *n.* infanticidio.

infantile *a.* infantil, pueril; ___ **paralysis** / parálisis ___.

infantilism *n.* infantilismo, manifestación de características infantiles en la edad adulta.

infarct, infarction *n.* infarto, necrosis de un área de tejido por falta de irrigación sanguínea (isquemia); **bland** ___ / ___ blando; **cardiac** ___ / ___ cardíaco; **cerebral** ___ / ___ cerebral; **hermorrhagic** ___ / ___ hemorrágico; **myocardial** ___ / ___ del miocardio; **pulmonary** ___ / ___ pulmonar.

infect *v.* infectar; infectarse.

infected *a.* infectado-a.

infection *n.* infección, invasión del cuerpo por microorganismos patógenos y la reacción y efecto que éstos provocan en los tejidos; **acute** ___ / ___ aguda; **airborne** ___ / ___ aerógena; **chronic** ___ / ___ crónica; **contagious** ___ / ___ contagiosa; **cross** ___ / ___ hospitalaria; **fungus** ___ / ___ de hongos parásitos; **massive** ___ / ___ masiva; **opportunistic** ___ / enfermedad oportunista infecciosa; **pyogenic** ___ / ___ piogénica; **secondary** ___ / ___ secundaria; **subclinical** ___ / ___ subclínica; **systemic** ___ / ___ sistémica; **water-borne** ___ / ___ hídrica.

infectious *a.* infeccioso-a, rel. a una infección; ___ **agent** / agente ___; ___ **disease** / enfermedad ___.

infecundity *n.* infecundidad, esterilidad.

infer *v.* inferir, deducir.

inferior *a.* inferior.

inferiority complex *n.* complejo de inferioridad.

infertility *n.* infertilidad, inhabilidad de concebir o procrear.

infestation *n.* infestación, invasión del organismo por parásitos.

infiltrate *v.* infiltrar, penetrar.

infiltration *n.* infiltración, acumulación de sustancias extrañas en un tejido o célula.

infirmary *n.* enfermería, establecimiento de salud, local donde se atiende a personas enfermas o lesionadas.

inflame *v.* inflamar; inflamarse.

inflammation *n.* inflamación, reacción de un tejido lesionado.

inflammatory *a.* inflamatorio-a, rel. a la inflamación.

inflation *n.* inflación, distensión.

inflection *n.* inflexión, torcimiento.

inflict *v.* infligir, causar sufrimiento.

inflow *n.* flujo, afluencia, entrada.

influenza *n.* influenza, infección viral aguda del tracto respiratorio.

inform *v.* informar, comunicar, avisar.

information *n.* información; informe.

infraclavicular *a.* infraclavicular, localizado debajo de la clavícula.

infraction *a.* infracción, fractura ósea incompleta sin desplazamiento.

infradiaphragmatic *a.* infradiafragmático-a, localizado debajo del diafragma.

infraorbital *a.* infraorbital, infraorbitario-a, localizado debajo de la órbita.

infrared rays *n. pl.* rayos infrarrojos.

infrascapular *n.* infraescapular, localizado debajo de la escápula.

infrequent *a.* infrecuente, raro-a.

infundibulum *n.* (*pl.* **infundibula**) infundíbulo, estructura en forma de embudo.

infusion *n.* infusión. 1. introducción lenta, por gravedad, de líquidos en una vena; 2. sumersión de un elemento en agua para obtener los principios activos solubles.

ingest *v.* ingerir.

ingestant, ingesta *n.* alimentación oral.

ingestion *n.* ingestión, proceso de ingerir alimentos.

ingredient *n.* ingrediente, componente.

ingrowing *a.* rel. a una parte que crece hacia adentro y no hacia afuera, en forma opuesta a lo normal.

ingrown nail *n.* uñero; uña encarnada, uña enterrada.

inguinal *a.* inguinal, rel. a la ingle; ___ **canal** / conducto, canal ___; ___ **hernia** / hernia ___; ___ **ligament** / ligamento ___; ___ **ring** / anillo ___.

inhalant *n.* inhalante, medicamento administrado por inhalación.

inhalation *n.* inhalación, aspiración de aire o vapor a los pulmones; **smoke** ___ / ___ de humo.

inhale *v.* inhalar, aspirar.

inherent *a.* inherente, rel. a una cualidad natural o innata.

inherit *v.* heredar.

inheritance *n.* herencia. V. **heredity.**

inherited *a.* heredado-a, rel. a la herencia.

inhibit *v.* inhibir; inhibirse, cohibirse.

inhibition *n.* inhibición, interrupción o restricción de una acción o hábito.

inhibitor *n.* inhibidor, agente que causa una inhibición.

initial *a.* inicial, primero-a.

initiate *v.* iniciar, comenzar, empezar.

inject *v.* inyectar, acto de introducir líquidos en un tejido, vaso o cavidad por medio de un inyector.

injection *n.* inyección, acción de inyectar una droga o líquido en el cuerpo.

injector *n.* inyector, jeringa, dispositivo que se usa para inyectar.

injure *v.* dañar; lastimar, herir.

injured *a. pp.* de **to injure,** lastimado-a, dañado-a; herido-a.

injury *n.* lesión, lastimadura; herida; ___-free / ileso-a.

ink *n.* tinta.

inlaid *a.* incrustado-a; embutido-a.

inlet *n.* entrada, acceso.

innate *a.* innato-a, inherente.

inner *a.* interior.

innervate *v.* inervar, estimular un área o parte con energía nerviosa.

innervation *n.* inervación. 1. acto de inervar; 2. distribución de nervios o de energía nerviosa en un órgano o área.

innocent *a.* inocente.

inoculable *a.* inoculable, que puede ser transmitido por inoculación.

inoculate *v.* inocular, inmunizar, vacunar.

inoculation *n.* inoculación, vacunación, inmunización, acción de administrar sueros, vacunas u otras sustancias para producir o incrementar inmunidad a una enfermedad determinada.

inoculum *n.* (*pl.* **inocula**) inóculo, la sustancia introducida por inoculación.

inoperable *a.* inoperable, que no puede tratarse quirúrgicamente.

inorganic *a.* inorgánico-a; que no pertenece a organismos vivos.

inosculating *n.* comunicación directa, anastomosis.

inotropic *a.* inotrópico-a, que afecta la intensidad o energía de las contracciones musculares.

inquest *n.* encuesta, investigación oficial.

insalubrious *a.* insalubre; antihigiénico-a.

insane *a.* loco-a, demente.

insanitary *a.* antihigiénico-a.

insanity *n.* locura, demencia.

insanity defense *n.* defensa por demencia.

insatiable *a.* insaciable, insatisfecho-a.

insect *n.* insecto.

insecticide *n.* insecticida.

insecurity *n.* inseguridad.

insemination *n.* inseminación, fertilización de un óvulo.

insensible *n.* insensible, que carece de sensibilidad.

inseparable *a.* inseparable.

insertion *n.* inserción; 1. acto de insertar; 2. punto de unión de un músculo y un hueso.

inside *prep.* por dentro, hacia adentro; adentro.

insider *n.* persona bien informada.

insidious *a.* insidioso-a, rel. a una enfermedad que se desarrolla gradualmente sin producir síntomas obvios.

insight *n.* conocimiento; penetración; *v.* **to get an ___ into** / formarse una idea de; hacer un estudio detenido.

insignificant *a.* insignificante, sin importancia.

insipid *a.* insípido-a, sin sabor; *pop.* soso-a.

insist *v.* insistir; **to ___ on** / ___ en; **to ___ that** /

___ en que.

in situ *L.* in situ. 1. en el lugar normal; 2. que no se extiende más allá del sitio en que se origina.

insolation *n.* insolación. *V.* **sunstroke.**

insoluble *a.* insoluble, que no se disuelve.

insomnia *n.* insomnio, desvelo.

inspection *n.* inspección.

install *v.* instalar, colocar.

installation *n.* instalación; montaje.

instant *n.* instante; *a.* instantáneo-a, inmediato-a; urgente.

instep *n.* empeine, parte anterior del pie.

instillation *n.* instilación, goteo de un líquido en una cavidad o superficie.

instinct *n.* instinto.

instinctive *a.* instintivo-a.

institution *n.* institución; fundación; establecimiento; [*mental*] asilo, manicomio; [*home for the aged*] asilo de ancianos.

instruct *v.* instruir, enseñar, dar instrucciones.

instrument *n.* instrumento.

insufficiency *n.* insuficiencia, falta de; **adrenal ___ / ___** suprarrenal; **cardiac ___ / ___** cardíaca; **coronary ___ / ___** coronaria; **hepatic ___ / ___** hepática; **mitral ___ / ___** mitral; **pulmonary valvular ___ / ___** pulmonar-valvular; **renal ___ / ___** renal; **respiratory ___ / ___** respiratoria; **valvular ___ / ___** valvular; **venous ___ / ___** venosa.

insufficient *a.* insuficiente.

insufflate *v.* insuflar, soplar hacia el interior de una cavidad, parte u órgano.

insula *n.* ínsula, lóbulo central del hemisferio cerebral.

insulin *n.* insulina. hormona secretada en el páncreas; ___ **dependent** / insulinodependiente.

insulinemia *n.* insulinemia, exceso de insulina en la sangre.

insurance *n.* seguro; compañía de seguros; *Mex.* aseguranza; **disability ___ / ___** por incapacidad; **life ___ / ___** de vida; **medical ___ / ___** médico; ___ **policy** / póliza de ___ .

insure *v.* asegurar; asegurarse.

intake *n. V.* **ingestion.**

intelligence *n.* inteligencia.

intelligent *a.* inteligente, listo-a.

intense *a.* intenso-a.

intensify *v.* intensificar.

intensity *n.* intensidad.

intensive *a.* intensivo-a.

intention *n.* intención. 1. meta o propósito; 2. proceso natural en la curación de heridas.

intentional *a.* intencional, a propósito.

interaction *n.* interacción; **drug ___ / ___** de medicamentos.

intercalated *a.* intercalado-a, colocado-a entre dos partes o elementos.

intercostal *a.* intercostal, entre dos costillas.

intercourse *n.* [*sexual*] coito, relaciones sexuales; intercambio, comunicación.

intercurrent *a.* intercurrente, que aparece

en el curso de una enfermedad y que la modifica.

interdigitation *n.* interdigitación, entrecruzamiento de partes esp. los dedos.

interest *n.* interés; *v.* to take an ___ in / interesarse por.

interfere *v.* interferir.

interference *n.* interferencia, anulación o colisión entre dos partes.

interferon *n.* interferón, proteína natural liberada por células expuestas a la acción del virus que se usa en el tratamiento de infecciones y neoplasmas.

interfibrillar *a.* interfibrilar, localizado entre fibrillas.

interim *L.* interim, entretanto.

interior *a.* interior.

interlobular *a.* interlobular, que ocurre entre dos lóbulos de un órgano.

intermediary *a.* intermediario-a, situado entre dos cuerpos.

intermediate *a.* intermedio-a, situado entre dos extremos; después del principio y antes del final.

intermittent *a.* intermitente, que no es continuo; ___ **positive-pressure breathing** / ventilación ___ bajo presión positiva; ___ **pulse** / pulso ___.

intern *n.* interno-a; médico-a interno-a.

internal *a.* interno-a, dentro del cuerpo; ___ **bleeding** / hemorragia ___.

internalization *n. psic.* internalización, proceso inconsciente por el cual una persona adapta las creencias y valores de otra persona o de la sociedad en que vive.

International Red Cross *n.* Cruz Roja Internacional, organización mundial de asistencia médica.

International unit (I.U.) *n.* unidad internacional, medida de una sustancia definida aceptada por la Conferencia Internacional de Unificación de Fórmulas (C.I.U.F.)

interpret *v.* interpretar, traducir oralmente.

interpretation *n.* interpretación.

interpreter *n.* intérprete.

interruption *n.* interrupción.

interstices *n. pl.* intersticios, intervalos o pequeños espacios.

interstitial *a.* intersticial, rel. a los espacios dentro de un tejido, órgano o célula.

interval *n.* intervalo; espacio; período de tiempo.

intervene *v.* intervenir; asistir; supervisar.

interventricular *a.* interventricular, localizado entre los ventrículos; ___ **optum** / tabique ___ del corazón.

intervertebral disk *n.* disco intervertebral.

interview *n.* entrevista.

intestinal *a.* intestinal, rel. a los intestinos; ___ **bypass surgery** / desviación quirúrgica ___; ___ **flora** / flora ___; ___ **juice** / jugo ___; ___ **obstruction** / obstrucción ___; ___ **perfora-**

tion / perforación ___.

intestine *n.* intestino, tubo digestivo que se extiende del píloro al ano; **large** ___ / ___ grueso; **small** ___ / ___ delgado.

intima *L.* (*pl.* **intimae**) íntima, la membrana o túnica más interna de las capas de un órgano tal como en un vaso capilar.

intimal *a.* íntimal, rel. a la íntima.

intolerance *n.* intolerancia, incapacidad de soportar dolor o los efectos de una droga.

intoxicate *v.* intoxicar.

intoxication *n.* intoxicación, envenenamiento o estado tóxico producido por una droga o sustancia tóxica.

intra-abdominal *a.* intrabdominal, localizado dentro del abdomen.

intra-aortic *a.* intraórtico-a, rel. a o situado dentro de la aorta.

intra-arterial *a.* intra-arterial, dentro de una arteria.

intra-articular *a.* intra-articular, dentro de una articulación.

intracapsular *a.* intracapsular, dentro de una cápsula.

intracellular *a.* intracelular, dentro de una célula o células.

intracranial *a.* intracraneal, dentro del cráneo.

intrahepatic *a.* intrahepático-a, dentro del hígado.

intralobular *a.* intralobular, dentro de un lóbulo.

intraluminal *a.* intraluminal. 1. dentro de la luz o estructura lumínica; 2. semejante al lumen de un vaso arterial o venoso.

intramuscular *a.* intramuscular, dentro del músculo.

intraocular *a.* intraocular, dentro del ojo; ___ **pressure** / presión ___.

intraoperative *a.* intraoperatorio-a, que tiene lugar durante un proceso quirúrgico.

intraosseous *a.* intraóseo-a, dentro de la sustancia ósea.

intrarenal *a.* intrarrenal, que ocurre dentro del riñón; ___ **failure** / insuficiencia ___.

intrauterine *a.* intrauterino-a, dentro del útero; ___ **device (IUD)** / dispositivo ___.

intravenous *a.* intravenoso-a, dentro de una vena; ___ **infusion** / infusión ___; ___ **injection** / inyección ___.

intraventricular *a.* intraventricular, dentro de un ventrículo.

intrinsic *a.* intrínseco-a, esencial, exclusivo-a. *V.* **inherent**.

intrinsic factor *n.* factor intrínseco, proteína normalmente presente en el jugo gástrico humano.

introducer *n.* intubador, divisa utilizada para intubar.

introitus *L.* introito, abertura o entrada a un canal o cavidad.

introspection *n.* introspección, análisis propio o de sí mismo-a.

introversion *psic.* inversion, introversión, acto de concentración de una persona en sí misma, con disminución del interés por el mundo externo.

intubation *n.* intubación, inserción de un tubo en un conducto o cavidad del cuerpo.

intussusception *n.* intususcepción, invaginación tal como la de una porción del intestino que causa una obstrucción intestinal.

in utero *L.* in utero, dentro del útero.

invade *v.* invadir, penetrar; atacar.

invaginate *v.* invaginar, replegar una porción de una estructura en otra parte de la misma.

invagination *n.* invaginación, proceso de inclusión de una parte dentro de otra.

invalid *a.* inválido-a; debilitado-a; incapacitado-a.

invariable *a.* invariable, que no cambia.

invasion *n.* invasión, acto de invadir.

invasive *a.* invasor-a, invasivo-a; que invade tejidos adyacentes; **non-___** / no ___ .

inverse, inverted *a.* inverso-a, invertido-a.

inversion *n.* inversión, proceso de volverse hacia adentro.

invert *v.* invertir.

investigation *n.* investigación, indagación.

investment *n.* revestimiento, cubierta.

invisible *a.* invisible, que no puede verse a simple vista.

in vitro *L.* in vitro, dentro de una vasija de vidrio, término aplicado a pruebas de laboratorio.

in vivo *L.* in vivo, en el cuerpo vivo.

involuntary *a.* involuntario-a.

involution *n.* involución, cambio retrógrado.

involutional melancholia *n. psic.* melancolía involucional, trastorno emocional depresivo que se observa en mujeres de 40 a 55 años y en hombres de 50 a 65 años.

involved *a.* envuelto-a en, metido-a en; **He is ___ in the case** / Él está ___ el caso.

iodine *n.* iodo, yodo. 1. elemento no metálico que pertenece al grupo halógeno usado como componente en medicamentos para contribuir al desarrollo y funcionamiento de la tiroides; 2. tintura de yodo usada como germicida y desinfectante.

iodism *n.* yodismo, envenenamiento por yodo.

iodize *v.* yodurar, tratar con yodo.

ion *n.* ion, átomo o grupo de átomos provistos de carga eléctrica.

ionization *n.* ionización, disociación de compuestos en los iones que los componen.

ionizing radiation *n.* radiación por ionización.

ipecac, syrup of *n.* jarabe de ipecacuana, emético y expectorante.

ipsilateral *a.* ipsilateral, ipsolateral, que afecta el mismo lado del cuerpo.

irascible *a.* irascible, que se irrita fácilmente.

iridectomy *n. círg.* iridectomía, extirpación de una parte del iris.

iridology *n.* iridología, estudio del iris y de los cambios que éste sufre en el curso de una enfermedad.

iris *n.* iris, membrana contráctil del humor acuoso del ojo situada entre el cristalino y la córnea, que regula la entrada de la luz.

iritis *n.* iritis, infl. del iris.

iron *n.* hierro; *v.* **to have an ___ constitution** / tener una constitución de hierro.

iron-deficiency anemia *n.* anemia por deficiencia de hierro.

iron lung *n.* pulmón de hierro, máquina que se usa para producir respiración artificial.

irradiate *v.* irradiar; exponer a o tratar por uso de radiación.

irradiation *n.* irradiación, uso terapéutico de radiaciones.

irrational *n.* irracional.

irreducible *a.* irreducible, que no puede reducirse.

irregular *a.* irregular.

irrelevant *a.* ajeno-a, no pertinente, que no tiene relación con lo que se discute; que no viene al caso.

irrigate *v.* irrigar, lavar con un chorro de agua.

irrigation *n.* irrigación, acto o proceso de irrigar.

irritability *n.* irritabilidad, propiedad de un organismo o tejido de reaccionar al ambiente.

irritable *n.* irritable, que reacciona con irritación a un estímulo.

irritate *v.* irritar.

irritation *n.* irritación, reacción extrema a un dolor o a una condición patológica.

ischemia *n.* isquemia, insuficiencia de riego sanguíneo a un tejido o parte; **silent ___** / ___ silenciosa.

ischemic *a.* isquémico-a, que padece de isquemia o rel. a la misma.

ischium *n.* (*pl.* **ischia**) isquion, parte posterior de la pelvis.

island *n.* isla, nombre dado a un grupo celular o a un tejido aislado.

islets of Langerhans *n.* V. **Langerhans, islets of.**

isolate *v.* aislar, separar.

isolated *a.* aislado-a, separado-a.

isolation *n.* aislamiento, proceso de aislar o separar; **___ ward** / sala de ___ .

isometric *a.* isométrico-a, de dimensiones iguales.

isoniazid *n.* isoniazida, medicamento antibacteriano usado en el tratamiento de tuberculosis.

isotonic *a.* isotónico-a, que tiene la misma tensión que otra dada; **___ exercise** / ejercicio ___ .

isotope *n.* isótopo, elemento químico que pertenece a un grupo de elementos que presentan propiedades casi idénticas, pero que difiere de éstos en el peso atómico.

issue *n.* emisión; cuestión; **___ of blood** / pérdida de sangre; **to avoid the ___** / esquivar la cuestión; *v.* brotar, fluir; emitir.

issued *a.* expedido-a, emitido-a.

issuing *n.* salida.

it *pron. neut. (pl.* **they**); **the best of** ___ / lo mejor; **the worst of** ___ / lo peor; **it's,** *contr.* de **it is** / eso es; es.

itch *n.* picazón.

itching *n.* sensación de picazón.

itself *pron. m.* (él) mismo, sí mismo; *f.* (ella) misma; sí misma.

ivy *n.* hiedra.

j *abbr.* joint / articulación.

jab *n.* pinchazo, punzada; golpe corto; *v.* pinchar; dar golpes cortos.

jacket *n.* forro; corsé, soporte del tronco y de la espina dorsal usado para corregir deformidades.

Jacksonian epilepsy *n.* epilepsia jacksoniana, epilepsia parcial sin pérdida del conocimiento.

jam *n.* conserva, compota; *v.* **to be in a ___** / estar en apuros.

jamais vu *Fr.* jamais vu, nunca visto, percepción de una experiencia familiar o conocida como si fuera una experiencia nueva.

jar *n.* jarro, frasco, pomo, recipiente de cristal.

jargon *n.* jerga, jerigonza; parafasia. *V.* **paraphasia.**

jasmine *n.* jazmín; **___ tea** / té de ___.

jaundice *n.* ictericia, derrame biliar por exceso de bilirrubina en la sangre que causa pigmentación amarillo-anaranjada de la piel y otros tejidos y fluidos del cuerpo; **obstructive ___** / ___ obstructiva, obstrucción de la bilis. *V.* **icterus.**

jaundiced *a.* ictérico-a, rel. a la ictericia o que padece de ella.

jaw *n.* mandíbula, quijada, maxilar inferior.

jawbone *n.* hueso maxilar de la mandíbula.

jaw-lever *n.* abrebocas. *V.* **gag.**

jealous *a.* celosa-a.

jealousy *n.* celos.

jejunal *a.* yeyunal, rel. al yeyuno.

jejunectomy *n. cirg.* yeyunectomía, excisión de todo el yeyuno o parte del mismo.

jejunostomy *n.* yeyunostomía, creación de una abertura permanente en el yeyuno a través de la pared abdominal.

jejunum *n.* yeyuno, porción del intestino delgado que se extiende del duodeno al íleon.

jelly *n.* jalea, sustancia gelatinosa; **contraceptive ___** / ___ anticonceptiva; **petroleum ___** / vaselina.

jerk *n.* sacudida, reflejo súbito, contracción muscular brusca; *a.* [*slang*] tonto-a, imbécil; *v.* sacudir, tirar de, mover bruscamente.

jest *n.* broma, chiste; *v.* bromear.

jet *n.* chorro; avión de propulsión.

jet lag *n.* estado de cansancio que sufren los viajeros aéreos después de jornadas largas a través de diferentes zonas de tiempo.

jitters *n.* [*slang*] nerviosidad.

job *n.* trabajo, empleo; [*task*] tarea.

jog *v.* correr acompasadamente como medio de ejercicio físico.

jogger *n.* corredor-a.

jogging *n.* acción de correr como medio de ejercicio.

join *v.* unir, juntar; [*as a member*] hacerse miembro, hacerse socio-a; [*meet*] encontrarse.

joint *n.* articulación, coyuntura, punto de unión entre dos huesos; **arthrodial ___** / artrodia, que permite un movimiento de deslizamiento; **ball-and-socket ___** / ___ esferoidea, que permite movimientos en varias direcciones; **hip ___** / ___ de la cadera; **knee ___** / ___ de la rodilla; **sacroiliac ___** / ___ sacroilíaca; **shoulder ___** / ___ del hombro.

joint capsule *n.* cápsula articular, cubierta en forma de bolsa que envuelve una articulación.

joint mice *n.* partículas sueltas de cartílago o hueso que se alojan generalmente en algunas articulaciones.

jolly *a.* alegre, jovial.

jolt *n.* sacudida, tirón.

journal *n.* diario.

jovial *n.* jovial, alegre.

jowl *n.* cachete, carrillo.

joy *n.* alegría.

judge *n.* juez, magistrado-a; *v.* juzgar, hacer juicio.

judgment *n.* juicio; decisión, opinión.

jug *n.* jarro.

jugular *a.* yugular, rel. a las venas yugulares.

jugular veins *n.* venas yugulares, venas que llevan la sangre de la cabeza y del cuello al corazón.

juice *n.* jugo, zumo, líquido extraído o segregado; **apple ___** / ___ de manzana; **carrot ___** / ___ de zanahoria; **gastric ___** / gástrico; **grape ___** / ___ de uva; **grapefruit ___** / ___ de toronja; **intestinal ___** / ___ intestinal; **pancreatic ___** / ___ pancreático; **pineapple ___** / ___ de piña; **plum ___** / ___ de ciruela.

juiciness *n.* jugosidad.

juicy *a.* jugoso-a.

jump *n.* salto, brinco; *v.* saltar, brincar.

jumpy *a.* inquieto-a, intranquilo-a.

junction *n.* unión, entronque, punto de contacto de dos partes.

junctura *n.* juntura; coyuntura.

junkie *a. slang,* [*rel. to drug addiction*], vicioso-a, narcómano-a, *Mex.* tecato-a.

jurisprudence, medical *n.* jurisprudencia médica, ciencia del derecho judicial que se aplica a la medicina.

just *a.* justo-a; preciso-a, exacto-a; **-ly** *adv.* justamente.

justice *n.* justicia.

justify *v.* justificar.

juvenile *a.* juvenil, joven; **___ delinquency** / delincuencia ___.

juvenile rheumatoid arthritis *n.* artritis reumatoidea juvenil; *V.* **rheumatoid arthritis.**

juxtaglomerular *a.* yuxtaglomerular, junto a un glomérulo.

juxtaglomerular apparatus *n.* aparato yuxtaglomerular, grupo de células localizadas alrededor de arteriolas aferentes del riñón, que intervienen en la producción de renina y en el metabolismo del sodio.

juxtaglomerular cells *n.* células yuxtaglomerulares, localizadas cerca de o junto a glomérulos del riñón.

juxtaposition *n.* yuxtaposición, aposición; posición adyacente.

K *abbr.* **kalium** / potasio.

k *abbr.* **kilogram** / kilogramo.

kala-azar *n.* kala-azar, infestación visceral por un protozoo.

kalemia *n.* potasemia, presencia de potasio en la sangre.

kaliuresis *n.* caliuresis, aumento en la excreción de potasio en la orina.

kallikrein *n.* calicreína, enzima potente de acción vasodilatadora.

kaolin *n.* caolín, silicato de aluminio hidratado, agente de cualidades absorbentes de uso interno y externo.

Kaposi's disease *n.* enfermedad de Kaposi, neoplasma maligno localizado en las extremidades inferiores de hombres adultos que se desarrolla rápidamente en casos de SIDA.

karyolysis *n.* cariolisis, disolución del núcleo de una célula.

karyolytic *a.* cariolítico-a, rel. a cariolisis o que la causa.

karyon *n.* carión, núcleo celular.

karyotype *n.* cariotipo, cromosoma característico de un individuo o de una especie.

keep *vi.* [*a record*] mantener; [*guard*] guardar; **to ___ down** / limitar; **to ___ from** / absternerse de, guardarse de, evitar; **to ___ off** / alejarse, apartarse; **to ___ on** / continuar; **to ___ quiet** / estarse quieto-a, quedarse callado-a; **to ___ up** / mantener, continuar.

keeping *n.* cuidado, custodia.

keloid *n.* queloide, cicatriz de tejido grueso rojizo que se forma en la piel después de una incisión quirúrgica o de una herida.

keloidosis *n.* queloidosis, formación de queloides.

kelp *n.* cenizas de un tipo de alga marina rica en yodo.

keratectomy *n.* *cirg.* queratectomía, incisión de una parte de la córnea.

keratin *n.* queratina, proteína orgánica insoluble que es un elemento componente de las uñas, la piel y el cabello.

keratinization *n.* queratinización, proceso por el cual las células se vuelven callosas por dépositos de queratina.

keratinous *a.* queratinosa-a, rel. a o de la naturaleza de la queratina.

keratitis *n.* queratitis, infl. de la córnea; **interstitial ___** / **___ intersticial**; **mycotic ___** / **___ micótica**, queratomicosis, infección fungal de la córnea; **trophic ___** / **___ trófica**, causada por el virus del herpes.

keratocele *n.* queratocele, hernia de la membrana anterior de la córnea.

keratohemia *n.* queratohemia, presencia de sangre en la córnea.

keratolysis *n.* queratolisis. 1. exfoliación de la epidermis; 2. anomalía congénita por la cual se muda la piel periódicamente; **___ neonatorum** / **___ neonatal**.

keratolytic *n.* queratolítico, agente que provoca exfoliación.

keratoma *n.* queratoma, callosidad, tumor córneo.

keratomalacia *n.* queratomalacia, degeneración de la córnea causada por deficiencia de vitamina A.

keratoplasty *n.* *cirg.* queratoplastia, cirugía plástica de la córnea.

keratoscope *n.* queratoscopio, instrumento para examinar la córnea.

keratoses *n.* queratoses, enfermedad no contagiosa de la piel con escamación y posible inflamación.

keratosis *n.* queratosis, condición callosa de la piel tal como callos y verrugas; **actinic ___** / **___ actínica**, lesión solar precancerosa; **blenorrhagic ___** / **___ blenorrágica**, manifestada en la palma de las manos y los pies con erupción escamosa.

keratotomy *n.* *cirg.* queratotomía, incisión a través de la córnea.

keratous *a.* queratoso-a, semejante a la córnea.

kernicterus *n.* kernícterus, forma de ictericia del recién nacido.

ketoacidosis *n.* cetoacidosis, acidosis causada por el aumento de cuerpos cetónicos en la sangre.

ketogenesis *n.* cetogénesis, producción de acetona.

ketone bodies *n.* cuerpos cetónicos o acetónicos, comúnmente llamados acetonas, productos desintegrados de las grasas en el catabolismo celular.

ketosis *n.* cetosis, producción excesiva de cuerpos acetónicos como resultado del metabolismo incompleto de ácidos lípidos; acidosis.

key *n.* llave; [*clue, reference*] clave.

kick *n.* patada, puntapié; *v.* patear, dar puntapiés; [*addiction*] **to ___ the habit** / [*to abstain or stay away*] dejar la droga.

kid *n.* [*child*] niño, niña, chiquillo, chiquilla.

kidney *n.* riñón, órgano par situado a cada lado de la región lumbar y que sirve de filtro al organismo; **artificial ___** / **___ artificial**; **___ failure** / fallo renal; **polycystic ___** / **___ poliquístico**; **___ stones** / piedras o cálculos renales, *pop.* piedras en los riñones.

kill *v.* matar; [*germs*] exterminar; **to ___ time** / pasar el tiempo.

kilo *n.* kilogramo, kilo.

kilometer *n.* kilómetro.

kind *n.* clase, tipo; *a.* bondadoso-a; *v.* **to be so ___ as to** / tener la bondad de; **-ly** *adv.* bondadosamente.

kindness *n.* bondad.

kindred *n.* parentesco.

kinesiology *n.* cinesiología, estudio de los músculos y los movimientos musculares.

kinesitherapy *n.* cinesiterapia, tratamiento por medio de movimiento o ejercicios.

kinesthesia *n.* cinestesia, experiencia sensorial, sentido y percepción de un movimiento.

kinetic *n.* cinético-a, rel. al movimiento.

kingdom *n.* reino, categoría en la clasificación de animales, plantas y minerales.

kinship *n.* [*family relationship*] parentesco.

kit *n.* equipo.

kitchen *n.* cocina.

klebsiella *n.* klebsiela, bacilo gram-negativo asociado con infecciones respiratorias y del tracto urinario.

Klebs-Löffler bacillus *n.* bacilo de Klebs-Löffler, bacilo de la difteria.

kleptomania *n. psic.* cleptomanía, deseo incontrolable de robar.

kleptomaniac *n., a,* cleptómano-a, persona afectada por cleptomanía; rel. a la cleptomanía.

knead *v.* amasar, sobar.

kneading *n.* amasijo, proceso de masaje y frotación.

knee *n.* rodilla, articulación del fémur, la tibia y la patela; ___ **dislocation** / dislocación de la ___; ___ **protector** / rodillera.

kneecap *n.* rótula.

knee jerk *n.* reflejo de la rodilla que se produce con el toque de un martillo de goma en el ligamento de la patela.

knife *n.* cuchillo.

knob *n.* protuberancia, bulto.

knock-knee *n. V.* **genus valgum.**

knot *n.* nudo; **surgical** ___ / ___ quirúrgico.

know *vi.* saber, [*to be acquainted*] conocer; **to** ___ **how to** / saber + *inf.;* **to** ___ **of** / tener noticias de, estar enterado-a de.

knowledge *n.* conocimiento; **to the best of my** ___ / a mi entender, por lo que sé; *v.* **to have** ___ **of** / saber.

knuckle *n.* nudillo.

Koch's bacillus *n.* bacilo de Koch, *Mycobacterium tuberculosis,* causa de la tuberculosis en los mamíferos.

kolpitis *n.* colpitis, infl. de la mucosa vaginal.

Kussmaul breathing *n.* respiración de Kussmaul, respiración jadeante y profunda vista en casos de acidosis diabética.

kwashiorkor *n.* Kwashiorkor, deficiencia proteínica o desnutrición durante la infancia que se manifiesta después del destete esp. en áreas tropicales y subtropicales.

kyphosis, hunchback *n.* cifosis, exageración en la curvatura posterior de la espina dorsal que da lugar a una corcova.

kyphotic *a.* cifótico-a; *pop.* corcovado-a, que sufre de una corcova.

L *abbr.* **liter** / litro.
l *abbr.* **left** / izquierdo-a; **lethal** / letal; **light** / ligero-a; **lower** / más bajo.
label *n.* etiqueta; *u.* poner etiquetas.
labial *a.* labial, rel. a los labios.
labial glands *n.* glándulas labiales, situadas entre la mucosa labial y el músculo orbicular de la boca.
labile *a.* lábil, inestable, frágil, que cambia o se altera fácilmente.
lability *n.* labilidad, condición de inestabilidad.
labium *n.* (*pl.* **labia**) labio; 1. borde carnoso; 2. estructura semejante a un labio.
labor *n.* parto; **active** ___ / ___ activo; **induction of** ___ / ___ inducido; **after** ___ / después del ___; **before** ___ / antes del ___; **complicated** ___ / ___ complicado; **contractions during** ___ / contracciones durante el ___; **dry** ___ / ___ seco; **during** ___ / durante el ___; **hard** ___ / ___ laborioso; **painless** ___ / ___ sin dolor; ___ **pains** / dolores de ___; ___ **room** / sala de ___; **stages of** ___ / etapas del ___; *u.* estar de parto; *V.* **childbirth.**
laboratory *n.* laboratorio; ___ **technician** / técnico de ___; ___ **findings** / resultados del análisis.
labored *a.* laborioso-a, trabajoso-a; ___ **breathing** / respiración jadeante.
laborious *a.* laborioso-a, trabajoso-a.
labyrinth *n.* laberinto. 1. red de conductos del oído interno cuya función relaciona la audición con el equilibrio del cuerpo; 2. conductos y cavidades que forman un sistema comunicándose entre sí.
labyrinthitis *n.* laberintitis. 1. infl. aguda o crónica del laberinto; 2. otitis interna.
lacerate *u.* lacerar, desgarrar.
laceration *n.* laceración, desgarro.
lachrymogenous *a.* lacrimógeno-a, que produce lágrimas.
lachrymose *a.* lacrimoso-a, lagrimoso-a.
lack *n.* falta, carencia; necesidad; falta de; ___ **of food** / ___ de alimentos; ___ **of medication** / falta de o carencia de medicina; ___ **of orientation** / ___ de orientación; *u.* carecer de; faltar; **they** ___ **everything** / carecen de todo.
lacrimal *a.* lagrimal, rel. a las lágrimas y a los órganos y partes relacionados con éstas; ___ **bone** / hueso ___; ___ **duct** / conducto ___; ___ **gland** / glándula ___; ___ **sac** / saco ___.
lacrimation *n.* lagrimeo, producción de lágrimas.
lactacidemia *n.* lactacidemia, exceso acumulado de ácido láctico en la sangre.
lactase *n.* lactasa, enzima intestinal que hidroliza la lactosa y produce dextrosa y galactosa.

lactation *n.* lactancia, crianza, secreción de leche.
lactial *a.* lácteo-a, rel. a la leche.
lactic acid *n.* ácido láctico.
lactiferous *a.* lactífero-a, que segrega y conduce leche.
lactocele *n.* lactocele. *V.* **galactocele.**
lacto-ovovegetarian *a.* lacto-ovovegetariano-a; que sigue una dieta de vegetales, huevos y productos lácteos.
lactose, lactine *n.* lactosa, lactina, azúcar de leche; ___ **deficiency** / intolerancia a la ___.
lacuna *L.* (*pl.* **lacunae**) lacuna, laguna, depresión pequeña tal como las cavidades del cerebro.
lady *n.* dama, sénora.
lag *n.* atraso, retraso; [*slow growth*] latencia; ___ **time** / período de latencia.
laid up *a.* inactivo-a; *pop.* en cama; enfermo-a.
laity *n.* [*nonprofessional*] lego.
La Leche League *n.* La Liga de la Leche, organización que promueve la lactancia materna.
lallation, lambdacism *n.* lalación, lambdacismo. 1. defecto y cambio fonético de la *l* por la *r*; 2. balbuceo, tartamudeo infantil.
Lamaze technique, Lamaze method *n.* método de Lamaze, procedimiento de parto natural con adiestramiento de la madre en técnicas respiratorias que facilitan el proceso del parto.
lamb *n.* cordero-a, oveja, borrego-a.
lamb chop *n.* chuleta de cordero.
lamb's wool *n.* lana de cordero.
lame *a.* cojo-a, lisiado-a; *u.* **to go** ___ / cojear, andar cojeando.
lamella *n.* laminilla. 1. capa fina; 2. disco que se inserta en el ojo para aplicar un medicamento.
lament *n.* lamento, queja; lamentarse, quejarse.
lamina *n.* (*pl.* **laminae**) lámina, placa o capa fina.
laminar *a.* laminar, laminado-a, rel. a láminas; formado por capas.
laminated *a.* laminado-a, que está formado por una o varias láminas.
laminectomy *n. cirg.* laminectomía, extirpación de una o varias láminas vertebrales.
lamp *n.* lámpara; **lamplight** / luz de una ___; **infrared** ___ / ___ infrarroja; **slit** ___ / ___ de hendidura; **sun** ___ / ___ solar.
lancet, lance *n.* lanceta, instrumento quirúrgico; *u.* abrir con una lanceta.
Landztainer's classification *n.* clasificación de Landztainer, diferenciación de grupos sanguíneos; O-A-B-AB.
language *n.* lenguaje.
languid *a.* lánguido-a, débil, flojo-a; decaído-a.
languidness *n.* languidez, decaimiento.
lanolin *n.* lanolina, sustancia purificada que se obtiene de la lana de la oveja y se usa en pomadas.
lantern *n.* linterna, farol.
lanugo *n.* lanugo, vellosidad, pelusilla suave que cubre el cuerpo del feto.

lap *n.* regazo, falda; [*sitting*] sentado-a en las piernas de; **mother's** ___ / el ___, la ___ de la madre.

laparoscope *n.* laparoscopio, instrumento usado para visualizar la cavidad peritoneal.

laparoscopy *n.* laparoscopía, examen de la cavidad peritoneal por medio de un laparoscopio.

laparotomy *n. cirg.* laparotomía, incisión y abertura del abdomen.

lapse *n.* [*time*] lapso, intervalo de tiempo.

lard *n.* manteca, grasa de origen animal.

large *a.* grande, grueso-a, abultado-a; ___ **intestine** / intestino grueso.

larger, largest *comp., sup.*, de **large** más grande; mayor; **the tumor is** ___ **now** / el tumor está más grande ahora.

larva *L.* (*pl.* **larvae**) larva, primera fase o forma de ciertos organismos tal como los insectos.

larval *a.* larval, larvado-a, rel. a una larva.

larvate *a.* larvado-a, rel. a un síntoma atípico o insidioso.

larvicide *n.* larvicida, agente que destruye las larvas, esp. las de los insectos.

laryngeal *a.* laríngeo-a; ___ **reflex** / reflejo ___, tos producida por irritación de la laringe.

laryngectomy *n. cirg.* laringectomía, extirpación de la laringe.

laryngitis *n.* laringitis; 1. infl. de la laringe; 2. afonía, ronquera.

laryngopharyngitis *n.* laringofaringitis, infl. de la laringe y la faringe.

larynogopharynx *n.* laringofaringe, porción inferior de la faringe.

laryngoplasty *n. cirg.* laringoplastia, reconstrucción plástica de la laringe.

laryngoscope *n.* laringoscopio, instrumento usado para examinar la laringe.

laryngoscopy *n.* laringoscopía, examen de la laringe; **direct** ___ / ___ directa, por medio de un laringoscopio; **indirect** ___ / ___ indirecta, por medio de un espejo.

laryngospasm *n.* laringoespasmo, espasmo de los músculos de la laringe.

laryngotomy *n. cirg.* laringotomía, incisión de la laringe.

larynx *n.* laringe. 1. parte del tracto respiratorio situada en la parte superior de la tráquea; 2. órgano de la voz.

laser *n.* laser. 1. sigla del inglés "Light Amplification by Stimulated Emission of Radiation" (amplificación de la luz por estimulación de emisión de radiación); 2. bisturí microquirúrgico usado en la cauterización de tumores.

laser beams *n. pl.* rayos de laser, rayos de luz por efecto radioactivo de calor intenso que se usan para destruir tejidos o separar partes.

lassitude *n.* lasitud, languidez, agotamiento.

last *a.* último-a; final, pasado-a; **the** ___ **treatment** / el ___ tratamiento; **the** ___ **word** / la ___ palabra; ___ **night** / anoche.

late *a.* tardío-a, último-a; *adv.* tarde; *v.* **to be** ___ /

atrasarse, retrasarse; **-ly** *adv.* últimamente, hace poco.

latency *n.* latencia, acto de permanecer latente; ___ **period** / período de ___.

latent *a.* latente, presente pero no activo-a; sin síntomas aparentes; sin manifestación.

later *a., comp.* de **late**; *adv.* más tarde, luego, después.

lateral *a.* lateral, rel. a un lado o costado.

lateroflexion *n.* lateroflexión, flexión lateral o de inclinación hacia un costado.

latest *a., sup.* de **late**, último; **at the** ___ / a más tardar; **the** ___ **drug on the market** / el medicamento más reciente en el mercado.

lather *n.* jabonadura, espuma de jabón.

latter *pron.* éste, ésta; el, la más reciente, el más moderno, la más moderna.

laugh *n.* risa; *v.* reír; **to** ___ **at** / reírse de, mofarse.

laughter *n.* risa, carcajada.

lavage *n.* lavado, irrigación de una cavidad.

lavatory *n.* [*basin*] lavatorio, lavabo, lavamanos; [*restroom*] inodoro, servicio, baño, excusado.

law *n.* ley, regla, norma.

lawsuit *n.* pleito legal, litigio.

lawyer *n.* abogado-a, *Mex.* licenciado-a.

lax *a.* laxo-a, suelto-a, relajado-a.

laxative *n.* laxante, laxativo, purgante suave.

laxity *n.* laxitud, aflojamiento, flojedad; relajación.

lay *vi.* poner, colocar; **to** ___ **aside** / desechar; apartar; **to** ___ **off** / suspender, despedir.

layer *n.* capa, estrato.

laying *n.* colocación, acto de colocar.

laziness *n.* pereza, holgazanería, haraganería.

lazy *a.* perezoso-a, flojo-a, holgazán, holgazana, haragán, haragana.

lazy eye *n.* ambliopía, falta de coordinación en la percepción de la profundidad visual.

lead *n.* 1. plomo; ___ **apron** / delantal de ___, usado como protección a radiaciones; ___ **poisoning** / envenenamiento por ___; 2. conductor, tal como la guía que se usa en una electrocardiografía; *vi.* conducir, llevar de la mano, guiar.

leading *a.* principal, primero-a, más importante.

leaf *n.* hoja.

leak *n.* [*of gas*] escape; [*water*] gotera, filtración; salirse, derramarse, escaparse.

lean *a.* [*meat*] magro-a, sin grasa; [*without flesh*] enjuto, flaco-a; seco-a; *v.* [*aptitude*] **to** ___ **toward** / tener propensión o disposición hacia algo o hacia alguien; [*on, against*] apoyarse, recostarse, arrimarse a; [*over*] inclinarse.

learn *vi.* aprender; [*to have knowledge of*] saber; [*to learn about something new*] tener noticias de, enterarse de.

learning *n.* aprendizaje; ___ **disability** / impedimento en el ___.

leather *n.* cuero, piel curtida.

leave *n.* [*of absence*] licencia, permiso de ausencia del trabajo; *vi.* [*to go away from*] salir; [*to give up*] dejar, renunciar; descontinuar, abandonar; **to ___ alone** / dejar en paz; **to ___ behind** / dejar atrás; **Nothing was left behind** / No se dejó nada; **to ___ off** / dejar.

lecithin *n.* lecitina, elemento esencial en el metabolismo de las grasas presente en los tejidos de los animales, esp. el tejido nervioso.

lecture *n.* conferencia, disertación.

ledge *n.* borde.

leech *n.* sanguijuela, gusano anélido acuático chupador de sangre; **artificial ___** / ventosa.

left *a.* izquierdo-a; **to the ___** / a la izquierda; **___-hand** / mano izquierda; **___ side** / lado **___**.

left-handed *a.* zurdo-a.

leg *n.* pierna, extremidad inferior que se extiende de la rodilla al tobillo; **___ injuries** / traumatismos de la ___; *v.* **to pull one's ___** / tomar el pelo; **to get back on one's ___-s** / levantarse; ponerse bien; recobrar la salud.

legal *a.* legal, legítimo-a, de acuerdo con la ley; **___ medicine, forensic medicine** / medicina ___; **___ suit** / litigio, demanda, pleito.

legislation, medical *n.* legislación médica.

legitimacy *n.* legitimidad.

legitimate *a.* legítimo-a, auténtico-a.

legume *n.* legumbre

leiomyofibroma *n.* leiomiofibroma, tumor benigno compuesto de tejido conectivo fibroso y muscular liso.

leiomyoma *n.* leiomioma, tumor benigno compuesto esencialmente de tejido muscular liso.

leiomyosarcoma *n.* leiomiosarcoma, tumor formado por leiomioma y sarcoma.

leisure *n.* holganza, ociosidad; **at ___** / a conveniencia, cómodamente; *a.* **___ hours** / tiempo libre, horas desocupadas.

lema *n.* legaña, lagaña, secreción de los ojos.

lemon *n.* [*fruit*] limón; [*tree*] limonero.

lemonade *n.* limonada.

lend *vi.* prestar; **to ___ a hand** / prestar ayuda, ayudar, dar ayuda.

length *n.* longitud, largo; extensión, distancia; **___ of time** / período de tiempo; **___ of stay** [*in a hospital*] / tiempo de internamiento.

lengthen *v.* alargar, extender, dilatar, prolongar.

lengthy *a.* largo-a; prolongado-a.

lenient *a.* indulgente, lenitivo-a; consentidor-a.

lens *n.* 1. lente; **achromatic ___** / ___ acromático; **adherent ___** / ___ adherido; **biconcave ___** / ___ bicóncavo; **biconvex ___** / ___ biconvexo; **bifocal ___** / ___ bifocal; **contact ___** / de contacto, lentillas; **dislocation of ___** / dislocación del ___; **implantation, intraocular** / ___-s intraoculares; **trifocal ___** / ___-s trifocales; 2. cristalino, lente transparente del ojo.

lent *a. pp.* de **to lend,** prestado-a.

lenticula *n.* lente pequeño.

lenticular *a.* lenticular, rel. a un lente.

lentil *n.* lenteja.

leper *a.* leproso-a, lazarino-a; que sufre de lepra.

leprosy *n.* lepra, enfermedad infecciosa conocida también como enfermedad de Hansen causada por el bacilo *Mycobacterium leprae* caracterizada por lesiones cutáneas de pústulas y escamas.

leptomeninges *n.* leptomeninges, las membranas más finas del cerebro; la piamadre y la aracnoide.

leptomeningitis *n.* leptomeningitis, infl. de las leptomeninges.

lesbian *n.* lesbiana, mujer homosexual.

lesbianism *n.* lesbianismo, homosexualidad femenina.

lesion *n.* lesión, herida, contusión.

less *a. comp.* menos, menor; **more or ___** / más o menos; **___ complicated** / ___ complicado; **___ difficult** / ___ difícil; **___ and ___** / cada vez menos; *adv.* menos, en grado menor; *sufijo* menos, sin.

lessen *v.* aliviar, aminorar, disminuir, acortar; **a pill to ___ the pain** / una pastilla para ___ el dolor.

lesser *a. comp.* de **less,** menor; más pequeño.

lesson *n.* lección, enseñanza, instrucción.

let *vi.* permitir, dejar, conceder; **to ___ down** / dejar bajar; dejar caer; desilusionar, abandonar; **let us + inf.** / vamos a + *inf.;* **to ___ be** / dejar tranquilo-a; **to ___ blood** / hacer sangrar; **to ___ go** / soltar; **to ___ in** / dejar entrar, admitir; **to ___ out** / dejar salir; **___ us go** / vámonos.

lethal *a.* letal, mortal; **___ dose (LD)** / dosis ___.

lethargic, lethargical *a.* letárgico-a, aletargado-a.

lethargy *n.* letargo, estupor.

letter *n.* letra; carta; **___ opener** / abrecartas.

lettuce *n.* lechuga.

leucine *n.* leucina, aminoácido esencial en el crecimiento y metabolismo.

leukapheresis *n.* leucaferesis, separación de leucocitos de la sangre de un paciente con subsecuente retransfusión al mismo paciente.

leukemia *n.* leucemia, cáncer de la sangre; **chronic ___** / ___ crónica; **lymphocytic ___** / ___ linfocítica.

leukemic *a.* leucémico-a, rel. a la leucemia o que padece de ella.

leukemoid *n.* leucemoide, semejante a la leucemia.

leukocyte *n.* leucocito, glóbulo blanco, célula importante en la defensa y reparación del organismo; **acidophil ___** / ___ acidófilo, que cambia de color con ácidos colorantes; **basophil ___** / ___ basófilo, que cambia de color con colorantes básicos; **lymphoid ___** / ___ linfoide, sin gránulos; **neutrophil ___** / ___ neutrófilo, de afinidad con colorantes neutros; **polymorphonuclear ___** / ___ polimorfonucleado, con núcleos de más de un lóbulo.

leukopenia *n.* leucopenia, número anormalmente bajo de glóbulos blancos.

leukoplakia *n.* leucoplasia, áreas de color opaco en la membrana mucosa de la lengua gen. de carácter precanceroso.

leukorrhea *n.* leucorrea, flujo vaginal blancuzco.

levator *n.* elevador, músculo que eleva o levanta una parte.

level *n.* nivel, plano; *v.* nivelar, ajustar; ___ **of health** / estado de salud.

leveling *n.* nivelación.

levocardia *n.* levocardia, transposición de las vísceras abdominales y conservación de la posición normal del corazón en el lado izquierdo del tórax.

levodopa *n.* levodopa, sustancia química usada en el tratamiento de la enfermedad de Parkinson.

levulose *n.* levulosa. *V.* **fructose.**

lewd *a.* lujurioso-a, deshonesto-a, libidinoso-a, obsceno-a.

lewdness *n.* lujuria, impudicia, sensualidad, lascivia.

liability *n.* riesgo, responsabilidad de pago.

liable *a.* responsable, sujeto-a a cargos.

liar *n., a.* embustero-a, mentiroso-a.

liberation *n.* liberación.

liberty *n.* libertad; **to be at ___ to** / tener ___ para.

librarian *n.* bibliotecario-a.

library *n.* biblioteca.

lice *n. pl.* piojos.

license, licence *n.* licencia, permiso; **medical** ___ / ___ para ejercer la medicina.

licensure *n.* autorización, permiso legal para ejercer la medicina o ejecutar actos sólo permitidos a médicos o personal médico.

lichen *n.* liquen, lesiones o erupciones de la piel no contagiosas de forma papular; ___ **planus** / ___ plano.

licit *a.* lícito-a, permitido-a.

lick *v.* lamer; golpear, *pop.* dar una tunda.

lid *n.* 1. párpado del ojo; 2. tapa, tapadera.

lidocaine *n.* lidocaína, anestésico.

lie *n.* mentira, embuste; ___ **detector** / polígrafo, detector de ___-s; *v.* mentir; *v.* tenderse; **to ___ down** / echarse, acostarse, descansar.

life *n.* vida, modo de vivir, existencia; ___ **expectancy** / expectativa de ___, promedio de ___; ___ **insurance** / seguro de ___; ___ **preservers, ___ support devices** / aparatos para prolongar la ___; ___**-saving measure** / medida para prolongar o salvar la ___; ___ **span** / longevidad; ___**-threatening** / que puede causar la muerte.

life insurance *n.* seguro, póliza de seguro; *Mex. A.* aseguranza.

lifeless *a.* muerto-a, sin vida.

lifetime *n.* toda la vida, curso de la vida; *a.* vitalicio-a.

lift *v.* levantar, alzar, elevar; ___ **your hand** / levante, levanta la mano; **to give one a ___** / ayudar, animar, alentar.

lifting *n.* acto de levantar, levantamiento.

ligament *n.* ligamento. 1. banda de fibras de tejido conjuntivo que protege las articulaciones y evita que sufran torceduras o luxaciones; 2.

banda protectora de fascias y músculos que conectan o sostienen vísceras.

ligate *v.* ligar, aplicar una ligadura.

ligature, ligation *n.* ligadura; acción o proceso de ligar.

light *n.* luz; lumbre; ___ **absorption** / absorción de la ___; ___ **adaptation** / adaptación de la ___; ___ **perception** / percepción de la ___; ___ **reflex** / reflejo de la ___; ___ **therapy** / fototerapia; *a.* ligero-a, liviano-a claro-a, pálido-a; ___**-headed** / [*dizzy*] mareado-a; **-ly** *adv.* ligeramente, levemente.

lighten *v.* iluminar, prender la luz; [*color*] aclarar.

lightening *n.* [*childbirth*] aligeramiento, descenso del útero en la cavidad pélvica, gen. en la etapa final del embarazo.

lighter *a. comp.* más ligero-a, más claro-a, más pálido-a.

likable *a.* agradable, amable, simpático-a.

like *a.* parecido-a, igual, semejante; **to look ___** / parecerse a; [*to look alike*] **The boy looks ___ the father** / El niño se parece al padre; *v.* **to ___ someone, something** / gustar, agradar; **I ___ this medicine** / Me gusta esta medicina; *prep.* como; *adv.* como si, del mismo modo.

lima beans *n. pl.* habas de lima.

limb *n.* 1. extremidad, miembro del cuerpo; 2. porción terminal o distal de una estructura; ___ **amputation** / amputación de una ___; ___ **rigidity** / rigidez de la ___ o del miembro.

limber *a.* flojo-a, flexible.

limbic *a.* marginal.

limbic system *n.* sistema límbico, grupo de estructuras cerebrales.

limbus *n.* limbo, filo o borde de una parte; ___ **corneae** / ___ de la córnea.

lime *n.* lima. 1. ___ **juice** / jugo, zumo de ___; 2. cal, óxido de calcio.

liminal *a.* liminal, casi imperceptible.

limit *n.* límite, frontera; **assimilation ___** / ___ de asimilación; **saturation ___** / ___ de saturación; ___ **of perception** / umbral perceptivo.

limitation *n.* limitación, restricción; ___ **of motion** / ___ de movimiento.

limited *a.* limitado-a, restricto-a; ___ **activity** / actividad ___; ___ **autopsy** / autopsia parcial.

limp *n.* cojera, flojera; *v.* cojear, renquear, renguear.

linden tea *n.* té de flores de tilo.

line *n.* línea; rasgo; arruga; límite o guía.

linear *a.* lineal, semejante a una línea.

linen *n.* lienzo, lino; **bed ___** / ropa de cama.

linger *v.* [*to suffer*] consumirse, padecer lentamente; [*to delay*] demorarse.

lingering *v.* prolongación, tardanza, morosidad; *a.* prolongado-a, retardado-a, moroso-a.

lingua *n.* (*pl.* **linguae**) lengua o estructura semejante a la lengua.

lingual *a.* lingual, rel. a la lengua.

lingula *n.* língula, proyección o estructura en forma de lengüeta.

liniment *n.* linimento, untura de uso externo.

lining *n.* túnica, capa, forro, cubierta, revestimiento.

linitis *n.* linitis, *V.* **gastritis.**

link *n.* eslabón, vínculo.

linkage *n.* vínculo, unión, asociación de genes.

lint *n.* 1. fibra de algodón; 2. partículas desprendidas de la ropa.

lip *n.* labio, parte externa de la boca.

lipectomy *n. cirg.* lipectomía, excisión de tejido graso; **submental** ___ / ___ submental, del cuello.

lipemia *n.* lipemia, presencia anormal de grasa en la sangre.

lipid, lipide *n.* lípido, sustancia orgánica que no se disuelve en el agua pero que es soluble en alcohol, éter o cloroformo.

lipodystrophy *n.* lipodistrofia, trastorno del metabolismo de las grasas.

lipoid *n.* lipoide, sustancia que se asemeja a la grasa.

lipoma *n.* lipoma, tumor de tejido adiposo.

lipomatosis *n.* lipomatosis. 1. condición causada por depósito excesivo de grasa; 2. lipomas múltiples.

lipomatous *a.* lipomatoso-a, obeso-a.

lipoproteins *n. pl.* lipoproteínas, proteínas combinadas con compuestos lípidos que contienen una concentración alta de colesterol.

liposarcoma *n.* liposarcoma, tumor maligno que contiene elementos grasos.

liposis *n.* obesidad, acumulación excesiva de grasa en el cuerpo.

liposoluble *a.* liposoluble, que se disuelve en sustancias grasas.

liposuction *n.* liposucción, proceso de extraer grasa por medio de alta presión al vacío.

lip reading *n.* lectura labial, interpretación del movimiento de los labios.

liquefy *v.* licuar, disolver; descoagular.

liquid *n.* líquido, fluido; ___ **balance** / balance de ___; ___ **retention** / retención de ___.

liquor *n.* 1. licor, líquido acuoso que contiene sustancias medicinales; 2. término general aplicado a algunos líquidos del cuerpo.

lisping *n.* ceceo, sustitución de sonidos debido a un defecto en la articulación de las palabras, tal como el sonido de la z por la c, o el sonido de la c por la s.

list *n.* lista; **casualty** ___ / lista de accidentados.

listen *v.* escuchar, atender, prestar atención.

listless *a.* apático-a, lánguido-a, sin ánimo; indiferente.

liter *n.* litro.

lithiasis *n.* litiasis, formación de cálculos, esp. biliares o del tracto urinario.

lithium *n.* litio, elemento metálico usado como tranquilizante para tratar casos severos de psicosis.

lithotomy *n. cirg.* litotomía, incisión en un órgano o conducto para extraer cálculos.

lithotripsy *n.* litotripsia, trituración de cálculos en el riñón, el uréter, la vejiga y la vesícula biliar.

lithotriptor *n.* litotriturador, aparato o mecanismo para triturar cálculos; **extracorporal shock wave** ___ / ___ extracorporal con ondas de choque.

litter *n.* [*stretcher*] camilla; *v.* tirar basura.

little *a.* [*size*] pequeño-a; [*quantity*] poco, muy poco, un poquito; ___ **by** ___ / poco a poco.

live *v.* vivir, existir; ___ **birth** / nacimiento con vida.

livelihood *n.* vida; existencia; subsistencia.

lively *a.* vivo-a; vivaracho-a, animado-a.

liver *n.* hígado, glándula mayor del cuerpo que segrega bilis y sirve de estabilizador y productor de azúcar, enzimas, proteínas y colesterol además de eliminar las sustancias tóxicas del organismo; ___ **circulation** / circulación hepática; ___ **cirrhosis** / cirrosis hepática; ___ **damage** / lesión hepática; **enlarged** ___ / ___ agrandado; ___ **failure** / insuficiencia hepática; ___ **function tests** / pruebas funcionales hepáticas; **infantile biliary** ___ **cirrhosis** / cirrosis biliar infantil; ___ **spots** / manchas hepáticas.

livid *a.* lívido-a; *pop.* amoratado-a.

lividity *n.* lividez, descoloración que resulta de la gravitación de sangre; **post mortem** ___ / ___ cadavérica.

living *n.* vida; con vida; modo de vivir; **cost of** ___ / costo de ___; ___ **expenses** / gastos de mantenimiento; ___ **under stress** / ___ agitada, ___ con estrés.

living will *n.* testamento hecho por una persona en completo estado de salud en el que dispone que en caso de peligro de muerte no se use ningún medio artificial para prolongarle la vida.

load *n.* carga, peso; ___ **dose** / dosis de ___; *v.* cargar, recargar.

loading *n.* carga por administración de una sustancia en una prueba metabólica; ___ **test** / prueba de carga.

loan *n.* préstamo; *v.* prestar.

lobar *a.* lobar, lobular, rel. a un lóbulo; ___ **pneumonia** / pulmonía ___.

lobby *n.* salón de entrada, sala de espera, vestíbulo.

lobe *n.* lóbulo, porción redondeada y más o menos delimitada de un órgano; **middle** ___ **syndrome** / síndrome del lóbulo medio del pulmón.

lobectomy *n. cirg.* lobectomía, excisión de un lóbulo; **complete** ___ / ___ completa; **left lower** ___ / ___ izquierda anterior; **partial** ___ / ___ parcial.

lobotomy *n. cirg.* lobotomía, incisión de un lóbulo cerebral con el fin de aliviar ciertos trastornos mentales.

lobster *n.* langosta.

lobular *a.* lobular, rel. a un lóbulo.

lobule *n.* lobulillo, lóbulo pequeño.

local *a.* local, rel. a una parte aislada; ___ **anesthe-**

sia / anestesia ___; ___ **application** / aplicación ___; ___ **recurrence** / reaparición ___.

localization *n.* localización. 1. rel. al punto de origen de una sensación; 2. determinación de la procedencia de una infección o lesión.

localize, locate *v.* localizar.

lochia *n.* loquios, flujo serosanguíneo del útero en las primeras semanas después del parto.

lock *n.* cerradura; *v.* cerrar, trancar; encerrar, cerrar con llave; encerrarse, trancarse; cerrarse.

lockjaw *n.* tétano; pasmo; V. **tetanus.**

locomotion *n.* locomoción.

loculated, locular *a.* locular, rel. a un lóculo.

loculus *n.* (*pl.* **loculi**) lóculo, cavidad pequeña.

locus *n.* 1. lugar, sitio; 2. localización de un gene en el cromosoma.

logagraphia *n.* logagrafía, incapacidad de reconocer palabras escritas o habladas.

logamnesia *n.* logamnesia, afasia sensorial.

logaphasia *n.* logafasia, afasia motora, gen. causada por una lesión cerebral.

logic *a.* lógico-a, acertado-a.

logical *a.* lógico-a, preciso-a, exacto-a.

logopedics *n.* logopedia, estudio y tratamiento de la voz.

loin *n.* flanco, ijar, ijada, parte inferior de la espalda y de los costados entre las costillas y la pelvis.

long *a.* largo-a, extenso-a, prolongado-a; ___ **ago** / hace tiempo; **How** ___ **ago?** / ¿Cuánto tiempo hace?; ___ **after** / mucho después; ___-**standing** / de larga duración; **not** ___ **before** / poco tiempo antes; ___-**distance** / larga distancia.

longevity *n.* longevidad, ancianidad, duración larga de la vida.

longing *n.* deseo, anhelo, ansia.

longitudinal *a.* longitudinal, a lo largo del eje del cuerpo.

longus *a.* largo-a, extenso-a.

look *n.* [*appearance*] aspecto, apariencia, cara; mirada, ojeada. *v.* mirar; revisar; **to** ___ **for** / buscar; **to take a** ___ **at** / mirar, echar una mirada; **to** ___ **bad** / tener mal aspecto; **to** ___ **through** / examinar con cuidado.

loop *n.* asa; estructura en forma de lazo semejante a la curvatura de una cuerda.

loose *a.* suelto-a, desatado-a, libre; ___ **bowels** / deposiciones blandas o aguadas; *v.* desatar, desprender, aflojar.

lordosis *n.* lordosis, aumento exagerado hacia adelante de la concavidad de la columna lumbar.

lose *vi.* perder.

loss *n.* pérdida; ___ **of balance** / ___ del equilibrio; ___ **of blood** / de sangre; ___ **of consciousness** / ___ del conocimiento; ___ **of contact with reality** / ___ del contacto con la realidad; ___ **of grip** / ___ de la retención; ___ **of hearing** / ___ de la audición; ___ **of memory** / ___ de la memoria; ___ **of motion** / ___ del

movimiento; ___ **of muscle tone** / ___ de la tonicidad muscular; ___ **of vision** / ___ de la visión; **at a** ___ / confundido-a.

lost *a. pp.* de to lose, perdido-a, desorientado-a, extraviado-a.

lotion *n.* loción, ablución.

loud *a.* ruidoso-a, escandaloso-a.

loupe *n.* lupa binocular, lente convexa de aumento usada esp. por cirujanos y oculistas.

louse *n.* (*pl.* **lice**) piojo, insecto parásito que se aloja en el pelo, trasmisor de enfermedades infecciosas tales como la fiebre tifoidea.

love *n.* amor, cariño, afecto; *v.* amar, querer; **to fall in** ___ / enamorarse; **to fall in** ___ **with** / enamorarse de.

low *a.* bajo-a; [*in spirits*] abatido-a; ___ **opinion** / mala opinión.

lower *a., comp.* de low, inferior; bajo-a; *v.* bajar, poner más bajo; [*in quantity, price*] reducir, disminuir; **to** ___ **the arm** / ___ el brazo.

loyal *a.* leal, fiel, constante.

lozenge *n.* pastilla que se disuelve en la boca.

lubricant *n.* lubricante, agente oleaginoso que al lubricar disminuye la fricción entre dos superficies; **oil-based** ___ / ___ oleaginoso; **water-based** ___ / ___ acuífero.

lubricate *v.* lubricar, untar, saturar una superficie con un líquido, especialmente aceite.

lubrication *n.* lubrificación, lubricación.

lucid *a.* lúcido-a, claro-a, inteligible; cuerdo-a.

lucidity *n.* claridad, esp. mental.

lucidness *n.* lucidez, claridad mental.

luck *n.* suerte, dicha; casualidad; **good** ___ / buena ___; **out of** ___ / de mala suerte; **worse** ___ / la peor ___.

lucky *a.* afortunado-a, dichoso-a; *v.* **to be** ___ / tener suerte.

lues *n.* lúes, sífilis.

luetic *a.* luético-a, sifilítico-a, rel. a o que padece de sífilis.

lukewarm *a.* tibio-a, templado-a; [*feelings*] indiferente.

lumbago *n.* lumbago, dolor en la parte inferior de la espalda.

lumbar *a.* lumbar, región de la espalda entre el tórax y la pelvis; ___ **puncture** / punción ___; ___ **vertebrae** / vértebras ___-es.

lumbriscosis *n.* lumbricosis, infestación por lombrices.

lumen *n.* lumen. 1. unidad de flujo luminoso; 2. espacio en una cavidad, canal, conducto u órgano.

Luminal *n.* Luminal, patente comercial de un compuesto de fenobarbital usado como sedante.

luminal *a.* luminal, rel. a la luz de un conducto.

luminescence *n.* luminosidad, emisión de luz sin producción de calor.

luminous *a.* luminoso-a, rel. a la luminosidad

lump *n.* bulto, protuberancia, chichón; [*in the throat*] nudo en la garganta; [*of sugar*] terrón de azúcar.

lumpectomy *n. cirg.* tumorectomía, extirpación de un tumor gen. de la mama.

lunacy *n.* locura, demencia.

lunar *a.* lunar, rel. a la luna.

lunatic *a.* lunático-a, demente, loco-a.

lunch *n.* almuerzo, comida del mediodía.

lung *n.* pulmón, órgano par de la respiración contenido dentro de la cavidad pleural del tórax que se conecta con la faringe a través de la tráquea y la laringe; ___ **abscess** / absceso pulmonar; **air containing** ___ / ___ aireado; ___ **cancer** / cáncer del ___; ___ **capacities** / volumen pulmonar; ___ **collapse** / colapso del ___; ___ **diseases** / neumopatías; ___ **elasticity** / elasticidad pulmonar; ___ **hemorrhage** / hemorragia pulmonar.

lungworm *n.* gusano nematodo que infesta los pulmones.

lupus *n.* lupus, enfermedad crónica de la piel de origen desconocido que causa lesiones degenerativas locales.

lupus erythematosus, discoid *n.* lupus eritematoso discoide, condición caracterizada por placas escamosas de bordes enrojecidos que causa irritación de la piel.

lupus erythematosus, systemic *n.* lupus eritematoso sistémico, condición caracterizada por episodios febriles que afecta las vísceras y el sistema nervioso.

lust *n.* lujuria, codicia, deseo incontenible.

luteal *a.* lúteo, rel. al cuerpo lúteo.

luteinizing hormone *n.* hormona luteinizante producida por la pituitaria anterior que estimula la secreción de hormonas sexuales por los testículos (testosterona) y el ovario (progesterona) e interviene en la formación de esperma y óvulos.

luxation *n.* luxación, dislocación.

lye *n.* lejía; ___ **poisoning** / envenenamiento por ___.

lying *a.* acostado-a; recostado-a; extendido-a.

lymph *n.* linfa, líquido claro que se encuentra en los vasos linfáticos; ___ **nodes** / ganglios linfáticos.

lymphadenectomy *n. cirg.* linfadenectomía, extirpación de vasos linfáticos y ganglios.

lymphadenitis *n.* linfadenitis, infl. de los ganglios linfáticos.

lymphadenopathy *n.* linfadenopatía, enfermedad que afecta los nódulos linfáticos; **axillary** ___ / ___ axilar; **cervical** ___ / ___ cervical; **generalized** ___ / ___ generalizada; **mediastinal** ___ / ___ mediastínica; **supraclavicular** ___ / ___ supraclavicular.

lymphangiectasis *n.* linfangiectasis, dilatación de los vasos linfáticos.

lymphangiogram *n.* linfangiograma, representación filmada de ganglios y vasos linfáticos usando un medio de contraste inyectado.

lymphangitis *n.* linfangitis, infl. de vasos linfáticos.

lymphatic *a.* linfático-a, rel. a la linfa; ___ **spaces** / espacios ___-s; ___ **system** / sistema ___ .

lymphedema *n.* linfedema, edema causado por una obstrucción en los vasos linfáticos.

lymphoblast *n.* linfoblasto, forma primitiva del linfocito.

lymphocyte *n.* linfocito, célula linfática; ___ **B cell** / ___ B, importante en la producción de anticuerpos.

lymphocyte T *n.* linfocitos de células T, linfocitos diferenciados en el timo que dirigen la respuesta inmunológica y alertan a las células B a responder a los antígenos; ___ **T helper** / ayudante de ___, inductores, aumentan la producción de anticuerpos de las células B; **cytotoxic** ___ / ___ citotóxicos, ayudan a exterminar células extrañas como en el rechazo de órganos transplantados; **supressor** ___ / represores de ___, detienen la producción de anticuerpos de las células B.

lymphocytosis *n.* linfocitosis, cantidad excesiva de linfocitos en la sangre periférica.

lymphogranulomatosis, Hodgkin's disease *n.* linfogranulomatosis, enfermedad de Hodgkin, granuloma infeccioso del sistema linfático.

lymphogranuloma venereum *n.* linfogranuloma venéreo, enfermedad viral trasmitida sexualmente que puede producir elefantiasis de los genitales y estrechez rectal.

lymphoid *a.* linfoide, que se asemeja al tejido linfático.

lymphoma *n.* linfoma, neoplasma del tejido linfático.

lymphomatoid *n.* linfomatoide, rel. a un linfoma o semejante a éste.

lymphopenia, lymphocytopenia *n.* linfopenia, linfocitopenia, disminución en el número de linfocitos en la sangre.

lymphoreticular *a.* linforreticular, rel. a células reticuloendoteliales de los nódulos linfáticos.

lymphosarcoma *n.* linfosarcoma, neoplasma maligno del tejido linfoide.

lysergic acid diethylamide (LSD) *n.* dietilamida del ácido lisérgico.

lysin *n.* lisina, anticuerpo que disuelve o destruye células y bacterias.

lysis *n.* lisis. 1. proceso de destrucción o disolución de glóbulos rojos, bacterias o cualquier antígeno por medio de lisina; 2. desaparición gradual de los síntomas de una enfermedad.

336

m *abbr.* **male** / hombre; **malignant** / maligno; **married** / casado-a; **mature** / maduro; **melts at** / se derrite a; **minute** / minuto; **molecular weight** / peso molecular; **morphine** / morfina.

macerate *v.* macerar; suavizar una materia por medio de inmersión en un líquido.

machine *n.* aparato, máquina.

macrocephalia *n.* macrocefalia, cabeza anormalmente grande.

macrocephalic *a.* macrocefálico-a, megalocefálico-a, de cabeza anormalmente grande.

macrocosm *n.* macrocosmo. 1. el universo como representación del ser humano; 2. el universo considerado como un todo.

macrocythemia *n.* macrocitemia, macrocitosis, glóbulos rojos anormalmente grandes.

Macrodantin *n.* Macrodantina, nombre comercial Furantoína, bactericida usado en el tratamiento de infecciones urinarias.

macroglossia *n.* macroglosia, agrandamiento excesivo de la lengua.

macrognathia *n.* macrognatia, mandíbula demasiado grande.

macromolecule *n.* macromolécula, molécula de tamaño grande tal como la de una proteína.

macrophage, macrophagus *n.* macrófago, célula mononuclear fagocítica; ___ **migration** / migración de ___-s.

macroscopic *a.* macroscópico-a, que se ve a simple vista, antónimo de microscópico.

macrospore *n.* macroespora, espora grande.

macula, macule *n.* mácula, pequeña mancha descolorida de la piel.

macula lutea, yellow spot *n.* mácula lútea, pequeña zona amarillenta situada en el centro de la retina.

macular *a.* macular, rel. a una mácula.

maculopapular *a.* maculopapular, rel. a máculas y pápulas.

mad *a.* [*insane*] loco-a, demente, perturbado-a; [*moody*] enojado-a, furioso-a; *v.* **to become** ___ / enloquecer; enloquecerse, enfurecerse; volverse loco-a; enojarse.

made *v., pret., pp.* de **to make,** hecho-a, producido-a.

madhouse *n.* manicomio, asilo de locos.

maggot *n.* larva de un insecto.

magistral *a.* magistral, rel. a medicamentos que se preparan de acuerdo a indicaciones médicas.

magma *n.* magma. 1. suspensión de partículas en una cantidad pequeña de agua; 2. sustancia viscosa compuesta de material orgánico.

magnesia *n.* magnesia, óxido de magnesio; **milk of** ___ / leche de ___.

magnesium *n.* magnesio; ___ **sulfate** / sulfato de ___.

magnet *n.* imán.

magnetic *a.* magnético-a; ___ **field** / campo ___.

magnetic resonance imaging *n.* imágenes por resonancia magnética, procedimiento por imágenes basado en el análisis cualitativo de la estructura química y biológica de un tejido.

magnetism *n.* magnetismo, propiedad de atracción y repulsión magnéticas.

magnetize *v.* magnetizar, imantar.

magnetoelectricity *n.* magnetoelectricidad, electricidad inducida por medios magnéticos.

magnification *n.* magnificación, ampliación de un objeto.

magnifier *n.* amplificador; vidrio de aumento.

magnify *v.* amplificar, agrandar, ampliar, aumentar.

magnifying glass *n.* lente de aumento; lupa.

magnitude *n.* magnitud.

mail *n.* correo, correspondencia; *v.* **to** ___ **a letter** / echar una carta al ___.

maim *v.* mutilar; estropear; lisiar.

main *a.* principal; esencial; **-ly** *adv.* principalmente, esencialmente.

maintenance *n.* mantenimiento; [*feeding*] alimentación; sostén, apoyo; [*of a building*] conservación, mantenimiento.

make *vi.* hacer; [*money*] ganar; **to** ___ **mistakes** / hacer errores; equivocarse; [*earn*] **How much do you** ___? / ¿Cuánto gana usted?, ¿cuánto ganas tú?; **to** ___ **believe** / fingir; **to** ___ **fun of** / burlarse de; **to** ___ **known** / declarar; **to** ___ **no difference** / no tener importancia; **to** ___ **a prescription** / llenar, preparar una receta; **to** ___ **sense** / tener sentido; **to** ___ **sure** / asegurarse; **to** ___ **up** [*time*] / recobrar el tiempo perdido; **to** ___ **up one's mind** / decidirse.

mal *n.* enfermedad, trastorno, desorden.

malabsorption syndrome *n.* síndrome de malabsorción, condición gastrointestinal con trastornos múltiples causada por absorción inadecuada de alimentos.

malacia *n.* malacia, reblandecimiento o pérdida de consistencia en órganos o tejidos.

malacoplakia *n.* malcoplaquia, formación de áreas blandas en la membrana mucosa de un órgano hueco.

maladjusted *a.* inadaptado-a, incapaz de adaptarse al medio social y de soportar tensiones.

malady *n.* enfermedad, trastorno, desorden.

malaise *n.* malestar, indisposición, molestia.

malar *a.* malar, rel. a la mejilla o a los pómulos.

malar bone *n.* pómulo, hueso en ambos lados de la cara.

malaria *n.* malaria, infección febril aguda a veces crónica causada por protozoos del género *Plasmodium* y trasmitida por el mosquito *Anófeles.*

malariacidal *a.* malaricida, que destruye parásitos de malaria.

malassimilation *n.* malasimilación, asimilación deficiente.

maldigestion *n.* indigestión.

male *n.* varón; hombre; macho; ___ **nurse** / enfermero.

malformation *n.* deformación, anomalía o enfermedad esp. congénita.

malfunction *n.* disfunción, funcionamiento defectuoso; *v.* funcionar mal.

malice *n.* malicia, malos deseos.

malicious *a.* malicioso-a.

malignancy *n.* 1. cualidad de malignidad; 2. tumor canceroso.

malignant *a.* maligno-a, pernicioso-a, de efecto destructivo.

malinger *v.* fingirse enfermo-a; fingir una enfermedad.

malingerer *n.* simulador-a, persona que finge o exagera los síntomas de una enfermedad.

malleable *a.* maleable.

malleolus *n.* (*pl.* **malleoli**) maléolo, protuberancia en forma de martillo tal como la que se ve a ambos lados de los tobillos.

mallet finger *n.* dedo en martillo; **mallet toe** / dedo del pie en martillo.

malleus *n.* (*pl.* **mallei**) malleus, uno de los huesecillos del oído medio.

malnourished *a.* desnutrido-a, malnutrido-a.

malnutrition *n.* malnutrición; mala alimentación; deficiencia nutricional.

malocclusion *n.* maloclusión, mordida defectuosa.

malposition *n.* posición inadecuada.

malpractice *n.* negligencia profesional.

malpresentation *n.* presentación anormal del feto durante el parto.

malrotation *n.* malarotación, rotación anormal o defectuosa de un órgano o parte.

malt *n.* malta; **malted milk** / leche malteada.

maltose *n.* maltosa, tipo de azúcar.

malunion *n.* malaunión, fijación imperfecta de una fractura.

mamma *n.* mama, glándulas secretoras de leche en la mujer localizadas en la parte anterior del tórax.

mammal *n.* animal mamífero.

mammalgia *n.* mamalgia, dolor en la mama.

mammaplasty, mammoplasty *n. cirg.* mamaplastia, mamoplastia, cirugía plástica de los senos; **augmentation** ___ / ___ de aumento; **reconstructive** ___ / ___ de reconstrucción; **reduction** ___ / ___ de reducción.

mammary *a.* mamario-a, rel. a los pechos o senos. ___ **glands** / glándulas ___-s.

mammectomy, mastectomy *n. cirg.* mamectomía, mastectomía, excisión de la mama o de una porción de la glándula mamaria.

mammillary *a.* mamilar, que se asemeja a un pezón.

mammillated *a.* mamilado-a, que presenta protuberancias similares a un pezón.

mammilliplasty *n. cirg.* mamiliplastia, operación plástica del pezón.

mammillitis *n.* mamilitis, infl. del pezón.

mammitis, mastitis *n.* mastitis, infl. de la mama.

mammogram *n.* mamograma, rayos X de la mama.

mammography *n.* mamografía, rayos X de la glándula mamaria.

mammoplasty *n. cirg.* mamoplastia, operación plástica de la mama.

man *n.* (*pl.* **men**) hombre.

manageable *a.* manejable; dócil.

manager *n.* administrador-a, gerente-a.

mandatory *a.* necesario-a, requerido-a.

mandible *n.* mandíbula, hueso de la quijada en forma de herradura.

mandibular *a.* mandibular, rel. a la mandíbula.

maneuver *n.* maniobra, movimiento preciso hecho con la mano.

mange *n.* sarna, roña.

mangy *a.* sarnoso-a, roñoso-a.

manhandle *v.* maltratar.

manhood *n.* virilidad; edad viril.

mania *n.* manía, trastorno emocional caracterizado por excitación excesiva, ansiedad y altas y bajas de espíritu.

maniac *a.* maníaco-a, persona afectada de manía.

manic-depressive psychosis *n.* psicosis maníaco-depresiva cíclica, condición caracterizada por estados de depresión y manía.

manifest *v.* manifestar; expresar; revelar; manifestarse, revelarse.

manifestation *n.* manifestación; revelación.

manikin *n.* maniquí, figura representativa del cuerpo humano.

manipulate *v.* manipular, manejar.

manipulation *n.* manipulación, tratamiento por medio del uso diestro de las manos.

manliness *n.* masculinidad, virilidad.

manly *a.* varonil.

manner *n.* manera, modo; hábito, costumbre; [*behavior*] **bad** ___-s / malos modales.

mannerism *n.* manerismo, expresión peculiar en la manera de hablar, de vestir o de actuar.

manometer *n.* manómetro, instrumento para medir la presión de líquidos o gases.

manslaughter *n.* homicidio sin premeditación.

mantle *n.* manto, capa.

manual *a.* manual, manuable.

manubrium *n.* (*pl.* **manubria**) manubrium, estructura en forma de mano.

many *a., pron.* muchos-as; tantos, tantas; **a great** ___ / muchos, muchas; **as** ___ **as** / tantos-as como, igual número de.

marasmus *n.* marasmo, emaciación debida a malnutrición, esp. en la infancia.

march *n.* marcha, progreso; *v.* marchar, poner en marcha.

margarine *n.* margarina.

margin *n.* margen, borde.

marginal *a.* marginal; **a** ___ **case** / un caso ___.

margination *n.* marginación, acumulación y adherencia de leucocitos a las paredes de los vasos capilares en un proceso inflamatorio.

marijuana, marihuana *n.* mariguana. *V.* **Cannabis sativa.**

marital *a.* matrimonial, marital; ___ **relations** / relaciones ___-es.

marjoram *n.* mejorana.

mark *n.* marca, seña, señal, signo; *v.* marcar; señalar.

marker *n.* marcador, indicador.

marmalade *n.* mermelada, conserva de frutas.

marriage *n.* matrimonio; [*ceremony*] boda, casamiento.

married *a.* casado-a; ___ **couple** / matrimonio; ___ **life** / vida conyugal, vida matrimonial.

marrow *n.* médula, tejido esponjoso que ocupa las cavidades medulares de los huesos; *pop.* tuétano; ___ **aspiration** / aspiración de la ___; ___ **cellularity** / celularidad medular; ___ **failure** / insuficiencia medular; ___ **infiltration** / infiltración medular; ___ **injury** / lesión medular; ___ **puncture** / punción de la ___ ósea; ___ **transplant** / transplante de la ___.

marsupialization *n. cirg.* marsupialización, conversión de una cavidad cerrada a una forma de bolsa abierta.

masculation *n.* masculación, desarrollo de características masculinas.

masculine *a.* masculino-a, viril.

masculinization *n.* masculinización. *V.* **virilización.**

mash *v.* mezclar ingredientes; amasar; **mashed** *a., pp.* de to mash, [*vegetables*] ___ **potatoes** / puré de patatas.

mask *n.* máscara. 1. cubierta de la cara; 2. aspecto de la cara, esp. como manifestación patológica; **death** ___ / mascarilla; **pregnancy** ___ / manchas en la cara durante el embarazo; **surgical** ___ / cubreboca.

masked *a.* enmascarado-a; oculto-a.

masochism *n.* masoquismo, condición anormal de placer sexual por abuso infligido a otros o a sí mismo-a.

mass *n.* masa, cuerpo formado de partículas coherentes.

massage *n.* masaje, proceso de manipulación del cuerpo por medio de fricciones; **cardiac** ___ / ___ cardíaco de resucitación; *v.* dar masaje, sobar.

masseter *n.* músculo masetero, músculo principal de la masticación.

masseur, masseuse *Fr.* masajista, persona que da masajes.

massive *a.* maciso-a, abultado-a.

mastadenitis *n.* mastadenitis, infl. de una glándula mamaria. *V.* **mastitis.**

mastadenoma *n.* mastadenoma, tumor de la mama, tumor del seno.

mastalgia *n.* mastalgia, *V.* **mammalgia.**

mastectomy *n. cirg.* mastectomía. *V.* **mammectomy.**

masticate *v.* masticar, mascar.

mastication, chewing *n.* masticación.

masticatory *a.* masticatorio-a, rel. a la masticación.

mastitis, cystic *n.* mastitis cística, enfermedad fibroquística de la mama.

mastoid *n.* mastoides, apófisis del hueso temporal; *a.* 1. mastoideo-a, rel. a la mastoides o que ocurre en la región del proceso mastoideo; 2. semejante a una mama.

mastoid antrum *n.* antro mastoideo, cavidad que sirve de comunicación entre el hueso temporal, el oído medio y las células mastoideas.

mastoid cells *n. pl.* células mastoideas, bolsas de aire en la prominencia mastoidea del hueso temporal.

mastoiditis *n.* mastoiditis, infl. de las células mastoideas.

mastopathy *n.* mastopatía, afección de las glándulas mamarias.

mastopexy *n.* mastopexia, corrección plástica del seno pendular.

masturbate *v.* masturbarse.

masturbation *n.* masturbación, autoestimulación y manipulación de los genitales para obtener placer sexual.

match *n.* semejante; [*by pairs*] pareja; [*game*] juego, partido; copia; *v.* igualar, asemejar, [*colors*] armonizar, hacer juego.

matching *n. a.* semejante, igual; ___ **pair** / compañero-a, pareja.

material *n.* materia; asunto; *a.* material; esencial.

maternal *a.* maternal, materno-a, rel. a la madre; ___ **fetal exchange** / intercambio materno-fetal; ___ **welfare** / bienestar materno.

maternity *n.* maternidad; ___ **hospital** / hospital de ___.

mating *n.* emparejamiento de sexos opuestos esp. para la reproducción.

matricide *n.* matricidio.

matrilineal *a.* de línea materna, descendiente de la madre.

matrix *n.* matriz; molde.

matter *n.* materia, sustancia; asunto; **gray** ___ / ___ gris; **as a** ___ **of fact** / en realidad; **What is the** ___? / ¿Qué pasa?, ¿qué ocurre?; **Let's take care of this** ___ / Vámos a hacernos cargo de este asunto.

mattress *n.* colchón.

maturate *v.* madurar; sazonar; supurar.

mature *a.* maduro-a; [*fruit*] sazonado-a.

maturity *n.* madurez; etapa de desarrollo completo.

maxilla *n.* maxila, hueso del maxilar superior.

maximum *a. sup.* máximo.

may *v. aux.* poder, [*possibility*] **it** ___ **be** / puede ser; [*permission*] ___ **I see you?** / ¿Puedo verlo-a?, ¿pudeo verte?; ___ **I come in?** / ¿Puedo entrar?

maybe *adv.* quizás, tal vez.

maze *n.* laberinto.

me *pron.* me, mí; **The doctor is going to see** ___ / El doctor me va a ver; **The medicine is for** ___ / La medicina es para mí; **Come with** ___ /

339

Venga, ven conmigo.

meager *a.* escaso-a, insuficiente, pobre.

meal *n.* comida; **at** __time / a la hora de la __ .

mean *n.* media, índice, término medio; __ **corpuscular hemoglobin** / índice corpuscular de hemoglobina; *a.* malo-a, desconsiderado-a, de mal humor.

meaning *n.* significado.

measles *n.* sarampión; *pop. Mex.* tapetillo de los niños, enfermedad sumamente contagiosa esp. en niños de edad escolar causada por el virus de la rubéola.

measles immune serum globulin *n.* suero de globulina preventivo contra el sarampión, se inyecta en uno de los cinco días siguientes a la exposición al contagio.

measles virus vaccine, live *n.* vacuna antisarampión de virus vivo, de uso en la inmunización contra el sarampión.

measure *n.* medida, dimensión, capacidad de algo; *u.* medir.

meat *n.* carne; **roast** __ / __ asada.

meatal *a.* meatal, concerniente al meato.

meatus *n.* meato, pasaje, abertura, apertura.

mechanic *n.* mecánico-a.

mechanical *a.* mecánico-a.

mechanism *n.* mecanismo. 1. respuesta involuntaria a un estímulo; **defense** __ / __ de defensa; 2. estructura semejante a una máquina.

meconium *n.* meconio. 1. primera fecalización del recién nacido; 2. opio.

medial *a.* medial, localizado-a hacia la línea media.

median *n.* mediana, intermedio; __ **plane** / plano medio.

mediastinal *a.* mediastínico-a, rel. al mediastino.

mediastinitis *n.* mediastinitis, infl. del tejido del mediastino.

mediastinoscopy *n.* mediastinoscopía, examen del mediastino por medio de un endoscopio.

mediastinum *n.* mediastino. 1. cavidad entre dos órganos; 2. masa de tejidos y órganos que separa los pulmones.

mediate *u.* mediar, interceder.

mediator *a.* mediador-a; intercesor-a.

medic *n.* técnico-a entrenado para dar primeros auxilios.

Medicaid *n.* Asistencia Médica, programa del gobierno de los Estados Unidos que provee asistencia médica a los pobres.

medical *n.* médico-a; medicinal, curativo-a; __ **assistance** / asistencia __ ; __ **examiner** / médico forense; __ **history** / hoja clínica; __ **records** / registros __-s; [*patient's record*] expediente del paciente; __ **staff** / cuerpo médico; __ **student** / estudiante de medicina.

Medicare *n.* Programa de asistencia médica del gobierno del los Estados Unidos a personas desde los 65 años de edad o a adultos incapacitados para trabajar.

medicate *u.* recetar, medicinar.

medication *n.* medicina, medicamento; *pop.* remedio.

medicinal *a.* medicinal, rel. a la medicina, o con propiedades curativas.

medicine *n.* medicina. 1. ciencia que se dedica al mantenimiento de la salud por medio de tratamienos de curación y prevención de enfermedades; **aerospace** __ / __ del espacio; **clinical** __ / __ clínica; **community** __ / __ comunal, al servicio de la comunidad; **environmental** __ / __ ecológica; **forensic** __ / __ forense; **legal** __ / __ legal; **nuclear** __ / __ nuclear; **preventive** __ / __ preventiva; **socialized** __ / __ socializada; **sports** __ / __ deportiva; **tropical** __ / __ tropical; **veterinary** __ / __ veterinaria; 2. una droga o medicamento; __ **chest** / botiquín.

medicine man *n.* curandero; **medicine woman** curandera.

medicolegal *a.* médicolegal, rel. a la medicina en relación con las leyes.

mediolateral *a.* mediolateral, rel. a la parte media y a un lado del cuerpo.

medium *n.* (*pl.* **media**) medio. 1. intermediario-a, elemento mediante el cual se obtiene un resultado; 2. sustancia que transmite impulsos; 3. sustancia que se usa en un cultivo de bacterias.

medulla *n.* médula, *pop.* tuétano, parte interna o central de un órgano; __ **ossium, bone marrow** / __ ósea; __ **oblongata** / __ oblongata, bulbo raquídeo, porción de la médula localizada en la base del cráneo.

medullar, medullary *a.* medular, rel. a la médula.

meet *n.* reunión; concurso; *vi.* encontrar; reunirse con; **I am glad to** __ **you** / Mucho gusto en conocerlo-a.

meeting *n.* reunión, junta; conferencia.

megabladder, megalocystis *n.* megalocisto, vejiga distendida.

megacephalic *a.* megacefálico-a. V. **macrocephalus.**

megacolon *n.* megacolon, colon anormalmente agrandado.

megaesophagus *n.* megaesófago, dilatación anormal de la parte inferior del esófago.

megalomania *n.* megalomanía, delirio de grandeza.

megavitamin *n.* megavitamina, dosis de vitamina en exceso de la cantidad normal requerida diariamente.

meibomian cyst *n.* quiste meibomiano, quiste del párpado.

meiosis *n.* meiosis, proceso de subdivisión celular que resulta en la formación de gametos.

melancholia *n. psic.* melancolía, depresión acentuada.

melancholic *a.* melancólico-a, rel. a la melancolía.

melanin *n.* melanina, pigmento oscuro de la piel, el pelo y partes del ojo.

melanocyte *n.* melanocito, célula que produce melanina.

melanoma *n.* melanoma, tumor maligno compuesto de melanocitos.

melanosis *a.* melanosis, condición que se caracteriza por la pigmentación oscura presente en varios tejidos y órganos.

melanuria *n.* melanuria, presencia de pigmentación oscura en la orina.

melena *n.* melena, masa de heces fecales negruscas y pastosas que contiene sangre digerida.

mellow *a.* dulce, suave, tierno-a.

melon *n.* melón.

melt *v.* derretir, disolver.

member *n.* miembro. 1. órgano o parte del cuerpo; 2. socio-a de una organización.

membrane *n.* membrana, capa fina que sirve de cubierta o protección a una cavidad, estructura u órgano; **elastic** ___ / ___ elástica; **mucous** ___ / ___ mucosa; **nuclear** ___ / ___ nuclear; **permeable** ___ / ___ permeable; **placental** ___ / ___ de la placenta; **semipermeable** ___ / ___ semipermeable; **synovial** ___ / ___ sinovial; **tympanic** ___ / ___ timpánica.

membranous *a.* membranoso-a, rel. a una membrana o de la naturaleza de ésta.

memorandum *n.* memorando, nota.

memorial *n.* memoria, recuerdo.

memorize *v.* memorizar, aprender de memoria.

memory *n.* memoria, retentiva, facultad de la mente para registrar y recordar experiencias; **good** ___ / buena ___; **bad** ___ / mala ___; **short-term** ___ / ___ inmediata; *v.* **to lose the** ___ / perder la ___; **to have memories from** / tener recuerdos de; **Do you have a good** ___? / ¿Tiene, tienes buena ___?

men *pl.* de **man**, hombres.

menace *n.* amenaza; *v.* amenazar, atemorizar.

menarche *n.* menarca, inicio de la menstruación.

mend *v.* reparar, componer, mejorar.

mendable *a.* reparable, componible.

Mendelism *n.* mendelismo, principios que explican la trasmisión genética de ciertos rasgos.

meningeal *a.* meníngeo-a, rel. a las meninges.

meninges *n. pl.* meninges, las tres capas de tejido conjuntivo que rodean al cerebro y a la médula espinal.

meningioma *n.* meningioma, neoplasma vascular gen. benigno de desarrollo lento que se origina en las meninges.

meningism *n.* meningismo, irritación congestiva de las meninges gen. de naturaleza tóxica con síntomas similares a los de la meningitis pero sin inflamación.

meningismus *L.* meningismus. *V.* **meningism.**

meningitic *a.* meningítico-a, rel. a las meninges.

meningitis *n.* meningitis, infl. de las meninges cerebrales o espinales; **cryptococcal** ___ / ___ criptocócica; **viral** ___ / ___ viral.

meningocele *n.* meningocele, protrusión de las meninges a través del cráneo o de la espina dorsal.

meningococcus *n.* meningococo, uno de los microorganismos causantes de la meningitis cerebral epidémica.

meningoencephalitis *n.* meningoencefalitis, cerebromeningitis, infl. del encéfalo y de las meninges.

meningoencephalocele *n.* meningoencefalocele, protrusión del encéfalo y de las meninges a través de un defecto en el cráneo.

meningomyelitis *n.* meningomielitis, infl. de la médula espinal y las membranas que la cubren.

meningomyelocele *n.* meningomielocele, protrusión de la médula espinal y las meninges a través de un defecto en la columna vertebral.

meniscectomy *n. cirg.* meniscectomía, extirpación de un menisco.

meniscus *n.* (*pl.* **menisci**) menisco, estructura cartilaginosa de forma lunar.

menometrorrhagia *n.* menometrorragia, menstruación irregular o excesiva.

menopause *n.* menopausia, cambio de vida en la mujer adulta, terminación de la etapa de reproducción y disminución de la producción hormonal.

menorrhagia *n.* menorragia, períodos o reglas muy abundantes.

menorrhalgia *n.* menorralgia, menstruación dolorosa.

menorrhea *n.* menorrea, flujo menstrual normal.

menses *n.* menses, menstruo, menstruación, período, regla.

menstrual *a.* menstrual, rel. a la menstruación; ___ **cycle** / ciclo ___; ___ **disorder** / trastorno ___.

menstruate *v.* menstruar.

menstruation *n.* menstruación, flujo sanguíneo periódico de la mujer.

mental *a.* mental, rel. a la mente; ___ **age** / edad ___; ___ **disorder** / trastorno ___; ___ **deficiency** / retraso ___; ___ **health** / salud ___; ___ **hygiene** / higiene ___; ___ **illness** / enfermedad ___; ___ **retardation** / retraso ___; ___ **test** / examen de capacidad ___.

mentality *n.* mentalidad, capacidad mental.

mentation *n.* actividad mental.

menthol *n.* mentol, sustancia que se obtiene del alcanfor de menta y que tiene efecto sedante.

mentum *n.* mentón, barbilla, prominencia de la barba.

merbromin *n.* merbromina, polvo rojo inodoro, soluble en agua, usado como germicida.

merciful *a.* misericordioso-a, compasivo-a.

merciless *a.* inhumano-a, despiadado-a.

mercurial *a.* mercurial, perteneciente o rel. al mercurio.

mercurochrome *n.* mercurocromo, nombre registrado de la merbromina.

mercury *n.* mercurio, metal líquido volátil; ___

poisoning / envenenamiento por ___.

mercy n. misericordia, compasión; ___ **killing** / eutanasia.

merge v. unir, unificar.

meridian n. meridiano, línea imaginaria que conecta los extremos opuestos del axis en la superficie de un cuerpo esférico.

mescaline n. mescalina, alcaloide alucinogénico, pop. peyote.

mesectoderm n. mesectodermo, masa de células que componen las meninges.

mesencephalon n. mesencéfalo, el cerebro medio en la etapa embrionaria.

mesenchyme n. mesénquima, red de células embrionarias que forman el tejido conjuntivo y los vasos sanguíneos y linfáticos en el adulto.

mesenteric a. mesentérico-a, concerniente al mesenterio.

mesentery n. mesenterio, repliegue del peritoneo que fija el intestino a la pared abdominal posterior.

mesial a. mesial V. **medial.**

mesion n. mesión, plano imaginario medio que divide el cuerpo en dos partes simétricas.

mesmerism n. mesmerismo, uso del hipnotismo como método terapéutico.

mesocardia n. mesocardia, desplazamiento anormal del corazón hacia el centro del tórax.

mesocolon n. mesocolon, mesenterio que fija el colon a la pared abdominal posterior.

mesoderm n. mesodermo, capa media germinativa del embrión situada entre el ectodermo y endodermo de la cual provienen el tejido óseo, el muscular, los vasos sanguíneos y linfáticos, y las membranas del corazón y abdomen.

mesothelium n. mesotelio, capa celular del mesodermo embrionario que forma el epitelio que cubre las membranas serosas en el adulto.

mess n. lío, confusión; v. **to make a** ___ / hacer un ___; desordenar, revolver, ensuciar.

message n. mensaje, recado.

messy a. revuelto-a, desordenado-a, sucio-a.

metabolic a. metabólico-a, rel. al metabolismo; ___ **rate** / índice ___.

metabolism n. metabolismo, suma de los cambios fisicoquímicos que tienen efecto a continuación del proceso digestivo; ___ **basal** / ___ basal, el nivel más bajo del gasto de energía; **constructive** ___ / anabolismo, asimilación; **destructive** ___ / ___ destructivo, catabolismo; **protein** ___ / ___ de proteínas, digestión de proteínas y conversión de éstas en aminoácidos.

metabolite n. metabolito, sustancia producida durante el proceso metabólico.

metacarpal a. metacarpiano-a, rel. al metacarpio.

metacarpus n. metacarpo, la parte formada por los cinco huesecillos metacarpianos de la mano.

metal n. metal; ___ **fume fever** / fiebre por aspiración de vapores metálicos.

metallic a. metálico-a, rel. a un metal o de la naturaleza de éste.

metamorphosis n. metamorfosis. 1. cambio de forma o estructura; 2. cambio degenerativo patológico.

metaphase n. metafase, una de las etapas de la división celular.

metaphysis n. metáfisis, zona de crecimiento del hueso.

metastasis n. metástasis, extensión de un proceso patológico de un foco primario a otra parte del cuerpo a través de los vasos sanguíneos o linfáticos como se observa en algunos tipos de cáncer.

metastasize v. metastatizar, esparcirse por metástasis.

metastatic a. metastásico-a, rel. a la metástasis.

metatarsal a. metatarsiano-a, rel. al metatarso.

metatarsus n. metatarso, la parte formada por los cinco huesecillos del pie situados entre el tarso y los dedos.

meteorism n. meteorismo, abdomen distendido causado por acumulación de gas en el estómago o los intestinos.

methadone n. metadona, droga sintética potente de acción narcótica menos intensa que la morfina.

methanol, wood alcohol n. metanol, alcohol de madera.

method n. método, procedimiento; proceso; tratamiento.

meticulous a. meticuloso-a.

metopic a. metópico-a, frontal, rel. a la frente.

metria a. metria, infl. del útero durante el puerperio.

metric a. métrico-a; ___ **system** / sistema ___.

metritis n. metritis, infl. de la pared uterina.

metroflebitis n. metroflebitis, infl. de las venas uterinas.

micrencephaly n. micrencefalia, cerebro anormalmente pequeño.

microabscess n. microabsceso, absceso diminuto.

microanatomy n. microanatomía, histología.

microbe n. microbio, microorganismo, organismo diminuto.

microbial, microbian a. microbiano-a, rel. a los microbios.

microbicide n. microbicida, agente exterminador de microbios.

microbiology n. microbiología, ciencia que estudia los microorganismos.

microcephaly n. microcefalia, cabeza anormalmente pequeña de origen congénito.

micrococcus n. micrococo, microorganismo.

microcolon n. microcolon, colon anormalmente pequeño.

microcosmus n. microcosmo. 1. universo en miniatura; 2. cualquier entidad o estructura considerada en sí misma un pequeño universo.

microcurie n. microcurie, unidad de radiación.

microfiche n. microficha, ficha en la que se acumulan datos para ser vistos bajo un lente amplificador.

microfilm n. microfilm, microfilme, película que contiene información reducida a un tamaño mínimo.

micrognathia n. micrognatia, mandíbula inferior anormalmente pequeña.

micrography n. micrografía, estudio microscópico.

microinvasion n. microinvasión, invasión de tejido celular adyacente a un carcinoma localizado que no puede verse a simple vista.

micromelia n. micromelia, extremidades anormalmente pequeñas.

micromelic a. micromélico-a, rel. a la micromelia.

micrometer n. micrómetro, instrumento para medir distancias cortas.

microorganism n. microorganismo, organismo que no puede verse a simple vista.

microphallus n. microfalo, pene anormalmente pequeño.

microscope n. microscopio, instrumento óptico con lentes que amplifican objetos que no pueden verse a simple vista; **electron** __ / __ electrónico; **light** __ / __ con luz o lumínico.

microscopic a. microscópico-a, rel. al microscopio.

microscopy n. microscopía, examen que se realiza con un microscopio.

microsome n. microsoma, elemento fino granular del protoplasma.

microsomia n. microsomía, cuerpo anormalmente pequeño de proporciones normales.

microsurgery n. microcirugía, operación efectuada con el uso de microscopios quirúrgicos e instrumentos minúsculos de precisión.

microtome n. micrótomo, instrumento de precisión que se usa en la preparación de secciones finas de tejido para ser examinadas bajo el microscopio.

microtomy n. microtomía, corte de secciones finas de tejido.

microwave n. microonda, onda corta electromagnética de frecuencia muy alta.

micturate v. orinar.

middle n. medio, centro; **in the __ of** / en el __ de.

middle age n. mediana edad, madurez.

middle ear n. oído medio, parte del oído situada más allá del tímpano.

middle finger n. el dedo cordial.

middle lobe syndrome n. síndrome del lóbulo medio del pulmón.

midget n. enano-a.

midgut n. intestino medio del embrión.

midline n. línea media del cuerpo.

midnight n. medianoche.

midplane n. plano medio.

midriff n. diafragma.

midsection n. sección media.

midstream specimen n. especimen de orina que se toma después de comenzar la emisión y poco antes de terminarse.

midwife n. comadrona, partera.

midyear n. mediados de año.

migraine n. migraña, jaqueca, ataques severos de dolor de cabeza que gen. se manifiestan en un solo lado acompañados de visión alterada y en algunos casos de náuseas y vómitos.

migration n. migración, movimiento de las células de un lugar a otro.

mild a. [pain] leve, tolerable; moderado-a, indulgente.

mildew n. moho, añublo.

miliary a. miliar, caracterizado-a por pequeños tumores o nódulos.

miliary tuberculosis n. tuberculosis miliar, enfermedad que invade el organismo a través de la sangre y se caracteriza por la formación de tubérculos diminutos en los órganos afectados.

milieu n. medio ambiente.

milk n. leche; **boiled __** / __ hervida; **condensed __** / __ condensada; **evaporated __** / __ evaporada; __ **of magnesia** / __ de magnesia; **skim __** / __ desnatada; **sterilized __** / __ esterilizada; **mother's __** / leche materna.

milking n. ordeño, maniobra para forzar sustancias fuera de un tubo.

milky a. lechoso-a, lácteo-a.

mimetic, mimic a. mimético-a, que imita.

mind n. mente, entendimiento; v. atender, tener en cuenta; **to bear in __** / tener presente; **to be out of one's __** / volverse loco-a; **to make up one's __** / decidirse; **to speak one's __** / dar una opinión; dar su parecer.

miner n. minero.

mineral n. mineral, elemento inorgánico; a. mineral; __ **water** (carbonated) / agua __ efervescente.

mineralization n. mineralización, depósitos de minerales en los tejidos.

mineralocorticoid n. mineralocorticoide, tipo de hormona liberada por la glándula suprarrenal que participa en la regulación del volumen de la sangre.

minimal a. comp. mínimo-a, más pequeño-a.

minimal dose n. dosis mínima, la menor dosis necesaria para producir un efecto determinado.

minimal lethal dose n. dosis letal mínima, la menor dosis de una sustancia que puede ocasionar la muerte.

minimize v. aliviar, atenuar, mitigar; reducir al mínimo; **This pill is to __ the pain** / Esta pastilla es para __ el dolor.

minister n. ministro; pastor.

minor n. [in age] menor de edad; a. [smaller, youngest] menor, más pequeño; **a __ problem**

/ un problema sin importancia; ___ **surgery** / cirugía menor.

minority *n.* minoría, minoridad.

mint *n.* [*herb*] menta.

minute *n.* [*time*] minuto, momento; *a.* menudo-a, mínimo-a, diminuto-a.

miosis *n.* miosis, contracción excesiva de la pupila.

miracle *n.* milagro, prodigio.

miraculous *a.* milagroso-a, prodigioso-a.

mirror *n.* espejo.

misadventure *n.* infortunio, desgracia; accidente.

misanthropy *n.* misantropía, aversión a la humanidad.

misbehave *v.* portarse mal, conducirse mal.

misbehaved *a.* malcriado-a, majadero-a; mal educado-a.

misbehavior *n.* mala conducta, mal comportamiento.

miscalculate *v.* hacer un error o falta; equivocarse.

miscalculation *n.* error, falta, equivocación.

miscarriage *n.* aborto, malparto, expulsión del feto por vía natural.

miscegenation *n.* mestizaje, cruzamiento de razas o de culturas.

miscible *a.* capaz de mezclarse o disolverse.

misdiagnosis *n.* diagnóstico equivocado o erróneo.

misery *n.* sufrimiento, pena; desesperación; miseria.

misfit *n.* mal adaptado-a; *v.* no sentar bien, desajustar.

misfortunate *a.* desdichado-a, desgraciado-a.

misfortune *n.* desdicha, desgracia.

misguide *v.* dirigir mal, aconsejar mal.

misguided *a.* mal aconsejado-a, mal dirigido-a.

misinform *v.* dar una información errónea.

misinformed *a.* mal informado-a.

misjudge *v.* juzgar mal, tener una opinión errónea.

misleading *a.* engañoso-a, descaminado-a, erróneo-a.

misogamy *n.* misogamia, aversión al matrimonio.

misogyny *n.* misoginia, aversión a las mujeres.

misplace *v.* extraviar, poner algo fuera de lugar.

miss *n.* señorita, jovencita; *v.* [*to fail, to overlook*] perder; **to** ___ **an appointment** / perder el turno; [*sentiment*] echar de menos; **to** ___ **one's family** / echar de menos a la familia; [*to skip*] **to** ___ **a period** / faltar la regla, faltar el período.

misshape *v.* deformar, desfigurar.

misshaped, misshapen *a.* deforme, desfigurado-a.

missing *a.* desaparecido-a; extraviado-a.

mission *n.* misión; destino.

mistake *n.* error, equivocación, desacierto, falta; *vi.* equivocar, entender mal, confundir; *vr.* equivocarse, confundirse.

mistaken *a. pp.* de **to mistake,** equivocado-a, desacertado-a, incorrecto-a.

mister *n.* señor.

mistimed *a.* inoportuno, fuera de tiempo.

mistranslation *n.* traducción incorrecta.

mistrustful *a.* desconfiado-a, receloso-a.

misunderstand *vi.* no comprender, entender mal.

mitigate *v.* mitigar, aliviar, calmar.

mitigated *a.* mitigado-a, aliviado-a, calmado-a; disminuido-a.

mitochondria *n.* mitocondria, filamentos microscópicos del citoplasma que constituyen la fuente principal de energía de la célula.

mitogen *n.* mitógeno, sustancia que induce mitosis celular.

mitogenesis, mitogenia *n.* mitogénesis, causa de la mitosis celular.

mitosis *n.* mitosis, división celular que da lugar a nuevas células y reemplaza tejidos lesionados.

mitral *a.* mitral, rel. a la válvula mitral o bicúspide; ___ **disease** / enfermedad de la válvula ___ del corazón; ___ **incompetence** / insuficiencia ___; ___ **murmur** / soplo; ___ **orifice** / orificio ___; ___ **valve insuficiency** / insuficiencia de la válvula ___; ___ **valve prolapse (MVP)** / prolapso de la válvula ___, cierre defectuoso de la válvula___.

mitral regurgitation *n.* regurgitación mitral, flujo sanguíneo retrógrado del ventrículo izquierdo a la aurícula izquierda causado por lesión de la válvula mitral.

mitral stenosis *n.* estenosis mitral, estrechez del orificio izquierdo aurículo-ventricular.

mitral valve *n.* válvula mitral, válvula aurículo-ventricular izquierda del corazón.

mittelschmerz *n.* dolor en el viente relacionado con la ovulación que ocurre gen. a mitad del ciclo menstrual.

mix *v.* mezclar, juntar, asociar.

mixed *a.* mezclado-a, asociado-a.

mixture *n.* mezcla, mixtura; poción.

mnemonics *n.* mnemónica, adiestramiento de la memoria por medio de asociación de ideas y otros recursos.

moan *n.* quejido, gemido, queja, lamento; *vr.* quejarse, lamentarse.

mobility *n.* movilidad.

mobilization *n.* movilización.

mobilize *v.* movilizar; movilizarse, moverse.

modality *n.* modalidad, cualquier método de aplicación terapéutica.

mode *n.* 1. moda, manera, valor repetido con mayor frecuencia en una serie; 2. modo.

model *n.* modelo, patrón, molde.

moderated *a.* moderado-a, mesurado-a; [*price*] módico, [*weather*] templado; ___ **temperature** / temperatura ___.

moderation *n.* moderación, sobriedad.

modern *a.* moderno-a, reciente.

modest *a.* modesto-a, recatado-a.

modification n. modificación, cambio.

modify v. modificar, cambiar.

modulation n. modulación, acto de ajustar o adaptar tal como ocurre en la inflexión de la voz.

moiety n. mitad, una de las porciones de un todo.

molar n. diente molar, muela.

mold n. moho, cualquier moho.

molding n. amoldamiento de la cabeza del feto para adaptarla a la forma y tamaño del canal del parto.

mole n. mancha, lunar.

molecular a. molecular, rel. a una molécula; __biology / biología __.

molecule n. molécula, unidad mínima de una sustancia.

molest v. dañar físicamente, vejar; humillar; asaltar.

mollusc, mollusk n. (pl. **mollusca.**) molusco.

moment n. momento, instante.

momentary a. momentáneo-a.

momentum L. momentum; ímpetu; fuerza de movimiento.

monarticular a. monarticular, que concierne o afecta a una sola articulación.

money n. dinero; moneda; divisas.

mongolism n. mongolismo. V. **Down syndrome.**

mongoloid a. mongoloide, rel. al mongolismo o que sufre del mismo.

moniliasis n. moniliasis. V. **candidiasis.**

monitor n. monitor. 1. instrumento electrónico usado para monitorear una función; 2. persona que supervisa una función o actividad; v. monitorear, chequear sistemáticamente con un instrumento electrónico una función orgánica, tal como los latidos del corazón.

monitoring n. monitoreo, acción de monitorear; **blood pressure** __ / __ de la presión arterial; **cardiac** __ / __ cardíaco; **fetal** __ / __ del corazón fetal.

monochromatic a. monocromático-a, de un solo color.

monoclonal a. monoclonal, rel. a un solo grupo de células; __ **antibodies** / anticuerpos __-es.

monocular a. monocular, rel. a un solo ojo.

monocyte n. monocito, glóbulo blanco mononuclear granuloso.

monogamy n. monogamia, unión matrimonial legal con una sola persona.

mononuclear a. mononuclear, que tiene un solo núcleo; __ **cell** / célula __.

mononucleosis n. mononucleosis, presencia de un número anormalmente elevado de leucocitos mononucleares en la sangre; **infectious** __ / __ infecciosa, infección viral aguda.

monosaccharide n. monosacárido, azúcar simple.

monotone n. monotonía.

monotonous a. monótono-a.

monozygotic twins n. pl. gemelos monocigóticos con características genéticas idénticas.

monster n. monstruo.

month n. mes.

monthly a. mensual; adv. mensualmente.

mood n. estado de ánimo, disposición, humor; v. **to be in a bad** __ / estar de mal __; **to be in a good** __ / estar de buen __; **to be in the** __ / tener deseos de; gr. modo.

moody a. malhumorado-a; propenso-a a cambios de ánimo.

moon n. luna; **moonlight** / luz de la __.

moonface n. cara de luna, cara llena redonda característica de pacientes sometidos a un tratamiento prolongado de un esteroide.

moonlighter n. persona que tiene más de un empleo.

moral a. moral, honesto-a, honrado-a.

morality n. ética, rectitud, moral.

morbid a. mórbido, insano-a, morbosa-a, rel. a una enfermedad.

morbidity n. morbidez, morbosidad, enfermedad.

mordacious a. mordaz, satírico-a.

more a. más; adv. más; **more and more** / cada vez __; **once** __ / una vez __; [before numeral] __ **than a hundred** / __ de cien; [before a verb] __ **than** / más de lo que; __ **than he needs** / más de lo que necesita.

moreover adv. además, además de eso; también.

morgue Fr. morgue, necrocomio, depósito temporal de cadáveres.

moribund a. moribundo-a, cercano-a a la muerte, agonizante.

morning n. mañana, madrugada; **Good** __ / buenos días, buen día; **early in the** __ / muy de __; **in the** __ / por la __, en la __; **stiffness** / rigidez matutina muscular y de las articulaciones; **tomorrow** __ / __ por la __.

morning sickness n. trastorno matutino de náuseas y vómitos que sufren algunas mujeres en la primera etapa del embarazo.

moron n. morón-a, persona con retraso mental de un cociente intelectual de 50 a 70.

morphine n. morfina, alcaloide que se obtiene del opio y se usa como analgésico y sedante.

morphinism n. morfinismo, condición morbosa ocasionada por la adicción a la morfina.

mortal a. mortal, mortífero-a, fatal, letal.

mortality n. mortalidad, mortandad. 1. estado de ser mortal; 2. índice de mortalidad.

mortify v. mortificar; mortificarse, sentirse mortificado-a.

mortuary n. mortuorio, funeraria.

morula n. mórula, masa esférica y sólida de células que resulta de la división celular del óvulo fecundado.

mosaic n. mosaico, la presencia en una persona de distintos tejidos adyacentes derivados de la misma célula como resultado de mutaciones.

mosquito n. mosquito.

most a. sup. de **more,** el, la más; lo más; el, la mayor; el mayor número de, la mayor parte de; adv. más, muy, a lo sumo; **-ly** sumamente, principalmente.

mother *n.* madre, mamá; **mother-in-law** / suegra.

motherhood *n.* maternidad.

motility *n.* movilidad.

motion *n.* movimiento; [*sign*] seña, indicación; moción; ___ **sickness** / mareo.

motionless *a.* sin movimiento, inmóvil.

motivate *v.* motivar, animar.

motivation *n.* motivación, estimulación externa.

motive *n.* motivo; ánimo, fuerza mayor.

motor *n.* motor, agente que produce o induce movimiento; *a.* motor-a, que causa movimiento.

motor development *n.* desarrollo motor.

motor neuron *n.* neurona motora, células nerviosas que conducen impulsos que inician las contracciones musculares.

mottled *a.* moteado-a, descolorido-a.

mountain *n.* montaña.

mourn *v.* estar de duelo; guardar luto.

mouse *n.* (*pl.* **mice**) ratón, [*small*] ratoncito.

moustache *n.* bigote.

mouth *n.* boca. 1. cavidad bucal; 2. abertura de cualquier cavidad; **by** ___ por vía bucal; **Open your** ___ / Abra, abre la boca.

mouthwash *n.* antiséptico bucal; enjuague.

move *n.* movimiento; paso; *v.* mover; mudar; **to** ___ **about, to** ___ **around** / caminar, andar, ir; **to** ___ **away** / irse, trasladarse, mudarse; **to** ___ **down** / bajar; ___ **your hand** / Mueva, mueve la mano; ___ **your fingers** / Mueva, mueve los dedos.

movement *n.* movimiento, moción, acción, maniobra; [*of the intestines*] evacuación, defecación.

much *a.* mucho-a; abundante; *adv.* excesivamente, demasiado, en gran cantidad; **as** ___ **as** / tanto como; **How** ___? / ¿Cuánto? **not as** ___ **as before** / no tanto como antes; **too** ___ / en exceso, demasiado; **How** ___ **does it hurt?** / ¿Cuánto le duele?

mucin *n.* mucina, glucoproteína, ingrediente esencial del mucus.

mucocele *n.* mucocele, dilatación de una cavidad ósea debida a una acumulación de secreción mucosa.

mucocutaneous *a.* mucocutáneo-a, rel. a la membrana mucosa y la piel.

mucoid *n.* mucoide, glucoproteína similar a la mucina; *a.* de consistencia mucosa.

mucomembranous *a.* mucomembranoso-a, rel. a la membrana mucosa.

mucosa *n.* mucosa, membrana mucosa. *V.* **mucous membrane.**

mucosal *a.* mucosal, rel. a cualquier membrana mucosa.

mucosity *n.* mucosidad.

mucous *a.* mucoso-a, flemoso-a; ___ **colitis** / colitis ___.

mucous membrane *n.* membrana mucosa, láminas finas de tejido celular que cubren aberturas o canales que comunican con el exterior.

mucus *n.* moco, mucosidad, sustancia viscosa segregada por las membranas y glándulas mucosas.

multicellular *a.* multicelular, que consiste de muchas células.

multifactorial *a.* multifactorial, rel. a varios factores.

multifocal *a.* multifocal, rel. a más de un foco.

multilocular *a.* multilocular, *V.* **multicellular.**

multiparity *n.* multiparidad. 1. condición de una mujer que ha tenido más de un parto logrado; 2. parto múltiple.

multiple *a.* múltiple, más de uno; ___ **organ failure** / fallo ___ de órganos; ___ **personality** / personalidad ___.

multiple sclerosis *n.* esclerosis múltiple, enfermedad progresiva lenta del sistema nervioso central causada por pérdida de la capa de mielina que cubre las fibras nerviosas del cerebro y de la médula espinal.

mummification *n.* momificación, conversión a un estado similar al de una momia tal como en la gangrena seca o en el estado de un feto que muere y permanece en la matriz.

mumps *n.* paperas, parotiditis, enfermedad febril aguda de alta contagiosidad que se caracteriza por la infl. de las glándulas parótidas y otras glándulas salivales.

mural *a.* mural, rel. a las paredes de un órgano o parte.

muriatic *n.* muriático, derivado de sal común; ácido muriático.

murmur *n.* soplo, ruido; sonido breve raspante, esp. un sonido anormal del corazón; **aortic** ___, **regurgitant** / ___ aórtico, regurgitante; **cardiac** ___ / ___ cardíaco; **continuous** ___ / ___ continuo; **diastolic** ___ / ___ diastólico; **functional** ___ / ___ funcional; **innocent** ___ / ___ inocente; **mitral** ___ / ___ mitral; **pansystolic** ___ / ___ pansistólico; **presystolic** ___ / ___ presistólico; **systolic** ___ / ___ sistólico.

Murmur	*Soplo*
aortic, regurgitant	aórtico, regurgitante
bronchial	bronquial
cardiac	cardíaco
continuous	continuo
crescendo	creciente
diastolic	diastólico
endocardial	endocardial
exocardial	exocardial
functional	funcional
mitral	mitral
pansystolic	pansistólico
presystolic	presistólico
systolic	sistólico

muscle *n.* músculo, tipo de tejido fibroso capaz de contraerse y que permite el movimiento de las partes y los órganos del cuerpo; **cardiac** ___ / ___ cardíaco; **flexor** ___ / ___ flexor; **involuntary, visceral** ___ / ___ involuntario, visceral; **loss of** ___ **tone** / pérdida de la tonicidad muscular; ___ **building** / desarrollo muscular; ___ **strain** / distensión muscular; ___ **toning** / tonicidad muscular; **striated, voluntary** ___ / ___ estriado, voluntario; ___ **relaxants** / relajadores musculares, medicamentos para aliviar espasmos musculares.

muscular *a.* muscular, musculoso-a, rel. al músculo; ___ **atrophy** / atrofia ___; ___ **contractions** / contracciones ___-es; ___ **dystrophy** / distrofia ___; ___ **rigidity** / rigidez ___.

muscularis *n.* muscularis, capa muscular de un órgano.

musculature *n.* musculatura; aparato muscular del cuerpo.

musculoskeletal *a.* musculoesquelético-a, rel. a los músculos y el esqueleto.

musculotendinous *a.* musculotendinoso-a, que está formado por músculo y tendón.

mushroom *n.* hongo, seta, champiñón; ___ **poisoning** / envenenamiento por ___-s.

mussel *n.* almeja.

must *v. aux.* deber, ser necesario, tener que; **You must take the medication** / Usted debe, tú debes tomar la medicina.

mustard *n.* mostaza.

mutagen *n.* mutágeno, sustancia o agente que causa mutación.

mutant *a.* mutante, rel. a un organismo que ha pasado por mutaciones.

mutation *n.* mutación, alteración, cambios espontáneos o inducidos en la estructura genética.

mute *n.* mudo-a.

mutilate *v.* mutilar, cortar, cercenar.

mutilation *n.* mutilación.

mutism *n.* mutismo, mudez.

mutter *v.* murmurar, musitar; decir entre dientes; *pop.* cuchichear.

my *a.* mi, mis; mío-a, míos-as.

myalgia *n.* mialgia, dolor muscular.

myasthenia *n.* miastenia, debilidad muscular; ___ **gravis** / ___ grave.

myatonia *n.* miatonía, deficiencia o pérdida del tono muscular.

mycetoma *n.* micetoma, infección causada por hongos parásitos que afectan a la piel, al tejido conjuntivo y a los huesos.

mycobacterium *L. Mycobacterium,* especie de bacterias gram-positivas en forma de bastoncillo que incluyen las causantes de la lepra y la tuberculosis.

mycology *n.* micología, estudio de hongos y de las enfermedades que ellos producen.

mycoplasmas *n. pl.* microplasmas, la más diminuta forma de organismos vivos libres a la cual pertenecen los virus que causan enfermedades como la pulmonía y la faringitis.

mycosis *n.* micosis, cualquier enfermedad causada por hongos.

mycotic *a.* micótico-a, rel. a la micosis.

mycotoxins *n. pl.* micotoxinas, toxinas producidas por hongos parásitos.

mydriasis *n.* midriasis, dilatación prolongada de la pupila del ojo.

mydriatic *a.* midriático-a, que causa dilatación de la pupila del ojo.

myectomy *n. cirg.* miectomía, extirpación de una porción de un músculo.

myelin *n.* mielina, sustancia de tipo grasoso que cubre las fibras nerviosas.

myelination, myelinization *n.* mielinización, crecimiento de mielina alrededor de una fibra nerviosa.

myelinolysis *n.* mielinólisis, enfermedad que destruye la mielina alrededor de ciertas fibras nerviosas; **acute** ___ / ___ aguda; ___ **transverse** / ___ transversa.

myelitis *n.* mielitis, infl. de la espina dorsal.

myelocele *n.* mielocele, hernia de la médula espinal a través de la columna vertebral.

myelocyte *n.* mielocito, leucocito granular de la médula ósea presente en la sangre en ciertas enfermedades.

myelocytic *a.* mielocítico-a, rel. a mielocitos; ___ **leukemia** / leucemia ___.

myelodysplasia *n.* mielodisplasia, desarrollo anormal de la columna vertebral.

myelofibrosis *n.* mielofibrosis, fibrosis de la médula ósea.

myelogenic, myelogenous *a.* mielógeno-a, que se produce en la médula.

myelogram *v.* mielograma, radiografía de la médula usando un medio de contraste.

myelography *n.* mielografía, radiografía de la columna vertebral con inyección de medio de contraste en la región subaracnoidea.

myeloid *n.* mieloide; *a.* rel. a la médula espinal o similar a la médula espinal o a la médula ósea; ___ **tissue** / médula roja.

myeloma *n.* mieloma. 1. cualquier tumor de la médula espinal u ósea; 2. tumor formado por el tipo de células que se encuentran en la médula ósea; **multiple** ___ / ___ múltiple.

myelomeningocele *n.* mielomeningocele, hernia de la médula espinal y de las meninges con protrusión a través de un defecto en el canal vertebral.

myelopathy *n.* mielopatía, cualquier condición patológica de la médula espinal o de la médula ósea.

myeloproliferative *a.* mieloproliferativo-a, que se caracteriza por una proliferación de la médula ósea dentro o fuera de la médula.

myelosuppression *n.* mielosupresión, inhabilidad de la médula ósea de producir glóbulos rojos y plaquetas.

myocardial, myocardiac *a.* miocárdico-a, rel. al miocardio; ___ **contraction** / contracción del miocardio; ___ **diseases** / miocardiopatías.

myocardial infarction *n.* infarto cardíaco, necrosis de células del músculo cardíaco debido a un bloqueo del abastecimiento de sangre que lo irriga, condición usu. conocida como "ataque al corazón."

myocardiography *n.* miocardiografía, trazado de los movimientos del músculo cardíaco.

myocardiopathy *n.* miocardiopatía, *V.* **cardiomyopathy.**

myocarditis *n.* miocarditis, infl. del miocardio.

myocardium *n.* miocardio, capa media de la pared cardíaca.

myoclonus *n.* mioclonus, contracción o espasmo muscular tal como se manifiesta en la epilepsia.

myocyte *n.* miocito, célula del tejido muscular.

myodystrophy *n.* miodistrofia, distrofia muscular.

myofibril *n.* miofibrilla, fibrilla diminuta delgada del tejido muscular.

myofibroma *n.* miofibroma, tumor compuesto de elementos musculares.

myofilament *n.* miofilamento, filamentos microscópicos que constituyen las fibrillas musculares.

myogenic *a.* miogénico-a, que se origina en un músculo.

myoglobin *n.* mioglobina, pigmento del tejido muscular que participa en la distribución de oxígeno.

myography *n.* miografía, gráfico que registra la actividad muscular.

myolysis *n.* miolisis, destrucción de tejido muscular.

myoma *n.* mioma, tumor benigno compuesto de tejido muscular.

myomectomy *n. cirg.* miomectomía. 1. excisión de una porción de un músculo o de tejido muscular; 2. extirpación de un tumor miomatoso localizado gen. en el útero.

myometrium *n.* miometrio, pared muscular del útero.

myonecrosis *n.* mionecrosis, necrosis del tejido muscular.

myoneural *a.* mioneural, rel. a una terminación nerviosa en un músculo; ___ **junction** / unión ___.

myopathy *n.* miopatía, cualquier enfermedad muscular.

myope *n.* miope, persona que tiene miopía.

myopia *n.* miopía, defecto del globo ocular por el cual los rayos de luz hacen foco enfrente de la retina, lo que causa dificultad para ver objetos a distancia.

myopic *a.* miope. 1. que padece de miopía; 2. rel. a la miopía.

myosin *n.* miosina, la proteína más abundante del tejido muscular.

myositis *n.* miositis, infl. de uno o de más músculos.

myotomy *n. cirg.* miotomía, sección o disección de un músculo.

myotonia *n.* miotonía, condición muscular con aumento en rigidez y contractibilidad muscular y disminución de relajamiento.

myringectomy, myringodectomy *n.* miringectomía, extirpación de la membrana timpánica o de una parte de ésta.

myringitis *n.* miringitis, infl. del tímpano.

myringoplasty *n. cirg.* miringoplastia, cirugía plástica de la membrana del tímpano.

myxedema *n.* mixedema, condición causada por deficiencia funcional de la tiroides.

myxoma *n.* mixoma, tumor compuesto de tejido conjuntivo.

N *abbr.* **nasal** / nasal; **nerve** / nervio; **nitrogen** / nitrógeno; **normal** / normal; **number** / número.

Nabothian cysts *n. pl.* quistes de Naboth, quistes pequeños gen. benignos formados por obstrucción de las glándulas secretoras de mucus del cuello uterino.

nail *n.* 1. uña de los dedos del pie o de la mano; ___ **scratch** / arañazo; ___ **biting** / comerse la uñas; **ingrown** ___ / uñero, ___ encarnada; 2. clavo. *V.* **pin.**

nailbed *n.* matriz de la uña, porción de epidermis que cubre la uña.

naive *a.* ingenuo-a; cándido-a; inocente.

naked *a.* desnudo-a, descubierto-a; *pop.* en cuero, en pelota; **with the** ___ **eye** / a simple vista; *v.* **to strip** ___ / desnudarse.

name *n.* nombre; [*first name and surname*] nombre completo, nombre y apellido; **What is your** ___? / ¿Cómo se llama usted?, ¿cómo te llamas tú?, ¿cuál es su, tu nombre?

nanism *n.* nanismo. *V.* **dwarfism.**

nap *n.* siesta; *v.* **to take a** ___ / echar una ___, dormir una ___.

nape *n.* nuca, cerviz, parte posterior del cuello; *pop.* pescuezo, cogote.

napkin *n.* servilleta.

narcissism *n.* narcisismo. 1. amor excesivo a sí mismo; 2. placer sexual derivado de la contemplación del propio cuerpo.

narcolepsy *n.* narcolepsia, padecimiento crónico de accesos de sueño.

narcoleptic *a.* narcoléptico-a, rel. a la narcolepsia o que padece de ella.

narcosis *n.* narcosis, estado inconsciente causado por un narcótico o droga.

narcotic *a.* narcótico-a, estupefaciente de efecto analgésico que puede producir adicción.

naris *n.* (*pl.* **nares**) naris, orificios o ventanas de la nariz.

narrow *a.* angosto-a, estrecho-a.

nasal *a.* nasal, rel. a la nariz; ___ **cavity** / cavidad ___; ___ **congestion** / congestión ___; ___ **drip** / goteo ___, *pop.* moquera; ___ **instillation** / instilación ___.

nascent *a.* 1. naciente, incipiente; 2. liberado de un compuesto químico.

nasogastric *a.* nasogástrico-a, rel. a la nariz y el estómago; ___ **tube** / tubo ___.

nasolabial *a.* nasolabial, rel. a la nariz y el labio.

nasopharynx *n.* nasofaringe, parte de la faringe localizada sobre el velo del paladar.

nasty *a.* agresivo-a, de mal carácter; ___ **illness** / enfermedad grave, seria; ___ **weather** / mal tiempo.

natal *a.* natal, rel. a la natalidad.

natality *a.* natalidad, índice de nacimientos en una comunidad.

natimortality *n.* mortinatalidad, porcentaje de nacimientos no viables o no logrados.

nationality *n.* nacionalidad.

native *a.* nativo-a, natural de, [*indigenous*] indígena, autóctono-a; ___ **born** / nacido-a en; oriundo-a de; ___ **tongue** / lengua materna.

nativity *n.* natividad, nacimiento.

natriuretic *n.* natriurético-a. *V.* **diuretic.**

natural *a.* natural; sencillo-a; ___ **childbirth** / parto ___; **-ly** *adv.* naturalmente.

nature *n.* naturaleza.

naturopath *n.* naturópata, persona que practica la naturopatía.

naturopathy *n.* naturopatía, tratamiento terapéutico por medio de recursos naturales.

naughtiness *n.* malacrianza, travesura, majadería.

naughty *a.* travieso-a, majadero-a.

nausea *n.* náusea, asco, ganas de vomitar.

nauseate *v.* dar o causar náuseas, dar asco; **to be nauseated** / tener náuseas.

nauseating *a.* nauseabundo-a.

nauseous *a.* nauseoso-a. 1. propenso a tener náuseas; 2. que produce náusea o asco.

navel *n.* ombligo.

navicular *a.* navicular, en forma de nave.

near *a.* cercano-a, próximo-a, a corta distancia; **a** ___ **relative** / un pariente ___; [*almost*] casi; *prep.* cerca de, junto a; [*at hand*] a la mano; [*toward*] ___ **the right** / hacia la derecha, cerca de la derecha; **-ly** *adv.* casi, por poco; **He, she** ___ **died** / él, ella por poco se muere.

nearsighted *a.* miope, corto-a de vista.

nearsightedness *n.* miopía. *V.* **myopia.**

neat *a.* pulcro-a, cuidadoso-a, aseado-a; [*very pleasing*] bueno-a.

nebulization *n.* nebulización, atomización, conversión de un líquido a una nube de vapor.

nebulizer *n.* nebulizador, atomizador de líquido.

nebulous *a.* nebuloso-a.

necessary *n.* necesidad; *a.* necesario-a, indispensable; **It is** ___ / Es necesario; **what is** ___ / lo necesario; **whatever is** ___ / lo que sea necesario.

necessity *n.* necesidad.

neck *n.* cuello, pescuezo. 1. parte del cuerpo que une la cabeza al tronco; 2. región de un diente entre la corona y la raíz.

necklace *n.* collar, gargantilla.

neck of uterus *n.* cuello uterino.

necrogenic *a.* necrógeno-a, rel. a la muerte; 2. que se forma o compone de materia muerta.

necrology *n.* necrología, estudio de estadísticas referentes a la mortalidad.

necrophilia *n.* necrofilia. 1. atracción mórbida por los cadáveres; 2. relación sexual con un cadáver.

necrophobia. *n.* necrofobia, temor anormal a la muerte y a los cadáveres.

necropsy *n.* nectropsia. *V.* **autopsy.**

necrose *v.* necrosar, causar o experimentar necrosis.

necrosis *n.* necrosis, muerte parcial o total de las células que forman un tejido tal como ocurre en la gangrena.

necrotic *a.* necrótico-a, rel. a la necrosis o a un tejido afectado por ésta.

necrotize *a.* necrosar, causar la muerte, producir necrosis.

need *n.* necesidad; **a person in** ___ / un-a necesitado-a; *v.* necesitar.

needle *n.* aguja; **hypodermic** ___ / ___ hipodérmica.

needless *a.* inútil, innecesario.

needy *a.* necesitado-a; pobre; *n. pl.* **the** ___ / los ___-s.

negation *n.* negación.

negative *a.* negativo-a; ___ **culture** / cultivo ___; **-ly** *adv.* negativamente.

negativism *n. psic.* negativismo, conducta caracterizada por una actuación opuesta a la sugerida.

neglect *n.* negligencia, descuido, desamparo.

neglectful *a.* negligente, descuidado-a.

negligence *n.* negligencia, descuido.

negligent *a.* negligente, descuidado-a.

neighbor *n.* vecino-a.

nemathelminth *n.* nematelminto, gusano intestinal de forma redondeada que pertenece al orden de los *Nemathelmintes*.

nematocide *n.* nematocida, agente que destruye nematodos.

Nematoda *L. Nematoda*, clase de gusanos del orden de los *Nemathelmintes*.

nematode *n.* nematodo, gusano de la clase *Nematoda*.

nematology *n.* nematología, estudio de los gusanos de la clase *Nematoda*.

neoarthrosis, nearthrosis *n.* neoartrosis, neartrosis, articulación artificial o falsa.

neologism *n.* neologismo. 1. *psic.* vocablos a los cuales el paciente mental atribuye nuevos significados no relacionados con el verdadero; 2. vocablo al cual se le atribuye un giro nuevo.

neomycin *n.* neomicina, antibiótico de espectro amplio.

neonatal *a.* neonatal, rel. a las primeras seis semanas después del nacimiento.

neonate *n.* neonato-a, recién nacido-a, de seis semanas o menos de nacido-a.

neonatologist *n.* neonatólogo-a, especialista en neonatología.

neonatology *n.* neonatología, estudio y cuidado de los recién nacidos.

neoplasia *n.* neoplasia, formación de neoplasmas.

neoplasm *n.* neoplasma, crecimiento anormal de tejido nuevo tal como un tumor.

neoplastic *a.* neoplástico-a, rel. a un neoplasma.

nephew *n.* sobrino.

nephralgia *n.* nefralgia, dolor en el riñón.

nephrectomy *n. cirg.* nefrectomía, extirpación de un riñón.

nephric *a.* néfrico-a, renal.

nephritic *n.* nefrítico-a, rel. a la nefritis o afectado por ella.

nephritis *n.* nefritis, infl. del riñón.

nephrocalcinosis *n.* nefrocalcinosis, depósitos de calcio en los túbulos renales que pueden causar insuficiencia renal.

nephrogram *n.* nefrograma, radiografía del riñón.

nephrolithiasis *n.* nefrolitiasis, presencia de cálculos renales.

nephrolithotomy *n. cirg.* nefrolitotomía, incisión en el riñón para extraer cálculos renales.

nephrology *n.* nefrología, estudio del riñón y de las enfermedades que lo afectan.

nephroma *n.* nefroma, tumor del riñón.

nephron *n.* nefrona, unidad funcional y anatómica del riñón.

nephropathy *n.* nefropatía, cualquier enfermedad del riñón.

nephropexy *n. cirg.* nefropexia, fijación de un riñón flotante.

nephrosclerosis *n.* nefroesclerosis, endurecimiento del sistema arterial y del tejido intersticial del riñón.

nephrosis *n.* nefrosis, afección renal degenerativa asociada con gran cantidad de proteína en la orina, niveles bajos de albúmina en la sangre y edema pronunciado.

nephrostomy *n. cirg.* nefrostomía, formación de una fístula en el riñón o en la pelvis renal.

nephrotic syndrome *n.* síndrome nefrótico, afección del riñón caracterizada por un exceso de pérdida de proteína.

nephrotomography *n.* nefrotomografía, tomografía del riñón.

nephrotomy *n. cirg.* nefrotomía, incisión en el riñón.

nephrotoxic *a.* nefrotóxico, que destruye células renales.

nephrotoxin *n.* nefrotoxina, toxina que destruye células renales.

nerve *n.* nervio, cada una de las fibras libres o fibras en haz que conectan al cerebro y la médula espinal con otras partes y órganos del cuerpo; ___ **block** / bloqueo del ___; ___ **cells** / neuronas; ___ **degeneration** / degeneración nerviosa; ___ **ending** / terminación del ___; ___ **fiber** / fibra nerviosa; **pinched** ___ / ___ pellizcado; ___ / ___ **tissue** / tejido nervioso.

nervous *a.* nervioso-a, ansioso-a, excitable; ___ **breakdown** / colapso ___, crisis ___; ___ **debility** / fatiga ___; ___ **disorder** / trastorno ___; ___ **impulse** / impulso ___; ___ **system** / sistema ___.

nervousness *n.* nerviosismo, nerviosidad.

nest *n.* nido de células, masa de células en forma de nido de pájaro.

nestiatria *n.* nestiatría, terapia con ayuno.

network *n.* red, encadenación; arreglo de fibras en forma de malla.

neural *a.* neural, rel. al sistema nervioso.

neuralgia *n.* neuralgia, dolor intenso a lo largo

de un nervio.

neuralgic *a.* neurálgico-a, rel. a la neuralgia.

neurapraxia *n.* neurapraxia, parálisis temporal de un nervio sin causar degeneración.

neurasthenia *n.* neurastenia, término asociado con un estado general de irritabilidad y agotamiento nervioso.

neurasthenic *a.* neurasténico-a, rel. a o con síntomas de neurastenia.

neurilemma *n.* neurilema, membrana fina que cubre una fibra nerviosa.

neurinoma *n.* neurinoma, neoplasma benigno de las capas que rodean un nervio.

neuritis *n.* neuritis, infl. de un nervio.

neuroanatomy *n.* neuroanatomía, estudio anatómico del sistema nervioso.

neuroblast *n.* neuroblasto, célula nerviosa primitiva.

neuroblastoma *n.* neuroblastoma, tumor maligno del sistema nervioso formado en gran parte por neuroblastos.

neurodermatosis *n.* neurodermatosis, erupción crónica cutánea de origen desconocido que se caracteriza por una picazón intensa en áreas localizadas.

neuroectoderm *n.* neuroectodermo, tejido embrionario del cual se deriva el tejido nervioso.

neuroendocrinology *n.* neuroendocrinología, estudio del sistema nervioso y su relación con las hormonas.

neurofibroma *n.* neurofibroma, tumor del tejido fibroso que cubre un nervio periférico.

neurofibromatosis *n.* neurofibromatosis, condición que se caracteriza por la manifestación de múltiples neurofibromas a lo largo de los nervios periféricos.

neuroglia *n.* neuroglia, células que sirven de sostén y constituyen el tejido intersticial del sistema nervioso.

neurohypophysis *n.* neurohipófisis, porción nerviosa posterior de la glándula pituitaria.

neuroleptic *n.* neuroléptico, agente tranquilizante; ___ **anesthesia** / anestesia con el uso de un ___.

neurologist *n.* neurólogo-a, especialista del sistema nervioso.

neurology *n.* neurología, rama de la medicina que estudia el sistema nervioso.

neuroma *n.* neuroma, tumor constituido principalmente por fibras y células nerviosas.

neuromuscular *a.* neuromuscular, rel. a nervios y músculos.

neuron *n.* neurona, célula que constituye la unidad básica funcional del sistema nervioso.

neuro-ophthalmology *n.* neurooftalmología, rama de la oftalmología que se especializa en la parte del sistema nervioso relacionada con la visión.

neuropacemaker *n.* neuromarcapasos, instrumento para estimular eléctricamente la médula espinal.

neuropathology *n.* neuropatología, ciencia que

estudia las enfermedades nerviosas.

neuropathy *n.* neuropatía, trastorno o cambio patológico en los nervios periféricos; **autonomic** ___ / ___ autónoma; **motor** ___ / ___ motor.

neuropharmacology *n.* neurofarmacología, estudio farmacológico del efecto de drogas en el sistema nervioso.

neurophysiology *n.* neurofisiología, fisiología del sistema nervioso.

neuropil *n.* neurópilo, red de fibras nerviosas (dendritas y neuritas) y de las células de la glia interrumpidas por sinapses en partes del tejido nervioso.

neuropsychopharmacology *n.* neurosicofarmacología, estudio de medicamentos y del efecto que causan en el tratamiento de trastornos mentales.

neuroradiology *n.* neurorradiología, radiología del sistema nervioso.

neurosis *n.* neurosis, condición que se manifiesta principalmente por ansiedad y por el uso de mecanismos de defensa.

neurosurgeon *n.* neurocirujano-a, especialista en neurocirugía.

neurosurgery *n.* neurocirugía, *cirg.* del sistema nervioso.

neurosyphilis *n.* neurosífilis, sífilis que afecta el sistema nervioso central.

neurotic *a.* neurótico-a, que sufre de neurosis.

neurotoxicity *n.* neurotoxicidad, acción tóxica destructiva del sistema nervioso.

neurotransmitter *n.* neurorregulador, sustancia química que modifica la transmisión de impulsos a través de una sinapsis entre nervios o entre un nervio y un músculo.

neurovascular *a.* neurovascular, rel. a los sistemas nervioso y vascular.

neutral *a.* neutral.

neutralization *n.* neutralización, proceso de anular o contrarrestar la acción de un agente.

neutralize *v.* neutralizar; contrarrestar.

neutropenia *n.* neutropenia. *V.* **agranulocytosis.**

neutrophil *n.* neutrófilo, leucocito-fagocito que se tiñe con colorantes neutrales.

neutrophilia *n.* neutrofilia, aumento de neutrófilos en la sangre.

neutrotaxis *n.* neutrotaxis, estimulación de neutrófilos con una sustancia que los atrae o repele.

never *adv.* nunca, jamás; ___ **fear** / pierda cuidado; ___ **mind** / no importa.

nevertheless *adv.* sin embargo, no obstante.

nevus *n.* (*pl.* **nevi**) nevo, lunar, marca de nacimiento.

new *a.* nuevo-a; **What is new?** / ¿Qué hay de ___?

newborn *n.* recién nacido-a; neonato-a.

news *n. pl.* noticias; **bad** ___ / malas ___; **good** ___ / buenas ___; *v.* **to break the** ___ / dar la noticia.

newspaper *n.* diario, periódico.

next *a.* próximo-a, siguiente; **Who is** ___? /

¿Quién es el, la ___? ___ **door** / al lado; **The table is** ___ **to the bed** / La mesa está al lado de la cama; ___ **of kin** / el pariente más cercano; ___ **to nothing** / casi nada.

nexus *n.* (*pl.* **nexus**) nexo, conexión, unión.

niacin *n.* ácido nicotínico.

nice *a.* delicado-a, fino-a, bueno-a; *adv.* finamente, delicadamente; **nicely done** / bien hecho.

niche *n.* nicho, depresión o defecto pequeño esp. en la pared de un órgano hueco.

nicotine *n.* nicotina, alcaloide tóxico, ingrediente principal del tabaco.

niece *n.* sobrina.

night *n.* noche; **by** ___ / de noche, por la noche; **Good** ___ / Buenas noches; **last** ___ / anoche; ___ **before last** / anteanoche.

nightfall *n.* atardecer, anochecer.

nightgown *n.* bata de dormir, camisa o camisón.

nightmare *n.* pesadilla.

night watch *n.* guardia nocturna.

nipple *n.* pezón; [*of male*] tetilla; [*nursing bottle*] mamadera, tetera; **cracked** ___ / ___ agrietado; **engorged** ___ / ___ enlechado.

nitric acid *n.* ácido nítrico.

nitrogen *n.* nitrógeno.

nitroglycerine *n.* nitroglicerina, nitrato de glicerina usado como vasodilatador esp. en la angina de pecho.

no *adv.* no, de ningún modo, de ninguna manera; **no good** / no vale; ___ **one** / nadie; **Say yes or** ___ / Diga, di que sí o que no.

Nocardia *n.* Nocardia, microorganismo grampositivo que causa nocardiosis.

nocardiosis *n.* nocardiosis, infección generalmente pulmonar causada por Nocardia que puede expandirse a varias partes del cuerpo.

nocturia, nycturia *n.* nocturia, nicturia, frecuencia aumentada de emisión de orina esp. durante la noche.

nocturnal *a.* nocturno-a, nocturnal, de noche; ___ **emission, emiction** / micciones ___s orinarse en la cama; emisión ___ involuntaria de semen.

nod *v.* inclinar la cabeza; aprobar.

node *n.* nudo, nódulo, ganglio; **lymphatic** ___ / ___ linfático.

nodose *a.* nudoso-a, formado por nódulos o protuberancias.

nodular *a.* nodular, semejante a un nudo.

nodule *n.* nódulo o nudo pequeño.

noise *n.* ruido; *v.* **to make** ___ / hacer ___.

noiseless *a.* callado-a, tranquilo-a.

noisy *a.* ruidoso-a, turbulento-a, bullicioso-a.

nomadic *a.* nómada, errante.

nomenclature *n.* nomenclatura, terminología.

non compos mentis *L.* non compos mentis, mentalmente incompetente.

none *pron.* nadie, ninguno-a.

noninvasive *a.* no invasor, que no se propaga o invade.

nonparous *a.* nulípara. *V.* **nulliparous.**

nonsense *n.* tontería, bobería, disparate.

nonspecific *a.* sin especificación.

nonviable *n.* que no puede sobrevivir.

noodle *n.* fideo, tallarín; pasta.

noon *n.* mediodía.

norm *n.* norma, regla.

normal *a.* normal, natural, regular.

normalization *n.* normalización, regreso al estado normal.

normocalcemia *n.* normocalcemia, nivel normal de calcio en la sangre.

normoglycemia *n.* normoglucemia, concentración normal de azúcar en la sangre.

normokalemia *n.* normopotasemia, nivel normal de potasio en la sangre.

normotensive *a.* normotenso-a, de presión arterial normal.

normothermia *n.* normotermia, temperatura normal.

normotonic *a.* normotónico-a, de tono muscular normal.

nose *n.* nariz; **bridge of the** ___ / tabique nasal, puente de la nariz; **running** ___ / nariz destilante; coriza.

nosebleed *n.* sangramiento por la nariz.

nosocomial *a.* nosocomial, rel. a un hospital o clínica; ___ **infection** / infección ___, enfermedad adquirida en un hospital.

nostalgia *n.* nostalgia, tristeza, añoranza.

nostril *n.* naris, fosa nasal, ventana o ala de la nariz.

not *adv.* no, de ningún modo; **Why not?** / ¿Por qué no?; ___ **at all** / de ninguna manera.

notch *n.* incisión, incisura, ranura, escotadura; **suprasternal** ___ / ___ supraesternal.

note *n.* nota, apunte, aviso; **progress** ___ **-s** / informe del progreso clínico; *v.* notar, apreciar; **to take** ___ **of** / tomar ___ de, darse cuenta de, observar.

nothing *n.* nada, niguna cosa; *adv.* en nada, de ningún modo, de ninguna manera.

notice *n.* aviso, informe, nota; observación; *v.* notar, hacer caso, observar.

noticeable *a.* notorio-a, que se distingue.

notification *n.* notificación, aviso, información.

notify *v.* avisar, informar, notificar; ___ **your doctor at once** / Avise a su médico en seguida.

notion *n.* noción, concepto, opinión.

notochord *n.* notocordio, sostén fibrocelular del embrión que se convierte más tarde en la columna vertebral.

noun *n.* nombre, sustantivo.

nourish *v.* alimentar, nutrir, sustentar.

nourishable *a.* nutritivo-a, alimenticio-a.

nourishing *a.* alimenticio-a, nutritivo-a.

nourishment *n.* alimento, nutrición, sustento.

novice *a.* principiante, novicio-a.

novocaine *n.* novocaína, anestésico.

now *adv.* ahora, ahorita, en este momento, actualmente; **from** ___ **on** / de ___ en adelante; **just** ___ / ___ mismo, hace un momento; ___ **and then** / de vez en cuando; ___ **then** /

ahora bien.

nowadays *adv.* hoy en día, al presente.

no way *adv.* de ningún modo, de ninguna manera.

nowhere *adv.* en ninguna parte; ___ **else** / en ninguna otra parte.

nubile *a.* núbil. rel. a la madurez sexual femenina.

nucha *n.* nuca, parte posterior del cuello.

nuchal brace *n.* braguero de cuello.

nuclear *a.* nuclear. 1. rel. al núcleo de la célula; 2. rel. a la fuerza atómica.

nuclear envelope *n.* envoltura nuclear, forma que toman las dos membranas nucleares que envuelven al núcleo de la célula al examinarse bajo el microscopio electrónico.

nucleated *a.* nucleado-a, que posee un núcleo.

nucleic acid *n.* ácido nucleico.

nucleolus *n.* nucléolo, pequeña estructura esférica en el núcleo celular.

nucleotide *n.* nucleótido, unidad estructural de ácido nucleico.

nucleus *n.* (*pl.* **nuclei, nucleuses**) núcleo, parte esencial de una célula; ___ **pulpous** / ___ pulposo, masa gelatinosa contenida dentro de un disco intervertebral.

nude *a.* desnudo-a, *pop.* en cuero, en cuero vivo.

nudity *n.* desnudez.

nuisance *n.* molestia, incomodidad, estorbo; **What a** ___! / ¡Qué lata!

null *a.* nulo-a, sin valor, inútil; ___ **hypothesis** / hipótesis ___.

nulligravida *n.* nuligrávida, mujer que nunca ha concebido.

nulliparous *n.* nulípara, mujer que nunca ha dado a luz un feto con vida.

numb *a.* [*extremity*] entumecido-a, adormecido-a; aturdido-a; **My fingers are** ___ / mis dedos están ___-s; **I feel** ___ / Me siento entumecido-a; me siento aturdido-a.

number *n.* número, cifra.

numbness *n.* [*in a part*] entumecimiento, adormecimiento; [*confusion*] aturdimiento, entorpecimiento.

numerous *a.* numeroso-a.

numskull *a.* mentecato-a, tonto-a.

nun *n.* monja, hermana religiosa.

nurse *n.* enfermero-a; ___ **aid** / asistente de ___; ___ **anesthetist** / ___ anestesista; **chief** ___, **head** ___ / jefe-a de ___ -s; **community health** ___ / ___ de salud pública; ___ **practitioner** / practicante de ___; **surgical** ___ / ___ de cirugía; *v.* [*care*] cuidar a una persona enferma; [*breast-feeding*] amamantar, dar el pecho, dar de mamar.

nursery *n.* guardería; [*in a hospital*] sala de niños recién nacidos.

nursing *n.* 1. cuidado de los enfermos; 2. lactancia.

nut *n.* [*fruit*] nuez; [*mad*] loco-a, maniático-a; [*screw*] tuerca.

nutrient *n.* alimento, nutriente, sustancia nutritiva.

nutriment *n.* nutrimento, alimento, sustancia nutritiva.

nutrition *n.* nutrición, mantenimiento, alimentación.

nutritious *a.* nutritivo-a, alimenticio-a, que proporciona nutrición.

nutritive *a.* nutritivo-a, sustancioso-a, alimenticio-a.

nutty *a.* abundante en nueces, con sabor a nueces; *pop.* [*crazy*] loco-a, chiflado-a.

nympha *n.* ninfa, labio interior de la vulva.

nymphomania *n.* *psic.* ninfomanía, fuego uterino, deseo sexual mórbido en la mujer.

nymphomaniac *a.* ninfómana, mujer afectada por ninfomanía.

nystagmus *n.* nistagmo, espasmo involuntario del globo ocular.

O *abbr.* **oculus** / ojo; **oral** / oral; **orally** / oralmente, por la boca; **oxygen** / oxígeno.

oath *n.* juramento, promesa; **Hippocratic** ___ / ___ hipocrático; **under** ___ / bajo ___; *v.* **to take an** ___ / jurar, prestar ___.

oatmeal *n.* harina de avena.

obedience *n.* obediencia.

obedient *a.* obediente.

obese *a.* obeso-a, excesivamente grueso-a.

obesity *n.* obesidad, grasa excesiva en al cuerpo.

obey *v.* obedecer; **You must** ___ / usted debe ___, tú debes ___.

obfuscation *n.* ofuscación, confusión mental.

object *n.* objeto, cosa; *v.* objetar, oponerse, tener inconveniente.

objective *n.* objetivo, propósito; *a.* objetivo-a, rel. a la percepción de fenómenos y sucesos tal como se manifiestan en la vida real; ___ **sign** / señal ___; ___ **symptoms** / síntomas ___ -s; **-ly** *adv.* objetivamente.

obligate *v.* obligar, exigir.

obligation *n.* obligación, deber, compromiso.

obligatory *a.* obligatorio-a.

oblique *a.* oblicuo-a, diagonal.

obliterate *v.* obliterar, anular, destruir.

obliteration *n.* obliteración, destrucción; oclusión por degeneración o por cirugía.

obscure *a.* oscuro-a; oculto-a, escondido-a.

observation *n.* observación, examen, estudio.

observe *v.* observar, estudiar, examinar.

obsession *n.* obsesión, preocupación excesiva con una idea o emoción fija.

obsessional *a.* obsesivo-a, rel. a una obsesión o causante de ésta.

obsessive-compulsive *n.* estado neurótico obsesivo-compulsivo con repetición morbosa de acciones como desahogo de tensiones y ansiedades.

obsolete *a.* obsoleto-a, anticuado-a, en desuso, inactivo-a.

obstacle *n.* obstáculo, *pop.* traba.

obstetric *a.* obstétrico-a, rel. a la obstetricia.

obstetrician *n.* obstetra, partero-a, tocólogo-a, especialista en obstetricia.

obstetrics *n.* obstetricia, rama de la medicina que se refiere al cuidado de la mujer durante el embarazo y el parto.

obstinate *a.* obstinado-a, *pop.* cabeza dura, cabeciduro-a.

obstipation *n.* obstipación, estreñimiento rebelde.

obstruct *v.* obstruir, impedir.

obstructed *a.* obstruido-a, tupido-a.

obstruction *n.* obstrucción, bloqueo, obstáculo, impedimento; **intestinal** ___ / ___ intestinal.

obstructive lung disease, chronic *n.* obstrucción crónica del pulmón que impide la entrada libre del aire a causa de un estrechamiento físico o funcional del árbol bronquial.

obtain *v.* obtener, adquirir, conseguir.

obturation *n.* obturación, obstrucción o bloqueo de un pasaje.

obturator *a.* obturador-a, bloqueador-a, que obstruye una abertura.

obtuse *a.* obtuso-a. 1. que le falta agudeza mental; 2. romo-a, mellado-a.

obvious *a.* obvio-a, evidente.

occasion *n.* ocasión, circunstancia, casualidad; *v.* causar, ocasionar.

occasional *a.* infrecuente, casual, accidental; **-ly** *adv.* a veces; de vez en cuando, ocasionalmente.

occipital *a.* occipital, rel. a la parte posterior de la cabeza; ___ **bone** / hueso ___; ___ **condyle** / cóndilo ___; ___ **lobe** / lóbulo ___.

occipitofrontal *a.* occipitofrontal. rel. al occipucio y la frente.

occipitoparietal *a.* occipitoparietal, rel. a los huesos y lóbulos occipital y parietal.

occipitotemporal *a.* occipitotemporal, rel. a los huesos occipital y temporal.

occiput *n.* occipucio, porción postero-inferior del cráneo.

occlusion *n.* oclusión, cierre, obstrucción.

occult *a.* oculto-a, desconocido-a; escondido-a.

occult blood *n.* sangre oculta, presencia de sangre en cantidad tan ínfima que no puede verse a simple vista.

occupation *n.* ocupación, trabajo, profesión, oficio; ___ **neurosis** / neurosis del trabajo, de la profesión.

occupational *a.* ocupacional, rel. a una ocupación; ___ **therapist** / terapeuta ___; ___ **therapy** / terapia ___.

occupy *v.* ocupar, llenar.

occurrence *n.* ocurrencia, suceso, acontecimiento; **of frequent** ___ / que sucede con frecuencia.

octogenarian *n.* octogenario-a, persona de ochenta años de edad o más; *a.* octogenario-a.

ocular *a.* ocular, visual, rel. a los ojos o a la vista.

oculist *n.* oculista. V. **ophthalmologist**.

oculogyric *a.* oculógiro-a, rel. a la rotación del globo ocular.

oculomotor *a.* oculomotor, rel. al movimiento del globo ocular.

oculus *L.* oculus, ojo, órgano de la visión.

odd *a.* extraño-a, irregular, raro-a, inexacto-a; **an** ___ **case** / un caso ___; ___ **or even** / nones o pares; **thirty** ___ **pills** / treinta píldoras más o menos, treinta y tantas píldoras; **at** ___ **times** / en momentos imprevistos, a horas imprevistas.

odontalgia *n.* odontalgia, dolor de dientes; dolor de muelas.

odontectomy *n.* *cirg.* odontectomía, extracción de una pieza dental.

odontogenesis *n.* odontogénesis, proceso de desarrollo dentario.

odontoid *a.* odontoideo-a, semejante a un diente.

odontologist *n.* odontólogo-a, dentista o cirujano-a dental.

odontology *n.* odontología, estudio de los dientes y del tratamiento de las enfermedades dentales.

odor *n.* olor.

odorless *a.* sin olor, inodoro-a.

odorous *a.* oloroso-a, fragante.

odynophobia *n. psic.* odinofobia, temor excesivo al dolor.

Oedipus complex *n.* complejo de Edipo, amor intenso del hijo a la madre acompañado de celos y antipatía al padre.

of *prep.* de; [*possession*] ___ **the** / del, de la; [*telling time*] menos; **Call at a quarter** ___ **six** / Llame, llama a las seis ___ cuarto.

off *adv.* fuera de aquí, lejos; ___ **and on** / a veces, a intervalos; ___ **the record** / confidencial; *v.* [*work*] **to be** ___ / ausente, [*without work*] sin trabajo; **The operation is** ___ / Se ha suspendido la operación; **to put** ___ / aplazar, posponer, diferir; **to turn** ___ / cerrar, apagar; *int.* ¡fuera!, ¡salga!, ¡sal!

offence, offense *n.* ofensa, agravio, afrenta.

offend *v.* ofender, insultar, agraviar.

offensive *a.* ofensivo-a.

offer *n.* oferta, ofrecimiento.

office *n.* oficina; **doctor's** ___ / consulta, consultorio; [*business*] ___ **hours** / horas de ___; horas de consulta.

official *a.* oficial, autorizado-a.

offspring *n.* descendencia, sucesión, hijos.

often *adv.* con frecuencia, frecuentemente, a menudo; **How** ___? / ¿Cuántas veces?; **as** ___ **as needed** / tantas veces como sea necesario; **not** ___ / pocas veces; **too** ___ / demasiadas veces.

oil *n.* aceite; **castor** ___ / ___ de ricino; **cod liver** ___ / ___ de hígado de bacalao; **mineral** ___ / ___ mineral; **olive** ___ / ___ de oliva; **salad** ___ / ___ para ensalada; *v.* aceitar, lubricar, engrasar, untar con aceite.

oily *a.* grasoso-a, grasiento-a, oleaginoso-a, lubricante.

ointment *n.* ungüento, pomada, unto, untura; medicamento oleaginoso semisólido de uso externo.

old *a.* viejo-a, anciano-a; antiguo-a; **an** ___ **man** / un anciano, un hombre ___; **an** ___ **method** / un método antiguo; **How** ___ **are you?** / ¿Cuántos años tiene, tienes?; **I am fifty years** ___ / Tengo cincuenta años; ___ **wives' tale** / cuento de ___.

oleaginous *a.* oleaginoso-a, aceitoso-a, derivado del aceite o rel. al mismo.

oleomargarine *n.* oleomargarina, margarina.

olfactory *a.* olfatorio-a, rel. al sentido del olfato.

oligohemia, oligemia *n.* oligohemia. *V.* **hypovolemia.**

oligohydramnios *n.* oligohidramnios, bajo nivel de líquido amniótico al término de la gestación.

oligomenorrhea *n.* oligomenorrea, deficiencia en la menstruación.

oligospermia *n.* oligospermia, disminución del número de espermatozoos en el semen.

oliguria *n.* oliguria, disminución en la formación de orina.

olive *n.* oliva. 1. materia gris localizada detrás de la médula oblongata; 2. color aceitunado, verde oliva; 3. árbol del olivo; 4. aceituna.

omen *n.* agüero.

omental *a.* omental, rel. a un omento o formado por él.

omentectomy *n. cirg.* omentectomía, extirpación total o parcial de un omento.

omentitis *n.* omentitis, infl. del omento.

omentum *n.* omento, repliegue del peritoneo que conecta el estómago con ciertas vísceras abdominales.

ominous *a.* ominoso-a, nefasto-a.

omission *n.* omisión; exclusión.

omit *v.* omitir, suprimir, excluir.

omnivorous *a.* omnívoro-a, que come alimentos de origen vegetal y animal.

omphalectomy *n. cirg.* onfalectomía, extirpación del ombligo.

omphalic *n.* onfálico-a, rel. al ombligo.

omphalitis *n.* onfalitis, infl. del ombligo.

omphalocele *n.* onfalocele, hernia congénita del ombligo.

on *prep.* sobre, encima, en, hacia; [*before inf.*] después de; al; ___ **an average** / por término medio; ___ **the contrary** / al contrario; ___ **the left foot** / en el pie izquierdo; ___ **the right eye** / en el ojo derecho; ___ **the table** / sobre la mesa, encima de la mesa; *adv.* ___ **account of** / a causa de; ___ **all sides** / por todos lados; *v.* **to be** ___ **call** / estar de guardia; **caught** ___ / atrapado-a en; ___ **condition that you come back** / con tal de que vuelva; **later** ___ / más tarde; **off and** ___ / a intervalos, de vez en cuando; ___ **and** ___ / continuamente, sin cesar, sin parar; ___ **purpose** / a propósito; [*function*] funcionando; **The machine is on** / El aparato está funcionando; *a.* [*clothing*] puesto-a; **She has the robe on** / Ella tiene la bata ___; [*after a verb*] **Go** ___! / ¡Siga, sigue!; ¡Continúe, continúa!

onanism *n.* onanismo, coito interrumpido.

once *n.* una vez; *adv.* **all at** ___ / al mismo tiempo, de pronto; **at** ___ / **en seguida, ahora mismo;** ___ **in a while** / algunas veces, de vez en cuando.

oncogenesis *n.* oncogénesis, formación y desarrollo de un tumor.

oncogenic *a.* oncogénico-a, rel. a la oncogénesis.

oncologist *n.* oncólogo-a. especialista en oncología.

oncology *n.* oncología, rama de la medicina que estudia los neoplasmas.

oncolysis *n.* oncólisis, destrucción de las células de un tumor.

oncotic *a.* oncótico-a, rel. a una tumefacción o la causa de ésta.

oncotomy *n. cirg.* oncotomía, incisión en un tumor, absceso o quiste.

one *n.* [*number*] uno; *a.* un, uno-a, solo, único-a; **just** ___ / solamente uno; **only** ___ **form** / una sola forma; **from** ___ **day to another** / de un día a otro; **He is** ___ **good patient** / él es un buen paciente; *pron.* **the only** ___ / el único, la única; **the** ___ **I have** / el que tengo; **this** ___ / éste; ___ **and all** / todos; ___ **of them** / ___ de ellos.

one-eyed *n.* tuerto-a.

oneiric *a.* onírico-a, rel. a los sueños.

oneirism *n.* onirismo, estado de ensoñación; soñar despierto.

onerous *a.* oneroso-a, gravoso-a.

oniomania *n. psic.* oniomanía, psicosis de urgencia de gastar dinero.

onion *n.* cebolla.

onlay *n.* injerto, esp. en la reparación de defectos óseos.

only *a.* único-a, solo-a; *adv.* sólo, solamente.

onomatomania *n. psic.* onomatomanía, repetición obsesiva de palabras.

onychectomy *n. cirg.* oniquectomía, extirpación de una uña.

onychia *n.* oniquia, infl. de la matriz de una uña.

onychosis *n.* onicosis, enfermedad o deformidad de las uñas.

oocyte *n.* oocito, ovocito, el óvulo antes de la madurez.

oogenesis *n.* oogénesis, formación y desarrollo del óvulo.

oophorectomy *n. cirg.* ooforectomía, excisión parcial o total de un ovario.

oophoritis *n.* ooforitis, infl. de un ovario.

oosperm *n.* oospermo, óvulo fecundado.

ooze *v.* exudar, supurar.

oozing *n.* exudado; supuración.

opacification *n.* opacificación, proceso de opacar.

opacity *n.* opacidad, falta de transparencia.

opaque *a.* opaco-a, sin brillo, que no deja pasar la luz.

open *a.* abierto-a, descubierto-a, destapado-a, libre de paso; ___ **heart surgery** / operación a corazón ___ ; *v.* abrir, descubrir, destapar, abrir paso; cortar, rajar.

opening *n.* abertua, orificio de entrada o salida.

open reduction *n.* reducción abierta, [*in fractures*] técnica de reducir fracturas con exposición de la dislocación o del hueso.

operable *a.* operable, que puede tratarse con cirugía.

operate *v.* operar, intervenir, proceder.

operating room *n.* sala de operaciones, quirófano.

operation *n.* operación, intervención quirúrgica, procedimiento quirúrgico.

operculum *n.* opérculo. 1. cubierta o tapadera; 2. una de las partes del cerebro que cubre la ínsula.

operon *n.* operon, sistema de genes combinados en el cual el gene operador regula las demás genes estructurales.

ophthalmia *n.* oftalmía. 1. conjuntivitis severa; 2. infl. interna del ojo.

ophthalmic *a.* oftálmico-a, visual, rel. al ojo; ___ **nerve** / nervio ___ ; ___ **solutions** / soluciones ___ -s.

ophthalmitis *n.* oftalmitis, condición inflamatoria del ojo.

ophthalmologist *n.* oftalmólogo-a, médico oculista especializado en trastornos y enfermedades de la vista.

ophthalmology *n.* oftalmología, rama de la medicina que trata del estudio del ojo y trastornos de la vista.

ophthalmoneuritis *n.* oftalmoneuritis, infl. del nervio óptico.

ophthalmopathy *n.* oftalmopatía, enfermedad de los ojos.

ophthalmoplasty *n.* oftalmoplastia, cirugía plástica del ojo.

ophthalmoplegia *n.* oftalmoplegia, parálisis de un músculo ocular.

ophthalmoscope *n.* oftalmoscopio, instrumento usado para visualizar el interior del ojo.

ophthalmoscopy *n.* oftalmoscopía, examen del ojo con un oftalmoscopio.

opiate *n.* opiáceo, opiato, cualquier droga derivada del opio; ___ **abstinence syndrome** / síndrome provocado por la abstinencia de opio o sus derivados.

opinion *n.* opinión, juicio, parecer; *v.* **to have an** ___ / opinar, hacer juicio, dar el parecer; **to be of the same** ___ / estar de acuerdo, acordar.

opinionated *a.* obstinado-a, inflexible.

opioids *n. pl.* drogas que no son derivadas del opio pero pueden producir efectos similares a éste.

opisthotonos *n.* opistótonos, espasmo tetánico de los músculos de la espalda por el cual los talones se viran hacia atrás y el tronco se proyecta hacia adelante.

opium *n.* opio, *Papaver somniferum*, narcótico, analgésico, estimulante venenoso y alucinógeno cuya adicción produce deteriorización física y mental; *slang* goma.

opiumism, opiomania *n.* opiomanía. 1. adicción al uso de opio o sus derivados; 2. condición física deteriorada por el uso de opio.

opponent *n.* oponente, antagonista, contrario-a; *a.* opuesto-a, contrario-a.

opportune *a.* oportuno-a, conveniente.

opportunist *n.* oportunista.

opportunistic *a.* oportunista.

opportunistic infectious disease *n.* enfermedad oportunista infecciosa, infección parasítica oportunista, producida por un microorganismo gen. no dañino, que no causa una enfermedad severa o prolongada pero se convierte en patógeno cuando la inmunidad del organismo ha sido ya quebrantada.

opportunity *n.* oportunidad, ocasión.

oppose *v.* oponer, resistir; oponerse, resistirse.

opposite *a.* opuesto-a, adverso-a, contrario-a.

opposition *n.* oposición, objeción.

oppress *v.* oprimir, afligir, agobiar; apretar.

oppression *n.* opresión, pesadez; **an** ___ **in the chest** / una ___, una sofocación en el pecho.

oppressive *a.* opresivo-a, sofocante, molesto-a, gravoso-a.

opsoclonus *n.* opsoclono, movimiento irregular del ojo, esp. relacionado con algunos casos de trastorno cerebral.

opsonin *n.* opsonina, anticuerpo que al combinarse con un antígeno hace que éste sea más suceptible a los fagocitos.

optic, optical *a.* óptico-a, rel. a la visión; ___ **disk** / disco ___, punto ciego de la retina; ___ **illusion** / ilusión ___; ___ **nerve** / nervio ___.

optics *n.* óptica, ciencia que estudia la luz y la relación de ésta con la visión.

optimist *a.* optimista.

optimum *a.* óptimo-a, el mejor, la mejor; ___ **temperature** / temperatura ___.

option *n.* opción, alternativa.

optometer *n.* optómetro, instrumento usado para medir el poder de refracción del ojo.

optometrist *n.* optometrista, optómetra, profesional que practica la optometría.

optometry *n.* optometría, práctica de examinar los ojos para determinar la agudeza visual y para la prescripción de lentes correctivos y otros auxilios visuales.

or *conj.* o, u (used instead of *o* before words beginning in *o* or *ho*).

oral *a.* oral, bucal, rel. a la boca; verbal, hablado; ___ **contraceptive** / píldora contraceptiva; ___ **diagnosis** / diagnóstico bucal; ___ **hygiene** / higiene bucal.

orange *n.* naranja; ___ **grove** / naranjal; **orange-ade** / naranjada.

orbicular *a.* orbicular, circular; ___ **muscle** / músculo ___, rodea una pequeña abertura tal como la de la boca.

orbit *n.* órbita, cavidad ósea de la cara que contiene los ojos.

orbital *a.* orbital. rel. a la órbita; ___ **fractures** / fracturas ___ -es.

orchidectomy *n. cirg.* orquidectomía, orquectomía, extirpación de un testículo.

orchiditis, orchitis *n.* orquiditis, orquitis, infl. de los testículos.

orchidopexy, orchiopexy *n. cirg.* orquidopexia, orquipexia, procedimiento por el cual se baja y se fija al escroto un testículo que no ha descendido.

orchiotomy *n.* orquiotomía, incisión en un testículo.

order *n.* orden, reglamento, disposición; **in** ___ **that** / para que, a fin de que; **in** ___ **to** / para;

v. ordenar, disponer, mandar; [*arrange*] arreglar; **to be in good** ___ / estar en buen estado; **to get out of** ___ / descomponerse.

orderly *n.* asistente de enfermero-a.

ordinary *a.* ordinario-a, corriente, común.

organ *n.* órgano, parte del cuerpo que realiza una función específica; **end** ___ / ___ terminal; ___ **displacement** / desplazamiento de un ___; ___ **transplant** / transplante de un ___.

organelle *n.* organelo, organito, órgano diminuto de los organismos unicelulares.

organic *a.* orgánico-a. 1. rel. a un órgano u órganos; 2. rel. a organismos de origen vegetal o animal; ___ **disease** / enfermedad ___.

organism *n.* organismo, ser vivo.

organization *n.* organización; asociación.

organize *v.* organizar, disponer, arreglar.

organogenesis *n.* organogénesis, desarrollo y crecimiento de un órgano.

orgasm *n.* orgasmo, clímax sexual.

orient *n.* oriente, este.

oriental *a.* oriental.

orientation *n.* orientación, dirección.

orifice *n.* orificio, salida, boquete, abertura.

origin *n.* origen, principio.

original *n.* original, prototipo; *a.* original; primitivo-a.

originality *n.* originalidad.

originate *v.* originar, engendrar; provenir de.

originator *n.* originador, productor.

oropharynx *n.* orofaringe, parte central de la faringe.

orphan *n.* huérfano-a.

orphanage *n.* orfanato, hospicio, asilo de huérfanos.

orthochromatic *a.* ortocromático-a, de color normal o que acepta coloración sin dificultad.

orthodontia *n.* ortodoncia, rama de la odontología que trata las irregularidades dentales por medio de procedimientos correctivos.

orthopeda, orthopedics *n.* ortopedia, rama de la medicina que trata de la prevención y corrección de trastornos en los huesos, articulaciones, músculos, ligamentos y cartílagos.

orthopedic *a.* ortopédico-a, rel. a la ortopedia; ___ **shoes** / calzado ___; ___ **surgery** / cirugía ___.

orthopedist *n.* ortopédico-a, ortopedista, especialista en ortopedia.

orthopnea *n.* ortópnea, dificultad para respirar excepto en posición erecta.

orthoscopic *a.* ortoscópico, rel. a los instrumentos que se usan para corregir distorsiones ópticas.

orthosis *n.* ortosis, corrección de una deformidad o impedimento.

orthotopic *a.* ortotópico-a, que ocurre en una posición normal o correcta.

os *L.* (*pl.* **ossa**) os, hueso.

oscillate *v.* oscilar; fluctuar.

oscillation *n.* oscilación, movimiento de vaivén, tal como el de un péndulo.

osmolar *a.* osmolar, de naturaleza o propiedad osmótica.

osmology *n.* osmología, estudio de los olores.

osmoreceptor *n.* osmorreceptor. 1. grupo de células cerebrales que reciben estímulos olfatorios; 2. grupo de células en el hipotálamo que responden a cambios en la presión osmótica de la sangre.

osmosis *n.* osmosis, difusión de un solvente a través de una membrana semipermeable interpuesta entre soluciones de concentración diferente.

osmotic *a.* osmótico-a, rel. a la osmosis.

osseous *a.* óseo-a, rel. a los huesos; ___ **tissue** / tejido ___.

ossicle *n.* huesillo, osículo.

ossific *a.* osífico-a, rel. a la formación del tejido óseo.

ossification *n.* osificación, proceso de desarrollo óseo.

ossification, ostosis *n.* osificación. 1. conversión de una sustancia en hueso; 2. desarrollo del hueso.

ossify *v.* osificar, transformarse en hueso.

osteal *a.* óseo-a, rel. a los huesos.

osteitis *n.* osteítis, ostitis, infl. de un hueso; ___ **fibrosa cystica** / ___ fibrosa cística, con degeneración fibrosa y manifestación de quistes y nódulos en el hueso.

ostensive *a.* ostensivo-a, evidente, aparente.

osteoarthritis *n.* osteoartritis, hipertrofia degenerativa del hueso y de las articulaciones esp. en la vejez.

osteoarthropathy *n.* osteoartropatía, enfermedad gen. dolorosa que afecta las articulaciones y los huesos.

osteoblast *n.* osteoblasto, célula desarrollada aisladamente en una lacuna de la sustancia ósea.

osteocarcinoma *n.* osteocarcinoma, cáncer del hueso.

osteocartillaginous *a.* osteocartilaginoso-a, rel. a la formación de huesos y cartílagos.

osteochondral *n.* osteocondral, rel. a o compuesto de hueso y cartílago.

osteochondritis *n.* osteocondritis, infl. del hueso y del cartílago.

osteoclast *n.* osteoclasto, célula gigante multinucleada que participa en la formación de tejido óseo y reemplaza al cartílago durante la osificación.

osteocyte *n.* osteocito, célula ósea desarrollada.

osteodystrophy *n.* osteodistrofia, hipertrofia múltiple degenerativa con formación defectiva del hueso.

osteogenesis *n.* osteogénesis. *V.* **ossification.**

osteoid *a.* osteoide, rel. o semejante a un hueso.

osteology *n.* osteología, rama de la medicina que estudia la estructura y funcionamiento de los huesos.

osteoma *n.* osteoma, tumor formado de tejido óseo.

osteomalacia *n.* osteomalacia, reblandecimiento de los huesos debido a la pérdida de calcio en la matriz del hueso.

osteomyelitis *n.* osteomielitis, infección del hueso y de la médula ósea.

osteonecrosis *n.* osteonecrosis, destrucción y muerte del tejido óseo.

osteopath *n.* osteópata, especialista en osteopatía.

osteopathy *n.* osteopatía. 1. sistema terapéutico médico con énfasis en la relación entre los órganos y el sistema muscular esquelético que hace uso de la manipulación como medio de corrección; 2. cualquier enfermedad de los huesos.

osteopenia *n.* osteopenia, disminución de la calcificación ósea.

osteophyte *n.* osteófito, prominencia ósea.

osteoporosis *n.* osteoporosis, pérdida en la densidad del hueso.

osteotomy *n. cirg.* osteotomía, cortar o serruchar un hueso.

ostial *a.* ostial, rel. o concerniente a un orificio o abertura.

ostium *L.* (*pl.* **ostia**) ostium, pequeña abertura.

ostomy *n. cirg.* ostomía, creación de una abertura entre un órgano y la piel como medio de salida exterior, tal como se efectúa en colostomías e ileostomías.

otalgia, otodynia, otoneuralgia *n.* otalgia, otodinia, otoneuralgia, dolor de oídos.

otectomy *n. cirg.* otectomía, extirpación del contenido estructural del oído medio.

other *a.* otro-a, diferente, nuevo-a; **every ___ day** / un día sí y otro no; *pron.* **the ___ one** / el otro, la otra; **the ___ ones** / los otros, las otras.

otherwise *adv.* de otra manera, de otro modo, por otra parte.

otic *a.* ótico-a, rel. al oído.

oticodinia *n.* oticodinia, vértigo causado por una enfermedad del oído.

otitis *n.* otitis, infl. del oído externo, medio o interno.

otolaryngologist *n.* otolaringólogo-a, especialista en otolaringología.

otolaryngology *n.* otolaringología, estudio de la garganta, nariz y oídos.

otologist *n.* otólogo-a, especialista en enfermedades del oído.

otology *n.* otología, rama de la medicina que estudia el oído, su función y las enfermedades que lo afectan.

otoneurology *n.* otoneurología, estudio del oído interno en su relación con el sistema nervioso.

otoplasty *n.* otoplastia, cirugía plástica del oído.

otorrhagia *n.* otorragia, sangramiento por el oído.

otosclerosis *n.* otosclerosis, sordera progresiva debida a la formación de tejido esponjoso en el laberinto del oído.

otoscope *n.* otoscopio, instrumento para examinar el oído.

otoscopy *n.* otoscopia, uso del otoscopio en un examen del oído.

ototomy *n. cir.* ototomía, incisión en el oído.

ototoxic *a.* ototóxico-a, que tiene efecto tóxico en el octavo par craneal o en los órganos de la audición.

ouch *int.* ¡ay!

ought *v.* deber, deber de + *inf.;* ser necesario, tener la obligación de + *inf.*

ounce *n.* onza.

oust *v.* expulsar, sacar, echar fuera.

out *adv.* afuera, fuera; [*light, appliance*] apagado-a [*unconscious*] inconsciente, sin conocimiento; ___ **of** / de; **three** ___ **of ten cases** / tres de diez casos; ___ **of work** / sin trabajo, sin empleo, desempleado-a; *v.* **to be** ___ / estar ausente; **to go** ___ / salir; **Get** ___! / ¡Salga!, ¡sal!

outbreak *n.* erupción; [*of an epidemic*] brote epidémico.

outbreathe *v.* dejar sin aliento; *pop.* dejar sin resuello.

outburst *n.* erupción; estallido; arranque; manifestación abrupta, brote.

outcome *n.* resultado, consecuencia; [*good*] éxito.

outdated *a.* anticuado-a.

outdo *vi.* superar, exceder.

outdoors *a.* al aire libre; externo-a; *adv.* afuera de la casa.

outer *a.* externo-a; exterior.

outfit *n.* traje, equipo, habilitación.

outflow *n.* derrame, salida, flujo.

outgoing *n.* salida, ida, partida; *a.* saliente, cesante; expansivo-a.

outgrow *vi.* sobrepasar, crecer más.

outgrowth *n.* excrecencia, bulto.

outlet *n.* orificio de salida; [*electric*] tomacorriente.

outlive *v.* sobrevivir, vivir más que; durar más.

outlook *n.* punto de vista, expectativa, opinión.

outnumber *v.* exceder en número.

outpass *v.* pasar más allá de; avanzar.

outpatient *n.* paciente externo, paciente de consulta externa, paciente no hospitalizado.

outpour *n.* derramamiento, chorro; *v.* chorrear, derramar, verter.

output *n.* rendimiento; producción; salida; ___ **failure** / fallo en el ___.

outrageous *a.* [*shocking*] atroz; increíble.

outright *a.* sincero-a, franco-a, cabal; *adv.* francamente, sinceramente.

outroot *v.* sacar de raíz, desarraigar, extirpar.

outside *n.* exterior, apariencia; *prep.* fuera de, más allá de.

outspoken *a.* franco-a, que habla sin rodeos.

outstretch *v.* extender, alargar, expandir.

outweigh *v.* pesar más que; exceder.

oval *a.* oval; rel. al óvulo.

oval window *n.* ventana oval; abertura del oído medio.

ovarian *a.* ovárico-a, rel. a los ovarios.

ovariectomy *n. cirg.* ovariectomía. *V.* **oophorectomy.**

ovary *n.* ovario, órgano reproductor femenino que produce el óvulo.

over *a.* acabado-a, terminado-a; *prep.* sobre, encima, por; a través de; *adv.* por encima, de un lado a otro; al otro lado; al revés; ___ **again** / otra vez; ___ **and** ___ **again** / muchas veces; *v.* [*years*] **to be** ___ / tener más de; **It is** ___ / ya se pasó, ya se acabó; **Turn** ___ / Vuélvase, vuélvete.

overact *v.* exagerar.

overanxious *a.* demasiado inquieto-a, excitado-a, muy ansioso-a.

overbearing *a.* insoportable.

overbite *n.* sobremordida.

overboil *v.* hervir demasiado, hervir más de lo necesario.

overburden *v.* agobiar, sobrecargar.

overcareful *a.* demasiado cuidadoso-a, *pop.* puntilloso-a.

overcharge *n.* precio excesivo, recargo de precio; *v.* sobrecargar, cobrar demasiado.

overclosure *n.* sobrecierre, cierre de la mandíbula antes de que los dientes superiores e inferiores se junten.

overcoat *n.* abrigo, sobretodo.

overcome *vi.* vencer, rendir; sobreponerse; **You must** ___ **this** / Debe sobreponerse, debes sobreponerte a esto; **You must** ___ **this sickness** / Debe, debes ___ a esta enfermedad.

overcompensation *n.* sobrecompensación, *psic.* intento exagerado de ocultar sentimientos de inferioridad o de culpa.

overcorrection *n.* sobrecorrección, acción de corregir en exceso un defecto visual por medio de lentes.

overdose *n.* dosis excesiva; dosis tóxica; sobredosis.

overdue *a.* retrasado-a, tardío-a.

overeat *vi.* comer con exceso; hartarse.

overexposure *n.* superexposición; exposición excesiva.

overextension *n.* sobreextensión.

overfeed *vi.* sobrealimentar, alimentar en exceso.

overflow *n.* rebosamiento; derramamiento; *pop.* desparramo.

overgrown *a.* demasiado crecido-a, muy grande o agrandado-a.

overgrowth *n.* proliferación excesiva.

overhear *vi.* oír por casualidad; alcanzar a oír.

overjoyed *a.* rebosante de alegría.

overnight *n.* velada, la noche completa; *adv.* durante la noche; la noche pasada.

overpowering *a.* abrumador-a; irresistible.

overproduction *n.* superproducción.

overreact *v.* reaccionar en exceso.

overresponse *n.* sobrerespuesta, reacción excesiva a un estímulo.

oversight *n.* descuido, equivocación, inadvertencia.

overtime *n.* tiempo suplementario; horas extras de trabajo.

overweigh *v.* pesar más que; sobrecargar.

overweight *n.* peso excesivo, sobrepeso.

overwhelm *v.* abrumar; colmar.

overwork *n.* trabajo excesivo, trabajo en exceso.

ovicular, ovoid *a.* ovicular, en forma de huevo.

oviduct *n.* oviducto, conducto uterino; trompas de Falopio.

ovotestis *n.* ovotestis, glándula hermafrodita que contiene tejido ovárico y testicular.

ovulation *n.* ovulación, liberación periódica del óvulo o gamete por el ovario.

ovulatory *a.* ovulatorio-a, rel. al proceso de ovulación.

ovum *n.* (*pl.* **ova**) óvulo, gamete fecundado.

oxalic acid *n.* ácido oxálico.

oxidant *a.* oxidante, que causa oxidación o rel. a ésta.

oxidation *n.* oxidación, combinación de una sus-tancia con oxígeno.

oxidize *v.* oxidar, combinar con oxígeno.

oximeter *n.* oxímetro, instrumento para medir la cantidad de oxígeno en la sangre.

oxygen *n.* oxígeno, elemento o gas incoloro e inodoro no metálico que circula libremente en la atmósfera; ___ **deficiency** / falta de ___; ___ **distribution** / distribución de ___; ___ **treatment** / tratamiento de ___.

oxygenation *n.* oxigenación, saturación de oxígeno.

oxygenator *n.* oxigenador, instrumento para oxigenar la sangre gen. usado durante cirugía.

oxygen tent *n.* cámara de oxígeno, tienda de oxígeno.

oxygen therapy *n.* terapia de oxígeno.

oxytocin *n.* oxitocina, ocitocina, hormona pituitaria que estimula las contracciones del útero.

oyster *n.* ostra, ostión.

P *abbr.* part / parte; **phosphorous** / fósforo; **plasma** / plasma; **population** / población; **positive** / positivo; **posterior** / posterior; **postpartum** / postpartum; **pressure** / presión; **psychiatry** / psiquiatría; **pulse** / pulso.

pabulum *L.* pabulum, alimento o sustancia alimenticia.

pace *n.* marcha, paso, el andar; *v.* andar, marchar.

pacemaker, pacer *n.* marcapasos, estabilizador del ritmo cardíaco; **internal __ / __** interno; **temporary __ / __** temporal.

pachyderma *n.* paquidermia. *V.* **elephantiasis.**

pachygyria *n.* paquigiria, circunvoluciones gruesas en la corteza cerebral.

pacifier *n.* chupete, tetera, teto.

pacify *v.* apaciguar, tranquilizar.

pack *n.* envoltura. 1. cubierta fría o caliente en la cual se envuelve el cuerpo; 2. compresa; *v.* [*to wrap*] envolver.

packing *n.* tapón, taponamiento. 1. acto de llenar una cavidad con gasa o algodón; 2. envoltura.

pad *n.* cojín, almohadilla; *v.* [*to fill*] rellenar.

padding *n.* relleno.

pain *n.* [*ache*] dolor; [*suffering*] sufrimiento, pena; [*colicky*] cólico; **burning __ / __** quemante, con ardor; **constant __ / __** constante, que no se quita; **dull __ / __** sordo; **flank __ / __** en el costado; **gnawing __ /** punzada; **localized __ / __** localizado; **mild __ / __** leve, dolorcito; **pressure-like __ / __** opresivo; **radicular __ /** radicular; **referred __ / __** referido, que se percibe en un lugar distinto al que se origina; **sharp __ / __** agudo; **severe __ / __** fuerte, severo; **subjective __ / __** subjetivo, sin causa física aparente; **a __ that comes and goes** / un __ que viene y va; **a __ that irradiates** / un __ que se

Pain	Dolor
burning	quemante
colicky	cólico
constant	constante
deep	profundo
dull	sordo
localized	localizado
mild	leve
oppresive	opresivo
piercing	penetrante
strong	fuerte
subjective	subjetivo
pressing	lancinante
referred	referido

corre; **a __ like a knife** / __ como un cuchillo, lancinante; **Where do you have the __?** / ¿Dónde tiene, tienes el __?; *v.* **to be in __** / tener __; [*to suffer*] sufrir, apenar, afligir; estar apenado-a; estar afligido-a. *V.* **Appendix B.**

painful *a.* doloroso-a, penoso-a, aflictivo-a.

painkiller *n.* calmante, sedante, remedio, pastilla para el dolor.

painless *a.* sin dolor; [*easy*] fácil.

paint *n.* pincelación, aplicación a la piel de una solución medicinal; *v.* pintar, aplicar una solución.

pair *n.* par, pareja.

pajama *n.* piyama, pijama.

palatable *a.* sabroso-a, apetitoso-a; gustoso-a.

palate *n.* paladar; velo del paladar; *pop.* cielo de la boca; **bony __ / __** óseo; **hard __ / __** duro; **soft __ / __** blando.

palatine *a.* palatino, rel. al paladar.

pale *a.* pálido-a, descolorido-a.

paleface *n.* rostro pálido, carapálida.

palindromic *a.* palindrómico-a, recurrente.

palliative *a.* paliativo-a, lenitivo-a, que alivia.

pallid *a.* pálido-a, descolorido-a.

pallor *n.* palidez.

palm *n.* palma, parte inferior de la mano; **__ oil** / aceite de __.

palmar *a.* palmar, rel. a la palma de la mano.

palpable *a.* palpable.

palpate *v.* palpar, acto de palpación.

palpation *n.* palpación, acto de tocar y examinar con las manos un área del cuerpo.

palpitate *v.* palpitar, latir.

palpitation *n.* palpitación, latido; pulsación; aleteo rápido.

palsy *n.* perlesía, parálisis, pédida temporal o permanente de la sensación, de la función o control de movimiento de una parte del cuerpo; **cerebral __ / __** cerebral, parálisis parcial y falta de coordinación muscular debida a una lesión cerebral congénita.

paludism *n.* paludismo, enfermedad infecciosa febril gen. crónica, transmitida por la picadura de un mosquito Anófeles infectado por un protozooario *Plasmodium.*

pamper *v.* mimar; malcriar.

pampered *a. pp.* de **to pamper,** mimado-a, consentido-a.

pamphlet *n.* folleto.

pampiniform *a.* pampiniforme, semejante a la estructura de un zarcillo de la vid.

panacea *n.* panacea, remedio para todas las enfermedades.

panarteritis *n.* panarteritis, infl. de las capas de una arteria.

panarthritis *n.* panartritis. 1. infl. de varias articulaciones del cuerpo; 2. infl. de los tejidos de una articulación.

pancreas *n.* páncreas, glándula del sistema digestivo que secreta externamente el jugo pancreático e interiormente la insulina y el glucagón.

pancreatalgia *n.* pancreatalgia, dolor en el páncreas.

pancreatectomy *n. cirg.* pancreatectomía, excisión parcial o total del páncreas.

pancreatic *a.* pancreático-a, rel. al páncreas; ___ cyst / quiste ___; ___ duct / conducto ___; ___ juice / jugo ___; ___ neoplasms / neoplasmas ___-s.

pancreaticoenterostomy *n. cirg.* pancreaticoenterostomía, anastomosis entre el conducto pancreático y el intestino.

pancreatin *n.* pancreatina, enzima digestiva del páncreas.

pancreatitis *n.* pancreatitis, infl. del páncreas; acute ___ / ___ aguda; hemorrhagic, acute ___ / ___ hemorrágica aguda.

pancytopenia *n.* pancitopenia, disminución anormal del número de células sanguíneas.

pandemic *a.* pandémico-a, de contagiosidad epidémica en un área geográfica extensa.

panendoscope *n.* panendoscopio, instrumento óptico usado para examinar la vejiga.

pang *n.* dolor agudo penetrante.

panglossia *n.* panglosia, verborrea.

panhidrosis *n.* panhidrosis, transpiración generalizada.

panhypopituitarism *n.* panhipopituitarismo, deficiencia de la pituitaria anterior.

panhysterectomy *n. cirg.* panhisterectomía, excisión total del útero.

panic *n.* pánico, temor excesivo; *u.* tener un miedo excesivo; sobrecogerse de pánico.

panicked *a. pp.* de to panic, sobrecogido-a de pánico; *pop.* muerto-a de miedo.

panniculitis *n.* paniculitis, infl. del panículo grasoso.

panniculus *n.* panículo, capa de tejido adiposo; ___ adiposus / ___ adiposo; ___ carnosus / ___ carnoso.

pannus *L.* pannus, paño, membrana de tejido granulado que cubre una superficie normal.

pansinusitis *n.* pansinusitis, infl. de los senos paranasales de un lado o de ambos.

pant *u.* jadear, resollar.

panting *n.* jadeo, respiración rápida.

pants *n. pl.* pantalones, calzones.

Papanicolaou test, Pap smear *n.* prueba de Papanicolaou (frotis, unto), recolección de mucosa de la vagina y del cuello uterino para detectar un cáncer incipiente.

papaya *n.* papaya, *Cuba* frutabomba.

paper *n.* papel; toilet ___ / ___ higiénico.

papilla *n.* (*pl.* papillae) papila, protuberancia esp. en la lengua.

papillary *a.* papilar, rel. a una papila.

papilledema *n.* papiledema, edema del disco óptico.

papilliforme *a.* papiliforme, similar a una papila.

papillitis *n.* papilitis, infl. del disco óptico.

papilloma *n.* papiloma, tumor epitelial benigno.

papillomatosis *n.* papilomatosis, presencia de múltiples papilomas.

papovavirus *n.* papovavirus, miembro de un grupo de virus de gran importancia en el estudio del cáncer.

papular *a.* papular, rel. a una pápula.

papule *n.* pápula, protuberancia en la piel compuesta de materia sólida.

papulosquamous *a.* papuloescamoso-a, rel. a pápulas y escamas; ___ skin diseases / enfermedades cutáneas ___s.

paracentesis *n.* paracéntesis, punción para obtener o eliminar líquido de una cavidad.

paraffin *n.* parafina.

parainfluenza viruses *n. pl.* virus de parainfluenza, virus asociados con infecciones respiratorias, esp. en los niños.

parallax *n.* paralaje, posición de desplazamiento aparente de un objeto de acuerdo con la posición del observador.

paralysis *n.* parálisis, pérdida parcial o total de movimiento o de función de una parte del cuerpo.

paralytic *a.* paralítico-a, inválido-a; impedido-a, rel. a o que sufre de parálisis; ___ ileus / parálisis del intestino.

paralyze *u.* paralizar, inmovilizar.

paralyzer *a.* paralizador, que causa parálisis.

paramagnetic *a.* paramagnético-a, rel. a una sustancia susceptible al magnetismo.

paramedic *n.* paramédico-a, profesional con entrenamiento para ofrecer asistencia médica esp. de emergencia.

parametrium *n.* parametrio, tejido celular suelto alrededor del útero.

paranasal *a.* paranasal, adyacente a la cavidad nasal.

paranasal sinuses *n. pl.* senos paranasales, cualquiera de las cavidades aéreas en los huesos adyacentes a la cavidad nasal.

paranoia *n. psic.* paranoia, trastorno mental caracterizado por delirio de persecución o de grandeza.

paranoid *a.* paranoico-a, persona afectada por paranoia.

parapancreatic *a.* parapancreático-a, adyacente al páncreas.

paraparesis *n.* paraparesis, parálisis parcial esp. de las extremidades inferiores.

paraphasia *n.* parafasia, tipo de afasia que se caracteriza por el uso incoherente de palabras.

paraphimosis *n.* parafimosis. 1. constricción del prepucio detrás del glande del pene; 2. retracción del párpado por detrás del globo ocular.

paraplegia *n.* paraplejía, parálisis de la parte inferior del tronco y de las piernas.

paraplegic *a.* parapléjico-a, rel. a, o afectado por paraplejía.

parapsychology *n.* parapsicología, estudio de fenómenos psíquicos tales como la telepatía y la percepción extrasensorial.

pararectal *a.* pararrectal, adyacente al recto.

parasite *n.* parásito, organismo que vive a expensas de otro.

parasitic *a.* parasítico-a, parasitario-a.

parasitism *n.* parasitismo, infección de parásitos.

parasitology *n.* parasitología, estudio de los parásitos.

parasternal *a.* parasterno-a, adyacente al esternón.

parasympathetic *a.* parasimpático, rel. a una de las dos ramas del sistema nervioso autónomo; ___ **nervous system** / sistema nervioso autónomo.

parasympatholytic *a.* parasimpatolítico, que destruye o bloquea las fibras nerviosas del sistema nervioso parasimpático.

parasystole *n.* parasístole, irregularidad en el ritmo cardíaco.

parathormone *n.* hormona paratiroidea, hormona reguladora del calcio.

parathyroid *n.* paratiroides, grupo de glándulas endocrinas pequeñas situadas junto a la tiroides; *a.* paratiroideo-a, localizado-a cerca de la tiroides; ___ **hormone** / hormona ___, reguladora de calcio.

parathyroidectomy *n. cirg.* paratiroidectomía, extirpación de una o más de las glándulas paratiroideas.

paratyphoid *n.* paratífica, fiebre similar a la tifoidea.

paravertebral *a.* paravertebral, situado-a al lado de la columna vertebral.

parched *a.* reseco-a.

paregoric *n.* paregórico, narcótico, calmante derivado del opio.

parenchyma *n.* parénquima, partes funcionales de un órgano.

parent *n.* padre o madre; *pl.* ___-s / padres.

parenteral *a.* parenteral, rel. a la introducción de medicamentos o sustancias en el organismo por otra vía que no sea la del canal alimenticio; ___ **hyperalimentation** / sobrealimentación intravenosa.

parenthood *n.* paternidad o maternidad.

paresis *n.* paresia, parálisis parcial o leve.

paresthesia *n.* parestesia, sensación de hormigueo o de calambre que se asocia a una lesión de un nervio periférico.

paretic *a.* parético-a, rel. o afectado por paresis.

parietal *a.* parietal, rel. al hueso parietal; rel. a la pared de una cavidad.

parietal bone *n.* hueso parietal, uno de los dos huesos situados en la parte superior y lateral del cráneo.

Parkinson's disease *n.* enfermedad de Parkinson, atrofia o degeneración de los nervios cerebrales que se manifiesta con temblores, debilidad muscular progresiva, cambios en el habla, la manera de andar y la postura.

parodynia *n.* parodinia, parto difícil.

paronychia *n.* paroniquia, infl. del área adyacente a la uña.

parotid *n.* parótida, glándula secretora de saliva localizada cerca del oído.

parotiditis *n.* parotiditis, parotitis. *V.* **mumps.**

paroxysm *n.* paroxismo, ataque. 1. espasmo o convulsión; 2. síntomas que se repiten y se intensifican.

pars *L.* pars, parte, porción.

parsley *n.* perejil.

part *n.* parte, porción; [*component of an instrument*] pieza; **-ly** *adv.* parcialmente, en parte.

parthenogenesis *n.* partenogénesis, reproducción en la cual el óvulo se desarrolla sin ser fecundado por un espermatozoo; **artificial** ___ / ___ artificial.

partial *a.* parcial; **-ly** *adv.* parcialmente.

participate *v.* participar, tomar parte.

particle *n.* partícula, porción ínfima de una materia.

particular *a.* particular; **-ly** *adv.* particularmente.

parturient *a.* parturienta, mujer que acaba de dar a luz o está en el acto de dar a luz.

parturifacient *n.* parturifaciente, droga que induce el parto.

parturition *n.* parto, alumbramiento.

parumbilical *a.* paraumbilical, adyacente al ombligo.

parvovirus *n.* parvovirus, grupo de virus patógenos que originan enfermedades en animales aunque no en personas.

pass *v.* pasar, aprobar; **to ___ away** / morir, fallecer; **to ___ on** / contagiar, pegar; **to ___ out** / desmayarse; **to ___ over** / pasar por, atravesar.

passage *n.* pasaje. 1. conducto o meato; 2. evacuación del intestino.

passion *n.* pasión, emoción intensa.

passionate *a.* apasionado-a.

passive *a.* pasivo-a; sumiso-a; inactivo-a, que no es espontáneo o activo; ___ **exercise** / ejercicio ___ .

passivity *n.* pasividad, estado anormal de dependencia de otros.

past *n.* pasado; *a.* pasado-a.

pasta *n.* pasta, preparación de sustancias medicinales gen. para aplicar a la epidermis.

pasteurization *n.* pasteurización, proceso de destrucción de microorganismos nocivos por medio de la aplicación de calor regulado.

patch *n.* placa, mancha. 1. pequeña porción de tejido que se caracteriza por pigmentación diferente a la del área que lo rodea; 2. parche, adhesivo aplicado para proteger heridas; ___ **test** / prueba alérgica.

patella *L.* patella, rótula.

patellectomy *n.* patelectomía, excisión de la patella.

patellofemoral *a.* patelofemoral, rel. a la rótula y el fémur.

patency *n.* permeabilidad. *V.* **permeability.**

patent *n.* patente, producto de marca autorizada o derecho exclusivo; ___ **medicine** / medicina de ___, ___ médico; *a.* patente; accesible;

abierto-a.

paternal *a.* paterno, rel. al padre.

paternity *n.* paternidad.

paternity test *n.* prueba de la paternidad, comparación del tipo sanguíneo de un niño o niña con el de un hombre para comprobar si éste puede ser el padre.

path *n.* vía, curso.

pathetic *a.* patético-a.

pathogen *n.* patógeno, agente capaz de producir una enfermedad.

pathogenesis *n.* patogénesis, origen y desarrollo de una enfermedad.

pathogenic *a.* patógeno-a, que causa una enfermedad.

pathognomonic *a.* patognomónico-a, rel. a un signo o síntoma característico de una enfermedad.

pathologic, pathological *a.* patológico-a, rel. a o producido por enfermedades.

pathology *n.* patología, ciencia que estudia la naturaleza y causa de las enfermedades.

pathophysiology *n.* patofisiología, estudio de los efectos de una enfermedad en los procesos fisiológicos.

pathway *n.* curso, comunicación; senda.

patience *n.* paciencia.

patient *n.* paciente, enfermo-a, ___'s care / cuidado del ___; ___ **discharge** / alta, egreso del ___; **private** ___ / ___ privado-a; **self-paying** ___ / ___ solvente; **-ly** *adv.* con paciencia, pacientemente.

patrilineal *a.* de descendencia paterna; rel. a rasgos heredados del padre.

patronize *v.* tratar con condescendencia.

pattern *n.* patrón, modelo, tipo.

patulous *a.* abierto-a, distendido-a.

pause *n.* pausa, interrupción; paro; **compensatory** ___ / ___ compensatoria; *v.* **to give** ___ / dar que pensar.

pay *vi.* pagar; **to** ___ **attention** / prestar atención; **to** ___ **in cash** / ___ al contado.

payment *n.* pago.

pea *n.* chícharo, guisante.

peace *n.* paz; ___ **of mind** / tranquilidad de espíritu; *v.* **to be at** ___ / estar en paz, tranquilizarse; **to keep, to hold one's** ___ / quedarse tranquilo-a.

peaceful *a.* pacífico-a; tranquilo-a, calmado-a.

peach *n.* melocotón, *H.A.* durazno.

peak *n.* [*sickness*] crisis, [*diagram*] cresta; cima, punta.

peanut *n.* maní, *Mex.* cacahuete; ___ **butter** / mantequilla de ___.

pear *n.* pera.

peau d'orange *Fr.* piel de naranja, condición cutánea que asemeja la cáscara de naranja y que es señal importante en el cáncer de la mama.

pectin *n.* pectina, carbohidrato que se obtiene de la cáscara de frutas cítricas y de manzana.

pectoral *a.* pectoral, rel. al pecho.

pectus *L.* pecho, tórax.

peculiar *a.* peculiar.

pedal *a.* pedal; rel. al pie.

pederasty *n.* pederastia, relación homosexual anal esp. entre un hombre adulto y un muchacho.

pediatric *a.* pediátrico-a, rel. a la pediatría.

pediatrician *n.* pediatra, médico-a especialista en enfermedades de la infancia.

pediatrics *n.* pediatría, rama de la medicina relacionada con el cuidado y desarrollo de los niños y el tratamiento de las enfermedades que los afectan.

pedicle *n.* pedículo, porción estrecha que conecta un tumor o colgajo con su base.

pediculosis *n.* pediculosis, infestación de piojos.

pedodontist *n.* dentista infantil.

pedophilia *n. psic.* pedofilia, atracción mórbida sexual de un adulto hacia los niños.

peduncle *n.* pedúnculo, conexión en forma de tallo.

pedunculated *a.* pediculado-a, pedunculado-a, rel. a o provisto de pedúnculo.

pedunculus *L.* pedúnculo.

peel *n.* [*fruits*] cáscara, hollejo, corteza; *v.* pelar; [*to shed skin*] despellejarse, pelarse.

peeling *n.* peladura, **chemical** ___ / ___ química. *V.* **exfoliation.**

pellagra *n.* pelagra, enfermedad causada por deficiencia de niacina y caracterizada por dermatitis, trastornos gastrointestinales y finalmente mentales.

pelvic *a.* pélvico-a, pelviano-a, rel. a la pelvis.

pelvic inflammatory disease *n.* enfermedad inflamatoria de la pelvis.

pelvis *n.* pelvis. 1. cavidad en la parte inferior del tórax formada por los huesos de la cadera, el sacro y el cóccix; 2. cavidad en forma de vasija o copa.

pemphigoid *a.* penfigoideo, semejante al pénfigo con diferencias clínicas.

pemphigus *L.* pénfigo, término usado para definir una variedad de dermatosis, cuya característica común consiste en la manifestación de ampollas que se infectan y revientan.

pendent, pending *a.* [*hanging*] pendiente, colgante, suspenso-a, dependiente; [*waiting*] pendiente.

pendulous *a.* pendular, que oscila o cuelga.

peneal, penial *a.* peneano-a, rel. al pene.

penetrate *v.* penetrar, pasar, atravesar.

penetrating *a.* [*as a pain*] penetrante, agudo-a.

penetration *n.* penetración. 1. acción de penetrar; 2. paso de radiación a través de una sustancia.

penicillin *n.* penicilina, antibiótico que se obtiene directa o indirectamente de un grupo de cultivos del hongo de la especie *Penicillium*.

penile *a. V.* **peneal.**

penis *n.* pene, parte exterior del aparato reproductor masculino que contiene la uretra y a través de la cual pasan el semen y la orina.

people *n.* [*of a nation*] pueblo; [*population*] población, personas, habitantes; gente.

pepper *n.* [*spice*] pimienta; pimiento.

peppermint *n.* hierbabuena, yerbabuena.

pepsin *n.* pepsina, enzima principal del jugo gástrico.

peptic *a.* péptico-a, rel. a la acción o a la digestión de los jugos gástricos.

peptic ulcer *n.* úlcera péptica, ulceración de las membranas mucosas del esófago, estómago o duodeno causada por acidez excesiva en el jugo gástrico y producida por tensión aguda o crónica; ___ **perforation** / perforación de la ___.

per *prep.* por; ___ **rectum** / ___ el recto, ___ vía rectal.

perceive *v.* darse cuenta de, percibir, advertir.

percentage *n.* porcentaje, tanto por ciento.

perception *n.* percepción, acción de reconocer conscientemente un estímulo sensorial; **extrasensory** ___ **(ESP)** / ___ extrasensorial.

perceptivity *n.* perceptibilidad, capacidad de percibir.

perceptual *a.* perceptivo-a, que recibe o transmite sensaciones.

percuss *v.* percutir, producir una percusión.

percussion *n.* percusión, procedimiento de palpación de toque firme en la superficie del cuerpo para producir sensaciones vibratorias que indiquen el estado de una parte interior determinada; **auscultatory** ___ / ___ auscultatoria.

percutaneous *a.* percutáneo-a, aplicado-a a través de la piel.

percutaneous transluminal angioplasty *n.* angioplastia transluminal percutánea, proceso de dilatación de una arteria por medio de un balón inflado a presión.

perfect *a.* perfecto-a, completo-a, acabado-a; **-ly** *adv.* perfectamente, completamente.

perfectionism *n.* *psic.* perfeccionismo, tendencia al fervor exagerado en la ejecución de actividades sin distinción de importancia entre las mismas.

perfectionist *a.* perfeccionista.

perforate *v.* perforar, abrir un agujero.

perforation *n.* perforación, agujero.

perform *v.* llevar a cabo, realizar, hacer; **to** ___ **an operation** / operar, intervenir quirúrgicamente.

perfusion *n.* perfusión, pasaje de un líquido o sustancia a través de un conducto.

perianal *a.* perianal, situado alrededor del ano.

pericardial, pericardiac *a.* pericárdico-a, pericardial, rel. al pericardio; ___ **effusion** / derrame ___; ___ **window** / resección ___, creación de una apertura en el pericardio.

pericardiectomy *n.* *cirg.* pericardiectomía, excisión parcial o total del pericardio.

pericarditis *n.* pericarditis, infl. del pericardio; **constrictive** ___ / ___ constrictiva; **fibrinous** ___ / ___ fibrinosa.

pericardium *n.* pericardio, membrana delicada de capa doble en forma de saco que envuelve el corazón y el inicio de los grandes vasos.

peril *n.* peligro, riesgo.

perimetrium *n.* perimetrio, membrana exterior del útero.

perinatal *n.* perinatal, rel. a o que ocurre antes, durante o inmediatamente después del nacimiento.

perinatologist *n.* perinatólogo-a, especialista en perinatología.

perinatology *n.* perinatología, estudio del feto y del recién nacido durante el período perinatal.

perineal *a.* perineal, rel. al perineo.

perinephric *a.* perinefrítico-a, rel. a o cercano al riñón.

perineum *n.* perineo, suelo pelviano delimitado anteriormente por la raíz del escroto en el hombre y la vulva en la mujer y posteriormente por el ano.

period *n.* período. 1. intervalo de tiempo; época; **incubation** ___ / ___ de incubación; **latency** ___ / ___ de latencia; 2. período, menstruación, menses, regla; 3. *gr.* punto.

periodic *a.* periódico-a.

periodical *n.* publicación, periódico.

periodontal *a.* periodontal, localizado alrededor de un diente.

periodontics *n.* periodoncia, rama de la odontología que estudia las enfermedades que atacan las áreas que envuelven los dientes.

periosteum *n.* periosteo, membrana fibrosa gruesa que cubre la superficie de los huesos excepto la superficie articular.

peripheral *a.* periférico-a, rel. a la periferia.

peripheral nervous system *n.* sistema nervioso periférico, nervios situados fuera del sistema nervioso central.

periphery *n.* periferia, parte de un cuerpo fuera del centro.

perishable *a.* perecedero-a, de fácil descomposición debido al contenido orgánico.

peristalsis *n.* peristalsis, contracciones ondulantes de estructuras tubulares tal como el canal alimenticio, cuyo movimiento fuerza el contenido almacenado hacia afuera en dirección descendente.

peristaltic *a.* peristáltico-a, rel. a la peristalsis.

peritoneal *a.* peritoneal, rel. al peritoneo; ___ **cavity** / cavidad ___.

peritoneoscopy *n.* peritoneoscopía. *V.* **laparoscopy.**

peritoneum *n.* peritoneo, membrana que cubre la pared abdominal y las vísceras.

peritonitis *n.* peritonitis, infl. del peritoneo.

peritonsillar *a.* periamigdalino-a, que rodea o está cerca de una amígdala.

periungual *a.* periungueal, localizado cerca de una uña.

periurethral *a.* periuretral, alrededor de la uretra.

perlèche *Fr.* perlèche, *pop.* boquera, infección en la comisura de los labios y manifestaciones de infl. y fisuras, gen. causada por desnutrición.

permanent *a.* permanente; **-ly** *adv.* permanentemente.

permeability *n.* permeabilidad, cualidad de ser permeable; **capillary** ___ / ___ capilar.

permeable *a.* permeable, que permite el paso de sustancias a través de una membrana u otras estructuras.

permissible *a.* permisible; permitido-a.

permit *n.* permiso, consentimiento; *v.* permitir, autorizar.

pernicious *a.* pernicioso-a, nocivo-a, destructivo-a.

peroxide, hydrogen *n.* peróxido de hidrógeno, agua oxigenada.

perpendicular *a.* perpendicular.

per rectum *L.* per rectum, por el recto, por vía rectal.

persecution *n.* persecución, acosamiento.

perseveration *n. psic.* perseveración, tipo de trastorno mental que se manifiesta con repetición anormal de palabras y acciones.

persist *v.* persistir, perseverar, insistir.

persistence *n.* persistencia, insistencia, constancia.

person *n.* persona.

persona *n. psic.* persona, personalidad adoptada que encubre la verdadera.

personal *a.* personal, privado-a.

personality *n.* personalidad, rasgos, características y conducta individual que distinguen a una persona de otras; **antisocial** ___ / ___ antisocial; **compulsive** ___ / ___ compulsiva; **extroverted** ___ / ___ extrovertida; **introverted** ___ / ___ introvertida; **neurotic** ___ / ___ neurótica; **paranoid** ___ / ___ paranoica; **psychopathic** ___ / ___ psicopática; **split** ___ / ___ desdoblada; **schizoid** ___ / ___ esquizoide.

personnel *n.* personal; **medical** ___ / equipo médico, cuerpo facultativo.

perspective *n.* perspectiva.

perspiration *n.* sudor, transpiración.

perspire *v.* sudar, transpirar.

persuade *v.* persuadir.

persuasion *n.* persuasión, técnica terapéutica que consiste en un acercamiento racional al paciente para orientarle en sus actuaciones.

pertaining *a.* perteneciente; referente a.

pertubation *n.* pertubación, acto de insuflar oviductos para hacerlos permeables.

perturbation *n.* perturbación. 1. sentimiento de inquietud; 2. variación anormal de un estado regular a otro.

pertussis, whooping cough *n.* pertusis, tosferina, enfermedad infantil infecciosa que se inicia con un estado catarral seguido de una tos seca persistente.

perversion *n.* perversión, desviación depravada, gen. de índole sexual.

pervert *n.* pervertido-a, persona que manifiesta alguna forma de perversión.

pervious *a.* pervio-a. *V.* **permeable.**

pes *L.* (*pl.* **pedes**) pes, pie o estructura similar a éste.

pessary *n.* pesario, instrumento que se introduce en la vagina para sostener el útero o como contraceptivo.

pessimism *n.* pesimismo, propensión a juzgar situaciones negativamente.

pessimist *n.* pesimista, persona que muestra pesimismo.

pessimistic *a.* pesimista.

pest *n.* 1. insectos nocivos; 2. peste. *V.* **plague.**

pesticide *n.* pesticida, exterminador de insectos y roedores.

pet *n.* 1. animal doméstico favorito; 2. niño-a mimado-a.

petechia *n.* (*pl.* **petechiae**) petequia, mancha hemorrágica pequeña que se manifiesta en la piel y las mucosas en casos de estado febril esp. en la tifoidea.

petit mal *Fr.* petit mal, ataque epiléptico benigno con pérdida del conocimiento pero sin convulsiones.

petrified *a.* petrificado-a, convertido-a en piedra.

peyote *n.* peyote, planta de la que se extrae la mescalina, droga alucinatoria.

phage *n.* bacteriófago. *V.* **bacteriophage.**

phagocyte *n.* fagocito, célula que ingiere y destruye otras células, sustancias y partículas extrañas.

phagocytic *a.* fagocítico-a, fagocitario-a, rel. a fagocitos.

phagocytosis *n.* fagocitosis, proceso de ingestión y digestión realizado por fagocitos.

phalanx *n.* (*pl.* **phalanxes, phalanges**) falange, uno de los huesos largos de los dedos de los pies o las manos.

phallic *a.* fálico, rel. al pene.

phantasm *n.* fantasma, ilusión óptica, aparición.

phantom *n.* fantasma, fantoma. 1. imagen mental; 2. patrón transparente del cuerpo y sus partes.

pharmaceutical *a.* farmacéutico-a, rel. a la farmacia.

pharmaceutics *n.* 1. farmacia; 2. preparaciones farmacéuticas.

pharmacist *n.* farmacéutico-a, boticario-a.

pharmacokinetics *n.* farmacocinética, estudio *in vivo* del metabolismo y acción de las drogas.

pharmacology *n.* farmacología, estudio de drogas, medicamentos, su naturaleza, origen, efectos y usos.

pharmacopeia *n.* farmacopea, compendio de drogas, agentes químicos y medicamentos regidos por una autoridad oficial que sirve de estándar en la preparación y dispensación de productos farmacéuticos.

pharmacy *n.* farmacia, botica.

pharyngitis *n.* faringitis, infl. de la faringe.

pharynx *n.* faringe, pasaje del aire de las fosas nasales a la laringe y de la boca al esófago en el tracto alimenticio.

phase *n.* fase, estado de desarrollo, estado transitorio.

phasic *a.* fásico-a, rel. a una fase.

phenobarbital *n.* fenobarbital, hipnótico, sedante, nombre comercial Luminal.

phenomenon *n.* (*pl.* **phenomena**) fenómeno. 1. evento o manifestación de cualquier índole; 2. síntoma objetivo de una enfermedad.

phenotype *n.* fenotipo, características visibles de un organismo como resultado de interacción entre el ambiente y los factores hereditarios.

phimosis *n.* fimosis, estrechamiento del orificio del prepucio que impide que éste pueda extenderse hacia atrás sobre el glande.

phlebitis *n.* flebitis, infl. de una vena, trastorno común esp. en las extremidades.

phlebogram *n.* flebograma, trazado del pulso venoso.

phlebolith *n.* flebolito, depósito calcáreo en una vena.

phlebotomy *n. cirg.* flebotomía, venotomía, incisión en una vena para sacar sangre.

phlegm *n.* flema. 1. mucus; 2. uno de los cuatro humores del cuerpo.

phlegmon *n.* flemón, infl. del tejido celular.

phobia *n.* fobia, temor exagerado e irracional.

phobic *a.* fóbico-a, rel. a la fobia.

phonation *n.* fonación, emisión de la voz.

phone *n.* teléfono; ___ **call** / llamada telefónica.

phonetic *a.* fonético-a, rel. a la voz y a los sonidos articulados.

phonetics *n.* fonética, ciencia que estudia la articulación de los sonidos y su pronunciación.

phoniatrics *n.* foniatría, estudio de la fonación.

phonocardiogram *n.* fonocardiograma, representación gráfica que describe los sonidos del corazón.

phonogram *n.* fonograma, representación gráfica de la intensidad de un sonido.

phonoscope *n.* fonoscopio, instrumento para registrar los sonidos del corazón.

phosphate *n.* fosfato, sal del ácido fosfórico.

phosphorus *n.* fósforo, elemento no metálico que se encuentra en alcaloides.

photocoagulation *n.* fotocoagulación, proceso usado en cirugía óptica por el cual un rayo intenso de luz controlada (laser) produce una coagulación localizada.

photophobia *n.* fotofobia, intolerancia a la luz.

phototherapy *n.* fototerapia, exposición a los rayos del sol o a una luz artificial con propósito terapéutico.

phrase *n. gr.* frase.

phrenetic *a.* frenético-a, maníaco-a.

phthiriasis *n.* ftiriasis. *V.* **pediculosis.**

phylaxis *n.* filaxis, autodefensa del organismo.

physic *n.* medicamento, esp. un catártico o purgante.

physical *a.* físico-a, rel. al cuerpo y su con-

dición; ___ **examination** / examen ___; ___ **fitness** / acondicionamiento ___; ___ **therapist** / terapeuta ___; ___ **therapy** / terapia ___.

physician *n.* médico-a; **attending** ___ / ___ de cabecera; **consulting** ___ / ___ consultante, consultor; **family** ___ / ___ de familia; ___ **on call** / ___ de guardia; **primary** ___ / ___ de asistencia primaria; **referring** ___ / ___ recomendante.

physiognomy *n.* fisionomía, semblante, rasgos faciales.

physiologist *n.* fisiólogo-a, especialista en fisiología.

physiology *n.* fisiología, ciencia que estudia las funciones de los organismos vivos y los procesos químicos o físicos que los caracterizan.

physiotherapy *n.* fisioterapia, tratamiento por medio de agentes físicos como agua, calor o luz.

physique *n.* físico, presencia, figura.

phytobezoar *n.* fitobezoar, concreción formada por fibra vegetal que se deposita en el estómago o el intestino y no se digiere.

pia mater *L.* piamáter, piamadre, membrana vascular fina, la más interna de las meninges.

pian *n. V.* **frambesia.**

pica *n.* pica, deseo insaciable de ingerir sustancias que no son comestibles.

pick *n.* [*axe*] pico; [*choice*] selección; *v.* seleccionar, escoger; **to** ___ **out** / sacar, entresacar; **to** ___ **up** / recoger; captar.

picture *n.* fotografía; lámina; retrato.

piece *n.* pedazo, parte.

pierce *v.* agujerear, perforar.

piercing *a.* penetrante, agudo-a.

pigeon-toed *a.* patizambo-a.

pigment *n.* pigmento, colorante.

pigmentation *n.* pigmentación, coloración.

piles *n. pl.* almorranas, hemorroides.

piliation *n.* piliación, formación y desarrollo de pelo.

pill *n.* pastilla, píldora; **birth control** ___ / la píldora, píldora de control del embarazo; **sleeping** ___ / sedativo, ___ para dormir; **pain** ___ / calmante, sedativo, ___ para el dolor.

pillar *n.* columna, pilar.

pillow *n.* almohada; [*inflatable*] almohadilla, cojín.

pilus *L.* (*pl.* **pili**) pilus, pelo.

pimple *n.* barrillo, [*blackhead*] espinilla, grano de la cara.

pin *n.* clavo ortopédico, pieza de metal o hueso que se usa para unir partes de un hueso fracturado.

pinch *n.* pellizco; *v.* pellizcar; comprimir, apretar.

pinched nerve *n.* nervio pellizcado.

pineal *a.* pineal, en forma de piña o cono.

pineal gland *n.* glándula o cuerpo pineal.

pink *a.* rosado-a, sonrosado-a.

pinkeye *n.* conjuntivitis catarral, oftalmia purulenta.

pinna *L.* pinna, pabellón de la oreja.

pipet, pipette *n.* pipeta, probeta, tubo de ensayo.

pit *n.* hueco, hoyo; [*seed*] semilla de frutas.

pitch *n.* tono, diapasón, cualidad de un sonido de acuerdo con la frecuencia de las ondas que lo producen.

pith *n.* médula, parte principal.

pitiful *a.* lastimoso-a, pobre.

pituitary gland *n.* glándula pituitaria. *V.* **hypophysis.**

pity *n.* lástima, compasión; **What a __!** / ¡Qué __!

pivot *n.* pivote, eje, parte que sostiene la corona de un diente.

place *n.* lugar, sitio; **in __ of** / en __ de; *v.* colocar; **to put in __** / colocar en su __.

placebo *n.* placebo, sustancia anodina sin valor medicinal gen. usada en experimentos por comparación; **__ controlled trial** / prueba controlada por __.

placenta *n.* placenta, órgano vascular que se desarrolla en la pared del útero a través del cual el feto se nutre de la madre por medio del cordón umbilical; **early, previa __** / **__ previa,** anterior al feto en relación con la apertura externa del cuello uterino, lo que puede causar una hemorragia grave.

placental *a.* placentario-a, de la placenta, rel. a la placenta; **__ insufficiency** / insuficiencia __.

plague *n.* peste. 1. peste bubónica, infección epidémica transmitida por la picadura de pulgas de ratas; 2. enfermedad epidémica que causa alta mortalidad.

plain *a.* común, ordinario-a.

plan *n.* plan, planificación; intento; *v.* planear.

plane *n.* plano. 1. superficie lisa y plana; 2. superficie relativamente lisa formada por un corte imaginario o un corte real a través de una parte del cuerpo; **axial __** / **__ axial; coronal __** / **__ coronal, frontal; sagittal __** / **__ sagital.**

planned parenthood *n.* planificación familiar.

planning *n.* planeamiento, planificación; organización; **family __** / **__ familiar.**

plant *n.* planta; **medicinal __** / **__,** yerba medicinal.

plantar *a.* plantar, rel. a la planta del pie; **__ reflex** / reflejo plantar. *V.* **Babinski's sign.**

plaque, placque *n.* placa; plaqueta. 1. cualquier superficie de la piel o membrana mucosa; 2. plaqueta sanguínea.

plasma *n.* plasma, componente líquido de la sangre y linfa que se compone en su mayor parte (91%) de agua; **__ proteins** / proteínas sanguíneas.

plaster *n.* yeso, emplaste, molde; **__ cast** / vendaje enyesado, tablilla de __.

plastic *n.* plástico; *a.* plástico-a.

plasticity *n.* plasticidad, capacidad para moldearse.

plastic surgery *n.* cirugía plástica, proceso quirúrgico para reparar o reconstruir estructuras del cuerpo.

plate *n.* placa. 1. estructura lisa tal como una lámina ósea; 2. pieza de metal que se usa como soporte de una estructura.

platelet *n.* plaqueta, elemento celular esencial en la coagulación de la sangre.

platinum *n.* platino.

Platyhelminthes *n.* Platelmintos, *phylum* de gusanos planos que incluye las clases *Cestoda* y *Trematoda.*

play *v.* jugar; [*an instrument*] tocar.

play therapy *n. psic.* terapia infantil aplicada en un ambiente de juguetes y juegos infantiles por medio de los cuales se estimula a los niños a revelar conflictos interiores.

please *int.* por favor; **Come in, __!** / ¡Entre, entra por favor!; *v.* gustar, agradar, satisfacer; tener placer, tener gusto en.

pleasing *a.* agradable, placentero-a, gustoso-a.

pleasure principle *n. psic.* principio del placer, conducta dirigida a satisfacer deseos propios y evadir el dolor.

pledget *n.* tapón de algodón absorbente o de gasa.

pleomorphism *n.* pleomorfismo, cualidad de asumir o tener formas diferentes.

plethora *n.* plétora, exceso de cualquiera de los líquidos del organismo.

plethysmography *n.* pletismografía, registro de las variaciones de volumen que ocurren en una parte u órgano en relación con la cantidad de sangre que pasa sobre los mismos.

pleura *n.* pleura, membrana doble que cubre los pulmones y la cavidad torácica; **parietal __** / **__ parietal; visceral __** / **__ visceral.**

pleural *a.* pleural, rel. a la pleura; **__ cavity** / cavidad __; **__ effusion** / derrame __.

pleuralgia *n.* pleuralgia, dolor en la pleura o en un costado.

pleurisy *n.* pleuresía, infl. de la pleura.

pleuritic *a.* pleurítico-a, rel. a o de la naturaleza de la pleuresía.

pleuritis *n.* pleuritis. *V.* **pleurisy.**

pleuroscopy *n.* pleuroscopía, examen de la cavidad pleural a través de una incisión en el tórax.

plexiform *a.* plexiforme, en forma de plexo o red.

plexus *n.* plexo, red de nervios o de vasos sanguíneos o linfáticos.

pliability *n.* flexibilidad; docilidad.

plica *n.* (*pl.* **plicae**) plica, doblez o pliegue.

plicate *v.* doblar, plegar.

plug *n.* tapón.

plumbism *n.* plumbismo, envenenamiento crónico con plomo.

plural *gr.* plural, más de uno en número.

pluripotent, pluripotential *a.* pluripotencial, que puede tomar más de un curso de acción.

pneumatic *a.* neumático-a, rel. al aire o a la respiración.

pneumatization *n.* neumatización, formación de cavidades llenas de aire en un hueso esp. en el hueso temporal.

pneumatocele *n.* neumatocele. 1. hernia de tejido pulmonar; 2. saco o tumor que contiene gas.

pneumococcal *a.* neumocócico-a, rel. a la neumonía o que la causa.

pneumococcus *n.* (*pl.* **pneumococci**) neumococo, microorganismo o tipo de bacteria gram-positiva que causa neumonía aguda y otras infecciones del tracto respiratorio superior.

pneumocystis carinii pneumonia *n.* neumonía neumocística carinii, tipo de pulmonía aguda intersticial causada por el bacilo *Pneumocysti carinii,* considerada una de las infecciones oportunistas comunes del SIDA.

pneumoencephalograpy *n.* neumoencefalografía, rayos X del cerebro por medio de aire o gas inyectado para permitir distinguir visualmente la corteza y los ventrículos cerebrales.

pneumomediastinum *L.* neumomediastinum, presencia de gas o de aire en los tejidos del mediastino.

pneumonia *n.* pulmonía, neumonía, enfermedad infecciosa causada por bacterias o virus presentes en el tracto respiratorio superior; **double** __ / __ doble; __, **lobar** / __ lobar; **staphylococcal** __ / __ estafilocócica.

pneumonic *a.* neumónico-a, rel. a los pulmones o a la neumonía.

pneumonitis *n.* neumonitis V. **pneumonia.**

pneumothorax *n.* neumotórax, acumulación de aire o gas en la cavidad pleural que resulta en colapso del pulmón afectado; **spontaneous** __ / __ espontáneo; **tension** __ / __ por tensión.

pocket *n.* saco, bolsa; [*clothing*] bolsillo.

pockmark *n.* marca, señal o cicatriz. 1. marca de una pústula; 2. señal que deja la viruela.

podiatrist *n.* podíatra, especialista en podiatría.

podiatry *n.* podiatría, diagnóstico y tratamiento de afecciones de los pies.

point *n.* punto, punta.

poison *n.* veneno; [*insect, reptile bite*] ponzoña; substancia tóxica; __ **ivy** / hiedra venenosa.

poisoning *n.* envenenamiento.

poisonous *a.* venenoso-a; tóxico-a.

polar *a.* polar, rel. a un polo.

polarity *n.* polaridad. 1. cualidad de poseer polos; 2. presentación de efectos opuestos en dos extremos o polos.

polarization *n.* polarización.

pole *n.* polo, 1. cada uno de los extremos opuestos de un cuerpo u órgano o de una parte esférica u oval.

policy *n.* póliza; reglamento; **insurance** __ / __ de seguros.

polio, poliomyelitis *n.* polio, poliomielitis,

parálisis infantil, enfermedad contagiosa que ataca el sistema nervioso central y causa parálisis en los músculos esp. de las piernas.

poliovirus *n.* poliovirus, agente causante de la poliomielitis.

polite *a.* cortés.

pollen *n.* polen.

pollute *v.* contaminar, corromper.

pollution *n.* polución, contaminación; **air** __ / __ del aire; **water** __ / __ del agua.

poly *n.* poli, leucocito polimorfonuclear.

polyarthritis *n.* poliartritis, infl. de varias articulaciones.

polyarticular *a.* poliarticular, que afecta varias articulaciones.

polyclinic *n.* policlínica, hospital general.

polycystic *a.* poliquístico-a, que está formado-a por varios quistes.

polycythemia *n.* policitemia, aumento excesivo de glóbulos rojos; **primary** __ / __ primaria; __ **rubra** / __ vera secundaria; __ vera. V. **erythrocythosis.**

polydactyly *n.* polidactilia, condición anormal de poseer más de cinco dedos en la mano o el pie.

polydipsia *n.* polidipsia, sed insaciable.

polygamy *n.* poligamia, práctica de poseer más de un cónyuge a la vez.

polygraph *n.* polígrafo, instrumento para obtener diversas pulsaciones arteriales y venosas simultáneamente.

polyhydramnios *n.* polihidramnios, exceso de líquido amniótico.

polymorphonuclear *a.* polimorfonucleado-a, que tiene un núcleo lobular complejo.

polymorphonuclear leukocyte *n.* leucocito polimorfonucleado, granulocito con núcleo de lóbulos múltiples.

polymyalgia *n.* polimialgia, condición caracterizada por dolor en distintos músculos; __ **rheumatica** __ / __ reumática.

polymyopathy *n.* polimiopatía, cualquier enfermedad que afecta varios músculos simultáneamente.

polymyositis *n.* polimiositis. V. **dermatomyositis.**

polyneuropathy *n.* polineuropatía, enfermedad que afecta varios nervios a la vez.

polyp *n.* pólipo, cualquier protuberancia o bulto que se desarrolla de una membrana mucosa.

polypectomy *n.* *cirg.* polipectomía, excisión de un pólipo.

polyposis *n.* poliposis, formación numerosa de pólipos.

polysaccharide *n.* polisacárido, carbohidrato que puede disolverse en agua.

polyunsaturated *a.* poli-no saturado, que denota un ácido graso.

polyvalent *a.* polivalente, que tiene efecto en contra de más de un agente.

pomade *n.* pomada, sustancia medicinal semisólida para uso externo.

pons *L.* pons, formación de tejido que sirve de

puente entre dos partes.

poor *a.* pobre, necesitado-a; deficiente; **in ___ condition** / en mala condición, en mal estado.

popliteal *a.* poplíteo-a, área posterior de la rodilla.

popper *n. pop.* nombre atribuido a algunas drogas adictivas.

population *n.* población, habitantes de un área.

porcine *a.* porcino-a, rel. al cerdo.

pore, porus *n.* poro, abertura diminuta tal como la de una glándula sudorípara.

pork *n.* cerdo, puerco; **___ chop** / chuleta o costilla de cerdo.

porosis *n.* porosis, formación de una cavidad.

porous *a.* poroso-a, permeable.

porphyria *n.* porfiria, defecto metabólico congénito que se caracteriza por exceso de porfirina en la sangre, en la orina y en las heces fecales, causando numerosos trastornos físicos y psiquiátricos.

porphyrin *n.* porfirina, compuesto que ocurre en el protoplasma y que es la base de los pigmentos respiratorios en los animales y las plantas.

porta *L.* porta, entrada, esp. la parte de un órgano por donde penetran vasos sanguíneos y nervios.

portacaval *a.* portacava, rel. a la vena porta y la vena cava inferior.

portal *a.* portal, rel. al sistema portal.

portal circulation *n.* circulación portal, curso por el cual la sangre entra al hígado por la vena porta y sale por la vena hepática.

portal hypertension *n.* hipertensión portal, aumento de la presión en la vena porta debido a una obstrucción.

portal vein *n.* vena porta, vena formada por varias ramas de venas que provienen de órganos abdominales.

portion *v.* porción.

position *n.* posición. 1. actitud o postura del cuerpo; **anatomic ___** / **___** anatómica; **central ___** / **___** central; **decubitus ___** / **___** decúbito; **deep ___** / **___** dentro de, profunda; **distal ___** / **___** distal; **genupectoral ___** / **___** genupectoral; **inferior ___** / **___** inferior; **lateral ___** / **___** lateral, de un lado; **lithotomy ___** / **___** de litotomía; **lying down ___** / **___** yacente, acostada; **medial ___** / **___** media; **posterior ___** / **___** posterior, detrás de; **prone ___** / **___** prona, boca abajo; **superficial ___** / **___** superficial; **superior ___** / **___** superior, encima de; **supine ___** / **___** supina, boca arriba; **upright ___** / **___** erecta; 2. posición y presentación del feto. *V.* **presentation.**

positive *a.* positivo-a, afirmativo-a.

positivity *n.* positividad, manifestación de una reacción positiva.

possess *v.* poseer, tener.

possessed *a.* poseído-a, dominado-a por una idea o pasión.

possession *n.* posesión.

possessive *n. gr.* adjetivo o pronombre posesivo; *a.* posesivo-a.

posterior *a.* posterior. 1. rel. a la parte dorsal o trasera de una estructura; 2. que continúa.

posthumous *a.* póstumo, que ocurre después de la muerte.

posthypnotic *a.* posthipnótico-a, que sigue al estado hipnótico.

post ictal *a.* post ictal, después de un ataque.

post mature *a.* postmaduro-a, rel. a un recién nacido después de un embarazo prolongado.

postmortem *L.* post mortem, después de la muerte; autopsia.

postnasal *a.* postnasal, detrás de la nariz.

postoperative *a.* postoperatorio-a, que ocurre después de la operación; **___ care** / cuidado **___**; **___ complication** / complicación **___**.

postpartum *L.* postpartum, después del parto; **___ blues** / estado de depresión que sigue al parto.

postpartum period, puerperium *n.* puerperio, período de aproximadamente seis semanas después del parto durante el cual los órganos de la madre vuelven a su estado normal.

postpartum psychosis *n.* psicosis del postpartum.

postpone *v.* posponer, demorar, aplazar.

postprandial *a.* postprandial, después de una comida.

postural *a.* postural, rel. a la postura del cuerpo; **___ hypotension** / hipotensión **___**, descenso de la presión arterial en posición erecta.

posture *n.* postura, posición del cuerpo.

potable *a.* potable, salubre, que puede beberse.

potassium *n.* potasio, mineral que se encuentra en el cuerpo combinado con otros, esencial en la conducción de impulsos nerviosos y actividad muscular.

potato *n.* patata, *H.A.* papa.

potbelly *n.* panza, barriga.

potency *n.* fuerza, potencia.

potent *a.* potente, fuerte; eficaz.

potential *a.* potencial, que existe en forma de cierta capacidad o disposición.

potion *n.* poción, dosis de líquido medicinal.

pouch *n.* bolsa, saco, cavidad.

poultice *n.* cataplasma, emplasto.

pound *n.* libra, medida de peso; *v.* machacar, golpear.

pour *v.* verter, vaciar, derramar.

poverty *n.* pobreza, carencia.

powder *n.* polvo; **powdered** *a.* en polvo.

power *n.* poder, fuerza.

pox *n.* enfermedad eruptiva de la piel caracterizada por manifestación de vesículas que se convierten en pústulas.

practical *a.* práctico-a.

practice *n.* práctica; costumbre; **private ___** / **___** privada; *v.* practicar.

prandial *a.* prandial, rel. a las comidas.

preagonal *a.* preagónico-a; moribundo-a, al

borde de la muerte.

preanesthetic *n.* preanestésico, agente preliminar que se administra con anticipación a la
anestesia general.

precancerous *a.* precanceroso-a, susceptible a o
que puede convertirse en un cáncer.

precarious *a.* precario-a.

precaution *n.* precaución.

precede *v.* preceder, anteceder.

precipitate *n.* precipitado, depósito de partes
sólidas que se asientan en una solución; *a.*
precipitado-a, que sucede con rapidez.

precise *a.* preciso-a, correcto-a.

precision *n.* precisión, exactitud.

precocious *a.* precoz, de un desarrollo más
avanzado que el normal para la edad; __ **child**
/ niño-a __.

precocity *n.* precocidad, desarrollo de rasgos
físicos o facultades mentales más avanzados
que lo normal en comparación con la edad
cronológica.

precursor *n.* precursor-a, predecesor-a, manifestación tal como la aparición de un síntoma o
señal antes de desarrollarse una enfermedad;
a. precursor-a, predecesor-a; preliminar.

predict *v.* predecir.

predictable *a.* predecible.

predispose *v.* predisponer.

predisposed *a.* predispuesto-a, que tiene susceptibilidad o tendencia a contraer una enfermedad.

predisposition *n.* predisposición, inclinación a
desarrollar una condición o enfermedad debido a factores genéticos, ambientales o psicológicos.

predominant *a.* predominante.

preeclampsia *n.* preeclampsia, condición tóxica que se ve en la última etapa del embarazo
y que se manifiesta con hipertensión, albuminuria y edema.

prefer *v.* preferir, seleccionar.

preferable *a.* preferible, favorito-a.

preference *n.* preferencia.

prefix *n. gr.* prefijo.

pregnancy *n.* embarazo, gravidez, estado de gestación; **ectopic** __ / __ ectópico; **extrauter-
ine** __ / __ extrauterino; **incomplete** __ /
__ incompleto; **interstitial** __ / __ intersticial; **false** __ / __ falso; **multiple** __ / __
múltiple; **prolonged** __ / __ prolongado;
surrogate __ / __ subrogado; **tubal** __ / __
tubárico.

pregnant *a.* embarazada, encinta, en estado de
gestación; grávida.

prehensile *a.* prensil, adaptado para agarrar o
asir.

prejudice *n.* prejuicio.

preliminary *a.* preliminar.

premature *a.* [*newborn*] prematuro-a, nacido antes de llegar a término.

prematurity *n.* prematurez, condición del feto
antes de alcanzar el término de treinta y siete

semanas de la gestación.

premedication *n.* premedicación. *V.* **preanesthetic.**

premenstrual *n.* premenstrual, antes de la
menstruación; __ **tension** / tensión __.

premonition *n.* premonición, presentimiento.

premunition *n.* premunición, inmunidad a una
infección específica debida a la presencia previa del agente que la causa en el organismo.

prenatal *a.* prenatal, anterior al nacimiento; __
care / cuidado __.

preoccupation *n.* preocupación.

preoccupied *a.* preocupado-a.

preoccupy *v.* preocupar; preocuparse.

preoperative care *n.* cuidado preoperatorio,
cuidado preliminar a la operación.

prep *abbr.* término que se usa esp. para referirse
a todo lo relacionado con el proceso preoperatorio.

preparation *n.* preparación. 1. acción de preparar algo; 2. un medicamento que se prepara
para ser administrado.

prepare *v.* preparar.

prepared childbirth *n.* parto natural. *V.* **natural
childbirth.**

preposition *n. gr.* preposición.

prepubescent *a.* prepubescente, anterior a la
pubertad.

prepuce *n.* prepucio, pliegue de piel sobre el
glande del pene.

prerenal *a.* prerrenal. 1. situado frente al riñón;
2. que tiene lugar en la circulación antes de
llegar al riñón.

presacral *a.* presacro, frente al sacro.

presbiopia *n.* presbiopía, presbicia, condición
de la visión que ocurre en la vejez a causa de
una deficiencia en la elasticidad del cristalino.

prescribe *v.* prescribir, recetar.

prescribed *a. pp.* de **to prescribe,** prescrito-a,
ordenado-a.

prescription *n.* receta; __ **tablet** / formulario.

presence *n.* [*looks*] presencia, aspecto; [*attendance*] asistencia.

present *n. gr.* tiempo presente; **at** __ / hoy, actualmente, por ahora; [*gift*] regalo, obsequio;
v. **to be** __ / asistir, estar presente; **-ly** *adv.*
ahora, actualmente.

presentation *n.* presentación. 1. reporte oral; 2.
posición del feto en el útero según se detecta
en un examen, o posición de salida en relación al canal del parto en el momento del
nacimiento; **breech** __ / __ de nalgas; **brow**
__ / __ de cejas o frente; **cephalic** __ / __
de cabeza; **face** __ / __ de cara; **footling**
/ __ de pies; **shoulder** __ / __ de hombro;
transverse __ / __ transversa.

preservation *n.* preservación, conservación.

preservative *n.* preservativo, conservador. 1.
agente que se añade a un alimento o medicamento para impedir el desarrollo de bacterias; 2. profiláctico.

preserve *v.* preservar, conservar.

press *v.* hacer presión, comprimir, oprimir.

pressor *a.* presor, que tiende a aumentar la presión sanguínea.

pressure *n.* presión, tensión, compresión; **arterial** ___ / ___ arterial, presión o tensión de la sangre sobre las paredes de los vasos capilares; **atmospheric** ___ / ___ atmosférica, la que ejerce la masa de aire alrededor de la tierra; **central venous** ___ / ___ central venosa, presión de la sangre en la aurícula derecha del corazón; **diastolic** ___ / ___ diastólica, presión arterial durante la diástole; **intracranial** ___ / ___ intracraneana o intracraneal, presión ejercida dentro de la cavidad craneana; **intrathoracic** ___ / ___ intratorácica, presión dentro del tórax; **partial** ___ / ___ parcial, la que ejerce uno de los gases de una composición mixta; **osmotic** ___ / ___ osmótica, *V.* osmosis; **pulse** ___ / ___ de pulso; **systolic** ___ / ___ sistólica, presión arterial durante la contracción de los ventrículos; **venous** ___ / ___ venosa, la de la sangre en las venas; *v.* hacer presión, presionar.

pressure point *n.* punto de presión, área donde puede sentirse el pulso o hacer presión para contener un sangramiento.

pressure sore *n.* úlcera de decúbito.

pretend *v.* pretender, fingir, aparentar.

preterit *gr.* préterito, tiempo pasado.

preterm *n.* pretérmino, lo que concierne a sucesos anteriores a completar el término de treinta y siete semanas en un embarazo.

prevalence *n.* prevalencia, número de casos en una población afectados por la misma enfermedad en un tiempo determinado.

prevent *v.* prevenir, precaver, evitar.

preventive *a.* preventivo-a; ___ **health services** / servicios de salud ___ .

prevertebral *a.* prevertebral, situado enfrente de una vértebra.

previous *a.* previo-a, anterior.

priapism *n.* priapismo, erección prolongada y dolorosa del pene a consecuencia de una enfermedad.

price *n.* precio, valor, costo.

prick *n.* pinchazo; punzada; picadura, aguijón; *v.* picar, punzar, aguijonear, pinchar.

prickly heat *n.* salpullido, sarpullido.

priest *n.* sacerdote, padre, cura.

primarily *adv.* primeramente; principalmente, primordialmente.

primary *a.* inicial, primario-a, rel. al contacto o atención de un caso en su principio; ___ **physician** / médico de cabecera, facultativo que atiende al paciente inicialmente, esp. un pediatra o médico de familia.

primary care *n.* atención inicial del paciente.

prime *a.* primero-a, principal; *v.* **to be in one's** ___ / estar en la flor de la vida.

primitive *a.* primitivo-a; embriónico-a.

primordial *a.* primordial, esencial.

principal *a.* principal, más importante.

principle *n.* principio. 1. ingrediente esencial de un compuesto químico; 2. regla; orden.

print *n.* impresión, marca.

prior *n.* antecesor, predecesor; *a.* previo-a; ___ **to** / anterior a, antes de.

priority *n.* prioridad, preferencia, precedencia.

prism *n.* prisma.

privacy *n.* vida privada; aislamiento.

private *a.* privado-a, particular, exclusivo-a; ___ **hospital** / clínica; ___ **practice** / consulta particular; ___ **room** / cuarto ___ ; **-ly** *adv.* privadamente.

privation *n.* privación, necesidad.

privilege *n.* privilegio, derecho.

privileged *a.* confidencial, privilegiado-a; reservado-a; ___ **information** / información ___ o reservada.

probability *n.* probabilidad.

probable *a.* probable, casi posible; **-ly** *adv.* probablemente.

probe *n.* sonda, instrumento flexible que se usa para explorar cavidades o conductos y para medir la penetración de una herida; **hollow** ___ / ___ acanalada.

problem *n.* problema; cuestión; trastorno; ___ **solving** / solución de ___ s.

problematic *a.* problemático-a; dificultoso-a.

procedure *n.* procedimiento; **clinical** ___ / ___ clínico; **invasive** ___ / ___ invasivo; **noninvasive** ___ / ___ no invasivo; **surgical** ___ / ___ quirúrgico; **therapeutic** ___ / ___ terapéutico.

proceed *v.* proceder, continuar, seguir adelante, avanzar.

process *n.* proceso, método, sistema.

procreate *v.* engendrar, procrear, reproducir.

procreation *n.* procreación, reproducción.

proctalgia *n.* proctalgia, dolor en el recto y el ano.

proctitis *n.* proctitis, infl. de la mucosa del recto y del ano.

proctologist *n.* proctólogo-a, especialista en proctología.

proctology *n.* proctología, estudio del colon, recto y ano, de las enfermedades que los afectan y su tratamiento.

proctoscope *n.* proctoscopio, espéculo rectal, tipo de endoscopio usado para examinar el recto.

procure *v.* procurar, tratar de obtener.

prodromal *a.* prodrómico-a, rel. a la fase inicial de una enfermedad.

prodrome *n.* pródromo, señal o síntoma preliminar.

produce *n.* producto, esp. vegetales, frutas y legumbres; producción; *v.* producir, crear; causar.

product *n.* producto; resultado, efecto.

production *n.* producción, rendimiento.

productive *a.* productivo-a, fecundo-a.

profession *n.* profesión, carrera, oficio.

professional *n.* profesional, facultativo-a; *a* profesional, facultativo-a; ___ **care** / cuidado ___ ;

___ help / asistencia médica, asistencia ___.

profile *n.* perfil, bosquejo, esbozo; **biochemical** ___ / ___ bioquímico; **physical** ___ / ___ físico.

profit *n.* beneficio, ganancia; ventaja.

profunda *L.* (*pl.* **profunda**) muy interior, en referencia esp. a algunas arterias.

profundus *L.* profundo, interior.

profuse *a.* profuso-a; abundante; **-ly** *adv.* profusamente; abundantemente.

progeny *n.* descendencia, prole.

progesterone *n.* progesterona, hormona esteroide segregada por los ovarios.

prognathous *a.* prognato-a, que tiene la mandíbula prominente.

prognose *v.* pronosticar o predecir el desarrollo de una enfermedad.

prognosis *n.* pronóstico, evaluación del curso probable de una enfermedad.

prognosticate *v.* pronosticar.

progress *n.* progreso; *v.* **to make** ___ / progresar, mejorar.

progressive *a.* progresivo-a, que avanza.

projection *n.* proyección. 1. protuberancia; 2. *psic.* mecanismo por el cual el (la) paciente atribuye inconscientemente a otras personas u objetos las cualidades y sentimientos propios que rechaza.

prolapse *n.* prolapso, caída de un órgano o parte.

proliferation *n.* proliferación, multiplicación en número por reproducción esp. de células similares.

proliferous, prolific *a.* prolífero-a, que se reproduce fácilmente.

prolong *v.* prolongar, extender; retardar.

prolongation *n.* prolongación, extensión.

prominence *n.* prominencia, proyección; *pop.* bulto.

promise *n.* promesa; *v.* prometer, dar la palabra.

promontory *n.* promontorio, elevación.

prompt *a.* puntual, a tiempo.

pronate *v.* pronar, poner el cuerpo o parte del mismo en posición prona.

prone *a.* acostado-a, postrado-a. 1. en posición acostada boca abajo; 2. con la mano virada, apoyada en el dorso; 3. propenso, susceptible a contraer una enfermedad.

pronoun *n. gr.* pronombre.

pronounce *v.* pronunciar, articular sonidos de letras.

pronunciation *n.* pronunciación.

proof *n.* prueba, comprobación; *v.* probar, demostrar.

propagate *v.* propagar, diseminar.

propagation *n.* propagación, reproducción.

proper *a.* propio-a, particular, apropiado-a.

property *n.* propiedad, cualidad, característica, atributo.

prophase *n.* profase, primera fase en la mitosis celular.

prophylactic *n.* profiláctico. 1. agente o método para evitar infecciones; 2. contraceptivo.

Properties	*Propiedades*
abundant	abundante
acid	ácido
bitter	amargo
chilly	frío
clammy	frío y pegajoso
cold	frío
dirty	sucio
dry	seco
dull	[*pain*] sordo; torpe
fat	gordo, grasoso
fresh	fresco
heavy	pesado; grueso; opresivo
hot	caliente; [*taste*] picante
light	ligero; claro; leve
liquid	líquido
long	largo
moist	húmedo; mojado
poor	pobre; deficiente; falto de
rich	rico; copioso
sharp	[*pain*] agudo, penetrante; [*tool*] afilado
short	[*length*] corto, falto de [*height*] bajo
skinny	flaco, delgado
slim	esbelto
sour	agrio
strong	fuerte, vigoroso
sweet	dulce, azucarado
tall	alto
tasteless	desabrido
thick	grueso, espeso
warm	tibio, calentico
wet	mojado

prophylaxis *n.* profilaxis, medidas para prevenir enfermedades o su propagación.

proportion *n.* proporción, tamaño determinado, medida.

proprietary medicine *n.* medicamento de patente.

proprioceptive *a.* propioceptivo-a, que recibe estímulos.

proprioceptor *n.* propioceptor, terminación nerviosa receptora que responde a estímulos y trasmite información de los movimientos y posiciones del cuerpo.

proptosis *n.* proptosis, desplazamiento de un órgano hacia adelante tal como el globo ocular.

proscribe *v.* prohibir, cancelar.

prosencephalon *n.* prosencéfalo, porción ante-

373

rior de la vesícula cerebral de la que se desarrollan el diencéfalo y el telencéfalo.

prostate *n.* próstata, glándula masculina que rodea el cuello de la vejiga y la uretra.

prostatectomy *n. cirg.* prostatectomía, excisión parcial o total de la próstata.

prostatic *a.* prostático-a, rel. a la próstata; ___ hypertrophy / hipertrofia ___, agrandamiento benigno de la próstata debido a la vejez.

prostatic specific antigen *n.* antígeno prostático específico, examen sanguíneo para evaluar los antígenos prostáticos específicos en la circulación.

prostatism *n.* prostatismo, trastorno debido a una obstrucción del cuello de la vejiga por agrandamiento de la próstata.

prostatitis *n.* prostatitis, infl. de la próstata.

prosthesis *n.* prótesis, reemplazo de una parte del cuerpo con un sustituto artificial.

prosthetics *n.* protética, rama de la cirugía que se dedica al reemplazo de partes del cuerpo.

prostitution *n.* prostitución.

prostrate *a.* postrado-a. 1. en posición prona o supina; 2. débil, abatido-a; *v.* postrar; abatir; *vr.* postrarse; abatirse, debilitarse.

prostration *n.* postración, debilidad, abatimiento.

protean *n.* proteico, que se manifiesta en distintas formas.

protect *v.* proteger, cuidar.

protection *n.* protección, cuidado.

protective *a.* protector-a.

protective isolation *n.* aislamiento protector, estado que se recomienda en casos de pacientes de baja resistencia o inmunidad.

protein *n.* proteína, complejo compuesto nitrogenado esencial en el desarrollo y preservación de los tejidos del cuerpo; ___ **balance** / balance de las ___-s; **concentration** / ___ concentración de ___.

proteinaceous *a.* proteináceo-a, de la naturaleza de o semejante a una proteína.

proteinemia *n.* proteinemia, proteínas en la sangre.

proteinosis *n.* proteinosis, acumulación en exceso de proteínas en los tejidos.

proteinuria *n.* proteinuria, presencia de proteínas en la orina.

prothrombin *n.* protrombina, una de las cuatro proteínas principales del plasma junto a la albúmina, la globulina y el fibrinógeno.

protocol *n.* protocolo, notas oficiales de un procedimiento.

protoplasm *n.* protoplasma, parte esencial de la célula que incluye el citoplasma y el núcleo.

prototype *n.* prototipo, modelo, ejemplo.

protozoon *n.* (*pl.* **protozoa.**) protozoo, organismo unicelular.

protraction *n.* protracción, tracción hacia afuera, como en la mandíbula.

protrude *v.* sobresalir; salirse de su lugar.

protruding *a.* saliente.

protuberance *n.* protuberancia, prominencia.

proud *a.* orgulloso-a, arrogante.

prove *v.* demostrar, comprobar, probar.

provide *v.* proveer, dar, abastecer.

providence *n.* providencia.

provision *n.* provisión, abastecimiento.

provisional *a.* provisional, interino; **-ly** *adv.* provisionalmente, por lo pronto.

proximal *a.* cerca del punto de referencia.

prune *n.* ciruela pasa.

pruriginous *a.* pruriginoso-a, rel. a prurigo.

prurigo *n.* prurigo, condición cutánea crónica inflamatoria que se caracteriza por pápulas pequeñas y picazón intensa.

pruritus *n.* prurito, comezón, picazón.

pseudoaneurysm *n.* pseudoaneurisma, condición semejante a la dilatación de un aneurisma.

pseudocyesis *n.* pseudociesis. V. **pseudopregnancy.**

pseudocyst *n.* pseudo quiste, formación semejante a la de un quiste.

pseudogout *n.* seudogota, condición artrítica recurrente con síntomas similares a los de la gota.

pseudopregnancy *n.* embarazo falso o imaginario.

psoriasis *n.* psoriasis, dermatitis crónica que se manifiesta con manchas rojas cubiertas de escamas blancas.

psyche *n.* psique, mente, proceso mental consciente o inconsciente.

psychedelic *a.* psicodélico-a, rel. a substancias o drogas que pueden inducir alteraciones perceptuales tales como alucinaciones y delirios.

psychiatric *a.* psiquiátrico-a, siquiátrico-a.

psychiatrist *n.* psiquiatra, siquiatra, especialista en psiquiatría.

psychiatry *n.* psiquiatría, rama de la medicina que estudia los trastornos mentales.

psychic *a.* psíquico-a, rel. a la mente o psique.

psychoactive *a.* psicoactivo-a, que afecta la condición mental.

psychoanalysis *n.* psicoanálisis, método de análisis psicológico creado por Sigmund Freud que se vale de la interpretación de los sueños y la libre asociación de ideas para hacer al paciente consciente de conflictos reprimidos y tratar de ajustar su conducta emocional.

psychoanalyst *n.* psicoanalista, analista.

psychoanalyze *v.* psicoanalizar, sicoanalizar.

psychobiology *n.* psicobiología, estudio de la psique en relación con otros procesos biológicos.

psychodrama *n.* psicodrama, método de terapia psíquica en el cual se dramatizan situaciones conflictivas de la vida del paciente con la participación de éste.

psychological *a.* psicológico-a, rel. a la psicología.

psychologist *n.* psicólogo-a, profesional que

practica la psicología.

psychology *n.* psicología, sicología, ciencia que estudia los procesos mentales y la conducta de un individuo.

psychomotor *a.* psicomotor-a, rel. a acciones motoras como resultado de actividades mentales.

psychopath *n.* psicópata, persona que padece de trastornos mentales.

psychopathology *n.* psicopatología, rama de la medicina que trata de las causas y naturaleza de las enfermedades mentales.

psychopharmacology *n.* psicofarmacología, estudio del efecto de drogas y medicamentos en la mente y la conducta.

psychophysiological *a.* psicofisiológico-a, rel. a la influencia mental sobre procesos físicos tal como se manifiesta en algunos desórdenes y enfermedades.

psychosis *n.* psicosis, trastorno mental severo de origen orgánico o emocional en el cual el paciente pierde contacto con la realidad y sufre de alucinaciones o aberraciones mentales; **alcoholic** ___ / ___ alcohólica; **depressive** ___ / ___ depresiva; **drug** ___ / ___ por drogas; **manic-depressive** ___ / ___ maníacodepresiva; **organic** ___ / ___ orgánica; **senile** ___ / ___ senil; **situational** ___ / ___ situacional; **toxic** ___ / ___ tóxica; **traumatic** ___ / ___ traumática.

psychosocial *a.* psicosocial, rel. a factores psicológicos y sociales.

psychosomatic *a.* psicosomático-a, rel. al cuerpo y a la mente; ___ **symptom** / síntoma ___. *V.* **psychophysiological.**

psychotherapy *n.* psicoterapia, tratamiento de trastornos mentales o emocionales por medios psicológicos tales como el psicoanálisis.

psychotic *a.* psicótico-a, rel. a o que sufre de una psicosis.

psychotropic drugs *n.* drogas psicotrópicas, compuestos químicos que afectan la estabilidad mental.

ptosis *Gr.* ptosis, prolapso de un órgano o parte, esp. visto en el párpado superior.

puberty *n.* pubertad, adolescencia, desarrollo de las características sexuales secundarias y comienzo de la capacidad reproductiva.

pubescense *n.* pubescencia, pubertad. 1. principio de la pubertad; 2. vellosidad, lanugo.

pubic *a.* púbico-a, rel. al pubis; ___ **hair** / vello ___.

pubis *n.* (*pl.* **pubes**) pubis, región púbica, enstructura ósea frontal de la pelvis.

public *a.* público-a.

public health *n.* salubridad pública, rama de la medicina que se dedica a la atención social, física y mental de los miembros de una comunidad.

pudendum *L.* (*pl.* **pudenda**) pudendum, órganos genitales externos, esp. los femeninos.

puerile *a.* pueril, infantil.

puerperal *a.* puerperal, concerniente al puerperio.

puerperium *n.* puerperio. *V.* **post partum.**

pull *n.* tirón; *v.* tirar, halar, arrancar, sacar; **to** ___ **in** / tirar hacia adentro; **to** ___ **oneself together** / calmarse; **to** ___ **through** [*as in a sickness*] / recuperarse; **to** ___ **up one's knees** / levantar las rodillas.

pulley *n.* polea.

pulmonary, pulmonic *a.* pulmonar, pulmónico-a, rel. al pulmón o a la arteria pulmonar; ___ **alveolar proteinosis** / proteinosis alveolar ___; ___ **artery wedge pressure** / presión diferencial de la arteria ___; ___ **edema** / edema ___; ___ **embolism** / embolia ___; ___ **emphysema** / enfisema ___; ___ **insufficiency** / insuficiencia ___; ___ **stenosis** / estenosis ___; ___ **valve** / válvula ___; ___ **vein** / vena ___.

pulp *n.* pulpa. 1. parte blanda de un órgano; 2. quimo; 3. pulpa dental, parte central blanda de un diente.

pulsatile *a.* pulsátil, de pulsación rítmica.

pulsation *n.* pulsación, latido rítmico tal como el del corazón.

pulse *n.* pulso, dilatación arterial rítmica que gen. coincide con los latidos cardíacos; **alternating** ___ / ___ alternante; **bigeminal** ___ / ___ bigeminado; **dorsalis pedis** ___ / ___ de la arteria dorsal del pie; **femoral** ___ / ___ femoral; **filiform** ___ / ___ filiforme; **full** ___ / ___ lleno; **peripheral** ___ / ___ periférico; **radial** ___ / ___ radial; **regular** ___ / ___ regular; ___ **pressure** / presión del pulso, diferencia entre la presión sistólica y la diastólica.

pulverize *v.* pulverizar, reducir a polvo, hacer polvo.

pump *n.* bomba; *v.* bombear; **to** ___ **out** / ___ hacia afuera, sacar por bomba.

pumping *n.* bombeo; **heart** ___ / ___ del corazón; **stomach** ___ / ___ estomacal.

punch *n.* sacabocados, instrumento quirúrgico que se usa para perforar o cortar un disco o un segmento de tejido.

punctuate *n.* puntuar, acto de perforar un tejido con un instrumento afilado.

puncture *n.* punción, perforación; *v.* punzar, pinchar; agujerear.

puncture wound *n.* herida por perforación con un instrumento afilado.

pungent *a.* pungentivo-a, acre; penetrante.

pupil *n.* pupila, abertura contráctil del iris que da entrada a la luz.

pupillary *a.* pupilar, rel. a la pupila.

pure *a.* puro-a, sin contaminación.

purgative *n.* purgante, catártico que causa evacuación.

purge *n.* purga, medicamento o catártico; *v.* purgar, forzar la evacuación de los intestinos por medio de un purgante.

purification *n.* purificación, destilación.

purify *v.* purificar, destilar.

375

purple *n.* color púrpura; morado.

purpose *n.* propósito, intención.

purposeful *a.* intencional, con intención; determinado-a.

purpura *n.* púrpura, condición caracterizada por manchas rojizas o de color púrpura en la piel, debidas al escape de sangre a los tejidos; **thrombocytopenic** ___ / ___ trombocitopénica.

purulence *n.* purulencia, pus.

purulent *a.* purulento-a, que está supurando.

pus *n.* pus, excreción, fluido amarillento espeso que se forma por supuración.

push *n.* empujón; pujo; ___ **button** / botón de llamada; *v.* [*as to bear down*] pujar.

pustule *n.* pústula, costra, elevación pequeña de la piel que contiene pus; *pop.* postilla.

put *vi.* poner; **to** ___ **in** / poner dentro de, echar en, meter; **to** ___ **off** / aplazar, cancelar; **to** ___ **on** [*clothes*] / ponerse la ropa, vestirse; **to** ___ **out** [*light, fire*] / apagar; **to** ___ **together** / unir, juntar; **to** ___ **up with** / aguantar, soportar, tolerar.

putrefaction *n.* putrefacción, condición de ser pútrido-a, corrompido-a.

putrid *a.* pútrido-a, corrompido-a.

pyelogram *n.* pielograma, radiografía de la pelvis renal y uréter usando un medio de contraste.

pyelolithotomy *n. cirg.* pielolitotomía, incisión para extraer un cálculo de la pelvis renal.

pyelonephritis *n.* pielonefritis, infl. del riñón y de la pelvis renal.

pyeloplastia *n. cirg.* pieloplastia, operación de reparación plástica de la pelvis renal.

pyelostomy *n. cirg.* pielostomía, formación o establecimiento de una abertura en la pelvis renal para desviar la orina hacia el exterior.

pyelotomy *n. cirg.* pielotomía, incisión de la pelvis renal.

pyloric *a.* pilórico, rel. al píloro.

pyloroplasty *n. cirg.* piloroplastia, reparación del píloro.

pylorus *n.* píloro, abertura u orificio circular entre el estómago y el duodeno.

pyocyte *n.* piocito, corpúsculo de pus.

pyoderma *n.* pioderma, cualquier enfermedad de la piel que presenta supuración.

pyogenic *a.* piógeno-a, purulento-a.

pyorrhea *n.* piorrea, periodontitis.

pyramid *n.* pirámide, estructura semejante a un cono, tal como la médula oblongata.

pyrectic, pyretic *a.* pirético-a, rel. a la fiebre.

pyretolysis *n.* piretolisis. 1. reducción de fiebre; 2. proceso de curación que se acelera con la fiebre.

pyrexia *n.* pirexia, condición febril.

pyrogen *n.* pirógeno, sustancia que produce fiebre.

pyromania *n.* piromanía, obsesión con el fuego; manía incendiaria.

pyuria *n.* piuria, presencia de piocitos en la orina.

q. abbr. **quantity** / cantidad; **quaque** / cada.

quack *n.* charlatán, persona que pretende tener cualidades o conocimientos para curar enfermedades.

quackery *n.* curanderismo, charlatanería.

quadrangle *n.* cuadrángulo, figura geométrica formada por cuatro ángulos.

quadrant *n.* cuadrante, cuarta parte de un círculo.

quadratus *L.* quadratus. 1. músculo de cuatro lados; 2. figura de cuatro lados.

quadriceps *n.* cuadríceps, músculo de cuatro cabezas, extensor de la pierna.

quadriplegia *n.* cuadriplegia, parálisis de las cuatro extremidades.

quadruplet *a.* cuádruple, cada uno de los cuatro hijos nacidos en un parto múltiple.

quake *n.* [*earthquake*] temblor de tierra, terremoto sismo, estremecimiento; *v.* temblar.

qualification *n.* calificación; [*competence*] capacidad.

qualified *a.* competente, capaz.

qualify *v.* calificar; capacitar.

qualitative *a.* cualitativo-a, rel. a cualidad o clase.

qualitative test *n.* prueba cualitativa.

quality *n.* cualidad, propiedad.

quantitative test *n.* prueba cuantitativa.

quantity *n.* cantidad.

quantum *L.* quantum, unidad de energía.

quarantine *n.* cuarentena, período de cuarenta días durante los cuales se restringen las actividades de personas o animales para prevenir la propagación de una enfermedad contagiosa.

quarrel *n.* pelea, riña, disputa, querella; *v.* reñir, disputar, pelear.

quartan *a.* cuartana, que recurre cada cuatro días tal como la fiebre palúdica.

quarter *n.* cuarto, cuarta parte de un todo.

quash *v.* suprimir, sofocar.

quaver *n.* vibración, temblor; *v.,* vibrar, temblar.

queasy *a.* nauseabundo-a; ___ **stomach** / naúseas, asco.

queer *a.* raro-a, excéntrico-a; [*slang*] homosexual, invertido, maricón.

queilotomy *n.* queilotomía. *V.* **cheilotomy.**

quench *v.* extinguir, apagar; [*thirst*] saciar.

query *n.* pregunta; duda.

quest *n.* indagación, búsqueda, pesquisa.

question *n.* pregunta; cuestión, problema; *v.* interrogar, preguntar.

quick *a.* rápido-a, ligero-a, [*alert*] listo-a; ___-**frozen** / congelado-a al instante; -**ly** *adv.* pronto, rápidamente, al instante.

quicken *v.* acelerar; animar, avivar, estimular.

quickening *n.* 1. animación; 2. percepción por la madre del primer movimiento del feto en el útero.

quiescent *a.* quiescente, en estado de reposo; inactivo-a.

quiet *a.* quieto-a, sosegado-a, tranquilo-a; *v.* calmar, tranquilizar.

quinidine *n.* quinidina, alcaloide derivado de una *Cinchona* que se usa en irregularidades cardíacas.

quinine *n.* quinina, alcaloide que se obtiene de la corteza de una *Cinchona* usado como antiséptico y antipirético esp. en el tratamiento de paludismo, tifoidea y malaria.

quininism *n.* quininismo, chinchonismo, intoxicación de sales de quinina.

quintan *n.* quintana, fiebre recurrente cada cinco días.

quintuplet *a.* quíntuple, cada uno de los cinco hijos nacidos en un parto múltiple.

quit *v.* disistir, dejar, parar.

quota *n.* cuota.

quotient *n.* cuociente, cociente, cifra que resulta de una división; **achievement** ___ / ___ de realización; **blood** ___ / ___ sanguíneo; **growth** ___ / ___ de crecimiento; **intelligence** ___ / ___ de inteligencia.

R *abbr.* **radioactive** / radioactivo; **resistance** / resistencia; **respiration** / respiración; **response** / respuesta, reacción.

rabbi *n.* rabí, rabino.

rabbit *n.* conejo-a; ___ **test** / prueba del embarazo.

rabbit fever *n.* fiebre de conejo. *V.* **tularemia.**

rabid *a.* rabioso-a, rel. a la rabia o afectado por ella.

rabies *n.* rabia. *V.* **hydrophobia.**

race *n.* raza, grupo étnico diferenciado por características comunes heredadas.

racemose *a.* racimoso-a, racimado-a, similar a un racimo de uvas.

rachicentesis *n.* raquicentesis, punción lumbar.

rachiotomy *n. cirg.* raquiotomía. *V.* **laminectomy.**

rachis *n.* raquis, la columna vertebral.

rachitic *a.* raquítico-a. rel. al raquitismo; débil, endeble.

rachitism, rhachitis, rachitis *n.* raquitismo, enfermedad por deficiencia que afecta el desarrollo óseo en los adolescentes, causada por falta de calcio, fósforo y vitamina D.

racial *a.* racial, étnico-a, de la raza; ___ **prejudice** / prejuicio ___; ___ **immunity** / inmunidad ___, tipo de inmunidad natural de los miembros de una raza.

rad *n.* rad. 1. dosis de radiación absorbida; 2. rad, *abbr.* de radix, raíz.

radial *a.* radial. 1. rel. al hueso del radio; 2. que se expande en todas direcciones a partir de un centro.

radiant *a.* radiante, que emite rayos.

radiate *v.* irradiar, expandirse.

radiation *n.* radiación. 1. emisión de materiales o partículas radioactivas; 2. propagación de energía; 3. emisión de rayos desde un centro común; ___ **dosage** / dosis de ___; ___ **hazards** / riesgos y peligros causados por una ___; ___ **therapy** / radioterapia; **electromagnetic** ___ / ___ electromagnética; **infrared** ___ / ___ por rayos infrarrojos; **ionizing** ___ / ___ ionizante; **ultraviolet** ___ / ___ de rayos ultravioleta.

radiation sickness *n.* enfermedad por radiación causada por exposición a rayos X o materiales radioactivos.

radical *n. gr.* raíz de una palabra; *a.* radical, dirigido a erradicar la raíz de una enfermedad o de todo tejido enfermo; ___ **treatment** / tratamiento ___.

radicle *n.* radícula, estructura semejante a una raíz.

radicular *a.* radical, rel. a la raíz u origen.

radiculectomy *n. cirg.* radiculectomía, excisión de la raíz de un nervio, esp. de la raíz de un nervio espinal.

radiculitis *n.* radiculitis, infl. de la raíz de un nervio.

radiculomyelopathy *n.* radiculomielopatía, enfermedad que afecta la médula espinal y la raíz de los nervios espinales.

radiculoneuritis, Guillain-Barré syndrome *n.* radiculoneuritis, síndrome de Guillain-Barré, infl. de las raíces de los nervios espinales.

radiculoneuropathy *n.* radiculoneuropatía, condición patológica de los nervios y sus raíces.

radiculopathy *n.* radiculopatía, cualquier enfermedad de las raíces de los nervios espinales.

radioactive *a.* radiactivo-a, rel. a la radiactividad o que la posee.

radioactive iodine excretion test *n.* prueba radiactiva del yodo, evaluación de la función de la tiroides por medio del uso de yodo radiactivo.

radioactivity *n.* radiactividad, propiedad de ciertos elementos de producir radiaciones.

radiobiology *n.* radiobiología, estudio del efecto de la radiactividad en tejidos vivos.

radiocarbon *n.* carbono radiactivo.

radiocardiography *n.* radiocardiografía, registro gráfico de una sustancia radioactiva durante su paso a través del corazón.

radiocurable *a.* radiocurable, que se puede curar por medio de radioterapia.

radiodermatitis *n.* radiodermatitis, dermatitis causada por la exposición a radiaciones.

radioelement *n.* radioelemento, cualquier elemento que tiene propiedades radiactivas.

radiography *n.* radiografía, uso de rayos X para producir imágenes en placas o en una pantalla fluorescente.

radioimmunity *n.* radioinmunidad, disminución de la sensibilidad a las radiaciones.

radioimmunoassay *n.* radioinmunoensayo.

radioisotope *n.* radioisótopo, isótopo radioactivo.

radiologic *a.* radiológico-a, rel. a la radiología.

radiologist *n.* radiólogo-a, especialista en radiología.

radiology *n.* radiología, ciencia que trata de los rayos X o rayos que provienen de sustancias radiactivas, esp. para uso médico.

radiolucent *a.* radiolúcido-a, que permite el paso de la mayor parte de rayos X.

radionecrosis *n.* radionecrosis, desintegración de tejidos por radiación.

radionuclear venography *n.* venografía radionuclear, estudio de las venas por medio de rayos gamma.

radionuclide imaging *n. V.* **scintigraphy.**

radiopaque *a.* radiopaco-a, que no deja pasar rayos X u otra forma de radiación; ___ **dye** / colorante ___.

radiopharmaceutical agents *n.* radiofármacos, drogas radiactivas usades en el tratamiento y diagnóstico de enfermedades.

radioreceptor *n.* radiorreceptor, receptor que recibe energía radiante como la de los rayos X, de la luz o del calor.

radioresistance *n.* radiorresistencia, resistencia a los efectos de una radiación.

radioresistant *a.* radiorresistente, que tiene la propiedad de resistir efectos radiactivos.

radioscopy *n.* radioscopía. *V.* **fluoroscopy.**

radiosensitive *a.* radiosensitivo-a, que es afectado por o que responde a un tratamiento de radiación.

radiotherapy *n.* radioterapia, tratamiento de una enfermedad por medio de rayos X o por otras sustancias radiactivas.

radish *n.* rábano.

radium *L.* radium, radio, elemento metálico radiactivo y fluorescente usado en algunas de sus variaciones en el tratamiento de tumores malignos; ___ **needle** / aguja de radio, divisa en forma de aguja que contiene radio usada en radioterapia.

radium therapy *n.* radioterapia, terapia con el uso de radio.

radius *n.* radio. 1. hueso largo del antebrazo; 2. línea recta que une el centro y cualquier punto de la circunferencia.

radon *n.* radón, elemento radiactivo gaseoso.

rage *n.* rabia, ira, cólera.

rain *n.* lluvia; *v.* llover.

raise *v.* levantar; [*increase*] aumentar, subir.

raisin *n.* pasa, uva seca.

rale *n.* estertor, sonido anormal originado en el pulmón que se percibe durante la auscultación; **coarse** ___ / ___ áspero; **crackling** ___ / ___ crujiente; **crepitant** ___ / ___ crepitante; **dry** ___ / ___ seco; **moist** ___ / ___ húmedo.

rambling *a.* sin orden ni concierto.

ramification *n.* ramificación, distribución en ramas.

ramify *v.* ramificar; ramificarse.

ramus *n.* (*pl.* **rami**) rama, bifurcación, división.

rancid *a.* rancio-a, de olor desagradable; que denota descomposición.

rancor *n.* rencor, resentimiento.

random control test *n.* prueba de control sin método.

range *n.* escala de diferenciación; ___ **of motion** / alcance de movimiento.

ranine *n.* ranino-a, rel. a la ránula o parte inferior de la lengua.

ranula *n.* ránula, quiste situado debajo de la lengua causado por la obstrucción de un canal glandular.

rape *n.* violación; *v.* violar, abusar sexualmente.

raphe *n.* rafe, línea de unión de dos mitades simétricas de una estructura tal como la lengua.

rapid *a.* rápido-a, veloz.

rapidity *n.* rapidez, velocidad.

rapport *n.* relación armoniosa.

raptus *L.* raptus, arrebato, ataque súbito violento.

rare *a.* raro-a; único-a; **-ly** *adv.* raramente, casi nunca.

rash, rasche *Fr. n.* rasche, erupción; **diaper** ___ / eritema de los pañales; **heat** ___ / salpullido; **hemorrhagic** ___ / ___ hemorrágica; **maculopapular** ___ / ___ maculopapular; **papular** ___ / ___ papular; **squamous** ___ / ___ escamosa.

raspberry *n.* frambuesa; ___ **mark** / marca de nacimiento de color rosado.

rasura *n.* rasura, raspadura, limadura.

rat *n.* rata.

rate *n.* índice, proporción; tasa; **birth** ___ / ___ de natalidad; **death** ___ / ___ de mortalidad; **at any** ___ / de todos modos; no obstante; **at the** ___ **of** / a razón de; **intrinsic** ___ / frecuencia intrínseca; *v.* estimar, evaluar, tasar.

rather *adv.* algo, un tanto; bastante; más bien.

ratify *v.* ratificar, confirmar.

rating *n.* evaluación; clasificación, determinación.

ratio *L.* (*pl.* **ratios**.) relación, proporción, razón, expresión de la cantidad de una sustancia en relación con otra.

ration *n.* ración, porción alimenticia.

rational *a.* racional, cuerdo-a, basado-a en la razón.

rationalization *n. psic.* racionalización, mecanismo de defensa por el cual se justifica la conducta o actividades propias con explicaciones que aunque razonables no se ajustan a la realidad.

rattlesnake *n.* serpiente de cascabel; ___ **poison** / veneno de la ___.

Rauwolfia serpentina *n. Rauwolfia serpentina*, planta tropical de la cual se obtiene la reserpina, extracto que se usa en el tratamiento de hipertensión y en algunos casos de trastornos mentales.

rave *v.* delirar, hablar irracionalmente.

raw *a.* crudo-a; [*skin*] en carne viva; [*fruit*] sin madurar; [*material*] materia prima.

ray *n.* rayo.

Raynaud's disease *n.* síndrome de Raynaud. *V.* **acrocyanosis.**

Raynaud's phenomenon *n.* fenómeno de Raynaud, síntomas asociados con el síndrome de Raynaud.

razor *n.* navaja, cuchilla.

reabsorb *v.* reabsorber.

reach *n.* alcance; **within** ___ / al ___ de; *v.* alcanzar, obtener.

react *v.* reaccionar, responder a un estímulo.

reaction *n.* reacción, respuesta; **allergic** ___ / ___ alérgica; **anaphylactic** ___ / ___ anafiláctica; **anxiety** ___ / ___ de ansiedad; **chain** ___ / ___ en cadena; **conversion** ___ / ___ de conversión; **immune** ___ / ___ inmune; **runaway** ___ / ___ de escape.

reactivate *v.* reactivar, volver a activar.

reactivation *n.* reactivación, el acto de volver a activar.

reactive *a.* reactivo-a, que tiene la propiedad de reaccionar o de causar una reacción.

379

reactive depression n. *psic.* reacción depresiva psicótica a consecuencia de una experiencia traumática.

reactivity n. reactividad, manifestación de una reacción.

read vi. leer; ___ **the letters** / Lea, lee las letras.

reader n. lector, lectora.

reading n. lectura; ___ **glasses** / anteojos, espejuelos, gafas para leer; ___ **disorders** / trastornos o impedimentos en la ___.

ready a. listo-a, preparado-a; v. **to get** ___ / prepararse, arreglarse.

reaffirm v. reafirmar, asegurar.

reagent n. reactivo, agente que produce una reacción.

reagin n. reagina, anticuerpo usado en el tratamiento de alergias que estimula la producción de histamina.

real a. real, verdadero-a, cierto-a; **-ly** adv. realmente, verdaderamente, ciertamente.

realistic a. verdadero-a, realista.

reality n. realidad.

reality principle n. principio de realidad, método de orientación del paciente hacia el mundo externo para provocar el reconocimiento de objetos y actividades olvidados, esp. dirigido a personas severamente desorientadas.

reality therapy n. terapéutica por realidad, método por el que se enfrenta al paciente con la realidad ayudándolo a aceptarla.

realize v. realizar; llevar a cabo; darse cuenta de.

reanimate v. reanimar, revivir.

rear a. posterior, trasero-a.

reason n. razón; justificación; v. razonar; justificar.

reasonable a. razonable; justificado-a; sensato-a; ___ **care** / cuidado justificado; ___ **charge** / honorarios ___-s; ___ **cost** / costo ___.

reassessment n. estimado; reevaluación; ___ **of the case** / reevaluación del caso.

reassure v. asegurar, alentar, restablecer la confianza.

reawaken v. volver a despertar.

rebel n. rebelde.

rebellion n. rebelión.

rebound n. rebote, regreso a una condición previa después que el estímulo inicial se suprime; v. rebotar, repercutir.

rebound phenomenon n. fenómeno de rebote, movimiento intensificado de una parte hacia adelante cuando se elimina la fuerza inicial contra la cual ésta hacía resistencia.

recalcification n. recalcificación, restauración de compuestos de calcio en los tejidos.

recall v. recordar; reclamar; hacer volver; acordarse de.

receipt n. recibo, carta de pago.

receive v. recibir, admitir; acoger; aceptar.

recent a. reciente; moderno; nuevo-a; **-ly** adv. recientemente, hace poco tiempo.

receptaculum L. (*pl.* **receptacula**) receptaculum, receptáculo, recipiente.

receptionist n. recepcionista.

receptive a. receptivo-a, acogedor-a.

receptor n. receptor, terminación nerviosa que recibe un estímulo y lo transmite a otros nervios; **auditory** ___ / ___ auditivo; **contact** ___ / ___ de contacto; **proprioceptive** ___ / ___ propioceptivo; **sensory** ___ / ___ sensorial; **taste** ___ / ___ gustativo; **temperature** ___ / ___ de temperatura.

recess n. suspensión; cavidad, espacio vacío.

recession n. recesión, retirada, retroceso patológico de tejidos tal como la retracción de la encía.

recessive a. recesivo-a. 1. que tiende a retraerse; 2. en genética, rel. al gene que permanece latente.

recidivism n. recidiva, reincidencia, tendencia a recaer en una condición, enfermedad o síntoma previo.

recipe n. receta, prescripción.

recipient n. 1. receptor; vasija; recipiente; 2. persona que recibe una transfusión, un implante de tejido o un órgano de un donante.

reciprocal a. recíproco-a, mutuo-a.

reciprocity n. reciprocidad.

reckless a. descuidado-a, imprudente.

recklessness n. descuido; indiferencia; imprudencia; temeridad.

reclaim v. reclamar.

reclamation n. reclamación.

recline n. reclinación; v. reclinar, inclinar; recostarse.

reclining a. recostado-a, inclinado-a.

recognition n. reconocimiento, estado de ser reconocido.

recognize v. reconocer; admitir.

recollection n. recuerdo, memoria.

recombination n. recombinación.

recommend v. recomendar; aconsejar.

recommendation n. recomendación.

recompense n. recompensa, compensación, reparación.

recompression n. recompresión, vuelta a la presión ambiental normal.

reconcile v. reconciliar; reconciliarse; resignarse, conformarse.

reconciliation n. reconciliación, conformidad.

reconsider v. recapacitar; volver a considerar.

reconstitution n. reconstitución, restitución de un tejido a la forma inicial.

reconstruct v. reconstruir, reparar, restablecer.

reconstruction v. reconstrucción.

record n. [*trace of an instrument*] registro; [*medical history*] historia clínica, expediente; informe; anotación; evidencia; v. registrar, inscribir; [*on tape*] grabar; **to go on** ___ / expresar públicamente; **off the** ___ / confidencialmente.

recorder n. anotador-a; archivero-a; registrador-a; **tape** ___ / grabador-a.

recoup v. recuperar; recobrar; recuperarse, recobrarse; restablecerse.

recourse n. recurso, auxilio.

recover u. recobrar, recuperar, restablecer; restablecerse, recobrarse, reponerse.

recovery n. recuperación, restablecimiento, recobro, mejoría; **past** ___ / sin remedio, sin cura; ___ **room** / sala de ___.

recreation n. recreo, pasatiempo, entretenimiento.

recrudescence n. recrudescencia, relapso, reaparición de síntomas.

rectal a. rectal, del recto, rel. al recto.

rectification n. rectificación, corrección; enmienda.

rectify u. rectificar, corregir, enmendar.

rectocele n. rectocele, hernia del recto con protrusión en la vagina.

rectosigmoid a. rectosigmoide, rel. al sigmoide y al recto.

rectovaginal a. rectovaginal, rel. a la vagina y el recto.

rectovesical a. rectovesical, rel. al recto y la vejiga.

rectum n. recto, la porción distal del intestino grueso que se extiende de la flexura sigmoidea al ano.

rectus L. (pl. **recti**) músculo recto; ___ **muscles** / músculos ___, grupo de músculos rectos tales como los situados alrededor del ojo y en la pared abdominal.

recumbent a. yacente, acostado-a, recostado-a, reclinado-a, recumbente; acostado-a de espaldas ___ **position** / posición ___.

recuperate u. recuperar, recobrar las fuerzas; recuperarse, reponerse.

recuperation n. recuperación, restablecimiento.

recur u. repetir, volver a ocurrir; recaer, repetirse.

recurrence n. recidiva. 1. reaparición de síntomas después de una remisión; 2. relapso, recaída.

recurrent a. recurrente, repetido-a.

red n. [color] rojo; ___ **cell** / glóbulo rojo, hematíe, eritrocito; **Congo** ___ / ___ Congo; **scarlet** ___ / ___ escarlata.

redden u. enrojecer, teñir de rojo.

reddish a. rojizo-a, enrojecido-a.

red-eyed a. de ojos enrojecidos; con los ojos inyectados.

red-faced a. ruborizado-a, con la cara encendida.

redhead a. pelirrojo-a.

red-hot a. muy caliente, candente.

redness n. enrojecimiento.

redress u. volver a vendar; poner un nuevo vendaje; remediar.

reduce u. reducir, rebajar; disminuir. 1. restaurar a la situación normal, tal como un hueso fracturado o dislocado; 2. disminuir la potencia al dar hidrógeno o quitarle oxígeno a un compuesto; 3. bajar de peso.

reducible a. reducible, susceptible a la reducción.

reducing exercises n. pl. ejercicios para adelgazar, ejercicios para bajar de peso.

reductase n. reductasa, enzima que actúa como catalítico en el proceso de reducción.

reduction n. reducción, disminución, acción de reducir.

reductor n. reductor, agente que causa reducción en otras sustancias.

reeducation n. reeducación, enseñanza con entrenamiento para recobrar funciones motoras o mentales.

refer u. referir, atribuir, asignar, referirse a.

reference n. referencia; ___ **values** / valores de ___.

referral n. recomendación; remisión; ___ **and consultation** / ___ y consulta.

refill n. repuesto; repetición; relleno; repetición de una receta; u. reponer; repetir; rellenar.

refine u. refinar, purificar.

reflect u. reflejar; **to** ___ **upon** / reflexionar.

reflection n. reflexión. 1. acomodamiento o vuelta hacia atrás tal como una membrana que después de llegar a la superficie de un órgano se repliega sobre sí misma; 2. rechazo de la luz u otra forma de energía radiante de una superficie; 3. introspección.

reflex n. reflejo, respuesta motora involuntaria a un estímulo; **Achilles tendon** ___ / ___ del tendón de Aquiles; ___ **action** / acto, acción ___; ___ **arch** / arco ___; **behavior** ___ / ___ adquirido; **chain** ___ / ___ en cadena; **conditioned** ___ / ___ condicionado; **instinctive** ___ / ___ instintivo; **patellar** ___ / ___ patelar o rotuliano; **radial** ___ / ___ radial; **rectal** ___ / ___ rectal; **stretch** ___ / ___ de estiramiento; **unconditioned** ___ / ___ no condicionado; **vagal** ___ / ___ vagal.

reflexogenic n. reflexógeno, agente que causa un reflejo.

reflux n. reflujo, flujo retrógrado.

reform n. reforma, cambio; u. reformar, cambiar; reformarse.

refract u. refractar, desviar. 1. cambiar una dirección tal como la de un rayo de luz al pasar de un medio a otro de diferente densidad; 2. rectificar anormalidades de refracción en el ojo y corregirlas.

refraction n. refracción, acto de refractar; **ocular** ___ / ___ ocular.

refractivity n. refractividad, habilidad de refractar.

refractory a. refractario-a. 1. resistente a un tratamiento; 2. que no responde a un estímulo.

refresh u. refrescar; renovar, revivir; refrescarse; renovarse.

refreshing a. refrescante.

refreshment n. refresco; refrigerio.

refrigerant a. refrigerante; antipirético-a.

refrigerate u. refrigerar, mantener en el frío.

refrigeration n. refrigeración, reducción del calor a una temperatura fría por medios externos.

refringent *a.* refringente, rel. a la refracción o que la causa.

refuge *n.* refugio; asilo; *v.* to take ___ / refugiarse.

refugee *n.* refugiado-a.

refuse *n.* desecho, basura; desperdicios.

regain *v.* recuperar, recobrar; to ___ consciousness / recobrar el conocimiento.

regard *n.* respeto, consideración; in ___ to / respecto a; regards / recuerdos.

regarding *prep.* respecto a.

regenerate *v.* regenerar.

regeneration *n.* regeneración, restauración, renovación.

regime *n.* régimen, regla, plan, esp. en referencia a una dieta o ejercicio físico.

region *n.* región, parte del cuerpo más o menos delimitada.

regional *a.* regional; ___ medical programs / programas médicos ___ -es.

registration *n.* registro, inscripción; [*courses*] matrícula.

regression *n.* regresión, retrogresión. 1. vuelta a una condición anterior; 2. apaciguamiento de síntomas o de un proceso patológico.

regret *n.* sentimiento de pesar; remordimiento; *v.* sentir, lamentar deplorar; I ___ to tell you / Siento decirle, decirte.

regrettable *a.* lamentable; infortunado-a.

regular *a.* regular, común, -ly *adv.* regularmente, con regularidad.

regularity *n.* regularidad, normalidad.

regulate *v.* regular, ordenar.

regulation *n.* regulación, norma o regla.

regulator *n.* regulador-a.

regurgitant *a.* regurgitante, rel. a la regurgitación.

regurgitate *v.* regurgitar.

regurgitation *n.* regurgitación. 1. acto de devolver o expulsar la comida de la boca; 2. flujo retrógrado de la sangre a través de una válvula defectuosa del corazón; aortic ___ / ___ aórtica; mitral ___ / ___ mitral.

rehabilitate *v.* rehabilitar, ayudar a recobrar funciones normales por medio de métodos terapéuticos.

rehabilitation *n.* rehabilitación, acto de rehabilitar.

rehabilitee *n., a.* rehabilitado-a.

rehydration *n.* rehidratación, restablecimiento del balance hídrico del cuerpo.

reimplantation *n.* reimplantación. 1. restauración de un tejido o parte; 2. restitución de un óvulo al útero después de extraerlo y fecundarlo *in vitro*.

reinfection *n.* reinfección, infección subsecuente por el mismo microorganismo.

reinforce *v.* reforzar; fortalecer.

reinfusion *n.* reinfusión, reinyección de suero sanguíneo o líquido cefalorraquídeo.

reinnervation *n.* reinervación, injerto de un nervio para restaurar la función de un músculo.

reinoculation *n.* reinoculación, inoculación subsecuente con el mismo microorganismo.

reject *n.* rechazar, rehusar.

rejection *n.* rechazo, reacción inmunológica de incompatibilidad a células de tejidos transplantados; acute ___ / ___ agudo; chronic ___ / ___ crónico; hyperacute ___ / ___ hiperagudo.

rejuvenate *v.* rejuvenecer; rejuvenecerse.

rejuvenescense *n.* rejuvenecimiento.

relapse *n.* recidiva, recaída, reincidencia; *v.* volver a sufrir una enfermedad o los síntomas de ésta después de cierta mejoría.

relapsing fever *n.* fiebre recurrente.

relate *v.* relacionar; establecer una relación; relacionarse.

related *a.* relacionado-a; emparentado-a.

relation *n.* relación; comparación.

relationship *n.* relación, parentesco, lazo familiar.

relative *n.* pariente, familiar; *a.* relativo-a; *gr.* pronombre relativo.

relax *v.* relajar el cuerpo, reducir tensión; relajarse; aflojar; descansar.

relaxant *n.* relajante, tranquilizante; droga que reduce la tensión.

relaxation *n.* relajación, acto de relajar o de relajarse; reposo, descanso.

relaxed *a.* relajado-a.

release *n.* información; liberación; *v.* soltar, librar, desprender; [*to inform*] informar, dar a conocer.

releasing hormone *n.* hormona estimulante.

reliability *n.* confiabilidad; calidad de confianza; precisión.

reliable *a.* [*person*] formal, responsable; seguro-a.

relief *n.* alivio, mejoría; ayuda, auxilio; What a ___! / ¡Ay, qué ___ !; *v.* to be on social ___ / recibir asistencia social.

relieve *v.* [*pain*] aliviar, mejorar.

religion *n.* religión.

religious *a.* religioso-a.

reluctance *n.* renuencia, aversión, disgusto.

reluctant *a.* renuente; resistente; contrario-a.

rely *v.* depender, contar con, confiar en.

remain *v.* permanecer; to ___ in bed / guardar cama.

remainder *n.* resto, residuo.

remains *n. pl.* restos, despojos.

remake *v.* rehacer.

remark *n.* observación, nota, advertencia; *v.* observar, indicar, advertir.

remarkable *a.* extraordinario-a, notable.

remedial *a.* remediador-a, reparador-a, curativo-a.

remedy *n.* remedio, cura, medicamento; *v.* remediar, curar.

remember *v.* recordar, acordarse; ___ correctly! / ¡Acuérdese, acuérdate bien!; Don't you ___? / ¿No se acuerda?, ¿no te acuerdas?

remind *v.* recordar, advertir.

remineralization *n.* remineralización, reemplazo de minerales perdidos en el cuerpo.

reminisce *v.* recordar; divagar.

reminiscense *n.* memoria, recordatorio, reminiscencia.

remission *n.* remisión. 1. disminución o cesación de los síntomas de una enfermedad; 2. período de tiempo durante el cual los síntomas de una enfermedad disminuyen.

remittent *a.* remitente, que se repite a intervalos.

remorse *n.* remordimiento.

remote *a.* remoto-a, distante.

removable *a.* separable, mudable.

removal *n.* extirpación, remoción.

remove *v.* sacar; quitar, extraer; extirpar.

renal *a.* renal, rel. a o semejante al riñón; ___ **clearance test** / prueba de aclaramiento o depuración ___; ___ **failure, acute** / insuficiencia ___ aguda; ___ **insufficiency** / insuficienca ___; ___ **papillary necrosis** / necrosis papilar ___; ___ **pelvis** / pelvis ___; ___ **transplantation** / transplante ___.

renew *v.* renovar.

renin *n.* renina, enzima segregado por el riñón que interviene en la regulación de la presión arterial.

renogram *n.* renograma, proceso de monitoreo del índice de eliminación sanguínea a través del riñón usando una sustancia radiactiva inyectada previamente.

renovate *v.* reformar, renovar.

reopen *v.* volver a abrir, abrir de nuevo.

repair *n.* reparación, restauración; *v.* reparar, restaurar.

repeat *n.* repetir, reiterar.

repellent *a.* repelente.

repercussion *n.* repercusión. 1. penetración o dispersión de una inflamación, tumor o erupción; 2. peloteo.

replace *v.* reemplazar, reponer, substituir.

replacement *n.* reemplazo, substitución, repuesto.

replete *a.* repleto-a, lleno-a en exceso.

replication *n.* reproducción, duplicación.

reply *n.* contestación, respuesta; *v.* contestar, responder.

repolarization *n.* repolarización, restablecimiento de la polarización de una célula o de una fibra nerviosa o muscular después de su depolarización.

report *n.* informe, reporte; *v.* informar, reportar.

reprehensible *a.* reprensible, reprobable, censurable.

repress *v.* reprimir.

repression *n.* represión. 1. inhibición de una acción; 2. *psic.* mecanismo de defensa por el que se eliminan del campo de la conciencia deseos e impulsos en conflicto.

reproduce *v.* reproducir; reproducirse.

reproducer *n.* reproductor.

reproduction *n.* reproducción; **sexual** ___ / ___ sexual.

reproductive *a.* reproductivo-a, rel. a la reproducción.

repudiate *v.* repudiar, repeler.

repugnant *a.* repugnante, repulsivo-a.

repulsion *n.* repulsión, aversión, repugnancia.

repulsive *a.* repulsivo-a, chocante.

reputation *n.* reputación, fama, nombre.

reputed *a.* reputado-a, distinguido-a, de buena fama.

request *n.* petición, encargo; solicitud; *v.* pedir, hacer una petición, [*of supplies*] encargar.

require *v.* requerir, solicitar.

required *a.* requerido-a, necesario-a; mandatorio-a.

requirement *n.* requerimiento.

requisite *n.* requisito.

rescind *v.* rescindir, anular; terminar.

rescue *v.* salvar, rescatar, librar; ___ **method** / método de ___, de salvamento.

research *n.* investigación, indagación, pesquisa; *v.* investigar, indagar, hacer investigaciones.

resect *n.* resecar. 1. cortar una porción de un órgano o tejido; 2. hacer una resección.

resection *n.* resección, extirpación de una porción de órgano o tejido; **bloc** ___ / ___ en bloque; **gastric** ___ / ___ gástrica; **transurethral** ___ / ___ transuretral; **wedge** ___ / ___ en cuña.

resectoscope *n.* resectoscopio, instrumento quirúrgico provisto de un electrodo cortante como el que se usa para la resección de la próstata a través de la uretra.

resectoscopy *n.* resectoscopía, resección de la próstata con un resectoscopio.

resemblance *n.* semejanza, parecido.

resemble *v.* tener semejanza; parecerse a.

resentment *n.* resentimiento, rencor.

reserpine *n.* reserpina, derivado de la *Rauwolfia serpentina* que se usa principalmente en el tratamiento de la hipertensión y de desórdenes emocionales.

reservation *n.* reservación, reserva.

reserve *n.* reserva, sustancia, objeto o idea que se guarda para uso futuro; *v.* reservar; conservar, guardar.

reserved *a.* reservado-a, [*personality*] reservado-a, callado-a.

reside *v.* residir, vivir.

residency *n.* residencia, período de entrenamiento médico especializado que se hace gen. en un hospital.

resident *n.* médico-a residente, que cursa una residencia.

residual *a.* residual, restante, remanente; ___ **function** / función ___; ___ **urine** / orina ___.

residue *n.* residuo; ___ **diet, high** / dieta de ___ alto; ___ **diet, low** / dieta de ___ bajo.

resign *v.* renunciar, resignar, desistir; resignarse.

resilience *n.* elasticidad. *V.* **elasticity.**

resilient *a.* elástico-a.

resin *a.* resina, sustancia vegetal insoluble en el

agua aunque soluble en alcohol y éter que tiene una variedad de usos medicinales y dentales.

res ipsa loquitur *L.* res ipsa loquitor, evidente, que habla por sí mismo.

resist *v.* resistir; rechazar.

resistance *n.* resistencia, oposición; capacidad de un organismo para resistir efectos dañinos; **initial** ___ / ___ inicial; **acquired** ___ / ___ adquirida; **peripheral** ___ / ___ periférica; *v.* **to offer** ___ / oponerse; hacer resistencia.

resistant *a.* resistente; **fast** ___ / resistencia a un colorante.

resolute *a.* resuelto-a, determinado-a.

resolution *n.* resolución. 1. terminación de un proceso inflamatorio; 2. habilidad de distinguir detalles pequeños y sutiles tal como se hace a través de un microscopio; 3. descomposición sin supuración.

resolve *v.* resolver. 1. encontrar una solución; 2. descomponer, analizar, separar en componentes.

resonance *n.* resonancia, capacidad de aumentar la intensidad de un sonido; **normal** ___ / ___ normal; **vesicular** ___ / ___ vesicular; **vocal** ___ / ___ vocal.

resonant *a.* resonante, que da un sonido vibrante a la percusión.

resorcinol *n.* resorcinol, agente usado en el tratamiento de acné y otras dermatosis.

resorption *n.* resorción, pérdida total o parcial de un proceso, tejido o exudado por resultado de reacciones bioquímicas tales como lisis y absorción.

resort *n.* recurso; **health** ___ / lugar de recuperación física; **the last** ___ / el último ___; *v.* acudir, pedir ayuda, recurrir.

resource *n.* recurso, medio.

respect *n.* respeto, consideración; *v.* respetar, considerar.

respectable *a.* respetable, acreditado-a.

respiration *n.* respiración, proceso respiratorio; **abdominal** ___ / ___ abdominal; **aerobic** ___ / ___ aeróbica; **accelerated** ___ / ___ acelerada; **anaerobic** ___ / ___ anaeróbica; **diaphragmatic** ___ / ___ diafragmática; **air hunger, gasping** ___ / ___ jadeante; **labored** ___ / ___ laboriosa.

respirator *n.* respirador, aparato para purificar el aire que se inhala o para producir respiración artificial; **chest** ___ / ___ torácico.

respiratory *a.* respiratorio-a, rel. a la respiración; ___ **care unit** / unidad de cuidado ___; ___ **quotient** / cociente ___; ___ **distress syndrome** / síndrome de dificultad ___; ___ **failure, acute** / insuficiencia ___ aguda; ___ **failure, chronic** / insuficiencia ___ crónica; ___ **function tests** / pruebas de función ___; ___ **system** / sistema ___; ___ **tract infections and diseases** / infecciones y enfermedades de las vías ___ -s.

respiratory center *n.* centro respiratorio, área

en la médula oblongata que regula los movimientos respiratorios.

response *n.* respuesta. 1. reacción o cambio de un órgano o parte a un estímulo; **immune** ___ / ___ inmune; 2. reacción de un paciente a un tratamiento.

responsibility *n.* responsabilidad.

responsible *a.* responsable.

rest *n.* descanso, reposo; residuo, resto; ___ **cure** / cura de reposo; *v.* decansar, reposar.

restenosis *n.* reestenosis, recurrencia de estenosis después de cirugía correctiva.

restful *a.* tranquilo-a, quieto-a.

resting *a.* inactivo-a, en reposo, en estado de descanso.

restitutio ad integrum *L.* restitutio ad integrum, recuperación total de la salud.

restoration *n.* restauración, restitución, restablecimiento, acción de restituir algo a su estado original.

restorative *n.* restaurativo, agente que estimula la restauración.

restore *v.* restituir, restablecer.

restraint *n.* restricción; confinamiento; ___ **in bed** / ___ en cama; **mechanical** ___ / ___ mecánica; **medicinal** ___ / ___ con uso de medicamentos.

restrict *v.* restringir, confinar.

restricted *a.* limitado-a, confinado; ___ **area** / área ___.

result *n.* resultado, conclusión.

resuscitate *v.* resucitar; reanimar.

resuscitation *n.* resucitación. 1. devolver la vida; reanimar el corazón; 2. respiración artificial.

resuscitator *n.* resucitador, aparato automático de asistencia respiratoria.

retain *v.* retener, guardar; quedarse con.

retainer *n.* [*dentistry*] aro, freno de retención.

retardate *a.* retardado-a, retrasado-a, atrasado-a.

retardation *n.* retraso, atraso, retardo anormal de una función motora o mental; **psychomotor** ___ / ___ psicomotor; *V.* **mental retardation.**

retch *n.* arcada, basca, contracciones abdominales espasmódicas que preceden al vómito.

rete *L.* (*pl.* retia) rete; red. *V.* **network.**

retention *n.* retención, conservación; **fluid** ___ / ___ de líquido; **gastric** ___ / ___ gástrica; ___ **enema** / enema de ___; **urinary** ___ / ___ urinaria.

reticular *a.* reticular, retiforme, en forma de red.

reticulation *n.* reticulación, disposición reticular.

reticulocyte *n.* reticulocito, célula roja inmadura, eritrocito en red o gránulos que aparece durante la regeneración de la sangre.

reticulocytopenia, reticulosis *n.* reticulocitopenia, reticulosis, disminución anormal del número de reticulocitos en la sangre.

reticulocytosis *n.* reticulocitosis, aumento en el número de reticulocitos.

reticuloendothelial system *n.* sistema reticuloendotelial, red de células fagocíticas (excepto leucocitos circulantes) esparcidas por todo el cuerpo que intervienen en procesos tales como la formación de células sanguíneas, destrucción de grasas, eliminación de células gastadas y restauración de tejidos que son participantes esenciales en el proceso inmunológico del organismo.

reticuloendothelioma *n.* reticuloendotelioma, tumor del sistema reticuloendotelial.

reticuloendothelium *n.* reticuloendotelio, tejido del sistema reticuloendotelial.

reticulohistiocytoma *n.* reticulohistiocitoma, agregación de células granulares y gigantes.

reticulopenia *n.* reticulopenia. *V.* **reticulocytopenia.**

reticulum *n.* retículo. 1. red de nervios y vasos sanguíneos; 2. tejido reticular.

Retin-A *n.* Retin-A, nombre comercial del ácido retinoico, medicamento usado en el tratamiento de acné.

retina *n.* retina, la capa más interna del ojo que recibe imágenes y transmite impulsos visuales al cerebro; **detachment of the ___** / desprendimiento de la ___.

retinal *a.* de la retina, retiniano-a; rel. a la retina; **___ degeneration** / deterioro retiniano, deterioración retiniana; **___ perforation** / perforación ___.

retinitis *n.* retinitis, infl. de la retina.

retinoblastoma *n.* retinoblastoma, tumor maligno de la retina gen. hereditario.

retinol *n.* retinol, vitamina A$_1$.

retinopathy *n.* retinopatía, cualquier condición anormal de la retina.

retinoscopy *n.* retinoscopía, determinación y evaluación de errores visuales de refracción.

retinosis *n.* retinosis, proceso degenerativo de la retina.

retire *v.* retirar; [*from work*] retirarse, jubilarse; [*to bed*] irse a acostar.

retired *a. pp.* de **to retire,** retirado-a; [*from work*] retirado-a, jubilado-a; [*withdrawn*] reservado-a; retirado-a; [*secluded*] alejado-a, apartado-a.

retiree *n.* jubilado-a; retirado-a.

retract *v.* retraer, retractar; retraerse, volverse hacia atrás.

retractile *a.* retráctil, retractable.

retraction *n.* retracción, encogimiento, contracción; acto de echarse hacia atrás; **clot ___** / ___ del coágulo; **uterine ___** / ___ uterina.

retractor *n.* retractor. 1. instrumento para separar los bordes de una herida; 2. tipo de músculo que retrae una parte u órgano.

retrieval *n.* recuperación de algo.

retroaction *n.* retroacción, acción retroactiva.

retroactive *a.* retroactivo-a, de acción retroactiva.

retroauricular *a.* retroauricular, rel. a o situado detrás de la oreja o aurícula.

retrocecal *a.* retrocecal, rel. a o situado detrás del ciego.

retrocession *n.* retroceso.

retroflexion *n.* retroflexión, flexión de un órgano hacia atrás.

retrograde *a.* retrógrado-a, que se mueve hacia atrás o retorna al pasado; **___ amnesia** / amnesia ___; **___ aortography** / aortografía ___; **___ pyelography** / pielografía ___.

retrogression *n.* retrogresión, regreso a un estado más primitivo de desarrollo.

retrolental *a.* retrolental, situado detrás del cristalino; **___ fibroplasia** / fibroplasia ___.

retroperitoneal *a.* retroperitoneano-a, rel. a o situado detrás del peritoneo.

retroplasia *n.* retroplasia. *V.* **anaplasia.**

retrospective *a.* retrospectivo-a; **___ study** / estudio ___.

retroversion *n.* retroversión, inclinación o vuelta hacia atrás; **___ of the uterus** / desplazamiento del útero hacia atrás.

retrovirus *n.* retrovirus, virus que pertenece al grupo ácido ARN, algunos de los cuales son oncogénicos; **human endogenous ___** / ___ endógeno humano.

retry *v.* ensayar de nuevo.

return *n.* regreso, retorno; *v.* regresar.

Retzius, space of *n.* espacio de Retzius, área entre la vejiga y los huesos del pubis.

reunion *n.* reunión, unión de partes o tejidos esp. en un hueso fracturado o partes de una herida al cicatrizar.

revascularization *n.* revascularización, proceso de restauración de la sangre a una parte del cuerpo después de una lesión o una derivación quirúrgica.

reversal *n.* reversión, restitución a un estado anterior.

review *n.* revisión, análisis, repaso; **___ of systems** / **___** de sistemas; [*literary*] reseña; *v.* repasar, volver a ver.

revise *v.* revisar, repasar, mirar con detenimiento.

revision *n.* revisión.

revitalize *n.* revitalizar, vivificar, volver a dar fuerzas.

revive *v.* revivir.

revulsion *n.* revulsión.

revulsive *a.* revulsivo-a, rel. a la revulsión o que la causa.

Reye's syndrome *n.* síndrome de Reye, enfermedad aguda que se manifiesta en niños y adolescentes con edema agudo en órganos importantes esp. en el cerebro y el hígado.

rhabdomyosarcoma *n.* rabdomiosarcoma, tumor maligno de fibras musculares estriadas que afecta gen. los músculos esqueléticos.

rhachitis *n.* raquitismo. *V.* **rickets.**

Rh blood group *n.* grupo sanguíneo Rh. *V.* **blood group.**

rheum, rheuma *n.* 1. reuma, secreción catarral o acuosa por la nariz; 2. reumatismo.

rheumatic *a.* reumático-a, rel. a o afectado por reumatismo.

rheumatic fever *n.* fiebre reumática, fiebre o condición acompañada de dolores en las articulaciones que puede dejar como secuela trastornos cardíacos y renales.

rheumatism *n.* reumatismo, enfermedad aguda crónica caracterizada por infl. y dolor en las articulaciones.

rheumatoid *a.* reumatoide, de naturaleza semejante al reumatismo.

Rh genes *n. pl.* genes Rh, determinantes de los distintos tipos sanguíneos Rh.

rhinal *a.* rinal, rel. a la nariz.

rhinitis *n.* rinitis, infl. de la mucosa nasal.

rhinolaryngitis *n.* rinolaringitis, infl. simultánea de las mucosas nasales y laríngeas.

rhinopharyngitis *n.* rinofaringitis, infl. de la nasofaringe.

rhinophyma *n.* rinofima, acné rosácea aguda en el área de la nariz.

rhinoplasty *n. cirg.* rinoplastia, cirugía plástica de la nariz.

rhinorrhea *n.* rinorrea, secreción mucosolíquida por la nariz.

rhinoscopy *n.* rinoscopía, examen de los pasajes nasales a través de la nasofaringe o de los orificios nasales.

rhizotomy *n. cirg.* rizotomía, división o transección de la raíz de un nervio.

rhodopsin *n.* rodopsina, pigmento de color rojo púrpura que se encuentra en los bastoncillos de la retina y que facilita la visión en luz tenue.

rhythm *n.* ritmo, regularidad en la acción o función de un órgano u órganos del cuerpo tal como el corazón.

rhythmical *a.* rítmico-a.

rhytidectomy *n.* ritidectomía, estiramiento de la piel de la cara por medio de cirugía plástica.

rib *n.* costilla, uno de los huesos de una serie de doce pares que forman la pared torácica.

riboflavin *n.* riboflavina, vitamina B$_2$, componente del complejo vitamínico B esencial en la nutrición.

ribonucleoprotein *n.* ribonucleoproteína, sustancia que contiene proteína y ácido ribonucleico.

rich *a.* [*wealth*] rico-a, opulento-a; [*food*] sabroso-a; muy sazonado-a, muy condimentado-a.

rickets *n.* raquitismo. *V.* **rachitism.**

rickettsia *n.* ricketsia, rickettsia, uno de los organismos gram-negativos que se reproducen solamente en células huéspedes de pulgas, piojos, garrapatas y ratones, y se transmiten a humanos a través de las mordidas de éstos.

ridge *n.* borde, reborde, elevación prolongada.

rifampicin *n.* rifampicina, sustancia semisintética, antibacteriana que se usa en el tratamiento de la tuberculosis pulmonar.

right *n.* justicia; derecho; *a.* derecho-a, rel. a la parte derecha del cuerpo; recto-a, correcto-a;

___ -**handed** / diestro-a, que usa con preferencia la mano derecha; **on the** ___ **side** / al costado o lado derecho; [*health*] sano-a; *v.* **to be in one's** ___ **mind** / estar en su juicio, estar cuerdo-a; **the** ___ **medication** / la medicina necesaria; **the** ___ **treatment** / el tratamiento adecuado; [*in a problem*] **taking the** ___ **direction** / la solución indicada; **Everything is all** ___ / Todo está bien; ___ **or wrong** / con o sin razón; *adv.* bien, correctamente; mismo; **It is going all** ___ / Todo sigue bien; ___ **here** / aquí mismo.

right to refuse treatment *n.* derecho a rehusar tratamiento, el derecho que tiene el (la) paciente de negarse a recibir tratamiento en contra de su voluntad.

right to treatment *n.* derecho a recibir tratamiento, el derecho que tiene el (la) paciente de recibir atención médica de una institución de salud que ha asumido la responsabilidad de tratar al paciente.

rights of the patient *n. pl.* derechos del paciente.

rigid *a.* rígido-a, tieso, inmóvil.

rigidity *n.* rigidez, tesura, inmovilidad, inflexibilidad; **cadaveric** ___ / ___ cadavérica, rigor mortis.

rigor *n.* rigor. 1. escalofrío repentino con fiebre alta; 2. tesura, inflexibilidad muscular.

ring *n.* anillo, círculo; *vi.* sonar; zumbar.

ringing *a.* resonante, retumbante; ___ **ears** / tintineo, zumbido, ruido en los oídos.

ringworm *n.* tiña.

rip *v.* rasgar, desgarrar.

ripe *a.* [*fruit*] maduro-a; [*boil, cataract*] madurado-a.

ripen *v.* madurar; madurarse.

ripening *n.* reblandecimiento, dilatación tal como la del cuello uterino durante el parto.

ripping *n.* laceración, rasgadura; descosedura.

rise *n.* ascensión, subida, salida, crecimiento; *vi.* ascender, subir; [*from bed*] levantarse o salir de la cama; **to** ___ **to one's feet** / ponerse de pie.

risk *n.* riesgo, peligro; ___ **of contamination** / riesgo o peligro de contaminación; ___ **factors** / factores de ___; **high-** ___ **groups** / grupos de alto ___; **potential** ___ / ___ posible. *v.* poner en peligro; arriesgarse.

risky *a.* arriesgado-a, peligroso-a.

risorious *n.* risorio, músculo que se inserta en la comisura de la boca.

ristocetin *n.* ristocetina, antibiótico que se usa en el tratamiento de infecciones producidas por un estreptococo gram-positivo.

Ritalin hydrochloride *n.* clorhidrato de Ritalin, estimulante y antidepresivo benigno.

ritual *n.* ritual, rito.

rivalry *n.* rivalidad; competencia.

roach *n.* cucaracha.

road *n.* camino, carretera; curso.

roast *a.* asado-a ___ **meat** / carne ___; *v.* asar, hornear.

386

robe *n.* [*dressing gown*] bata.

robust *a.* robusto-a, vigoroso-a.

rod *n.* bastoncillo; varilla.

rodent *n.* roedor; *a.* roedor-a; __ **ulcer** / úlcera __ roedora, que destruye poco a poco.

rodenticide *n.* rodenticida, agente que destruye roedores.

roentgenography *n.* radiografía.

role *n.* [*theatre*] papel; *v.* **to play the** __ **of** / hacer el __ de.

role model *n.* prototipo, modelo.

roll *n.* panecillo; *v.* rodar.

Romberg's sign *n.* signo de Romberg, oscilación del cuerpo que indica inhabilidad de mantener el equilibrio en posición erecta, con los pies juntos y los ojos cerrados.

rongeur *Fr.* rongeur, fórceps o pinzas para extraer astillas de hueso y tejidos endurecidos.

room *n.* cuarto, sala; **bath** __ / __ de baño; **delivery** __ / sala de partos; **operating** __ / sala de operaciones, quirófano; **the patient's** __ / __ del paciente; **recovery** __ / sala de recuperación; __ **temperature** / temperatura ambiente; **waiting** __ / sala de espera.

root *n.* raíz; radical.

Rorschach test *n.* prueba de Rorschach, prueba psicológica por la cual se revelan rasgos de la personalidad a través de la interpretación de una serie de borrones de tinta.

rosary *n.* rosario, estructura que se asemeja a cuentas enlazadas.

rosemary *n.* romero.

roseola *n.* roséola, condición de la piel caracterizada por manchas rosáceas de varios tamaños.

rosette *F.* rosette, células en formación semejante a una rosa.

rose water *n.* agua de rosa.

rostral *a.* rostral, rel. o semejante a un rostro.

rostrum *L.* rostro. 1. cara; 2. pico, proyección.

rosy *a.* rosado-a, de color de rosa.

rot *v.* podrirse, pudrirse, echarse a perder.

rotary *a.* rotatorio-a; giratorio-a.

rotate *v.* rotar, girar, voltear.

rotation *n.* rotación; **fetal** __ / __ de la cabeza del feto.

rotator *n.* rotador; *a.* rotador-a.

rotten *a.* podrido-a, putrefacto-a, corrompido-a; [*tooth*] cariado-a.

rough *a.* [*surface, skin*] áspero-a, escabroso-a; [*character*] rudo-a. grosero-a; *v.* **to have a** __ **time** / pasarla mal.

round *a.* redondo-a, circular; __ **-shouldered** / cargado de espaldas; **all year** __ / todo el año.

route *n.* ruta.

routine *n.* rutina, hábito, costumbre; *a.* rutinario-a.

rub *n.* 1. fricción, frote, frotación, masaje; 2. sonido producido por el roce de dos superficies secas que se detecta en auscultación; *v.* frotar, hacer penetrar un ungüento o pomada en la piel; friccionar; **to** __ **off** / limpiar frotando; borrar; **to** __ **down** / dar un masaje.

rubber *n.* goma; __ **bulb** / perilla de __; __ **gloves** / guantes de __.

rubbing *n.* masaje.

rubbing alcohol *n.* alcohol para fricciones.

rubefacient *n.* enrojecedor, agente que enrojece la piel.

rubella *n.* rubéola, sarampión alemán; *pop. Mex.* pelusa, enferemedad infecciosa viral que se manifiesta con dolor de garganta, fiebre y una erupción rosácea y que puede ocasionar serios trastornos fetales si la madre la contrae durante los primeros tres meses del embarazo.

rubella virus vaccine, live *n.* vacuna de virus vivo contra la rubéola.

rubescent *a.* ruborizado-a, que se enrojece.

rubor *n.* rubor, enrojecimiento de la piel.

rudiment *n.* rudimento. 1. órgano parcialmente desarrollado; 2. órgano o parte que ha perdido total o parcialmente su función anterior.

ruga *n. L.* (*pl.* **rugae**) arruga, pliegue.

rugose *a.* arrugado-a, lleno-a de arrugas.

rugosity *n.* rugosidad, arruga.

rule *n.* régimen, regla, precepto; __ / __s **and regulations** / según el reglamento; **as a** __ / por lo general; *v.* gobernar, administrar; **to** __ **out** / prohibir, desechar; **to be ruled by one's emotions** / dejarse llevar por las emociones.

rumble *n.* ruido sordo; estruendo.

run *n.* carrera; *vi.* correr, hacer correr; **to** __ **a fever** / tener calentura.

rupture *n.* [*hernia*] ruptura; [*bone*] rotura, fractura; [*boil*] reventazón; *v.* reventar, romper, fracturar; abrirse, reventarse, romperse, fracturarse.

rush *n.* precipitación, agolpamiento, torrente; oleada; **with a** __ / de golpe, de repente; *v.* darse prisa; **to** __ **in** / entrar de golpe, entrar con precipitación.

rusty *a.* oxidado-a.

rye *n.* centeno.

S *abbr.* **sacral** / sacral; **section** / sección; **stimulus** / estímulo; **subject** / sujeto; **sulphur** / sulfuro, azufre.

s *abbr.* **second** / segundo; **singular** / singular.

Sabin vaccine *n.* vacuna de Sabin, vacuna oral contra la poliomielitis.

sac *n.* saco, bolsa; estructura u órgano en forma de saco o bolsa.

saccades *n.* sacades. *V.* **nystagmus.**

saccharide *n.* sacárido, compuesto químico que pertenece a una serie de carbohidratos que incluye los azúcares.

saccharine *n.* sacarina, sustancia sumamente dulce, agente dulcificante artificial, *a.* sacarino-a, azucarado-a.

saccule *n.* sáculo, saco o bolsa pequeña.

saclike *a.* en forma de saco.

sacral *a.* sacral, rel. al sacro o situado cerca de éste; ___ **nerves** / nervios ___-es; **plexus** ___ / plexo ___ .

sacralization *n.* sacralización, fusión de la quinta vértebra lumbar con el sacro.

sacrifice *n.* sacrificio; *v.* sacrificar.

sacroiliitis *n.* sacroilitis, infl. de la articulación sacroilíaca.

sacrolumbar *a.* sacrolumbar, rel. a las regiones sacral y lumbar.

sacrum *n.* sacro, hueso triangular formado por cinco vértebras fusionadas en la base de la espina dorsal y entre los dos huesos de la cadera.

sad *a.* triste, desconsolado-a.

saddle back *n.* espalda caída. *V.* **lordosis.**

sadism *n.* sadismo, perversión por la cual se obtiene placer sexual infligiendo dolor físico o psicológico a otros.

sadist *n.* sadista, persona que practica sadismo.

sadistic *a.* sádico-a, rel. al sadismo.

sadness *n.* tristeza, melancolía.

sadomasochism *n.* sadomasoquismo, derivación de placer sexual infligiendo dolor físico a sí mismo o a otros.

sadomasochist *n.* sadomasoquista, persona que practica sadomasoquismo.

safe *a.* seguro-a, sin peligro; sin riesgo; **-ly** *adv.* seguramente.

safety *n.* seguridad, protección; ___ **pin** / imperdible.

sag *v.* perder elasticidad, perder la forma; combarse; pandearse; [*to weaken*] debilitarse.

sage *n.* salvia.

sagittal *a.* sagital, semejante a una saeta; ___ **plane** / plano ___, paralelo al eje longitudinal del cuerpo.

said *a. pp.* de **to say,** dicho; dicho-a, citado-a, antes mencionado.

salacious *a.* lascivo-a, libidinoso-a.

salad *n.* ensalada.

salary *n.* sueldo, salario.

salicylate *n.* salicilato, cualquier sal de ácido salicílico; ___ **poisoning** / envenenamiento por aspirina.

salicylic acid *n.* ácido salicílico, ácido cristalino blanco derivado del fenol.

salicylism *n.* salicilismo, condición tóxica causada por ingestión excesiva de ácido salicílico.

salient *a.* saliente, pronunciado-a.

saline *a.* salino-a; ___ **solution** / solución ___; agua destilada con sal; ___ **cathartic** / purgante ___ .

saliva *n.* saliva, secreción de las glándulas salivales que envuelve y humedece el bolo alimenticio en la boca y facilita la deglución.

salivant *a.* salivoso-a, rel. a la saliva.

salivary glands *n. pl.* glándulas salivales o salivares.

salivation *n.* salivación. 1. acto de secreción de saliva; 2. secreción excesiva de saliva.

Salk vaccine *n.* vacuna de Salk, vacuna contra la poliomielitis.

sallow *a.* pálido-a, lívido-a.

salmon *n.* salmón.

salmonella *n.* Salmonela, género de bacterias gram-negativas de la familia *Enterobacteriaceae* que causan fiebres entéricas, otras infecciones gastrointestinales y septicemia.

salmonellosis *n.* salmonelosis, infección causada por ingestión de comida contaminada por bacterias del género Salmonella.

salpingectomy *n. cirg.* salpingectomía, extirpación de una o de ambas trompas de Falopio.

salpingitis *n.* salpingitis, infl. de las trompas de Falopio.

salpingo-oophorectomy *n. cirg.* salpingo-ooforectomía, extirpación de un ovario y un tubo uterino.

salpingoplasty *n. cirg.* reparación plástica de las trompas de Falopio.

salpinx *Gr.* (*pl.* **salpinges**) trompa, estructura similar a la trompa de Eustaquio o a la trompa de Falopio.

salt *n.* sal, cloruro de sodio; **iodized** ___ / ___ yodada; **noniodized** ___ / ___ corriente; **smelling** ___-**s** / ___-es aromáticas; ___ **shaker** / salero; ___-**free diet** / dieta libre de ___ o sin ___; **low-** ___ **diet** / dieta hiposódica; *v.* salar, echar sal; [*to season with*] condimentar con sal, sazonar.

salty *a.* salado-a, salobre, salino-a.

salubrious *a.* salubre, saludable.

salutary *a.* saludable.

salve *n.* ungüento, pomada.

same *a.* mismo-a, idéntico-a, igual.

sample *n.* espécimen, muestra; *v.* probar; sacar o tomar una muestra.

sampling *n.* muestreo; hacer muestras; selección partitiva; **random** ___ / ___ al azar.

sanatorium *n.* sanatorio, institución de rehabilitación física o mental.

Sanitary towel : paño higiénico compresa higiénica

sanction *n.* sanción, pena.

sand *n.* arena.

sandy *a.* arenoso-a.

sane *a.* sano-a; [*mentally*] cuerdo-a.

sanguine *a.* sanguíneo-a. 1. rel. a la sangre; 2. de complexión rosácea, con disposición alegre.

sanguineous *a.* sanguíneo-a, rel. a la sangre o de abundante sangre.

sanguinolent *a.* sanguinolento-a, que contiene sangre.

sanitarian *n.* sanitario-a, persona entrenada en problemas de salubridad.

sanitarium *n.* sanatorio, institución de salud de rehabilitación física o mental.

sanitary *a.* higiénico-a; ___ **napkin** / servilleta ___ absorbente, toalla ___ .

sanitation *n.* saneamiento, sanidad.

sanity *n.* cordura, sensatez, bienestar mental.

sap *n.* savia, jugo natural de algunas plantas.

saphenous *a.* safeno-a, rel. a las venas safenas.

saphenous veins *n. pl.* venas safenas, dos venas superficiales de la pierna.

sapphism *n.* safismo, lesbianismo.

saprophyte *n.* saprófito, organismo vegetal que vive en materia orgánica pútrida.

sarcoidosis *n.* sarcoidosis. *V.* **Schaumann's disease.**

sarcoma *n.* sarcoma, neoplasma maligno formado por tejido conectivo.

sardonic laugh *n.* risa sardónica, contracción espasmódica de los músculos risorios en forma de una sonrisa.

sat *a., pp.* de **to sit,** sentado-a.

satellite *n.* satélite, estructura asociada con otra o situada cerca de ella.

satiate *v.* saciar.

satiated *a.* saciado-a.

satiety *n.* saciedad, hartura, hartazgo.

satisfactory *a.* satisfactorio-a.

satisfied *a.* satisfecho-a, contento-a.

satisfy *v.* satisfacer.

saturate *v.* saturar; empapar.

saturated *a.* saturado-a, empapado-a, incapaz de absorber o recibir una sustancia más allá de un límite; ___ **solution** / solución ___ .

saturation *n.* saturación, acto de saturar; ___ **index** / índice de ___ ; ___ **time** / tiempo de ___ .

sauce *n.* salsa; [*dressing*] aderezo.

sausage *n.* salchicha; chorizo.

save *v.* salvar, [*energy, money*] ahorrar; [*time*] aprovechar el tiempo.

say *vi.* decir; **You don't say!** / ¡No me diga!, ¡no me digas!

scab *n.* costra, escara.

scabies *n.* sarna, infección cutánea parasitaria muy contagiosa que causa picazón.

scald *n.* escaldadura, quemadura de la piel causada por vapor o por un líquido caliente; *v.* lavar en agua hirviendo, quemar con un líquido caliente.

scale *n.* 1. escala, balanza; 2. escama, costra, lámina que se desprende de la piel seca.

scaling *n.* peladura.

scalp *n.* cuero cabelludo; ___ **dermatoses** / dermatosis del ___ .

scalpel *n.* escalpelo; bisturí, instrumento quirúrgico.

scaly *a.* escamoso-a.

scan, scintiscan *n.* escán; rastreo, proceso que reproduce la imagen de un tejido u órgano específico usando un detector de la sustancia radiactiva tecnecio 99 m. inyectada como medio de contraste; **bone** ___ / ___ de los huesos; **brain** ___ / ___ del cerebro; **heart** ___ / ___ cardíaco; **lung** ___ / ___ pulmonar; **thyroid** ___ / ___ de la tiroide.

scanner *n.* escáner, dispositivo explorador.

scanning *n.* escanografía, escrutinio y registro por medio de un instrumento de detección de la emisión de ondas radiactivas de una sustancia específica que ha sido inyectada y que se concentra en partes o tejidos en observación.

scant *a.* escaso-a, parco-a, insuficiente.

scanty *a.* escaso-a, limitado-a, no abundante.

scaphoid *a.* escafoide, en forma de bote esp. en referencia al hueso del carpo y al del tarso.

scapula *n.* escápula, hueso del hombro.

scar *n.* cicatriz, marca en la piel; *v.* cicatrizar.

scare *v.* asustar, atemorizar.

scarification *n.* escarificación, acto de hacer punturas o raspaduras en la piel.

scarlet feber, scarlatina *n.* escarlatina, enfermedad contagiosa aguda caracterizada por fiebre y erupción con enrojecimiento de la piel y la lengua.

scatology *n.* escatología. 1. estudio de las heces fecales; 2. obsesión con el excremento y las inmundicias.

scatter *v.* esparcir, diseminar; dispersar, desparramar.

scattered *a.* esparcido-a, diseminado-a; desparramado-a, regado-a; derramado-a.

scene *n.* escena, escenario.

scent *n.* olor; aroma, perfume.

Schaumann's disease *n.* enfermedad de Schaumann, enfermedad crónica manifestada con pequeños tubérculos esp. en los pulmones, los nódulos linfáticos, los huesos y la piel.

schedule *n.* horario; *v.* hacer un horario; programar.

schema *n.* esquema, plan, planeamiento.

schematic *a.* esquemático-a, rel. a un esquema.

Schilling test *n.* prueba de Schilling; uso de vitamina B_{12} radiactiva en el diagnóstico de anemia perniciosa primaria.

schistosoma *n.* *Schistosoma,* esquistosoma, duela, especie de trematodo cuyas larvas entran en la sangre del huésped por contacto con agua contaminada a través del tubo digestivo o la piel.

schistosomiasis *n.* esquistosomiasis, infestación producida por la duela.

schizoid *a.* esquizoide, semejante a la esquizofrenia.

schizophrenia *n. psic.* esquizofrenia, desintegración mental que transforma la personalidad con varias manifestaciones psicóticas tales como alucinaciones, retraimiento y distorsión de la realidad.

schizophrenic *a.* esquizofrénico-a, rel. a la esquizofrenia o que padece de ella.

sciatica *n.* ciática, neuralgia que se irradia a lo largo del nervio ciático.

sciatic nerve *n.* nervio ciático, nervio que se extiende desde la base de la columna vertebral a lo largo del muslo y se ramifica en la pierna y el pie.

scintigraphy *n.* escintigrafía, técnica de diagnóstico que emplea radioisótopos para obtener una imagen bidimensional de la distribución de un radiofármaco en un área designada del cuerpo.

scintillate *v.* escintilar, centellear, brillar.

scintiscan *n.* escintiescán, gammagrama, registro de la imagen bidimensional de la distribución interior de un radiofármaco en un área seleccionada previamente para fines de diagnóstico.

scirrhous *a.* escirroso-a, duro-a, rel. a un escirro.

scirrhus *n.* escirro, tumor canceroso duro.

scissors *n. pl.* tijeras.

sclera, sclerotica *n.* esclerótica, parte blanca del ojo compuesta de tejido fibroso.

scleritis *n.* escleritis, infl. de la esclerótica.

sclerosing solutions *n. pl.* soluciones esclerosantes.

sclerosis *n.* esclerosis, endurecimiento progresivo de los tejidos y órganos; **Alzheimer's** ___ / ___ de Alzheimer; **amyotrophic lateral** ___ / ___ lateral amiotrófica; **arterial** ___ / ___ arterial; **multiple** ___ / ___ múltiple.

sclerotherapy *n.* escleroterapia, tratamiento con una solución química que se inyecta en las várices para producir esclerosis.

sclerotic *a.* esclerótico-a, rel. a la esclerosis o afectado por ella.

scoliosis *n.* escoliosis, desviación lateral pronunciada de la columna vertebral.

scoop *n.* paletada, cucharada.

scorch *v.* chamuscar, quemar, abrasar.

score *n.* valoración, evaluación; *v.* llevar la cuenta; [*in a game*] anotar.

scorpion *n.* escorpión, alacrán; ___ **sting** / picadura de ___.

scotoma *n.* (*pl.* **scotomata**) escotoma, área del campo visual en la cual existe pérdida parcial o total de la visión.

scotopia *n.* escotopia, visión nocturna, adaptación visual a la oscuridad.

scotopic *a.* escotópico-a, rel. a la escotopia; ___ **vision** / visión ___.

scrape *n.* raspadura, rasponazo, raspado; *v.* raspar, rasguñar.

scraper *n.* descarnador, raspador.

scratch *n.* rasguño, arañazo; *v.* raspar, rascar, rascarse; ___ **test** / prueba del rasguño, gen. para uso en pruebas alérgicas.

scream *n.* grito, chillido; *v.* gritar, chillar.

screech *v.* chillar.

screen *n.* pantalla; *v.* examinar sistemáticamente un grupo de casos; escrutar; **toxicology** ___ / protocolo toxicológico.

screening *n.* escrutinio, averiguación, selección; **biochemical** ___ / serie selectiva bioquímica; **multiphasic** ___ / ___ múltiple; **prescriptive** ___ / ___ prescrito.

screw *n.* tornillo, rosca.

scribble *n.* garabato.

scrofula *n.* escrófula, tuberculosis de la glándula linfática.

scrofuloderma *n.* escrofuloderma, *pop.* lamparón, tipo de escrófula cutánea.

scrotal *a.* escrotal, rel. al escroto.

scrotum *n.* escroto, saco o bolsa que envuelve o contiene los testículos.

scrub *v.* limpiar, fregar, restregar; ___ **nurse** / enfermera de cirugía.

scrubbing *n.* limpieza rigurosa de las manos y brazos antes de la cirugía.

scruple *n.* escrúpulo.

scrupulous *a.* escrupuloso-a.

scrupulousness *n.* escrupulosidad.

scum *n.* espuma; escoria.

scurvy *n.* escorbuto, enfermedad causada por deficiencia de vitamina C que se manifiesta con anemia, encías sangrantes y un estado general de laxitud.

seal *n.* sello; *v.* cerrar herméticamente.

seam *n.* costura, línea de costura.

search *n.* búsqueda, investigación; registro; *v.* buscar, registrar; investigar.

seasickness *n.* mareo; mareo por movimiento.

season *n.* estación; temporada; *v.* [*cooking*] sazonar.

seasoned *a.* sazonado-a; ___ **foods** / alimentos ___-s.

seat *n.* asiento; localidad.

sebaceous *a.* sebáceo-a, seboso-a, rel. al sebo o de la naturaleza de éste; ___ **cyst** / quiste ___; ___ **gland** / glándula ___.

seborrhea *n.* seborrea, secreción excesiva de las glándulas sebáceas.

sebum *n.* sebo, secreción espesa que segregan las glándulas sebáceas.

second *n.* segundo; *a.* segundo-a.

secondary *a.* secundario-a.

secretagogue, secretogogue *n.* secretogogo, agente que estimula la secreción glandular.

secrete *v.* secretar, segregar.

secretion *n.* secreción. 1. producción de un tejido o sustancia como resultado de una actividad glandular; **purulent** ___ / ___ purulenta; 2. sustancia producida por secreción.

secretory *a.* secretorio-a, que tiene la propiedad de secretar.

section *n.* sección, porción, parte; *v.* cortar;

seccionar.

sectioning *n.* partición, división, corte.

secure *a.* seguro-a; *v.* asegurar.

security *n.* seguridad; ___ **measures** / medidas de ___.

sedation *n.* sedación, acción o efecto de calmar o sedar; *v.* **to put under** ___ / dar un sedante, calmante o soporífero.

sedative *n.* calmante, sedante, agente con efectos tranquilizantes.

sedentary *a.* sedentario-a. 1. de poca actividad física; 2. rel. a la posición sentada.

sediment *n.* sedimento, materia que se deposita en el fondo de un líquido.

sedimentation *n.* sedimentación, acción o proceso de depositar sedimentos; ___ **rate** / índice de ___.

see *vi.* ver; **to** ___ **to it** / atender, ver que, hacer que; **I see!** / ¡Ya veo!; **Let's** ___ / Vamos a ver.

seed *n.* semilla, simiente.

seeing *n.* vista, visión.

seen *a., pp.* de **to see**, visto-a.

segment *n.* segmento, porción, sección.

segmentation *n.* segmentación, acto de dividir en partes.

seizure *n.* ataque repentino, acceso; ___ **activity** / actividad convulsiva.

seldom *adv.* rara vez, con rareza, raramente.

select *v.* seleccionar, escoger.

selection *n.* selección, elección.

self *n.* el yo; *pron.* uno-a mismo-a; *a.* sí mismo-a; mismo-a; propio-a; ___**-assurance** / confianza en ___; ___**-centered** / egoísta, egocéntrico-a; ___**-conscious** / concentrado-a en ___, cohibido-a; ___**-contained** / autónomo; [*personality*] reservado-a; ___**-contamination** / autocontaminación; ___**-control** / dominio de ___; ___**-defense** / defensa propia; ___**-delusion, deception** / engaño a ___; ___**-denial** / abnegación; ___**-determination** / autodeterminación; ___**-distrust** / falta de confianza en ___; ___**-esteem** / amor propio, reconocimiento de valores propios; ___**-identity** / conciencia de la identidad del yo; ___**-induced** / auto-inducido-a; ___**-medication** / automedicación; ___**-pity** / compasión por ___; *v.* **to be** ___**-sufficient** / valerse por ___.

selfish *a.* egoísta.

sella turcica *n.* silla turca, depresión en la superficie superior del esfenoide que contiene la hipófisis.

semantics *n.* semántica, estudio del significado de las palabras.

semen *n.* semen, esperma, secreción espesa blanca segregada por los órganos reproductivos masculinos.

semester *n.* semestre.

semicoma *n.* semicoma, estado comatoso leve.

semidisintegration *n.* semidesintegración, tiempo requerido por una sustancia radiactiva para perder la mitad de la radioactividad por desintegración.

seminal *a.* seminal, rel. a una semilla o que consiste de una semilla.

seminiferous *a.* seminífero-a, que produce semen.

semiotic *n.* semiótico-a, rel. a los síntomas o señales de una enfermedad.

semiotics *n.* semiótica, rama de la medicina que trata de las señales y síntomas de una enfermedad.

send *vi.* enviar, mandar.

senescence *n.* senescencia, senectud, proceso de envejecimiento.

senile *a.* senil, rel. a la vejez esp. en lo que afecta a las funciones mentales y físicas.

senility *n.* senilidad, cualidad de ser senil.

senior citizen *n.* persona mayor; jubilado-a.

sensation *n.* sensación, percepción de una estimulación por un órgano sensorial.

sense *n.* sentido, facultad de percibir por medio de los órganos sensoriales; ___ **of hearing** / ___ del oído; ___ **of smell** / ___ del olfato; ___ **of sight** / ___ de la vista; ___ **of taste** / ___ del gusto; ___ **of touch** / ___ del tacto; **common** ___ / ___ común; ___ **of humor** / ___ del humor; *v.* sentir.

sensibility *n.* sensibilidad, capacidad de recibir sensaciones.

sensitive *a.* sensitivo-a, sensible.

sensitivity *n.* sensibilidad, susceptibilidad.

sensitivity training *n.* entrenamiento de la sensibilidad o capacidad sensorial.

sensitization *n.* sensibilización, acto de hacer sensible o sensorial.

sensorial *a.* sensorial, sensitivo-a; que se percibe por los sentidos.

sensorimotor *a.* sensitivomotor, rel. a las actividades motoras y sensitivas del cuerpo.

sensory *a.* sensorial, sensorio-a, rel. a las sensaciones o los sentidos; ___ **aphasia** / afasia ___.

sensory threshold *n.* umbral sensorial.

sensual *a.* sensual, carnal.

sensuous *a.* sensual.

sentiment *n.* sentimiento.

separate *v.* separar, dividir.

separation *n.* separación, división; selección.

sepsis *L.* sepsis, condición tóxica producida por una contaminación bacteriana.

septal *a.* septal, rel. a un septum; ___ **deviation** / desviación ___.

septate *a.* septado-a, rel. a una estructura dividida por un septum.

septic *n.* séptico-a, rel. a la sepsis; ___ **shock** / choque ___.

septicemia, blood poisoning *n.* septicemia, envenenamiento de la sangre, invasión de la sangre por microorganismos virulentos.

septum *L.* (*pl.* **septa**) septum, tabique o membrana que divide dos cavidades o espacios; **ventricular** ___ / ___ ventricular.

sequela *n.* (*pl.* **sequelae**) secuela, condición que resulta de una enfermedad, lesión o tratamiento.

sequence *n.* secuencia, sucesión.

sequester *v.* secuestrar, aislar.

sequestration *n.* secuestro, aislamiento. 1. acto de aislar; 2. formación de un sequestrum.

sequestrum *n.* sequestrum, secuestro, fragmento de un hueso necrosado que se separa de un hueso sano adyacente.

serene *a.* sereno-a, tranquilo-a.

serial *a.* en serie.

series *n.* serie, grupo de especímenes en una secuencia.

serious *a.* serio-a; complicado-a; **-ly** *adv.* seriamente.

seroconversion *n.* seroconversión, desarrollo de anticuerpos como respuesta a una infección o a la administración de una vacuna.

serologic, serological *a.* serológico-a, rel. a un suero; ___ **test** / prueba ___.

serology *n.* serología, ciencia que estudia las propiedades de los sueros.

seroma *n.* seroma, acumulación gen. subcutánea de suero sanguíneo que produce una hinchazón que se asemeja a un tumor.

seronegative *a.* seronegativo-a, que presenta una reacción negativa a pruebas serológicas.

seropositive *a.* seropositivo-a, que presenta una reacción positiva a pruebas serológicas.

seropositivity *n.* seropositividad, resultado positivo en un examen serológico.

serosa *n.* membrana serosa.

serosanguineous *a.* serosanguíneo-a, de naturaleza serosa y sanguínea.

serotype *n.* serotipo, tipo de microorganismo que se determina por las clases y combinaciones de antígenos presentes en la célula.

serotyping *n.* determinación del serotipo.

serous *a.* seroso-a, que produce o contiene suero.

serpiginous *n.* serpiginoso-a, sinuoso-a, de movimiento semejante a una serpiente.

serrated *a.* serrado-a, endentado-a, con proyección similar a los dientes de un serrucho.

serum *n.* suero, líquido seroso. 1. elemento del plasma que permanece líquido y claro después de la coagulación; 2. cualquier líquido seroso; 3. suero inmune de animales o personas que se inocula para producir inmunizaciones pasivas o temporales.

sesamoid *a.* sesamoideo, semejante a una pequeña masa o semilla incrustada en una articulación o cartílago.

sessile *a.* sésil, insertado o fijo en una base ancha que carece de pedúnculo.

session *n.* sesión.

set *n.* conjunto, equipo; grupo; instrumentos y accesorios; [*surgical*] instrumental quirúrgico; **it is all** ___ / todo está arreglado; *vi.* poner, colocar; [*a broken bone*] encasar, fijar, ajustar; ___ **a fracture** / componer una fractura.

setback *n.* recaída; retraso, contrariedad.

setting *n.* [*environment*] ambiente; montaje.

settle *v.* asentar, fijar; asegurar.

settlement *n.* [*account*] arreglo, ajuste.

sever *v.* cortar, romper; separar.

several *a.* varios-as, muchos-as, algunos-as.

severe *a.* grave, severo-a.

severe combined immunodeficiency disease *n.* enfermedad grave de inmunodeficiencia combinada, una de las enfermedades genéticas raras que se caracteriza por el desarrollo defectivo de las células que generan anticuerpos.

sew *vi.* coser.

sewage *n.* aguas de alcantarilla, cloacas.

sewing *n.* costura, puntada.

sex *n.* sexo; ___ **determination** / determinación del ___; ___ **disorders** / trastornos o anomalías sexuales; ___ **distribution** / distribución según el ___.

sex-linked *a.* 1. relacionado con el sexo; 2. que se refiere a cromosomas sexuales o es transmitido por ellos.

sexual *a.* sexual, rel. al sexo; ___ **behavior** / conducta ___; ___ **characteristics** / características ___-es; ___ **development** / desarrollo ___; ___ **intercourse** / relaciones ___-es, coito; ___ **life** / vida ___; ___ **maturity** / madurez ___; **-ly** *adv.* sexualmente; ___ **transmitted disease** / enfermedad transmitida ___.

sexuality *n.* sexualidad, características de cada sexo.

shade *n.* sombra.

shadow *n.* sombra; opacidad.

shaft *n.* caña, *V.* **diaphysis.**

shake *vi.* agitar; [*hands*] dar la mano; [*from cold*] temblar, tiritar de frío; ___ **well before using** / agítese bien antes de usarse.

shaken *a.* sacudido-a; afectado-a; debilitado-a.

shakes *n. pl.* temblores, *pop.* tembladera; escalofríos; fiebre intermitente.

shaky *a.* vacilante, temeroso-a; [*untrustworthy*] que no merece confianza.

shall *v. aux.* deber.

Sexual Disorders	*Trastornos Sexuales*
erotomania	erotomania
exhibitionism	exhibicionismo
fetishism	fetichismo
frotteurism	froterismo
masochism	masoquismo
nymphomania	ninfomanía
paraphilia	parafilia
pedophilia	pedofilia
sadism	sadismo
satyromania	satiromanía
transvestic fetishism	fetichismo trasvestido
voyeurism	voyeurismo, mironismo

shaman *n.* curandero.

shamanism *n.* curanderismo.

shame *n.* vergüenza; **What a ___!** / ¡Qué pena!, ¡Qué lástima!; *v.* avergonzar.

shameful *a.* vergonzoso-a, penoso-a.

shank *n.* canilla de la pierna.

shape *n.* forma, aspecto; condición [*health*] **in bad ___** / enfermo-a; destruido-a; **out of ___** / deformado-a, imperfecto; [*physically*] desajuste físico; *v.* formar, moldear.

sharp *a.* [*pain*] agudo-a; [*instrument*] afilado-a.

shave *v.* afeitar; afeitarse.

shears *n. pl.* tijeras.

sheath *n.* cubierta, capa o membrana protectora.

shed *vi.* [*blood, tears*] derramar; [*light*] dar, esparcir; difundir; [*skin, hair*] mudar; pelar; soltar; descamar.

shedding *n.* [*hair*] exfoliación; [*skin*] peladura.

sheep *n.* oveja, carnero.

sheet *n.* lámina, hoja de metal; [*bedclothes*] sábana.

shelf *n.* anaquel, estructura en forma horizontal alargada.

shell *n.* cáscara; concha marina.

shellfish *n.* molusco; marisco.

shield *n.* escudo, cubierta.

shift *n.* cambio de posición, desviación; [*work period*] turno; *v.* cambiar, desviar.

shigellosis *n.* shigelosis, disenteria bacilar.

shinbone *n.* espinilla, borde anterior de la tibia.

shingles *n.* culebrilla, herpes zóster, erupción inflamatoria de la piel con vesículas o ampollas gen. localizadas en el tronco.

shirt *n.* camisa; **under___** / camiseta.

shiver *n.* estremecimiento, escalofrío, temblor; *v.* tener escalofríos; tiritar de frío; estremecerse.

shock, choc *Fr. n.* shock, choque, estado anormal generado por una insuficiencia circulatoria sanguínea que puede causar descenso en la presión arterial, pulso rápido, palidez, temperatura anormalmente baja y debilidad; **anaphylactic ___** / **___** anafiláctico; **endotoxic** / **___** endotóxico; **septic ___** / **___** séptico; **___ therapy, electric** / terapia electroconvulsiva.

shoe *n.* zapato, calzado; **orthopedic ___-s** / calzado ortopédico.

short *a.* corto-a; [*time*] breve; [*height*] bajo-a; **in a ___ time** / en breve, dentro de poco; **on ___ notice** / en corto plazo; **___ of breath** / falto-a de respiración; sin resuello.

shortage *n.* carencia, falta, déficit.

shorten *v.* acortar.

shortsightedness, nearsightedness *n.* *V.* **myopia.**

shot *n.* tiro, disparo; [*wound*] balazo; [*injection*] inyección.

should *v. aux., cond., pret.* de **shall**, deber.

shoulder *n.* hombro, unión de la clavícula, la escápula y el húmero.

shout *n.* grito, alarido; *v.* gritar.

show *vi.* mostrar, enseñar, manifestar; revelar.

shower *n.* ducha; *v.* ducharse, darse una ducha.

shrimp *n.* camarón.

shrink *n. pop.* psiquiatra o alienista, psicólogo; *vi.* encoger; encogerse.

shudder *v.* estremecerse.

shunt *n.* desviación, derivación; *v.* desviar, derivar.

shut *vi.* cerrar.

shy *a.* tímido-a, temeroso-a; cauteloso-a.

sialadenitis, sialoadenitis *n.* sialoadenitis, infl. de una glándula salival.

sialogogue *n.* sialagogo, agente que estimula la secreción salival.

sialogram *n.* sialograma, rayos X del conducto de la glándula salival.

sick *n., a.* enfermo-a; **___ leave** / licencia por enfermedad.

sickly *a.* enfermizo-a, achacoso-a, endeble.

sickness *n.* enfermedad, dolencia, mal.

side *n.* lado, costado; **by the ___ of** / al ___ de; **right ___** / **___** derecho; **left ___** / **___** izquierdo; **___ effect** / efecto secundario, reacción gen. adversa a un medicamento, tratamiento o droga.

sideways *a.* de lado.

sieve *n.* colador; *v.* colar, pasar por un tamiz.

sight *n.* vista; **at first ___** / a primera ___.

sigmoid *a.* sigmoide, sigmoideo. 1. que tiene forma de *s*; 2. rel. al colon sigmoide.

sigmoidoscope *n.* sigmoidoscopio, instrumento tubular largo que se usa para examinar la flexura sigmoide.

sigmoidoscopy *n.* sigmoidoscopía, uso de un sigmoidoscopio para examinar la flexura sigmoide.

sign *n.* señal, signo, indicación, manifestación objetiva de una enfermedad; **vital ___-s** / signos vitales.

signature *n.* 1. firma; 2. parte de una receta médica que contiene las instrucciones.

significance *a.* significado; **of no ___** / sin importancia.

significant *a.* importante, significativo-a.

signify *v.* significar.

sign language *n.* lenguaje mímico por señales. *V.* **dactilology.**

silence *n.* silencio.

silent *a.* silencioso-a.

silicon *n.* silicio, elemento no metálico encontrado en la tierra.

silicone *n.* silicón, silicona, compuesto orgánico que se usa en lubricantes, productos sintéticos, cirugía plástica y en prótesis.

silicosis *n.* silicosis, inhalación de partículas de polvo.

silk *n.* seda.

silly *a.* tonto-a.

silver *n.* plata; **___ nitrate** / nitrato de ___.

similar *a.* similar, semejante, parecido-a.

simmer *v.* cocer a fuego lento.

simple *a.* simple, sencillo-a; **-ly** *adv.* simplemente, meramente.

simplify *v.* simplificar.

simulate *v.* fingir, simular, pretender.

simulation *n.* simulación, fingir un síntoma o enfermedad.

since *adv.* desde; ___ **then; ever** ___ / ___ entonces; ___ **when?** / ¿___ cuándo?

sinew *n. V.* **tendon.**

single *a.* sencillo-a, simple, solo-a; [*unmarried*] soltero-a.

singular *a.* singular, único.

singultus *n. L.* hipo.

sinoatrial *a.* sinoatrial, rel. a la región del seno auricular.

sinoatrial, sinoauricular node *n.* nódulo sinusal o senoauricular, localizado en la unión de la vena cava y la aurícula derecha, y que se considera el punto de origen de los impulsos que estimulan los latidos del corazón.

sinogram *n.* sinograma, radiografía de un seno paranasal usando un medio de contraste.

sinuous *a.* sinuoso-a, ondulado-a.

sinus *L.* sinus, seno, cavidad de abertura estrecha; ___ **rhythm** / ritmo sinusal.

sinusal *a.* sinusal, rel. a un sinus.

sinusitis *n.* sinusitis, infl. de la mucosa de un seno o cavidad, esp. los senos paranasales.

sinusoid *n.* sinusoide, conducto diminuto que lleva sangre a los tejidos de un órgano; *a.* rel. a un sinus.

sip *n.* sorbo, trago; *v.* sorber.

siphon *n.* sifón.

sister *n.* hermana; ___-**in-law** / cuñada.

sit *vi.* sentar, asentar; **to** ___ **down** / sentarse.

situated *a.* situado-a, localizado-a.

situation *n.* situación, localización.

situs *L.* situs, posición, sitio.

size *n.* tamaño; [*garments*] talla.

skeletal *a.* esquelético-a.

skeleton *n.* esqueleto, armazón ósea del cuerpo.

skew *n.* movimiento oblicuo-a, movimiento sesgado-a, de lado.

skill *n.* destreza, habilidad.

skin *n.* piel, epidermis, cutis; *pop.* pellejo; **sagging facial** ___ / cutis colgante; ___ **cancer** / cáncer de la ___; ___ **diseases** / enfermedades de la ___, dermatosis; ___ **graft** / injerto de la ___; ___ **rash** / erupción cutánea, urticaria; ___ **tests** / pruebas cutáneas; ___ **ulcer** / úlcera cutánea.

skinny *a.* flaco-a, delgado-a, descarnado-a.

skip *v.* omitir, pasar por alto; [*jump*] saltar.

skirt *n.* falda.

skull *n.* cráneo; calavera, estructura ósea de la cabeza; ___ **fractures** / fracturas del ___; **base of the** ___ / base del ___.

slant *n.* inclinación, plano inclinado; *v.* inclinar; [*words*] distorsionar; inclinarse.

slanted *a.* oblicuo-a, inclinado-a; sesgado-a.

slap *n.* bofetada, manotazo; *v.* pegar, dar una bofetada, dar un manotazo.

sleep *n.* sueño; ___ **apnea** / apnea intermitente

que ocurre durante el sueño; **balmy** ___ / ___ reparador; ___ **cycles** / ciclos del ___; ___ **disorders** / trastornos del ___; ___ **stages** / fases del ___; **twilight** ___ / ___ crepuscular; *vi.* dormir; dormirse; **to** ___ **soundly** / ___ profundamente.

sleepiness *n.* somnolencia, adormecimiento.

sleeping pill *n.* soporífero, somnífero, pastilla para dormir.

sleeping sickness *n.* enfermedad del sueño, dolencia aguda endémica de África que se manifiesta con fiebre, letargo, escalofríos, pérdida de peso y debilidad general, causada por un protozoo transmitido por la picadura de la mosca tsetse.

sleepwalking *n.* sonambulismo.

sleeve *n.* manga; **Put up your** ___ / Súbase, súbete la manga.

slender *a.* esbelto-a; delgado-a.

slice *n.* pedazo, tajada, rebanada.

slide *n.* diapositiva, laminilla; [*specimen holder*] portaobjeto.

slight *a.* ligero-a, leve; ___ **fever** / fiebrecita, fiebre ___.

slim *a.* delgado-a; esbelto-a; insuficiente; **a** ___ **chance** / poco probable.

slimy *a.* viscoso-a; enlodado-a.

sling *n.* cabestrillo, soporte de vendaje.

slippery *a.* resbaladizo-a, resbaloso-a.

slit *n.* incisión, hendidura, rajadura; *v.* **to make a** ___ / hacer una incisión, hacer una hendidura; rajar, cortar en tiras.

slope *n.* inclinación; declive; *v.* estar inclinado-a; estar en declive.

slough *n.* esfacelo, masa de tejido muerto que se ha desprendido de un tejido vivo.

slow *a.* lento-a, pausado-a, despacioso-a; [*clock*] atrasado, retrasado; *v.* **to** ___ **down** / ir más despacio; tener más calma; **-ly** *adv.* lentamente, pausadamente, más despacio.

sluggish *a.* flojo-a, inactivo-a, de movimiento lento.

small *a.* pequeño-a; **smaller** *comp.* / más pequeño; **smallest** *sup.* / el menor, el más pequeño.

smallpox *n.* viruela, enfermedad infecciosa viral que se manifiesta con un cuadro febril agudo y erupción de ampollas y pústulas diseminadas por todo el cuerpo.

smart *a.* inteligente, listo-a.

smear *n.* frotis, unto; *v.* untar, embarrar.

smegma *n.* esmegma, secreción producida por las glándulas sebáceas vista esp. en los órganos genitales exteriores.

smell *n.* 1. olor, aroma; **penetrating** ___ / ___ penetrante; 2. sentido del olfato; *v.* oler, percibir un olor.

smile *n.* sonrisa; *v.* sonreír.

smiling *a.* risueño-a.

smog *n.* mezcla de niebla y humo.

smoke *n.* humo; ___ **inhalation** / inhalación de ___; ___ **screen** / cortina de ___; *v.* fumar; **Do**

not __ here / No fume, no fumes aquí.
smooth a. liso-a; [cutis] suave, terso-a, delicado-a.
snake n. serpiente, culebra; __-bite / mordedura de __; __ venom / ponzoña de __; poisonous __ / __ venenosa.
snap n. chasquido, ruido cardíaco relacionado con la apertura de una válvula del corazón, gen. la válvula mitral; opening __ / __ de apertura.
sneeze n. estornudo; v. estornudar.
sniff v. olfatear, oler; absorber por la nariz; resoplar.
sniffle n. catarro nasal; v. sorber repetidamente por la nariz.
snooze v. adormecerse.
snore n. ronquido; v. roncar.
snort v. aspirar a través de la mucosa nasal.
snow n. nieve; v. nevar.
snuff v. inhalar; resoplar hacia adentro; to __ up / tomar por la nariz.
so adv. así, de este modo, de esta manera; __ that / de manera que; not __ much / no tanto; it is not __ / no es __; so-so / más o menos, regular.
soak v. remojar, empapar; to __ in, to __ up / absorber, chupar.
soap n. jabón; v. enjabonar; to __ oneself / enjabonarse.
sob n. sollozo; v. sollozar.
sober a. sobrio-a, serio; v. to get __ / dejar de beber, dejar de tomar bebidas alcohólicas.
sociable a. sociable, amigable.
social a. social, sociable; __ behavior / conducta o comportamiento __; __ security / seguro __; __ work / asistencia __; __ worker / trabajador-a __.
socialization n. socialización, adaptación social.
socialized a. socializado-a; __ medicine / medicina __.
society n. sociedad; organización social.
sociobiology n. sociobiología, ciencia que estudia los factores genéticos como determinantes de la conducta.
sociologist n. sociólogo-a, especialista en sociología.
sociology n. sociología, ciencia que trata de las relaciones sociales y de los fenómenos de tipo social.
sociopath n. sociópata, persona caracterizada por una conducta antisocial.
sock n. media, calcetín.
socket n. hueco, [of a bone] fosa; [electric] enchufe.
soda n. soda, carbonato de sodio; baking __ / bicarbonato de sodio.
sodium n. sodio, elemento metálico alcalino que se encuentra en los líquidos del cuerpo.
sodomite n. sodomita, persona que comete sodomía.
sodomy n. sodomía, término que denota relación sexual entre hombres; bestialidad o felación.

soft a. blando-a, suave, delicado-a; [metals] flexible, maleable; __ diet / dieta __; __ drinks / refrescos, bebidas no alcohólicas; -ly adv. suavemente, blandamente.
soften v. ablandar, suavizar.
softening n. reblandecimiento, ablandamiento; suavidad.
soggy a. saturado-a, empapado-a.
soil n. tierra, terreno; [dirt] suciedad.
solace n. consuelo; solaz; esparcimiento; v. consolar; alegrar.
solar a. solar, rel. al sol.
sole n. suela, planta del pie.
solid a. sólido-a, macizo-a; [person] serio-a, formal.
soluble a. soluble.
solution n. solución.
solvent n. solvente, líquido que disuelve o es capaz de producir una solución.
somatic a. somático-a, rel. al cuerpo.
somatization n. somatización, psic. proceso de conversión de experiencias mentales en manifestaciones corporales.
some a. alguno-a; algún, algo de, un poco de; unos, unos cuantos, unas, unas cuantas, algunos-as.
somebody n. alguien; __ else / otra persona.
somehow adv. de algún modo, de alguna manera.
something n. alguna cosa, algo; __ else / otra cosa.
somnambulance, somnambulism n. somnambulismo.
somnambule n. sonámbulo-a, persona que anda mientras está dormida.
somniferous n. soporífero.
somnolence n. somnolencia.
son n. hijo; __-in-law / yerno; sonny / hijito.
sonogram n. sonograma, registro de una imagen producida por ultrasonido.
sonography n. sonografía. V. ultrasonography.
sonolucent a. sonoluciente, [ultrasonography] que puede dar paso a las ondas sonoras sin reflejarlas de nuevo en la fuente de origen.
sonorous a. sonoro-a, resonante, con un sonido vibrante.
soon adv. pronto, dentro de poco, en poco tiempo.
soothe v. calmar, aliviar, mitigar; suavizar.
sophistication n. sofisticación, adulteración de una sustancia.
soporific n. soporífico, agente que produce el sueño.
sore a. [feeling] adolorido-a, doloroso-a, con dolor; __ eyes / malestar en los ojos, ojos adoloridos; __ throat / dolor de garganta; __ all over / malestar general, dolor en todo el cuerpo; __ wound / llaga, úlcera; herida; v. to be sore / estar adolorido-a.
sorrow n. pena, aflicción, pesar, dolor.
sorrowful a. apenado-a, afligido-a, apesadumbrado-a, adolorido-a.

sorry *a.* apesadumbrado-a; arrepentido-a; **I am** ___ / Lo siento; *v.* **to be** ___ / arrepentirse de; **to be** ___ **for (someone)** / tener lástima de (alguien).

sort *n.* clase, especie, género; **all** ___**-s of** / una variedad de; **out of** ___**-s** / malhumorado-a, indispuesto-a; *v.* separar, clasificar, distribuir.

soul *n.* alma, espíritu.

sound *n.* sonido, ruido; ruido de soplo percibido por auscultación; *v.* sonar.

soup *n.* sopa.

sour *a.* agrio-a, ácido, avinagrado-a.

source *n.* origen; foco; fuente.

sourness *n.* acedía, agrura, acidez.

south *n.* sur.

soy *n.* soja, soya.

space *n.* área, espacio, segmento, lugar.

spacial *a.* espacial, rel. al espacio.

span *n.* lapso, instante, momento; tiempo limitado; intervalo; distancia.

Spanish *n.* [*language*] español; / [*native*] español-a; *a.* español-a; **Spanish-American** / hispanoamericano-a.

spasm *n.* espasmo, convulsión, contracción muscular involuntaria.

spasmodic *a.* espasmódico-a.

spastic *a.* espástico-a, convulsivo-a, espasmódico-a. 1. de naturaleza espasmódica; ___ **colon** / colon espasmódico o espástico; 2. que sufre espasmos.

spasticity *n.* espasticidad, aumento en la tensión normal de un músuclo que causa movimientos rígidos y dificultosos.

spatula *n.* espátula.

speak *vi.* hablar; ___ **slowly** / Hable, habla despacio; ___ **louder** / Hable, habla más alto.

special *a.* especial, único-a; extraordinario-a; **-ly** *adv.* especialmente.

specialist *n.* especialista.

specialize *v.* especializarse.

specialty *n.* especialidad.

species *n.* (*pl.* **species**) especie, clasificación de organismos vivos pertenecientes a una categoría biológica.

specific *a.* específico-a; determinado-a; preciso-a.

specify *v.* especificar.

specimen *n.* espécimen, muestra.

speck *n.* mácula, mancha.

spectacles *n. pl.* lentes, espejuelos, gafas.

spectrum *n.* (*pl.* **spectra**) espectro. 1. amplitud en la actividad de un antibiótico contra variedades de microorganismos; 2. serie de imágenes que resultan de la refracción de radiación electromagnética; 3. banda matizada de rayos solares discernibles a simple vista o con un instrumento sensitivo.

speculate *v.* argumentar, especular.

speculum *n.* espéculo, instrumento para dilatar un conducto o cavidad.

speech *n.* habla, lenguaje; ___ **defect** / defecto del ___; ___ **disorder** / trastorno del ___; ___

therapy / terapéutica del ___.

spell *n.* ataque súbito; *v.* **to have a** ___ / tener un ataque o acceso de; deletrear; **to** ___ **a word** / deletrear una palabra.

spend *vi.* [*money*] gastar, [*energy*] gastar, consumir; [*time*] pasar.

sperm *n.* esperma, semen; ___ **count** / espermiograma *V.* **semen.**

spermatic *a.* espermático, rel. al esperma.

spermaticidal, spermaticide *n.* espermaticida, que destruye o causa la muerte de espermatozoos.

spermatocele *n.* espermatocele, quiste del epidídimo que contiene espermatozoos.

spermatogenesis *n.* espermatogénesis, proceso de formación y desarrollo de espermatozoos.

spermatoid *a.* espermatoide, con apariencia de semen.

spermatorrhea *n.* espermatorrea, pérdida involuntaria de esperma.

spermatozoid, spermatozoon *n.* (*pl.* **spermatozoa**) espermatozoo, célula sexual masculina que fertiliza el óvulo.

spermicidal *n.* espermicida *V.* **spermaticidal.**

spermiogram *n.* espermiograma, evaluación de los espermatozoides en el proceso de determinación de la esterilidad.

sphenoid *n.* esfenoide, hueso situado en la base del cráneo.

sphere *n.* esfera. 1. estructura en forma de globo; 2. ambiente sociológico.

spherical *a.* esférico-a, rel. a una esfera.

spherocyte *n.* esferocito, eritrocito de forma esférica.

spherocytosis *n.* esferocitosis, presencia de esferocitos en la sangre.

spheroid *n.* esferoide, de forma esférica.

spherule *n.* esfera diminuta.

sphincter *n.* esfínter, músculo circular que abre y cierra un orificio.

sphincteroplasty *n. cirg.* esfinteroplastia, operación plástica de un esfínter.

sphincterotomy *n. cirg.* esfinterotomía, corte de un esfínter.

sphygmomanometer *n.* esfigmomanómetro, instrumento para determinar la presión arterial.

spica *n.* espica, tipo de vendaje.

spice *n.* especia, condimento.

spicular *a.* espicular, en forma de aguja.

spicule *n.* espícula, cuerpo en forma de aguja.

spider *n.* araña; **black** ___ / araña negra.

spike *n.* espiga; [*in a graphic*] cresta o elevación brusca.

spill *n.* derrame; *v.* derramar, verter.

spina *n.* spina, espina. 1. protuberancia en forma de espina; 2. la espina o columna vertebral.

spina bifida *n.* espina bífida, malformación congénita en el cierre de un conducto de la estructura ósea de la espina vertebral, con o sin protrusión de las meninges medulares, gen. a nivel lumbar; **occult** ___ / ___ oculta, sin protrusión.

spinach *n.* espinaca.

spinal *a.* espinal, raquídeo-a, rel. a la médula espinal o a la espina o columna vertebral; ___ **anesthesia** / anestesia raquídea; ___ **canal** / canal raquídeo; ___ **cord** / médula ___; ___ **fluid** / líquido cefalorraquídeo; ___ **fusion** / fusión ___; ___ **puncture** / punción ___; ___ **shock** / choque ___; ___ **stenosis** / estenosis ___.

spinal column *n.* columna o espina vertebral, estructura ósea formada por treinta y tres vértebras que rodean y contienen la médula espinal.

spinal cord *n.* médula espinal, columna de tejido nervioso que se extiende desde el bulbo raquídeo hasta la segunda vértebra lumbar y de la cual parten todos los nervios que van al tronco y a las extremidades; ___ **compression** / compresión de la ___.

spindle *n.* huso. 1. estructura o célula en forma de rodillo; 2. forma que toman los cromosomas durante la mitosis y la meiosis.

spine *n.* columna o espina vertebral; *pop.* espinazo.

spine-shaped *a.* espinoso-a, acantoso-a.

spinous *a.* espinoso-a, en forma de espina.

spiral *a.* espiral, que se envuelve alrededor de un centro o axis.

spirit *n.* 1. espíritu, alma; 2. solución alcohólica de una sustancia volátil.

spiritual healing *n.* cura mental, cura espiritual.

spirochetal *a.* espiroquetósico-a, rel. a espiroquetas.

spirochete *n.* espiroqueta, microorganismo espiral de la especie *Spirochaetales* que incluye el microorganismo causante de la sífilis.

spirometer *n.* espirómetro, instrumento que se usa para medir la cantidad de aire que se inhala y la que se expele del pulmón.

spirometry *n.* espirometría, medida de la capacidad respiratoria tomada por medio de un espirómetro.

spit *n.* saliva, escupo; *vi.* escupir, expectorar.

spittle *n.* saliva; expectoración; salivazo, escupitazo.

splanchnic *a.* esplácnico-a, rel. a las vísceras o que llega a éstas; ___ **nerves** / nervios ___-s.

spleen *n.* bazo, órgano vascular linfático, situado en la cavidad abdominal; **accesory** ___ / ___ accesorio.

splenectomy *n. cirg.* esplenectomía, excisión del bazo.

splenic *a.* esplénico-a, rel. al bazo.

splenoportography *n.* esplenoportografía, radiografía de las venas esplénica y cava usando un medio de contraste radiopaco inyectado en el bazo.

splenorenal *a.* esplenorrenal, rel. al bazo y al riñón.

splenorenal shunt *n.* derivación esplenorrenal, anastomosis de la vena o arteria esplénica a la vena renal esp. en el tratamiento de la hipertensión portal.

splint *n.* férula, tablilla, soporte de madera, metal, plástico, vidrio de fibra o yeso usado para dar apoyo, inmovilizar un hueso fracturado o proteger una parte del cuerpo.

splinter *n.* espina; esquirla; astilla.

split *n.* división, desunión; abertura; *v.* dividir, desunir, separar; dividirse, separarse.

splitting *n.* fragmentación; desdoblamiento.

spoil *v.* echar a perder.

spoken *v. pp.* de **to speak,** hablado.

spoken language *n.* lenguaje hablado.

spondylitis *n.* espondilitis, infl. de una o más vértebras; **ankylosing** ___ / anquilosante, reumatoide.

spondylolisthesis *n.* espondilolistesis, desplazamiento anterior de una vértebra sobre otra, gen. la cuarta lumbar sobre la quinta o ésta sobre el sacro.

spondylolysis *n.* espondilólisis, disolución o destrucción de una vértebra.

spondylopathy *n.* espondilopatía, cualquier enfermedad que afecta las vértebras.

spondylosis *n.* espondilosis. 1. anquilosis vertebral; 2. toda lesión degenerativa de la columna vertebral.

sponge *n.* esponja; *v.* esponjar, remojar con una esponja.

spongy *a.* esponjoso-a; poroso-a.

spontaneous *a.* espontáneo-a.

spoon *n.* cuchara.

spoonful *n.* cucharada.

sporadic *a.* esporádico-a, infrecuente.

spore *n.* espora, célula reproductiva unicelular.

sporicide *n.* esporicida, agente que destruye esporas.

sport *n.* 1. mutación; 2. deporte; ___ **medicine** / medicina del deporte.

spot *n.* mancha, marca, pápula; **blind** ___ / punto ciego; **liver** ___ / ___ hepática; *v.* [*stain*] manchar; [*notice*] notar.

spotting *n.* manchas de flujo vaginal sanguinolento.

sprain *n.* torcedura, esguince, torsión de una articulación con distensión y laceración parcial de los ligamentos; *v.* torcer; torcerse; **to** ___ **one's ankle** / el tobillo.

spray *n.* atomizador de líquido para rociar; *v.* rociar con un líquido.

spread *n.* extensión, diseminación, esparcimiento; *a.* extendido-a, esparcido-a; diseminado-a; *vi.* diseminar; esparcir, extender; diseminarse, esparcirse, extenderse.

sprue *n.* esprue, enfermedad digestiva crónica caracterizada por la inhabilidad de absorber alimentos que contienen gluten.

spur *n.* espolón, protuberancia esp. de un hueso; **calcaneal** ___ / ___ calcáneo.

spurious *a.* espurio-a, falso-a.

sputum *n.* esputo, flema; **bloody** ___ / ___ sanguinolento.

squamous *a.* escamoso-a; ___ **cell** / célula ___.

square *n.* cuadrado; *a.* cuadrado-a; correcto-a, justo, -a.

squash *n.* calabaza; *v.* aplastar; estrujar.

squat *v.* agacharse; sentarse en cuclillas; acuclillarse.

squeak *n.* chirrido; *v.* chirriar, rechinar.

squeal *n.* chillido, alarido; *v.* chillar.

squeeze *v.* apretar, comprimir; [*cloth, fruit*] exprimir.

squint *n.* estrabismo; acción de encoger los ojos como protección contra una luz intensa, o para tratar de ver mejor. *V.* **strabismus.**

stab *n.* puñalada; *v.* apuñalar, acuchillar.

stability *n.* estabilidad, permanencia, seguridad.

stabilization *n.* estabilización, acto de hacer algo estable.

stabilize *v.* estabilizar, evitar cambios o fluctuaciones.

stabilizer *n.* estabilizador, agente que estabiliza.

stable *a.* estable, que no fluctúa.

staff *n.* personal de una institución.

stage *n.* [*sickness*] estadío, etapa o período de transición durante el desarrollo de una enfermedad; fase; **in a recuperating** ___ / en una ___ de recuperación.

stagger *v.* escalonar, saltear, distribuir con una secuencia; vacilar; tambalear; tambalearse.

staging *n.* estadificación, clasificación de la extensión y gravedad durante el proceso de una enfermedad.

stagnation *n.* estancación, estancamiento, falta de circulación en los líquidos.

stain *n.* 1. colorante, tinte; 2. mancha, mácula.

staining *n.* coloración, tintura.

stalk *n.* tallo, estructura alargada que se asemeja al tallo de una planta.

stammer *n.* tartamudeo, balbuceo; *v.* tartamudear, balbucear.

stand *n.* sitio, puesto, situación; *vi.* ponerse o estar de pie; sostenerse; **to** ___ **back** / retroceder; ___ **on your toes** / pararse en la punta de los pies; **to** ___ **still** / no moverse, estarse quieto-a.

standalone *n.* estandona, droga esteroide anabólica.

standard *n.* estándar, norma, criterio, pauta a seguir; lo normal, lo usual o común; ___ **of care** / atención o cuidado ___; ___ **deviation** / desviación ___; ___ **error** / error ___; ___ **procedure** / procedimiento ___, procedimiento usual establecido.

standardization *n.* estandarización, uniformidad; normalización.

standing *n.* [*position*] de pie; [*pending*] vigente; ___ **orders** / órdenes o reglamento vigente.

standstill *n.* paro, cese de actividad.

stapedectomy *n. cirg.* excisión del estribo para mejorar la audición.

stapes *n.* estribo, el más interno de los hueseci-

llos del oído.

staphylococcal *a.* estafilocócico-a, rel. a o causado por estafilococos; ___ **food poisoning** / intoxicación alimenticia por estafilococos.

staphylococcemia *n.* estafilococemia, presencia de estafilococos en la sangre.

Staphylococcus *Gr.* estafilococo. 1. especie de bacteria gram-positiva que puede causar diferentes clases de infecciones; incluye parásitos que se alojan en la piel y las mucosas; 2. término aplicado a cualquier micrococo patológico.

staphylotoxin *n.* estafilotoxina, toxina producida por estafilococos.

staple *n.* presilla, grapa; *v.* presillar, engrapar.

star *n.* estrella.

starch *n.* almidón, fécula, elemento principal de los carbohidratos.

starchy *a.* feculento-a; almidonado-a; ___ **foods** / alimentos ___-s, almidones que contienen carbohidratos.

stare *n.* mirada fija; *v.* mirar fijamente.

start *n.* comienzo, principio, inicio; *v.* empezar, comenzar, iniciar; hacer andar o funcionar un aparato; [*motor*] arrancar, poner en marcha.

starvation *n.* desnutrición, inanición, hambre, privación de alimentos.

starve *v.* pasar hambre, privar de alimentos.

stasis *n.* estasis, estancamiento de la circulación de un líquido tal como la sangre y la orina en una parte del cuerpo.

state *n.* estado, condición; **nutritional** ___ / ___ nutricional.

station *n.* estación; **nursing** ___ / puesto de enfermeras.

stationary *a.* estacionario-a, estacionado-a, que permanece en una posición fija.

statistics *n.* estadística.

stature *n.* estatura, altura.

status *L.* status, estado o condición; ___ **asthmaticus** / ___ asmaticus, condición de un ataque de asma agudo; ___ **epilepticus** / ___ epiléptico, serie de ataques sucesivos con pérdida del conocimiento.

stay *v.* permanecer; quedarse; **to** ___ **awake** / desvelarse; **to** ___ **in bed** / ___ en cama, guardar cama.

steam *n.* vapor.

stearine *n.* estearina, componente blanco y cristalino de las grasas.

steatorrhea *n.* esteatorrea, exceso de grasa en las heces fecales.

stellate *a.* estrellado-a, semejante a una estrella.

stem *n.* tallo, pedúnculo, estructura semejante al tallo de una planta; **brain-**___ / ___ encefálico; ___ **cell** / célula madre.

stenosed *a.* estenosado-a, rel. a una estenosis.

stenosis *n.* estenosis, estrechamiento o contracción anormal de un pasaje; **aortic** ___ / ___ aórtica; **pyloric** ___ / ___ pilórica.

stenotic *a.* estenósico-a, producido por o caracterizado por estenosis.

step n. paso; [stairs] escalón, peldaño; ___ **by** ___ / paso a paso; v. **to** ___ down / bajar; reducir; **to** ___ **in** / entrar; intervenir; **to** ___ **up** / subir; apurar, acelerar.

stereoradiography n. estereorradiografía, radiografía tridimensional.

stereotaxis n. estereotaxia, técnica de localización de áreas cerebrales usadas en procedimientos neurológicos.

stereotype n. estereotipo; cliché.

sterile a. estéril. 1. que no es fértil; 2. aséptico-a; que no contiene ni produce microorganismos.

sterility n. esterilidad, incapacidad de concebir o procrear.

sterilization n. esterilización. 1. procedimiento que impide la reproducción; 2. destrucción completa de microorganismos; **dry heat** ___ / ___ por calor seco; **vapor** ___ / ___ por vapor; **gas** ___ / ___ por gas.

sterilize v. esterilizar.

sternal a. esternal, rel. al esternón; ___ **puncture** / punción ___.

sternocostal a. esternocostal, rel. al esternón y las costillas.

steroid n. esteroide, compuesto orgánico complejo del cual se derivan varias hormonas como el estrógeno, la testosterona y la cortisona.

stertor n. estertor. V. **rale.**

stethoscope n. estetoscopio, instrumento médico usado en la auscultación.

stew n. guisado, cocido; v. guisar, cocer.

sticky a. pegajoso-a.

stiff a. tieso-a, rígido-a; ___ **neck** / cuello ___.

stigma n. estigma, huella. 1. señal específica de una enfermedad; 2. marca o señal en el cuerpo.

still a. inmóvil, quieto-a, tranquilo-a.

stillbirth n. nacimiento sin vida.

stillborn a. mortinato-a, muerto-a al nacer.

Still's disease n. enfermedad de Still, artritis reumatoidea juvenil.

stimulant n. estimulante, agente que produce una reacción.

stimulate v. estimular; motivar; excitar.

stimulation a. estimulación; motivación.

stimulus n. (pl. **stimuli**) estímulo, cualquier agente o factor que produce una reacción; **conditioned** ___ / ___ condicionado; **subliminal** ___ / ___ sublimado.

sting n. picadura; **bee-**___ / picadura de abeja; **wasp** ___ / ___ de avispa.

stink n. olor desagradable, mal olor.

stippling n. punteado, condición de apariencia con manchas.

stipulate n. negociar, estipular.

stir n. movimiento; excitación; v. revolver, agitar.

stirrup bone n. estribo. V. **stapes.**

stitch n. punto de sutura; v. dar puntos.

stock n. caldo.

stocking n. medias; **elastic** ___ / calceta, media elástica.

stocky a. robusto-a.

stoma n. estoma, abertura hecha por cirugía, esp. en la pared del abdomen.

stomach n. estómago, órgano en forma de saco que forma parte del tubo digestivo; ___ **ulcer** / úlcera gástrica; ___**-ache** / dolor de ___; **on an empty** ___ / en ayunas; ___ **pump** / bomba estomacal; ___ **pumping** / lavado de ___; v. pop. soportar, tolerar.

stomachal a. estomacal, rel. al estómago; ___ **tonic** / tónico ___.

stomal n. estomal, rel. a un estoma.

stomatitis n. estomatitis, infl. de la mucosa de la boca; **aphthous** ___ / ___ aftosa.

stone n. piedra, cálculo.

stool n. heces fecales, excremento; ___ **fat** / grasa fecal; ___ **softener** / copro-emoliente.

stop n. parada, alto, interrupción; v. detener, parar, interrumpir; **to make a** ___ / hacer alto, hacer una parada; detenerse, pararse.

stoppage n. bloqueo; obstrucción; taponamiento.

storm n. tormenta; intensificación repentina de síntomas de una enfermedad.

strabismus n. estrabismo, alineamiento anormal de los ojos debido a una deficiencia muscular; pop. bizquera.

straight a. derecho-a, recto-a; estirado-a, erguido-a.

straightjacket n. camisa de fuerza.

strain n. esfuerzo, torcedura, V. **sprain;** [inherited trait] rasgo, cepa; v. forzar; **to** ___ **the eyes** / forzar la vista; **to** ___ **a muscle** / torcer un músculo; [filter] colar, pasar; esforzarse demasiado.

strainer n. colador, coladera.

strand n. filamento, hilo; fibra delicada.

strange a. extraño-a, raro-a; extranjero-a; no relacionado-a con un organismo o situado-a fuera del mismo.

strangle v. estrangular.

strangulated n. estrangulado-a; constreñido-a; ___ **hernia** / hernia ___.

strangulation n. estrangulación. 1. asfixia o sofocación gen. causada por obstrucción de las vías aéreas; 2. constricción de un órgano o estructura debida a compresión.

strap n. faja, banda, correa, tira; v. poner una faja; amarrar, atar.

stratification n. estratificación, formación en capas.

stratified a. estratificado-a, colocado-a en capas; ___ **epithelium** / epitelio ___.

stratum n. estrato; capa.

strawberry n. fresa; ___ **mark** / marca en forma de ___.

stream n. chorro, flujo, corriente.

strength n. fuerza, vigor, resistencia.

strep throat n. infección y dolor de garganta causados por un estreptococo.

streptococcal a. estreptocócico-a, rel. a estreptococos, ___ **infections** / infecciones ___-s.

streptococcemia *n.* estreptococemia, infección de la sangre debida a la presencia de estreptococos.

streptococcus *n.* estreptococo, género de microorganismo de la tribu *Streptococceae*, bacterias gram-positivas que se agrupan en pares o cadenas y que causan enfermedades serias.

streptomycin *n.* estreptomicina, antibiótico que se usa contra infecciones bacterianas.

stress *n.* estrés, tensión emocional, compulsión. 1. factor químico, físico o emocional que provoca un cambio como respuesta inmediata o demorada en las funciones del cuerpo o en sus partes; ___ **test** / prueba de esfuerzo; 2. *gr.* énfasis, acento tónico.

stretch *n.* tirón, estirón, esfuerzo; *v.* extender, alargar, estirar; **to ___ forth, to ___ out** / estirarse, extenderse, alargarse; ___ **receptor** / receptor de estiramiento.

stretcher *n.* camilla, andas; dilatador, extendedor.

stretching *n.* dilatación, estiramiento.

stria *n.* lista, fibra.

striated *a.* estriado-a, enlistado-a; ___ **muscle** / músculo ___ .

stricken *a.* afectado-a súbitamente; afligido-a.

strict *a.* estricto-a; exacto-a.

stricture *n.* estrechez, estrechamiento, constricción.

stridor *L.* stridor, estridor, ruido sordo respiratorio.

strike *n.* golpe, ataque repentino; *vi.* golpear, atacar súbitamente.

string *n.* cuerda, cordel.

string bean *n.* habichuela verde.

stroke *n.* 1. embolia cerebral, apoplejía; ataque súbito; 2. choque, golpe.

stroking *n.* acto de frotar suavemente.

stroma *n.* estroma, armazón de tejido que sirve de soporte a un órgano.

strong *a.* fuerte, fornido-a, robusto-a; ___-**minded** / determinado-a, decidido-a.

structural *a.* estructural, rel. a la estructura de un órgano.

structure *n.* estructura; orden.

struggle *n.* lucha, esfuerzo; *v.* luchar, esforzarse.

struma *L.* estruma, engrosamiento de la tiroides; *pop.* bocio.

strychnine *n.* estricnina, alcaloide cristalino muy venenoso.

stubborn *a.* obstinado-a, testarudo-a, caprichoso-a; *v.* **to become ___** / obstinarse, encapricharse.

student *n.* estudiante; **medical ___** / ___ de medicina.

study *n.* estudio; **double-blind ___-ies** / ___-s de doble incógnita, de doble desconocimiento; *v.* estudiar.

stuff *n.* material, elemento; *v.* embutir, llenar, empaquetar; **to ___ oneself** / hartarse.

stump *n.* muñón, parte que queda de una extremidad amputada.

stun *v.* aturdir, pasmar.

stupid *n.* estúpido-a, imbécil.

stupidity *n.* estupidez.

stupor *n.* estupor, letargo.

sturdy *a.* fuerte, vigoroso-a.

stutter *v.* tartamudear.

stuttering *n.* tartamudeo.

sty *n.* orzuelo, condición inflamatoria de las glándulas sebáceas del párpado.

styloid *a.* estiloide, de forma larga y puntiaguda.

subacromial *a.* subacromial, rel. al acromión o localizado debajo de éste.

subacute *a.* subagudo-a, rel. a una condición que no es ni aguda ni crónica.

subarachnoid *a.* subaracnoideo-a, que ocurre debajo de la membrana aracnoidea o de posición inferior a ésta; ___ **hemorrhage** / hemorragia ___ ; ___ **space** / espacio ___ .

subatomic *a.* subatómico-a, menor que un átomo.

subcapsular *n.* subcapsular, situado debajo de una cápsula.

subclavian, subclavicular *a.* subclavicular, localizado debajo de la clavícula; ___ **steal syndrome** / síndrome del secuestro ___ ; ___ **artery** / arteria ___ ; ___ **vein** / vena ___ .

subclinical *a.* subclínico-a, sin manifestación clínica.

subconscious *n. psic.* subconsciente, subconsciencia, donde se lleva a cabo la elaboración de procesos mentales que afectan la conducta y que no son reconocidos en un nivel consciente; *a.* subconsciente, parcialmente consciente.

subcostal *a.* subcostal, debajo de las costillas.

subculture *n.* subcultivo, cultivo de bacterias que se deriva de otro.

subcutaneous *a.* subcutáneo-a, debajo de la piel.

subdivide *v.* subdividir.

subdue *a.* sumiso-a, dominado-a, subyugado-a; *v.* dominar, subyugar.

subdural *a.* subdural, situado debajo de la dura madre; ___ **hematoma** / hematoma ___ ; ___ **space** / espacio ___ .

subependymal *a.* subependimario-a, situado debajo del epéndimo.

subhepatic *a.* subhepático-a, situado debajo del hígado.

subject *n.* sujeto. 1. término usado en referencia al paciente; 2. tópico; 3. *gr.* sujeto del verbo.

subjective *a.* subjetivo-a; ___ **symptoms** / síntomas ___-s.

sublethal dose *a.* dosis subletal, cantidad insuficiente de una sustancia para causar la muerte.

sublimate *n.* sublimado, sustancia adquirida por sublimación; *v.* sublimar, depurar.

sublimation *n.* sublimación. 1. cambio de un estado sólido a vapor; 2. *psic.* término freudiano que se refiere al proceso de transferir un impulso o deseo instintivo a una conducta aceptada socialmente.

sublingual *a.* sublingual, situado-a debajo de la lengua; __ **gland** / glándula __.

subluxation *a.* subluxación, dislocación incompleta.

submandibular *a.* submandibular, debajo de la mandíbula.

submental *a.* submental, debajo del mentón.

submerge *v.* sumergir, colocar debajo de un líquido.

submission *n.* sumisión, sometimiento.

submit *v.* someter; someterse.

submucosa *n.* submucosa, capa de tejido celular situado debajo de una mucosa.

subnormal *a.* subnormal, menos que el promedio normal.

subphrenic *a.* subfrénico-a, situado-a debajo del diafragma; __ **abscess** / absceso __.

subscapular *a.* subescapular, debajo de la escápula.

subscription *n.* subscripción, parte de la receta médica que da instrucciones para la preparación de un medicamento.

subside *v.* menguar, apaciguar, bajar, cesar.

subsist *v.* subsistir, sobrevivir.

substance *n.* sustancia, líquido; droga; __ **abuse** / abuso de drogas; __ **dependence** / dependencia de drogas; __ **withdrawal syndrome** / síndrome de abstinencia de drogas; **ground** __ / __ fundamental.

substantive *n. gr.* substantivo, sustantivo, nombre.

substernal *a.* subesternal, debajo del esternón.

substitute *n.* sustituto-a; reemplazo; *v.* sustituir, reemplazar.

substitution *n.* substitución, __ **therapy** / terapia por __.

substratum *n.* sustrato, fundación, base en la que vive un organismo.

substructure *n.* subestructura, soporte o material que sirve de base.

subtile, subtle *a.* sutil, delicado-a; inadvertido-a, desapercibido-a.

subungual *a.* subungual, debajo de una uña.

succeed *v.* tener éxito, salir bien; lograr.

success *n.* éxito, acierto, triunfo.

successful *a.* afortunado-a, de excelente resultado.

successive *a.* sucesivo-a, consecutivo-a.

succus *L.* succus, jugo.

such *a.* tal, semejante; **in __ manner** / en __ forma.

suck *v.* chupar, [*mother's milk*] mamar; **to __ out** / chupar sacando; vaciar, extraer.

sucrose *n.* sucrosa, sacarosa que se obtiene de la caña de azúcar o la remolacha.

suction *n.* succión, aspiración; __ **device** / dispositivo de __.

sudden *a.* súbito-a, imprevisto-a, repentino-a; __ **death** / muerte __.

sudor *n.* sudor, secreción de las glándulas sudoríparas.

sudorific *a.* sudorífico-a, que promueve el sudor.

sudoriparous *a.* sudoríparo-a, que secreta sudor; __ **gland** / glándula __.

sue *v.* demandar, poner pleito.

suffer *v.* sufrir, padecer; **to __ from** / padecer de.

suffering *n.* sufrimiento, padecimiento.

sufficient *a.* suficiente; **-ly** *adv.* suficientemente.

suffix *n. gr.* sufijo.

suffocate *v.* sofocar, asfixiar; faltar la respiración.

suffocation *n.* asfixia, paro de la respiración.

suffusion *n.* sufusión, infiltración de un líquido del cuerpo en los tejidos circundantes.

sugar *n.* azúcar, carbohidrato que consiste esencialmente de sucrosa; **beet __, cane __** / sucrosa; **fruit __** / fructosa; **grape __** / glucosa; **milk __** / lactosa.

suggest *v.* sugerir, indicar, aconsejar.

suggestion *n.* sugerencia, consejo, indicación; sugestión.

suggestive *a.* sugestivo-a, rel. a la sugestión o que sugiere.

suicidal *a.* suicida, rel. al suicidio o con tendencia al mismo.

suicide *n.* suicidio; suicidarse; **attempted __** / tentativa o intento de __.

sulcus *L.* (*pl.* **sulci**) sulcus, depresión leve, sisura.

sulfacetamide *n.* sulfacetamida, sulfonamida antibacteriana.

sulfa drugs *n.* sulfa, medicamentos del grupo sulfonamida, antibacterianos.

sulfate *n.* sulfato, sal de ácido sulfúrico.

sulfonamides *n. pl.* sulfonamidas, grupo de compuestos orgánicos sulfuro-bacteriostáticos.

sulfur *n.* azufre, sulfuro.

sulfuric *a.* sulfúrico-a, rel. al sulfuro.

sullen *a.* malhumorado-a; resentido-a.

summary *n.* sumario, historia clínica del paciente; __ **of hospital records** / sumario del expediente.

summation *n.* suma total, acción o efecto acumulativo.

sun *n.* sol; __ **-bathing** / baño de __; __ **-burn** / quemadura de __, eritema solar; __ **-burnt** / quemado-a, tostado-a por el sol; *v.* **to __ -bathe** / tomar el __.

sunscreen *n.* bloqueador solar.

sunspot *n.* mancha de sol.

sunstroke *n.* insolación.

superb *a.* magnífico-a, superior.

super ego *L.* el yo, término freudiano que se refiere a la parte de la psique que concierne a los valores sociales, morales y éticos.

superfecundation *n.* superfecundación, fertilización sucesiva de dos óvulos que pertenecen al mismo ciclo menstrual en dos actos sexuales distintos.

superfemale *n.* superhembra, organismo femenino que tiene más del número necesario de cromosomas que determinan el sexo.

superficial *a.* superficial, rel. a la superficie; **-ly** *adv.* superficialmente.

superinfection *n.* superinfección, infección subsecuente producida gen. por un microorganismo diferente que ocurre durante el curso de una infección presente.

superior *n.* superior, más alto; [*position*] hacia arriba; al exterior.

superiority complex *n.* complejo de superioridad.

supernatural *a.* sobrenatural.

supernumerary *a.* supernumerario-a, en número mayor que el normal.

superolateral *a.* superolateral, en posición superior y lateral.

supersaturate *v.* supersaturar, saturar excesivamente, añadir una sustancia en una cantidad mayor de la que puede ser disuelta normalmente por un líquido.

supersaturated *a.* supersaturado-a.

supersensitiveness *n.* supersensibilidad, hipersensibilidad.

supersonic *a.* supersónico-a, ultrasónico, rel. a ondas de frecuencia demasiado alta para ser captadas por el oído humano.

superstition *n.* superstición.

superstitious *a.* supersticioso-a.

supervise *v.* supervisar, dirigir.

supervisor *n.* supervisor-a, jefe-a.

supine *a.* supino-a, de posición acostada de espalda, boca arriba y con la palma de la mano hacia arriba.

supper *n.* cena, la comida.

supplant *v.* reemplazar, substituir.

supplement *n.* suplemento; *v.* complementar.

supplemental *a.* suplemental, adicional.

supply *n.* abastecimiento; **supplies** / artículos de ___, provisiones; *v.* proveer, surtir, abastecer.

support *n.* soporte, sostén.

suppose *v.* suponer.

suppository *n.* supositorio, medicamento semisólido que se inserta en una cavidad natural del cuerpo (vagina, recto).

suppression *n.* supresión. 1. fallo súbito del cuerpo en la producción de una excreción o secreción normal; 2. en psicoanálisis, la inhibición de una idea o deseo.

suppurate *v.* supurar, excretar.

suppuration *n.* supuración, formación o salida de pus.

suppurative *a.* supurativo-a, rel. a la supuración.

supraclavicular *a.* supraclavicular, situado-a encima de la clavícula.

supraglottic *a.* supraglótico-a, situado encima de la glotis.

suprapubic *a.* suprapúbico-a, localizado-a encima del pubis; ___ **catheter** / cáteter ___; ___ **cystostomy** / cistostomía ___.

supratentorial *a.* supratentorial, que ocurre encima del tentorio.

sural *a.* sural, rel. a la pantorrilla.

sure *a.* seguro-a, decidido-a; positivo-a.

surface *n.* superficie; porción o límite exterior de una estructura; ___ **tension** / tensión superficial.

surfactant *n.* surfactante, agente tensoactivo que modifica la tensión superficial de un líquido.

surgeon *n.* cirujano-a.

surgery *n.* cirugía, rama de la medicina que comprende procesos operatorios de reparación, diagnosis de enfermedades y corrección de estructuras del cuerpo; **ambulatory** ___ / ___ ambulatoria; **arthroscopic** ___ / ___ artroscópica; **chest** ___ / ___ cardiotorácica; **conservative** ___ / ___ conservadora; **corrective** ___ / ___ correctiva; **cytoreductive** ___ / ___ citorreductiva; **major** ___ / ___ mayor; **minor** ___ / ___ menor; **orthopedic** ___ / ___ ortopédica; **oral** ___ / ___ oral; **plastic** ___ / ___ plástica; **radical** ___ / ___ radical; **reconstructive** ___ / ___ reconstructiva.

surgical *a.* quirúrgico-a; ___ **dressing** / vendaje ___ protector; ___ **equipment** / equipo ___; ___ **flaps** / colgajos ___-s; ___ **incision** / incisión ___; ___ **instruments** / instrumentos ___-s; ___ **mesh** / malla ___; ___ **resident** / residente de cirugía.

surname *n.* apellido, nombre de familia.

surpass *v.* sobrepasar, exceder.

surplus *n., a.* sobrante, excedente.

surprise *n.* sorpresa.

surrogate *a.* subrogado-a, que sustituye algo o a alguien; *v.* subrogar, sustituir.

surveillance *n.* vigilancia.

survey *n.* encuesta; cuestionario.

survival *n.* supervivencia.

survive *v.* sobrevivir.

survivor *n.* sobreviviente.

survivorship *n.* supervivencia; anualidad, renta o pensión anual.

susceptibility *n.* susceptibilidad.

susceptible *a.* susceptible.

suspect *a.* sospechoso-a.

suspend *v.* suspender, cancelar.

Surgery	*Cirugía*
ambulatory	ambulatoria
arthroscopic	artroscópica
chest	cardiotorácica
cytoreductive	citorreductiva
conservative	conservadora
corrective	correctiva
major	mayor
minor	menor
orthopedic	ortopédica
oral	oral
plastic	plástica
radical	radical
reconstructive	reconstructiva

suspicion n. sospecha.

sustain v. sostener, mantener; [a wound] sufrir una herida.

sustained a. sostenido-a; ininterrumpido-a; sufrido-a.

suture n. sutura; puntada; línea de unión; **absorbable surgical** ___ / ___ absorbible quirúrgica; **bolster** ___ / ___ compuesta; **catgut** ___ / ___ de catgut; **purse-string** ___ / ___ en bolsa de tabaco; **uninterrupted continuous** ___ / ___ continua, de peletero; **vertical mattress** ___ / ___ de colchonero.

swab n. escobillón; v. limpiar, fregar.

swaddling band n. fajero.

swallow n. trago; deglución; v. tragar, deglutir.

swallowing n. deglución.

Swan-Ganz catheter n. cáteter de Swan-Ganz, sonda flexible que contiene un balón cerca de la punta y que se emplea para medir la presión sanguínea en la arteria pulmonar.

swaying n. vaivén, movimiento acompasado.

sweat n. sudor, secreción de las glándulas sudoríparas; **cold** ___ / ___ -es fríos; **night** ___-s / ___-es nocturnos; v. sudar; hacer sudar.

sweated a. pp. de **to sweat**, sudoriento-a; sudoroso-a.

sweat glands n. pl. glándulas sudoríparas.

sweating n. sudor, perspiración, transpiración.

sweaty a. sudado-a, sudoroso-a.

sweep vi. barrer; recoger; limpiar.

sweet a. dulce, azucarado-a; [tempered] dulce, agradable, gentil.

sweet basil n. albahaca.

sweetener n. dulcificante.

sweeten v. endulzar, azucarar.

sweets n. pl. golosinas, dulces.

swell vi. hinchar, abultar, entumecer, agrandar; hincharse, entumecerse, agrandarse.

swelling n. hinchazón; tumefacción; pop. bulto, chichón.

swift a. ligero-a; fácil, sin complicación; **a** ___ **operation** / una operación fácil, sin complicaciones.

swim vi. nadar.

swimmer n. nadador-a; ___**'s ear** / otitis del ___.

switch n. [instrumento] cambio; conector eléctrico; v. cambiar; **to** ___ **on** / conectar; **to** ___ **off** / desconectar; cambiar.

swollen a. pp. de **to swell**, hinchado-a.

swoon n. desmayo, síncope; v. desfallecer; desmayarse, desvanecerse.

syllable n. gr. sílaba.

Sylvian aqueduct n. acueducto de Silvius, conducto estrecho que conecta los ventrículos cerebrales tercero y cuarto.

symbiosis n. simbiosis, unión estrecha de dos organismos que pertenecen a especies diferentes.

symbiotic a. simbiótico-a, rel. a la simbiosis.

symbol n. símbolo, representación o señal que sustituye o representa en la práctica otra cosa o idea.

symbolism n. simbolismo. 1. uso de símbolos en la práctica para dar una representación a las cosas; 2. psic. anormalidad mental por la cual el paciente percibe todos los sucesos y cosas como símbolos de sus propios pensamientos.

symmetrical a. simétrico-a.

symmetry n. simetría, correspondencia perfecta entre partes de un cuerpo colocadas en posición opuesta a un centro o axis.

sympathectomy n. cirg. simpatectomía, extirpación de una porción del simpático.

sympathetic a. simpático-a, rel. al sistema nervioso simpático.

sympathetic nervous system n. sistema nervioso simpático, abastecedor de los músculos involuntarios, formado por nervios motores y sensoriales.

sympatholytic a. simpatolítico-a, que ofrece resistencia a la actividad producida por la estimulación del sistema nervioso simpático.

sympathomimetic a. simpatomimético-a, que puede causar cambios fisiológicos similares a los causados por el sistema nervioso simpático.

sympathy n. simpatía, asociación, relación. 1. afinidad; 2. relación entre dos órganos afines por la cual una anomalía en uno afecta al otro; 3. afinidad entre la mente y el cuerpo que causa que se afecten entre sí.

symphysis n. sínfisis, articulación en la cual las superficies óseas adyacentes se unen por un fibrocartílago; **pubic** ___ / ___ púbica.

symptom n. síntoma, manifestación o indicio de una enfermedad según se percibe por el paciente; **constitutional** ___ / ___ constitucional; **delayed** ___ / ___ demorado; **objective** ___ / ___ objetivo; **pathognomic** ___ / ___ patognómico; **presenting** ___ / ___ presente; **prodromal** ___ / ___ prodrómico; **withdrawal** ___ / ___ de supresión.

symptomatic a. sintomático-a, de la naturaleza de un síntoma o rel. a éste.

symptomatology n. sintomatología, conjunto de síntomas que se refieren a una enfermedad o a un caso determinado.

symptom complex n. complejo de síntomas concurrentes que caracterizan una enfermedad.

synapse n. sinapsis, punto de contacto entre dos neuronas donde el impulso que pasa por la primera neurona origina un impulso en la segunda.

synapsis n. sinapsis, aparejamiento de cromosomas homólogos al comienzo de la meiosis.

synaptic a. sináptico-a, rel. a la sinapsis.

synarthrosis n. sinartrosis, articulación inmóvil en la cual los elementos óseos están fusionados.

synchondrosis n. sincondrosis, articulación inmóvil de superficies unidas por tejido cartilaginoso.

syncopal a. sincopal, rel. a un síncope.

syncope *n.* síncope, desmayo o pérdida temporal del conocimiento.

syncytial *a.* sincitial, rel. a un sincitio o que lo constituye.

syncytium *n.* sincitio, masa protoplasmática nucleada que resulta de la fusión celular.

syndactylism *n.* sindactilia, anomalía congénita que consiste en la fusión de dos o más dedos de la mano o los pies.

syndrome *n.* síndrome, síntomas y señales que caracterizan una enfermedad; **acquired immune deficiency ___ (AIDS) / ___** de inmunodeficiencia adquirida (SIDA); **adipose ___ / ___** adiposo; **adrenogenital ___ / ___** suprarrenogenital; **battered children ___ / ___** de niños maltratados; **congenital rubella ___ / ___** congénito de rubéola; **dumping ___ / ___** de vaciamiento gástrico rápido; **hepatorenal ___ / ___** hepatorrenal; **malabsorption ___ / ___** de malabsorción gastrointestinal; **middle lobe ___ / ___** del lóbulo medio del pulmón; **nephrotic ___ / ___** nefrótico; **respiratory stress ___ / ___** de dificultad respiratoria; **scalded skin ___ / ___** de escaldadura, quemadura de la epidermis; **sick sinus ___ / ___** del seno carotídeo; **subclavian steal ___ / ___** del secuestro subclavicular; **sudden death ___ / ___** de muerte súbita; **multiple transfusion ___ / ___** de transfusión múltiple; **toxic shock ___ / ___** de choque tóxico, envenenamiento de la sangre causado por estafilococos; **withdrawal ___ / ___** de privación.

synechia *n.* sinequia, unión o adherencia anormal de tejidos u órganos esp. referente al iris, al cristalino y a la córnea.

synergic *n.* sinérgico-a, que posee la propiedad de actuar en cooperación.

synergism *n.* sinergismo, correlación o unión armoniosa entre dos o más estructuras o sustancias.

synovia *n.* sinovia, líquido que lubrica las articulaciones y los tendones.

synovial *a.* sinovial, rel. a la membrana sinovial; **___ bursa** / bursa ___; ; **cyst** / quiste ___.

synovial fluid *n.* líquido sinovial, líquido viscoso transparente.

synovitis *n.* sinovitis, infl. de la membrana sinovial; **dry ___ / ___** seca; **purulent ___ / ___** purulenta; **serous ___ / ___** serosa.

synovium *n.* membrana sinovial.

synthesis *n.* síntesis, composición de un todo por la unión de las partes.

synthesize *u.* sintetizar, producir síntesis.

synthetic *a.* sintético-a, rel. a una síntesis o producido por ésta.

syntonic *a.* sintónico-a, rel. a un tipo de personalidad estable que se adapta normalmente al ambiente.

syphilis *n.* sífilis, enfermedad venérea contagiosa que se manifiesta en lesiones cutáneas, usu. transmitida por contacto directo.

syphilitic *n. a.* sifilítico-a, rel. a la sífilis o causado por ella.

syphilology *n.* sifilología, rama de la medicina que se dedica al tratamiento y diagnosis de la sífilis.

syphiloma *n.* tumor sifilítico.

syringe *n.* jeringa, jeringuilla; **disposable ___ / ___** desechable; **glass cylinder ___ / ___** con tubo de cristal; **hypodermic ___ / ___** hipodérmica.

syringobulbia *n.* siringobulbia, presencia de cavidades en la médula oblongata.

syringocele *n.* siringocele. 1. conducto central de la médula espinal; 2. meningomielocele que contiene una cavidad en la médula espinal ectópica.

syringomyelia *n.* siringomielia, enfermedad crónica progresiva de la columna vertebral caracterizada por cavidades llenas de líquido en la región cervical y que a veces se extiende a la médula oblongata.

syrinx *Gr.* (*pl.* **syringes**) syrinx. 1. fístula; 2. tubo o conducto.

syrup *n.* jarabe, almíbar.

system *n.* sistema, grupo de partes u órganos combinados que constituyen un conjunto que desempeña una o más funciones vitales en el organismo; **cardiovascular ___ / ___** cardiovascular; **digestive ___ / ___** digestivo; **endocrine ___ / ___** endocrino; **genitourinary ___ / ___** genitourinario; **hematopoietic ___ / ___** hematopoyético; **immune ___ / ___** de inmunidad; **lymphatic ___ / ___** linfático; **nervous ___ / ___** nervioso; **osseous ___ / ___** óseo; **portal ___ / ___** portal; **respiratory ___ / ___** respiratorio; **reticuloendothelial ___ / ___** reticuloendotelial.

systematic *a.* sistemático-a, que se ajusta a un régimen o sistema.

systematization *n.* sistematización, acción de seguir un sistema.

systematize *n.* sistematizar, hacer una síntesis.

systemic *a.* sistémico-a; que afecta el cuerpo en general; **___ circulation** / circulación ___.

systole *n.* sístole, contracción del corazón esp. de los ventrículos; **atrial ___ / ___** auricular; **premature ___ / ___** prematura; **ventricular ___ / ___** ventricular.

systolic *a.* sistólico-a, rel. a la sístole; **___ murmur** / soplo ___; **___ pressure** / presión ___.

T *abbr.* **absolute temperature** / temperatura absoluta; **T+, increased tension** / tensión aumentada; **T−, diminished tension** / tensión disminuida.

tabacism *n.* tabaquismo, intoxicación aguda o crónica causada por una excesiva inhalación de polvo de tabaco.

tabes *n.* tabes, deterioro progresivo del organismo o de una parte del mismo debido a una enfermedad crónica.

tabetic *a.* tabético-a, rel. a tabes o que padece de éste.

table *n.* tabla. 1. capa o lámina ósea; 2. mesa; **examination** ___ / ___ de reconocimiento; **operating** ___ / ___ de operaciones; 3. tabla, colección de datos o de referencia con una variante determinada.

tablespoon *n.* cuchara; ___-**ful** *n.* cucharada; *V.* **Appendix C.**

tablet *n.* tableta, comprimido, dosis en un compuesto sólido; **enteric coated** ___ / ___ de capa entérica.

taboo, tabu *n.* tabú, prohibición; *a.* prohibido-a.

tabular *a.* tabular, dispuesto en forma de tabla o cuadro.

tabulate *v.* tabular, hacer tablas o listas.

tache *n.* tacha, mancha, peca; imperfección.

tachyarrhythmia *n.* taquiarritmia, forma de arritmia acompañada de pulso rápido.

tachycardia *n.* taquicardia, aceleración de la actividad cardíaca, gen. a una frecuencia de más de 100 por minuto en una persona adulta; **atrial** ___ / ___ auricular; **ectopic** ___ / ___ ectópica; **paroxysmal atrial** ___ / ___ auricular paroxística; **sinus** ___ / ___ sinusal; **supraventricular** ___ / ___ supraventricular; **ventricular** ___ / ___ ventricular.

tachypnea *n.* taquipnea, respiración anormalmente acelerada.

tact *n.* tacto; diplomacia, discreción.

tactful *a.* discreto-a.

tactic *n.* táctica.

tactile *a.* táctil, palpable; rel. al sentido del tacto; ___ **discrimination** / discriminación ___; ___ **system** / sistema ___.

tactless *a.* indiscreto-a.

taenia, tenia *n.* tenia, parásito de la clase *Cestoda* que en la etapa adulta vive en el intestino de los vertebrados.

tag *n.* [*label*] etiqueta.

tail *n.* [*appendage*] cola, rabo.

taint *n.* [*stain*] mancha, mácula; *v.* manchar, podrirse o causar putrefacción; corromperse.

take *vi.* [*to get*] tomar; [*to seize*] coger, agarrar; [*to carry something, to take someone*] llevar; [*to remove*] quitar; **to** ___ **notes** / anotar; **to** ___ **a trip** / viajar; **to** ___ **a walk** / dar un paseo; **to be taken ill** / enfermarse.

talar *a.* talar, rel. al tobillo.

talc *n.* talco.

talcum *n.* polvo.

tale *n.* [*story*] cuento; [*gossip*] *pop.* chisme.

talent *n.* talento, habilidad.

talk *n.* charla, plática; *v.* charlar, hablar, platicar.

tall *a.* alto-a; elevado-a.

talon *n.* talón, parte posterior de un diente molar.

talotibial *a.* talotibial, rel. al talón y la tibia.

talus *n.* (*pl.* **tali**) talón, astrágalo, tobillo.

tambour *n.* tambor. 1. tímpano del oído medio; 2. instrumento de precisión que se usa para registrar y transmitir movimientos ligeros tales como las contracciones peristálticas.

tampon *n.* tapón, gasa o algodón prensado que se aplica o inserta en la vagina u otra cavidad para absorber secreciones.

tamponade *Fr.* taponamiento, aplicación de tapones a una herida o cavidad para detener una hemorragia o absorber secreciones; **balloon** ___ / ___ por balón insuflable; **cardiac** ___ / ___ cardíaco, compresión aguda del corazón causada por un exceso de sangre acumulada en el pericardio.

tangible *a.* tangible.

tangle *n.* enredo, confusión; *v.* enredarse; confundirse.

tangled *a.* enredado-a; confundido-a.

tangy *a.* [*smell*] fuerte, penetrante.

tantrum *n.* rabieta; *pop.* berrinche, pataleta.

tap *n.* punción, perforación; acto de perforar un tejido con un instrumento afilado; **bloody** ___ / ___ lumbar hemática; **spinal** ___ / ___ lumbar; *v.* tocar ligeramente; punzar, perforar, hacer una punción; ___ **water** / agua corriente.

tape *n.* [*audiotape*] cinta magnética; [*adhesive*] esparadrapo; ___ **recorder** / grabadora.

tapeworm *n.* tenia, solitaria. *V.* **taenia.**

tarantula *n.* tarántula, araña negra venenosa.

tardive *Fr.* tardío, retardado-a, que tarda en aparecer.

target *n.* 1. [*area*] blanco; 2. objetivo de una investigación; 3. célula "en diana" u órgano afectado por un agente definido (droga u hormona).

tarsal *a.* tarsal, tarsiano-a. 1. rel. al tarso; 2. rel. al tejido conectivo que soporta el párpado del ojo.

tarsal bones *n. pl.* huesos del tarso.

tarsometatarsal *a.* tarsometatarsiano-a, rel. al tarso y al metatarso.

tarsus *n.* tarso, parte posterior del pie situada entre los huesos de la pierna y los huesos metatarsianos.

tart *a.* agrio-a, ácido-a.

task *n.* tarea, labor, trabajo.

taste *n.* gusto; ___ **buds** / papilas gustativas; **in good** ___ / de buen ___; *v.* probar, saborear.

tasteful *a.* gustoso-a, sabroso-a.

tasteless *a.* insípido-a, sin sabor.

tasty *a.* gustoso-a, apetitoso-a, sabroso-a.

tattooing *n.* tatuaje, diseño con colorantes permanentes en la epidermis.

taught *pret., pp.* de **to teach**, enseñado.

tax *n.* impuesto, contribución; **tax-exempt** *a.* exento de impuesto; *v.* imponer; cargar, abrumar.

taxis *L.* taxis. 1. manipulación o reducción de una parte u órgano para llevarlo a la posición normal; 2. reflejo direccional del movimiento de un organismo en respuesta a un estímulo.

T cells *n. pl.* linfocitos T, linfocitos diferenciados en el timo que dirigen la respuesta inmunológica y que asisten a los linfocitos B a responder a antígenos; **helper** ___ / ___ inductores, ayudantes, estimulantes de la producción de anticuerpos formados por células que se derivan del linfocito B; **cytotoxic** ___ / ___ citotóxicos, destructores de células extrañas al cuerpo (como en el caso de órganos transplantados); **suppressor** ___ / ___ supresores de la producción de anticuerpos formados por células que se derivan del linfocito B.

tea *n.* té.

teach *vi.* enseñar.

team *n.* equipo; grupo asociado; *v.* **to** ___ **up** / asociarse en cooperación.

teamwork *n.* esfuerzo coordinado; trabajo en coordinación.

tear *n.* lágrima; desgarramiento, desgarro; ___ **gas** / gas lacrimógeno; *vi.* rasgar, desgarrar, romper; **to** ___ **off** / arrancar; **to shed** ___-s / lagrimear llorar.

tear duct *n.* conducto lacrimal.

tearful *a.* lagrimoso-a.

tearing *n.* lagrimeo.

tease *v.* rasgar, separar un tejido o espécimen con agujas para examinarlo bajo el microscopio.

teaspoon *n.* cucharita; ___-ful / cucharadita.

teat *n.* tetilla. 1. glándula mamaria; 2. pezón.

technetium 99m *n.* technecio 99m., radioisótopo que emite rayos gamma, de uso frecuente en medicina nuclear.

technician *n.* técnico-a, persona entrenada en la administración de tratamientos o pruebas de laboratorio y que gen. actúa bajo la supervisión de un facultativo; **dental** ___ / ___ dental; **electrocardiographic** ___ / ___ electrocardiógrafo-a; **emergency medical** ___ / ___ de emergencia; **medical laboratory** ___ / laboratorista; **radiologic** ___ / ___ radiólogo-a; **respiratory therapy** ___ / ___ de terapia respiratoria.

technique *n.* técnica, método o procedimiento.

technologist *n.* tecnólogo-a, persona experta en tecnología.

technology *n.* tecnología, ciencia que trata de la aplicación de procedimientos técnicos.

tectorium *L.* tectorium, membrana que cubre el órgano de Corti.

tectum *L.* tectum, estructura en forma de techo.

tedious *a.* tedioso-a, aburrido-a, engorroso-a.

teenage *n.* adolescencia.

teenager *n.* jovencito-a de trece a diecinueve años de edad.

teeth *n. pl.* dientes; **deciduous** ___ / ___ de leche o primera dentición; **permanent** ___ / ___ permanentes; **secondary** ___ / ___ secundarios; **wisdom** ___ / ___ cordales, *pop.* muelas del juicio.

teething *n.* dentición.

tegument *n.* tegumento, la piel.

telangiectasia *n.* telangiectasia, telangiectasis, condición causada por dilatación de los vasos capilares y arteriolas que puede formar un angioma.

telemedicine *n.* telemedicina, uso de la televisión como medio de asistencia en el cuidado de la salud.

telemetry *n.* telemetría, información transmitida electrónicamente a distancia.

telencephalon *n.* telencéfalo, porción anterior del encéfalo.

telepathy *n.* telepatía, comunicación aparente de pensamientos de una persona a otra por medios extrasensoriales.

telephone *n.* teléfono; ___ **call** / llamada telefónica; *v.* telefonear, llamar por teléfono.

teleradiography *n.* telerradiografía, rayos X tomados a dos o más metros de distancia del objetivo para disminuir distorsiones.

television *n.* televisión; ___ **set** / televisor.

tell *vi.* decir; relatar, contar.

telophase *n.* telofase, fase final de un proceso.

temper *n.* carácter, disposición; temple, humor; genio; *v.* **to have bad** ___ / tener mal ___; **to have good** ___ / tener buen ___.

temperament *n.* temperamento, combinación de la constitución física, mental y emocional de una persona que la distingue de otras.

temperate *a.* moderado-a; sobrio-a, abstemio-a.

temperature *n.* temperatura. 1. grado de calor o frío según se mide en una escala específica; 2. calor natural de un cuerpo vivo; 3. fiebre o calentura; **absolute** ___ / ___ absoluta; **ambient** ___ / ___ ambiental; **axillary** ___ / ___ axilar; **body** ___ / ___ del cuerpo; **critical** ___ / ___ crítica; **maximum** ___ / ___ máxima; **minimum** ___ / ___ mínima; **normal** ___ / ___ normal; **oral** ___ / ___ oral; **rectal** ___ / ___ rectal; **subnormal** ___ / ___ subnormal.

tempest *n.* tempestad, tormenta.

template *n.* patrón, molde.

temple *n.* sien, superficie lisa a cada lado de la parte lateral de la cabeza.

temporal *a.* temporal. 1. rel. a la sien; ___ **bone** / hueso ___; ___ **lobe** / lóbulo ___; 2. rel. al tiempo.

temporary *a.* temporal; pasajero-a; [*transition period*] interino-a; transitorio-a.

temporomandibular joint *n.* articulación temporomaxilar, rel. a la articulación entre la mandíbula y el hueso temporal.

tempting *a.* tentador-a; atractivo-a.

tenacious *a.* tenaz, persistente; determinado-a.

tend *v.* cuidar, atender; vigilar.

tendency *n.* tendencia.

tender *a.* sensitivo-a al tacto o la palpación; ___ **points** / puntos neurálgicos; [*soft*] blando-a, tierno-a.

tenderness *n.* blandura; delicadeza. 1. sensibilidad, condición sensible al tacto o palpación; 2. ternura.

tendinitis, tendonitis *n.* tendinitis, tendonitis, infl. de un tendón.

tendinous *a.* tendinoso-a, rel. a o semejante a un tendón.

tendon *n.* tendón, tejido fibroso que sirve de unión a los músculos y los huesos y a otras partes; **deep ___ reflexes** / reflejos profundos de los ___-es; ___ **jerk** / tirón tendinoso; ___ **reflex** / reflejo tendinoso.

tenesmus *n.* tenesmo, condición dolorosa e ineficaz al orinar o defecar.

tennis elbow *n.* codo de tenista.

tenosynovitis *n.* tenosinovitis, infl. de la vaina que cubre un tendón.

tense *a.* tenso-a, rígido-a, tirante, en estado de tensión.

tenseness *n.* tensión.

tension *n.* tensión. 1. acto o efecto de estirarse o ser extendido; 2. grado de estiramiento; 3. sobreesfuerzo mental, emocional o físico; **premenstrual ___** / ___ premenstrual; 4. expansión de un gas o vapor; **surface ___** / ___ superficial.

tension headache *n.* dolor de cabeza causado por una tensión nerviosa mental.

tensor *n.* tensor, músculo que estira o hace tensión.

tent *n.* tienda, cámara esp. para cubrir un espacio en el cual se incluye al paciente; **oxygen ___** / ___ o cámara de oxígeno.

tentaculum *n.* tentáculo, tipo de gancho quirúrgico para sujetar o prensar una parte.

tentative *a.* tentativo-a, experimental, sujeto-a a cambios.

tentorial *a.* tentorial, rel. a un tentorium.

tentorium *L.* tentorium, estructura que se asemeja a una tienda.

tenuous *a.* tenue, delicado-a.

tepid *a.* tibio-a.

teratogen *n.* teratógeno, agente que causa teratogénesis.

teratogenesis *a.* teratogénesis, producción de anomalías severas en el feto.

teratoid *a.* teratoide. 1. semejante a un monstruo; 2. que proviene de un embrión malformado; ___ **tumor** / tumor ___.

teratology *n.* teratología, estudio de malformaciones en el feto.

teratoma *n.* teratoma, neoplasma que deriva de más de una capa embrionaria y por lo tanto se compone de tejidos de distintas clases.

teres *L.* teres, término empleado para describir ciertos tipos de músculos o ligamentos alargados y cilíndricos.

term *n.* término. 1. período de tiempo de duración efectiva o limitada tal como en el embarazo; 2. vocablo.

terminal *a.* terminal, final.

terminal illness *n.* enfermedad maligna que causa la muerte.

terminate *v.* terminar, acabar.

termination *n.* terminación.

terminology *n.* terminología, nomenclatura.

ternary *a.* ternario-a, que se compone de tres elementos.

Terramycin *n.* Terramicina, nombre comercial de un antibiótico derivado de la tetraciclina.

terrible *a.* terrible.

terror *n.* terror, pánico.

tertian *a.* terciano-a, que se repite cada tercer día; ___ **fever** / fiebre ___.

tertiary syphilis *n.* sífilis terciaria, el estado más avanzado de la sífilis.

test *n.* prueba; examen; análisis; **antinuclear antibody ___** / ___ antinuclear de anticuerpo; **double-blind ___** / ___ de doble incógnita; **creatinine clearance ___** / ___ de aclaramiento de creatinina; **endurance ___** / ___ de resistencia; **fat stool ___** / ___ de grasa fecal; **follow-up ___** / ___ subsecuente; **glucose tolerance ___** / ___ de tolerancia a la glucosa; **liver function ___** / ___ de función hepática; **outcome of ___** / resultado de la ___; **pregnancy ___** / ___ del embarazo; **random ___** / ___ de control sin método; **respiratory function ___** / ___ de función respiratoria; **skin ___** / ___ cutánea; **scratch ___** / ___ de rasguño, ___ de alergia; **screening ___** / ___ eliminatoria; **single-blind ___** / ___ de ciego simple; **stress ___** / ___ de esfuerzo; **thyroid function ___** / ___ de función tiroidea; **timed ___** / ___ de tiempo limitado o medido; **treadmill ___** / ___ de esfuerzo; ___ **tube** / tubo de ensayo; ___ **type** / ___ de tipo, prueba visual de letras; **visual ___** / ___ visual; **visual field ___** / ___ visual de campimetría.

testament *n.* testamento.

tester *n.* probador, ensayador.

testicle *n.* testículo, una de las dos glándulas reproductivas masculinas que produce espermatozoos y la hormona testosterona; **ectopic ___** / ___ ectópico; **undescended ___** / ___ no descendido.

testicular *a.* testicular, rel. al testículo; ___ **tumors** / tumores ___-es.

testify *v.* declarar, testificar.

testis *L.* (*pl.* **testes**) testis, testículo.

testosterone *n.* testosterona, hormona producida en el testis estimulante del desarrollo de algunas características masculinas secundarias tales como el vello facial y la voz grave; ___ **implant** / implante de ___.

test-tube baby *n.* fertilización *in vitro*, embarazo en probeta o que resulta de un óvulo fecundado fuera de la madre en el laboratorio y reimplantado en el útero.

tetanic *a.* tetánico-a, rel. al tétano; ___ **antitoxin** / antitoxina ___; ___ **convulsion** / convulsión ___; ___ **toxoid** / toxoide ___.

tetanus, lockjaw *n.* tétano, enfermedad infecciosa aguda causada por el bacilo del tétano gen. introducido a través de una lesión y que se manifiesta con espasmos musculares y rigidez gradual de la mandíbula, el cuello y el abdomen.

tetanus immune globulin *n.* globulina inmune contra el tétano.

tetany *n.* tetania, afección neuromuscular que se manifiesta con espasmos intermitentes de los músculos voluntarios asociada con deficiencia paratiroidea y disminución del balance de calcio.

tetracycline *n.* tetraciclina, antibiótico de espectro amplio usado para combatir microorganismos gram-positivos y gram-negativos, ricketsia y cierta variedad de virus.

tetrad *n.* tétrada, grupo de cuatro elementos similares.

tetralogy *n.* tetralogía, término aplicado a una combinación de cuatro factores o elementos.

tetraplegia *n.* tetraplejía, parálisis de las cuatro extremidades.

tetraploid *n.* tetraploide, que posee cuatro grupos de cromosomas.

tetravalent *n.* tetravalente, que posee una valencia química igual a cuatro.

texture *n.* textura, composición de la estructura de un tejido.

thalamic *a.* talámico-a, rel. al tálamo.

thalamus *n.* tálamo, una de las dos estructuras formadas por masas de materia gris que se encuentran en la base del cerebro y que constituyen el centro principal por donde los impulsos sensoriales pasan a la corteza cerebral.

thalassemia *n.* talasemia, grupos de anemias hipocrómicas causadas por factores genéticos que producen reducción o fallo en la síntesis total de hemoglobina; **major** ___ / ___ mayor; **minor** ___ / ___ menor.

thalassotherapy *n.* talasoterapia, tratamiento de una enfermedad por medio de baños de mar o exposición al aire marino.

thalidomide *n.* talidomida, sedativo e hipnótico, causante probado de malformaciones en niños de madres que tomaron la droga durante el embarazo.

than *conj.* que; *comp.* que. V. grammar section.

thanatology *n.* tanatología, rama de la medicina que trata de la muerte en todos sus aspectos.

thank *v.* dar gracias; agradecer.

thankful *a.* agradecido-a.

thanks *n. pl.* gracias; agradecimiento, gratitud.

thaw *n.* deshielo, descongelación; *v.* descongelar, deshelar, derretir.

theca *n.* teca, envoltura o capa que actúa esp.

como protectora de un órgano.

thecoma *n.* tecoma, tumor ovárico gen. benigno.

thenar *a.* tenar, rel. a la palma de la mano; ___ **eminence** / eminencia ___; ___ **muscles** / músculos ___-es.

theoretical *a.* teórico-a, rel. a una teoría.

theory *n.* teoría. 1. conocimientos relacionados con un tema sin verificación práctica de los mismos; 2. especulación u opinión que no ha sido probada científicamente.

therapeutic *a.* terapéutico-a. 1. que tiene propiedades curativas; 2. rel. a la terapéutica; ___ **indications** / indicaciones ___-s.

therapeutics *n.* terapéutica, rama de la medicina que estudia tratamientos y curaciones.

therapist *n.* terapeuta, persona experta en una o más áreas de aplicación de tratamientos en el campo de la salud; **physical** ___ / ___ físico; **speech** ___ / finiatra, logopeda.

therapy *n.* terapia, terapéutica, tratamiento de una enfermedad; **adjuvant** ___ / ___ adjunta; **anticoagulant** ___ / ___ anticoagulante; **behavior** ___ / ___ de conducta; **component** ___ / ___ componente; **electroconvulsive (E.C.T.)** / electrochoque; **x-ray** ___ / radioterapia; **external beam** ___ / ___ por radiación externa; **group** ___ / ___ de grupo; **hormone** ___ / ___ hormonal; **inhalation** ___ / ___ por inhalación; **maintenance** ___ / ___ de sostén o mantenimiento; **occupational** ___ / ___ ocupacional; **palliative** ___ / ___ paliativa; **physical** ___ / fisioterapia; **shock** ___ / ___ por choque; **supportive** ___ / ___ de apoyo; **systemic** ___ / ___ sistémica.

thermal, thermic *a.* termal, térmico-a, rel. al calor o producido por éste.

thermistor *n.* termistor, tipo de termómetro para medir cambios mínimos en la temperatura.

thermocoagulation *n.* termocoagulación, coagulación de tejidos por medio de corrientes de alta frecuencia.

thermodynamics *n.* termodinámica, ciencia que trata de la relación entre el calor y otras formas de energía.

thermograph *n.* termógrafo, detector infrarrojo que registra variaciones de la temperatura corporal según reacciona a los cambios de la circulación sanguínea.

thermography *n.* termografía, registro obtenido con un termógrafo.

thermometer *n.* termómetro, instrumento usado para medir el grado de calor o frío; **Celsius** ___ / ___ de Celsius o centígrado; **clinical** ___ / ___ clínico; **Fahrenheit** ___ / ___ de Fahrenheit; **rectal** ___ / ___ rectal; **self-recording** ___ / ___ de registro automático.

thermonuclear *a.* termonuclear, rel. a reacciones termonucleares.

thermoregulation *n.* termorregulación, regulación del calor o de la temperatura; termotaxis.

thermos *n.* termo.

thermostat *n.* termostato, instrumento regulador de temperaturas.

thermosterilization *n.* termoesterilización, esterilización por medio del calor.

thermotaxis *n.* termotaxis. 1. mantenimiento de la temperatura del cuerpo; 2. reacción de un organismo al estímulo del calor.

thermotheraphy *n.* termoterapia, uso terapéutico del calor.

thesis *n.* (*pl.* **theses**) tesis; postulado.

thick *a.* grueso-a; macizo-a; [*liquid*] espeso-a.

thicken *v.* engrosar, espesar; condensar.

thickness *n.* espesor, densidad; consistencia.

thigh *n.* muslo, porción de la extremidad inferior entre la cadera y la rodilla; ___ **bone** / fémur.

thin *a.* delgado-a, flaco-a; [*liquid*] aguado-a, aclarado-a; [*light*] ligero-a.

thing *n.* cosa, objeto.

think *vi.* pensar; [*believe*] creer; **to ___ it over** / pensarlo bien; **to ___ nothing of** / tener en poco; **to ___ through** / considerar; **to ___ well of** / tener buena opinión de.

thinner *n.* solvente, diluyente.

third degree burn *n.* quemadura de tercer grado.

thirst *n.* sed.

thirsty *a.* sediento-a; *v.* **to be ___** / tener sed.

thoracentesis *n.* toracentesis, punción y drenaje quirúrgicos de la cavidad torácica.

thoracic *a.* torácico-a, rel. al tórax; ___ **cage** / caja o pared ___; ___ **cavity** / cavidad ___; ___ **duct** / conducto ___; ___ **injuries** / traumatismos ___-s; ___ **neoplasms** / neoplasmas ___-s.

thoracicoabdominal *a.* toracicoabdominal, rel. al tórax y al abdomen.

thoracolumbar *a.* toracolumbar, rel. a las vértebras torácicas y lumbares.

thoracoplasty *n. cirg.* toracoplastia, cirugía plástica del tórax por medio de excisión de costillas para provocar la caída de un pulmón afectado.

thoracostomy *n. cirg.* toracostomía, incisión en la pared del tórax usando la abertura como drenaje.

thoracotomy *n. cirg.* toracotomía, incisión de la pared torácica.

thorax *n.* tórax, el pecho.

Thorazine *n.* Torazina, sedante y antiemético.

thorough *a.* completo-a, minucioso-a, acabado-a; **-ly** *adv.* completamente, minuciosamente, a fondo.

thought *n.* pensamiento, concepto, idea; *a., pp.* de **to think,** pensado.

thoughtful *n.* atento, solícito-a, esmerado-a.

thread *n.* hilo; fibra, filamento; línea fina. 1. material de sutura; 2. cualquier filamento fino semejante a un hilo; *v.* enhebrar, ensartar; ___**-like** / hiliforme, fibroso-a, filamentoso-a.

threat *n.* amenaza.

threaten *v.* amenazar.

threshold *n.* umbral. 1. grado mínimo necesario de un estímulo para producir un efecto; 2. dosis mínima que puede producir un efecto; **absolute ___** / ___ absoluto; **auditory ___** / ___ auditivo; ___ **of consciousness** / ___ de la consciencia; ___ **dose** / dosis mínima; **renal ___** / ___ renal; **sensory ___** / ___ sensorio.

thrill *n.* "thrill", estremecimiento, vibración o ruido especial que se siente por palpación; **aneurysmal ___** / ___ aneurismal; **aortic ___** / ___ aórtico; **arterial ___** / ___ arterial; **diastolic ___** / ___ diastólico; **presystolic ___** / ___ presistólico; **systolic ___** / ___ sistólico; *v.* emocionar, excitar; *v.* emocionarse, excitarse.

thrive *v.* prosperar, progresar.

throat *n.* garganta, área que incluye la faringe y la laringe.

throat culture *n.* muestra de cultivo del mucus extraído de la garganta y detección en el laboratorio de la presencia o no de agentes infecciosos en el mismo.

throb *n.* latido, pulsación, palpitación; *v.* latir, palpitar, pulsar.

throbbing *a.* palpitante.

thrombectomy *n. cirg.* trombectomía, extracción de un trombo.

thrombin *n.* trombina, enzima presente en la sangre extravasada que cataliza en la conversión de fibrinógeno en fibrina.

thrombinogen *n.* trombinógeno. *V.* **prothrombin.**

thromboangiitis *n.* tromboangiitis, infl. de un vaso sanguíneo con trombosis; trombosis de un vaso sanguíneo.

thrombocyte *n.* trombocito, plaqueta.

thrombocytopenia *n.* trombocitopenia, disminución anormal del número de las plaquetas sanguíneas.

thrombocytopenic *a.* trombocitopénico-a, rel. a la trombocitopenia.

thrombocytosis *n.* trombocitosis, aumento excesivo de plaquetas en la sangre.

thromboembolism *n.* tromboembolia, obstrucción de un vaso sanguíneo por un coágulo desprendido del lugar de origen.

thrombogenesis *n.* trombogénesis, formación de cóagulos o trombos.

thrombolysis *n.* trombólisis, lisis o disolución de un coágulo.

thrombolytic *a.* trombolítico-a, rel. a un trombo o que causa la disolución de éste.

thrombophlebitis *n.* tromboflebitis, dilatación de la pared de una vena asociada con trombosis.

thrombosed *a.* trombosado-a, rel. a un vaso sanguíneo que contiene un trombo.

thrombosis *n.* trombosis, formación, desarrollo y presencia de un trombo; **biliary ___** / ___ biliar; **cardiac ___** / ___ cardíaca; **coronary ___** / ___ coronaria; **embolic ___** / ___ embólica; **traumatic ___** / ___ traumática; **venous ___** /

___ venosa.

thrombotic *a.* trombótico-a, rel. a la trombosis o que padece de ella.

thrombus *n.* (*pl.* **thrombi**) trombo, coágulo que causa una obstrucción vascular parcial o total.

throw *vi.* tirar; arrojar.

thrush *n.* muguet, afta, infección fungosa de la mucosa oral que se manifiesta con placas blancas en la cavidad bucal y la garganta.

thumb *n.* dedo pulgar; ___ **sucking** / chuparse el dedo gordo.

thumbnail *n.* uña del pulgar.

thymectomy *n. cirg.* timectomía, extirpación del timo.

thymic *a.* tímico-a, rel. al timo.

thymocyte *n.* timocito, linfocito que se origina en el timo.

thymoma *n.* timoma, tumor que se origina en el timo.

thymus *n.* timo, glándula situada en la parte inferior del cuello y anterosuperior de la cavidad torácica que desempeña un papel de importancia en la función inmunológica.

thyroglobulin *n.* tiroglobulina. 1. iodina que contiene glicoproteína secretada por la tiroides; 2. sustancia que se obtiene de tiroides porcinas y se administra como suplemento en el tratamiento de hipertiroidismo.

thyroglossal *a.* tirogloso-a, rel. a la tiroides y a la lengua.

thyroid *n.* glándula tiroides, una de las glándulas endocrinas situadas delante de la tráquea y constituida por dos lóbulos laterales conectados en el centro; ___ **function tests** / pruebas del funcionamiento de la ___; *a.* tiroideo-a, rel. a la tiroides; ___ **cartilage** / cartílago ___; ___ **hormones** / hormonas ___-as; ___ **storm** / tormenta ___, crisis ___.

thyroidectomy *n. cirg.* tiroidectomía, extirpación de la tiroides.

thyroidism *n.* tiroidismo, condición por exceso de secreción tiroidea.

thyroiditis *n.* tiroiditis, infl. de la tiroides.

thyroid-stimulating hormone *n.* hormona estimulante de la secreción tiroidea. *V.* **thyrotropin.**

thyromegaly *n.* tiromegalia, agrandamiento de la tiroides.

thyroparathyroidectomy *n. cirg.* tiroparatiroidectomía, excisión de la tiroides y la paratiroides.

thyrotoxicosis *n.* tirtoxicosis, trastorno causado por hipertiroidismo que se manifiesta con agrandamiento de la tiroides, aumento en el metabolismo, taquicardia, pulso rápido e hipertensión.

thyrotropin *n.* tirotropina, hormona estimulante de la tiroides secretada por el lóbulo anterior de la pituitaria; ___ **releasing hormone** / hormona estimulante de ___.

thyroxine *n.* tiroxina, hormona producida por la tiroides que contiene yodo; se obtiene sintéti-

camente de la tiroides de animales y se usa en el tratamiento de hipotiroidismo.

tibia *n.* tibia, hueso triangular anterior de la pierna situado debajo de la rodilla.

tibial *a.* tibial, rel. a la tibia o localizado cerca de ella.

tic *Fr.* tic, espasmo súbito o involuntario de un músculo que ocurre esp. en la cara; **convulsive** ___ / ___ convulsivo; **coordinated** ___ / ___ coordinado; **douloureux** ___ / ___ doloroso; **facial** ___ / ___ facial.

tick *n.* garrapata, acárido chupador de sangre transmisor de enfermedades; ___ **bite** / picadura de ___.

tickle *n.* cosquilleo; *v.* hacer cosquillas, consquillear; sentir un cosquilleo.

tickling *n.* cosquilla.

tidal *a.* rel. al volumen de inspiración y expiración.

tidiness *n.* aseo, pulcritud; limpieza.

tidy *a.* aseado-a, pulcro-a; limpio-a.

tie *n.* ligadura, lazo; conexión *v.* amarrar, atar, enlazar; **to be tied up** / estar muy ocupado-a.

tight *a.* [*fitted*] apretado-a, ajustado-a; [*airtight*] hermético-a; tirante; **a** ___ **situation** / una situación grave; ___ **squeeze** / *pop.* aprieto; *v.* **to hold on** / agarrarse bien.

tighten *v.* apretar, ajustar.

time *n.* tiempo, medida de duración; **bleeding** ___ / ___ de sangramiento; **coagulation** ___ / ___ de coagulación; **a limited** ___ / ___ limitado; ___ **exposure** / ___ de exposición; ___ **frame** / espacio de ___; ___ **lag** / ___ de latencia; **perception** ___ / ___ de percepción; **prothrombin** ___ / ___ de protrombina; **at** ___**s** / a veces; **at the same** ___ / a la vez; **behind** ___ / atrasado-a; **for some** ___ / por algún ___; **for the** ___ **being** / por el momento, por ahora; **from** ___ **to** ___ / de vez en cuando; **in due** ___ / a su debido ___; **on** ___ / a tiempo; **What is it?** / ¿Qué hora es?; **At what** ___? / ¿A qué hora?; *v.* marcar, medir el tiempo; **to set the** ___ / medir el tiempo.

timed *pp.* tiempo medido.

timely *a.* oportuno-a.

timer *n.* regulador de tiempo, minutero.

timid *a.* tímido-a.

tincture *n.* tintura, extracto de origen animal o vegetal que contiene alcohol.

tinea *L.* tinea, tiña, infección cutánea fungosa; ___ **capital** / ___ capitis; ___ **pedis** / ___ pedis, *pop.* pie de atleta; ___ **versicolor** / ___ versicolor.

tingle *n.* hormigueo, comezón, sensación de picazón.

tinnitus *n.* zumbido, chasquido, sonido que se siente en el oído.

tint *n.* tinte, colorante; *v.* teñir, colorar, dar color.

tiny *a.* diminuto-a.

tip *n.* punta, extremo; [*light touch*] toque ligero.

tired *a.* cansado-a, fatigado-a.

tiredness *n.* cansancio, fatiga.

tireless *a.* incansable, infatigable.

tiresome *a.* pesado-a, tedioso-a.

tiring *a.* agotador-a, que cansa o fatiga.

tissue *n.* tejido, grupo de células similares de función determinada unidas por una sustancia intercelular que actúan conjuntamente; **adipose** ___ / ___ adiposo; **bone** ___, **bony** ___ / ___ óseo; **cartilaginous** ___ / ___ cartilaginoso; **connective** ___ / ___ conectivo; **epithelial** ___ / ___ epitelial; **endothelial** ___ / ___ endotelial; **erectile** ___ / ___ eréctil; **fibrous** ___ / ___ fibroso; **glandular** ___ / ___ glandular; **granulation** ___ / ___ de granulación; **lymphoid** ___ / ___ linfoide; **mesenchymal** ___ / ___ mesenquimatoso; **muscular** ___ / ___ muscular; **nervous** ___, **nerve** ___ / ___ nervioso; **scar** ___ / ___ cicatrizante; **subcutaneous** ___ / ___ subcutáneo.

tissue typing *n.* tipificación, clasificación por tipo; tipificación de tejido.

titer, titre *n.* título, la cantidad de una sustancia que se requiere para producir una reacción con un volumen determinado de otra sustancia.

titrate *v.* titular, determinar por titulación.

titration *n.* titulación, determinación de volumen usando soluciones estandarizadas de valor conocido.

toadstool *n.* seta venenosa; hongo venenoso.

toast *n.* tostada.

tobacco *n.* tabaco, planta americana de la *Nicotiana tabacum* cuyas hojas preparadas contienen nicotina, sustancia tóxica perjudicial a la salud; ___ **smoke pollution** / contaminación por humo de ___; ___ **use disorder** / trastorno por uso de ___.

tocograph *n.* tocógrafo, instrumento para estimar la fuerza de las contracciones uterinas.

tocometer *n.* tocómetro. V. **tocograph.**

today *adv.* hoy.

Tissue	*Tejido*
adipose	adiposo
bone, bony	óseo
cartilaginous	cartilaginoso
connective	conectivo
endothelial	endotelial
epithelial	epitelial
erectile	eréctil
fibrous	fibroso
glandular	glandular
granulation	de granulación
lymphoid	linfoide
mesenchymal	mesenquimatoso
muscular	muscular
nervous	nervioso
scar	cicatrizante
subcutaneous	subcutáneo

toddler *n.* niño-a que comienza a caminar.

toe *n.* dedo del pie.

toe drop *n.* caída de los dedos del pie.

toe nail *n.* uña de un dedo del pie.

toilet *n.* 1. servicio, inodoro; 2. limpieza relacionada con un procedimiento médico o quirúrgico; ___ **paper** / papel higiénico.

toilet training *n.* entrenamiento de los niños para controlar el acto de orinar y el de defecar.

tolerable *a.* tolerable.

tolerance *n.* tolerancia, capacidad de soportar una sustancia o un ejercicio físico sin sufrir efectos dañinos, tal como el uso de una droga o una actividad física prolongada.

tolerant *a.* tolerante.

tolerate *v.* tolerar.

tomato *n.* tomate; ___ **soup** / sopa de ___.

tomogram *n.* tomograma, radiografía seccionada de una parte del cuerpo.

tomograph *n.* tomógrafo, máquina radiográfica que se usa para hacer una tomografía.

tomography *n.* tomografía, técnica de diagnóstico por la cual se hacen radiografías de un órgano por secciones del mismo a profundidades distintas; **computerized axial** ___ **(CAT)** / ___ axial computarizada (TAC); **positron emission** ___ / ___ de emisión por positrón.

tomorrow *adv.* mañana; **day after** ___ / pasado ___.

tone *n.* tono. 1. grado normal de vigor y tensión en el funcionamiento de los órganos y músculos de un cuerpo sano; **muscular** ___ / ___ muscular; 2. cualidad definida de un sonido o voz.

tongue *n.* lengua; ___ **depressor** / depresor de ___; **dry** ___ / ___ seca; **geographic** ___ / ___ geográfica; **black hairy** ___ / ___ negra velluda, lengua infectada de hongos parásitos; **red** ___ / ___ roja o enrojecida; **sticky** ___ / ___ pegajosa.

tonic *n.* tónico, reconstituyente que restaura la vitalidad del organismo; *a.* tónico-a. 1. que restaura el tono normal; 2. caracterizado-a por una tensión continua.

tonicity *a.* tonicidad, cualidad normal de tono o tensión.

tonight *adv.* esta noche.

tonoclonic *a.* tonoclónico-a, rel. a espasmos musculares que son tónicos y clónicos.

tonometer *n.* tonómetro, instrumento usado para medir la tensión o presión esp. intraocular.

tonometry *n.* tonometría, medida de la presión o tensión.

tonsil *n.* amígdala, tonsila; **cerebellar** ___ / ___ cerebelosa; **lingual** ___ / ___ lingual; **palatine** ___ / ___ palatina; **pharyngeal** ___ / ___ faríngea.

tonsillar *a.* tonsilar, rel. a una tonsila; ___ **crypt** / cripta ___ o amigdalina; ___ **fossa** / fosa amigdalina.

tonsillectomy *n. cirg.* amigdalectomía, extirpación de las amígdalas.

tonsillitis *n.* amigdalitis, infl. de las amígdalas.

tonsilloadenoidectomy *n. cirg.* tonsiloadenoi-dectomía, extirpación de las adenoides y las amígdalas.

tonus *L.* tonus. *V.* **tone.**

too *adv.* además; también; asimismo; demasiado.

tooth *n.* (*pl.* **teeth**) diente; **impacted** ___ / ___ impactado; ___ **unerupted** / ___ no erup-cionado.

toothache *n.* dolor de muelas.

toothbrush *n.* cepillo de dientes.

toothpaste *n.* pasta de dientes, dentífrico.

tophaceous *a.* tofacio, rel. a un tofo o de natu-raleza arenosa.

tophus *n.* tofo. 1. depósito de sal de ácido úrico en los tejidos, gen. visto en casos de gota; 2. cálculo dental.

topical *a.* tópico-a, rel. a un área localizada.

topographic anatomy *n.* anatomía topo-gráfica.

torment *n.* tormento; *v.* atormentar.

torpid *a.* tórpido-a, torpe en los movimientos.

torpor *n.* embotamiento; estancamiento, inac-tividad física.

torque *Fr.* torque, fuerza rotatoria.

torsion *n.* torsión, rotación de una parte sobre su propio eje longitudinal; **ovarian** ___ / ___ ovárica; **testicular** ___ / ___ testicular.

torso *n.* torso, el tronco humano.

torticollis *n.* torticolis, espasmo tonicoclónico de los músculos del cuello que causa torsión cervical e inmovilidad de la cabeza.

tortuous *a.* tortuoso-a; torcido-a; sinuoso-a.

torture *n.* tortura, gran sufrimiento; castigo.

torus *L.* (*pl.* **tori**) torus, eminencia, protuberan-cia, abultamiento.

total *a.* total; completo-a; *v.* sumar, añadir.

totipotency *n.* totipotencia, habilidad de una célula de regenerarse o desarrollarse en otro tipo de célula.

totipotent *a.* totipotente, que puede generar totipotencia.

touch *n.* 1. sentido del tacto, percepción a través de la piel o de las membranas mucosas; 2. [*act of touching*] toque; *v.* tocar, palpar.

touch-up *n.* retoque.

tourniquet *n.* torniquete, dispositivo usado para aplicar presión sobre una arteria y contener la salida de la sangre.

towel *n.* toalla.

toxemia *n.* toxemia, condición tóxica provocada por la absorción de toxinas que provienen de un foco infeccioso.

toxic *a.* tóxico-a, venenoso-a, rel. a un veneno o de naturaleza venenosa.

toxicity *n.* toxicidad, cualidad de ser venenoso.

toxicological *a.* toxicológico-a, rel. a la toxi-cología.

toxicologist *n.* toxicólogo-a, especialista en toxi-cología.

toxicology *n.* toxicología, estudio de los venenos

o sustancias tóxicas, los efectos que causan en el organismo y su tratamiento; ___ **screen** / protocolo toxicológico.

toxicosis *n.* toxicosis, estado morboso debido a un veneno.

toxin *n.* toxina, veneno, sustancia nociva de origen animal o vegetal; **bacterial** ___ / ___ bacteriana.

toxin-antitoxin *n.* toxina antitoxina, mezcla casi neutra de toxina diftérica y antitoxina que se usa en inmunizaciones contra la difteria.

toxoid *n.* toxoide, toxina desprovista de toxici-dad que al introducirse en el organismo causa la formación de anticuerpos; *a.* toxoide, de naturaleza tóxica o venenosa; **diphtheria** ___ / ___ diftérico; **tetanus** ___ / ___ tetánico.

toxoplasma *n. Toxoplasma,* género de parásito protozoario.

toxoplasmosis *n.* toxoplasmosis, infección causada por un microorganismo de la familia *Toxoplasma* que invade los tejidos, con sín-tomas leves de malestar o posible infl. de las glándulas linfáticas; puede ocasionar daños a la vista y al sistema nervioso central.

toy *n.* juguete.

trace *n.* rastro, vestigio. 1. cantidad diminuta de un elemento químico; 2. marca visible; *v.* trazar; rastrear, investigar.

tracer *n.* trazador, radioisótopo que al intro-ducirse en el cuerpo crea un rastro que puede detectarse.

trachea *n.* tráquea, conducto respiratorio entre la parte extrema inferior de la laringe y el comienzo de los bronquios.

tracheal *a.* traqueal, rel. a la tráquea; ___ **stenosis** / estenosis ___.

tracheitis *n.* traqueítis, infl. de la tráquea.

tracheoesophageal *a.* traqueoesofágico-a, rel. a la tráquea y al esófago.

tracheomalasia *n.* traqueomalasia, reblandeci-miento de los cartílagos traqueales.

tracheostenosis *n.* traqueostenosis, estrechez de la tráquea.

tracheostomy *n. cirg.* traqueostomía, incisión en la tráquea para permitir el paso de aire en caso de obstrucción.

tracheotomy *n. cirg.* traqueotomía, incisión en la tráquea a través de la piel y los músculos del cuello.

trachoma *n.* tracoma, infección viral contagiosa de la conjuntiva y la córnea que se manifiesta con fotofobia, dolor, lagrimeo y, en casos severos, ceguera total.

tracing *n.* trazo, gráfica descriptiva que hace un instrumento al registrar un movimiento.

tract *n.* tracto, tubo, vía, vías, sistema alargado compuesto de tejidos y órganos que actúan coordinadamente para desempeñar una función; **alimentary** ___ / ___ alimenticio; **ascending** ___ / ___ ascendiente; **biliary** ___ / ___ biliar; **digestive** ___ / ___ digestivo; **geni-tourinary** ___ / ___ genitourinario; **olfactory**

___ / vía olfatoria; **pyramidal** ___ / ___ piramidal; **respiratory** ___ / ___ o vía respiratoria.

traction *n*. tracción. 1. acto de tirar o halar; 2.
fuerza que tira con tensión; **cervical** ___ / ___
cervical; **lumbar** ___ / ___ lumbar.

tractor *n*. tractor, instrumento o máquina usada
para aplicar tracción.

trademark *n*. marca registrada.

tragus *n*. (*pl*. **tragi**) trago, protuberancia triangular en la parte externa del oído.

train *v*. entrenar; entrenarse.

trained nurse *n*. enfermero-a graduado-a.

training *n*. entrenamiento; adiestramiento.

trait *n*. rasgo o característica; **acquired** ___ / ___
adquirido; **inherited** ___ / ___ heredado.

trance *n*. *psic*. trance, condición semejante a un
estado hipnótico que se caracteriza por la disminución de la actividad motora.

tranquil *a*. tranquilo-a, sereno-a.

tranquility *n*. tranquilidad, descanso.

tranquilizer *n*. tranquilizante, calmante.

transabdominal *a*. transabdominal, a través del
abdomen o de la pared abdominal.

transaxial *a*. transaxial, a través del axis de una
estructura o parte.

transcapillary *a*. transcapilar, que ocurre a
través de las paredes de los capilares.

transcript *n*. expediente; copia.

transcutaneous *a*. transcutáneo-a, a través de la
piel; ___ **electrical nerve stimulation** / estimulación eléctrica ___ de un nervio.

transducer *n*. transductor, dispositivo que convierte una forma de energía a otra.

transect *v*. cortar transversalmente.

transection *n*. corte transversal a través del eje
largo de un órgano.

transfer *v*. transferir, cambiar.

transfer, transference *n*. transferencia. 1. *psic*.
reorientación que hace el paciente de sentimientos negativos o positivos (esp. reprimidos inconscientemente) hacia otra persona,
esp. el psicoanalista; 2. transmisión de síntomas o fluidos de una parte a otra del cuerpo.

transferrin *n*. transferrina, globulina beta en el
plasma de la sangre que fija y transporta el
hierro.

transfixion *n*. *cirg*. transfixión, acto de atravesar
y cortar al mismo tiempo los tejidos blandos de
dentro hacia afuera como en la extirpación de
tumores o en amputaciones.

transform *v*. transformar, cambiar la apariencia,
carácter o estructura.

transformation *n*. transformación, cambio de
forma o apariencia.

transfusion *n*. transfusión, acto de transferir un
fluido a una vena o arteria; **blood** ___ / ___ de
sangre; **direct** ___ / ___ directa; **exchange** ___
/ exsanguino-transfusión; **indirect** ___ / ___
indirecta.

transillumination *n*. transiluminación, paso de
luz a través de un cuerpo.

transitional *a*. transitorio-a, rel. a transición o

cambio.

transitory *a*. transitorio-a, pasajero-a.

translate *v*. traducir.

translator *n*. traductor-a; intérprete.

translocation *n*. translocación, desplazamiento
de un cromosoma o parte del mismo hacia
otro cromosoma.

translucent *a*. translúcido-a, que deja pasar la
luz.

transmigration *n*. transmigración, paso de un
lugar a otro tal como las células sanguíneas en
diapédesis.

transmissible *a*. transmisible, trasmisible, que
puede transmitirse.

transmission *n*. transmisión, acto de transmitir
o transferir tal como una enfermedad contagiosa o hereditaria; ___ **by contact** / ___ por
contacto; **droplet** ___ / ___ por instilación;
pathogen ___ / ___ patógena; **placental** ___ /
___ placentaria.

transmit *v*. transmitir, trasmitir, contagiar; conducir.

transmural *a*. transmural, que ocurre o se administra a través de una pared.

transmutation *n*. transmutación. 1. transformación, cambio evolutivo; 2. cambio de una sustancia en otra.

transocular *a*. transocular, que pasa a través de
la órbita ocular.

transonance *n*. transonancia, resonancia transmitida.

transorbital *a*. transorbital, que ocurre o que
pasa a través de la cavidad ósea del ojo.

transparency *n*. transparencia; [*slide*] diapositiva.

transparent *a*. transparente.

transpiration *n*. transpiración, perspiración.

transpire *v*. transpirar; [*to perspire*] sudar, transpirar; [*to happen*] suceder, acontecer.

transplacental *a*. transplacental, a través de la
placenta.

transplant *n*. trasplante. 1. acto de transferir un
órgano o tejido de un donante a un recipiente, o de una parte del cuerpo a otra para
sustituir una parte enferma o restituir un órgano a su función normal; 2. parte artificial o
natural que se usa como reemplazo; *v*. transplantar.

transplantation *n*. transplantación, trasplantación, acto de hacer un trasplante; **autoplastic**
___ / ___ autoplástica; **heteroplastic** ___ / ___
heteroplástica; **heterotopic** ___ / ___ hete-
rotópica; **homotopic** ___ / ___ homotópica.

transpleural *a*. transpleural, que ocurre o se administra a través de la pleura.

transport *n*. transporte, movimiento de materiales en el cuerpo esp. a través de la membrana celular.

transportation *n*. transporte.

transposition *n*. transposición. 1. desplazamiento de un órgano o parte a una posición
opuesta; 2. cambio genético de un cromosoma

413

a otro que resulta a veces en defectos genéticos.

transposition of great vessels *n.* transposición de los grandes vasos, anomalía congénita en la cual la aorta sale del ventrículo derecho mientras que el tronco pulmonar sale del ventrículo izquierdo.

transsexual *a.* transexual. 1. persona que tiene una urgencia psicológica de pertenecer al sexo opuesto; 2. persona que ha cambiado de sexo sometiéndose a una operación quirúrgica.

transudate *n.* trasudado, fluido que ha pasado a través de una membrana o ha sido expulsado como resultado de una inflamación.

transurethral *a.* transuretral, que ocurre o se administra a través de la uretra.

transvaginal *a.* transvaginal, a través de la vagina.

transversal *a.* transversal.

transverse *a.* transversal, atravesado-a; ___ **plain** / plano ___.

transvestism *n.* trasvestismo, adopción de modales del sexo opuesto, esp. la manera de vestir.

transvestite *n.* transvestido-a, transvestita, persona que practica el transvestismo.

trapezius *n.* trapecio, músculo trangular plano esencial en la rotación de la escápula.

trash *n.* basura, desecho.

trauma *n.* trauma. 1. lesión física causada por un agente externo; 2. *psic.* estado emocional severo.

traumatic *a.* traumático-a, rel. a un trauma.

traumatism *n.* traumatismo.

traumatize *v.* traumatizar, lesionar, lastimar.

traumatized *a.* traumatizado.

traumatology *n.* traumatología, rama de la cirugía que trata del cuidado de lesiones y heridas.

travel *n.* viaje; *v.* viajar, hacer un viaje.

treadmill *n.* [*physical fitness*] rueda de andar.

treatment *n.* tratamiento, método o procedimiento que se usa en la cura de enfermedades, lesiones y deformaciones; ___ **plan** / plan o método de ___; **preventive** ___ / ___ preventivo; **symptomatic** ___ / ___ sintomático.

tree *n.* 1. árbol; 2. estructura anatómica semejante a un árbol.

Trematoda *n. Trematoda,* clase de gusanos parásitos de la especie de los *Platyhelminthes* que incluye la duela y los gusanos planos que infectan el organismo humano.

trematode *n.* trematodo, gusano parásito de la clase *Trematoda.*

tremble *n.* temblor, estremecimiento, movimiento involuntario oscilatorio; *v.* temblar; estremecerse.

tremendous *a.* tremendo a, formidable.

tremor *n.* temblor, estremecimiento; **alcoholic** ___ / ___ alcohólico; **coarse** ___ / ___ lento y acentuado; **continuous** ___ / ___ continuo; **es-**

sential ___ / ___ esencial; **fine** ___ / ___ de variaciones rápidas; **flapping** ___ / ___ de aleteo; **intention** ___ / ___ intencional; **intermittent** ___ / ___ intermitente; **muscular** ___ / ___ muscular; **physiological** ___ / ___ fisiológico; **rest** ___ / ___ de reposo.

tremulous *a.* trémulo-a, afectado-a por un estremecimiento o que posee las características de un temblor.

trench *n.* trinchera, zanja, foso; ___ **back** / rigidez y dolor de espalda; ___ **fever** / fiebre de ___, fiebre remitente transmitida por piojos; ___ **foot** / pie de ___, infección en los pies por exposición al frío; ___**-mouth** / infección con ulceración de las mucosas de la boca y la faringe.

trend *n.* tendencia; dirección.

Trendelenburg position *n.* posición de Trendelenburg, posición del paciente en la cual la cabeza descansa en un nivel más bajo que el tronco y las extremidades inferiores.

trepan *n.* trépano, instrumento usado en la trepanación; *v.* trepanar, perforar el cráneo con un trépano.

trepanation *n. cirg.* trepanación, perforación del cráneo con un instrumento especial para reducir el aumento de la presión intracraneal causada por fractura, acumulación de sangre o pus.

trephination *n. cirg.* trefinación, acto de cortar un tejido o un hueso dando un corte circular o de disco, operación gen. efectuada en el cráneo.

treponema *n.* treponema, parásito de la orden *Spirochaetales* que invade a humanos y animales; ___ **pallidum** / ___ pallidum, parásito causante de la sífilis.

treponemiasis *n.* treponemiasis, infección causada por espiroquetas del género *Treponema.*

triad *n.* triada, grupo de tres elementos que se relacionan entre sí.

triage *Fr.* triage, clasificación y evaluación de víctimas en acontecimientos catastróficos para establecer prioridades según la urgencia del tratamiento y aumentar así el número de sobrevivientes.

trial *n.* prueba, ensayo.

triangle *n.* triángulo.

triangular *a.* triangular.

tribe *n.* tribu, categoría biológica en taxonomía.

triceps *L.* tríceps, músculo de tres porciones o cabezas; ___ **reflex** / reflejo del ___.

Trichinella *n. Trichinella,* género de gusanos nematodos, parásitos de animales carnívoros.

trichinosis *n.* triquinosis, enfermedad adquirida por la ingestión de carne cruda o mal cocinada, esp. de cerdo, que contiene larvas enquistadas de *Trichinella spiralis.*

trichitis *n.* triquitis, infl. de los bulbos pilosos.

trichobezoar *n.* tricobezoar, concreción o bezoar formado de pelo que se aloja en el intestino o el estómago.

Trichomonas *n. Trichomonas*, parásitos proto-zoarios que se alojan en el tubo digestivo y en el tracto genitourinario de vertebrados; ___ **vaginalis** / ___ vaginalis, agente causante de la vaginitis.

trichomoniasis *n.* trichomoniasis, infestación por *Trichomonas*.

trichromatic *a.* tricromático-a, compuesto de tres colores.

tricky *a.* engañoso-a; complicado-a.

tricuspid *a.* tricúspide. 1. que posee tres puntas o cúspides; 2. rel. a la válvula tricúspide del corazón; ___ **atresia** / atresia ___; ___ **murmur** / soplo ___.

trifocal *a.* trifocal; ___ **lenses** / lentes ___-es.

trigeminal *a.* trigeminal, rel. al nervio tri-gémino; ___ **cough** / tos ___ / ___ **neuralgia** / neuralgia ___; ___ **pulse** / pulso ___.

trigeminal nerve *n.* nervio trigémino. *V.* **cranial nerves.**

trigeminus *L.* trigeminus, nervio trigémino.

trigger *n.* desencadenamiento; impulso o reac-ción que inicia otros eventos; ___ **points** / pun-tos de ___; *v.* desencadenar, iniciar.

trigger zone *n.* área sensitiva que al recibir un estímulo ocasiona una reacción en otra parte del cuerpo.

triglycerides *n. pl.* triglicéridos, combinación que resulta de una molécula de glicerol con tres moléculas de ácidos grasos diferentes; la presencia elevada de triglicéridos se considera un factor importante en el desarrollo de enfer-medades cardiovasculares.

trigone *n.* trígono, área de forma triangular.

trigonitis *n.* trigonitis, infl. del trígono de la ve-jiga urinaria.

trimester *n.* trimestre.

trip *n.* 1. viaje; 2. *slang,* uso de drogas alucina-torias.

triphasic *a.* trifásico-a, que se produce en tres fases o variaciones, esp. en referencia a las corrientes eléctricas.

triple *a.* triple, que consiste de tres componentes.

triplopia *n.* triplopia, trastorno visual por el cual se producen tres imágenes del mismo objeto.

trismus *Gr.* trismus, espasmo de los músculos de la masticación debido a una condición pa-tológica.

trisomic *a.* trisómico-a, caracterizado por tri-somía.

trisomy *n.* trisomía, trastorno genético por el cual una persona posee tres cromosomas homólogos por célula en lugar de dos (diploide), lo cual causa deformaciones fetales serias.

triturate *v.* triturar.

triumph *n.* triunfo, éxito; *v.* triunfar, tener éxito.

trochanter *n.* trocánter, una de las dos promi-nencias exteriores localizadas bajo el cuello del fémur; **greater** ___ / ___ mayor; **lesser** ___ / ___ menor.

trochlea *n.* tróclea, estructura que sirve de polea.

trochlear nerve *n.* nervio troclear. *V.* **cranial nerves.**

trophic *a.* trófico-a, rel. a la nutrición.

tropical *a.* tropical; ___ **diseases** / enfermedades ___-es; ___ **medicine** / medicina ___.

tropism *n.* tropismo, tendencia de una célula u organismo a reaccionar de una forma definida (positiva o negativa) en respuesta a estímulos externos.

trouble *n.* aflicción, calamidad, problema; **What is the trouble?** / ¿Qué sucede?, ¿qué pasa? *v.* **to be in** ___ / estar en un apuro; **to be worth the** ___ / valer la pena.

troubled *a.* afligido-a, inquieto-a; preocupado-a.

trough *n.* canal o zanja.

trousers *n. pl.* pantalones.

true *a.* verdadero-a, cierto-a, real; verídico-a.

true pelvis *n.* pelvis verdadera o menor, parte inferior contráctil de la pelvis.

truncal *a.* troncal, truncado-a, rel. al tronco.

truncate *a.* truncado-a, que tiene una parte cercenada; amputado-a; *v.* truncar, cortar, amputar.

truncus *L.* truncus, tronco, torso, el cuerpo hu-mano con exclusión de la cabeza y las extremi-dades.

truss *n.* braguero, faja para mantener una her-nia reducida en su lugar; *v.* ligar, amarrar.

trust *n.* confianza, fe; *v.* confiar, creer en.

truth *n.* verdad; realidad; ___ **serum** / suero de la ___.

truthful *a.* veraz, verdadero-a; **-ly** *adv.* verdadera-mente, realmente.

try *n.* prueba, ensayo; *v.* probar, ensayar, hacer una prueba; intentar; **to** ___ **out** / probar, someter a prueba; **to** ___ **on** / probarse.

Trypanosoma *n. Tripanosoma*, género de pará-sito protozoario que se aloja en la sangre y es transmitido a los vertebrados por insectos vec-tores.

trypanosomal *a.* tripanosómico-a, rel. a un tri-panosoma o que es afectado por éste.

trypanosomiasis *n.* tripanosomiasis, cualquier infección causada por un parásito flagelado del género *Tripanosoma*.

trypsin *n.* tripsina, enzima formada por el tripsinógeno presente en el jugo pancreático.

trypsinogen *n.* tripsinógeno, sustancia inactiva segregada por el páncreas en el duodeno para formar tripsina.

tryptophan *n.* triptófano, aminoácido cristalino presente en las proteínas, esencial a la vida animal.

tsetse fly *n.* mosca tsetsé, insecto del sur de África, transmisor de la enfermedad del sueño.

tub *n.* tina, bañera.

tubal *a.* tubárico-a; ___ **pregnancy** / embarazo ectópico en una trompa de Falopio; ___ **liga-tion** / ligadura o ligazón de las trompas.

tube *n.* tubo, conducto, trompa; **drainage** ___ / ___ de drenaje; **endotracheal** ___ / ___ endotraqueal; **inhalation** ___ / ___ de inhalación; **intestinal decompression** ___ / sonda intestinal; **nasogastric** ___ / ___ nasogástrico; **tracheotomy** ___ / ___ de traqueotomía; **thoracostomy** ___ / ___ de toracostomía.

tuber *L. pl.* **tubera**) tuber, tuberosidad; nódulo.

tubercle *n.* tubérculo. 1. nódulo pequeño; 2. pequeña prominencia de un hueso; 3. lesión producida por el bacilo de la tuberculosis.

tubercular *a.* tubercular, caracterizado por lesiones tuberosas.

tuberculin *n.* tuberculina, compuesto preparado del bacilo de la tuberculosis usado en las pruebas de diagnóstico de infecciones de la tuberculosis.

tuberculin test *n.* prueba de la tuberculina.

tuberculocidal *a.* tuberculocida, que destruye el bacilo de la tuberculosis.

tuberculosis *n.* tuberculosis, infección bacteriana aguda o crónica causada por el germen *Mycobacterium tuberculosis* que gen. afecta los pulmones pero que también puede afectar otros órganos; ___ **in childhood** / ___ infantil; **meningeal** ___ / ___ meníngea; **pulmonary** ___ / ___ pulmonar; **spinal** ___ / ___ espinal; **urogenital** ___ / ___ urogenital.

tuberculous *a.* tuberculoso-a, rel. a o que padece de tuberculosis o que puede causarla.

tuberculum *L.* tuberculum, tubérculo.

tuberosity *n.* tuberosidad, elevación o protuberancia.

tuberous *a.* tuberoso-a, semejante a una tuberosidad.

tuberous sclerosis *n.* esclerosis tuberosa, enfermedad familiar marcada por ataques convulsivos, deficiencia mental progresiva y formación de múltiples tumores cerebrales cutáneos.

tuboabdominal pregnancy *n.* embarazo tuboabdominal.

tubo-ovarian *a.* tuboovárico-a, rel. a la trompa de Falopio y el ovario; ___ **abscess** / absceso ___.

tuboplasty *n. cirg.* tuboplastia, reparación plástica de un conducto esp. de una trompa de Falopio.

tubule *n.* túbulo, conducto o canal pequeño; **collecting** ___ / ___ colector; **renal** ___ / ___ renal; **seminiferous** ___ / conduto seminífero.

tuft *n.* penacho, copete.

tug *n.* tirón; estirón; *v.* halar; estirar.

tugging *n.* tirón, acción de estirar con fuerza o tensión.

tularemia *n.* tularemia, fiebre de conejo, infección transmitida a las personas por la picadura de un insecto vector o contraída en la manipulación de carne infectada.

tumefaction *n.* tumefacción, tumescencia, proceso de hinchazón.

tumefy *v.* entumecerse, hincharse.

tumid *a.* túmido-a, hinchado-a.

tummy *n.* pancita, barriguita.

tumor *n.* tumor. 1. bulto o hinchazón; 2. crecimiento espontáneo de tejido nuevo en masa que no tiene propósito fisiológico alguno; **diffuse** ___ / ___ difuso; **inflammatory** ___ / ___ inflamatorio; **medullary** ___ / ___ medular; **necrotic** ___ / ___ necrótico; **nonsolid** ___ / ___ no sólido; **radioresistant** ___ / ___ radiorresistente; **radiosensitive** ___ / ___ radiosensitivo; **scirrhous** ___ / ___ escirroso; **undifferentiated** ___ / ___ no diferenciado.

tumoricidal *a.* tumoricida, que destruye células tumorales.

tumorigenesis *n.* tumorigénesis, formación de tumores.

tumor makers, serum *n. pl.* sustancias en el plasma sanguíneo indicativas de la posible presencia de un tumor maligno.

tumorous *a.* tumoroso-a, que tiene la apariencia de un tumor.

tumor virus *n.* virus tumoroso, capaz de producir cáncer.

tuna *n.* [*fish*] atún.

tunic *n.* túnica, membrana protectora; ___ **adventitia** / ___ adventicia; ___ **albuginea** / cápsula albugínea; ___ **externa** / ___ externa; ___ **interna** / ___ interna; ___ **media** / ___ media; ___ **mucosa** / ___ mucosa; ___ **muscularis** / ___ muscular; ___ **serosa** / ___ serosa; ___ **vaginalis** / ___ vaginal.

tunnel *n.* túnel, canal o conducto estrecho; **carpal** ___ / ___ del carpo; **flexor** ___ / ___ flexor; **tarsal** ___ / ___ tarsiano.

tunnel vision *n.* visión en túnel, trastorno frecuente en casos de glaucoma avanzado que produce al paciente una disminución visual considerable tal como si mirara a través de un túnel.

turbid *a.* turbio-a, túrbido-a; nebuloso-a.

turbinated *a.* aconchado-a. 1. en forma de concha o cúpula; 2. rel. a los cornetes nasales.

turgid *a.* túrgido-a; hinchado-a, distendido-a.

turgor *n.* turgor. 1. distensión; 2. tensión celular normal.

turn *n.* vuelta, giro; turno; *v.* voltear, virar, dar vuelta, torcer; **to** ___ **back** / volver, regresar, retroceder; **to** ___ **down** / doblar; desaprobar, rechazar; [*when referring to one's body*] volverse, darse vuelta, virarse; **to** ___ **into** / volverse, convertirse en, transformarse; **to** ___ **out** / resultar; **to** ___ **pale** / palidecer; **to** ___ **red** / enrojecerse.

turned-down *a.* vuelto-a; doblado-a hacia abajo; desaprobado-a; rechazado-a.

turned-up *a.* vuelto-a, doblado-a hacia arriba.

Turner's syndrome *n.* síndrome de Turner, trastorno endocrino congénito que se manifiesta con deficiencia ovárica, amenorrea, estatura baja y la presencia de cromosomas X solamente.

turning *n.* 1. versión, término obstétrico refe-

416

rente a la manipulación del feto en el útero para facilitar el parto; 2. vuelta; *a.* giratorio-a; **the __ point** / la crisis, el momento decisivo.

turnover *n.* cambio; *a.* cambiado-a de posición; *v.* voltear, cambiar de posición; transferir.

tussis *L.* tussis, tos.

tussive *a.* tusivo-a, rel. a la tos o causado por ésta.

T wave *n.* onda T, parte del electrocardiograma que representa la repolarización de los ventrículos.

tweezers *n. pl.* pinzas, tenacillas.

twice *adv.* dos veces; __ **as much,** __ **as many** / el doble.

twig *n.* terminación o rama diminuta de un nervio o de una arteria.

twilight *n.* crepúsculo; __ **sleep** / sueño crepuscular; __ **state** / estado de somnolencia.

twinge *n.* punzada, dolor agudo.

twinkle *n.* guiñada, pestañeo; *v.* guiñar un ojo; pestañear, parpadear; **in a** __ / en un momento, en un instante.

twins *n. pl.* gemelos, mellizos, jimaguas, uno de dos hijos nacidos de un mismo embarazo; **dizygotic** __ / __ dicigóticos; **identical** __ / __ idénticos; **monozygotic** __ / __ monocigotos; **Siamese** __ / __ siameses; **true** __ / __ verdaderos.

twist *n.* torsión, torcedura; sacudida, contorsión; peculiaridad; *v.* [*an ankle*] torcer, virar, doblar.

twitch *n.* tic nervioso espasmódico; sacudida.

tympanectomy *n. cirg.* timpanectomía, excisión de la membrana timpánica.

tympanic *a.* timpánico-a, resonante; rel. al tímpano __ **membrane** / membrana __; __ **resonance** / resonancia __.

tympanites *n.* timpanitis, distensión del abdomen causada por acumulación de gas en los intestinos.

tympanitic *a.* timpanítico-a, rel. a la timpanitis o afectado por ésta.

tympanoplasty *n.* timpanoplastia, reconstrucción del oído medio.

tympanotomy *n.* timpanotomía, incisión de la membrana timpánica.

tympanum *n.* tímpano, oído medio.

type *n.* tipo, género, clase, modelo o ejemplar distintivo.

typhlitis *n.* tiflitis, infl. del ciego.

typhoid *a.* tifoideo-a, rel. al tifo o semejante a éste.

typhoid fever *n.* fiebre tifoidea, infección abdominal aguda que es causada por una bacteria de la clase *Salmonella* y que se manifiesta con infl. abdominal, postración, fiebre alta y dolor de cabeza.

typhus *n.* tifus, tifo, infección aguda causada por una *Rickettsia* que se manifiesta con fiebre alta, intensos dolores de cabeza y delirio.

typhus vaccine *n.* vacuna tífica.

typical *a.* típico-a, conforme a un tipo.

typing *n.* tipificación de tejidos, determinación por tipos; **blood** __ / determinación del grupo sanguíneo.

U *abbr.* unit / unidad; **uranium** / uranio; **urology** urología.

udder *n.* ubre, glándula mamaria de la vaca y otros animales mamíferos.

ugliness *n.* fealdad.

ugly *a.* feo-a.

ulcer *n.* úlcera, llaga o lesión en la piel o en la membrana mucosa con desintegración gradual de los tejidos; **chronic leg varicose** ___ / ___ varicosa crónica de la pierna; **decubitus** ___ / ___ por decúbito; **duodenal** ___ / ___ del duodeno; **gastric** ___ / ___ gástrica; **peptic** ___ / ___ péptica; **perforating** ___ / ___ perforante; **varicose** ___ / ___ varicosa; **vesical** ___ / ___ vesical.

ulcerate *v.* ulcerar; ulcerarse.

ulcerated *a.* ulcerado-a, de la naturaleza de una úlcera o afectado por ella.

ulceration *n.* ulceración, supuración; proceso de formación de una úlcera.

ulcerative *a.* ulcerativo-a, rel. a una úlcera o caracterizado-a por una condición ulcerosa; ___ **colitis** / colitis ___.

ulcerogenic *a.* ulcerógeno-a, que produce úlceras.

ulcerous *a.* ulceroso-a, rel. a una úlcera o que la padece.

ulerythema *n.* uleritema, dermatitis eritematosa caracterizada por la formación de cicatrices.

ulna *n.* cúbito. *V.* **cubitus.**

ulnar *n.* ulnar, rel. al cúbito o a los nervios y arterias relacionados con éste.

ulocarcinoma, ulocarcinomata *n.* ulocarcinoma, ulocarcinomata, cáncer de las encías.

ultimate *a.* último-a, final; fundamental.

ultracentrifuge *n.* ultracentrífuga, aparato de fuerza centrífuga que separa y sedimenta las moléculas de una sustancia.

ultrafiltration *n.* ultrafiltración, proceso de filtración que deja pasar pequeñas moléculas pero impide el paso de moléculas mayores.

ultramicroscope *n.* ultramicroscopio, microscopio de campo oscuro capaz de hacer visibles objetos que no se distinguen en un microscopio de luz común.

ultrasonic *a.* ultrasónico-a, supersónico-a; ___ **diagnosis** / diagnóstico por ultrasonido.

ultrasonogram *n.* ultrasonograma, imagen producida por medio de ultrasonografía.

ultrasonography *n.* ultrasonografía, técnica de diagnóstico que emplea ultrasonido para producir imágenes de una estructura o de tejidos del cuerpo.

ultrasound *n.* ultrasonido, ondas de frecuencia superior a las del oído humano que se usan en ultrasonografía en procedimientos terapéuticos y de diagnóstico.

ultrasound imaging *n.* imágenes por ultrasonido, captación de imágenes de órganos o tejidos del cuerpo por medio de ultrasonido empleando técnicas de reflejo (ecograma).

ultrastructure *n.* ultraestructura, estructura diminuta que solamente puede distinguirse bajo un microscopio electrónico.

ultraviolet *a.* ultravioleta, que se extiende más allá de la zona violeta del espectro; ___ **rays** / rayos ___; ___ **therapy** / terapia de radiación ___.

ululation *n.* ululación, emisión de gritos o alaridos incoordinados de tipo histérico esp. de pacientes mentales.

umbilical *a.* umbilical, rel. al ombligo; ___ **notch** / ligamento ___; ___ **hernia** / hernia ___.

umbilical cord *n.* cordón umbilical, estructura que sirve de conexión entre el feto y la placenta durante la gestación.

umbilicus, navel *n.* ombligo, depresión en el centro del abdomen que marca el punto de inserción del cordón umbilical.

unable *a.* incapaz, inhábil.

unacceptable *a.* inaceptable, no aprobado-a.

unaccustomed *a.* no usual, no acostumbrado-a, desacostumbrado-a.

unadulterated *a.* natural, puro-a, sin mezcla, no adulterado-a.

unaffected *a.* no afectado-a.

unanimous *a.* unánime.

unanswered *a.* por contestar, no contestado-a.

unassisted *a.* sin ayuda, sin auxilio, desamparado-a.

unattached *a.* suelto-a, sin conexión.

unattended *a.* desatendido-a.

unavoidable *a.* inevitable.

unaware *a.* sin conocimiento de causa; que ignora.

unbearable *a.* insoportable, intolerable, insufrible, imposible de soportar.

unbeliever *a.* incrédulo-a.

unbiased *a.* imparcial, sin prejuicios.

Ulcer	*Úlcera*
chancroidal	chancroide
chronic	crónica
chronic leg varicose	varicosa crónica de la pierna
decubitus	por decúbito
duodenal	duodenal
gastric	gástrica
hemorrhagic	homorrágica
indolent	indolente
marginal	marginal
mycotic	micótica
peptic	péptica
perforating	perforante
phagedenic	fagedénica
syphilitic	sifilítica
vesical	vesical

unclog *v.* desbloquear, permeabilizar; destupir, destapar.

uncomfortable *a.* incómodo-a, molesto-a, desagradable.

uncommon *a.* poco común, raro-a, extraño-a.

unconditioned reflex *n.* reflejo no condicionado o natural.

unconditioned response *n.* respuesta no condicionada o reacción no restringida.

unconscious *a.* inconsciente. 1. que ha perdido el conocimiento; 2. que no responde a estímulos sensoriales.

unconsciousness *n.* inconsciencia, pérdida del conocimiento.

uncooperative *a.* poco dócil; que no coopera.

uncover *v.* destapar, descubrir, poner al descubierto.

unction *n.* unción, aplicación de un ungüento o aceite.

unctuous *a.* untuoso-a, oleaginoso-a; grasoso-a.

undecided *a.* indeciso-a, indeterminado-a.

undefined *a.* indefinido-a.

under *a.* inferior; *prep., adv.* debajo, menos, menos que; bajo; ___ **observation** / bajo observación; ___ **treatment** / bajo tratamiento.

underage *a.* menor de edad.

underclothing *n.* ropa interior.

underdeveloped *a.* subdesarrollado-a; en desarrollo.

underdevelopment *n.* subdesarrollo.

underestimate *v.* subestimar; menospreciar.

underfed *a.* desnutrido-a, mal alimentado-a.

undergo *vi.* someterse a; sufrir, padecer, soportar; **to** ___ **surgery** / someterse a una operación.

underline *v.* subrayar.

undermine *v.* dañar, debilitar.

undernourished *a.* desnutrido-a; malnutrido-a.

undernutrition *a.* desnutrición.

undershirt *n.* camiseta.

underside *n.* el lado de abajo.

undersigned *n.* el abajo firmante.

understand *vi.* comprender, entender.

understood *a. pp.* de **to understand,** convenido-a, entendido-a, comprendido-a.

undertake *vi.* emprender, iniciar, tomar la iniciativa.

underway *n.* en camino; bajo estudio.

underwear *n.* ropa interior.

underweight *n.* falta de peso, peso deficiente; bajo de peso; de peso insuficiente.

undesirable *a.* indeseable, inaceptable, aborrecido-a.

undetected *a.* no detectado-a, no descubierto-a, inadvertido-a.

undetermined *a.* indeterminado-a.

undeveloped *a.* no desarrollado-a, sin manifestación.

undifferentiation *n.* indiferenciación. *V.* **anaplasia.**

undigested *a.* no digerido-a, no asimilado-a.

undiluted *a.* no diluido-a, sin diluirse, concen-

trado-a.

undiminished *a.* sin disminución.

undisclosed *a.* no revelado-a, no dado-a a conocer.

undo *vi.* deshacer, desatar; desabrochar.

undress *v.* desvestirse; quitarse la ropa.

undulant *a.* ondulante; ___ **fever** / fiebre ___ . *V.* **brucellosis.**

undulated *a.* ondulado-a, de borde ondulado o irregular.

uneasy *a.* inquieto-a.

unengaged *a.* desencajado-a, fuera de lugar.

unequal *a.* desigual; desproporcionado-a.

unexpected *a.* inesperado-a, imprevisto-a.

unfinished *a.* incompleto-a, sin terminar.

unfit *a.* inepto-a, inhábil, incapaz.

unfitness *n.* ineptitud, incapacidad, incompetencia.

unforeseen *a.* inesperado-a, imprevisto-a.

unfortunate *a.* infeliz, desafortunado-a, desgraciado-a.

unfriendly *a.* poco amistoso-a, poco amigable.

ungrateful *a.* desagradecido-a, ingrato-a.

ungual *a.* ungueal, rel. a una uña.

unguent *n.* ungüento, medicamento preparado para uso externo.

unhappy *a.* infeliz, desgraciado-a.

unharmed, unhurt *a.* ileso-a; *pop.* sano-a y salvo-a.

unhealthy *a.* [*environment*] insalubre, malsano-a; [*person*] enfermizo-a, achacoso-a.

uniarticular *a.* uniarticular, rel. a una sola articulación.

unibasal *a.* unibásico-a, rel. a una sola base.

unicellular *a.* unicelular, de una sola célula.

uniform *n.* [*garment*] uniforme; *a.* uniforme; invariable.

unigravida *a.* unigrávida, mujer embarazada por primera vez.

unilateral *a.* unilateral, rel. a un solo lado.

uninsured *a.* no asegurado-a, sin seguro.

union *n.* unión. 1. acción de unir dos cosas en una; 2. juntura de dos partes cortadas (amputadas) de un hueso o de los bordes de una herida.

uniovular *a.* uniovular, que se desarrolla de un solo óvulo.

uniparous *a.* unípara, mujer que tiene un parto simple.

unipolar *a.* unipolar, de un solo polo, tal como las células nerviosas.

unique *a.* único-a; solo-a; que se distingue de otros.

unit *n.* unidad. 1. estándar de medida; 2. (IU) unidad internacional (UI). *V.* **international unit;** 3. unidad fisiológica, la más mínima división de un órgano capaz de realizar una función; **motor** ___ / ___ motora.

unite *v.* unir; reunir.

united *a.* unido-a.

unity *n.* unidad; unión.

universal *a.* universal, general; ___ **antidote** /

antídoto ___ .

universal donor *n.* donante universal, persona que pertenece al grupo de sangre tipo O, de factor RH negativo, cuya sangre puede ser dada a personas con sangre tipo ABO con poco riesgo de complicaciones.

universal recipient *n.* recipiente universal, persona que pertenece al grupo de sangre AB.

universe *n.* universo.

university *n.* universidad.

unjust *a.* injusto-a.

unkind *a.* despiadado-a, sin bondad.

unlawful *a.* ilegal, ilícito-a.

unlicensed *a.* no acreditado-a, sin licencia o sin permiso.

unlikely *a.* improbable, dudoso-a.

unlucky *a.* desafortunado-a.

Unna's paste boot *n.* bota de pasta de Unna, compresión que se usa en el tratamiento de úlceras varicosas en la pierna, con vendajes en espiral aplicados y cubiertos con la pasta medicinal de Unna.

unnecessary *a.* innecesario-a.

unobstructed *a.* abierto-a, suelto-a; libre; no obstruido.

unofficial *a.* sin autorización; no oficial, se dice de una droga o medicamento no aprobado por la farmacopea o los formularios vigentes autorizados.

unopened *a.* cerrado-a, tapado-a, sin abrir.

unorganized *a.* desorganizado-a; no estructurado; sin orden.

unreal *a.* ilusorio-a, imaginario-a.

unreasonable *a.* irrazonable, intransigente.

unrest *n.* desasosiego, inquietud; intranquilidad.

unsalted *a.* sin sal, que le falta sal.

unsanitary *a.* insalubre, malsano.

unsaturated *a.* no saturado-a.

unstable *a.* inestable.

untiring *a.* incansable.

untreated *a.* no tratado-a.

unwanted *a.* no deseado-a.

up *prep., adv.* arriba, en lo alto.

update *v.* [*to improve*] modernizar; [*documents*] poner al día; arreglar.

upgrade *v.* mejorar.

upgrowth *n.* crecimiento, desarrollo, maduración.

upper *n. pop.* droga estimulante, esp. una anfetamina; *a. comp.* superior, más alto-a.

upper airway obstruction *n.* obstrucción en el conducto aéreo superior.

upper GI *n.* examen radiográfico del estómago y duodeno con ingestión de una sustancia que sirve de medio de contraste.

upper jaw *n.* mandíbula superior.

upper respiratory infection *n.* infección del tracto respiratorio superior.

upper respiratory tract *n.* aparato respiratorio superior compuesto de la nariz, los conductos nasales y la nasofaringe.

upset *a.* indipuesto-a; nervioso-a; disgustado-a; *v.*

trastornar; enfadar.

uptake *n.* absorción, fijación o incorporación de alguna sustancia a un organismo vivo; ___ **and storage** / captura (toma) y almacenamiento.

uranium *n.* uranio, elemento metálico pesado.

urate *n.* urato, sal de ácido úrico.

urea *n.* urea, producto del metabolismo de las proteínas, forma en la cual el nitrógeno se excreta por la orina.

ureal *a.* ureico-a, rel. o concerniente a la urea.

urelcosis *n.* urelcosis, ulceración de las vías urinarias.

uremia *n.* uremia, condición tóxica causada por insuficiencia renal que produce retención en la sangre de sustancias nitrogenadas, fosfatos y sulfatos.

uremic *a.* urémico-a, rel. a la uremia o causado por ella.

ureter *n.* uréter, uno de los conductos que llevan la orina del riñón a la vejiga.

ureteral *a.* ureteral, uretérico-a, rel. o concerniente al uréter.

ureterectasis *n.* ureterectasis, dilatación anormal del uréter.

ureterectomy *n. cirg.* ureterectomía, extirpación parcial o total del uréter.

ureteritis *n.* ureteritis, infl. del uréter.

ureterocele *n.* ureterocele, dilatación quística de la porción distal intravesical del uréter debida a una estenosis del orificio ureteral.

ureterocystoneostomy *n. cirg.* ureterocistoneostomía. *V.* **ureteroneocystostomy.**

ureterocystostomy *n. cirg.* ureterocistostomía, transplantación de un uréter a otra parte de la vejiga.

ureterography *n.* ureterografía, radiografía del uréter usando un medio radiopaco.

ureteroheminephrectomy *n. cirg.* ureteroheminefrectomía, resección de la porción de un riñón y el uréter en ciertos casos de duplicación del tracto urinario superior.

ureterohydronephrosis *n.* ureterohidronefrosis, distensión del uréter y del riñón debida a una obstrucción.

ureteroiliostomy *n.* ureteroiliostomía, anastomosis del uréter a un segmento aislado del íleon.

ureterolithiasis *n.* ureterolitiasis, desarrollo de un cálculo ureteral.

ureterolithotomy *n. cirg.* ureterolitotomía, incisión del uréter para extraer un cálculo.

ureteroneocystostomy *n. cirg.* ureteroneocistostomía. *V.* **ureterocystoneostomy.**

ureteronephrectomy *n. cirg.* ureteronefrectomía, excisión del riñón y su uréter.

ureteroplasty *n.* ureteroplastia, cirugía plástica del uréter.

ureteropyeloplasty *n. cirg.* ureteropieloplastia, cirugía plástica del uréter y la pelvis renal.

ureterosigmoidostomy *n. cirg.* ureterosigmoidostomía, implantación del uréter en el colon sigmoideo.

ureterostomy *n. cirg.* ureterostomía, formación de una fístula permanente para drenar un uréter.

ureterotomy *n. cirg.* ureterotomía, incisión de un uréter.

ureteroureterostomy *n. cirg.* ureteroureterostomía, anastomosis de dos uréteres o de dos extremos del mismo uréter.

urethra *n.* uretra, canal o conducto urinario.

urethral *a.* uretral, rel. a la uretra; ___ **stricture** / estrechez ___.

urethralgia *n.* uretralgia, dolor en la uretra.

urethrectomy *n. cirg.* uretrectomía, excisión parcial o total de la uretra.

urethritis *n.* uretritis, infl. aguda o crónica de la uretra.

urethrography *n.* uretrografía, rayos X de la uretra usando una sustancia radiopaca inyectada.

urethroscope *n.* uretroscopio, instrumento para visualizar el interior de la uretra.

urethrotome *n.* uretrótomo, instrumento quirúrgico empleado en una uretrotomía.

urethrotomy *n. cirg.* uretrotomía, incisión efectuada para aliviar una estrechez uretral.

urgent *a.* urgente.

uric acid *n.* ácido úrico, producto del metabolismo de las proteínas presente en la sangre y excretado en la orina.

uricemia *n.* uricemia, exceso de ácido úrico en la sangre.

uricosuria *n.* uricosuria, presencia excesiva de ácido úrico en la orina.

urinal *n.* orinal, vasija en que se recoge la orina; *pop.* taza, pato.

urinalysis *n.* urinálisis, examen de orina.

urinary *a.* urinario-a, rel. o concerniente a la orina. ___ **calculi** / cálculos ___-s; ___ **infection** / infección renal o ___; ___ **sediments** / sedimentos ___-s.

urinary bladder *n.* vejiga urinaria, órgano muscular en forma de saco que recoge la orina que secretan los riñones.

urinary system *n.* sistema urinario, órganos y conductos que participan en la producción y excreción de la orina.

urinary tract *n.* vías urinarias; ___ **infections** / infecciones de las ___.

urinate *n.* orinar, mear.

urination *n.* orina, acto de emisión de la orina; **frequent** ___ / orinar con frecuencia, micción frecuente; *Mex. A. pop.* meadera; **difficult** ___ / orinar con dificultad, micción difícil; **painful** ___ / orinar con dolor, micción dolorosa.

urine *n.* orina, orín, *pop.* aguas menores, líquido ambarino secretado por los riñones que se almacena en la vejiga y se elimina en la uretra; **clear** ___ / ___ clara; **dark** ___ / ___ turbia; **midstream** ___ / espécimen de ___ a mitad del chorro; **murky, hazy** ___ / ___ turbia; ___ **culture** / cultivo de ___; ___ **sediment** / sedimento de ___; ___ **specimen** / espécimen,

Urine, Anomalies	*Orina, anomalías*
acute retention (inability to urinate)	retención aguda (incapacidad de orinar)
abnormal color	color anormal
abnormal odor	olor anormal
blood in urine	sangre en la orina
changes in stream	cambios en el chorro
frequent urination	micción frecuente
involuntary urine leak	escape o goteo involuntario de orina
little or no urination	escasa o ninguna cantidad de orina
painful urination	micción dolorosa
urge incontinence	micción imperiosa

muestra de ___; **clean voided** ___ / ___ limpia al salir.

uriniferous *a.* urinífero-a, que contiene o conduce orina.

urinogenital *a.* urinogenital. *V.* **urogenital.**

urinoma *n.* urinoma, tumor o quiste que contiene orina.

urobilinogen *n.* urobilinógeno, pigmento derivado de la reducción de bilirrubina por acción de bacterias intestinales.

urodynamics *n.* urodinámica, estudio del proceso activo patofisiológico de la micción.

urodynia *n.* urodinia, micción dolorosa.

urogenital *a.* urogenital, rel. a la vía urinaria o al tracto urinario y genital; ___ **diaphragm** / diafragma ___.

urogram *n.* urograma, rayos X hechos por urografía.

urography *n.* urografía, rayos X de una parte de las vías urinarias con el uso de una sustancia radiopaca inyectada; **excretory or descending** ___ / ___ excretora o descendiente; **retrograde** ___ / ___ retrógrada.

urokinase *n.* urocinasa, enzima presente en la orina que se emplea en la disolución de coágulos.

urolithiasis *n.* urolitiasis, formación de cálculos urinarios y trastornos asociados con su presencia.

urologist *n.* urólogo-a, especialista en urología.

urology *n.* urología, estudio y tratamiento de las enfermedades del aparato genitourinario en el hombre y del tracto urinario en la mujer.

uropathy *n.* uropatía, enfermedades de las vías urinarias.

uropyourether *n.* uropiouréter, acumulación de orina y pus en la pelvis renal.

urticaria *n.* urticaria, erupción cutánea gen. alérgica que se manifiesta con ronchas rosáceas, se acompaña de picazón intensa y puede producirse por un factor interno o externo.

421

usage *n.* uso, costumbre.

use *n.* uso, utilidad, provecho; *v.* usar, emplear; **off-label** ___ / ___ no aprobado.

useful *a.* útil, provechoso-a, práctico-a.

usual *a.* usual, de costumbre; **-ly** *adv.* usualmente, generalmente.

uterine *a.* uterino-a, rel. al útero o matriz; ___ **bleeding** / sangramiento ___, sangramiento no relacionado con la menstruación; ___ **cancer** / cáncer del útero o de la matriz; ___ **prolapse** / prolapso ___; ___ **rupture** / rotura ___.

uterosalpingography *n.* uterosalpingografía, examen de rayos X de la matriz y la trompa de Falopio usando una sustancia radiopaca inyectada.

uterovaginal *a.* uterovaginal, rel. al útero y a la vagina.

uterovesical *a.* uterovesical, rel. al útero y la vejiga urinaria.

uterus *n.* útero, matriz, órgano muscular femenino del aparato reproductivo que contiene y nutre al embrión y feto durante la gestación; **didelphys** ___ / ___ didelfo.

uvea *n.* úvea, túnica vascular del ojo formada por el iris, el cuerpo ciliar y la coroide.

uveitis *n.* uveítis, infl. de la úvea.

uvula *n.* úvula, *pop.* campanilla, estructura colgante en el centro posterior del paladar blando.

U wave *n.* onda U, onda positiva que sigue a la onda T en el electrocardiograma.

V *abbr.* **valve** / válvula; **vein** / vena; **vide** (see) / vea; **vision** / visión; **volume** / volumen.

vacation *n.* vacaciones.

vaccinate *v.* vacunar, inocular.

vaccination *n.* vacunación, inoculación de una vacuna.

vaccine *n.* vacuna, preparación de microorganismos atenuados o muertos que se introduce en el cuerpo para establecer una inmunidad en contra de la enfermedad específica causada por dichos microorganismos; **BCG** ___ / ___ del bacilo Calmette-Guerin, contra la tuberculosis; **DTP (diphtheria, tetanus, pertussis)** ___ / ___ triple contra la difteria, tétano y pertusis (tos ferina); **influenza** ___ / ___ contra la influenza; **measles virus, inactivated** ___ / ___ antisarampión, inactivada; **measles virus, live attenuated** ___ / ___ antisarampión de virus vivo, atenuada; **pneumococcal polyvalent** ___ / ___ antineumocócica polivalente; **poliovirus, live oral trivalent** ___ / ___ antipolio trivalente o de Sabin; **Salk's antipoliomyelitis** ___ / ___ antipoliomielítica de Salk; **rabies** ___ / ___ antirrábica; **smallpox** ___ / ___ antivariolosa, antivariólica; **typhus** ___ / ___ antitífica; **typhoid** ___ / ___ contra la tifoidea.

vaccinia *n.* vaccina, virus causante de la viruela bovina del cual se obtiene la vacuna contra la viruela.

vacillate *v.* vacilar; fluctuar.

vacillating *a.* vacilante, oscilante, fluctuante.

vacuity *n.* vacuidad, vacío.

vacuole *n.* vacuola, pequeña cavidad o espacio en el protoplasma celular que contiene líquido o aire.

vacuolization *n.* vacuolización, formación de vacuolas.

vacuum *L.* vacuum, vacío, espacio desprovisto de materia o aire; *v.* extraer el polvo con una aspiradora; ___ **packed** / envasado-a al vacío.

vagal *a.* vagal, rel. al nervio vago o neumogástrico.

vagina *n.* vagina. 1. conducto en la mujer que se extiende del útero a la vulva; 2. estructura semejante a una vaina.

vaginal *a.* vaginal. 1. que posee forma de vaina; 2. rel. a la vagina.

vaginismus *L.* vaginismus, contracción dolorosa espasmódica de la vagina.

vaginitis *n.* vaginitis, infl. de la vagina; **bacterial** ___ / ___ bacteriana.

vagolytic *a.* vagolítico, rel. al nervio vago.

vagotomy *n.* *cirg.* vagotomía, interrupción del nervio vago.

vagrant *a.* errante; suelto-a; libre.

vague *a.* vago-a, indefinido-a; **-ly** *adv.* vagamente.

vagus *n.* vago, nervio neumogástrico.

vain *a.* vano-a, vanidoso-a; **-ly** *adv.* vanamente, en vano.

valgus *L.* valgus, doblado o torcido hacia afuera.

valid *a.* válido-a, valedero-a.

validity *n.* validez.

valient *a.* valiente.

vallecula *n.* valécula, depresión, surco o fisura esp. en referencia a estructuras anatómicas.

valley fever *n.* fiebre del valle. *V.* **coccidioidomycosis.**

valorization *n.* valorización, evaluación.

Valsalva's maneuver *n.* maniobra, experimento de Valsalva, procedimiento para demostrar la permeabilidad de la trompa de Eustaquio o de ajustar la presión del oído medio mediante una espiración forzada con la boca y la nariz tapadas.

valuable *a.* valioso-a, valuable.

value *n.* valor.

valve *n.* (*pl.* **valvae**) válvula, valva, estructura membranosa en un canal u orificio que al cerrarse temporalmente impide el reflujo del contenido que pasa a través de ella; **aortic** ___ / ___ aórtica; **aortic-semilunar** ___ / ___ aórtica semilunar; **atrioventricular left** ___ / ___ auriculoventricular izquierda; **atrioventricular right** ___, **tricuspid** / ___ auriculoventricular derecha, tricúspide; **bicuspid or mitral** ___ / ___ bicúspide o mitral; **ileocecal** ___ / ___ ileocecal; **pulmonary** ___ / ___ pulmonar; **pyloric** ___ / ___ pilórica.

valvulae conniventes *n.* *pl.* válvulas conniventes, pliegues circulares membranosos localizados en el intestino delgado que retardan el paso del contenido alimenticio en el intestino.

valvuloplasty *n.* *cirg.* valvuloplastia, operación plástica de una válvula.

valvulotome *n.* valvulótomo, instrumento quirúrgico que se usa para seccionar una válvula.

vapor *n.* vapor, gas.

vaporization *n.* vaporización. 1. acción o efecto de vaporizar; 2. uso terapéutico de vapores.

vaporize *v.* vaporizar, convertir una sustancia en gas o vapor.

vaporizer *n.* vaporizador, dispositivo para convertir una sustancia en vapor y aplicarla a usos terapéuticos.

variability *n.* variabilidad.

variable *n.* variable, factor que puede variar; *a.* que puede cambiar.

variant *n.* variante, objeto esencialmente igual a otro pero que difiere en la forma; *a.* variable, inconstante, que cambia o varía.

variation *n.* variación, diversidad en las características de objetos que se relacionan entre sí.

varicella *n.* varicela. *V.* **chickenpox.**

varicocele *n.* varicocele, condición varicosa de las venas del cordón espermático que produce una masa blanda en el escroto.

varicoid *a.* varicoide, que se asemeja a una várice.

varicose *a.* varicoso-a, rel. a las várices o que se

les asemeja; ___ **veins** / venas ___-s.

varicotomy *n. cirg.* varicotomía, excisión de una vena varicosa.

variety *n.* variedad.

variola *n.* variola, viruela.

variolic, variolous *a.* variólico-a, rel. a la viruela.

varioliform *a.* varioliforme, semejante a la viruela.

varix *n.* (*pl.* **varices**) várice, vena, arteria o vaso linfático aumentado o dilatado.

varus *L.* varus, doblado o torcido hacia adentro.

vary *v.* variar, cambiar; cambiarse; desviarse.

vas *L.* (*pl.* **vasa**) vas, vaso.

vascular *a.* vascular, rel. a vasos sanguíneos; ___ **system** / sistema ___, todos los vasos del cuerpo esp. los sanguíneos.

vascularization *n.* vascularización, formación de vasos sanguíneos nuevos.

vasculature *n.* vasculatura, disposición de los vasos sanguíneos en un órgano o parte.

vasculitis *n.* vasculitis. *V.* **angiítis.**

vasculopathy *n.* vasculopatía, cualquier enfermedad de los vasos sanguíneos.

vas deferens *L.* vas deferens, conducto excretor de espermatozoides.

vasectomy *n. cirg.* vasectomía, excisión parcial y ligadura de los conductos deferentes para impedir la salida de espermatozoides en el semen, procedimiento gen. usado como contraceptivo.

vaseline *n.* vaselina.

vasoactive *a.* vasoactivo, que afecta los vasos sanguíneos.

vasoconstrictive *a.* vasoconstrictivo-a, que causa constricción en los vasos sanguíneos.

vasodilation *n.* vasodilatación, aumento del calibre de los vasos sanguíneos.

vasodilator *n.* vasodilatador, agente que causa vasodilatación; *a.* vasodilatador-a; que causa vasodilatación.

vasomotor *n.* vasomotor, agente que regula las contracciones y la dilatación de los vasos sanguíneos; *a.* vasomotor-a, que causa dilatación o contracción en los vasos sanguíneos.

vasopressin *n.* vasopresina, hormona liberada por la pituitaria posterior que aumenta la reabsorción de agua en el riñón elevando la presión arterial.

vasopressor *n.* vasopresor, agente que produce constricción en los vasos sanguíneos; *a.* que tiene efecto vasoconstrictivo.

vasospasm *n.* vasoespasmo; **coronary** ___ / ___ coronario. *V.* **angiospasm.**

vasotonic *a.* vasotónico, rel. al tono de un vaso.

vasovagal *a.* vasovagal, rel. a los vasos y al nervio vago.

vasovagal syncope *n.* síncope vasovagal, desmayo súbito breve debido a un trastorno vasomotor y vagal.

vastus *L.* vastus, dilatado-a, agrandado-a, extendido-a.

Vater's ampulla *n.* ámpula de Váter, punto de entrada en el duodeno de los conductos excretores biliar y pancreático.

veal *n.* carne de ternera; ___ **chop** / chuleta de ___.

vector *n.* vector, portador, organismo microbiano transmisor de agentes infecciosos.

vegan *n.* vegetariano en el sentido estricto de la palabra.

vegetable *n.* vegetal.

vegetarian *n.* vegetariano-a, persona cuya dieta consiste principalmente en vegetales; *a.* rel. a los vegetales.

vegetarianism *n.* vegetarianismo, método de alimentación que consiste mayormente en una dieta de vegetales y frutas.

vegetation *n.* vegetación, crecimiento anormal de verrugas o excrecencias en una parte del cuerpo tal como se ve en la endocarditis.

vegetative *a.* vegetativo-a. 1. rel. a funciones de crecimiento y nutrición; 2. rel. a funciones corporales involuntarias o inconscientes.

vehicle *n.* vehículo. 1. sustancia sin acción terapéutica que acompaña a un agente activo en una preparación medicinal; 2. agente de transmisión.

veil *n.* velo. 1. membrana o cubierta fina que cubre una parte del cuerpo; 2. parte de la membrana amniótica que cubre la cara del feto; 3. alteración ligera de la voz.

vein *n.* vena, vaso fibromuscular que lleva la sangre de los capilares al corazón.

vena *L.* vena.

vena cava *n.* vena cava, una de las dos venas mayores, la vena cava inferior y la vena cava superior, que devuelven la sangre desoxigenada a la aurícula derecha del corazón.

venal *a.* venal, rel. a las venas.

venepuncture *n.* venipuntura, punción de una vena.

venereal *a.* venéreo-a, que resulta a consecuencia del acto sexual; ___ **disease (VD)** / enfermedad venérea.

venin, venine *n.* venina, sustancia tóxica del veneno de serpientes.

venin-antivenin *n.* veninantivenina, suero antídoto contra el veneno de serpientes.

venisection *n.* venisección. *V.* **phlebotomy.**

venoconstriction *n.* venoconstricción, reducción de las paredes venosas.

venogram *n.* venograma, radiografía de las venas usando un medio de contraste.

venography *n.* venografía, gráfica e información de un venograma.

venom *n.* veneno, sustancia tóxica.

venomous *a.* venenoso-a, tóxico-a.

veno-occlusive *a.* venoclusivo-a, rel. a una obstrucción venosa.

venotomy *n. cirg.* venotomía. *V.* **phlebotomy.**

venous *a.* venoso-a, rel. a las venas; ___ **blood** / sangre ___; ___ **congestion** / congestión ___; ___ **return** / retorno ___; ___ **sinus** / seno ___;

___ **thrombosis** / trombosis ___.

vent *Fr.* vent, abertura.

ventilate *v.* ventilar, airear.

ventilation *n.* ventilación. 1. circulación de aire fresco en una habitación; 2. oxigenación de la sangre; 3. *psic.* expresión franca de conflictos emocionales internos.

ventilator *n.* ventilador; respirador artificial.

ventral *a.* ventral, abdominal, rel. al vientre o a la parte anterior del cuerpo humano.

ventricle *n.* ventrículo, cavidad pequeña esp. una estructura del corazón, el cerebro o la laringe; **fourth** ___ **of the brain** / cuarto ___ cerebral; **left** ___ **of the heart** / ___ izquierdo del corazón; **larynx** ___ / ___ de la laringe; **lateral** ___ **of the brain** / ___ lateral del cerebro; **right** ___ **of the heart** / ___ derecho del corazón; **third** ___ **of the brain** / tercer ___ del cerebro.

ventricular *a.* ventricular, rel. a un ventrículo.

ventricular septal defect (VSD) *n.* defecto del tabique ventricular.

ventriculitis *n.* ventriculitis, infl. de un ventrículo.

ventriculography *n.* ventriculografía. *V.* **pneumoencephalography.**

ventriculotomy *n.* *cirg.* ventriculotomía, incisión de un ventrículo.

ventrodorsal *a.* ventrodorsal, rel. a las superficies ventral y dorsal.

venule *n.* vénula, vena diminuta que conecta los vasos capilares con venas mayores.

verb *gr.* verbo.

verbatim *L.* verbatim, al pie de la letra, palabra por palabra.

verdict *n.* veredicto, fallo.

verge *n.* anillo anal; margen; límite; borde; **on the** ___ **of** / a punto de.

verification *n.* verificación.

verify *v.* comprobar, verificar.

vermicide *n.* vermicida, vermífugo, agente destructor de vermes (gusanos).

vermiform *a.* vermiforme, que tiene la apariencia de un gusano.

vermiform appendix *n.* apéndice vermiforme.

vermilion border *n.* borde bermellón, el margen rosado expuesto del labio.

vermis *L.* vermis. 1. gusano parásito; 2. estructura semejante a un gusano tal como el lóbulo medio del cerebelo.

vernix *L.* barniz; ___ **caseosa** / unto sebáceo, secreción que protege la piel del feto.

verruca *n.* (*pl.* **verrucae**) verruga; ___ **filiformis** / ___ filiforme; **plantaris (plantar wart)** ___ / ___ plantaris; **vulgaris** ___ / ___ vulgaris.

verrucous *a.* verrugoso-a.

versatile *a.* versátil, polivalente; que tiene una variedad de aplicaciones.

version *n.* versión. 1. cambio de dirección de un órgano tal como el útero; 2. cambio de posición del feto en el útero que facilita el parto; **bimanual** ___ / ___ bimanual; **bipolar** ___ /

___ bipolar; **cephalic** ___ / ___ cefálica; **combined** ___ / ___ combinada; **external** ___ / ___ externa; **spontaneous** ___ / ___ espontánea.

vertebra *n.* (*pl.* **vertebrae**) vértebra, cada uno de los treinta y tres huesos que forman la columna vertebral; **cervical** ___ / ___ cervical; **coccygeal** ___ / ___ coccígea; **lumbar** ___ / ___ lumbar; **sacral** ___ / ___ sacra; **thoracic** ___ / ___ torácica.

vertebral *a.* vertebral, rel. a las vértebras; ___ **artery** / arteria ___; ___ **canal** / conducto ___; ___ **ribs** / costillas ___-es.

vertebrate *n.* vertebrado, que posee columna vertebral o una estructura semejante.

vertebrobasilar *a.* vertebrobasilar, rel. a las arterias vertebral y basilar.

vertex *n.* (*pl.* **vertices**) vértice. 1. cúspide de una estructura, tal como el punto extremo de la cabeza; 2. punto en que concurren los lados de un ángulo.

vertical *a.* 1. vertical, de posición erecta; 2. rel. al vértice; **-ly** *adv.* verticalmente.

vertiginous *a.* vertiginoso-a, rel. al vértigo.

vertigo *n.* vértigo, sensación de rotación en la que se cree que uno gira alrededor del mundo exterior o que éste gira alrededor de uno; **labyrinthine** ___ / ___ laberíntico.

verumontanitis *f.* verumontanitis, infl. del verumontanum.

verumontanum *L.* verumontanum, elevación en la uretra en el punto de entrada de los conductos seminales.

vesical *a.* vesical, rel. a una vejiga o semejante a ella.

vesication *n.* vesicación. 1. formación de ampollas; 2. una ampolla.

vesicle *n.* vesícula. 1. pequeña ampolla; 2. bolsa pequeña de la capa exterior de la piel que contiene líquido seroso.

vesicoureteral *a.* vesicoureteral, rel. a la vejiga urinaria y el uréter.

vesicovaginal *a.* vesicovaginal, rel. a la vejiga urinaria y la vagina.

vesicular *a.* vesicular, rel. a las vesículas.

vessel *n.* vaso, conducto o canal portador de un fluido tal como la sangre y la linfa; **blood** ___ / ___ sanguíneo; **collateral** ___ / ___ colateral; **great** ___-s / grandes ___-s; **lymphatic** ___ / ___ linfático.

vestibular *a.* vestibular, rel. a un vestíbulo; ___ **nerve** / nervio ___.

vestibule *n.* vestíbulo, cavidad que da acceso a un conducto.

vestige *n.* vestigio, resto de una estructura que en una etapa previa de la especie o el embrión, tuvo un desarrollo completo.

vestigial *a.* vestigial, rel. a vestigio; rudimentario-a.

vet *n.* *pop.* veterinario-a.

veterinarian *n.* veterinario-a, persona especializada en veterinaria; *a.* veterinario-a, rel. a la veterinaria.

veterinary medicine *n.* veterinaria, ciencia que trata de la prevención y cura de enfermedades y lesiones de animales, esp. domésticos.

via *L.* vía, tracto, conducto.

viability *n.* cualidad de ser viable.

viable *a.* viable, capaz de sobrevivir, término que se usa gen. en referencia al feto o al recién nacido.

viaduct *n.* viaducto.

vial *n.* frasco, ampolleta.

vibration *n.* vibración, oscilación.

vibrative, vibratory *a.* vibratorio-a, que produce vibración u oscila; ___ **sense** / sentido ___.

vicarious *a.* vicario-a, que asume el lugar de otro.

vice *n.* vicio; falta, defecto.

vicinity *n.* proximidad, vecindad; barrio.

vicious *a.* [*ridden by vice*] vicioso-a, depravado-a; **-ly** *adv.* viciosamente, malvadamente.

victim *n.* victima.

vide *L.* véase.

video *n.* video; ___ **tape** / videocinta.

view *n.* vista; **in** ___ **of** / en vista de; *v.* mirar, examinar.

viewpoint *n.* punto de vista.

vigil *n.* vigilia. 1. estado de respuesta consciente a un estímulo; 2. insomnio.

vigilance *n.* vigilancia, estado alerta o de atención.

vigor *n.* vigor, fortaleza.

vigorous *a.* vigoroso-a; fuerte; **-ly** *adv.* vigorosamente.

villous *a.* velloso-a, velludo-a.

villus *n.* (*pl.* **villi**) vellosidad, vello, proyección filiforme que crece en una superficie membranosa; **aracnoid** ___ / ___ aracnoidea; **chorionic** ___ / ___ coriónicas; **intestinal** ___ / ___ intestinal.

vinegar *n.* vinagre.

violaceous *a.* violáceo-a.

violate *v.* violar, abusar sexualmente.

violence *n.* violencia.

violent *a.* violento-a.

violet *n.* color violeta; *a.* violeta.

viper *n.* víbora.

viral *a.* viral, rel. a un virus.

viremia *n.* viremia, presencia de un virus en la sangre.

virgin *n.* virgen. 1. sustancia sin contaminación; 2. persona que no ha realizado el acto sexual.

virginal *a.* virginal.

virginity *n.* virginidad.

virile *a.* viril, varonil.

virility *n.* virilidad. 1. potencia sexual; 2. estado de poseer características masculinas.

virilization *n.* virilización, masculinización, proceso por el cual se desarrollan en la mujer características masculinas gen. debido a un trastorno hormonal o al suplemento artificial de hormonas masculinas.

virion *n.* virión, partícula viral madura que constituye la forma extracelular infecciosa de un virus.

virology *n.* virología, ciencia que estudia los virus.

virtual *a.* virtual, de existencia aparente, no real.

virulence *n.* virulencia. 1. poder de un organismo de causar determinadas enfermedades en el huésped; 2. cualidad o estado de ser virulento.

virulent *a.* virulento-a, nocivo-a, extremadamente tóxico.

virus *n.* virus, microorganismo ultramicroscópico capaz de causar enfermedades infecciosas; **attenuated** ___ / ___ atenuado; **Cocsackie** ___ / ___ de Cocsackie; **cytomegalic** ___ / ___ citomegálico; **ECHO** ___ / ___ ECHO; **enteric** ___ / ___ entérico; **herpes** ___ / ___ herpético; **pox** ___ / ___ variólico o de Pox; **respiratory syncytial** ___ / ___ sincitial respiratorio; **tumor** ___ / ___ oncogénico.

viscera *n.* *pl.* vísceras, órganos internos del cuerpo, esp. del abdomen.

visceral *a.* visceral, rel. a las vísceras.

visceromegaly *n.* visceromegalia, agrandamiento anormal de una víscera.

viscosity *n.* viscosidad, cualidad de ser viscoso, esp. la propiedad de los líquidos de no fluir libremente debido a la fricción de las moléculas.

viscous *a.* viscoso-a, gelatinoso-a, pegajoso-a.

viscus *L.* (*pl.* **viscera**) víscera.

visible *a.* visible, aparente, evidente; **-ly** *adv.* visiblemente, evidentemente; aparentemente.

vision *n.* visión. 1. sentido de la vista; 2. capacidad de percibir los objetos por la acción de la luz a través de los órganos visuales y los centros cerebrales con que se relacionan; **achromatic** ___ / ___ acromática; **binocular** ___ / ___ binocular; **central** ___ / ___ central; **chromatic** ___ / ___ cromática; **day** ___ / ___ diurna; **double** ___ / ___ doble, diplopia; **field of** ___ / ___ campo visual; **night** ___ / ___ nocturna; **peripheral** ___ / ___ periférica.

visit *n.* visita; *v.* visitar, ir de visita.

visiting hours *n.* horas de visita.

visual *a.* visual, rel. a la visión; ___ **acuity** / acuidad ___; ___ **field** / campo ___.

visualization, imagery *n.* visualización, proceso de crear imágenes como ayuda al tratamiento de curación.

Vision	*Visión*
achromatic	acromática
binocular	binocular
central	central
day	diurna
double	doble, diplopia
night	nocturna
peripheral	periférica

visualize *v.* visualizar. 1. crear una imagen visual de algo; 2. hacer visible, tal como copiar la imagen de un órgano en una radiografía.

vital *a.* vital, rel. a la vida o esencial en el mantenimiento de la misma; ___ **capacity** / capacidad ___; ___ **signs** / signos ___-es; ___ **statistics** / estadística demográfica.

vitality *n.* vitalidad. 1. cualidad de vivir; 2. vigor mental o físico.

vitalize *v.* vitalizar, dar vida; reanimar.

vitamin *n.* vitamina, uno de los compuestos orgánicos que se encuentran en pequeñas cantidades en los alimentos y que son esenciales en el desarrollo y funcionamiento del organismo.

vitaminic *a.* vitamínico-a, rel. a las vitaminas.

vitiate *v.* viciar; infectar.

vitiligo *n.* vitíligo, trastorno epidérmico benigno que se manifiesta con manchas blancas en partes expuestas del cuerpo.

vitreous *a.* vítreo-a, vidrioso-a, casi transparente, hialino; ___ **chamber** / cámara ___; ___ **body** / cuerpo ___; ___ **humor** / humor ___.

vivifying *a.* vivificador, vivificante.

vivisection *n.* vivisección, corte o sección realizada en animales con fines investigativos.

vocabulary *n.* vocabulario.

vocal *a.* vocal, oral, rel. a la voz o producido por ella.

vocal cords *n. pl.* cuerdas vocales; órgano esencial de la voz; **false** ___ / ___ superiores o falsas; **true** ___ / ___ inferiores o verdaderas.

vocalization *n.* vocalización.

vocation *n.* vocación, profesión.

voice *n.* voz.

voiced *a.* dicho-a, expresado-a; producido-a por la voz.

void *a.* nulo-a, vacío-a; inválido-a, sin efecto; *v.* anular, invalidar; evacuar, eliminar.

volatile *a.* volátil, que se evapora fácilmente.

volition *n.* volición, voluntad, poder de determinación.

volume *n.* volumen. 1. espacio ocupado por una sustancia o un cuerpo; 2. cantidad, intensidad; **blood** ___ / ___ sanguíneo; **expiratory air re-**serve ___ / ___ de reserva expiratoria o aire de reserva; **heart** ___ / ___ cardíaco; **residual** ___ / ___ residual; **stroke** ___ / ___ sistólico; **tidal** ___ / ___ de ventilación pulmonar.

volumetric *a.* volumétrico, rel. a la medida de volumen.

voluntary *a.* voluntario-a; ___ **muscle** / músculo ___.

volunteer *a.* voluntario-a.

voluptuous *a.* voluptuoso-a, provocador-a, sensual; **-ly** *adv.* voluptuosamente.

volvulus *a.* vólvulo, obstrucción intestinal causada por torsión o anudamiento del intestino en torno al mesenterio.

vomer *n.* vómer, hueso impar que forma parte del tabique medio de las fosas nasales.

vomit *n.* vómito; *v.* vomitar.

vomiting *n.* manifestación de vómitos.

vomitive *n.* vomitivo.

von Recklinghausen's disease *n.* enfermedad de von Recklinghausen. *V.* **neurofibromatosis.**

voracious *a.* voraz.

voracity *n.* voracidad.

vortex *n.* (*pl.* **vortices**) vórtice, estructura de forma espiral.

voucher *n.* comprobante.

vowel *n.* vocal.

voyeur *Fr.* voyeur, persona que practica voyeurismo.

voyeurism *n.* voyeurismo, perversión sexual por la cual la contemplación de actos u órganos sexuales induce erotismo.

vulnerability *n.* vulnerabilidad.

vulnerable *a.* vulnerable, propenso a accidentes o enfermedades.

vulva *L.* vulva, conjunto de los órganos femeninos externos del aparato genital.

vulval *a.* vulvar, rel. a la vulva.

vulvectomy *n. cirg.* vulvectomía, excisión de la vulva.

vulvitis *n.* vulvitis, infl. de la vulva.

vulvovaginal *a.* vulvovaginal, rel. a la vulva y la vagina.

W *abbr.* **water** / agua; **weight** / peso.

waddle *n.* marcha tambaleante, andar anserino.

wail *v.* lamentarse; gemir.

waist *n.* cintura; talle.

waistband *n.* cinto, cinturón.

waistline *n.* cintura.

wait *v.* esperar, aguardar; **to __ on** / servir, atender a.

waiting *n.* espera; demora; **__ room** / sala de __.

waive *v.* diferir, posponer.

wake *vi.* despertar; **to __ up** / despertar; despertarse.

walk *n.* paseo; caminata; *v.* caminar, andar; **to __ up and down** / caminar de un lado a otro.

walker *n.* andador, andaderas, aparato que se usa para ayudar a caminar.

walking cast *n.* molde de yeso que se adapta para caminar.

wall *n.* pared; tabique; **__ tooth** / diente molar.

walled-off *a.* encapsulado-a.

wander *v.* vagar; [*to lose one's way*] desviarse, perderse, extraviarse.

wandering *a.* errante, errático-a; desviado-a; **__ cell** / célula __; **__ goiter** / bocio móvil; **__ pain** / dolor __; **__ tooth** / diente desviado.

want *n.* necesidad, falta, carencia; *v.* querer, desear; necesitar; carecer de.

war *n.* guerra.

ward *n.* sala de hospital; **__ diet** / dieta hospitalaria; **isolation __** / sala de aislamiento; **__ of the state** / bajo custodia, bajo tutela del estado.

warfarin *n.* warfarina, anticoagulante, nombre genérico de Coumadin, medicamento usado en la prevención de trombosis e infartos.

warm *a.* caluroso-a; caliente; [*lukewarm*] tibio-a; [*character*] afectuoso-a, expresivo-a; *v.* **to be __** / tener calor, [*not very hot but feverish*] tener destemplanza; [*weather*] hacer calor; **to __ to** / simpatizar con; **to __ up** / calentar; *adv.* **-ly** afectuosamente, con entusiasmo.

warm-up *n.* [*physical fitness*] calentamiento.

warn *v.* prevenir, advertir, avisar.

warning *n.* advertencia; aviso; [*hard lesson*] escarmiento; **__ signal** / advertencia; señal premonitoria; **__ symptoms** / síntomas premonitorios.

warp *n.* torcedura; torcimiento; *v.* torcer; retorcer; perder la forma.

warranty *n.* garantía.

wart *n.* verruga. *V.* **verruca.**

warty *a.* verrugoso-a, rel. a verrugas.

was *pret.* de **to be.**

wash *n.* lavado, baño, lavadura; **mouth-__** / enjuague; *v.* lavar; **to __ away** / quitar con una lavadura; [*oneself*] lavarse.

washbasin *n.* lavamanos, palangana, vasija.

washcloth *n.* toallita de manos; paño de lavarse.

washed-out *a.* descolorido-a, desteñido-a.

washstand *n.* lavabo, lavamanos.

wasp *n.* avispa; **__ sting** / picadura de __.

Wasserman test *n.* prueba de Wasserman, análisis serológico de la sífilis.

waste *n.* desperdicio, residuo, gasto inútil; merma, pérdida; **__ of time** / pérdida de tiempo; *v.* desperdiciar, desgastar, malgastar; **to __ away** / demacrarse, consumirse.

wastebasket *n.* cesto de basura.

wasted *a.* desgastado-a, malgastado-a; [*person*] demacrado-a; consumido-a.

wasting *n.* agotamiento, consunción, pérdida de funciones vitales.

watch *n.* reloj de pulsera o bolsillo; vigilia; *v.* cuidar, observar, esperar; tener cuidado; **to __ one's step** / cuidarse, tener cuidado; **__ out!** / ¡Cuidado!

water *n.* agua, líquidos del cuerpo; infusión; **__ bag** / bolsa de __; **__ bed** / cama de, colchón de __; **__ blister** / ampolla acuosa; **__-cooled** / enfriado-a por __; **__ faucet** / grifo, pila, llave; **__ intake** / ingestión o toma de __; **__ level** / nivel del __; **__ pill** / diurético; **__ pollution** / contaminación del __; **__ purification** / purificación del __; **__-tight** / hermético, impermeable; **__-soluble** / soluble en __, que se disuelve en __; **__ supply** / abastecimiento de __; *v.* **to be in deep __** / tener dificultades; **to give __** / dar __; **to wash with __** / lavar con __; [*plants*] **to __** / regar; humedecer; mojar.

watered *a.* aguado-a; diluido-a.

water-electrolyte balance *n.* equilibrio hidroelectrolítico.

water-electrolyte imbalance *n.* desequilibrio hidroelectrolítico

water-hammer pulse *n.* pulso en martillo de agua.

water intoxication *n.* intoxicación acuosa, retención excesiva de agua.

watery *a.* acuoso-a, aguado-a, húmedo-a; **__ eyes** / ojos llorosos.

wave *n.* onda, ondulación; ademán de la mano. 1. movimiento o vibración ondulante que tiene una dirección fija y prosigue en una curva de ondulación; 2. representación gráfica de una actividad tal como la obtenida en un encefalograma; **brain __-s** / __-s cerebrales; **electromagnetic __-s** / __-s electromagnéticas; **excitation __** / __ de excitación; **high-frequency __** / __ de alta frecuencia; **__ length** / longitud de __; **short __** / corta; **ultrasonic __-s** / __-s ultrasónicas; *v.* hacer señales o ademanes con la mano.

waved *a.* ondulado-a, ondeado-a.

wavy *a.* ondulado-a.

wax *n.* cera. 1. cera producida por abejas; 2. secreción cerosa; **ear __** / __ del oído. *V.* **cerumen;** 3. sustancia de origen animal, vegetal o mineral que se emplea en preparaciones de pomadas y ceratos; **depilatory** __ / __ depilatoria.

waxy *a.* ceroso-a, céreo-a; [*applied wax*] encerado-a.

way *n.* vía, camino; pasaje; __ **of life** / manera de vivir; costumbres; __ **out** / salida; **by the** __ / a propósito; **in no** __ / de ningún modo; **out of the** __ / fuera de curso, desviado-a; lejano-a; **that** __ / por allí; **the other** __ **around** / por el contrario; *v.* **to make** __ / abrir paso.

weak *a.* débil, flojo-a, endeble, enclenque. poco fuerte.

weaken *v.* debilitar; desfallecer; debilitarse; deteriorarse.

weakness *n.* debilidad, debilitamiento, flojera, flaqueza.

wealth *n.* riqueza, abundancia.

wealthy *a.* rico-a, acaudalado-a, adinerado-a.

wean *n.* destetar, quitar el pecho de la madre.

weaning *n.* destete.

weanling *n.* el, la recién destetado-a, desmamado-a.

wear *n.* uso, gasto, deterioro, deteriorización; *vi.* usar, llevar puesto; desgastar; **to** __ **out** / gastar; gastarse; desgastarse.

wearing *n.* desgaste; pérdida; decaimiento.

weary *a.* cansado-a, fatigado-a.

weather *n.* [*climate*] tiempo; __ **forecasting** / pronóstico del __ .

web *n.* red, membrana; **pulmonary arterial** __**-s** / __ de membranas arteriopulmonares.

webbed *n.* unido-a por una telilla o membrana.

wedge *n.* cuña.

weight *n.* peso; **birth** __ / __ al nacer; __ **gain** / aumento de __ ; __ **loss** / pérdida de __ .

welcome *n.* bienvenida; *a.* bienvenido-a; agradable; deseado-a; *v.* dar la bienvenida, recibir con agrado; **You are** __ / De nada; para servirle; no hay de que; **a** __ **surprise** / una sorpresa agradable.

welfare *n.* bien, bienestar; salud; asistencia; __ **benefits** / beneficios de asistencia social; __ **work** / trabajo de asistencia social; __ **worker** / trabajador-a social.

well *a.* bueno-a, en buena salud; **wellbeing** / bienestar; *adv.* bien, favorablemente, felizmente; **all is** __ / todo va bien.

welt *n.* verdugón, roncha.

Western Blot, immunoblot *n.* Western Blot, "inmunoblot", prueba subsecuente para confirmar la infección por el virus VIH, en pacientes con evidencia de exposición, indicada por un ensayo enzimático inmuno-sorbente (ELISA).

wet *a.* mojado-a, humedecido-a; *v.* mojar, humedecer.

wet dream *n.* emisión seminal nocturna.

Wharton's duct *n.* conducto de Wharton, conducto excretorio de la glándual submaxilar.

wheal *n.* roncha.

wheat *n.* trigo; __ **germ** / germen de __ .

wheel *n.* rueda; *v.* hacer rodar.

wheelchair *n.* silla de ruedas.

wheezing *n.* respiración sibilante.

when *pron.* cuándo; **Since** __? / ¿Desde __?; *conj.* cuando; si.

whenever *adv.* cuando quiera; siempre que; __ **is needed** / siempre que se necesite; __ **you wish** / siempre que lo desee.

while *adv.* mientras, un rato, algún tiempo; **for a** __ / temporalmente; **not for a** __ / por ahora no.

whimper / *n.* quejido, lloriqueo; *v.* sollozar, lloriquear.

whine *n.* quejido, gemido, lamento; *v.* gemir, quejarse, lamentarse.

whiplash injury *n.* lesión de latigazo.

Whipple's disease *n.* enfermedad de Whipple, trastorno causado por la acumulación de depósitos lípidos en los tejidos linfáticos e intestinales.

whirlpool bath *n.* baño de remolino.

whisper *n.* susurro, cuchicheo; *v.* susurrar, cuchichear.

whistle *n.* silbido; *v.* silbar.

white *n.* color blanco; __ **of the egg** / clara de huevo; *a.* blanco-a; __ **corpuscle** / leucocito, glóbulo __ .

white matter *n.* sustancia blanca, tejido nervioso formado en su mayor parte por fibras mielínicas y que constituye el elemento conductor del cerebro y de la médula espinal.

whiteness *n.* blancura.

whitish *a.* blanquecino-a; blancuzco-a.

whole *n.* total, conjunto; **as a** __ / en conjunto; *a.* todo-a; **the** __ **day** / todo el día.

wholesome *a.* sano-a, saludable.

whoop *n.* estridor, sonido que caracteriza la respiración después de un ataque de tos ferina.

whooping cough *n.* tos ferina. *V.* **pertussis.**

whorl *n.* espiral. 1. disposición de fibras en forma esférica, esp. las fibras cardíacas; 2. tipo de huella digital.

wide *a.* ancho-a; **three feet** __ / de tres pies de ancho; amplio-a; extenso-a; __ **open** / muy abierto; **-ly** *adv.* ampliamente, extensamente.

widen *v.* ensanchar, extender.

widespread *a.* extendido-a; muy difundido-a; general.

widow *n.* viuda.

widower *n.* viudo.

width *n.* anchura, ancho.

wife *n.* esposa.

wig *n.* peluca.

will *n.* voluntad, determinación, deseo; testamento; *v.* querer, ordenar, mandar.

Wilms' tumor *n.* tumor de Wilms, neoplasma del riñón que se desarrolla rápidamente y usu. se ve en la infancia.

Wilson's disease *n.* enfermedad de Wilson, enfermedad hereditaria que se manifiesta con serios trastornos hepáticos y cerebrales.

win *vi.* ganar, vencer.

wind *n.* viento, aire; flato, ventosidad.

windburn *n.* quemadura por el viento.

window *n.* ventana.

windpipe *n.* tráquea; *pop.* gaznate.

wine *n.* vino.

wing *n.* ala.

wink *n.* pestañeo; *v.* pestañear.

winter *n.* invierno.

wire *n.* alambre.

wisdom teeth *n.* cordales, muelas del juicio.

wise *n.* cuerdo, prudente.

with *conj.* con.

withdraw *vi.* retirar, suprimir, descontinuar; privar de; **to __ a product from the market** / descontinuar o suprimir un producto.

withdrawal *n.* supresión, retracción; introversión; privación.

withdrawal syndrome *n.* síndrome de privación de una droga adictiva como resultado de la supresión de la misma.

withdrawal treatment *n.* tratamiento de desintoxicación.

within *prep.* dentro de, en el interior de; a distancia de; al alcance de; cerca de; **__ an hour** / __ una hora.

without *prep.* sin, falto de, fuera de; *adv.* fuera, afuera; exterior.

withstand *vi.* resistir, soportar, sufrir.

woman *n.* (*pl.* **women**) mujer.

womb *n.* matriz, útero. *V.* **uterus.**

wonder *n.* maravilla, prodigio, admiración; admirarse, asombrarse.

wonderful *a.* maravilloso-a, asombroso-a, estupendo-a, excelente.

wood *n.* madera.

word *n.* vocablo, palabra, término.

work *n.* trabajo, empleo, ocupación; *v.* trabajar.

workshop *n.* laboratorio o taller de trabajo.

workup *n.* 1. preparación del paciente para la aplicación de un tratamiento; 2. obtención de los datos pertinentes a un caso.

worm *n.* lombriz, gusano.

wormlike *a.* vermicular, vermiforme.

wound *n.* herida, lesión; **contused __ / __** contusa, lesión subcutánea; **gunshot __ / __** de bala; **penetrating __ / __** penetrante; **puncture __ / __** de punción, con un instrumento afilado; **__ debridement** / desbridamiento de __.

wrinkle *n.* arruga; *v.* arrugarse.

wrinkled *a.* arrugado-a.

wrist *n.* carpo, muñeca. *V.* **carpus; __ drop** / muñeca caída.

write *vi.* escribir.

writing *n.* escritura, acto de escribir.

wrong *n.* error, falsedad; *a.* equivodaco-a; erróneo-a; incorrecto-a; **the __ treatment** / un tratamiento __; **the __ side** / el lado afectado, el lado incorrecto; *v.* **to be __** / no tener razón, estar equivocado-a; **to go __** / [*to fail to understand*] interpretar mal; equivocarse; **-ly** *adv.* mal; incorrectamente, equivocadamente.

X *abbr.* **xanthine** / xantina.

xanthic *a.* amarillento-a, rel. a la xantina.

xanthine *n.* xantina, grupo de substancias tales como la cafeína estimulantes del sistema nervioso central y del corazón.

xanthochromia *n.* xantocromía, color amarillento visto en placas de la piel o en el líquido cefalorraquídeo.

xanthochromic *a.* xantocrómico-a, de apariencia amarillenta o relacionado-a con la xantocromía.

xanthoderma *n.* xantoderma, color amarillento de la piel.

xanthoma *n.* xantoma, formación tumoral de placas o nódulos en la piel.

xanthosis *n.* xantosis, descoloración amarillenta de la piel debida a ingestión excesiva de alimentos tales como la zanahoria y la calabaza.

X chromosome *n.* cromosoma X, cromosoma sexual diferencial que determina las características del sexo femenino.

xenograft *n.* xenoinjerto; ___ **rejection** / rechazo de ___. *V.* **heterograft.**

xenon *n.* xenón, elemento gaseoso, radioisótopo que se encuentra en pequeñas cantidades en el aire atmosférico.

xenon-133 *n.* xenón 133, radioisótopo de xenón usado en la fotoescanción del pulmón.

xenophobia *n.* xenofobia, temor excesivo o aversión a algo o a alguien extraño o extranjero.

xenotransplant *n.* xenotransplante, proceso de transplantar un órgano o parte de una especie a otra.

xeroderma *n.* xeroderma, piel excesivamente seca.

xerography *n.* xerografía. *V.* **xeroradiography.**

xeromammography *n.* xeromamografía, xerorradiografía de la mama.

xerophthalmia *n.* xeroftalmia, sequedad excesiva de la conjuntiva causada por deficiencia de vitamina A.

xeroradiography *n.* xerorradiografía, registro de imágenes electrostáticas por medio de un proceso en seco usando placas cubiertas con un elemento metálico tal como el selenio.

xerosis *n.* xerosis, sequedad anormal presente en la piel, ojos y membranas mucosas.

xerostomia *n.* xerostomía, excesiva sequedad en la boca debida a una deficiencia de secreción salival.

xiphoid *a.* xifoide, en forma de espada, similar al apéndice xifoide o ensiforme.

xiphoid process *n.* apéndice xifoide, formación cartilaginosa que se une al cuerpo del esternón.

X-linked *a.* rel. a caracteres genéticos que se relacionan con el cromosoma X.

x-rays *n.* rayos X (equis), radiografía. 1. ondas electromagnéticas de alta energía de radiación que se usan para penetrar tejidos y órganos del cuerpo y para registrar densidades en una placa o pantalla; 2. placa fotográfica o fluorescente que obtiene la imagen de estructuras internas del organismo.

Y *abbr.* **y/o year-old** / de un año de edad.

yaw *n.* lesión primaria de la frambesia.

yawn *n.* bostezo; *v.* bostezar.

yaws *n. pl.* V. **frambesia.**

Y chromosome *n.* cromosoma Y, cromosoma sexual diferencial que determina las características sexuales del sexo masculino.

year *n.* año; **at the beginning of the** ___ / a principios de ___; **at the end of the** ___ / al final del ___; **every** ___ / todos los ___-s; **last** ___ / el ___ pasado; **New Year** / Año Nuevo; **once a** ___ / una vez al ___; **-ly** *adv.* anualmente.

yeast *n.* levadura, hongo diminuto capaz de provocar fermentación que se usa en la nutrición como fuente de vitaminas y proteínas.

yell *n.* grito, alarido; *v.* gritar.

yellow *n.* color amarillo; *a.* amarillo-a.

yellow body *n.* cuerpo amarillo. V. **corpus luteum.**

yellow fever *n.* fiebre amarilla, enfermedad endémica de regiones tropicales debida a un virus que es transmitido por la picadura del mosquito hembra *Aedes Aegypti* y que se manifiesta con fiebre, ictericia y albuminuria.

yellowish *a.* amarillento-a.

yesterday *adv.* ayer.

yet *conj.* todavía; no obstante, sin embargo.

yield *n.* rendimiento; producción; *v.* producir, rendir.

yoga *n.* yoga, sistema de creencias y práctica de meditación y autodominio a través del cual se trata de alcanzar un estado de unión entre el yo y el universo.

yogurt *n.* yogur, leche fermentada por la acción del *Lactobacillus bulgaricus* a la que se le atribuyen valores nutritivos y terapéuticos.

yolk *n.* 1. yema del huevo; 2. conjunto de sustancias que nutren al embrión.

young *a.* joven; juvenil.

youngster *n.* jovencito-a, muchacho-a.

youth *n.* juventud, mocedad.

Z *abbr.* **z** zero / cero; **zone** / zona.

zero population growth (ZPG) *n.* crecimiento cero de población, condición demográfica que existe en un período de tiempo determinado en el cual la población permanece estable, sin aumentar ni disminuir.

zinc *n.* zinc, elemento metálico cristalino de propiedad astringente.

zinc ointment *n.* pomada de zinc.

Zollinger-Ellison syndrome *n.* síndrome de Zollinger-Ellison, condición manifestada por hipersecreción gástrica, hiperacidez y ulceración péptica del estómago e intestino delgado.

zona *n.* zona. 1. área o capa espcífica; 2. herpes zóster.

zone *n.* zona, estructura anatómica en forma de banda.

zoograft *n.* zooinjerto, injerto que proviene de tejido animal.

zoster *n.* zóster. *V.* **herpes zoster, shingles.**

zygoma *n.* cigoma, zigoma, prominencia ósea que forma un arco en la unión del hueso malar y el temporal.

zygote *n.* cigoto, óvulo fertilizado, célula fecundada por la unión de dos gametos.

Appendix A
Communicating
with Patients

Apéndice A
Comunicación
con los pacientes

Question Formats: English / Formatos para preguntas: Español

The following questions to elicit client/subject information can be changed to fit different formats. Many questions can be personalized by including the patient's name. Some questions can be expanded to request more information. In others, adopting a multiple choice format provides definite answers. Here are some examples.

A) Affirmative-negative answers: Make a statement and ask the patient to answer **Yes** or **No.**

B) Give information and ask the patient to evaluate his/her condition accordingly.

C) Provide several answers and ask the patient to select an answer applicable to his/her needs or condition.

A) Limiting the patient to an affirmative or negative answer.

Example 1. The question "How do you feel now?" can be changed to

I feel fine now. Yes ☐ No ☐

Example 2. Expanding a question to obtain more information (see question 14).

Do you have any children? Yes ☐ No ☐
If yes, how many children do you have? ____

How old are they?

Name	*Age*
_____	___
_____	___

B) Horizontal or vertical scales are used with statements in many questionnaires to evaluate moods, physical condition, habits, and effects of medication or treatment. These statements require the patient's self-evaluation and can be expanded to elicit in-depth information.

Example 1. On a scale from 1 to 10, indicate how you feel.

very ill ├┼┼┼┼┼┼┼┼┤ very well
        1 2 3 4 5 6 7 8 9 10

Example 2. You are almost at the end of your treatment. If the top step on the ladder represents complete recovery and the bottom line represents no improvement, rate your present condition.

Las siguientes preguntas para obtener información del cliente/sujeto se pueden cambiar para conformarse a distintos formatos. Muchas preguntas pueden ser personalizadas introduciendo el nombre del paciente. Es posible ampliar algunas preguntas para obtener más información. Otras pueden adaptarse al formato de múltiples respuestas para obtener respuestas más precisas. A continuación siguen algunos ejemplos.

A) Para obtener respuestas afirmativas y negativas: Haga una declaración y pídale al paciente que conteste **Sí** o **No.**

B) Ofrezca información y permita que el paciente evalúe sus propias necesidades o su condición.

C) Ofrezca varias respuestas e indique al paciente que seleccione la respuesta que corresponda mejor a sus necesidades o a su condición.

A) Respuestas afirmativas o negativas: Limitando al paciente a responder **Sí** o **No.**

Ejemplo 1. Cambie la pregunta "¿Cómo se siente ahora?" a

Ahora me siento bien. Sí ☐ No ☐

Ejemplo 2. Ampliación de la pregunta para obtener más información (ver la pregunta 14).

¿Tiene hijos? Sí ☐ No ☐
Si la respuesta es **Sí,** ¿cuántos hijos tiene usted?
____

¿Qué edades tienen?

Nombre	*Edad*
_____	___
_____	___

B) Las escalas verticales y horizontales se usan junto con declaraciones en muchas encuestas para evaluar el estado emocional o físico, los hábitos y los efectos de tratamientos o de medicamentos. Las declaraciones solicitan una evaluación propia del paciente y pueden ampliarse para obtener información más precisa.

Ejemplo 1. En una escala de 1 a 10 indique cómo se siente ahora.

muy mal ├┼┼┼┼┼┼┼┼┤ muy bien
        1 2 3 4 5 6 7 8 9 10

Ejemplo 2. Usted está casi al final de su tratamiento. Si el escalón más alto de la escalerilla representa su recuperación completa y la línea de abajo representa una falta absoluta de progreso, evalúe su condición actual.

437

I am on step # ___ .

Estoy en el escalón # ___ .

Example 3. If you feel you are near the bottom of the ladder, where do you hope to be in six months from now?

Ejemplo 3 Si usted se encuentra al principio de la escalera, ¿dónde espera encontrarse en seis meses a esta fecha?

Step # ___

Escalón # ___

C) A multiple choice group can help the patient focus responses more precisely or elicit specific facts.

C) Un grupo de preguntas que pueden guiar al paciente a dar respuestas más específicas.

Example 1. Select the answer that best describes how you feel now.

Ejemplo 1. Seleccione la respuesta que describe mejor su estado de salud presente.

I now feel

Ahora me siento

___ completely well
___ better
___ so-so
___ ill
___ very ill
___ worse

___ completamente bien
___ mejor
___ regular
___ mal
___ muy mal
___ peor

Example 2. To find specific facts (see question 13 below).

Ejemplo 2. Para obtener datos específicos (ver la pregunta 13 del cuestionario).

Marital status (Check one.)

Estado Civil. Marque con X la respuesta que le corresponda.

___ single
___ married
___ living with partner
___ separated
___ divorced
___ widowed

___ soltero-a
___ casado-a
___ convivo con un-a compañero-a
___ separado-a
___ divorciado-a
___ viudo-a

Interrogative Words	Palabras interrogativas
how many, how much	¿cuánto; cuánto-a, cuántos, cuántas?
what?	¿qué?
when?	¿cuándo?
where?	¿dónde?
where to?	¿adónde?
where from?	¿de dónde?
who?	¿quién?, ¿quiénes?
whom?	¿a quién?, ¿a quiénes?
which?	¿cuál?, ¿cuáles?
whose?	¿de quién?, ¿de quiénes?
why?	¿por qué?

Personal Data / Datos personales

- **name** / nombre
- **age** / edad
- **address** / domicilio, dirección
- **family members** / familiares

Questioning the Patient / Preguntas al paciente

English

1. Are you the patient?
2. Who is the patient?
3. What is your name?
4. How old are you?
5. How old is the patient?
6. What is your telephone number?
7. What is your address?
8. Is this your permanent address?
9. How long have you lived at the present address?
10. Are your parents living?
11. What is your father's name?
12. What is your mother's name?
13. Are you

    ___ single?
    ___ married?
    ___ divorced?
    ___ separated?
    ___ living with partner?
    ___ widow?
    ___ widower?

14. What is your spouse's name?
15. Do you have children? ___
    How many? ___
16. Do they live with you?
17. Do you live alone?
18. Name, address and telephone of a person who can be notified in case of an emergency.

Spanish

1. ¿Es usted el (la) paciente?
2. ¿Quién es el (la) paciente?
3. ¿Cómo se llama usted?
4. ¿Qué edad tiene usted?
5. ¿Cuántos años tiene el paciente?
6. ¿Cuál es su teléfono?
7. ¿Cuál es su dirección?
8. ¿Es ésta su dirección permanente?
9. ¿Cuánto tiempo hace que vive en la dirección actual?
10. ¿Viven sus padres?
11. ¿Cómo se llama su padre?
12. ¿Cómo se llama su madre?
13. ¿Es usted . . .

    ___ soltero-a?
    ___ casado-a?
    ___ divorciado-a?
    ___ está separado-a?
    ___ convive con alguien?
    ___ viudo-a?

14. ¿Cómo se llama su esposo-a?
15. ¿Tiene hijos? ___
    ¿Cuántos? ___
16. ¿Viven con usted?
17. ¿Vive solo-a?
18. Nombre, dirección y teléfono de una persona a quien podamos avisar en caso de emergencia.

Financial Facts / Finanzas y pagos

- **medical insurance** / seguro médico
- **occupation** / ocupación
- **paying the bill** / pago de la cuenta

English

1. Do you have medical insurance?

Spanish

1. ¿Tiene usted seguro médico?

439

2. What is the name of your insurance company?
3. What is the number of your policy?
4. Do you have more than one insurance policy?
5. What is your occupation?
6. Where do you work?
7. Name and address of your employer?

8. What is your social security number?
9. Do you receive any worker's compensation?
10. Are you self-supporting?
11. Who supports you?
12. Are you eligible for Medicare?
13. What is your Medicare number?

14. Who is responsible for this bill?
15. How do you want to pay for this bill?
16. Will you pay for this bill in a lump sum or would you like to make other arrangements?

2. ¿Cómo se llama la compañía de seguro?
3. ¿Cuál es el número de su póliza?
4. ¿Tiene más de un seguro médico?
5. ¿En qué trabaja usted?
6. ¿Dónde trabaja?
7. ¿Nombre y dirección de la empresa en que trabaja?
8. ¿Cuál es el número de su seguro social?
9. ¿Recibe alguna compensación laboral?
10. ¿Se mantiene con sus propios recursos?
11. ¿Quién se hace cargo de sus gastos?
12. ¿Tiene derecho a recibir Medicare?
13. ¿Cuál es el número de su tarjeta de Medicare?
14. ¿Quién es responsable por esta cuenta?
15. ¿Cómo quiere pagar la cuenta?
16. ¿Va a pagar esta cuenta en su totalidad o quisiera hacer otros arreglos?

Chief Complaint / Queja principal

• **present illness** / enfermedad actual.
• **date and time of onset of illness** / comienzo de la enfermedad.
• **characteristics of illness** / características de la enfermedad.
• **frequency of illness** / frecuencia de la enfermedad.

English

1. What brings you here?
2. How do you feel right now?
3. When did this problem begin?
4. Have you lost any weight recently?
5. Is this problem preventing you from working?
6. Is this problem affecting your regular activities?
7. Have you had this problem (symptom, discomfort) before?
8. Did it start suddenly or gradually?
9. Do you have this problem constantly?
10. Every day?
    How many times a day
11. When do you feel worst

    ____ in the morning
    ____ in the afternoon
    ____ at night?

12. Does it make you feel

    ____ weak
    ____ tired
    ____ exhausted?

13. Do you have fever?
14. Are you in pain?
15. Have you seen a doctor since you became ill?
16. Is your family aware of this problem?

Spanish

1. ¿Cuál es la causa de su visita?
2. ¿Cómo se siente en este momento?
3. ¿Cuando le comenzó este problema?
4. ¿Ha bajado de peso recientemente?
5. ¿Este trastorno (problema, condición) le impide trabajar?
6. ¿Este problema afecta sus actividades diarias?
7. ¿Ha tenido este malestar, (síntoma, trastorno) antes?
8. ¿Le empezó de pronto o gradualmente?
9. ¿Tiene este trastorno continuamente?
10. ¿Todos los días?
    ¿Cuántas veces al día?
11. ¿Cuándo se siente peor

    ____ por la mañana
    ____ por la tarde
    ____ por la noche?

12. ¿Lo (la) hace sentirse

    ____ cansado-a
    ____ débil
    ____ fatigado-a?

13. ¿Tiene fiebre (calentura)?
14. ¿Tiene dolor?
15. ¿Ha consultado a algún médico desde que se enfermó?
16. ¿Está su familia al tanto de este problema?

440

17. Are you taking any medication now?
18. Have you done or taken anything that seems to help you?
19. Have you ever been hospitalized on account of this problem?

17. ¿Está tomando ahora alguna medicina?
18. ¿Ha hecho o tomado algo que le mejore?
19. ¿Ha tenido que ingresar en el hospital debido a este problema?

Medical History / Historia clínica

General Questions / Preguntas generales
Family History / Historia médica familiar
Patient's Past Medical History / Historia clínica del paciente
Review of Systems / Repaso por aparatos

- **eyes, ears, nose, and throat** / ojos, oídos, nariz y garganta
- **cardiopulmonary** / cardiopulmonar
- **gastrointestinal** / gastrointestinal
- **genitourinary system** / aparato genitourinario
- **urinary system** / sistema urinario
- **skin** / piel
- **musculoskeletal system** / sistema musculoesquelético
- **neurological system** / sistema neurológico

General Questions / Preguntas generales

English

1. Have you gained weight recently?
2. Have you lost weight recently?
3. Do you have any pain?
4. Where does it hurt?
5. Is the pain

    ___ sharp
    ___ severe
    ___ mild
    ___ dull?

6. Can you describe the pain?
7. Do you tire easily?
8. Do you feel dizzy?
9. Do you generally sleep well?
10. How many hours do you sleep?
11. Do you sleep during the day?
12. Do you take any pills to help you to sleep?
13. How long have you had this pain?
14. Are you taking any medication?
15. Are you taking any sedatives?
16. Do you have nausea?
17. Have you fainted at any time?
18. Have you felt dizzy or fainted after eating or exercising?
19. Do you suffer from headaches?

Spanish

1. ¿Ha aumentado de peso últimamente?
2. ¿Ha bajado de peso recientemente?
3. ¿Tiene algún dolor?
4. ¿Dónde le duele?
5. ¿Es el dolor

    ___ agudo
    ___ fuerte
    ___ leve
    ___ sordo?

6. ¿Puede describir el dolor?
7. ¿Se cansa fácilmente?
8. ¿Se siente mareado-a?
9. ¿Duerme bien generalmente?
10. ¿Cuántas horas duerme?
11. ¿Duerme durante el día?
12. ¿Toma alguna pastilla para dormir?
13. ¿Cuánto tiempo hace que tiene el dolor?
14. ¿Está tomando alguna medicina?
15. ¿Está tomando algún calmante?
16. ¿Tiene nauseas?
17. ¿Se ha desmayado alguna vez?
18. ¿Se ha desmayado o mareado después de comer o hacer ejercicio?
19. ¿Padece de dolores de cabeza?

441

Family History; Past Medical History/
Historia familiar; historia clínica previa

Note: You may include questions 1–9 from **Personal Data** to obtain more complete data. /
Puede incluir las preguntas 1–9 de **Datos personales** para obtener más información.

English

1. Do you have any children?
2. How old were you when you had your first child?
3. Do your children live with you?
4. Are your parents living?
5. Are they in good health?
6. Is your father living?

[*If the answer is Yes*]
7. What is his health like?

[*If the answer is No*]
8. What did he die of?
9. How old was he when he died?
10. Is your mother living?
11. What is her health like?
12. What did she die of?
13. Did any of your parents, grandparents, or close relatives die of or have any of the following diseases?

___ cancer
___ blood disease
___ diabetes
___ epilepsy
___ glaucoma
___ heart disease
___ high blood pressure
___ mental retardation
___ insanity
___ tuberculosis

14. Have you ever been hospitalized?
why?
for how long?
how many times?
15. Have you ever had any of the following illnesses?

___ amebic dysentery
___ allergies
___ anemia
___ appendicitis
___ arthritis
___ asthma
___ conjunctivitis
___ cancer
___ chicken pox
___ chorea
___ chronic laryngitis
___ chronic tonsilitis
___ cirrhosis

Spanish

1. ¿Tiene usted hijos?
2. ¿Cuántos años tenía cuando tuvo su primer hijo o hija?
3. ¿Viven sus hijos con usted?
4. ¿Viven sus padres?
5. ¿Tienen buena salud?
6. ¿Vive su padre?

[*Si la respuesta es afirmativa*]
7. ¿Cómo está de salud?

[*Si la respuesta es negativa*]
8. ¿De qué murió?
9. ¿Qué edad tenía cuando murió?
10. ¿Vive su madre?
11. ¿Cómo está de salud?
12. ¿De qué murió?
13. ¿Murió o padeció alguno de sus padres, abuelos o familiares inmediatos de una de estas enfermedades?

___ cáncer
___ enfermedad de la sangre
___ diabetes
___ epilepsia
___ glaucoma
___ enfermedad del corazón
___ la presión alta
___ retraso mental
___ demencia, locura
___ tuberculosis

14. ¿Ha tenido que hospitalizarse?
¿por qué?
¿por cuánto tiempo?
¿cuántas veces?
15. ¿Ha tenido alguna de las enfermedades siguientes?

___ disenteria amebiana
___ alergias
___ anemia
___ apendicitis
___ artritis
___ asma
___ conjuntivitis
___ cáncer
___ varicela
___ corea
___ laringitis crónica
___ amigadalitis crónica
___ cirrosis hepática

442

___ cystitis	___ cistitis
___ diabetes	___ diabetes
___ diphtheria	___ difteria
___ diverticulitis	___ diverticulitis
___ ear infections	___ infecciones en los oídos
___ emphysema	___ enfisema
___ epilepsy	___ epilepsia
___ gallbladder attack	___ ataque vesicular
___ gallstones	___ cálculos en la vesícula
___ goiter	___ bocio
___ gonorrhea	___ gonorrea
___ hay fever	___ fiebre del heno
___ heart disease	___ enfermedad del corazón
___ hepatitis	___ hepatitis
___ high blood pressure	___ presión arterial alta
___ jaundice	___ ictericia
___ measles; German measles	___ sarampión; sarampión alemán, rubéola
___ mononucleosis	___ mononucleosis
___ mumps	___ paperas
___ scarlet fever	___ escarlatina
___ syphilis	___ sífilis
___ tuberculosis	___ tuberculosis
___ typhoid fever	___ fiebre tifoidea
___ valley fever	___ fiebre del valle
___ peptic ulcers	___ úlceras pépticas

16. Have any of your immediate relatives been addicted to

___ alcohol
___ tobacco
___ drugs?

17. Have you ever been addicted to

___ alcohol
___ tobacco
___ drugs?

18. Has anyone in your family died of a heart attack?
19. Is there any sickness that seems to be repeated in your family?
20. Have any of your siblings died?
21. How old was he (she)?
22. Where have you lived for most of your life?

16. ¿Algún familiar inmediato ha sido adicto a

___ bebidas alcohólicas
___ tabaco
___ drogas?

17. ¿Ha tenido alguna vez adicción a

___ bebidas alcohólicas
___ tabaco
___ drogas?

18. ¿Algún familiar cercano ha muerto de un ataque al corazón?
19. ¿Hay alguna enfermedad que se repita en su familia?
20. ¿Ha muerto alguno de sus hermanos?
21. ¿Cuántos años tenía?
22. ¿Dónde ha vivido la mayor parte de su vida?

Sensory Organs / Órganos de los sentidos
Mouth, Throat, Ears, Eyes, Skin /
La boca, la garganta, los oídos, los ojos, la piel

English	Spanish
1. Have you noticed any bleeding from your gums or mouth?	1. ¿Ha notado si las encías o la boca le sangran?
2. Does your tongue feel sore? Is any part of your mouth sore?	2. ¿Se siente la lengua adolorida? ¿Le duele otra área de la boca?
3. Do you have swelling or lumps in the mouth?	3. ¿Tiene alguna hinchazón o bola en la boca?
4. Do you have difficulty swallowing?	4. ¿Tiene dificultad al tragar?
5. Do you suffer from sore throats? how frequently?	5. ¿Padece de dolor de garganta? ¿con qué frecuencia?
6. Do you have any dripping or drainage in the back of the throat?	6. ¿Tiene alguna supuración o flema en la parte posterior de la garganta?
7. Are you often hoarse?	7. ¿Tiene ronquera frecuentemente?
8. Have you noticed any swelling in your neck?	8. ¿Ha notado alguna hinchazón en el cuello?
9. Have you ever had nosebleeds?	9. ¿Ha tenido sangramiento por la nariz?
10. Do you have any difficulty hearing?	10. ¿Tiene alguna dificultad para oír?
11. Do you have ringing in your ears? ___ right ear ___ left ear ___ both	11. ¿Tiene zumbido o tintineo en los oídos? ___ en el derecho ___ en el izquierdo ___ en ambos
12. Have you noticed any secretion from your ears?	12. ¿Ha notado alguna secreción por los oídos?
13. Do you have earaches?	13. ¿Padece de dolor de oído?
14. Have you noticed any change in your vision?	14. ¿Ha notado algún cambio en la vista?
15. Do you wear glasses or contact lenses? ___ for close-up ___ for distance ___ for reading ___ all the time	15. ¿Usa espejuelos o lentes de contacto? ___ para ver de cerca ___ para distancia ___ para leer ___ siempre
16. Have you noticed any redness or swelling in your eyes?	16. ¿Se ha notado los ojos enrojecidos o hinchados?
17. Do you have double vision?	17. ¿Tiene visión doble?
18. Do you see spots or flashes of light?	18. ¿Ve alguna vez manchas o luces?
19. Have you had pain in your eyes?	19. ¿Ha tenido dolor en los ojos?
20. Do you have any discharge from your eyes?	20. ¿Le supuran los ojos?
21. Have your eyes ever been affected by any sickness or accident?	21. Ha sido su vista afectada por alguna enfermedad o accidente?
22. Do you have blurred vision?	22. ¿Se le nubla la vista?
23. Do you have a burning feeling in your eyes?	23. ¿Le arden los ojos?
24. Do you have to strain your eyes to see better?	24. ¿Tiene que forzar la vista para ver mejor?
25. When was your last vision test?	25. ¿Cuándo fue la última vez que se hizo un examen de la vista?

444

Cardiopulmonary System / Sistema cardiopulmonar

English	Spanish

1. Have you ever had an electrocardiogram?
2. Have you ever noticed rapid heartbeats?
3. Have you ever had chest pain?
4. How long did it last?
5. In what part of the chest?
6. Does it radiate to any part of your body?

   ___ arm
   ___ shoulder
   ___ neck
   ___ back

7. Do you cough?

   ___ a little
   ___ a lot
   ___ a dry cough

8. Does your chest hurt when you cough?
9. Do you have any swelling in your legs or ankles?
10. Do you have high blood pressure?
11. Do you bleed easily?
12. Do you smoke?
    For how long have you smoked?
13. How many cigarettes per day?
14. Have you tried to stop?
15. Have you ever had lung disease?

16. Have you ever had any heart trouble?
17. Do you have frequent colds?
18. Do you cough up any phlegm?
19. What does it look like?
20. What color is it?

   ___ clear
   ___ white
   ___ yellow
   ___ green
   ___ dark
   ___ brown

21. Have you ever coughed up blood?
22. Have you had any trouble breathing?
23. Are you short of breath

   ___ at night
   ___ after meals
   ___ when you exercise
   ___ when you walk
   ___ even resting?

24. Have you noticed any particular sound in your breathing?
25. Is there any position that makes your breathing

   ___ easier
   ___ worse

Spanish

1. ¿Se le ha hecho alguna vez un electrocardiograma?
2. ¿Ha notado alguna vez si tiene palpitaciones?
3. ¿Ha tenido alguna vez dolor en el pecho?
4. ¿Cuánto tiempo le duró?
5. ¿En que parte del pecho?
6. ¿Se le corre a alguna parte del cuerpo?

   ___ el brazo
   ___ el hombro
   ___ el cuello
   ___ la espalda

7. ¿Tiene tos?

   ___ poca tos
   ___ mucha tos
   ___ una tos seca

8. ¿Le duele el pecho cuando tose?
9. ¿Se le hinchan las piernas o los tobillos?
10. ¿Tiene la presión alta?
11. ¿Tiene tendencia a sangrar?
12. ¿Fuma?
    ¿Cuánto tiempo hace que fuma?
13. ¿Cuántos cigarros al día?
14. ¿Ha tratado de dejar de fumar?
15. ¿Ha tenido alguna enfermedad de los pulmones?

16. ¿Ha tenido algún problema del corazón?
17. ¿Tiene catarros frecuentes?
18. ¿Tose con flema?
19. ¿Cómo es la flema?
20. ¿De qué color es la flema?

   ___ clara
   ___ blanca
   ___ amarilla
   ___ verde
   ___ oscura
   ___ marrón o chocolate?

21. ¿Alguna vez ha tenido sangre al toser?
22. ¿Ha tenido dificultad para respirar?
23. ¿Le falta la respiración

   ___ por la noche
   ___ después de comer
   ___ al hacer ejercicio
   ___ cuando camina
   ___ aun si descansa?

24. ¿Ha notado algún sonido diferente al respirar?
25. ¿Hay alguna posición que le haga respirar

   ___ mejor
   ___ peor

445

Gastrointestinal System / Aparato o sistema digestivo

English	Spanish

1. Is there any food that disagrees with you?
2. Do you have heartburn?
3. Do you suffer from stomachaches?

___ before eating
___ while eating
___ after eating

4. Do you suffer from indigestion?
5. Do you drink or eat between meals?
6. Do you drink coffee?
   How many cups a day?
7. Do you eat fried or fatty foods?
8. Do you burp a lot?
9. How much milk do you drink? What kind?

___ 2%
___ skim
___ whole

10. At what time do you eat breakfast?
11. At what time do you eat your last meal of the day?
12. Do you try to eat a balanced meal every day?
13. What kind of food do you generally eat more?

___ meats
___ vegetables
___ bread and cereals
___ fruits

14. Do you eat a good breakfast every day?
15. Are you constipated?
16. Do you have a bowel movement every day?

17. Are your stools normal? What color are they?
18. Do you have diarrhea?
19. Have you noticed any blood or mucous in the stools?

Spanish

1. ¿Le cae mal algún alimento?
2. ¿Tiene ardor en el estómago?
3. ¿Padece de dolores de estómago?

___ antes de comer
___ mientras come
___ después de comer

4. ¿Padece de indigestión?
5. ¿Come o toma líquidos entre las comidas?
6. ¿Toma café?
   ¿Cuántas tazas al día?
7. ¿Come comidas fritas o grasosas?
8. ¿Eructa mucho?
9. ¿Cuánta leche toma? ¿De qué clase?

___ desnatada
___ natural

10. ¿A qué hora se desayuna?
11. ¿A qué hora hace su última comida del día?
12. ¿Trata de comer una comida balanceada todos los días?
13. ¿Qué clase de alimentos generalmente come más?

___ carnes
___ vegetales
___ panes y cereales
___ frutas

14. ¿Toma un buen desayuno todos los días?
15. ¿Padece de estreñimiento?
16. ¿Elimina (obra, está al corriente) todos los días?
17. ¿Ha notado si la evacuación tiene un color normal?
18. ¿Tiene diarrea?
19. ¿Ha notado sangre o mucosidad en las heces fecales?

Musculoskeletal System / Sistema musculoesquelético

English	Spanish

1. Do you have pain in your joints?
2. Do you have pain in the neck or back?
3. Do your muscles hurt?
4. Do you feel general muscle weakness?
5. Have you noticed any swelling on a bone?
6. Do you have pain in your bones?
7. Have you ever had a fracture or a sprain? How long ago? What bone or part was affected?

Spanish

1. ¿Le duelen las articulaciones?
2. ¿Tiene dolor en el cuello o la espalda?
3. ¿Le duelen los músculos?
4. ¿Siente debilidad muscular general?
5. ¿Ha notado hinchazón en algún hueso?
6. ¿Siente dolor en los huesos?
7. ¿Ha tenido alguna vez una fractura o luxación? ¿Cuando le sucedió? ¿Que hueso o parte le afectó?

446

Neurological System / Sistema neurológico

English

Spanish

1. Do you have any feeling of tingling or numbness?
2. Do you forget things easily?
3. Is your memory worse than before?
4. Do you have good balance?
5. Do you have any difficulty walking?
6. Do you have difficulty moving

___ towards the right
___ towards the left?

7. Have you ever lost consciousness?
8. More than once?
9. Do you walk without difficulty?
10. Do you need any walking device

___ cane
___ walker

to maintain your balance?
11. Do you feel like falling sometimes?

12. Is your memory

___ good
___ bad
___ not as good as it used to be?

13. Can you feel this?
14. Can you smell this?
15. Does any particular food taste different to you?

1. ¿Tiene alguna sensación de hormigueo o entumecimiento?
2. ¿Olvida las cosas con facilidad?
3. ¿Tiene la memoria peor que antes?
4. ¿Tiene buen equilibrio?
5. ¿Tiene alguna dificultad para caminar?
6. ¿Tiene dificultad en moverse

___ hacia la derecha
___ hacia la izquierda?

7. ¿Ha perdido el conocimiento alguna vez?
8. ¿Más de una vez?
9. ¿Camina sin dificultad?
10. ¿Necesita alguna ayuda

___ bastón
___ caminador

para mantener el equilibrio?
11. ¿Siente algunas veces como si fuera a caerse?

12. ¿Es su memoria

___ buena
___ mala
___ no tan buena como antes?

13. ¿Puede sentir esto?
14. ¿Puede oler esto?
15. ¿El sabor de algún alimento en particular le parece diferente?

Skin / Piel

English

Spanish

1. Do you have any sores or blisters?
2. Do you have any mole that is red or itchy?

3. Do you have a skin rash?
4. Since when have you had this eruption?
5. Have you noticed any change?
6. Have you noticed any unusual spots in your skin?
7. Do you use any cosmetics that cause redness or swelling to your skin?
8. Have you had any severe burns?

9. Does anything make you itchy?
10. Is your skin very sensitive to the sun's rays?
11. Do you use any sunblockers (creme or lotion) if you are going to be exposed to the sun?
12. Have you noticed any discoloration on your skin?

1. ¿Tiene algunas llagas o ampollas?
2. ¿Tiene algún lunar que se pone rojo o le pica?
3. ¿Tiene alguna erupción?
4. ¿Desde cuándo ha tenido esta erupción?
5. ¿Ha notado algún cambio?
6. ¿Ha notado alguna mancha peculiar en la piel?
7. ¿Usa cosméticos que le causen enrojecimiento o hinchazón en la piel?
8. ¿Ha tenido alguna vez una quemadura grave?
9. ¿Hay algo que le da picazón?
10. ¿Es su piel muy sensitiva a los rayos del sol?
11. ¿Usa algún bloqueador de raoys del sol (crema o loción) si va a estar expuesto-a a los rayos del sol?
12. ¿Ha notado algún cambio de color en la piel?

447

Genitourinary System / Aparato genitourinario

(To female patients)

English	Spanish

1. How old were you when you had your first period?
2. When was your last period?
3. Are your periods difficult?

4. How long does your period last?
5. Do you ever bleed between periods?

6. Do you have any discharge from the vagina?
7. What does it look like?
8. Do you have any itching or burning in the genital area?
9. Have you ever had a venereal disease?
10. Have you ever had any trouble with your breasts?

___ secretion
___ pain
___ swelling
___ a lump

11. Have you learned how to examine your breasts?
12. Do you examine your breasts regularly?
13. Do you have any discharge from your breasts?
14. Have you noticed any mass or lump in your breasts?
15. Are you pregnant?
16. Have you ever been pregnant? How many times?
17. Have you ever had a miscarriage? How many times?
18. Have you ever had an induced abortion? How many times?

19. Do you have any problem during intercourse?
20. Do you have any pain during intercourse?

21. Do you use any type of birth control?
22. How many live births have you had?
23. Did you have any stillbirths?

Spanish:

1. ¿Qué edad tenía cuando tuvo la primera regla (período)?
2. ¿Cuándo tuvo la última regla?
3. ¿Son sus periodos difíciles? (¿Es la regla dificultosa?)
4. ¿Cuántos días le dura el periodo?
5. ¿Tiene algún sangramiento después de pasar la regla?
6. ¿Tiene algún flujo o secreción en la vagina?
7. ¿Cómo es?
8. ¿Tiene alguna picazón o ardor en alguna parte interior?
9. ¿Ha tenido alguna enfermedad venérea?
10. ¿Ha tenido alguna vez algún trastorno en los senos?

___ secreción
___ dolor
___ hinchazón
___ una bolita

11. ¿Ha aprendido a examinarse los senos?
12. ¿Se autoexamina los senos regularmente?
13. ¿Tiene alguna secreción en los senos?
14. ¿Ha notado algún bulto o bolita en los senos?
15. ¿Está embarazada, (en estado? encinta?)
16. ¿Ha estado embarazada alguna vez? ¿Cuántas veces?
17. ¿Ha tenido alguna vez un malparto? ¿Cuántas veces?
18. ¿Ha tenido alguna vez un aborto inducido? ¿Cuántas veces?
19. ¿Tiene algún problema o dificultad en las relaciones sexuales?
20. ¿Tiene dolor durante las relaciones sexuales?
21. ¿Usa algún tipo de anticonceptivo?
22. ¿Cuántos embarazos se le han logrado?
23. ¿Tuvo algún parto no logrado?

(To male patients)

1. Do you have any discharge from the penis?
2. Do you have pain in the testicles?
3. Do you have pain or swelling in the scrotum?
4. Are you unable to have an erection?
5. Do you have a satisfactory sex life?
6. Have you had any venereal disease?
7. Have you fathered any children?

Spanish:

1. ¿Tiene alguna secreción por el pene?
2. ¿Tiene dolor en los testículos?
3. ¿Tiene dolor o hinchazón en el escroto?
4. ¿Se la dificulta tener una erección?
5. ¿Está satisfecho con su vida sexual?
6. ¿Ha tenido alguna enfermedad venérea?
7. ¿Ha tenido hijos?

448

Urinary System / Aparato o sistema urinario

English

Spanish

1. Do you have any trouble urinating?
2. Do you have to get up to urinate during the night? How many times?
3. Do you have back or flank pain?

4. Do you have pain or burning when urinating?
5. Is the color of the urine

____ yellow
____ murky
____ milky
____ pale
____ reddish?

6. Do you have blood in the urine?
7. Are you unable to control your urination?
8. Do you urinate too often?
9. Do you pass a little or a lot of urine regularly?
10. Do you have difficulty starting to urinate?
11. Do you have difficulty maintaining a continuous flow of urine?
12. Have you ever had any kidney problem?
13. Have you ever passed stones?

1. ¿Tiene dificultad cuando orina?
2. ¿Tiene que levantarse por la noche a orinar? ¿Cuántas veces?
3. ¿Tiene algún dolor en la espalda o en el costado?
4. ¿Tiene dolor o ardor cuando orina?

5. ¿Es la orina

____ amarilla
____ turbia
____ lechosa
____ sin color
____ rojiza?

6. ¿Tiene sangre en la orina?
7. ¿No puede controlar la salida de orina?
8. ¿Orina con demasiada frecuencia?
9. ¿Orina mucho o poco regularmente?

10. ¿Tiene dificultad al comenzar a orinar?
11. ¿Tiene dificultad en mantener el chorro?

12. ¿Ha padecido de los riñones?
13. ¿Ha expulsado cálculos?

Labor and Delivery / Labores del parto

English

Spanish

1. When is the expected date of delivery?
2. Are you having pains?
3. When did they start?
4. Are your pains spaced at regular intervals?

5. How long does the pain last?
6. How much time is there between pains?
7. Has your water broken?

8. Push. Push more. Do not push.
9. Do not push until we tell you.
10. Breathe in and out.
11. Breathe slowly when you have the contractions.
12. Breathe normally.
13. Breathe slowly and then rapidly.
14. Are you going to breastfeed your baby?
15. We are going to prepare you for the delivery.
16. I am going to do a vaginal examination to determine the progress of the labor.
17. I am going to have to do a cesarean section.
18. You have a fine baby.

1. ¿Cuál es la fecha supuesta del parto?
2. ¿Tiene ya dolores?
3. ¿Cuándo le comenzaron?
4. ¿Ocurren los dolores a intervalos regulares?

5. ¿Cuánto le dura el dolor?
6. ¿Cuánto tiempo pasa entre cada dolor?
7. ¿Se le rompió la fuente (la bolsa de aguas)?
8. Puje. Puje más. No puje más.
9. No puje hasta que le digamos.
10. Respire para adentro y para afuera.
11. Respire lentamente cuando tenga las contracciones.
12. Respire normalmente.
13. Respire lenta y luego rápidamente.
14. ¿Va a darle el pecho al nene?
15. Vamos a prepararla para el parto.
16. Voy a hacerle un examen vaginal para determinar el progreso del parto.
17. Le vamos a tener que hacer una cesárea.
18. Tiene un bebé precioso.
Tiene una bebita preciosa.

The Newborn / El recién nacido

Practical vocabulary including characteristics, health care, anomalies, and the most common congenital disorders.

Vocabulario práctico referente a características, cuidado de la salud, anomalías, y trastornos congénitos más comunes.

Characteristics	*Características*
full-term	nacido(-a) a término completo
premature	prematuro
body weight at birth	peso al nacer
body length	largo del cuerpo
body temperature at birth	temperatura tomada al nacer
normal breathing	respiración normal
vital signs normal	signos vitales normales
face features	rasgos faciales
breastfed	(lactante) toma el pecho de la madre
bottle-fed	toma el biberón
normal patterns of sleep	patrones normales de sueño
normal cry	llanto normal
nurses well	toma el pecho bien
crying when hungry or wet	llora cuando tiene hambre o está mojado-a
weight gain normal	aumento de peso normal
normal growth and development	crecimiento y desarrollo normales
weight loss	pérdida de peso
time sleeping	tiempo durmiendo
time awake	tiempo despierto
movements	movimientos
alertness	expresión viva
lifts his/her head	levanta la cabeza
umbilical cord drop	caída del cordón umbilical
taking vitamins with formula	toma vitaminas en la fórmula
suckling well from breast or bottle	tomando bien el pecho o chupando el biberón

Baby's Health Care	*Cuidado de la salud del bebé*
initial health profile	perfil inicial de la salud
daily reassessment of feeding	evaluación diaria de la alimentación
urine and stool patterns	patrones de orina y defecación
circumcision	circuncisión
frequency of feedings	frecuencia en la toma del pecho o del biberón
time taken in nursing	tiempo que pasa tomando el pecho
daily amount of formula	cantidad diaria de fórmula
time awake	tiempo despierto(-a)
daily sleeping time	tiempo de sueño diario
results from physical examination	resultados del examen físico
heart rate	frecuencia cardíaca
pulse	pulso
bathing	baño
select formula under doctor's advice	seleccionar la fórmula según recomendación del doctor
careful preparation of formula	cuidado en la preparación de la fórmula
burp the baby after nursing or during bottle feedings	sacar el viento (ayudar al bebé a eructar después de darle el pecho o el biberón)

450

Baby's Health Care

safety habits followed (bed covers, clothing, bottle caps)
avoid overdressing the baby
keep the room warm
change diapers to avoid skin rash

check bowel movements
keep a regular schedule for bathing
check the baby while he/she sleeps
doctor's examination six weeks after birth

Cuidado de la salud del bebé

hábitos de seguridad (ropa de cama y de vestir; tapas seguras del biberón)
evitar ponerle demasiada ropa
mantener la habitación con una temperatura normal
cambio de pañales (culero, tapico) para evitar una erupción
observar las defecaciones
asignar una hora especial para su baño
observar al bebé cuando está dormido
examen médico seis semanas después del nacimiento

Anomalies / Anomalías

Anomalies	Anomalías
abdominal swelling	inflamación abdominal
blood in the stools	sangre en las deposiciones
cyanosis	cianosis
colic	cólico
constipation	estreñimiento
convulsions	convulsiones
cradle cap	costra láctea
diaper rash	eritema, erupción
diarrhea sudden and explosive	diarrea explosiva y súbita
Down syndrome	síndrome de Down
dry scales	escama seca
excessive crying	llanto excesivo
feeding problems	problemas de alimentación
inadequate gaining	aumento inadecuado de peso
increasing fussiness	mayor intranquilidad
infantile spasms	espasmos infantiles
infections	infecciones
intolerance to lactose	intolerancia a la lactosa
jaundice	ictericia
Marfan's syndrome	síndrome de Marfan
milk allergy	alergia a la leche
nasal congestion	congestión nasal
seborrheic eczema	eczema infantil
skin irritation	irritaciones en la piel
sudden jerk	contracción brusca
vaginal bleeding	sangramiento vaginal
weight loss	pérdida de peso

Congenital Disorders / Trastornos congénitos

Congenital Disorders	Trastornos congénitos
cleft palate	paladar hendido
hare lip	labio leporino
club foot	pie en garra
atrial septal defect	defecto septal auricular
aortic stenosis	estenosis aórtica
heart murmurs	soplos cardíacos
Marfan's syndrome	síndrome de Marfan
Down syndrome	síndrome de Down
transposition of the great vessels	transposición de los grandes vasos
Fallot's tetralogy	tetralogía de Fallot

Vocabulary of the Newborn

awake despierto-a; **to wake up** despertarse

baby *n.* bebito-a; el bebé, nene

baby's body cuerpecito del bebé

baby's clothes ropita del bebé

bathing aseo, baño; **to bathe the baby** bañar al bebé

birth nacimiento; **to be born** nacer

bottle n. biberon; botella

bottle feed dar el biberón

burp eructo; **to burp** eructar;

burping the baby sacar el viento; ayudar a eructar

change cambio; **to change** cambiar

colic cólico

cradle cuna

cradle cap costra láctea

cry llanto; **to cry** llorar

date of birth fecha de nacimiento

diaper pañal, braga, *M.A.* pavico, zapeta

female hembra; **female baby** hembrita

fontanel fontanela, mollera

little arm bracito

little ear orejita

little eye ojito

little foot piecesito

little hand manita

little head cabecita

little leg piernita, piernecita

little mouth boquita

male varón; **male baby** varoncito

milk leche

to nurse amamantar, dar el pecho

pediatrician pediatra

schedule horario, hora especial asignada

sleep sueño; **to sleep** dormir

small face carita

suck chupar

umbilical cord cordón umbilical

vomit vómito; **to vomit** vomitar

wean destete; **to wean** destetar

to weigh pesar

weight peso

How much does he/she weigh ¿Cuánto pesa?

How old is the baby? ¿Cuánto tiempo (meses, días, semanas) tiene?

At the Doctor's Office / En el consultorio médico

English

1. Have you ever seen the doctor before?
2. Please fill out this form.
3. Please sit down, and we will call you shortly.
4. Follow me, please.
5. Please get on the scale.
6. Now I am going to take your blood pressure.
7. Please undress and put on this gown.
8. Would you like to use the bathroom?
9. The doctor will be here shortly.
10. Breathe

    ___ normally
    ___ deeply
    ___ hold your breath

11. Cough lightly.
12. Does it hurt here when I touch you?
13. Show me where it hurts.
14. You may get dressed now.
15. The doctor would like to see you in

    ___ a week
    ___ a month
    ___ 6 months
    ___ a year

16. Would you like to make the appointment now?
17. Would you like to take care of your bill now?

Spanish

1. ¿Ha visto al doctor alguna vez antes?
2. Por favor, llene esta planilla.
3. Siéntese, por favor, y le llamaremos dentro de un ratico.
4. Sígame, por favor.
5. Por favor, súbase a la báscula.
6. Ahora le voy a tomar la presión arterial.
7. Por favor, desvístase y póngase esta bata.
8. ¿Quisiera usar el servicio?
9. El doctor vendrá dentro de poco.
10. Respire

    ___ normalmente
    ___ profundamente
    ___ aguante la respiración

11. Tosa ligeramente.
12. ¿Le duele aquí cuando le toco?
13. Indíqueme dónde le duele.
14. Ya se puede vestir.
15. El doctor le quiere ver dentro de:

    ___ una semana
    ___ un mes
    ___ 6 meses
    ___ un año

16. ¿Quisiera hacer el turno ahora (ahorita)?
17. ¿Quisiera pagar su cuenta ahora?

Medication and Treatment / Medicamentos y tratamientos

English

1. I will prescribe some medication that should

   ___ alleviate the discomfort
   ___ relieve the pain
   ___ help us determine the problem

2. Take the medicine

   ___ twice a day
   ___ three times a day
   ___ four times a day
   ___ before meals
   ___ after meals
   ___ first thing in the morning
   ___ before going to bed
   ___ with some solid food
   ___ with milk or juice

3. Always shake the bottle well.

Spanish

1. Le voy a recetar una medicina que le va a:

   ___ aliviar el malestar
   ___ mejorar el dolor
   ___ ayudarnos a determinar cuál es el problema

2. Tome la medicina

   ___ dos veces al día
   ___ tres veces al día
   ___ cuatro veces al día
   ___ antes de las comidas
   ___ después de las comidas
   ___ al levantarse
   ___ al acostarse
   ___ con algo de comer
   ___ con leche o jugo

3. Siempre agite bien la botella.

4. Apply to the area

___ an ice pack
___ a heating pad

5. Take a warm Sitz bath

___ once a day
___ twice a day
___ three times a day

6. When you lie down, raise the feet above the level of the heart.
7. You should

___ lose weight
___ exercise more
___ stop smoking
___ avoid salt in your diet
___ eat a more balanced diet
___ eat more vegetables
___ eat more fruit and fiber

8. We still don't know what is causing your illness.
9. It is necessary that you have

___ a blood test
___ some laboratory tests
___ a urinalysis
___ a mammogram
___ a sonogram
___ an x-ray
___ a scan
___ therapy

10. We will make the necessary arrangements with

___ the laboratory
___ the hospital
___ the therapist

11. Take the written orders with you.
12. It is advisable to put you in the hospital for further tests.
13. You will need an operation.
14. Your

___ husband
___ wife
___ son
___ daughter

will need an operation
15. It is not a serious operation.
16. It is a somewhat serious operation.
17. Take your hospitalization and insurance papers with you.
18. We still do not have the results of the tests.

4. Póngase en la parte afectada

___ una bolsa de hielo
___ una almohadilla eléctrica

5. Dése un baño de asiento caliente

___ una vez al día
___ dos veces al día
___ tres veces al día.

6. Cuando se acueste, levante los pies por encima del nivel del corazón.
7. Usted debe

___ bajar de peso
___ hacer más ejercicio
___ dejar de fumar
___ no comer comidas con sal
___ hacer una dieta más balanceada
___ comer más vegetales
___ comer más fruta y fibra

8. No hemos podido determinar todavía la causa de su enfermedad.
9. Es necesario que se haga

___ un análisis de sangre
___ unas pruebas de laboratorio
___ un análisis de orina
___ un mamograma
___ un sonograma
___ una radiografía
___ un escán
___ terapia

10. Nosotros haremos los arreglos necesarios con

___ el laboratorio
___ el hospital
___ el (la) terapista

11. Lleve las órdenes médicas consigo.
12. Es conveniente hospitalizarlo-a para hacerle pruebas adicionales.
13. Usted va a necesitar una operación.
14. Su

___ esposo
___ esposa
___ hijo
___ hija

va a necesitar una operación.
15. No es una operación difícil.
16. Es una operación de cierta gravedad.
17. Lleve consigo al hospital las órdenes del médico y la póliza de seguro.
18. Todavía no tenemos el resultado de las pruebas.

Indications for Laboratory and X-ray Examination / Indicaciones para pruebas de laboratorio y radiografías

English

1. You cannot drink or eat anything before the test.
2. You can brush your teeth, but do not drink water.
3. Before the test you should not

   ___ eat
   ___ drink water or any other liquid
   ___ smoke
   ___ chew gum
   ___ take any medicine
   ___ suck any pills or candy

4. You should eat at least two hours before taking a catharctic.
5. You should eat a light supper the night before the test (operation).
6. You should not eat any greasy foods.
7. You must take these tablets which are especially for this test.
8. The tablets contain a substance that we can trace during the test and that will help make a diagnosis.
9. You must follow these directions exactly as you are told.

Spanish

1. Tiene que estar en ayunas (sin beber ni comer nada) antes de la prueba.
2. Se puede lavar los dientes, pero no tome agua.
3. Antes del examen no debe

   ___ comer
   ___ tomar agua ni ningún otro líquido
   ___ fumar
   ___ masticar chicle
   ___ tomar ninguna medicina
   ___ chupar ninguna pastilla o caramelo

4. Debe comer por lo menos dos horas antes de tomar un purgante.
5. Debe comer una comida ligera la noche antes de la prueba (operación).
6. No debe comer comidas grasosas.
7. Debe tomarse estas pastillas que son especialmente para la prueba.
8. Las tabletas contienen una substancia que se puede rastrear durante la prueba y que ayudará a hacer el diagnóstico.
9. Debe seguir estas instrucciones al pie de la letra.

X-ray and Laboratory Examination / Examen radiológico y de laboratorio

English

1. What type of test are you here for?
2. Do you have the written orders from the doctor?
3. Have you had anything to eat or drink this morning?
4. Have you had anything to eat or drink after twelve o'clock midnight?
5. Have you ever had an x-ray examination that required

   ___ an injection
   ___ swallowing any pills
   ___ special medication

   before the x-ray was taken?
6. Are you allergic to any medication?
7. Are you presently taking any medication?
8. Do you suffer from or have you ever suffered from asthma?
9. Do you suffer from any allergies?
10. This is part of the test.
11. I have to take an x-ray.
12. Breathe deeply.

Spanish

1. ¿Qué clase de prueba (análisis) se vino a hacer?
2. ¿Trae las indicaciones del doctor por escrito?
3. ¿Viene en ayunas?
4. ¿Ha comido o bebido (tomado) algo después de las doce de la noche?
5. ¿Le han hecho alguna vez una radiografía que haya requerido

   ___ una inyección
   ___ tomar alguna pastilla
   ___ un medicamento especial

   antes de hacerse la placa?
6. ¿Es alérgico-a a alguna medicina?
7. ¿Está tomando actualmente alguna medicina?
8. ¿Padece o ha padecido alguna vez de asma?
9. ¿Padece usted de alguna alergia?
10. Esto es parte del examen.
11. Tengo que tomarle una placa.
12. Respire profundamente.

455

13. Breathe deeply and hold your breath.

14. You can breathe normally.
15. I have to take one more x-ray.
16. Please wait to make sure that I don't need to take another one.
17. We are going to take a series of x-rays.
18. After the first x-rays, we will give you a liquid to drink.
19. Drink this liquid, please.
20. After the test, you can have something to eat.
21. We are going to give you a barium enema.
22. We are going to turn off the light.
23. This is not going to hurt you but it may be unpleasant.
24. This light is used to examine your intestine.
25. You can use the bathroom here.
26. I am going to inject this into your vein.
27. In this test I am going to take fluid from your spine.
28. This is a cold solution.
29. This machine is to take the mucous from your lungs.
30. I am going to insert this tube to

___ take out the phlegm that is bothering you
___ help you void

31. We are going to draw some blood from

___ the vein
___ the finger
___ the ear

32. Leave the cotton (the Band-aid) in place for a few minutes.
33. Call tomorrow to find out the results of the test.
34. We will call to notify you.

13. Respire profundamente y aguante la respiración.

14. Puede respirar normalmente.
15. Tengo que sacarle una placa más.
16. Por favor espere para comprobar si tengo que sacar otra placa.
17. Le vamos a sacar una serie de placas.
18. Después de las primeras placas le daremos a tomar un líquido.
19. Tómese este líquido, por favor.
20. Después de la prueba puede comer algo.
21. Le vamos a poner un enema de bario.
22. Vamos a apagar la luz.
23. Esto no le va a causar dolor pero puede causar cierta molestia.
24. Esta luz es para examinarle el intestino.
25. Puede usar el servicio (el baño) aquí.
26. Voy a inyectarle esta sustancia en la vena.
27. En esta prueba le voy a sacar líquido de la columna.
28. Esta solución está fría.
29. Esta máquina es para extraer mucosidades de los pulmones.
30. Voy a ponerle esta sonda

___ para sacarle la flema que le molesta

___ para ayudarle a orinar

31. Le vamos a extraer sangre

___ de la vena
___ del dedo
___ de la oreja

32. Déjese el algodón (la curita) puesto-a por unos minutos.
33. Llame mañana para saber el resultado de la prueba.
34. Le llamaremos para notificarle.

Ambulance and Emergency Room / Ambulancia y sala de emergencia

English

1. Calm down, the ambulance is on its way.

2. To what hospital do you want to go?

3. To what hospital shall we take him, her?

4. Do you understand what I am saying?
5. What is your name?
6. What day of the week is it?
7. Who is your doctor?
8. Has you doctor been notified?
9. Are you in pain?
10. Are you having any problem breathing?
11. Have you fainted or lost consciousness at any time?

Spanish

1. Cálmese, por favor, la ambulancia está en camino.

2. ¿A qué hospital quiere que lo (la) llevemos?

3. ¿A qué hospital quiere que lo (la) llevemos?

4. ¿Entiende lo que le digo?
5. ¿Cómo se llama?
6. ¿Qué día de la semana es hoy?
7. ¿Quién es su médico?
8. ¿Le han avisado a su médico?
9. ¿Tiene dolor?
10. ¿Tiene dificultad para respirar?
11. ¿Se demayó o perdió el conocimiento en algún momento?

12. Are you taking any medication?
13. How many pills did you take?
14. Are you allergic to any medications?
15. When did the accident occur?
16. Where did it happen?
17. Have you had a tetanus shot?
18. When was the last time?
19. Have you been hospitalized before?

___ When?
___ For what reason?
___ Here?
___ Where?

[*To a female patient*]
20. Do you know if you are pregnant?
21. Could you be pregnant?

12. ¿Está tomando alguna medicina?
13. ¿Cuántas pastillas tomó?
14. ¿Es alérgico-a a alguna medicina?
15. ¿Cuándo ocurrió el accidente?
16. ¿Dónde ocurrió?
17. ¿Se le ha inyectado contra el tétano?
18. ¿Cuándo fue la última vez?
19. ¿Ha sido hospitalizado-a alguna vez?

___ ¿Cuándo?
___ ¿Por qué motivo?
___ ¿Aquí?
___ ¿Dónde?

[*A una mujer*]
20. ¿Sabe usted si está embarazada?
21. ¿Es posible que usted esté embarazada?

Hospitalization / Hospitalización

English

1. Do you have the written doctor's orders with you?
2. It is necessary to complete some paper work before you are admitted.
3. Sit in this wheelchair, please.
4. We are taking you to your room.
5. We suggest you don't keep any valuables in your room because the hospital is not responsible for lost items.
6. We need a signed consent for your surgery.
7. Push this button for assistance.
8. Call if you need

___ to use the bedpan
___ a sleeping pill
___ something for the pain
___ something to drink
___ an extra pillow or blanket

9. You can get out of bed.
10. You must stay in bed.
11. I am the nurse.
12. I need to take your

___ pulse
___ temperature
___ blood pressure

13. I am going to take a sample of blood.
14. I need to give you a shot.
15. I am going to give you an intravenous feeding.
16. This will not hurt.
17. Someone will come to take you to

___ the x-ray room
___ the laboratory
___ the rehabilitation room

Spanish

1. ¿Tiene las indicaciones del doctor consigo?
2. Necesitamos obtener cierta información antes de ingresarlo, -la.
3. Siéntese en esta silla de ruedas, por favor.
4. Lo (la) vamos a llevar a su cuarto.
5. Le aconsejamos que no deje objetos de valor en el cuarto ya que el hospital no se hace responsable por cualquier pérdida de objetos.
6. Necesitamos una autorización firmada para su operación.
7. Apriete este botón si necesita algo.
8. Llame si necesita

___ usar el bacín
___ una pastilla para dormir
___ algo para aliviar el dolor
___ algo para tomar
___ una almohada o una frazada (cobija) adicional

9. Puede bajarse de la cama.
10. Debe quedarse en la cama.
11. Soy el (la) enfermero-a.
12. Tengo que tomarle

___ el pulso
___ la temperatura
___ la presión arterial

13. Voy a tomarle una muestra de sangre.
14. Tengo que ponerle una inyección.
15. Voy a ponerle un suero en la vena.
16. No le va a doler.
17. Alguien va a venir a llevarlo-a

___ a la sala de rayos X
___ al laboratorio
___ a la sala de rehabilitación

Surgery / Cirugía

English   Spanish

1. I am going to prepare you for surgery
2. I am going to give you an enema.
3. I am going to shave you.
4. Your surgery is scheduled for

    ___ later
    ___ this afternoon
    ___ tomorrow morning
    ___ tomorrow afternoon

5. The anesthetist will be here to talk to you and ask you some questions

    ___ soon
    ___ later
    ___ before surgery

6. We will give you a sedative before taking you to the operating room.
7. Would you like us to notify your family of the time of the operation?
8. After the operation you will be taken to the recovery room.
9. When you wake up you may have

    ___ a tube in your throat to help you breathe
    ___ a tube in the bladder to help you urinate
    ___ a tube in the stomach so you will not vomit

10. After surgery you will be given IV until you start eating and drinking.

11. Your doctor will be here

    ___ soon
    ___ later
    ___ tomorrow

12. You will be discharged

    ___ later
    ___ tomorrow
    ___ in a week

13. Call your doctor's office and make an appointment

    ___ in a week
    ___ in ten days

14. Call us if you need help, but if it is an emergency, call 911.

1. Voy a prepararlo-a para la operación.
2. Le voy a hacer un lavado intestinal.
3. Lo (la) voy a rasurar.
4. La cirugía va a ser

    ___ más tarde
    ___ esta tarde
    ___ mañana por la mañana
    ___ mañana por la tarde

5. El (la) anestesista vendrá a hablar con usted y a hacerle algunas preguntas

    ___ dentro de un ratico
    ___ más tarde
    ___ antes de la operación

6. Le vamos a dar un calmante antes de llevarlo-a a la sala de operaciones.
7. ¿Quiere que le hagamos saber a su familia a qué hora es la operación?
8. Después de la operación lo (la) llevarán a la sala de recuperación.
9. Al despertarse tal vez tenga

    ___ un tubo en la garganta para ayudarlo-a a respirar
    ___ un tubo en la vejiga para que pueda orinar
    ___ un tubo en el estómago para que no vomite

10. Después de la cirugía se le pondrá un suero hasta que usted empiece a alimentarse.

11. Su médico vendrá a verle

    ___ pronto
    ___ más tarde
    ___ mañana

12. Le van a dar de alta

    ___ más tarde
    ___ mañana
    ___ dentro de una semana

13. Llame a la consulta de su médico y pida turno para dentro de

    ___ una semana
    ___ diez días

14. Llame aquí si necesita asistencia, pero si se trata de una emergencia, llame al 911 (nueve uno uno).

Anesthesia / Anestesia

English

1. I am the anesthetist.
2. I need to ask you some questions.
3. Are you allergic to anything? To what?
4. Are you allergic to any medication? Which?
5. Are you taking any medication? Which?
6. How long have you been taking it?
7. Have you been taking aspirin for any reason?
8. Are you taking any diuretic?
9. Have you had surgery before?

10. What kind of an operation was it?
11. Do you remember what kind of anesthesia you had?
12. Did you have any trouble with the anesthesia?
13. What kind of trouble?
14. Today we are going to give you the following anesthesia. (**V. anesthesia**)
15. Try to relax.

Spanish

1. Soy el (la) anestesista.
2. Tengo que hacerle algunas preguntas.
3. ¿Es alérgico-a a algo? ¿A qué?
4. Es usted alérgico-a a alguna medicina? ¿A cuál?
5. ¿Está tomando alguna medicina? ¿Cuál?
6. ¿Por cuánto tiempo la ha estado tomando?
7. ¿Ha estado tomando aspirina por algún motivo?
8. ¿Toma algún diurético?
9. ¿Ha tenido alguna operación anteriormente?

10. ¿Qué tipo de operación fue?
11. ¿Recuerda usted que clase de anestesia le dieron?
12. ¿Tuvo alguna dificultad con la anestesia?
13. ¿Qué tipo de dificultad?
14. Hoy le vamos a dar la siguiente anestesia. (**V. anestesia**)
15. Trate de relajarse.

Commands / Ordenes
Positions and Body Movements / Posiciones y movimientos del cuerpo

English

1. Stand here.
2. Stand here and do not move.
3. Sit on the table.
4. Lie down on the table

    ____ on your back
    ____ face down
    ____ on your right side
    ____ on your left side

5. Put your knees against your chest and let your chin touch your chest.
6. Put your arms around this machine.

7. Do not get up, remain lying down.
8. Raise your head.
9. Raise your hands.
10. Raise your right hand.
11. Raise your left hand

    ____ higher
    ____ lower

12. Open your hand.
13. Close your hand.
14. Extend your fingers.
15. Close your fingers one at a time.
16. Lift your right leg.
17. Lift your left leg.
18. Can you move the leg?

Spanish

1. Párese aquí.
2. Párese aquí y no se mueva.
3. Siéntese sobre la mesa.
4. Acuéstese sobre la mesa

    ____ boca arriba
    ____ boca abajo
    ____ sobre el lado derecho
    ____ sobre el lado izquierdo

5. Acerque las rodillas al pecho lo más posible y deje que la barbilla toque el pecho.
6. Ponga los brazos alrededor de esta máquina.

7. No se levante, quédese acostado-a.
8. Levante la cabeza.
9. Levante las manos.
10. Levante la mano derecha.
11. Levante la mano izquierda

    ____ más hacia arriba
    ____ más hacia abajo

12. Abra la mano.
13. Cierre la mano.
14. Extienda los dedos.
15. Cierre uno por uno los dedos.
16. Levante la pierna derecha.
17. Levante la pierna izquierda.
18. ¿Puede mover la pierna?

459

19. Bend over.
20. Bend over backwards.
21. Raise your buttocks (hips).

22. Put your hands behind your head.
23. Extend your arms, and bringing them towards the front, touch the tips of your index fingers together.
24. Bend your arm.
25. Extend your arm.
26. Squeeze my hand.
27. Squeeze my hand as hard as you can.

28. Make a fist.
29. Open your mouth.
30. Rinse your mouth.

19. Dóblese.
20. Dóblese hacia atrás.
21. Levante las nalgas (las asentaderas, caderas).
22. Ponga las manos detrás de la cabeza.
23. Extienda los brazos y, trayéndolos hacia el frente, toque las puntas de los dedos índice.
24. Doble el brazo.
25. Extienda el brazo.
26. Apriéteme la mano.
27. Apriéteme la mano lo más fuerte que pueda.
28. Cierre el puño.
29. Abra la boca.
30. Enjuáguese la boca.

Questions on HIV and AIDS / Preguntas sobre el VIH y el SIDA

1. What are the symptoms of AIDS?
2. What is the difference between HIV and AIDS?
3. How does one get infected by HIV?

4. Is HIV contagious?
5. Can one be infected through

____ saliva?
____ sexual intercourse?
____ blood transfusion?

6. Can one get the virus from food prepared by an infected person?

7. Can one be infected by using the same utensils (glasses, spoons, or other objects) used by an infected person?

8. Can one be infected by the bite of a mosquito or by any other type of bite?

9. Is the use of condoms a safe protection?

10. Is there any other type of protection?
11. What are the safe sex rules to follow?

1. ¿Cuáles son los síntomas del SIDA?
2. ¿Cuál es la diferencia entre el VIH y el SIDA?
3. ¿Cómo puede una persona infectarse con el VIH?
4. ¿Es el VIH contagioso?
5. ¿Se puede contraer la infección a través de

____ la saliva?
____ del acto sexual?
____ una transfusión de sangre?

6. ¿Se puede contraer la infección a través de comida preparada por una persona infectada?

7. ¿Se puede contraer la infección a través del uso de los mismos utensilios (vasos, cucharas u otros objetos) que han sido usados por una persona infectada?

8. ¿Se puede contraer el virus a través de la picadura de un mosquito o de cualquier otro tipo de picada o mordedura?

9. ¿Es el uso de condones una protección segura?

10. ¿Hay algún otro tipo de protección?
11. ¿Cuál sería un comportamiento sexual sin riesgo?

Included in *"high-risk groups"* are gays, drug addicts who inject drugs, and hemophilliacs, children born to addicts who inject drugs, female and male prostitutes, and heterosexuals who engage in sexual activity with multiple partners who might belong to any of the preceding groups.

Incluidos entre *"los grupos de mayor riesgo"* están los homosexuales, drogadictos que se inyectan (intercambian agujas y jeringuillas infectadas), los hemofílicos, los hijos de adictos a drogas inyectadas, hombres y mujeres que practican la prostitución, y cualquier persona heterosexual que lleva una vida sexual activa con posibles miembros de los grupos descritos anteriormente.

12. What does a positive test result mean?

13. Is the test always right?

14. Will test results be confidential?

15. Is this test the only way to confirm if a person is infected by HIV?

16. Is there a cure for AIDS?

12. ¿Qué significa un resultado positivo a la prueba?

13. ¿Es siempre definitivo el resultado de la prueba?

14. ¿Son confidenciales los resultados de las pruebas?

15. ¿Es esta prueba la única manera de saber si una persona está infectada por el virus del VIH?

16. ¿Hay alguna cura para el SIDA?

Persons infected with HIV recently may not show HIV antibodies in their bloodstream for months. A person that may have been exposed to the virus should have repeated tests for best results. / Una persona recientemente infectada con VIH puede no presentar anticuerpos contra el VIH en la corriente sanguínea por varios meses. Para mayor seguridad una persona expuesta al virus VIH debe repetir la prueba sucesivamente.

HIV and AIDS Related General Observations / Observaciones generales relacionadas con el VIH y el SIDA

HIV seronegative means that the test did not show HIV antibodies in the bloodstream. / **VIH seronegativo** quiere decir que la prueba no indicó la presencia de anticuerpos VIH en la corriente sanguínea.

1. You should be tested for HIV if

   a) you think you may have had any kind of sexual contact with an infected person.

   b) you have used intravenous drugs and exchanged needles or syringes with an infected person.

1. Usted debe hacerse la prueba del VIH si

   a) ha tenido cualquier tipo de contacto sexual con una persona que cree que está infectada.

   b) ha usado drogas intravenosas y ha compartido agujas o jeringuillas con personas infectadas.

HIV seropositive means that there are HIV antibodies in the bloodstream. / **VIH seropositivo** quiere decir que existen anticuerpos contra el VIH en la corriente sanguínea.

2. It is very important to follow safe sexual conduct.

3. You are capable of being infected by the virus even if you are exposed only once.

2. Es sumamente importante evitar una conducta sexual arriesgada.

3. Usted puede ser infectado(-a) por el virus aunque haya estado expuesto(-a) una sola vez.

Serostatus unknown refers to any person that has never been tested for HIV infection. / **Seroestado desconocido** indica que la persona nunca ha tenido una prueba de VIH.

4. If the result of the test is positive, you should be under the care of an AIDS knowledgeable health professional.

5. It would be helpful if you would join a support group.

4. Si el resultado de la prueba es positivo usted debe estar bajo el cuidado de un inmunólogo o profesional de salud con conocimientos del tratamiento del SIDA.

5. Sería beneficioso que usted se asociara a un grupo de sostén.

461

ELISA (*enzyme linked immunosorbent assay*) detects the presence of HIV antibodies in the bloodstream perhaps years before the patient develops signs of infection. / ELISA (*estudio inmunosorbente enzimático*) es una prueba que se realiza para detectar anticuerpos contra el VIH presentes en la corriente sanguínea, quizás años antes de que el paciente presente algún síntoma.

6. For prevention, remember that there are three risky ways to contract AIDS:

   • unprotected sexual activity with several partners or with someone at risk

   • injection of drugs using contaminated needles
   • blood transfusions

7. Protection

   • control of sexual behavior
   • use of safer sex techniques when engaging in sexual relations
   • avoiding having multiple sexual partners
   • never assuming that a healthy looking sexual partner is not infected if his/her sexual behavior is risky

   • having a monogamous relationship with an uninfected partner
   • abstaining from risky sexual activity

6. Como prevención, recuerde que hay tres formas arriesgadas de contraer el SIDA:

   • actividad sexual sin protección con varios compañeros o con alguien que no evita riesgos
   • inyección de drogas con agujas contaminadas
   • transfusiones de sangre

7. Protección

   • actividad sexual controlada
   • uso de técnicas sexuales de prevención en las relaciones sexuales
   • evitar actividades sexuales con más de una persona
   • nunca asumir que la apariencia saludable de un(-a) compañero-a sexual indica que no esté infectado-a por el virus, siempre que mantenga una conducta sexual arriesgada
   • mantener una relación sexual monógama con una person no infectada
   • abstención de actividades sexuales arriesgadas

Appendix B
Common Medical Disorders: Signs, Symptoms, Tests and Treatments

---

Apéndice B
Trastornos médicos comunes: Signos, síntomas, pruebas y tratamientos

Signs and Symptoms in Most Common Disorders and Diseases / Señales y síntomas en desórdenes y enfermedades más comunes

English	Spanish
abscess in	**absceso**
brain	cerebral
breast	de la mama
kidney	del riñón
(throat) tonsilar	amigdalino (garganta)
abnormal color in feces, stools	color anormal en las heces fecales o excremento
black	ennegrecido
pale	pálido
red	rojizo
white	blanquecino
abnormal color in the urine	**cambios anormales en el color de la orina**
coffee	pardo-negrusco
pale	casi sin color
pink, reddish	rosáceo, rojo
yellow-orange	amarillo-anaranjado
abnormal fatigue	**cansancio excesivo**
abnormal odor in urine	**olor anormal en la orina**
aromatic	aromático
foul	fétido
abnormal walking	**marcha, andar anormal**
accummulation of fluids in	**acumulación de líquido en**
abdomen	el abdomen
joints	las articulaciones
tissues	los tejidos
absent periods	**falta de menstruación**
aging, premature	**envejecimiento prematuro**
anxiety	**ansiedad**
apathy	**apatía**
atrophy of muscles	**atrofia muscular**
asphyxiating episodes	**ataques de asfixia**
attention span, limited	**capacidad de atención limitada**
backache	**dolor de espalda**
low	en la parte baja
bad breath, halitosis	**mal aliento, halitosis**
baldness	**calvicie**
behavior	**conducta**
belligerent	agresiva, violenta
excited	excitada
belching	**eructos, eructación**
black-and-blue marks	**morados, moretones**
blackheads	**espinillas**
bleeding from	**sangramiento [sangrar por]**
the ear	el oído
the gums	las encías
the mouth	la boca
the nose	la nariz

English	Spanish
the vagina	la vagina
under the skin	debajo de la piel (sangramiento subcutáneo)
a wound	una herida
blemishes	**manchas**
blindness	**ceguera**
blind spots	**puntos ciegos**
blisters	**ampollas**
blood clot	**coágulo**
blood flow	**flujo de sangre**
copious	abundante
scanty	escaso, con manchas
blood in	**presencia de sangre en**
the feces	las heces fecales
the urine	la orina
bloodshot eye	**ojo inyectado**
bluish skin	**piel amoratada**
blurring	**vista nublada**
body odor	**olor fuerte a sudor**
boil	**grano, comedón**
bones	**huesos**
calcium loss	pérdida de calcio
deformity	deformidad
fractures	fracturas
spontaneous fractures	fracturas expontáneas
bowlegs	**piernas arqueadas**
breathing	**respiración**
abnormal breathing	respiración anormal
choking sensation	sensación de ahogo
difficulty in exhaling	dificultad al exhalar
difficulty in inhaling	dificultad al aspirar
bronzed skin	**piel bronceada**
bruised body	**contusiones en el cuerpo**
bulbous red nose	**nariz roja y bulbosa**
burning feeling	**ardor; sensación quemante**
cardiac arrest	**paro cardíaco**
cardiac arrythmia	**arritmia cardíaca**
change in bowel habits	**cambio en el hábito de defecar, obrar**
chapped lips	**labios resecos**
chills	**escalofríos**
severe	intensos
cleft lip	**labio leporino**
cleft hands	**manos en garra**
clenched teeth	**dientes apretados**
clotting of blood	**coagulación de la sangre**
clubbed fingers	**dedos en maza**
coated tongue	**lengua pastosa**
coldness in extremities	**frialdad de manos y pies**
collapse	**colapso**
collapsing	**colapso**
knee	de la rodilla
lung	del pulmón
coma	**coma**
common cold	**catarro, resfriado**

English	Spanish
constipation	**estreñimiento**
extended	continuado
constriction of the penis	**constricción del pene**
contractions of	**contracciones**
a muscle	de un músculo
the uterus	del útero
convulsions	**convulsiones**
coordination loss	**pérdida de la coordinación**
corns	**callos**
cough	**tos**
dry	seca
excessive	excesiva
coughing up blood	expectoración de sangre
coughing up bloody phlegm	expectoración de flema sanguinolenta
crack in the corner of the mouth	**grieta en la comisura del labio**
cracked lips	**labios agrietados**
cramps	**calambre**
cross-eye	**estrabismo, bizquera**
cyanosis	**cianosis**
cyst	**quiste**
dandruff	**caspa**
deafness	**sordera**
deformity of	**deformidad de**
the bones	los huesos
the fingers	los dedos
the joints	las articulaciones
the muscles	los músculos
dehydration	**deshidratación**
delirium	**delirio**
depression	**depresión**
desintegration of nails	**desintegración de las uñas**
diaper rash	**eritema de los pañales**
diarrhea	**diarrea**
bloody	con sangre
constant	constante
explosive	explosiva
light colored	de color pálido
frothy	espumosa
10 to 20 times daily	de diez a viente veces al día
severe	grave
difficulty in	**dificultad al**
breathing	respirar
defecting	defecar, obrar
urinating	orinar
swallowing	tragar
dilated pupil	**dilatación de la pupila**
dimpling	**formación de depresiones u hoyuelos**
discharge from	**supuración por**
the ear	el oído
the eye	el ojo
the nipples	los pezones
the penis	el pene
the vagina	la vagina

467

English	Spanish
discoloration around the eye	cambio de color de la piel alrededor del ojo
discomfort	molestia
discomfort in passing water	dificultad, molestia al orinar
distended abdomen	abdomen, vientre distendido
distortion of (visual)	distorsión visual de
color	color
size	tamaño
shape	forma
dizziness	mareo
double vision	visión doble
dribbling	goteo
drowsiness	amodorramiento
dry mouth	boca seca
dyspepsia	dispepsia
earache	dolor de oído
echoing sounds	repetición de sonidos
edema	edema
emaciation	emaciación, enflaquecimiento
emotional instability	inestabilidad emocional
empty bladder	vejiga vacía (no se forma orina)
enlarged	agrandamiento, engrosamiento
abdomen	del abdomen
eyeball	del globo del ojo
feet	de los pies
heart	del corazón
lymph nodes	de los nódulos linfáticos
erection difficulties	dificultad en la erección
euphoria	euforia
excessive urination	micción excesiva
exhaustion	agotamiento
eyeball	globo ocular
rolled upward	virado hacia arriba
palsied	paralizado
protruding	protuberante
failure to gain weight	no poder aumentar de peso
failure to lose weight	no poder adelgazar
fainting	desmayo
false labor pains	dolores de parto falsos
fatigue	cansancio excesivo, fatiga
feminization	feminización
fever	fiebre, calentura
erratic	errática
high	alta
intermittent	intermitente
persistent	persistente
recurrent	recurrente
fissured tongue	leguna fisurada
flabby skin	piel flácida
flatfoot	pie plano
flushing	rubor
foul breath	aliento fétido
foul taste	sabor (muy) desagradable

English	Spanish
fragility of bones	fragilidad de los huesos
freckles	pecas
frigidity	frigidez
frostbite	quemadura de frío, congelación
furred tongue	lengua saburral
growing pains	dolores de crecimiento
hard nodules	nódulos endurecidos
in the face	en la cara
in the head	en la cabeza
hardening of the skin	endurecimiento de la piel
harelip	labio leporino
headache	dolor de cabeza
excrutiating and throbing	agudísimo y palpitante
pounding	demoledor
hearing loss	pérdida de la audición
heart attack	ataque al corazón
heartbeat	latido del corazón
extra	extra
irregular	irregular
skipped	intermitente
slow	lento
heartburn	ardor en el estómago
heart pain	dolor en el corazón
heart palpitation	palpitación
heavy breasts	senos pesados
height loss	disminución en la estatura
hemorrhage after menopause	hemorragia después de la menopausia
hiccups	hipo
hissing in the ear	zumbido en los oídos
hoarseness	ronquera
hot flashes	fogaje, bochorno
incontinence	incotinencia
of feces	de heces focales
of urine	de la orina
indigestion	indigestión
inflammation	inflamación
insensibility	insensibilidad
insensitivity to heat or cold	insensibilidad térmica al frío o al calor
insomnia	insomnio
intercourse, painful	coito doloroso
irregular periods	menstruación irregular
jaundice	ictericia
lack of appetite	falta de apetito
large	agrandamiento
head	de la cabeza
limbs	de las extremidades
tongue	de la lengua
lesion	lesión
lethargy	letargo
limping	cojera
listlessness	falta de ánimo, apatía
locked jaw	mandíbula cerrada
locked knee	rodilla bloqueada

469

English	Spanish
loose teeth	**dientes flojos**
loss of	**pérdida**
appetite	del apetito
balance	del equilibrio
bladder control	del control de la vejiga
consciousness	del conocimiento
control of muscle tonicity	del control de la tonicidad muscular
coordination	de la coordinación
feeling	del sentido del tacto
libido	de la libido
luster in hair	del brillo del pelo
luster in nails	del brillo de las uñas
peripheral vision	de la visión periférica
smell	del olfato
voice	de la voz
low birth weight	**peso bajo al nacer**
lumps in	**bultos, masa en**
breast	el seno, la mama
joints	(el área de) las articulaciones
neck	el cuello
pubic area	el pubis
magenta tongue	**lengua magenta**
malocculsion	**maloclusión**
masculinization	**masculinización**
memory loss	**pérdida de la memoria**
menstruation problems	**problemas de la menstruación**
mental ability impairment	**deterioro de la habilidad mental**
moles	**lunares**
mouth breathing	**respiración por la boca**
muscular incoordination	**falta de coordinación muscular**
nasal speech	**habla nasal**
night blindness	**ceguera nocturna**
night urination	**micción nocturna**
numbness	**entumecimiento**
obstruction	**obstrucción**
odor	**olor, aroma**
oozing	**excreción**
pain	**dolor**
dull	sordo
fulminant	fulminante
gripping	opresivo, con sensación de agarrota-miento
lancinating	lancinante
intense	intenso, agudo
irradiating	que se irradia, que se corre
mild	leve
persistant	persistente
severe	severo
painful gums	**encías dolorosa**
painful swelling	**hinchazón dolorosa**
paleness	**palidez**
paleness around the mouth	**palidez alrededor de la boca**
pallor	**palidez**

470

English	Spanish
palpitations	palpitaciones
palsy	parálisis
paralysis	parálisis
peeling of the skin	peladura, descamación de la piel
pimples	granos, barros
pins and needles sensation	cosquilleo, hormigueo
polyps	pólopos
postnasal drip	goteo postnasal
premature aging	envejecimiento prematuro
premature beat	latido prematuro
premature ejaculation	eyaculación prematura
premature menopause	menopausia prematura
premenstural tension	tensión premenstrual
profuse sweating	sudor excesivo
prominence of blood vessels	prominencia de vasos capilares
prostration	postración
protrusion from vagina	protrusión a través de la vagina
puffiness	hinchazón, intumescencia, [abogotamiento]
of the face	de la cara
of the legs	de las piernas
pulmonary	pulmonar
abscess	absceso
edema	edema
embolism	embolia
infarction	infarto
tuberculosis	tuberculosis
pyorrea	piorrea
rapid heartbeat	latidos rápidos
rapid loss of vision	pérdida percipitada de la visión
rapid loss of weight	rápida pérdida de peso
rapid pulse	pulso rápido
rash	erupción, ronchas
red spots (tiny)	pequeñas manchas rojas
red and swollen joints	articulaciones inflamadas y enrojecidas
relapse	recaída
restlessness	intranquilidad
retraction of the nipple	retracción del pezón
rigidity	rigidez
ringing in the ears	zumbido en los oídos
salivaction, excessive	salivación excesiva
salivation and difficulty in swallowing	salivación excesiva y dificultad al tragar
scaled ulcer	llaga con costra
scanty urine	escasez de orina
seizures	ataques, episodios
semiconscious state	estado seminconsciente
shock	shock, choque
shortness of breath	falta de respiración
skin	piel
clammy	pegajosa
cold	fría
moist	húmeda
skin discoloration	cambio de color de la piel
ashen	cenicienta

English	Spanish
brownish	cetrina
darkening	oscurecimiento
pale	pálida
pallor (face)	palidez (en la cara)
reddening	enrojecimiento
reddening (flushing)	rubor
yellow-white	blanco-amarillenta
slow clotting blood	**coagulación lenta**
slow growth	**crecimiento retardado**
slow loss of vision	**pérdida gradual de la visión**
slow pulse	**pulso lento**
slow speech	**habla despaciosa**
smarting	**escozor**
sneezing	**estornudo**
snoring	**ronquido**
softening of	**reblandecimiento de**
the bones	los huesos
the nails	las uñas
soft ulcerating tumor	**tumor ulceroso blando**
sore	**llaga**
sore, hard crusted	**llaga de costra dura**
to be sore	**estar adolorido-a**
sore throat	**dolor de garganta**
spasm	**espasmo**
spastic gait	**marcha espástica**
spasticity	**espasticidad**
speech difficulties	**trastornos del habla**
split nails	**uñas partidas**
sticky mucus	**mucosidad pegajosa**
stiffening	**rigidez**
stiff neck	**cuello rígido**
stools	**heces fecales**
hard and dark	oscuras y duras
clay-colored	de color arcilloso
bulky and greasy	deposición abundante y grasienta
black and tarry	oscuras y viscosas
pencil shaped	heces fecales largas y finas
persistently bloody	con persistente presencia de sangre
stuttering	**tartamudeo**
subnormal temperature	**temperatura subnormal**
sudden stoppage of flow (urine)	**para súbito del chorro (orino)**
swallowing difficulty	**dificultad al tragar**
swelling	**hinchazón**
inside the mouth	dentro de la boca
of the ear canal	del conducto auditivo
of face; of eyes	de la cara; de los ojos
of feet	de los pies
of hands	de las manos
of the lymph nodes	de los ganglios
tachycardia	**taquicardia**
tingling	**cosquilleo**
total lack of urination	**ausencia de orina**
tremor of	**temblor en**

English	Spanish
the fingers	los dedos
the hands	las manos
the lips	los labios
tumor	**tumor**
twitch	**sacudida nerviosa, "tic nervioso"**
ulcer	**úlcera, llaga**
unawareness of surroundings	**no saber donde uno se encuentra**
unconsciousness	**pérdida del conocimiento**
unresponsiveness	**sin dar una respuesta sensible; sin dar de sí**
urgent urination	**micción imperiosa**
urination, decreased	**deficiencia de orina**
urination, weak stream	**chorro de orina débil**
vaginal bleeding	**sangramiento vaginal**
vaginal discharge	**flujo vaginal**
varicose veins	**venas varicosas**
vertigo	**vértigo, vahido**
vomiting	**vómitos, náuseas**
black	de colo oscuro
occasional	ocasionales
bloody	sanguinolentos, con sangre
waddling gait	**marcha, andar tambaleante**
warts	**verrugas**
weak muscles	**debilidad en los músculos**
weakness	**debilidad**
weight	**peso**
loss	pérdida de
gain	aumento de
wheezing	**respiración sibilante**
worms	**gusanos, lombrices, parásitos**
in instestine	en el intestino
in stool	en el excremento
wrist fracture	**fractura de la muñeca**
yawing	**bostezo**

Trauma: Emergency Problems / Trauma: Problemas de emergencia

Penetrating Wounds gunshot wounds knife or stab wounds blunt instrument injury wounds produced by animal bites: dogs, cats, rodents, wild animals, African bees, black widow spiders, snakes, scorpions, jellyfish, octopuses, sponges, etc.	*Heridas Penetrantes* heridas de bala heridas de cuchillo o puñalada heridas de instrumento despuntado lesiones producidas por picaduras o mordidas de animales: perros, gatos, roedores, animales salvajes, abejas africanas, serpientes, arañas negras, escorpiones, aguamala, pulpos, esponjas, etc.

Burns	*Quemaduras*
acid burns	quemaduras por ácido
fire burns	quemaduras por fuego
frostbite	quemadura de frío
radiation burns	quemaduras por radiación
sunburns	quemadura de sol

Skin Burns	*Possible effects*	*Quemaduras de la piel*	*Efectos posibles*
first-degree burns (scalds)	painful erythema, scalds	quemaduras de primer grado (escaldadura)	eritema doloroso, escaldaduras
second-degree burns (damage lower layer; superficial or deep)	blisters, scars	quemaduras de segundo grado (dañan la segunda capa cutánea)	ampollas, cicatrices
third-degree burns (go into the subcutaneous layer; destruction of epidermis and dermis)	hard and charred burns, inhalation of vapors, stridor, shock, possible airway obstruction	quemaduras de tercer grado (penetran la capa subcutánea; destrucción de la epidermis y la dermis)	quemaduras duras y chamuscadas; aspiración de vapores, estridor, shock, posible obstrucción del conducto respiratorio
fourth-degree burns (involving skin, muscle and bones)	same damage as third-degree burns, involving a higher % of the body	de cuarto grado (comprenden la piel, músculos y huesos)	igual daño que las quemaduras de tercer grado, cubren un % mayor del cuerpo

Substances Causing Toxic Effects by Inhalation, Ingestion or by Direct Contact / Sustancias que causan efectos tóxicos por aspiración, ingestión, o por contacto directo

Substance	Sustancia
alcohols (ethanol, methanol)	alcoholes (etanol, metanol)
alkalis (i.e., ammonia)	alcalíes (p. ej., amoníaco)
arsenic	arsénico
boric acid	ácido bórico
carbon monoxide	monóxido de carbono
cleaners (toilet, ovens, pools)	limpiadores (de servicios, hornos, piscinas)
contaminated seafood, ciguatera	pescado contaminado, ciguatera
cyanide	cianuro
herbicides	herbicidas
metals (iron, lead)	metales (hierro, plomo)
muriatic acid	ácido muriático
mushrooms	setas (hongos)
overdose of medications (salicylates, neuroleptics, antidepressants, etc.)	sobredosis de medicamentos (salicilatos, neurolépticos, tranquilizantes, opiáceos, etc.)
paint thinners, antifreeze, etc.	aguarrás, trementina, anticongelante
plants (hemlock, morning glory, daffodil, hyacinth, ivy, oleander)	plantas (cicuta, gloria de la mañana, narciso trompón, jacinto, hiedra venenosa, adelfa)
shellfish	mariscos contaminados
strong acids	ácidos fuertes

Fractures / Fracturas

Bone Fractures	Fracturas óseas
avulsion	por avulsión
blow-out	por estallamiento
closed	cerrada
conmminuted	conminuta
complete	completa
compressed	por compresión
depressed	con hundimiento
greenstick	de tallo verde
hairline	de raya fina
impacted	impactada
open	expuesta
pathologic	patológica
spiral	espiral
stress	de sobrecarga

Foreign Bodies Penetrating the Body / Cuerpos extraños que penetran el cuerpo

Organ or Part	Caused by	Consequences	Órgano o parte	Causa	Consecuencias
abdomen	stick	abrasions	abdomen	astilla	abrasiones
chest	knives	hemorrhage	tórax	cuchillos	hemorragia
eye, ear, throat	sharp instruments	infections	ojo, oído, garganta	instrumentos afilados	infecciones
extremities	bullet, projectile	lacerations	extremidades	bala, proyectil	laceraciones
skull	splinter	scratches, wounds	cráneo	espina	rasgullos, heridas

Some Complications due to Foreign Bodies
abdominal: internal hemorrhage; infection
chest: infection complications, hemorrhage

eye: scratches, abrasions, lacerations, infection
ear and nose: pain and pus
pharynx: occlusion of the airway
stomach and bowel: discomfort, pain; sharp objects may cause vomiting, gastro-intestinal hemorrhage
urethral: discharge, pain and bleeding
vaginal: lacerations, infection, bleeding

Ciertas complicaciones debidas a cuerpos extraños
abdominal: hemorragia intestinal; infecciones
tórax complicaciones de infecciones, hemorragia
ojo: rasguño, abrasión, desgarramiento, infección
oído y nariz: dolor y secreción purulenta
faringe: oclusión del conducto respiratorio
estómago e intestino: molestia y dolor; la ingestion de objetos afilados puede causar vómitos, hemorragia intestinal
uretral: flujo, dolor y sangramiento
vaginal: laceraciones, infección, sangramiento

Airway Foreign Bodies / Cuerpos extraños en el conducto respiratorio

Way	Symptoms	Vía	Síntomas
penetrating through puncture wounds by swallowing	cough, chest pain, dyspnea, gasping for air, stridor, unable to speak, unable to swallow normally	penetración a través de heridas o laceraciones al tragar	tos, dolor en el pecho, disnea, jadeo, estridor, dificultad al hablar, dificultad al tragar

Toxic Effects by Inhalation, Ingestion or by Direct Contact / Efectos tóxicos por aspiración, ingestión o por contacto directo

Effect	Efecto
abdominal pain	dolor abdominal
airway obstruction	obstrucción del conducto respiratorio
allergies	alergias
arrhythmias	arritmias
asphyxia	asfixia
bronchospasm	broncoespasmo
burns	quemaduras
collapse	colapso
coma	coma
confusion	confusión
dizziness	mareo
dehydration	deshidratación
dyspnea	disnea
edema of the pharynx and larynx	edema de la faringe y la laringe
hoarseness	ronquera
intoxication	intoxicación
muscle spasms	espasmo muscular
pulmonary edema	edema pulmonar
respiratory failure	fallo respiratorio
stridor	estridor

Drug Addiction / Adicción a las drogas

Addictive Drugs	Drogas adictivas	Addictive Drugs	Drogas adictivas
alcohol	alcohol	heroin	heroína
amphetamines	anfetaminas	marihuana	marijuana
barbiturates	barbitúricos	morphine	morfina
cocaine	cocaína	nicotine	nicotina
hallucinogens	halucinógenos		

Loss of Consciousness / Pérdida del conocimiento

Caused by Seizures	Debido a ataques
alcohol or other drug withdrawal	privación de alcohol o de otra droga
drug abuse	adicción a las drogas
epilepsy	epilepsia
febrile convulsions	convulsiones febriles
head trauma	contusión cerebral
metabolic problems	problemas metabólicos

Caused by Coma	Debido a coma
diabetic	diabético
traumatic: head, massive hemothorax	traumático: cerebral, hemotórax masivo
hyperglycemic	hiperglicémico
hypoglycemic	hipoglicémico
drug overdose	sobredosis

477

Eye Emergencies / Emergencias de la vista

Symptom	Síntoma
abrasion, scrape	abrasión o desgarramiento
perforating injury	herida con perforación
swelling and pain	hinchazón y dolor
chemical penetration	penetración de una sustancia química
foreign body piercing	penetración de cuerpo extraño
eye discharge with pus and redness	enrojecimiento y supuración con pus
severe constant pain	dolor constante y fuerte
sudden red or pink colored vision	visión súbita de color rojo o rosada
sudden blindness or double vision	ceguera o visión doble súbita

Chest Pain / Dolor en el pecho

Possible causes	Symptoms	Causa posible	Síntomas
myocardial infarction, heart attack	chest pain in the center of the chest behind the sternum; sweating, possible nausea and vomiting.	infarto del miocardio, ataque al corazón	dolor en el pecho que puede correrse al cuello, al maxilar y al brazo; sudor y posiblemente náuseas y vómitos
angina pectoris	chest pain with a sensation of pressure, sweaty brow; pain radiates to the left shoulder and down, and sometimes to the arm	angina de pecho	dolor en el pecho con sensación de presión, sudores en la frente; el dolor se radia al hombro izquierdo y a veces al brazo
pericarditis	chest pain, dull or sharp, rapid breathing, cough	pericarditis	dolor sordo o agudo en el pecho, respiración rápida, tos

Other Emergencies / Otras emergencias

Other Emergencies	Otras emergencias
cardiopulmonary resuscitation	resucitación pulmonar
emergency delivery	urgencia de parto
vaginal bleeding	sangramiento vaginal
hypertension	hipertensión
child abuse	niños maltratados
sexual assault	violación sexual
drowning	ahogamiento
suicide	suicidio

Medical Tests / Pruebas médicas

Cardiovascular Problems / Problemas cardiovasculares

Test	Prueba
angiography ☑	angiografía (coronaria, pulmonar, etc.,) ☑
aortography	aortografía
arterial blood gases ☑	gases en sangre arterial ☑
arteriography	arteriografía
cardiac catheterization	cateterización cardíaca
chest films ☑	radiografías del tórax ☑
CT scanning (computerized tomography)	TC (tomografía computarizada)
EKG (electrocardiogram) ☑	ECG (electrocardiograma) ☑
echocardiography	ecocardiografía
endomyocardial biopsy	biopsia endomiocárdica
enzyme tests	pruebas de enzimas
exercise stress tests	pruebas de esfuerzo
gammagraphy ☑	gammagrafía ☑
MRI magnetic resonance imaging ☑	IRM imágenes de resonancia magnética ☑
venography	venografía

☑ Tests marked above may also be indicated in pulmonary studies.
☑ Las pruebas señaladas arriba también pueden ser indicadas en estudios pulmonares.

Respiratory Problems / Problemas respiratorios

Test	Prueba
acid-fast stain	tinción fijada en ácido
bronchography	broncografía
bronchoscopy	broncoscopía
gammagraphy (lung)	gammagrafía pulmonar
Gram stain	tinción de Gram
lung scans	escán pulmonar
needle aspiration biopsy	biopsia de aspiración con aguja
respiratory function tests	pruebas de función respiratoria
serologic studies	estudios serológicos
serum electrolytes	electrólitos en suero
skin testing	pruebas cutáneas
sputum culture	cultivo de esputo
Wright stain	tinción de Wright

Work-up / Estudios, radiografías y análisis

arterial blood gases	gases en sangre arterial
biochemical profile	pruebas selectivas bioquímicas
biopsy ☑	biopsia pulmonar
CBC complete blood count ☑	recuento hemático total ☑
chest films ☑	radiografías torácicas ☑
electrocardiogram	electrocardiograma
ESR (erythrocyte sedimentation rate)	índice de eritrosedimentación
hematocrit ☑	hematócrito ☑
protein electrophoresis	electroforesis proteica ☑
serum creatinine or BUN ☑	creatinina sérica o BUN ☑
serum potassium	potasio sérico
urinalysis ☑	análisis de orina ☑

☑ All tests marked above are done in addition to tests administered for specific problems.
☑ Todas las pruebas señaladas arriba se hacen además de pruebas administradas por problemas específicos.

Other Tests for Specific Problems / Otras pruebas, de problemas específicos

barium x-ray examinations	radiografía con bario
bone marrow biopsy	biopsia de la médula ósea
bone scan	escán óseo
cervical smear test	prueba de unto
cholecistography	colecistografía
chromosome analysis	análisis cromosomático
coagulation time	tiempo de coagulación
colonoscopy	colonoscopía
gastroscopy	gastroscopía
hysterosalpingography	histerosalpingografía
intravenous pyelography	pielografía intravenosa
kidney imaging	imágenes renales
laparoscopy	laparoscopía
liver function tests	pruebas de función hepática
liver scan	escán hepático
mammography	mamografía
mediastinoscopy	mediastinoscopía
occult blood (fecal)	sangre oculta fecal
pregnancy tests	pruebas de embarazo
prostatic specific antigen	antígeno prostático específico
semen analysis	análisis del semen
thyroid function tests	pruebas de función tiroidea
ultrasound scanning	escán de ultrasonido
HIV serology	serología de VIH

Recommendations to the patient / Recomendaciones al paciente

Preparation for a C.T. scan / Preparación para un escán (exploración) de T.C.

You cannot eat or drink anything 4 to 8 hours before the test.

No puede comer o beber líquidos de 4 a 8 horas antes de la prueba.

1. Change into a hospital gown.
2. You will be secured on the table by a strap.
3. You will receive a contrast medium by mouth or by injection.
4. Sometimes you may receive the contrast medium before your test.
5. You will be moved into the scanner; it will scan your body from 30 to 60 minutes.
6. You must remain still to prevent the images from blurring.
7. During the scan you may be asked to hold your breath for a few seconds.
8. You may hear some noises made by the x-ray machine.
9. Remain still. They may need more images to complete the exam.
10. During the test you can usually talk to the technician over an intercom if necessary.

1. Póngase esta bata.
2. Le ayudarán a sujetarse a la mesa con un cinturón de seguridad.
3. Le administrarán un medio de contraste si es necesario, oralmente o inyectado.
4. A veces se administra el medio de contraste antes de la prueba.
5. Pasará al interior del escáner (explorador), el cual explorará su cuerpo de 30 a 60 minutos.
6. No se mueva para prevenir que las imágenes salgan borrosas.
7. Durante la exploración es posible que le indiquen que aguante la respiración por unos segundos.
8. Es posible que oiga los ruidos que hace la máquina de rayos X.
9. No se mueva. Es posible que necesiten tomar más imágenes para completar el examen.
10. Durante la prueba generalmente puede hablar con el/la técnico(a) por el intercomunicador.

Preparation for an MRI / Preparación para una exploración de IRM

1. Follow instructions given about eating, drinking, and medications.
2. Someone may accompany you.
3. Sign the consent form.
4. Use the bathroom before the test.
5. Remove jewelry, eyeglasses, and clothing with zippers or metal buttons. You will be given a hospital gown.
6. You will be checked with a metal detector.
7. You will be given a contrast medium by injection.
8. Let the technician know if you feel very nervous or if you have an upset stomach or other problem.
9. They will place you on a table.
10. The table will slide into the interior of the machine.
11. Relax and remain still.
12. You will not feel anything except for some sounds coming from the machine.

1. Siga las instrucciones que le den sobre comidas, líquidos y medicinas.
2. Alguien le puede acompañar a la prueba.
3. Firme el consentimiento.
4. Vaya al servicio antes de la prueba.
5. Quítese las prendas, espejuelos, ropa con "zipers" (cremalleras) o botones metálicos. Le darán una bata del hospital.
6. Le chequearán con un detector de metales.
7. Le inyectarán un medio de contraste.
8. Infórmele al tecnico si se siente muy nervioso(a) o si tiene náuseas o cualquier otro problema.
9. Le colocarán sobre una mesa.
10. La mesa pasará al interior de la máquina.
11. Relájese y permanezca sin moverse.
12. No sentirá nada con excepción de los sonidos que hace la máquina.

Medications / Medicamentos

Medications	Main Use	Medicamentos	Uso principal
antacid	to treat acidity	antiácido	para tratar la acidez
analgesic	pain reliever	analgésico	para aliviar el dolor
anticonvulsant	to prevent or treat convulsions	anticonvulsivo	para prevenir o tratar convulsiones
anticoagulant	to prevent blood clotting	anticoagulante	para prevenir la coagulación sanguínea
antibiotic	to treat bacterial infection	antibiótico	para tratar infecciones bacterianas
antidepressant	to treat depression	antidepresivo	para tratar la depresión
antidiarrheal	to treat diarrhea	antidiarreico	para tratar la diarrea
antiemetic	to prevent or alleviate nausea and/or vomiting	antiemético	para prevenir o aliviar la náusea y/o vómito
anti-inflammatory	to counteract or suppress inflamation	antiinflamatorio	para contrarrestar o suprimir la inflamación
antiseptic	to inhibit infection or putrefaction	antiséptico	para impedir la infección o putrefacción
antihypertensive	to lower blood pressure	antihipertensivo	para bajar la presión arterial
antioncotic	to treat tumefaction	antioncótico	para tratar la tumefacción
antitussive	to relieve or reduce the cough	antitusivo, béquico	para remediar o reducir la tos
bronchodilator	to expand the air passages of the lungs or dilate the bronchi as in the treatment of asthma or other respiratory disorders	broncodilatador	para expandir los conductos respiratorios o dilatar los bronquios como en el tratamiento de asma y otros trastornos respiratorios
cathartic	to treat constipation by stimulating bowel movements	catártico, purgante	para tratar el estreñimiento estimulando la evacuación

Medications	Main Use	Medicamentos	Uso principal
decongestant	to reduce congestion or swelling	descongestionante	para reducir la congestión o hinchazón
diuretic	to increase urine production	diurético	para aumentar la producción de orina
emetic	to cause vomiting	emético	para promover el vómito
expectorant	to promote expectoration	expectorante	para promover la expectoración
hypnotics or soporifics	to induce sleep	hipnóticos o soporíferos	para inducir el sueño
laxative	to prevent or treat constipation	laxante	para tratar o prevenir el estreñimiento
stimulant	to stimulate or produce a reaction	estimulante	para estimular o provocar una reacción
tranquilizer	to treat stress and anxiety	tranquilizante	para tratar el estrés y la ansiedad
vasodilator	to cause vasodilation	vasodilatador	para causar la vasodilatación

Etiology of Common Diseases

Disease	Transmission	Incubation	Contagion Period	Symptoms
Chicken pox, Varicella	by direct contact or by respiratory droplets	7–21 days	from onset of symptoms until pocks are gone	fever, discomfort, patches of red spots that appear first in the upper part of the body and then, to a lesser degree, on the arms and legs; the vesicles fill with fluid, rupture, and disappear without leaving any scars
Diphtheria	by contact with carrier or by contaminated milk	2–6 days	from onset of symptoms to 4–6 weeks thereafter	weakness, sore throat, fever, rapid pulse, grayish membrane covering the throat and tonsils
German measles, Rubella	by direct contact or by inhaling infected droplets	2–3 weeks	one week before rash appears	slight fever, swelling of the neck glands, and a rash of flat, pink spots
Measles	by direct contact or inhaling infected droplets	7–14 days	10–14 days before symptoms appear until rash is gone	high fever, nasal congestion, conjunctivitis, dry cough, tiny red spots, first in mouth, then spreading throughout the body
Mumps, parotitis	by direct contact or by inhaling infected droplets	12–24 days	one day before symptoms appear until swelling goes down	from medium to high fever, headache, swelling of the parotid glands (below and in front of the ear), painful chewing and swallowing
Roseola infantum	undetermined, believed to be caused by a virus	undetermined	undetermined	sudden, high fever that lasts for about three days and that may cause convulsions, rash, and swelling of the lymph glands
Scarlet fever, scarlatina	contact with carrier	24 hours to 3 days	from onset to one day after antibiotic treatment begins	sudden onset of fever, sore and infected throat, rash on neck and chest, strawberry tongue
Viral colds	contact with carrier or infected secretion	1–2 days after exposure	for duration	headache, nasal congestion, cough, sneezing, hoarseness, watering eyes

Etiología de enfermedades comunes

Enfermedad	Transmisión	Incubación	Período de contagio	Síntomas
La china, varicela	por contacto directo o por destilación o aspiración de microgotas infectadas	7–21 días	desde la aparición de los síntomas hasta que las pústulas desaparecen	fiebre, malestar, grupos de pápulas rojizas que surgen primero en la porción superior del cuerpo y, en menor grado, en las piernas y brazos; las pápulas se llenan de fluido, revientan y no dejan cicatriz
Difteria	por contacto directo o a través de leche contaminada	2–6 días	desde el momento en que aparecen los síntomas hasta 4–6 semanas después	debilidad, dolor de garganta, fiebre, pulso rápido, membrana grisácea que cubre la garganta y las amígdalas
Sarampión alemán, rubéola	por contacto directo o por destilación o aspiración de microgotas infectadas	2–3 semanas	una semana antes de la erupción	fiebre ligera, infl. de las glándulas del cuello y erupción de pequeñas máculas rosáceas
Sarampión	por contacto directo o por destilación o aspiración de microgotas infectadas	7–14 días	desde 10–14 días antes de la aparición de los síntomas hasta que éstos desaparecen	fiebre alta, congestión nasal, conjuntivitis, tos seca, pequeñas, máculas rojas que surgen en la boca y luego se difunden por todo el cuerpo
Paperas, parotiditis	por contacto directo o por destilación o aspiración de microgotas infectadas	12–24 días	un día antes de la aparición de los síntomas hasta que la hinchazón desaparece	fiebre alta, dolor de cabeza, hinchazón de las glándulas parótidas (debajo y por delante de la oreja), dolor al masticar y al tragar
Roséola infantil	indeterminada, se cree que es de origen viral	indeterminada	indeterminada	fiebre alta súbita que dura unos tres días y que puede dar lugar a convulsiones, erupción cutánea e infl. de los ganglios
Fiebre escarlata, escarlatina	por contacto con el (la) portador-a	desde 24 horas hasta 3 días después	desde que aparecen los síntomas hasta un día después de empezar el tratamiento con antibióticos	fiebre súbita, garganta adolorida y enrojecida, erupción cutánea en el cuello y pecho, lengua aframbuesada
Catarros virales	contacto con el (la) portador-a o con secreción infectada	1–2 días después de estar expuesto	durante todo el curso del catarro	dolor de cabeza, congestión nasal, tos, estorndos frecuentes, ronquera, ojos aguados, llorosos

Sexually Transmitted Diseases (STD) / Enfermedades por contagio sexual (venéreas)

Sickness	Transmission	Enfermedad	Contagio
candidiasis, *Candida albicans,* fungus, yeast infection; thick, creamy discharge	sexual contact, use of towels or clothing belonging to an infected person, or caused by a low pH in the vagina	**candidiasis,** *Cándida albicans,* infección fungosa caracterizada por flujo cremoso	contacto sexual, el uso de toallas o ropa interior de una persona infectada, o pH bajo de la vagina
chlamydia, *Chlamydia Trachomatis,* causative agents of urethritis, lymphogranuloma, prostatitis, salpingitis, newborn conjunctivitis	sexual contact; newborns may be infected during childbirth	**clamidia,** *Chlamydia Trachomatis,* agente causante de uretritis, linfogranuloma, prostatitis, salpingitis, conjuntivitis del neonato	contacto sexual rectal, oral o vaginal, o de la madre al feto durante el parto
condyloma acuminatum, venereal warts	sexual contact or by using towels belonging to an infected person	**condiloma acuminatum,** verrugas venéreas	contacto sexual o por el uso de toallas de una persona infectada
genital herpes virus type 2; causing blisters and sores on the genitals	anal, oral, vaginal sexual contact at the outbreak of the disease; touching blisters and sores; can be transmitted to the newborn at birth	**herpes de los genitales,** *virus de tipo 2;* causante de ampollas y úlceraciones en los genitales	contacto sexual anal, oral o vaginal; de la madre a la criatura durante el parto; por contacto con ampollas y ulceraciones
gonorrhea, gonococcus *Neisseria,* infection invading the genitourinary tract, pharynx and anus	anal, oral, vaginal sexual contact; from mother to child during childbirth; period of incubation from 3 to 5 days	**gonorrea,** gonococo *Neisseria,* infección que invade el tracto genitourinario, la faringe y el recto	contacto sexual rectal, oral o vaginal; de la madre durante el parto; período de incubación de 3 a 5 días
hepatitis: A-, B-, C-, and D-type viruses inflammation of the liver; other serious disorders are also present	sexual contact, transfusion of contaminated blood; contact through abrasions, tiny cuts, or wounds with the blood of an infected person; or by the mother at childbirth or through breast-feeding; **hepatitis B** usually involves oral-anal sex	**hepatitis: víruses de tipo A, B, C y D** (delta) inflamación del hígado, manifestándose otros trastornos serios	por contacto sexual, tranfusión de sangre contaminada; contacto a través de heridas o abrasiones con la sangre de una persona infectada; por la madre durante el parto o la lactancia; la **hepatitis B** generalmente resulta de contacto sexual oral-anal
HPV virus, *human papilomavirus,* considered a strong cocarcinogen; generally present with other STD diseases	venereal disease, characterized by warts, can expand by autoinoculation in the genitals and anus	**HPV virus,** *papilomavirus humano,* considerado un posible cocarcinógeno; generalmente presente con otras enfermedades venéreas	enfermedad venérea, caracterizada por verrugas o condilomas en los genitales y el ano que se expanden por autocontagio

486

Sickness	Transmission	Enfermedad	Contagio
pubic lice, "crabs," *pthirus pubis;* discomfort produced by itching	sexual contact, transmitted in bed linen, towels, toilet seats	**el piojo púbico,** *pthirus pubis,* malestar por intensa picazón	contacto sexual, transmitido en toallas, y ropa de cama y asiento de retrete, (inodoro)
syphilis, *Treponema pallidum,* 10 to 90 day incubation period; ulceration, warts in the genital area; invades the bloodstream to different organs	anal, oral, vaginal sexual contact, by sores through mucous membranes or abrasions or by touching a chancre; from mother to child; in pregnancy can cause stillbirth or congenital syphilis	**sífilis,** *Treponema pallidum,* de 10 a 90 días de incubación; úlcera primera, verrugas en el área genital; se extiende por vía sanguínea a diferentes órganos	contacto sexual rectal, oral, vaginal, por contacto con ulceraciones a través de membranas mucosas o al tocar un chancro; durante el embarazo puede causar sífilis congénita o muerte al feto
trichomoniasis, *Trichomonas vaginalis,* causes foul-smelling vaginal discharge, itching, burning	sexual activity, infected semen on washcloths, bedclothes	**tricomoniasis,** *trichomonas vaginalis,* causa flujo vaginal de olor desagradable, picazón, ardor	actividad sexual, semen infeccioso en toallas o ropa de cama

Muscles and Actions / Músculos y acciones

Name	Action	Nombre	Acción
occipitofrontal	draws scalp backward and forward; raises the eyebrows	occipitofrontal	mueve el cuero cabelludo hacia atrás y hacia adelante; levanta las cejas
buccinator	compresses the cheek and retracts the angle of the mouth	buccinador	comprime el cachete y retracta el ángulo de la boca
sternocleidomastoid	flexes the vertebral column and rotates the head to the opposite side of the muscle that is being contracted	esternocleidomastoideo	flexiona la columna vertebral y rota la cabeza hacia el lado opuesto del músculo que se contrae
trapezius	draws back the head of the humerus; rotates the scapula	trapecio	mueve la cabeza del húmero hacia atrás; rota la escápula
deltoid	abducts, flexes, and extends the arm	deltoides	abduce, flexiona y extiende el brazo
biceps (of arm)	flexes the articulation of the elbow and turns the forearm	bíceps (braquial)	flexiona la articulación del codo y gira el antebrazo
triceps (of arm)	extends the forearm and the arm	tríceps (braquial)	extiende el antebrazo y el brazo
latissimus dorsi	adducts, extends, and rotates the arm	dorsal ancho	aduce, extiende y rota el brazo

487

Name	Action	Nombre	Acción
pectoral, greater	adducts, flexes, and rotates the arm medially	pectoral mayor	aduce, flexiona y rota el brazo hacia adentro
pectoral, smaller	draws shoulder forward and downward, raises the ribs, and acts as an inhaling muscle	pectoral menor	baja y lleva el hombro hacia adelante, eleva las costillas y actúa como músculo inspirador
psoas, greater	flexes, adducts, and rotates the thigh	psoas mayor	flexiona, aduce y rota el muslo
psoas, smaller	assists the greater psoas	psoas menor	asiste al psoas mayor
oblique of abdomen, external	lowers the ribs, flexes the thorax, and presses the abdominal viscera	oblicuo mayor del abdomen	baja las costillas, flexiona el tórax y comprime las vísceras abdominales
gluteus maximus	extends and rotates the thigh	glúteo mayor	extiende y rota el muslo
gluteus medius	abducts and rotates the thigh	glúteo mediano	abduce y rota el muslo
gluteus minimum	abducts and extends the thigh	glúteo menor	abduce y extiende el muslo
quadriceps	extends the leg and flexes the muscle over the pelvis	cuadríceps	extiende la pierna y flexiona el muslo sobre la pelvis
soleus	extends and rotates the foot	sóleo	extiende y rota el pie

Physical Fitness / Acondicionamiento físico

Vocabulary / Vocabulario

aerobic	aeróbico-a
cardiovascular	cardiovascular
cool down	enfriarse, enfriamiento
endurance	resistencia
equipment	equipo
exercise	ejercicio
flexibility	flexibilidad
muscle tone	tono muscular
strengthening	fortalecer, fortalecimiento
strength training	programa de fortalecimiento
stretching out	estirarse, estiramiento
treadmill	rueda de andar
warm up	calentarse, calentamiento
weights	pesas
workout	programa de ejercicio

General Observations and Recommendations / Observaciones y recomendaciones generales

Exercise helps you in many ways.	El ejercicio lo beneficia de muchas maneras.
It keeps your lungs and heart healthy.	Mantiene los pulmones y el corazón saludables.
It helps the blood flow in your body.	Ayuda la circulación de la sangre.
It improves your muscle tone.	Aumenta la tonicidad muscular.
It alleviates arthritic pain.	Alivia el dolor artrítico.
Strengthens the bones and stimulates the production of hormones.	Fortalece los huesos y estimula la producción de hormonas.
It helps to keep your weight down.	Ayuda a mantener un buen peso.
It makes you feel good.	Le hace sentirse bien.
Do exercises that you like.	Haga ejercicios que le gusten.
Do exercises a few times a week.	Haga los ejercicios varias veces a la semana.
Talk to your doctor about a good exercise program for you.	Consulte con su médico en cuanto a un programa de ejercicios que sea bueno para usted.

Exercises / Ejercicios

Warming up and Cooling Down Exercises / Ejercicios de calentamiento y de enfriamiento

rotate your neck	gire el cuello
raise your shoulders	alce los hombros
make fists	cierre y abra el puño
stretch the calves and arms	estire las pantorrillas y los brazos
rotate your ankles	gire los tobillos
breathe deeply	respire profundamente

489

Common Exercises and Sports / Ejercicios y deportes comunes

neck stretches	estirar el cuello
arm stretches	estirar los brazos
arm circles	rotar los brazos
rise on your toes	pararse de puntillas
waist bends	doblar la cintura
weight lifting	levantar peso
bicycling	ciclismo
jogging	correr rítmicamente
swimming	natación
walking	caminar
brisk walking	caminar rápidamente

Taking Care of Your Back / El cuidado de la espalda

Maintain a good posture.	Mantenga una postura correcta.
When lifting, allow the legs to do the work.	Cuando levante algún peso, deje que las piernas hagan el esfuerzo.
Bend your knees, not your back.	Doble las rodillas, no la espalda.
Don't stand or sit in the same position for long periods of time.	No mantenga la misma posición por largo tiempo.
Sleep on your side with legs pulled in towards the chest.	Duerma sobre el costado con las piernas dobladas hacia el pecho.
Watch your weight.	Mantenga un buen peso.
Talk to your doctor about a good exercise program for you.	Consulte a su médico sobre un programa de ejercicios que sea adecuado para usted.

Number of Calories Burnt During Some Exercises / Número de calorías que se queman durante algunos ejercicios

Exercise	Ejercicio	Calories per Hour / Calorías por hora
aerobics	aeróbica, aerobic	360–480
bicycling	montar en bicicleta	410
jogging	correr	650–700
swimming	nadar	275–500
walking	caminar	300–440
weight lifting	levantar peso	480

USDA Pyramid with Food Groups and Proportions / Pirámide del USDA de grupos alimenticios y raciones diarias[1]

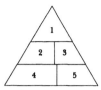

Groups	Grupos	Servings p.d. / Raciones p.d.
1. bread, rice, cereal, pasta	1. pan, arroz, cereal, pasta	6–11 p.d.
2. vegetables	2. vegetales	3–5 p.d.
3. fruits	3. frutas	2–4 p.d.
4. meat, poultry, fish, dry beans, nuts	4. carne, aves, pescado, frijoles secos, nueces	2–3 p.d.
5. fats, oils, sweets	5. grasas, aceites, dulces	to add at discretion / añadir a discreción

[1]USDA, United States Dietary Allowances / Raciones de la dieta alimenticia diaria por el Departamento de Salud del gobierno de los Estados Unidos de América.

Therapeutic Diets	Dietas terapéuticas
balanced	balanceada
bland	blanda
carbohydrate-free	libre de carbohidratos
cholesterol-free	libre de colesterol
dried	limitada en líquido
diabetic	diabética
fat-free	libre de grasa
gluten-free	libre de gluten
high-calorie	rica en calorías
high-fiber	alta en fibra
high-potency	con vitaminas
liquid	líquida
low-calorie	baja en calorías
low-carbohydrate	baja en carbohidratos
low-salt	baja en sal
pureed	en puré
macrobiotic	macrobiótica
sodium-restricted	limitada en sodio (sal)
soft	semisólida
weight reduction	de reducción de peso
with proteins	con proteínas

Nutrients	Nutrientes
carbohydrates[1]	carbohidratos[1]
fats[1]	grasas[1]
minerals[2]	minerales[2]
proteins[1]	proteínas[1]
vitamins[2]	vitaminas[2]

[1]macronutrients
[2]micronutrients

Sources of Vitamins and Minerals

Vitamin A: fish, liver, egg yolk, butter, yellow fruits

Vitamin D: fish liver oils, liver, egg yolk, butter

Vitamin E: vegetable oil, wheat germ, leafy vegetables, margarine, egg yolk, legumes

Vitamin K, K$_1$, K$_2$: pork, liver, vegetable oils,

Vitamin B$_6$ group: spinach, organ meats, fish, legumes, whole-grain cereals, sweet potatoes, avocado

Vitamina B$_{12}$: liver, meats, egg yolk, milk and dairy products

Vitamina C (ascorbic acid): citric fruits, tomatoes, green peppers, cabbage

Fatty Acids: vegetable oils (corn, sunflower, canola), margarine

Folic Acid: fresh green vegetables, fruits, gizzards, kidneys, liver

Biotin: legumes, liver, nuts, cauliflower, egg yolk

Niacin (niacinamide, nicotinic acid): dried yeast, liver, meat, fish, legumes, whole grain cereal

Thiamine (vitamin B$_1$): potatoes, legumes, pork, liver, enriched cereals

Riboflavin (vitamin B$_2$): milk, cheese, liver, eggs, enriched cereals

Potassium: bananas, apricots, peaches, prunes, raisins, milk

Calcium: milk, milk products, meat, fish, eggs, beans, fruits, vegetables

Copper: liver, shellfish, whole grains, nuts, poultry

Magnesium: dark green vegetables, dairy products, nuts, meat, whole grain cereals

Phosphorus: dairy products, meat, fish, poultry, legumes, grains, nuts

Iron: Meats, spinach, radishes

Sodium: beef, pork, cheese, olives, sauerkraut

Zinc: dairy products, liver, wheat bran, shellfish

Fuentes de vitaminas y minerales

Vitamina A: pescado, hígado, yema de huevo, mantequilla, frutas amarillas

Vitamina D: aceite de hígado de pescado, hígado, yema de huevo, mantequilla

Vitamina E: aceite vegetal, germen de trigo, hojas de vegetales, margarina, yema de huevo, legumbres

Vitamina K, K$_1$, K$_2$: cerdo, hígado, aceites vegetales

Grupo de B$_6$: espinaca, vísceras, pescado, cereales de grano, boniato, aguacate, legumbres

Vitamina B$_{12}$: hígado, carnes, yema de huevo, leche y derivados

Vitamina C (ácido ascórbico): frutas cítricas, tomate, ají verde, repollo

Acidos grasos: aceites vegetales (de maíz, girasol, canola)

Acido fólico: vegetales frescos, frutas, molleja de ave, riñones, hígado

Biotina: legumbres, hígado, nueces, repollo, yema de huevo

Niacina (niacinamida, ácido nicotínico): levadura en polvo, hígado, carne, pescado, legumbres, cereales de grano

Tiamina (vitamina B$_1$): papas, legumbres, cerdo, hígado, cereales enriquecidos

Riboflavina (vitamina B$_2$): leche, quesos, hígado, huevos, cereales enriquecidos

Potasio: plátanos, albaricoque, durazno (melocotón), ciruelas pasas, pasas, leche

Calcio: leche y sus derivados, carnes, pescado, huevos, frijoles, frutas, vegetales

Cobre: hígado, mariscos, granos enteros, nueces, carne de ave

Magnesio: verduras verdes, productos lácteos, nueces, carne, cereales de granos enteros

Fósforo: productos lácteos, carne, pescado, carne de ave, legumbres, granos enteros, nueces

Hierro: Carnes, espinaca, rábanos

Sodio: carne de res, cerdo, queso, aceitunas, col agria

Zinc: productos lácteos, hígado, salvado, mariscos

Why Are Vitamins Essential?

Vitamin A: helps to have good vision, healthy hair, skin and nails; fights infection

Vitamin D: calcium absorbent, helps to maintain healthy bones and teeth

Vitamin E: important in the formation of red blood cells, and building tissues and muscle development

Vitamin K, K_1, K_2: intervenes in the formation of prothrombin and other coagulation factors

Vitamin B_6 group: of great importance in the metabolism and absorption of proteins

Vitamin B_{12}: effective in pernicious anemia, aids in formation of genetic materials (DNA and RNA)

Vitamin C (ascorbic acid): aids in the formation of collagen; helps prevent infection and bleeding of the gums

Fatty Acids: precursors of prostaglandins, builders of many lipids

Folic Acid: maturation of RBCs, helpful to prevent anemia, intervenes in the formation of genetic material

Biotin: aids in body growth, amino acid and fatty acid metabolism

Niacin (niacinamide, nicotinic acid): helps in carbohydrate metabolism

Thiamine (vitamin B_1): aids in peripheral and central nerve cell functions, and to metabolize carbohydrates into energy

Riboflavin (vitamin B_2): aids to metabolize carbohydrates, proteins, and fats

Potassium: necessary to keep acid-base balance, muscle activity, water retention

Calcium: blood coagulation, bone and teeth formation, transmission of nerve impulses

Copper: necessary in the synthesis of hemoglobin, component of digestive enzymes

Magnesium: aids to synthesize protein; formation of bones and teeth

Phosphorus: helps metabolize calcium, protein, and glucose; formation of bones and teeth

Sodium: acid-base balance, blood pH, muscle activity

Iron: needed to maintain the correct level of hemoglobin in the blood

Zinc: aids metabolism of proteins

¿Por qué son esenciales las vitaminas?

Vitamina A: ayuda a tener buena visión, pelo, piel y uñas saludables; combate infecciones

Vitamina D: absorbente del calcio, ayuda a mantener los huesos y dientes

Vitamina E: importante en la formación de glóbulos rojos y en el desarrollo de los tejidos y músculos

Vitamina K, K_1, K_2: intervienen en la formación de la protrombina y otros factores de coagulación

Grupo de B_6: de gran importancia en el metabolismo y la absorción de las proteínas

Vitamina B_{12}: efectiva en la anemia perniciosa, ayuda a la formación de materiales genéticos (DNA y RNA)

Vitamina C (ácido ascórbico): ayuda a la formación de colágeno; ayuda a prevenir infecciones y sangramiento de las encías

Acidos grasos: precursores de prostaglandinas, constructores en varios lípidos

Acido fólico: maduración de RBCs, ayuda a prevenir la anemia, necesario en la formación de elementos genéticos

Biotina: ayuda al crecimiento, metabolismo de aminoácidos y acidos grasos

Niacina (niacinamida, ácido nicotínico): ayuda en el metabolismo de carbohidratos

Tiamina (vitamina B_1): esencial en las funciones de las células nerviosas y periféricas y en el metabolismo de carbohidratos

Riboflavina (vitamina B_2): ayuda a metabolizar carbohidratos, proteínas y grasas

Potasio: necesario al balance ácido-básico, a la actividad muscular, en la retención de agua

Calcio: coagulación de la sangre, formación de dientes y huesos, transmisión de impulsos nerviosos

Cobre: necesario en la síntesis de hemoglobina, componente de enzimas digestivas

Magnesio: ayuda en la síntesis de las proteínas; formación de huesos y dientes

Fósforo: ayuda a metabolizar el calcio, las proteínas y la glucosa; esencial en la formación de huesos y dientes

Sodio: balance ácido-básico, pH sanguíneo actividad muscular

Hierro: necesario para mantener el nivel correcto de hemoglobina en la sangre

Zinc: ayuda en el metabolismo de las proteínas

Water + Values

Contains important minerals

Acts as a regulator of body temperature

Plays an important role in digestion

A major component of plasma

A provider of nutrients to the cells

Works as a helper to empty body waste

Comprises about two thirds of the human body

Agua + Valores

Contiene minerales importantes

Actúa como reguladora de la temperatura corporal

Desempeña un papel importante en la digestión

Es un componente mayor del plasma

Es proveedora de nutrientes a las células

Trabaja como ayudante en procesos corporales de eliminación

Comprende cerca de las dos terceras partes del cuerpo humano

493

Methods of Food Preparation / Métodos de preparación de alimentos

baked	asado, horneado
boiled	hervido
broiled	asado a la parrilla
cooked	cocinado
cut	cortado, tajado
defrosted	descongelado
drained	secado; colado
enriched	enriquecido; aumentado con
fried	frito
grilled	a la brasa
peeled	pelado; (*naranja*) mondada
pickled	en encurtido, escabeche
raw	crudo; sin cocinar; (*fruta*) verde
salted	salado
scraped	raspado
skimmed	descremada
sliced	en rebanadas, en tajadas
steamed	cocinado al vapor
stewed	guisado, estofado
sweetened	endulzado, azucarado
unpeeled	sin pelar
unsalted	sin sal
unsweetened	sin azúcar
well-done	bien cocinado

Food Additives	*Aditivos a los alimentos*
allergens	alérgenos
chemicals	sustancias químicas
colorings	colorantes
contaminants from natural sources	contaminantes de fuentes naturales
minerals	minerales
natural toxins	toxinas naturales
nutrients	sustancias nutritivas
preservatives	preservativos
toxicants	tóxicos producidos en la elaboración

Food Processing	*Procesamiento de los alimentos*
blanching	blanqueamiento
canning	enlatado; en conserva
dehydration	deshidratación
freezing	congelación
homogenization	homogeneización
pasteurization	pasteurización
refining	refinación, purificación

494

Nutrition Vocabulary / Vocabulario de la nutrición

Foods: Fruits, Vegetables, Meats, Breads and Beverages / Alimentos: Frutas, vegetales, carnes, panes y bebidas

Fruits	Frutas
avocado	aguacate
apple	manzana
apricot	albaricoque
banana	plátano
blueberry	mora azul
blackberry	zarzamora
cantaloupe	cantalú (melón)
coconut	coco
cranberry	arándano
cherry	cereza
date	dátil
fig	higo
grape	uva
guava	guayaba
grapefruit	toronja
lemon	limón
mango	mango
melon	(green) sandía
nectarine	nectarina
orange	naranja
papaya	papaya, frutabomba
peach	durazno, melocotón
pear	pera
pineapple	piña
plum	ciruela
prune	ciruela pasa
raisins	pasas
raspberry	frambuesa
strawberry	fresa
tangerine	mandarina
watermelon	melón de agua

Fruits are rich in potassium, carbohydrates, fiber, and vitamins A and C.
Las frutas son ricas en potasio, carbohidratos, fibra y vitaminas A y C.

Vegetables	Vegetales
artichoke	alcachofa
asparagus	espárrago
avocado	aguacate
basil	mejorana
bean	frijol; S.A: habichuela
beets	remolacha, betabel
brussel sprouts	colecita de Bruselas
broccoli	brocol
cabbage	repollo
capers	alcaparras
carrot	zanahoria
cauliflower	coliflor
celery	apio
coriander	cilantro
cumin	comino
corn	maíz, elote
cucumber	pepino
eggplant	berenjena
endive	escarola, endivia
fennel	hinojo
garlic	ajo
ginger	gengibre
green bean	habichuela
kale	col rizada
leek	puerro
lentil	lentejav
lettuce	lechuga
mushrooms	hongos, champiñones
olives	aceitunas
onions	cebollas
parsley	perejil
peas	guisantes, arvejas
potato	papas, patatas
rice	arroz
rosemary	romero
spinach	espinaca
squash	calabaza
sweet potato	camote, boniato
tomato	tomate
yam	batata, boniato
watercress	berro

Fat
fatty acids
unsaturated fats: —most vegetable fats
saturated fats: —animal fats
ácidos grasos
sin grasas saturadas—la mayoría de las grasas vegetales
grasas saturadas—grasas de animales

Calculation of the % of Fat in Foods / Cálculo del % de grasas en los alimentos
fat grams × 9 (calories) = #   gramos de grasa × 9 (calorías) = #
divided by 235 calories = % of fat   # dividido por 235 calorías = % de grasa

---

Fat + Values   Grasas + Valores
- Helps in the absorption of vitamins A, D, E, and K
- Stored in adipose tissue, helping to maintain cell membranes.

- Ayuda a la absorción de las vitaminas A, D, E y K
- Se almacena en el tejido adiposo; ayuda a mantener las membranas celulares.

Negative Factors / Factores negativos

- Saturated fats increase the danger of building up cholesterol in the artery walls.
Las grasas saturadas aumentan el peligro de almacenar colesterol en las paredes de las arterias.
- Fat production of calories is more than double that of protein or carbohydrates. If the production of calories is not consumed (i.e., exercises), body fat will increase.
La producción de calorías de las grasas es más del doble que la producida por las proteínas o los carbohidratos. Si la producción de calorías no se consume (p.ej., ejercicios, trabajo activo) la grasa en el cuerpo aumenta.

Meats	*Carnes*
beef	res
chicken, hen	pollo, gallina
lamb	carnero
pork	cerdo, puerco
fish	pescado
turkey	pavo
duck	pato
shellfish	*mariscos*
clams	almejas
crab	cangrejo
lobster	langosta
mussels	mejillones
oysters	ostras
shrimp	camarón

Breads and Cereals	*Panes y cereales*
barley	cebada
buttermilk bread	pan de suero
cheese bread	pan de queso
cookies	galleticas
cornbread	pan de maíz
crackers	galletas
egg bread	pan de huevo
oat bran	salvado de avena
French bread	pan francés
potato bread	pan de papas
rolls	panecitos
sweet rolls	panecitos dulces
tortillas	tortillas
white bread	pan blanco
whole-grain bread	pan de grano entero
whole-wheat toast	pan de trigo, pan negro

Milk Products	*Productos lácteos*
butter	mantequilla
cheese	queso
cottage cheese	requesón
cream	crema
ice cream	helado
margarine	margarina
milk	leche
yogurt	yogur

496

Beverages	Bebidas
beer	cerveza
bouillon	caldo claro de carne
broth	caldo
carbonated drinks	sodas
chocolate	chocolate
coffee	café
consomme	consomé
fruit juices	jugos de fruta
gelatin	gelatina
ice	hielo
lemonade	limonada
milk	leche
condensed milk	leche condensada
evaporated milk	leche evaporada
skim milk	leche descremada
mineral water	agua mineral
sherbet	sorbete
tea; herbal tea	té negro; té de hierbas
thirst-quencher beverages	bebidas que matan la sed
water (mineral)	agua mineral
water (spring)	agua de manantial
wine	vino

Food Qualities	Cualidades de los alimentos	Food Qualities	Cualidades de los alimentos
acid	ácido	peeled	pelado
bitter	amargo	washed	lavado
bloody	algo crudo, con sangre	strained	escurrido
cold	frío	soft	blando
dry	seco, escurrido	rich	rico
enough	suficiente	savory	sabroso, apetitoso
healthy	saludable	seasoned	sazonado
fresh	fresco	sharp	algo crudo, poco hecho
frozen	congelado	sour	agrio
ground	molido	spoiled	dañado, contaminado
highly priced	muy caro	spicy	picante, muy condimentado
light	ligero	sticky	pegajoso
nutritious	nutritivo	strong	fuerte
liquified	licuado	sweet	dulce
kneeded	amasado	tasty	sabroso, de buen gusto
mashed	en puré; machacado	unpeeled	sin pelar
old	viejo	warm	caliente

Note: Adjectives ending in -o form the feminine by dropping the -o and adding -a.

Appendix C
Systems of
Measurements

Apéndice C
Sistemas de medidas

Weights and Measures / Pesos y medidas

All equivalents are approximate. / Todas las equivalencias son aproximadas.

Liquid Measure doses	*Líquidos: Capacidad dosis (sistema métrico)*	
1 quart / cuarto = 0.946 liter / litro	1000	cc.*
1 pint / pinta = 0.0473 liter / litro	500	cc.
8 fluid ounces / onzas	240	cc.
3.5 fluid ounces / onzas	100	cc.
1 fluid ounce / onza	30	cc.
4 fluid drams / dracmas	4	cc.
15 minims, drops / gotas	1	cc.
1 minim, drop / gota	0.06	cc.
1 teaspoonful / cucharadita de café	4	cc.
1 teaspoonful / cucharadita de postre	8	cc.
1 tablespoonful / cucharada sopera	15	cc.
1 teacupful / media taza	120	cc.
1 cup / taza	240	cc.

*cc. *abbr.* cubic centimeters / centímetros cúbicos

Solids	*Sólidos*	
1 pound / libra	373.24	grams / gramos
1 ounce / onza	30	grams / gramos
4 drams / dracmas	15	grams / gramos
1 dram / dracma	4	grams / gramos
60 grains / granos = 1 dram / dracma	4	grams / gramos
30 grains / granos = 0.5 dram / dracma	2	grams / gramos
15 grains / granos	1	gram / gramo
10 grains / granos	0.6	grams / gramos
1 grain / grano	60	milligrams / miligramos
$3/4$ grain / grano	50	mg.*
$1/2$ grain / grano	30	mg.
$1/4$ grain / grano	15	mg.
$1/10$ grain / grano	6	mg.

*mg. *abbr.* milligrams / miligramos

Other Liquid Measures	*Otras medidas líquidas*	
1 barrel / barril	119.07	liters / litros
1 gallon / galón = 8 pints / pintas (*Ingl.*)	3.785	L*
4 quarts / cuartos	3.785	L
1 liter / litro	2.113	pints / pintas
1 quart / cuarto	0.946	L
1 pint / pinta	0.473	L

*L *abbr.* liter / litro.

Avoirdupois Weights	*Peso avoirdupois (comercio)*	
1 ton / tonelada	1016	kilograms / kilos
1 hundredweight = 112 pounds / libras	50.80	kilograms / kilos
2.20 pounds / libras	1	kilogram / kilo
1 pound / libra = 16 ounces / onzas	0.453	kilograms / kilo
1 ounce / onza	28.34	grams / gramos

501

Length		Longitud	
1	mile / milla	1.60	kilometers / kilómetros
1	yard / yarda = 3 feet / pies	0.914	meters / metros
1	foot / pie = 12 inches / pulgadas	0.304	meter / metro
1	inch / pulgada	25.4	milimeters / milímetros
0.04	inch / pulgada	1	milimeter / milímetro
0.39	inch / pulgada	1	centimer / centímetro
39.37	inches / pulgadas	1	meter / metro

Temperature / Temperatura

Fahrenheit (°F)	Centígrado (°C)
32°F freezing point (sea level / nivel del mar)	0°C punto de congelación
212°F boiling point	100°C punto de ebullición
Normal Body Temperature	Temperatura normal del cuerpo
Children: 99°F	Niños: 37.2°C
Adults: 98.6°F	Adultos: 37.0°C

Conversion to °C		Conversión a °F	
subtract 32	−32	multiplique por 9	× 9
multiply by 5	× 5	divida entre 5	÷ 5
divide by 9	÷ 9	añada +32	+32

Cardinal Numerals / Números cardinales

0 cero / zero	30 treinta / thirty
1 uno (un, una) / one	40 cuarenta / forty
2 dos / two	50 cincuenta / fifty
3 tres / three	60 sesenta / sixty
4 cuatro / four	70 setenta / seventy
5 cinco / five	80 ochenta / eighty
6 seis / six	90 noventa / ninety
7 siete / seven	100 ciento, cien / one hundred
8 ocho / eight	101 ciento uno / one hundred and one
9 nueve / nine	110 ciento diez / one hundred and ten
10 diez / ten	200 doscientos / two hundred
11 once / eleven	300 trescientos / three hundred
12 doce / twelve	400 cuatrocientos / four hundred
13 trece / thirteen	500 quinientos / five hundred
14 catorce / fourteen	600 seiscientos / six hundred
15 quince / fifteen	700 setecientos / seven hundred
16 diez y seis, dieciséis / sixteen	800 ochocientos / eight hundred
17 diez y siete, diecisiete / seventeen	900 novecientos / nine hundred
18 diez y ocho, dieciocho / eighteen	1,000 mil / one thousand
19 diez y nueve, diecinueve / nineteen	1,010 mil diez / one thousand and ten
20 veinte / twenty	1,500 mil quinientos / one thousand five hundred
21 veinte y uno, veintiuno / twenty-one	2,000 dos mil / two thousand
	1,000,000 un millón / one million

Note: Uno and ciento and its multiples are the only cardinal numbers that change form. Uno drops the -o when it precedes a masculine singular noun: one liter of water / un litro de agua; but it does not drop the -o in: one out of ten / uno de cada diez.
Ciento changes to cien before nouns and before mil and millón: one hundred cases / cien casos; one hundred thousand cases / cien mil casos.

Multiples of **ciento** agree in gender and number with the nouns they modify: two hundred cases / **doscientos casos;** two hundred pills / **doscientas píldoras.**

Ordinal Numerals / Números ordinales

The ordinals first to tenth

English	Masculine	Feminine
first	1º primero	primera
second	2º segundo	segunda
third	3º tercero	tercera
fourth	4º cuarto	cuarta
fifth	5º quinto	quinta
sixth	6º sexto	sexta
seventh	7º séptimo	séptima
eighth	8º octavo	octava
ninth	9º noveno	novena
tenth	10º décimo	décima

Primero and **tercero** drop the -o before masculine singular nouns.

the first year / **el primer año**
the third day / **el tercer día**

Note: If a cardinal number and a numeral are used to qualify the same noun, the cardinal always precedes the ordinal.

the first three patients / **los tres primeros pacientes**
Take the first two pills now. / **Tome las dos primeras pastillas ahora.**

In reference to dates, the ordinal **primero** is used for the first day of the month; the cardinal is used for the other dates.

Fractions / Fracciones

$\frac{1}{2}$	a, one half / medio, la mitad
$\frac{1}{3}$	a, one third / un tercio, una tercera parte
$\frac{1}{4}$	a, one fourth / un cuarto, una cuarta parte
$\frac{1}{5}$	a, one fifth / un quinto, una quinta parte
$\frac{1}{6}$	a, one sixth / un sexto, una sexta parte
$\frac{1}{8}$	a, one eighth / un octavo, una octava parte
$\frac{1}{10}$	a, one tenth / un décimo, una décima parte
$\frac{3}{5}$	three fifths / tres quintos
$\frac{5}{8}$	five eighths / cinco octavos
$\frac{7}{10}$	seven tenths / siete décimos
0.1	a, one tenth / un décimo
0.01	a, one hundredth / un centésimo
0.001	a, one thousandth / un milésimo

Time / El Tiempo

Days of the Week / Días de la semana

Days	Días
Monday	lunes
Tuesday	martes
Wednesday	miércoles
Thursday	jueves
Friday	viernes
Saturday	sábado
Sunday	domingo

You must return on **Monday.** / Debe volver el **lunes.**
On **Thursdays** the office is closed. / Los **jueves** la consulta está cerrada.
The test will be next **Friday.** / La prueba será el próximo **viernes.**

Note: Days of the week and months of the year are not capitalized in Spanish. / En inglés los días de la semana y los meses del año se escriben con mayúscula.

Seasons and Months of the Year / Estaciones y meses del año

Spring	Primavera
March	marzo
April	abril
May	mayo

Your operation will be in May. / Su operación será en mayo.

Summer	Verano
June	junio
July	julio
August	agosto

It is very hot in the summer. / Hace mucho calor en el verano.

Autumn	Otoño
September	septiembre
October	octubre
November	noviembre

Make your next appointment for May. / Haga la próxima cita para mayo.
April is a bad month for allergies. / Abril es un mes malo para las alergias.
I saw the patient last September. / Vi al paciente el pasado mes de septiembre.

Winter	Invierno
December	diciembre
January	enero
February	febrero

Do you have many colds in the winter? / ¿Tiene muchos resfriados en el invierno?

504

Time of Day / La hora

What time is it?	¿Qué hora es?
At what time?	¿A qué hora?
It is . . .	Es la . . . (Son las . . .)
At	a la, a las
in the morning	por la mañana
in the afternoon	por la tarde
in the evening (at night)	por la noche

Es la una	**A la una** tomo la medicina. / I take the medication **at one.**
Son las dos	**A las dos** llegaré al hospital. / I will arrive at the hospital **at two.**
Son las dos y media	**A las dos y media** tengo una consulta. / I have an appointment **at two-thirty.**
Son las cuatro	**A las cuatro** voy a la farmacia. / I am going to the pharmacy **at four.**
Son las once	**A las once** hablé con la enfermera. / I spoke to the nurse **at eleven.**
Son las doce	**A mediodía** como el almuerzo. / I eat lunch **at noon.**

Expressions of time / Expresiones de tiempo

General Terms	Términos generales	General Terms	Términos generales
night	noche	daily	díario, diariamente
midnight	medianoche	2 weeks	dos semanas, quince días
mid-morning	media mañana	annual	anual
evening	tardecita	bimester	bimestre
sunset	atardecer	century	siglo
morning	mañana	date	fecha
day	día	decade	década
sunrise, dawn	amanecer, la aurora	monthly	mensual, mensualmente
afternoon	tarde	trimester	trimestre
night	noche	twice a day	dos veces al día
noon	mediodía	weekly	semanal, semanalmente

Phrases	Frases
after lunch	después del almuerzo
at bedtime	al acostarse
at dinner time	a la hora de la cena
before breakfast	antes de desayunar
during meals	durante las comidas
one week from today	en una semana, en siete días

Timing Tests and Medications / Tiempo marcado en pruebas y medicinas

liquid intake 24 hours	toma líquida de 24 horas
first morning specimen	espécimen de primera hora en la mañana
timed specimen	espécimen de tiempo marcado
fasting blood test	prueba sanguínea en ayunas
one teaspoon every three hours	una cucharadita cada tres horas
one pill a day	una pastilla al día

Stages of Life / Etapas de la vida

Ages	*Edades*
pre-born, fetus	prenacido(a), feto
newborn	neonato, recién nacido(a)
parvulum	párvulo(a)
toddler	el pequeño, la pequeña
child, childhood	niño(a), la niñez
puberty, adolescence	la pubertad, la adolescencia
adult	adulto(a), mayor de edad
young man, young woman, youth	el joven, la joven, la juventud
maturity, middle age	la madurez, la mediana edad
old man, old woman; old age	el anciano, el señor mayor; la anciana, la señora mayor; la vejez
date of birth	fecha de nacimiento
date of death	fecha de fallecimiento

Appendix D
Verb Tables

Apéndice D
Tablas de verbos

Verb Tables / Tablas de verbos

Regular Verbs / Verbos regulares

Simple Tenses

Infinitive	*tomar*	*comer*	*admitir*
	to take, to drink	to eat	to admit
-ndo form (gerund)	tomando	comiendo	admitiendo
-do form (pp.)	tomado	comido	admitido

	tomar	*comer*	*admitir*
Indicative			
Present	tomo	como	admito
	tomas	comes	admites
	toma	come	admite
	tomamos	comemos	admitimos
	tomáis	coméis	admitís
	toman	comen	admiten
Preterit	tomé	comí	admití
	tomaste	comiste	admitiste
	tomó	comió	admitió
	tomamos	comimos	admitimos
	tomasteis	comisteis	admitisteis
	tomaron	comieron	admitieron
Imperfect	tomaba	comía	admitía
	tomabas	comías	admitías
	tomaba	comía	admitía
	tomábamos	comíamos	admitíamos
	tomabais	comíais	admitíais
	tomaban	comían	admitían
Future	tomaré	comeré	admitiré
	tomarás	comerás	admitirás
	tomará	comerá	admitirá
	tomaremos	comeremos	admitiremos
	tomaréis	comeréis	admitiréis
	tomarán	comerán	admitirán
Condicional	tomaría	comería	admitiría
	tomarías	comerías	admitirías
	tomaría	comería	admitiría
	tomaríamos	comeríamos	admitiríamos
	tomaríais	comeríais	admitiríais
	tomarían	comerían	admitirían
Subjunctive			
Present	tome	coma	admita
	tomes	comas	admitas
	tome	coma	admita
	tomemos	comamos	admitamos
	toméis	comáis	admitáis
	tomen	coman	admitan

Imperfect (-ra)	tomara	comiera	admitiera
	tomaras	comieras	admitieras
	tomara	comiera	admitiera
	tomáramos	comiéramos	admitiéramos
	tomarais	comierais	admitierais
	tomaran	comieran	admitieran
Imperfect (-se)	tomase	comiese	admitiese
	tomases	comieses	admitieses
	tomase	comiese	admitiese
	tomásemos	comiésemos	admitiésemos
	tomaseis	comieseis	admitieseis
	tomasen	comiesen	admitiesen

	Root-Vowel Changing Verbs		
Infinitive	*apretar*	*mostrar*	*entender*
	to squeeze	to show	to understand
-ndo form (*gerund*)	apretando	mostrando	entendiendo
-do form (*pp.*)	apretado	mostrado	entendido

Indicative			
Present	aprieto	muestro	entiendo
	aprietas	muestras	entiendes
	aprieta	muestra	entiende
	apretamos	mostramos	entendemos
	apretáis	mostráis	entendéis
	aprietan	muestran	entienden
Subjunctive			
Present	apriete	muestre	entienda
	aprietes	muestres	entiendas
	apriete	muestre	entienda
	apretemos	mostremos	entendamos
	apretéis	mostréis	entendáis
	aprieten	muestren	entiendan

Note: Use **apretar** as a model to conjugate: **cerrar** / to close: **comenzar** / to begin; **despertar** / to wake up; **empezar** / to begin; **pensar** / to think; **sentar** / to settle, to fit; **sentarse** / to sit down.

Other verbs like **mostrar** are: **acordar** / to agree; **acordarse** / to remember; **acostarse** / to lie down; **apostar** / to bet; **encontrar** / to find; **encontrarse** / to run across, to meet; **probar** / to test; to taste; **recordar** / to remember; **rogar** / to beg; **volar** / to fly.

Other verbs like **entender** are: **atender** / to attend; **defender** / to defend; **encender** / to light, to set fire to; **perder** / to lose.

Infinitive	*volver*	*sentir*	*dormir*	*repetir*
	to return	to feel	to sleep	to repeat
-ndo form (*gerund*)	volviendo	sintiendo	durmiendo	repitiendo
-do form (*pp.*)	vuelto	sentido	dormido	repetido

510

Indicative Present				
	vuelvo	siento	duermo	repito
	vuelves	sientes	duermes	repites
	vuelve	siente	duerme	repite
	volvemos	sentimos	dormimos	repetimos
	volvéis	sentís	dormís	repetís
	vuelven	sienten	duermen	repiten
Subjunctive Present				
	vuelva	sienta	duerma	repita
	vuelvas	sientas	duermas	repitas
	vuelva	sienta	duerma	repita
	volvamos	sintamos	durmamos	repitamos
	volváis	sintáis	durmáis	repitáis
	vuelvan	sientan	duerman	repitan

Note: Other verbs that follow the same changes: **mover** / to move; **disolver** / to dissolve; **doler** / to hurt; **moler** / to grind; **morder** / to bite; **promover** / to promote; and other verbs formed by adding a prefix to **volver. Volver** and its derivatives have an irregular past participle as does **disolver** (**disuelto**).

Verbs conjugated like **sentir: advertir** / to advise, to take notice; **consentir** / to consent; **convertir** / to convert; **digerir** / to digest; **divertirse** / to have a good time; **herir** / to wound, hurt, stab; **hervir** / to boil; **mentir** / to lie; **preferir** / to prefer; **referir** / to refer.

Like **dormir** are: **dormirse** / to fall asleep, and **morir** / to die.

Use **repetir** as a model verb for: **competir** / to compete; **concebir** / to conceive; **derretir** / to melt; **conseguir** / to obtain; **medir** / to measure; **pedir** / to ask, to request; **reír** / to laugh.

Irregular Verbs / Verbos irregulares

The following verbs and their compound forms have irregularities that do not allow their inclusion in any of the previous classifications. For the twenty irregular verbs listed here only the tenses with irregular forms are given. Apply the rules for regular verbs to tenses not given here. Only the singular forms are given when the ordinary rules of those tenses are followed in their formation. The auxiliary verb **haber** belongs to this group.

Irregular Verb Conjugations / Conjugación de los verbos irregulares

Infinitive Present participle Past Participle	Indicative		Subjunctive	Conditional
andar / to walk andando andado	**present** ando andas anda andamos andáis andan	**preterit** anduve anduviste anduvo anduvimos anduvisteis anduvieron	**imperfect** anduviera anduvieras anduviera anduviéramos anduvierais anduvieran	
caer / to fall cayendo caído	**present** caigo	**preterit** cayó cayeron	**imperfect** cayera cayeras cayera cayéramos cayerais cayeran	

511

Infinitive Present participle Past Participle	Indicative			Subjunctive		Conditional
dar / to give dando dado	present doy das da damos dais dan	preterit di diste dio dimos disteis dieron		present dé des dé demos deis den	imperfect diera dieras diera diéramos dierais dieran	
decir / to tell diciendo dicho	present digo dices dice decimos decís dicen	preterit dije dijiste dijo dijimos dijisteis dijeron	future diré dirás dirá diremos diréis dirán	present diga digas diga digamos digáis digan	imperfect dijera dijeras dijera dijéramos dijerais dijeran	conditional diría dirías diría diríamos diríais dirían
estar / to be estando estado	present estoy estás está	preterit estuve estuviste estuvo		present esté estés esté	imperfect estuviera estuvieras estuviera	
hacer / to do, make haciendo hecho	present hago	preterit hice hiciste hizo	future haré harás hará	present haga hagas haga	imperfect hiciera hicieras hiciera	conditional haría harías haría
ir / to go yendo ido	present voy vas va vamos vais van	preterit fui fuiste fue fuimos fuisteis fueron	imperfect iba ibas iba ibamos ibais iban	present vaya vayas vaya vayamos vayáis vayan	imperfect fuera fueras fuera fuéramos fuerais fueran	
oír / to hear oyendo oído	present oigo oyes oye oímos oís oyen	preterit oí oíste oyó oímos oísteis oyeron		present oiga oigas oiga	imperfect oyera oyeras oyera	
poder / to be able pudiendo podido	present puedo puedes puede podemos podéis pueden	preterit pude pudiste pudo pudimos pudisteis pudieron	future podré podrás podrá podremos podréis podrán	present pueda puedas pueda podamos podáis puedan	imperfect pudiera pudieras pudiera pudiéramos pudierais pudieran	conditional podría podrías podría podríamos podríais podrían
poner / to put poniendo puesto	present pongo pones pone	preterit puse pusiste puso pusimos pusisteis pusieron	future pondré pondrás pondrá	present ponga pongas ponga pongamos pongáis pongan	imperfect pusiera pusieras pusiera	conditional pondría pondrías pondría
querer / to want queriendo querido	present quiero quieres quiere queremos queréis quieren	preterit quise quisiste quiso quisimos quisisteis quisieron	future querré querrás querrá querremos querréis querrán	present quiera quieras quiera queramos queráis quieran	imperfect quisiera quisieras quisiera quisiéramos quisierais quisieran	conditional querría querrías querría querríamos querríais querrían

Infinitive Present participle Past Participle	Indicative			Subjunctive		Conditional
saber / to know sabiendo sabido	**present** sé sabes sabe	**preterit** supe supiste supo	**future** sabré sabrás sabrá	**present** sepa sepas sepa	**imperfect** supiera supieras supiera	**conditional** sabría sabrías sabría
salir / to leave saliendo salido	**present** salgo		**future** saldré saldrás saldrá	**present** salga salgas salga		**conditional** saldría saldrías saldría
ser / to be siendo sido	**present** soy eres es somos sois son	**preterit** fui fuiste fue fuimos fuisteis fueron	**imperfect** era eras era éramos erais eran	**present** sea seas sea seamos seáis sean	**imperfect** fuera fueras fuera fuéramos fuerais fueran	
tener / to have teniendo tenido	**present** tengo tienes tiene tenemos tenéis tienen	**preterit** tuve tuviste tuvo tuvimos tuvisteis tuvieron	**future** tendré tendrás tendrá tendremos tendréis tendrán	**present** tenga tengas tenga tengamos tengáis tengan	**imperfect** tuviera tuvieras tuviera tuviéramos tuvierais tuvieran	**conditional** tendría tendrías tendría tendríamos tendríais tendrían
venir / to come viniendo venido	**present** vengo vienes viene venimos venéis vienen	**preterit** vine viniste vino vinimos vinisteis vinieron	**future** vendré vendrás vendrá vendremos vendréis vendrán	**present** venga vengas venga vengamos vengáis vengan	**imperfect** viniera vinieras viniera viniéramos vinierais vinieran	**conditional** vendría vendrías vendría vendríamos vendríais vendrían
ver / to see viendo visto	**present** veo ves ve vemos veis ven		**imperfect** veía veías veía veíamos veíais veían	**present** vea veas vea veamos veáis vean		

513

Abbreviations

I.N.R. — International Normalised Ratio
(both languages the same)   (blood)

E C G —   PR ⎫ — stet
          a QRS ⎬
            QRS ⎭   Mr Lyall — 860579.
                              (2006)
                        Lucinda at Newcastle
                        Uni from Ochler.

Spanish   (see inside front cover) English
             volumen corpuscular medio
V.C.M.   ~~medial~~ corpuscular volume ← M.C.V.
             mean?
H.C.M.   C.H.C.

C.H.C.M.   M.C.H.C.

Cay a dos   Band Neutrophils

V.P.M.   ~~median~~ platelet volume   M.P.V.

** ufc/ml   ~~of~~ cfu/ml

L.O.E.   S.O.L.s

V.I.   ventriculo izquierdo
A I   atrio   "
I.T.   insuficiencia tricúspida
(see green notebook for others from Valencia)

        Ankle brachial index — A.B.I.
        arterial B.P. measured
        by Echo-Doppler.

respiratory problems — they get nebulisers
                    + drugs eg. anti.